R. Gupta's®

POPULAR MASTER GUIDE

LL.B

Three Year Degree Course

Entrance Examination

Useful for CUET, Delhi University; Allahabad University; Banaras Hindu University; Punjab University; Bharati Vidyapeeth Pune; Bangalore University; University of Lucknow; Aligarh Muslim University; Chaudhary Charan Singh University, Meerut (CCS University); Maharishi Dayanand University, Rohtak; Chandigarh University; Mumbai University; Kerala University, Thiruvananthapuram; Calicut University; Sri Venkateswara University, Tirupati; Guwahati University; Himachal Pradesh University, Shimla; Jammu University; Kashmir University and Other reputed Universities/Institutes of India

By
RPH Editorial Board

2027 EDITION

RAMESH PUBLISHING HOUSE, NEW DELHI

Published by
O.P. Gupta *for* Ramesh Publishing House
Admin. Office
12-H, New Daryaganj Road, Opp. Officers Mess,
New Delhi-110002 ✆ 23275224, 23245124
E-mail: info@rameshpublishinghouse.com
For Online Shopping: www.rameshpublishinghouse.com

Showroom
- Balaji Market, Nai Sarak, Delhi-110006 ✆ 23282525 📱 9354373464
- 4457, Nai Sarak, Delhi-110006

Book Code: R-832

ISBN: 978-93-5012-592-2

Price: ₹ 640

Printed at: B.K. Offset, Delhi

CONTENTS

Special Note : *Some Universities may include/exclude one or two different topics/ subjects in their Entrance Examination than those given in this book. Students are advised to refer to the prospectus of the university for which they are applying, to get the complete and final information.*

Previous Years' Paper

LL.B. (3 Years Course)

Entrance Exam, 2025*

(Exam held on 29-06-2025)

1. The word economics is derived from which Greek word?

A. Oikos B. Oeconomicus
C. Ekklesiastikas D. Oikonomia

2. A campaign launched in April 2010, with a view to clean the river Ganges has been named as:

A. Nirmal Ganga-Sparsh Ganga
B. Namami Gange
C. Pavitra Ganga
D. Swargashram Ganga

3. Who among the following was the founder of Pushyabhuti Dynasty?

A. Pushyabhuti B. Prabhakar
C. Aditya Vardhan D. Harshavardhan

4. Bhagwati sutra is related to which of the following religions?

A. Buddhism B. Jainism
C. Hinduism D. Sikhism

5. Which word is the odd man out?

A. Trivial B. Unimportant
C. Important D. Insignificant

6. All the shrubs in the garden are flowering shrubs; some of the shrubs in the garden are rosy shrubs; all rosy shrubs in the garden are flowering shrubs. If the first two statements are true, the third statement is:

A. False B. True
C. Uncertain D. None of these

7. Please, come ______ the bathroom.

A. Out of B. Over
C. On D. In

8. The rain comes ______ the cloud.

A. In B. Near
C. From D. Under

9. The Stars ______ counted.

A. can B. can be
C. cannot be D. must

10. X introduced Y saying, "he is the husband of the granddaughter of the father of my father". How is the Y related to X?

A. Brother B. Uncle
C. Co-brother D. Brother-in-law

11. Three of the following four words are alike in certain way and one is different. Select the odd one.

A. Goggle B. Spectacles
C. Bifocal D. Optical reader

12. Select the option that is related to the third term in the same way as the second term is related to the first term:

IVORY : ZWSPJ : CREAM :

A. NFDQB B. ISNFDB
C. DSFCN D. BQDZL

1. D	2. A	3. A	4. B	5. C	6. B
7. A	8. C	9. C	10. D	11. D	12. B

* Conducted by Panjab University.

13. In the following question, select the related word pair from the given alternatives:

Tuberculosis : Lungs : Typhoid :

A. Liver
B. Intestine
C. Lungs
D. Brain

14. Find the Odd one out from the given set of numbers:

14, 28, 35, 46, 56, 84

A. 56
B. 84
C. 35
D. 46

15. Who was the Chairman of the drafting committee of the Constitution of India?

A. Dr. B.R. Ambedkar
B. K.M. Munshi
C. B.N. Rau
D. Mohammad Saadullah

16. Concepts of "Fundamental rights", "judicial review" and "Independence of judiciary" is borrowed from:

A. USA
B. UK
C. USSR
D. France

17. Full Form of NATO is:

A. North Atlantic Treaty Organisation
B. North American Treaty Organisation
C. North African Treaty Organisation
D. None of these

18. The pigeon-hole theory for the Law of Tort is given by:

A. Salmond
B. Winfield
C. Austin
D. Bentham

19. The Latin term "Ubi jus ibi remedium" means:

A. Where there is a right, there is a remedy
B. Where there is no right, there is a remedy
C. Where there is right, there is no remedy
D. Where there is no right, there is no remedy

20. The number of permanent members of the UN Security Council is:

A. 7
B. 5
C. 6
D. 10

21. The theme for International Women's Day 2025 is:

A. "For ALL Women and Girls: Right, Equality, Empowerment"
B. "Invest in women: Accelerate progress"
C. "Digital: Innovation and Technology for Gender Equality"
D. None of the above

22. What is the name of AI chatbot of "X"?

A. Chat GPT
B. DeepSeek
C. Grok
D. Gemini

23. Donald Trump is ______ and ______ President of USA?

A. 45th and 47th
B. 44th and 45th
C. 45th and 46th
D. 43rd and 45th

24. Mount Lewotobi Laki-Laki was recently in the news. It is located in:

A. Philippines
B. USA
C. Indonesia
D. Australia

25. ______ was honoured with the Outstanding/ Lifetime Achievement in Indian Cinema award at the International Indian Film Academy Awards (IIFA) 2025?

A. Rakesh Roshan
B. Sanjay Leela Bhansali
C. Vinod Chopra
D. Rajkumar Hirani

26. Choose the most appropriate answer from the below given idioms/phrases:

"Once in a Blue Moon"

A. Often
B. Rarely
C. Repeatedly
D. Both B and C

13. B	**14.** D	**15.** A	**16.** A	**17.** A	**18.** A	**19.** A
20. B	**21.** A	**22.** C	**23.** A	**24.** C	**25.** A	**26.** B

27. Palaeontology is the scientific study of:

A. Plants and Animals
B. Insects
C. Rocks and Mountains
D. Fossils

28. 1 milli meter is equal to:

A. 0.5 cm B. 0.1 cm
C. 0.2 cm D. 0.3 cm

29. A Puisne Judge of a High Court is:

A. Judge other than Chief Justice
B. The Chief Justice
C. A temporary Judge
D. A retired Judge

30. What is the meaning of Chattel?

A. Any property
B. Immovable property
C. Movable property
D. Cattel

31. Which of the products got GI Tag in "Agriculture" area from the state of Meghalaya?

A. Khasi Mandarin B. Memong Narang
C. Chak Hao D. A and B

32. Motilal Chimanlal Setalvad was the first:

A. Attorney general of India
B. Chairman of the Law Commission of India
C. Chairman of the Bar Council of India
D. All of the above

33. "Budget" is known as:

A. Annual Financial Statement
B. Annual Budget
C. Annual Financial Budget
D. Financial Statement of the year

34. A prominent example of "transformative constitutionalism" in India can be seen in the case of:

A. Joseph Shine vs. Union of India
B. Independent Thought vs. Union of India
C. Navtej Singh Johar vs. Union of India
D. Suresh Kumar Kaushal vs. Naz Foundation

35. International Day of Yoga was first celebrated on:

A. 21st June, 2016
B. 21st June, 2015
C. 22nd June, 2016
D. 22nd June, 2015

36. A, B, C, D, E and F are standing in a circle and looking at the centre. Only D is between A and B. Only F is between A and C. E is just left of B. Who is only one standing between E and F?

A. A B. C
C. D D. B

37. A man is facing south-west. If he turns 90 degrees in the anticlockwise direction and then 135 degrees in the clockwise direction, which direction is he facing now?

A. West B. North-East
C. North-West D. East

38. Which of the following gases initiates a chain reaction that breaks down ozone in the upper atmosphere?

A. Nitrogen Oxide
B. Carbon Dioxide
C. Hydrogen Sulphide
D. Chlorine

39. If VARANASI is coded as WCUESGQ, then the code of KOLKATA will be:

A. LOQOZEH B. HLZEOOQ
C. ZELHOQO D. LQOOFZH

40. How much cash prize has BCCI announced for the Indian winning team of ICC Champions Trophy 2025?

A. ₹ 52 Crore B. ₹ 55 Crore
C. ₹ 58 Crore D. ₹ 50 Crore

27. D	**28.** B	**29.** A	**30.** C	**31.** D	**32.** D	**33.** A
34. C	**35.** B	**36.** B	**37.** A	**33.** D	**39.** D	**40.** C

41. What is India's rank in the World Happiness Report 2025?

A. 117th B. 118th
C. 119th D. 120th

42. "Talking twenty to the dozen" means:

A. Talking hurriedly and rapidly
B. Talking without making sense
C. Talking about groceries
D. None of these

43. Which one is synonym for "Legal"?

A. Inclusive B. Frugal
C. Statutory D. Pragmatic

44. The antonym of "Skeptical" is:

A. Gullible B. Certain
C. Credulous D. Doubtful

45. Jitendra Pal Singh was recently appointed as India's Ambassador to which country?

A. United States B. Israel
C. France D. Germany

46. Who is the author of *Pride* and *Prejudice*?

A. Charlotte Brontë B. Emily Brontë
C. Jane Austen D. Mary Shelley

47. Which of the following plays was written by William Shakespeare?

A. The Importance of Being Earnest
B. Doctor Faustus
C. Othello
D. Waiting for Godot

48. Who wrote the famous poem *Daffodils*?

A. John Keats
B. Percy Bysshe Shelley
C. William Wordsworth
D. Lord Byron

49. The study of human societies and cultures is known as:

A. Sociology B. Anthropology
C. Philosophy D. Political Science

50. The Industrial Revolution began in which country?

A. United States B. France
C. Germany D. Great Britain

51. Which social scientist developed the theory of classical conditioning?

A. Sigmund Freud B. B.F. Skinner
C. Ivan Pavlov D. Jean Piaget

52. The study of how human populations change over time is called:

A. Sociology B. Demography
C. Anthropology D. Psychology

53. Which of the following soils is most suitable for cotton cultivation?

A. Laterite soil B. Alluvial soil
C. Black soil D. Red soil

54. Which state has the largest forest cover in India by area?

A. Arunachal Pradesh
B. Madhya Pradesh
C. Chhattisgarh
D. Maharashtra

55. The Treaty of Chittor (1615) was signed between which two rulers?

A. Jahangir and Maharana Amar Singh
B. Akbar and Maharana Pratap
C. Aurangzeb and Chhatrapati Raja Sambha Ji
D. Shah Jahan and Raja Udai Singh

56. Which Delhi Sultan introduced the Persian festival of Nowruz in India?

A. Balban
B. Alaudin Khilji
C. Mohammad Bin Tughlaq
D. Firoz Shah Tughlaq

57. Which one of the following Gupta emperors is known as the 'Napoleon of India'?

A. Chandragupta I B. Samudragupta
C. Kumaragupta D. Skandagupta

41. B	**42.** A	**43.** C	**44.** B	**45.** B	**46.** C	**47.** C	**48.** C	**49.** B
50. D	**51.** C	**52.** B	**53.** C	**54.** B	**55.** A	**56.** A	**57.** B	

58. The imperial capital of Mauryan empire during the reign of Ashoka was:

A. Tosali B. Ujjain
C. Suvarnagiri D. Patliputra

59. What is the total area of India in lakh square kilometres?

A. 30.8 B. 31.8
C. 32.8 D. 33.8

60. The MacMohan Line demarcates India's legal border with which of the following countries?

A. Pakistan B. Bhutan
C. China D. Myanmar

61. Who was the Governor-General of India during the time of 1857 revolt?

A. Lord Canning
B. Lord Denning
C. Lord Mountbatten
D. Lord Minto

62. The special Olympics World Summer Games 2019 were held in:

A. Dubai B. Abu Dhabi
C. Doha D. Muscat

63. What is "injunction"?

A. Monetary compensation
B. Court order
C. Criminal penalty
D. Legal presumption

64. Which of these is a source of law?

A. Opinions B. Statutes
C. Feelings D. Hopes

65. What is "negligence" in Tort Law?

A. Intentional harm
B. Failure to exercise reasonable care
C. Breach of contract
D. Criminal act

66. "Caveat emptor" means

A. Let the seller beware
B. Let the buyer beware
C. Let the witness beware
D. Let the judge beware

67. If all cats are mammals, and all mammals are animals, then all cats are:

A. Plants B. Animals
C. Reptiles D. Insects

68. If "TABLE" is coded as "UBAMD," then "CHAIR" is coded as:

A. DIBSJS B. SIDBJ
C. SBIDJ D. DIBJS

69. What comes next in the sequence: A, C, F, J:

A. M B. N
C. O D. P

70. A statement that is always true is called a:

A. Contradiction B. Contingency
C. Tautology D. Paradox

71. Which organization recently launched the quantum processor 'Willow'?

A. Amazon B. Meta
C. Google D. Microsoft

72. What is the primary objective of the Gobardhan Portal?

A. To promote solar energy systems.
B. To streamline the setup process for Biogas/Compressed Biogas plants in India.
C. To facilitate rural electrification projects.
D. To develop irrigation systems.

73. Which countries are involved in the AUKUS submarine deal?

A. India, US and China
B. US, UK and Australia
C. Ukraine, France and Germany
D. Russia, Australia and Malaysia

58. D	**59.** C	**60.** C	**61.** A	**62.** B	**63.** B	**64.** B	**65.** B
66. B	**67.** B	**68.** D	**69.** C	**70.** C	**71.** C	**72.** B	**73.** B

74. The P-800 Onyx Missile is developed by which country?

A. China B. Japan
C. Russia D. India

75. Which country recently declared a national emergency on drug abuse?

A. Sierra Leone B. Guinea
C. Mali D. Nigeria

76. Which state won the 56th National Kho Kho Championship 2023-24?

A. Uttar Pradesh B. Karnataka
C. Maharashtra D. Madhya Pradesh

77. Jonatan Christie, who recently won his first Asian Badminton Championship, belongs to which country?

A. Vietnam B. Thailand
C. Singapore D. Indonesia

78. What is the capital of Australia?

A. Sydney B. Melbourne
C. Canberra D. Perth

79. What is the chemical symbol for gold?

A. Ag B. Fe
C. Au D. Cu

80. What is the largest desert in the world?

A. Sahara Desert
B. Arabian Desert
C. Gobi Desert
D. Antarctic Polar Desert

81. What is the currency of Japan?

A. Won B. Yuan
C. Yen D. Ringgit

82. What is the primary gas in Earth's atmosphere?

A. Oxygen B. Carbon dioxide
C. Nitrogen D. Argon

83. Which city is known as the "Silicon Valley" of India?

A. Mumbai B. Delhi
C. Bengaluru D. Chennai

84. Which country is known as the "Rainbow Nation"?

A. Brazil B. India
C. South Africa D. Mexico

85. Which sentence is grammatically correct?

A. Me and him went to the store
B. He and I went to the store
C. Him and me went to the store
D. I and him went to the store

86. What does the idiom "to kick the bucket" mean?

A. To succeed B. To fail
C. To die D. To celebrate

87. What is a homophone?

A. Words with similar meanings
B. Words with opposite meanings
C. Words that sound the same but have different meanings
D. Words that are spelled the same

88. The principle of "pacta sunt servanda" in international law refers to:

A. The right to self-determination
B. The obligation to perform treaty obligations in good faith
C. The immunity of state officials
D. The prohibition of the use of force

89. What is the principle of "state sovereignty"?

A. The right of states to intervene in the internal affairs of other states
B. The supreme authority of a state within its own territory
C. The obligation of states to join international organizations
D. The duty of states to provide foreign aid

74. C	**75.** A	**76.** C	**77.** D	**78.** C	**79.** C	**80.** D	**81.** C
82. C	**83.** C	**84.** C	**85.** B	**86.** C	**87.** C	**88.** B	**89.** B

growing public health crisis, particularly among youth, and to strengthen rehabilitation and law-enforcement measures.

76. The state of Maharashtra won the 56th National Kho Kho Championship 2023–24. The championship showcased high-level competition among teams from across India, and Maharashtra demonstrated consistent performance and dominance throughout the tournament. This victory further strengthened the state's reputation in traditional Indian sports.

77. Jonatan Christie, who won his first Asian Badminton Championship, belongs to Indonesia. He is one of Indonesia's leading shuttlers and has represented his country in several international tournaments. This victory marked a significant milestone in his career and highlighted Indonesia's strength in badminton.

78. The capital of Australia is Canberra, not Sydney or Melbourne as commonly assumed. Canberra was purposefully designed and selected as a neutral location between the two major cities. It serves as the political and administrative centre of the country and houses the Australian Parliament.

79. The chemical symbol for gold is Au, which is derived from the Latin word *Aurum* meaning shining dawn or glow. Gold is a precious metal known for its high value, resistance to corrosion, and extensive use in jewellery and electronics.

80. The largest desert in the world is the Antarctic Polar Desert. Although commonly people think of hot deserts like the Sahara, Antarctica is classified as a desert because it receives extremely low precipitation. It is the coldest and driest region on Earth.

81. The official currency of Japan is the Yen. It is symbolised by the sign ¥ and is widely used in domestic as well as international trade. The Yen is issued by the Bank of Japan and is one of the most traded currencies in the world's foreign exchange markets. It plays a major role in Asia's financial systems and global economics.

82. The primary gas in Earth's atmosphere is Nitrogen. It makes up about 78% of the total atmospheric composition, which helps in diluting Oxygen and preventing rapid combustion. Nitrogen is essential for the nitrogen cycle and supports plant growth indirectly through soil nutrients. This dominance makes it the most abundant atmospheric gas.

83. Bengaluru is known as the "Silicon Valley of India" due to its large concentration of IT companies, startups, and software industries. It houses major global tech firms and is a hub for innovation, research, and development. The city significantly contributes to India's digital economy and technological advancement.

84. South Africa is known as the "Rainbow Nation" because of its rich cultural, racial, and ethnic diversity. The term was popularised after the end of apartheid to symbolise unity and harmony among people of different backgrounds. It reflects the nation's inclusive identity and democratic transformation.

85. The grammatically correct sentence is "He and I went to the store." In formal English, subject pronouns (he, I, she, we) are used when they perform the action in a sentence. The other options incorrectly use object pronouns like me and him as subjects, which is grammatically wrong.

86. The idiom "to kick the bucket" is a commonly used informal expression that means to **die**. It is a figurative phrase and does not relate to any physical bucket. This idiom is often used in casual or humorous contexts to refer to death without using the word directly, making the expression less harsh.

87. A homophone refers to words that sound the same when spoken but have different meanings and often different spellings. Examples include *pair and pear*, or *sea and see*. These words can create confusion in writing if not used correctly, which is why understanding homophones is important in English grammar.

88. The principle of *pacta sunt servanda* is a fundamental rule in international law which means that treaties must be honoured and performed in good faith. It ensures that countries respect and fulfil their international agreements. This principle forms the basis of trust and cooperation between states in global relations.

89. The principle of 'state sovereignty' refers to the supreme authority of a state over its own territory and internal affairs. It means that no external power has the right to interfere in a nation's domestic matters without consent. This concept is central to international law and the independence of nations.

90. The concept of *jus cogens* refers to peremptory norms of international law that are binding on all states and cannot be violated or set aside. These rules are considered so fundamental that no treaty or agreement can override them. Examples include prohibitions against genocide, slavery, and torture.

91. The Kyoto Protocol on climate change is an international environmental agreement adopted under the United Nations Framework Convention on Climate Change (UNFCCC), not under the World Trade Organization (WTO). The WTO deals mainly with global trade rules and agreements such as TRIPS, GATS, and the Agreement on Agriculture. Therefore, the Kyoto Protocol is not covered by the WTO framework.

92. The Most-Favoured-Nation (MFN) principle requires WTO member countries to treat all other WTO members equally in terms of trade. This means that if a country grants a special trade concession (like reduced tariffs) to one member, it must offer the same concession to all other WTO members. This principle promotes fairness and prevents discrimination in international trade.

93. The WTO's dispute settlement system is designed to resolve trade disputes between member governments in a peaceful and structured manner. It provides a legal process where countries can challenge unfair trade practices and seek rulings based on WTO rules. This system helps maintain stability and predictability in global trade relations.

94. The chemical symbol for table salt is NaCl, which stands for sodium chloride. It is a compound formed by the reaction of sodium (Na) and chlorine (Cl). Table salt is widely used in cooking and food preservation and also plays an essential role in maintaining the body's electrolyte balance.

95. The hardest natural substance found on Earth is diamond. It ranks highest on the Mohs scale of hardness and is capable of cutting or scratching all other natural materials. Due to its exceptional hardness and brilliance, diamond is widely used in jewellery as well as industrial cutting tools.

96. The unit of force is the Newton. It is named after Sir Isaac Newton and is defined as the force required to accelerate a mass of one kilogram by one metre per second squared. In physics, force is measured as a push or pull acting on an object, and Newton is the standard SI unit used worldwide for this purpose.

97. The scientific study of the universe is called Astronomy. It deals with the study of celestial bodies such as stars, planets, galaxies, comets, and other cosmic phenomena. Astronomy also explores the origin, structure, and evolution of the universe, helping humans understand outer space and its laws.

98. The unit of electric current is the Ampere. It measures the rate of flow of electric charge through a conductor. One ampere is defined as the flow of one coulomb of charge per second and is a fundamental unit in electrical and electronic systems.

99. The scientific name for the voice box is the Larynx. It is an organ located in the throat responsible for producing sound and enabling speech. The larynx also plays an important role in breathing and protecting the airway during swallowing.

100. The primary cause of ozone layer depletion is Chlorofluorocarbons (CFCs). These man-made chemicals release chlorine atoms into the atmosphere, which break down ozone molecules. This process weakens the ozone layer, allowing harmful ultraviolet rays to reach the Earth's surface.

Previous Years' Paper

LL.B. (3 Year Course)

Entrance Exam, 2024

(Exam held on 23-06-2024)

1. How many UNESCO Heritage sites are there in India?

A. 52 B. 32

C. 42 D. 22

2. Which country has the Iron Dome air defence system?

A. USA B. Israel

C. Germany D. India

3. What is the name of the rocket that launched Chandrayaan-3?

A. LVM-3 B. GSLV MKIII

C. PSLV-XL D. None of the above

4. On October 9, 2022, which village was declared as the first round the clock solar powered village in India?

A. Mandali B. Modhera

C. Matarasan D. None of the above

5. Justice DY Chandrachud is:

A. 48th CJI B. 49th CJI

C. 50th CJI D. 51th CJI

6. Where is world's tallest Nataraja statue situated?

A. Pragati Maidan B. Bharat Mandapam

C. Rae-Bareli D. None of these

7. When is World Asthma Day observed?

A. 7th May B. 8th May

C. 9th May D. 10th May

8. Which of the following is not matching in the group?

A. Amrita Sher-Gil

B. S.H. Raza

C. M.F. Hussain

D. S.P. Balasubrahmanyam

9. Which of the following countries of Southeast Asia, India shares a maritime boundary?

A. Indonesia B. Malaysia

C. Singapore D. Vietnam

10. 'Chandipur-on-sea' is situated in which among of the following States?

A. Odisha B. Andhra Pradesh

C. West Bengal D. Tamil Nadu

11. Which of the following has India's first Smart Tribal Village been inaugurated?

A. Gujarat

B. Tamil Nadu

C. Jammu & Kashmir

D. Chhattisgarh

12. What is the common name of Calcium Sulphate Hemihydrate?

A. Bleaching Powder

B. Sloaked lime

C. Plaster of Paris

D. Detergent

1. C	**2.** B	**3.** A	**4.** B	**5.** C	**6.** B	**7.** *	**8.** D
9. A	**10.** A	**11.** C	**12.** C				

* *Conducted by Panjab University.*

13. British scientist J.J. Thomson was awarded the Nobel Prize in Physics in 1906 for the discovery of the:

A. Electron B. Proton
C. Neutron D. Radioactivity

14. Which of these is NOT an allotropic form of carbon?

A. Diamond B. Graphite
C. Fullerene D. None of these

15. Which of the following group of elements contain the noble gas?

A. s-block B. p-block
C. d-block D. f-block

16. What is the pH of human blood?

A. 8.2 B. 7.4
C. 6.5 D. 7

17. Who among the following established the 'Mahila Seva Mandal' and the 'Native Female School' in Pune?

A. Aruna Asaf Ali
B. Jhalkar Bai
C. Savitribai Phule
D. Sarla Devi Chaudharni

18. The 'doctrine of proportionality' is applied by the judiciary to test:

A. The reasonable balance between laws and government actions.
Validity of a Constitution Amendment Act.
C. Encroachment by the central government in the legislative jurisdiction of states.
D. Validity of the speaker's decision on the anti-defection laws.

19. The Jataka tales, a collection of Buddhist fables, originated in which Indian Language?

A. Hindi B. Urdu
C. Pali D. Bengali

20. The autobiography titled 'Wings of fire' belongs to:

A. Mahatma Gandhi
B. Rabindranath Tagore
C. Jawaharlal Nehru
D. A.P.J. Abdul Kalam

21. Name the woman medical officer who got deployed at Siachen, the world's highest battlefield, marking a significant stride towards gender inclusivity in India's armed forces is:

A. Captain Payal Chabbra
B. Captain Geetika Kaul
C. Captain Beena Tiwari
D. None of these

22. Which among the following is not a carnivorous plant?

A. Pitcher plant
B. Venus fly trap
C. Waterwheel plant
D. Marsh mallow

23. 'Best Long Documentary Award' at the South Asian Film Festival of Montreal 2023 won by:

A. Gujrat
B. Gauri
C. Scam
D. Bharat Mata Ki

24. Gandhi Peace Prize award was instituted by Government of India in:

A. 2005 B. 2000
C. 1998 D. 1995

25. Who received 'Lifetime Achievement Award' at Filmfare Awards 2024?

A. Dharmendra
B. David Dhawan
C. Karan Johar
D. Siddharatha Roy Kapur

13. A	**14.** D	**15.** *	**16.** B	**17.** C	**18.** A	**19.** C	**20.** D
21. B	**22.** D	**23.** B	**24.** D	**25.** B			

26. Which institution announced special awards for artists above 75 years of age?
A. Sangeet Natak Akademi
B. Lalit Kala Akademi
C. Sahitya Kala Akademi
D. ICCR

27. India announced a USD 250 million line of credit to ________ country for the modernization of its agricultural sector and to enhance bilateral ties in areas of defence, trade, health care.
A. Kenya B. Tanzania
C. South Africa D. Uganda

28. The process by which ammonia is converted into nitrate is:
A. Nitrogen-fixation B. Ammonification
C. Denitrification D. Nitrification

29. Hair is mainly used for which of the following?
A. Defence B. Coloration
C. Insulation D. Sensation

30. The origin of Lassa and Ebola is:
A. Humans B. Fruit bats
C. Primates D. Pigeons

31. Japan hosted _____ G7 Summit in 2023.
A. 49th B. 48th
C. 47th D. 46th

32. _______ two cities jointly secured the cleanest city title at the Swachh Survekshan Awards 2023, with one of them winning the accolade for the seventh time.
A. Varanasi and Surat
B. Kerala and Indore
C. Indore and Varanasi
D. Indore and Surat

33. The Kashi Tamil Sangaman 2023 was inaugurated on December 17, 2023 at:
A. Varanasi B. Coimbatore
C. Mathura D. None of these

34. What is the name of the joint military exercise conducted between Indian and US Army Special Forces?
A. Garula Shield
B. Vajra Prahar
C. Surya Talwar
D. Shakti

35. The term "Acid" as defined under Explanation 1 of Section 326B of the IPC 1860 includes:

Any substance which is:
A. Acidic in nature
B. Of corrosive character
C. Is of burning in nature and capable of causing bodily injury leading to scar or disfigurement or temporary or permanent disability
D. All of the above

36. Which of the following statements regarding abetment under Indian Penal Code is correct?
A. Abetment of an offence requires the act to be committed by the abettor directly.
B. Abetment may involve instigation, engagement in conspiracy, or intentional aid to commit an offence.
C. Abetment is not considered an offence under Indian Penal Code.
D. Abetment can only occur if the person abetted has the same guilty intention or knowledge as the abettor.

37. Under Indian Penal Code, the unlawful assembly consists of how many persons?
A. Two or more B. Three or more
C. Four or more D. Five or more

38. ________ is no longer a criminal offence as the Supreme Court of India scrapped Section 497 of Indian Penal Code, 1860.
A. Dacoity B. Adultery
C. Bribery D. Petty theft

26. A	**27.** A	**28.** D	**29.** *	**30.** *	**31.** A	**32.** D	**33.** A
34. B	**35.** D	**36.** B	**37.** D	**38.** B			

39. The headquarter of United Nations is situated in:
A. Paris
B. The Hague
C. New York
D. More than one of the above

40. The most recent state to join the United Nations Organisation, which was recognized as an independent nation in 2011 is:
A. Sweden B. South Sudan
C. Spain D. Sri Lanka

41. In 2006, the ______ was changed and renamed as Human Rights Council.
A. Humanitarian Council
B. UN Commission on Human Rights
C. Humanitarian Commission
D. Human Rights Commission

42. In which year did the UN General Assembly adopted the resolution called 'Uniting for Peace Resolution'?
A. 1951 B. 1950
C. 1968 D. 1967

43. How many Articles and Chapters are there in the Charter of the United Nations Organisation in total?
A. 110 Articles and 20 Chapters
B. 111 Articles and 19 Chapters
C. 115 Articles and 25 Chapters
D. 114 Articles and 28 Chapters

44. According to the theory of 'social utilitarianism' as propounded by Ihering:
A. Greatest number of people should get greatest pleasure.
B. The essential body of legal rules is always based upon the social "facts" of law.
C. A balance is to be struck between the competing interests in society.
D. Law is a means to social ends.

45. "The spirit of the common law" is a significant work of:
A. Montesquieu B. Dicey
C. Austin D. Roscoe Pound

46. Which school of juris is concerned with "positus"?
A. Sociological B. Analytical
C. Historical D. Realist school

47. Who wrote the book "law and the modern mind"?
A. Gray B. Holmes
C. Jerome Frank D. Llewellyn

48. Under Section 6(c) of Hindu Minority and Guardianship Act, the natural guardian of a married minor girl is:
A. Father B. Mother
C. Husband D. None of these

49. One person is said to be an agnate of another:
A. Two are related by blood or adoption wholly through males
B. Two are related by blood or adoption but not wholly through males
C. Two are related by blood or adoption but wholly through females
D. None of the above

50. A marriage may be solemnized between any two Hindus, if:
A. Neither party has a spouse living at the time of marriage.
B. The bridegroom has completed the age of 21 years and the bride, the age of 18 years at the time of marriage.
C. The parties are not sapindas of each other, unless the custom or usage governing each of them permits of a marriage between the two.
D. All of the above

39. C	**40.** B	**41.** B	**42.** B	**43.** B	**44.** D	**45.** D	**46.** B
47. C	**48.** C	**49.** A	**50.** D				

51. An adoption can be made by:
A. A Hindu Male
B. A Hindu Female
C. Both (A) and (B)
D. Only (A) and not (B)

52. The Panjab & Haryana High Court quashed Haryana's 75% private job reservation law, declaring ______ Act unconstitutional.
A. The Employee's State Insurance Act, 1948
B. SC reservation Act, 1976
C. The Haryana State Employment of Local Candidates Act, 2020
D. None of the above

53. The Sabarimala Temple case dealt with the entry of women aged:
A. Below 10 years B. 10-18 years
C. 18-30 years D. 10-50 years

54. Who among the following Vice-Presidents in India resigned from his office to contest the elections of President?
A. Fakhruddin Ali Ahmed
B. V.V. Giri
C. R. Venkataraman
D. None of these

55. The Exchange of enclaves between India and Bangladesh was executed through ______ amendment.
A. 100th B. 101th
C. 102nd D. 99th

56. The procedure for amendment of the Indian Constitution has been borrowed from:
A. Constitution of France
B. Constitution of USA
C. Constitution of Germany
D. Constitution of South Africa

57. Fundamental duties inserted in the Constitution of India on the recommendations of:
A. Swaran Singh Committee
B. Nehru Committee
C. Mandal Committee
D. Gadgill Committee

58. The Constitution (fifty-ninth) Amendment Act was made in the year of:
A. 1987 B. 1986
C. 1988 D. 1985

59. Which of the following Articles in the constitution of India contains the expression 'mother tongue'?
A. Article 350 B. Article 350A
C. Article 351A D. Article 360

60. Which amendment of Indian Constitution provides for the establishment of National Commission for Scheduled Castes and Scheduled Tribes?
A. 90th B. 89th
C. 91st D. 88th

61. AI for Good Global Summit, 2023 was held in Geneva from:
A. July 6-7 B. July 1-4
C. July 7-10 D. July 10-13

62. Which country hosted the ASEAN countries conference on Traditional Medicines?
A. Thailand B. India
C. Sri Lanka D. Myanmar

63. Which country hosted the Sustainable Development Goals (SDGs) Summit in September, 2023?
A. New Delhi B. New York
C. Paris D. Nairobi

64. In a certain code, RAT is written as 12 and RAN as 6, then RAG is written in the same code as:
A. 6 B. 7
C. 8 D. 9

51. C	**52.** C	**53.** D	**54.** B	**55.** A	**56.** D	**57.** A	**58.** C
59. B	**60.** *	**61.** A	**62.** B	**63.** B	**64.** C		

65. A is the son of C; C and Q are sisters; Z is the mother of Q and P is the son of Z. Which of the following statements is true?
A. P and A are cousins
B. P is the maternal uncle of A
C. Q is the maternal grandfather of A
D. C and P are sisters

66. If RAMON is written as 12345 and DINESH as 675849, then HAMAM will be written as:
A. 92233 B. 92323
C. 93322 D. 93232

67. Consider the following relationship among members of a family of six persons A, B, C, D, E, F:
(*a*) The number of males equals that of females.
(*b*) A & E are sons of F.
(*c*) D is the mother of two, one boy & one girl.
(*d*) B is the son of A.
(*e*) There is only one married couple in the family at present.
Which one of the following inferences can be drawn from the above?
A. A, B & C are all females
B. A is husband of D
C. E & F are children of D
D. D is the daughter of F

68. A boy asked Shruti what is her relation to Aman? To which she said, "Aman is the only brother of my son-in-law's wife." What is the relation between Shruti and Aman?
A. Mother and Son B. Father and Son
C. Aunt and Nephew D. None of these

69. What is the new award instituted to honour scientists in India?
A. PM Vigyan Puraskar
B. Rashtriya Vigyan Puraskar
C. Bharat Vigyan Puraskar
D. Deen Dayal Vigyan Puraskar

70. Who is called the 'Father of Green Revolution' in India?
A. Verghese Kurian B. M.S. Swaminathan
C. Dhayan Chand D. Vikram Sarabhai

71. Jon Fosse who won the 2023 Nobel Prize in Literature, is from which country?
A. USA B. Germany
C. Norway D. Australia

72. A is the sister of B whose father is D. If the wife of D is E whose only son C has 2 sisters. Then identify how is B related to E?
A. Mother B. Sister
C. Son D. Daughter

73. Who formed Swaraj Party?
A. Udham Singh B. Bhagat Singh
C. C.R. Dass D. Lala Lajpat Rai

74. Which state is earlier known as 'Magadha'?
A. Punjab B. Uttar Pradesh
C. Himachal Pradesh D. Bihar

75. "The mound of the dead" is the local name of:
A. Harappan Civilization
B. Mohenjo-Daro
C. Sumerian Civilization
D. None of these

76. What is the lifespan of RBCs in human body?
A. 120 days B. 12 days
C. 10 days D. 20 days

77. Find the antonym for 'Ubiquitous'.
A. Scarce B. Abundant
C. Pervasive D. Limited

78. Identify the sentence with the correct use of the modal verb 'can'.
A. She cans play piano
B. He can to swim
C. They can't make it to the meeting
D. I can travels to the world

65. B	**66.** B	**67.** B	**68.** A	**69.** B	**70.** B	**71.** C	**72.** D
73. C	**74.** D	**75.** B	**76.** A	**77.** *	**78.** C		

79. Identify the antonym for the word 'Generous'.
A. Selfish B. Gracious
C. Benevolent D. Altruistic

80. The principle that when Act was not done at the desire of the promisor and hence no consideration was laid down in:
A. Abdul Aziz v. Masum Ali
B. Dutton v. Poole
C. Tweedle v. Atkinson
D. Durga Prasad v. Baldeo

81. 'Moses v. Macferlan' is a case relating to:
A. Theory of unjust enrichment
B. The right of lien
C. Test of agency
D. Doctrine of frustration

82. Voidable contract is one:
A. Which is lawful
B. Which is invalid
C. Which is valid if it is not avoided by the party entitled to do so
D. Which is unlawful

83. When the agreement is caused by coercion, fraud or misrepresentation the agreement is:
A. Illegal B. Unenforceable
C. Void D. Voidable

84. One who can use both hands:
A. Ambivert B. Ambidextrous
C. Martinet D. Introvert

85. Which one of the following is a correct sentence?
A. Ram is more tall than Sham
B. Ram is not more tall than Sham
C. Ram is taller than Sham
D. Ram is taller to Sham

86. Choose the correct synonym of **Germinate**.
A. Decay B. Breed
C. Produce D. Sprout

87. Choose the correct plural form of **underlined** word:
The <u>nucleus</u> of atoms consists of **protons** and neutrons.
A. Nucleuses B. Nuclei
C. Nucleous D. None of these

88. Complete the blank with the right **proposition.**
Rajnish has not slept _______ yesterday.
A. through B. by
C. since D. on

89. Choose the option that contains the **right** proposition to complete the sentence:
His mother shouted _______ him when **he** came home late.
A. on B. over
C. for D. at

90. Choose the correct meaning of the **idiom** used in a sentence:
He is feeling a bit under the weather.
A. Not able to do something as well **as** before
B. Feeling slightly ill
C. To loose control
D. None of the above

91. Choose the correct meaning of the **below** mentioned idiom:
Queer the pitch
A. Postpone something for later
B. Ruin someone's plans/mood
C. Spoil a plan
D. None of these

92. Choose the correct meaning of the **idiom** used in a sentence:
Break a leg in your exam today
A. Very calm and composed
B. Focus closely so
C. In good health
D. Good luck

79. A	**80.** D	**81.** A	**82.** C	**83.** D	**84.** B	**85.** C	**86.** D
87. B	**88.** C	**89.** D	**90.** B	**91.** *	**92.** D		

93. Substitute one word for study of languages:
A. Philology B. Anthropology
C. Lithography D. Biology

94. Fair comment is regarded as a defense for the tort of:
A. Nuisance
B. Abuse of legal procedure
C. Defamation
D. None of these

95. Which of the following is not an exception to Rylands v. Fletcher?
A. Act of God
B. Act of third party
C. Plaintiff's own default
D. Absolute Privilege

96. The rule of Absolute Liability was laid down in:
A. M.C. Mehta v. Union of India
B. Donoghue v. Stevenson
C. Wilkinson v. Downtown
D. None of the above

97. "Tort is a civil wrong for which the remedy is a common law action for unliquidated damages, and which is not exclusively the breach of a contract or the breach of a trust or other merely equitable obligation." This definition was given by:
A. Fraser B. Winfield
C. Salmond D. Limitation Act, 1963

98. If there is a contract between A and B and as a result of the breach of contract by A, injury is caused to C. 'C', who is a stranger to the contract, bring an action against A, whose breach of contract with B has also resulted in the commission of tort against C, this was laid down in:
A. Haynes v. Harwood
B. Padmavati v. Dugganaika
C. Ushaben v. Bhagyalaxmi Chitra Mandi
D. Donoghue v. Stevenson

99. "*Volenti non fit injuria*" means:
A. Defense of consent
B. Act of God
C. Private defence
D. Mistake

100. Jacob Mathew v. State of Punjab is a landmark case related to:
A. Deficiency of educational services
B. Medical negligence
C. Contributory negligence
D. Composite negligence

EXPLANATORY ANSWERS

1. (C): India has 42 UNESCO World Heritage sites as of the latest update. This number includes both cultural and natural heritage sites that are recognized for their universal value and significance, according to the United Nations Educational, Scientific and Cultural Organization (UNESCO).

2. (B): The Iron Dome is an air defense system developed by Israel. It is designed to intercept and destroy short-range rockets and artillery shells fired from distances of 4 to 70 kilometers away. The system was first deployed by Israel in 2011 and has since been integral to its defense strategy against missile threats.

3. (A): The rocket that launched Chandrayaan-3, India's third lunar exploration mission, was the GSLV Mk-III, also known as LVM-3. This rocket, developed by the Indian Space Research Organisation, is currently India's most powerful launch vehicle and is designed to carry heavier payloads into higher orbits.

93. A **94.** C **95.** D **96.** A **97.** C **98.** D **99.** A **100.** B

4. (B): Modhera was declared the first round-the-clock solar-powered village in India on October 9, 2022. Located in Gujarat, this initiative is part of India's commitment to increasing the use of renewable energy sources.

5. (C): Justice DY Chandrachud is the 50th Chief Justice of India. He succeeded Uday Umesh Lalit and assumed office on November 9, 2022. His tenure is noted for various landmark judgments and the emphasis on enhancing the technological infrastructure of the Indian judiciary.

6. (B): The world's tallest Nataraja statue is located at Bharat Mandapam, which is part of the Delhi International Trade Fair area, Pragati Maidan in New Delhi, India. This statue is a representation of Lord Shiva as Nataraja, the Lord of Dance, and is a significant cultural and religious symbol in Hinduism.

8. (D): Amrita Sher-Gil, S.H. Raza, and M.F. Hussain were all prominent painters, known for their contributions to Indian art. S.P. Balasubrahmanyam, however, was a celebrated Indian musician and playback singer, not a painter.

9. (A): India shares a maritime boundary with Indonesia among the options provided. This boundary is situated in the Andaman Sea and the Indian Ocean, facilitating significant maritime interaction between the two nations. Malaysia, Singapore, and Vietnam do not share direct maritime borders with India.

10. (A): Chandipur-on-sea is located in the state of Odisha, on the east coast of India. This location is well-known for its unique beach that recedes up to 5 kilometers during low tide, providing a distinctive natural phenomenon and attracting tourists and researchers.

11. (C): India's first Smart Tribal Village has been inaugurated in Jammu & Kashmir. This initiative is part of broader efforts to integrate technology with rural development, providing advanced infrastructural benefits like internet connectivity and sustainable energy solutions to tribal communities.

12. (C): The common name of Calcium Sulphate Hemihydrate is Plaster of Paris. This compound is used primarily in building materials, especially for plastering walls and creating architectural moldings, due to its ability to harden quickly when mixed with water.

13. (A): British scientist J.J. Thomson was awarded the Nobel Prize in Physics in 1906 for the discovery of the electron. His experiments with cathode rays led to the identification of the electron as a subatomic particle, which was a pivotal development in the field of atomic physics.

14. (D): All the options given—Diamond, Graphite, and Fullerene—are allotropic forms of carbon, which means they are different structural variations of the same element. Therefore, the correct answer is "None of these," as all listed options are indeed allotropes of carbon.

16. (B): The pH of human blood is typically around 7.4. This slightly basic pH is crucial for maintaining homeostasis and ensuring that enzymatic reactions occur under optimal conditions within the body.

17. (C): Savitribai Phule, along with her husband Jyotirao Phule, was a pioneer in women's education in India. She established the 'Mahila Seva Mandal' and the 'Native Female School' in Pune, focusing on educating women and girls at a time when such initiatives were rare and revolutionary for women's rights in India.

18. (A): The 'doctrine of proportionality' is applied by the judiciary to ensure that laws and government actions maintain a reasonable balance and do not excessively infringe on individuals' rights or freedoms. This doctrine is used to assess whether the measures taken are appropriate and necessary in relation to the aim pursued.

19. (C): The Jataka tales, which are a collection of stories concerning the previous births of Gautama Buddha, were originally composed in the Pali language. These tales are an important part of Buddhist literature and serve to teach moral lessons and the virtues of Buddhist philosophy.

20. (D): The autobiography titled 'Wings of Fire' was authored by Dr. A.P.J. Abdul Kalam, who was an esteemed scientist and the 11th President of India.

21. (B): Captain Geetika Kaul is the woman medical officer who was deployed at Siachen, the world's highest battlefield. This deployment marks a significant step toward gender inclusivity in the Indian armed forces, highlighting the increasing roles and recognition of women in areas previously dominated by male personnel.

22. (D): Among the options given, the Marsh mallow is not a carnivorous plant. While the Pitcher plant, Venus fly trap, and Waterwheel plant are all carnivorous, capturing and digesting insects to obtain nutrients, the Marsh mallow is a non-carnivorous plant known for its medicinal properties and is commonly found in wet areas.

23. (B): The 'Best Long Documentary Award' at the South Asian Film Festival of Montreal 2023 was won by the documentary titled 'Gauri.' This film likely covered impactful themes or narratives that resonated well with the jury and audience, securing its win at the festival.

24. (D): The Gandhi Peace Prize was instituted by the Government of India in 1995. This international award is named after Mahatma Gandhi and is awarded to individuals and institutions for their contributions towards social, economic, and political transformation through non-violence and other Gandhian methods.

25. (B): At the Filmfare Awards 2024, the 'Lifetime Achievement Award' was received by David Dhawan. This award recognizes his extensive career and significant contributions to the Indian film industry, particularly in the genre of comedy, where he has directed many successful films.

26. (A): The Sangeet Natak Akademi announced special awards for artists above 75 years of age. This prestigious institution is dedicated to promoting the performing arts in India, including music, dance, and drama.

27. (A): India announced a USD 250 million line of credit to Kenya for the modernization of its agricultural sector and to enhance bilateral ties in areas of defense, trade, and healthcare. This financial aid aims to support Kenya's agricultural advancements and strengthen the collaborative efforts between the two nations in various key sectors, reflecting India's commitment to fostering development and cooperation with African countries.

28. (D): The process by which ammonia is converted into nitrate is known as nitrification. This is a two-step process involving different types of bacteria. Initially, ammonia is oxidized to nitrite by ammonia-oxidizing bacteria (AOB), and subsequently, nitrite is converted to nitrate by nitrite-oxidizing bacteria (NOB). This biochemical process is crucial for the nitrogen cycle in ecosystems, helping to convert nitrogen into forms that can be absorbed by plants.

31. (A): Japan hosted the 49th G7 Summit in 2023. The G7, or Group of Seven, is an intergovernmental organization consisting of

Canada, France, Germany, Italy, Japan, the United Kingdom, and the United States.

32. (D): Indore and Surat jointly secured the cleanest city title at the Swachh Survekshan Awards 2023. Notably, Indore won this accolade for the seventh consecutive time, underlining its sustained efforts in urban sanitation and waste management.

33. (A): The Kashi Tamil Sangaman 2023 was inaugurated on December 17, 2023, in Varanasi. This event was designed to strengthen cultural ties between Tamil Nadu and Varanasi, highlighting the shared historical and spiritual heritage of these regions.

34. (B): The joint military exercise conducted between Indian and US Army Special Forces is named Vajra Prahar. This annual exercise is designed to enhance the interoperability and cooperation between the special forces of the two nations, focusing on a variety of tactics including counter-terrorism and high-intensity conflict scenarios.

35. (D): Under Explanation 1 of Section 326 B of the IPC 1860, the term "Acid" includes any substance of a corrosive character, acidic in nature, and capable of causing bodily injury leading to scar, disfigurement, or temporary or permanent disability. This comprehensive definition is aimed at addressing the severity and varying circumstances of acid attacks.

36. (B): Abetment under the Indian Penal Code correctly involves instigation, engagement in conspiracy, or intentional aid to commit an offence. This broad definition ensures that all forms of encouragement or support to commit a crime are covered under the law, not just direct participation.

37. (D): Under the Indian Penal Code, an unlawful assembly consists of five or more persons. This group must intend to conduct themselves in a manner that disturbs the public peace or that involves any use of force or show of force against people or property.

38. (B): Adultery is no longer a criminal offence, as the Supreme Court of India scrapped Section 497 of the Indian Penal Code, 1860.

39. (C): The headquarters of the United Nations is situated in New York City, USA. The UN, established in 1945, is an international organization aimed at fostering international peace and security.

40. (B): The most recent state to join the United Nations Organization, which was recognized as an independent nation in 2011, is South Sudan. Following its independence from Sudan after a long conflict, South Sudan became the 193rd member state of the UN.

41. (B): In 2006, the UN Commission on Human Rights was changed and renamed as the Human Rights Council. This transformation was aimed at addressing criticisms and enhancing the efficiency and effectiveness of the global human rights monitoring body.

42. (B): The UN General Assembly adopted the resolution called 'Uniting for Peace Resolution' in 1950. This resolution allows the General Assembly to take action in maintaining international peace and security when the Security Council is unable, primarily due to the veto power of any of its five permanent members.

43. (B): The Charter of the United Nations Organisation comprises 111 Articles and is organized into 19 Chapters. This foundational document sets out the rights and obligations of member states, and the structure and functioning of the UN bodies.

44. (D): According to the theory of 'social utilitarianism' as propounded by Ihering, law is a means to social ends. This perspective emphasizes that law should serve to achieve societal goals, rather than just reflecting abstract principles or individual interests, focusing on the practical impacts of laws within society.

45. (D): "The Spirit of the Common Law" is a significant work of Roscoe Pound. In this work, Pound expounds on his legal philosophy, particularly his views on how the common law has evolved and its implications for society, reflecting his foundational role in the sociological school of jurisprudence.

46. (B): The Analytical school of jurisprudence is concerned with "positus," focusing on the law as it is — that is, laws that are enacted and enforced, rather than moral arguments or societal impacts. This school, often associated with thinkers like John Austin, prioritizes the structure and nature of law in its analysis.

47. (C): Jerome Frank wrote the book "Law and the Modern Mind." Frank was a leading figure in the American legal realist movement, and his work often addressed the complexities of legal reasoning and the uncertainties inherent in the judicial process.

48. (C): Under section 6(c) of the Hindu Minority and Guardianship Act, the natural guardian of a married minor girl is her husband. This provision recognizes the husband as the primary caretaker and guardian in the context of the legal framework governing Hindu marriages in India.

49. (A): One person is said to be an agnate of another if the two are related by blood or adoption wholly through males. This concept is significant in various legal and cultural contexts, where lineage and inheritance through the male line are recognized and given legal relevance.

50. (D): A marriage may be solemnized between any two Hindus, if all the conditions listed in options A, B, and C are met. These conditions ensure that the marriage is legally valid and socially acceptable, including aspects such as the absence of a living spouse, age requirements, and non-violation of prohibitions against marrying within certain close relationships or kinship networks, known as sapindas.

51. (C): An adoption can be made by both a Hindu male and a Hindu female as specified under the Hindu Adoption and Maintenance Act, 1956. The Act allows any adult Hindu, whether male or female, who is of sound mind and not disqualified by law, to legally adopt a child.

52. (C): The Punjab & Haryana High Court quashed Haryana's 75% private job reservation law, specifically the Haryana State Employment of Local Candidates Act, 2020, declaring it unconstitutional.

53. (D): The Sabarimala Temple case dealt with the entry of women aged between 10 to 50 years. The Supreme Court of India lifted the traditional ban on the entry of women of menstrual age into the temple, considering it a discriminatory practice against women, thereby ensuring equality before the law as enshrined in the Constitution.

54. (B): V.V. Giri resigned from his office as Vice-President of India to contest the elections of President. He is notable for taking this step to actively engage in the presidential race, which he subsequently won, serving as the President of India from 1969 to 1974.

55. (A): The exchange of enclaves between India and Bangladesh was executed through the 100th amendment of the Indian Constitution. This amendment, enacted in 2015, facilitated the operationalization of the 1974 India-Bangladesh Land Boundary Agreement.

56. (D): The procedure for amendment of the Indian Constitution has been borrowed from the Constitution of South Africa. This influence is particularly evident in the requirement of a two-thirds majority in Parliament for amendments, similar to the South African model, which aims at ensuring a broad consensus in the legislative process for constitutional changes.

57. (A): Fundamental duties were inserted in the Constitution of India based on the recommendations of the Swaran Singh Committee. Established in 1976, the committee suggested the inclusion of a specific chapter in the Constitution outlining the fundamental duties of the citizens towards the state to promote a conscious and active citizenry.

58. (C): The Constitution (fifty-ninth) Amendment Act was made in the year 1988. This amendment was significant for allowing the imposition of emergency in Punjab due to the internal disturbances at the time. It also enabled the suspension of some fundamental rights during the emergency period.

59. (B): Article 350A in the constitution of India contains the expression 'mother tongue'. This article obligates every state and local authority to provide adequate facilities for instruction in the mother tongue at the primary stage of education to children belonging to linguistic minority groups, ensuring the preservation and promotion of cultural and linguistic heritage.

61. (A): The AI for Good Global Summit, 2023 was held in Geneva from July 6-7. This event, organized annually by the International Telecommunication Union in partnership with other UN organizations, focuses on leveraging artificial intelligence to address global challenges and achieve the Sustainable Development Goals.

62. (B): India hosted the ASEAN countries conference on Traditional Medicines. The conference aimed to explore and share knowledge on traditional medicines among ASEAN countries, reflecting India's significant historical and contemporary contributions to this field and promoting cooperation in alternative medicine practices.

63. (B): The Sustainable Development Goals (SDGs) Summit in September 2023 was hosted by New York. This summit, part of the United Nations General Assembly high-level week, focuses on reviewing progress towards the SDGs, addressing challenges, and planning further actions to achieve these global goals by 2030.

64. (C): Given in a certain code,

RAT = 12

$\Rightarrow 18 + 1 + 20 = 39 \Rightarrow 3 + 9 = 12$

and RAN = 6

$\Rightarrow 18 + 1 + 14 = 33 \Rightarrow 3 + 3 = 6$

Similarly, RAG = ?

$\Rightarrow 18 + 1 + 7 = 26 \Rightarrow 2 + 6 = 8$

$\therefore$ RAG = 8

So, RAG is written as 8.

65. (B):

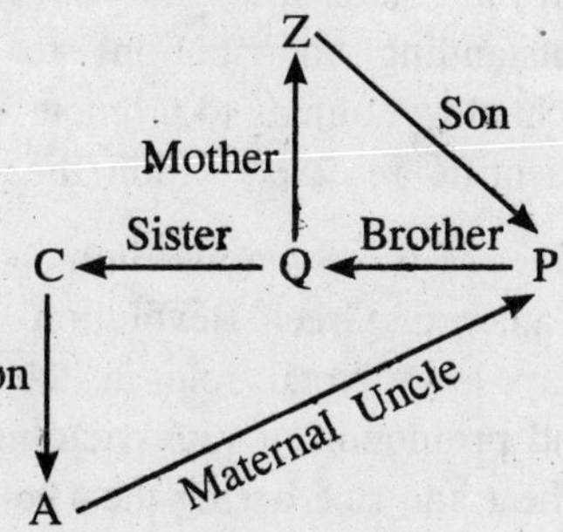

Here, P is the maternal uncle of A.

66. (B): Given,

R A M O N and D I N E S H

↓ ↓ ↓ ↓ ↓ ↓ ↓ ↓ ↓ ↓ ↓

1 2 3 4 5 6 7 5 8 4 9

Similarly, H A M A M

↓ ↓ ↓ ↓ ↓

9 2 3 2 3

So, HAMAM will be written as 92323.

67. (B):

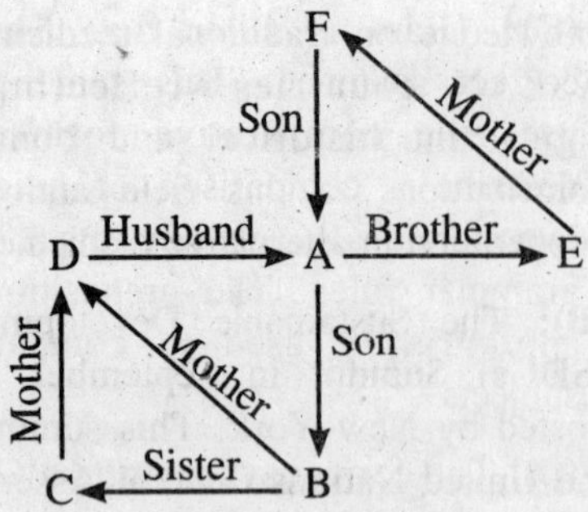

Here, A is the husband of D.

68. (A):

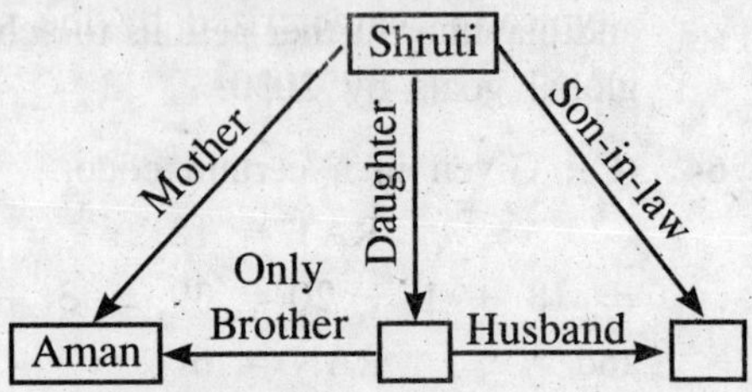

Here, mother and son is the relation between Shruti and Aman.

69. (B): The new award instituted to honour scientists in India is called the Rashtriya Vigyan Puraskar. This award recognizes outstanding contributions to science and technology, aiming to promote and encourage scientific research within the country.

70. (B): M.S. Swaminathan is called the 'Father of Green Revolution' in India. He played a pivotal role in the development and promotion of high-yielding varieties of wheat and rice during the 1960s and 1970s, which significantly increased food production and averted famine in India, transforming the agricultural landscape.

71. (C): Jon Fosse, who won the 2023 Nobel Prize in Literature, is from Norway. He is renowned for his minimalist style and has been a major figure in European literature, known especially for his plays and novels. His work often explores existential themes and the complexities of human relationships.

72. (D):

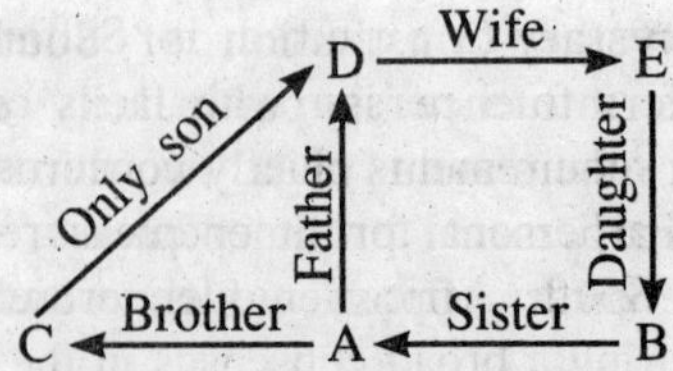

Here, B is the daughter of E.

73. (C): The Swaraj Party was formed by C.R. Dass, along with Motilal Nehru, in 1923. This was after the dissatisfaction with the non-cooperation movement led by Mahatma Gandhi, which was abruptly called off following the Chauri Chaura incident.

74. (D): The state earlier known as 'Magadha' is Bihar. This ancient kingdom played a significant role in the historical and cultural development of India and was known for its contributions to early Indian politics, religion, and philosophy.

75. (B): "The mound of the dead" is the local name for Mohenjo-Daro, one of the major cities of the ancient Indus Valley Civilization. Located in present-day Pakistan, Mohenjo-Daro was one of the world's earliest major urban centers, known for its advanced urban planning and civil engineering.

76. (A): The lifespan of RBCs (Red Blood Cells) in the human body is approximately 120 days. These cells are crucial for transporting oxygen from the lungs to various parts of the body and returning carbon dioxide back to the lungs for exhalation.

78. (C): "They can't make it to the meeting" is the sentence with the correct use of the modal verb 'can'. The negative form 'can't' (cannot) is properly used here to indicate inability or impossibility in the context of attendance.

79. (A): The antonym for 'Generous', which means showing a readiness to give more of something, especially money, than is strictly necessary or expected, is 'Selfish'. 'Selfish' refers to a person who lacks consideration for others and is chiefly concerned with their own personal profit or pleasure, making it the direct opposite of generous.

80. (D): In the case of 'Durga Prasad v. Baldeo', the principle established was that if an act is not done at the desire of the promisor, then there is no consideration. This Indian contract law case emphasized that for consideration to be valid, it must be done at the promisor's request, aligning with the legal requirements for forming a valid contract.

81. (A): 'Moses v. Macferlan' is a landmark case relating to the theory of unjust enrichment. The judgment by Lord Mansfield laid down foundational principles for the claim of money had and received to the plaintiff's use, establishing that a person who receives money wrongfully at another's expense should repay it, aligning with the broader principles of equity and justice.

82. (C): A voidable contract is one which is valid until one of the parties entitled to do so chooses to avoid it. This option describes the nature of voidable contracts accurately, where the validity of the contract depends on the continued acceptance of the contract terms by the aggrieved party.

83. (D): When an agreement is caused by coercion, fraud, or misrepresentation, it is considered voidable. This legal provision allows the party whose consent was affected by such undue influences to decide whether to proceed with or void the agreement, giving them the right to seek redress or affirmation of the contract.

84. (B): One who can use both hands with equal skill is described as 'Ambidextrous'. This term specifically refers to the ability to use both hands with comparable proficiency, often in contexts involving manual dexterity or fine motor skills.

85. (C): "Ram is taller than Sham" is the correct sentence. This sentence correctly uses the comparative form "taller" to describe a comparison of height between two individuals, adhering to standard English grammar rules. The preposition "than" is appropriately used to compare the two subjects.

86. (D): The correct synonym for 'Germinate' is 'Sprout'. Germination refers to the process in which a seed develops into a new plant, typically characterized by the sprouting of a seedling from a seed.

87. (B): The correct plural form of the underlined word 'nucleus' is 'nuclei'. In scientific and technical contexts, 'nucleus' refers to the central and most important part of an object, movement, or group, forming the basis for its activity and growth. 'Nuclei' is the standard plural form in both common usage and scientific terminology.

88. (C): The correct preposition to complete the sentence "Rajnish has not slept _______ yesterday" is 'since'. This preposition is used to indicate the point in time from which a particular period began, which in this case is 'yesterday'. It correctly conveys that Rajnish hasn't slept at any point after yesterday began.

89. (D): In the sentence "His mother shouted _______ him when he came home late," the correct preposition is 'at'. This preposition is used to indicate direction or orientation, particularly in verbal exchanges, and is commonly used with verbs of communication like 'shouted' to indicate the target of the action.

90. (B): "He is feeling a bit under the weather" means 'Feeling slightly ill'. This idiom is commonly used to describe a person who is not feeling well, typically due to minor illnesses. It suggests a less than optimal health condition but not severely ill.

92. (D): "Break a leg" is an idiomatic expression commonly used to wish someone good luck, especially before they perform or have a significant event such as an exam. The phrase originated in theatre as a way of wishing performers good luck without saying those exact words, which is considered bad luck.

93. (A): "Philology" is the study of languages, especially their historical development and relationships. It involves the examination of literary texts and written records, the establishment of their authenticity and original form, and the determination of their meaning. Thus, philology is the correct term for the study of languages.

94. (C): "Fair comment" is regarded as a defense for the tort of defamation. This legal principle allows individuals to make statements that are opinion-based, provided they are on matters of public interest and are not made maliciously.

95. (D): "Absolute Privilege" is not an exception to the rule established in Rylands v. Fletcher. The Rylands v. Fletcher rule states that a person who keeps hazardous materials on their property is liable for any damage caused if those materials escape. The recognized exceptions to this rule include Act of God, act of a third party, plaintiff's own default, and statutory authority.

96. (A): The rule of Absolute Liability was laid down in M.C. Mehta v. Union of India. This landmark judgment by the Supreme Court of India evolved from the principle of strict liability established in Rylands v. Fletcher.

97. (C): The definition of tort as a civil wrong for which the remedy is a common law action for unliquidated damages, and which is not exclusively the breach of a contract, the breach of a trust, or other merely equitable obligation was given by Salmond. This definition emphasizes that torts are civil wrongs that are redressable by damages and are distinct from contractual or equitable wrongs.

98. (D): The case of Donoghue v. Stevenson laid down the principle where a party can bring an action for negligence even if there was no direct contractual relationship with the defendant. This foundational case in the development of modern law of negligence involved a woman who became ill after consuming a ginger beer that contained a decomposed snail, though she had not purchased the bottle herself. It established the "duty of care" owed to one's neighbors—defined as those who might foreseeably be affected by one's actions. The principle from this case is relevant in situations where a breach of contract with one party also results in the commission of a tort against a third party, as it broadens the scope of duty beyond direct contractual relationships.

99. (A): "Volenti non fit injuria" means the defense of consent. This legal doctrine holds that a person who knowingly and voluntarily consents to and takes on a risk cannot claim damages for the harm that results from it. This principle is commonly applied in cases where individuals engage in dangerous sports or activities.

100. (B): Jacob Mathew v. State of Punjab is a landmark case related to medical negligence. The Supreme Court of India clarified the standards and scope for criminal liability of doctors, emphasizing that a high degree of negligence is necessary to warrant criminal prosecution, thus protecting medical professionals from frivolous lawsuits while ensuring accountability.

Previous Years' Paper

LL.B. (3 Year Course)
Entrance Exam, 2023*

1. Who wrote the book India Wins Freedom?
A. Akhilesh Tilotia
B. Amitav Ghosh
C. Maulana A.K. Azad
D. A.B. Vajpayee

2. World Milk Day is celebrated on:
A. 1 June B. 3 June
C. 5 June D. 7 June

3. Rearing of silkworms for the production of silk fiber is known as:
A. Sericulture B. Aquaculture
C. Apiculture D. Pisciculture

4. 'Sattriya' is the Classical Dance of which state?
A. Arunachal Pradesh
B. Assam
C. Rajasthan
D. Bihar

5. Which festival is also known as 'Mahakumbh of the East'?
A. Hornbill Festival B. Moatsu Mong
C. Ambubachi Mela D. Bihu Festival

6. Who has taken the historic task of decorating the original manuscript of the Constitution of India?
A. Nandalal Bose
B. Abanindranath Tagore
C. Prem Behari Lal
D. Rabindranath Tagore

7. In which of the following years were the first Oscar awards presented?
A. 1920 B. 1923
C. 1929 D. 1933

8. What is the Milk of Rubber plant called?
A. Latex B. Reisen
C. Rubber D. Polymer

9. Scientific name of Neem is?
A. *Azadirachta indica*
B. *Ocimum tenuiflorum*
C. *Mangifera indica*
D. *Ficus religiosa*

10. The Tropic of Cancer passes through which state?
A. Madhya Pradesh
B. Maharashtra
C. Karnataka
D. Odisha

11. Which is the world's first airport to fully run on solar power?
A. Dubai B. Vancouver
C. Cochin D. Zurich

12. Who led Mahad Satyagraha?
A. Mahatma Gandhi
B. Dr. B.R. Ambedkar
C. Acharya Vinoba Bhave
D. Bal Gangadhar Tilak

1. C	**2.** A	**3.** A	**4.** B	**5.** C	**6.** A
7. C	**8.** A	**9.** A	**10.** A	**11.** C	**12.** B

*Conducted by Panjab University, Chandigarh

13. The provision for establishment of Supreme Court of Calcutta was made in which Act?
A. Regulating Act of 1773
B. Indian Council Act, 1861
C. Charter Act of 1813
D. Pitt's India Act, 1784

14. Who discovered the *x*-ray?
A. Maxwell B. Wilhelm Rontgen
C. Faraday D. Hertz

15. In the human body, fats are stored in the
A. Epidermis B. Adipose tissue
C. Liver D. Epithelium

16. What does airbag, used for safety of car driver, contain?
A. Sodium bicarbonate
B. Sodium azide
C. Sodium nitrite
D. Sodium peroxide

17. Ten-rupee note contains the signature of:
A. Finance Secretary, Government of India
B. Chairman, Reserve Bank of India
C. Finance Minister, Government of India
D. Governor, Reserve Bank of India

18. Gilt-edged market is:
A. Bullion market
B. Market of government securities
C. Market of guns
D. Market of pure metals

19. Who was the first woman to become a Chief Election Commissioner of India?
A. V.S. Ramadevi B. G.D. Das
C. S.K. Bedi D. R.M. Nikam

20. In which year the first General Election was held in India after Independence?
A. September 1947 – January 1948
B. March 1948 – July 1948
C. January 1950 – May 1950
D. October 1951 – February 1952

21. When was the last earth summit held?
A. 2012 B. 2014
C. 2016 D. 2018

22. During the Election of President in 2022, President Droupadi Murmu clear edge over:
A. Nitish Kumar
B. Yashwant Sinha
C. Mallikarjun Kharge
D. Jairam Ramesh

23. Assamese __________ got GI Tag.
A. Kati Bihu B. Gamocha
C. Chaklang D. Siraj

24. Who is the President of Indian Olympic Association Executive Council?
A. Ms. M.C. Mary Kom
B. Ms. P.T. Usha
C. Ms. Rajlaxmi Singh Deo
D. Lt. Gen. Harpal Singh

25. Full form of FSSAI is:
A. Food Safety and Standards Authority of India
B. Food Security and Standards Authority of India
C. Food Safety and Standards Association of India
D. Food Security and Safety Authority of India

26. Lviv is in which Country:
A. Russia B. Ukraine
C. Georgia D. Armenia

27. Chernobyl is famous for:
A. Nuclear Power Plant failure
B. Gold Mine
C. Coal Mine
D. Hydro Power Plant Failure

28. First woman to win olympic medal for India:
A. Mary Kom B. Saina Nehwal
C. K. Malleshwari D. P.V. Sindhu

13. A	**14.** B	**15.** B	**16.** B	**17.** D	**18.** B	**19.** A	**20.** D
21. A	**22.** B	**23.** B	**24.** B	**25.** A	**26.** B	**27.** A	**28.** C

29. The first Asian Games were held in:
A. Manila B. Tokyo
C. Jakarta D. New Delhi

30. Full form of INTERPOL
A. International Criminal Police Organ
B. International Criminal Police Organisation
C. Internal Criminal Police Office
D. International Crime Prevention Organisation

31. A continuous process of change is known as:
A. Flux B. Dynamism
C. Metamorphosis D. Transformation

32. People who belong to the same country:
A. Patriots B. Comrades
C. Compatriots D. Natives

33. Reasoning method involving two statements from which a conclusion is reached:
A. logism B. syllogism
C. rhetoric D. rhapsody

34. A person between 90 and 100 years old.
A. septuagenarian B. nonagenarian
C. centenarian D. octogenarian

35. Choose the one which best expresses the similar meaning of 'Bequeath':
A. Disclose B. Scold
C. Surround D. Give

36. A hater of marriage:
A. Misogamist B. Celibate
C. Betrothed D. Elope

37. Engaged to be married:
A. Betrothed B. Banns
C. Trousseau D. Misogamist

38. A man having more wives at a time:
A. Polyandry B. Polygamy
C. Group Family D. None of these

39. Ante-diluvium means:
A. Old time B. Up-to-date
C. A to Z D. None of these

40. He doesn't work with hands, he works ______ the machine.
A. with B. by
C. at D. on

41. If E = 5 and HOTEL = 12 then LAMB will be
A. 7 B. 10
C. 26 D. 28

42. One day, Tim left the home and cycled for 10 km southwards, turned right and cycled 5 km. Then he again turned right cycled 10 km and turned left and cycled 10 km. How many kilometers will he have to cycle to reach his home straight?
A. 10 km B. 15 km
C. 20 km D. 25 km

43. Jessi walks 10 kilometres towards north. From there, he walks 6 kilometres towards South. Then, he walks 3 kilometres towards East. How far and in which direction is he with reference to his starting point?
A. 5 kilometres West
B. 5 kilometres North-East
C. 7 kilometres East
D. 7 kilometres West

44. If INDIA is written as 914491, the DELHI will be written as?
A. 45389 B. 451289
C. 45489 D. 451279

45. A number consists of three digits whose sum is 10. The middle digit is equal to the sum of the other two and the number will be increased by 99 if its digits are reversed. The number is:
A. 145 B. 253
C. 370 D. 352

29. D	**30.** B	**31.** A	**32** C	**33.** B	**34.** C	**35.** D	**36.** A	**37.** A
38. B	**39.** A	**40.** C	**41.** A	**42.** B	**43.** B	**44.** B	**45.** B	

46. If the number obtained by interchanging the digits of two number is 18 more than the original number and the sum of the digits is 8, then what is the original number?

A. 26 B. 35

C. 53 D. None of these

47. The ratio 5:4 expressed as percentage is equal to:

A. 12.5% B. 40%

C. 80% D. 125%

48. P, Q and R are three typists who working simultaneously can type 216 pages in 4 hours. In one hour, R can type as many pages more than Q as Q can type more than P. During the period of 5 hours, R can type as many pages as P can during 7 hours. How many pages does each of them type per hour?

A. 14,17,20 B. 15,17,22

C. 15,18,21 D. 16,18,22

49. A can complete a piece of work in the same amount of time as B and C together take to complete the same work. A and B together can complete that work in 10 days and C alone can complete it in 50 days. How many days will it take for B to complete the work alone?

A. 20 B. 24

C. 25 D. 26

50. Three persons are walking from a place A to B. Their speed are in the ratio of 4:3:5. The time ratio to reach B by these persons will be:

A. 4:3:5 B. 5:3:4

C. 15:9:20 D. 15:20:12

51. Lila is more studious than Kim. Kim is not as studious as Pooja. Kajal is not as studious as Kim or Pooja. Who is in the last degree of being studious?

A. Lila B. Kim

C. Pooja D. Kajal

52. The time by a watch is 1:30. If the hour points towards west, in which direction will the minute hand point?

A. North-East B. North-West

C. South-East D. South-West

53. The mother of five students, A, B, C, D and E have different professions, i.e., teaching, music, medicine, law and architecture. A's mother is not an architect but E's mother is a singer. B's mother teaches while C's mother practice medicine. D's mother is not a lawyer. Whose mother is a lawyer?

A. A B. B

C. C D. E

54. If A=5, B=6, C=7, D=8, then the numbers 16, 5, 27, 29, 9, 22, 23 will give a word

A. Teacher B. Lawyers

C. Crawler D. Trainer

55. If every 2 out of 3 readymade shirts need alterations in the sleaves, every 3 out of 4 needs alterations in collars and every 4 out of 5 need it in the body, how many alterations will be required for 60 shirts?

A. 24 B. 123

C. 133 D. 143

56. In a class, 20% of the members own two cars each, 40% of the remaining members own three cars each and the remaining members own only one car each. Which of the following statements is definitely true from the given statements?

A. Only 20% of the total members own three cars each.

B. 48% of the total members own only one car each.

C. 60% of the total members own at least two cars each.

D. 80% of the total members own at least one car.

46. B **47.** D **48.** C 49 C **50.** D **51.** D **52.** A **53.** A **54.** B **55.** C **56.** B

57. A total of 324 coins of 20 paisa and 25 paisa make a sum of ₹ 71. The number of 25 paisa coins is:

A. 120 B. 124
C. 144 D. 200

58. A man wears socks of two colours – black and brown. He has altogether 20 black socks and 20 brown socks in the drawer. Supposing he has to take out the socks in the dark, how many must he take out to be sure that he has a matching pair?

A. 3 B. 20
C. 39 D. None of these

59. Abba cut a cake into two halves and cut one half into smaller pieces of equal size. Each of the small pieces is 20 grams in weight. If she has seven pieces of the cake in all with her, how heavy was the original cake?

A. 120 g B. 140 g
C. 240 g D. 280 g

60. At the end of a business conference the ten people present all shake hands with each other once. How many handshakes will be there altogether?

A. 20 B. 45
C. 55 D. 90

61. 'B' happened to be a member of unlawful assembly. A factional fight ensured during which 'B' was injured and retired to the side, later on a man was killed. Now:

A. 'B' is guilty of murder being member of unlawful assembly.
B. 'B' is not guilty of murder as he ceased to be a member of unlawful assembly at the time when the murder was committed.
C. B is not guilty of murder, but lesser offence.
D. None of the above

62. Which of the following is not an ingredient of abetment?

A. instigating
B. engaging in conspiracy
C. intentional aiding
D. enticement

63. Which one of the following is an essential ingredient of sedition?

A. Dishonest intention
B. Mala fide intention
C. Words spoken must cause public disorder by acts of violence
D. Exciting disaffection towards the Government.

64. Which from the following is correct:

A. When two or more persons by fighting in a public place, disturb the public peace, they are said to commit an affray.
B. When five or more persons by fighting in a public place, disturb the public peace, they are said to commit an affray.
C. When five or more persons by fighting in a private place, disturb the public, they are said to commit an affray.
D. When two or more persons by fighting in a private place, disturb the public, they are said to commit an affray.

65. The act of God causes injury to no one means:

A. Actus dei nemini facit injuriam
B. ad hominem
C. Ut res magis valet quam pereat
D. Fraus et jus nunquam cohabitant

66. Which is incorrect from the following that "a Hindu male shall not adopt except with the consent of his wife unless the ______".

A. wife has renounced the word
B. wife has become insolvent
C. wife has ceased to be a Hindu
D. wife has been declared by a court to be of unsound mind.

57. B	**58.** A	**59.** C	**60.** B	**61.** B	**62.** D	**63.** D	**64.** A	**65.** A	**66.** B

67. As per The Hindu Adoptions and Maintenance Act, 1956 maintenance includes ______.

A. provision for food, clothing, residence, education and medical attendance, entertainment and treatment;

B. provision for food, clothing, residence, education and medical attendance, transportation and treatment;

C. provision for food, clothing, residence, education and medical attendance and treatment;

D. all of the above;

68. Which from the following is not a form of marriage under Muslim Law?

A. Tavih marriage B. Sahih marriage

C. Batil marriage D. Fasid marriage

69. Which of the following is not a tort?

A. Defamation

B. Negligence

C. Culpable Homicide

D. Nuisance

70. A loud bass beat that can be heard through an apartment wall (from another apartment) at midnight can be classified as

A. Nuisance

B. Trespass

C. Interference with contractual relations

D. Conversion

71. What is meant by the term "actionable per se"?

A. Actionable only in the civil courts

B. A tort of strict liability

C. Actionable without proof of damage

D. Actionable at the instance of the injured party on

72. The pigeon-hole theory for the law of tort was given by:

A. Winfield B. Lord Macaulay

C. Salmond D. Austin

73. The main difference between libel and slander is that:

A. Libel concerns adults only; slander, minors only

B. Libel concerns minors only; slander, adults only

C. Libel concerns those things spoken; slander, those things in print.

D. Libel concerns those things in print; slander, those things spoken

74. 'Consensus ad idem', means:

A. Contract caused by mistake of one party as to matter of fact

B. Both the parties to an agreement are under a mistake

C. An agreement upon the same thing in the same sense

D. None of the above

75. X owes ₹ 15,000 to Y and Y accepts ₹ 12,000 in full and final settlement of the outstanding due. This is called:

A. Cancellation B. Remission

C. Alteration D. Concession

76. If the finder of goods does not return the goods to true owner. He will be guilty of ____

A. Fraud

B. Criminal misappropriation of goods

C. Extortion

D. Theft.

77. Liquidated damages is essentially a:

A. Payment of money stipulated as a warning to the attending party.

B. Payment of compensation determined by the court.

C. Compensation arbitrarily determined by the aggrieved party.

D. Genuine covenanted pre-estimate of damage.

67. C	**68.** A	**69.** C	**70.** A	**71.** C	**72.** C
73. D	**74.** C	**75.** B	**76.** B	**77.** D	

78. When an acceptance may be revoked:
A. An acceptance may be revoked at any time before the communication of the acceptance is complete as against the proposer, but not afterwards.
B. An acceptance may be revoked at any time before the communication of the acceptance is complete as against the acceptor, but not afterwards.
C. An acceptance may be revoked at any time before the communication of the acceptance is incomplete as against the acceptor, but not afterwards.
D. An acceptance may be revoked at any time after the communication of the acceptance is complete as against the acceptor, but not afterwards.

79. Which one of the following Articles of the Indian Constitution belongs to a different category?
A. Article 14 B. Article 15
C. Article 16 D. Article 19

80. What does the writ of Quo warranto mean?
A. It is issued when an office holder is found to misuse his duties.
B. It is issued when a court wants to order a lower court or similar authority to transfer some matter pending before it to other courts or other authorities.
C. It is issued by higher courts when they find that lower courts have made judgements beyond their powers of jurisdiction.
D. It is issued when the court finds that the office holder is illegally holding that position.

81. Who said this: "There is nothing to be ashamed of in borrowing. It involves no plagiarism. Nobody holds any patent rights in the fundamental ideas of a Constitution."
A. Dr. Rajendra Prasad
B. Pt. Jawaharlal Nehru
C. Dr. B.R. Ambedkar
D. N. Gopalaswami

82. Which one of the following Constitutional Amendments introduced the anti-defection provision in the Constitution for the first time?
A. 54th Amendment
B. 53rd Amendment
C. 52nd Amendment
D. 51st Amendment

83. Which amendment of the Constitution was challenged in Janhit Abhiyan vs Union of India?
A. 85th Constitution Amendment
B. 92nd Constitution Amendment
C. 103rd Constitution Amendment
D. 105th Constitution Amendment

84. On which day Doctrine of Basic Structure was lay down?
A. 15th April 1973
B. 18th April 1973
C. 24th April 1973
D. 30th April 1973

85. Ninth Schedule of the Constitution was added by which Constitution Amendment?
A. 1st Constitution Amendment
B. 11th Constitution Amendment
C. 42nd Constitution Amendment
D. 44th Constitution Amendment

86. Article 21-A of Constitution of India was added by which Constitution Amendment?
A. 84th Constitution Amendment
B. 85th Constitution Amendment
C. 86th Constitution Amendment
D. 87th Constitution Amendment

87. Who is the founder of the historical school?
A. Savigny B. Kelson
C. Grotius D. Duguit

78. B	**79.** D	**80.** D	**81.** C	**82.** C	**83.** C	**84.** C	**85.** A	**86.** C	**87.** A

88. Who said that "Public Policy is an unruly horse where once you stride on it you do not know where it's going to take you."
A. Justice Borrough
B. Blackstone
C. Stammler
D. Montesquieu

89. Who wrote the book "the concept of law?"
A. Blackstone B. Duguit
C. Bentham D. Hart

90. Who made a statement that "certainty of law is a myth?"
A. Jerome Frank B. Julius Stone
C. Bentham D. Paton

91. According to whose theory, "Law is not universal in its nature; like language it varies with people and age"?
A. Bentham's theory
B. Austin's theory
C. Savigny's theory
D. Montesquieu's theory

92. How many official languages does the United Nations have?
A. 5 B. 6
C. 7 D. 4

93. In which year was the UNO awarded the Nobel Peace Prize?
A. 1975 B. 1990
C. 2001 D. 2008

94. Who was the first Indian to be the President of U.N. General Assembly?
A. Natwar Singh
B. V.K. Krishna Menon
C. Smt. Vijay Laxmi Pandit
D. Romesh Bhandari

95. The non-permanent members of the Security Council shall be elected for:
A. Two years B. Five years
C. Nine years D. Ten years

96. Contract is a ________ obligation.
A. Moral B. Constitutional
C. Civil D. Administrative

97. When is the communication of a proposal complete according to Section 4 of Indian Contract Act, 1872?
A. When it is delivered by the proposer
B. When the person to whom is it made accepts the proposal
C. When it comes to the knowledge of the person to whom it is made
D. When it comes to the knowledge anyone in the common company of the person to whom it is made.

98. Under the Hindu Marriage Act, the spinda relationship extends in the line of ascent, to:
A. two degrees through the mother and three degrees through the father
B. three degrees through the mother and four degrees through the father
C. three degrees through the mother and five degrees through the father
D. five degrees through the mother and seven degrees through the father

99. The Supreme Court has set up a five-judge Constitution bench to hear petitions seeking legal recognitions of same sex marriages. The bench is set up by Chief Justice of India. Who among the following is not the member for the said constitutional bench?
A. Justice Sanjay Kishan Kaul
B. Justice Ravindra Bhat
C. Justice Hima Kohli
D. Justice Y.V. Chandrachud

100. The legal Maxim 'Res ipsa loquitur' means:
A. Things are not what they seem
B. Things shall remain as they were
C. Things speak for itself
D. Things cannot be explained

88. C	**89.** D	**90.** A	**91.** C	**92.** B	**93.** C	**94.** C
95. A	**96.** C	**97.** C	**98.** C	**99.** D	**100.** C	

ANSWERS

1. (C): Maulana Abul Kalam Azad wrote India Wins Freedom, which is a personal account of the partition from his perspective. The book includes his experiences during India's independence and his ideas on freedom and liberty. It covers the events between 1935 and 1948 that shaped the destiny of the new nation. Azad was a prominent figure in the Independence movement, and served as Congress President from 1940 to 1946 and India's first education minister from 1947 to 1958.

2. (A): World Milk Day is celebrated on June 1st every year to recognize the importance of milk as a global food. The Food and Agriculture Organization (FAO) of the United Nations established the day in 2001 to promote milk's advantages and use worldwide.

3. (A): The rearing of silkworms for the production of silk fiber is known as sericulture. Sericulture is an agro-based industry that involves breeding and rearing silkworms to produce raw silk. The silk fiber is obtained from the cocoons spun by silkworms. The cocoons are exposed to steam, sun, or boiled to separate the silk fiber. India is the only country that produces all four of the most well-known commercial silks.

4. (B): Sattriya dance is the enchanting classical dance form of Assam. It originated in the 15th century AD and is deeply connected to the state's cultural and religious heritage. The dance form was developed as a part of Bhaona, one-act plays created by the saint Mahapurusha Sankaradeva. Themes depicted in Sattriya performances are often to Krishna, an avatar of Vishnu, and stories from the epics Mahabharata and Ramayana.

5. (C): The Ambubachi Mela is known as the "Mahakumbh of the East" and is one of the largest gatherings in eastern India. It's an annual Hindu festival that takes place in June at the Kamakhya Temple in Guwahati, Assam. The festival celebrates the yearly menstruation cycle of the temple's presiding goddess, Devi Kamakhya. It's believed that during the monsoon rains, devotees can access the creative and nurturing power of Mother Earth's "menses" at the festival site.

6. (A): The historic task of decorating the original manuscript of the Constitution of India was undertaken by Nandalal Bose. He was a renowned Indian painter and one of the pioneers of modern Indian art. His artistic contributions to the Constitution of India manuscript are highly celebrated. Renowned for his mastery in both traditional Indian and modern artistic techniques, Bose infused the manuscript with intricate designs, motifs, and illustrations inspired by India's rich heritage and diverse cultural traditions.

7. (C): The first Academy Awards, later known as the Oscars, were presented in 1929 at a private dinner at the Hollywood Roosevelt Hotel in Los Angeles, California. The ceremony honored films released between August 1, 1927 and July 31, 1928, and was hosted by Douglas Fairbanks, president of the Academy of Motion Picture Arts and Sciences (AMPAS). The 15-minute ceremony was attended by 270 people and featured 12 award categories.

8. (A): The milky substance found within a rubber plant is called latex. It's a distinct substance from the plant's sap and functions as a type of internal transport system, carrying essential nutrients and other compounds throughout the plant. In the case of rubber trees (from which most commercial rubber is derived), latex is the source of the raw material used to produce all those rubber bands, gloves, and tires we use in everyday life.

9. (A): The scientific name for the neem tree is *Azadirachta indica*. It is also known as the Indian lilac, nimtree, or dogoyaro in Nigeria. The neem tree is a member of the mahogany family, Meliaceae, and is native to the Indian subcontinent and most African countries. Neem has antibacterial and antifungal properties, and is commonly used in shampoos, soaps, creams, toothpastes, and mouthwashes.

10. (A): Madhya Pradesh, a central Indian state, is one of the states through which the Tropic of Cancer passes. It runs through the southern part of the state, crossing regions such as Khandwa, Betul, and Chhindwara districts. This geographical feature is significant because it divides India into two climatic zones: the tropical zone to the south and the subtropical zone to the north.

11. (C): Cochin International Airport in India is the world's first airport to fully run on solar power. In 2015, the airport installed 46,000 solar panels across 45 acres near its cargo complex, which produce 12 megawatts (MW) of power to run the airport's operations.

12. (B): Dr. B.R. Ambedkar led the Mahad Satyagraha on March 20, 1927 in Mahad, Maharashtra, India. The nonviolent protest aimed to give untouchables the right to use water from a public tank in Mahad, which was off-limits to lower castes. The Mahad Satyagraha was a significant step towards achieving social justice, equality, and civil rights for the Dalit community in India. March 20 is observed as Social Empowerment day in India.

13. (A): The Regulating Act of 1773 established the Supreme Court of Judicature at Fort William in Calcutta. The act was passed in June 1773 by the British Parliament and was the first parliamentary authorization to define the powers of the East India Company in India. The Supreme Court was established to hear and determine complaints for crimes and suits or actions in Bengal, Bihar, and Orissa.

14. (B): Wilhelm Conrad Röntgen, a German physicist, discovered X-rays on November 8, 1895. He named them X-rays because the nature of the radiation was unknown at the time. Röntgen published a paper about the discovery, titled "On a new kind of rays", on December 28, 1895. X-rays are a form of high-energy electromagnetic radiation with wavelengths ranging from 10 nanometers to 10 picometers.

15. (B): Fats are stored in the human body in adipose tissue, also known as body fat. Adipose tissue is a central metabolic organ that regulates the body's energy homeostasis. During periods of high energy intake, adipocytes, or specialized fat cells, store energy in the form of fat (triglycerides). When the body is deprived of energy, these triglycerides can be mobilized as free fatty acids. During starvation or fasting, adipose tissue breaks down to provide energy to the body.

16. (B): Sodium azide is the chemical found in car airbags that converts to nitrogen gas when an electrical charge is triggered by impact. Sodium azide is a colorless, crystalline solid that is highly soluble in water and is also used as a preservative in laboratory reagents and biologic fluids. It is highly toxic and acutely poisonous. Airbags are passive safety features that are designed to reduce or prevent injuries to drivers and passengers in a crash.

17. (D): In India, the ten-rupee note features the signature of the Governor, Reserve Bank of India (RBI). The RBI is entrusted with the vital responsibility of managing the country's monetary policy and issuing currency notes. This signature signifies the RBI's authorization and guarantees the legitimacy of the ten-rupee note for financial transactions.

18. (B): The gilt-edged market is synonymous with the market for government securities, particularly bonds issued by governments. These securities are considered extremely safe investments because they are backed by the government's credit, hence the term "gilt-edged," which implies high security and reliability. Investors often turn to this market for stable returns and low risk, making it a fundamental component of the financial landscape.

19. (A): The first woman to become the Chief Election Commissioner of India was V.S. Ramadevi. She held this prestigious position from November 26, 1990, to December 11, 1990. V.S. Ramadevi was a remarkable figure who also served as the first woman Governor of Karnataka and the first and only woman Secretary-General of the Rajya Sabha.

20. (D): The first General Election in India after Independence was held from October 1951 to February 1952. This election marked a significant milestone in India's democratic journey as it was the first time that the entire Indian population, regardless of caste, creed, or gender, had the opportunity to participate in the electoral process. The election was conducted to elect members of the Lok Sabha (House of the People) and the various state legislative assemblies.

21. (A): The term "Earth Summit" is often used to refer to a series of major United Nations conferences focused on international cooperation regarding environmental issues and sustainable development. The most recent Earth Summit, Rio+20, took place in Rio de Janeiro, Brazil in 2012. It aimed to renew political commitment for sustainable development, assess progress since the 1992 Rio Earth Summit, and address new and emerging challenges.

22. (B): In the 2022 Presidential Election in India, President Droupadi Murmu secured a clear advantage over Yashwant Sinha, who was the nominee from the opposition. Murmu, a former Jharkhand governor and the BJP's parliamentary board nominee, made history by becoming the first Tribal woman to be President of India.

23. (B): The Assamese Gamocha, also known as the Gamosa, received the Geographical Indication (GI) tag on December 13, 2022. The GI tag protects the Gamocha from imitations and promotes the local weavers and their traditional weaving techniques. The Gamocha is a handwoven rectangular cotton cloth with red borders and different designs and motifs. It is a significant cultural symbol and identity of Assam, and is used in various ways in daily life.

24. (B): P.T. Usha was appointed as the President of the Indian Olympic Association (IOA) on December 10, 2022. She is the first-ever woman to hold the IOA presidency in history. Usha became the first Indian woman to reach the final of an Olympic event. She is the youngest Indian sprinter, at 16, to compete in the Olympics at the 1980 Moscow Games and won the first medal of the 1982 Asian Games in track and field.

25. (A): The full form of FSSAI is Food Safety and Standards Authority of India. It is an autonomous statutory body that is responsible for maintaining food safety and standards in India. FSSAI is a regulatory body that enforces strict standards and regulations to ensure the quality and safety of food products in India and to safeguard public health.

26. (B): Lviv, is a city in Ukraine, near the border with Poland. It is one of the largest cities in Ukraine and serves as the administrative center of Lviv Oblast (province). Lviv has a rich history and cultural heritage, with influences from various cultures including Ukrainian, Polish, Austrian, and Jewish. Lviv is also renowned for its vibrant cultural scene, with numerous festivals, museums, theaters, and art galleries attracting visitors from around the world.

27. (A): Chernobyl is famous for the nuclear power plant disaster that occurred on April 26, 1986. It was the result of a catastrophic accident during a safety test at the Chernobyl Nuclear Power Plant in the Ukrainian Soviet Socialist Republic, which is now Ukraine. The explosion and subsequent fire released large amounts of radioactive particles into the atmosphere, making it one of the worst nuclear disasters in history.

28. (C): Karnam Malleswari is the first Indian woman to win an Olympic medal, a bronze in weightlifting at the 2000 Sydney Olympics. Malleswari also became the first Indian woman to win the weightlifting World Championship in 1994.

29. (D): The first Asian Games were held in New Delhi, India from March 4–11, 1951. The games featured six sports: association football, athletics, basketball, cycling, swimming, and weight lifting, and 11 participating nations. The Asian Games, also known as Asiad, are a continental multi-sport event held every four years. The first Prime Minister of India, Nehru, advocated for the games to help reestablish bonds between Asian countries and contribute to peace in Asia.

30. (B): INTERPOL stands for International Criminal Police Organization. It is an inter-governmental organization that works with police in 195 member countries to make the world safer. INTERPOL coordinates police activities of participating nations against international criminals. It provides police with the ability to share and access data about crimes and criminals, as well as a variety of technical and operational support.

31. (A): Flux refers to a continuous process of change or movement, often characterized by fluctuation, variation, or transition from one state to another. It implies a state of constant motion or flow, where things are in a state of flux if they are continually changing or evolving. This term is commonly used in various contexts, including physics, chemistry, biology, and sociology, to describe dynamic systems or phenomena that exhibit ongoing change or instability.

32. (C): Compatriots are individuals who share the same country of origin or nationality. They are united by their common citizenship and often share cultural, social, and historical ties. The term emphasizes a sense of belonging and solidarity among people who identify with the same nation-state. Compatriots may feel a strong sense of kinship and camaraderie with each other, as they share common experiences, traditions, and values associated with their homeland.

33. (B): Syllogism is a logical reasoning method that uses deductive reasoning to reach a conclusion from two or three statements. The word syllogism comes from the Greek word syllogismos, which means "conclusion, inference". In a syllogism, the two statements are a major and a minor, and the conclusion is the main point of the argument.

34. (C): A centenarian is a person who is between 90 and 100 years. The term is often used to describe people who are long-lived, as life expectancy worldwide is typically less than 100 years. Living to be a centenarian is not only a testament to good health and longevity but also reflects the experiences and wisdom gained over a lifetime of living.

35. (D): The word that best expresses a similar meaning to "bequeath" is "give". "Bequeath" means to leave or pass on (property, possessions, etc.) by will or formal declaration, which is similar to giving something to someone as a gift or inheritance.

36. (A): A person who hates, avoids, or opposes marriage is called a misogamist. The word "misogamy" comes from the Greek words mis meaning "hate" and gamy meaning "marriage". It can also be defined as an intense dislike or a feeling of dislike that demands action.

37. (A): "Betrothed" is a term used to describe someone who is engaged to be married. When two people become engaged, they have agreed to marry each other at some point in the future. During the period of engagement, they are often referred to as the betrothed or the engaged couple.

38. (B): Polygamy is the term for when a man is married to more than one woman at the same time. Polygamy is rare worldwide and is usually found in a few regions. In India, polygamy is portrayed in a neutral light by all major religions, and the separation between religion and land laws has also contributed to its lack of prohibition.

39. (A): Ante-diluvium means "old time". It is an adjective that refers to something that is very old, old-fashioned, or out of date. It's essentially a way of indicating a very ancient or primordial time, before a significant cataclysmic event.

40. (C): In this context, "at" can indeed be a suitable preposition. "He doesn't work with hands, he works at the machine" implies his physical location where he interacts with the machine to complete tasks, likely using his mind and not manual labour.

41. (A): H O T E L

$\downarrow \quad \downarrow \quad \downarrow \quad \downarrow \quad \downarrow$

$8 + 15 + 20 + 5 + 12$

$= 60 \div 5$

$= 12$

Here, total number is divided by the total number of letters present in the word.

Hence,

L A M B

$\downarrow \quad \downarrow \quad \downarrow \quad \downarrow$

$12 + 1 + 13 + 2$

$= 28 \div 4 = 7.$

42. (B):

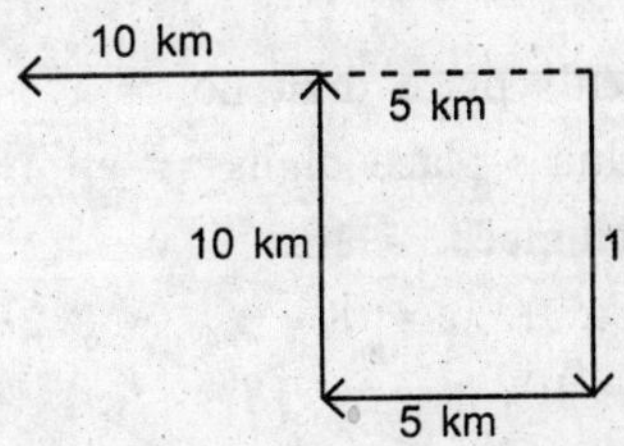

He will have cycle to 15 km to reach his home straight.

43. (B): In right triangle ACD,

$$AD^2 = (4)^2 + (3)^2$$
$$= 16 + 9$$
$$= 25$$
$$AD = 5 \text{ km}$$

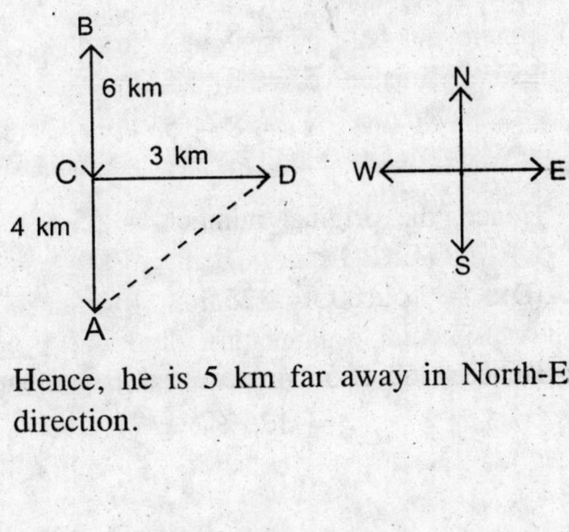

Hence, he is 5 km far away in North-East direction.

44. (B): Given,

I	N	D	I	A
↓	↓	↓	↓	↓
9	14	4	9	1

Similarly,

D	E	L	H	I
↓	↓	↓	↓	↓
4	5	12	8	9

Hence, Delhi will be written as 451289.

45. (B): Let the middle digit be x. then

$2x = 10$ or $x = 5$

The number is either 253 or 352 since, the number increased on reversing the digits, So the hundred's digit is smaller than the unit's digit.

Hence, required number = 253

46. (B): Let ten's place digit no = x

and Unit's place digits = y

$\therefore$ Number = $10x + y$

Now, $x + y = 8$ ...(i)

$10y + x - 10x - y = 18$

$9y - 9x = 18$

$y - x = 2$ ...(ii)

Solving (i) and (ii), then we get

$$x + y = 8$$
$$y - x = 2$$
$$2y = 10$$

$\Rightarrow y = 5$

Putting the value of y in (i)

$x + y = 8$

$\Rightarrow x + 5 = 8$

$\therefore x = 8 - 5$

$= 3$

Hence, the original number = 35.

47. (D): $\frac{5}{4} \times 100 = 125\%$

Hence, ratio of 5 : 4 expressed as percentage

= 125%

48. (C): $\therefore$ (P + Q + R)'s 4 hrs work

= 216 pages

$\therefore$ (P + Q + R)'s 1 hr work = $\frac{216}{4}$

= 54 pages

Clearly, each of them type per hr

= 15, 18, 21 pages.

49. (C) : (A + B + C)'s 1 day work

$$= \frac{1}{10} + \frac{1}{50}$$

$$= \frac{5+1}{60}$$

$$= \frac{6}{50} = \frac{3}{25}$$

2 A's 1 day work = $\frac{3}{25}$

A's 1 day work = $\frac{3}{50}$ [$\because$ A = B + C]

B's 1 day work = $\frac{1}{10} - \frac{3}{50}$

$$= \frac{5-3}{50}$$

$$= \frac{2}{50} = \frac{1}{25}$$

Hence, B alone can do this work in 25 days.

50. (D) : Ratio of their speed = 4 : 3 : 5

Ratio of their time taken = $\frac{1}{4} : \frac{1}{3} : \frac{1}{5}$

$$= \frac{15}{60} : \frac{20}{60} : \frac{12}{60}$$

= 15 : 20 : 12

53. (A): E's mother is Singer

B's mother is Teacher

C's mother practice medicine

D's mother is not a lawyer

Clearly, A's mother is lawyer.

54. (B): $\therefore$ A = 5, B = 6, C = 7, D = 8

16	5	27	29	9	22	23	will give a word
↓	↓	↓	↓	↓	↓	↓	
L	a	w	y	e	r	s	

55. (C): Number of alterations in 1 shirt

$$= \frac{2}{3} + \frac{3}{4} + \frac{4}{5}$$

$$= \frac{40 + 45 + 48}{60}$$

$$= \frac{133}{60}$$

Hence, number of alterations in 60 shirts

$$= \frac{133}{60} \times 60$$

$$= 133$$

56. (B): Let total members = 100

$$\frac{20}{100} \times 100 = 20 \times 2 = 40 \text{ cars}$$

Remaining members = 80

$$\frac{40}{100} \times 80 = 32 \times 3 = 96 \text{ cars}$$

Remaining, 80 − 32 = 48 members

48 × 1 = 48 cars

Hence, (B) statement is definitely true.

57. (B): Let the number of 20 paise coins = x

Then, the no. of 25 paise coins = 324 − x

$$\Rightarrow \frac{1}{5}x + \frac{1}{4}(324 - x) = 71$$

$$\Rightarrow \frac{4x + 5(324 - x)}{20} = 71$$

$$\Rightarrow 4x + 1620 - 5x = 1420$$

$$\Rightarrow -x = 1420 - 1620$$

$$= -200$$

$$\Rightarrow x = 200$$

Hence, no. of 25 paise coins

$$= 324 - 200$$

$$= 124.$$

58. (A): As man draws out socks in dark, so in his first draws might be he draws out black or brown. As there are only two colour socks.

Let us assume that in his first draws he draws black colour.

Now to complete his pair he has to draw one more time.

In his second draw he get a black or brown as he is pulling out in dark.

Let he got a brown colour in the second draw then he got a pair or socks of different colour.

Also there is a chance he take out a black colour. Then in this case his pair of socks will be completed but as getting out of two consecutive black socks is not possible every time.

So, Let he tries another chance.

In his third draw he will get a sock of either black or brown colour.

If he gets black colour in third draw then in combining first and third he got pair of black colour.

But if he gets in third draws brown colour then combining second and third he got pair of brown colour socks.

Therefore, from above we see that to surely get pair of socks of the same colour, man has to draw socks minimum three times.

So, the correct option is (A).

59. (C): The weight of the original cake

$$= (20 \times 6 + 120) \text{ grams}$$

$$= (120 + 120) \text{ grams}$$

$$= 240 \text{ grams}$$

60. (B): Number of handshakes = ${}^{10}C_2$

$$= \frac{10!}{2! \times 8!}$$

$$= \frac{10 \times 9 \times 8!}{2 \times 8!}$$

$$= 5 \times 9$$

$$= 45$$

61. (B): According to legal principles, individuals cannot be held responsible for crimes committed by an unlawful assembly if they have withdrawn from the assembly before the commission of the crime. In this scenario, 'B' retired to the side before the murder occurred, thus ceasing to be a member of the unlawful assembly at the time of the murder. As a result, 'B' cannot be held guilty of murder based on the timing of their withdrawal from the unlawful assembly.

62. (D): Enticement is not an ingredient of abetment, but instigating, engaging in conspiracy, and international aiding are. According to the Indian Penal Code, abetment can be committed by instigation, conspiracy, or intentional aiding. Abetment by instigation occurs when someone causes or attempts to cause something to be done by willfully misrepresenting or concealing a material fact.

63. (D): Sedition involves acts or expressions that aim to excite disaffection or feelings of hatred or contempt towards the government or authorities. This can include speeches, writings, or actions that provoke rebellion or disobedience against the established order. The crucial aspect of sedition is the intention to undermine the authority of the government or to create unrest or disorder within the society.

64. (A): Affray is a legal term that refers to a situation where two or more individuals engage in a physical altercation in a public place, causing disturbance and fear among the public. It involves fighting in a public setting, such as a street or a park, and is considered a breach of the peace. The key aspect of affray is that it occurs in a public place and disrupts the public order, leading to potential harm or intimidation of bystanders.

65. (A): This Latin phrase translates to "The act of God causes injury to no one." It is a legal principle indicating that natural disasters or unforeseeable events, often referred to as "acts of God," do not create liability for damages or injuries.

66. (B): According to Hindu law, a Hindu male shall not adopt except with the consent of his wife unless the wife has become insolvent, meaning she has lost her mental capacity or competency to make decisions due to financial difficulties. In such circumstances, the husband may proceed with the adoption without the wife's consent, as her financial situation affects her ability to participate in the decision-making process.

67. (C): The Hindu Adoptions and Maintenance Act, 1956 defines maintenance as the provision for the essential needs of the dependent. This includes ensuring access to food, clothing, residence, education, medical attendance, and treatment. Maintenance aims to support the well-being and livelihood of the dependent individual, ensuring they have the necessary resources for a decent standard of living.

68. (A): Tavih marriage does not appear to be a recognized form of marriage under Muslim law. There are four kinds of Muslim marriages: Sahih, Batil, Fasid and Muta. Essentially, a valid marriage must adhere to the specific conditions and ceremonies outlined by the relevant Muslim sect.

69. (C): Culpable Homicide falls under criminal law, not tort law. It refers to the unlawful killing of another person and can have varying degrees depending on the intent and circumstances. In criminal law, the focus is on punishing the offender and protecting society. The other options—defamation, negligence, and nuisance—are all examples of torts, which are civil wrongs that result in harm or injury to another person or their property, giving rise to a legal liability for the person who commits the tort.

70. (A): Nuisance, in legal terms, refers to any activity or condition that interferes with the use and enjoyment of someone's property or land. In the context of the scenario described, the loud bass beat that penetrates through the apartment wall at midnight disrupts the peace and quiet of the neighbouring apartment, affecting the residents' ability to relax or sleep. This interference with their right to enjoy their property without disturbance constitutes a nuisance under the law.

71. (C): "Actionable per se" refers to a legal concept where an action or behaviour is inherently wrongful or harmful, and therefore, gives rise to a cause of action without the need for the plaintiff to prove specific damages. In other words, certain actions are considered wrongful or harmful in themselves, regardless of whether they result in tangible harm, and can be grounds for legal action.

72. (C): Sir John Salmond was a renowned jurist who advocated for a more closed and categorized approach to the law of torts. According to his theory, there are established categories of wrongs (like pigeon holes) that define what can be considered a tort. If a specific harm doesn't fit neatly into one of these categories, there's no remedy available under tort law.

73. (D): The main difference between libel and slander lies in the form of communication. Libel refers to defamatory statements or content that is published or broadcasted in written or visual form, such as newspapers, magazines, or online platforms. Slander, on the other hand, involves defamatory statements that are spoken or orally communicated. Therefore, libel pertains to statements in print, while slander pertains to spoken statements.

74. (C): "Consensus ad idem" is a Latin term that translates to "agreement to the same thing." In legal terms, it refers to the meeting of minds between parties to a contract, where both parties understand and agree to the same terms and intentions of the contract.

75. (B): When Y accepts a lesser amount, ₹ 12,000, in full and final settlement of the outstanding due of ₹ 15,000, it is known as "remission." Remission occurs when a creditor accepts a lesser sum than what is actually owed by the debtor in full satisfaction of the debt. This can be beneficial for both parties: X gets to settle the debt for a lesser amount, and Y avoids the potential hassle and cost of collecting the entire amount, especially if there's a chance they might not be able to collect it in full.

76. (B): Criminal misappropriation of goods involves dishonestly taking possession of movable property and using it as one's own or dishonestly using or disposing of that property in violation of any direction of law prescribing the mode in which such property is to be used or disposed of, with the intention of causing wrongful gain or loss to any person.

77. (D): Liquidated damages refer to a predetermined amount of compensation agreed upon by the parties to a contract, which represents a genuine estimate of the potential losses or damages that might occur in the event of a breach of contract. These damages are agreed upon and specified within the contract itself, based on a reasonable assessment of potential harm or loss.

78. (B): In contract law, an acceptance is considered complete when it is communicated to the offeror or proposer. Therefore, in option B, the acceptance can be revoked by the acceptor at any time before the communication of acceptance is complete, meaning before it reaches the offeror. Once the acceptance is communicated it becomes binding on both parties, and it cannot be revoked. This principle ensures that once an acceptance is communicated and becomes binding, both parties are obligated to fulfill the terms of the contract.

79. (D): Article 19 falls under a different category. It pertains to the Right to Freedom, freedom of speech and expression, freedom to assemble peacefully, freedom to form associations or unions, freedom to move freely throughout the territory of India, and freedom to reside and settle in any part of the territory of India. However, Articles 14, 15, and 16 of the Indian Constitution all pertain to the Fundamental Rights guaranteed to citizens. They ensure equality before the law, prohibit discrimination on various grounds, and provide for equality of opportunity in matters of public employment.

80. (D): The writ of Quo Warranto is a legal remedy used to challenge the legality of a person holding a public office or position. It essentially questions the authority of the individual to hold the office or position. If the court finds that the person is holding the position unlawfully or without proper authority, it may issue the writ of quo warranto, compelling the individual to justify their right to hold the office or position.

81. (C): Dr. B.R. Ambedkar, the principal architect of the Indian Constitution, made this statement during the Constituent Assembly debates. Ambedkar believed that borrowing ideas and principles from other constitutions is not a sign of weakness but rather a pragmatic approach to creating an effective and functional constitution. He argued that fundamental ideas of a constitution, such as democracy, equality, and justice, are universal and not subject to copyright or patent rights.

82. (C): The 52nd Amendment Act of 1985 was introduced to address the issue of political defections in India. It added the Tenth Schedule to the Indian Constitution, commonly known as the Anti-Defection Law. This amendment aimed to curb the problem of legislators switching parties for personal gain or political reasons, which often led to instability in governments and undermined democratic principles.

83. (C): The Janhit Abhiyan vs Union of India case primarily challenged the constitutional validity of the 103rd Constitution Amendment Act, which introduced the 10% reservation for economically weaker sections (EWS) in educational institutions and government jobs.

84. (C): On 24th April 1973, the Supreme Court of India, in the landmark case of Kesavananda Bharati vs. State of Kerala, established the Doctrine of Basic Structure. This doctrine asserts that certain fundamental features of the Constitution are immutable and cannot be amended by the Parliament through its amending powers under Article 368 if such amendments alter or destroy the basic structure of the Constitution.

85. (A): The Ninth Schedule of the Constitution was added by the First Constitution Amendment Act of 1951. This amendment was introduced to address legal challenges to land reform laws and other social welfare legislations aimed at abolishing zamindari system, tenancy reforms, and other agrarian reforms. The purpose of including these laws in the Ninth Schedule was to provide them with protection from judicial review and challenges on the grounds of violation of fundamental rights.

86. (C): The 86th Constitution Amendment Act of 2002 introduced Article 21-A to the Constitution of India. This amendment aimed to provide free and compulsory education to all children in the age group of 6 to 14 years as a fundamental right. Article 21-A enshrines the right to education and places an obligation on the State to ensure that every child receives education in a manner that ensures his or her full development and the fulfillment of his or her potential.

87. (A): Friedrich Karl von Savigny is considered the founder of the historical school of jurisprudence. Savigny was a German jurist and legal scholar who believed that a nation's customary law is its living law, and that the role of jurisprudence is to uncover this law. He argued that the legal system's coherence is often due to a lack of understanding of its history and origins. The historical school of jurisprudence is a 19th century legal theory that posits that law develops over time to reflect a society's values, traditions, and customs.

88. (C): Friedrich Stammler, a German legal philosopher, is credited with this quote. This statement encapsulates the idea that public policy, once set into motion, can have unpredictable and far-reaching consequences. Stammler's quote highlights the complexity and dynamic nature of public policy, suggesting that once decisions are made and actions are taken, their outcomes may not always align with initial expectations.

89. (D): "The Concept of Law" was written by H.L.A. Hart, a British legal philosopher. Published in 1961, this influential work is considered one of the most important contributions to legal philosophy in the 20th century. In the book, Hart presents a comprehensive analysis of the nature of law, exploring fundamental questions such as the relationship between law and morality, the nature of legal obligation, and the role of authority in legal systems.

90. (A): Jerome Frank, an American legal philosopher and judge, made the statement "certainty of law is a myth." This statement reflects Frank's skepticism towards the notion that law can provide absolute certainty or predictability in its outcomes. Frank argued that legal decisions are influenced by a variety of factors, including judicial discretion, social context, and individual biases, which can introduce uncertainty into the legal process.

91. (C): Savigny's theory, also known as the Historical School of jurisprudence, posits that law is not a static, universal set of principles, but rather a product of the historical, cultural, and social context in which it arises. According to Savigny, law evolves organically over time and is shaped by the customs, traditions, and values of the people within a particular society. He compared law to language, suggesting that, like language, it is subject to change and variation across different cultures and historical periods.

92. (B): The United Nations has six official languages: Arabic, Chinese, English, French, Russian, and Spanish. English and French are the working languages of the United Nations Secretariat and are used in day-to-day professional exchanges. The UN's six translation services are responsible for producing parliamentary documentation, correspondence, publications, and other documents in the six official languages.

93. (C): The United Nations (UN) and its Secretary-General Kofi Annan were jointly awarded the Nobel Peace Prize in 2001. The Norwegian Nobel Committee recognized the UN and Annan for their work in "creating a more peaceful and better organized world". The committee also noted that the UN is a leader in international efforts to achieve peace and security, and to address the world's economic, social, and environmental challenges.

94. (C): Smt. Vijay Laxmi Pandit, an Indian diplomat and politician, became the first Indian to be elected as the President of the

United Nations General Assembly in 1953. Her election to this prestigious position marked a significant milestone for India's diplomatic representation on the global stage. She was known for her strong advocacy of peace, disarmament, and the rights of developing nations during her tenure as President of the General Assembly.

95. (A): The non-permanent members of the United Nations Security Council are elected by the General Assembly to serve a term of two years. Each year, five non-permanent members are elected, with their terms staggered to ensure continuity and representation from different regions of the world. The purpose of having non-permanent members is to provide broader representation within the Security Council and to enhance the legitimacy of its decisions by including a diverse range of perspectives.

96. (C): A contract is a civil obligation because it arises from agreements made between parties. In civil law systems, contractual obligations are governed by the principles of contract law, which establish the rights and duties of the parties involved in the agreement. When parties enter into a contract, they voluntarily assume certain obligations and responsibilities towards each other, such as the obligation to perform specific actions, provide goods or services, or refrain from certain behaviours.

97. (C): Section 4 of the Indian Contract Act, 1872, deals with the communication of proposals. It states that the communication of a proposal is complete when it comes to the knowledge of the person to whom it is made. This means that for a proposal to be considered effectively communicated, it must be brought to the attention of the intended recipient. Once the proposal is known to the person to whom it is addressed, the communication is deemed complete, and the recipient can then consider the proposal and respond to it accordingly.

98. (C): Sapinda relationship refers to the degrees of kinship within which marriage is prohibited due to the close blood relationship between the parties. According to the Act, a person is said to be within the sapinda relationship of another if they are related to each other in the line of ascent, either by blood or adoption, within a certain number of degrees. Specifically, under the Hindu Marriage Act:

- The sapinda relationship extends to three degrees of ascent through the mother.
- The sapinda relationship extends to five degrees of ascent through the father.

99. (D): Justice Y.V. Chandrachud is not a member of the five-judge Constitution bench set up by the Chief Justice of India to hear petitions seeking legal recognition of same-sex marriages. This means that he is not part of the bench that will deliberate on the issue and make decisions regarding the legal status of same-sex marriages in India. The other options listed (Justices Sanjay Kishan Kaul, Ravindra Bhat, and Hima Kohli) are likely to be members of the bench tasked with hearing these petitions.

100. (C): "Res ipsa loquitur" is a Latin phrase commonly used in law to describe a principle where the occurrence of an accident or injury itself suggests negligence or fault. Literally translated, it means "the thing speaks for itself." This legal doctrine is often applied in cases where the circumstances surrounding an accident or injury strongly imply negligence on the part of the defendant, even in the absence of direct evidence of negligence.

Previous Years' Paper (Solved)

CUET—LL.B., Entrance Exam, 2022

Subject Code: PGQP40

(Online exam held on 06-09-2022)

1. Which of the following is a one-word substitute for 'the study of sound and sound waves'?

A. Chronology B. Acoustics
C. Alchemy D. Autistics

2. Which of the following is a one-word substitute for 'easily deceived'?

A. Fallible B. Permeable
C. Gullible D. Pliable

3. Choose the correct sentence.

A. I go there briefly.
B. I go there little time.
C. I go there very seldom.
D. I go there seldomly.

4. Choose the most appropriate option to complete the sentence:

I wanted to borrow Mohan's umbrella, but he refused

A. lending me. B. lending it to me.
C. to lend it to me. D. to lend me.

5. Which of the following words will be the correct choice for the blank?

I told him ______ his face that he was a liar.

A. to B. on
C. at D. in

6. Given below are four sentences in jumbled order. Select the option that gives their correct order.

(*a*) The lid can be sealed on to the vessel by means of a rubber ring.

(*b*) It consists of a very strong vessel, made of aluminium alloy with a lid that fits tightly on the top.

(*c*) At the centre of the lid there is a vent or hole through which steam can escape.

(*d*) A pressure cooker is a vessel in which food is cooked in steam under pressure.

Choose the ***correct*** answer from the options given below:

A. (*d*), (*a*), (*b*), (*c*) B. (*a*), (*d*), (*c*), (*b*)
C. (*d*), (*b*), (*c*), (*a*) D. (*d*), (*c*), (*b*), (*a*)

7. Choose the correct sentence.

A. You're getting married, aren't you?
B. You're getting married, are you?
C. You're getting married, won't you?
D. You're getting married, will you?

8. Which of the following is a one-word substitute for 'one who has no money'?

A. Bankrupt B. Pauper
C. Orphan D. Derelict

9. In the sentence given below a part is italicised. Which choice as a replacement will improve the sentence?

If the countries *go after war*, many people will die needlessly.

A. go for war B. go to war
C. go in war D. go at war

10. Which of the following is a one-word substitute for 'one who enjoys food with pleasure'?

A. Gourmet B. Gourmand
C. Glutton D. Omnivorous

11. Find out the correct meaning of the following idiom:

To burn your bridges

A. To burn down one's house
B. To exhaust all the resources
C. To make it impossible to go back
D. To leave a job

12. Choose the option which is opposite in meaning to the following word:

Cognizance

A. Tidiness B. Ignorance
C. Adulteration D. Disheveled

13. Identify the correct indirect speech form of the sentence from the options given below:

Riddhi said, "Let it rain, I have to go".

A. Riddhi said that she did not care for the rain and she had to go.
B. Riddhi suggests that she does not care for the rain and she has to go.
C. Riddhi persisted that she did not care for the rain and she had to go.
D. Riddhi proposed that she did not care for the rain and she has to go.

14. Given below are two statements:

Statement I : Fun can never take the indefinite article, but a definite article is quite common.

Statement II : Very, not much, is used before too.

In the light of the above statements, choose the *correct* answer from the options given below:

A. Both Statement I and Statement II are true
B. Statement I is false, but Statement II is true
C. Statement I is true, but Statement II is false
D. Both Statement I and Statement II are false

15. Given below are two statements:

Statement I : Abroad is never preceded by an article.

Statement II : Also is used only in positive sentences.

In the light of the above statements, choose the *correct* answer from the options given below:

A. Both Statement I and Statement II are false
B. Both Statement I and Statement II are true
C. Statement I is true, but Statement II is false
D. Statement I is false, but Statement II is true

16. Choose the correct sentence:

A. What I hated most were the insects everywhere.
B. What I hated most was the insects everywhere.
C. What I hated most was the insect everywhere.
D. What I hated most were the insect everywhere.

17. Match List-I with List-II.

List-I (Word)	List-II (Synonym)
(*a*) Abstinence	I. Weak
(*b*) Infamous	II. Disgraceful
(*c*) Feeble	III. Exposed
(*d*) Vulnerable	IV. Avoidance

Choose the *correct* answer from the options given below:

	(*a*)	(*b*)	(*c*)	(*d*)
A.	III	I	IV	II
B.	II	IV	III	I
C.	IV	III	II	I
D.	IV	II	I	III

18. Match List-I with List-II.

List-I (Word)	List-II (Antonym)
(*a*) Bane	I. Calm
(*b*) Fray	II. Approve
(*c*) Blame	III. Boon
(*d*) Terrific	IV. Moderate

Choose the *correct* answer from the options given below:

	(*a*)	(*b*)	(*c*)	(*d*)
A.	III	I	II	IV
B.	IV	III	I	II
C.	II	IV	I	III
D.	III	IV	I	II

19. Given below are four sentences in jumbled order. Select the option that gives their correct order.

(*a*) I was hoping to find a photocopier shop.

(*b*) As I browsed, I felt the bookshop attendant's eyes on me.
(*c*) Some years ago, on a whim, I walked into a small shopping complex on Church Street in Bangalore.
(*d*) Instead, on the ground floor, I discovered a small second-hand bookshop.

Choose the ***correct*** answer from the options given below:

A. (*c*), (*b*), (*a*), (*d*) B. (*c*), (*a*), (*d*), (*b*)
C. (*a*), (*d*), (*c*), (*b*) D. (*b*), (*c*), (*a*), (*d*)

20. Choose the most appropriate option for completing the following paragraph:

The West has two fixed notions about India. One is that it is a romantic land, full of holy men, maharajas, palaces and elephants: the other is of India as a land of horrors—a place of intolerable poverty and squalor, hunger and disease ...

A. How can one country have two such contradictory images?
B. Who has the strength to face not God but–himself?
C. Should we be serving an urgent need?
D. Does not it amount to suppression, the suppression of a whole country?

21. From among the following, choose the antonym of 'knowledge'.

A. Deceit B. Ignorance
C. Folly D. Stupidity

Directions (Qs. No. 22-25): *Read the following passage and answer four questions that follow:*

No nation or culture is truly independent in terms of its intellectual life, and all depends to some extent on an exchange of knowledge. The more "modern" a nation is in terms of involvement with technology, industrialization and current political and social thought, the more dependent it tends to be on an international network of creation and distribution of knowledge. This international network operates in many ways. Books and journals are circulated across international boundaries, films are exported from one country to another, educational advice is given, experts circulate knowledge on a wide range of topics, students travel beyond their countries, and translations of publications from one language to another are commissioned.

22. The passage mainly proposes that all modern nations and cultures are:

A. self-sufficient B. technocratic
C. knowledgeable D. interdependent

23. The writer primarily links distribution of modern knowledge to:

(*a*) technology (*b*) religion
(*c*) language (*d*) industry

Choose the ***correct*** answer from the options given below:

A. (*a*) and (*b*) only B. (*a*) and (*c*) only
C. (*b*) and (*d*) only D. (*a*) and (*d*) only

24. The concluding clause of the passage is in:

A. Passive voice B. Direct speech
C. Active voice D. Imperative form

25. Which of the following is a one-word substitute for 'an inheritance from father'?

A. Patrimony B. Alimony
C. Acrimony D. Simony

26. Lok Sabha and Rajya Sabha are convened together for resolving a deadlock between them under the chairmanship of:

A. The President
B. The Vice-president
C. The Lok Sabha Speaker
D. The Chief Election Commissioner

27. Which High Court has the jurisdiction over the union territory of Andaman and Nicobar Islands?

A. Madras High Court
B. Karnataka High Court
C. Kerala High Court
D. Calcutta High Court

28. Which team has won the Uber cup 2022 by defeating the defending and 15 times Champion China?

A. India B. Japan
C. Thailand D. South Korea

29. Which of the following systems is followed by RBI for issuing currency?
A. Proportionate system
B. Simple deposit system
C. Minimum reserve system
D. Fixed fiduciary issue system

30. Which of the following Asian countries has been facing violent protests by its citizens over economic crisis recently?
A. Bangladesh B. Maldives
C. Nepal D. Sri Lanka

31. Which of the following procedures of parliament has not been borrowed from any country and has been evolved by parliament of India by itself?
A. Quorum B. Starred questions
C. Zero hour D. Question hour

32. Recently, in a major shift in its trade policy, India has opened up its central government procurement market to _______ under the Free Trade Agreement (FTA).
A. Saudi Arabia
B. Thailand
C. Canada
D. The United Arab Emirates

33. Consider the following statements about the dance form of Kuchipudi:
(*a*) Kuchipudi is one of the eight classical styles of Indian dance.
(*b*) Kuchipudi derives its roots from the ancient Hindu-Sanskrit text of Natya Shastra and is a dance-drama.
(*c*) Kuchipudi derives its name from a village in Tamil Nadu.
(*d*) It is largely devoted to the Hindu God Shiva.
(*e*) The dance-drama has the components of Dharavu, Nritta, Nritya and Natya

Choose the ***correct*** answer from the options given below:
A. (*a*), (*b*) and (*e*) only
B. (*a*) and (*d*) only
C. (*b*) and (*c*) only
D. (*a*), (*b*) and (*d*) only

34. Consider the following statements about gravitational waves.
(*a*) Gravitational waves are formed when a star explodes in a supernova, when two stars orbit each other and when two black holes merge.
(*b*) They travel at the speed of light, squeeze and stretch anything in their path.
(*c*) The concept of gravitational waves was given by Isaac Newton.
(*d*) The first gravitational wave was accidentally detected by LIGO in 2015.

Choose the ***correct*** answer from the options given below:
A. (*d*) only B. (*a*) and (*d*) only
C. (*a*) and (*c*) only D. (*c*) only

35. Arrange the following changes in the constitution through amends in the chronological order.
(*a*) Made Sikkim a full-fledged state of Indian Union.
(*b*) Integrated Puducherry in the Indian Union.
(*c*) Included Sindhi as official language in the Eighth Schedule.
(*d*) Accorded a special status to the union territory of Delhi by designating it as the national capital area.
(*e*) Integrated Goa, Daman, and Diu in the Indian Union.

Choose the ***correct*** answer from the options given below:
A. (*c*), (*b*), (*e*), (*a*), (*d*)
B. (*e*), (*d*), (*a*), (*c*), (*b*)
C. (*e*), (*b*), (*c*), (*a*), (*d*)
D. (*d*), (*a*), (*b*), (*c*), (*e*)

36. Arrange the following events in the making of Indian constitution in chronological order.
(*a*) The constitution of India was adopted by the constituent assembly.
(*b*) Appointment of Dr. Rajendra Prasad as President of the assembly.
(*c*) Adoption of objective Resolution presented by Pandit Jawaharlal Nehru by the constituent assembly.

(*d*) Last meeting of the constituent assembly.
(*e*) The constituent assembly met for the first time.

Choose the ***correct*** answer from the options given below:

A. (*c*), (*b*), (*e*), (*a*), (*d*)
B. (*e*), (*d*), (*a*), (*c*), (*b*)
C. (*e*), (*b*), (*c*), (*a*), (*d*)
D. (*d*), (*a*), (*b*), (*c*), (*e*)

37. Given below are two statements: One is labelled as Assertion (A) and the other is labelled as Reason (R).

Assertion (A) : Folk music is fast disappearing from the cultural tapestry in India.

Reason (R) : Folk music is not supported by modern technologies and media.

In the light of the above statements, choose the ***correct*** answer from the options given below:

A. Both (A) and (R) are true and (R) is the correct explanation of (A)
B. Both (A) and (R) are true, but (R) is NOT the correct explanation of (A)
C. (A) is true, but (R) is false
D. (A) is false, but (R) is true

38. Given below are two statements: One is labelled as Assertion (A) and the other is labelled as Reason (R).

Assertion (A) : The current generation of youths does not read books.

Reasons (R) : The youths have adequate visual material to watch and gain knowledge.

In the light of the above statements, choose the ***correct*** answer from the options given below:

A. Both (A) and (R) are true and (R) is the correct explanation of (A)
B. Both (A) and (R) are true, but (R) is NOT the correct explanation of (A)
C. (A) is true, but (R) is false
D. (A) is false, but (R) is true

39. Match List-I with List-II.

List-I	**List-II**
(*a*) Kalidasa	I. Chhatrapati Shivaji
(*b*) Bana Bhatta	II. Vikramaditya
(*c*) Chandra Bardai	III. Harshavardhana
(*d*) Parmanand	IV. Prithviraj Chauhan

Choose the ***correct*** answer from the options given below:

	(*a*)	(*b*)	(*c*)	(*d*)
A.	I	II	III	IV
B.	II	III	IV	I
C.	IV	III	II	I
D.	III	I	IV	II

40. Match List-I with List-II.

List-I (Dance form)	**List-II (States of origin)**
(*a*) Sattriya	I. Andhra Pradesh
(*b*) Mohiniyattam	II. West Bengal
(*c*) Kuchipudi	III. Assam
(*d*) Gauriya Nritya	IV. Kerala

Choose the ***correct*** answer from the options given below:

	(*a*)	(*b*)	(*c*)	(*d*)
A.	II	I	IV	III
B.	IV	III	II	I
C.	I	II	III	IV
D.	III	IV	I	II

41. Given below are two statements.

Statement I : Tuberculosis is caused by viruses that most often affect the lungs.

Statement II : TB is spread from person to person through the air.

In the light of the above statements, choose the ***most appropriate*** answer from the options given below:

A. Both Statement I and Statement II are correct.
B. Both Statement I and Statement II are incorrect.
C. Statement I is correct, but Statement II is incorrect.
D. Statement I is incorrect, but Statement II is correct.

42. Given below are two statements:

Statement I : Lighting is a very rapid and massive discharge of electricity in the atmosphere.

Statement II : Inter Cloud or Intra Cloud (IC) lightning are invisible and harmful.

In the light of the above statements, choose the ***most appropriate*** answer from the options given below:

A. Both Statement I and Statement II are correct.
B. Both Statement I and Statement II are incorrect.
C. Statement I is correct, but Statement II is incorrect.
D. Statement I is incorrect, but Statement II is correct.

43. Who has been conferred with the prestigious Royal Gold medal 2022, the world's highest honour in the field of architecture?

A. Hafeez contractor
B. Brinda Somaya
C. Balkrishna Vithaldas Doshi
D. Raj Rewal

44. The festival commomerating Buddha's birth, enlightenment and death is called:

A. Vaisakh B. Buddha Jayanti
C. Buddha Purnima D. Buddha Vaisakhi

45. Identify the correct combination of the members of QUAD.

(*a*) India (*b*) Vietnam
(*c*) Japan (*d*) Australia
(*e*) USA (*f*) South Korea

Choose the ***correct*** answer from the options given below:

A. (*a*), (*b*), (*c*), (*d*) only
B. (*a*), (*d*), (*e*), (*f*) only
C. (*a*), (*b*), (*e*), (*f*) only
D. (*a*), (*c*), (*d*), (*e*) only

46. Given below are two statements:

Statement I : ALU is an important component of CPU that is used to perform various arithmetic and logical operations in the computer system.

Statement II : Integer arithmetic refers to various arithmetic operations involving integer operands only.

In the light of the above statements, choose the ***correct*** answer from the options given below:

A. Both Statement I and Statement II are true
B. Both Statement I and Statement II are false
C. Statement I is true, but Statement II is false
D. Statement I is false, but Statement II is true

47. Good quality video and higher resolution image are achieved through:

A. AVI B. Quicktime
C. MPEG D. None of these

48. Match List-I with List-II.

List-I	**List-II**
(*a*) Open a document	I. CTRL + W
(*b*) Close a document	II. CTRL + O
(*c*) Help	III. CTRL + F2
(*d*) Print preview	IV. F1

Choose the ***correct*** answer from the options given below:

	(*a*)	(*b*)	(*c*)	(*d*)
A.	I	II	IV	III
B.	II	I	IV	III
C.	II	I	III	IV
D.	IV	I	II	III

49. Which keys are used to open the properties dialog box for the selected file or folder?

A. Alt + Enter B. Shift + Enter
C. Alt + P D. Shift + P

50. MICR stands for:

A. Metallic Ink Character Reader
B. Magnetic Ink Card Reader
C. Magnetic Ink Character Recognition
D. Metallic Info Card Recognition

51. Identify the first computer virus:

A. Creeper B. Tinba
C. Crypto locker D. Conficker

52. Find the odd one out (related to MS Word):

A. Web Layout B. Outline
C. Slide View D. Print Layout

53. Which one is not a Network Topologies?
A. Ring B. Bus
C. Star D. Umbrella

54. Which software is used to create and manage database?
A. MS Access B. MS Excel
C. Out look D. One note

55. Which technique is used to encrypt the data?
A. Block chaining B. Big data analytics
C. Cloud computing D. AR/VR

56. Let A and B be two clocks. Clock A loses 3 minute in a day and clock B gains 2 minutes per day. If clock B is 10 minutes ahead of clock A then how many days will it take clock B to be 45 minutes ahead of clock A?
A. 3 days B. 7 days
C. 10 days D. 9 days

57. What is the remainder of 16^{12345} divided by 5?
A. 0 B. 1
C. 2 D. 3

58. Ram's present age is one-third of the age of his father. 5 years ago, his age was one-fifth of his father' age. What are the present ages of Ram and his father?
A. 10 years and 31 years
B. 12 years and 36 years
C. 10 years and 30 years
D. 15 years and 45 years

59. What is the area of a right angle triangle whose base is 1/7 times of its height?
A. $x^3/14$ B. $x/14$
C. $x^2/14$ D. $x^2/7$

60. If 0.25 : x : : 5 : 3, then value of x is:
A. 0.013 B. 0.015
C. 0.150 D. 0.130

61. Which one of the following forms a set?
A. {x : x is fine best cricket player of the world}
B. {x : x is three best scientists of the world}
C. {x : x is prime factors of 100}
D. {x : x is ten best businessmen of the world}

62. Let 2% and 5% be two successive discounts on shoes. What is the single discount equivalent to these two successive discounts?
A. 5.5% B. 6%
C. 6.9% D. 7.2%

63. Two pipes P and Q alone can fill a tank in 30 minutes and 45 minutes respectively. A third pipe R can empty filled tank in 20 minutes. First, pipes P and Q are together opened, then, after 5 minutes pipe R is also opened. How many minutes are required to fill the tank completely?
A. 115 minutes B. 125 minutes
C. 135 minutes D. 145 minutes

64. A 15% stock yields 20%. What is the market value of the stock of the face value ₹ 100?
A. ₹ 57 B. ₹ 55
C. ₹ 75 D. ₹ 97

65. A cab travels at 70km/h from Prayagraj to Varanasi and at 90 km/h from Varanasi to Prayagraj. What is the average speed of cab for entire journey?
A. $78\frac{3}{4}$ km/h B. $87\frac{3}{4}$ km/h
C. $78\frac{3}{5}$ km/h D. 80 km/h

66. Ram is twice as efficient as Shyam. If both complete a work in 20 days then time taken by each to complete the same work, individually is:
A. 30 days and 60 days
B. 20 days and 40 days
C. 10 days and 20 days
D. 5 days and 10 days

67. How much time will it take for an amount of ₹ 1,200 to yield ₹ 144 as simple interest at the rate 3% per annum?
A. 3 years B. 4 years
C. 4.5 years D. 5 years

68. Ram and Shyam invest in a business in the ratio 1 : 3. After donation of 10% of the total profit. Ram's share is ₹ 900. What was the total profit?
A. ₹ 6,050 B. ₹ 4,000
C. ₹ 3,500 D. ₹ 1,000

69. A 200 m long train, with a speed of 90 km/h, crosses a 180 m long train, which is moving with speed of 100 km/h in opposite direction. How much time, they will take to cross each other?

A. 2.1 sec B. 1.2 sec
C. 2.7 sec D. 7.2 sec

70. If $\frac{x+y}{x-y}=\frac{1}{4}$ and $\frac{2-x}{y-2}=\frac{1}{3}$ then $3x + 4y$ is equal to:

A. 2.0 B. 1.5
C. 1.7 D. 3.5

71. What should be the ratio of milk and water, which yields a gain of 15% by selling it at cost price?

A. 10 : 5 B. 20 : 5
C. 20 : 3 D. 10 : 3

72. What is the weight of a right circular cone of height 14 cm and base radius 7 cm? The material used for cone weight 6 g/cm^3.

A. 4.31 kg B. 4.41 kg
C. 4.81 kg D. 4.91 kg

73. The LCM of two numbers is 28 and their product is 112 then what is the HCF?

A. 3 B. 4
C. 7 D. 10

74. If α, β and γ denote the principal, rate of interest per annum and time respectively. What is the amount if interest is compounded half yearly?

A. $\alpha\left(1+\frac{\beta}{200}\right)^{2\gamma}$ B. $\beta\left(1+\frac{\beta}{200}\right)^{2\gamma}$

C. $\gamma\left(1+\frac{\beta}{200}\right)^{2\alpha}$ D. $\alpha\left(1+\frac{\gamma}{200}\right)^{2\beta}$

75. If 4 men can do a work in 8 days while 10 women can do it in 10 days. In how many days can 6 men and 5 women complete the same work?

A. 5.5 days B. 6 days
C. 9 days D. 2 days

76. What is the area of a square, which is circumscribed by a circle of radius 5 unit?

A. 50.5 sq. unit B. 25 sq. unit
C. 50 sq. unit D. 100 sq. unit

77. A sum of money is to be distributed among 4 persons in the proportion of 3 : 3 : 2 : 5. If second person gets ₹ 500 more than third person then what is the share of fourth person?

A. ₹ 500 B. ₹ 1,500
C. ₹ 2,500 D. ₹ 3,500

78. If output of 2 men is equal to that of 4 women who can complete a task in 10 days working together. How much time would 3 men and 3 women together take a complete the same task?

A. $5\frac{4}{9}$ days B. $4\frac{1}{3}$ days

C. $7\frac{1}{5}$ days D. $4\frac{4}{9}$ days

79. Two partners P and Q invest in a company in the ratio of 2 : 1. If Q's share in the total profit is ₹ 1,500 then what was the total profit?

A. ₹ 4,000 B. ₹ 4,500
C. ₹ 5,500 D. ₹ 5,550

80. The loss after selling a commodity for ₹ 225 is same as the profit after selling it for ₹ 415. What is the cost of the commodity?

A. ₹ 230 B. ₹ 203
C. ₹ 320 D. ₹ 200

81. The question given below consists of a statement, followed by three arguments numbered I, II and III. You have to decide which of the arguments is a strong argument and which is a weak argument.

Statement: Should India make efforts to promote cottage industries?

Arguments:

I. Yes, it will address the rural unemployment in India to some extent.

II. Yes, it will address the problem of excess migration to cities.

III. No, the population of India is so large that the supply can hardly meet the demand.

Choose the ***most appropriate*** answer from the options given below:

A. Only argument I is strong
B. Only argument II is strong
C. Both arguments I and II are strong
D. All arguments I, II and III are strong

82. The question given below consists of a statement, followed by three arguments numbered I, II and III. You have to decide which of the arguments is a strong argument and which is a weak argument.

Statement: Should a famous actor be entitled to right to privacy in personal matters?

Arguments:

I. Yes, in personal matters, a famous actor has an equal right to privacy as any other member of society.
II. No, when a person voluntarily chooses a profession which puts him in limelight, he should not complain about lack of privacy.
III. No, loss of privacy is a fair price to pay for the fame and money that a famous actor gets.

Choose the ***most appropriate*** answer from the options given below:

A. Only argument I is strong
B. Only argument II is strong
C. Both arguments I and II are strong
D. All arguments I, II and III are strong

83. In the following question, two statements numbered I and II are given:

I. The birth rate in the district has been decreasing for the last five years.
II. The district administration has conducted extensive door to door family planning campaigns among the uneducated poor.

Choose the ***most appropriate*** answer from the options given below:

A. Statement I is the cause and statement II is its effect
B. Statement II is the cause and statement I is its effect
C. Both the statements I and II are independent causes
D. Both the statements I and II effects of independent causes

84. In the following question, two statements numbered I and II are given:

I. Spherical shape has the least possible surface area and highest surface tension.
II. Raindrop has a spherical shape.

Choose the ***most appropriate*** answer from the options given below:

A. Statement I is the cause and statement II is its effect
B. Statement II is the cause and statement I is its effect
C. Both the statements I and II are independent causes
D. Both the statements I and II are effects of independent causes

85. In the following question, two statements numbered I and II are given:

I. Part of straight stick which is partially immersed in water appears to be bent.
II. Pool of water appears to be less deep than it really is.

Choose the ***most appropriate*** answer from the options given below:

A. Statement I is the cause and statement II is its effect
B. Statement II is the cause and statement I is its effect
C. Both the statements I and II are independent effects
D. Both the statements I and II are effects of independent causes

86. In the following question, two statements numbered I and II are given:

I. Microfinance is important to small and individual business.
II. Small and individual business do not have access to traditional financial resources from major institutions.

Choose the ***most appropriate*** answer from the options given below:

A. Statement I is the cause and statement II is its effect
B. Statement II is the cause and statement I is its effect

C. Both the statements I and II are independent effects
D. Both the statements I and II are effects of independent cause

87. The question given below consists of a statement, followed by two conclusions numbered I and II. You have to assume everything in the statement to be true, then consider the two conclusions together and decide which of them logically follows beyond a reasonable doubt from the information given in the statement.

Statement: The Earth takes 24 hours to rotate through 360 degrees longitude.

Conclusions:

I. Two places that are 15 degrees of longitude apart have a di. erence of one hour.

II. If a person was travelling 180 degrees longitude east to west, he would lose a day.

Choose the ***most appropriate*** answer from the options given below:

A. Only conclusion I follows
B. Only conclusions II follows
C. Both conclusions I and II follow
D. Neither I nor II follows

88. The question given below consists of a statement, followed by two conclusions numbered I and II. You have to assume everything in the statement to be true, then consider the two conclusions together and decide which of them logically follows beyond a reasonable doubt from the information given in the statement.

Statement: When a person has a prolonged exposures to very cold temperature, he is unable to think clearly or move well.

Conclusions:

I. When a body begins to lose heat faster than it's produced, it leads to exhaustion of body's stored energy.

II. Body temperature that is too low affects the brain.

Choose the ***most appropriate*** answer from the options given below:

A. Only conclusion I follows
B. Only conclusion II follows
C. Both conclusions I and II follows
D. Neither I nor II follows

89. In the question below is given a statement followed by two assumptions numbered I and II. You have to consider the statement and the following assumptions and decide which of the assumptions is implicit in the statement.

Statement: Parents are not legally responsible for children above the age of 18 years.

Assumptions:

I. Parents become incapable of bearing such responsibility by the time children become adults.

II. Children become mature and thus capable of making decisions and bearing their own responsibility by the time they become adults.

Choose the ***most appropriate*** answer from the options given below:

A. Only assumption I is implicit
B. Only assumption II is implicit
C. Neither I nor II is implicit
D. Both I and II are implicit

90. In the question below is given a statement followed by two assumptions numbered I and II. You have to consider the statement and the following assumptions and decide which of the assumptions is implicit in the statement.

Statement: Driving under the influence of alcohol and/or narcotic substance is prohibited in law.

Assumptions:

I. Being under such influence impairs one's ability to use one's common sense and think long term.

II. Being under such influence slows one's reaction time and makes it difficult for one's brain to process information.

Choose the ***most appropriate*** answer from the options given below:

A. Only assumption I is implicit

B. Only assumption II is implicit
C. Neither I nor II is implicit
D. Both I and II are implicit

91. The question given below consists of a statement, followed by two conclusions numbered I and II. You have to assume everything in the statement to be true, then consider the two conclusions together and decide which of them logically follows beyond a reasonable doubt from the information given in the statement.

Statement: Sand is not very good at retaining heat.

Conclusions:

I. Sandy deserts are very hot during the day when sand releases heat into the air, and is reheated by the sun.

II. Sandy deserts are very cold at night when sand has released heat into the air and cannot be reheated by the sun.

Choose the ***most appropriate*** answer from the options given below:

A. Only conclusion I follows
B. Only conclusion II follows
C. Both conclusions I and II follows
D. Neither I nor II follows

92. In the question below is given a statement followed by two assumptions numbered I and II. You have to consider the statement and the following assumptions and decide which of the assumptions is implicit in the statement.

Statement: Schools admit children living within a certain radius.

Assumptions:

I. The closer the homes of children are to their school, the easier it is for schools to collect fees.

II. The closer the homes of children are to their school, the easier it is for schools to drop children home in medical emergency.

Choose the ***most appropriate*** answer from the options given below:

A. Only assumption I is implicit
B. Only assumption II is implicit
C. Neither I nor II is implicit
D. Both I and II are implicit

93. Cardiologist is to heart as Pulmonologist is to:

A. Kidney B. Lung
C. Bones D. Pancreas

94. Floriculture is to flowers as Sericulture is to:

A. Vegetables B. Seeds
C. Milk D. Silk

95. Fiction is to Literature as Alliteration is to

A. Cinema B. Dress
C. Cuisine D. Figure of speech

96. Which of the following forms a consistent group?

(*a*) Dance (*b*) Opera
(*c*) Painting (*d*) Play
(*e*) Instrumental Music

Choose the ***correct*** answer from the options given below:

A. (*a*), (*b*), (*c*) and (*d*) only
B. (*a*), (*b*), (*c*) and (*e*) only
C. (*a*), (*b*), (*d*) and (*e*) only
D. (*a*), (*c*), (*d*) and (*e*) only

97. Which of the following forms a consistent group?

(*a*) Anthracite (*b*) Graphite
(*c*) Peat (*d*) Flint
(*e*) Bituminous

Chosse the ***correct*** answer from the options given below:

A. (*a*), (*b*), (*c*) and (*e*) only
B. (*a*), (*b*), (*d*) and (*e*) only
C. (*a*), (*c*), (*d*) and (*e*) only
D. (*b*), (*c*), (*d*) and (*e*) only

98. Which of the following forms a consistent group?

(*a*) Hygrometer (*b*) Barometer
(*c*) Thermometer (*d*) Glucometer

Choose the ***correct*** answer from the options given below:

A. (*a*), (*b*), (*c*) and (*d*) only
B. (*a*), (*b*), (*c*) and (*e*) only
C. (*a*), (*b*), (*d*) and (*e*) only
D. (*a*), (*c*), (*d*) and (*e*) only

99. If the following statements are True.

All poets are idealists; some idealists are philosophers; and some poets are not philosophers.

Which of the following statements can be inferred as True?

(*a*) Some idealists are poets
(*b*) No philosophers are poets
(*c*) Some philosophers are idealists
(*d*) Some poets are not idealists
(*e*) All idealists are poets

Choose the ***correct*** answer from the option given below':

A. (*a*), (*b*) and (*c*) only
B. (*b*), (*c*) and (*e*) only
C. (*a*) and (*c*) only
D. (*b*) and (*d*) only

100. If the following statements are True:

All snakes are reptiles; and some snakes are poisonous creatures; but some poisonous creatures are not snakes.

Which of the following statements can be inferred as True?

(*a*) Some snakes are not reptiles
(*b*) Some reptiles are not poisonous creatures
(*c*) No poisonous creatures are snakes
(*d*) Some reptiles are snakes
(*e*) All poisonous creatures are snakes

Choose the ***correct*** answer from the options given below:

A. (*a*), (*b*) and (*c*) only
B. (*b*), (*c*) and (*e*) only
C. (*a*) and (*c*) only
D. (*b*) and (*d*) only

ANSWERS

1	**2**	**3**	**4**	**5**	**6**	**7**	**8**	**9**	**10**
B, D	C	C	C	A, B	C	A, B	B	B	A, B
11	**12**	**13**	**14**	**15**	**16**	**17**	**18**	**19**	**20**
C, D	B	C	D	B	A	D	A	B	A
21	**22**	**23**	**24**	**25**	**26**	**27**	**28**	**29**	**30**
B	D	D	A	A	C	D	D	C	D
31	**32**	**33**	**34**	**35**	**36**	**37**	**38**	**39**	**40**
C	D	A	*	*	C	B	D	B	D
41	**42**	**43**	**44**	**45**	**46**	**47**	**48**	**49**	**50**
D	*	C	*	D	A	C	B	A	B, C
51	**52**	**53**	**54**	**55**	**56**	**57**	**58**	**59**	**60**
A	C	D	A	A	B	B	C	C	C
61	**62**	**63**	**64**	**65**	**66**	**67**	**68**	**69**	**70**
C	C	C	C	A	A	B	B	D	A
71	**72**	**73**	**74**	**75**	**76**	**77**	**78**	**79**	**80**
C	A	B	A	*	C	C	D	B	C
81	**82**	**83**	**84**	**85**	**86**	**87**	**88**	**89**	**90**
C	A	B	A	*	B	C	C	B	D
91	**92**	**93**	**94**	**95**	**96**	**97**	**98**	**99**	**100**
C	C	B	D	D	C	A	*	C	D

Previous Paper (Solved)

LL.B. (Three Year Degree Course)

Entrance Examination, 2021*

1. Which of the following books is correctly matched to the author?

A. Rabindranath Tagore—The Collector's Wife

B. Jyotiba Phule—Such A Long Journey

C. Salman Rushdie—A Fine Balance

D. Khushwant Singh—Train To Pakistan

2. On August 15, 1947, the cabinet of Independent India consisted of:

(*a*) Bhimrao Ramji Ambedkar as the first Minister of Law.

(*b*) Sardar Vallabhbhai Patel as the first Minister of Defence.

Which of the above statement(s) is true:

A. Both B. Neither

C. (*a*) only D. (*b*) only

3. Russian revolution took place in the year ......

A. 1919 B. 1914

C. 1917 D. 1916

4. Three-banded rosefinch has been found recently in the state of

A. Assam

B. Nagaland

C. Arunachal Pradesh

D. Sikkim

5. Financial Inclusion Index is to be released by which of the following body?

A. NITI Aayog

B. Reserve Bank of India

C. National Bank for Agriculture and Rural Development

D. Small Industries Development Bank of India

6. Which among the following launched the Online Dispute Resolution Handbook?

A. National Development Council

B. National Consumer Disputes Redressal Commission

C. NITI Aayog

D. National Women Commission

7. Mental Wellbeing Digital platform MANAS stands for

A. Mental Health and Normalcy Augmentation System

B. Maternal Health and Normalcy Augmentation System

C. Mental Health and Non-Augmentation System

D. None of the these

8. Who among the following has not won the Rajiv Gandhi Khel Ratna Award 2020?

A. Rani Rampal B. Manika Batra

C. Vinesh Phogat D. Shikhar Dhawan

9. Who among the following has not won the Arjuna Award 2020?

A. Dutee Chand B. Ishant Sharma

C. Aditi Ashok D. Virat Kohli

10. Which of the following is correctly matched?

A. Mizoram – Aizawl

B. Manipur – Itanagar

C. Sikkim – Shillong

D. Meghalaya – Kohima

11. .... is the classical dance form of Kerala.

A. Bharatanatyam B. Sattriya

C. Kuchipudi D. Kathakali

*Conducted by NTA for Three year LL.B. Course Admission in University of Delhi.

12. The words "except the State of Jammu and Kashmir" have been omitted in section 1 of the Indian Penal Code, 1860 by:

A. Jammu and Kashmir Reorganisation Act, 2019.

B. Jammu and Kashmir Reorganisation Act, 2018.

C. Jammu and Kashmir Organisation Act, 2019.

D. Jammu and Kashmir Organisation Act, 2018.

13. X goes to a shop for buying an item costing ₹ 10. X gives a ₹ 10 coin to the shopkeeper, but the shopkeeper refuses to sell the item as he does not accept the ₹ 10 coin, arguing that ₹ 10 coin is not accepted in his locality. What legal option X has in this situation?

A. To file a case in the court against the Reserve Bank of India for circulating a coin which is refused by some

B. To file a police complaint against the shopkeeper for refusing a valid legal tender issued by the Reserve Bank of India

C. To file a Public Interest Litigation for declaring ₹ 10 coin as invalid

D. X has no legal option

14. A person who helps another person in the commission of an offence is a/an:

A. Abettor B. Instigator

C. Accomplice D. Friend

15. Principle: Whoever causes death by doing an act with the intention of causing death, or with the intention of causing such bodily injury as is likely to cause death commits the offence of murder.

Facts: A, knowing that Z is labouring under such a disease that a blow is likely to cause his death, strikes him with the intention of causing bodily injury. Z dies in consequence of the blow. A is liable for:

A. Culpable homicide not amounting to murder as another person with same blow would not have died.

B. Culpable homicide not amounting to murder as it was not certain the blow would kill Z.

C. Culpable homicide amounting to murder as A had intention of causing such bodily injury that is likely to cause death of Z owing to his disease.

D. Culpable homicide amounting to murder as A had intention of causing Z's death.

16. Who among the following has the power to issue an order under section 144 of the Criminal Procedure Code, 1973 (CrPC):

A. Commissioner of Police

B. Director General of Police

C. District Magistrate

D. Public Prosecutor

17. A puts jewels into a box belonging to Z, with the intention that they may be found in that box, and that this circumstance may cause Z to be convicted of theft. A has committed the offence of:

A. Lying

B. Giving false evidence

C. Fabricating evidence

D. Cheating

18. Which among the following offence is committed when a person voluntarily obstructs another so as to prevent the latter in proceeding in any direction in which that person has a right to proceed?

A. Wrongful confinement

B. Criminal use of force

C. Wrongful restraint

D. Assault

19. Principle: Nothing is an offence by reason of any harm which it may cause to a person for whose benefit it is done in good faith, even without that person's consent, if the circumstances are such that it is impossible for that person to signify consent.

Facts: Z is carried off by a tiger. A fires at the tiger knowing it to be likely that the shot may kill Z, but not intending to kill Z, and in good faith intending Z's benefit. A's ball gives Z a mortal wound.

A has committed:

A. Offence as A's ball has given Z a mortal wound.

B. Offence as he knew the shot may kill Z.

C. Offence as A did not fire for the benefit of Z.

D. No offence as A fired at the tiger in good faith for the benefit of Z and did not intend to kill Z.

20. In all robbery there is:

A. Only Extortion

B. Either theft or extortion

C. Only Theft

D. Both theft and extortion

21. Who chaired the First Law Commission that prepared the first draft of the Indian Penal Code?

A. Warren Hastings B. Thomas Macaulay

C. William Bentinck D. Charles Hardinge

22. Criminal Procedure falls under which of the following lists of the Indian Constitution?

A. State List B. Union List

C. Concurrent List D. List of States

23. Principle: Whoever, intending to take dishonestly any movable property out of the possession of any person without that person's consent, moves that property in order to such taking, is said to commit theft.

Facts: A sees a ring belonging to Z lying on a table in Z's house. Not venturing to misappropriate the ring immediately for fear of search and detection, A hides the ring in a place where it is highly improbable that it will ever be found by Z, with the intention of taking the ring from the hiding place and selling it when the loss is forgotten.

A has committed:

A. Theft at the time of first moving the ring

B. Theft at the time when he comes back to take the ring

C. No offence

D. Criminal misappropriation

24. How many places of sitting the National Green Tribunal has?

A. One B. Three

C. Four D. Five

25. The World Commission on Environment and Development in its report titled .... defined sustainable development as 'development that meets the needs of the present without compromising the ability of future generations to meet their own needs'. Choose the correct answer from options below.

A. Brundtland Report

B. Our Common Future

C. Agenda 21

D. Caring For the Earth : A Strategy for Sustainable Living

26. What is the main objective of the United Nations Framework Convention on Climate Change (UNFCCC)?

A. Decrease of oxygen

B. Stabilisation of greenhouse gases

C. Increase of greenhouse gases

D. Increase of temperature

27. World Environmental Day is celebrated on

A. December 10 B. April 30

C. June 5 D. August 15

28. Advocate M.C. Mehta is known in the context of

A. Public interest environmental litigations

B. Challenging the election of former Prime Minister Mrs Indira Gandhi

C. Challenging the Aadhaar project

D. Challenging the law that prohibited entry of women to Sabarimala temple in Kerala

29. Noise pollution was included in the Air (Prevention and Control of Pollution) Act, 1981 as pollution in the year ....

A. 1981 B. 1987

C. 1982 D. 2000

30. A person sold a watch for ₹ 1520 and thereby losses 5%. In order to gain 10% she has to sell the watch for

A. ₹ 1660 B. ₹ 1760

C. ₹ 1600 D. ₹ 1680

31. B is to the North of A, C is to the East of A, E is to the south of C, and D is to the West of A. Then, what is the position of D in relation to C?

A. South B. South-West
C. South-East D. West

32. Of the three numbers, the first is half of the second and twice the third. The average of these numbers is 42. The smallest of these numbers is

A. 36 B. 18
C. 12 D. 24

33. Four members have to be nominated to a Committee and there are six candidates, A, B, C, D, E and F. The following conditions apply:

(*a*) If A is nominated, then D does not find any place

(*b*) If B is nominated, then either E or F has to be nominated, but not both

(*c*) If C is nominated, then both D and B have to be nominated.

Which one of the following is an acceptable combination?

A. A, B, C and E B. A, B, C and D
C. B, C, E and F D. B, C, D and F

34. What is the next number in this sequence?

1, 3, 9, 23, 53,

A. 100 B. 115
C. 155 D. 125

35. What is the next number in this sequence?

1, 1, 2, 3, 5, 8, ?

A. 12 B. 13
C. 15 D. 14

36. "Only the party who has suffered damage or injury can approach the court of law".

The above rule is based on the principle of:

A. *Locus standi* B. *Modus operandi*
C. *Quid pro quo* D. *Status quo*

37. Which of the following is not a Directive Principle of State Policy in the Constitution of India?

A. Organization of village panchayats
B. Equal pay for equal work for both men and women
C. To develop the scientific temper, humanism and the spirit of enquiry and reform
D. Protection of monuments and places and objects of national importance

38. Remedy of restitution of conjugal rights is available under the Hindu Marriage Act, 1955 to:

A. Husband only
B. Wife only
C. Both wife and husband
D. Divorced wife only

39. Geeta is a Jain and Shyam is a Hindu. Their marriage can be solemnized under:

A. Special Marriage Act, 1954
B. Hindu Marriage Act, 1955
C. Either 1 or 2
D. Neither 1 nor 2

40. Which one of the following is not a source of Muslim Law?

A. Quran B. Sunnat
C. Shruti D. Ijma

41. In which of the following cases has the Supreme Court of India made it mandatory for candidates contesting elections to the legislatures and their spouses to declare their source of income at the time of filing nominations?

A. Lok Prahari v. Union of India
B. Jan Chaukidar v. Union of India
C. People's Union for Democratic Rights v. Union of India
D. People's Union for Civil Liberties v. Union of India

42. In which of the following cases did the Supreme Court of India hold that seeking votes in the name of voters' religion amounts to a corrupt practice?

A. Abhiram Singh v. C.D. Commachen
B. Prabhakaran v. Jayarajan
C. Lily Thomas v. Union of India
D. S. Subramaniam Balaji v. Govt. of Tamil Nadu

43. Consider the following and identify the correct statement(s).

(*a*) A President of India is not eligible for re-election

(*b*) Lok Sabha is the Upper House of Parliament

(*c*) Total number of High Courts in India at present is 25

(*d*) There is no constitutional provision for Deputy Prime-Minister in the Constitution of India

Choose the correct option(s) from the options given below

A. (*a*) and (*b*) only B. (*b*) and (*c*) only
C. (*c*) and (*d*) only D. (*d*) only

44. The question regarding disqualification of the Speaker of the Lok Sabha under the X Schedule of the Constitution of India is referred for the decision to:

A. Deputy Chairperson of the Rajya Sabha
B. Deputy Speaker of the Lok Sabha
C. The President of India
D. A member elected for this purpose by the Lok Sabha

45. The electoral college that elects the President of India comprises of:

A. All members of both the Houses of Parliament
B. Elected members of both the Houses of Parliament and of State Legislative Assemblies of the states
C. All members of both Houses of Parliament and State Legislative Assemblies
D. All members of both Houses of Parliament and State Legislative Assemblies and Councils

46. The usual process of a valid Agreement includes of different stages:

(*a*) Acceptance (*b*) Agreement
(*c*) Consideration (*d*) Offer

Arrange the above in sequence and choose the correct answer from the options given below:

A. (*d*), (*c*), (*a*), (*b*) B. (*d*), (*b*), (*a*), (*c*)
C. (*d*), (*a*), (*c*), (*b*) D. (*d*), (*b*), (*c*), (*a*)

47. From whom is an offer addressed to when a product is kept on the shelf of a shop with a price tag attached?

A. Shopkeeper B. Shop Attendant
C. Manufacturer D. Customer

48. Legal Principle: Any contract made for an unlawful consideration is void in law.

Facts: Mr. X agrees to pay ₹ 1000 to Mr. Z for giving false evidence in the Court.

Choose the correct answer:

A. The contract is voidable at the option of Mr. Z due to the risk involved in it.
B. The contract is void due to unlawful consideration.
C. The contract is valid and Mr. Z must perform it.
D. The contract is voidable at the option of Mr. X.

49. The active concealment of the facts while entering into a contract is considered:

A. Mistake B. Misrepresentation
C. Fraud D. Coercion

50. Mr. X entered into contract with A to deliver 10 kgs of mangoes to Mr. A on 20th July. On 18th July, Mr. X refused to perform the contract. This is an instance of:

A. Abandonment of contract
B. Remission of contract
C. Breach of contract
D. Anticipatory breach of contract

51. The subsequent changes made in the nature of contract is known as:

A. Novation B. Alteration
C. Rescission D. Repudiation

52. If a company enters into a contract beyond the scope of its object, it becomes:

A. Intra vires B. Infra vires
C. Ultra vires D. Ultimo vires

53. Which among the following is entitled to be protected through copyright?

A. Facts
B. Ideas
C. Expressions
D. Methods of operation

54. The maximum term of protection for a literary work of an individual author under the Copyright Act, 1957 is:
A. 60 years
B. Lifetime of the author plus 60 years
C. Lifetime of the author plus 70 years
D. 20 years

55. An invention is protected by
A. Copyright B. Trademark
C. Industrial design D. Patent

56. Consider the following statements about Intellectual Property (IP) and identify correct statement(s).
(*a*) IP refers to the creations of the mind such as inventions, literary, artistic works
(*b*) IP includes patents and copyright
(*c*) IP does not include trademarks
(*d*) IP does not include industrial designs

Choose the correct answer from the options given below:
A. (*a*) and (*c*) only B. (*b*) and (*d*) only
C. (*a*) only D. (*a*) and (*b*) only

57. Match List-I with List-II

List-I	List-II
(*a*) Albert Einstein	(*i*) Television
(*b*) Alexander Fleming	(*ii*) Theory of Relativity
(*c*) Charles Darwin	(*iii*) Penicillin
(*d*) John Logie Baird	(*iv*) Theory of Evolution

Choose the correct answer from the options given below:

	(*a*)	(*b*)	(*c*)	(*d*)
A.	(*ii*)	(*iii*)	(*iv*)	(*i*)
B.	(*ii*)	(*iv*)	(*i*)	(*iii*)
C.	(*ii*)	(*i*)	(*iv*)	(*iii*)
D.	(*ii*)	(*iv*)	(*iii*)	(*i*)

58. Given below are two statements, one is labelled as Assertion (A) and the other is labelled as Reason (R)

Assertion (A): The writing material of a pencil is generally made up of Graphite.

Reason (R): Graphite is a good conductor of electricity.

In light of the above statements, choose the correct answer from the options given below
A. Both (A) and (R) are true and (R) is the correct explanation of (A)
B. Both (A) and (R) are true, but (R) is NOT the correct explanation of (A)
C. (A) is true, but (R) is false
D. (A) is false, but (R) is true

59. Who among the following is called the 'Father of Artificial Intelligence'?
A. John McCarthy
B. Charles Babbage
C. John Brunner
D. JP Eckert

60. Histology is the study of:
A. Fungi B. Bones
C. Tissue D. Virus

61. Read the statements and choose the correct answer from the options given below:
(*a*) The chemical name of baking soda is Sodium Carbonate.
(*b*) Baking soda forms alkaline solution with water.

Which of the above statements are true:
A. Both are true B. Neither is true
C. Only (*a*) is true D. Only (*b*) is true

62. Choose the correctly matched option given below:
A. The Nobel Prize in Chemistry 2020: William D. Nordhaus and Paul M. Romer
B. The Nobel Prize in Physiology or Medicine 2020: Alvin E. Roth and Lloyd S. Shapley
C. The Sveriges Riksbank Prize in Economic Sciences 2020: Paul R. Milgrom and Robert B. Wilson
D. Nobel Prize in Physics 2020 : Abhijit Banerjee and Esther Duflo

63. The Finance Minister presented the Government of India's Budget for the year 2021-2022 in the Parliament on:

A. 1 January 2021 B. 1 February 2021
C. 1 March 2021 D. 31 March 2021

64. Nora-al-Matroushi is the first female_______ from ______. Choose the correct answer from the options below:
A. Astronaut, Bangladesh
B. Astronaut, UAE
C. Lawyer, Iran
D. Lawyer, Israel

65. Read the statements and choose the correct answer from the options given below.
(*a*) The Chairperson of the NITI Aayog is the Prime Minister of India.
(*b*) Minister of Defence is an ex-officio member of NITI Aayog.

Which of the above statements are true:
A. Both are true B. Neither is true
C. Only (*a*) D. Only (*b*)

66. Office of Economic Adviser (OEA) is an attached office of the:
A. Department of Economic Affairs, Ministry of Finance, Government of India
B. Department of Expenditure, Ministry of Finance, Government of India
C. Department of Commerce, Ministry of Commerce & Industry, Government of India
D. Department for Promotion of Industry and Internal Trade, Ministry of Commerce & Industry, Government of India

67. Which among the following is the apex body responsible for implementing India's flagship public health insurance/assurance scheme called 'Ayushman Bharat Pradhan Mantri Jan Arogya Yojana'?
A. All India Institute of Medical Sciences
B. Health department of different states
C. National Health Authority
D. National Health Mission

68. The Nobel Peace Prize for 2020 was awarded to ....
A. World Health Organisation
B. World Food Programme
C. United Nations Development Programme
D. United Nations Environment Programme

69. The Nobel Prize in Physiology or Medicine is awarded by ....
A. The Nobel Assembly at Karolinska Institutet, Stockholm, Sweden
B. The Royal Swedish Academy of Sciences, Stockholm, Sweden
C. The Swedish Academy, Stockholm, Sweden
D. The Committee of the Norwegian Parliament

70. Read the statements and choose the correct answer from the options given below.
(*a*) Kangana Ranaut won the best female actor award as per the National Film Awards 2020.
(*b*) She was awarded the National Film Award for her work in *Manikarnika* and *Judgementall Hai Kya.*

Which of the above statements are true:
A. Both (*a*) and (*b*) are true
B. Neither (*a*) nor (*b*) is true
C. Only (*a*) is true
D. Only (*b*) is true

71. Given below are three statements

Statement I: India is a federal polity.

Statement II: India's federal model is different from the federal model of the United States of America.

Statement III: Federalism implies horizontal distribution of power between the executive, legislature and the judiciary.

In light of the above statements, choose the correct answer from the options given below
A. Statement I is true
B. Statements II and III are true
C. Statements I and II are true
D. Statements I, II and III are true

72. Read the following statement(s) in the context of the 'Socially and Educationally Backward Classes Act, 2018' [The Act] passed by the Maharashtra legislature:

Statement I: The Act has been challenged on the ground that it violates the maximum limit of 50 per cent imposed on reservations

Statement II: The limit of 50 per cent on reservation is expressly mentioned in the text of the Article 16 of the Constitution of India, 1950

Statement III: According to the Supreme Court judgment of Indra Sawhney v Union of India (1992), the State governments can provide reservation beyond 50 per cent in 'exceptional circumstances'.

Statement IV: The limit of 50 per cent on reservation is not mentioned expressly in the text of Article 16 of the Constitution of India, 1950

Which of the above-mentioned statement(s) is correct:

A. I and II only
B. II, III and IV only
C. I, III and IV only
D. III and IV only

73. Which of the following principles can be located in the Constitution of India?

(*a*) Separation of Power
(*b*) Federalism
(*c*) Parliamentary Sovereignty
(*d*) Secularism

Choose the correct answer from the options given below:

A. (*a*), (*b*) and (*d*) only
B. (*a*), (*b*) and (*c*) only
C. (*b*), (*c*) and (*d*) only
D. (*c*) and (*d*) only

74. According to the text of Articles 19(1)(a) and 19(2) of the Constitution of India, 1950, the State can make laws to restrict freedom of speech and expression on which of the following ground(s):

(*a*) Hate Speech
(*b*) Contempt of Court
(*c*) Defamation
(*d*) Decency or morality

Choose the correct answer from the options given below:

A. (*a*), (*b*) and (*c*) only
B. (*a*), (*b*) and (*d*) only
C. (*b*) and (*d*) only
D. (*b*), (*c*) and (*d*) only

75. Under the Citizenship (Amendment) Act, 2019, persons belonging to Hindu, Sikh, Buddhist, Jain, Parsi or Christian community from certain specified countries are not be treated as illegal migrants. Which are those countries?

(*a*) Afghanistan
(*b*) Bangladesh
(*c*) Pakistan
(*d*) Myanmar

Choose the correct answer from the options given below:

A. (*c*) only
B. (*b*) and (*c*) only
C. (*a*), (*b*) and (*c*) only
D. (*a*), (*b*), (*c*) and (*d*)

76. Which of the following statement(s) is not true about the role and status of the Governor in India?

(*a*) The Governor is elected by the State Legislature.
(*b*) The Governor is appointed by the President of India.
(*c*) A person who has completed the age of thirty years can be a Governor.
(*d*) The same person cannot be appointed as the Governor of two or more states.

Choose the correct answer from the options given below:

A. (*a*), (*b*) and (*d*) only
B. (*a*) and (*d*) only
C. (*a*), (*c*) and (*d*) only
D. (*a*) and (*c*) only

77. Which among the following states does not have veto power in the United Nations Security Council?

A. The United States of America
B. Germany

C. Russia
D. The United Kingdom

78. Which International organization is hearing the case of Gambia v. Myanmar commonly referred to as the *Rohingya Genocide* case?
A. African Court on Human and Peoples' Rights
B. International Court of Justice
C. International Criminal Court
D. United Nations High Commissioner for Refugees

79. Which of the following countries has not signed the statute of the International Criminal Court?
A. Germany B. Brazil
C. Australia D. China

80. The World Health Organization (WHO) headquarters is situated in
A. Paris B. Geneva
C. The Hague D. Washington DC

81. Which of the following countries is not a member of the South Asian Association for Regional Cooperation (SAARC)?
A. Bhutan B. Bangladesh
C. Myanmar D. Afghanistan

82. Which of the following alliance is created to provide collective security?
A. ASEAN B. NATO
C. SAARC D. NAFTA

83. Which organ of the United Nations has accomplished its mandate and ceased to be operational?
A. Trusteeship Council
B. General Assembly
C. International Court of Justice
D. Economic and Social Council

84. The recent Supreme Court judgment Nitisha v. Union of India (2021) of India held that:
A. The Hindu Succession Act, 1956 discriminated between men and women
B. Denial of entry in religious places to women violated right to equality
C. The Indian Army's policy on the Grant of Permanent Commission to women violated right to equality
D. The offence of adultery under the Indian Penal Code, 1860 violates the right to equality

85. Who was the first chief justice of the Supreme Court of India?
A. H.J. Kania
B. M. Patanjali Sastri
C. Mehr Chand Mahajan
D. Bijan Kumar Mukherjea

86. Who among the following was the shortest serving chief justice of the Supreme Court of India?
A. Kamal Narain Singh
B. Madhukar Hiralal Kania
C. Lalit Mohan Sharma
D. Mohammad Hidayatullah

87. Which among the following schedules of the Constitution of India deals with the distribution of legislative power between the Parliament and state legislatures?
A. Schedule I
B. Schedule III
C. Schedule V
D. Schedule VII

88. Article 1 of the Constitution of India defines India as:
A. Federal State
B. Unitary State
C. Union of States
D. Quasi-Federal State

89. Which among the following is related to the issuing of first compulsory licensing on pharmaceutical patent in India?
A. Bayer v. Natco
B. Novartis v. Union of India & Others
C. Novartis v. Cipla
D. Merk v. Glenmark

90. Which of the following is not a nature of 'torts'?
A. It is a civil wrong
B. It is only a wrong against individual

C. There must be a wrongful act
D. It is mainly developed from common law principles

91. Which of the following statements is not true?
A. Duty under tort is fixed by law
B. Duty under tort is a moral duty
C. Duty under tort is not fixed by the parties
D. Duty under tort is towards the whole world

92. Ms. Shilpa Sheg separated from Mr. Arun Sheg through a decree of divorce. Then after she married to Mr. Kunal Vesth but continued with 'Sheg' title of her earlier husband without any malice. Mr. Arun Sheg filed a suit for removal of 'Sheg' title from the name of Ms. Shilpa Sheg. Continuing the "Sheg" title by Ms. Shilpa is
A. a tort because it is a violation of the right of Mr. Arun
B. not a tort because it is not a violation of the right of Mr. Arun
C. a tort because it is a violation of duty by Ms. Shilpa
D. a crime

93. Mr. A lets out his crane and driver to Mr. B for carrying B's business under a contract providing that the driver shall be the servant of Mr. B. The crane driver by his negligence injured a person walking on the road. Who will be liable for the negligence of the driver?
A. Mr. A
B. Mr. B
C. Both Mr. A and B
D. Only the Driver

94. The enforcement of which of the following Fundamental Rights guaranteed by the Constitution of India, 1950, cannot be suspended due to the Proclamation of Emergency on account of war or external aggression?
A. Right to freedom of speech and expression
B. Right to life and personal liberty
C. Right to religion
D. Right to equality

95. Which of the following rights are a part of freedom of speech and expression guaranteed by the Constitution of India, 1950?
(*a*) Exercise of freedom of speech and expression through the medium of internet
(*b*) Right to information
(*c*) Right to broadcast
(*d*) Right to remain silent

In light of the above statements, choose the correct answer from the options given below
A. (*a*), (*b*) and (*c*) only
B. (*b*), (*c*) and (*d*) only
C. (*a*), (*b*) and (*d*) only
D. (*a*), (*b*), (*c*) and (*d*)

Directions (Qs. No. 96-100): *Read the passage and answer the following questions:*

In short, to give life "is to frame and make a living creature, fashion the parts, and mould and suit them to their uses; and having proportioned and fitted them together, to put into them a living soul." Parents do not fashion the child and most commonly, do not even intend to create it; they do so as a by-product of the instinctive desires God has placed in them. In response to Filmer's claims, Locke states, "They who say the father gives life to children, are so dazzled with the thoughts of monarchy, that they do not, as they ought, remember God, who is "the Author and Giver of Life." Parents have fiduciary responsibility for their children on Locke's account, but it expires upon their maturity. Parents are obliged to provide for their children "not as their own workmanship, but the workmanship of their own maker."

This is why Locke insists that although children are not born in a "state of equality, though they are born to it." Adults have "a sort of rule and jurisdiction over them when they come into the world, and for some time after; but it is a temporary one." The bonds of children's subjection "are like the Swadling Cloths they are wrapt up in, and supported by, in the weakness of their Infancy." Developing age and reason loosen these bonds, "till at length they drop quite off, and leave a man at his own free disposal." The power to command "ends with nonage." Thereafter, although "honour and respect, support and defense, and whatsoever gratitude can oblige a man to, for the highest benefits he is naturally capable of, be always due from a son to his parents; yet all this puts no sceptre into the father's hand, no sovereign power of commanding." The only legitimate sanction at the parent's disposal is the power to withhold inheritance, or "to bestow it with a more sparing or liberal hand, according as the behaviour of this or that child hath comported with his will and humor." Parents are to "inform the mind, and govern the actions of their yet ignorant nonage, till reason shall take its place, and ease them of that trouble." This treatment of children reflects an inclusive view of the right to make decisions for oneself: the only justifiable basis for paternalism is incapacity.

One reason that Locke's view of moral equality has had staying power since he wrote is that the obvious secular analogue of his claim that we are all God's property is that we are nobody's property. The workmanship model persisted in the western intellectual consciousness long after it was cut loose from its Lockean theological moorings. If we abandon the theology yet still embrace the workmanship ideal as most in the Enlightenment tradition since Locke—be they conservatives, liberals, or radicals—have done, the logic of his argument against Filmer continues to hold. Indeed, it can be extended: parents cannot own children because they do not make them, but by the same token nor can anyone else own them. In this way the egalitarian logic of his argument against Filmer extends beyond their theological disagreements.

96. According to Locke, who is the creator of life?

A. Parents B. Mother
C. Monarch D. God

97. Adult's rule and jurisdiction over children...

(*a*) Is temporary.
(*b*) Is based on infancy of the child.
(*c*) Never ends with nonage.
(*d*) Can be justified as paternalism based on incapacity.

Choose the correct answer from the **options** given below:

A. (*a*), (*b*), (*c*) and (*d*)
B. (*a*) and (*b*) only
C. (*a*), (*b*) and (*c*) only
D. (*a*), (*b*) and (*d*) only

98. The reason that Locke's theory has survived the test of time is:

(*a*) That we all are God's property.
(*b*) That we all are nobody's property.
(*c*) That his theory was secular.
(*d*) That his theory's secular analogue **is** accepted by intellectuals.

Choose the correct answer from the **options** given below:

A. (*b*) and (*c*) only
B. (*a*) and (*c*) only
C. (*a*), (*b*) and (*d*) only
D. (*b*) and (*d*) only

99. "Parents are to "inform the mind, and **govern** the actions of their yet ignorant nonage**, till** reason shall take its place, and ease **them of** that trouble." Who is having this troub**le and** what is the trouble?

(*a*) Children, inability to make decision**s**
(*b*) Parents, informing the child and gover**ning** their actions
(*c*) God, fashioning a child
(*d*) Locke, explaining the theory

Choose the correct answer from the **options** given below:

A. (*d*) only
B. (*c*) and (*d*) only
C. (*a*), (*b*) and (*c*) only
D. (*b*) only

100. This passage can have its "Title" as:

A. Child is the Father of Man
B. Infancy of Child
C. Theory of Moral Equality
D. Filmer's Theory

ANSWERS

1	2	3	4	5	6	7	8	9	10
D	C	C	C	B	C	A	D	D	A
11	**12**	**13**	**14**	**15**	**16**	**17**	**18**	**19**	**20**
D	A	B	A	C	C	C	C	D	B
21	**22**	**23**	**24**	**25**	**26**	**27**	**28**	**29**	**30**
B	C	A	D	B	B	C	A	B	B
31	**32**	**33**	**34**	**35**	**36**	**37**	**38**	**39**	**40**
D	B	D	B	B	A	C	C	C	C
41	**42**	**43**	**44**	**45**	**46**	**47**	**48**	**49**	**50**
A	A	C	D	B	C	*	B	C	D
51	**52**	**53**	**54**	**55**	**56**	**57**	**58**	**59**	**60**
B	C	C	B	D	D	A	B	A	C
61	**62**	**63**	**64**	**65**	**66**	**67**	**68**	**69**	**70**
D	C	B	B	A & C	D	C	B	A	*
71	**72**	**73**	**74**	**75**	**76**	**77**	**78**	**79**	**80**
C	C	A	D	C	C	B	B	D	B
81	**82**	**83**	**84**	**85**	**86**	**87**	**88**	**89**	**90**
C	B	A	C	A	A	D	C	A	B
91	**92**	**93**	**94**	**95**	**96**	**97**	**98**	**99**	**100**
B	B	A	B	D	D	D	D	D	C

Previous Paper (Solved)

LL.B. (Three Year Degree Course)

Entrance Examination, 2020*

Directions (Qs. No. 1-5): *Read the passage and answer the following questions:*

What I have tried to do is to discern and articulate the natural laws of a particular kind of human undertaking, which I have described as "the enterprise of subjecting human conduct to the governance of rules". These natural laws have nothing to do with any "brooding omnipresence in the skies". Nor have they the slightest affinity with any such proposition as that the practice of contraception is a violation of God's law. They remain entirely terrestrial in origin and application.

They are not "higher" laws; if any metaphor of elevation is appropriate they should be called "lower" laws. They are like the natural laws of carpentry, or at least those laws respected by a carpenter who wants the house he builds to remain standing and serve the purpose of those who live in it.

Though these natural laws touch one of the most vital of human activities they obviously do not exhaust the whole of man's moral life. They have nothing to say on topics as polygamy, the study of Marx, the worship of God, the progressive income tax, or the subjugation of women. If the question be raised whether any of these subjects, or others like them, should be taken as objects of legislation, that question relates to what I have called the external morality of law.

As a convenient (though not wholly satisfactory) way of describing the distinction being taken we may speak of a procedural, as distinguished from a substantive natural law. What I have called the internal morality of law is in this sense a procedural version of natural law, though to avoid misunderstanding the word 'procedural' should be assigned a special and expanded sense so that it would include, for example, a substantive accord between official action and enacted law. The term 'procedural' is, however, broadly appropriate as indicating that we are concerned, not with the substantive aims of legal rules, but with the ways in which a system of rules for governing human conduct must be constructed and administered if it is to be efficacious and at the same time remain what it purports to be.

1. The passage is an explanation of....

1. Legal Morality
2. The Worship of God
3. Natural Law
4. God's Law

Choose the correct option from below.

A. 1, 2, 3 & 4 B. 1 and 3 only
C. 2 and 3 only D. 3 only

2. The procedural version of natural law relates to:

A. Internal morality
B. External morality
C. Objects of legislation
D. Human activities

3. Natural laws, according to this passage, are:

1. the ones, having brooding omnipresence in the skies
2. terrestrial in origin and application
3. higher laws
4. lower laws

Choose the correct option from below:

A. Both 1 and 3 B. 1, 2 and 3 only
C. Both 2 and 3 D. Both 2 and 4

*Conducted by NTA for Three year LL.B. Course Admission in University of Delhi.

4. The term 'procedural' means and includes:
1. A substantive accord between official action and enacted law
2. Administration of a system of rules for governing human conduct
3. Construction of a system of rules for governing human conduct
4. External morality

Choose the correct option from below.
A. 1, 2, 3 & 4 B. 1, 2 and 3 only
C. 2 and 3 only D. 4 only

5. The enterprise of subjecting human conduct to the governance of rules relates to:
1. Natural laws
2. God's laws
3. Objects of legislation
4. Higher laws

Choose the correct option from below.
A. 1, 2, 3 & 4 B. 1 only
C. Both 2 and 3 D. 4 only

6. According to the World Bank's 'Ease of Doing Business rankings', benchmarked to May 2019, India is ranked at:
A. 89 B. 75
C. 63 D. 91

7. The difference between total revenue and total expenditure of a government is termed as:
A. Fiscal deficit
B. Revenue deficit
C. Primary deficit
D. Monetised deficit

8. In 2019, the Sveriges Riksbank Prize in Economic Sciences in memory of Alfred Nobel was awarded to:
A. Richard H. Thaler
B. William D. Nordhaus
C. Paul M. Romer
D. Michael Kremer

9. As per law, the monetary policy framework in India shall be operated by:
A. NITI Aayog
B. Reserve Bank of India
C. Department of Economic Affairs
D. Department of Revenue

10. The head office of the Securities and Exchange Board of India is located at:
A. Delhi
B. Kolkata
C. Mumbai
D. Chennai

11. Who among the following was not a recipient of a Nobel Prize?
A. Madam Marie Curie
B. Abhijeet Banerjee
C. Mahatma Gandhi
D. Mother Teresa

12. Which of the following represents the correct order of organising Tennis Grand Slams in an year (from January to December)?
A. Australian Open, French Open, Wimbledon, US Open
B. US Open, Wimbledon, Australian Open, French Open
C. Australian Open, Wimbledon, French Open, US Open
D. Wimbledon, French Open, US Open, Australian Open

13. Who among the following was not in the list of Bharat Ratna awardees in 2019?
A. Pranab Mukherjee
B. Bhupen Hazarika
C. Nanaji Deshmukh
D. Deen Dayal Upadhyay

14. Who won the Dadasaheb Phalke Award, 2019?
A. Rajnikant B. Amitabh Bachchan
C. Bhupen Hazarika D. None of these

15. Who among the following are the recipients of the Rajiv Gandhi Khel Ratna Award, 2019?
A. Virat Kohli and Cheteswar Pujara
B. Deepa Malik and Bajrang Punia
C. Fouaad Mirza and Gaurav Singh Gill
D. Pooja Dhanda and Gurmeet Singh Sandhu

16. Who among the following was the recipient of Raman Magsaysay Award, 2019?
A. Ravish Kumar
B. Arnab Goswami
C. Sandip Pandey
D. Punya Prasun Bajpai

17. Which country won the FIFA World Cup Final 2018?
A. Croatia B. France
C. Brazil D. Germany

18. Where was the ICC Women's T20 World Cup 2020 organised?
A. England B. South Africa
C. Australia D. West Indies

19. Who among the following have won the best actress and best actor awards for 66th National Film Awards 2019?
A. Keerthy Suresh, Ayushmann Khurana, Vicky Kaushal
B. Deepika Padukon, Ayushmann Khurana, Akshay Kumar
C. Kangana Ranaut, Vicky Kaushal, Swanand Kirkere
D. Keerthy Suresh, Akshay Kumar, Swanand Kirkere

20. Which of the following city was granted cleanest capital city award as per the Swachh Survekshan Awards 2019?
A. Lucknow B. Mumbai
C. Panaji D. Bhopal

21. Who won the Ranji Trophy 2019-20?
A. Saurashtra B. Vidarbha
C. Delhi D. Karnataka

22. 'Vyom Mitra' is ________.
A. An unmanned aerial vehicle to observe air quality
B. A nanosatellite developed by India in association with Japan
C. A humanoid which will be sent by ISRO in space.
D. An indigenously designed aircraft to rescue people from natural disasters.

23. Which of the following reports is/are released by the World Bank?
(*a*) Women, Business and the Law
(*b*) The World's Women
(*c*) Economic Freedom Index
Choose the correct answer from the options given below:
A. (*a*) only B. (*c*) only
C. (*a*) and (*c*) only D. (*a*) and (*b*) only

24. Consider the following statements regarding Bharat Interface for Money (BHIM) and answer the following question.
1. It is a payment interface developed by Reserve Bank of India (RBI) to allow real-time fund transfer.
2. It allows for the linking of multiple bank accounts and the option of applying in Initial Public Offer (IPO).

Which of the statements given above is/are correct?
A. 1 only
B. 2 only
C. Both 1 and 2
D. Neither 1 nor 2

25. Which among the following releases the Human Capital Index?
A. World Bank
B. International Monetary Fund
C. United Nation Development Program
D. World Economic Forum

26. '*Mohiniyattam*', a classical solo dance, originated in:
A. Odisha B. Kerala
C. Tamil Nadu D. None of these

27. Which among the following stands for USB in relation to laptops and computers?
A. Unique Storage Bus
B. Universal Series Bus
C. Universal Serial Bus
D. Unique Series Bus

28. Which one of these is not a specialized agency of the United Nations?
A. International Civil Aviation Organization
B. International Labour Organization
C. Food and Agricultural Organization
D. World Trade Organization

29. Which Indian Judge was a member of the International Criminal Tribunal for the Far East (Tokyo Tribunal)?
A. Judge Radha Binod Paul
B. Judge Nagendra Singh
C. Judge Dalveer Bhandari
D. Judge Hiralal J. Kania

30. Which one of the following is a tripartite UN agency?
A. International Civil Aviation Organization
B. International Maritime Organization
C. International Labour Organization
D. International Criminal Court

31. Which one of the following was established by the Rome Statute?
A. International Criminal Court
B. International Criminal Tribunal for Rwanda
C. International Crimes Tribunal, Bangladesh
D. Special court for Sierra Leone

32. Which one of the following is not a principal organ of the United Nations?
A. Trusteeship Council
B. General Assembly
C. Human Rights Council
D. Security Council

33. In India, the writ of *prohibition* may be issued, when there is ________.
A. Both an absence of jurisdiction or excess of jurisdiction & violation of principles of natural justice
B. Violation of principles of natural justice
C. An absence of jurisdiction or excess of jurisdiction
D. A request to produce the body of the person

34. Which Schedule of the Constitution of India, 1950 prescribes the forms of oaths or affirmations for constitutional functionaries?
A. Sixth Schedule B. Second Schedule
C. Fifth Schedule D. Third Schedule

35. Who declared a state of emergency in India under Article 352 of the Constitution of India in the year 1975?
A. Indira Gandhi
B. Giani Zail Singh
C. Fakhruddin Ali Ahmed
D. Sanjay Gandhi

36. Who among the following has a casting vote over a bill in a joint parliamentary session?
A. Chairman of Rajya Sabha
B. Speaker of Lok Sabha
C. Deputy Speaker of Rajya Sabha
D. President of India

37. Exchange of Enclaves between India and Bangladesh was executed through:
A. 100th Constitutional Amendment Act
B. 101st Constitutional Amendment Act
C. 102nd Constitutional Amendment Act
D. 99th Constitutional Amendment Act

38. Article 44 of the Constitution of India is related to:
A. Uniform Civil Code for citizens
B. Provision of early childhood care and education to children below the age of 6 years
C. The duty of the state to raise the level of nutrition
D. Organization of agriculture and animal husbandry

39. Supreme Court of India's judgement in Justice K.S. Puttaswamy (Retd.) and Anr. *v* Union of India and Ors is related to:
A. Right to Privacy B. 2G Spectrum
C. Coal gate Scam D. Section 377 of IPC

40. Indian legal system confers citizenship in the following manner:
(*a*) By Birth (*b*) By Descent
(*c*) By Naturalisation (*d*) By Registration

Choose the correct option:
A. (*a*) and (*b*) only
B. (*b*) and (*c*) only
C. (*a*), (*b*) and (*c*) only
D. All of these

41. The Citizenship (Amendment) Act, 2019 provides for special provisions for citizenship for migrants from the following countries:
(*a*) Myanmar (*b*) Afghanistan
(*c*) Bangladesh (*d*) Pakistan

Choose the correct answer from the options given below
A. (*a*), (*c*) and (*d*) only
B. (*b*), (*c*) and (*d*) only
C. (*a*), (*b*) and (*c*) only
D. All of these

42. According to the Constitution of India, which of the following fundamental rights cannot be suspended during national emergency?
A. Article 19 and 21
B. Article 14 and 21
C. Article 14 and 19
D. Article 20 and 21

43. The pardoning power of the Governor of a state includes:
(*a*) Power to pardon a sentence of life imprisonment
(*b*) Power to grant pardon where the punishment or sentence is by Court Martial
(*c*) Power to remit a sentence
Choose the correct answer from the options given below:
A. (*a*) and (*c*) only B. (*b*) and (*c*) only
C. (*a*) only D. All of these

44. Which among the following recommended the inclusion of Fundamental Duties in the Constitution of India?
A. Swaran Singh Committee
B. Nehru Committee
C. Gadgill Committee
D. Mandal Commission

45. Which of the following option(s) are available for a party aggrieved by a decision of the Supreme Court of India?
(*a*) Curative Petition
(*b*) Review Petition
(*c*) Writ Petition
(*d*) Public Interest Litigation
Choose the *correct* answer from the options given below:
A. (*a*) and (*b*) only B. (*b*), (*c*) and (*d*) only
C. (*b*) and (*c*) only D. All of these

46. Under Article 25 of the Constitution of India, the right to profess, practice and propagate religion is subject to the following restrictions:
(*a*) Public Interest
(*b*) Morality
(*c*) Health
(*d*) Other Provisions of Part III (Fundamental Rights) of the Constitution of India
Choose the *correct* answer from the options given below:
A. (*a*) and (*b*) only
B. (*b*), (*c*) and (*d*) only
C. (*b*) and (*c*) only
D. All of these

47. The provision relating to *ex post facto law* is embodied in:
A. Article 20 (1)
B. Article 20 (2)
C. Article 20 (3)
D. Article 13 (2)

48. Which of the following terms was inserted in the Preamble of the Constitution of India through the 42nd Constitutional Amendment Act?
A. Sovereign B. Democratic
C. Secular D. Unity

49. Which of the following grounds can be invoked to restrict freedom of speech and expression according to the Constitution of India?
(*a*) Sovereignty and Integrity of India
(*b*) Friendly relations with foreign States
(*c*) Security of the State
(*d*) Contempt of Court
Choose the *correct* answer from the options given below:
A. (*a*), (*b*) and (*d*) only
B. (*b*), (*c*) and (*d*) only
C. (*a*), (*b*) and (*c*) only
D. All of these

50. Which is not true with regard to "common intention" under the Indian Penal Code?
A. Acts done by several persons
B. Pre-arranged plan
C. Prior meeting of minds
D. Membership of an unlawful assembly

51. Which of the following is an offence under the Indian Penal Code?
A. Marital rape
B. Adultery
C. Stalking
D. Both Marital rape and Stalking

52. Which chapter of the Indian Penal Code deals with general exceptions?
A. Chapter III B. Chapter IV
C. Chapter V D. Chapter VI

53. When a man inserts, to any extent, any object or a part of the body, not being his penis, into the vagina, the urethra or anus of a woman or makes her to do so with him or any other person, he commits:
A. Rape B. Sexual Harassment
C. Sexual Assault D. None of these

54. The Doctrine of Rarest of Rare was established in:
A. Bachan Singh *v.* State of Punjab
B. Mithu *v.* State of Punjab
C. Shatrughan Singh Chauhan *v.* Union of India
D. None of these

55. *Mens rea* is not a necessary condition for:
A. Kidnapping B. Murder
C. Theft D. Wrongful Restraint

56. The Maxim *'ignorantia facti excusat, ignorantia juris non excusat'* means:
A. Ignorance of fact excuses, ignorance of law does not excuse
B. Ignorance of law excuses, ignorance of fact does not excuse
C. Ignorance due to which mistake occurs is excused if done in good faith
D. Ignorance due to which a vital mistake occurs, is not excused even if done in good faith

57. Under the Indian Penal Code, nothing is considered to be an offence if it is done by a child under_____ years of age.
A. Six B. Seven
C. Eight D. Nine

58. The right of private defence under the Indian Penal Code is available for the protection of:
A. Other humans only
B. Only self
C. Self and other humans
D. Only property

59. X threatens to publish a defamatory libel concerning Y unless Y gives you money. He thus induces Y to give him money. Here X has committed the offense of:
A. Defamation
B. Mischief
C. Criminal Intimidation
D. Extortion

60. In *Navtej Singh Johar case,* dealing with transgenders' issues, the Supreme Court of India asked the Centre to include them in:
A. Other Backward Classes
B. Scheduled Castes/Tribes
C. Economically Backward Classes
D. None of these

61. 'A' in his madness, attempts to kill 'B'. 'B' hits 'A' with an iron rod seriously injuring him. Choose the correct option from below.
A. 'B' has no right of private defence since 'A' is mad
B. 'B' has right of private defence though 'A' is mad
C. 'B' is guilty of inflicting grievous injury on 'A'
D. None of these

62. The Fundamental Duties towards environment were imposed on the citizens in the year:
A. 1978 B. 1974
C. 1976 D. 1992

63. Bharat Stage Emission Standards (BSES) are set by the:
A. Central Pollution Control Board
B. Ministry of Environment, Forest and Climate Change
C. Ministry of Transport and Highways
D. Supreme Court of India

64. The Blue Flag, a certification that a beach, marina, or sustainable boating tourism operator meets its stringent standards, is awarded by:
A. Ministry of Environment, Forest and Climate Change
B. Foundation for Environmental Education (FEE)
C. United Nations
D. International Seabed Authority

65. The United Nations Conference on Environment and Development (UNCED) is also known as the:
A. Earth Summit B. Paris Convention
C. Kyoto Protocol D. Montreal Protocol

66. Which among the following is an international treaty related to the protection of the ozone layer?
A. Kyoto Protocol
B. Paris Agreement
C. Montreal Protocol
D. Aarhus Convention

67. The United Nations Programme on Reducing Emissions from Deforestation and Forest Degradation (or UN-REDD Programme) is a collaborative programme of the.....
(*a*) Food and Agriculture Organization of the United Nations (FAO)
(*b*) United Nations Development Programme (UNDP)
(*c*) United Nations Environment Programme (UNEP)

Choose the *correct* answer from the options given below:
A. (*a*) and (*c*) only B. (*b*) and (*c*) only
C. None D. All of these

68. Which of the following is a legal effect of adoption?
A. An adopted child shall be deemed to be the child of his or her adoptive father or mother.
B. All the ties of the child in the family of his or her birth shall be deemed to be severed.
C. Both A and B
D. None of these

69. Under Muslim law, a legal guardian may:
A. Sell the movable property in the interest of the child
B. Exercise right of pre-emption on behalf of the child
C. Acknowledge a debt on behalf of the child
D. All of these

70. Which among the following is not a ground for divorce under the Special Marriage Act, 1954?
A. Adultery
B. Desertion
C. Mental disorder
D. Irretrievable breakdown of marriage

71. Degrees of prohibited relationships is applicable between two persons if they are related by:
A. Full blood
B. Half or uterine blood
C. Adoption
D. All of these

72. Which of the following is provided in section 7 of the Hindu Marriage Act, 1955?
A. Registration
B. Ceremonies for solemnising a Hindu marriage
C. Adoption of child
D. All of these

73. The manager of Waqf is known as:
A. Mujwar B. Mutawalli
C. Khadim D. Sajjada Nashin

74. Which Amendment of the Constitution of India reduced the voting age from 21 years to 18 years?
A. 73rd Constitutional Amendment
B. 69th Constitutional Amendment
C. 61st Constitutional Amendment
D. 83rd Constitutional Amendment

75. The Election Commission of India does not have the power to:
A. Register a political party
B. Re-register a political party
C. Conduct election to State Legislatures
D. None of these

76. Who elects the representatives of the states in Rajya Sabha?
A. Elected members of State Legislative Assemblies
B. All registered voters in India
C. Elected Members of Parliament
D. Elected members of State Legislative Assemblies and Parliament

77. Which practices among the following constitute 'corrupt practice' in the Parliamentary election?
A. Bribery
B. Procuring assistance of the government servants
C. Promoting the feeling of hatred and enmity between different classes of citizens on ground of religion, caste etc.
D. All of these

78. What can be the maximum number of representatives of States and Union Territories in the Council of States?
A. 238 B. 240
C. 245 D. 250

79. An agreement consists of reciprocal promises between at least.....
A. Four parties
B. Six parties
C. Three parties
D. Two parties

80. Who among the following does not have the capacity to enter into a contract?
A. Corporation
B. Minor
C. A person convicted of an offence
D. All of these

81. The age of majority for entering into a contract under the Indian Contract Act, 1872 is:
A. 18 years
B. 21 years
C. 16 years
D. 25 years

82. A contract of insurance is an example of:
A. Quasi Contract
B. Contingent Contract
C. Both
D. None of these

83. Agreement of social nature is unenforceable because it lacks:
A. Intention to create moral relationship
B. Intention to create social relationship
C. Intention to create legal relationship
D. Intention to create an agreement

84. Doctrine of privity of contract implies:
A. Only those persons who are party to a contract can enforce the same
B. Only those persons who are not party to a contract can enforce the same
C. Only those persons who are known to the promisor can enforce the contract
D. Only those persons who are known to the promisee can enforce the contract

85. In India, provisions of the Indian Contract Act, 1872 apply to:
A. Citizens B. Persons
C. Companies D. All of these

86. Product patent in India was introduced in:
A. 2004 B. 2005
C. 2003 D. 2006

87. Industrial design specifically refers to:
A. Form of expression
B. Functionality
C. Form of expression with aesthetic appeal
D. Invention

88. Which among the following combinations is not mentioned under the TRIPS?
A. Patents, Trademarks and Copyright
B. Patents, Trademarks and Industrial Designs
C. Patents, Copyright and Data Exclusivity
D. Patents, Copyright and Undisclosed Information

89. Intellectual property rights are ________ in their enforcement.
A. Territorial
B. Regional
C. International
D. All of these

90. The trade-related intellectual property disputes are settled by:
A. WIPO
B. WTO
C. ICJ
D. World Economic Forum

91. The formula of making *Coca-Cola* is protected under:
A. Copyright B. Trademarks
C. Trade Secrets D. None of these

92. In the following question, choose the correct alternative which can replace the question mark.

Ignominous : Honourable : : Cajole : ?

A. Notorious B. Coax
C. Bully D. Filch

93. In the following question, choose the correct alternative which can replace the question mark.

Condign : Deserved : : Veracity : ?

A. Mercy B. Boring
C. Obloquy D. Accuracy

94. Complete the series.

RESTITUTION, ESTITUTIO, TITUTIO, ITUTI,

A. UTI B. TUT
C. ITU D. TI

95. If A × B means A is to the north of B; A + B means A is to the south of B; A % B means A is to the west of B; A – B means A is to the east of B; then in P % Q + R – S, S is in which direction with respect to Q?

A. South-West B. South-East
C. North-East D. North-West

Directions (Qs. No. 96 and 97): *Read the passage and answer the following questions:*

Nine diplomats R, S, T, U, V, W, X, Y and Z are sitting around a table facing the centre. Z sits 5th to the right of X. T is not an immediate neighbour of either X or Z. S sits between Y and V. T sits 4th to the left of V. U sits 2nd to the right of W. Y is not an immediate neighbour of Z.

96. Which of the following is U's position with respect to S in the anti-clockwise direction starting from S?

A. 3rd to the Left B. 4th to the Left
C. 5th to the Right D. 7th to the Right

97. Three of the following pairs are alike based on their seating positions in the above arrangement and so form a group. Find the odd one out.

A. TR B. ZS
C. YW D. UV

98. Read the passage and answer the following one question:

A wildlife sanctuary contains animals of at least two of the following six kinds—nilgai, chinkara, black buck, wild boar, leopards, jackals. No other kinds of animals are in the sanctuary. The following conditions must hold:

1. Jackals are not in the sanctuary if Chinkaras are
2. Black bucks are not in the sanctuary if Wild boars are
3. Either wild boar or jackal, but not both, are in the sanctuary
4. Jackals are in the sanctuary if Nilgais, Leopards, or both are in the sanctuary.

If there are no wild boars in the sanctuary, then which one of the following is a kind of animal that cannot be in the sanctuary.

A. Nilgai B. Chinkara
C. Black buck D. Jackal

99. Given A ÷ B means A is father of B, A × B means A is wife of B, A + B means A is the brother of B, A – B means A is the daughter of B.

If, E ÷ F × G + H, then how is H related to F?

A. Brother-in-law B. Brother
C. Father D. Father-in-law

100. Choose the odd one out.

A. FCDE B. UQRS
C. KGHI D. PLMN

ANSWERS

1	2	3	4	5	6	7	8	9	10
B	A	D	B	B	C	A	D	B	C
11	**12**	**13**	**14**	**15**	**16**	**17**	**18**	**19**	**20**
C	A	D	B	B	A	B	C	A	D

21	22	23	24	25	26	27	28	29	30
A	C	A	B	A	B	C	D	A	C
31	**32**	**33**	**34**	**35**	**36**	**37**	**38**	**39**	**40**
A	C	A	D	C	B	A	A	A	D
41	**42**	**43**	**44**	**45**	**46**	**47**	**48**	**49**	**50**
B	D	A	A	A	B	A	C	A	D
51	**52**	**53**	**54**	**55**	**56**	**57**	**58**	**59**	**60**
C	B	A	A	A	A	B	C	D	A
61	**62**	**63**	**64**	**65**	**66**	**67**	**68**	**69**	**70**
B	C	A	B	A	C	D	C	D	D
71	**72**	**73**	**74**	**75**	**76**	**77**	**78**	**79**	**80**
D	B	B	C	B	A	D	A	D	B
81	**82**	**83**	**84**	**85**	**86**	**87**	**88**	**89**	**90**
A	B	C	A	D	B	C	C	A	B
91	**92**	**93**	**94**	**95**	**96**	**97**	**98**	**99**	**100**
C	C	D	A	D	C	D	B	A	A

EXPLANATORY ANSWERS

6. Ease of Doing Business rankings have been released by World Bank on October 24. In the list of Ease of Doing India has ranked 63rd for 2019-20. India's ranking has improved by 14 places as India was ranked 77 in the list of 2018-19.

India has joined the top-10 reforming countries in terms of economy for the third consecutive year. Ease of doing business has come in the ranking of ease of doing business at a time when the country is a victim of the economic slowdown.

7. Fiscal Deficit: It is the gap between the government's expenditure requirements and its receipts.

This equals the money the government needs to borrow during the year. A surplus arises if receipts are more than expenditure.

- **Fiscal Deficit = Total expenditure – (Revenue receipts + Non-debt creating capital receipts).**
- It indicates the total borrowing requirements of the government from all sources.
- From the financing side: Gross fiscal deficit = Net borrowing at home + Borrowing from RBI + Borrowing from abroad.
- The gross fiscal deficit is a key variable in judging the financial health of the public sector and the stability of the economy.

8. Abhijit Banerjee, Esther Duflo and Michael Kremer won The Sveriges Riksbank Prize in Economic Sciences in Memory of Alfred Nobel 2019 for their experimental approach to alleviating global poverty.

9. Monetary Policy Framework: The modified RBI Act provides the legislative mandate explicitly to the Reserve Bank of India in order to operate the policy framework of the country. The monetary policy framework aims to set the policy repo rate as per the assessment of the present and developing macroeconomic situation. The agenda also aims at modulating liquidity conditions to adjust the money market rates at/around the repo rates.

10. Securities and Exchange Board of India (SEBI) was first established in 1988 as a non-statutory body for regulating the securities market. It became an autonomous body on 30 January, 1992 and was accorded statutory powers with the passing of the SEBI Act, 1992 by the Indian Parliament. SEBI has its headquarters at the business district of Bandra Kurla Complex in Mumbai and has Northern, Eastern, Southern and Western Regional Offices in New Delhi, Kolkata, Chennai, and Ahmedabad respectively.

The SEBI is managed by its members, which consists of the following:

- The chairman is nominated by the Union Government of India.
- Two members, *i.e.,* Officers from the Union Finance Ministry.
- One member from the Reserve Bank of India.
- The remaining five members are nominated by the Union Government of India, out of them at least three shall be whole-time members.

11. Mahatma Gandhi was nominated for Nobel Peace Prize in 1937, 1938, 1939, and 1947. Gandhi Ji became a strong choice for this prize only after India got independence. He was nominated again in 1948 and it was sure that he would get the prize this time. But few days before the final announcement of the Nobel Peace Prize, he was assassinated by N.R. Godse.

12. The Grand Slam tournaments, also referred to as majors, are the world's four most important annual tennis events. The tournaments offer the most ranking points, prize money, public and media attention, the greatest strength and size of field, and greater number of "best of" sets for men, which is 5. The Grand Slam itinerary consists of the Australian Open in mid January, the French Open from late May to early June, Wimbledon in late June to early July, and the US Open in August-September. Each tournament is played over a two-week period.

13. **Bharat Ratna** – 'Jewel of India' is the highest civilian award of the country. It is conferred for exceptional Service to the nation in various fields such as Science arts, literature and recognition of public service of the highest order. The award can be granted posthumously and since its establishment, seven awards were granted posthumously. The Bharat Ratna Awardees in 2019 are: 1. Pranab Mukherjee; 2. Bhupen Hazarika (Posthumously); 3. Nanaji Deshmukh (Posthumously).

15. The Rajiv Gandhi Khel Ratna, officially known as Rajiv Gandhi Khel Ratna Award in Sports and Games, is the *highest sporting honour of the Republic of India*. The award is named after Rajiv Gandhi, former Prime Minister of India who served the office from 1984 to 1989. It is awarded annually by the Ministry of Youth Affairs and Sports. Rajiv Gandhi Khel Ratna Award Launched in 1991 to 1992, the cash award of ₹ 7.5 lakh for honouring the outstanding sportsperson in a year for his/her achievement in sports. Rajiv Gandhi Khel Ratna 2019: Sh. Bajrang Punia (Wrestling); and Ms. Deepa Malik (Para Athletics).

16. **Ravish Kumar** is an Indian journalist, author and media personality. He is the Senior Executive Editor of NDTV India. He hosts a number of programmes including the channel's flagship weekday show *Prime Time*, *Hum Log*, *Ravish Ki Report* and *Des Ki Baat*.

He has been twice conferred with Ramnath Goenka Excellence in Journalism Award for the *Best Journalist of the Year* and became the fifth Indian journalist to receive the Ramon Magsaysay Award in 2019.

17. The 2018 FIFA World Cup Final was a football match that took place on 15 July, 2018 to determine the winners of the 2018 FIFA World Cup. It was the final of the 21st FIFA World Cup, a quadrennial tournament contested by the men's national teams of the member associations of FIFA. The match was played by France and Croatia, and held at the Luzhniki Stadium in Moscow, Russia.

18. The 2020 ICC Women's T20 World Cup was the seventh ICC Women's T20 World Cup tournament. It was held in Australia between 21 February and 8 March, 2020. The final took place at the Melbourne Cricket Ground on International Women's Day. Hosts Australia won the tournament, beating India by 85 runs, to win their fifth title.

19. The 66th National Film Awards ceremony was the award ceremony which took place in 2019 to honour the best films of 2018, in the Indian cinema. The declaration of awards was delayed due to 2019 Indian general election. The list of **Award winners** under the **different categories** is mentioned as under:
• **Best Feature Film:** Hellaro (Gujarati Film) • **Best non feature film:** Son Rise by Vibha Bakshi and The Secret Life of Frogs by Ajay and Vijay Bedi • **Best Director:** Adhitya Dhar for Uri : The Surgical Strike • **Best Actor:** Ayushmann Khuranna for Andhadhun and Vicky Kaushal for Uri : The Surgical Strike • **Best Actress:** Keerthy Suresh for Mahanati • **Best Supporting Actor:** Swanand Kirkire for Chumbhak.

27. **Universal Serial Bus** (**USB**) is an industry standard that establishes specifications for cables and connectors and protocols for connection, communication and power supply (interfacing) between computers, peripherals and other computers. A broad variety of USB hardware exists, including eleven different connectors, of which USB-C is the most recent.

32. The main bodies of the United Nations are the General Assembly, the Security Council, the Economic and Social Council, the Trusteeship Council, the International Court of Justice, and the UN Secretariat. All were established under the UN Charter when the Organization was founded in 1945.

38. **Article 44:** Uniform civil code for the citizens. The State shall endeavour to secure for the citizens a uniform civil code throughout the territory of India.

44. 42nd Amendment Act of 1976 added 10 Fundamental Duties to the Indian Constitution. 86th Amendment Act, 2002 later added 11th Fundamental Duty to the list. Swaran Singh Committee in 1976 recommended Fundamental Duties, the necessity of which was felt during the internal emergency of 1975-77. The Fundamental Duties are dealt with Article 51A under Part-IV A of the Indian Constitution.

95. P % Q + R – S

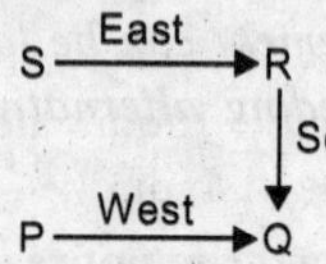

Here, S is in North-West direction with respect to Q.

96.

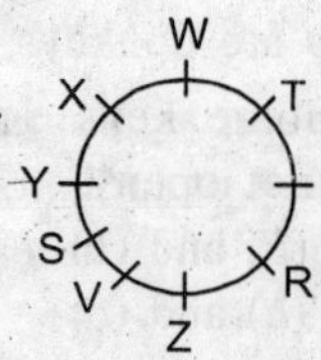

Here, U is 5th to the right of S.

97. Here, TR, ZS and YW are alike each pair between one diplomate

∴ The odd one = UV (Two diplomats between U and V).

99. Given, E ÷ F × G + H

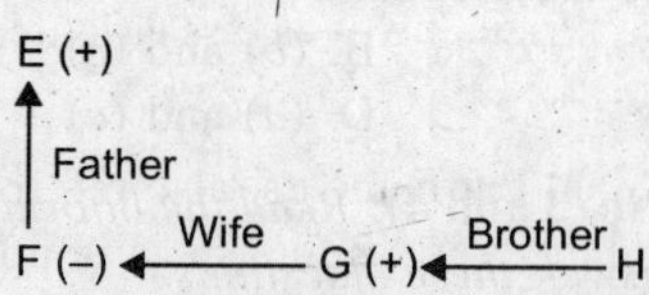

Here, H is the Brother-in-law of F.

100. A. 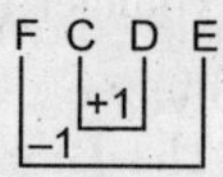

B. 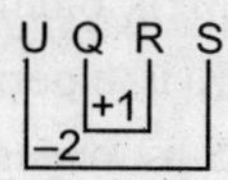

C. 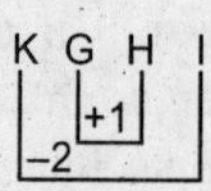

D. 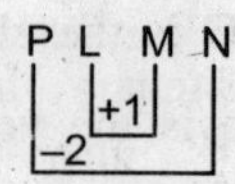

Here, Option (A) is odd one.

Previous Paper (Solved)

LL.B. (Three Year Degree Course)

Entrance Examination, 2019*

Directions (Qs. No. 1 and 2): *Question given below has a set of three statements. Choose the alternative where the third statement can be logically deduced from both the preceding alternatives, but not just from one of them.*

1. (*a*) Many teachers are not readers. All singers are teachers. All singers are not readers

(*b*) Some giraffes are donkeys. Some giraffes are sheep. Some sheep are donkeys.

(*c*) All locks are keys. Some keys do not open. Some locks do not open

A. (*c*) only   B. (*b*) and (*c*)
C. (*b*) only   D. (*a*) and (*c*)

2. (*a*) Few mathematicians are scientists. Some scientists play. Few mathematicians play

(*b*) Rabbit is a flower. Some flowers are made of chromoplasts. Rabbit is made of chromoplast.

(*c*) No elephant eats grass. All lions eat grass. No lions are elephants.

A. (*c*) only   B. (*b*) and (*c*)
C. (*b*) only   D. (*a*) and (*c*)

Directions (Qs. No. 3 and 4): *Read the information carefully and answer these questions.*

(*i*) A is older than S.
(*ii*) M is older than A but younger than K.
(*iii*) K is elder than S.
(*iv*) S is younger than M.
(*v*) G is the eldest.

3. Who is the youngest?
A. A   B. S
C. M   D. K

4. Age wise, who is in the middle?
A. A   B. S
C. M   D. K

Directions (Qs. No. 5 and 6): *Read the following information carefully and answer the questions given below.*

The sum of the incomes of U and V is more than that of X and Y taken together. The sum of the incomes of U and X is the same as that of V and Y taken together. Moreover U earns half as much as the sum of the incomes of V and Y.

5. Whose income is the highest?
A. Y
B. X
C. U
D. V

6. Which statement is correct?
A. V and Y together earn half of what X earns
B. U earns equal to X
C. U earns more than X
D. Y earns less than X

7. Which of the following is correct?
A. Both FIFA, 2014 - Brazil, FIFA, 2018 - Russia & FIFA, 2022 - Qatar & FIFA, 2010 - South Africa, FIFA, 2018 - Russia & FIFA, 2022 - Qatar
B. FIFA, 2014 - Brazil, FIFA, 2018 - Russia & FIFA, 2022 - Qatar
C. FIFA, 2010 - South Africa, FIFA, 2018 - Russia & FIFA, 2022 - Qatar
D. None of these

*Conducted by NTA for Three year LL.B. Course Admission in University of Delhi.

8. Which one of the following does not constitute the electoral college for electing the President of India?
A. Elected members of Rajya Sabha
B. Elected members of the Legislative Council
C. Elected members of the Legislative Assembly of each state
D. Elected members of Lok Sabha

9. A watch reads 4:30. If the minute hand points towards north east, then the hour hand will point towards the:
A. South-west B. North-west
C. South D. South-east

10. As per VII Schedule of the Constitution of India, the power to enact laws on residuary matters lies with:
A. State legislature B. None
C. Parliament D. The President

11. The doctrine of 'Transferred Malice' is contained in which Section of the IPC, 1860?
A. Section 304A B. Section 149
C. Section 34 D. Section 301

12. The doctrine of 'double jeopardy' enshrined in Article 20 (2) means:
A. punishment once awarded cannot be enhanced in appeal or revision
B. no one can be prosecuted and punished more than once for the same offence
C. one can be prosecuted several times for the same offence
D. one can be prosecuted more than once, but punished only once

13. The electoral college that elects the Vice President of India comprises of:
A. Members of both Houses of Parliament
B. Elected members of both Houses of Parliament
C. Elected members of both Houses of Parliament and State Legislative Assemblies
D. Elected members of both Houses of Parliament and State Legislative Assemblies and Legislative Councils

14. A First Information Report (FIR) for a cognizable offence may be lodged by:
A. Victim
B. Family member of the victim
C. All of these
D. Police officer

15. Sarkaria Commission was concerned with:
A. Electoral Reforms
B. Financial Reforms
C. Centre-State Relations
D. Judicial reforms

16. The Right of private defence of the body extends to the voluntarily causing of death, if the offence which occasions the exercise of right is:
A. an assault with the intention of kidnapping or abducting
B. an assault with intention of escaping with stolen property immediately after the theft
C. an assault reasonably causing an apprehension that simple injury will be caused
D. of arresting a person who is running away after having committed an offence of voluntarily causing hurt

17. The anti-defection law in India is contained in:
A. The X Schedule of the Constitution of India
B. The VII Schedule of the Constitution of India
C. The IV Schedule of the Constitution of India
D. The IX Schedule of the Constitution of India

18. Art. 51A of the Constitution of India provides for the Fundamental Duties of:
A. Public Servants
B. Prime Minister and his Council of Ministers
C. Citizens of India
D. All those who run public and private sectors

19. Proceedings to be in *camera* means:
A. Proceedings in public
B. Proceedings in private
C. Proceedings recorded in camera
D. None of these

20. A general offer is an offer which:
A. None of these
B. Cannot be termed as a contract
C. Contains all the essentials of a valid contract
D. Can be accepted by anyone

21. World Intellectual Property Day is celebrated on:
A. 23rd September
B. 26th April
C. 4th August
D. 21st June

22. The principle of quantum meruit is applicable when:
A. When the contract is indivisible and something in relation to contract is done
B. When an act is done graciously
C. The contract is divisible, and some parts are performed
D. Both the contract is divisible, and some parts are performed and when the contract is indivisible and something in relation to contract is done

23. The President gives his resignation to the:
A. Prime Minister
B. Speaker of Lok Sabha
C. Vice President
D. Chief Justice

24. How many times the President of India can seek re-election to his post?
A. Any number of times
B. 2 times
C. Once
D. 3 times

25. The charge of impeachment against the President of India for his removal can be preferred by:
A. Rajya Sabha
B. Lok Sabha
C. Speaker of Lok Sabha and Chairman of Rajya Sabha
D. Both Houses of Parliament

26. 'Achilles heel' means:
A. a food disease
B. a kind of fungus
C. a painful spot
D. a weak point

27. The word 'plagiarist' refers to a person who:
A. Is a professional boxer
B. Uses language and thoughts of another author without authorization and the representation of that author's work as one's own, without crediting the original author
C. Is called by courts to give testimony in cases relating to fingerprints
D. Is a collector of old and antique stamps of different countries

28. Basic structure of Constitution can be amended:
A. By 2/3rd majority
B. By simple majority
C. By special majority and ratification by half of states
D. None of these

29. The right to protect one's own person and property against the unlawful aggression of others is known as:
A. an act done by the consent of the other
B. none of these
C. the right of private defence
D. volenti non fit injuria

30. Fraud occurs when:
A. Both acts are done with the intention to deceive another party & active concealment of facts
B. Active concealment of facts
C. An act is done with the intention to deceive another party
D. None of these

31. Under Patent Act, 1970 Patent is granted for:
A. 5 years
B. 10 years
C. 20 years
D. 15 years

32. An agreement in restraint of marriage is:
A. Void B. Illegal
C. Voidable D. Valid

33. X + Y > U + V and Y + U > X + V, then it is definite that:
A. V > Y B. X > V
C. Y > V D. U > V

34. Who is equivalent of Attorney General in State?
A. Judge of the High Court
B. Advocate General
C. Chief Minister
D. None of these

35. Who among the following is the First Iraqi National to have received the Nobel Peace Prize?
A. Reem Alasadi
B. Jenna Krajeski
C. Najiba Ahmed
D. Nadia Murad Basee Taha

36. Under Trade Marks Act, 1999 the trademark is granted for:
A. 10 years, but may be renewed from time to time subject to the provisions of the Act
B. 20 years, but may be renewed from time to time subject to the provisions of the Act
C. 15 years, but may be renewed from time to time subject to the provisions of the Act
D. 5 years, but may be renewed from time to time subject to the provisions of the Act

37. *Caveat Venditor* means:
A. Buyer beware
B. Seller beware
C. None of these
D. Manufacturer beware

38. In which landmark judgment did the Supreme Court of India decriminalized homosexuality:
A. Navtez Singh Johar v. Union of India, 2018
B. Maneka Gandhi v. Union of India, 1978
C. Hussainara Khatoon v. State of Bihar, 1979
D. Nilabati Behera v. State of Orissa, 1993

39. The name of the Union given in the Constitution is:
A. Hindustan *i.e.* Bharatvarsha
B. Bharatdesh *i.e.* India
C. India *i.e.* Bharat
D. India *i.e.* Hindustan

40. 'A' threatens his wife and son to commit suicide in case they did not execute a deed in his favour.

This will amount to:
A. None of the above B. Both the above
C. Undue influence D. Coercion

41. Two young persons, A & B fight with each other. A was having a blade with which 'A' inflicts injury on the face of B leaving a scar on the cheek of B. A is guilty of offence of causing
A. simple hurt by rash or negligent act
B. simple hurt
C. grievous hurt by rash or negligent act
D. grievous hurt

42. In which of the following cases was the judgment popularly known as Jallikattu verdict pronounced?
A. Federation of Indian Animal Protection Organisation v. UOI
B. Gauri Maulekhi v. UOI
C. Animal Welfare Board of India v. A. Nagaraja
D. Nair, NR and others v. UOI

43. In which of the cases the relationship of principal and agent exists:
A. Both Relationship between partners & Relationship between employer and employee
B. Relationship between husband and wife
C. Relationship between employer and employee
D. Relationship between partners

44. In which year Right of Children to Free and Compulsory Education, Act was enacted by Parliament of India?
A. 2008 B. 2009
C. 2007 D. 2005

45. In which one of the following judgments the Constitutional Bench of the Supreme Court of India, the 'rarest of rare' principle in the award of death penalty was first laid down?
A. Bachan Singh v. State of Punjab (1980)
B. Gopalanachari v. State of Kerala (1980)
C. Tukaram v. State of Maharashtra (1979)
D. Dr. Upendra Baxi v. State of UP (1983)

46. The three lists in the Seventh Schedule of the Constitution of India represent:
A. Principle of Division of Power
B. Principle of Separation of Power
C. Doctrine of Cooperative Federalism
D. Rule against non-arbitrariness

47. Five people, A, C, D, F and G are sitting around a table. A is sitting to the left of G. One person is sitting between G and D. C is sitting to the left of A:

Choose the correct option:
A. F is sitting between C and D
B. F is sitting between A and G
C. F is sitting between G and D
D. F is sitting to the right of D

48. *Non est factum* means:
A. None of these
B. Document executed under fraud
C. Document executed under misrepresentation
D. It is not my deed

49. Malimath Committee is associated with reforms in the field of:
A. Education
B. Domestic relations
C. Labour Welfare
D. Criminal Law

50. In the year 2002 the Competition Act was enacted. This Act replaces:
A. Prevention of Corruption Act, 1988
B. Monopolies and Restrictive Trade Practices Act, 1969
C. Consumer Protection Act, 1986
D. Protection of Civil Rights Act, 1955

51. On 9th March 2018, a Constitution Bench of the Supreme Court of India confirmed that the right to die with dignity is a fundamental right while allowing passive euthanasia and living will. This judgment is known as:
A. Common Cause v. UOI
B. Supreme Court Advocates-On-Record Association v. UOI
C. P. Rathinam v. UOI
D. Justice KS Puttaswamy v. UOI

52. The essentials of a valid custom are:
A. All of these
B. Consistency
C. Antiquity
D. Certainty

53. The essential characteristic of a tort is, violation of:
A. right in rem (a right vested in some determinate person and available against the world at large)
B. right in personam (a right available only against some determinate person or property)
C. none of these
D. a contractual right

54. Theft and Extortion are listed under the IPC as offences against:
A. Public order and tranquillity:
B. Property
C. All of these
D. Body

55. Flog a dead horse means:
A. To try to get work out of someone who is already exhausted
B. To beat a horse to death
C. Cruelty to animals
D. Waste effort on something when there is no chance of succeeding

56. Representation of members in House of People in India is based on:
A. Community
B. Population
C. Area of the State
D. Literacy of State

57. Who authored the book 'Indian Philosophy'?
A. Shashi Tharoor
B. William Shakespeare
C. Charles Dickens
D. Sarvepalli Radhakrishnan

58. The term used to describe an accused who seeks pardon from the court by agreeing to testify against all others involved in the crime is:
A. Hostile witness
B. None of these
C. Accomplice
D. Approver

59. When both the parties are under a mistake of fact essential to the contract, the contract is:
A. Void
B. Voidable
C. None of these
D. Does not affect its validity

60. Article 360 of Constitution of India has been invoked in India:
A. Never invoked B. Once
C. Twice D. Thrice

61. Article 20 and Article 21 has been taken from the purview of Article 359 of the Constitution of India by:
A. The Constitution (42nd Amendment) Act
B. The Constitution (43rd Amendment) Act
C. The Constitution (59th Amendment) Act
D. The Constitution (44th Amendment) Act

62. Find the average of prime numbers between 20 and 50:
A. 40.5 B. 39.8
C. 37.6 D. 35.8

63. 'Z' takes away a golden chain of his wife which was given by her father as Stridhan, without her consent, and gifts it to his girlfriend. 'Z' is guilty of:
A. not guilty of theft as the property was temporarily taken away
B. not guilty of theft as the chain was their joint property
C. guilty of theft
D. guilty of criminal misappropriation

64. The power of the President of India to issue an ordinance is a:
A. Quasi-judicial power
B. Judicial power
C. Executive power
D. Legislative power

65. Complete the series:

A	D	G
D	I	N
I	P	?

A. Y B. W
C. X D. V

66. Complete the series:

H	K	Q
C	G	O
E	J	?

A. N B. L
C. T D. P

67. Who among the following is famous for Bharatnatyam?
A. Madhavi Mudgal
B. Sonal Mansingh
C. Birju Maharaj
D. Yamini Krishnamurti

68. For the philosophy underlying our Constitution, the historic 'Objectives Resolution' was moved in the Constituent Assembly on 13th December 1946 by:
A. Dr. S. Radhakrishnan
B. Dr. Rajendra Prasad
C. Dr. B.R. Ambedkar
D. Jawaharlal Nehru

69. 'A', a person of unsound mind, attempts to kill 'B'. 'B' hits 'A' with an iron rod seriously injuring him.
A. 'B' has right of private defense though 'A' is a person of unsound mind
B. 'B' has no right of private defense since 'A' is a person of unsound mind
C. 'B' is guilty of inflicting grievous injury on 'A'
D. None of these

70. 'A' agrees to Pay 'B' Rupees 1000 if it rains today, 'B' will pay him Rupees 1000 if it does not rain. Which kind of agreement is this?
A. Voidable Agreement
B. Contingent Agreement
C. Wagering Agreement
D. None of the above

71. 'Proper respect is shown to National Anthem by standing up when the National Anthem is sung. It will not be right to say that disrespect is shown by not joining in the singing.' It has been held in:
A. Ram Jawaya Kapur v. U.O.I.
B. Keshavananda Bharati v. U.O.I.
C. Bijoi Emmanuel v. State of Kerala
D. Surya Narain v. U.O.I.

72. Abhiram Singh v. CD Commachen (2017) is a judgment of the Supreme Court dealing with which of the following issues?
A. Proper and adequate access to public places for visually disabled persons
B. Seeking votes in the name of religion amounts to a corrupt practice
C. Linkage of IT returns with Aadhaar
D. Compensation to Uphaar tragedy victims

73. The 262nd Law Commission of India report deals with:
A. Electoral Reforms
B. 2015 Model Bilateral Investment Treaty
C. Amendment of Arbitration and Conciliation Act 1996
D. Abolition of death penalty

74. In taking and recording evidence, the language of every Court within the State other than the High Court shall be:
A. Determined by the respective State Government
B. Hindi or English
C. Hindi
D. English

75. General exceptions are laid down in the Indian Penal Code in:
A. Chapter VI B. Chapter VIII
C. Chapter IV D. Chapter IV and VI

76. Choose the correct spelling:
A. surveillance B. surveilance
C. surveilence D. survellience

77. Choose the correct spelling:
A. Connoiseur B. Connoisseur
C. Conoissuer D. Connoissuer

78. What do you mean by "candidate losing the deposit" after the poll result is announced?
A. A defeated candidate who fails to secure more than one third of the valid votes polled in the constituency will lose his security deposit
B. A defeated candidate who fails to secure more than one sixth of the valid votes polled in the constituency will lose his security deposit
C. A defeated candidate who fails to secure more than one fourth of the valid votes polled in the constituency will lose his security deposit
D. A defeated candidate who fails to secure minimum 600 valid votes polled in the constituency will lose his security deposit

79. What is the product of all numbers in the dial of a telephone?
A. 1,59,450 B. 1,59,480
C. None of these D. 1,58,480

80. What kind of damages are available for breach of contract?
A. Vindictive Damages
B. Unliquidated Damages
C. All these
D. Liquidated Damages

81. Which of the following laws has not been amended by the Criminal Law (Amendment) Act, 2018?
A. Sexual Harassment of Women at Workplace (Prevention, Prohibition and Redressal) Act, 2013
B. Indian Penal Code, 1860
C. Protection of Children from Sexual Offences Act (POCSO), 2012
D. Criminal Procedure Code, 1973

82. Which of the following are included as fundamental duties under Constitution of India?

I. To abide by the Constitution and respect for its ideals and institutions.

II. To uphold and protect the Sovereignty, Unity and Integrity of India.

III. To ensure the rule of law in the country

IV. To safeguard public property and to abjure violence.

A. I, II, IV B. I, III, IV
C. I, II, III, IV D. I, II, III

83. Which of the following is an inchoate crime?
A. Public nuisance
B. Culpable homicide
C. Riot
D. Criminal attempt

84. Which of the following writs called bulwark of personal freedom?
A. Habeas Corpus
B. Quo Warranto
C. Mandamus
D. Certiorari

85. Which of the following is ***not*** an essential ingredient of Criminal Breach of Trust?
A. Negligence
B. Entrustment
C. Misappropriation/ conversion
D. Dishonest intention

86. Which of the set is said to be the Golden triangle of Indian Constitution?
A. Articles 14, 15 and 16
B. Articles 20, 21 and 22
C. Article 14, 19 and 21
D. Preamble, Fundamental Right and Directive Principles

87. Capacity to contract relates to:
A. None of these
B. Competence of the parties to enter into contract
C. Intention of the parties to enter into contract
D. Age of parties to contract

88. Clause (4) of Article 15 has been added to the Constitution of India by:
A. The Constitution (Second Amendment) Act
B. The Constitution (Sixth Amendment) Act
C. The Constitution (First Amendment) Act
D. The Constitution (Fourth Amendment) Act

89. 'A' agrees to sell his house to 'B', 'A' has two houses. The agreement is:
A. Void
B. Both Void and Valid
C. Voidable
D. Valid

90. The writ of prohibition may be issued, when there is:
A. Both an absence of jurisdiction or access of jurisdiction and violation of principles of natural justice
B. Violation of principles of natural justice
C. An absence of jurisdiction or access of jurisdiction
D. Request to produce the body of the person

91. The first Constitutional Amendment was challenged in the case:
A. Sajjan Singh v. State of Rajasthan
B. None of these
C. Sankari Prasad v. UOI
D. Both Sankari Prasad v. UOI & Sankari Prasad v. UOI

92. The President of the India can consult the Supreme Court of India:
A. To seek advice before he imposes emergency in any state
B. When a question of law of public importance arises
C. In order to do complete justice when a death penalty convict seeks clemency from the President
D. Against any decision taken by the Prime Minister and his council of ministers

93. The average of five consecutive numbers is 16. Find the smallest of these numbers:
A. 20 B. 8
C. 12 D. 14

94. The Preamble of Indian Constitution envisages what kinds of justice?
A. Political B. Economic
C. Social D. All of these

95. As per the Constitution of India the sovereignty of India lies with:
A. The Parliament of India
B. The Supreme Court of India
C. The People of India
D. The Constitution of India

96. Bt. in 'Bt. Brinjal' is:
A. Virus B. None of these
C. Antibiotic D. Bacterium

97. Who is the first Indian woman appointed as Judge of ITLOS (International Tribunal for the Law of the Sea)?
A. Ruma Pal B. Flavia Agnes
C. Indira Banerjee D. Neeru Chadha

98. Who is the Director General of International Atomic Energy Agency (IAEA)?
A. Mohamed Elbardei
B. Mahmoud Mekki
C. Luther Rangreji
D. Yukia Amano

99. Under the Indian Penal Code, 1860 dislocation of tooth constitutes the offence of:
A. Assault B. Simple hurt
C. None of these D. Grievous hurt

100. One card is drawn from a pack of 52 cards. What is the probability that the card drawn is either a black card or a queen?
A. $\frac{7}{13}$ B. $\frac{1}{2}$
C. $\frac{1}{52}$ D. $\frac{15}{26}$

ANSWERS

1	2	3	4	5	6	7	8	9	10
A	A	B	C	D	B	A	B	*	C
11	**12**	**13**	**14**	**15**	**16**	**17**	**18**	**19**	**20**
D	B	A	C	C	A	A	C	B	D
21	**22**	**23**	**24**	**25**	**26**	**27**	**28**	**29**	**30**
B	*	C	A	D	D	B	D	C	A
31	**32**	**33**	**34**	**35**	**36**	**37**	**38**	**39**	**40**
C	A	C	B	D	A	B	A	C	D
41	**42**	**43**	**44**	**45**	**46**	**47**	**48**	**49**	**50**
*	C	A	B	A	A	C	D	D	B
51	**52**	**53**	**54**	**55**	**56**	**57**	**58**	**59**	**60**
A	A	A	B	D	B	D	D	A	A
61	**62**	**63**	**64**	**65**	**66**	**67**	**68**	**69**	**70**
D	D	C	D	B	C	D	D	A	C
71	**72**	**73**	**74**	**75**	**76**	**77**	**78**	**79**	**80**
C	B	D	A	C	A	B	B	C	D
81	**82**	**83**	**84**	**85**	**86**	**87**	**88**	**89**	**90**
A	A	D	A	A	C	B	C	A	A
91	**92**	**93**	**94**	**95**	**96**	**97**	**98**	**99**	**100**
C,D	B	D	D	C	D	D	D	D	A

EXPLANATORY ANSWERS

3. $G > K > M > A > S$

↑ eldest (G) ... ↑ youngest (S)

Hence, S is the youngest.

4. $G > K > M > A > S$

↑ Middle (M)

Hence, Age wise M is on the middle.

5.
$$U + V > X + Y \quad ...(i)$$
$$U + X = V + Y \quad ...(ii)$$
$$U = \frac{V+Y}{2} \quad ...(iii)$$

From equation (*ii*) and (*iii*)
$$U + X = 2U$$
$$U = X$$

Now, from equation (*i*)
$$V > Y$$

From equation (*i*) and (*ii*),
$$V + Y + V - X > X + Y$$
$$\Rightarrow \quad 2V + Y - X > X + Y$$
$$2V > 2X$$
$$V > X$$

Hence, V's income is the highest.

6.
$$U + V > X + Y \quad ...(i)$$
$$U + X = V + Y \quad ...(ii)$$
$$U = \frac{V+Y}{2} \quad ...(iii)$$

From equation (*ii*) and (*iii*),
$$U + X = 2U$$
$$U = X$$

Hence, 'U' earns equal to X.

8. The President is indirectly elected by means of an electoral college consisting of the elected members of the Parliament of India and the Legislative assemblies of the States of India and the Union territories of Delhi and Puducherry. The number and value of votes are based on the population in 1971 rather than the current population, as a result of the 42nd Amendment, and extended by the 84th Amendment, with the intention to encourage family planning programs in the states by ensuring that states are not penalized for lowering their population growth.

The Vice President is elected by a different electoral college, consisting of members (elected as well as nominated) of the Lok Sabha and Rajya Sabha.

The presidential electoral college is made up of the following:

- elected members of the Rajya Sabha (upper house of the Parliament of India);
- elected members of the Lok Sabha (lower house of the Parliament of India);
- elected members of each state's State Legislative Assembly (lower house of the state legislature); and
- elected members of each union territory possessing a Legislative assembly (*i.e.*, Delhi and Puducherry).

10. The Constitution of India has provided for a division of powers between the Central and state governments. *Under the Seventh Schedule, there are three lists – the Union, State and Concurrent.*

- The *Union List* has a range of subjects under which the Parliament may make laws. This includes defence, foreign affairs, railways, banking, among others.
- The *State List* lists subjects under which the legislature of a state may make laws. Public order, police, public health and sanitation; hospitals and dispensaries, betting and gambling are some of the subjects that come under the state.
- The *Concurrent List* includes subjects that give powers to both the Centre and state governments. Subjects like Education including technical education, m 'ical education and universities, popu ion

control and family planning, criminal law, prevention of cruelty to animals, protection of wildlife and animals, forests etc. However, given that there can be conflict when it comes to *laws passed by Parliament and state legislatures on the same subject, the Constitution provides for a central law to override a state law.*

11. Section 301, Indian Penal Code embodies what the English authors describe as the doctrine of transfer malice or the transmigration of motive. Section 301 of IPC provided that if a person, by doing anything which he intends or knows to be likely to cause death, commits culpable homicide by causing the death of any person, whose death he neither intends nor knows himself to be likely to cause, the culpable homicide committed by the offender is of the description of which it would have been, if he had caused the death of the person whose death he intended or knew himself to be likely to cause. This provision clearly shows that if the killing took place in the course of doing an act which a person intends or knows to be likely to cause death, it ought to be treated as if real intention of the killer had been actually carried out.

12. A partial protection against double jeopardy is a Fundamental Right guaranteed under Article 20 (2) of the Constitution of India, which states "No person shall be prosecuted and punished for the same offence more than once". This provision enshrines the concept of *autrefois convict*, that no one convicted of an offence can be tried or punished a second time. However, it does not extend to *autrefois acquit*, and so if a person is acquitted of a crime he can be retried. In India, protection against *autrefois acquit* is a statutory right, not a fundamental one. Such protection is provided by provisions of the Code of Criminal Procedure rather than by the Constitution.

15. Sarkaria Commission was set up in June 1983 by the central government of India. The Sarkaria Commission's charter was to examine the relationship and balance of power between state and central governments in the country and suggest changes within the framework of Constitution of India. The Commission was so named as it was headed by Justice Rajinder Singh Sarkaria, a retired judge of the Supreme Court of India. The other two members of the committee were Shri B. Sivaraman and Dr. SR Sen.

17. The *Tenth Schedule was inserted in the Constitution in 1985 by the 52nd Amendment Act.* It *lays down the process by which legislators may be disqualified on grounds of defection by the Presiding Officer of a legislature* based on a petition by any other member of the House.

- The decision on question as to disqualification on ground of defection is referred to *the Chairman or the Speaker of such House, and his decision is final.*
- The *law applies to both Parliament and state assemblies.*

18. The fundamental duties were incorporated in Part IV-A of our constitution by 42nd Constitutional Amendment Act, 1976. Presently we have 11 fundamental duties in our constitution under article 51-A, which are statutory duties and are enforceable by law. The idea behind the incorporation of the fundamental rights was to emphasize the obligation of the citizen in exchange of the comprehensive fundamental rights enjoyed by them. **Article 51 'A'** contained in Part IV A of the Constitution deals with Fundamental Duties. Fundamental Duties are **taken from the Constitution of Russia.**

19. In-camera proceeding is used in sensitive cases essentially to protect the privacy of the parties. Simply put, 'in-camera' proceeding is a proceeding carried out in private, in the absence of the public and the press. Essentially the proceedings are conducted through video conferencing to safeguard the privacy and protection of the accused. The public and the media are excluded from such proceedings for the purposes of sensitivity.

21. World Intellectual Property Day is observed annually on 26 April. The event was established by the World Intellectual Property Organization (WIPO) in 2000 to "raise awareness of how patents, copyright, trademarks and designs impact on daily life" and "to celebrate creativity, and the contribution made by creators and innovators to the development of societies across the globe". 26 April was chosen as the date for World Intellectual Property Day because it coincides with the date on which the Convention establishing the World Intellectual Property Organization entered into force in 1970.

23. Article 56 of the Indian Constitution makes it clear that the term of the President is five years from the date on which he enters the office. His term may terminate earlier (*i*) by resignation addressed to the Vice-President, or (*ii*) removal by impeachment for violation of the Constitution.

33. $X + Y > U + V$ ...(*i*)

$Y + U > X + V$ ...(*ii*)

On adding, we get,

$$(X + Y) + (Y + U) > (U + V) + (X + V)$$

$$2Y > 2V$$

$$Y > V$$

Hence, option (C) is correct.

47.

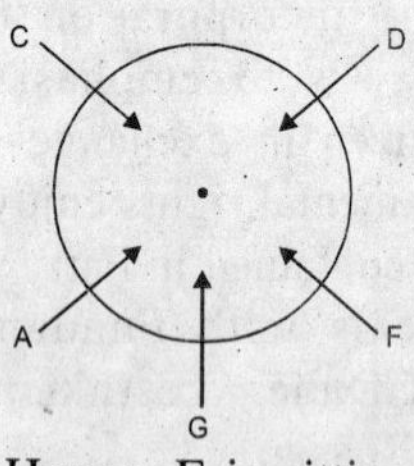

Hence, F is sitting between G and D.

62. The Prime numbers between 20 and 50 are 23, 29, 31, 37, 41, 43, 47

∴ Required Average

$$= \frac{23+29+31+37+41+43+47}{7} = \frac{251}{7}$$

$= 35.8.$

65. Column I Column II Column III

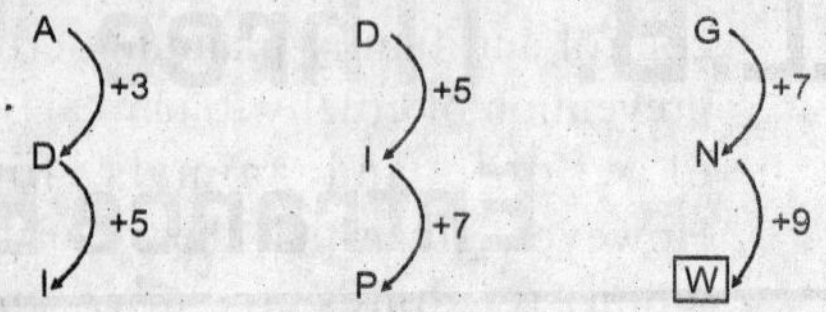

66.

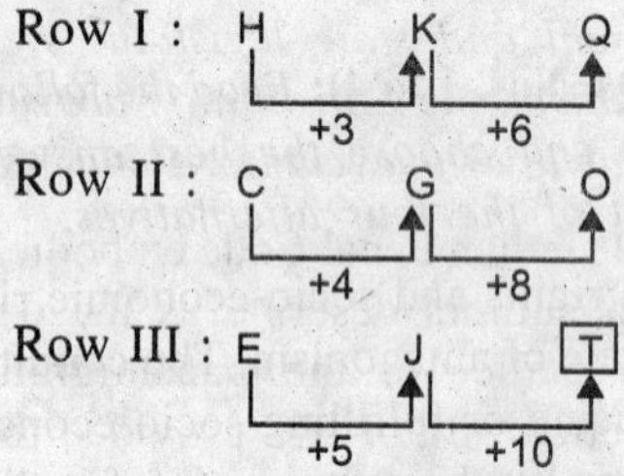

93. Let the first five consecutive numbers are $x, x + 1, x + 2, x + 3, x + 4$

We have, Average = 16

$$\therefore \frac{x+(x+1)+(x+2)+(x+3)+(x+4)}{5} = 16$$

$$\frac{5x+10}{5} = 16$$

$$5x + 10 = 80$$

$$5x = 70 \Rightarrow x = 14$$

Hence, the smallest number = 14.

100. Probability that the drawn card is Black

$$P(A) = \frac{26}{52} = \frac{1}{2}$$

Probability that the drawn card is Queen

$$P(B) = \frac{4}{52} = \frac{1}{13}$$

Probability that the drawn card is Black and Queen

$$P(A \cap B) = \frac{2}{52} = \frac{1}{26}$$

∴ Required probability that the drawn card either a black or a queen

$$P(A \cup B) = P(A) + P(B) - P(A \cap B)$$

$$= \frac{1}{2} + \frac{1}{13} - \frac{1}{26}$$

$$= \frac{13+2-1}{26} = \frac{14}{26} = \frac{7}{13}.$$

Previous Paper (Solved)

LL.B. (Three Year Degree Course) Entrance Examination, 2018*

Directions (For Qs. Nos. 1 to 4): *Read the following passage carefully and choose the best answer to each question out of the four alternatives:*

Civil and political rights and socio-economic rights do not exist in a state of antagonism. The conditions necessary for realising or fulfilling socio-economic rights do not postualte the subversion of political freedom. The reason for this is simple. Socio-economic entitlements must yield true benefits to those for whom they are intended. This can be achieved by eliminating rent-seeking behaviour and by preventing the capture of social welfare benefits by persons who are not entitled to them. Capture of social welfare benefits can be obviated only when political systems are transparent and when there is a free flow of information. Opacity ensures benefit to those who monopolize scarce economic resources. On the other hand, conditions where civil and political freedoms flourish ensure that governmental policies are subject to critique and assessment. It is this scrutiny which sub-serves the purpose of ensuring that socio-economic benefits actually permeate to the underprivileged for whom they are meant. Conditions of freedom and a vibrant assertion of civil and political rights promote a constant review of the justness of socio-economic programmes and of their effectiveness in addressing deprivation and want. Scrutiny of public affairs is founded upon the existence of freedom. Hence civil and political rights and socio-economic rights are complementary and not mutually exclusive.

1. According to the passage, assertion of rights ______.

A. is frowned upon

B. must be discouraged

C. promotes just social policies

D. is desirable

2. Which of the following statements best conveys the idea of the passage?

1. Civil and political rights and social and economic rights are opposed to each other.
2. Political freedom must be compromised to realize rights.
3. Existence of criticism of government is a proof of vibrant assertion of civil and political rights.
4. Transparency ensures equitable distribution of resources.

Choose the correct code:

A. 2 and 4 B. 1 and 2

C. 1 and 3 D. 3 and 4

3. According to the passage capture of social benefits ______.

A. ensures accountability

B. must be discouraged to ensure equitable distribution of resources

C. is an evil necessity

D. should be encouraged to maintain free flow of information

4. Opacity means:

A. Ostensible B. Transparent

C. Unclear D. Opal like

5. A is the mother of D and sister of B. B has a daughter C who is married to F. G is the husband of A. How is G related to D?

A. Son B. Father

C. Uncle D. Husband

6. If the price of a book is first decreased by 25% and then increased by 20%, then the net change in the price will be:

A. 30 B. 20

C. 10 D. 40

*Conducted by University of Delhi (18-06-2018).

7. Which among the following is correctly matched?

A. Indian Law Institute – Bhopal
B. Central Institute of Indian Languages – Chandigarh
C. Film and Television Institute of India – Chennai
D. National Insurance Academy – Pune

8. Which among the following languages was added to the Eighth Schedule of the Constitution of India, 1950 through 92nd Amendment Act of 2003?

A. Manipuri B. Nepali
C. Maithili D. Konkani

9. Britishers established Fort St. George as a trading outpost of East India Company in:

A. Varanasi B. Chandigarh
C. Chennai D. Jaipur

10. Which among the following cities does not have a bench of the National Green Tribunal?

A. Ahmedabad B. Chennai
C. Pune D. Kolkata

11. Which among the following was chosen as the Oxford Dictionaries Word of the Year in 2017?

A. Vape B. Post-truth
C. Emoji D. Youthquake

12. Which amongst the following is a committee constituted to inquire into allegations of corruption in Indian Premier League?

A. Satyajit Ray Committee
B. Shyam Benegal Committee
C. Justice Mukul Mudgal Committee
D. Justice Khosla Committee

13. In India, the National Voter's Day is celebrated on

A. 25th December
B. 25th January
C. 17th March
D. 17th January

14. If A > B, B > C and C > D, then which of the following conclusions is definitely wrong?

A. D < A B. C < B
C. A < D D. B < A

15. Who won the Gold Medal for India in the Women's 10 metre air pistol event at the XXI Commonwealth Games, 2018?

A. Manika Batra
B. Punam Yadav
C. Pooja Sahasrabudhe
D. Manu Bhaker

16. In a class of 45 students, one of the student ranks 20th. When two more students take admission then his rank gets one place down. What is his position from the bottom?

A. 28 B. 26
C. 25 D. 27

17. Which Schedule of the Constitution of India, 1950 prescribes the forms of oaths or affirmations for constitutional functionaries?

A. Sixth Schedule B. Second Schedule
C. Fifth Schedule D. Third Schedule

18. Which provision of the Constitution of India, 1950 deals with legislative powers of the President?

A. Article 123 B. Article 73
C. Article 139 D. Article 59

19. Which provision of the Constitution of India prohibits employment of children below the age of fourteen years to be employed in factories?

A. Article 23 B. Article 17
C. Article 27 D. Article 24

20. Who among the following is the current member of the International Law Commission from India?

A. Nagender Singh B. P.S. Rao
C. Aniruddha Rajput D. Dalbir Bhandari

21. The product of the ages of X and Y is 240. If twice the age of Y is more than X's age by 4 years, what is the age of Y?

A. 18 B. None of these
C. 12 D. 16

22. Two numbers are in the ratio of 3 : 7. If 5 is subtracted from the numbers, the ratio becomes 4 : 11. The numbers are:

A. 18, 42 B. 12, 28
C. 9, 16 D. 21, 49

23. "Do unto others as you would have them do unto you" means:
A. People tend to want whatever they don't have.
B. Don't do mean things to people.
C. If someone offers you a gift, don't question it.
D. Don't trust other people to do important things for you.

24. Who headed the group of experts on Privacy constituted by the Planning Commission?
A. Justice Arijit Pasayat
B. Justice M.B. Shah
C. Justice M.N. Venkatachalia
D. Justice A.P. Shah

25. Who amongst the following judges of the Supreme Court of India never served as a High Court judge?
A. Justice A.M. Khanwilkar
B. Justice Uday Umesh Lalit
C. Justice Kurian Joseph
D. Justice Abhay Manohar Sapre

26. In which of the following judgements did the Supreme Court of India set aside the practice of talaq-e-biddat *i.e.*, triple talaq?
A. Fazlunbi *Vs.* K. Khader Vali
B. Mohd. Ahmed Khan *Vs.* Shah Bano Begum
C. Bai Tahira *Vs.* Ali Hussain Fissali Chothia
D. Shayara Bano *Vs.* Union of India

27. The name of the largest river island of the world located in India is
A. Cijuli B. Pajuli
C. Khajuli D. Majuli

28. In which state the Sasan Ultra Mega Power Project is located?
A. Tamil Nadu B. Uttar Pradesh
C. Madhya Pradesh D. Maharashtra

29. Identify the correct statement:
A. Only taking of dowry is prohibited under law.
B. Only giving of dowry is prohibited under law.
C. Dowry is legally allowed with the consent of involved parties.
D. Giving as well as taking dowry is prohibited under law.

30. The recently launched 'Laqshya' programme is aimed at
A. Reducing malnutrition in children below ten years of age
B. Reducing maternal mortality rates
C. Elimination of tuberculosis by 2025
D. Improving quality of life in rural areas

31. X is wife of Y. Y is uncle of Z. B is sister of Y. How is B related to X?
A. Sister-in-Law B. Cousin
C. Brother D. Uncle

32. A judge of the Supreme Court of India after retirement can practice in
A. Supreme Court of India only
B. High Court
C. National Green Tribunal
D. None of these

33. Four tests—French, Hindi, English and Sanskrit are to be conducted on four consecutive days, not necessarily in the same order. The English test is held before the test which is conducted after Hindi. Sanskrit test is conducted exactly after two tests are held. Which is the last test held?
A. French B. Sanskrit
C. Hindi D. English

34. The headquarters of the World Trade Organization is located in
A. Geneva B. London
C. New York D. Nairobi

35. First UNESCO mixed heritage site of India is
A. Kangchendzonga National Park
B. Kaziranga National Park
C. Dachigam National Park
D. Bharatpur Bird Sanctuary

36. Renu, Sheena, Heena and Seema are sitting around a table. Renu is just right to the Sheena. Heena is left to Seema. Who amongst the following facing each other?
A. Renu – Sheena B. Renu – Seema
C. Sheena – Seema D. Heena – Renu

37. If B is coded as 2 and RATE is coded as 44 in a code language, how would you code NATION in that code language?
A. 74 B. 75
C. 72 D. 73

38. There are two groups of birds. If one bird moves from first group to the second group, the number of birds in the second group becomes double of the first group. If one bird moves from second group to the first group, the number of birds in both the groups becomes equal. How many birds were there in group 1 and 2 initially (respectively)?
A. 9, 5 B. 5, 7
C. 7, 5 D. 5, 9

39. Hari's commute never bothered him because there were always seats available on the train and he was able to spend 40 minutes comfortably reading newspapers. Ever since the train schedule changed, the train has become extremely crowded, and by the time the doors open at his station, there isn't a seat to be found. Which of the following inference is correct?
A. Hari's commute is less comfortable since the train schedule changed
B. Many commuters will complain about the new train schedule.
C. Hari is likely to look for a new job closer to his home.
D. Hari would be better off taking the bus to work.

40. European Court of Human Rights is located in
A. Hamburg B. Strasbourg
C. Luxembourg D. St. Petersburg

41. 'Earth Hour' is a global initiative of the
A. UN Development Programme
B. Earth Day Organization
C. World Wide Fund for Nature
D. UN Environment Programme

42. Arrange these mountain ranges from North to South
1. Satpura 2. Nilgiri
3. Vindhyas 4. Aravalis

Codes:

A.	1	4	3	2
B.	4	3	1	2
C.	4	1	3	2
D.	4	1	2	3

43. Which of the following is/are principal organ/s of the United Nations?
1. International Court of Justice
2. United Nations Development Programme
3. United Nations Economic and Social Council
4. United Nations Environment Programme
A. Only 1 B. All of these
C. 1, 2 and 4 D. 1 and 3

44. Who among the following can attend the meetings of both Houses of Parliament while being not a member of either House?
A. Solicitor General of India
B. Attorney General of India
C. Chief Election Commissioner
D. Comptroller and Auditor General of India

45. Who among the following is known as the 'Frontier Gandhi'?
A. Maulana Abul Kalam Azad
B. Maulana Shaukat Ali
C. Sir Syed Ahmed Khan
D. Khan Abdul Ghaffar Khan

46. Who among the following was not conferred Bharat Ratna?
A. Atal Bihari Vajpayee
B. Nelson Mandela
C. Homi J. Bhabha
D. Khan Abdul Ghaffar Khan

47. Who among the following was not a member of the Constituent Assembly of India?
A. Lakshmi Sehgal
B. Rajkumari Amrit Kaur
C. Hansa Mehta
D. Sarojini Naidu

48. Who amongst the following did not serve as the Chairman of the Law Commission of India?
A. Mr. M.C. Setalvad
B. Justice B.P. Jeevan Reddy

C. Justice A.P. Shah
D. Justice V.R. Krishna Iyer

49. "Behind the eight ball" means __________.
A. in safety B. in extravagance
C. in comfort D. in trouble

50. Who is the author of the book titled "Why I am a Hindu"?
A. Rakesh Sinha
B. Shashi Tharoor
C. Gopal Krishna Gandhi
D. Justice R. Banumathi

51. Inter-state river water disputes in India are to be decided by
A. Central Water Commission
B. Ministry of Water Resources
C. High Courts
D. None of the these

52. What is the meaning of *ex facie*?
A. Making the face down
B. Beside the face of it
C. Behind the face it
D. On the face of it

53. Who proposed the idea of Constituent Assembly of India in 1934?
A. Dr. B.R. Ambedkar
B. S.N. Mukherjee
C. Dr. Rajendra Prasad
D. M.N. Roy

54. Which of the following is explicitly prescribed as a Directive Principle of State Policy under the Constitution of India?
A. Organisation of village panchayats
B. Promotion of co-operative societies
C. Participation of workers in management of industries
D. All of these

55. Which of the following rivers does not flow into the Bay of Bengal?
A. Godavari B. Periyar
C. Kaveri D. Krishna

56. Which of the following smart cities has become the India's first city to run on 100% Renewable Energy during Daytime?
A. Chandigarh B. Puducherri
C. Gwalior D. Diu

57. Which of the following does not fall in the List I—Union List of the Seventh Schedule to Constitution of India?
A. Naval, military and air force works
B. Public health and sanitation
C. Sanctioning of cinematograph films for exhibition
D. Banking

58. Which of the following is not placed at Hague?
A. Permanent Court of Arbitration
B. International Tribunal for the Law of the Sea
C. International Court of Justice
D. International Criminal Court

59. Which of the following is not a Fundamental Duty under Article 51A of the Constitution of India?
A. To value and preserve the rich heritage of our composite culture
B. To safeguard public property and to abjure violence
C. To respect and propagate political values
D. To cherish and follow the noble ideals which inspired our national struggle for Freedom

60. Which of the following statement best explains the phrase 'Devil's Advocate'?
A. Expressing contentious opinion
B. Expressing discontentment
C. Arguing for the sake of argument
D. Arguing for the guilty

61. Which of the following fundamental right is not available to a foreigner in India?
A. Freedom of Speech and Expression
B. Right to Life and Liberty
C. Right to equality
D. Right against Ex post facto laws

62. In the following question, there is a certain relation between two given words on one side :: Choose the suitable words to be put on the other side from the given alternatives.
Glutton : Willpower :: ______ : ______
A. Platoon : Squad B. Charlatan : Hoax
C. Savant : Gumption D. Coward : Courage

63. In the following question, there is a certain relation between two given words on one side:: Choose the suitable word to be put on the other side from the given alternatives.
Inflexible: Limber :: Failure: ________

A. Achievement B. Expunge
C. Trouble D. Murmur

64. Find out which part of the sentence given below has an error: Demi has not completed her homework, isn't it?

A. her homework B. No fault
C. isn't it D. has not completed

65. Find out which part of the sentence given below has an error:
My Mother asked me that what I was doing.

A. that what I was doing
B. asked me
C. My mother
D. No fault

66. Choose the correct inference:
People who are bald are generally happy. Asif is bald. Therefore, Asif is happy.

A. Can't be determined
B. False
C. Probably true
D. True

67. Choose the correct inference:
The presence of calcium in milk makes it white. Egg is white. Therefore, egg also contains calcium:

A. TRUE
B. Can't be determined
C. FALSE
D. Probably true

68. Choose the correct inference:
Identify the odd one out

A. Tree B. Leaf
C. Branch D. Stem

69. Choose the correct inference:
Identify the odd one out

A. RAM = 18113 B. SUA = 19211
C. HOP = 81516 D. MAP = 13115

70. Choose the correct collective noun.
A ______ of ships.

A. Army B. Fleet
C. Belt D. Pack

71. Choose the correct collective noun.
A ________ of baboons.

A. Herd B. Congress
C. Pack D. Meeting

72. Choose the word that is nearest in meaning to the given word:
Abrogate

A. Revoke informally B. Revoke formally
C. Accept informally D. Accept formally

73. Choose the word that is nearest in meaning to the given word:
Extol

A. Glorify B. Dishonour
C. Provoke D. Announce

74. Choose the most appropriate option to fill in the blanks:
I have never seen ______ painting before.

A. as beautiful B. so beautiful
C. such a beautiful D. any beautiful

75. Choose the most appropriate option to fill in the blanks.
They ______ learning classical music next year.

A. will have been B. will be
C. will D. will have to

76. Fill in the missing word:
Insect : Disease :: War : ?

A. Army B. Victory
C. Destruction D. Weapon

77. Fill in the missing word:
Distance : Metre :: Force : ?

A. Dioptre B. Joule
C. Watt D. Newton

78. Arrange the words given below in a meaningful sequence:

1. Chaitra 2. Falgun
3. Magh 4. Bhadrapad
5. Aashadh

A. 1, 2, 5, 4, 3 B. 1, 2, 3, 4, 5
C. 1, 3, 4, 2, 5 D. 1, 5, 4, 3, 2

79. Statements: In a one day cricket match, the total runs made by a team were 300. Out of these 240 runs were made by bowlers.

Conclusions:

I. The opening batsmen were bowlers.

II. 80% of the team consists of bowlers.

A. Both Conclusions I and II follow
B. Neither Conclusion I nor II follows
C. Only Conclusion II follows
D. Only Conclusion I follows

80. Complete the series:
BAY, EDV, HGS, KJP, _____

A. NMQ B. NMP
C. NMM D. NMO

81. Complete the series:
REF, SGH, _____, UKL

A. TIJ B. VJT
C. MNT D. VXZ

82. Complete the series:
BCB, DED, FGF, HIH, ____

A. IJI B. JHJ
C. JKJ D. HJH

83. Complete the series:
53, 53, 40, 40, 27, 27, ____

A. 12 B. 14
C. 53 D. 27

84. Complete the series:
E64, _____, K16, N8, Q4

A. H32 B. G23
C. F32 D. J23

85. Complete the series:
70, 68, 66, 63, 61, 59, 56, 54, _______.

A. 52 B. 51
C. 50 D. 53

86. Complete the series:
192, 48, ____, 3

A. 11 B. 13
C. 12 D. 14

87. Apply the principle to the facts and choose the most appropriate option:

Principle 1: When a person voluntarily consents to infliction of some harm upon himself/herself, he/she cannot complain for the harm suffered and his/her consent acts as a good defence against him/her.

Principle 2: The consent may be express or implied.

Facts: The plaintiff was a spectator at Formula One Car race. Despite due care by the organisers, there was a collision between two cars during the race and one of the cars was thrown among the audience, gravely injuring Hasan. Hasan was paralysed waist down due to this injury.

Decision:

A. Organisers are liable to compensate Hasan as even though he agreed to take the risk of being injured, he did not agree to be paralysed.
B. Organisers are liable to compensate Hasan as he did not expressly consent to being gravely injured.
C. Organisers are liable to compensate Hasan for the harm caused to him, as he did not voluntarily agree to be gravely injured.
D. Organisers are not liable to compensate as Hasan impliedly took the risk of injury. The danger of car collision is inherent in Formula 1 Car Race. The possibility of spectators being injured by such collision is foreseeable.

88. Apply the principle to the facts and choose the most appropriate option:

Principle: If the offeror has prescribed a particular mode or manner of acceptance, the acceptance must be made in the prescribed manner only. In the event of the acceptor not following the prescribed mode of acceptance, no valid contract comes into existence.

Facts: Arora Enterprises made an offer to buy desks from Bharucha Co. Ltd. According to the terms of the contract, the acceptance was to be made through e-mail. Bharucha Co. and Ltd. sent the acceptance through post. Arora Enterprises received this letter but entered into contract with Abdulla Enterprises. Bharucha Co. Ltd. sued Arora Enterprises for breach of contract.

Decision:

A. Bharucha Co. Ltd can successfully sue Arora Enterprises as it has conveyed its acceptance and fulfilled essential conditions required by contract.

B. Arora Enterprises can be sued as it entered into contract with Abdulla Enterprises after receiving the acceptance of Bharucha Co. Ltd.

C. Arora Enterprises cannot be sued, as the acceptance was invalid.

D. The acceptance is valid as what is necessary is that the acceptance must reach the offeror.

89. Apply the principle to the facts and choose the most appropriate option:

Principle: A contract to do an act, which, after the contract is made becomes impossible is void when the act becomes impossible.

Facts: Sheela owned a two storey building. She agreed to lease the property to Harleen for a period of 1 year for a rent of fifty thousand rupees per month. The contract was signed by both the parties on April 30, 2015. It was agreed that the lease period would start from May 5, 2015. On May 3, 2015, a massive fire broke out and the building was completely destroyed.

Decision:

A. The contract is void as the subject matter of the contract has ceased to exist.

B. The contract is void as the fire broke out two days before the start of the lease period.

C. The contract is valid as the performance of the contract does not depend on the existence of the subject matter of contract, *i.e.* the building.

D. The contract is valid as it was already signed before the fire broke out.

90. Apply the principle to the facts and choose the most appropriate option:

Principle: Unreasonable interference with a person's use or enjoyment of land constitutes nuisance.

Facts: A brick grinding machine was installed by Mihir adjoining the premises of George who was a medical practitioner. The dust from the machine used to enter George's medical chamber and cause inconvenience to the patients.

Decision:

A. George cannot sue Mihir for nuisance as every nuisance is not inconvenience.

B. George cannot sue Mihir for nuisance as Mihir has a right to use his property as he deems fit.

C. George cannot sue Mihir for nuisance as the use of land by George was not illegal.

D. George can sue Mihir for nuisance as the dust interfered with the physical comfort of George and his patients.

91. One who studies elections and trends in voting is known as:

A. Demagogue

B. Odontologist

C. Psephologist

D. Numismatic

92. Right to Property is a

A. Fundamental Right

B. Not recognized in India

C. None of these

D. Legal Right

93. 'Operation Cactus' recently in the news refers to:

A. Indian army's cross border strike in Myanmar

B. India's nuclear project in Pokhran

C. India's military intervention in Maldives in 1988

D. India's Surgical Strikes on terror launch pads in PoK in 2016

94. Recently the UN General Assembly passed a resolution rejecting the Israeli claim of Jerusalem as its new capital. Which among the following countries voted against the resolution to support the Israeli claim?

A. Guatemala

B. India

C. Cuba

D. Sri Lanka

95. Fundamental Duties were added in the Constitution of India on the recommendation of:
A. Malimath Committee
B. Santhanam Committee
C. Sarkaria Committee
D. Swaran Singh Committee

96. Murugappa Gold Cup is related to which of the following sports?
A. Wrestling B. Swimming
C. Kabaddi D. Hockey

97. The President of India can be impeached on the ground of:
A. Both Violation of the Constitution of India and Proved misbehaviour or incapacity
B. Proved misbehaviour or incapacity
C. Violation of the Constitution of India
D. None of these

98. The Vice-President of India may be removed from his office by:
A. Resolution of the House of the People and duly approved by President.
B. Resolution of the Council of States and agreed to by the House of the People.
C. Resolution of the Council of States only.
D. The President of India upon the advice of the Council of Ministers.

99. As per the XIV Finance Commission Report how much is the State Governments' share in taxes?
A. 42% B. 40%
C. 41% D. 44%

100. Under the 'Adopt a Heritage' project, which corporate house has signed MoU to maintain historic site "Red Fort"?
A. Larsen & Tourbo
B. Dalmia Bharat Ltd.
C. Tata Motors
D. Tata Consultancy Services

ANSWERS

1	2	3	4	5	6	7	8	9	10
C	D	B	C	B	C	D	C	C	A
11	**12**	**13**	**14**	**15**	**16**	**17**	**18**	**19**	**20**
D	C	B	C	D	D	D	A	D	C
21	**22**	**23**	**24**	**25**	**26**	**27**	**28**	**29**	**30**
C	D	B	D	B	D	D	C	D	B
31	**32**	**33**	**34**	**35**	**36**	**37**	**38**	**39**	**40**
A	D	A	A	A	B	D	B	A	B
41	**42**	**43**	**44**	**45**	**46**	**47**	**48**	**49**	**50**
C	C	D	B	D	C	A	D	D	B
51	**52**	**53**	**54**	**55**	**56**	**57**	**58**	**59**	**60**
D	D	D	D	B	D	B	B	C	A
61	**62**	**63**	**64**	**65**	**66**	**67**	**68**	**69**	**70**
A	D	A	C	A	C	B	A	D	B
71	**72**	**73**	**74**	**75**	**76**	**77**	**78**	**79**	**80**
B	B	A	C	B	C	D	D	B	C
81	**82**	**83**	**84**	**85**	**86**	**87**	**88**	**89**	**90**
A	C	B	A	A	C	D	C	A	D
91	**92**	**93**	**94**	**95**	**96**	**97**	**98**	**99**	**100**
C	D	C	A	D	D	C	B	A	B

EXPLANATORY ANSWERS

5. 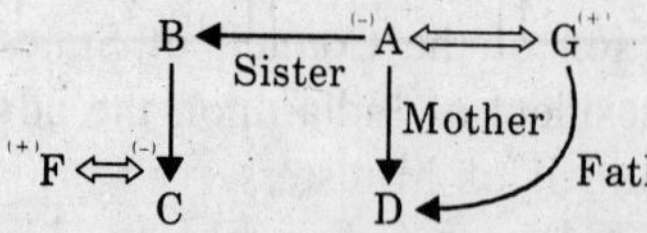

6. Let the initial price of the book = ₹ 100

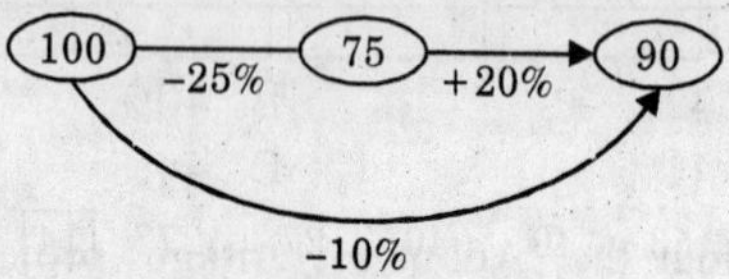

14. A > B, B > C and C > D

A > B > C > D

1. D < A (True)
2. C < B (True)
3. A < D (False)
4. B < A (True)

16. Total students = 45 + 2 = 47

Rank from Top = 20 + 1 = 21

Rank from Bottom = Total – Rank from Top + 1

= 47 – 21 + 1 = 27

21. Let the age of X and Y are P and Q years respectively,

According to question,

$$P \times Q = 240 \quad ...(1)$$

$$2Q - P = 4 \quad ...(2)$$

put $P = \frac{240}{Q}$, in equation (2)

$$2Q - \frac{240}{Q} = 4$$

$$2Q^2 - 240 = 4Q$$

$$2Q^2 - 4Q - 240 = 0$$

$$Q^2 - 2Q - 120 = 0$$

$$Q^2 - 12Q + 10Q - 120 = 0$$

$$Q(Q - 12) + 10(Q - 12) = 0$$

$$(Q + 10)(Q - 12) = 0$$

Q = –10 (Neglect)

Q = 12

∴ Y age is 12 years

22. Let two numbers are $3x$ and $7x$ respectively.

Then, $\frac{3x-5}{7x-5} = \frac{4}{11}$

$$33x - 55 = 28x - 20$$

$$5x = 35$$

$$x = 7$$

∴ The Numbers are 21 and 49.

31. 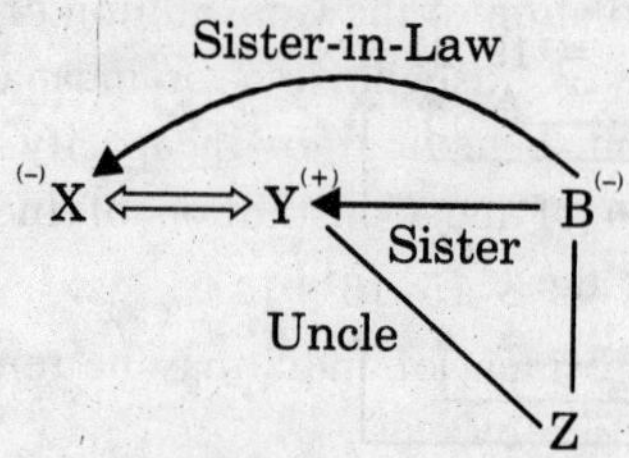

33. I. English

II. Hindi

III. Sanskrit

IV. French (Last Test)

36. 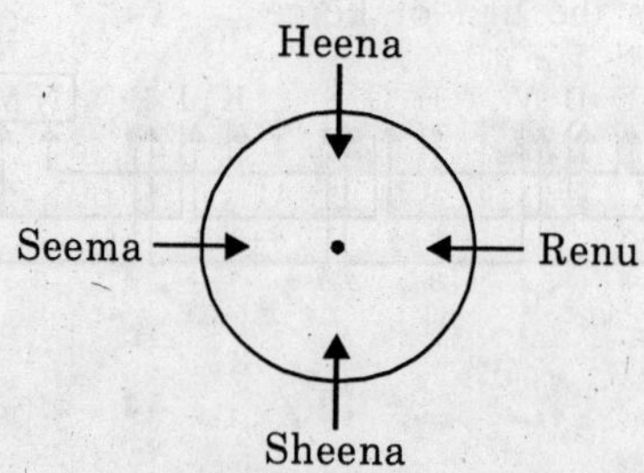

37. As, B → 2

RATE → 18 + 1 + 20 + 5 = 44

Similarly,

NATION = 14 + 1 + 20 + 9 + 15 + 14 = 73

38. Let initially the number of birds in group 1 and group 2 are x and y resepctively.

Case 1 : $2(x - 1) = (y + 1)$

$$2x - y = 3 \quad ...(1)$$

Case 2 : $x + 1 = y - 1$

$$x - y = 2 \quad ...(2)$$

90. The concept of "jus cogens" refers to:

A. Rules of customary international law that are binding on all states and cannot be derogated from
B. Non-binding recommendations of international organizations
C. Bilateral agreements between two states
D. Rules of international commercial law

91. Which of the following agreements is NOT covered by the WTO?

A. Agreement on Trade-Related Aspects of Intellectual Property Rights (TRIPS)
B. General Agreement on Trade in Services (GATS)
C. Kyoto Protocol on climate change
D. Agreement on Agriculture

92. The "Most-Favoured-Nation" (MFN) principle requires member countries to:

A. Offer the same trade concessions to all WTO members
B. Provide preferential treatment to developing countries
C. Impose higher tariffs on goods from non-member countries
D. Restrict trade with countries that violate human rights

93. The WTO's dispute settlement system is primarily designed to:

A. Impose criminal sanctions on member states
B. Encourage bilateral negotiations between member states
C. Resolve trade disputes between member governments
D. Promote free movement of labour

94. What is the chemical symbol for table salt?

A. KCl B. NaCl
C. $CaCl_2$ D. $MgSO_4$

95. What is the hardest natural substance?

A. Steel B. Gold
C. Diamond D. Quartz

96. What is the unit of force?

A. Joule B. Watt
C. Newton D. Pascal

97. What is the scientific study of the universe called?

A. Geology B. Biology
C. Astronomy D. Chemistry

98. What is the unit of electric current?

A. Volt B. Ohm
C. Ampere D. Datt

99. What is the scientific name for the voice box?

A. Trachea B. Larynx
C. Bronchus D. Alveoli

100. What is the primary cause of ozone layer depletion?

A. Carbon monoxide
B. Chlorofluorocarbons (CFCs)
C. Sulfur dioxide
D. Nitrogen oxides

EXPLANATORY ANSWERS

1. The term *economics* has its roots in ancient Greek language. It is derived from the word *Oikonomia*, which is a combination of two Greek words: *Oikos* meaning "house" or "household" and *Nomos* meaning "law" or "management." Together, *Oikonomia* literally means "household management." Over time, this concept evolved to represent the systematic study of how resources are produced, distributed, and consumed in society, which is what we now call economics.

90. A	**91.** C	**92.** A	**93.** C	**94.** B	**95.** C
96. C	**97.** C	**98.** C	**99.** B	**100.** B	

2. The campaign launched in April 2010 to clean and de-pollute the river Ganga was named Nirmal Ganga-Sparsh Ganga. This initiative was an ambitious programme that aimed to restore the purity of the river by reducing pollution levels, improving sanitation practices, and creating awareness among the people living along the river banks. The campaign began from Gangotri and focused on rejuvenating the sacred river through coordinated efforts involving government agencies and local communities. The programme Namami Gange was introduced later in 2014 as a more comprehensive and large-scale mission by the Union Government.

3. The Pushyabhuti Dynasty was founded by Pushyabhuti, who laid the foundation for a prominent ruling family in North India. This dynasty later gained significant historical importance during the reign of Harshavardhan, one of the most powerful rulers of the 7th century. Pushyabhuti established the initial power base and lineage from which the dynasty expanded.

4. The Bhagwati Sutra is a major canonical text of Jainism, particularly belonging to the Shwetambara sect. It contains detailed philosophical discussions, religious teachings, and dialogues between Lord Mahavira and his disciples. It plays a crucial role in explaining Jain doctrines, ethics, and spiritual practices.

5. The words Trivial, Unimportant, and Insignificant all describe something that has little value, meaning, or significance. In contrast, Important conveys the idea of something that is significant or valuable. Since its meaning is opposite to the others, it is clearly the odd man out in the group.

6. From the first statement, it is clear that all shrubs in the garden are flowering shrubs. The second statement says that some shrubs are rosy shrubs. Since these rosy shrubs are also shrubs of the same garden, and all shrubs are already stated to be flowering, it logically follows that all rosy shrubs are flowering shrubs as well. Therefore, the third statement is a direct and valid conclusion based on the first two.

7. The sentence "Please, come ______ the bathroom." requires a preposition that shows movement from inside a place to the outside. The phrase *out of* correctly expresses this idea of exiting or leaving an enclosed space. Other options like *over*, *on*, and *in* do not logically fit the context of coming from inside the bathroom to outside, making them grammatically incorrect here.

8. The sentence "The rain comes ______ the cloud." refers to the origin or source of rain. Rain forms in clouds due to condensation and then falls to the earth. The preposition *from* is used to indicate source or point of origin, which makes the sentence scientifically and grammatically correct. The other options do not convey this meaning.

9. The sentence "The stars ______ counted." needs a verb form that expresses impossibility. Since stars are countless and spread across an immeasurable universe, it is not practically possible to count them. Therefore, the passive form *cannot be* counted correctly expresses this idea. The other options either change the meaning or make the sentence grammatically incomplete.

10. Let us carefully analyse the relationship:

"He is the husband of the granddaughter of the father of my father."

- Father of my father = Grandfather
- Granddaughter of my grandfather = My sister (or female cousin)
- Husband of that granddaughter = Husband of my sister

The husband of one's sister is called a **brother-in-law**. Hence, Y is related to X as a brother-in-law.

11. The words *goggle, spectacles, and bifocal* are all types of eyewear used by people, mainly for vision correction or protection of the eyes. An *optical reader*, however, is not eyewear; it is a device/machine used for scanning or reading printed marks or text (like OMR or barcode readers). So it does not belong to the same category as the other three.

12. This is a coding-decoding problem based on a fixed logical pattern.

From the given pair IVORY : ZWSPJ, the coding rule can be understood as follows:

First, the letters of the word are arranged in descending order according to their alphabetical positions.

IVORY → I(9), V(22), O(15), R(18), Y(25)

Descending order: Y, V, R, O, I → YVROI

Next, each letter is moved one step forward in the English alphabet:

Y → Z

V → W

R → S

O → P

I → J

Thus, IVORY becomes ZWSPJ, which matches the given code.

Now applying the same rule to CREAM:

C(3), R(18), E(5), A(1), M(13)

Descending order: R, M, E, C, A → RMECA

Shifting each letter one step forward:

R → S

M → N

E → F

C → D

A → B

This produces the code ISNFDB as per the given options, which follows the established pattern accurately.

13. Tuberculosis (TB) is a disease that mainly affects the lungs, so the first pair is Tuberculosis : Lungs. Typhoid, on the other hand, is an infectious disease that primarily affects the *intestine* (especially the small intestine). Therefore, the correct analogous pair is Typhoid : Intestine.

14. Look at the numbers: 14, 28, 35, 46, 56, 84.

$$14 = 2 \times 7$$
$$28 = 4 \times 7$$
$$35 = 5 \times 7$$
$$56 = 8 \times 7$$
$$84 = 12 \times 7$$

All of these are multiples of 7 except 46. Since 46 is not divisible by 7, it is the odd one out.

15. The Drafting Committee of the Constitution of India was responsible for preparing the draft of the Constitution. The Chairman of this committee was Dr. B. R. Ambedkar, who played a crucial role in framing and structuring the Constitution and is often called the "Chief Architect of the Indian Constitution."

16. The concepts of Fundamental Rights, Judicial Review, and Independence of Judiciary in the Indian Constitution have been borrowed from the Constitution of the United States of America. These features ensure protection of individual liberties and empower the courts to interpret the Constitution and strike down unconstitutional laws, which are the key principles of the American constitutional system.

17. NATO stands for North Atlantic Treaty Organisation. It is an intergovernmental military alliance established in 1949 with the main objective of ensuring collective security and mutual defence among its member countries. According to Article 5 of the NATO treaty, an armed attack against one member is considered an attack against all, requiring collective response. It plays an important role in maintaining peace and stability in the North Atlantic region and beyond.

18. The Pigeon-hole theory in the Law of Torts was given by Salmond. According to this theory, the Law of Tort consists of specific and defined categories of wrongs. For a civil wrong to be considered a Tort, it must fit into one of these pre-existing categories or "pigeon-holes." If a wrong does not fall under any recognised category, it cannot be treated as a Tort under this approach.

19. The Latin maxim "Ubi jus ibi remedium" is a fundamental principle of law. It literally translates to "Where there is a right, there is a remedy." This means that if a person's legal right is violated, the law must provide a way to enforce that right or compensate for its infringement. It ensures that legal rights are meaningful and not merely theoretical.

20. The United Nations Security Council (UNSC) is one of the principal organs of the United Nations responsible for maintaining international peace and security. It consists of 15 members in total, out of which five are permanent members: the United States, the United Kingdom, France, Russia, and China. These five countries hold special powers including the right to veto any substantive resolution.

21. The theme for International Women's Day 2025 is "For ALL Women and Girls: Rights, Equality, Empowerment." This theme highlights the importance of creating an inclusive world where every woman and girl enjoys equal rights and opportunities. It focuses on removing discrimination, promoting leadership, and empowering women socially, politically, and economically. The theme also aligns with global efforts to strengthen gender justice and equality across all sectors of society.

22. The AI chatbot of the platform "X" (formerly Twitter) is called Grok. It is developed by xAI, a company founded by Elon Musk, and is designed to provide conversational responses with real-time access to information from X. Grok is known for its witty and slightly humorous tone while also offering intelligent assistance. It represents the integration of artificial intelligence into social media platforms.

23. Donald Trump holds the distinction of being both the 45th and 47th President of the United States. He first served as the 45th President from 2017 to 2021 and later returned to office in 2025 as the 47th President. This makes him one of the few American presidents to serve non-consecutive terms. His political career continues to have significant national and global impact.

24. Mount Lewotobi Laki-Laki is a volcano located in Indonesia, specifically on the island of Flores in the East Nusa Tenggara province. It has recently been in the news due to increased volcanic activity and eruptions. These eruptions have led to safety warnings, evacuations, and disruptions in nearby regions. The volcano is closely monitored due to its potential impact on surrounding communities.

25. The Outstanding/Lifetime Achievement in Indian Cinema award at IIFA 2025 was presented to Rakesh Roshan. He is a veteran actor, director, and producer who has made remarkable contributions to Hindi cinema. He is best known for blockbuster films like Koi Mil Gaya and the Krrish series. The award recognises his decades-long influence and dedication to the Indian film industry.

26. The idiom "Once in a Blue Moon" is used to describe something that happens very rarely or on very unusual occasions. It refers to an event that occurs so infrequently that it is almost exceptional. The phrase originates from the rare astronomical event when two full moons appear in a single month. Therefore, it clearly conveys the idea of something happening only occasionally.

27. Palaeontology is a scientific discipline that deals with the study of fossils, which are the preserved remains or impressions of ancient plants and animals. It helps scientists understand prehistoric life, evolutionary changes, and the geological history of the Earth. By examining fossils, palaeontologists reconstruct past environments and extinct species. Hence, fossils are the central focus of palaeontology.

28. One millimetre is a unit of measurement in the metric system used to measure very small lengths. Since 1 centimetre equals 10 millimetres, dividing 1 cm by 10 gives the value of 1 millimetre. Therefore, 1 mm is equal to 0.1 cm. This conversion is commonly used in scientific and mathematical calculations.

29. A Puisne Judge of a High Court is any judge who serves under the Chief Justice and is not the head of the court. The word "puisne" means junior or subordinate in status. These judges perform regular judicial duties and decide cases but do not hold the administrative authority of the Chief Justice. Thus, the term refers to all High Court judges other than the Chief Justice.

30. The term "Chattel" is a legal word used to describe movable property that can be physically transferred from one place to another. It includes items like furniture, vehicles, jewellery, and other personal goods. It does not include land or buildings, which are considered immovable property. Therefore, chattel specifically means movable property.

31. The state of Meghalaya has received GI (Geographical Indication) tags for two agricultural products – Khasi Mandarin and Memong Narang. These products are unique to the climatic conditions and traditional farming practices of the region. The GI tag helps protect their authenticity and boosts the local farmers' economic prospects by giving them national and international recognition.

32. Motilal Chimanlal Setalvad was a highly distinguished legal personality in India. He served as the first Attorney General of India, the first Chairman of the Law Commission of India, and also played a key role in shaping legal reforms in the country. His contribution to the Indian legal system was pioneering and influential, making him the correct choice for all given positions.

33. In official terms, the "Budget" is known as the Annual Financial Statement under Article 112 of the Indian Constitution. It presents the estimated receipts and expenditure of the Government for a financial year. This statement outlines how the government plans to collect revenue and allocate funds for various development and administrative purposes.

34. A prominent example of *transformative constitutionalism* in India is seen in the case of Navtej Singh Johar vs. Union of India. In this landmark judgment, the Supreme Court decriminalised consensual homosexual acts by partially striking down Section 377 of the IPC. The judgment transformed social and legal norms by promoting equality, dignity, and individual liberty, reflecting the dynamic nature of the Constitution.

35. The International Day of Yoga was first celebrated on 21st June 2015. This day was declared by the United Nations following a proposal by India, recognising yoga as a practice that promotes physical, mental, and spiritual well-being. Since then, it has been observed worldwide to spread awareness about the benefits of yoga and healthy living.

36. "Only D is between A and B" means that around the circle the three must appear as A – D – B or B – D – A with exactly one person (D) between A and B.

"Only F is between A and C" means A – F – C or C – F – A, again with exactly one person (F) between A and C.

Combining these two local sequences around A, we can place them as: C – F – A – D – B (in order around the circle).

Now, "E is just left of B". Since everyone is facing the centre, "left" means clockwise. So E is immediately clockwise from B, giving the full clockwise order: C – F – A – D – B – E. From this arrangement, going clockwise from E to F, we pass only C in between. So the only one standing between E and F is C.

37. The man starts facing south-west. Think of directions as angles: East (0°), North (90°), West (180°), South (270°), so South-West is 225°. He first turns 90° anticlockwise, i.e., 225° + 90° = 315°, which is South-East. Then he turns 135° clockwise, so 315° − 135° = 180°, which corresponds to West. So finally, he is facing West.

38. In the upper atmosphere (stratosphere), chlorine atoms released mainly from chlorofluorocarbons (CFCs) initiate chain reactions that destroy ozone molecules. A single chlorine atom can break down many ozone (O_3) molecules before it is deactivated, which makes chlorine particularly harmful to the ozone layer. Therefore, among the options given, chlorine is the gas directly associated with starting the ozone-depleting chain reaction.

39. In the code, each letter of the word is shifted forward in the alphabet by increasing steps. For KOLKATA:

K → L (+1)
O → Q (+2)
L → O (+3)
K → O (+4)
A → F (+5)
T → Z (+6)
A → H (+7)

So, KOLKATA becomes LQOOFZH, which matches option D.

40. After India won the ICC Champions Trophy 2025, the BCCI officially announced a cash reward of ₹ 58 crore for the team, including players, coaching and support staff, and the Men's Selection Committee. This amount was declared as a recognition of their unbeaten run in the tournament and their victory in the final against New Zealand.

41. In the World Happiness Report 2025, India has been placed at the 118th position among the ranked countries. This report evaluates nations based on factors such as income level, social support, life expectancy, freedom, generosity, and perception of corruption. Despite being one of the fastest-growing economies, India's low ranking reflects challenges related to overall well-being and quality of life indicators. The report is annually published by the UN Sustainable Development Solutions Network.

42. The idiom "Talking twenty to the dozen" refers to speaking very fast and continuously. It is used when someone talks rapidly, often without pause, usually due to excitement, nervousness, or enthusiasm. The phrase does not imply nonsense talk but rather speed and volume in conversation. Hence, it specifically highlights hurried speech.

43. The word "Legal" means something that is permitted or authorised by law. The closest synonym among the given options is "Statutory," which refers to something established or regulated by statute (law). The other options do not relate to law or legality. Therefore, "Statutory" correctly matches the meaning of "Legal."

44. The word "Skeptical" means having doubt or not easily believing something. Its antonym should express certainty or firm belief. Among the options, "Certain" best fits as it means confident and sure without doubt. While "credulous" also suggests belief, "certain" is the most accurate opposite in this context.

45. Jitendra Pal Singh, a senior Indian Foreign Service (IFS) officer, was recently appointed as India's Ambassador to Israel. He has served in several important diplomatic positions and brings extensive experience in international relations. His appointment strengthens India's diplomatic engagement and strategic partnership with Israel in areas such as defence, technology, and trade.

46. Pride and Prejudice is a classic romantic novel written by Jane Austen. It was first published in 1813 and explores themes such as marriage, morality, social class, and misunderstandings in 19th-century England. The story mainly focuses on the character Elizabeth Bennet and her relationship with Mr. Darcy. Jane Austen is widely regarded as one of the greatest English novelists.

47. Among the given options, Othello was written by William Shakespeare. It is a tragic play that centres on jealousy, betrayal, and manipulation, particularly revolving around the character of Othello and Iago. The other plays listed were written by different authors such as Oscar Wilde, Christopher Marlowe, and Samuel Beckett.

48. The famous poem Daffodils (also known as I Wandered Lonely as a Cloud) was written by William Wordsworth. This poem describes the beauty of nature and the joyful sight of daffodils swaying in the breeze. It reflects Wordsworth's love for natural scenery and his belief in nature's healing power.

49. The study of human societies, cultures, traditions, and social relationships is known as Anthropology. It focuses on understanding how humans live, behave, and evolve in different environments and cultural settings. While Sociology studies society in general, Anthropology goes deeper into cultural and evolutionary aspects.

50. The Industrial Revolution began in Great Britain in the late 18th century. It marked a major shift from hand production to machine-based manufacturing, leading to rapid industrial growth. Innovations such as the steam engine and mechanised textile production transformed the economy and society. From Britain, it later spread to other parts of the world.

51. The theory of classical conditioning was developed by Ivan Pavlov, a Russian physiologist. He demonstrated this theory through his famous experiment with dogs, where he showed how a neutral stimulus (like a bell) could be associated with a natural response (salivation). Over time, the dogs began to salivate at the sound of the bell alone. This experiment became the foundation of behavioural learning theory.

52. The study of how human populations change over time is known as Demography. It deals with population size, growth, density, distribution, birth rates, death rates, and migration. Demographers analyse these trends to understand social, economic, and planning issues. This field is crucial for government policy and development planning.

53. Black soil is the most suitable for cotton cultivation. It is also known as "Regur soil" and is rich in lime, potash, and magnesium. This soil has high moisture-retaining capacity, which is essential for cotton crops. It is mainly found in the Deccan Plateau region of India.

54. Madhya Pradesh has the largest forest cover in India by total area. It is often referred to as the "Tiger State" of India due to its extensive forested regions and wildlife reserves. The state's vast forest area plays a significant role in biodiversity conservation and ecological balance. It has consistently ranked first in forest cover according to government reports.

55. The Treaty of Chittor (1615) was signed between Mughal Emperor Jahangir and Maharana Amar Singh of Mewar. The treaty ended the long-standing conflict between the Mughals and the Rajputs of Mewar. It allowed Mewar to retain its internal autonomy while accepting Mughal supremacy. This agreement marked an important moment in Mughal-Rajput relations.

56. The Persian festival of Nowruz was introduced in India by Ghiyas-ud-din Balban, a powerful ruler of the Mamluk (Slave) Dynasty who reigned from 1266 to 1287 AD. Balban adopted Persian customs to strengthen royal authority and create a sense of divine kingship. Along with Nowruz, he also introduced court rituals such as *sijda* (prostration) and *paibos* (kissing the Sultan's feet) to impose strict discipline and enhance the grandeur of the monarchy. The celebration of Nowruz symbolised the Persian New Year and was used to reinforce the majestic and authoritative image of the Sultan.

57. Samudragupta is known as the "Napoleon of India" because of his brilliant military skills and extensive conquests. This title was given by the British historian V.A. Smith after studying his victorious campaigns recorded in the Allahabad Pillar Inscription. He undertook both northern (Digvijaya) and southern (Dharma Vijay) expeditions, expanding the Gupta Empire far and wide. Besides being a great warrior, he was also a patron of art, music, and literature.

58. The imperial capital of the Mauryan Empire during the reign of Ashoka was Patliputra (modern Patna). It served as the political, administrative, and military headquarters of the empire. From Patliputra, Ashoka issued his famous rock and pillar edicts that spread the message of Dhamma, peace, and moral conduct. The city was a major centre of governance and learning in ancient India.

59. The total geographical area of India is approximately 32.8 lakh square kilometres. This vast land area makes India the seventh-largest country in the world. It includes a wide variety of physical features such as the Himalayas, Indo-Gangetic plains, Thar desert, Deccan plateau, and long coastal regions. This diversity contributes to India's rich climate and ecological variation.

60. The McMahon Line forms the legal boundary between India and China. It was drawn in 1914 during the Shimla Convention between British India and Tibet. India recognises this line as its official border, especially in Arunachal Pradesh, while China disputes its validity. The McMahon Line remains a significant point of discussion in India-China border relations.

61. Lord Canning was the Governor-General of India at the time of the Revolt of 1857. He played a crucial role during this turbulent period and later became the first Viceroy of India after the British Crown took direct control from the East India Company in 1858. His tenure focused on restoring order and introducing administrative reforms to stabilise British rule in India.

62. The Special Olympics World Summer Games 2019 were held in Abu Dhabi, United Arab Emirates. This was the first time the games were hosted in the Middle East and North Africa region. The event promoted inclusivity and showcased the talents of athletes with intellectual disabilities from around the world, marking a significant milestone for global sports and social awareness.

63. An "injunction" is a court order that directs a person to either do or refrain from doing a specific act. It is commonly used to prevent harm or maintain the status quo until a final decision is made. Injunctions are an important remedy in civil law to protect rights and prevent irreparable damage.

64. A source of law refers to the origin from which legal rules are derived. Among the given options, *statutes* are formal written laws enacted by a legislative body and form a primary source of law. They provide binding legal authority and govern the legal system of a country.

65. In Tort Law, "negligence" refers to the failure to exercise reasonable care that a prudent person would in similar circumstances. This lack of care results in unintended harm or injury to another person. Negligence forms the basis for many civil liability cases where compensation is claimed for damages caused by carelessness.

66. The Latin phrase *Caveat emptor* translates to "Let the buyer beware." It means that the buyer is responsible for carefully examining the goods before purchasing them. If the buyer fails to inspect and later finds defects, the seller is generally not liable. This principle is commonly applied in sales and contract law to protect sellers from unwarranted claims.

67. This question is based on logical reasoning. Since all cats are mammals, and all mammals are animals, it logically follows that all cats must also be animals. This conclusion is derived directly from the two given premises and is universally true. Therefore, cats fall under the category of animals.

68. This coding question follows a letter-shifting rule, where each letter of the original word is replaced by the next letter in the English alphabet. In other words, every letter moves one step forward (+1 position). This type of coding is very commonly used in reasoning questions. Let us apply this rule clearly to the word CHAIR:

- C → D (next letter after C)
- H → I (next letter after H)
- A → B (next letter after A)
- I → J (next letter after I)
- R → S (next letter after R)

So, when each letter is shifted forward by one position, CHAIR becomes DIBJS. This matches exactly with option D.

Despite minor inconsistency in the example TABLE → UBAMD, the options themselves clearly support a simple forward shift pattern, and DIBJS is the only fully logical and accurate result.

69. The sequence follows an increasing pattern of steps:

A (+2) → C,
C (+3) → F,
F (+4) → J.

The next step should increase by 5. Therefore, J + 5 = O. This maintains the progressive pattern of increasing alphabetical jumps.

70. A *tautology* is a statement that is always true regardless of the truth or falsehood of its individual components. It is true by virtue of its logical structure. For example, "It will rain or it will not rain" is always true. Hence, a statement that is always true is called a *tautology*.

71. The quantum processor named Willow was launched by Google as part of its advanced quantum computing programme. This processor is designed to improve stability, speed, and error correction in quantum systems, which are capable of solving extremely complex problems far beyond the ability of classical computers. Willow represents another major step by Google towards achieving practical and scalable quantum computing.

72. The Gobardhan Portal was launched to streamline and simplify the establishment of Biogas and Compressed Biogas (CBG) plants across India. It acts as a single-window system for registration, coordination, and monitoring of waste-to-energy projects. The portal supports sustainable development by promoting the use of organic waste such as cattle dung and crop residue to generate clean energy.

73. The AUKUS submarine deal is a trilateral security partnership involving the United States, the United Kingdom, and Australia. Under this agreement, the US and UK will help Australia acquire nuclear-powered submarines to strengthen its naval capabilities. The pact focuses on enhancing defence cooperation in the Indo-Pacific region amid rising strategic challenges.

74. The P-800 Onyx Missile is a supersonic cruise missile developed by Russia. It is designed primarily for anti-ship warfare and has the capability to evade modern air defence systems due to its high speed and low-flight trajectory. This missile is considered a powerful component of Russia's naval strike arsenal.

75. Sierra Leone declared a national emergency on drug abuse due to the rapid rise in consumption of a dangerous synthetic drug known as "Kush." The government took this step to combat the

equn. (1) to eqn. (2), we get

$$x = 5$$

put $x = 5$ in equation (1)

$$2 \times 5 - y = 3$$

$$y = 7$$

$\therefore$ No. of Birds in group 1 and 2 are 5 and 7 respectively.

68. Except (A) Tree, all others are the parts of tree.

69. (i) R A M = 18 1 13

(ii) S U A = 19 21 1

(iii) H O P = 8 15 16

(iv) M A P = 13 1 ~~15~~ 16 (Odd One)

77. As Metre is the unit of Distance, similarly Newton is the unit of Force.

80. B A Y E D V H G S K J P [N M M]

+3 +3 +3 +3

+3 +3 +3 +3

–3 –3 –3 –3

81. R E F S G H [T I J] U K L

+1 +1 +1

+2 +2 +2

+2 +2 +2

82. B C B D E D F G F H I H [J K J]

+2 +2 +2 +2

+2 +2 +2 +2

+2 +2 +2 +2

83. 53 53 40 40 27 27 [14]

–13 –13 –13

–13 –13

84. E 64 [H 32] K 16 N 8 Q 4

+3 +3 +3 +3

÷2 ÷2 ÷2 ÷2

85. 70 68 66 63 61 59 56 54 [52]

–2 –2 –3 –2 –2 –3 –2 –2

86. 192 48 [12] 3

÷4 ÷4 ÷4

Previous Paper (Solved)

LL.B. (Three Year Degree Course) Entrance Examination, 2017*

1. When was Article 21A (right to education) inserted in part of the constitution?
A. 2000 B. 2002
C. 2003 D. 2005

2. How many members can the President nominate to the Rajya Sabha ?
A. 10 B. 12
C. 14 D. 16

3. Who decides on the issue whether a Bill is a Money Bill or not?
A. President of India
B. Speaker of Lok Sabha
C. Chairman of Rajya Sabha
D. Finance Minister

4. What is 'Carbon Footprint'?
A. A kind of fossil
B. A measure to know the availability of petroleum product
C. Amount of carbon dioxide released into atmosphere
D. Analysis to know the breathing problems

5. Who amongst the following was not a Chief Justice of India?
A. Justice P.N. Bhagwati
B. Justice R.M. Lodha
C. Justice Krishna Iyer
D. Justice J.S. Verma

6. Who was the first Leader of Opposition on Lok Sabha?
A. Jagjivan Ram B. Ram Suhag Singh
C. Y.B. Chavan D. Sharad Pawar

7. When a convict is temporarily released from the prison for a fixed period of time, it is called.....
A. Parole B. Bail
C. Discharge D. Acquittal

8. From the constitution of which country, the procedure for amendment of the constitution has been borrowed by India?
A. Constitution of France
B. Constitution of United States
C. Constitution of Germany
D. Constitution of South Africa

9. How many languages are there in the Eighth Schedule of the Constitution of India?
A. 17 B. 18
C. 20 D. 22

10. The Legislative Assembly of each states shall consist of........
A. Not more than five hundred fifty and not less than fifty members
B. Not more than five hundred and not less than sixty members
C. Not more than four hundred and not less than seventy members
D. Not more than and not less than as many members as decided by Parliament.

11. The 'Collegium system' is ....
A. A process to appoint judges in the High Court and the Supreme Court of India.
B. A process to elect the Speaker of the Lok Sabha
C. A process to elect President and Vice-President of India.
D. A process to elect Leader of the Opposition party in the Lok Sabha

12. Under the Prevention of Children from Sexual Offence Act, 2012, 'child' means ....
A. Any child who had not completed 18 years of age
B. A male child who has not completed 16 years of age and female child who has not completed 18 years of age.

*Conducted by University of Delhi (02-07-2017).

C. Any child who is not under guardianship
D. Any person who has not attained the level of maturity and behaves like a child

13. Which of the following statements is incorrect about Money Bill?
A. On the question whether a Bill Money Bill or not, the decision of the Pı dent is final.
B. A Bill is not to be deemed a Money Bill by reason only that it provides for the imposition, abolition, remission, alternation or regulation of any tax by any local authority or body.
C. A Money Bill shall not be introduced in a Legislative Council.
D. If the Legislative Assembly does not accept any of the recommendations of the Legislative Council, the Money Bill shall be deemed to have been passed by both houses in the form in which it was passed by Legislative Assembly.

14. Who presides over joint sitting of both houses of Parliament?
A. President
B. Prime Minister
C. Chairman of Rajya Sabha
D. Speaker of Lok Sabha

15. "To provide free local aid to an accused" is covered under ....
A. Directive Principles of State Policy
B. Fundamental rights
C. Discretion of the State
D. Moral rights

16. In the United States, the residuary power lies with ....
A. States
B. Federal Government
C. States and federal government depending upon the subject matter as the constitution did not define it in clear and cogent terms
D. Local Government

17. Under which of the following provisions of the Constitution of India 1950, the Supreme Court may grant special leave to appeal from any judgement, decree, determination, sentence or order?
A. Article 131 B. Article 134
C. Article 136 D. Article 143

18. Justice social, economic and political is.....
A. A Directive Principle of States Policy taken into account while making law
B. An ideal enshrined in the Preamble to the Constitution of India
C. Guaranteed by Fundamental Rights in the Constitution of India
D. Guaranteed by Supreme Court through its writ jurisdiction

19. Which of the following amendments, amended the Preamble to the Constitution of India 1950?
A. 42nd Amendment
B. 43rd Amendment
C. 44th Amendment
D. 24th Amendment

20. Which among the following writs literally means "what is your authority"?
A. Mandamus B. Quo Warranto
C. Certiorari D. Habeas Corpus

21. When was the first world Tsunami Awareness Day observed across the world?
A. 5 November, 2016
B. 1 January, 2017
C. 15 March, 2016
D. 13 April, 1017

22. Mr. Donald Trump is .... President of the United States.
A. 53rd B. 45th
C. 65th D. 39th

23. Who is the first Indian–American named as US Ambassador to the United Nations?
A. Seema Verma B. Preeti Bansal
C. Nikki Haley D. Preet Baharara

24. Where was worlds's first hydrogen– powered and zero–emission passenger train named Coradia ilint unveiled in November, 2016?
A. Germany B. France
C. Netherlands D. Japan

25. Who won Asian Women's Hockey Champions Trophy 2016 which was held in Singapore?

A. Spain B. India
C. Pakistan D. Australia

26. When was demonetization of ₹ 500 and ₹ 1,000 notes announced by Prime Minister of India?

A. 6 November, 2016
B. 7 November, 2016
C. 8 November, 2016
D. 9 November, 2016

27. Find out the incorrect match :

Group A	*Group B*
A. Tim Cook	Apple
B. Sundar Pichai	Google
C. Kunal Bahl and Rohit Bansal	Snapdeal
D. Brian Acton	Amazon

28. In February–March 2017, Vidhan Sabha elections were conducted in five states. Which were these states?

A. U.P., Uttarakhand, Tripura, Goa, Punjab
B. U.P., Uttarakhand, Manipur, Puducherry, Punjab
C. U.P., Uttarakhand, Manipur, Himachal Pradesh, Punjab
D. U.P., Uttarakhand, Manipur, Goa, Punjab

29. Who among the following was the Chief Guest at the 15th Pravasi Bharatiya Divas Convention held at Bengaluru on 8th January, 2017?

A. Antonio Costal
B. Kailash Purryag
C. Mahendra Pal Chaudhry
D. Dilma Rousseff

30. With which of the following, India is actively involved to sell its indigenously developed surface-to-air missile system?

A. Japan B. Mauritius
C. Vietnam D. Mongolia

31. Who won Malaysia Master Grand Prix Gold Title in January, 2017?

A. PV Sindhu
B. Pompawee Chochuwong
C. Saina Nehwal
D. Carolina Marin

32. YAHOO was proposed to be renamed as........

A. VERIZON B. ALTABA
C. ALIBABA D. MARISSA

33. How many teams will participate in FIFA World Cup in 2018?

A. 32 B. 36
C. 42 D. 48

34. Recently, the Prime Minister of India has announced that pregnant women in 650 districts will get........ directly in bank accounts to money medical expenses, etc.

A. ₹ 10,000 B. ₹ 7,000
C. ₹ 6,000 D. ₹ 5,000

35. According to World Bank, India's 2016-17 economic growth estimate was........

A. 6.8% B. 7%
C. 7.6% D. 8.2%

36. Recently, who amongst the following has taken over as the chairman of the United Nation Board of Auditors?

A. Vinod Rai
B. Raghuram Rajan
C. Anthony Lake
D. Shashi Kant Sharma

37. What was the most common password in 2016 throughout the world?

A. 123456 B. 654321
C. abcdefg D. abc123

38. Zaira Wasim, who was in limelight recently, is..........

A. A close associate of Malala Yousafzai
B. A renowned human rights activist
C. An actress in Hindi movie *Dangal*
D. A Brand Ambassador of Beti Bachao Beti Padhao programme

39. Who is the present Chairman of Tata Sons?

A. Ratan Tata
B. Cyrus Mistry
C. Rajesh Gopinath
D. Natarajan Chandrasekharan

40. The Ringling Bros. and Barnum & Bailey Circus has recently announced that it will end its circus show, which stared around 150 years back. To which country do they belong?

A. United Kingdom
B. United States
C. Netherlands
D. Denmark

41. The last man to walk on moon died in January, 2017. Who was he?

A. Neil Armstrong
B. Buzz Aldrin
C. Eugene Cernan
D. James Irwin

42. In World Economic Forum's Inclusive Development Index in 2017, India ranked .... among 79 developing economies.

A. 37th B. 60th
C. 5th D. 28th

43. Who was the Prime Minister of Britain when India got Independence?

A. Clement Atlee
B. Sir Winston Churchill
C. Sir Stafford Cripps
D. Lord Mountbatten

44. Find out the incorrect match:

Group A	*Group B*
A. Hezbollah	Lebanon
B. Al Shabab	Somalia
C. Boko Haram	Rwanda
D. Hamas	West Bank and Gaza Strip

45. A robot journalist named 'Xiao Nan' made its debut in a Chinese newspaper in January, 2017 with a 300 character long article. In how much time the article was written by it?

A. 1 second B. 5 seconds
C. 60 seconds D. 90 seconds

46. The outgoing US President Barack Obama commuted the 35 year prison sentence of a whistleblower army officer who lacked state secrets to Wiki Leaks in 2010. What is his/her name?

A. Anatoly Kucherena
B. Edward Snowden
C. Chelsea Manning
D. Maria Haley

47. Currently who holds the record for fastest 50, 100 and 150 runs in one day International cricket matches?

A. Lance Klusener
B. Chris Gayle
C. Virat Kohli
D. De Villiers

48. The Qinghai–Tibet railway in China is the highest railway in the world. Its highest point reaches an altitude of............

A. 5072 meters B. 4763 meters
C. 4087 meters D. 3965 meters

49. Which of the following states has recently declared a second capital?

A. Maharashtra
B. Jammu and Kashmir
C. Uttarakhand
D. Himachal Pradesh

50. When was the Union Budget presented this year?

A. February, 1 B. February, 28
C. March, 1 D. March, 15

Directions (Qs. 51-59): *Read the following passage carefully and choose the best answer to each question out of the four alternatives given.*

Legislation is the prime source of law and consists in the declaration of legal rules by a competent authority. A parliamentary legislature frames new law such as Act of Parliament, and arnends or repeals old laws. Legislature delegates law-making power bodies. Delegated legislation may open to challenge for irregularity of process; and the legislature usually has the right to withdraw delegated power if it sees fit. Most legislatures have their power restricted by the nation's constitution, and Montesquieu's there of the separation of power typically restricts a legislate power's legislation. Although the legislature has the power to legislate, it is the court which has the power to interpret statutes. Similarly although parliament has the power to legislate, it is usually the executive who decides on legislative programme. Judicial precedent is based on the doctrine of decisis and mostly associated with jurisdictions based on the English common law but the concept has been adopted in part by civil law system precedent in the accumulated principle of law derived from centuries of decision judgement passed by judges in important cases are recorded and has been a significant source of law. A judicial precedent is a judgement or decision a court of law cited as an authority for deciding a similar state of fact the same manner or as the same principle or by analogy. Equity is the case law developed by the court of chancery which is now defunct. Equity prevails over common law, but its application is discretionary. Equity's main judicature reforms in the 1870s effected a procedural fusion of the two bodies of law ending their institutional separation. The reforms did not affect any substantive fusion, however. Judicial or academic reasoning which assumes the contrary has been described as a "fusion fallacy". A custom as a law is not written, but is a rule whereby if a practice can be shown to have existed for a very long time, such as "since time immemorial", it becomes a source of law.

51. The doctrine of stare decisis is associated with............... .
A. Judicial precedent
B. Delegated Legislation
C. Customs
D. Legislation

52. Who has the supreme power to interpret statutes?
A. Parliament B. Court
C. Legislature D. Executive

53. Judicial precedent is associated mainly with jurisdictions based on........ .
A. Continental law
B. Canon law
C. English common law
D. Civil law

54. To which of the following courts, though now non-operational, does equity owe its origin?
A. Curia Regis B. House of Lords
C. Privy Council D. Court of Chancery

55. Who may delegate law-making powers to lower bodies?
A. Executive B. Judiciary
C. Convention D. Legislature

56. A judgement of a court of law cited as an authority is useful for decision later case which has......... .
A. A fundamental similarity in the area of dispute
B. A similar state of fact
C. The same parties before the court
D. Its origin in the same place

57. Which two areas of law were amalgamated in the later part of nineteenth century?
A. Equity and Custom
B. Common law and equity
C. Common law and civil law
D. Civil law and equity

58. A practice which has been followed for a very long period of time becomes a source of law as............ .
A. Legislation B. Equity
C. Precedent D. Custom

59. Probate is one of the contributions of ....
A. Equity B. Common law
C. Customary law D. Civil law

Directions (Qs. 60 and 61) : *Choose the most appropriate option to replace the expression in the brackets:*

60. Ramesh was a noble man who always feared law. He was arrested on (false and exaggerated) charges.
A. Law-abiding B. Trumped-up
C. Mistaken D. Free-and-clear

61. Risham never bothered about right and wrong in his life. He often teamed with others to do petty crimes. He was charged with (disobeying the orders of the judge) when he was late for court.
A. Disturbing the peace
B. Contempt of court
C. Contributory negligence
D. Vicarious liability

Directions (Qs. 62-65) : *Choose the most appropriate option to fill in the blanks:*

62. A lyre was played in ancient Rome. The lyre is a.........
A. Stringed instrument in the harp classes
B. Wind instrument in the wind class
C. Percussion instrument in the leap class
D. A combination of wind and percussion instruments

63. The president has a .... of .... around him where he makes public appearances.
A. Catalyst, individuals
B. Barrier, catalyst
C. Hedge, protection
D. Derrick, limits

64. .... the green room now?
A. Whos in B. Whose in
C. Who's in D. Whos' in

65. The rumours were .... and she welcomed the opportunity to .... them.
A. Appealing, demystify
B. Fabricated, demystify
C. Fabricated, refute
D. Pertinent, enjoy

Directions (Qs. 66 and 67) : *Choose the word that is most near in meaning to the given word.*

66. MUTABILITY
A. Calculable B. Movable
C. Tenacity D. Fragility

67. CREDULOUS
A. Movables B. Imaginable
C. Ardent D. Sceptical

Directions (Qs. 68-70) : *In each of the following questions, there is a certain relation between two given words on one side and choose the most suitable word/ words to be put on the other side from the given alternatives.*

68. COPYRIGHT : BOOK :: .... : ....
A. Tool : measurement
B. Addendum : chapter
C. Letter : alphabet
D. Deed : property

69. SENTENCE : WORDS :: .... : ....
A. Manuscript : editor
B. Paragraph : punctuation
C. Collage : paper strips
D. Novel : index

70. GLADE : .... :: CASTLE : MOAT
A. Greenish B. Woods
C. Royalty D. Water

71. Pick the odd one out:
A. Lake B. River
C. Pond D. Ocean

72. Pick the odd one out:
A. Lion B. Rabbit
C. Dolphin D. Shark

73. Bhubaneswar is to Odisha as Kohima is to....................
A. Meghalaya B. Nagaland
C. Assam D. Sikkim

74. Kennel is to dog as stable is to ....
A. Horse B. Bird
C. Pig D. Buffalo

75. Fill in the missing number:
5,11, ... , 47
A. 24 B. 25
C. 27 D. 23

76. If 7 : 21 :: x :123, then x is equal to which of the following?
A. 41 B. 49
C. 34 D. 35

77. If COURT = 50 and POLICE = 60, then LAWYER = ?
A. 50 B. 60
C. 70 D. 45

78. If AbzY : CdxW, then GhvU : ....?
A. IjtS B. RsPq
C. SrQp D. Hijk

Directions (Qs. 79-83) : *Study the following information to answer the questions given below:*

In a certain code 'negligence of child rights' is written as 'mi ki va se', 'education of child' is written as 'ki de va', 'abusive environment of child' is written as 'va li ki fo' and 'effective environment of child' as 'ki li re va'.

79. What is the code for 'child'?

A. va B. ki
C. re D. yu

80. What is the code for 'environment'?

A. li B. hi
C. ki D. re

81. What is the code for 'education'?

A. ki B. hi
C. va D. de

82. What does 'ki' stand for?

A. of B. negligence
C. environment D. child

83. Which of the following may represent 'effective child education'?

A. va li mi B. ki va li
C. mi ki li D. re va de

84. On a certain day, clouds were observed in the sky. It rained later in the day. Which of the following statements are correct?

A. If the sky is cloudy, it will rain.
B. If the sky is cloudy, it is likely to rain.
C. There is no connection between the two events.
D. Insufficient information

85. In a measure to reduce accidents because of drunken driving, the traffic department created a campaign to create awareness. Which of the following is a convincing argument in this context?

A. Drunken driving increases the likelihood of accident as alcohol affects physical and mental efficiency.
B. Drunken driving leads to death.
C. Drunken driving is uncivilized.
D. Drunken driving can damage your car.

86. Ram can do a work in 60 days and the same work Sohan can finish in 40 days. If both of them work together, then in how many days will the work be over?

A. 24 B. 32
C. 50 D. 100

87. Gita sold her watch to Sita for ₹ 800 at a loss of 20%. The same watch was sold to Gita by Shakti at 20% loss. What is the actual price of the watch?

A. ₹ 1000 B. ₹ 1250
C. ₹ 1500 D. ₹ 1700

88. A goods train is 800 meters long and it is running at a constant speed of 60 km/per hour. If it takes 120 seconds to pass a bridge, then calculate the length of the bridge.

A. 1450 m B. 1200 m
C. 1600 m D. 1800 m

89. A man bought 2 pens for ₹ 65. He sold one of them at a gain of 7% and other at a loss of 6%. On the whole, he neither gained nor suffered loss. The cost of the pens were respectively:

A. ₹ 35, ₹ 30 B. ₹ 32, ₹ 33
C. ₹ 33,₹ 32 D. ₹ 30, ₹ 35

90. The average age of 30 boys in a class is 15.2 years. If 15 more boys join the class, the average age of the class is reduced by half a year. The average age of new comers is:

A. 13.0 years B. 12.3 years
C. 13.7 years D. 14.0 years

91. **PRINCIPLE** : Whoever, by words, or by signs or otherwise brings or attracts to bring into hatred or contempt or excites disaffection towards the Government established by law in India shall be punished with imprisonment by the law of on sedition.

FACTS : X made the following two statements at a public gathering.

I. This is a government of scoundrels, bootleggers, fools. Throw them out this time by voting against them. They don't deserve to be in power.

II. Kill all these corrupts and rascals who are running this nation, whether they are leaders of the ruling party or the government servants. Come help me to clean this nation from these evils.

DECISION:

A. X is not guilty of sedition for having made the statements I and II as he was exercising his fundamental right of freedom of speech and expression.

B. X is guilty of sedition for having made the statements I and II.

C. X is guilty of sedition for making statement I only.

D. X is guilty of sedition for making statement II only.

92. PRINCIPLE: An agreement is enforceable at law if parties competent to contract enter into it with free consent, for consideration.

FACTS: An extraordinary intelligent and matured boy of 17 years enters into an agreement with a man to sell his new phone for a sum of ₹ 5,000. He accepts the money but later on changes his mind and refuses to deliver his phone. The man files a suit for a specific performance.

DECISION:

A. The man will get the phone as it was a valid agreement

B. The man will not succeed as the consideration was too low.

C. The man will not succeed as the boy did not enter the agreement with free consent.

D. The man will not succeed as the agreement was not valid.

93. PRINCIPLE: A master is liable for those acts of his servant which are committed in the course of employment.

FACTS: A travelling agency asked its driver to drop a customer at the Delhi University. After dropping the customer, when he was returning to the office of agency, he found his girlfriend on the way who was waiting for a bus to her residence which is one kilometre away from the office of agency. The driver offered her the lift. On the way, the car met with an accident and the girl got severely injured. She now claims compensation from the agency.

DECISION:

A. The girl will succeed as the driver was driving in the course of employment.

B. The girl will not succeed as the driver was not driving in the course of employment.

C. The girl will not succeed on the basis of strict liability of the agency.

D. The girl will not succeed as she took free lift from her boyfriend. She would rather be liable to pay the fare to the agency and be prosecuted.

94. PRINCIPLE: When any person with an intention to cause damage to the public or to any person, causes distribution of any property, he is said to have committed the offence of mischief.

FACTS: The workers of Ubzuki Mobiles went on strike for the payment of bonus to them. In order to force the management to pay the bonus to of the workers, Mr. X threw a stone with full force and damaged the premises of the company. Did X commit any offence?

DECISION:

A. X committed the offence of mischief.

B. As X was on strike with other workers to get their demands fulfilled he didn't commit any offence.

C. X was right as the management was not fulfilling their legitimate demands and this was the only way to make their voice heard.

D. X didn't commit any offence, as the labour laws of India allow the workers to get their legitimate demands fulfilled from the management. X is, therefore, immune from any legal action.

95. When was the Constitution of India adopted?

A. 26 November, 1948

B. 26 November, 1949

C. 26 January, 1950

D. 26 January, 1949

96. Which of the following articles of the Constitution of India, 1950 provides for the right to property?

A. Article 31 B. Article 43

C. Article 31 A D. Article 300 A

97. According to Article 1 clause (1) of the Constitution of India 1950, "India that is ....., shall be a Union of States".
A. Bharat
B. Hindustan
C. Republic of India
D. Democratic Republic of India

98. The President of India exercise his powers...........................
A. Through Vice-President
B. Either directly or through officers subordinate to him
C. Through Cabinet Minister
D. Through Prime Minister

99. How can Governor of a State be removed?
A. By President of India anytime.
B. By impeachment by that State Legislature.
C. By the Union Government at the request of the Chief Minister.
D. By Supreme Court on a writ petition filed against the Governor.

100. Which of the following Articles of the Constitution of India 1950, provides that the law declared by Supreme Court is binding on all courts?
A. Article 32 B. Article 141
C. Article 129 D. Article 372

ANSWERS

1	2	3	4	5	6	7	8	9	10
B	B	B	C	C	B	A	D	D	B
11	**12**	**13**	**14**	**15**	**16**	**17**	**18**	**19**	**20**
A	A	A	D	A	A	C	B	A	B
21	**22**	**23**	**24**	**25**	**26**	**27**	**28**	**29**	**30**
A	B	C	A	B	C	D	D	A	C
31	**32**	**33**	**34**	**35**	**36**	**37**	**38**	**39**	**40**
C	B	A	C	B	D	A	C	D	B
41	**42**	**43**	**44**	**45**	**46**	**47**	**48**	**49**	**50**
C	B	A	C	A	C	D	A	D	A
51	**52**	**53**	**54**	**55**	**56**	**57**	**58**	**59**	**60**
A	B	C	*	D	B	B	D	A	B
61	**62**	**63**	**64**	**65**	**66**	**67**	**68**	**69**	**70**
B	A	C	C	C	C	D	D	C	B
71	**72**	**73**	**74**	**75**	**76**	**77**	**78**	**79**	**80**
*	*	B	A	D	A	B	A	A	A
81	**82**	**83**	**84**	**85**	**86**	**87**	**88**	**89**	**90**
D	A	D	B	A	A	B	B	D	C
91	**92**	**93**	**94**	**95**	**96**	**97**	**98**	**99**	**100**
D	D	B	A	B	D	A	B	A	B

EXPLANATORY ANSWERS

1. Spurred by the Unnikrishnan judgement and a public demand to enforce the right to education, successive governments from 1993 worked towards bringing a constitutional amendment to make education a fundamental right. That led to the 86th amendment in December, 2002 which inserted the article 21A in the Constitution:

Right to education (21A) : "The State shall provide free and compulsory education to all children of the age of six to fourteen years in such manner as the State may, by law, determine."

2. Article 80 of the Constitution lays down the maximum strength of Rajya Sabha as 250, out of which 12 members are nominated by the President and 238 are representatives of the States and of the two Union Territories.

3. To make sure that Rajya Sabha doesn't amend the bill by adding some non-money matters (known as Financial Bill), the Lok Sabha Speaker certifies the bill as a money bill before sending it to the upper house, and the decision of the Speaker is binding on both the Houses.

4. Carbon footprint is the amount of carbon dioxide released into the atmosphere as a result of the activities of a particular individual, organization, or community.

6. The Leader of the Opposition is the politician who leads the official opposition in either House of the Parliament of India. The post received statutory recognition through the Salary and Allowances of Leaders of Opposition in Parliament Act, 1977 which defines the term "Leader of the Opposition" as that member of the Lok Sabha or the Rajya Sabha who, for the time being, is the Leader of that House of the Party in Opposition to the Government having the greatest numerical strength and recognised, as such, by the Chairman of the Rajya Sabha or the Speaker of the Lok Sabha. As in the given question Alphabet "L" and "O" are given in capital that could mean that the question is referring to recognized opposition leader and thus the answer would be C, *i.e.* Y.B. Chavan.

The second possibility is the opposition leader of 1st Lok Sabha was A.K. Gopalan, until then the post of opposition of leader was not recognized.

The third possibility could be option B, as in 4th Lok Sabha election the Indian National Congress (INC) satisfied the criteria of 10% of vote and thus Dr. Ram Suhag Singh is elected as the Opposition leader.

7. Parole refers to the temporary or permanent release of a prisoner before the expiry of a sentence, on the promise of good behaviour.

11. The Supreme Court of India's collegium system, which appoints judges to the nation's constitutional courts, has its genesis in, and continued basis resting on, three of its own judgements which are collectively known as the Three Judges Cases.

12. The Protection of Children from Sexual Offences Act, 2012, has been passed by the Lok Sabha on 22nd May, 2012. The act defines a child as any person below the age of 18 years and provides protection to all children under the age of 18 years from the offences of sexual assault, sexual harassment and pornography.

14. The joint sitting of the Parliament is called by the President and is presided over by the Speaker or, in his absence, by the Deputy Speaker of the Lok Sabha or in his absence, the Deputy-Chairman of the Rajya Sabha.

18. B – Though the answer could be A also, as the same language is present in both DPSPs and Preamble.

20. The word Quo-Warranto literally means "by what warrants?" or "what is your authority"? It is a writ issued with a view to restrain a person from holding a public office to which he is not entitled. The writ requires the concerned person to explain to the Court by what authority he holds the office. If a person has usurped a public office, the Court may direct him not to carry out any activities in the office or may announce the office to be vacant. Thus, High Court may issue a writ of quo-warranto if a person holds an office beyond his retirement age.

27. Brian Acton is the co-founder (with Jan Koum) of WhatsApp, a mobile messaging application which was acquired by Facebook Inc. in February 2014.

33. The final tournament will involve 32 national teams, which include 31 teams determined through qualifying competitions and the automatically qualified host team. A total of 64 matches will be played in 12 venues located in 11 cities. The final will take place on 15 July in Moscow at the Luzhniki Stadium.

54. D – Official answer key gives C, but the passage clearly states "Equity is the case law developed by the Court of Chancery which is now defunct."

60. Trumped up means an excuse or a false accusation.

61. The contempt of court is an offence of being disobedient to or disrespectful of a court of law and its officers.

62. Lyre is a stringed instrument like a small U-shaped harp with strings fixed to a crossbar, used especially in ancient Greece. Modern instruments of this type are found mainly in East Africa.

66. Mutability refers to liability or tendency to change, which is opposite to Tenacity.

67. Credulous refers to having or showing too great a readiness to believe things, which is opposite to being skeptical.

68. One's can prohibit others copying the book content by obtaining the authority through copyrighting the book. Likewise one can prohibit others from claiming ownership over their property by obtaining authority over it through deed.

69. The sentence is the collection of words, likewise the collage is the collection of paper stripes.

70. The Castle is surrounded by Moat likewise Glade is surrounded by Woods.

71. B – Official answer key gives D but we feel answer should be B because river is the only moving body of water, the remaining are not. If the intention was to differentiate between freshwater and saltwater bodies, there are many saltwater lakes too, so that would fail.

72. B or D – The answer would be B if the differentiator is herbivores vs carnivores, but the answer would be D if the differentiator is mammals vs non-mammals.

73. The relation is between states and their capitals.

74. The relation is between the animals and their shelters.

75. The series would be as follows:

$5 \times 2 + 1 = 11$

$11 \times 2 + 1 = 23$

$23 \times 2 + 1 = 47$

Thus, option D is correct.

76. The relation would be as follows:

$7 \times 3 = 21$

$41 \times 3 = 123$

78. The pattern is following first 2 increasing order alphabets and next 2 decreasing order alphabets.

For Qs. 79 to 83 :

(1) "Negligence of child right" is coded as " mi ki va se"

(2) "education of child" is coded as "ki de va"

(3) "abusive environment of child" is coded as "va li ki fo"

(4) "effective environment of child" is coded as "ki li re va"

The code "ki va" is common to all of the code with word "of child". education – "de"

By comparing (3) and (4) we can conclude that "environment" –> "li"

In 4th code what left is "Effective" –> "re"

79. A – The ambiguity in (ki va) = (of child) is saved purely by options in Q 83

84. Having cloudy day doesn't guarantee raining, hence the option B is correct.

86. Let the total amount of work to be done be 120 units (L.C.M. of 60 and 40).

Ram can finish the work in 60 days, so his per day work is 2 units.

Similarly, Sohan can finish the work in 40 days, so his per day work is 3 units.

Working together the work done per day by Sohan and Ram = 2 + 3 = 5 units

To complete 120 units of work they together take 120/5 = 24 days.

87. Let's consider that the cost price for Geeta be 'x'.

As given in the question,

$(80 \times x) / 100 = 800$

$x = 1000$

The cost price for Geeta would be the selling price for Shakti.

Let's consider that the actual price of watch be 'w'

$(80 \times w)/100 = 1000$

$w = 1250$

Thus, the actual cost of the watch is ₹ 1,250.

88. As given in the question,

Speed = 60 km/hr = 50/3 m/sec

Time = 120 sec

Distance = $L_1 + L_2 = 800 + x$

Using the formula, Speed = Distance/Time

$50/3 = (800 + x)/120$

$2000 = 800 + x$

Therefore, $x = 1200$

The length of the bridge is 1200 meters.

89. Let's consider, the price of both pens were 'x' and 'y'.

As given in the question,

$x + y = 65$ ... (1)

$x + y = (107 \times x)/100 + (94 \times y)/100$

$6500 = 107x + 94(65 - x)$

$6500 = 107x + 94 \times 65 - 94x$

$6500 = 6110 + 13x$

$390 = 13x$

$x = 30$

$y = 65 - 30 = 35$

Therefore, the cost of the two pens are ₹ 30 and ₹ 35.

Previous Paper (Solved)

LL.B. (Three Year Degree Course) Entrance Examination, 2016*

Directions (Q. 1 to 7): *Read the following passage carefully and choose the most appropriate answer to each question out of the four alternatives given.*

Thomas Edison was born in 1847 in Milan, Ohio. He was nicknamed "Al" at an early age. At the age of 11, Edison moved to Michigan where he spent the remainder of his childhood. Thomas Edison struggled at school, but learned to love reading and conducting experiments from his mother who taught him at home. At the age of 15, Edison became a "tramp telegrapher", sending and receiving messages via Morse code, an electronically-conveyed alphabet using different clicks for each letter. In 1870, Edison moved to New York City and improved the stock ticker. He soon formed his own company that manufactured the new stock tickers. He also began working on the telegraph, and invented a version that could send four messages at once. Edison then moved with his family to New Jersey where he started his famous laboratory. In 1877, Edison, with the help from "muckers", individuals from around the world looking to make fortunes in America, invented the phonograph. The phonograph was a machine that recorded and played back sounds. In 1878, Edison invented the light bulb as well as the power grid system, which could generate electricity and deliver it to homes through a network of wires. He subsequently started the Edison Electric Light Company in October of 1878. Edison continued to invent or improve products and make significant contributions to X-ray technology, storage batteries and motion pictures (movies). Edison was a prolific inventor, holding 1,093 USA patents in his name, as well as many patents in the United Kingdom, France, and Germany.

1. As per the above paragraph, which of the following was the first accomplishment of Thomas Edison?
   A. Inventing tin foil
   B. Inventing an improved stock ticker
   C. Inventing the light bulb
   D. Inventing an improved X-ray
2. A phonograph is most similar to:
   A. A record player
   B. A walkie-talkie
   C. A television
   D. A microphone
3. In which state did Thomas Edison not live?
   A. Michigan B. New York
   C. Ohio D. Massachusetts
4. Which of the following describes Morse Code most appropriately?
   A. A system of clicks that stand for current
   B. A system of clicks that stand for letters
   C. A system of clicks that stand for words
   D. A system of clicks that stands for signals
5. Who is a "mucker"?
   A. Someone from Thomas Edison's family
   B. Someone from another country
   C. Someone from another country hoping to make a fortune in America
   D. Someone from another country hoping to find a home in America
6. Which of the following is not included in Thomas Edison's inventions?
   A. The first phonograph
   B. The improved stock ticker
   C. A power system that could deliver electricity to homes
   D. The first storage battery
7. How many patents Edison registered worldwide?
   A. 1093
   B. More than 1093
   C. 957
   D. None of the above

*Conducted by University of Delhi (22-06-2016).

8. Select the word closely related to platitude:
A. Trite remark
B. Concerned feeling
C. Disdainful attitude
D. Protest

9. Select the word closely related to buttress:
A. Negate B. Buttering
C. Mock D. Strengthen

Directions (Q. Nos. 10 to 14): *Choose the most appropriate word(s) among the four given alternatives to fill in the gap(s).*

10. My mother asked me to demonstrate a ____ of common sense to make the right decision.
A. Modicum B. Fractious
C. Disdain D. Culpability

11. Although leprosy is not a highly contagious disease, those who have contracted it have always been pariahs and have been ______ by others.
A. Accepted B. Admonished
C. Sheltered D. Ostracized

12. The film's hero, a pearl diver, naively expects that the purchasers will compete amongst themselves to pay him the best price for his pearl, but instead they ______ to ______ him.
A. work...help
B. plan...incentivise
C. refuse...deceive
D. collude...swindle

13. After hours of acrimonious arguments the negotiations reached a(n) ______; neither side was willing to compromise.
A. Solution B. Resolution
C. End D. Impasse

14. Punishment for transgressions of the law ceases to have a deterrent effect if the punishment is frequently __________.
A. Changed B. Arbitrary
C. Lenient D. Commuted

Directions (Q. Nos. 15 to 19): *In the following questions four alternatives are given for the idiom/phrase* **bold and underlined** *in the sentence. Choose the alternative which most appropriately expresses the meaning of the idiom/phrase.*

15. Professor Giri said, "We will have to "**cover a lot of ground**" in this course." What did he mean by "cover a lot of ground"?
A. We have to skip a large part of syllabus
B. We have to complete a lot of material
C. We have to start from basics
D. We have to travel a lot

16. Ramesh said to me, You **"have the floor."** What does this mean?
A. You have practically won
B. You have full right to disagree
C. You have full permission to speak your mind now
D. You have tenancy rights over the property's floor

17. "To play second fiddle" means:
A. To support the role and view of another person
B. To act like a minor criminal
C. To deceive your superior
D. To play the second musical instrument

18. "Hanging fire" means:
A. Going to be sacrificed
B. Going on slowly
C. Being hotly debated
D. Going to be burnt soon

19. "Go out on a limb" means:
A. Being at two places at the same time
B. Put oneself in an isolated or disadvantageous position
C. Going somewhere without being noticed
D. Fracturing one's own limb

Directions (Q. Nos. 20 to 26): *Choose the most appropriate word that is nearly opposite in meaning to the given word.*

20. CORROBORATE :
A. Deny B. Differentiate
C. Affirm D. Create artificially

21. ARCHAIC :
A. Novel

B. Somber
C. Soft
D. Archeological finding

22. ARBITRARY :
A. Customary B. Mediate
C. Legitimate D. Desperate

23. AFFABLE :
A. Friendly B. Surely
C. Winsome D. Livid

24. ADULATE :
A. Moderate B. Admire
C. Lambaste D. Adulterate

25. RECANT :
A. Noisy B. Militarise
C. Reuse D. Assert

26. EXCORIATE :
A. Diminish B. Excommunicate
C. Abandon D. Acclaim

Directions (Q. Nos. 27 to 31): *In each of the following questions, there is a certain relation between two given words on one side of::*

Choose the suitable word/words to be put on the other side from the given alternatives.

27. Club : Golf :: ______ : ______
A. Candid : Disingenuous
B. Racket : Tennis
C. Author : Book
D. Ball : Soccer

28. Plaint : Rigid :: ______ : ______
A. Petulant : Adulterated
B. Moist : Wet
C. Excessive : Overgrown
D. Crass : Refined

29. Arguing : Litigation :: Courting : ______
A. Romance B. Judiciary
C. Adjudication D. Dispute

30. Plaintiff : Defendant :: ______ : ______
A. Court : Law B. Victim : Accused
C. Judge : Jury D. Husband : Wife

31. Tax : Exemption :: ______ : ______
A. Crime : Punishment
B. Disease : Immunity
C. Trial : Forfeit
D. Fine : Money

32. Select the word most closely related to buttress:
A. Obliterate B. Confuse
C. Overlook D. Support

33. Who won the T-20 Cricket World Cup for Women in 2016?
A. India B. Australia
C. West Indies D. England

34. On 23rd April 2016, _____ death anniversary of William Shakespeare was celebrated.
A. 200th B. 300th
C. 350th D. 400th

35. In which of the following States, President's Rule was imposed in 2016?
A. Assam B. Nagaland
C. Arunachal Pradesh D. Tripura

36. With which of the following, the recent Panama Papers Leak controversy primarily relates?
A. Money laundering and evasion of tax
B. Destabilize the political parties in several countries
C. To cheat on World Bank and IMF
D. To conduct terrorist attacks in many countries

37. When was Zika virus first isolated?
A. 1947 B. 1987
C. 1996 D. 2016

38. The term "Dirty Snowball" is related to _____
A. Comets
B. Meteorites
C. Space debris primarily from space crafts
D. Asteroids

39. Who is the author of "To Kill a Mockingbird"?
A. Chetan Bhagat B. Harper Lee
C. Paulo Coelho D. Agatha Christie

40. The 30th anniversary of which of the following disasters falls in 2016?
A. Chernobyl Nuclear Disaster
B. Bhopal Gas Disaster
C. Delhi Oleum Gas Disaster
D. Fukushima Nuclear Disaster

41. Where is the headquarters of European Union?
A. Paris B. Brussels
C. Rome D. Strasbourg

42. Which of the following is the incorrect match?

Group A	Group B
A. The Alchemist	Paulo Coelho
B. The Old Man and the Sea	Ernest Hemingway
C. Harry Potter and the Philosopher's Stone	J.K. Rowling
D. Our impossible Love	Jeff Kinney

43. Who was the First Speaker of Lok Sabha?
A. Sardar Hukum Singh
B. Bali Ram Bhagat
C. G.V. Mavalankar
D. Sir Shadi Lal

44. Which of the following pairs is incorrect?

A. Telephone	Graham Bell
B. Small Pox Vaccination	Eduard Jener
C. Diesel Engine	Carnot
D. Ball Point	John J. Loud

45. "*Sare Jahan Se Achchha Hindostan Hamara*" was written by ______.
A. Bankim Chandra Chatterjee
B. Ram Prasad Bismil
C. Rabindra Nath Tagore
D. Iqbal

46. "Sunny Days" is the autobiography of ______.
A. Sachin Tendulkar B. Sunil Gavaskar
C. Sunny Deol D. Shrikant

47. "Silicon Valley of India" refers to ______
A. Bengaluru B. Pune
C. Gurgaon D. Hyderabad

48. Who was the Chief Guest on the occasion of 67th Republic Day of India?
A. Barack Obama
B. Francois Hollande
C. Xi Jinping
D. David Cameron

49. Who among the following cricketers scored the fastest century in the Test matches?
A. Brendon McCullum B. AB de Villiers
C. Chris Gayle D. Virat Kohli

50. A referendum on whether United Kingdom should remain a member of the European Union or leave it, is to take place on ______.
A. July 28, 2016
B. September 30, 2017
C. October 15, 2018
D. June 23, 2016

51. Who is Raul Castro?
A. President of Columbia
B. President of Peru
C. President of Cuba
D. President of Panama

52. Who is the present Prime Minister of Nepal?
A. Khadga Prasad Sharma Oli
B. Girija Prasad Koirala
C. Sushil Koirala
D. Madhav Kumar Nepal

53. The total number of States in India is ______.
A. 29 B. 27
C. 25 D. 21

54. Who among the following won the Fields Medal in 2014 for his/her achievement in Mathematics?
A. Shakuntala Devi
B. Manjul Bhargava
C. Venkatraman Ramakrishnan
D. Raghuram Rajan

55. Who among the following is the co-founder of the popular social networking site, Twitter?
A. Charles Babbage
B. Jack Dorsey
C. Bill Gates
D. Mark Zuckerberg

56. Who has recently been appointed as the Chairman of Banks Board Bureau (BBB)?
A. Vinod Rai
B. J.B. Rao
C. Upendra Kumar Sinha
D. K. Narayanmurthy

57. The Indira Gandhi International Airport of New Delhi has been ranked at number ___ position in 25-40 Million Passengers Per Annum (MPPA) category in 2015 in ASQ Survey.

A. 1 B. 2
C. 3 D. 4

58. The branch of medicine concerned with the study of cancer is:

A. Oncology B. Cardiology
C. Pathology D. Ophiology

59. Acquired Immuno Deficiency Syndrome (AIDS) is caused by:

A. Protozoa B. Virus
C. Fungus D. Bacteria

60. The recommendations of Justice Lodha Committee primarily relates to ______.

A. BCCI
B. Reservation for the Jat people
C. Reform in the labour sector
D. Pathankot incident

61. Find the incorrect match:

	Group A	Group B
A.	Mukul Rohtagi	Attorney General of India
B.	Ravi Shankar Prasad	Law Minister of India
C.	H.L. Dattu	Chairperson, NHRC
D.	T.S. Thakur	Chief Justice of India

62. Who among the following former Secretary Generals of the United Nations died in February 2016?

A. Kofi Annan
B. U. Thant
C. Javier Perez de Cuellar
D. Boutros Boutros Ghali

63. Find the incorrect match:

	Group A	Group B
A.	Neither Roses Nor Thorns	H.R. Khanna
B.	My Life : Law and Other Things	M.C. Setalvad
C.	Roses in December : an Autobiography	M.C. Chagla
D.	Before Memory Fades : an Autobiography	V.R. Krishna Iyer

64. Who among the following was not the Chief Justice of India?

A. Justice P. Sathasivam
B. Justice Altamas Kabir
C. Justice S.H. Kapadia
D. Justice M. Jagannadha Rao

65. When did World Trade Organisation (WTO) come into force?

A. January 1994 B. January 1995
C. January 1996 D. January 1998

66. How many nations are currently members of the United Nations?

A. 191 B. 192
C. 193 D. 194

67. The Supreme Court of India comprises of the Chief Justice and ______ other Judges.

A. 24 B. 25
C. 29 D. 30

68. Who is the Chairperson of Law Commission of India?

A. Justice Cyriac Joseph
B. Justice B.S. Chauhan
C. Justice K.G. Balakrishnan
D. Justice S.H. Kapadia

69. Legal Principle : No person shall be prosecuted and punished for the same offence more than once.

Facts : Suresh harasses his colleague Nimita in the office. Nimita makes a complaint to her employer and also to the police station. Following the recommendations of the departmental committee, the employer terminates the services of Suresh. The police also arrested him and prosecution started. He defended that he cannot be punished twice. Which of the following options is correct?

A. He cannot be prosecuted.
B. He can be prosecuted because departmental proceedings are different from prosecution.
C. It is the sole discretion of the court to prosecute him or not to prosecute him as he has already paid a price by losing his job.
D. The court has to prosecute only if the departmental committee has recommended his prosecution.

70. Recently, Rahul Raj Singh, the boyfriend of TV actress Pratyusha Banerjee was arrested for _______.
A. Her murder
B. Her suicide
C. Abetting her suicide
D. Her culpable homicide

71. Which of the following countries recently blocked Indian efforts to list Jaish-e-Mohammed chief Masood Azhar as a terrorist at the UN sanction committee?
A. France
B. Germany
C. United Kingdom
D. China

72. Which of the following is not a subject matter of protection under the Copyright Act, 1957?
A. Computer Programme
B. Industrial designs
C. Work of architecture
D. Film script

73. Which of the following is protectable under the Patent law?
A. Discovery B. Idea
C. Invention D. All the above

74. Under which of the following statutes, the Tirupathi Laddu has been protected?
A. Copyright Act, 1957
B. Trade Marks Act, 1999
C. The Plant Varieties and Farmers Rights Act, 2001
D. The Protection of Geographical Indications of Goods Act, 1999

75. The Directive Principles of State Policy are normally given effect by _______.
A. Laws made by the Government
B. Judgements of the courts
C. Orders of executives
D. Doing nothing as effect has already been given by the Constitution itself

76. A writ by which the decision of the lower court is quashed by High Court or Supreme Court because it was based on irregular procedure is known as _______.
A. Mandamus B. Prohibition
C. Certiorari D. Quo Waranto

77. What is the meaning of Caveat Emptor?
A. Let the buyer beware
B. A legal action or trial
C. An offence in which arrest can be made without a warrant
D. The obligation of proving the case

78. The International Criminal Court does not have jurisdiction with respect to _______.
A. Crime of genocide
B. Crimes against humanity
C. Crime of terrorism
D. Crime of aggression

79. Where is the Seat of International Court of Justice?
A. Rome B. The Hague
C. Nuremberg D. Geneva

80. The international humanitarian law relating to civilian persons in the time of war was codified in a comprehensive manner in _______.
A. Geneva Convention
B. Hague Convention
C. Madrid Convention
D. Vienna Convention

81. Remarks of a judge, which are casual and are not directly relevant to the case at band are known as _______.
A. *Autrefois acquit*
B. *Ratio decidendi*
C. *Obiter dicta*
D. *Stare decisis*

82. Which of the following statements is incorrect?
A. Tort is a civil wrong.
B. Every civil wrong is not a tort.
C. In tort, normally liquidated damages are granted.
D. Law of tort is independent of criminal law.

83. Violation of a legal right without causing any harm, loss or damage to the plaintiff is known as _______.

A. *Injuria sine damno*
B. *Damnum sine injuria*
C. *Res ipsa loquitur*
D. Qui facit per aliumfacit *per se*

84. In which of the following cases, the rule of strict liability was initially laid down?
A. *Rylands* v. *Fletcher*
B. *M.C. Mehta* v. *Union of India*
C. *Ponting* v. *Noakes*
D. *Box* v. *Jubb*

85. In which of the following circumstances, there shall be no vicarious liability?
A. Liability of the principal for the tort of his agent.
B. Liability of partners for each other's tort.
C. Liability of the master for the tort of his servant.
D. Liability of the teacher for the tort of his student.

86. Which of the following is not a defence in case of torts?
A. *Volenti non fit injuria*
B. Act of God
C. Non-commercial motive
D. Statutory authority

87. Which of the following statements is incorret with respect to defamation?
A. Defamation is caused when a person causes injury to another person's reputation without any lawful justification.
B. Defamation is a crime, not a tort.
C. Defamation may be caused by Libel or Slander or both
D. Statements made under the defence of absolute privilege *e.g.*, in *Parliamentary proceedings* are not actionable.

88. The territorial waters may extend upto ____.
A. 12 nautical miles from the baseline of the coastal States
B. 24 nautical miles from the baseline of the coast. States
C. 50 nautical miles from the baseline of the coastal States
D. 200 nautical miles from the baseline of the coastal States

89. A person who obtains money from other person at gun point commits the offence of _____.
A. Theft B. Robbery
C. Cheating D. Extortion

90. Who is presently an Indian Judge in the International Court of Justice?
A. Justice R.M. Lodha
B. Justice H.L. Dattu
C. Justice Dalvir Bhandari
D. Justice Nagendra Singh

91. The Fourth Schedule of Constitution of India Deals with _______.
A. Allocation of Seats in the Council of States
B. Allocation of Seats in the House of People
C. Languages
D. Forms of Oath or Affirmation

92. Who was the first Law Minister of Independent India?
A. Maulana Abul Kalam Azad
B. K.N. Katju
C. B.R. Ambedkar
D. C. Rajagopalachari

93. Ordinance is promulgated by the:
A. Governor
B. President
C. Parliament
D. Both A and B

94. _______ may by law alter the name of any State.
A. Union Council of Ministers
B. Parliament
C. Lok Sabha
D. Rajya Sabha

95. Bharat Ratna, Padma Vibhushan, Padma Bhushan, and Padma Shri are _______.
A. Titles
B. Awards
C. To be added as suffixes or prefixes to the names of the recipients
D. Both A and C

96. Narco analysis test without consent is ______.
A. permitted in all cases
B. prohibited
C. within the discretion of the judge
D. within the discretion of investigating officer

97. The word 'secular' was added to the Preamble of the Constitution in the year ______.
A. 1978 B. 1976
C. 1975 D. 1979

98. Right to privacy is a ______.
A. Part of personal liberty
B. Right to be let alone
C. Fundamental right
D. All of the above

99. Uniform civil code is a ______.
A. Directive Principle
B. Fundamental Duty
C. Fundamental Right
D. None of the above

100. Respect for national flag is a ______.
A. Fundamental Right
B. Directive Principle
C. Fundamental Duty
D. Fundamental Duty only for government functionaries

101. Reservation for women representation is introduced in ______.
A. Panchayats
B. Parliament
C. Legislative assemblies
D. All of the above

102. Public health is an item in the ______.
A. State List B. Union List
C. Concurrent List D. None of the above

103. CAG is appointed by ______.
A. The Prime Minister of India
B. The President of India
C. The Parliament of India
D. Finance Minister

104. Writ of habeas corpus is a/an ______.
A. Constitutional remedy
B. Legislative remedy
C. Executive remedy
D. Quasi judicial remedy

105. Who presides over the joint session of Parliament?
A. Parliamentary Affairs Minister
B. The Prime Minister
C. The Speaker of Lok Sabha
D. The Vice President

106. Under the Constitution of India raising the level of nutrition of people has been provided as a ______.
A. Fundamental Duty
B. Directive Principle
C. Duty of Medical Council of India
D. None of the above

107. **Assertion (A):** A void contract is not necessarily illegal.
Reason (R): Every illegal contract is void.
A. Both (A) and (R) are individually true and (R) is the correct explanation of (A).
B. Both (A) and (R) are individually true but (R) is not the correct explanation of (A).
C. (A) is true but (R) is false
D. (A) is false but (R) is true

108. What is the duration of 'zero hour' in Lok Sabha?
A. Three hours B. Half-an-hour
C. One hour D. Unspecified

109. The rule of evidence which forbids a person from denying the truth of a statement made earlier by him is known as ______.
A. Estoppel
B. *Res judicata*
C. Mcnaughten rule
D. Contradiction

110. The nature of relationship a doctor shares with his patient is ______.
A. Moral B. Customary
C. Statutory D. Fiduciary

111. The First Official Language Commission, as required under Article 344 of the Constitution, was constituted by the President in:

A. 1950 with K.M. Munshi as its Chairman
B. 1955 with B.G. Kher as its Chairman
C. 1960 with M.C. Chhagla as its Chairman
D. 1965 with Humayun Kabir as its Chairman

112. Indian Evidence Act was drafted by:
A. TB Maculay
B. Huxley
C. James F. Stephen
D. Henry Summer Maine

113. A Dying Declaration is admissible ______.
A. Only in criminal proceedings
B. Only in civil proceedings
C. Both in civil and criminal proceedings
D. Only in quasi judicial proceedings

114. The Rule of absolute liability was first laid down in India in MC Mehta v. Union of India which pertained to the ______.
A. Bhopal Gas Tragedy case
B. Oleum Gas Leak case
C. Uphaar Cinema Tragedy case
D. Burning of school in Tamil Nadu

115. Which of these is not correctly matched?
A. Blasphemy : Speaking Against God
B. Libel : Written Defamation
C. Slander : Spoken Defamation
D. Tort : Liquidated Damages

116. **Assertion (A) :** The Indian Constitution was adopted on 26th November, 1949.
Reason (R) : Law Day is celebrated in India on 26th November every year.
A. Both (A) and (R) are individually true and (R) is the correct explanation of (A).
B. Both (A) and (R) are individually true but (R) is not the correct explanation of (A).
C. (A) is true, but (R) is false
D. (A) is false, but (R) is true

117. Who is known as father of international law?
A. Grotius B. Hobbes
C. Oppenheim D. Lauterpatch

118. The idea of Preamble to Constitution has been borrowed from?
A. USA B. Japan
C. UK D. Australia

119. Who can be appointed as a Director of a company?
A. Any juristic person
B. Only an individual
C. Any artificial person
D. All of the above

120. Which of the following is not an example of intellectual property?
A. Right on the contents of a book
B. Right on the logo of a company
C. Right on the manufacturing process of a drug
D. Right on the discovery of a plant species

121. An 'encumbrance' in legal parlance is a _____.
A. Charge on property
B. Gift of property
C. Right in rem
D. Right against perpetuity

122. Any two people, irrespective of their religion, caste and creed can solemnize a marriage, commonly known as civil marriage under:
A. Indian Christian Marriage Act
B. The Family Courts Act
C. Special Marriage Act
D. Hindu Marriage Act

123. Which one of the following Constitutional Amendments was based on the recommendations of the Swaran Singh Committee?
A. 24th amendment
B. 39th amendment
C. 42nd amendment
D. 44th amendment

124. Under the Indian constitution, certain payments like emoluments to the President and judges of the supreme Court do not require any parliament sanction as such, but are nevertheless shown separately in the budget. These are drawn from:
A. Grant-in-aid
B. Contingency Fund
C. Consolidated Fund of India
D. Public accounts

125. "Directive principle of state policy is the conscience of the Constitution which embody the social philosophy of the constitution" was said by:

A. Granville Austin

B. K.C. Wheare

C. A.V. Dicey

D. B.R. Ambedkar

126. Official languages of the United Nations include:

A. English, Chinese and Japanese

B. English, Russian and German

C. English, Persian and French

D. English, Russian and French

127. United Nations day is celebrated on:

A. 24 October B. 26 January

C. 25 August D. 25 December

128. Trafficking in human beings is ______ in the Constitution of India.

A. Prohibited

B. Permitted in certain circumstances only

C. Regulated

D. Permitted

129. Law of Torts deals with:

A. Defamation B. Trespass

C. Negligence D. All of the above

130. Section 66A of the Information Technology Act was struck down by the Supreme Court on the ground of violation of ______.

A. Personal liberty

B. Equality

C. Free speech and expression

D. All of the above

131. The book "The Indian Constitution and Social Revolution : Right to Property since Independence" was written by:

A. Soli Sorabjee B. Krishna Ananth

C. D.D. Basu D. None of the above

132. The first Law Commission of independent India was set up under the Chairmanship of:

A. T.V. Venkatarama Aiyar

B. P.B. Gajendragadkar

C. M.C. Setalvad

D. K.V.K. Sundaram

133. "*Amicus curiae*" refers to:

A. Friend to the court

B. Amicable settlement out of court

C. Case pending in a court

D. None of the above

134. Who is CEO of NITI Aayog in India?

A. Ashok Chawla

B. Amitabh Kant

C. Sudhir Mittal

D. Augustene Peter

135. The Members of the National Human Rights Commission are appointed by:

A. The President of India

B. Chairperson of National Human Rights Commission

C. The Chief Justice of India

D. The Prime Minister of India

136. Third Schedule to the Constitution of India deals with:

A. List of States and Union Territories

B. Languages

C. Panchayati Raj

D. Forms of Oaths or Affirmations

137. Protection from 'double jeopardy' means:

A. No person shall be prosecuted and compelled to be a witness in the same case simultaneously.

B. No person shall be sued for a civil wrong and prosecuted for an offence simultaneously.

C. No person shall be prosecuted and punished for the same offence more than once.

D. No person shall be prosecuted for two offences simultaneously.

138. Which of the following statutes has been enacted for the protection of wild animals, birds and plants?

A. Environment Protection Act

B. Forest Conservation Act

C. Wildlife Protection Act

D. Biological Diversity Act

139. Mahesh is an excellent swimmer, he finds Ramesh, child of 4 years of age drowning in the river Yamuna. He could have saved the child by jumping into the river. But he did not do so and Ramesh drowned and died. Mahesh is guilty of:

A. Murder

B. Culpable homicide not amounting to murder

C. Abetment to sucide

D. No offence

140. Mohit started from his office towards East. After covering a distance of 8 km he turned towards left and covered a distance of 6 km. What is the shortest distance now from his office?

A. 12 km B. 8 km

C. 10 km D. 6 km

141. All the faces of a cube are painted with red colour. Then it is cut into 125 small equal cubes. How many small cubes will be formed having no face coloured?

A. 27 B. 16

C. 36 D. 25

142. ||–; |–|, –||, ?

A. |–| B. –||

C. ||– D. – –|

143. If 'rule' is written as 15 18 9 2, then how would 'evidence' be written?

A. 312 21 32166 78

B. 2 19 6 12 2 11 26 2

C. 4 4 23 22 13 25

D. 3 45 65 23 22 100

144. If MONARCH is written as OQPCTEJ, what is represented by MKPIFQO?

A. EMPEROR B. KINGDOM

C. EMPIRE D. MONARCHY

145. Pick the odd one out:

A. Book B. Page

C. Tissue D. E-book

146. Pick the odd one out:

A. Judge

B. Advocate General

C. Attorney General

D. Solicitor General

147. Pick the odd one out:

A. Hovercraft B. Military Tank

C. Aircraft D. Submarine

148. Pradeep is shorter than Anu. Viraj is shorter than Pradeep. Sanam is the same height as Pradeep. Who is the tallest?

A. Anu B. Pradeep

C. Viraj D. Insufficient data

149. In the above question, later another boy Gambhir joins the group. Gambhir is 10.5 cm taller than Viraj. Now who is the tallest?

A. Insufficient data

B. Gambhir

C. Anu

D. Pradeep

150. Fill in the missing number:

17, 19, 23, 29, ... ?

A. 31 B. 35

C. 39 D. 37

151. Fill in the missing number:

1, 1, 2, 3, 5, 8, ..., 21

A. 21 B. 8

C. 11 D. 13

152. What number will come next?

$\frac{1}{2}, \frac{1}{4}, \frac{1}{8}, \ldots$

A. 1/16 B. 1/10

C. 1/12 D. 1

153. A man walked 20 km west, then 10 km North, and then 5 km West. Which one of the following statements is true regarding his current location?

A. It is to the North West of his original location.

B. It is 35 km to the North West of his original location.

C. It is 25 km to the West of his original location.

D. It is 10 km to the North of his original location.

Directions (Q. Nos. 154 to 156): Identify the choice that most appropriately completes the second set so that it expresses the same relationship as the first set.

154. Kettle is to tea as Battery is to ______.

A. Bulb B. Speed
C. Electricity D. Heat

155. Tyre is to car as _____ is to foot.

A. Shoe B. Toes
C. Ankles D. Heel

156. Pride is to lion as school is to ______ .

A. Fish B. Self-esteem
C. Students D. Dignity

Directions (Q. Nos. 157 to 159): *Identify the essential part of the item given, that is, from the given choices, select the part without which the given item cannot exist.*

157. Violin :

A. Strings B. Box
C. Teacher D. Music

158. Court :

A. Files B. Witness
C. Judge D. Gavel

159. Zoo :

A. Cages B. Visitors
C. Animals D. Guards

160. A village on the Indo-Nepalese border was found to have been infiltrated by Maoists and other radicals. While the central administration acknowledged the locals' support as the reason for the difficulty in sanitizing the region, it still sent out three teams to do a study before sending in a strike force: one was a fact-finding team of lawyers and sociologists, another a surveillance team and the third, a logistics team. The investigators found out that the locals were denied equality of law and justice, the surveillance and logistics teams found out that there were excellent and foolproof opportunities seasonwise to neutralize the Maoists.

Which of the following statements do you find logical?

A. Sending in a strike force at the earliest would solved the problem forever.

B. Ensuring equality of law and justice to the villagers was a long-term and inexpensive solution.

C. Educating the villagers against the dangers of supporting the radicals would be a better solution.

D. There is no need of any action, the problem would solve by itself.

161. A tourist was shopping in a foreign country. She wanted to buy silk scarfs. Using her guide book for the country's language she found that:

Silk worm is chee chan; scarf is jee; and earth worm is mik chan

How would she say 'silk scarf' to the shop keeper?

A. Mik jee B. Chee jee
C. Mik chan D. None of the above

Directions (Q. Nos. 162 to 163): *You must match definitions to situations. There is one definition and four possible choices to each question. Select the choice that provides the most appropriate example for the definition given in the question. Answer these questions based only on the given definitions.*

162. Violating an apartment lease. Definition: This occurs when the tenant does something that is prohibited by the legal document that he/she signed with the landlord. Which of the following is the most appropriate example of violating an apartment lease?

A. Tina has decided to move to another city, so she calls her landlord to tell him that she is not interested in renewing her lease when it expires next month.

B. Manu writes to his landlord with complaints about the apartment he has rented for a year.

C. Vinod signed a legally binding document that requires him to pay a monthly rent for his apartment and he has failed in this for the last three months.

D. Leroy feels that his landlord is not maintaining properly the apartment which he has rent. He consults his attorney about the possible courses of action.

163. A Guarantee is an assurance about the quality of a product that is given (1) is writing by the manufacturer, or (2) verbally by the person selling the product.

Which is the most apporpriate example of a Guarantee?

A. The salesman advises Kamala to be sure to buy a vacuum cleaner with a guarantee.

B. Som buys a used digital camera from his colleague who promises to refund Som's money if the camera does not perform as expected.

C. The auto reseller specializes in refurbishing and selling used cars.

D. Madhab purchases a refrigerator with the highest consumer ratings.

164. Find out the odd one from the given four states.

A. Karnataka B. Maharashtra
C. Kerala D. Haryana

165. If '1 A B + C C A = 2 9 5', then the value of B is:

A. 9 B. 6
C. 8 D. 4

166. How many times will you write the digit 2, if you write all the numbers from 201 to 300?

A. 99 B. 119
C. 131 D. 20

167. Some groups of letters are given; three of them are alike in some manner, while one is different. Find out the odd one out.

A. BQPR B. AOCQ
C. IWKY D. ESGU

168. In a certain code SQUARE is written as 21 19 23 3 20 7 and CIRCLE is written as 5 11 20 5 14 7. How is RECTANGLE written in the same code?

A. 20 5 3 20 1 14 9 14 7
B. 20 7 5 22 3 16 9 14 7
C. 20 7 3 22 1 16 7 14 7
D. 20 7 5 20 3 14 7 14 7

169. $3x + y = 19$, and $x + 3y = 1$. Find the value of $2x + 2y$.

A. 10 B. 20
C. 16 D. 18

170. Sharma family went out for a picnic and took three different types of sandwiches with them. Vegetable, grilled and cheese sandwiches were made in a ratio of 5 to 7 to 8. If a total of 120 sandwiches were made, how many grilled sandwiches were made?

A. 42 B. 168
C. 158 D. 48

171. A pot contains exactly 12 litres of milk. If milk is drained from the pot until it holds exactly 6 liters of milk less than the quantity drained away, how many liters of milk were drained away?

A. 3 B. 6
C. 9 D. None of the above

172. It has been demonstrated by many surveys that students who attend school where teacher/student ratio is low get the best quality education. As a result, when my children are ready to attend school, I'll make sure that they attend a school with a very small student population.

Which of the following identifies the greatest flaw in the reasoning above?

A. Students should themselves take advantage of the low teacher/student ratio by choosing small classes.

B. Basic intelligence should be considered the result of childhood environment, not school education.

C. In school of large student population, bullying of weaker students is the norm.

D. A very small student population does not by itself, ensure a low teacher/student ratio.

173. Ramesh has fifteen years of typing experience; therefore, if you are looking for an efficient typist to key in your data into the new system, you need look no further. The speaker assumes that:

A. Ramesh will fit well into the new office environment

B. Fifteen years of practice ensures typing efficiency

C. Ramesh is a fast and accurate typist

D. Ramesh's job profile is the best that the new employer could probably get

174. The rate of violent crime in the state of Antigua is up 40 per cent from last year. The fault lies entirely in the judicial system: Recently the judges' sentences have been so lenient that criminals can now do almost anything without fear of a long and assured prison term.

The argument above would be weakened if it were true that:

A. 35 per cent of the police in Antigua have been laid off in the last year due to budget cuts.

B. In a recent poll 70 per cent of the population in Antigua opposes capital punishment.

C. 90 per cent of the other states in the country have in fact lower crime rates than does this state.

D. White collar crime in Antigua has also increased by over 20 per cent in the last year.

175. Complete the narration below:

Some scholars have suggested that long-term prisoners, on release from jail, be given a reasonable state pension to reduce the likelihood of their resorting to crime. A section of populace instinctively rejects this suggestion as it feels that it would be like rewarding criminal activity. The supporters of the prisoners' pension scheme have criticized those who reject this possibility, by claiming that for the critics ______.

A. Welfare of individual is also important

B. Emotion is more important than justice

C. Post-sentence behaviour is not important

D. Punishment for criminals is more important than crime prevention

ANSWERS

1 B	2 A	3 D	4 B	5 C	6 D	7 B	8 A	9 D	10 A
11 D	12 D	13 D	14 D	15 B	16 C	17 A	18 B	19 B	20 A
21 A	22 C	23 B	24 C	25 D	26 D	27 B	28 D	29 A	30 B
31 B	32 D	33 C	34 D	35 C	36 A	37 A	38 A	39 B	40 A
41 B	42 D	43 C	44 C	45 D	46 B	47 A	48 B	49 A	50 D
51 C	52 A	53 A	54 B	55 B	56 A	57 A	58 A	59 B	60 A
61 B	62 D	63 D	64 D	65 B	66 C	67 D	68 B	69 B	70 C
71 D	72 B	73 C	74 D	75 A	76 C	77 A	78 C	79 B	80 A
81 C	82 C	83 A	84 A	85 D	86 C	87 B	88 A	89 B	90 C

91	92	93	94	95	96	97	98	99	100
A	C	D	B	B	B	B	D	A	C
101	**102**	**103**	**104**	**105**	**106**	**107**	**108**	**109**	**110**
A	A	B	A	C	B	B	D	A	D
111	**112**	**113**	**114**	**115**	**116**	**117**	**118**	**119**	**120**
B	C	C	B	D	B	A	A	B	D
121	**122**	**123**	**124**	**125**	**126**	**127**	**128**	**129**	**130**
A	C	C	C	A	D	A	A	D	C
131	**132**	**133**	**134**	**135**	**136**	**137**	**138**	**139**	**140**
B	C	A	B	A	D	C	C	D	C
141	**142**	**143**	**144**	**145**	**146**	**147**	**148**	**149**	**150**
A	C	B	B	D	A	A	A	A	D
151	**152**	**153**	**154**	**155**	**156**	**157**	**158**	**159**	**160**
D	A	A	C	A	A	A	C	C	B
161	**162**	**163**	**164**	**165**	**166**	**167**	**168**	**169**	**170**
B	C	B	D	C	B	A	B	A	A
171	**172**	**173**	**174**	**175**					
C	D	B	A	D					

EXPLANATORY ANSWERS

37. **Zika virus** is a member of the virus family *Flaviviridae*. It is spread by daytime-active *Aedes* mosquitoes, such as *A. aegypti* and *A. albopictus*. Its name comes from the Zika Forest of Uganda, where the virus was first isolated in 1947. Zika virus is related to the dengue, yellow fever, Japanese encephalitis, and West Nile viruses.

38. A **comet** is an icy small Solar System body that, when passing close to the Sun, warms and begins to evolve gasses, a process called outgassing.

A comet is an icy body that releases gas or dust. They are often compared to dirty snowballs. Comets contain dust, ice, carbon dioxide, ammonia, methane and more.

39. ***To Kill a Mockingbird*** is a novel by Harper Lee published in 1960. It was immediately successful, winning the Pulitzer Prize, and has become a classic of modern American literature. The plot and characters are loosely based on the author's observations of her family and neighbours, as well as on an event that occurred near her hometown in 1936, when she was 10 years old.

40. Ukraine is marking the 30th anniversary of the Chernobyl nuclear disaster, which permanently poisoned swathes of eastern Europe and highlighted the shortcomings of the secretive Soviet system.

In the early hours of April 26, 1986, a botched test at the nuclear plant in then - Soviet Ukraine triggered a meltdown that spewed deadly clouds of atomic material into the atmosphere, forcing tens of thousands of people from their homes.

41. The **European Union** (**EU**) is a politico-economic union of 28 member states that are located primarily in Europe. The headquarter of European Union is Brussels. EU policies aim to ensure the free movement of people, goods, services, and capital within the internal market, enact legislation in justice and home affairs, and maintain common policies on trade, agriculture, fisheries, and regional development.

43. The **First Lok Sabha** was constituted on 17 April 1952 after India's first general election. The 1st Lok Sabha lasted its full tenure of five years and was dissolved on 4 April 1957.

G.V. Mavalankar (27 November 1888 – 27 February 1956) popularly known as ***Dadasaheb*** was an independence activist, the President (from 1946 to 1947) of the Central Legislative Assembly, then Speaker of the Constituent Assembly of India, and later the first Speaker of the Lok Sabha, the lower house of the Parliament of India.

45. ***'Sare Jahan Se Achcha Hindostan Hamara'*** is an Urdu language patriotic song written by Muhammad Iqbal. Iqbal was a lecturer at the Government College, Lahore at that time, and was invited by a student Lala Har Dayal to preside over a function. Instead of delivering a speech, Iqbal sang *Saare Jahan Se Achcha*.

47. The **Silicon Valley of India** is a nickname of the Indian city of Bangalore. As Bangalore is on the Mysore Plateau, the area is also sometimes referred to as "Silicon Plateau". The name signifies Bangalore's status as a hub for information technology companies in India and is a comparative reference to the original Silicon Valley, the major hub for information technology companies in the United States and in the world.

50. The **United Kingdom European Union membership referendum**, also known as the **EU referendum** and the **Brexit referendum**, took place on 23 June 2016 in the United Kingdom and Gibraltar to gauge support for the country either remaining a member of, or leaving, the European Union (EU).

51. **Raul Castro** is a Cuban politician, who has been President of the Council of State of Cuba and the President of the Council of Ministers of Cuba since 2008. Castro previously exercised presidential powers in an acting capacity from 2006 to 2008. Castro is Commander in Chief of the Armed Forces, and has also been First Secretary of the Central Committee of the Communist Party of Cuba since 2011. Castro is the nation's highest ranking general.

55. **Twitter** is an online news and social networking service where users post and read short 140-character messages called "tweets". Registered users can post and read tweets, but those who are unregistered can only read them.

Twitter was created in March 2006 by Jack Dorsey, Noah Glass, Biz Stone, and Evan Williams and launched in July, whereby the service rapidly gained worldwide popularity.

56. **Banks Board Bureau** is an autonomous body of Union Government of India tasked to improve the governance of Public Sector Banks, recommend selection of chiefs of government owned banks and financial institutions and to help banks in developing strategies and capital raising plans. Vinod Rai has been appointed the chairman of the Bank Board Bureau.

58. The branch of medicinel is concerned with the study, diagnosis, and treatment of cancer and tumors.

59. Acquired Immuno Deficiency Syndrome (AIDS) is an advanced stage of infection with the human immunodeficiency virus (HIV). Following initial infection, a person may not notice any symptoms or may experience a brief period of influenza - like illness. Typically, this is followed by a prolonged period with no symptoms. As the infection progresses, it interferes more with the immune system, increasing the risk of common infections like tuberculosis, as well as other opportunistic infections, and tumors that rarely affect people who have working immune systems.

60. The Court had appointed the committee in January 2015 to look into the functioning of the Indian board and suggest changes to its constitution.

On January 4, 2016, RM Lodha, the former Chief Justice of India, unveiled the three-man committee's recommendations, which shook the hierarchy of BCCI and its member associations. Consequently, the BCCI and various state associations approached the Supreme Court raising objections to the recommendations.

The final order of the two-judge bench comprising TS Thakur, the Chief Justice of India, and Justice Ibrahim Kalifulla, signed off on most of the Lodha proposals, setting in motion a major revamp of the way cricket is run in India.

64. List of Chief Justice of India

S.No.	Name	Period of office	
1	H.J. Kania	26-Jan-50	6-Nov-1951
2	M. Patanjali Sastri	7-Nov-51	3-Jan-54
3	Mehr Chand Mahajan	4-Jan-54	22-Dec-54
4	Bijan Kumar Mukherjea	23-Dec-54	31-Jan-1956
5	Sudhi Ranjan Das	1-Feb-56	30-Sep-59
6	Bhuvaneshwar Prasad Sinha	1-Oct-59	31-Jan-64
7	Prahlad Balacharya Gajendragadkar	1-Feb-64	15-Mar-66
8	Amal Kumar Sarkar	16-Mar-66	29-Jun-66
9	Koka Subba Rao	30-Jun-66	11 April 1967
10	Kailas Nath Wanchoo	12-Apr-67	24-Feb-68
11	Mohammad Hidayatullah	25-Feb-68	16-Dec-70
12	Jayantilal Chhotalal Shah	17-Dec-70	21-Jan-71
13	Sarv Mittra Sikri	22-Jan-71	25-Apr-73
14	Ajit Nath Ray	26-Apr-73	27-Jan-77
15	Mirza Hameedullah Beg	28-Jan-77	21-Feb-78
16	Yeshwant Vishnu Chandrachud	22-Feb-78	11-Jul-85
17	Prafullachandra Natwarlal Bhagwati	12-Jul-85	20-Dec-86
18	Raghunandan Swarup Pathak	21-Dec-86	18 June 1989
19	Engalaguppe Seetharamiah Venkataramiah	19-Jun-89	17-Dec-89
20	Sabyasachi Mukharji	18-Dec-89	25-Sep-1990
21	Ranganath Misra	26-Sep-90	24-Nov-91
22	Kamal Narain Singh	25-Nov-91	12-Dec-91
23	Madhukar Hiralal Kania	13-Dec-91	17-Nov-92
24	Lalit Mohan Sharma	18-Nov-92	11-Feb-93
25	Manepalli Narayana Rao Venkatachaliah	12-Feb-93	24-Oct-94
26	Aziz Mushabber Ahmadi	25-Oct-94	24-Mar-97
27	Jagdish Sharan Verma	25-Mar-97	17-Jan-98
28	Madan Mohan Punchhi	18-Jan-98	9-Oct-98
29	Adarsh Sein Anand	10-Oct-98	11-Jan-01
30	Sam Piroj Bharucha	11-Jan-01	6-May-02
31	Bhupinder Nath Kirpal	6-May-02	8-Nov-02
32	Gopal Ballav Pattanaik	8-Nov-02	19-Dec-02
33	V.N. Khare	19-Dec-02	2-May-04
34	S. Rajendra Babu	2-May-04	1-Jun-04
35	Ramesh Chandra Lahoti	1-Jun-04	1-Nov-05
36	Yogesh Kumar Sabharwal	1-Nov-05	13-Jan-07
37	K.G. Balakrishnan	13-Jan-07	11-May-10
38	S.H. Kapadia	12-May-10	28-Sep-12
39	Altamas Kabir	29-Sep-12	18-Jul-13
40	P. Sathasivam	19-Jul-13	26-Apr-14
41	Rajendra Mal Lodha	27-Apr-14	27-Sep-14
42	H.L. Dattu	28-Sep-14	2-Dec-15
43	T.S. Thakur	3-Dec-15	3-Jan-17
44	J.S. Khehar	4-Jan-17	27-Aug-17

65. The **World Trade Organization** (**WTO**) is an intergovernmental organization which regulates international trade. The WTO officially commenced on 1 January 1995 under the Marrakesh Agreement, signed by 123 nations on 15 April 1994, replacing the General Agreement on Tariffs and Trade (GATT), which commenced in 1948.

66. The **United Nations** (**UN**) is an intergovernmental organization to promote international co-operation. A replacement for the ineffective League of Nations, the organization was established on 24 October 1945 after World War II in order to prevent another such conflict. At its founding, the UN had 51 member states; there are now 193. The headquarters of the United Nations is in New York City.

67. The **Supreme Court of India** is the highest judicial forum and final court of appeal under the Constitution of India, the highest constitutional court, with the power of constitutional review. It comprises the Chief Justice of India and 30 other judges. It has original, appellate and advisory jurisdictions.

On January 28, 1950, India's Supreme Court succeeded the Federal Court of India which was established by Government of India Act 1935 and the Privy Council, which was highest judicial body in the country during British Era. The organisation, independence, jurisdiction, powers and functions of the Supreme Court are provided in articles 124 to 147 in Part V of the Constitution of India.

68. Justice Balbir Singh Chauhan, a former judge of the Supreme Court was appointed Chairman of the 21st Law Commission on 10 March.

Law Commission of India is an executive body established by an order of the Government of India. Its major function is to work for legal reform. Its membership primarily comprises legal experts, who are entrusted a mandate by the Government. The Commission is established for a fixed tenure and works as an advisory body to the Ministry of Law and Justice.

72. Copyright is a form of intellectual property protection granted under Indian law to the creators of original works of authorship such as literary works (including computer programs, tables and compilations including computer databases which may be expressed in words, codes, schemes or in any other form, including a machine readable medium), dramatic, musical and artistic works, cinematographic films and sound recordings.

Copyright law protects expressions of ideas rather than the ideas themselves. Under section 13 of the Copyright Act 1957, copyright protection is conferred on literary works, dramatic works, musical works, artistic works, cinematograph films and sound recording. For example, books, computer programs are protected under the Act as literary works.

73. The Patents Act 1970, along with the Patents Rules 1972, came into force on 20th April 1972, replacing the Indian Patents and Designs Act 1911. Patents refer to enforceable exclusive rights granted to the inventor in exchange for his/her making their invention public. In India, an invention pertaining to a new product/process, involving an inventive step and capable of industrial application can be patented. Patents are a form of intellectual property. An inventor can also appoint an assignee who acts on his/her behalf and incurs both the rights and the liabilities.

75. Part IV, Articles 36-51 of the Indian constitution constitutes the Directive Principles of State Policy which contain the broad directives or guidelines to be followed by the State while establishing policies and laws. The legislative and executive powers of the state are to be exercised under the purview of the Directive Principles of the Indian Constitution.

Inspired by the Constitution of Ireland, the Directive Principles contain the very basic philosophy of the Constitution of India, and that is the overall development of the nation through guidelines related to social justice, economic welfare, foreign policy, and legal and administrative matters. The Directive Principles of State Policy are normally given effect by Laws made by the Government.

77. ***Caveat emptor*** is Latin for "Let the buyer beware. Generally, *caveat emptor* is the contract law principle that controls the sale of real property after the date of closing, but may also apply to sales of other goods.

78. The **International Criminal Court** is an intergovernmental organization and international tribunal that sits in The Hague in the Netherlands. The ICC has the jurisdiction to prosecute individuals for the international crimes of genocide, crimes against humanity, and war crimes.

79. See explanation of 78.

80. **International humanitarian law (IHL)** is the law that regulates the conduct of war. It is that branch of international law which seeks to limit the effects of armed conflict by protecting persons who are not participating in hostilities, and by restricting and regulating the means and methods of warfare available to combatants.

The **Geneva Conventions** comprise four treaties, and three additional protocols, that establish the standards of international law for the humanitarian treatment in war.

81. ***Obiter dicta*** is Latin for a word said "by the way", that is, a remark in a judgement that is "said in passing". It is a concept derived from English common law, whereby a judgement comprises only two elements: *ratio decidendi* and *obiter dicta.* For the purposes of judicial precedent, *ratio decidendi* is binding, whereas *obiter dicta* are persuasive only.

Obiter dicta are remarks or observations made by a judge that, although included in the body of the court's opinion, do not form a necessary part of the court's decision.

83. *Injuria sine damno* means violation of a legal right without causing any harm, loss or damage to the plaintiff. It is just reverse to the maxim damnum sine injuria.

In case of injuria sine damno the loss suffered by the plaintiff is not relevant for the purpose of a cause of action. It is relevant only for assessing the amount of damages. If the plaintiff has suffered no harm and yet the wrongful act is actionable, nominal damages may be awarded.

84. In India, absolute liability is a standard of tort liability which stipulates that where an enterprise is engaged in a hazardous or inherently dangerous activity and harm results to anyone on account of an accident in the operation of such hazardous or inherently dangerous activity resulting, for example, in escape of toxic gas the enterprise is strictly and absolutely liable to compensate all those who are affected by the accident and such liability is not subject to any of the exceptions which operate vis-à-vis the tortious principle of strict liability under the rule in *Rylands* v. *Fletcher*.

86. General Defences to Torts

1. The defence of Consent
2. When plaintiff is the wrongdoer
3. Inevitable Accident
4. Act of God
5. Act in relation to Private Defence
6. Necessity
7. Act in respect to Statutory Authority

88. Territorial waters or a **territorial sea** as defined by the 1982 United Nations Convention on the Law of the Sea, is a belt of coastal waters extending at most 12 nautical miles (22.2 km; 13.8 mi) from the baseline (usually the mean low-water mark) of a coastal state. The territorial sea is regarded as the sovereign territory of the state, although foreign ships (civilian) are allowed innocent passage through it, or transit passage for straits; this sovereignty also extends to the airspace over and seabed below. Adjustment of these boundaries is called, in international law, maritime delimitation.

91. Fourth Schedule contains provisions as to the allocation of seats in the Council of States.

93. Normally, parliament has powers to make laws and it alone can pass laws on Union list matters. However there may be some conditions when the parliament is not in session and it becomes necessary to make laws. In these cases our constitution under **Article 123** gives special legislative powers to President of India by promulgating ordinance under certain circumstances. Thus if both the houses of parliament is not in session and it becomes necessary to make laws then president can make laws within the powers provided by the Constitution of India.

The law making power in state is vested in the state assembly. But there may be situations when state assembly is not in session and it is necessary to make laws for the state. In these circumstances **Article 213** of the constitution provides that Governor of the state can promulgate ordinance.

96. Narco analysis test without consent is prohibited. The narco analysis test is conducted by mixing 3 grams of Sodium Pentothal or Sodium Amytal dissolved in 3000 ml of distilled water. Narco Test refers to the practice of administering barbiturates or certain other chemical substances, most often Pentothal Sodium, to lower a subject's inhibitions, in the hope that the subject will more freely share information and feelings. A person is able to lie by using his imagination. In the narco Analysis Test, the subject's inhibitions are lowered by interfering with his nervous system at the molecular level.

A few democratic countries, India most notably, still continue to use narco analysis. This has come under increasing criticism from the public and the media in that country. Narco analysis is not openly permitted for investigative purposes in most developed and/or democratic countries. In India, the narco analysis test is done by a team comprising of an anesthesiologist, a psychiatrist, a clinical/forensic psychologist, an audio-videographer, and supporting nursing staff. The forensic psychologist will prepare the report about the revelations, which will be accompanied by a compact disc of audio-video recordings. The strength of the revelations, if necessary, is further verified by subjecting the person to polygraph and brain mapping tests.

97. With the 42nd Amendment of the Constitution of India enacted in 1976, the Preamble to the Constitution asserted that India is a secular nation. However, neither India's constitution nor its laws define the relationship between religion and state.

98. Right to privacy was earlier recognized as "implicit" in the right to life and liberty – guaranteed by Article 21 of the constitution. However, implicit rights have been subject to judicial scrutiny time and again. As per current judicial pronouncements, the right to privacy is a fundamental right enforceable against state as held by the Supreme Court in *R. Rajagopal* v. *State of Tamil Nadu*. Further, the right to privacy could also be extended against private persons through the law of torts (torts are law dealing with 'civil wrongs').

99. **Uniform civil code** is the proposal to replace the personal laws based on the scriptures and customs of each major religious community in India with a common set governing every citizen. These laws are distinguished from public law and cover marriage, divorce, inheritance, adoption and maintenance. Article 44 of the Directive Principles in India sets its implementation as duty of the State.

100. Part IV-A was added by the 42nd Amendment Act, 1976. It encompasses Part IV, Article 51A enumerating Ten Fundamental Duties of the Citizens of India.

Under this Article, it shall be the duty of every citizen of India

(*i*) To abide by the Constitution and respect the National Flag and the National Anthem;

(*ii*) To cherish and follow the noble ideals which inspired our national struggle for freedom;

(*iii*) To protect the sovereignty, unity and integrity of India;

(*iv*) To defend the country and receive national services;

(*v*) To promote the spirit of common brotherhood amongst all the people of India;

(*vi*) To preserve the rich heritage of our composite culture;

(vii) To protect and improve the natural environment;

(*viii*) To develop the scientific temper and spirit of inquiry;

(*ix*) To safeguard public property;

(*x*) To strive towards excellence in all spheres of individual and collective activity.

(*xi*) To provide opportunities for education to his child or, as the case may be, ward between age of 6 and 14 years;

The 11th point was adopted by 86th Constitutional Amendment Act, 2002.

103. The CAG is appointed by the President of India by a warrant under his hand and seal. The CAG, before taking over his office, makes and subscribes before the President an oath or affirmation:

1. to bear true faith and allegiance to the Constituion of India;

2. to uphold the sovereignty and integrity of India;
3. to duly and faithfully and to the best of his ability, knowledge and judgement perform the duties of his office without fear or favour, affection or ill-will; and
4. to uphold the Constitution and the laws.

He holds office for a period of six years or upto the age of 65 years, whichever is earlier. He can resign any time from his office by addressing the resignation letter to the President. He can also be removed by the President on same grounds and in the same manner as a judge of the Supreme Court. In other words, he can be removed by the President on the basis of a resolution passed to that effect by both the Houses of Parliament with special majority, either on the ground of proved misbehaviour or incapacity.

104. Habeas Corpus: It is a Latin term which literally means 'to have the body of'. It is an order issued by the court to a person who has detained another person, to produce the body of the latter before it. The court then examines the cause and legality of detention. It would set the detained person free, if the detention is found to be illegal. Thus, this writ is a bulwark of individual liberty against arbitrary detention.

The writ of *habeas corpus* can be issued against both public authorities as well as private individuals. The writ, on the other hand, is not issued where the *(a)* detention is lawful, *(b)* the proceeding is for contempt of a legislature or a court, *(c)* detention is by a competent court, and *(d)* detention is outsite the jurisdiction of the court.

105. Joint sitting is an extraordinary machinery provided by the Constitution to resolve a deadlock between the two Houses over the passage of a bill. A deadlock is deemed to have taken place under any one of the following three situations after a bill has been passed by one House and transmitted to the other House:

1. if the bill is rejected by the other House;
2. if the Houses have finally disagreed as to the amendments to be made in the bill; or
3. if more than six months have elapsed from the date of the receipt of the bill by the other House without the bill being passed by it.

The Speaker of Lok Sabha presides over a joint sitting of the two Houses and the Deputy Speaker, in his absence. If the Deputy Speaker is also absent from a joint sitting, the Deputy Chairman of Rajya Sabha presides. If he is also absent, such other person as may be determined by the members present at the joint sitting, presides over the meeting. It is clear that the Chairman of Rajya Sabha does not preside over a joint sitting as he is not a member of either House of Parliament.

106. Article 47 says that the State shall regard the raising of the level of nutrition and the standard of living of its people and the improvement of public health as among its primary duties and, in particular, the State shall endeavour to bring about prohibition of the consumption except for medicinal purposes of intoxicating drinks and of drugs which are injurious to health. Most of the social development programmes such as National Health Mission, Mid Day Meal scheme, ICDS etc. which target the women, children, weaker sections of the society are inspired by Articles 45, 46 and 47.

108. Unlike the question hour, the zero hour is not mentioned in the Rules of Procedure. Thus it is an informal device available to the members of the Parliament to raise matters without any prior notice. The zero hour starts immediately after the question hour and lasts until the agenda for the day (*i.e.*, regular business of the House) is taken up. In other words, the time gap between the question hour and the agenda is known as zero hour. It is an Indian innovation in the field of parliamentary procedures and has been in existtence since 1962.

109. **Estoppel** is a collective name given to a group of legal doctrines in common law legal systems whereby a person is prevented from making assertions that are contradictory to his or her prior position on certain matters before the court - the person is said to be "estopped".

110. *Fiduciary* derives from the Latin word for "confidence" or "trust". The bond of trust between the patient and the physician is vital to the diagnostic and therapeutic process. It forms the basis for the physician-patient relationship. In order for the physician to make accurate diagnoses and provide optimal treatment recommendations, the patient must be able to communicate all relevant information about an illness or injury. Physicians are obliged to refrain from divulging confidential information. This duty is based on accepted codes of professional ethics, which recognize the special nature of physician-patient relationships.

111. **Official Languages Commission** is a commission which was constituted by the President of India in pursuance to the provisions stated in the Article-344 of the Indian Constitution. This commission was constituted on June 7, 1955 vide a notification of the Ministry of Home Affairs, Government of India. The First Official Language Commission, as required under Article-344 of the Constitution, was constituted by the President in 1955 with B.G. KHER as its Chairman.

112. The **Indian Evidence Act**, originally passed in India by the Imperial Legislative Council in 1872, during the British Raj, contains a set of rules and allied issues governing admissibility of evidence in the Indian courts of law.

The law is mainly based upon the firm work by Sir James F. Stephen, who could be called the founding father of this comprehensive piece of legislation.

113. In the law of evidence, the **dying declaration** is testimony that would normally be barred as hearsay but may in common law nonetheless be admitted as evidence in Criminal law trials because it constituted the last words of a dying person.

117. Hugo Grotius was a Dutch *wunderkind* of the 17th Century. He was a child prodigy who entered university at age 11, a member of an important diplomatic delegation from his native Holland to France at age 15, awarded a French doctor of laws at age 16, an Attorney General of The Netherlands at age 24. He is now remembered as the "father of international law." Adam Smith described him in 1762 as "the first... to give the world anything like a regular system of natural jurisprudence."

118. Sources of the Constitution at a Glance

	Sources	*Features Borrowed*
1.	Government of India Act of 1935	Federal Scheme, Office of governor, Judiciary, Public Service Commissions, Emergency provisions and administrative details.
2.	British Constitution	Parliamentary government, Rule of Law, legislative procedure, single citizenship, cabinet system, prerogative writs, parliamentary privileges and bicameralism.
3.	US Constitution	Fundamental rights, independence of judiciary, judicial review, impeachment of the president, removal of Supreme Court and high court judges and post of vice-president, Preamble.

4.	Irish Constitution	Directive Principles of State Policy, nomination of members to Rajya Sabha and method of election of president.
5.	Canadian Constitution	Federation with a strong Centre, vesting of residuary powers in the Centre, appointment of state governors by the Centre, and advisory jurisdiction of the Supreme Court.
6.	Australian Constitution	Concurrent List, freedom of trade, commerce and inter-course, and joint sitting of the two Houses of Parlimant.
7.	Weimar Constitution of Germany	Suspension of Fundamental Rights during Emergency.
8.	Soviet Constitution (USSR, now Russia)	Fundamental duties and the ideal of justice (social, economic and political) in the Preamble.
9.	French Constitution	Republic and the ideals of liberty, equality and fraternity in the Preamble.
10.	South African Constitution	Procedure for amendment of the Constitution and election of members of Rajya Sabha.
11.	Japanese Constitution	Procedure established by Law.

121. An **encumbrance** is a right to, interest in, or legal liability on real property that does not prohibit passing title to the property but that diminishes its value. Encumbrances can be classified in several ways. They may be financial or non-financial.

122. The **Special Marriage Act, 1954** is an Act of the Parliament of India enacted to provide a special form of marriage for the people of India and all Indian nationals in foreign countries, irrespective of the religion or faith followed by either party. The Act originated from a piece of legislation proposed during the late 19th century.

124. **Consolidated Fund of India** is the chief account of the Government of India. The inflow to this fund is by way of taxes like Income Tax, Central Excise, Customs and also non-tax revenues which arise to the government in connection with the conduct of its business. Loans raised by issue of treasury bills are also received in this fund. The government meets all its expenditure including loan repayments from this fund. No amount can be withdrawn from the fund without the **authorisation from the Parliament.** This fund is formed under the provision of Article-266 (1) of the Indian Constitution.

126. The current official and working languages of the United Nations are:

- Arabic
- Chinese
- English
- French
- Russian
- Spanish

127. UN Day marks the anniversary of the entry into force in 1945 of the UN Charter. With the ratification of this founding document by the majority of its signatories, including the five permanent members of the Security Council, the United Nations officially came into being. 24 October has been celebrated as United Nations Day since 1948. In 1971, the United Nations General Assembly recommended that the day be observed by Member States as a public holiday.

128. Articles 23 & 24 of Indian Constitution deal with the Right against Exploitation. Article

23 prohibits the traffic in human beings and forced labor such as begar.

The Human Trafficking is the illegal trade in human beings for the purposes of commercial sexual exploitation, prostitution or forced labor. It is the modern form of slavery.

132. The first Law Commission of independent India was established in 1955 for a three year term. The Chairman of this Commission was Mr. M.C. Setalvad, who was also the First Attorney General of India.

133. *Amicus curiae* is a legal Latin phrase, literally translated as "friend of the court", that refers to someone, not a party to a case, who volunteers to offer information on a point of law or some other aspect of the case to assist the court in deciding a matter before it. The information may be a legal opinion in the form of a brief, testimony that has not been solicited by any of the parties, or a learned treatise on a matter that bears on the case. The decision whether to admit the information lies with the discretion of the court.

135. The National Human Rights Commission (NHRC) is an autonomous statutory body established in 1993 according to the provisions of the Protection of Human Rights Act. The Commission is composed of a chairperson and six members. The chairperson has to have been a chief justice of the Supreme Court. The Member of the National Human Rights Commission are appointed by the President of India.

The purpose of the NHRC is, suo moto or through the petition of a person, to investigate the violation of human rights or the failures of the state or other to prevent a human rights violation.

138. The **Wildlife Protection Act, 1972** is an Act of the Parliament of India enacted for protection of plants and animal species. Before 1972, India only had five designated national parks. Among other reforms, the Act established schedules of protected plant and animal species; hunting or harvesting these species was largely outlawed.

148. Anu

|

Pradeep, Sonam

|

Viraj

Hence, Anu is the tallest.

149. Insufficient data

150. 17 → 19 → 23 → 29 → [37]

+ 2, + 4, + 6, + 8

Hence, the missing number is 37.

151. 1, 1, 2, 3, 5, 8, [13], 21

1 + 1 = 2

1 + 2 = 3

2 + 3 = 5

3 + 5 = 8

5 + 8 = 13

8 + 13 = 21

Hence, missing number is 13.

152. $\frac{1}{2}$ → $\frac{1}{4}$ → $\frac{1}{8}$ → [$\frac{1}{16}$]

$\times\frac{1}{2}$, $\times\frac{1}{2}$, $\times\frac{1}{2}$

Hence, next number will come $\frac{1}{16}$.

153. 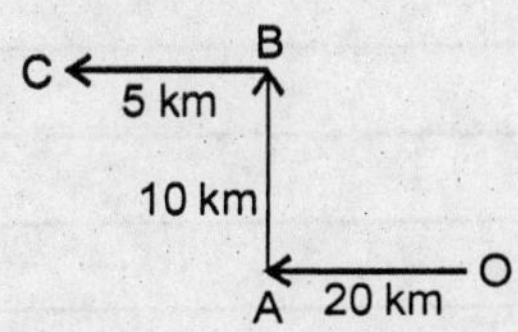

Hence, option (A) is correct.

It is to the North West of his original location.

154. Kettle is to tea as Battery is to electricity.

155. Tyre is to car as shoe is to foot.

156. Pride is to lion as school is to dignity.

YOUR SPACE

Previous Paper (Solved)

LL.B. Entrance Examination, 2015*

1. The youngest recipient of the Bharat Ratna is:
   A. Sachin Tendulkar
   B. Acharya Vinoba Bhave
   C. BR Ambedkar
   D. JRD Tata
2. Typhoon Haiyan devastated parts of which Island not on recently?
   A. The Phillipines
   B. Japan
   C. Indonesia
   D. Srilanka
3. Which was the first country to abolish capital punishment?
   A. United States of America
   B. Australia
   C. Netherlands
   D. Venezuela
4. The latest and the 29th state of India is:
   A. Vijayawada B. Telengana
   C. Seemandhra D. Warrangal
5. What is the pH value of human blood?
   A. 7.40 B. 8.40
   C. 9.40 D. 6.40
6. Planning Commission has been scrapped and replaced by a new think tank called:
   A. National Institution for Transforming India Ayog
   B. National Rural Development Commission
   C. National Commission for Progress and Development
   D. National Research and Development Commission
7. In the epic Ramayana, which bird tried to present Ravana from carrying Sita away?
   A. Kak Bhashundi B. Jayant
   C. Jatayu D. Garuda
8. Match the following Ragas with the time they are played:
   (a) Raga Deepak 1. Rainy-Season
   (b) Raga Malkauns 2. Evening
   (c) Raga Bhairavi 3. Morning
   (d) Raga Megha 4. Midnight
   A. (a)-1, (b)-2, (c)-3, (d)-4
   B. (a)-4, (b)-3, (c)-2, (d)-1
   C. (a)-4, (b)-2, (c)-3, (d)-1
   D. (a)-2, (b)-4, (c)-3, (d)-1
9. Who was the first English Writer to win the Nobel Prize in Literature?
   A. Rudyard Kipling
   B. Rabindranath Tagore
   C. Orhan Pamuk
   D. Sir Winston Churchil
10. What is the NASDAQ?
    1. World's first electronic stock market
    2. World's largest shipping fleet
    3. World's highest postal office
    4. Another name for New York Stock Exchange
    A. 1 and 4 are correct B. Only 1 is correct
    C. Only 4 is correct D. All are incorrect
11. One rupee note in India was issued by:
    A. Reserve Bank of India
    B. Union Government of India
    C. Governor of Reserve Bank of India
    D. Central Bank of India
12. As per United Nations Report, which 2 countries will lead global urban population growth between 2010 and 2050?
    A. Nigeria and USA
    B. India and China
    C. Ukraine and Brazil
    D. Pakistan and Bangladesh

* *Conducted by University of Delhi (07-06-2015)*

13. Who wrote "Crusader or Conspirator - Coalgate and other Truths"?
A. Vijay Seshadri B. P.C. Parakh
C. Sanjaya Baru D. R.K. Yadav

14. Which of the following works has not been authored by Nobel Laureate Gabriel Garcia Marquez, who died recently?
A. One Hundred Years of Solitude
B. The Autumn of the Patriarch
C. Love in the time of Cholera
D. Life is What You Make It

15. Identify the correct person:
1. His epitaph reads, "Good friend, for Jesus sake forbeare, To digg the dust encloased here ...."
2. He died in Strafford-Upon-Avon, UK
3. He was a literary genius and World famous Playwright
4. He died in 1616

Who is he?
A. William Shakespeare
B. Christopher Caudwell
C. Samuel Coleridge
D. William Wordsworth

16. Which one of the followings is not a World Heritages to?
A. Red Fort B. Safdarjung Tomb
C. Qutub Minar D. Humayun's Tomb

17. World's highest post office is located in:
A. Hikkim in Himachal Pradesh
B. Sikkim
C. Tawang in Arunachal Pradesh
D. Musoorie in Uttarakhand

18. Shashi Tharoor's book 'The Great Indian Nobel' uses a plot of which epic/literary creation:
A. Ramayana B. Mahabharata
C. Meghdootam D. Katha Sarita Sagara

19. Who is the present Secretary General of the United Nations?
A. Boutros Boutros Ghali
B. Kofi Annan
C. Ban Ki Moon
D. Javier Perez de Cuellar

20. Which of the following is a land-locked country?
A. Nepal B. Bangladesh
C. South Africa D. Pakistan

21. Which of the following has child welfare as its primary goal?
A. UNESCO B. UNCTAD
C. UNICEF D. UNCITRAL

22. Which Hindi writer is known as Agyeya?
A. Sachchidananda Hirananda Vatsyayana
B. Phanishwar Nath Renu
C. Nagarjun
D. None of the above

23. Who wrote the book 'Asian Drama'?
A. Graham Green
B. Garbriel Garcia Marquez
C. Gunnar Myrdal
D. Milan Kundera

24. The countries which have concluded Teesta Water sharing Agreement are:
A. China and India
B. Bhutan and India
C. India and Nepal
D. Bangladesh and India

25. Entomology is the science that studies:
A. Behavior of human beings
B. Insects
C. The origin and history of technical and scientific terms
D. The formation of rocks

26. How many squares are in a chess board?
A. Thirty six B. Sixty four
C. Twenty four D. Forty eight

27. The Southern-most point of Indian territory is:
A. Kanyakumari B. Trivandrum
C. Indira point D. Chennai

28. The book "Crime and Punishment" is written by:
A. Fyodor M. Dostoyevsky
B. John K. Galbraith
C. Oliver Goldsmith
D. Lewis Carroll

29. The first Dada Saheb Phalke Award was won by:

A. Devika Rani
B. Ashok Kumar
C. Leela Chitnis
D. Dara Singh

30. Mauritius a country in Indian Ocean is located in the continent of:

A. Asia B. Africa
C. Europe D. Australia

Directions (Q. 31 to 40): *Read the passage given below and answer the following questions:*

Once upon a time, there was a royal elephant which used to reside in the premises of the king's palace. The elephant was very dear to the king so he was well-fed and well treated. There was also a dog who lived near the elephant's shed. He was very weak and skinny. He was always fascinated by the smell of rich sweet rice being fed to the royal elephant. One day, the dog could no longer resist the aroma of the rice and somehow managed to sneak into the elephant's shed. He ate the grains of sweet rice that fell from the elephant's mouth. He liked the rice so much, that he started going there daily to eat the rice. For days, the huge elephant didn't notice the small dog as he was busy enjoying the delicious food. Gradually, the dog grew bigger and stronger eating such rich food. Finally the elephant noticed him and allowed him access to the food. The elephant enjoyed the company of the dog and started sharing his food with him. They also started spending time with each other and soon became good friends. They ate together, slept together and played together. While playing, the elephant would hold the dog in his trunk and swing him back and forth. Soon neither of them was happy without the other. They became great friends and didn't want to be separated from each other.

Then one day, a man saw the dog and asked the elephant-keeper, "I want to buy this dog. What price do you want for it?" The elephant keeper didn't own the dog but sold it and extracted a sum of money from this deal. The man took the dog to his home village, which was quite for away. The King's elephant became very sad after this incident. He missed his friend a lot and started neglecting everything. He didn't want to do anything without his dear friend, so, he stopped eating, drinking and even bathing. Finally, the elephant-keeper reported this to the King; however he didn't mention anything about the dog. The King had a wise minister, who was known for his keen understanding of animals. The King ordered the minister, "Go to the elephant shed and find out the reason for the elephant's condition". The intelligent minister went to the elephant shed and found the elephant very sad. He examined the elephant and asked the elephant keeper, "There is nothing wrong with this elephant's body, then why does he look so sad? I think this elephant is grief-stricken, possibly due to the loss of a dear friend.

Do you know if this elephant shared a close friendship with anyone? The elephant-keeper said, "There was a dog who used to eat, sleep and play with the elephant. He was taken by a stranger three days ago". The minister went back to the King and said. Your majesty, in my opinion, the royal elephant is not sick, but he is lonesome without his dear friend, the dog". The King said, "You're right, friendship is one of the most wonderful things of life. Do you know where that dog is?" The Minister replied, "elephant keeper has informed me that a stranger took him away and he doesn't know his whereabouts". They King asked, "How can we bring back my elephant's friend and make him happy again?" The Minister suggested, "Your Majesty, make a declaration that whoever has the dog that used to live at the royal elephant's shed will be penalized". The King did the same and the man who had taken the dog, instantly turned him loose when he heard the proclamation. As soon as he was freed, the dog ran back as fast as he could to the elephant's shed. The elephant was so delighted to see the dog that he picked his friend up with his trunk and swung him back and forth. The dog wagged his tail while the elephant's eyes sparkled with happiness. The King was content to see the elephant happy once again and rewarded the Minister for his wise judgment.

31. What was the Minister's diagnosis of the elephant's condition?
A. The elephant hated his keeper
B. The elephant was lonely
C. The elephant was starving
D. The elephant had hurt his leg and was in pain

32. What method did the Minister suggest to the King to get back the dog?
A. To declare that whoever had that particular dog would be punished
B. To keep a bowl of rice for the dog in the elephants shed so that he could be lured back to the palace
C. To command the elephant keeper to look for the dog in the Village
D. To persuade the elephant to call out to the dog

33. Why had the elephant become very sad?
A. He no longer got his daily bowl of rice
B. He was unhappy with the King for having sold the dog
C. He missed his friend the dog
D. He was sold to an unknown man by his keeper

34. What did the elephant-keeper do to the dog?
A. He sold the dog to an unknown man for a price
B. He hit the dog as the dog was eating the elephant's food
C. He killed the dog
D. He complained to the King about the dog

35. Which of the following would be the most appropriate title for the passage?
A. Friends and Enemies
B. The King and the Minister
C. The elephant-keeper
D. The Bond of Friendship

36. Why was the elephant taken care of?
A. He was a very loyal elephant
B. He was the strongest elephant in the Kingdom
C. He was weak and the King had a lot of sympathy for him
D. None of these

37. Why did the dog start going to the elephant's shed every day?
A. He liked the elephant a lot and wanted to become friends with him
B. He was being fed by the King everyday
C. He was fond of the elephant's shed
D. He liked the taste of the rice being fed to the elephant

38. What did the dog do once he was set free?
A. He ate rice to his heart's content
B. He thanked the King for his kindness
C. He ran away from the Kingdom to a place faraway
D. He ran back to his friend the elephant

39. What of the following can definitely be said about the elephant keeper?
1. He was greedy
2. He was insensitive
3. He was brave
A. Only 1
B. Only 2
C. Only 1 and 2
D. Only 2 and 3

40. Seeing the elephant happy the King rewarded the:
A. Minister B. Dog
C. Elephant-keeper D. Owner of Dog

Directions (Q. 41 to 45): *Fill in the blanks.*

41. A wife on legal separation from her husband may be entitled to ....
A. debt B. alimony
C. compensation D. damages

42. The body part between the neck and the abdomen is called ....
A. thorax B. cardiac
C. viscera D. stomach

43. You currently have all the newest software programmes. The reason your computer is running so slow is that you have old .... You may have to buy more physical memory, perhaps, a bigger hard drive if you want your computer to run faster.
A. warehouses B. software
C. wires D. hardware

44. The new teacher loves poems and makes us ....

A. heartily learn them
B. learn them heartily
C. learn them by heart
D. learning by heart them

45. The guerillas attacked the village. Nobody was left alive. They .... all the inhabitants.

A. disposed B. shielded
C. perturbed D. slaughtered

Directions (Q. 46 to 49): *There is a certain relation between given words. From the given alternatives choose a pair depicting similar relationship.*

46. Whale : Mammal as

A. Oak : Tree B. Coat : Tie
C. Flower : Leaf D. Ant : Hill

47. Bee : Hive as

A. Dog : Show B. Rider : Bicycle
C. Cow : Barn D. Horse : Carriage

48. Ornithologist : Birds as

A. Botanist : Animals
B. Archaeologist : Fishes
C. Zoologist : Animals
D. Anthropologist : Insects

49. Habits : Instincts as

A. Work : Play
B. Training : Heredity
C. Acquired : Cultivated
D. Birds : Animals

50. Give the meaning of *quid pro quo*

A. quit the job
B. favourable opinion
C. revenge
D. something in return

51. POLYGLOT—is someone who

A. has more than one spouse
B. drinks too much
C. plays more than one sport
D. speaks many languages

52. Only one of these words cannot be changed to another by changing – 'ful to – less', e.g., hopeful to – hopeless. Which one is it?

A. eventful B. fearful
C. woeful D. stressful

Directions (Q. 53 to 55): *There is a certain relation between two given words on one side of sign :: . One word is given on the other side of sign :: . Choose the suitable word to be put with the given word from the following alternatives.*

53. Arguing : Litigation :: Courting : ......

A. Judiciary
B. Adjudication
C. Romance
D. Arbitration

54. Aircraft : Air :: Satellite : ......

A. Telecommunication
B. Television
C. Cables
D. Outerspace

55. White : Peace :: Red : ......

A. Cleanliness B. Martyr
C. Roses D. Violence

56. Which of the following words cannot be formed from the letters of the word "STRANGE"

A. Ranges B. Gangster
C. Angels D. Grants

57. Find out the word that cannot be formed from the letters of "METAMORPHOSIS".

A. Tomato B. Rotation
C. Oasis D. Sister

58. What is the opposite of "Worthy"?

A. ugly B. undeserving
C. valuable D. dishonourable

59. What is the opposite of "Hapless"?

A. kind B. significant
C. lucky D. distinct

60. What is the opposite of "Audacity"?

A. cowardice B. patricide
C. bravado D. admonition

61. Ram purchased a mobile phone and sold it to Shyam at 10% profit. Then Shyam sold it back to Ram at a loss of 10%. What is the outcome in the hands of Ram?

A. 2% profit B. 1% profit
C. 2% loss D. 1% loss

62. The ratio of ages of Ram and Gopal is 2:5 and the ratio of the ages of Gopal and Vishnu is 3:4. What would be the ratio of the ages of Ram, Gopal and Vishnu?

A. 2:3:4 B. 3:4:5
C. 6:10:15 D. 6:15:20

63. Suppose X is the husband of Y and W is the daughter of X. Again Z is the husband of W and N is the daughter of Z. The relationship of N to Y is:

A. Daughter B. Grand daughter
C. Cousin D. Niece

64. The sum of three numbers is 132. If the first number be twice the second and third number be one-third of the first, then the second number is:

A. 32 B. 36
C. 48 D. 60

65. Find the odd one from the following:

A. Solar cell
B. Solar energy
C. Hydro power
D. Thermal energy

66. Find the odd one from the following:

A. 17 B. 32
C. 33 D. 20

67. FGK is related to HIM as TIM is related to ....?

A. VZA B. NLP
C. VKO D. MPQ

68. Fill in the missing part: 5, 11, ..., 47, 95

A. 25 B. 23
C. 42 D. 47

69. Fill in the missing part: 100, 48, ..., 9

A. 40 B. 41
C. 22 D. 26

70. From the choices given, select the most critical components of a school:

A. test
B. blackboard
C. students
D. library

71. In a post-graduate class, 5 students have law degrees, 3 have engineering degrees, and 2 have both law and engineering degrees. How many students are there in the class?

A. 6 B. 10
C. 8 D. 7

72. .... is to Yacht, as Wing is to Airplane.

A. Mast B. Diesel
C. Pole D. Compass

73. As per a recent World Bank report, which country has overtaken Japan to become the world's 3rd largest economy in terms of PPP (Purchasing Power Parity)?

A. India B. China
C. Brazil D. Indonesia

74. Shyam said, "This girl is the wife of the grandson of my mother". Who is Shyam to the girl?

A. Father
B. Grandfather
C. Husband
D. Father-in-law

75. Sum of two different positive integers is 11 and the sum of their squares is 61. What is the ratio of these integers?

A. 1:2 B. 5:2
C. 5:6 D. 3:2

76. Fifty persons can assemble 40 machines in 30 days. How long will 25 persons take to assemble 20 machines?

A. 15 days B. 25 days
C. 30 days D. 45 days

77. Point out which entry does not form a class with the other entries in the following options:

A. house
B. mortgage
C. hypothecation
D. immovable property

78. Point out which entry does not form a class with the other entries in the following options:

A. Law
B. Court
C. Morality
D. Judge

79. Point out which entry does not form a class with the other entries in the following options:
A. Freedom of speech
B. Right to equality
C. Freedom of religion
D. Right to make contract

80. STATEMENT: Most of the students of Navodaya Vidyalaya are of outstanding merit. Mark the most correct inference drawn.
A. Some of the students are of outstanding merit.
B. There is no student in the vidyalaya who is not outstanding.
C. There are some students in Navodaya Vidyalaya who are below outstanding merit.
D. All students are of outstanding merit.

81. In a certain code 'na pa ka so means 'birds fly very high', 'ri so la pa' means birds are very beautiful' and 'ti me ka bo' means 'the parrots could fly'. Which of the following is the code for 'high' in that language?
A. na B. ka
C. bo D. so

82. If the digits in the number 86435192 are arranged in ascending order, what will be the difference between the digits which are second from the right and fourth from the left in the new arrangement?
A. One B. Two
C. Three D. Four

Directions (Q. 83 to 85): *Read the following data and use it for answering the questions that follow:*

Four people A, B, C and D have together got ₹ 1000 with them. A and B have got as much money as C and D put together. A has got more money than B. C has about half as money as D has. A has ₹ 5 more than D.

83. How much money does B have?
A. ₹ 11.66 B. ₹ 13.50
C. ₹ 32.30 D. ₹ 10.30

84. Who has got the most money?
A. A
B. B
C. C
D. Cannot be determined

85. Who has got the second biggest sum?
A. A B. B
C. C D. D

86. One number is twice the second number, second is twice the third and the third is twice the fourth. How many times is the first number of the fourth number?
A. 8 times B. 4 times
C. 6 times D. 1/4 times

87. "Picture" is related to "see" in the same way as "food" is related to:
A. Cook B. Energy
C. Eat D. Heat

88. Plato said 'that government is the best government which governs least'. This statement contradicts from which of the following options?
A. Good governance means no governance
B. An able government legislates on every aspect of citizen's life
C. A good governance is more liberal
D. A citizen enjoys only rights but not duties

89. If INDIA is written as 914491 then DELHI will be written
A. 45389 B. 451289
C. 45489 D. 451279

90. Raju is standing facing north. He goes 30 meter ahead and turns left and goes for 15 meter. Now he turns right and goes for 50 meter, and finally turns to his right and walks. In which direction is he heading?
A. North B. East
C. South D. West

91. The maxim "de minimus non curat lex" means
A. Law would not take action in serious matter
B. Law would not take action on small and trifling matter
C. Law does not ignore any act which causes the slightest harm
D. Law would take action in small and trifling act

92. When a women is changing her clothes in a trial room, A captures the image through hidden camera and uploads on internet what offence is committed by A?

A. Rape B. Sexual assault
C. Voyeurism D. Stalking

93. The Supreme Court recognized transgenders as third gender with all rights" is in the case of:

A. NAZ foundation v. Govt. of NCT (Delhi)
B. NALSA v. Union of India
C. Baljit Singh v. State of Haryana
D. Vajresh Venkatray v. State of Karnataka

94. Which Article deals with Uniform civil Code in Constitution of India?

A. 42 B. 43
C. 44 D. 45

95. The test of creamy layer in reservation policy in India is not applicable to:

A. SC B. ST
C. OBC D. Both (A) and (B)

96. The first cyber police station whose jurisdiction covers all offences committed under Information Technology Act 2000, was set up at:

A. Bangalore B. New Delhi
C. Cochin D. Jaipur

97. Precedent is binding and authoratative on later cases is based on the principle of law known as:

A. judicial sanctity B. stare decisis
C. status de manerio D. binding decision

98. The 39th Constitutional Amendment laid that election of any person to Lok Sabha holding the office of Prime Minister cannot be challenged before a Court of Law, but only before an authority established by Parliament. This was declared unconstitutional by the Supreme Court in:

A. Keshavananda Bharati case
B. Maneka Gandhi case
C. Indira Gandhi v. Raj Narain case
D. None of the above

99. Lawyers are officers of the court and are constituted into an independent profession under the:

A. Constitution of India
B. Indian Penal Code
C. Civil Procedure Code
D. The Advocates Act

100. Supreme Court's advisory jurisdiction is provided under .... of the Constitution:

A. Article 123 B. Article 124
C. Article 143 D. Article 226

101. Census takes place in India:

A. every 20 years B. every 10 years
C. every 15 years D. every 5 years

102. The first Law Commission was established in India under the chairmanship of:

A. Lord Canning
B. Lord Macaulay
C. Lord William Bentick
D. Lord Dalhousie

103. The doctrine of Basic Structure about amendment of Constitution was propounded by the Supreme Court in:

A. Sajjan Singh case B. Golak Nath case
C. Kesvananda Bharati case
D. A.K. Gopalan case

104. Which one of the following is covered in the intellectual property rights?

A. Art of driving a motor car
B. Ownership in a motor car
C. Invention of a new motor car
D. Possession of a motor car

105. The origin of Fundamental rights in Constitution of India can be tracked to .... of Indian National Congress.

A. Karachi session
B. Tripura session
C. Madras session
D. Nagpur session

106. Constitution Day of India is celebrated on ....

A. 26 October B. 26 November
C. 26 January D. 15 August

107. The Chairman of National Human Rights Commission of India is:
A. Justice K.G. Balakrishnan
B. Justice A.S. Anand
C. Justice Rajendra Babu
D. None of the above

108. International law consists of
A. A body of customary and conventional rules of law as well as general principles of law
B. A body of conventional rules only
C. Is body of customary rules only
D. A body of general principles of law

109. President is the head of the Union Executive such power has been given to him by
A. Constitution of India
B. Parliament
C. Special Commission appointed from time to time for this purpose
D. Supreme Court of India

110. A Colonel in Indian Army is equal to .... in Indian Navy.
A. Commandar B. Captain
C. Commodore D. Rear Admiral

111. The prime responsibility of maintaining international peace and security is on the Security Council consisting of 15 members, out of which 5 are permanent members and 10 non-permanent members. The non-permanent members of Security Council are elected by General Assembly for a term of:
A. 1 year B. 2 years
C. 3 years D. 5 years

112. General Election for Lok Sabha in India is normally held
A. every 5 years
B. every 6 years
C. every 4 years
D. at the desire of President of India

113. When a person is prosecuted for committing a criminal offence, the burden of proof is on:
A. Himself B. Prosecution
C. Court D. Police

114. Acceptance of a proposal if done by e-mail is
A. valid after Information Technology Act, 2000
B. valid if proposal directs to send acceptance by e-mail
C. valid if acceptance is acted upon by the proposer
D. all the above are correct

115. Sex determination tests have been banned under
A. Pre-Conception & Pre Natal Diagn ostic Techniques (Prohibition of Sex Selection) Act,
B. SDT (Prohibition) Act
C. Ultra-sound Control Act
D. Medical Termination of Pregnancy Act

116. Right to vote in India is based on the principle of
A. Restricted franchise
B. Hereditary privilege
C. Universal adult franchise
D. Educational qualifications

117. If a person goes away secretly, or evades the jurisdiction of the Court, he is
A. Absconding B. Abrogating
C. Absenting D. Abomining

118. The Headquarters of World Trade Organization (WTO) is at:
A. Geneva (Switzerland)
B. Washington D.C. (U.S.A.)
C. London (United Kingdom)
D. Beijing (China)

119. The Headquarters of world FAO (Food and Agriculture Organization) is at:
A. Geneva (Switzerland)
B. Rome (Italy)
C. Washington D.C. (USA)
D. Vienna (Austria)

120. Which organization is popularly called the "World Bank"?
A. International Monetary Fund
B. International Bank of Reconstruction and Development
C. International Development Agency
D. International Finance Corporation

121. Who was appointed first President of the National Consumer Dispute Redressal Commission after the Consumer Protection Act was passed in the year 1986?
A. Justice Balakrishna Eradi
B. Justice Rama Rao
C. Justice Krishna lyer
D. Justice Balachandran

122. The United Nations University (UNU) is at:
A. Geneva (Switzerland)
B. The Hague (The Neitherlands)
C. Tokyo (Japan)
D. New York (USA)

123. A right available against world at lage is:
A. right in personam B. right in rem
C. right in pleno D. right in situ

124. An order of the court directing a person not to do something or refrain from doing a particular thing is called:
A. Inhibition B. injunction
C. intortunuim D. infans

125. Election petitions are heard by
A. High Courts and Supreme Court
B. Election Tribunals
C. Election Commission
D. Special Courts

126. Who among the following is the guardian of the public purse?
A. Parliament
B. Public Accounts Committee
C. President
D. Comptroller and Auditor-General

127. In India the case of "Hung Parliament" occurs when?
A. after a general election two major Political parties get equal number of seats
B. after a general election no party or a formation of political parties gets an absolute majority in Lok Sabha
C. after a general election every party claims to form a government
D. It refers to the results of elections to Rajya Sabha alone

128. The Presence of one or more employees an/or other persons who are protesting an action or labour dispute, for influencing employees or customers or visitors to withhold the action work or business is called:
A. Strike
B. Picketing
C. Serjeanty
D. Piscary

129. What is plea bargaining?
A. A procedure by which a defendant/accused pleads guilty in exchange for a lesser sentence
B. A conference between opposing lawyers to settle claim
C. A conference between opposing lawyers and judge to determine the time a case should be heard
D. None of the above

130. A document issued by Court, calling upon the person to whom it is directed to attend before the judge
A. Summons B. Call
C. Bailiff D. Bond

131. An act in excess of the authority conferred by law is:
A. *Intra vires* B. Illegal
C. *Ultra vires* D. Extra-legal

132. Fourth Estate refers to:
A. Prime Minister's Estate
B. President's Estate
C. Supreme Court
D. Press and Media

133. The book 'Roses in December has been written by an eminent jurist. He is:
A. M. Hidayatullah
B. M.C. Chhagla
C. V.R. Krishna lyer
D. A.S. Anand

134. The first woman Governer of India was:
A. Padmaja Naidu
B. Sarojini Naidu
C. Vijayalaxmi Pandit
D. Sharada Mukherjee

135. The President of India nominates two Anglo Indians members to:
A. Union Executive
B. Council of States
C. Legislative Assembly
D. House of People

136. Which officer of the Government of India has the right to take part in the proceedings of Parliament of India even though he is not a member?
A. Vice-President
B. Attorney-General for India
C. Comptroller and Auditor-General
D. Election Commissioner

137. It is the duty of the State to safeguard forests and wildlife under:
A. Article 48 of Constitution of India
B. Article 48A of Constitution of India
C. Article 49 of Constitution of India
D. Article 50 of Constitution of India

138. Who among the following is the Chief Justice of India?
A. Justice Altamas Kabir
B. Justice H.L. Dattu
C. Justice S.H. Kapadia
D. Justice Dalver Bhandari

139. Who among the following does not hold his/her office at the pleasure of the President of India?
A. Chairman of UPSC
B. Attorney-General for India
C. Speaker of Lok Sabha
D. Comptroller and Auditor-General of India

140. "In any event, whatever system of Government we may establish here it must fit in with the temper of the people and be acceptable to them". It was said by
A. Dr. B.R. Ambedkar
B. Jawaharlal Nehru
C. D.D. Basu
D. Mahatma Gandhi

141. The concept of Public Interest Litigation which became popular in India originated in:
A. UK B. Australia
C. Canada D. USA

142. Total number of ministers including Prime Minister shall not exceed .... % of the total number of members of Lok Sabha.
A. 10% B. 14%
C. 15% D. 18%

143. Which state of India has a Civil Code which is Common for all?
A. Jammu and Kashmir
B. Goa
C. Mizoram
D. Nagaland

144. The present Chairman of Law Commission of India is:
A. Justice D.K. Jain B. Justice P.V. Reddy
C. Justice M.J. Rao D. Justice A.P. Shah

145. When the offices of both the President and Vice-President of India are vacant, then their functions will be discharged by
A. Prime Minister
B. Home Minister
C. Chief Justice of India
D. Speaker

146. What is true with rights of private defence in Criminal Law?
A. Private defence of property of self or any other person and private defence of body of self or of any other person
B. Private defence of property and body of self
C. Private defence of body of self only
D. Private defence of property of self only

147. A Lok Adalat is different from other courts
A. Because its decisions cannot be challenged in any Court of Law
B. Because the system is developed by the judges
C. Because the Parliamentary Act guides it
D. None of the above

148. The General Assembly of UNO is the:
A. Supplemental organ of United Nations
B. Main deliberative organ of United Nation
C. Not an organ of the United Nations
D. Specialized agency of United Nations

149. Who is the Chairman of Press Council of India?

A. Justice Chandramauli K. Prasad
B. Justice K.T. Thomas
C. Justice A.K. Ganguly
D. Justice Markanday Katju

150. Under the Contempt of Courts Act, 1971 the accused may be discharged or punishment may be remitted on:

A. Apology made to the satisfaction of court
B. Apology has no place in the Act
C. Apology that reduces punishment
D. None of the above

151. Sati pratha was declared illegal in British India during the regime of:

A. Lord Cornwallis
B. Lord William Bantinck
C. Lord Ripon
D. Raja Ram Mohan Roy

152. LEGAL PRINCIPLE: The violation of legal right without damage gives rise to tort.

FACTUAL SITUATION: X runs Medical coaching centre and charges ₹ 2 lakhs per annum as fee. Y started another Medical coaching centre and started charging ₹ 1 lakh per annum fee for competing with X. This act of Y compelled X to reduce his charge to such ₹ 1 lakh.

QUESTION: Can X claim damages from Y?

A. Yes, he can as Y violated his legal right
B. No, X has reduced the fee on his own
C. Yes because as there was damages there was legal injury
D. No because though there was damage but there was no legal injury

153. LEGAL PRINCIPLE: Every agreement in restraint of marriage of any person is void.

FACTUAL SITUATION: X entered into an agreement with a banker and deposited ₹ 5 lakhs with the banker. The terms of the agreement provided that X's son Y shall be the beneficiary of the deposited amount only if he marries after he attains the age of 21.

QUESTION: Is agreement between X and Banker void?

A. Yes, since the agreement is restraining the marriage of Y
B. Yes, because Y has right to marry only when he is eligible to cast his vote
C. No, agreement is valid and enforceable
D. None of the above

154. LEGAL PRINCIPLE: Agreements the meaning of which is not certain, or not capable of being made certain, are void.

FACTUAL SITUATION: A purchased cards for a certain prince coupled with a promise to give ₹ 100 more to the seller if the cards are proved lucky.

A. This is a valid agreement
B. This agreement is void for uncertainty because it is not possible to precisely determine whether the cards brought good luck to A
C. The agreement is partially valid and partially void
D. The agreement is voidable

155. LEGAL PRINCIPLE: It is settled that ignorance of law is not excuse but ignorance of fact may be excused.

FACTUAL SITUATION: X; a foreign national was carrying child pornographic material with him and was apprehended when he reached India. It is an offence to possess child pornographic material in India. X did not know this law.

QUESTION: Can X be prosecuted in India?

A. X cannot be prosecuted because he had actually no knowledge about the Indian law.
B. X cannot be prosecuted because ignorance of fact is excusable.
C. X can be prosecuted because ignorance of law is not excusable.
D. It is always in the discretion of court to decide in cases involving foreigners.

156. The law that protects authors of books or articles by giving exclusive rights is known as:

A. Copyright law B. Patent law
C. Trade mark law D. Design law

157. Where has been established High Court for the state of Uttranchal

A. Nainital B. Dehradun
C. Pauri Garwal D. Ranchi

158. According to the amendment in Negotiable Instruments Act, the physical cheque is no more required to be sent to drawee bank because:

A. of difficulty in sending cheques to paying branch
B. Cheque in the electronic form is sent to paying bank
C. difficulties caused by loss of physical cheque
D. law permits truncation of cheques by sending electronic image of cheque to the paying bank in electronic form.

159. '*Persona non grata*' means

A. An unwelcome person
B. Personal favour which is illegal
C. Prisoners of war
D. Person not eligible for subsidies or grants

160. LEGAL PRINCIPLES: Legal aid is a right and not a charity.

FACTUAL SITUATION: A person facing a criminal charge in a criminal trial pleads that he is unable to engage an advocate for reasons of proverty and that he should be provided with a lawyer at State expenses to defend him. Decide

A. State is bound to provide him a lawyer as it is a matter of his right
B. State may refuse to pay the expenses of lawyer to a criminal
C. State may deny on the ground of unavailability of lawyer or lack of finance.
D. State may provide him a lawer on the condition that he will return to the government the fee payable to the advocate within a reasonable period

161. LEGAL PRINCIPLES: A contingent contract is a contract to do or not to do something, if some event, collateral to such contract, does or does not happen.

FACTUAL SITUATION: A agrees to pay B a sum of ₹ 15 lakhs if B marries C latest by 31st March 2015. Due to unavailability of marriage hall, B could marry C only on 7th April 2015. B claims ₹ 15 lakhs from A.

A. B can successfully claim ₹15 lakhs from A
B. B cannot claim ₹ 15 lakhs from A as B married C after the prescribed date
C. B cannot only claim ₹ 15 lakhs but also special damages from A for having married C
D. B can claim ₹ 15 lakhs from A only when C also joins B in the claim

162. LEGAL PRINCIPLE: Acts done by children below 12 years of age are not offences if they are not mature enough to understand the nature and consequences of the acts.

FACTUAL SITUATION: Sahil, a child of 10 years of age, finds a gold coin in his uncle's home. He gives the coin to his sister Rachna who is eight years old. The uncle reports the matter to the police. The police conducts a search. During the investigation the police finds the gold coin kept in the toys of Rachna. Rachna tells the police that Sahil had given the coin to her.

DECISION:

A. Sahil is guilty of theft
B. Rachna is guilty of theft
C. Both Sahil and Rachna are guilty of theft
D. Neither Sahil nor Rachna is guilty of theft

163. For which among the following posts there is no provision in Constitution of India?

A. Deputy Speaker
B. Prime Minister
C. Deputy Prime Minister
D. Vice-President

164. Income Tax in India is
1. Indirect tax
2. Progressive tax
3. Direct tax
4. Proportional tax

A. 1 and 2 B. 1 and 4
C. 2 and 3 D. 3 and 4

165. Who among the following became the first Indian member of the British Parliament?
A. C. Rajagopalachari
B. Vijayalaxmi Pandit
C. Dadabhai Naoroji
D. Maulana Azad

166. Both the President and the Governors of India have power to promulgate Ordinances. The statement is
A. True
B. False
C. Only if the concerned Parliament and legislature is not is session
D. Depends on circumstances

167. Which amongst the following international organizations deals with 'Refugees':
A. UNESCO B. UNICEF
C. UNHCR D. UNCTAD

168. The Headquarters of European Parliament's Secretariat is at:
A. Paris B. Luxembourg
C. Geneva D. Vienna

169. The 25-member NATO is based at:
A. Brussels B. London
C. Geneva D. Paris

170. Evergreening of Patents means
A. granting patents to harmful products
B. granting patents for 100 year
C. patenting the forest products in perpetuity
D. granting protection to improved inventions having no substantial significance

171. The first lady in India who became the Chief Minister of a State
A. Nandini Satpathy
B. Sheela Dikshit
C. Sucheta Kripalani
D. J. Jayalalitha

172. Parliament can legislate on any subject in the State List
A. For the implementation of international treaties or agreements
B. If the Rajya Sabha declares by two-third majority resolution that it is expedient to do so in national interest
C. If the legislatures of two or more States request it to do so for them
D. In all the above cases

173. Theft is an offence relating to
A. Movable Property only
B. Immovable Property only
C. Movable and Immovable Property only
D. Cash and Ornaments only

174. A notification inviting tender for goods is:
A. A promise
B. An invitation to make an offer
C. A Proposal
D. None of these

175. In India, the "right to free education" in Constitution emanates from:
A. Articles 29 and 30
B. Article 14
C. Article 21A
D. Article 19

ANSWERS

1	2	3	4	5	6	7	8	9	10
A	A	D	B	A	A	C	D	A	B
11	**12**	**13**	**14**	**15**	**16**	**17**	**18**	**19**	**20**
B	B	B	D	A	B	A	B	C	A
21	**22**	**23**	**24**	**25**	**26**	**27**	**28**	**29**	**30**
C	A	C	D	B	B	C	A	A	B

31	32	33	34	35	36	37	38	39	40
B	A	C	A	D	D	D	D	C	A
41	42	43	44	45	46	47	48	49	50
B	A	D	C	D	A	C	C	B	D
51	52	53	54	55	56	57	58	59	60
*	*	C	D	D	C	B	B	C	A
61	62	63	64	65	66	67	68	69	70
B	D	B	B	A	A	C	B	C	C
71	72	73	74	75	76	77	78	79	80
A	A	A	D	C	C	C	C	D	C
81	82	83	84	85	86	87	88	89	90
A	D	A	A	D	A	C	B	B	B
91	92	93	94	95	96	97	98	99	100
B	C	B	C	D	A	B	C	D	C
101	102	103	104	105	106	107	108	109	110
B	B	C	C	A	B	D	A	A	B
111	112	113	114	115	116	117	118	119	120
B	A	B	D	A	C	A	A	B	B
121	122	123	124	125	126	127	128	129	130
A	C	B	B	A	D	B	B	A	A
131	132	133	134	135	136	137	138	139	140
C	D	B	B	D	B	B	B	*	B
141	142	143	144	145	146	147	148	149	150
D	C	B	D	C	A	A	B	A	A
151	152	153	154	155	156	157	158	159	160
B	D	C	B	C	A	A	D	A	A
161	162	163	164	165	166	167	168	169	170
B	D	C	C	C	C	C	B	A	D
171	172	173	174	175					
C	D	A	B	C					

SOME SELECTED EXPLANATORY ANSWERS

61. Let cost price of mobile phone = ₹ 100

C.P. for Shyam = 100 + 10 = ₹ 110

$$\text{Loss} = \frac{10}{100} \times 110 = 11$$

S.P. for Shyam = 110 − 11 = ₹ 99

∴ C.P. for Ram = ₹ 99

Profit = 100 − 99 = ₹ 1

$$\text{Profit } \% = \frac{1}{100} \times 100 = 1\%.$$

62. Ram : Gopal = 2 : 5

Gopal : Vishnu = 3 : 4

∴ Ram : Gopal : Vishnu = 6 : 15 : 20.

63.

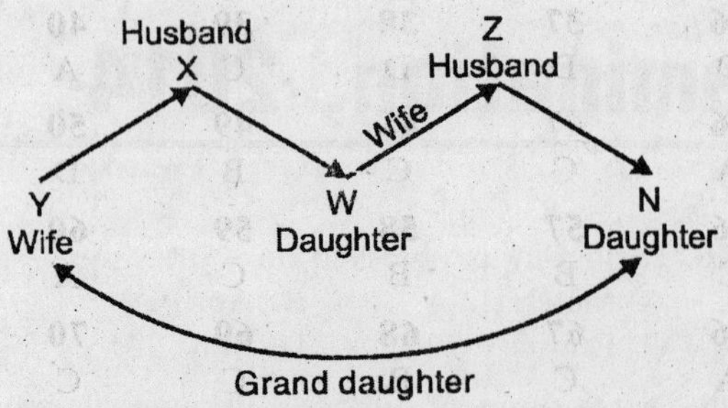

Hence, the relationship between N to Y is Grand daughter.

64. Let first no. $= 2x$

2nd no. $= x$

3rd no. $= \frac{2x}{3}$

According to the question,

$$2x + x + \frac{2x}{3} = 132$$

$$\Rightarrow \quad 6x + 3x + 2x = 396$$

$$\Rightarrow \quad 11x = 396$$

$$\Rightarrow \quad x = \frac{396}{11} = 36$$

Hence, the second number = 36.

68.

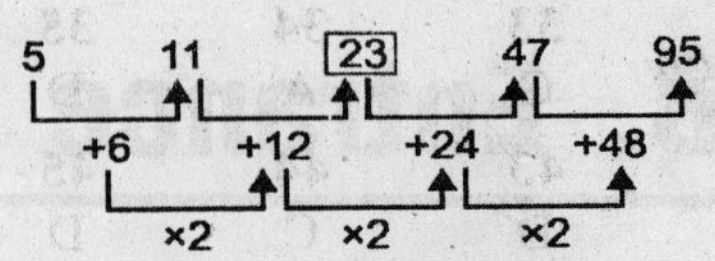

Hence, the missing part = 23.

69.

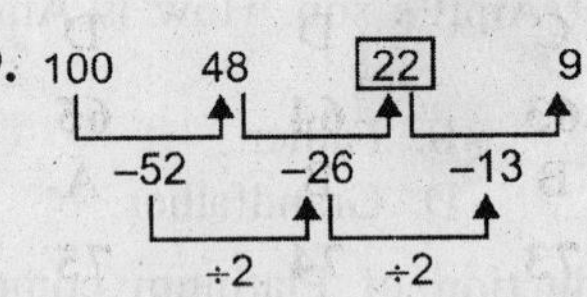

Hence, the missing part = 22.

71.

$$n(A \cup B) = n(A) + n(B) - n(A \cap B)$$
$$= 5 + 3 - 2$$
$$\therefore \quad n(A \cup B) = 6$$

Hence, there are 6 students in the class.

75. Let integers are 5 and 6

$$5 + 6 = 11$$

and $(5)^2 + (6)^2 = 25 + 36 = 61$

Required ratio = 5 : 6.

82. Given number = 86435192

Ascending order = 12345689

Required difference = 8 − 4 = 4.

Previous Paper (Solved)

LL.B. Entrance Examination, 2014

1. Ravi is brother of Amit's son. How is Amit related to Ravi?
A. Cousin B. Father
C. Son D. Grandfather

2. 80% of the production of Platinum comes from this country
A. India B. Latin America
C. China D. Africa

3. The square root of 289 is –
A. 13 B. 17
C. 27 D. 23

4. Find 12% of 5000
A. 620 B. 600
C. 680 D. 720

5. The average age of A, B and C is 25 years. The ratio of their ages is 3 : 5 : 7. Find the age of A
A. 21 years B. 18 years
C. 15 years D. Data inadequate

6. Rio declaration and agenda - 21 are the main achievements of:
A. Earth Summit 1992
B. Earth Summit +5 (1997)
C. Earth Summit – 2, 2002
D. Conference on Human Environment 1972

7. Where is the permanent secretariat of South Asian Association for Regional Cooperation (SAARC) located?
A. Nepal B. Bhutan
C. Bangladesh D. Maldives

8. Which of the following is India's first indigenously developed missile?
A. Akash B. Agni
C. Prithvi D. Trishul

9. "Survey of India" one of the oldest institutions in the country, is situated at
A. Pune B. Kolkatta
C. Dehradun D. Hyderabad

10. Earth Day is observed on –
A. March 22 B. April 22
C. February 22 D. May 22

11. Networking of libraries through electronic media is known as
A. Inflibnet B. Libinfnet
C. Internet D. HTML

12. Feedback of a message comes from
A. Satellite B. Media
C. Audience D. Communicator

13. Kanha National Park is for –
A. Lion B. Cheeta
C. Elephant D. Panda

14. The Mathematical study of population is known as
A. Polarography B. Osteology
C. Liminography D. Demography

15. Medical science used for investigating crimes is known as–
A. Criminal Medicine
B. Epistemological science
C. Forensic science
D. Ontological science

16. Parliament of India consists of
A. Lok Sabha, Rajya Sabha and President of India
B. Lok Sabha and Prime Minister of India
C. Lok Sabha and Vice President
D. Rajya Sabha, Prime Minister and other ministers

17. "Vande mataram" song is part of Literary work of –
A. Gitanjali B. Anand Math
C. Utsarg D. None of the above

18. International Labour Organization has its headquarters at –
A. The Hague B. Geneva
C. New York D. London

19. On which of the following rivers is the world's longest dam built?
A. Krishna B. Godavari
C. Mahanadi D. Sutlej

20. The study of the meaning and origin of words is called–
A. Anthropology B. Aetiology
C. Entomology D. Etymology

21. Gorima is taller than Sarita but not taller than Reena. Reena and Tanya are of the same height, Gorima is shorter than Anu. Among all the girls, who is the shortest?
A. Anu B. Reena and Tanya
C. Gorima D. Sarita

22. Find the odd one out. Mercury : Saturn : Pluto
A. Mars B. Earth
C. Planets D. Jupiter

23. The author of the book "My Country My Life" is –
A. Sonia Gandhi B. L.K. Advani
C. Jaswant Singh D. Pervez Musharraf

24. Which country of the following is known as Gaul?
A. Britain B. Ireland
C. Iceland D. France

25. In which state of India is the maximum number of Airports situated?
A. Maharashtra B. Madhya Pradesh
C. Himachal Pradesh D. Gujarat

26. Dakshin gangotri is the name of–
A. The place where the river ganga originates
B. The nuclear submarine acquired by the Indian Navy
C. A tributary of the Ganga
D. The first permanent research station established by India in Antarctica

27. The person known as flying Sikh
A. Harbhajan Singh
B. Gurpreet Singh
C. Navjoth Singh Siddhu
D. Milka Singh

28. 9, 16, 23, 30, 37, 44, 51, - - ?
A. 59, 66 B. 56, 62
C. 58, 66 D. 58, 65

29. In the following question some words are given which are related in some way. The same relationship exists among the words in one of the four alternatives given under it. Find the correct alternatives. France : Spain : Germany
A. Japan : China : Turkey
B. Sri Lanka : Japan : India
C. Iraq : Kuwait : Iran
D. Canada : California : Mexico

30. Which of the following is not included within the meaning of intellectual property?
A. Patents
B. Copyrights
C. Trademark
D. Property of an intellectual

31. Who among the following has been appointed as new Prime Minister of Egypt in February 2014?
A. Ibrahim Mehlib B. Hazlem-el-Beblawi
C. Ibrahim Sharif D. Abdel Fatah al-sisi

32. Which among the following States has got Krishi Karman Award 2014 for food grain production of more than 10 million tonnes?
A. Madhya Pradesh B. Uttar Pradesh
C. Punjab D. Rajasthan

33. Tungurahva Volcono, which is active recently, is located in which country?
A. Ecuador B. Phillippines
C. Indonesia D. Chile

34. India celebrates February 13 as National Women's day. In whose memory this day is celebrated?
A. Annie Besant B. Sarojini Naidu
C. Indira Gandhi D. Kasturi Bai

35. Which of the following countries will host 2018 winter Olympics?
A. South Korea B. Japan
C. Singapore D. Netherland

36. As per 2014 environmental performance index released recently India ranks
A. 140 B. 155
C. 165 D. 168

37. The Indian, who has been awarded the 2014 Marconi prize, a Nobel equivalent for technology engineers
A. Joseph Paulraj B. Naveen Natarajan
C. Sumitraraj Gupta D. Jagadish Singh

38. The "Yellow Rust" is a dreaded caused by
A. Bacteria B. Virus
C. Fungus D. Virus and Fungus

39. According to world wide cost of living index 2014, the city ranked as the world's most expensive city is
A. Singapore B. New York
C. Moscow D. Tokyo

40. The 'Crimean Tatars' or 'Crimians', who are in news recently, are Muslim Ethnic groups natives of
A. Russia B. Ukraine
C. Romania D. Turkey

41. 'Watson' is an artificially intelligent computer system capable of answering questions posed in natural language developed by ....
A. Google B. IBM
C. Microsoft D. Dell

42. The Government of India has decided to set up a new major port at Dugga Raja Patnam, located in
A. Andhra Pradesh B. Karnataka
C. Tamil Nadu D. Kerala

43. Which among the following countries has passed a bill which permits child euthanasia without any age limit?
A. Brazil B. Belgium
C. Switzerland D. Poland

44. Every year, the World Cancer Day is being observed on
A. January 31 B. February 1
C. February 4 D. February 6

45. Shirley Temple, who passed away recently, is a popular
A. Singer B. Child Artist
C. Author D. Painter

46. During March 2014, the India-Pakistan International Trade Fair was organized at
A. Faridabad B. Jalandhar
C. New Delhi D. Noida

47. The Beaufort sea is a part of
A. Pacific Ocean B. Atlantic Ocean
C. Arctic Ocean D. Indian Ocean

48. The first Indian State to observe 'The Child Protection Day'
A. Tripura B. Sikkim
C. Assam D. Meghalaya

49. Which among the following movies has bagged the best picture award at the 86th Oscar Awards 2014?
A. 12 years a slave B. Gravity
C. American Hustle D. Frozen

50. TDRA satellite, recently launched by NASA is a
A. Navigation satellite
B. Communication Satellite
C. Remote sensing Satellite
D. Space exploring Satellite

51. Telangana is the .... State of the Republic of India.
A. 27th B. 28th
C. 29th D. 30th

52. Himalayan glaciers lost in four decades, as per report of January 2014.
A. 23% B. 20%
C. 18% D. 15%

53. India is now the worlds .... internet user
A. Largest B. Second Largest
C. Third Largest D. Fourth Largest

54. In which of the following countries, UNICEF launched the 'End violence against children' initiative on 31st July 2013
A. India B. Pakistan
C. Bangladesh D. Myanmar

55. 'The Clean India' campaign at the world heritage site, Tajmahal, was launched by
A. Sri Jaipal Reddy
B. Sri Anand Sharma
C. Sri K. Chiranjeevi
D. Sri Ajit Singh

56. The most dominant currency in International trade is
A. Japanese Yen B. Euro
C. U.S. Dollar D. British Pound

57. .... Lok Sabha elections held during 2014.

A. 15th B. 16th
C. 17th D. 18th

58. The Czeck priest, Philosopher who has won the 2014 Templeton prize

A. Chris Herlinger B. Tomas Halis
C. Graham Green D. Bully Graham

59. For how many years, Hyderabad is envisaged as the common capital for Andhra Pradesh and Telangana as per Andhra Pradesh Reorganisation Act, 2014

A. 5 years B. 7 years
C. 10 years D. 12 years

60. The largest solar power plant in India till March 2014 is located in

A. Gujarat B. Rajasthan
C. Madhya Pradesh D. Tamil Nadu

61. 'Jai Hind' in India is the salutation given by

A. R.N. Tagore
B. M.K. Gandhi
C. Subhash Chandra Bose
D. Bankim Chandra Chatterjee

62. Dr. Ambedkar described this article as the "Heart and Soul of the Constitution"

A. Article 32 B. Article 21
C. Article 19 D. None of the above

63. Right to property was removed from the fundamental rights during the tenure of ....

A. Morarji Desai B. Rajiv Gandhi
C. Charan Singh D. Indira Gandhi

64. What is the maximum strength prescribed for Lok Sabha?

A. 543 B. 545
C. 550 D. 552

65. The first lady who became a judge of the Supreme Court

A. Leeila Seth B. Fathima Beevi
C. Sujata Manohar D. Rumapal

66. The ratio of width to the length of National Flag is ....

A. 3 : 4 B. 2 : 3
C. 1 : 2 D. 5 : 6

67. January 26th is celebrated as Republic Day and the same day is also observed as ....

A. Law Day B. Customs Day
C. Women's Day D. Children's Day

68. The oldest High Court in India is

A. Bombay High Court
B. Calcutta High Court
C. Madras High Court
D. Allahabad High Court

69. The International Court of Justice is a ....

A. Principal Organ of UNO
B. European Union Organisation
C. Subsidiary Organ of UNO
D. Independent institution by itself

70. What is the source of international law?

A. Custom
B. Treaties
C. General Principles of law
D. All of the above

71. The Malimath Committee report deals with

A. reform of criminal justice administration
B. Reform of stock markets
C. Review of laws relating to divorce
D. None of the above

72. Who wrote the first book on the Constitution of India?

A. B.R. Ambedkar B. Durgadas Basu
C. H.M. Seervai D. Jawaharlal Nehru

73. The term of office of the Governor of State is

A. Two years B. Three years
C. Four years D. Five years

74. To whom does the President address his letter of resignation?

A. Prime Minister
B. Chief Justice of India
C. Parliament
D. Vice-President

75. The Union Government enjoys exclusive powers in

A. Union List
B. Concurrent List
C. State List
D. Union List and State List

76. The President of the United States of America is elected every ....

A. Two years B. Three years
C. Four years D. Five years

77. Who is legally competent to declare war?

A. President of India
B. Chief Justice of India
C. Prime Minister of India
D. Law Minister of India

78. The Union Territory of Andaman and Nicobar Islands comes in the Jurisdiction of the High Court of

A. Madras B. Calcutta
C. Kerala D. Andhra Pradesh

79. The Law relating to Prisoners of war has been codified by ....

A. Hague conventions
B. Vienna conventions
C. Geneva conventions
D. None of the above

80. The first State in India created on linguistic basis is

A. Madhya Pradesh B. Andhra Pradesh
C. Gujarat D. Maharashtra

81. The Joint session of Parliament is presided over by the ....

A. President
B. Vice-President
C. Speaker of the Lok Sabha
D. Deputy Speaker of the Lok Sabha

82. The Head Quarters of the United Nations (UN) is located at

A. Los Angeles B. Washington
C. New York D. San Francisco

83. In Lok Sabha elections, the election compaign stops .... hours before the polling time.

A. 72 B. 48
C. 24 D. 36

84. List III of the 7th Schedule of the Indian Constitution deals with

A. Concurrent List
B. State List
C. Union List
D. List of Union Territory

85. Domestic Violence Act was passed in the year

A. 2005 B. 2007
C. 2010 D. 2014

86. Protection of Children from Sexual Offences Act was passed in the year

A. 2012 B. 2010
C. 2009 D. 2014

87. In an attempt to put a lid on Benami Transactions, the Union Cabinet has approved of the replacement of the Benami Transactions (Prohibition) Act 1988 with which of the following new laws, which will make Benami properties liable for confiscation.

A. Benami Transactions (Prosecution) Bill, 2011
B. Benami Transactions (Prohibition) Bill, 2011
C. Benami Accounts (Prohibition) Bill, 2011
D. Black Money Transactions (Prohibition) Bill, 2011

88. Use of violence by a member of unlawful assembly, in furtherance of their common object will constitute an office of

A. rioting B. assault
C. affray D. None of above

89. How many Schedules does the Constitution of India comprise?

A. Nine B. Ten
C. Eleven D. Twelve

90. The sanctioned strength of judges in the Supreme Court of India including the Chief Justice is

A. 25 B. 27
C. 30 D. 31

91. The headquarters of the Central Information Commission is at

A. Mumbai B. Ahmedabad
C. Calcutta D. New Delhi

92. A Finance Commission is constituted every .... years.

A. Two B. Three
C. Four D. Five

93. The Rajya Sabha has to return the Money Bill passed by the Lok Sabha within a period of .... days.

A. 10 B. 14

C. 20 D. 25

94. The Supreme Court, while refusing to stop the commissioning the .... power plant, stated that it has no power over such matters, unless the Constitution is tampered within the process.

A. Mundra B. Sasam

C. Trombay D. Kudankulam

95. The Union Cabinet cleared which of the following bills on 14th March 2013.

A. Criminal Law (Amendment) Bill

B. Protection of Women Bill from Sexual Harassment Bill

C. The Agricultural Bio security Bill

D. The North Eastern Council Bill

96. The decision that ruled that the Basic structure of the Constitution shall not be altered

A. Keshavananda Bharathi case

B. Golaknath case

C. Shankari Prasad case

D. Sajjansingh case

97. Which of the following is known as the wage price spiral?

A. The cycle of higher wages, higher prices

B. The cycle of lower wages, lower prices

C. The cycle of higher wages, lower prices

D. The cycle no wage increase, higher prices

98. Indian citizenship cannot be acquired by

A. Birth B. Descent

C. Registration D. Property Rights

99. The members of the Lok Sabha are elected for a term of .... years.

A. Two B. Three

C. Four D. Five

100. Uniform Civil Code stands for

A. Abolition of customary law

B. Globalization of legal system

C. Equality before law

D. Uniform family law for all religious groups

101. Constitution of India has come into effect in the year

A. 1947 B. 1950

C. 1949 D. 1948

102. Judges of the Supreme Court are selected by –

A. The Chief Justice of India

B. A panel of seniormost judges of the Supreme Court

C. The Union Law Minister

D. None of the above

103. The Supreme Court on 10th July 2013, struck down Section .... of the Representation of the People's Act

A. 8 (4) B. 9 (4)

C. 9 (2) D. 8 (2)

104. Which of the following bills was passed by the Lok Sabha on 29th August 2013

A. The Land Acquisition Bill

B. The Constitution (Scheduled Castes) Order Amendment bill

C. Governors (Emoluments, Allowances and Privileges) Amendment Bill

D. None of these

105. Limitation period for promissory note

A. 1 Year B. 2 Years

C. 3 Years D. 4 Years

106. Which of the following is the full form of FDI in banking and finance?

A. Foreign Direct Investment

B. Foreign Deposit Insurance

C. Foreign Daily Investment

D. Foreign Debt Investment

107. The National Food Security Bill was cleared by the .... on the 19th March, 2013.

A. Lok Sabha B. Rajya Sabha

C. President D. Union Cabinet

108. Which one of the following is not a feature of Indian Constitution?

A. Presidential form of Government

B. Independence of Judiciary

C. Federal Government

D. Republican form of Government

109. Which one of the following rights cannot be suspended during National Emergency
A. Right to Equality
B. Right to Life and Personal Liberty
C. Freedom of Religion
D. Freedom of Speech and Expression

110. Human Rights Day is observed on
A. 4th June B. 10th December
C. 24th October D. 6th August

111. Finance Commission is a ....
A. Statutory Authority
B. Non-Statutory Authority
C. Constitutional Authority
D. Judicial Authority

112. The Universal Declaration of Human Rights is an
A. International Treaty
B. Act of Parliament
C. UN General Assembly Resolution
D. None of the above

113. The Indian Prime Minister is appointed by
A. President
B. The Parliament
C. The leader of the largest party in Parliament
D. The council of states

114. The first general election in India was held in the year
A. 1952 B. 1950
C. 1953 D. 1954

115. Lok Adalat is
A. Court
B. Alternate Dispute Resolution Agency
C. Panchayat of elders
D. Union of citizens

116. The concept of 'Sarvodaya' is associated with
A. M.K. Gandhi
B. Jaya Prakash Narayan
C. Vinoba Bhave
D. Jawaharlal Nehru

117. New states can be created in the Union of India by the
A. President of India
B. Parliament by law
C. Parliament by amending the Constitution
D. Inter-State Council

118. President of India can make laws during recess of Parliament through
A. States B. Ordinances
C. Bills D. Notifications

119. Which one of the following is a Constitutional right and not a fundamental right?
A. Right to freedom of expression
B. Right to freedom of religion
C. Right to property
D. Right to move freely

120. The Indian Election Commission was established on
A. August 15, 1947 B. January 25, 1950
C. January 26, 1950 D. August 14, 1947

ANSWERS

1	2	3	4	5	6	7	8	9	10
B	D	B	B	C	A	A	C	C	B
11	**12**	**13**	**14**	**15**	**16**	**17**	**18**	**19**	**20**
A	C	B	D	C	A	B	B	C	D
21	**22**	**23**	**24**	**25**	**26**	**27**	**28**	**29**	**30**
D	C	B	D	A	D	D	D	C	D
31	**32**	**33**	**34**	**35**	**36**	**37**	**38**	**39**	**40**
A	A	A	B	A	B	A	C	A	B
41	**42**	**43**	**44**	**45**	**46**	**47**	**48**	**49**	**50**
B	A	B	C	B	B	C	C	A	B

51	52	53	54	55	56	57	58	59	60
C	D	C	B	C	C	B	B	C	C
61	**62**	**63**	**64**	**65**	**66**	**67**	**68**	**69**	**70**
C	A	A	D	B	B	B	B	A	D
71	**72**	**73**	**74**	**75**	**76**	**77**	**78**	**79**	**80**
A	B	D	D	1	C	A	B	C	B
81	**82**	**83**	**84**	**85**	**86**	**87**	**88**	**89**	**90**
C	C	B	A	A	A	B	A	D	D
91	**92**	**93**	**94**	**95**	**96**	**97**	**98**	**99**	**100**
D	D	B	D	A	A	A	D	D	D
101	**102**	**103**	**104**	**105**	**106**	**107**	**108**	**109**	**110**
B	B	A	A	C	A	D	A	B	B
111	**112**	**113**	**114**	**115**	**116**	**117**	**118**	**119**	**120**
C	C	A	A	B	C	B	B	C	B

SOME SELECTED EXPLANATORY ANSWERS

1.

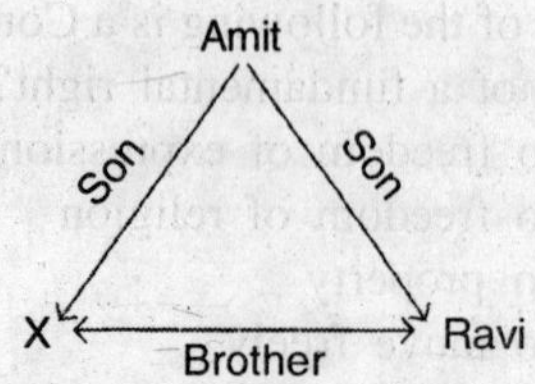

Hence, Amit is father of Ravi

3. Let $X^2 = 289$

or, $X = \sqrt{289} = \sqrt{17 \times 17}$

$\therefore$ $X = 17$

4. $5000 \times \frac{12}{100} = 600$

5. From given question,
Ages of A, B and C are $3x$, $5x$ and $7x$ respectively

Here, $\frac{3x + 5x + 7x}{3} = 25$

$15x = 75$

$x = 5$

Hence, Age of A = $3x$ = 15 years

7. Head office of SAARC is located in Kathmandu, Nepal.

12. Facebook is a social networking site where we feed/text our messages.

13. Kanha National Park is famous for its Cheeta.

21. Girls arrangement according to increasing height.
Sarita < Gorima < Anu < Reena = Tanya
or,
Sarita < Gorima < Reena = Tanya ≤ Anu
Hence, shortest among all the girls is Sarita

22. All are names of different planet, where as planet is name of class or pronoun.

28. 9, 16, 23, 30, 37, 44, 51 58 65
+7 +7 +7 +7 +7 +7 +7 +7

69. The six major (primary) organs of the UNO are:

(*i*) General assembly
(*ii*) Security Council
(*iii*) Economic and Social Council
(*iv*) Trusteeship Council
(*v*) Secretariat
(*vi*) International Court of Justice

Previous Paper (Solved)

LL.B–ENTRANCE EXAMINATION, 2013

1. Legal Principle: Every person is entitled to freedom of conscience and to profess, practice and propagate his religion subject to public order, morality and health.

Factual Situation: *X*, a Muslim sacrifices a cow on Bakra-Id believing it to be a part of his religious rites. However, there was a law of general prohibition on slaughter of cows. *X*, was prosecuted for slaughtering cow.

A. *X* cannot be prosecuted as killing of cow on Bakra-Id has the Muslim religious sanction.

B. *X* can be prosecuted as the state has a right to regulate the freedom of the religion in the interests of the public order.

C. *X* can be prosecuted as the slaughtering of cow hurts other community's religious sentiments.

D. *X* can be prosecuted, as the slaughtering of cow is cruelty to animals.

2. Under which Article of the Constitution of India has untouchability been abolished and its practice prohibited?

A. Article 17 B. Article 19
C. Article 20 D. Article 21

3. A judgment passed by the Supreme Court of India can be reviewed only by the:

A. President
B. Prime Minister
C. International Court of Justice
D. Supreme Court itself

4. Total number of ministers including Prime Minister shall not exceed ______ % of the total number of members of Lok Sabha.

A. 20 B. 14
C. 15 D. 18

5. A marriage is said to be child marriage if:

A. The girl is below 18 years and the boy is below 20 years.
B. The girl and the boy are below 21 years.
C. The girl is below 20 years and the boy below 21 years.
D. The girl is below 18 years and the boy below 21 years.

6. The founding member of the movement for Right to Information is:

A. Anna Hazare B. Aruna Roy
C. Arvind Kejriwal D. Arundathi Roy

7. The reservation of seats for women in Panchayat Raj institutions is:

A. 50% of total seats
B. 33% of total population
C. Proportionate to women population
D. 33% of total seats

8. Electoral disputes arising out of Presidential and Vice-Presidential elections are settled by:

A. Central Election Tribunal
B. Joint Committee of Parliament
C. Election Commission of India
D. Supreme Court of India

9. Ignorance of law is:

A. Excused
B. Not excused
C. Many times excused
D. All of these

10. Choose the Fundamental Rights available to Indian citizens but not to aliens.

I. Freedom of speech and expression

II. Equality before the law

III. Right of minorities

IV. Protection of life and liberty

A. I and III B. I and IV
C. II and IV D. II and III

11. The present Chairperson of the National Human Rights Commission of India is:
A. Justice A.S. Anand
B. Justice P.N. Bhagwati
C. Justice K.G. Balakrishnan
D. Justice Swatantra Kumar

12. Mr. Samay was severely hurt while working in his factory and fell unconscious. He was rushed to a hospital by his fellow workers. In the hospital (at emergency/casualty ward) the doctors opined that he should be operated immediately. While conducting preliminary examinations, he was found to be HIV positive. The doctors are in a dilemma regarding what should they do first.
A. Doctor should operate first.
B. Doctors should inform his family members.
C. Doctors should inform his employers.
D. Doctors should not inform anyone because it would violate patient's right of privacy.

13. Principle: When one person signifies to another his willingness to do or abstain from doing anything, with a view to obtaining the assent of that person to such an act or abstinence, he is said to have made a proposal.

Fact: Ram telegraphed to Shyam: "*Will you sell me your bullet bike? Telegram the lowest price.*" Shyam replied by telegram: "*Lowest price for bike is ₹1 lakh.*" *Ram immediately sent his consent through telegram stating: "I agree to buy the bike for ₹1 lakh asked by you.*" Shyam refused to sell the bike.
A. He cannot refuse to sell the bike because the contract has already been made.
B. He can refuse to sell the bike because it was only invitation to offer and not the real offer.
C. It was not a valid offer because willingness to enter into a contract was absent.
D. None of these

14. Sheela, an adult married woman, agreed to live in adultery with Rahul and also agreed to serve him as his housekeeper. In return, Rahul, an adult agreed to pay Sheela ₹5000 per month for living in adultery and ₹5000 per month for housekeeping. The agreement is:
A. Valid as the parties are adults and so capable of contracting.
B. Voidable as Sheela is a married woman.
C. Contingent as Sheela may or may not perform the agreement.
D. Unlawful as being opposed to public policy.

15. Rania applied for the post of Director in an organization. The governing body of the organization passed a resolution appointing him to the post. Afterwards, one of the members of the governing body informed him privately of the resolution. Subsequently, the resolution was rescinded by the governing body. Rania files a suit for breach of contract and claims damages. Which one of the following is the correct legal proposition in the case?
A. Rania cannot claim damages as she had not resigned from her existing post in anticipation of getting the appointment letter.
B. Rania cannot claim damages as there was no proper communication of acceptance.
C. Rania can claim damages as governing body cannot rescind the resolution once passed and communicated.
D. Rania can claim damages as there was private communication.

16. Y makes an attempt to steal some jewels by breaking open a box and finds, after opening the box, that there is no jewel in it. Choose the appropriate answer.
A. Y is not guilty of attempt to theft because the box was empty
B. Y is guilty of attempt to commit theft
C. Y is guilty of trespass
D. Y is not guilty of any offence

17. _______ is NOT a Central Government tax.
A. Income Tax B. Custom Duty
C. Land Revenue D. Service Tax

18. A patent is granted for a:
A. New expression
B. New invention
C. New combination
D. New discovery

19. JNNURM means:
A. Jawaharlal Nehru National Urban Renewal Mission
B. Jawaharlal Nehru Natural Urban Mission
C. Jawaharlal Nehru National Urban Rural Mission
D. None of these

20. Full form of TRIPS is:
A. Traffic related aspects of international ports
B. Technology related aspects of intellectual property rights
C. Trade related aspects of intellectual property rights
D. Trade related aspects of industrial property rights

21. WTO is the successor of:
A. NAM B. IMF
C. GATS D. GATT

22. Who described international law as positive morality?
A. Vladimir Lenin
B. Mao Zodong
C. Alexander Dworkin
D. John Austin

23. A draft is a/an ________ instrument.
A. Transferable B. Negotiable
C. Inchoate D. Non-refundable

24. Out of the following which statute is older than the others?
A. Indian Contract Act
B. Indian Penal Code
C. Transfer of Property Act
D. Companies Act

25. A film is protected under _____ Act.
A. Trade marks B. Patents
C. Copyright D. Cinematograph

26. The word "Ltd." after the name of a business enterprise denotes:
A. That it is a limited liability company.
B. That it is an unlimited liability company.
C. That it has issued limited shares.
D. That it has limited number of members.

27. Lawyers are officers of the Court and are constituted into an independent profession under the:
A. Constitution of India
B. Indian Penal Code
C. Civil Procedure Code
D. Advocates Act

28. In relation to a case the term *res subjudice* means that:
A. The case has been decided by a court
B. The case decided by a lower court could be appealed to a higher court
C. A case has been dismissed by a court
D. The case is pending before a court

29. Who is associated with drafting of the Indian Penal Code?
A. Thomas Macaulay
B. Frederic Pollock
C. Firdaus Kanga
D. Henry S. Maine

30. What does UNESCO deal with?
A. International economic, social and community matters
B. International ecclesiastical matters
C. International educational, scientific and cultural matters
D. International elections of societies and communities

31. Sexual intercourse with a girl under _____ is rape even if she had given her consent.
A. 15 years B. 18 years
C. 12 years D. 16 years

32. A lady wanted to buy a railway ticket but finding crowd near the ticket window at the station, asked Raju, who was near the window, to get a ticket for her and handed him money for the same. Raju took the money and instead of getting the ticket, ran away with it. What offence has been committed by Raju.
A. No offence
B. Criminal breach of trust
C. Criminal misappropriation
D. Theft

33. Z is carried off by a tiger. X fires at the tiger, knowing that the shot might kill Z, but with no intention to kill Z, and in good faith trying to save Z. X's shot, however, gives Z a mortal wound. Choose the correct option:

A. X has committed an offence of a grievous nature.

B. X has no moral duty to save Z therefore he can be held liable.

C. X has not committed any offence, as the act was in good faith and for the benefit of Z.

D. None of these

34. Remarks of a judge, which are made casually and are not relevant to the case in hand, are known as:

A. *Obiter dicta*

B. *Ratio decidendi*

C. Precedent

D. Binding source of law

35. The principle that agreements must be respected in good faith, is known as:

A. *Pacta dant legem contractri*

B. *Pactum de non petendo*

C. *Raison d'etre*

D. *Pacta sunt servanda*

36. "Justice must not only be done but also appear to be done, and may I add, must be paid for being done." Who is the author of this statement?

A. Henry Cecil B. Francis Bacon

C. Voltaire D. Seneca

37. Fiduciary relationship means a relationship based on:

A. Money B. Contract

C. Trust D. None of these

38. Contract is said to have three essentials. Which one among the following is not an essential in the formation of contract?

A. Offer B. Acceptance

C. Consideration D. Damages

39. 'Ecomark' is issued by:

A. Indian Standards Organisation

B. Bureau of Indian Standards

C. International Standards Organisation

D. The Trade Marks Office

40. Right to education is added as Article 21A in the Constitution of India by:

A. 86th Constitutional Amendment, 2002

B. 88th Constitutional Amendment, 2003

C. 89th Constitutional Amendment, 2003

D. 90th Constitutional Amendment, 2003

41. First Lokpal Bill had been introduced in the Parliament of India in the year:

A. 1962 B. 1964

C. 1966 D. 1968

42. Which among the following Vice-Presidents in India resigned from his office to contest for the post of President?

A. V.V. Giri

B. Fakhruddin Ali Ahmad

C. N. Sanjeeva Reddy

D. R. Venkataraman

43. A National Emergency in India remains in operation, with the approval of Parliament for:

A. Maximum of 1 year

B. Indefinite period

C. Maximum of 2 years

D. Maximum 3 years

44. Which among the following Indian Constitutional Amendments included 4 more languages in the Eighth Schedule to the Constitution of India?

A. 89th Amendment, 2003

B. 90th Amendment, 2003

C. 91st Amendment, 2003

D. 92nd Amendment, 2003

45. Constitution Amending Bill passed by the Parliament of India also requires to be ratified by the Legislatures of not less than half of the States in regard to the:

A. Fundamental Rights

B. Fundamental Duties

C. Representation of States in Parliament

D. Constitutional remedies

46. As per Constitutional requirement the parliament of India shall meet as least:

A. Once a year

B. Twice a year

C. Thrice a year

D. Four times a year

47. Chairman of Central Sixth Pay Commission in India was:
A. Justice B.N. Srikrishna
B. Justice B.N. Kripal
C. Justice L.K. Majumdar
D. Justice V.N. Khare

48. In which of the following cases the Constitution of India allows an exception to the rule of equality?
A. President and Governor
B. Prime Minister and Chief Minister
C. Union Law Minister and Law Minister of a State
D. Deputy Prime Minister and Deputy Chief Minister

49. Article 1 of the Constitution of India declares India as:
A. Federal State
B. Quasi-federal State
C. Unitary State
D. Union of the States

50. A Panchayat Samiti at the block level in India is only a/an:
A. Advisory body
B. Consultative committee
C. Co-ordinating and supervisory authority
D. Administrative authority

51. When the offices of both the President and Vice-President of India are vacant, then their functions will be discharged by:
A. Prime Minister
B. Home Minister
C. Chief Justice of India
D. Speaker

52. Parliament or a State Legislature in India can declare a seat vacant, if a member absents himself without notice from the session for more than:
A. 30 days B. 60 days
C. 90 days D. 120 days

53. Which country among the following is the first country in Europe to guarantee animal rights in its Constitution?
A. Belgium B. Germany
C. Switzerland D. Belgrade

54. Kothari Commission relates to:
A. Sports
B. Cultural
C. Education
D. Backward classes

55. Permission to vote in India by postal ballot is given to:
1. Members of the Armed Forces
2. Foreign Service personnel posted abroad
3. Officials on election duty
4. Candidates who are touring their constituencies
A. 2, 4 B. 1, 3
C. 1, 2, 3 D. 2, 3

56. The concept of Public Interest Litigation which has become quite popular in India originated in:
A. UK B. Australia
C. Canada D. USA

57. Right to property was removed from the list of Fundamental Rights from the Constitution of India during the tenure of:
A. Morarji Desai B. Rajiv Gandhi
C. Charan Singh D. Indira Gandhi

58. The current strength of Lok Sabha and State Assemblies in India is to be frozen up to:
A. 2026 B. 2016
C. 2018 D. 2015

59. Petitions to the Supreme Court of India under Article 32 of Constitution are subject to the rule of '*Res Judicata*' except:
A. *Quo Warranto*
B. *Certiorari*
C. *Habeas Corpus*
D. *Prohibition*

60. Which of the following fundamental rights, guaranteed by the constitution of India, 1950 cannot be suspended during emergency?
A. Freedom of speech and expression under Article 19(1)(a)
B. Right to Constitutional remedies under Articles 32 and 226
C. Right under Articles 21 and 22
D. Right under Articles 20 and 21

61. In which landmark judgment did the Supreme Court of India lay down guidelines against sexual harassment of women at workplace?
A. *Nilabati Behera v. State of Orissa*
B. *Hussainara Khatoon v. State of Bihar*
C. *Maneka Gandhi v. Union of India*
D. *Vishakha v. State of Rajasthan*

62. Clemency of capital punishment is granted by:
A. Jail superintendent
B. Prime Minister
C. Chief Justice of Supreme Court
D. President of India

63. To be tried under Juvenile Justice (Care and Protection) Act, 2000 the accused must be below the age of:
A. 18 B. 16
C. 14 D. 12

64. A hung Parliament is a Parliament:
A. Which meets in between two regular sessions.
B. In which no political party gets an absolute majority.
C. In which joint sessions of both the houses of the parliament take place.
D. Constituted for emergency purpose.

65. The official language of a Supreme Court is:
A. Hindi
B. English
C. Any language convenient to the client
D. All of the above

Directions (Q. Nos. 66 to 71): *Each of the next six questions consists of two statements, one labelled as 'Assertion' (A) and other as 'Reason' (R). You are to examine these two statements carefully and select the correct answer.*

66. Assertion (A): A void contract is not necessarily illegal.

Reason (R): Every illegal contract is void.
A. Both A and R are individually true and R is the correct explanation of A.
B. Both A and R are individually true but R is not the correct explanation of A.
C. A is true but R is false.
D. A is false but R is true.

67. Assertion (A): X, because of unsound state of mind and not knowing the nature of the act, attacks Y, who in self defense and in order to ward off the attack, hits him thereby injuring him. Y has not committed an offence.

Reason (R): Y had a right of private defense against X under Section 98 of the Indian Penal Code.
A. Both A and R are individually true and R is the correct explanation of A.
B. Both A and R are individually true but R is not the correct explanation of A.
C. A is true but R is false.
D. A is false but R is true.

68. Assertion (A): Austin's concept of law is known as imperative theory.

Reason (R): Austin emphasized on the commanding character of law.
A. Both A and R are individually true and R is the correct explanation of A.
B. Both A and R are individually true but R is not the correct explanation of A.
C. A is true but R is false.
D. A is false but R is true.

69. Assertion (A): The essence of joint liability under Section 149 of the IPC is that the criminal act must have been done with a view to fulfil the common object of an unlawful assembly.

Reason (R): Any sudden and provocative act done by a member of an unlawful assembly would render the other members of that assembly liable.
A. Both A and R are individually true and R is the correct explanation of A.
B. Both A and R are individually true but R is not the correct explanation of A.
C. A is true but R is false.
D. A is false but R is true.

70. Assertion (A): In the event of violation of any legal right (tort) the aggrieved party is entitled to recover unliquidated damages.

Reason (R): The object of awarding damages to the aggrieved party is to put him in the same position in which he would have been if the wrong would not have been committed. Damages are therefore, assessed on that basis.

A. Both A and R are individually true and R is the correct explanation of A.
B. Both A and R are individually true but R is not the correct explanation of A.
C. A is true but R is false.
D. A is false but R is true.

71. Assertion (A): The Constitution of India provides for the appointment of a Governor for a period of five years.

Reason (R): The governor holds office during the pleasure of the President.

A. Both A and R are true and R is the correct explanation of A.
B. Both A and R are true but R is not the correct explanation of A.
C. A is true but R is false.
D. A is false but R is true.

72. Which of the following countries was hit by a massive earthquake, measuring 7.6 magnitude on the Richter scale, on 31st August 2012?

A. Malaysia B. Indonesia
C. Thailand D. Philippines

73. Which State is famous for its bandhni, tie and dye technique?

A. Kerala
B. Haryana
C. Gujarat
D. Andhra Pradesh

74. On 16 May 2012 India declared to set up a $2 billion swap facility for ______ member nations.

A. SAARC B. Euro zone
C. BRICS D. ASEAN

75. Pranab Kumar Mukherjee, 76 was declared elected as ________ President of India on 22nd July 2012.

A. 10th B. 11th
C. 12th D. 13th

76. As per United Nations Report, which 2 countries will lead global urban population growth between 2010 and 2050.

A. Nigeria and USA
B. India and China
C. Ukraine and Brazil
D. Pakistan and Bangladesh

77. What is an anagram?

A. The result of rearranging the letters of a word or phrase to produce a new word or phrase
B. A geometrical shape with 'n' number of sides
C. A telegraph transmitted via analogous mode
D. A technique for constructing holograms

78. Metals that can be easily beaten into sheets are known as:

A. Beatable B. Ductile
C. Polymers D. Malleable

79. With which country does India share the longest border?

A. Bangladesh B. China
C. Nepal D. Pakistan

80. In which police station was the FIR relating to the assassination of Mahatma Gandhi registered?

A. Parliament Street Police Station
B. Tuglaq Road Police Station
C. Daryaganj Police Station
D. None of the above

81. Who is the author of the book "A Judge's Miscellany"?

A. Justice H.R. Khanna
B. Justice Dalveer Bhandari
C. Lord M.R. Dennings
D. Justice M. Hidayatullah

82. Where is the painting, Mona Lisa displayed?

A. Louvre, Paris
B. National Gallery of London
C. Luxembourg, Paris
D. Orsay, Paris

83. Münchausen Syndrome refers to:

A. A mental disorder in which the affected person fakes or exaggerates illness to gain attention and treatment.
B. A condition in which the affected person is excessively worried or preoccupied about having illness.

C. A disorder involving a fear of being negatively evaluated by others or being embarrassed because of impulsive acts.
D. An eating disorder involving a compulsion to eat or avoid eating.

84. Which modern Indian historian has described the events of 1857 as "neither first nor National nor War of Independence"?
A. V.D. Savarkar
B. Dadabhai Naoroji
C. R.C. Majumdar
D. S.N. Sen

85. Which Organization has won 2012 Noble Peace Prize?
A. European Union B. UNO
C. Red Cross D. IMF

86. Who among the following is the present Chief Information Commissioner under Right to Information Act, 2005?
A. Wajahat Habibullah
B. Satyanand Mishra
C. M.L. Sharma
D. Annapurna Dixit

87. First woman Prime Minister in the world was of:
A. Sri Lanka B. Bhutan
C. India D. Nepal

88. Sunita Williams spent ______ days in space.
A. 190 B. 192
C. 195 D. 198

89. Who among the following players won Australian Open Men's Single Title, 2013?
A. Bob Bryan
B. Novak Djokovic
C. Gisela Dulko
D. Daniel Nestor

90. Company showing apparent concern on environment by fake methods and shortcuts to appear as environment friendly organizations is called ____.
A. Green lighting B. Moon lighting
C. Green washing D. Rainbow warrior

91. According to 2011 census, which is the second most populous state in India?
A. Bihar B. West Bengal
C. Maharashtra D. Andhra Pradesh

92. Who among the following proposed the concept of Earth Hour?
A. Jim O'Neil
B. Theodore Levitt
C. Baruch Blumbers
D. Andy Ridley

93. Edward Roberts is associated with:
A. HIV
B. IVF
C. Global Warming
D. Nano Technology

94. Which of the following banks has celebrated Platinum Jubilee in July 2012?
A. SBI B. PNB
C. IOB D. BOI

95. World Heritage committee declared which natural site in India as a World Heritage site in July 2012?
A. The Nilgiris
B. The Aravali Ranges
C. Western ghats
D. Eastern ghats

96. Which country is providing huge grant to UNICEF to ensure India remains Polio free?
A. UK B. Russia
C. USA D. Japan

97. Shivnarine Chanderpaul secured place in the 10000 runs club in cricket in April 2012. He belongs to:
A. West Indies B. Sri Lanka
C. India D. Bangladesh

98. As per agreement on 10 July 2012, the World Bank will extend additional credit of $ 100 million to which Indian state, towards implementation of "Rural Livelihood" project namely "Jeevika".
A. Andhra Pradesh B. Bihar
C. Rajasthan D. Maharashtra

99. Finacle is a banking solutions software which was awarded, "Core Banking Technology", provider of the year award in July 2012. Finacle is from which software company?
A. Wipro B. TCS
C. Infosys D. Cognizant

100. With Parliament voting favourably in July 2012, Russia will be joining which world organization soon?

A. WTO B. IBRD
C. IMF D. UNCTAD

101. The Principal Bench of the Central Administrative Tribunal is at:

A. New Delhi B. Kolkata
C. Mumbai D. Chennai

Directions (Q. Nos. 102 to 111): *Read the passage given below and answer questions.*

Working overseas is always a challenge for any professional and if you are an Indian, always strive to give your best as Indians have always been considered intelligent, hardworking, talented and spiritual. Indians have always excelled in a competitive working environment and working overseas was something many Indians desired but few achieved till the information technology boom opened several white-collar job opportunities for them in global markets. However, securing employment abroad may be an achievement but retaining it, is quite a challenge as a professional required constant demonstration of professionalism and exacting standards of competence. Then, there is this challenge of working in an alien environment coupled with numerous other variables like culture, people, work ethics, local regulations, etc. that one is expected to cope up with to be successful on the job. Change, thus, becomes inevitable as one moves into a new work environment and the best way to tackle change is to be prepared for it, and adapt to it rapidly. Let us dwell on some key factors that could be useful when adapting to a foreign environment.

Each country is a mix of cultural and social influences that make it unique. Religious belief, way of speaking and behaviour, customs and traditions would all come across as very different. Also, home sickness and loneliness, all aspects of life and livelihood appear confusing, alien and difficult to comprehend. Privacy is highly valued in most countries which tends to translate into loneliness for most expatriates. One should experience the new culture and try different forms of entertainment and make friends among people coming from different cultural backgrounds. When you start work it is a good idea to be observant. Absorb as much as you can about systems in the organization and adjust accordingly.

Must you speak the language of the country you are in? Yes, you should be at least conversational. Co-workers want to speak their own language and will not be entirely comfortable if they cannot understand you. Even within the same language English, pronunciation can be a problem.

Westerners are particular about time so always make sure that you stick to time for meetings, attending offices and even social gatherings. Superiors at work and seniors are addressed by their first name. 'Sir' and 'Madam' are not much in vogue. Mix with a wide variety of people. Respect others' cultural background and keep clear of racist or sexist remarks and beliefs. Adapt to the local culture and traditions and be aware of the local favourites, they are good social conversation breakers.

Layoffs may be a stigma in India since it is relatively unheard of in white-collar jobs but the term 'job security' does not exist in developed world. Accept this as a part of the work hazard and do not let it affect your performance. Keep updating skills and knowledge constantly so that current skills are readily accepted in the job market, if you need to move on. Cost of medical services can prove to the prohibitive. Opt for health insurance cover at all time. If you travel a lot, consider travel and household insurance too. It is useful to be registered with the nearest Indian mission so that you can be easily reached in case of an eventuality.

102. An appropriate title for the passage is:

A. "Higher studies in foreign countries"
B. "The problems of getting a job abroad"
C. "Why Indians should not go abroad"
D. "How Indians can be successful in a foreign country"

103. While taking up a job in a foreign country, one should:

A. Be ready to face the change in culture
B. Be willing to try different varieties of food
C. Be conversational in the language of the country
D. All of the above

104. According to the passage, Indians have been successful overseas because:
A. India is a poor nation.
B. There is no job opportunity in India.
C. Indians are lazy in their own land.
D. Indians are considered intelligent, hardworking, talented and spiritual.

105. When you go to meet Westerners, you must stick to time because:
A. Westerners are particular about time.
B. Westerners are busy people.
C. To show that Indians always stick to time.
D. None of the above

106. 'Job Security' does not exist in developed world. So you must be prepared to move on by:
A. Looking for jobs elsewhere.
B. Updating skills and knowledge.
C. Returning to India.
D. Feel miserable and fight with the management.

107. In the early stages one tends to get lonely in a foreign country because:
A. Foreigners are hostile towards Indians.
B. Indians are not friendly people.
C. You are busy with your work.
D. Privacy is highly valued in most countries.

108. Health insurance is a must in a foreign land because:
A. Medical expenses are high.
B. You can fall ill very often.
C. You can save some money.
D. None of the above

109. What are the challenges in retaining an employment abroad?
A. Professionalism, competence and working in an alien culture.
B. Cost of living and loneliness.
C. Lack of facilities in the offices.
D. Sexual harassment.

110. What is the main theme of the passage?
A. Job opportunities in foreign countries.
B. How you can enjoy a holiday abroad.
C. The importance of being an NRI.
D. Challenges for working overseas.

111. The best way to tackle change is:
A. by avoiding it.
B. be prepared for it and adapt to it rapidly.
C. by changing places.
D. All of the above

Directions (Q. Nos. 112 and 113): *Each question has a pair of capitalised words followed by 4 pair of words. Choose the pair of words that do NOT express a relationship similar to that expressed by the capitalised pair.*

112. SPECTATORS : MATCH
A. Battalion : soldiers
B. Congregation : temple
C. Crew : vessel
D. Crowd : thoroughfare

113. PUNCTILIOUS : SLAPDASH
A. Mundane : exciting
B. Euphoric : despondent
C. Muddled : organised
D. Doleful : sombre

Directions (Q. Nos. 114 and 115): *Choose the correct option to fill the blanks.*

114. I Like to watch _____ play badminton in my garden:
A. them B. they
C. she D. he

115. She practiced hard ______ she could perform well.
A. unless B. hence
C. so that D. for

116. Identify the correct sentences from the options given below:
A. He has been giving alms to the poor since the last ten years.
B. He was giving alms to the poor for the last ten years.
C. He is giving alms to the poor for the last ten years.
D. He has been giving alms to the poor since 1999.

117. If a person says, "All of our knowledge brings us closer to ignorance", he implies:
A. The more we learn, the less we know.
B. Too much knowledge leads to ignorance.

C. The more we learn the more we realize how little we know.

D. Ignorance is the stepping stone to knowledge.

118. Pugnacious is to fight as garrulous is to:

A. Thought B. Fact
C. Speech D. Silence

119. Antonym for the word passionate is:

A. Dispassionate
B. Non-passionate
C. Unpassionate
D. None of the above

120. Difference between empathy and sympathy is that:

I. In empathy focus is on feeling the same as someone else.

II. In sympathy focus is on both the feelings and expression of feelings.

A. I is correct B. II is correct
C. Both are correct D. Both are incorrect

121. Choose the odd one out:

A. Whale : Mammal
B. Salamander : Insect
C. Snake : Reptile
D. Frog : Amphibian

122. Choose the correct option.

I. My shoes are much better than that of yours.

II. Rahul as well as his friends is going for the trip.

A. I is correct B. II is correct
C. Both are correct D. Both are incorrect

123. Choose the odd one out:

A. Sacrosanct B. Sacrilege
C. Sanctify D. Sanctimonious

124. There seems to be no solution _____ the food problem of many underdeveloped countries.

A. of B. for
C. to D. in

125. Make ______ while the sun shines.

A. a fortune B. hay
C. straw D. rainbows

126. A _____ by the Principal disciplined the rowdy schoolboys.

A. censor B. censure
C. direction D. suggestion

127. He ____ a lie if he ever said that he liked you.

A. was telling
B. have been telling
C. would have told
D. would have been telling

128. _____ the room, the door suddenly swung and hit her in the face.

A. On entering
B. Entering
C. As she entered
D. While entering

129. I must dispense _____ your services.

A. of B. in
C. at D. with

130. Choose the most appropriate sentence from the following:

A. All the employees must report immediately to the concerned heads of the department.
B. All the employees must report immediately to the heads of the departments concerned.
C. All the employees must report immediately to the concerned heads of the departments.
D. All the employees must report immediately to the heads of the department concerned.

131. Choose the word with the correct spelling.

A. Benidiction B. Solicitude
C. Psycophancy D. Intution

132. Choose the word which is closest in meaning to the word SHREWD.

A. Erudite B. Profound
C. August D. Artful

133. Which word is the opposite of "Hypothesize"?

A. Posit B. Conjecture
C. Refute D. Speculate

134. Concurrence means all of the following except:

A. Agreement B. Accord
C. Harmony D. Consensus

135. Radical is related to Moderate in the same way as Revolution is related to:
A. Change B. Chaos
C. Peace D. Reformation

136. If a person makes a statement: "I never speak the truth". The person can be said to be ____.
Choose the appropriate words to fill in the blank.
A. Lying
B. Lying as well as speaking the truth
C. Making a logically contradictory statement
D. Partially speaking the truth and partially lying

137. The HCF and the LCM of two numbers are equal. What can be said about the numbers?
A. They are prime
B. They are co-primes but not primes
C. They are equal
D. None of these

138. Ashok got 30% of the maximum marks in an exam and failed by 10 marks. Bala got 40% of maximum marks in it and got 10 marks more than the pass mark. Find the maximum marks.
A. 150 B. 200
C. 100 D. 250

139. Ajay and Vijay have some marbles. If Ajay gives 5 marbles to Vijay, he would have twice the number of marbles Vijay would have. If Vijay gives 15 marbles to Ajay, Ajay would have 8 times the marbles that Vijay would have. Find the number of marbles with Vijay.
A. 20 B. 30
C. 25 D. 35

140. P sells a table to Q at a profit of 10% and Q sells it to R at a profit of 12%. If R pays ₹246.40 for it, then how much had P paid for it?
A. 200 B. 300
C. 248 D. 346

141. If 0.06% of a number is 84, then 30% of that number is:
A. 25.2 B. 420
C. 42000 D. 2520

142. A sum was divided among P, Q & R. R got double than P who got double than Q. If the difference between the shares of Q and R is ₹3675.00, then the sum in rupees is:
A. 4900 B. 8575
C. 11025 D. 7350

143. One-third of one-fourth of a number is 12. Then the number is:
A. 96 B. 144
C. 108 D. 36

144. If the ratio of the areas of two squares is 25 : 36, then the ratio of their perimeters is:
A. 5 : 6 B. 25 : 36
C. 6 : 5 D. 36 : 25

145. Out of the total income, X spends 20% on house rent and 70% of the remaining amount of household expenditure. If X saves ₹1800, the total income is:
A. ₹8000 B. ₹9500
C. ₹7500 D. ₹8500

146. In a factory, the production of scooters rose to 48,400 from 40,000 in 2 years. The rate of growth per annum is:
A. 20% B. 10%
C. 30% D. 8%

147. War : Death : : Smoke : ?
A. Burning B. Pollution
C. Fire D. Cigarette

148. A and B are young ones of C. If C is the father of A but B is not the son of C. How are B and C related?
A. Niece and Uncle
B. Daughter and Father
C. Niece and Uncle
D. Daughter and Mother

149. Find the odd one out:
A. Stale : fresh B. Truth : lie
C. Slow : sluggish D. Teach : learn

150. In a family there are husband wife, two sons and two daughters. All the ladies were invited to a dinner. Both sons went out to play. Husband did not return from office. Who was at home?

A. Only wife was at home
B. All ladies were at home
C. Only sons were at home
D. No body was at home

151. There are five books A, B, C, D and E placed on a table. If A is placed below E, C is placed above D, B is placed below A and D is placed above E, then which of the following books touches the surface of the table?

A. C B. B
C. A D. E

152. Three ladies X, Y and Z marry three men A, B and C. X is married to A, Y is not married to an engineer, Z is not married to a doctor, C is not a doctor and A is a lawyer. Then which of the following statements is correct?

A. Y is married to C who is an engineer
B. Z is married to C who is a doctor
C. X is married to a doctor
D. None of these

153. If BAD is written as YZW and SAME as HZNV, then LOVE will be coded as:

A. ROWN B. OJUV
C. OLEV D. NOPL

154. JE, LH, OL, SQ, _____

A. WV B. WX
C. VW D. XW

155. In a certain code, COMPUTER is written as RFUVQNPC. How is MEDICINE written in the same code?

A. EOJDJEFM B. EOJDEJFM
C. MFEJDJOE D. MFEDJJOE

156. If ROSE is coded as 6821, CHAIR is coded as 73456 and PREACH is coded as 961473, what will be the code for SEARCH?

A. 216473 B. 246173
C. 214673 D. 214763

157. Appreciation is related to Reward in the same way as Disgrace is related to _______

A. Crime B. Guilt
C. Allegation D. Punishment

158. Here are some words translated from an artificial language:

slar means jump
slary means jumping
slarend means jumped

Which word could mean "playing"?

A. Clargslarend B. Clergy
C. Ellaclarg D. Slarmont

159. Statement: All windows are doors. No door is wall.

Conclusions:

I. No window is wall.
II. No wall is door.

A. Only conclusion I follows
B. Only conclusion II follows
C. Neither I nor II follows
D. Both I and II follow

160. Y is in the East of X which is in the North of Z. If P is in the South of Z, then in which direction of Y, is P?

A. North B. South
C. South East D. None of these

161. A boy rode his bicycle northward, then turned left and rode 1 km and again turned left and rode 2 km. He found himself 1 km west of his starting point. How far did he ride northward initially?

A. 3 km B. 1 km
C. 2 km D. 4 km

162. Complete the series: 120, 99, 80, 63, 48, ____.

A. 35 B. 33
C. 31 D. 37

163. Which one of the following is always found in 'Bravery'?

A. Power B. Courage
C. Knowledge D. Experience

164. If banana is apple, apple is grapes, grapes is mango, mango is nuts, nuts is guava, which of the following is a yellow fruit?

A. Mango B. Guava
C. Apple D. Nuts

165. If P is to the South of Q, R is to the east of Q then what direction is P with respect to R?

A. NE B. NW
C. SW D. SE

166. A father's age is 4 times the age of his elder son and 5 times the age of his younger son. When the elder son lived to three times his present age, then father's age will exceed his younger son's age by 3 years. What is the age of the father?

A. 40 B. 32
C. 30 D. None of these

167. If 63 + 25 = 16, 12 + 18 = 12 and 23 + 17 = 13, then 54 + 22 =

A. 13 B. 17
C. 19 D. 20

168. Which word does NOT belong with the others?

A. Wing B. Beak
C. Fin D. Rudder

169. Georgia is older than her cousin Marsha. Marsha's brother Bart is older than Georgia. When Marsha and Bart are visiting with Georgia, all three like to play a game of Monopoly. Marsha wins more often than Georgia does.

When he plays Monopoly with Marsha and Georgia, Bart often loses.

A. Of the three, Georgia is the oldest
B. Of the three, Marsha is the youngest
C. Georgia hates to lose at Monopoly
D. None of these

170. Disclosure always involves:

A. Exposition B. Display
C. Agents D. Secrets

171. The taxis playing in Wasseypur have the following fare structure: ₹20 for the first 2 km. ₹5 for every km in excess of 2 km. and upto 10 km, and ₹8 for every km in excess of 10 km. Bullock carts on the other hand charge ₹2 per km. Sardar Khan takes a taxi from the Wasseypur railway station to his home. On the way, at a distance of 14 km from the railway station, he meets Faizal Khan, and gets down from the taxi to talk to him. Later he takes a bullock cart to reach home. He spent a total of ₹102 to reach his home from the railway station. How far is his home from the railway station?

A. 17 B. 18
C. 19 D. 20

172. Prof. Mandal walks to the market and comes back in an auto. It takes him 90 minutes to make the round trip. If he takes an auto both ways it takes him 30 minutes. On a Sunday, he decides to walk both ways. How long would it take him?

A. 100 minutes B. 120 minutes
C. 150 minutes D. None of these

173. February 4th and March 10th fall on Monday in a particular year. Find the number of Sundays in the month of April, in the same year.

A. 5
B. 4
C. Cannot be determined
D. None of these

174. A certain number of students are staying in a hostel. A part of the hostel charges is fixed, irrespective of the number of occupants, and the remaining part varies directly as the number of occupants. When there were 50 occupants, each occupant had to pay ₹90. If there are 40 occupants, each will pay ₹100. If each occupant is paying ₹150, then find the number of occupants in the hostel.

A. 20 B. 15
C. 32 D. 45

175. Ram, Shyam and Tarun ran a race. The average of the speeds of the three was half the sum of the average speed of Ram and Shyam and the average speed of Shyam and Tarun. If the speeds of the three are distinct, then who among the following CANNOT be the winner?

A. Ram
B. Shyam
C. Tarun
D. Cannot be determined

ANSWERS

1	2	3	4	5	6	7	8	9	10
B	A	D	C	D	B	A	D	B	A
11	**12**	**13**	**14**	**15**	**16**	**17**	**18**	**19**	**20**
C	A	B	D	B	B	C	B	A	C
21	**22**	**23**	**24**	**25**	**26**	**27**	**28**	**29**	**30**
D	D	B	B	C	A	D	D	A	C
31	**32**	**33**	**34**	**35**	**36**	**37**	**38**	**39**	**40**
B	B	C	A	D	A	C	D	B	A
41	**42**	**43**	**44**	**45**	**46**	**47**	**48**	**49**	**50**
D	A	B	D	C	B	A	A	D	C
51	**52**	**53**	**54**	**55**	**56**	**57**	**58**	**59**	**60**
C	B	B	C	D	D	A	A	C	D
61	**62**	**63**	**64**	**65**	**66**	**67**	**68**	**69**	**70**
D	D	A	B	B	B	A	A	C	A
71	**72**	**73**	**74**	**75**	**76**	**77**	**78**	**79**	**80**
A	D	C	A	D	B	A	D	A	B
81	**82**	**83**	**84**	**85**	**86**	**87**	**88**	**89**	**90**
D	A	C	C	A	B	A	C	B	C
91	**92**	**93**	**94**	**95**	**96**	**97**	**98**	**99**	**100**
C	D	B	C	B	D	A	B	C	A
101	**102**	**103**	**104**	**105**	**106**	**107**	**108**	**109**	**110**
A	D	A	D	A	B	D	A	A	D
111	**112**	**113**	**114**	**115**	**116**	**117**	**118**	**119**	**120**
B	A	D	A	C	D	C	C	A	A
121	**122**	**123**	**124**	**125**	**126**	**127**	**128**	**129**	**130**
B	B	B	C	B	B	C	C	D	B
131	**132**	**133**	**134**	**135**	**136**	**137**	**138**	**139**	**140**
B	D	C	C	C	C	C	B	C	A
141	**142**	**143**	**144**	**145**	**146**	**147**	**148**	**149**	**150**
C	B	B	A	C	B	B	B	C	D
151	**152**	**153**	**154**	**155**	**156**	**157**	**158**	**159**	**160**
B	D	C	D	A	C	D	B	D	D
161	**162**	**163**	**164**	**165**	**166**	**167**	**168**	**169**	**170**
C	A	B	D	C	D	A	B	B	D
171	**172**	**173**	**174**	**175**					
C	C	B	A	B					

SOME SELECTED EXPLANATORY ANSWERS

137. Given that HCF = LCM

Product of two numbers = HCF × LCM

= HCF × HCF

This is only possible when two numbers are equal.

138. Let the maximum marks is x.

According to the question,

$$(x)\times\frac{30}{100}+10 = (x)\times\frac{40}{100}-10$$

$$0.4x - 0.3x = 10 + 10$$

$$0.1\,x = 20$$

$$x = \frac{20}{0.1} = 200.$$

139. Let Vijay and Ajay have x and y marbles respectively.

According to the question,

$$y - 5 = 2\{x + 5\}$$

$$\Rightarrow \quad 2x - y = -15 \qquad ...(i)$$

Again, $8(x - 15) = y + 15$

$$\Rightarrow \quad 8x - y = 135 \qquad ...(ii)$$

From (*i*) and (*ii*)

$$6x = 135 + 15$$

$$6x = 150$$

$$x = 25$$

Hence, Vijay has 25 marbles.

140. Let P had paid ₹x for the same table.

$$\text{S.P. of P} = x+\frac{10x}{100}=\frac{11x}{10}$$

$$\text{S.P. of Q} = \frac{11x}{10}\times\frac{112}{100}=\frac{154x}{125}$$

According to the problem,

$$\frac{154x}{125} = 246.40$$

$$x = \frac{246.40\times 125}{154} = 200.$$

Hence P had paid ₹200.

141. Let that number is x.

According to the question,

$$x\times\frac{0.06}{100} = 84$$

$$x = \frac{84\times 100\times 100}{6}$$

$$= 140000$$

$$30\%\text{ of } x = \frac{140000\times 30}{100} = 42000.$$

142. Let Q got ₹x

Then, P got ₹$2x$ and R got ₹$4x$.

According to the question,

$$4x - x = 3675$$

$$3x = 3675$$

$$\Rightarrow \quad x = ₹1225$$

Sum of rupees = $x + 2x + 4x = 7x$

= 7 × 1225 = ₹8575.

143. Let the number is x,

According to the question,

$$x\times\frac{1}{3}\times\frac{1}{4} = 12$$

$$x = 12 \times 3 \times 4 = 144.$$

144. Area of square = $(\text{side})^2$

Perimeters of square = 4 × side

Ratio of perimeter = ratio of square root of their areas

$$= \sqrt{\frac{25}{36}} = \frac{5}{6}.$$

145. Let total income of X is ₹P.

$$\text{House rent} = P\times\frac{20}{100} = \frac{P}{5}$$

$$\text{Remaining amount} = P-\frac{P}{5}=\frac{4P}{5}$$

$$\text{Household expenditure} = \frac{4P}{5}\times\frac{70}{100}=\frac{14P}{25}$$

$$\text{Remaining amount } \frac{4P}{5}-\frac{14P}{25}=\frac{6P}{25}$$

According to the question,

$$\frac{6P}{25} = 1800$$

$$6P = 1800 \times 25$$

$$P = \frac{1800 \times 25}{6} = ₹7500.$$

146. From complex interest formula

$$A = P\left(1+\frac{r}{100}\right)^t$$

where r is rate of growth per annum

$$48400 = 40000\left(1+\frac{r}{100}\right)^2$$

$$\left(\frac{1+r}{100}\right)^2 = \frac{48400}{40000}$$

$$\left(\frac{1+r}{100}\right) = \sqrt{\frac{484}{400}} = \frac{22}{20}$$

$$\frac{r}{100} = 1.1 - 1$$

$$r = 0.1 \times 100 = 10\%.$$

147. War always gives death and casualty. Similarly, smoke always causes pollution.

148.

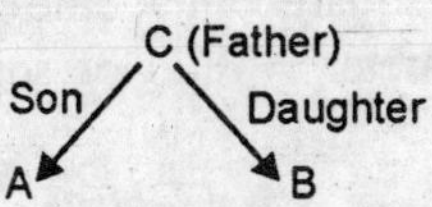

B and C are related as daughter and father.

149. Stale: fresh, Truth : lie and Teach : learn are examples of antonyms. Whereas Slow : Sluggish is an example of synonyms.

150. No body was at home.

151. Arrangement of books on the table is like this:

C — Top

D

E

A

B — Bottom

Table floor

152.

Ladies	Men	Profession
X	A	Lawyer
Y	B	Doctor
Z	C	Engineer

153.

A	B	C	D	E	F	G	H	I	J	K	L	M
Z	Y	X	W	V	U	T	S	R	Q	P	O	N

From above arrangement of English alphabets, we can code LOVE as OLEV.

154.

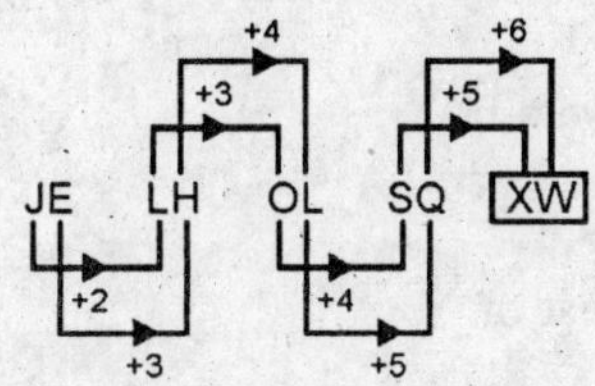

155.

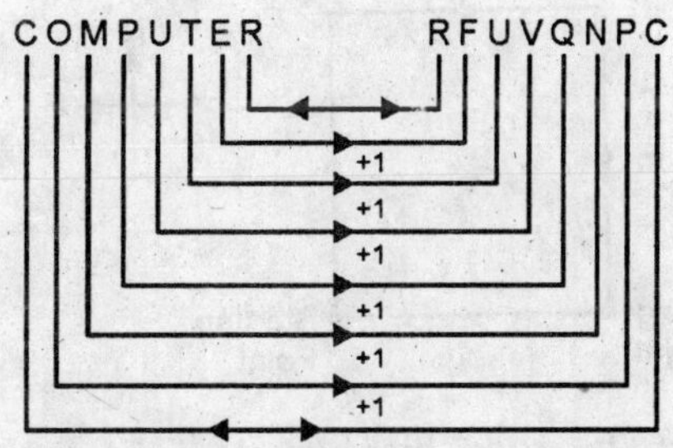

Similarly,

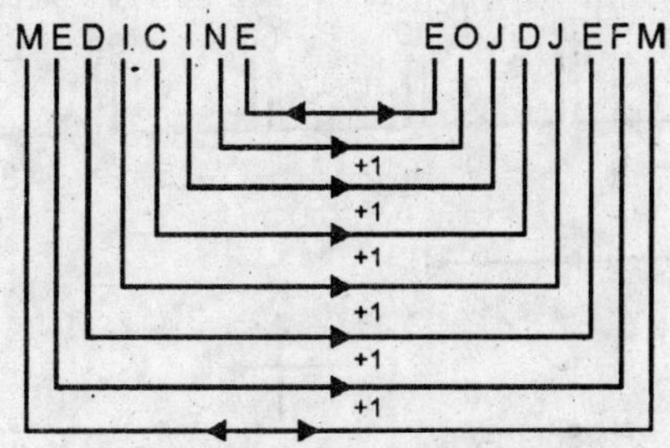

156.

R	O	S	E		C	H	A	I	R		P	R	E	A	C	H
↓	↓	↓	↓		↓	↓	↓	↓	↓		↓	↓	↓	↓	↓	↓
6	8	2	1		7	3	4	5	6		9	6	1	4	7	3

Similarly

S E A R C H
↓ ↓ ↓ ↓ ↓ ↓
2 1 4 6 7 3

159.

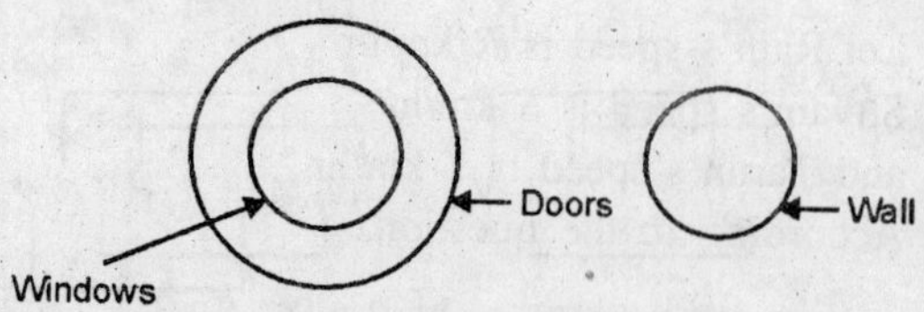

No door is wall and all windows are doors. So no window is wall.

160.

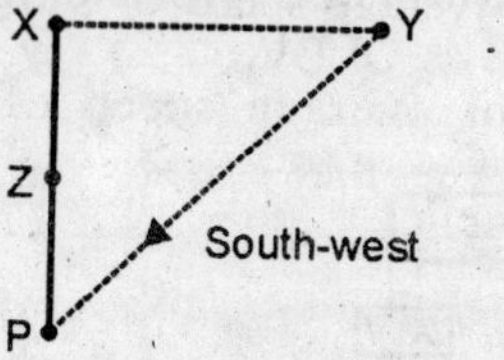

P is in south-west of Y.

161.

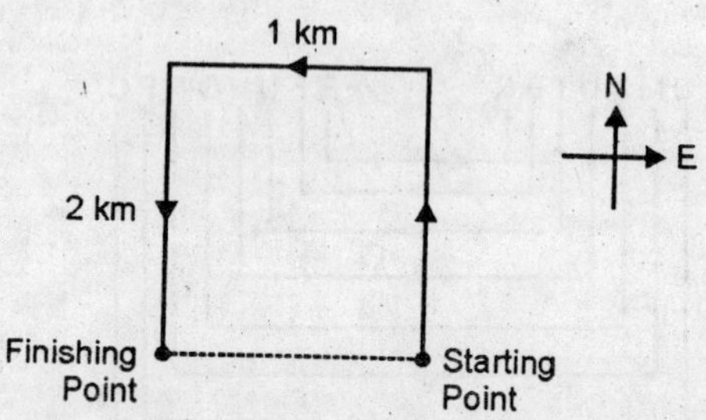

Hence, he rode his bicycle initially by distance 2 kms.

162.

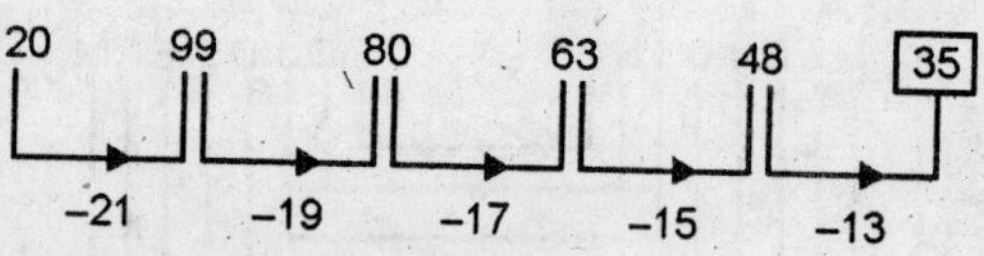

165.

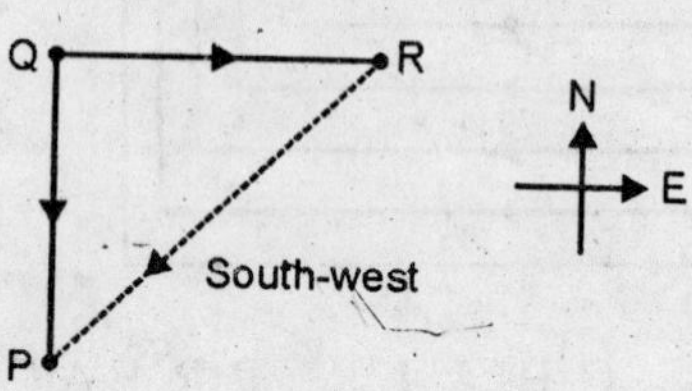

P is in south-west of R.

166. Let father's age is x years, elder son's age is y years and younger son's age is z years.

Given that

$$x = 4y = 5z$$

Ages, after $3y$ years,

$$x + 3y = z + 3y + 3$$

$$x - z = 3$$

or $$x - \frac{x}{5} = 3$$

or $$\frac{4x}{5} = 3$$

$$x = \frac{15}{4} \text{ years.}$$

Hence, father age is $\frac{15}{4}$ years.

This is a non-practical value.

167.

$$63 + 25 = 16$$

$$(6 + 3)\ (2 + 5) = 16$$

$$12 + 18 = 12$$

$$(1 + 2)\ (1 + 8) = 12$$

and $$23 + 17 = 13$$

$$(2 + 3)\ (1 + 7) = 13$$

Similarly,

$54 + 22$

$$(5 + 4)\ (2 + 2) = 13.$$

169. Bart > Georgia > Marsha

Here, of the three, Marsha is the youngest.

171. Taxi charge paid by Khan for first 14 km of travelling

$$= \begin{cases} 20 = 20 & \text{for distance } d \le 2 \text{ km} \\ 5 \times 8 = 40 & \text{for distance } 2 < d \le 10 \text{ km} \\ 8 \times 4 = 32 & \text{for distance } 10 < d \le 14 \text{ km} \end{cases}$$

$= 20 + 40 + 32 =$ ₹ 92

Per km charge for bullock cart = ₹ 2 distance travelled by bullock so that he paid ₹ 10 to bullock cart

$= \frac{10}{2} = 5$ km

Distance of his home from station

$= 14 + 5 = 19$ kms.

172. Let speed of Auto = x km/min.
his walking speed = y km/min
and distance of market from him = d km
According to the question,

$$\frac{d}{y} + \frac{d}{x} = 90$$

and $$\frac{2.d}{x} = 30$$

$$\Rightarrow \quad \frac{d}{x} = 15$$

so, $$\frac{d}{y} = 90 - 15$$

$= 75$ minutes

when he walks both ways

Time required $= \frac{2d}{y} = 150$ minutes.

175. Let Ram's speed is R km/hr
Shyam's speed is S km/hr
and Tarun's speed is T km/hr
According to the question,

$$\frac{R+S+T}{3} = \frac{1}{2}\left[\frac{R+S}{2} + \frac{S+T}{2}\right]$$

$\frac{R+S+T}{3}$ = Average speed of sum of average speed of Ram and Shyam and Shyam and Tarun

Hence, Shyam can't be the winner.

Previous Paper (Solved)

LL.B–ENTRANCE EXAMINATION, 2012

Directions: *In each of the following questions, out of the given alternatives, choose the one which best expresses the meaning of the given word:*

1. VAGUE
   A. Inadequate
   B. Insignificant
   C. Nebulous
   D. Meaningless

2. FATIGUE
   A. Sleepy B. Weariness
   C. Drowsiness D. Sweating

3. DEBONAIR
   A. Confident B. Elegant
   C. Charming D. Stylish

4. CARVE
   A. Acquire B. Cover
   C. Drive D. Achieve

Directions: *In each of the following questions, find out the best alternative for the given words/ sentences:*

5. The act of killing one's wife:
   A. Avicide B. Uxoricide
   C. Genocide D. Canicide

6. To hold something in leash:
   A. To restrain B. To discourage
   C. To disappoint D. To dismiss

7. A post without any compensation or remuneration:
   A. Voluntary
   B. Sinecure
   C. Honorary
   D. Non Participating

8. A short usually amusing story about some real person/event:
   A. Anecdote B. Allegory
   C. Tale D. Antidote

Directions: *Each of the following sentences is followed by four prepositions. Fill in the blanks with appropriate prepositions:*

9. Don't lament .... your misfortunes.
   A. over B. with
   C. to D. about

10. Don't be surprised .... and think like that.
    A. at B. about
    C. with D. on

11. He is not content .... this amount.
    A. on B. by
    C. at D. with

12. If you want to succeed let there be no .... in your effort.
    A. let up B. let off
    C. let on D. let by

Directions: *Each of the following questions contains four words. One of the four words is correctly spelled. Pick the correctly spelled word:*

13. A. Amiable B. Aly
    C. Alow D. Alot

14. A. Bonny B. Boaste
    C. Bounc D. Bridl

15. A. Outwit B. Outskarts
    C. Overcaste D. Overhal

16. A. Haggard B. Hagle
    C. Halmark D. Hampar

Directions: *In each of the following questions, a related pair of words is followed by four pairs of words. Select the pair that best expresses a relationship similar to that expressed in the original pair.*

17. OFFHAND : PREMEDITATION
    A. Aboveboard : Guile
    B. Thrifty : Precocious
    C. Evanescent : Transition
    D. Upright : Integrity

18. SCURRY : MOVE
A. Sleep : Drowse
B. Agenda : Meeting
C. Chatter : Talk
D. Chant : Sing

19. SKIRT : ISSUE
A. Siege : Vulnerability
B. Feud ; Acrimony
C. Sweep : Election
D. Dodge : Encounter

20. CURDLE : MILK
A. Underlying : Foundation
B. Fertilizer : Crop
C. Clot : Blood
D. Brew : Beer

Directions : *One word substitution.*

21. Fear of open spaces:
A. Obsession
B. Agoraphobia
C. Hallucination
D. Somnambulism

22. Government by priest or government which has its State religion:
A. Aristocracy B. Oligarchy
C. Theocracy D. Sacerdotal

23. Of the sense of touch is:
A. Tannery
B. Tactile
C. Olfactory
D. None of the above

24. A severe deserved punishment is:
A. Retribution B. Revisionism
C. Repartee D. Abdication

25. The system of putting plants and animals into various classes:
A. Topiary B. Ornithology
C. Taxonomy D. Agronomy

Directions: *Replace the bold phrase/word with a suitable idiom/word from the given choices.*

26. Prohibition is **gall and wormwood** to distillers.
A. Opportunity B. Mayhem
C. Abominable D. Heaven

27. The girls **hit it off right away.**
A. Got along very well
B. Clobbered
C. Became agitated
D. Cracked the plan

28. You **have to hustle** to get there on time.
A. Jostle
B. Catch a bus
C. Get ready
D. Get a move on

Directions: *Fill in the blanks.*

29. Retirement can either be a .... to age or an opportunity for new adventure.
A. surrender B. defeat
C. setback D. victory

30. Your treatment of your servant is .... mean.
A. golden B. nobly
C. flexibly D. nontoriously

31. Gangotri is .... by mountains on three sides.
A. hidden B. kept
C. flanked D. located

32. His performance did not come .... my expectation.
A. to B. upto
C. off D. near

33. Past civilization often saw comets as .... of death and doom.
A. portentous B. usherers
C. harbingers D. precursors

Directions: *Replace the underlined word with a word that will not alter the meaning.*

34. A <u>scurrilous</u> attack on her character.
A. Disparaging B. Vain
C. Oblique D. Slatternly

35. Rage against the new rules.
A. Pillage B. Ram
C. Culminate D. Fulminate

36. In a row of children facing north Ojas is fourth to the left of Abu who is tenth from the left end. Aashi is second to the right of Abu and eighth from the right end of the row. Total how many children are there in the row?
A. 19 B. 20
C. 21 D. 18

37. A lady and a gentleman are shopping in the market when the lady's friend happens to meet them. The friend asks the lady "who is the gentleman with you?" The lady replies: "the gentleman's mother-in-law and my mother-in-law are related as mother and daughter." The lady is the gentleman's ....?

A. wife B. daughter
C. daughter-in-law D. sister-in-law

38. Pointing to a photograph Nikita said 'She is the only grand daughter of my grandmother's daughter'. How is the girl in photograph related to Nikita?

A. Sister
B. Niece/daughter
C. Aunt
D. Cannot be determined

39. If 'A' is substituted by 26, 'B' by 25 and so on up to 'Z' which is substituted by 1, what will be the sum of the numbers substituted for the word 'FRAY'?

A. 57 B. 58
C. 60 D. 56

40. A is Y's brother. S is T's mother and A's aunt. How is T related to A?

A. Sister
B. Cousin
C. Aunt
D. Cannot be determined

41. Raja started from point A and travelled 8 kms towards the north to point B, he then turned right and travelled 7 kms to point C, from point C he took the first right and drove 5 kms to point D, he took another right and travelled 7 kms to point E, and finally turned right and travelled for another 3 kms to point F. What is the distance between point F and B?

A. 3 kms B. 2 kms
C. 28 kms D. 29 kms

42. In a certain code FIGHT is coded as GJFIU and WRITE is coded as XSHUF; then how will JUDGE be coded in the same code?

A. KVCHF B. HFEKV
C. KVEHF D. VKCFH

43. As North Pole is related to Magnet, in the same way .... is related to Battery.

A. Terminal B. Power
C. Energy D. Cell

44. Find the missing number in the following series.

6, 12, 21, ..., 48.

A. 40 B. 33
C. 38 D. 45

45. What is the missing number in this series?

6 7 5 8 4 9 ...

A. 11 B. 10
C. 2 D. 3

46. In the following question one term in the number series is wrong. Find out the wrong term.

8, 14, 26, 48, 98, 194, 386

A. 14 B. 48
C. 98 D. 194

47. A long rope has to be cut to make 23 small pieces. If it is double folded to start with how many times does it need to be cut?

A. 9 B. 23
C. 11 D. 12

48. Peyush earns twice as much in November as in each of the other months. What part of his entire year's earning does he earn in November?

A. 2/11 B. 2/13
C. 3/14 D. 1/6

49. In a certain code CHANDIGARH is written as DNAHCHRAGI. How is SIKKIM written in that code?

A. TJKJKM B. TJLLJN
C. MIKKIS D. KISMIK

50. When Rajeev was born, his father was 32 years older than his brother and his mother was 25 years older than his sister. If Rajeev's brother is 6 years older than Rajeev and his mother is 3 years younger than his father, how old was Rajeev's sister when Rajeev was born?

A. 15 years B. 7 years
C. 17 years D. 10 years

51. Reptile is to lizard as flower is to........... .

A. petal B. bud

C. marigold D. fish

52. Complete the following series:

A_5QR, A_4QS, A_3QT, ..., A_1QV

A. A_2QW B. A_2QV_2

C. A_2QU D. A_2Q_3U

Directions: *In each of the following number series, look for a pattern or relationship between the numbers, and fill in the missing number.*

53. 1, 2, 2, 5, 5, ...

A. 25 B. 19

C. 10 D. 26

54. 1, 8, 27, ...

A. 16 B. 10

C. 28 D. 64

55. 34, 39, 37, 38, 40, 37, ...

A. 43

B. 35

C. 33

D. 45

56. 69, 58, 71, 60, ...

A. 71 B. 73

C. 72 D. 70

Directions: *Each question has a word followed by four answer choices. Choose the word that is a necessary part of the leading word.*

57. School

A. Students B. Benches

C. Class rooms D. Building

58. Crops

A. Food B. Laborers

C. Harvest D. Irrigation

Directions: *The following terms are from an artificial language, with their English meanings. In the questions that follow, select the appropriate English translation of the artificial language.*

59. Ing Tor: Bus factory; igat ngot: has not; ngot e aut: not a car; e Ing: a bus. What does the word "aut Tor" mean in English?

A. not a car B. Car factory

C. not a bus D. a bus

60. If in addition to the above word meanings, if "aut boushp" means "car workshop", what does "Ing boushp" mean?

A. Car factory B. Bus factory

C. Bus workshop D. Car shop

Directions: *Fill in the relationships, based on the relationship that the question mentions.*

61. Sea is to whales as Road is to:

A. Tar B. Driving

C. Kerbs D. Cars

62. Book is to author as judgment is to:

A. Jury B. Judge

C. Advocate D. Defendant

63. Centimeter is to Meter as Kilobyte is to:

A. Computer Memory

B. Gigabyte

C. Information storage

D. Memory

64. Fill in the blank:

DBF, DEF_2, DE_2F_2, ... $D_2E_2F_3$

A. $D_2E_2F_2$ B. $D_2E_3F_3$

C. DEF_3 D. DE_3F_3

65. ABC, CBA, DBE, EBD, ...

A. ABD B. CBD

C. FBG D. GBF

66. Which word does not belong with others?

A. Treaty B. Legislation

C. Pact D. Right

67. Which word does not belong with others?

A. Jasmine B. Rose

C. Hibiscus D. Petals

68. Pen is to poet as needle is to:

A. Cloth B. Sewing

C. Tailor D. Burton

69. (*i*) Class A has higher enrollment than class B.

(*ii*) Class C has lower enrollment than class B.

(*iii*) Class A has lower enrollment than class C.

If the first two statements are true, the third statement is:

A. True

B. False

C. Partially true and partially false

D. None of the above

70. Oats has more fibre than corn but less fibre than bran.
Corn has more fibre than rice but less fibre than wheat.
Rice has the lowest fibre content.
If the first two statements are true, the third statement is:
A. True
B. False
C. Partially true and partially false
D. None of the above

71. The length of the year is greatest on the:
A. Mercury B. Earth
C. Jupiter D. Pluto

72. The largest producer of sugar in the world is:
A. Brazil B. Indonesia
C. Mexico D. Cuc.

73. The State in India with largest coastline is:
A. Tamil Nadu B. Kerala
C. Andhra Pradesh D. Maharashtra

74. The weight of the cricket ball is approximately:
A. 3 oz B. 4 oz
C. 5 oz D. 6 oz

75. The National Game of Canada is:
A. Cricket B. Football
C. Ice Hockey D. Tennis

76. At which place the 2014 Common Wealth Games will take place:
A. Beijing B. London
C. Glasgow D. Canada

77. How many foreign players can be part of playing 11 in IPL Cricket Tournament organized in India?
A. 3 B. 4
C. 5 D. 6

78. Name the first Arabic writer awarded Nobel Prize for Literature:
A. Salman Rushdie B. Gen Gaddafi
C. Naguib Mah Fouz D. Yasser Arafat

79. Sphygomomanometer is used to test:
A. Hormones Action
B. Brain Tumour
C. Functions of Intestines
D. Blood Pressure

80. Which British Governor General introduced postage stamp in India?
A. Lord Dalhousie
B. Lord Ripon
C. Lord Canning
D. Lord William Bentick

81. What is the Saudi Arabian currency called?
A. Dirham B. Peso
C. Dinar D. Riyal

82. In which of the following States the Legislative Council has been dispensed with?
A. Bihar B. Uttar Pradesh
C. West Bengal D. Odisha

83. Diphtheria is a disease affecting:
A. eyes B. throat
C. liver D. pancreas

84. In which of the following countries Chairman is the Head of the State?
A. Myanmar B. Nepal
C. Mauritius D. Bhutan

85. Which of the following Scams was not unearthed in 2010-11 in India?
A. 2G B. CWG
C. Adarsh D. Provident Fund

86. Which country has become the first country in the world to make broadband internet access a legal right of all citizens?
A. UK B. New Zealand
C. Finland D. Switzerland

87. The border of which two countries is known as 49th parallel line?
A. Germany & France
B. USA & Canada
C. South Korea & North Korea
D. Germany & Poland

88. International Women's Day is observed on:
A. 9th January B. 8th March
C. 1st February D. 25th March

89. Which Committee/Commission made recommendations to make civil services more efficient and decorrupted?
A. Kothari Commission
B. Niyogi Committee
C. Balwant Rai Committee
D. P.C. Hota Committee

90. What is the unit for temperature in the metric system?
A. Fahrenheit B. Kelvin
C. Degree D. Celsius

91. Where is Secretariat of SAARC located?
A. Colombo B. Islamabad
C. New Delhi D. Kathmandu

92. Who wrote the book "Ignited Minds: Unleashing the Power Within India"?
A. A.P.J. Abdul Kalam
B. Atal Bihari Vajpayee
C. L.K. Advani
D. Arjun Singh

93. Who amongst the following won the election for the post of Chief Executive of Hong Kong?
A. Kim Joong-Keun B. Leung Chun-ying
C. Henry Tang D. Albert Ho

94. Where did the Second Summit on Nuclear Security take place?
A. Seoul B. Washington
C. New Delhi D. Sydney

95. The SGPC and Akali Dal are appealing for mercy of .... who is on death row for the killing of Punjab Chief Minister in 1995.
A. Balwant Singh Rajoana
B. Kehar Singh
C. Gurdarshan Singh Bajwa
D. Kuldeep Singh

96. Name the MLA who has been abducted by Maoists in Odisha?
A. Lal Bihari Himirika
B. Hema Gamang
C. Surjya Narayan Patro
D. Jhina Hikaka

97. The recent controversy between India and China is related to:
A. Arabian Sea
B. South China Sea
C. Bay of Bengal
D. Middle-East region

98. Name the two children who were placed under foster care due to lack of parental care in 2011 in Norway.
A. Ankit and Aradhya
B. Abhijit and Anushka
C. Abhigyan and Aishwarya
D. Akhil and Asmita

99. Name the IPS Officer who was killed in Madhya Pradesh in March 2012?
A. Narender Kumar B. Rajbir Singh
C. S.K. Sharma D. Ravinder Kumar

100. Kurdistan is primarily known for:
A. Uranium stocks B. Oil reserves
C. Dry fruit products D. Fertiliser

Directions: *Given below are the statements of facts of the case. After statement of facts, legal principles are given. Apply the principles to the facts of the case and select the most appropriate answer from among the four alternatives.*

101. FACTS: The residents of the adjoining slums were persistently using the park for defecation. On the order of the chairman of the DDA the park was fenced and electric current was run on the wires on the top. A trespassing slum dweller touched a live wire and was electrocuted. Can the chairman be held liable for an offence of causing death by negligence?

PRINCIPLE: Whoever causes the death of any person by doing any rash or negligent act not amounting to culpable homicide, shall be punished with imprisonment of either description for a term which may extend to two years or with fine or with both.
A. No, because getting a public park electrically wired is no rash act
B. Administrative actions are immune to any liability
C. Yes, because getting a public park electrically wired is a rash and negligent act
D. None of the above

102. FACTS: A sets fire, by night, to an inhabited house in a large town, for the purpose of facilitating a robbery and this causes death of a person. A pleaded that he has intended the robbery but not the causing of death and became sorry for the death caused by his act.

Is A liable for causing the death voluntarily?

PRINCIPLE: A person is said to cause an effect "voluntarily" whereby he intended to cause it or by means which, at the time of employing those means, he knew or had reason to believe, to be likely to cause it.

A. A is liable for causing the death voluntarily though he has not intended to cause death of anyone, because he has set fire in an inhabited house not in abandoned house and it is quite natural that in such house people must be there during night.
B. A is not liable because he has not intended the murder of anyone.
C. A is not liable for murder but is liable for robbery only.
D. A is not responsible for murder because he has not killed anyone by his own hands.

103. FACTS: Certain persons transferred a tea estate to an incorporated company and claimed exemptions from "*ad valorem*" duty on the ground that they themselves were shareholders in the company.

PRINCIPLE: An incorporated company under the Companies Act has a separate entity and corporate liability.

A. The shareholders are liable to pay as the company is a separate legal person.
B. The shareholders are not liable to pay as it is a transfer from them in one name to themselves under another name.
C. The shareholders are liable because everybody has a duty to pay on a transfer or conveyance.
D. The shareholders will not pay, the company would pay on their behalf.

104. FACTS: Sahil, a child of 10 years of age, find a gold coin in his uncle's home. He gives the coin to his sister Rachna who is 8 years old. The uncle reports the matter to the police. The police conducts a search. During the investigation the police finds the coin kept in the toys of Rachna. Rachna tells the police that Sahil had given coin to her.

PRINCIPLE: Acts done by children below 12 years of age are not offences if they are not mature enough to understand the nature and consequences of the acts.

A. Sahil is guilty of theft.
B. Rachna is guilty of theft.
C. Both Sahil and Rachna are guilty of theft.
D. Neither Sahil nor Rachna is guilty of theft.

105. FACTS: Ajay runs the 'Indian Circus.' The circus has an interesting night show. Two motor cyclists, Ramesh and Suresh, rotate their motorcycles inside a big iron globe in complete darkness. And the audience, especially, the children gives a big clap. One day it so happens that during one night show an accident occurs inside the globe. Ramesh and Suresh collide with each other and Ramesh loses both his legs. His parents claim compensation from Ajay, the proprietor of the circus.

PRINCIPLE: An employer is responsible for any accident or loss caused to his employees, during the course of employment.

A. Ajay is not liable to pay any compensation because he cannot be held responsible for the accident.
B. Ajay is liable to pay compensation because he is the employer and the accident occurred during the course of employment.
C. Ajay is not liable to pay compensation but he can pay some amount to Ramesh if he has sympathy for him.
D. None of the above

106. FACTS: A farmhouse is located in South Delhi on 2 acre plot of land. The owner of the farmhouse keeps a specially trained ferocious dog to guard his property. He also employes a dog-handler to handle this dog and instructs all his other employees to avoid the dog. A sign is also put up on the gate saying "Beware of the Dog". On the afternoon of 26th January, a group of poor boys playing cricket in a nearby park hit the ball into the farmhouse. A 14-year-old boy enters the farmhouse to get the ball. The dog attacks the boy and he dies of the injuries. The family of the boy sues farmhouse owner for damages.

PRINCIPLES: (*i*) An occupier is not responsible to a trespasser except in respect of willful act intended to cause harm or done with reckless disregards. (*ii*) Master is liable for the acts of the employee/servant.

A. The owner is liable because the dog has a vicious or savage propensity and he had knowledge of the same.

B. The owner should pay the damages because he is rich and the boy killed was poor.

C. The owner is not liable because the boy was a trespasser.

D. The owner is not liable because a 14-year-old boy ought to have known about the presence of the ferocious dog.

107. FACTS: Charu while driving her car at a high speed, knocked down Seema, a middle aged woman who was walking on the road. Seema got her leg fractured as a result of this accident. As Seema was suffering from diabetes, her leg had to be amputated. Seema filed a suit against Charu for damages for the loss of her leg.

PRINCIPLE: A person is liable for all direct consequences of his act, which he could have reasonably foreseen as naturally flowing from his act.

A. Charu is liable as the loss of leg is directly attributable to her act.

B. Charu is not liable because she did not know Seema was suffering from diabetes.

C. Charu is liable because she could have reasonably foreseen the loss of leg of Seema.

D. Charu is not liable since a diabetes patient like Seema ought not to have walked on the road.

108. Endosulfan is banned in India under the:

A. Environment Protection Act, 1986

B. Hazardous Chemical Rules, 2000

C. Convention on Persistent Organic Pollutants, 2001

D. All of the above

109. Gram Nyayalaya Act, 2008 refers to:

A. Access to justice to citizens at door steps

B. Informal settlement of disputes

C. Free legal services

D. All of the above

110. Which among the following has been added as a fundamental right in the Constitution of India by 86th Amendment?

A. Right to information

B. Right to employment

C. Right to food security

D. Right to education

111. Special leave to appeal by the Supreme Court is available from the decision of:

A. Any court or tribunal

B. Any court, tribunal or administrative authority

C. Any court or tribunal relating to armed forces

D. Administrative tribunals only

112. Who was the Chariperson of the Committee on Review of the Working of the Constitution?

A. Subhash C. Kashyap

B. Justice Venkatachaliah

C. L.K. Advani

D. Justice B.N. Kirpal

113. Under which provision of the Constitution, the Supreme Court reviews its own judgments?

A. Article 132 B. Article 137

C. Article 139 D. Article 141

114. What does the phrase "*lex est norma recti*" mean?

A. Law is a rule of right

B. Law rules the rights

C. Law is a rule of State

D. Law follows equity

115. The Headquarters of the International Court of Justice is situated at:

A. Geneva B. Vienna

C. Rome D. The Hague

116. When was the International Monetary Fund established?

A. 1945 B. 1946

C. 1947 D. 1950

117. Sachar Committee Report refers to:
A. Reservation for minorities
B. Backwardness among the Muslim community
C. Judicial reform
D. Election reform

118. Wetland conservation is an obligation undertaken by India in:
A. Ramsar Convention, 1971
B. Convention on Biological Diversity, 1992
C. Convention on Migratory Species, 1979
D. U.N. Convention on Law of the Sea, 1982

119. Press Council of India is:
A. Statutory body
B. Constitutional body
C. Self-regulatory body
D. Private Association

120. Who said that democracy is a "government of the people, by the people and for the people"?
A. Abraham Lincoln B. Woodrow Wilson
C. Aristotle D. Plato

121. The Supreme Court being the highest court of appeal, is the most superior judiciary, but the various High Courts exercise a jurisdiction even wider than that of the Supreme Court under:
A. Article 32 of the Constitution
B. Article 141 of the Constitution
C. Article 164 of the Constitution
D. Articles 226 and 227 of the Constitution

122. Schedule X of the Constitution deals with:
A. Law protected from judicial review of the courts
B. Disqualification on ground of defection
C. Union and its territory
D. Union, State and Concurrent lists

123. Who amongst the following can attend the Session of the Parliament but has no right to vote?
A. Attorney General of India
B. Comptroller General of India
C. Chief Justice of India
D. Chief of the Indian Army

124. In India, right to vote is:
A. Fundamental right
B. Statutory right
C. Constitutional right
D. Moral right

125. Which of the following was merged with the Union of India?
A. Sikkim B. Goa
C. Puducherry D. Daman and Diu

126. Who headed the first Commission on Backward Classes?
A. B.P. Mandal
B. Kaka Saheb Kalekar
C. M.H. Mandal
D. S.P. Mandal

127. Who prepares National Income Estimates?
A. Central Statistical Organisation
B. National Sample Survey Organisation
C. Indian Statistical Institute
D. Planning Commission

128. Who said "litigation is a game in which the Court is the umpire"?
A. Salmond B. Pollock
C. Dicey D. Blackstone

129. Who called Directive Principles as a "cheque on bank payable at the convenience of the bank"?
A. B.R. Ambedkar B. H.M. Seervai
C. K.T. Shah D. Jawaharlal Nehru

130. India became a member of the UNO in the year:
A. 1950 B. 1945
C. 1947 D. 1948

131. A temporary tax levied to obtain revenue is called:
A. Excise Duty B. Sales tax
C. Surcharge D. Cess

132. The Uniform Civil Code was discussed at length in the case of:
A. Golak Nath case
B. Keshavanand Bharti case
C. Shah Bano case
D. Indira Sawhney case

133. Which of the following female judges has not been a judge of the Supreme Court?
A. Ruma Pal B. Gyan Sudha Mishra
C. Ranjana Desai D. Leela Seth

134. Pochampally saree is protected under:
A. Patents law
B. Trademark law
C. Designs law
D. Geographical indications law

135. In which year, the age of voting as universal adult franchise was lowered from 21 to 18 years?
A. 1985 B. 1988
C. 1990 D. 1991

136. What is the minimum age to be appointed as a Governor of a State in India?
A. 25 Years B. 35 Years
C. 21 Years D. 18 Years

137. What is the name of the first Chief Justice of India?
A. B.N. Mukherjee B. H.J. Kania
C. B.R. Ambedkar D. Aslam Khan

138. The Parliament has power to amend all parts of the Constitution except:
A. Fundamental rights and duties
B. Emergency provisions
C. Provisions regarding the Supreme Court
D. The Basic structure

139. Guidelines issued by the Supreme Court regarding sexual harassment at workplace against women in the historic *Vishakha's* case are law and binding on all courts in India by virtue of:
A. Art. 141 of the Constitution
B. Art. 146 of the Constitution
C. Art. 147 of the Constitution
D. Art. 144 of the Constitution

140. Palimony is a term used to describe court ordered financial settlement in disputes relating to:
A. Partners in live-in-relations
B. Environmental issues
C. Consumer affairs
D. Human rights violations

141. Which of the following is not a principle of natural justice?
A. *Audi alteram partern*
B. *Pacta sunt servanda*
C. Justice, equity and good conscience
D. Judges to be above suspicion

142. The line demarcating the boundaries of India and China is known as:
A. McMohan line B. Durand line
C. Radcliffe line D. 24th parallel

143. Which of the following is the principal subject of private international law?
A. Nation states
B. Individuals
C. Societies
D. Multinational companies

144. Tribal People were referred to as 'Adivasis' for the first time by:
A. M.K. Gandhi B. B.R. Ambedkar
C. Vinoba Bhave D. Vallabhbhai Patel

145. The Commission which enquired into and submitted report regarding the Godhra train carnage is:
A. Chelliah Commission
B. Wanchoo Committee
C. Rangrajan Committee
D. Nanavati Commission

146. Fiduciary relationships are relationships based on:
A. Financial terms B. Contracts
C. Both A and B D. Trust

147. The right of minorities conferred in Article 30(1) of the Constitution is with respect to the establishment of:
A. Educational Institution of their choice
B. Charitable Hospitals and Dispensaries
C. Place of worship to practice their religion
D. Rest Houses

148. The phrase 'de facto' means
A. all the facts
B. all the facts and figures
C. bona fide
D. for all practical purposes

149. The Supreme Court has held that hoisting the national flag atop the private buildings is a fundamental right of every citizen under:
A. Article 14 of the Constitution
B. Article 19(1)(a) of the Constitution
C. Article 21 of the Constitution
D. Article 25 of the Constitution

150. Which one of the following statements is correct? Parliament can make a law with respect to a matter in the State list in the national interest if:
A. The Rajya Sabha passes a resolution by a two-thirds majority
B. Parliament passes a resolution
C. A State makes a request
D. The President of India gives permission

151. For a valid Muslim marriage
A. offer and acceptance must be at the same place
B. offer and acceptance must be at the same time
C. offer and acceptance must be at the same time and place
D. offer and acceptance may be at different times and at different places

152. A void agreement means:
A. Agreement not enforceable by law
B. Agreement illegal in nature
C. Agreement not acceptable to Court of law
D. Agreement violating legal procedure

153. A, without the request of anybody, extinguishes the fire of B's godown. A suffers injury thereby. If B promises to compensate A for the whole amount he has spent on his treatment, then the contract is:
A. Valid and enforceable
B. Unenforceable because of lack of intention to create binding contract by the parties.
C. Void for want of consideration
D. Voidable at B's option

154. Which of the following defences is not available to the accused in a criminal case?
A. Infancy
B. Self-defence
C. Involuntary intoxication
D. Consent of the other party to the death

155. In criminal proceedings, acquittal refers to:
A. Being cleared of a charge or accusation
B. Pronounced guilty of a charge or accusation
C. Conviction for a lesser offence, as part of a plea bargain
D. Taking a lenient view, considering the honest past record of an accused

156. Which offence does not require a minimum of five persons?
A. Dacoity
B. Riots
C. Unlawful Assembly
D. Robbery

157. The procedure for amendment of the Indian Constitution was borrowed from the:
A. Constitution of USA
B. Constitution of USSR
C. Constitution of Germany
D. Constitution of South Africa

158. The Writ of Prohibition can be issued to:
A. Constitutional Authority
B. Statutory Authority
C. Non-Statutory Authority
D. All of the above

159. The President is bound to summon Parliament:
A. Within 6 months from the last sitting of former session
B. Within 3 months from the last sitting of former session
C. Within 4 months from the last sitting of former session
D. Within 12 months from the last sitting of former session

160. X, a doctor, informs his patient Y that Y was suffering from cancer. Hearing this Y dies of heart failure. X has committed:
A. culpable homicide not amounting to murder

B. no crime because he (X) communicated in good faith

C. the crime of killing Y because X knew that Y could die after hearing the news

D. the murder of Y

161. When does Supreme Court gives advice to the President on a matter of law or fact?

A. Only when the President seeks such advice

B. On its own

C. Only if the issue poses a threat to the unity and integrity of India

D. Only if the matter relates to the violation of fundamental rights of the citizens

162. A Muslim man under personal laws cannot marry:

A. a Jew

B. a Christian

C. an idolatress or a fire-worshipper

D. All of the above

163. What is the meaning of this Latin phrase "*audi alteram partem*"?

A. No one shall be judge in his own cause

B. No one shall be condemned unheard

C. Rights are associated with duties

D. None of the above

164. In which of the following countries, an effort was made to ban a translated version of Bhagavad Gita?

A. France B. Philippines

C. China D. Russia

165. Who is accused in the Israeli Embassy car attack which took place in New Delhi?

A. Syed Mohammad Kazmi

B. Suleman Mustafa

C. Iqbal Khan

D. Salim Iqbal

166. The Intelligence Bureau (IB) enjoys:

A. Constitutional status

B. Statutory status

C. Autonomous body under Parliament

D. None of the above

167. Which of the following is a correct pair?

A. United Nations Organisation–1946

B. Universal Declaration of Human Rights–1948

C. Constitution of India–1951

D. World Trade Organisation–1996

168. A marriage between a boy of below 21 years of age and a girl of below 18 years of age is:

A. Void B. Valid

C. Voidable D. Irregular

169. In which of the following, copyright does not subsist?

A. Industrial designs

B. Artistic works

C. Computer software

D. Sound recording

170. When did International Criminal Court come into existence?

A. 1998 B. 2000

C. 2001 D. 2002

171. Under which Chapter of the United Nations Charter, the Security Council can take enforcement action?

A. Chapter VI B. Chapter VII

C. Chapter VIII D. Chapter XII

172. Which of the following companies has recently been issued compulsory licence under Indian Patents Act, 1970?

A. Natco Pharma

B. Cipla

C. Dr. Reddy's Laboratories

D. Ranbaxy

173. Which of the following has adopted a resolution against Sri Lanka for war crimes?

A. United Nations Human Rights Council

B. International Committee of the Red Cross

C. International Criminal Court

D. Security Council of the United Nations

174. Which of the following grounds has been proposed for divorce in Hindu Marriage Act, 1955 and Special Marriage Act, 1954?

A. Cruelty

B. Abstention of sexual intercourse by spouse

C. Irretrievable breakdown of marriage

D. Desertion

175. What is the term used for the principles laid down in a judgement?

A. *Obiter dicta* B. *Ratio decidendi*

C. *Jus cogens* D. Interpretation

ANSWERS

1	2	3	4	5	6	7	8	9	10
C	B	B	B	B	A	C	A	A	B
11	**12**	**13**	**14**	**15**	**16**	**17**	**18**	**19**	**20**
D	A	A	A	A	A	D	C	D	C
21	**22**	**23**	**24**	**25**	**26**	**27**	**28**	**29**	**30**
B	C	B	A	C	B	A	A	A	D
31	**32**	**33**	**34**	**35**	**36**	**37**	**38**	**39**	**40**
C	B	C	C	D	A	C	B	B	B
41	**42**	**43**	**44**	**45**	**46**	**47**	**48**	**49**	**50**
B	A	A	B	D	B	C	D	D	D
51	**52**	**53**	**54**	**55**	**56**	**57**	**58**	**59**	**60**
C	C	D	D	A	B	A	C	B	C
61	**62**	**63**	**64**	**65**	**66**	**67**	**68**	**69**	**70**
D	B	B	A	D	D	D	C	B	A
71	**72**	**73**	**74**	**75**	**76**	**77**	**78**	**79**	**80**
D	A	C	D	C	C	B	C	D	A
81	**82**	**83**	**84**	**85**	**86**	**87**	**88**	**89**	**90**
D	C	B	A	D	C	B	B	D	D
91	**92**	**93**	**94**	**95**	**96**	**97**	**98**	**99**	**100**
D	A	B	A	A	D	B	C	A	B
101	**102**	**103**	**104**	**105**	**106**	**107**	**108**	**109**	**110**
C	A	A	D	B	D	A	C	A	D
111	**112**	**113**	**114**	**115**	**116**	**117**	**118**	**119**	**120**
B	B	B	A	D	A	B	A	A	A
121	**122**	**123**	**124**	**125**	**126**	**127**	**128**	**129**	**130**
D	B	A	B	A	B	A	B	C	B
131	**132**	**133**	**134**	**135**	**136**	**137**	**138**	**139**	**140**
C	C	D	B	B	B	B	D	D	A
141	**142**	**143**	**144**	**145**	**146**	**147**	**148**	**149**	**150**
B	A	B	B	D	D	A	A	B	A
151	**152**	**153**	**154**	**155**	**156**	**157**	**158**	**159**	**160**
C	B	A	D	A	D	D	D	A	A
161	**162**	**163**	**164**	**165**	**166**	**167**	**168**	**169**	**170**
A	D	B	D	A	D	B	A	D	D
171	**172**	**173**	**174**	**175**					
B	A	A	C	B					

SOME SELECTED EXPLANATORY ANSWERS

36. 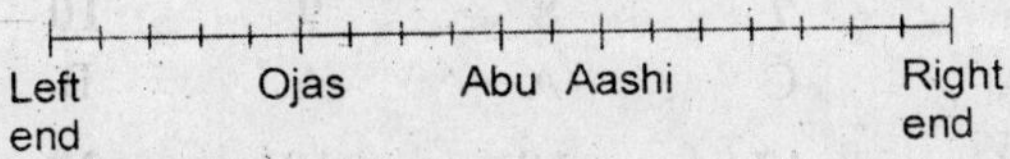

Hence, total number of children = 19.

37. 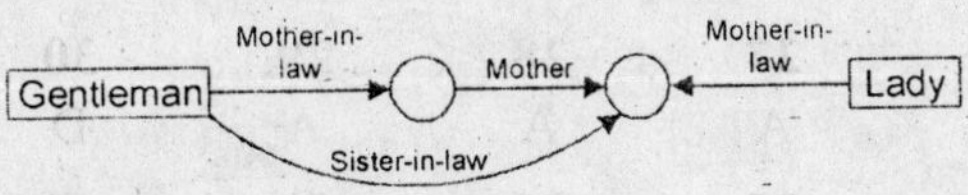

Hence, the lady is daughter-in-law of the gentleman.

38. 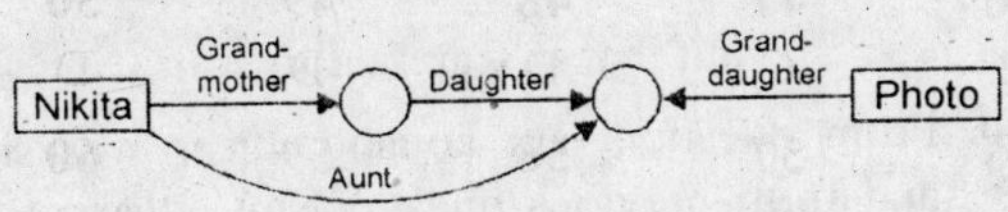

Hence, the girl in the photograph is niece of Nikita.

39. From question,

The required sum = 21 + 9 + 26 + 2 = 58

40. 

Hence, T is cousin of A.

41. 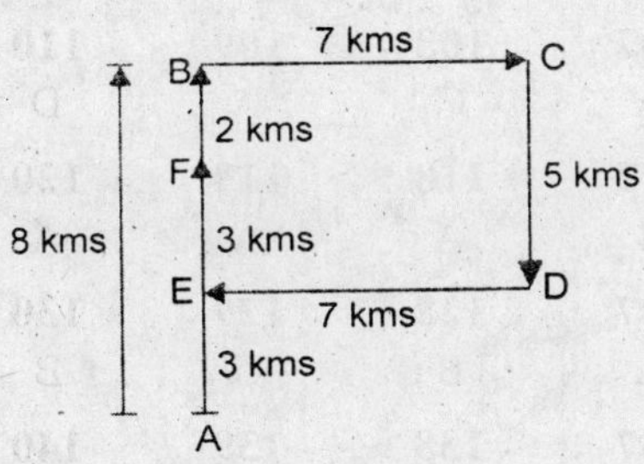

According to the figure,
distance between F and B = 2 kms.

42. 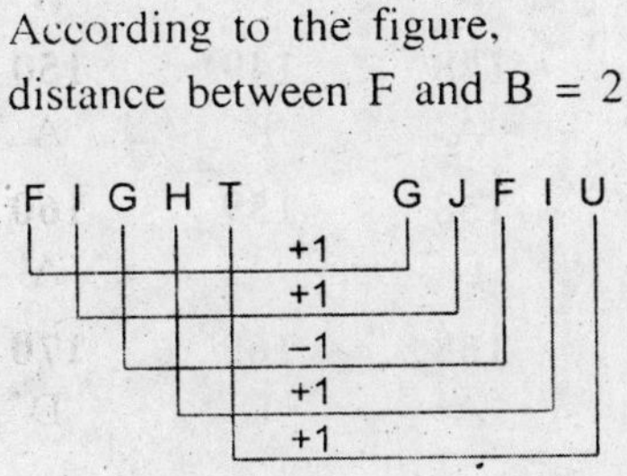

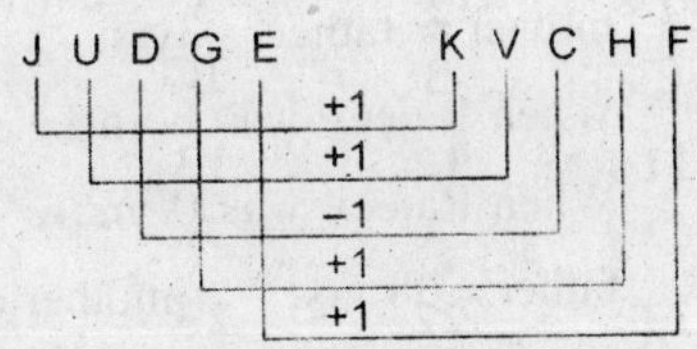

44. 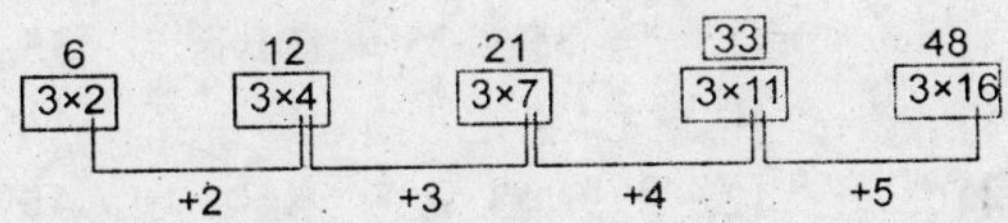

45. 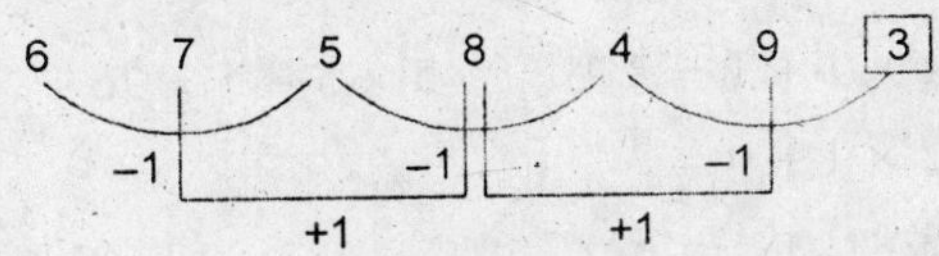

46.

$8 \times 2 - 2 = 14$ $\quad$ $50 \times 2 - 2 = 98$

$14 \times 2 - 2 = 26$ $\quad$ $98 \times 2 - 2 = 194$

$26 \times 2 - 2 = \boxed{50}$ $\quad$ $194 \times 2 - 2 = 386$

Hence, 48 is the wrong term.

47. 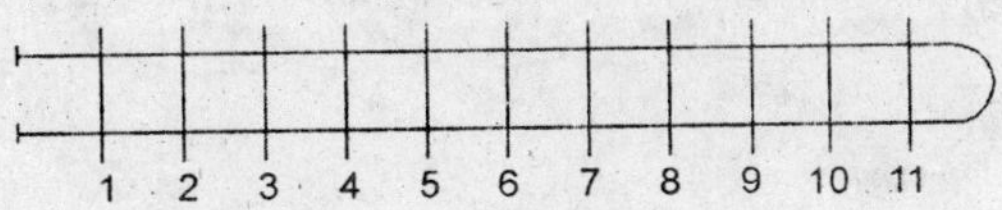

49. 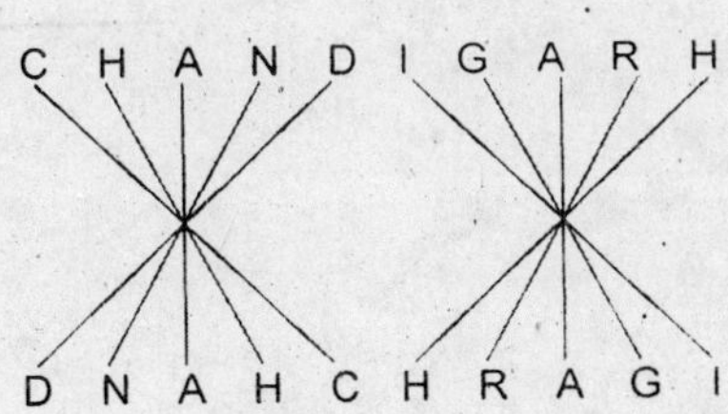

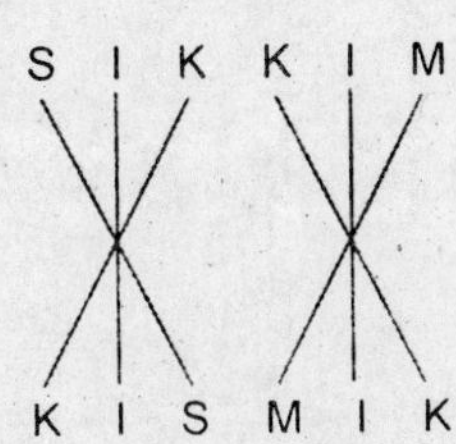

50. From question,

borther = Rajeev + 6 yrs.

father = brother + 32 yrs = Rajeev + 38 **yrs.**

mother = father – 3yrs.

When Rajeev was born i.e.,

When Rajeev was 0 yrs.

father = 38 yrs. $\therefore$ mother = 38 – 3 = 35 **yrs.**

Since, Sister = Mother – 25 yrs.

= 35 – 25 = 10 yrs.

52. A_5 Q R A_4 Q S A_3 Q T A_2 Q U A_1 Q V

53. 1 × 1 + 1 = 2 5 × 5 + 1 = 26

2 × 1 + 0 = 2

2 × 2 + 1 = 5

5 × 1 + 0 = 5

54. 1 8 27 [64]

1^3 2^3 3^3 4^3

55. 34 39 37 38 40 37 [43]

+3 +1 +3 +1 +3

56. 69 58 71 60 [73]

+2 +2 +2

59. [Ing] Tor —— [Bus] factory

igat (ngot) —— has (not)

(ngot) (e) aut —— (not) (a) car

(e) [Ing] —— (a) [bus]

Hence, Bus = Ing, factory = Tar, igat = **has**

ngot = not, a = e car = aut

$\therefore$ aut Tor = Car factory

60. From question, aut boushp = car **workshop** and from previous question aut = car

Hence, boushp = workshop

$\therefore$ Ing boushp = Bus workshop.

64. $D_1E_1F_1$ $D_1E_1F_2$ $D_1E_2F_2$ $D_2E_2F_2$ $D_2E_2F_3$ $D_2E_3F_3$

65. A B C C B A D B E E B D [G B H]

+2 +2

+3 +3

Previous Paper (Solved)

LL.B–ENTRANCE EXAMINATION, 2011

Instructions: *Each correct answer will get 4 marks. Each incorrect answer will incur a penalty of 1 mark. There will be no penalty, if a question is not attempted.*

1. The meaning of which of the following maxims is "where there is a right, there is a remedy"?

A. *ubi jus ibi remedium*
B. *damnum sine injuria*
C. *injuria sine damnum*
D. *ex turpi causa oritur non action*

2. A member of the Indian Parliament or State Legislature cannot be arrested in civil action within a period of .... days before and after the session.

A. 40 B. 45
C. 50 D. 55

3. A finds a watch on the floor of a State Transport bus while leaving it as the last passenger. He picked it up and put it in his pocket, instead of returning it to the State Transport authorities. Next day he sold the watch. *A* is liable for

A. theft
B. extortion
C. criminal misappropriation
D. criminal breach of trust

4. Power to punish for its contempt makes a High Court in India

A. a court of contempt
B. a court of record
C. a court of original jurisdiction
D. a court of appellate jurisdiction

5. LEGAL PRINCIPLE: A person can be benefited under private defence in case of intoxication.

FACTUAL SITUATION: Ram Lal got drunk voluntarily and on his way to home assaulted a policeman.

Which of the following is *correct?*

A. Ram Lal cannot be liable because he was drunk
B. Ram Lal cannot be liable because he gets benefit under private defence
C. Ram Lal can be liable because he got drunk voluntarily
D. None of the above

6. Election Commission of India is a

A. constitutional body
B. political body
C. quasi-judicial and quasi-political body
D. Both A and B

7. Article 32 of the Constitution of India empowers the Supreme Court and Article 226 empowers the High Courts to issue orders, directions and prerogative writs for the enforcement of fundamental rights. This right is known as

A. right to protect rights
B. right to enforce the rights
C. right to constitutional remedies
D. None of the above

8. Article 1 of the Indian Constitution declares India as

A. Unitary State
B. Union of States
C. Federal State
D. Quasi-Federal State

9. The Writ of *Prohibition* and *Certiorari* are available against

A. Legal and Semi-legal authorities
B. Implied authorities
C. Non-statutory authorities
D. Judicial or *quasi*-judicial authorities

10. 'What cannot be done directly cannot be done indirectly.' This statement epitomizes the doctrine of

A. colourable legislation
B. pith and substance
C. implied powers
D. ancillary powers

11. Rights which husband and wife have against each other are called

A. family rights
B. conjugal rights
C. spousal rights
D. matrimonial rights

12. The term 'Fourth Estate' refers to

A. Judiciary
B. Parliament
C. President's Estate
D. Press

13. 'Negligence' means

A. doing an act with the intention to cause harm to others
B. doing an act with forgetfulness
C. not doing an act with the intention to cause harm to others
D. doing an act by failing to take reasonable care

14. Who among the following has been the Chief Justice of India and has acted as the President of India?

A. Justice M. Hidayatullah
B. Justice S.V. Chandrachud
C. Justice P. Shastri
D. Justice P.B. Gajendragadkar

15. In tort, the remedy is

A. liquidated damages
B. unliquidated damages
C. punishment
D. judicial review

Directions (Qs. 16-21): *Read the following passage carefully and answer the questions that follow:*

Mystics in India say that the whole universe is just a sound. That way sound represents the basic energy of the universe. Sounds have a great impact on us and different sounds have different effect on people. Yesterday, walking back from party, I started to cross the street when I heard the sound of a coin dropping. It wasn't much but, as I turned, my eyes caught the heads of several other people turning too. A lady had dropped what appeared to be a one Rupee coin. The tinkling sound of a coin dropping on pavement is a definite attention-getter. Whatever the coin is, no one ignores the sound of it. It got me thinking about sounds again. We are besieged by so many sounds that attract varying degrees of attention. People in Mumbai seldom turn to look when a fire brigade vehicle, a police car or an ambulance comes screaming along the street. Even the loud siren is hardly heard there. It is often ignored. But at home in my village of Dinapur, it's different. The distant howl of a police car, an emergency vehicle or a fire siren brings me to my feet if I'm seated and brings me to the window if I'm in bed. The loudest sounds do not necessarily have the greatest impact on us; rather it's the quietest sounds that attract our attention the most. In the middle of the night, I can hear a dripping tap a hundred yards away through closed doors. I've been hearing little creaking noises and sounds which my imagination turns into footsteps in the middle of the night for thirty years in our house. How come I never heard those sounds in the daytime? I'm quite clear in my mind what the good sounds are and what the bad sounds are. I've turned against whistling, for instance. I used to think of it as the mark of a happy worker but lately I've been associating the whistler with a nervous person making compulsive noises. The gentle sounds of meditation music bring to my mind the patterns of the vast sky and through which I could peep into the ocean of my consciousness.

16. The sound of a coin dropping makes people

A. think of money
B. look at each other
C. pay attention to it
D. stop crossing the street

17. People in Mumbai

A. pay attention to emergency sirens
B. are used to sirens
C. are attracted by sounds
D. don't ignore loud sounds

18. How does the author relate to sounds at night?
A. He imagines sounds that do not exist
B. He exaggerates quiet sounds
C. He thinks taps should be turned off at night
D. He feels it's rather quiet at night

19. The author dislikes the sound of whistling because
A. it makes him sick
B. it makes him sad
C. it reminds him of stressed people
D. he doesn't like workers

20. What kind of sounds does the author find pleasant?
A. Tinkling sound of a coin dropping
B. Clinking sound of keys
C. Tapping of typewriter
D. Sounds of meditation music

21. How does the author feel about sounds in general?
A. They make him feel at home
B. He thinks that sounds are part of our lives
C. He thinks that sounds should be ignored
D. He feels that the entire universe is permeated with sounds.

22. A male Hindu marrying a second wife while the first marriage is subsisting, commits
A. an offence of bigamy
B. no offence
C. no offence if the permission of the first wife was taken in writing
D. no offence if the first wife chooses not to file a case against him

23. The term 'palimony' means
A. alimony from parents
B. maintenance from friends
C. court orders financial settlement amongst people in a live-in relationship
D. maintenance to old parents by children

24. A marriage amongst minors is considered to be legally
A. Invalid B. Void *ab initio*
C. Voidable D. Valid

25. The body of Sathya Sai Baba has been buried in
A. Sai Kulwanth Hall
B. Prem Sai Hall
C. Sai Jaswanth Hall
D. Sai Ram Hall

26. Who among the following has been declared as new Prime Minister of the Tibetan Government-in-exile?
A. Samdhong Rimpoche
B. Lobsang Sangay
C. Dalai Lama
D. Wang Chu

27. Which of the following is *not* protected by Copyright Act?
A. Computer databases
B. Invention
C. Musical work
D. Dramatic work

28. In legal parlance the term *'mens rea'* means
A. main culprit
B. monopolies and restrictive trade practices
C. measure of culpability
D. mental element in crime

29. Who among the following *does not* hold his office at the pleasure of the President?
A. Chairman of the UPSC
B. Speaker of the Lok Sabha
C. Attorney-General for India
D. Comptroller and Auditor-General of India

30. When master is held liable for the wrongful acts of his servant, the liability is called
A. Vicarious liability
B. Strict liability
C. Tortuous liability
D. Absolute liability

31. National Law Day is observed every year on
A. March 1 B. April 30
C. June 16 D. November 26

32. Which of the following States is a permanent member of the Security Council (UN)?
A. France B. Germany
C. Japan D. South Korea

33. A contract to which a minor is a party, is known as

A. Void *ab initio*
B. Voidable at the option of minor
C. Voidable at the option of other party
D. Valid

34. What does the 'Polluter Pays' principle mean?
A. Absolute liability to compensate the victims of pollution
B. Absolute liability to the cost of reversing the damaged ecology
C. Both A and B
D. Both A and B, provided the polluter was negligent and did not take reasonable care.

35. In which of the following cases, the Supreme Court held that Basic Structure of Constitution cannot be changed?
A. Golaknath case
B. Keshavananda Bharati case
C. Minerva Mills case
D. D.K. Basu v. State of West Bengal

36. What does the principle of vicarious liability mean?
A. A person is liable for his act
B. A person is liable for the act of another
C. A person is liable for the act of his master
D. None of the above

37. LEGAL PRINCIPLE: Any act done in the exercise of right of private defence shall not be an offence. The right to private defence in no case extends to the inflicting of more harm than it is necessary to inflict for the purpose of private defence.

FACTUAL SITUATION: Rajan saw a thief jumping the boundary wall and entering his house in the night. He picked up the sword and hid in a corner. The moment the person entered the house, he hit the person with sword and cut his head. Did Rajan commit the offence of killing the thief?

DECISION:
A. Yes, because he exceeded the right of private defence
B. No, he has not committed any offence because he exercised his right of private defence
C. Yes, because the thief should have been given an opportunity to run away from there
D. No, criminals should not be dealt with any leniency

38. LEGAL PRINCIPLE: A person is liable for all the injurious consequences of his careless act.

FACTUAL SITUATION: Ramesh, a snake charmer, was exhibiting his talents to a group of people. One of the snakes escaped and bit a child who had to be hospitalized for two days for treatment.

DECISION:
A. Ramesh is liable to compensate the child's family for his careless act
B. Ramesh is not liable to compensate the child's family because he exercised due care and did not do it wilfully
C. Ramesh is not liable to compensate the child's family because it is the duty of the spectators to take adequate care
D. Ramesh is not liable to compensate the child's family because it was a mere accident

39. LEGAL PRINCIPLE: Contractual liability is completely irrelevant to the existence of liability in tort.

FACTUAL SITUATION: Sudhir purchased a bottle of soft drink from a retailer. As he consumed more than half of the contents of the bottle, he found decomposed remains of a cockroach in the bottle. He vomited and fell sick on the thought of what he has consumed. He sued the manufacturer of soft drink for negligence, though there is no contractual duty on the part of manufacturer.

DECISION:
A. Sudhir cannot sue the retailer as he did not commit any mistake
B. Sudhir cannot sue the manufacturer for negligence as there was no contract between them
C. Sudhir can definitely sue the retailer as it was his duty to check the products before he sells them

D. Sudhir can sue the manufacturer as he had a duty to ensure that bottles did not contain any such material

40. LEGAL PRINCIPLE. An act of God is an operation of natural forces so unexpected that no human foresight or skill could reasonably be expected to anticipate it.

FACTUAL SITUATION: The Surya Club was celebrating its 50th anniversary and arranged for a concert by a leading musical group. The event was to be organized in Great Palace auditorium in the coastal area. All the tickets were sold out. On the day of the event, the tsunami destroyed many of the buildings including the auditorium. People who purchased the tickets asked for refund from the Club as the show could not take place.

DECISION:

A. The management of the Auditorium must refund the cost of tickets as they got money from the Club

B. The Club must refund the cost of tickets as the people were not at fault

C. The Club is not liable to refund the ticket but the ticket holders can demand the show to be organized at a later point of time

D. Neither the management of the Auditorium nor the Club is liable to refund the money

41. LEGAL PRINCIPLE: The occupier of the premises owes a duty of care to all his invitees and visitors.

FACTUAL SITUATION: Gopal was running a dairy from his farm house. People used a part of his farm as a short-cut to get to a nearby railway station. Gopal did not approve of this, and put up a notice that "Trespassers will be prosecuted." However, since a number of these people were also his customers he tolerated them. One day, a person who was using this short-cut was attacked by a bull belonging to the farm. The injured person filed a suit against Gopal.

DECISION:

A. Gopal is liable for having kept a bull on his farm

B. Gopal is not liable in view of the clear notice against trespassers

C. Gopal is liable because in fact he allowed the people to use his premises

D. Gopal is not liable to the people other than his customers

42. LEGAL PRINCIPLE: A person is guilty of culpable homicide amounting to murder if the act by which the death is caused is done with the intention to cause death.

FACTUAL SITUATION: *A* was hiding behind a bush to catch some rabbits. *B* also came to the same place for hunting with his gun. When *B* noticed some movements behind the bush he thought it was an animal and fired a shot due to which *A* was killed. Can *B* be prosecuted for murder?

DECISION:

A. *B* would not be liable for murder because he did not have the intention to kill *A* (but for culpable homicide amounting to murder)

B. *B* shall be liable for murder because he should have taken care to find out the target before shooting

C. *B* shall not be liable for murder because *B* was not expected to identify the target before shooting

D. *B* shall be liable for murder because for whatever reasons *A* was killed

43. LEGAL PRINCIPLE: Law of Contract mandates that two or more people are free to create mutual rights and duties provided such rights and duties are not opposed to public policy.

FACTUAL SITUATION: *A* enters into an agreement with *B* under which *B* undertakes to kill *A* when he is asleep. For this act, *A* deposited ₹ 1 lakh with a bank, which *B* could withdraw once he has performed the aforesaid task. *B* kills *A* according to the terms of the agreement.

DECISION:

A. *B* must get ₹ 1 lakh because he has performed his task

B. *B* must be prosecuted because he has killed *A*

C. *B* must not be prosecuted because *A* has consented to be killed

D. *B* must be prosecuted for killing *A* but he should get ₹ 1 lakh as agreed by *A*

44. LEGAL PRINCIPLE: Every partner in a partnership firm is liable for the acts of every other partner during the course of business of the partnership.

FACTUAL SITUATION: *A*, a partner in the firm XYZ with another partner *B* takes loan from a bank for the partnership firm. *A* misuses the fund for his personal e. *B* is very resourceful person. Can the bank demand the entire money from *B?*

DECISION:

A. No, because *A* has misused the money for his personal use

B. Yes, because both are partners in the same firm

C. No, because *B* has not taken any loan

D. No, because *B* has another partner in his firm.

45. LEGAL PRINCIPLE: Nothing is an offence, which is done by accident or misfortune and without any criminal intention or knowledge in the doing of a lawful act in a lawful manner by lawful means and with proper care and caution.

FACTUAL SITUATION: *A* is a woodcutter. One day when he was at work a number of children flocked to him, and asked him to make a cricket bat for them. Without listening to them he continued to chop woods using a heavy axe. Suddenly a piece of chopped wood flew and struck one child who was standing just two feet away from him as a result of which the child lost his one eye. Is *A* liable for the injury caused to the boy?

A. *A* is liable for causing injury to child

B. *A* is not liable because it was merely an accident

C. *A* is not liable because children flocked to him

D. *A* is liable because he has the knowledge that the boys standing near him may get hurt

46. LEGAL PRINCIPLE: If a person without any authority prevents a person to proceed to any direction and is kept confined, he commits an offence of criminal confinement.

FACTUAL SITUATION: The Municipal Board allowed X to hold a marriage party blocking a part of a public road. The marriage party blocked most of the roads and did not allow *A*, a passerby, to cross the road. He brings a charge of criminal confinement against the head of the marriage party and other associates. Can *A* succeed?

A. *A* cannot succeed because *X* has got previous permission from the Municipal Board and has blocked part of the public road

B. *A* can succeed because he has authority to walk on public road

C. *A* cannot succeed because he must have to wait upto end of marriage party

D. *A* shall succeed because no one is allowed to use public property for the personal benefit

47. Which of the following countries became the first country to allow Euthanasia?

A. The Netherlands

B. United Kingdom

C. Australia

D. United States of America

48. How many Schedules are there in the Constitution of India?

A. 7 B. 8

C. 10 D. 12

49. *A* obtained a sum of ₹ 50,000 by putting *B* in fear of death. Which of the following offences was committed by *A?*

A. Cheating B. Robbery

C. Mischief D. Extortion

50. The United Nations Organization is based on the principle of

A. the solidarity of the members

B. the sovereign equality of the members

C. international peace and good governance of the members

D. economic and social well being of its members

51. Which one of the following taxes is *not* levied by the Union Government?

A. Income-Tax B. Service Tax

C. Wealth Tax D. Value Added Tax

52. Remarks of a judge, which are made casually and are not relevant to the case-in-hand, are known as

A. Obiter dicta

B. Ratio decidendi

C. Precedent

D. Binding source of law

53. A writ issued by Supreme Court against a person who claims or usurps any office to enquire by what authority he supports his claim, is known as

A. *Mandamus* B. *Quo Warranto*

C. *Certiorari* D. *Habeas corpus*

54. The principle that agreements must be respected in good faith, is known as

A. *Pacta dant legem contractri*

B. *Pactum de non petendo*

C. *Raison d'etre*

D. *Pacta sunt servanda*

55. Who among the following can be parties to a case before the International Court of Justice?

A. Individuals and States

B. States and International Organisations

C. Ony States

D. All the above

56. Which of the following organizations regulate the international trade?

A. WTO B. UNO

C. GATT D. UNCTAD

57. The Directive Principles of State Policy are aimed at

A. securing political freedom

B. securing social and economic freedom by appropriate action

C. executive supremacy

D. judicial supremacy

58. Which of the following is known as Commission for Centre-State Relations?

A. Venkatachaliah Commission

B. Mandal Commission

C. Rangarajan Commission

D. Sarkaria Commission

59. Who wrote 'Das Capital'?

A. Karl Marx B. Jawaharlal Nehru

C. Lenin D. R.K. Narayanan

60. Match the following:

List I	***List II***
(a) Theft	(i) A matrimonial remedy
(b) Divorce	(ii) A civil wrong
(c) Defamation	(iii) A civil remedy
(d) Injunction	(iv) An offence under Indian Penal Code

Code:

	(a)	(b)	(c)	(d)
A.	(i)	(ii)	(iii)	(iv)
B.	(iv)	(ii)	(i)	(iii)
C.	(iv)	(i)	(ii)	(iii)
C.	(iii)	(i)	(iv)	(ii)

61. Who among the following was associated with the reservation stir of Gujjars in Rajasthan?

A. Suresh Meena

B. Bhairon Singh Shekhawat

C. Ram Niwas Mirdha

D. Colonel Bainsla

62. Which of the following legislations regulates electronic commerce?

A. Copyright Act, 1957

B. Trade Mark Act, 1999

C. Contract Act, 1872

D. Information Technology Act, 2000

63. Who is *ex-officio* Chairman of Rajya Sabha?

A. President

B. Vice-President

C. Prime Minister

D. Head of Opposition Party in Lok Sabha

64. Which of the following statements is *not* correct?
- A. Preamble of the Constitution is not justiciable
- B. Directive Principles of State Policy are positive obligations of State towards citizens
- C. Fundamental Rights are negative obligations of the State
- D. Fundamental Duties are enforceable

65. Which of the following amendments to the Constitution took away the Right of Property from Fundamental Rights?
- A. 42nd amendment B. 44th amendment
- C. 43rd amendment D. 45th amendment

66. *Lex fori* means
- A. the law of the place
- B. the law of the court in which case is tried
- C. the law of the place where contract is made
- D. None of the above

67. Ignorance of law is
- A. not an excuse in Indian law
- B. an excuse in Indian law
- C. no such principle is followed in Indian law
- D. partly an excuse in Indian law

68. An accused below the age of 18 years can be tried for committing an offence under
- A. Indian Penal Code
- B. Juvenile Justice (Care and Protection of Children) Act, 2000
- C. Being a minor, he cannot be tried
- D. Both A and B

69. Economic justice, an important objective of the Constitution of India is embeded in the
- A. Preamble
- B. Directive Principles of State Policy
- C. Fundamental Rights
- D. Both A and B

70. A political party is officially accorded the status of an opposition party in Lok Sabha only if it secures at least
- A. 4% of the seats B. 5% of the seats
- C. 10% of the seats D. 15% of the seats

71. The Competition Act was passed in the year 2002 to replace
- A. The Monopolies and Restrictive Trade Practices Act, 1969
- B. The Consumer Protection Act, 1986
- C. The Sale of Goods Act, 1930
- D. Unlawful Activities (Prevention) Act, 1967

72. A person is said to be vicariously liable when
- A. he is liable for his wrongful acts
- B. he is not liable even though he committed wrongful acts
- C. he is liable for the wrongful acts of others
- D. he is liable though no wrongful act has been done

73. A Hindu boy wants to marry a Muslim girl. They can solemnize their marriage under the
- A. Special Marriage Act
- B. Hindu Marriage Act
- C. Muslim Law
- D. Any of these

74. The negligence of a medical practitioner resulted in the loss to a patient. The patient wants to seek compensation from the doctor. He can approach
- A. Consumer Disputes Redressal Forum
- B. Civil Court
- C. Criminal Court
- D. Either A or B

75. Sagotra marriage in Hindu Law is
- A. Legal
- B. Illegal
- C. Permitted with the consent of Khap Panchayat
- D. Permitted with the consent of parents

76. When an interest in immovable property is transferred as a security for the payment of debt or performance of a promise it is called
- A. Pledge B. Lease
- C. Mortgage D. Surety

77. Which Article of the Constitution of India provides that Government of India can sue and be sued in the name of 'Union of India'?
- A. Article 32 B. Article 248
- C. Article 299 D. Article 300

78. Slander is of

A. Permanent form B. Transient form
C. Strict form D. None of these

79. Administrative law is concerned with the powers of the

A. President B. Legislature
C. Judiciary D. Executive

80. The doctrine of 'Rule of Law' is based on

A. Equality before the law
B. Equal protection of the laws
C. Positive discrimination
D. Exclusion of discretionary powers

81. On whom lies the burden of proof where there is a plea for self-defence?

A. Accused B. Prosecution
C. Complainant D. State

82. The Delhi High Court's decision in *Naz Foundation* case to decriminalize same gender consensual sex is regarding which section of the Indian Penal Code?

A. Section 375 B. Section 376
C. Section 377 D. Section 378

83. A lawyer appointed by the court to represent the interests of a person unable to hire a lawyer for himself is known as

A. *Forma pauperis* B. *Doli incapax*
C. *Amicus curiae* D. *Furious voluntas*

84. The term *sine a die* means

A. Indefinitely
B. Inadequate
C. Signature by a person on death bed
D. Continuously

85. Where are juvenile delinquents sent?

A. Borstal
B. Asylum
C. Reformative Centre
D. Protective custody

86. A Bill authorizing expenditure by the Government is called

A. Money Bill
B. Finance Bill
C. Appropriation Bill
D. Expenditure Bill

87. Which of the following is *not* an organ of the United Nations?

A. International Court of Justice
B. UNESCO
C. Trusteeship Council
D. Economic and Social Council

88. Who is the present Secretary-General of the United Nations?

A. Javier Perez de Cuellar
B. Kofi Annan
C. Boutros Boutros Ghali
D. Ban Ki Moon

89. From which of the following Lists of the Seventh Schedule of the Constitution, the Parliament derives legislative competence?

A. Only List I
B. From List I and List II
C. From List I, List II and List III
D. From List I and List III

90. In which of the following cases, the Supreme Court laid down guidelines on sexual harassment of working women at work places?

A. D.K. Basu v. State of West Bengal
B. Vishaka v. State of Rajasthan
C. Nilabati Behera v. State of Orissa
D. Both B and C

91. A contract enforceable at the instance of one party is known as

A. Void contract
B. Valid contract
C. Voidable contract
D. Illegal contract

Directions (Qs. 92-102): *Fill in the blank by looking at both the letter pattern and the number pattern.*

92. TCD, UEF, VGH, ..., XKL

A. ZMN B. VJI
C. WIJ D. WIL

93. EZFS, GZHS, IZJS, ..., MZNS

A. OZPS B. KZMS
C. LZMS D. KZLS

94. ABC, ABC_1, AB_1C_1, ...$A_1B_1C_2$

A. $A_1B_1C_1$ B. ABC_2
C. A_2BC_2 D. A_1B_2C

95. $Z_5QR, Z_4QS, Z_3QT, ... Z_1QV$

A. Z_2QW B. Z_2QV_2

C. Z_2QU D. Z_2Q_3U

96. A tree always has ....

A. root B. leave

C. flower D. stem

97. Wonder always has ....

A. amazement B. person

C. beautiful D. sadness

98. A bus always has ....

A. driver B. conductor

C. engine D. petrol

99. 'Frank' is to 'indirect' as 'honest' is to ....

A. candid B. wicked

C. truthful D. untruthful

100. 'Pride' is to 'lion' as 'shoal' is to ....

A. fish B. student

C. lady D. self-esteem

101. 'Mammal' is to 'monkey' as 'flower' is to ....

A. petal B. bud

C. dahlia D. fish

102. 'Marathon' is to 'race' as 'hibernation' is to ....

A. winter B. bear

C. summer D. sleep

103. Which of the following declarations was adopted by the BRIC countries recently to promote Global Food Security?

A. Moscow Declaration

B. Doha Declaration

C. Delhi Declaration

D. Kabul Declaration

104. At present, India is following

A. Fixed exchange rate

B. Floating exchange rate

C. Pegged up exchange rate

D. Pegged down exchange rate

105. "Between the Assassinations" is a book written by

A. Shobha De B. Kiran Desai

C. Chetan Bhagat D. Aravind Adiga

106. Who won the ICC Cricketer of the Year Award of 2010?

A. Sachin Tendulkar

B. Yuvraj Singh

C. MS Dhoni

D. Virender Sehwag

107. Who amongst the following has been described as "the leader other leaders love" by the Newsweek List of 10 Most Respected World Leaders of 2010?

A. Ms. Pratibha Patil

B. Dr. Manmohan Singh

C. Barack Obama

D. Dalai Lama

108. Which of the following match is *not correct?*

A. Julia Gillard — Prime Minister of Australia

B. Dilma Rousseff — President of Brazil

C. Sheikh Hasina — Prime Minister of Bangladesh

D. Liu Xiaobo — President of China

109. Tsunamis are not caused by

A. Hurricanes

B. Earthquakes

C. Undersea landslides

D. Volcanic eruptions

110. Itching due to insect bite is caused by

A. formic acid B. acetic acid

C. lactic acid D. malic acid

111. What is the chemical name of vinegar?

A. Acetic acid B. Citric acid

C. Pyruvic acid D. Malic acid

112. Which of the following plants *cannot* be multiplied by cuttings?

A. Bryophyllum B. Banana

C. Marigold D. Rose

113. Which one of the following is always associated with 'justice'?

A. kindness B. legitimate

C. nobility D. diminutiveness

114. Which of the following diagrams indicates the best relation between Men, Fathers and Doctors?

A. 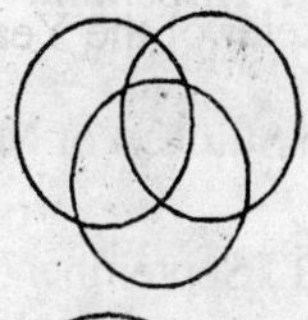 B. 

C.  D. 

115. Which of the following diagrams indicates the best relation between Lawyer, Writer and Actor?

A. 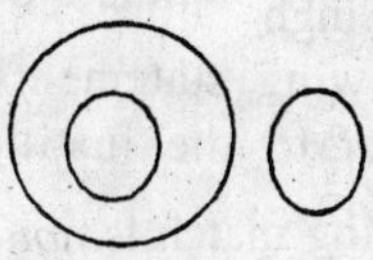 B. 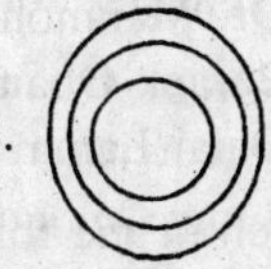

C. 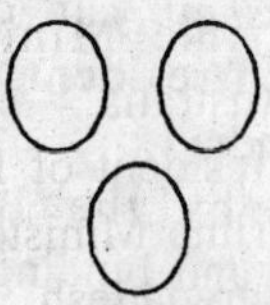 D. 

116. In a certain code REPORT is written as SDONQU, how is PERSON written in that code?

A. QDQRNP B. QDQRNM
C. ODQRNP D. None of these

117. In a certain code "7 8 6" means "study very hard", "9 5 8" means "hard work pays" and "6 4 5" means "study and work", which of the following is the code for "very"?

A. 8
B. 6
C. 7
D. Cannot be determined

118. Parthvi ranked 8th from the top and 37th from the bottom in a class. How many students are there in the class?

A. 47 B. 46
C. 45 D. 44

119. "Furniture" is related to "Table" in the same way as "Stationery" is related to

A. Store B. Chair
C. Office D. Pencil

120. If Nirali's mother is the only daughter of Akhil's mother, how is Akhil related to Nirali?

A. Maternal Uncle B. Father
C. Brother D. Grandfather

121. "Needle" is related to "Thread" in the same way as "Pen" is related to

A. Write B. Ink
C. Cap D. Paper

122. 'Paddy' is related to 'Field' in the same way as 'Steel' is related to

A. Factory B. Iron
C. Ore D. Wagon

123. Tejas said to Anish, "That boy playing cricket is the younger of the two brothers of the daughter of my father's wife." How is the boy playing cricket related to Tejas?

A. The boy is Tejas's brother
B. The boy is Tejas's uncle
C. The boy is Tejas's nephew
D. The boy is Tejas's son

124. If Ram is the brother of Savita; Savita is the sister of Shyam; and Shyam is the father of Laxman, how is Laxman related to Ram?

A. Laxman is Ram's brother
B. Laxman is Ram's nephew
C. Laxman is Ram's uncle
D. Cannot be determined

125. Which of the following diagrams indicates the best relation between Earth, USA and Hawaii?

A.  B. 

C. 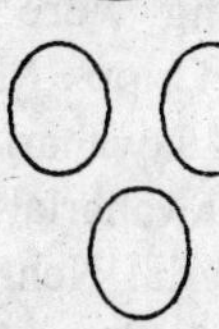 D. 

126. Which of the following diagrams indicates the best relation between Court, Lawyer and Judge?

A.  B. 

C. 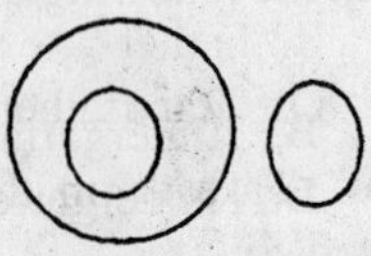 D. 

127. The largest 4 digit number exactly divisible by 88 is

A. 9984 B. 9944
C. 9848 D. 8888

128. Which of the following is a prime number?

A. 33 B. 89
C. 93 D. 15

129. Which of the following numbers is divisible by each one of 3, 7, 9 and 11?

A. 3792 B. 939
C. 37911 D. 2079

130. The difference between the place values of two sevens in the numeral 98734571 is

A. 699930 B. 69930
C. 600003 D. 699990

131. Pointing to a boy playing in the park Shatin said, "He is the son of the only son of my mother." How is Shatin related to that boy?

A. Shatin is the father of the boy
B. Shatin is the cousin of the boy
C. Shatin is the maternal uncle of the boy
D. Shatin is the brother of the boy

132. Which of the following is a proposed Nuclear Power Plant?

A. Narora B. Kaiga
C. Tarapur D. Jaitapur

133. Who among the following were official Congress negotiators with Cripps Mission?

A. Dr. Rajendra Prasad and Jawaharlal Nehru
B. Mahatma Gandhi and Jawaharlal Nehru
C. Sardar Patel and Jawaharlal Nehru
D. Jawaharlal Nehru and Maulana Azad

134. Who amongst the following *did not* go to space?

A. Anousheh Ansari B. Yuri Gagarin
C. Dennis Tito D. Rajender Sharma

135. Which of the following cities is *not* known for nuclear disaster?

A. Fukoshima B. Hiroshima
C. Chernobyl D. Moscow

136. When was Ms. Aung San Suu Kyi of Myanmar released from detention?

A. March 2010 B. September 2010
C. November 2010 D. January 2011

137. Who amongst the following Governor-Generals created the covenanted Civil Service of India which later came to be known as the Indian Civil Service?

A. Cornwallis B. Warren Hastings
C. Wellesley D. William Bentinck

138. Which of the following statements is not correct with respect to the institution of Banking *Ombudsman*?

A. The Banking *Ombudsman* can consider complaints from Non-resident Indians having accounts in India
B. The orders passed by the Banking *Ombudsman* are final and binding on the parties concerned
C. The Banking *Ombudsman* is appointed by the Reserve Bank of India
D. The service provided by the Banking *Ombudsman* is free of any fee

139. The International Development Association, a lending agency, is administered by the

A. International Bank for Reconstruction and Development
B. International Monetary Fund
C. United Nations Development Programme
D. United Nations Industrial Development Organization

Directions (Qs. 140-145): *In the following questions a word is given followed by four options. Pick the word having the opposite meaning to the given word.*

140. Depart

A. Hover B. Nebulous
C. Hirsute D. Neophyte

141. Valley

A. Hibernal B. Niggardly
C. Hypocritical D. Hummock

142. Prodigal
A. Hibernal B. Husbandry
C. Hyperbole D. Hortatory

143. Interesting
A. Intrepid B. Inundate
C. Inured D. Irksome

144. Applicable
A. Irrelevant B. Deleterious
C. Irreparable D. Inundate

145. Drain
A. Intransigent B. Inundate
C. Defile D. Defalcate

Directions (Qs. 146-150): *In the following questions, an idiomatic expression has been used, followed by some alternatives. Choose the one which best expresses its meaning.*

146. Pinky aced her English test.
A. Pinky fell dizzy during her English test
B. Pinky did very well in the English test
C. Pinky failed in the English test
D. Pinky was just average in her English test

147. I am feeling a bit under the weather.
A. I am walking in bad weather
B. I am walking in rain
C. I am walking under clouds
D. I am feeling a bit ill and lack energy

148. Vikram is a good egg.
A. Vikram is a person who could be relied on
B. Vikram is the name of a chicken
C. Vikram is smart and handsome
D. Vikram belongs to a noble family

149. John Doe refers to
A. An unidentified male
B. The famous sportsman John Doe
C. The legendary hero who fought in battles along with Robin Hood
D. A stupid person who can't understand jokes

150. To be tight fisted means
A. To keep your fist in your pocket
B. To be always ready to pick up a fight
C. To be frugal and not spend money
D. To argue fervently

Directions (Qs. 151-156): *In the following questions identify the correct word.*

151. A. Kindergarden B. Kintergartan
C. Kindergartan D. Kindergarten

152. A. Acommodation B. Accommodation
C. Accomodation D. Acomodation

153. A. Questionaire B. Questionneire
C. Questionnaire D. Questionnair

154. A. Massacre B. Masacre
C. Massecre D. Massacar

155. A. Embarrass B. Embarras
C. Embbarras D. Embarraas

156. A. Coincidence B. Coinsidence
C. Coninsidense D. Coincedence

Directions (Qs. 157-159): *Identify the pair that is closest in relationship to the given pair.*

157. Thunder: Storm ::
A. Portent : Catastrophe
B. Hurricane : Cyclone
C. Tornado : Gale
D. Earthquake : Convulsion

158. Embezzle : Trust ::
A. Admonish : Caution
B. Adjudge : Belief
C. Perjure : Oath
D. Adulterate : Faith

159. Kiln : Bricks ::
A. Silo : Crops B. Factory : Tiles
C. Furnace : Metals D. Oven : Cakes

Directions (Qs. 160-164): *Fill in the blanks with the words from the choices given below.*

160. My friend doesn't speak Sanskrit very well. I don't ....
A. neither B. either
C. also D. too

161. What............ in Delhi yesterday?
A. were you doing
B. did you do
C. you did
D. did you

162. ...., 'Tintin' appeals to many adult readers, too.

A. Though it is written for children
B. Though for children written
C. Though written for children
D. Though it were written for children

163. Exceeding speed limit and .... safety belts are two common causes of automobile deaths.
A. not to wear
B. don't wear
C. not having worn
D. failing to wear

164. She asked me how big................
A. is your apartment
B. my apartment was
C. was my apartment
D. is my apartment

Directions (Qs. 165-170): *In the following questions a group of words is given. Out of the group identify the one which doesn't match with the character of the group.*

165. A. Rogue B. Mendicant
C. Hooligan D. Vagabond

166. A. Communism B. Totalitarianism
C. Bolshevism D. Hedonism

167. A. Augment B. Auguration
C. Hunch D. Apprehension

168. A. Meander B. Deviate
C. Bend D. Seer

169. A. Confession B. Perjury
C. Deception D. Deceitfulness

170. A. illicit B. illusive
C. Adulterous D. Felonious

171. Who amongst the following is not a poet?
A. M. Zahur Khayyam
B. John Milton
C. Virgil
D. John Keats

172. In India, which of the following is regulated by the Forward Markets Commission?
A. Equity Futures Trading
B. Currency Futures Trading
C. Commodities Futures Trading
D. Commodities Futures and Financial Futures Trading

173. The reason for red soil is
A. abundance of magnesium
B. accumulated humus
C. presence of ferric oxides
D. abundance of phosphates

174. What causes wind to deflect toward left in the Southern Hemisphere?
A. Temperature
B. Pressure
C. Magnetic field
D. Rotation of the Earth

175. Which of the following is *not* a feature of Limited Liability Partnership firm?
A. It is corporate body with perpetual succession
B. Partners should be less than 20
C. Internal governance may be decided by mutual agreement among partners
D. Partnership and management need not be separate

ANSWERS

1	2	3	4	5	6	7	8	9	10
A	A	C	B	C	A	C	B	D	A
11	12	13	14	15	16	17	18	19	20
B	D	D	A	B	C	B	B	C	D
21	22	23	24	25	26	27	28	29	30
B	A	C	B	A	B	B	D	B	A
31	32	33	34	35	36	37	38	39	40
A	A	A	C	B	B	A	A	D	C

41	42	43	44	45	46	47	48	49	50
B	A	B	B	D	A	A	D	D	B
51	52	53	54	55	56	57	58	59	60
D	A	B	D	C	A	B	D	A	C
61	62	63	64	65	66	67	68	69	70
D	D	B	D	B	B	A	D	D	C
71	72	73	74	75	76	77	78	79	80
A	C	A	A	A	A	D	B	D	D
81	82	83	84	85	86	87	88	89	90
A	C	C	A	C	C	B	D	D	B
91	92	93	94	95	96	97	98	99	100
C	C	D	A	C	D	A	C	B	A
101	102	103	104	105	106	107	108	109	110
C	D	A	B	D	A	B	D	A	A
111	112	113	114	115	116	117	118	119	120
A	B	B	B	C	D	C	D	D	A
121	122	123	124	125	126	127	128	129	130
B	A	A	B	A	D	B	B	D	A
131	132	133	134	135	136	137	138	139	140
A	D	D	D	D	C	C	B	A	D
141	142	143	144	145	146	147	148	149	150
D	B	D	A	B	B	D	A	A	C
151	152	153	154	155	156	157	158	159	160
D	B	C	A	A	A	A	D	D	B
161	162	163	164	165	166	167	168	169	170
A	A	D	C	B	D	A	D	A	B
171	172	173	174	175					
A	C	C	D	B					

~~~~~~~~
~~~~~~~~

Previous Paper (Solved)

LL.B.–Entrance Exam, 2010

1. Safdar Hashmi was associated with:
A. Painting B. Journalism
C. Street theatre D. Higher education

2. Which country is estimated to have the third largest population in the world?
A. Pakistan
B. Bangladesh
C. Indonesia
D. United States of America

3. In which sport is a 'sand-iron' used?
A. Hockey B. Wrestling
C. Golf D. Beach Volleyball

4. The Abel Prize is awarded in the field of:
A. Biology B. Economics
C. Geography D. Mathematics

5. Which of the following aircraft's primary role is very high-altitude reconnaissance?
A. Lockheed U-2 B. F-117 Nighthawk
C. F-22 Raptor D. F-35 Lightning II

6. The Census of India, 2011, commenced on, the 1st April 2010 is:
A. 30th B. 25th
C. 20th D. 15th

7. Which music band recently won a court battle against EMI that may force the latter to stop selling the band's individual songs as downloads?
A. Queen B. Abba
C. Pink Floyd D. Guns & Roses

8. How many public sector enterprises have been conferred the status of Navratna by the Government of India, as of November, 2009?
A. Nine B. Twelve
C. Twenty Seven D. Eighteen

9. Which of the following awards is focused towards television?
A. Academy Awards
B. Emmy Awards
C. Golden Globe Awards
D. Grammy Awards

10. In which movie did Toby Stephens play the role of Captain William Gordon?
A. The Rising-Mangal Pandey
B. Rang De Basanti
C. Veer
D. Shatranj Ke Khiladi

11. Who wrote the poem, Gunga Din?
A. Rabindra Nath Tagore
B. T.S. Eliot
C. Rudyard Kipling
D. Mulk Raj Anand

12. What was the name of the rocket powered aircraft which completed first privately funded human spaceflight?
A. X-15
B. Space Ship One
C. Space Ship Alpha
D. Space Odyssey One

13. Which Indian scientist's article was translated to German by Albert Einstein and submitted on his behalf to the Zeitschrift fur Physik?
A. Satyendra Nath Bose
B. Homi Jehangir Bhabha
C. Jagdish Chandra Bose
D. Vikram Sarabhai

14. What is the main activity of the 'Institute for Works of Religion' at Vatican City?
A. Restoring old religious relics
B. Banking
C. Spreading religious information
D. Religious education

15. Who was referred to as the 'Godfather of World Music' by the Beatles guitarist George Harrison?
A. Ustad Amjad Ali Khan
B. Ustad Ghulam Ali Khan
C. Pandit Kumar Gandharava
D. Pandit Ravi Shankar

16. Which is the only United States' Naval Base that is located in a country with which the United States has no diplomatic relations?
A. Guantanamo Bay Naval Base
B. U.S. Fleet Activities Yokosuka
C. Naval Air Station Sigonella
D. Naval Station Rota

17. Which state is known as the Spice Garden of India?
A. Jammu & Kashmir
B. Punjab
C. Kerala
D. Uttar Pradesh

18. The mascot adopted in a campaign to raise civic awareness in Delhi, in the run up to the 2010 Commonwealth games has been named:
A. Delhi Ki Beti B. Shera
C. Delhi Ki Shaan D. None of these

19. Which annual fair in Rajasthan is famous for its camel trading?
A. Surajkund Mela B. Kumba Mela
C. Urs D. Pushkar Mela

20. Which city was described by Jawahar Lal Nehru as the 'Oxford of the East'?
A. Colombo B. Shanghai
C. Pune D. Banaras

21. Chilli pepper and tobacco were introduced in India by the
A. Portuguese B. British
C. Spanish D. French

22. Which of the following countries is to host the 2011 World Robot Olympiad?
A. China
B. United States of America
C. Israel
D. United Arab Emirates

23. 'Durand Line' is the boder separating:
A. India and Pakistan
B. Pakistan and Afghanistan
C. Pakistan and Nepal
D. India and Nepal

24. Which country is known as the 'Land of Cakes'?
A. England B. Belgium
C. Scotland D. France

25. Who, along with Shane Bond, was the highest bid player in the auction leading to 2010 edition of the Indian Premier League cricket tournament?
A. Kieron Pollard B. Kevin Pietersen
C. Sachin Tendulkar D. Wayne Parnell

26. Aspirin is a common name for:
A. Propanolol
B. Acetylsalicylic Acid
C. Neomycin Sulfate
D. A combination of all the above

27. Who is the Chief Justice of India?
A. Justice K.G. Balakrishnan
B. Justice Altamas Kabir
C. Justice P. Sathasivam
D. Justice S.H. Kapadia

28. According to latest surveys, the population of tigers in India has been reported to have dwindled to approximately:
A. 3642 B. 1411
C. 1165 D. 1657

29. Which Taliban leader, implicated in the assassination of Benazir Bhutto, was reportedly killed in a 2009 strike by a United States' Predator drone?
A. Baitullah Mehsud
B. Omar Saeed Sheikh
C. Wali-ur-Rehman
D. Mullah Mohammed Omar

30. Who is the present Union Minister for Human Resource Development?
A. Dr. Veerappa Moilly
B. Shri Kapil Sibal
C. Shri Arjun Singh
D. Dr. M.M. Joshi

31. Who was awarded the 19th Saraswati Samman for 2009?
A. Vijay Tendulkar
B. Amitabh Bacchan
C. Sunil Gangopadhyay
D. Surjit Patar

32. Who is the Chairman of the Bar Council of India?
A. Shri Gopal Subramaniam
B. Shri Ram Jethmalani
C. Shri P.P. Rao
D. Shri N.R. Madhava Menon

33. In March, 2010, a city/town declared spitting of Paan (Betal leaf) as illegal, inviting fine for criminal damage. Where is this city located?
A. Uttar Pradesh B. Maharashtra
C. Ottawa D. London

34. The Delhi Technological University was formerly known as the:
A. I.I.T., Delhi
B. Aryabhat Polytechnic, Delhi
C. Delhi College of Engineering
D. Indraprastha University

35. The Gulf separating Finland and Sweden is known as the:
A. Gulf of Bothnia B. Gulf of Lions
C. Gulf of Genoa D. Gulf of Venice

36. Groundwater confined between two impermeable layers is called:
A. Artesian well B. Artesian
C. Trapper water D. Artisan

37. Which of the following is a country located in the continent of Europe?
A. Libya B. Venezuela
C. Algeria D. Albania

38. Which is the oldest mountain range in India?
A. Satpura B. Aravali
C. Vindhya D. Himalaya

39. Nephrons are a part of human:
A. Nervous System
B. Respiratory System
C. Excretory System
D. Endocrine System

40. Which of the following is incorrect about BT Brinjal developed by Monsanto and Mahyco?
A. It requires more fertilizer than ordinary Brinjal plant.
B. It is a transgenic variety of Brinjal.
C. It contains genes from the soil bacterium Bacillus thuringiensis.
D. It is claimed to have higher resistance against pests.

41. In a eukaryotic cell, DNA may be stored in:
A. Nucleus B. Mitochondria
C. Chloroplast D. All of the above

42. Which car maker announced the recall of nearly 100,000 units of its recently launched hatchback models citing fuel tank problems?
A. Maruti Suzuki India Ltd.
B. Hyundai Motors India Ltd.
C. General Motors Corporation
D. Chevrolet

43. The body of a shark has no:
A. Gills B. Liver
C. Bones D. Fins

44. Who is associated with the remark, "the law, in its majestic equality, forbids rich and poor alike to sleep under bridges, to beg in the streets, and to steal their bread"?
A. Anatole France B. Glanville Williams
C. Charles Dickens D. Victor Hugo

45. Which Bill, reportedly laying down a code of conduct for judges of the higher judiciary was referred to a Group of Ministers for scrutiny in March, 2010?
A. The Supreme Court (Number of Judges) Amendment Bill
B. Judges (Inquiry) Bill
C. Judges (Declaration of Assets and Liabilities) Bill
D. Judicial Standards and Accountability Bill

46. An observer in a leading national daily remarked on the passage of Women's Reservaton Bill through Rajya Sabha as bipartisan consensus and an extraordinary act of political selflessness whereby a particular party put the interests of the nation above its own. In terms of numbers, how many members voted in favour and against the Bill, respectively?

A. 245 to None
B. 186 to 1
C. 232 to 1
D. The entire strength of 233 members voted in favour

47. Interpreting Articles 72 and 161 of the Constitution of India in relation to a criminal statute, a Bench of the Supreme Court of India had, in a judgement dated 22.03.2010, held that:

A. The clemency power of the Executive is absolute, remains unfettered and cannot be restricted by the provision of a Statute.
B. Section 377 of the Indian Penal Code, insofar as it criminalizes consensual sexual acts of adults in private is violative of the Constitution of India.
C. Once possession is established, the person who claims that it was not a conscious possession has to establish it.
D. Both (A) and (C)

48. In India, making a direct marketing telephone call, which a person has opted not to receive, is prohibited under:

A. Unsolicited Direct Marketing Act
B. Unsolicited Communications Regulations
C. Telecom Unsolicited Commercial Communications Regulations
D. Telecom Unsolicited Commercial Calls Regulations

49. Under the Indian Penal Code, an act may be an offence under the Code, but for the existence of a justification which may form a defence. Which of the following is not such a defence?

A. Act done by a child under seven years of age
B. Act done by a person of unsound mind
C. Act done by a child of immature understanding, above seven years and under twelve in age.
D. Act done outside the territorial limits of India.

50. The Penal Code in force in the territory of Jammu & Kashmir is known as the:

A. Indian Penal Code
B. Macaulay Penal Code
C. Ranbir Penal Code
D. Jammu & Kashmir Penal Code

51. Which one of the following measures was proposed in December,. 2009 for speedy resolution of commercial disputes valuing Rs. five crores and above, by an Act of Parliament?

A. Setting up Commercial Lok Adalats
B. Creation of a commercial division in the High Courts
C. Mandatory reference to arbitration, where commercial contract contains an arbitration clause
D. All of the above

52. A judgement relating to the Protection of Women against Domestic Violence Act, 2005, delivered on 22nd March 2010 by the High Court of Delhi has held that:

A. The Act operates prospectively
B. The Act operates retrospectively
C. The relief under this Act may be sought even for acts committed prior to October, 2006
D. Both (B) and (C)

53. Which of the following is a well known law firm in India?

A. AZB & Partners
B. TATA Consultancy
C. Leo Burnett India Pvt. Ltd.
D. Goldman Sachs Group, Inc.

54. Which of the following describes most closely the act of downloading Bollywood film songs for free, from websites over the internet?

A. Attempt to hack a computer system
B. Exercise of freedom of speech and expression
C. Breach of implied contract
D. Violation of intellectual property rights

55. Which of the following is not a feature of the criminal justice system in India?
A. Innocent until proven guilty
B. Right against self-incrimination
C. Preponderance of probability
D. Proof beyond reasonable doubt

56. Which High Court exercised jurisdiction over Delhi, prior to the establishment of the High Court of Delhi?
A. High Court of Gujarat
B. High Court of Punjab
C. High Court of Allahabad
D. High Court of Himachal Pradesh

57. Which of the following bodies was instrumental in setting up permanent and continuous Lok Adalat in Delhi, to resolve disputes pertaining to bodies such as the M.C.D., N.D.M.C., B.S.E.S., N.D.P.L., M.T.N.L., etc.?
A. Delhi Legal Services Authority
B. Bar Council of India
C. Bar Association of Delhi
D. Indian Council of Arbitration

58. Under which provision of the Code of Criminal Procedure may a Court make a proclamation requiring a person to appear at a specified place, if the Court has a reason to believe that the person has absconded?
A. Section 40 B. Section 42
C. Section 73 D. Section 82

59. Any proceedings for removal of a judge of any High Court in India may be initiated only by:
A. an order of the President of India
B. a notice of motion for presenting an address to the President, praying for the removal of a Judge, signed by requisite number of members of the Parliament
C. address by each house of the Parliament, supported by the requisite number of Members of Parliament
D. constitution of a Committee for the purpose of making an investigation into the grounds on which the removal of the Judge is prayed for.

60. In a recent case involving Toyota and Prius Auto Industries, Toyota was seeking an interim order to restrain Prius Auto Industries from using the word Prius, claiming its exclusive right to use it in view of its car named Prius. While denying this relief, a single Judge of the High Court of Delhi, by a judgement delivered on 19.03.2010, held that:
A. Prius was not an invented word
B. Toyota had approached the court too late
C. Prius Auto Industries was the registered owner of the trademark 'Prius', since 2002.
D. All of the above

61. In India, "identity theft" has been made punishable under the:
A. Indentity Theft Assumption and Deterrence Act
B. Information Technology Act
C. Indian Penal Code
D. Prize Chits and Money Circulation Schemes (Banning) Act

62. Which of the following enactments is proposed to ensure supply of the least a minimum quantity of food grains to families living Below Poverty Line (BPL) in India?
A. Food Safety Enhancement Act
B. Food Safety Act
C. Essential Services Maintenance Act
D. National food Security Act

63. In a Civil Writ Petition, a 'stay' may refer to:
A. A court order restraining an action until a future event occurs, or the order is revoked/modified
B. A court order directing an individual to remain present during the court proceedings
C. A court order to compel the presence of a witness at a specified place, if the court has a reason to believe that the person has absconded
D. Both (A) and (B)

64. Which of the following developments is associated with a March, 2010 judgement of the High Court of Delhi, relating to the role of women in the Indian armed forces?

A. Opportunities to women officers to operate in combat areas
B. Eligibility of women officers for Permanent Commission
C. Reservation for women in Indian armed forces
D. Both (A) and (B)

65. In criminal proceedings, acquittal refers to:
A. Being cleared of a charge or accusation
B. Pronounced guilty of a charge or accusation
C. Conviction for a lesser offence, as part of a plea bargain
D. Taking a lenient view, considering the honest past record of an accused

66. The legal branch of the Indian Army is known as:
A. Army Legal Corps
B. Judge Advocate General Branch
C. Court Martial Branch
D. Armed Forces Legal Corps

67. A clause in the World Anti-Doping Code, which was reportedly a cause of concern for Indian cricketers, is popularly referred to as:
A. Endorsements Clause
B. Roundabout Clause
C. Whereabouts Clause
D. No-notice Drugs Test Clause

68. To provide affordable access to justice to the citizens of India at the grass roots level, at their doorsteps, a body was established by an Act of the Parliament that came into force on 2nd October 2009. What this statutory body is called?
A. Nyaya Panchayat B. Gram Nyayalaya
C. Gram Panchayat D. Lok Adalat

69. The Right of Children to Free and Compulsory Education Bill was enacted to give effect to:
A. Article 14 of the Constitution of India
B. Article 45 of the Constitution of India
C. Article 21A of the Constitution of India
D. Article 21 of the Constitution of India

70. What is the closest meaning of the expression, 'ex aquo et bono'?
A. In equity and good conscience
B. For the public good
C. The thing speaks for itself
D. In good faith

71. Consider the following statement: "Reading is an activity involving the use of visual apparatus by means of which printed letters are recognized". This definition would be weakened most by pointing out that:
A. 'Skimming' is a form of reading.
B. An illiterate may recognize letters.
C. Some printed letters are difficult to interpret.
D. Seeing is necessary for reading.

72. History abounds with examples where chieftains have refused to transfer their military units to other chieftains who requested such transfer. The refusals occurred even when the chieftain who received the request for assistance was in a relatively safe place and even when the requesting chieftain's clan was under attack. Each of the reasons below, if true, supports the decision of the chieftain who refuses to share his forces, except one. Mark the one.
A. Greatest chieftains have emerged as victors in battles where they were outnumbered by the enemy.
B. War and peace are unpredictable and situations may change in a short time.
C. The chieftain with a larger army retains greater influence in the region.
D. Armies on the move are unnecessarily exposed to danger.

73. Which of the following is an anagram for the word "dormitory"?
A. Hostel B. Dirty Room
C. Dorm D. My Door

74. You are a qualified lawyer. A husband approaches you, seeking your professional services, for divorce proceedings. Ideally, what should you do?
A. Explain the difficulties involved in the proceedings for divorce.
B. Advise him to convince his wife for a mutual, uncontested divorce.

C. Refuse to be engaged in the case, since it is against professional conduct of a lawyer set by the Bar Council of India.

D. Advise him to approach for conciliation proceedings.

75. F.I.R. stands for First Information Report. As per the High Court of Delhi, if at the time of registration of F.I.R. by the police, it appears that crime was committed outside the jurisdiction of that Police Station, the Police after registration of such F.I.R. should transfer the F.I.R. to the Police Station having jurisdiction. Such F.I.R. made at the first instance has been termed as:

A. Preliminary F.I.R.
B. Zero F.I.R.
C. Daily Diary (D.D.) Numbe
D. Investigatory F.I.R.

76. A student of the University of Delhi has to pass in __________ Papers with at least __________ in each paper for the award of LL.B. Degree:

A. 30, 45 B. 25, 40
C. 32, 48 D. 35, 50

77. Point out the correct sentence:

A. Before joining as a lecturer, I used to work as a Lab Assistant for about five years.
B. Before joining as a Lecturer, I have working as a Lab Assistant for about five years.
C. Before joining as a lecturer, I worked as a Lab Assistant for about five years.
D. Before joining as a Lecturer, I have been working as a Lab Assistant for about five years.

78. Read the following sentences carefully:

(a) Most days my father _________ get up first and make breakfast.
(b) When I was training for the marathon, I ________ run over 100 kms. a week.
(c) We went to Agra to see the Taj where we ________ regularly.

Which one of the following verbs can complete all three sentences?

A. will B. would
C. shall D. used to

79. Fill in the blank with correct option : I ______ at 6 a.m. but _____ to be up by 5.00.

A. normally get up ...... I have some times
B. normally get up ...... sometimes have
C. get normally up ...... sometimes I have
D. get normally up ..... I sometimes have

80. __________ people trying to get into the football stadium.

A. There were too much
B. It was too many
C. There was too many
D. There were too many

81. PRINCIPLE: Justice must not only be done, but also be seem to be done.

FACTS: A judge is a shareholder in a Company, which is a party to a case before him. The integrity of the judge is above suspicion. Both the opposing counsels affirm their faith in the impartiality of the judge. The case is at the stage of final arguments. The judge, however, recuses himself from the case, on the ground of his shareholding. Which of the following is the most appropriate statement in the light of the Principle cited here?

A. The judge should have continued hearing the case since he was an honest judge.
B. The judge should have continued hearing since the counsels of both the parties had requested him to do so and, had thus agreed to adjudication by him.
C. Had the judge continued to hear the case, its outcome might have appeared to be prejudiced, even though it would not have been so.
D. The judge could have lost objectivity in the case and therefore recused from it.

82. 'M' was driving his fancy sports car at the speed of 120 kmph, after consuming alcohol. He lost control of the car and ran over 3 persons leading to their death. 'M' escaped the accident with injuries. What offence, if any, has 'M' committed under the Indian Penal Code?

A. 'M' is not guilty of any offence since he was incapable of judgment by reason of intoxication caused against his will.
B. 'M' is guilty of causing death by doing a rash or negligent act.
C. 'M' has committed the offence of culpable homicide since he caused ealth by doing an act with the intention of causing such bodily injury as is likely to cause death,
D. 'M' is guilty of committing murder since he did an act by which the death was caused and which was done with the intention of causing death.

83. PRINCIPLE: The word 'offence' denotes a thing made punishable by the Indian Penal Code. 'A' prevents 'B' from proceeding in any direction and keeps him/her confined to a place. 'A' has committed an offence of criminal confinement. According to the Indian Penal Code, whoever instigates a person to do a thing, is said to abet such a thing.

FACTS: 'L', in an interview to a magazine, articulated her views in favour of living together without a nuptial knot. aggrieved by the same, 'X' filed a criminal complaint against 'L', for abetting criminal confinement. Can 'L' be prosecuted and convicted for the same?

A. Yes, because the comments of 'L' could have encouraged people to live together without entering into a nupital bond.
B. Yes, because the comments of 'L' in fact encouraged certain individuals to live together without entering into a nupital bond.
C. No, because two adult people wanting to live together is not an offence.
D. No, because the comments of 'L' were not directed towards any particular person, and anybody acting on them, did so at his/her own risk.

84. On 1st April, 2010, 'P' and 'Q', friends of 'X', decided to pull a prank on her. They wore black masks to cover their faces and proceeded in an un-numbered car, towards the road that 'X' tood her regular morning walk. As 'X' was taking her morning walk, they brought the car to a halt next to her and proceeded to forcefully get her in it. 'A' bystander, 'Y', watching this, opened fire on 'P' and 'Q' with his licensed gun and cuased grievous injuries to them.

A. 'Y' is guilty of causing grievous hurt as he had no right to intermeddle in the private affairs of the friends and he was neither a public authority nor a police official.
B. 'Y' is not guilty of any offence because he had a right to protect the body of any other person, besides his own.
C. 'Y' is not guilty of any offence because he had a reasonable apprehension that 'X' was being assaulted with an intention of abduction.
D. Both (B) and (C)

85. PRINCIPLE I : According to Section 494 of the Indian Penal Code, whoever, having a husband or wife living, marries in any case in which such marriage is void by reason of its taking place during the life of such husband or wife, shall be punished with imprisonment of either description for a term which may extend to seven years, and shall also be liable to fine.

PRINCIPLE II : Hindu law, as contained in the Hindu Marriage Act, enforces monogramy. Polygamy is permitted under the Muslim Law.

Facts: Jitendar, a Hindu, was married to Meen, also a Hindu. Jitender and Sunita, another Hindu girl, converted to Islam and got married.

QUESTION: Is jitender guilty of the offence under Section 494 of the Indian Penal code?

A. No, becasue Jitender converted to Islam which permits more than one wife.
B. No, because Jitendar and Sunita convertded to Islam and married, with mutual consent.

C. Yes, because Jitendar had a wife living. He married again. The said marriage was void by reason of its taking place during the life of the first wife, in terms of Section 494, IPC.
D. Both (A) and (B)

86. In which city is Khuda Baksh Oriental Public Library situated?
A. Delhi B. Kolkata
C. Lucknow D. Patna

87. Kuchipudi is a dance form owing its origin to:
A. Kerala B. Andhra Pradesh
C. Orissa D. Tamil Nadu

88. When was the National Anthem of India first sung?
A. 25th December, 1909
B. 26th December, 1910
C. 27th December 1911
D. 28th December 1912

89. The first woman President of India hails from which city of India?
A. Jalna B. Jalgaon
C. Amravati D. Sangli

90. The rank of Colonel in the Indian Army is equivalent to which rank in the Indian Navy?
A. Captain B. Commodore
C. Commander D. Lieutenant

91. In which city is the headquarter of Zoological Survey of India situated?
A. Delhi B. Thiruvanantpuram
C. Kolkata D. Guwahati

92. Mount Harriat National Park is located in:
A. Andaman Nicobar Islands
B. Madhya Pradesh
C. Andhra Pradesh
D. Arunachal Pradesh

93. Who is the present Prime Minister of Malaysia?
A. Mohamed Nasheed
B. Ahmadinejad
C. Najib Rajak
D. Saad Hariri

94. Which of the folloiwng is the National aquatic animal of India?
A. Ganges crocodile
B. River dolphin
C. Blue whale
D. Olive Ridley turtle

95. Which team won the Sultan Azlan Shah Cup in 2009 held in Kuala Lumpur?
A. Pakistan B. New Zealand
C. India D. Australia

96. Which of the following is the capital of Croatia?
A. Zagreb B. Nicosia
C. Nuuk D. Roseau

97. Point out the incorrect match:
A. Mary Kom — Rajiv Gandhi Khel Ratna Award
B. Sinimol Paulose — Arjuna Award
C. P. Gopichand — Dronacharya Award
D. Jaydev Bisht — Dhyan Chand Award

98. Mark the correct pair:
A. Yamo wind — Uganda
B. Zonda wind — Japan
C. Austru wind — Austria
D. Laventer wind — Canada

99. Who wrote the Seva Sadan?
A. Rabindra Nath Tagore
B. Munshi Premchand
C. Rama Krishna Paramhansa
D. Sister Nivedita

100. Match the correct pair :
A. Syphilis — Treponema pallidum
B. Chancroid — Orthomyxoviridae
C. Influenza — Haemophilus ducreyi
D. Polio — Legionella

101. Name the officer of Indian army who initiated an inquiry into the Sukna land case?
A. Gen. V.K. Singh
B. Gen. Deepak Kapoor
C. Gen. Padmanabhan
D. Gen. B.C. Joshi

102. Who is the head of the National Advisory Council?
A. Manmohan Singh
B. Montek Singh
C. Sonia Gandhi
D. Pranab Mukherji

103. Which of the following country is ***not*** a member of North Atlantic Treaty Organisation (NATO)?

A. Argentina B. Croatia
C. Albania D. Canada

104. Name the book for which Aravind Adiga won the Booker Prize in 2008?

A. The Crouching Tiger, Hidden Dragon
B. Red Tide Rising
C. The Remains of the Day
D. The White Tiger

105. At a given time of the day, a 9-feet high pole casts a shadow of 15 feet. At the same time, an adjacent tree casts a shadow of 40 feet. How tall is the tree?

A. 12 feet B. 64 feet
C. 24 feet D. 20 feet

106. A's initial salary was increased by 40%. However, during the period of recession, his salary was reduced by 20%. On the whole:

A. A's salary increased over his initial salary by 12%.
B. A's salary increased over his initial salary by 20%.
C. A's salary decreased over his initial salary by 12%.
D. A's salary returned to the same level as his initial salary.

107. A man is 5 years elder to his wife who is now three times the age of her daughter. If the daughter's age is 10 years, what was the age of the man when the daughter was born?

A. 30 B. 25
C. 45 D. 40

Questions 108 to 110 are based on the following facts:

A law firm comprises of 6 cubicles, separated from each other by 6 feet high partitions; sound and smells therefore permeate to adjacent cubicles. You have been assigned the task of allotting the cubicles to six employees of the firm.

Ramesh is the secretary and telephone operator and needs to use the telephone quite often during the course of the day. All the employees generally maintain silence.

Manish and Brij need adjacent cubicles since they need to consult often.

Hemant is the senior partner and needs to be allotted cubicle 5 which faces a window.

Dinesh requires silence in cubicle next to his.

Tarun, Manish and Dinesh are smokers.

Hemant is allergic to cigarette smoke.

108. The three employees who are smokers should be allotted cubicles numbered:

A. 1, 2, 6
B. 4, 6, 1
C. 1, 2, 3
D. Cannot be accommodated in the same office.

109. Ideally, Manish should be allotted cubicle number:

A. 1 B. 6
C. 4 D. 3

110. All other things remaining same, which of the following events may lead to a request for change of cubicle?

A. Hemant operating a portable radio-set in his cubicle.
B. Ramesh needing silence in cubicles adjacent to his.
C. Tarun taking over the duties of Ramesh.
D. None of the above.

111. How is 3/17 expressed as a percentage?

A. 15.23% B. 17.64%
C. 19.5% D. 23.6%

112. A man is facing west. He turns 45 degrees in clockwise direction and then another 180 degrees in the same direction and then 270 degrees in the anticlockwise direction. What direction is he facing now?

A. South B. South East
C. West D. South West

113. What is the missing number in the series, 7, 15, 32, —, 138, 281 ?

A. 64 B. 67
C. 35 D. 45

114. It takes a moving train 30 seconds to cross a stationary engine. To compute the speed of the train, which of the following should be known?

A. The length of the stationary engine.
B. The length of the moving train.
C. The length of the moving engine.
D. Both the length of the stationary engine as well as the length of the moving train.

115. A pole has been affixed in a riverbed. One-half of the pole is buried in the riverbed. One-third of it is covered by water. 8 feet of it projects out of water. What is the total length of the pole in feet?
A. 48 B. 13
C. 18 D. 12

116. Which word would complete the following sequence:
DIRECT, ROLE, OCCIDENTAL, DARE, ... ?
A. DRAGON B. ARMOUR
C. ARMY D. PROVOKE

117. Since October 2009, which is the highest Court of appeal for England and Wales?
A. The Supreme Court of the United Kingdom
B. The House of Lords
C. The High Court of Justiciary
D. The Privy Council

118. Which odorant is commonly added to household Liquefied Petroleum Gas, to easily detect its leakage?
A. Methane B. Propane
C. Benzinol D. Mercaptan

119. Which football club did Lionel Messi play for in the 2009-10 UEFA Champions League?
A. Barcelona B. Lyon
C. Arsenal D. Manchester United

120. Which Indian company acquired the Megasari Makmur Group of Indonesia in 2010?
A. Reliance Industries Ltd.
B. Godrej Consumer Products Ltd.
C. TATA Motors Ltd.
D. Mittal Steel Company N.V.

121. Which of the following spots reportedly witnesses the largest sale of ice-cream in India?
A. Juhu Beach, Mumbai
B. Gateway of India, Mumbai
C. Marina Beach, Chennai
D. India Gate, Delhi

122. A joint team of scientists from Russia and U.S. was recently reported to have created the element to fill the gap in the periodic table of chemical elements. The element was called:
A. Element 117 B. Element 118
C. Ununoctium D. Eka-radon

123. Which organization shifted some of its operations from mainland China to Hong Kong in March 2010, due to censorship issues?
A. Microsoft B. Google
C. Dell D. Wipro

124. The word "economics" is derived from which Greek word?
A. Oikos B. Oeconomicus
C. Ekklesiastikos D. Oikonomia

125. Which of the following is primarily a digital book reader?
A. Apple I-Pod B. Sandisk Sansa
C. Amazon Kindle D. Nokia N95

126. Who is the author of *"The General Theory of Employment, Interest and Money"* (1936)?
A. Milton Friedman
B. John Maynard Keynes
C. Adam Smith
D. Thomas Friedman

127. Goods that are used in production of other goods and services are called:
A. Capital goods
B. Consumer goods
C. Homogenous goods
D. Consumable goods

128. Which among the following storage media has the maximum storage capacity?
A. Digital Video Disc (DVD)
B. Compact Disc (CD)
C. Vinyl Record
D. Blu Ray Disc

129. Around which year did the Persian scholar Al-Beruni visit India?
A. 1220 AD B. 1000 AD
C. 1030 AD D. 1347 AD

130. Who was the last ruler of the Aztec Empire of Mexico?
A. Montezuma II B. Cuauhtemoc
C. Hernan Cortes D. Quetzalcoatl

131. A firm is an oligopolistic industry if:
A. it is run by members of the same family.
B. it considers the actions of competitors when determining its pricing policy.
C. it produces a product identical to the product produced by its rivals.
D. it controls the pricing and promotion policy of the market.

132. The title of "Vikramaditya" was assumed by:
A. Chandragupta II B. Kanishka
C. Samudragupta D. Harshavardhana

133. Which of the following rulers is considered as a contemporary of the poet, Tulsidas?
A. Sher Shah Suri B. Shah Jahan
C. Babur D. Akbar

134. Which of the following movie was based on a video game?
A. Chronicles of Riddick
B. Max Payne
C. Spiderman 2
D. James Bond 007 : All or Nothing

135. The British East India Company was formally dissolved by an Act of the Parliament of the United Kingdom, called:
A. East India Merger & Acquisition Act
B. Goverment of India Act
C. East India Stock Dividend Redemption Act
D. Companies Act

136. What is the latest client operating system for PC from Microsoft as of March, 2010 called?
A. Windows 7
B. Windows CE
C. Windows Server 2008
D. Windows Vista

137. 'Bay of Pigs' refers to:
A. Slaughter of pigs in Egypt, in an attempt to prevent outbreak of swine flu
B. Argentine ivasion and occupation of the Falkalnd Islands leading to the Falklands War
C. Unsuccessful attempt by United States' backed Cuban exiles to overthrow the government of the Cuban premier, Fidel Castro
D. The combined territorial waters of four countries of southern Eurpoe: Portugal, Italy, Greece and Spain

138. What does a phillumenist collect?
A. Candles B. Matchboxes
C. Newspapers D. Light bulbs

139. In Roman Catholic Church, what is the title given to a person who is appointed to oppose a candidate's claim for canonization?
A. Church Defendant B. Hell's Angel
C. Church Prosecutor D. Devil's Advocate

140. What is the Commonwealth Games, 2010 mascot called?
A. Sheru B. Shera
C. Cheetah D. Jigrr

141. Which of the following is ***not*** considered a component of microeconomics?
A. Demand
B. Supply
C. Market equilibrium
D. Rate of inflation

142. Which of the following has developed the software platform, Maemo?
A. Nokia B. Dell
C. Microsoft D. Sony

143. What is the title of the film documenting Michael Jackson's preparations for his scheduled 2009-10 concert series?
A. I'll Be There B. Thriller
C. This is IT D. Heal the World

144. Who, among the following, was referred to as the 'Mozart of Madras' by the Time magazine?
A. Ilayaraja
B. A. R. Rahman
C. Santha P. Nair
D. S. P. Balasubrahmanyam

145. What is the name of the web browser developed by Google Inc?
A. Chrome B. Safari
C. Firefox D. Mozilla

146. Who is the present Chief of Army Staff?
A. Deepak Kapoor
B. P. V. Naik
C. V. K. Singh
D. Nirmal Kumar Verma

147. At which position did the Indian hockey team finish, in the 2010 Men's Hockey World Cup held at Delhi?

A. Ninth B. Tenth
C. Seventh D. Eighth

148. Venkatraman Ramakrishnan was awarded the 2009 Nobel Prize in Chemistry for:

A. studies of the structure and function of the ribosome
B. studies of the structure and function of the chromosome
C. studies of chemical processes on solid surfaces
D. studies of the structure and function of DNA

149. Which ad-agency was associated with the creation of animated creatures, 'Zoozoo', for promotion of Vodafone's services?

A. FCB-Ulka Advertising Ltd.
B. Ogilvy & Mather Ltd.
C. Mudra Communications Ltd.
D. Percept Advertising Ltd.

150. By which controversial instrument did the (then) President of Pakistan, Pervez Musharraf, grant powers to the Government to withdraw prosecution against politicians accused of various crimes, ostensibly to end their political victimization?

A. National Reconciliation Ordinance
B. National Coalition to Protect Political Freedom
C. President's power to grant pardon, Article 45 of the Constitution of the Islamic Republic of Pakistan
D. Universal Declaration of Human Rights

151. Which instrument aboard the Chandrayaan-1 detected the presence of water on the moon's surface?

A. Hydrophilic Receptor
B. Moon Mineralogy Mapper
C. Radiation Dose Monitor
D. X-ray Spectrometer

152. What is Satyam Computer Services Ltd. known as, since its takeover?

A. TCS Satyam B. Infosys Satyam
C. Wipro Satyam D. Mahindra Satyam

153. Where was Christ born, according to the Gospels of Mathew and Luke?

A. Jordan B. Nazareth
C. Bethlehem D. Jerusalem

154. A campaign launched in April, 2010, with the view to clean the river Ganga has been named as:

A. Sparsh Ganga
B. Nirmal Ganga
C. Pavitra Ganga
D. Swargashram Ganga

155. Who created the cartoon character Tintin?

A. Bill Watterson B. John Calvin
C. Charles M. Schulz D. Herge

156. Which two water bodies does the Panama Canal link?

A. Mediterranean Sea and Red Sea
B. Atlantic Ocean and Indian Ocean
C. Atlantic Ocean and Pacific Ocean
D. Pacific Ocean and Arctic Ocean

157. Which of the following has NASA proposed to 'retire from service' by the end of the year, 2010?

A. Ares I and Ares V
B. Discovery, Atlantis and Endeavor
C. International Space Center
D. All of the above

158. The speed of light in vacuum may be expressed in Mach numbers as, approximately:

A. Mach 90 B. Mach 9,000
C. Mach 9,00,000 D. Mach 90,000,000

159. Where would be zero degrees latitude and zero degrees longitude located?

A. Atlantic Ocean B. Sahara desert
C. North Pole D. South Pole

160. In the Rime of the Ancient Mariner, whom does the mariner stop to recite his story?

A. Doctor hastening to a medical emergency
B. Nobleman going to the House of Lords
C. Guest on his way to a wedding
D. Sailor returning to his ship

161. Which part of human body is completely deviod of blood supply?

A. Brain B. Cornea
C. Intestine D. Thyroid

162. Under what capacity is Hillary Clinton serving in the adminstration of President Barack Obama?
A. Secretary of State
B. Senator for New York
C. Defense Secretary
D. Secretary for External Affairs

Question 163 to 167 are based on the following passage:

PASSAGE

I entered the room where the corpse lay, and was led up to the coffin. How can I describe my sensations on beholding it? I feel yet parched with horror, nor can I reflect on that terrible moment without shuddering and agony, that faintly reminds me of the anguish of the recognition. The trial, the presence of the magistrate and witnesses, passed like a dream from my memory, when I saw the lifeless form of Henry Clerval stretched before me. I gasped for breath; and, throwing myself on the body, I exclaimed, "Have my murderous machinations deprived you also, my dearest Henry of life? Two, I have already destroyed; other victims await their destiny: but you, Clerval, my friend, my benefactor"

The human frame could no longer support the agonizing suffering that I endured, and I was carried out of the room in strong convulsions. A fever succeeded to this. I lay for two months on the point of death; my ravings, as I afterwards heard, were frightful; I called myself the murderer of William, of Justine, and of Clerval. Sometimes I entreated my attendants to assist me in the destruction of the fiend by whom I was tormented; and, at others, I felt the fingers of the monster already grasping my neck, and screamed aloud with agony and terror. Fortunately, as I spoke my native language, Mr. Kirwin alone understood me; but my gestures and bitter cries were sufficient to affright the other witnesses. Why did I not die? More miserable than man ever was beofre, why did I not sink into forgetfulness and rest? Death snatches away many blooming children, the only hopes of their doting parents; how many brides and youthful lovers has been one day in the bloom of health and hope, and the next a prey for worms and the decay of the tomb! Of what materials was I made, that I could thus resist so many shocks, which, like the turning of the wheel, continually renewed the torture?

163. The narrator's ravings could have been taken as an admission of guilt of being responsible for the death Henry Clerval, but for the fact that:
A. He was speaking in his native language
B. He was suffering immensely
C. He was physically ill
D. He was mentally unsound

164. The word 'machination' means:
A. Inventing a new machine
B. A crafty scheme
C. Foul intention
D. Understanding the working of something or someone

165. The narrator appears to make several references to his own suffering, but ignores the suffering undergone by those he claimed to have murdered, or others bereaved by the deaths. Considering this, the style of the passage may best be described as:
A. Ironical
B. Comical
C. Satirical
D. Self Centered

166. Describe the emotions of the narrator as can be sensed from the above passage:
A. Humiliation and pain
B. Grief and loss
C. Guilt and despair
D. Both (B) and (C)

167. What does the use of phrases such as 'parched with horror', 'shuddering and agony', 'I gasped for breath' suggest to the reader:
A. The mental torture that the narrator is undergoing.
B. The violent body language of the narrator.
C. The mental torments of the narrator expressed by a violent body language.
D. The hallucinations in the mind of the narrator, arising out of his grief.

Questions 168 to 175 are based on the following passage:

PASSAGE

(I) I savor the remotness and the rare times I'm alone on this muscular river in southern Utah, a precious ribbon of wild water between reservoirs and the suck holes of industry and agriculture.

(II) Officially, I'm here to have my peace disturbed. Floaters must have a permit to run this stretch of river. During the peak season a ranger checks lottery-drawn launch dates and a short list of gear related to safety and environmental protection. The permit system allows the federal agency in charge to hold numbeers of floaters to a maximum of about 10,000 a year, set in 1979, when use increased 250 per cent in just three seasons. Each year since, the actual number of people down the river has hovered close to this ceiling, which the agency believes is the river's capacity for a 'quality wilderness experience' socially if not physically, however, "wilderness experience" seems to have become an illusion if not irrelevant. Right now I'm the voluntary ranger managing both the illusion and the irrelevance.

(III) Most people accept the permit system as a panacea for the explosion in numbers of river runners and the consequences for a fragile riparian corridor. Others find regulation about as painless as an IRS audit.

(IV) They see the Southwest as a region of federally neutered rivers where a person is no longer free to kill himself in a four-foot rubber ducky pulling an inner tube piled with beans, testosterone, and a small machete. ...

(V) The boat ramp is swarming with people and vehicles to be shuttled to the take-out. Someone's dog is throwing up what appears to be rabbit parts. I'm approached by a pickup driven by a man waving a spray nozzle and hose hooked to a large barrel of allegedly lethal chemicals. He's from county weed control, he says. Have I seen the loathsome pepperweed? Not a leaf, I lie.

(VI) Cheerfully I sign the permit of the outfitter who specializes in theme river trips—stress management seminars, outings for the crystal fondlers or fingernail technicians of East Jesus, New Jersey, overcoming, at last, their irrational fear of Nature. Today's load is priests troubled by a lapsed faith—pale, anxious, overweight fellows in the early stages of heatstroke. I also check gear and answer questions about bugs, snakes, scorpions, camps, rapids and Indians (one side of the river is reservation land). Do I live here fulltime? they ask. No, I respond, except for an occasional shift at the put-in, I'm on the river eight days out of sixteen, six months a year.

(VII) ... Some rafts look as if they barely survived World War II.

(VIII) Others are outfitted with turbo-dynamic chrome-plated throw lines, heat-welded vinyl dry-bags, cargo nets spun from the fibers of dew-fed arachnids from Borneo, horseshoes, volleyball sets, sauna tents, coffinsized cooers stuffed with sushi, a small fleet of squirt boats, whining packs of androgynous progeny who prefer to be at home fulfilling their needs electronically. All of this gear is color-coordinated with SPF 14 sunscreen and owned by business majors in Styrofoam pith helmets and Lycra body gloves, in which they were placed at birth. Once loaded, their boats are pieces of personal architecture, stunning but nevertheless stuck on the sandbar six feet out from the boat ramp after a dramatic send-off.

168. Paragraphs V and VI describe the characteristics of the rafters. Which of the following characteristics is NOT described in those paragraphs?
A. Physical appearnace
B. Response to nature
C. Occupations
D. Conversation

169. The description, "androgynous progency who prefer to be at home fulfilling their needs electronically" refers to:
A. Pets not accustomed to outdoor life.
B. Rafters' preference to rafts with modern electronic gadgetry.
C. Rafters with battered rafts envying the ones with modern equipment.
D. Children who would rather be playing video games.

170. The effect of the last sentence of the passage may be described as:
A. Comic anti-climax B. Allegory
C. Symbolic conclusion D. Relief

171. Paragraph VI makes a reference to:
A. Native Americans
B. "Non-Resident Indians"
C. Immigrants
D. Mexicans

172. The narrator uses all the following tones of voice, *except*:
A. Amused B. Satirical
C. Cheerful D. Arrogant

173. Which of the following best describes the primary purpose of the passage?

A. To describe everyday life around American 'adventure camps'.

B. To prtest against exploitation of natural resources.

C. To satirize aspects of the 'back to the nature' movement.

D. To judge the vanity in poeple.

174. The author of the aforesaid passage may be best described as:

A. Narrator of the events of the past.

B. An ecologist concerned at the exploitation of the river.

C. A ranger making an official report of the events.

D. A commentator on contemporary American customs.

175. Which of the following is NOT employed in the Paragraph III of the above passage ("Most people accept permit ... IRS audit")?

A. Pun B. Simile

C. Metaphor D. Hyperbole

ANSWERS

1	2	3	4	5	6	7	8	9	10
C	D	C	D	A	D	C	D	B	A
11	12	13	14	15	16	17	18	19	20
C	B	A	B	D	A	D	A	D	C
21	22	23	24	25	26	27	28	29	30
A	D	B	D	A	B	D	B	A	B
31	32	33	34	35	36	37	38	39	40
D	A	D	C	A	B	D	B	C	A
41	42	43	44	45	46	47	48	49	50
D	A	C	A	D	B	A	C	D	C
51	52	53	54	55	56	57	58	59	60
B	D	A	D	C	B	A	D	B	D
61	62	63	64	65	66	67	68	69	70
B	D	A	B	A	B	C	B	C	A
71	72	73	74	75	76	77	78	79	80
B	A	B	D	B	A	C	D	B	D
81	82	83	84	85	86	87	88	89	90
C	B	C	D	C	D	B	C	B	A
91	92	93	94	95	96	97	98	99	100
C	A	C	B	C	A	D	A	B	A
101	102	103	104	105	106	107	108	109	110
B	C	A	D	C	A	B	C	D	C
111	112	113	114	115	116	117	118	119	120
B	D	B	D	A	B	A	D	B	B
121	122	123	124	125	126	127	128	129	130
D	A	B	D	C	B	A	D	C	B
131	132	133	134	135	136	137	138	139	140
B	A	D	B	C	A	C	B	D	B
141	142	143	144	145	146	147	148	149	150
D	A	C	B	A	C	D	A	B	A
151	152	153	154	155	156	157	158	159	160
B	D	C	A	D	C	A	C	A	C
161	162	163	164	165	166	167	168	169	170
B	A	A	B	A	D	C	B	D	A
171	172	173	174	175					
A	D	C	D	A					

Previous Paper (Solved)
LL.B. ENTRANCE EXAM., 2009

1. Besides Indian scientific instruments, the Chandrayan carried instruments from various other space agencies. Which, among the following, is not one of them?
A. Bulgarian Academy of Sciences (BAS)
B. National Aeronautics and Space Administration (NASA)
C. European Space Agency (ESA)
D. Russian Federal Space Agency (RFSA)

2. Who provided the earliest evidence of the Big Bang model of the Universe?
A. Einstein B. Fred Hoyle
C. Edwin Hubble D. Newton

3. Which of the following is used as a tool for tracking human ancestry through females?
A. Y-chromosome
B. Nuclear DNA
C. Mitochondrial DNA
D. X-chromosome

4. Which of the following is not a Kingdom under the Five Kingdom taxonomical classification?
A. Animalia B. Plantae
C. Monera D. Archaea

5. Which telecom operator was the first to announce third-generation (3G) telecom services in India?
A. Bharti Airtel
B. Reliance Communications
C. MTNL
D. TATA Infocomm

6. Which team won the Indian Premier League Tournament in 2008?
A. Chennai Supper Kings
B. Rajasthan Royals
C. Bangalore Royal Challengers
D. Deccan Chargers

7. What is the aerobatics demonstration team of Indian Navy known as?
A. Sea Hawks B. Surya Kiran
C. Sagar Pawan D. Blue Angels

8. Water retaining plants adapted to arid climates are known as:
A. Phylloclades B. Hemiepiphytes
C. Cactii D. Succulents

9. Who created the 'Common Man' associated with the Times of India?
A. R.K. Narayan B. R.K. Narayanan
C. R.K. Laxman D. K.R. Narayanan

10. Which event has been described as "the effective birth of economics as a separate discipline", by the New Encyclopaedia Britannica?
A. The emergence of the 18th century French Physiocrats.
B. The publication of Adam Smith's "The Wealth of Nations".
C. The development of Keynesian Economics.
D. The codification of economic formulae in the city States of Sumer.

11. Edible mushroom is a form of:
A. Animal B. Plant
C. Lower life form D. Fungus

12. 'Nitrogen fixation' refers to:
A. Fixing achievable targets for reducing nitrogen pollution in the atmosphere.
B. Developing means to synthesize and produce Nitrogen on a mass scale.
C. The process by which Nitrogen is converted from its natural form in the atmosphere to Nitrogen compounds.
D. The procedure for optimal utilization of Nitrogen based fertilizers in field.

13. Jacques Yves Cousteau is credited with:
A. liberating Paris in the Second World War

B. developing French naval warfare techniques
C. pioneering marine conservation
D. undertaking High Sea adventure trips

14. Which, among the following, is not a literary piece by R.K. Narayan?
A. The Man Eater of Malgudi
B. The Guide
C. Swami and Friends
D. Malgudi Junction

15. Which of the following establishments in India was modelled on the lines of the United States WestPoint?
A. The National Defence Academy
B. The National Academy of Sciences
C. The Indian Administrative Services
D. The Defence Research and Development Organisation

16. Who, among the following fictional characters, is not a creation of Satyajit Ray?
A. Feluda
B. Byomkesh Bakshi
C. Professor Shonku
D. Topshe

17. Which British doctrine is considered as one of the reasons leading to the First War of Independence, also known as the Sepoy Mutiny?
A. Doctrine of Lapse
B. Doctrine of Contributory Negligence
C. Doctrine of Incompetence
D. Doctrine of Frustration of Purpose

18. The vermiform appendix in humans is an example of:
A. Reflex action mechanism
B. Digestive System Organ
C. Vestigial Organ
D. Cognitive Behavioural Organ

19. Which phyto-hormones influence plant growth?
A. Auxin B. Gibberellin
C. Pheromone D. Lignin

20. Cell wall in plants is composed of:
A. Cambium B. Cellulose
C. Lignin D. Cytokinin

21. The policy of British East India Company in India during the period of 1813 – 1858 is described as:
A. Policy of Ring Fence
B. Policy of Annexation by Lapse
C. Policy of Subordinate Isolation
D. Policy of Subordinate Union

22. Which modern Indian historian has described the events of 1857 as "neither first nor National nor War of Independence"?
A. V. D. Savarkar B. Dadabhai Naoroji
C. S. N. Sen D. R. C. Majumdar

23. The airspace over one of the following was declared a 'no-fly zone' in December 2008, thereby prohibiting all flying activity up to a height of 10,000 feet over it. Choose the correct location.
A. Parliament of India
B. Satish Dhawan Space Centre, Sriharikota
C. Kalpakkam Nuclear Power Plant
D. Rashtrapati Bhavan

24. Who is the Governor of Reserve Bank of India?
A. Dr. D. Subbarao B. Dr. Rakesh Mohan
C. Dr. Y. V. Reddy D. Dr. Bimal Jalan

25. Which of the following offices has never been held by Prime Minister Manmohan Singh?
A. Finance Minister
B. Governor, Reserve Bank of India
C. Honorary Professor, Delhi School of Economics
D. Member, Lok Sabha

26. Op-Ed, with reference to a newspaper article, refers to:
A. Opinion Editorial
B. Opposite Editorial
C. Opinion Educational
D. Operative Editorial

27. "Stability 2008" refers to:
A. Russian strategic military exercise
B. Economic bailout package envisaged by the Obama regime
C. United Nations endeavour to bring peace to Somalia

D. Measures to maintain ecological balance in tropical rain forests

28. Who, among the following Indians, purchased the sword of Tipu Sultan at an auction in London?

A. Sanjay Khan B. Anil Ambani
C. Vijay Mallya D. Ratan Tata

29. Which of the following is one of the ten forces that 'flattened the world' in the opinion of Thomas L. Friedman in his book, "The World is Flat"?

A. Nuclear weapons B. Lunar landing
C. Netscape D. Television

30. Who was crowned the 57th Miss Universe at Miss Universe 2008?

A. Riyo Mori B. Dayana Mendoza
C. Rebeca Moreno D. Taliana Vargas

31. Who among the following has not won a medal in individual event at the Olympics?

A. Rajyavardhan Rathore
B. Abhinav Bindra
C. Leander Paes
D. Anjali Bhagat

32. Who among the following was the recipient of Padma Bhushan for distinguished services in sports?

A. Harbhajan Singh
B. Mahendra Singh Dhoni
C. Abhinav Bindra
D. Balbir Singh Khullar

33. Philadelphia chromosome is reported in patients suffering from:

A. Insomina B. Kidney Stone
C. Leukaemia D. Mental disorders

34. The Global Potato Conference 2008 was held at:

A. Lima, Peru
B. New Delhi, India
C. Mexico City, Mexico
D. Sao Paulo, Brazil

35. Which of the following is not a video gaming console?

A. Wii B. Playstation
C. X-Box D. Macbook

36. Which law was enacted in the United States in 2008, for the bailout of the U.S. financial system?

A. Emergency Economic Stabilization Act of 2008
B. Troubled Asset Relief Act of 2008
C. Energy Improvement and Extension Act of 2008
D. Mental Health Parity and Addiction Equity Act of 2008

37. Who led the FIDE Men's Chess ratings as on 1st February 2009?

A. Anatoli Karpov B. Viswanathan Anand
C. Veselin Topalov D. Vassily Ivanchuk

38. The *de facto* administrative captial of LTTE was located at:

A. Jaffna B. Kilinochchi
C. Vanni D. Elephant Pass

39. Which Pakistan based group was designated by the United Nations Security Council as a terrorist organization following the November, 2008 Mumbai attacks?

A. Lashkar-e-Taiba B. Jamaat-ud-Dawah
C. Jamaat-e-Islami D. Jaish-e-Mohammed

40. Which temple witnessed a stampede in September 2008?

A. Chamunda Devi Temple, Jodhpur, Rajasthan
B. Jagannath Temple, Puri, Orissa
C. Tirupati Temple, Tirupati, Andhra Pradesh
D. Chamunda Devi, Kangra, Himachal Pradesh

41. Name the oil tanker that was hijacked by Somali pirates in November, 2008?

A. MV. Elizabeth B. MV Sirius Star
C. Seabourn Spirit D. Achille Lauro

42. The Great Fire of Rome is associated with

A. Maximus Quintus
B. Tacitus
C. Pliny the Elder
D. Lucius Domitius

43. Which of the following is not a wireless data transfer technology?

A. EDGE B. GPRS
C. Bluetooth D. 3GP

44. Human saliva contains enzymes necessary for breakdown of:

A. Proteins B. Starch
C. Cellulose D. Vitamins

45. Which of the following substance is an anticoagulant?

A. Heparin B. Tannin
C. Fibrin D. Thrombin

46. The first metal used by man was:

A. Iron B. Copper
C. Aluminium D. Bronze

47. Where is the Large Hadron Collider (LHC) particle accelerator located?

A. Switzerland and France
B. Germany
C. United States of America and Mexico
D. Sweden

48. Which of the following is not a private space tourism venture?

A. Virgin Galactic B. Intercosmos
C. MirCorp D. Bigelow Aerospace

49. Where is the world's highest waterfall located?

A. Canada & United States
B. Argentina
C. Sri Lanka
D. Venezuela

50. The chemicals used in tear gas are known as

A. Mustard gas
B. Lachrymatory agents
C. Nitrous oxide
D. Nerve agents

51. On what date did Rakesh Sharma launch aboard Soyuz T-11 towards its destination, the Salyut 7 space station?

A. 13th January 1984
B. 23rd April 1984
C. 2nd April 1984
D. 26th January 1982

52. Polio virus is primarily transmitted via:

A. Contaminated food and water
B. Mosquito bite
C. Contaminated air
D. Mother to foetus

53. Which road in Delhi is known as the Fleet Street of India?

A. Kasturba Gàndhi Marg
B. Race Course Road
C. Bahadur Shah Zafar Road
D. Parliament Street

54. Which of the following is popularly known as the 'Siamese Fighting Fish'?

A. Betta B. Pirhana
C. Tuna D. Guppy

55. Which car maker is reportedly building the Presidential car for President of United States, Barack Obama?

A. Ford Motor Company
B. General Motors
C. Mercedes-Benz
D. Rolls Royce

56. Treatment of Dengue fever may require:

A. Platelet transfusion
B. Antibiotics
C. Administration of propanolol
D. All of the above

57. Which of the following popular fictional characters is not the public face of a superhero?

A. Peter Parker B. Bruce Wayne
C. Clark Kent D. Paul Drake

58. Which of the following countries conducted its first anti-satellite weapon test in the year 2007?

A. United States of America
B. Russia
C. Iran
D. China

59. 'Bar' is a unit of:

A. Humidity B. Alcohol content
C. Pressure D. Depth

60. Who is considered the inventor of detective fiction?

A. Arthur Conan Doyle
B. Agatha Christie
C. Erle Stanley Gardner
D. Edgar Allan Poe

61. Which term is being served by Smt. Sheila Dixit as the Chief Minister of Delhi?

A. Second B. Fourth
C. First D. Third

62. Which State among the following witnessed the largest polling percentage in the State Elections in 2008?

A. Jammu & Kashmir
B. Meghalaya
C. Mizoram
D. Delhi

63. With which of the following did the State Bank of India enter into a Joint-venture Agreement for undertaking general insurance business?

A. New India Assurance Ltd.
B. Insurance Australia Group
C. Lehman Brothers Holdings Inc.
D. Allianz

64. With which country did India sign an extradition treaty in November, 2008?

A. Egypt B. Sri Lanka
C. Portugal D. Nepal

65. The 14th Conference of Parties to the U.N. Framework Convention of Climate Change was held at:

A. Bali, Indonesia
B. Pozanan, Poland
C. Montreal, Canada
D. Buenos Aires, Argentina

66. Balwant Rai Mehta Committee Report, 1957 is associated with:

A. Tax Reforms
B. Planning Commission
C. National Defence
D. Panchayati Raj

67. Which was the first element to be discovered through synthesis?

A. Neptunium B. Plutonium
C. Technetium D. Promethium

68. AIDS stands for:

A. Acquired Immuno Deficiency Syndrome
B. Acquired Immunity Deficiency Syndrome
C. Acquired Immuno Disease Syndrome
D. Acquired Immuno Deficiency Symptoms

69. Which party won the December 2008 general elections in Bangladesh?

A. Awami League coalition
B. Bangladesh Nationalist Party (BNP) coalition
C. Jamaat-e-Islami Bangladesh
D. Bangladesh Jatiya Party

70. Who was the Chief Guest at the 60th Republic Day celebrations?

A. Nursultan Nazarbayev
B. Nicolas Sarkozy
C. Jacques Chirac
D. Vladimir Putin

71. The Indo-Sri Lanka Peace Accord was entered into under the leadership of:

A. Indira Gandhi and J.R. Jayewardene.
B. Rajiv Gandhi and J.R. Jayewardene.
C. Rajiv Gandhi and Ranasighe Premadasa.
D. Rajiv Gandhi and Chandrika Kumaratunga.

72. What time zone does India fall into?

A. GMT + IST B. GMT + 5.5
C. GMT + 3.5 D. GMT – 3.5

73. Which of the following events is associated with 'Smiling Buddha'?

A. The nuclear weapons test conducted by India in 1998.
B. The launch of Chandrayan.
C. The launch of PSLV-II.
D. The nuclear weapons test conducted by India in 1974.

74. Which event led to Rabindranath Tagore's renouncement of his knighthood?

A. Civil Disobedience Movement
B. Jallianwalla Bagh massacre
C. Morley Minto Reforms
D. Chauri Chaura

75. The concept of 'General Will' was advocated by:

A. Hume B. Hegel
C. Kant D. Rousseau

76. Which of the following is associated with the business of retail supply and distribution of electricity in Delhi?

A. Delhi Power Company Ltd.
B. BSES Yamuna Power Ltd.
C. Delhi Transco Ltd.
D. Delhi Electricity Regulatory Commission

77. How many Olympic Gold medals has the American swimmer, Michael Phelps won in his career till date?

A. Eight B. Fourteen
C. Nineteen D. Twelve

78. What is the Super WASP?

A. UK's extra-solar planet detection program
B. Genetically engineered giant Wasp
C. Anti ballistic missile shield
D. Long range tracking radar

79. Multiple allelism controls inheritance of:

A. Blood groups
B. PKU
C. Sickle cell anaemia
D. Colour blindness

80. Name the antimicrobial substance found in tears, saliva, sweat etc.:

A. Enzyme B. Lysozyme
C. Pepsin D. Co-Enzyme

81. Root nodule rhizobia in legumes are an example of:

A. Parasitism B. Symbiosis
C. Predation D. Commensalism

82. Which of the following is associated with Marx's economics?

A. Theories of Surplus Value
B. Essay on the Principle of Population
C. On the Principles of Political Economy and Taxation
D. Okishio's theorem

83. The movie 'A Fistful of Dollars' was based on which movie?

A. Sholay
B. Yojimbo
C. The Good, The Bad and The Ugly
D. Support Your Local Gunfighter

84. What is the unit for temperature in the metric system?

A. Fahrenheit B. Kelvin
C. Degrees D. Celsius

85. Where is the painting, Mona Lisa displayed?

A. Louvre, Paris
B. National Gallery of London
C. Luxembourg, Paris
D. Orsay, Paris

86. Aristotle argued for the existence of a divine being described as:

A. God
B. Prime Mover
C. The Being
D. Spiritual Entity of Soul

87. Which art movement was led by Pablo Picasso?

A. Cubism B. Futurism
C. Fauvism D. Impressionism

88. Carl Jung, the Swiss psychologist is regarded as founder of which school of psychology?

A. Ego psychology
B. Cultural-historical psychology
C. Evolutionary psychology
D. Analytical psychology

89. The chromosomal abnormality due to the presence of one abnormal 21st chromosome (Total 47) in man is called:

A. Down's Syndrome
B. Turner's Syndrome
C. Klinefetter's Syndrome
D. Edward's Syndrome

90. Who is the highest Civil servant of the Union Government?

A. Attorney-General B. Cabinet Secretary
C. Home Secretary D. Principal Secretary

91. Which Company acquired a majority shareholding in one of India's largest drugmaker, Ranbaxy?

A. Zenotech Laboratories Ltd.
B. Cipla

C. Pfizer
D. Daiichi Sankyo

92. Which Company was in news for the gruesome death of its CEO at the hands of its agitating employees in September, 2008?
A. Gilera B. Graziano
C. Bernardelli D. Gaggia

93. In which year was State of Israel admitted as a member of the United Nations?
A. 1950 B. 1949
C. 1948 D. 1952

94. Name the author of the book, "Sea of Poppies".
A. William Dalrymple
B. Amitav Ghosh
C. Chetan Bhagat
D. Salman Rushdie

95. Which country won the UEFA European Football Championship in 2008?
A. Brazil B. Argentina
C. Germany D. Spain

96. Who won the 2008 Man Booker Prize?
A. Steve Toltz B. Aravind Adiga
C. Chetan Bhagat D. Amitav Ghosh

97. Bone marrow transplants are effective in cases of:
A. Thalassemia B. Leukemia
C. Anemia D. Diabetes

98. The Chandrayan has detected the presence of one of the following elements in the lunar soil.
A. Aluminum B. Copper
C. Iron D. Uranium

99. Choose the most appropriate word to fill in the blanks.
The General's __________ at the battlefield paid off.
A. Gamut B. Gambit
C. Movement D. Commands

100. The speaker made a ______argument against the proposed law.
A. perspicuous B. perspicacious
C. precipitous D. conspicuous

101. A_______by the Principal disciplined the rowdy schoolboys.
A. Censor B. Censure
C. Direction D. Suggestion

102. Since the Parliament was not in session, the President promulgated a/an_____in view of the urgency.
A. Ordnance B. Order
C. Ordinance D. Statute

103. Studies have revealed that a female Whale spends considerable time nursing its newborn_______.
A. Whale B. Brood
C. Calf D. Pre-Toothed whale

104. Aamir______made 14 films and I think his latest is the best.
A. has B. made
C. had made D. was making

105. Sorry, we're late. We______the wrong turning.
A. were taking B. took
C. had taken D. are taking

106. Next week I_______Akash for 20 years.
A. will have known
B. am knowing
C. will have been knowing
D. know

107. Following the earthquake, ______in the area______major repair work.
A. each buildings.....need
B. each of buildings.....needs
C. every building.....needs
D. every building.....need

108. The radio station is owned by the Entertainment Group.,______Chairman is Mr. Vishal Wadhwa.
A. who's B. whose
C. that's D. which

109. Jack______leave the hospital only six hours after the operation.
A. could B. can
C. is able to D. was able to

110. Choose the correct sentence.
A. He described me the situation.
B. He describe the situation to me.

C. He described the situation to me.

D. I was described the situation.

111. Who______was coming to see me this morning?

A. did you say B. did you say that

C. you did say D. you said

112. I______our anniversary and I______how to make it up to her.

A. completely forgot...don't just know

B. completely forgot...just don't know

C. forgot completely...don't just know

D. forgot completely...just don't know

Questions 113 to 117 are based on the following passage:

"You've been in love, of course! If not, you've got it to come. Love is like the measles; we all have to go through it. Also like the measles, we take it only once. One never need be afraid of catching it a second time. The man who has had it can go into the most dangerous places and play the most foolhardy tricks with perfect safety. He can picnic in shady woods, ramble through leafy aisles, and linger on mossy seats to watch the sunset. He fears a quiet country-house no more than he would his own club. He can join a family party to go down the Rhine. He can, to see the last of a friend, venture into the very jaws of the marriage ceremony itself. ...

No, we never sicken with love twice. Cupid spends no second arrow on the same heart. Love's handmaids are our life-long friends. Respect, and admiration, and affection, our doors may always be left open for, but their great celestial master, in his royal progress, pays but one visit and departs. We like, we cherish, we are very, very fond of-but we never love again. A man's heart is a firework that once in its time flashes heavenward. Meteor-like, it blazes for a moment and lights with its glory the whole world beneath. Then the night of our sordid commonplace life closes in around it, and the burned-out case, falling back to earth, lies useless and uncared for, slowly smoldering into ashes".

113. In the opinion of the author, love is like measles because :

(a) Each one of us has to go through it.

(b) It happens only once in life.

(c) It makes a person reckless.

(d) It is painful.

A. (a), (b) and (d)

B. (a), (b) and (c)

C. (a) and (b)

D. All of them are correct.

114. The writing style of the author may be described as:

A. Romantic B. Melodramatic

C. Satirist D. Somber

115. Choose the word having the same meaning as "ramble".

A. Saunter B. Tumble

C. Shamble D. Rally

116. What, according to the author, are the emotions that accompany love?

A. Admiration and affection

B. Courage and fearlessness

C. Sickness

D. Foolhardiness

117. In which of the following ways is a man's heart been described as being similar to a firework?

A. A firework lights up the sky.

B. A firework flashes only momentarily and falls back to earth.

C. Having lighted up once, it is of no further use.

D. All of the above.

118. Choose the word having the same meaning as "obsequious".

A. Subservient B. Obscene

C. Rude D. Observant

119. Choose the word having the same meaning as "averse".

A. Adverse B. Unfavourable

C. Opposed D. Reversed

120. Choose the word having the same meaning as "apposite".

A. Inapt B. Opposite
C. Relevant D. Casual

121. Choose the word having a meaning opposite of "sequester".
A. Cloister B. Isolate
C. Unify D. Distribute

122. Choose the word having a meaning opposite of "sagacious".
A. Sanguine B. Capricious
C. Facetious D. Foolish

123. Choose the word having a meaning opposite of "erudite".
A. Calm B. Scholarly
C. Ignorant D. Filthy

124. Cognition refers to:
A. the ability to recognize
B. the reflex to a condition
C. the faculty of perception
D. an inclination towards seeking recognition

Choose the most appropriate answer to each Factual Situation given in Question Nos. 125 to 127 within the scope of the Principle mentioned.

125. PRINCIPLE: A person, who lawfully brings on his land something which though harmless, but will do mischief if it escape, must keep it at his peril, and if he does not, he is answerable for all the damage.

FACTUAL SITUATION: 'A' was the owner of a mill. In order to supply it with water he constructed a reservoir upon nearby land by employing engineers and contractors. 'B' was the owner of coal mines, under lands, close to but not adjoining the premises on which the reservoir was constructed. The contractors, while excavating for the bed of the reservoir, came upon abandoned shafts and filled them with soil not suspecting that they were abandoned mine shafts. The reservoir was completed and partly filled. Within days the bed of the reservoir gave way and burst, leading to flow of water through the channels connected with B's mine. Is 'A' liable to pay damages for loss caused to 'B'?

A. 'A' is not liable because there was no negligence on his part. He was not aware that the reservoir bed was connected to B's mines.
B. 'A' is liable to pay damages to 'B' because he brought the water on his property which would have caused mischief if it escaped and it did escape.
C. 'A' is not liable because 'B' never informed him the existence of B's mines.
D. 'A' is liable because he hired the services of unqualified engineers.

126. PRINCIPLE: Cheating is defined as deceiving any person to deliver any property and it includes the dishonest concealment of facts. Cheating by personation means a person cheating another by pretending to be some other person, or by knowingly substituting one person for another, or representing that he or any other person is a person other than he or such other person really is.

FACTUAL SITUATION: 'A' while leaving a restaurant mistakingly picked up the umbrella of 'B' instead of his own. The next day he decided to return to the restaurant with the umbrella, hoping to find the real owner. 'C', who had never seen 'B' in person and had only communicated with 'B' through letters was on his way to the restaurant to meet 'B'. Since 'B' and 'C' had never met, it was agreed between them to identify each other at the pre-appointed spot, the restaurant door, by the clothing of 'C' and umbrella of 'B' which they had described to each other in detail. 'C' saw 'A' at the door of the restaurant and identified the umbrella. Thinking 'A' to be 'B', 'C' delivered a parcel labelled Mr. B to 'A'. 'A' received the same without protest and promptly returned home without looking for 'B'. Is 'A' guilty of cheating by personation?

A. 'A' is not guilty because he was going to return the umbrella to the real owner and handing over 'B's' packet to 'A' was 'C's' mistake.

B. 'A' is not guilty because he was overcome by a sudden temptation.

C. 'A' is guilty because he was aware of the mistaken identity and that the parcel was not meant for him but for 'B'.

D. 'A' is guilty because the parcel might have been valuable to 'B'.

127. PRINCIPLE: A consumer is a person who buys any goods or services for a consideration and uses the goods for non-commercial purposes. Exclusive use of the goods for the purposes of earning his livelihood, by means of self-employment is not considered as commercial use. A consumer can approach a consumer forum if there is a deficiency in goods or service.

FACTUAL SITUATION: 'A', a taxi driver received a car music system for free, from an electronics company through a draw of lots and installed the same in his taxi. Some time later, the music system stopped working. 'A' approached the electronics company for a replacement but the company kept delaying. Can 'A' sue the company in a consumer forum?

A. Yes, 'A' is not using the music system for any commercial purpose. He is just plying a taxi for earning his livelihood.

B. Yes 'A' there is a deficiency in goods since the music system became non-functional.

C. No, 'A' is using his taxi for ferrying passengers which is a commercial purpose. Hence he is not a consumer.

D. No, 'A' is not a consumer since he has not paid any consideration for the music system.

128. For the first time, in the history of the Supreme Court of India, a sitting judge of the Supreme Court was questioned by Central Bureau of Investigation in a corruption case relating to multi-crore Ghaziabad Provident Fund scam. Who was the Judge?

A. Justice Y. K. Sabharwal

B. Justice Tarun Chatterjee

C. Justice Summit Mukherjee

D. Justice Nirmal Yadav

129. Dr. Hari Singh Gaur was the first Dean, Faculty of Law and the Vice Chancellor of:

A. Dr. Hari Singh Gaur University

B. University of Delhi

C. University of Lucknow

D. None of the above

130. Which of the following bodies had approached the Supreme Court of India seeking permission to interrogate the deposed Chairman of Satyam Computer Services?

A. Registrar of Companies

B. Securities and Exchange Board of India

C. Reserve Bank of India

D. Central Bureau of Investigation

131. How many persons were nominated for award of Ashok Chakra on 26th January 2009?

A. 9 B. 10

C. 11 D. 12

132. Which politician considered responsible for Babri Masjid demolition has apologised for his role in the demolition?

A. Ms. Uma Bharati

B. Mr. Madan Lal Khurana

C. Mr. Kalyan Singh

D. None of the above

133. Which is the University whose Faculty of Law has been given first rank among all Faculties having three-year LL.B. Degree course?

A. National Law School, University, Bangalore

B. University of Delhi

C. University of Hyderabad

D. W.B. National University of Juridical Sciences, Kolkata

134. According to a survey conducted by the Union Ministry of Labour and Employment, ______workers lost their job between October and December, 2008 in India on account of recession.

A. Three lakh B. Four lakh

C. Five lakh D. Seven lakh

135. The phrase 'de facto' means:
A. all the facts
B. all the facts and figures
C. bona fide
D. for all practical purposes

136. The expression "to assume air on" means:
A. to assume inferiority
B. to fill oneself with airy things
C. to affect humility
D. to have a haughty opinion about oneself

137. Which one of the following is associated with mentally or emotionally disturbed?
A. Psychological B. Psychopathic
C. Psychoanalytical D. Psychotherapic

138. The prediction by palm-reading is called:
A. Chironomy B. Chirography
C. Chiropidy D. Chiromancy

139. Neuralgia is associated with:
A. Record of heart beats
B. Mental imbalance
C. Nerve pain
D. Inflammation of the nerves

140. "FOB" in contaracts of carriage referst to
A. Fresh on Board B. Free on Board
C. Fresh off Boat D. Free off Board

141. Dishonour of a cheque is an offence under:
A. Section 138 of the Negotiable Instruments Act
B. Section 420 of the Indian Penal Code
C. Section 73 of the Contract Act
D. Section 41 of the Code of Criminal Procedure

142. A Lease Agreement is a form of:
A. Promissory note
B. Bill of Exchange
C. License
D. Contract

143. Which of the following is not an Alternate Dispute Redressal Mechanism?
A. Mediation B. Lok Adalat
C. Arbitration D. Plea Bargaining

144. The owner and landlord of a flat, allotted to him by the Delhi Development Authority, may recover possession of the flat from his tenant by taking recourse to the law. Which of the following may not have any bearing on such recovery of possession?
A. Delhi Rent Control Act, 1958
B. Agreement to Lease for a fixed term
C. Indian Contract Act, 1872
D. Public Premises (Eviction of Unauthorized Occupants) Act, 1971

145. Which of the following is not related to protection of rights of consumers?
A. 24th December
B. Jago Grahak, Jago
C. 15th March
D. All of them are related to consumer protection.

146. The 44th Amendment Act of 1978 to the Constitution of India:
A. Deleted the Fundamental Right to acquire, hold and dispose off property.
B. Introduced the Fundamental Right to free and compulsory education.
C. Deleted Fundamental Right to work
D. Suspended the Fundamental Right to constitutional remedies.

147. Who declared a state of emergency in India under Article 352 of the Constitution of India in the year 1975?
A. Indira Gandhi
B. Giani Zail Singh
C. Fakhruddin Ali Ahmed
D. Sanjay Gandhi

148. Who is the Solicitor General of India?
A. Milon K. Bannerjee
B. Goolam E. Vahnavati
C. Harish Salve
D. Soli Sorabjee

149. Following a ruling of the Delhi High Court, which among the following is not a criteria for designating an advocte as Senior Advocate: (a) ability (b) standing at Bar (c) 12 years of uninterrupted law practice (d) special knowledge or experience of law (e) money:

A. (b), (c) and (e) B. (e)
C. (b) and (c) D. (c) and (e)

150. The Bill for Welfare of Domestic Help has been passed by the State Legislature of:
A. Orissa B. Delhi
C. Bihar D. Maharashtra

151. Which Bill of Parliament seeks to give effect to Article 21A of the Constitution of India?
A. Right of Education Bill, 2008
B. Central Universities Bill, 2008
C. Limited Liability Partnership Bill, 2008
D. National Investigation Agency Bill, 2008

152. The Rules restricting the display of use of tobacco products in films and television programmes was recently struck down by the High Court of Delhi, being violative of:
A. Article 19(1)(a) of the Constitution of India.
B. Article 21 of the Constitution of India.
C. Section 5A of the Cinematograph Act, 1952.
D. Article 14 of the Constitution of India.

153. Against which of the following Indian establishments has a class action lawsuit been filed recently in the United States District Court, Southern District of New York?
A. Price Waterhouse Coopers
B. Satyam Computer Services Ltd.
C. Maytas Infra Ltd.
D. All of the above

154. Which judge of the Supreme Court of India was recently reported to have equated a terrorist with an animal and thus deserving of animal rights instead of human rights, in his speech?
A. Justice Arijit Pasayat
B. Justice B. N. Agarwal
C. Justice S. B. Sinha
D. Justice S. H. Kapadia

155. Who founded the doctrine of Utilitarianism?
A. John Austin
B. Holmes
C. Jeremy Bentham
D. Ronald Dworkin

156. Which of the following is not related to legal research?
A. www. manupatra.com
B. Black's Law Dictionary
C. Boyle's Law
D. Law of the Sea

157. Which of the following is considered the first international crime?
A. Piracy on the High Seas
B. Violation of Human Rights
C. Slavery
D. Software Piracy

158. Under which Article of the Constitution of India is the law down by Supreme Court binding on all courts?
A. Article 32 B. Article 141
C. Article 226 D. Article 124

159. Driving without a valid "Pollution Under Control Certificate" is punishable under the provisions of:
A. The Motor Vehicles Act, 1988
B. The Air (Prevention and Control of Pollution) Act, 1981
C. The Environment (Protection) Act, 1986
D. The Public Liability Insurance Act, 1991

160. Who appoints the Attorney General of India?
A. Chief Justice of India
B. Ministry of Law and Justice, Government of India
C. President of India
D. President of India in consultation with the Chief Justice of India

161. The only University in India covered in the first "Top 500 World University Rankings" for the year 2007 published by the Times Higher Education Supplement was:
A. University of Bombay
B. Punjab University
C. Shantiniketan
D. University of Delhi

162. An arrested person under the Indian Constitution does not have a fundamental right to ______.

A. travel abroad

B. practise any profession

C. get assistance of a legal practitioner of his choice if arrested under preventive detention law

D. challenge an arbitrary law

163. How many official languages have been recognised under the Constitution of India?

A. 14 B. 18

C. 20 D. 22

164. Which of the following is not true about LED?

A. It is an abbreviation for Light Emitting Diode.

B. It can emit light of various colours.

C. It is a type of superconductor.

D. It can emit light of infrared and ultra-violet frequencies.

165. Which of the following bodies is not set up under the Constitution of India?

A. Finance Commission

B. Union Public Service Commission

C. Supreme Court of India

D. National Human Rights Commission

166. Which documentary film won an Oscar during 81st Academy Awards 2009?

A. Slumdog Millionaire

B. Smile Pinki

C. Pinki Sonkar

D. Smile Train

167. The Child Labour (Prohibition and Regulation) Act, as amended in 2006, prohibits the employment of children under the age of ____ years as domestic servants.

A. 12 B. 18

C. 16 D. 14

168. Which of the following theories of crime is based on the works of Henry McKay and Clifford R. Shaw of the Chicago School thought?

A. Social disorganization theory

B. Strain theory

C. Rational choice theory

D. Routine activity theory

169. What is meant by the expression "Separation of Powers"?

A. Division of powers and spheres of authority between the police and the army at local and national level.

B. Model of governance dividing the powers and responsibilities of the State between its Executive, Legislature and a Judiciary.

C. Provision under the Constitution of India for separate High Courts for each State of the country.

D. Division of rights and liabilities between the Central Government, State Governments and the citizens of India through the Constitution of India read with the Right to Information Act.

170. Who is the author of the book "A Bunch of Old Letters"?

A. Pt. Jawahar Lal Nehru

B. Mahatma Gandhi

C. Smt. Indira Nehru Gandhi

D. Shri K.C. Pant

171. Which University had established Faculty of Law in 1924?

A. Allahabad University

B. Aligarh Muslim University

C. Banaras Hindu University

D. University of Delhi

172. Which is the present Law Commission of India?

A. 13th B. 16th

C. 18th D. 21st

173. Which of the following is entrusted with a statutory duty of laying down the standards of professional conduct an etiquette for advocates in India?

A. Bar Association of India

B. Bar Council of India

C. Delhi Bar Council

D. Supreme Court of India

174. What is an extradition treaty?

A. A treaty for surrender of an alleged or convicted criminal by one nation to another.

B. A treaty for ensuring fair trial of an alleged or convicted criminal transferred by one nation to another.

C. A treaty for international trial of an alleged or convicted criminal.

D. A treaty for trial of an alleged or convicted criminal by a nation, for crime committed or allegedly committed in another nation.

175. Who among the following is an accused in the Uphaar cinema fire case?

A. Vikas Yadav B. Sushil Ansal

C. Sanjeev Nanda D. Manu Sharma

ANSWERS

1	2	3	4	5	6	7	8	9	10
D	C	D	D	C	B	C	D	C	C
11	**12**	**13**	**14**	**15**	**16**	**17**	**18**	**19**	**20**
D	C	C	D	A	B	A	C	B	B
21	**22**	**23**	**24**	**25**	**26**	**27**	**28**	**29**	**30**
A	D	C	A	D	A	A	C	B	B
31	**32**	**33**	**34**	**35**	**36**	**37**	**38**	**39**	**40**
D	C	C	B	D	A	B	A	B	A
41	**42**	**43**	**44**	**45**	**46**	**47**	**48**	**49**	**50**
B	B	A	B	A	B	A	D	D	B
51	**52**	**53**	**54**	**55**	**56**	**57**	**58**	**59**	**60**
C	A	D	A	B	A	C	D	C	D
61	**62**	**63**	**64**	**65**	**66**	**67**	**68**	**69**	**70**
D	B	B	A	A	D	A	A	A	A
71	**72**	**73**	**74**	**75**	**76**	**77**	**78**	**79**	**80**
C	B	D	B	D	B	B	A	A	B
81	**82**	**83**	**84**	**85**	**86**	**87**	**88**	**89**	**90**
B	D	B	B	A	C	D	D	A	B
91	**92**	**93**	**94**	**95**	**96**	**97**	**98**	**99**	**100**
D	B	B	B	D	B	C	C	B	B
101	**102**	**103**	**104**	**105**	**106**	**107**	**108**	**109**	**110**
B	C	C	A	C	A	C	B	A	C
111	**112**	**113**	**114**	**115**	**116**	**117**	**118**	**119**	**120**
A	B	C	A	A	A	D	A	C	C
121	**122**	**123**	**124**	**125**	**126**	**127**	**128**	**129**	**130**
D	D	C	C	B	C	B	B	B	B
131	**132**	**133**	**134**	**135**	**136**	**137**	**138**	**139**	**140**
C	C	B	B	C	D	B	B	C	B

141	142	143	144	145	146	147	148	149	150
A	D	D	D	A	A	C	B	B	D
151	152	153	154	155	156	157	158	159	160
A	C	B	A	A	C	C	B	A	D
161	162	163	164	165	166	167	168	169	170
D	A	D	D	D	B	D	C	B	A
171	172	173	174	175					
D	C	B	A	B					

INDIAN POLITY

1

Constitutional Development of India

The Constitution of India, as opted by the Constituent Assembly in 1949, was not something absolutely new. It was, to a great extent, influenced by the Government of India Act of 1935 that was passed by the British Parliament. In order to understand and appreciate the Constitution, it is necessary to glance at the constitutional development during the British rule in India.

The foundation of British authority in India was laid down through the establishment of East India Company in England under a Charter of the British Queen Elizabeth. Under the Charter the Company was given an exclusive right of trading with India. In the beginning, the Company was purely a trading organization, but later on due to political circumstances, it acquired territorial power.

REGULATING ACT OF 1773

With the expansion of political power of the Company, it was felt in England that the affairs of the Company needed some regulation. As a result, the Regulating Act of 1773 came into being. Some of the salient features of the Act were as follows :

- Subjected the Company's actions to the supervision of the British Government.
- End of Dual government.
- Governor of Bengal to be the Governor-General of British territories of India.
- Establishment of Supreme Court in Calcutta.
- The servants of the Company were forbidden to engage in private trade, accept presents or bribes, etc.

PITT'S INDIA ACT OF 1784

- The commercial and political activities of the Company were now separated. Board of Control of six members (including two cabinet ministers) set-up to guide and supervise the affairs of the Company in India.
- Three members will be there in Governor-General's Executive Council.
- Secret Committee of three Directors were to look into political and military affairs. [Governor-General and the council were forbidden to declare war and make treaties without the sanction of secret committee].
- Madras and Bombay Presidencies were subordinated to the Governor-General-in-Council of Bengal in all matters.
- This act gave the British Government a measure of control over the Company's affairs. In fact, the Company became a subordinate department of the State.

CHARTER ACT OF 1793

- Company given monopoly of trade for 20 more years.
- Expenses and salaries of the Board of Control to be charged on Indian revenue.
- The Governor-General and the Governors could now over-ride the decisions of their respective Councils.
- All laws were to be translated in Indian languages.

- It laid the foundation of government, by written laws, interpreted by courts.

CHARTER ACT OF 1813

- Company deprived of its trade monopoly in India except in tea and trade with China. This made the Company more of an administrative body. All Englishmen could trade in India subject to few restrictions.
- A sum of ₹ 1 lakh earmarked annually for education of Indians.
- Further, Christian missionaries were also permitted to come to India and preach their religion.

CHARTER ACT OF 1833

- End of Company's monopoly even in tea and trade with China. Company was asked to close its commercial business at the earliest.
- All restrictions on European immigration into India and acquisition of land and property in India by them were removed, legalizing European colonization of India.
- Governor-General of Bengal to be Governor-General of India; all powers, administrative and financial, were centralized in the hands of the Governor-General-in-Council. (1st Governor-General of India—Lord William Bentinck).
- President of Board of Control became the minister for Indian affairs.
- A law member (without power to vote) was added to the Executive Council of the Governor-General. Macaulay was the first Law member. This increased the Council's strength to four, with it began the Indian Legislature.
- A law commission was constituted for codification of laws.
- The Act threw open to all, irrespective of religion, place of birth, descent and colour, services under the Company.

CHARTER ACT OF 1853

- The Act renewed the powers of the Company and allowed it to retain the possession of Indian territories in trust for the British Crown but not for any specified period.
- The number of members of the Court of Directors was reduced from 24 to 18 of which 6 were to be nominated by the Crown.
- The Law member was made a full member of the Governor-General's Executive Council.
- Legislation was treated for the first time as separate from executive functions.
- Questions could be asked and the policy of the Executive Council could be discussed, though the Executive Council could veto a bill of the Legislative Council.
- Recruitment to Civil Services was based on open annual competition examination (excluding Indians).

GOVERNMENT OF INDIA ACT, 1858

- Rule of Company in India ended and that of the Crown began.
- System of Dual government ended. Court of Directors and Board of Control abolished and substituted them with a post of Secretary of State (a member of the British cabinet). He was assisted by a 15-member council (called Indian Council). He was to exercise the powers of the Crown.
- Secretary of State governed India through the Governor-General.
- Governor-General received the title of Viceroy. He represented Secretary of State and was assisted by an Executive Council, which consisted of high officials of the Government.
- A unitary and highly centralized administrative structure was created.

INDIAN COUNCILS ACT, 1861

- A fifth member, who was to be a jurist, was added to the Viceroy's Executive Council.
- 6-12 additional members to be added to the Executive Council for legislation purpose. This implied that Viceroy's Executive Council, which was so long composed of officials, would now include certain additional non-official members. Some of non-official seats were offered to natives of high ranks. Thus, a minute element of 'popular' participation was introduced in the legislative process. The additional members, though, had little powers.
- The Executive Council was now to be called Central Legislative Council.
- Viceroy could issue ordinances in case of emergency.

INDIAN COUNCILS ACT, 1892

- Two improvements in both the Central and the Provincial Legislative Councils were suggested.
- Though the majority of the official members was retained, the non-official members were to be nominated by the Bengal Chamber of Commerce and Provincial Legislative Councils. [The non-official members of the Provincial Councils were to be nominated by certain local bodies such as universities, district boards, municipalities]. Indian leaders like G.K. Gokhale, Ashutosh Mukherjee, Ras Bihari Ghosh and S.N. Banerjee found their way in the Legislative Council.
- The Councils were to have the powers to discuss the annual statement of revenue and expenditure (*i.e.* the budget) and of addressing questions to the Executive). They could also put questions, within certain limits, to the Government on matters of public interest after giving six days notice.

INDIAN COUNCILS ACT, 1909

- Morley was the Secretary of State, while Minto was the Indian Viceroy.
- Legislative Councils, both at the Centre and in the Provinces, were expanded.
- With regard to Central Government, an Indian member was taken in the Executive Council of the Governor-General.
- The size of the Provincial Legislative Councils were enlarged by including elected non-official members so that the official majority was gone. Their functions were also increased. Now, they could move resolutions on Budget and on some matters of public issues.
- An element of election was also introduced in the Central Legislative Council, but the official majority was maintained.
- The most notable and retrograde change introduced was that Muslims were given separate representation. Thus, communal representation was introduced.

GOVERNMENT OF INDIA ACT, 1919

- Dyarchy system introduced in the provinces. It was considered to be a substantial step towards transfer of power to the Indians). The Provincial subjects of administration were to be divided into two categories : Transferred and Reserved.
- The Transferred subjects were to be administered by the Governor with the aid of ministers responsible to the Legislative Council. The Governor and the Executive Council were to administer the reserved subjects without any responsibility to the legislature.
- *Devolution Rules* : Subjects of administration were divided into two categories—Central and Provincial. Subjects of all India importance (like railways and finance) were brought under the category of Central, while matters relating to the

administration of the provinces were classified as Provincial.

- The Provincial Legislature was to consist of one House only (Legislative Council).
- The number of Indians in the Governor-General's Executive Council was raised to three in a Council of eight. The Indian members were entrusted with departments such as Law, Education, Labour, Health and Industries.
- The Centre was now to have a Bicameral Legislature for the first time. It actually happened after 1935 Act.
- Communal representation extended to Sikhs, Christians, Anglo-Indians, etc. Secretary of State to be henceforth paid salary out of the British revenue.

GOVERNMENT OF INDIA ACT, 1935

- Provided for the establishment of All-India Federation consisting of the British provinces and the Princely States. The joining of Princely States was voluntary and as a result the federation did not come into existence.
- Dyarchy was introduced at the Centre (*e.g.,* Department of Foreign Affairs and Defence were reserved for the Governor-General).
- The other Federal subjects were to be administered by the Governor- General with the assistance and advice of a Council of Ministers to be chosen by him (but to include representatives of Princely States and minorities, and to be responsible to the Central Legislature). Residuary powers were to be with the Governor-General only.
- The Federal Legislature (Central Legislature) was to have two chambers (bicameral)—the Council of State and the Federal Assembly. The Council of State was to be a permanent body with one-third of its membership being vacated and renewed triennially. The Federal Assembly's duration was fixed for five years.
- It made a 3-fold division of powers: Federal (Central) Legislative List Provincial Legislative List and the Concurrent Legislative List. Residuary legislative powers were subject to the discretion of the Governor-General. Even if a bill was passed by the Federal Legislature, the Governor-General could veto it, while even Acts assented to by the Governor- General could be disallowed by the King-in-Council.
- Provincial autonomy replaced Dyarchy in Provinces *i.e.,* the distinction between Reserved and Transferred subjects was abolished and full responsible government was established, subject to certain safeguards. They were granted separate legal identity.
- The Governor was the head of the Provincial Executive and was expected to be guided by the advice of the popular ministries. However, the Act gave arbitrary powers to the Governors to act in their 'discretion' in certain matters.
- The Act also provided for a Federal Court (which was established in 1937), with original and appellate powers) to interpret the Constitution. A Federal Bank (the Reserve Bank of India) was also established. The Indian Council of Secretary of State was abolished.
- Principle of separate electorate was extended to include Anglo-Indians, Indian Christians and Europeans.
- Burma (now Myanmar) and Aden were separated from India and two new provinces Orissa (now Odisha) and Sind were created.

INDIAN INDEPENDENCE ACT, 1947

- The division of British India into the two new and fully sovereign dominions of India and Pakistan, with effect from 15 August 1947.
- The partition of the provinces of Bengal and Punjab between the two new countries.

- ❖ The establishment of the office of Governor-General in each of the two new countries, as representative of the Crown.
- ❖ The conferral of complete legislative authority upon the respective Constituent Assemblies of the two new countries.
- ❖ The termination of British suzerainty over the princely states, with effect from 15 August 1947 (this was intended to encourage the various rulers to accede to one or other of the two new countries).
- ❖ The dropping of the use of the title "Emperor of India") by the British monarch (this was subsequently done by King George VI by royal proclamation on 22 June 1948).
- ❖ The Act also made provision for the division of joint property, etc. between the two new countries, including in particular the division of the armed forces.

This marked the end of the British rule in India and the emergence of a free India.

Interim Government (1946)

Members	***Portfolios Held***	***Members***	***Portfolios Held***
Jawaharlal Nehru	External Affairs & Commonwealth Relations	C.H. Bhabha	Works, Mines & Power
Sardar Vallabhbhai Patel	Home, Information & Broadcasting	Liaquat Ali Khan	Finance
Dr. Rajendra Prasad	Food & Agriculture	Abdur Rab Nishtar	Posts & Air
Dr. John Mathai	Industries & Supplies	Asaf Ali	Railways & Transport
Jagjivan Ram	Labour	C. Rajagopalachari	Education & Arts
Sardar Baldev Singh	Defence	I.I. Chundrigar	Commerce
		Ghaznafar Ali Khan	Health
		Joginder Nath Mandal	Law

First Cabinet of Free India (1947)

Members	***Portfolios Held***
Jawaharlal Nehru	Prime Minister, External Affairs & Commonwealth Relations, Scientific Research
Sardar Vallabhbhai Patel	Home, Information & Broadcasting, States
Dr. Rajendra Prasad	Food & Agriculture
Maulana Abul Kalam Azad	Education
Dr. John Mathai	Railways & Transport
R.K. Shanmugham Chetty	Finance
Dr. B.R. Ambedkar	Law
Jagjivan Ram	Labour
Sardar Baldev Singh	Defence
Raj Kumari Amrit Kaur	Health
C.H. Bhabha	Commerce
Rafi Ahmed Kidwai	Communication
Dr. Shyama Prasad Mukherji	Industries & Supplies
V.N. Gadgil	Works, Mines & Power

***

2

Constituent Assembly and Its Working

COMPOSITION OF THE CONSTITUENT ASSEMBLY

The Constituent Assembly was constituted in Nov. 1946 under the scheme formulated by the Cabinet Mission Plan. The features of the scheme were :

1. The Total strength of the Constituent Assembly was to be 389.
2. Each province and princely state (or group of states in case of small states) were to be allotted seats in proportion to their respective population. Roughly, one seat was to be allotted for every million population.
3. The representatives of princely states were to be nominated by the heads of the princely states.

The elections to the Constitutent Assembly (for 296 seats allotted to the British Indian Provinces) were held in July-August 1946. The Indian National Congress won 208 seats, the Muslim League 73 seats, and the small groups and independents got the remaining 15 seats. However, the 93 seats allotted to the princely states were not filled as they decided to stay away from the Constitutent Assembly. The Assembly included all important personalities of India at that time, with the exception of Mahatma Gandhi and M.A. Jinnah.

The Constituent Assembly held its first meeting on December 9, 1946. The Muslim League boycotted the meeting and insisted on a separate state of Pakistan. The meeting was thus attended by only 211 members. Dr. Sachchidanand Sinha, the oldest member, was elected as the temporary President of the Assembly, following the French practice.

Later, on December 11, 1946, Dr. Rajendra Prasad and H.C. Mukherjee were elected as the President and Vice-President of the Assembly respectively. Sir B.N. Rau was appointed as the Constitutional advisor to the Assembly.

The Constituent Assembly had 11 sessions over two years, 11 months and 18 days. The Constitution-makers had gone through the constitutions of about 60 countries, and the Draft Constitution was considered for 114 days. The total expenditure incurred on making the Constitution amounted to Rs. 64 lakh.

On January 24, 1950, the Constituent Assembly held its final session. It, however, did not end, and continued as the provisional parliament of India from January 26, 1950 till the formation of new Parliament after the first general elections in 1951-52.

COMMITTEES OF THE CONSTITUENT ASSEMBLY

The Constituent Assembly appointed a number of committees to deal with different tasks of constitution-making. Out of these, eight were major committees and the others were minor committees. The names of these committees and their chairmen are given below :

Major Committees

1. Drafting Committee—Dr. B.R. Ambedkar.

2. Steering Committee—Dr. Rajendra Prasad.
3. Rules of Procedure Committee—Dr. Rajendra Prasad.
4. Union Powers Committee—Jawaharlal Nehru.
5. Union Constitution Committee—Jawaharlal Nehru.
6. Provincial Constitution Committee—Sardar Patel.
7. Advisory Committee on Fundamental Rights and Minorities—Sardar Patel.
   This committee had two sub-committes:
   (a) Fundamental Rights Sub-Committee—J.B. Kripalani
   (b) Minorities Sub-Committee—H.C. Mukherjee.
8. States Committee (Committee for Negotiating with States)—Jawaharlal Nehru.

Minor Committees

1. House Committee—B. Pattabhi Sitaramayya.
2. Finance and Staff Committee—A.N. Sinha.
3. Credentials Committee—Alladi Krishnaswamy Ayyar.
4. Committee on the Functions of the Constituent Assembly—G.V. Mavalankar.
5. Order of Business Committee—Dr. K.M. Munshi.
6. Ad-hoc Committee on the National Flag—Dr. Rajendra Prasad.
7. Special Committee to Examine the Draft Constitution—Alladi Krishnaswamy Ayyar.

Drafting Committee

Among all the committees of the Constituent Assembly, the most important committee was the Drafting Committee set up on August 29, 1947. It was this committee that was entrusted with the task of preparing a draft of the new Constitution. It consisted of seven members. They were :

1. Dr. B.R. Ambedkar (Chairman)
2. Dr. K.M. Munshi
3. Syed Mohammad Saadullah
4. N. Gopalaswamy Ayyangar
5. N. Madhava Rau (He replaced B. L. Mitter who resigned due to ill-health)
6. T. T. Krishnamachari (He replaced D.P. Khaitan who died in 1948)
7. Alladi Krishnaswamy Ayyar

The Drafting Committee, after taking into consideration the proposals of the various committees, prepared the first draft of the Constitution of India, which was published in February 1948. The people of India were given eight months to discuss the draft and propose amendments. In the light of the public comments, criticisms and suggestions, the Drafting Committee prepared a second draft, which was published in October 1948.

The Drafting Committee took less than six months to prepare its draft. In all it sat only for 141 days.

Some provisions of the Constitution pertaining to citizenship, elections, provisional parliament, temporary and transitional provisions, and short title contained in Articles 5, 6, 7, 8, 9, 60, 324, 366, 367, 379, 388, 391, 392 and 393 came into force on November 26, 1949 itself.

The remaining provisions (the major part) of the Constitution came into force on January 26, 1950. This day is referred to in the Constitution as the 'date of its commencement', and celebrated as the Republic Day.

January 26 was specifically chosen as the 'date of commencement' of the Constitution because of its historical importance. It was on this day in 1930 that *Purna Swaraj* day was celebrated, following the resolution of the Lahore Session (December 1929) of the INC.

With the commencement of the Constitution, the Indian Independence Act of 1947 and the Government of India Act of 1935, with all enactments amending or supplementing the latter Act, were repealed. The Abolition of Privy Council Jurisdiction Act (1949) was however continued.

Criticism of the Constituent Assembly

1. Took long time.
2. Not a Representative Body.
3. Not a Sovereign Body.
4. Lawyer–Politician Domination.
5. Dominated by Congress.
6. Dominated by Hindus.

Statewise Membership of the Constituent Assembly of India as on December 31, 1947

Name	*No. of Members*	*Name*	*No. of Members*
A. Provinces (Indian Provinces)—229		Jodhpur	2
Madras	49	Kolhapur	1
Bombay	21	Kotah	1
West Bengal	19	Mayurbhanj	1
United Provinces	55	Mysore	7
East Punjab	12	Patiala	2
Bihar	36	Rewa	2
C.P. and Berar	17	Travancore	6
Assam	8	Udaipur	2
Orissa	9	Sikkim and Cooch Behar Group	1
Delhi	1	Tripura, Manipur and Khasi States Group	1
Ajmer-Merwara	1	U.P. States Group	1
Coorg	1	Eastern Rajputana States Group	3
B. Indian States (Princely States)—70		Central India States Group (including Bundelkhand and Malwa)	3
Alwar	1	Western India States Group	4
Baroda	3	Gujarat States Group	2
Bhopal	1	Deccan and Madras States Group	2
Bikaner	1	Punjab States Group	3
Cochin	1	Eastern States Group I	4
Gwalior	4	Eastern States Group II	3
Indore	1	Residuary States Group	4
Jaipur	3	**Total**	**299**

***

3

The Constitution of India : Preamble

One of the first tasks which the Constiuent Assembly did was the formulation of the objectives and the guiding principles that were to be the basis of the Constitution and reflect the democratic spirit of the Constitution.

In its resolution of June 24, 1946 the working committee of the Congress decided that the Congress should join the Assembly with a view to framing the Constitution for a free, united and democratic India.

At the session held in November 1946, on the eve of the meeting of the Constituent Assembly, the Congress adopted a resolution declaring that : "it stands for an independent sovereign republic wherein all powers and authority are derived from the people and for a Constitution wherein social objectives are laid down to promote freedom, progress and equal opportunity for all the people of India..."

In the early drafts of the Union Constitution, the Preamble was a somewhat formal affair. As provided by B.N. Rau's memorandum on the Union Constitution, dated 30th May, 1947 it was :

> *"We the people of India, seeking to promote the common good, do hereby, through our chosen representatives, enact, adopt and give to ourselves this constitution".*

Later, the Drafting Committee felt that the Preamble should be restricted to defining the essential features of the new State and its basic socio-political objectives and that the other matters dealt with in the resolution could be more appropriately provided for in the substansive parts of the Constitution.

Accordingly, the preamble, as formulated by the committee and included in its February 1948 Draft of the Constitution, read as follows :

> *"We, the people of India, having solemnly resolved to constitute India into a Sovereign Democratic Republic and to secure to all its citizens. Justice—social, economic and political, Liberty of thought, expression, belief, faith and worship;*
>
> *Equality of status and of opportunity; and to promote among all;*
>
> *Fraternity assuring the dignity of the individual and the unity of the Nation;*
>
> *In our Constituent Assembly this....of....(...day of May 1948, A.D.). do hereby adopt, enact and give to ourselves this Constitution."*

The Drafting Committee considered certain modifications to be neccessary although, generally it had tried, "to embody in the Preamble the spirit and, as far as possible, the language of the Objective Resolutions."

Thus, the phrase "Independent Sovereign Republic" was substituted by "Sovereign Democractic Republic", since independence was implied in the word 'sovereign'. A new clause about 'fraternity' was added, as, in the opinion of the committee, the need for fraternal concord and goodwill in India was never greater than at that time and this particular aim of the Constitution required to be emphasized through a special mention in the Preamble.

The Preamble was adopted by the Assembly without any alteration. Subsequently the words and figure "this twenty-sixth day of November 1949", were introduced in the last paragraph to indicate the date on which the Constitution was finally adopted by the Constituent Assembly.

The Preamble continued to be the same, till the year 1976 when by the 42nd Amendment, the phrase "Sovereign Democratic Republic" was replaced by "Sovereign Socialist Secular Democratic Republic" and "unity of the Nation" by "unity and integrity of the Nation."

Therefore, now, the present form of the Preamble is as follows :

> *"We the people of India having solemnly resolved to constitute India into a Sovereign, Socialist, Secular, Democratic, Republic and to secure to all its citizens.*
>
> *Justice–social, economic and political, Liberty of thought, expression, belief, faith and worship.*
>
> *Equality of status and of opportunity, and to promote among them all; Fraternity assuring the dignity of the individual and the unity and integrity of the Nation;*
>
> *In our Constituent Assembly this twenty-sixth day of November, 1949, do hereby adopt, enact and give to ourselves this Constitution."*

OBJECTIVES OF THE PREAMBLE

Sovereignty

Sovereignty is one of the foremost elements of any independent State. It means absolute independence, i.e., a government which is not controlled by any other power : internal or external. A country cannot have its own constitution without being sovereign. India is a sovereign country. It is free from external control. It can frame its policies. India is free to formulate its own foreign policy.

Socialist

The word socialist was not there in the Preamble of the Constitution in its original form. In 1976, the 42nd Amendment to the Constitution incorporated 'Socialist' and 'Secular', in the Preamble. The word 'Socialism' had been used in the context of economic planning. It signifies major role in the economy. It also means commitment to attain ideals like removal of inequalities, provision of minimum basic necessities to all, equal pay for equal work.

When you read about the Directive Principles of the State Policy, you will see how these ideals have been incorporated as well as partly, implemented in the Constitution.

Secularism

The term secular, as interpreted by the courts in India, means that 'the State' shall not discriminate between different religions and all shall be treated equally. In the context of secularism in India, it is said that 'India is neither religious, nor irreligious nor anti-religious.' Now what does this imply? It implies that in India there will be no 'State' religion—the 'State' will not support any particular religion out of public fund. This has two implications, (a) every individual is free to believe in, and practice, any religion he/she belongs to, and, (b) State will not discriminate against any individual or group on the basis of religion.

Democratic

The term democratic implies that the Governments are elected and accountable for their deeds to the people of India. Elections have to be held at regular intervals and people are allowed to exercise their franchise freely and fairly. It also means that there shall prevail the rule of law and no one could act arbitrarily.

In fact the Democratic principles of the country flow from this memorable last line of the Preamble. Democracy is generally known as government of the people, by the people and for the people.

Effectively this means that the Government is elected by the people, it is responsible and accountable to the people. The democratic principles are highlighted with the provisions of universal adult franchise, elections, fundamental rights, and responsible government.

Republic

The term Republic implies that the Head of the State gets his office by election by the people and not by hereditary claims. The Preamble declares India as a Republic. It means that the head of the State is the President who is indirectly elected and he is not a hereditary ruler as in case of the British Monarch. Under chapter of Union Executive you will read in detail about the election of the President of India.

Justice

Though it is not easy to give a precise meaning of the term justice, by and large, it can be stated that the idea of justice is equated with equity and fairness. Social justice, therefore, would mean that all sections of society, irrespective of caste, creed, sex, place of birth, religion or language, would be treated equally and no one would be discriminated on any of these grounds. Similarly, economic justice would mean that all the natural resources of the country would be equally available to all the citizens and no one would suffer from any undeserved want. Similarly, Political justice entitles all the citizens equal political rights such as right to vote, right to contest elections and right to hold public office etc.

Liberty

The Preamble also keeps liberty of thought, expression, belief, faith, and worship as its ideals. It means that the citizens would be free to follow a religion of their own choice and express their views freely and frankly. 'The State' would not interfere in all these matters. Though freedom from want has not been guaranteed in the Fundamental Rights, certain directives to the State have been mentioned in the Directive Principles.

Equality

The Preamble also provides for equality of status and opportunity. It implies that all the citizens would be able to make full use of their talents without any interruption and develop their personality to the maximum extent possible. Similarly equality of opportunities implies that regardless of the socio-economic situations into which one is born, he/she will have the same chance as everybody else to develop his/her talents and choose means of livelihood.

Fraternity, Dignity, Unity and Integrity

Lastly, the Preamble also aims at developing fraternity assuring the dignity of individual and the unity and integrity of the nation. It means that the common brotherhood, to be developed in India, would be based on the dignity of the individual without any consideration of his status in society. Similarly, such a brotherhood should also lead to the unity and integrity of the nation. In nutshell, the Preamble aims at a social order wherein the people would be sovereign, the government would be elected by and accountable to people, the powers of the government shall be restricted by the rights of people and people would have ample opportunities to develop their talents. Though the Preamble is not technically enforceable through courts of law, it is useful in interpreting the various provisions of the Constitution and acts as a beacon in conflicting situations

SIGNIFICANCE OF THE PREAMBLE

The Preamble embodies the basic philosophy and fundamental values—political, moral and religious—on which the Constitution is based. It contains the grand and noble vision of the Constituent Assembly, and reflects the dreams and aspirations of the founding fathers of the Constitution.

M. Hidayatullah, a former Chief Justice of India, observed, 'Preamble resembles the Declaration of Independence of the United States of America, but is more than a declaration. It is the soul of our Constitution, which lays down the pattern of our political society. It contains a solemn resolve, which nothing but a revolution can alter.

One of the controversies about the Preamble is as to whether it is a part of the Constitution or not. In the *Berubari Union case* (1960), the Supreme Court said that the Preamble shows the general purposes behind the several provisions in the Constitution, and is thus a key to the minds of the makers of the Constitution. Further, where the terms used in any article are ambiguous or capable of more than one meaning, some assistance at interpretation may be taken from the objectives enshrined in the Preamble. Despite this recognition of the significance of the Preamble, the Supreme Court specifically opined that Preamble is *not* a part of the Constitution.

In the *Kesavananda Bharati case* (1973), the Supreme Court rejected the earlier opinion and held that Preamble is a part of the Constitution. It observed that the Preamble is of extreme importance and the Constitution should be read and interpreted in the light of the grand and noble vision expressed in the Preamble.

The question as to whether the Preamble can be amended under Article 368 of the Constitution arose for the first time in the historic case of *Kesavananda Bharati* (1973). It was urged that the Preamble cannot be amended as it is not a part of the Constitution. The petitioner contended that the amending power in Article 368 cannot be used to destroy or damage the basic elements or the fundamental features of the Constitution, which are enshrined in the Preamble.

The Supreme Court, however, held that the Preamble is a part of the Constitution. The Court stated that the opinion tendered by it in the *Berubari Union* (1960) in this regard was wrong, and held that the Preamble can be amended, subject to the condition that no amendment is done to the 'basic features'. In other words, the Court held that the basic elements or the fundamental features of the Constitution as contained in the Preamble cannot be altered by an amendment under Article 368.

The Preamble has been amended only once so far, in 1976, by the 42nd Constitutional Amendment Act, which has added three new words—Socialist, Secular and Integrity—to the Preamble, This amendment was held to be valid.

Sources of Constitution

Source	*Features Borrowed*
Government of India Act, 1935	Federal Scheme, Office of governor, Judiciary, Public Service Commissions, Emergency provisions and administrative details.
British Constitution	Parliamentary government, Rule of Law, legislative procedure, single citizenship, cabinet system, prerogative writs, parliamentary privileges and bicameralism.
US Constitution	Fundamental rights, independence of judiciary, judicial review, impeach- ment of the president, removal of Supreme Court and high court judges and post of vice-president.
Irish Constitution	Directive Principles of State Policy, nomination of members to Rajya Sabha and method of election of president.
Canadian Constitution	Federation with a strong Centre, vesting of residuary powers in the Centre, appointement of state governors by the Centre, and advisory jurisdiction of the Supreme Court.

Source	*Features Borrowed*
Australian Constitution	Concurrent List, freedom of trade, commerce and inter-course, and joint sitting of the two Houses of Parliament.
Weimar Constitution of Germany	Suspension of Fundamental Rights during Emergency.
Soviet Constitution	Fundamental duties and the ideal of justice (social, economic and political) in the Preamble.
French Constitution	Republic and the ideals of liberty, equality and fraternity in the Preamble.
South African Constitution	Procedure for amendment of the Constitution and election of members of Rajya Sabha.
Japanese Constitution	Procedure established by Law.

SALIENT FEATURES OF THE INDIAN CONSTITUTION

The salient features of the Indian Constitution which directly and indirectly flows from the Preamble, indicating the faith of framers in the ideals, objectives and goals as mentioned in our Constitution.

Framed by the People of India

This Constitution has been framed by the representatives of the people of India through a Constituent Assembly during 1946-1949. Prior to it, the British Parliament enacted all the constitutions. The Constituent Assembly, however, was elected indirectly by the Provincial Legislative Assemblies that were themselves elected on a restricted franchise. The representatives of the princely states were the nominees of their rulers. In spite of it, the Constituent Assembly could be called a representative body because the then ruling party at the Centre had decided to give representation to all sections of society as well as to all shades of opinion.

Derived from Various Sources

It is a unique document that was derived from various sources. Our constitution makers were inspired to draft the provisions regarding Fundamental Rights and Supreme Court from the U.S.A, Directive Principles of State Policy from Ireland, Emergency from Germany, Distribution of legislative powers from Canada, and Parliamentary Institutions from the United Kingdom. Besides, they borrowed extensively from the Government of India Act, 1935.

A Written Constitution

The Indian Constitution is mainly a written constitution. A written constitution is framed at a given time and comes into force or is adopted on a fixed date as a document. Our constitution was framed over a period of 2 years, 11 months and 18 days, it was adopted on 26th November, 1949 and enforced on January 26, 1950.

Certain conventions have gradually evolved over a period of time which have proved useful in the working of the constitution. The British Constitution is an example of unwritten constitution. It is to be noted though, that a written constitution is 'mainly' an enacted document, there could be bodies or institutions which may not be included in the constitution but form an important part of governance. In Indian context one can mention the Planning Commission. It is very important body for country's planning and development. But, the planning commission was set up in March 1950, not by an Act of Parliament, nor as a Part of the Constitution of India. It was set up by a cabinet resolution. The Indian constitution is the lengthiest in the world. The original constitution had 395 Articles and 8 Schedules, while, the constitution of USA has only 7 Articles.

Sovereignty of the People

The Constitution declares the people of India to be the supreme authority. Prior to it, the supreme authority lay in the British Parliament. Even the Indian Independence Act, 1947 through which India got independence recognized the supremacy of the British Parliament. The term Sovereignty implies that the people of India are not subordinate to any other external agency. The membership of the Commonwealth of Nations, sometimes, is misinterpreted as a limitation on the sovereignty of the people of India. This, however, is not correct. The Commonwealth has now undergone a sea-change. It is now purely a voluntary association of independent sovereign States.

Republican Polity

The Constitution provides for the republican form of polity in India. Prior to it, the British king was the Head of the State who owed his office to the laws of inheritance. It is note-worthy that in Ancient India there existed republican governments in a number of parts for about one thousand years. But in modern times there was not a single territory where republican form of government prevailed.

Secular Polity

This Constitution provides for a secular polity in India. Though the term secular has not been defined in the Constitution anywhere, the substance of secularism can be deduced from various provisions of the Constitution. It has been used in the sense of absence of discrimination on grounds of religion and equal respect for all religions. Prior to it, the Government of India Act, 1935 had provided for a separate department of Ecclesiastical Affairs.

A Combination of Rigidity and Flexibility

The Indian Constitution is a unique example of combination of rigidity and flexibility. A constitution may be called rigid or flexible on the basis of its amending procedure. In a rigid constitution, amendment of the constitution is not easy. The Constitutions of USA, Switzerland and Australia are considered rigid constitutions. While, the British Constitution is considered flexible because amendment procedure is easy and simple. The Constitution of India provides for three categories of amendments. In the first category, amendment can be done by the two houses of Parliament simple majority of the members present and voting of before sending it for the President's assent. In the second category amendments require a special majority. Such an amendment can be passed by each House of Parliament by a majority of the total members of that House as well as by the 2/3rd majority of the members present and voting in each house of Parliament and send to the President for his assent which cannot be denied. In the third category besides the special majority mentioned in the second category, the same has to be approved also by at least 50% of the State legislatures. Thus, you see that the Indian Constitution provides for the type of amendments ranging from simple to most difficult procedure depending on the nature of the amendment.

Federal Polity

India has adopted a federal structure. In a federation there are two distinct levels of governments. There is one government for the whole country which is called the Union or Central Government. Also there is government for each Unit/State. The United States of America is a federation whereas the United Kingdom (Britain) has a unitary form of government. In a unitary structure there is only one government for the whole country and the power is centralised.

The Constitution of India does not use the term 'federal state'. It says that India is a 'Union of States'. There is a distribution of powers between the Union/Central Government and the State Governments. Since India is a federation, such distribution of functions becomes necessary. There are three lists of powers such as Union List, State List and the Concurrent List. These lists have been explained in Lesson 8 in detail. On the basic of this distribution, India may be called a federal system.

The supremacy of the judiciary is an essential feature of a federation so that the constitution could be interpreted impartially. In India, the Supreme Court has been established to guard the constitution. However, in case of Indian federalism, more powers have been given to the Union Government in administrative, legislative, financial and judicial matters. In fact, The Indian federal set up stands out with certain distinctive unitary features. The makers of our constitution while providing for two sets of government at the centre and in the states provided for division of powers favouring the Central Government, appointment of the Head of the State government by the Central Government, single unified judiciary, single citizenship indicate the unitary nature of our federalism. Therefore, it is said that India has a quasi-federal set up.

Parliamentary Democracy

India has a parliamentary form of democracy. This has been adopted from the British system. In a parliamentary democracy there is a close relationship between the legislature and the executive. The Cabinet is selected from among the members of legislature. The cabinet is responsible to the latter. In fact the Cabinet holds office so long as it enjoys the confidence of the legislature. In this form of democracy, the Head of the State is nominal. In India, the President is the Head of the State. Constitutionally the President enjoys numerous powers but in practice the Council of Ministers headed by thc Prime Minister, which really exercises these powers. The President acts on the advice of the Prime Minister and the Council of Ministers.

Fundamental Rights and Fundamental Duties

Every human being is entitled to enjoy certain rights which ensure good living. In a democracy all citizens enjoy equal rights. The Constitution of India guarantees those rights in the form of Fundamental Rights. Fundamental Rights are one of the important features of the Indian Constitution. Fundamental Rights are justiciable and are protected by the judiciary. In case of violation of any of these rights one can move to the court of law for their protection. Fundamental Duties were added to our Constitution by the 42nd Amendment. It lays down a list of ten Fundamental Duties for all citizens of India. While the rights are given as guarantees to the people, the duties are obligations which every citizen is expected to perform.

Directive Principles of State Policy

The Constitution provides for the Directive Principles of State Policy. No previous constitution had such a provision. Though the Instrument of Instructions attached to the Government of India Act, 1935, appears to be analogous to the Directives, the aims and objects of the two are very different. It is to be noted that the leaders of the Indian National Movement had made various promises regarding the Fundamental Rights that the citizens of free India would enjoy.

But when India got independence in 1947, the leaders realised that they did not possess sufficient means to grant those rights, particularly economic and social rights, immediately. But at the same time they did not want to go back upon their promises. They, therefore, decided to put the Fundamental Rights into two categories:

(i) those that were granted immediately.

(ii) those that would be granted in future if and when they were capable to do so.

The first were included in Chapter Ill entitled Fundamental Rights and the second were included in Chapter IV entitled Directive Principles of State Policy. The rights included in Chapter IV are nonenforceable through courts of law but they are the fundamental principles of governance which 'the State' (*i.e.* the Government and Parliament of India; the Government and the Legislature of each of the States and all local or other authorities within the territory of India or under the control of Government of India) is required to take cognisance of.

Single Integrated Judicial System

India has a single integrated judicial system. The Supreme Court stands as the apex court of the judicial system. Below the Supreme Court are the High Courts. The High Courts control and supervise the lower courts. The Indian judiciary, thus, stands like a pyramid with the lower courts as the base, High Courts in the middle and the Supreme Court at the top.

Independence of Judiciary

Indian judiciary is independent an impartial. The Indian judiciary is free from the influence of the executive and the legislature. The judges are appointed on the basis of their qualifications and cannot be removed easily.

Judicial Review

The Constitution provides for the judicial review of the Acts of Legislatures (of both, the Union and

States) as well as of the activities of the executives (Union and State). Prior to it, there was no such provision. This provision keeps the legislative and the executive branches of governments under restraint and they cannot exercise their authority arbitrarily.

Single Citizenship

In a federal state usually the citizens enjoys double citizenship as is the case in the USA. In India, there is only single citizenship. It means that every Indian is a citizen of India, irrespective of the place of his/her residence or place of birth. He/she is not a citizen of the Constituent State like Jharkhand, Uttaranchal or Chattisgarh to which he/she may belong to but remains a citizen of India. All the citizens of India can secure employment anywhere in the country and enjoy all the rights equally in all the parts of India.

Universal Adult Franchise

It provides for the universal adult franchise. Prior to it all the constitutions provided for restricted franchise. According to the Government of India Act, 1935, which granted the largest amount of franchise, only 14% of the people had a right to vote. It is noteworthy that most of the western democracies had taken a number of decades to grant such a right to their citizens.

Emergency Provisions

› Constitution makers also foresaw that there d be situations when the government could not un as in ordinary times. To cope with such ations, the Constitution elaborates on emergency provisions. There are three types of emergency : (a) emergency caused by war, external aggression or armed rebellion; (b) emergency arising out of the failure of constitutional machinery in states; and (c) financial emergency.

Recognition of Hindi as an Official Language

The Constitution recognizes Hindi as the official language of the Indian Union. Prior to it, English was the only official language of India. Besides Hindi, the Constitution also recognizes seventeen other Indian languages as regional languages.

Parts of the Constitution and its Subject Matters

Parts	*Subject Matter*
I	The Union and its Territory
II	Citizenship
III	Fundamental Rights
IV	Directive Principles of State Policy
IV-A	Fundamental Duties
V	The Union Government Chapter I — The Executive Chapter II — Parliament Chapter III — Legislative Powers of President Chapter IV — The Union Judiciary Chapter V — Comptroller and Auditor-General of India
VI	The State Governments Chapter I — General Chapter II — The Executive Chapter III — The State Legislature Chapter IV — Legislative Powers of Governor Chapter V — The High Courts Chapter VI — Subordinate Courts
VIII	The Union Territories
IX	The Panchayats
IX-B	The Co-operative Societies
IX-A	The Municipalities
X	The Scheduled and Tribal Areas
XI	Relations between the Union and the States
XII	Finance, Property, Contracts and Suits
XIII	Trade, Commerce and Intercourse within the Territory of India
XIV	Services under the Union and the States
XIV-A	Tribunals
XV	Elections
XVI	Special Provisions relating to SCs, STs, OBCs and Anglo-Indians
XVII	Official Language
XVIII	Emergency Provisions
XIX	Miscellaneous
XX	Amendment of the Constitution
XXI	Temporary, Transitional and Special Provisions
XXII	Short Title, Commencement, Authoritative Text in Hindi and Repeals

* * *

4

Federalism in India

Article 1, of our Constitution describes India as a 'Union of States'. The fathers of the Constitution as a matter of fact, deliberately used the word Union instead of Federation. They held that the unity and integrity of India could be emphasized better by the term "Union than by the word federation." Dr. Ambedkar, the Chairman of the Drafting Committee, clearly pointed out the significance of the term 'Union of States' in the Constituent Assembly when he observed. The Drafting Committee used this term to make it clear that though India was to be federation, the federation was not the result of an agreement by the States to join in a federation, and that the Federation not being the result of an agreement, no State has the right to secede from it. "The Federation is a Union because it is indestructible."

FEDERAL FEATURES

Although the term 'federation' is not used in our Constitution, but it is definitely federal in form. It possesses all the formal characteristics of a federal Constitution.

Supremacy of the Constitution

Though there is no express declaration of the supremacy of the Constitution as is in the Constitution of the United States of America yet the Indian Constitution is the Supreme law, of the land. Its provisions are binding on all governments. Neither the Union Government nor the Government of any State can override or contravene them. All authorities are expected to function under it and be loyal to it. No law inconsistent with any of its provisions can prevail. The President of India, the Governors of the States and all other important officers have to take an oath or affirmation to act according to the Constitution. In short no one in the country is above the constitution.

Distribution of Powers

Like many other federal constitutions of the world, the Indian Constitution also makes a distribution of the legislative powers between the Union and the States, the jurisdiction of each being demarcated by the Union, State and Concurrent Lists. The Union List contains 100 subjects which are under the exclusive jurisdiction of the Union Parliament. The items of State List (61 in number) are ordinarily within the competence of the State Legislatures. The 52 subjects of the Concurrent List are placed under the jurisdiction of both the Union and the State. The Union and the State Government derive powers from the Constitution and are free within their respective spheres.

Independent Judiciary

It is the pre-requisite of the federal polity that there should be an independent judicial tribunal to finally interpret the Constitution and to maintain its sanctity. The Court should also act as the guardian of the Constitution and see that it is not violated either by the Federal or State Governments. The Indian Constitution fulfils this requirement of the federal principle. It provides for a Supreme Court and the State High Courts which are empowered to declare any law passed by the Union Parliament and State Legislatures ultravires if it contravenes any of the provisions of the Constitution. The Supreme Court has also the power to keep the Central and State Governments within their respective spheres.

Written and More or Less Rigid Constitution

A federal constitution is necessarily a written constitution. The Indian Constitution is also a written one. In it even the coventions of the parliamentary system of government are reduced to writing. It is also rigid in so far as the method of amendment for some of its provisions is not easy. Neither the Union Government nor the State Governments acting unilaterally can change them. These provisions can be amended by the method prescribed in the Constitution and this method is different from that of ordinary legislation.

REASONS FOR ADOPTION OF FEDERAL SYSTEM

Though the fathers of the Constitution fully realised the importance of a strong Central Government, yet they did not favour the establishment of a full fledged unitary form of government. On the other hand, they preferred a federal polity for India, and there were many cogent reasons for that. In the first place, in a country of the size of India where some of the Provinces are large in area and population than the largest European powers outside the former Soviet Union, no form other than a federal one would have been feasible. Secondly, provincial problems, especially those associated with land tenure, irrigation, forestry, show marked differences, arising from the continental character of India, and these can be best administered by Provincial authorities. Thirdly, the maintenance of law and order over so vast a territory cannot be effectively achieved except by provincial machinery. Fourthly, the wide differences in custom, in personal laws and in property rights in land also demand that the states should be invested with powers which would make it possible for the administration to be run without too much interference from the Centre. Finally, the long distances do not favour the centralisation of the judicial administration. In view of all these peculiar problems and difficulties, the fathers of the Constitution decided in favour of the Federation which alone promised to provide for their satisfactory solution.

UNITARY FEATURES

Though the constitution possesses some formal characteristics of a federal constitution yet it is conspicuously unitary in spirit. It sets up a highly centralized structure of government which does not conform to the federal principle. To quote K.M. Panikkar, "the federal doctrine has been attempted and the central authority is strengthened in the new Indian Constitution. The theory of co-ordinate powers of the centre and the units would hardly apply to the Indian Federation when the centre is invested with such extraordinary powers and the provinces reduced frankly to a position of subordination. The strong unitary bias of the Constitution is evident from its following features.

Distribution of Powers in Favour of the Centre

The Indian Constitution has no doubt, made an elaborate division of the legislative powers, between the Union and the States. But the entire scheme of distribution of powers displays a strong tendency towards a high degree of centralization. The most important subjects like Defence of India, Naval, Military and Air Forces, Railways, Currency, Foreign Affairs etc. are all placed in the Union List, which is also the longest of the three. Besides, the Parliament has an exclusive jurisdiction with respect of matters include in this list. It has also the power to legislate on items which are placed in the State List and one ordinarily within the competence of the State legislation. The subjects of the concurrent List are, no doubt, under the jurisdiction of both Union and States but the legislation passed by the Union Legislature must prevail over the State legislation. Further, the Constitution vests all residency powers of legislation in the Central Government. This power includes the power, of making laws, imposing any taxes not mentioned in either of the State or Concurrent List. Parliament is also empowered to establish additional courts for the better administration of laws made by it on any matter included in the Union List. Besides, Parliament has the exclusive power of legislation to give effect to any treaty; agreement or convention with any other country or international body. Thus the Union Government or Centre has been made very strong under the Indian Constitution and it has vast powers vis-a-vis the States.

Single Citizenship

The Indian Constitution has established a single and uniform citizenship for the whole of India. The citizen owe allegiance only to the Indian Union. This is in striking contrast to the system of double citizenship that prevails in some federal states. For example, in the United States of America, a citizen of the United States is at the same time also a citizen of one of the states. Besides, the state in the USA often discriminate in favour of their own citizen and give them certain privileges which they may deny or grant on more difficult terms to them who are not their citizen or residents. The Indian Constitution does not recognize this dual citizenship.

Integrated Judicial System

One of the important characteristics of a federal polity is a dual judiciary, one set of judges enforcing the state laws and the other federal laws. In the United States of America, the states have their own judicial systems unrelated to and uncoordinated with the federal judiciary. Australia, too, follows the same patterns, but in India, though there are High Court in the States, the Judiciary is one and integrated. It enforces both States and the Union laws. The Supreme Court at Delhi is at the apex of the different court in the country and is not only a Federal Court but also the highest Court of Appeal.

Parliament can Redistribute the Territories of the States

It is the essence of the federal principle that the states or units should be given equal participation in matters relating to the alterations in their boundaries. The Constitution of the United States and Australia strictly denied for it. In United States of America, the boundaries of a state cannot be altered without its consent. In Australia too, alterations in boundaries of a State can only be made : (i) with the consent of the legislature of the states (ii) by the approval of the majority of the electors of the state voting upon the question. But in India the parliament can by a unilateral action make or unmake the territories of the States of the Union of India change the shape of the existing states or abolish some and substitute other units for them. This is, obviously, a great deviation from the federal principle.

Unitary in Emergencies

A typical federation cannot be changed into a unitary form except by amending the constitution. But the Indian Constitution can be both unitary as well as federal according to the requirements of time and circumstances. In normal times, it is designed to work on federal principle, but in times of national emergencies, it can be converted into a unitary one without the need of a formal amendment. While the Proclamation of emergency is in operation, the Parliament gets the power to legislate for the whole or any part of the territory of India with respect to any of the matters enumerated in the State list and the executive authority of the Union Government extends to the giving of directions to the State Governments as to how they should exercise their powers.

Appointment of Governors by the President

The Governor of a state in the United States of America is elected by the people of the state. But the Governor of a state in India is nominated by the President and is expressly given the authority of watching over all-India interest. He also holds office during the pleasure of the President. This is also a great limitation on the federal principle. The Governor of a state in case of conflict of loyalties-loyal to the President who appoints him and during whose pleasure the Governor holds office and loyalty to the state of which he is the head—the

Governor is likely to please the President even if involves sacrificing the interest of the state.

Supremacy of the Union in the Amendment of the Constitution

The provisions dealing with the amendment of the Constitution also emphasis the supremacy of the Union over the State Governments. Many of the important provisions of the Constitution can be amended by the Parliament if two-thirds majorities in both houses support the move. It is only in case of a few specified provisions that constitutional amendment requires the concurrence of at least half of the States. Besides, the State in India have no independent power of constitutional amendment. Even a decision to abolish the State Legislative Council requires an Act of Parliament. Thus there is unequal partnership of the central and regional governments in so far as the process of constitutional amendment is concerned.

NEED FOR STRONG CENTRE

The Indian Constitution creates a very strong centre, perhaps the strongest in any-federal system in the government. The fathers of the Constitution had enough jurisdiction in making the centre so powerful. India at the time of framing the constitution was passing through most uncertain time she was faced with the problems of national security, resettlement of refugees, communalism, provincialism and accession of Kashmir. To tackle these problems successfully and effectively, she obviously needed a strong Central Government. It was also held by the Constituent Assembly that if unity of India, achieved after so much struggle, was to be preserved, the fissiparous tendencies inherent in the Indian situation, which has led to the disruption of previous empires, would have to be carefully kept under check and those forces which had contributed to that unity, such as a common legal system, the growth of common economy, the maintenance of all-India civil services, the subordination of principal administration etc. would have to remain within the sphere of Central Government. This consideration also called for altering the balance in favour of the Central Government.

It was pointed out by some that, "If the backwardness of India in industry, technological skill, agricultural production and the numerous other economic factors which render her ineffective in the world, are to be remedied and the crucial problem of transforming her form an under-developed area into a great modern nation solved, by raising the standard of living, of health, of education and of general welfare, then the planning of all this has to be under a central direction unhampered by the statutory rights of the State Government." Under the influence of these sound and weighty arguments, the fathers of the Constitution created a very strong centre for the Indian Union.

DIVISION OF POWERS

For the proper understanding of the Indian federal system it is essential to examine the provisions of the Constitution which have bearing on the relations between the Union and the States. Our Constitution has made elaborated provisions with respect to their legislative, administrative and financial relations.

The Constitution has divided the legislative authority between the Union and the States and has drawn up three Lists for the purpose the Union List, the State List and the Concurrent List. The scheme of distribution is almost the same as in the Government of India Act, 1935 and seeks to cover every possible matter likely to fall within the spheres of governmental authority.

The Union List: The Union List contains 100 items and is the longest of the three list. The subjects included in the List are of all-India importance such as Defence, Foreign Affairs, United Nations, War and Peace, Citizenship, Railways, Currency, Posts and Telegraphs, Wirless and Broadcasting, Union Public Services etc. Since all these subjects are of common interest to the Union, they call for uniformity of legislation with respect to them. As such Parliament alone has power to make laws with regard to any of matters enumerated in the Union List.

The State List: The State List consists of such subjects as public order, police administration or justice, prisons, public health, agriculture, etc. The total numbers of these items is 61 and they are primarily of local interests. The State Legislature has the exclusive powers of legislation with regard to everyone of the items included in this List.

Concurrent List : The inclusion of List III or the Concurrent List, in the Constitution gives a particular significance to the distribution of legislative power in the Indian federal scheme. The Concurrent List consists of 52 items, such as criminal law and procedure, civil procedure, marriage, contracts, port trusts, welfare of labour, economic and social planning. These subjects are obviously such as may at some time require legislations by Parliament and at other by a State Legislature. The provision of a Concurrent List has two distinct advantages. In certain matters in which Parliament may not find it necessary or expedient to make laws, a State can take the initiative, and if other States follow and the matter assumes national importance, Parliament can intervene and bring about a uniform piece of legislation to cover the entire Union Territory.

NATIONAL DEVELOPMENT COUNCIL

Since India is a federal state, it was soon realised that the states must have their representation in the Planning Commission. As a result, the National Development Council (NDC) came into being in August 1952 to:

- Review the working of the National Plan from time to time.
- Consider important questions of social and economic policies affecting national development plans.
- Recommend measures for the achievement of the aims and targets set out in the National Plan, including measures to secure the active participation and cooperation of the people, improve efficiency of the administrative service, ensure fullest development of the less advance regions and sections of the community and, through sacrifices borne equally by all citizens, build up resources for national development.

The NDC consists of the prime minister as its chairman, the chief ministers (or their nominees) of all states and members of the NITI Aayog. The plan is prepared by the NITI Aayog and after that it is placed before the NDC for its approval. It is here that the union and the state governments are involved in the decision-making process. The Plan is presented to the Parliament for its final approval after it is passed by the NDC.

ZONAL COUNCIL

Each zonal council, consists of the Chief Minister and two other minister of each of the States in the zone and the Administrator in the case of a Union Territory. Zonal Councils have been established by the States Reorganisation Act, 1956 to advise on matters of common interest to each of the five zones into which the territory of India has been divided—Northern, Southern, Eastern, Western and Central.

(i) **The Central Zone,** comprising the States of Uttar Pradesh, Madhya Pradesh, Chhattisgarh and Uttarakhand.

(ii) **The Northern Zone,** comprising the States of Haryana, Himachal Pradesh, Punjab, Rajasthan and Union Territories of Jammu & Kashmir, Ladakh, Delhi & Chandigarh.

(iii) **The Eastern Zone,** comprising the States of Bihar, West Bengal, Odisha and Jharkhand.

(iv) **The Western Zone,** comprising the States of Gujarat, Maharashtra, Goa and the Union Territory of Dadra & Nagar Haveli and Daman & Diu.

(v) **The Southern Zone,** comprising the States of Andhra Pradesh, Telangana, Karnataka, Tamil Nadu, Kerala and the Union Territory of Puducherry.

Besides these, there is the North Eastern Council set up in 1972, to deal with the common problems of Assam, Meghalaya, Manipur, Nagaland,

Sikkim, Tripura, Arunachal Pradesh and Mizoram.

The main functions of the Zonal councils are:

- To achieve an emotional integration of the people.
- To help in arresting the growth of acute state consciousness in the form of regionalism, linguism and the like.
- To help in removing the after-effects of separation.
- To enable the centre and states in economic and social matters and to cooperate and exchange ideas and experience for evolving uniform policies.
- To cooperate with each other in the speedy and successful execution of development plans.
- To secure some kind of political equilibrium between different regions of the country.

***

5

Citizenship

Before the commencement of the Constitution the Indian were subjects of the Crown and the British Citizenship and Status of Aliens Act, 1914-48 applied to India as with respect to other countries of the British Commonwealth of Nations. The Act was modified in 1948 but under it there was no such thing as Indian Citizenship. The legislation on the subject in India was confined to a small enactment relating to naturalization was passed in 1926 which was meant for the benefit of persons coming to India from abroad.

It was on 26th November, 1949 when the Constituent Assembly adopted the Constitution of India, bringing into force at once the provisions relating to citizenship.

The Constitution provides for a single citizenship. Following categories of persons became citizens of India at the commencement of the Constitution:

(1) Persons born and domiciled in India.

(2) Persons domiciled in India and either of whose parents was born in India.

(3) Persons domiciled in India and residing in India ordinarily for a period of at least five years.

(4) Certain categories of people, who had migrated from Pakistan to India.

(5) Indians residing abroad but who make an application to acquire Indian citizenship.

The Constitution confers the following rights and privileges on the citizens of India (and denies the same to aliens):

1. Right against discrimination on grounds of religion, race, caste, sex or place of birth (Article 15).
2. Right to equality of opportunity in the matter of public employment (Article 16).
3. Right to freedom of speech and expression, assembly, association, movement, residence and profession (Article 19).
4. Cultural and educational rights (Articles 29 and 30).
5. Right to vote in elections to the Lok Sabha and state legislative assembly.
6. Right to contest for the membership of the Parliament and the state legislature.
7. Eligibility to hold certain public offices, that is, President of India, Vice-President of India, judges of the Supreme Court and the high courts, governor of states, attorney general of India and advocate general of states.

Along with the above rights, the citizens also owe certain duties towards the Indian State, as for example, paying taxes, respecting the national flag and national anthem, defending the country and so on.

METHODS FOR ACQUIRING INDIAN CITIZENSHIP

The Parliament passed Citizenship Act in 1955, providing for following methods for acquiring Indian citizenship:

(1) Citizenship by birth;

(2) Citizenship by descent;
(3) Citizenship by registration;
(4) Citizenship by naturalisation; and
(5) Citizenship by incorporation of territory.

The Central Government has the discretion to waive off any or all the conditions of citizenship if it thinks that the applicant has rendered distinguished service to the cause of science, art, philosophy, literature, world peace or human progress in general.

Amendment of Citizenship Act (1955)

In 1986, the Indian Citizenship Act was amended to restrict acquisition of citizenship by refugees coming to India from Bangladesh, Sri Lanka and other countries. It provided that persons born in India (i) on or after 26 January 1950, but prior to 26 November 1986 and (ii) on or after the commencement of the Amending Act, 1986, shall be citizens of India by birth only if either of their parents is a citizen of India at the time of his birth. The period for acquisition of citizenship through registration has also been increased from 6 months to 5 years.

Citizenship (Amendment) Bill (1992)

A bill seeking to eliminate discrimination against women in the matter of citizenship of their children received parliamentary approval on 30 November 1992. Under the Bill, a person born outside India would be deemed to be an Indian citizen if either of his/her parents were Indian. The provision in the principal Bill of 1955 only applied to those born to Indian male citizens.

The Citizenship Act (2003)

There has been persistent demand and expectations for dual citizenship for persons of Indian origin living in North America, Europe, Australia, New Zealand, Singapore and few other countries. On the occasion of first Pravasi Bhartiya Diwas on 9 January 2003, former Prime Minister of India Atal Bihari Vajpayee made an announcement for grant of dual citizenship of People of Indian Origins (PIOs). To translate that announcement into a reality, the necessary legislation was introduced by the Government of India in Parliament in May 2003. The Indian Parliament on 22 December 2003 passed a Bill to grant dual citizenship to the PIO. The Bill received the President's assent on 7 January 2004.

Citizenship Amendment Act, 2019 (CAA)

The Act seeks to amend the Citizenship Act, 1955 to make Hindu, Sikh, Buddhist, Jain, Parsi and Christian undocumented immigrants from Afghanistan, Bangladesh and Pakistan, eligible for citizenship of India. In other words, the Act intends to make it easier for persecuted people from India's neighbouring countries to become citizens of India. The legislation applies to those who were "forced or compelled to seek shelter in India due to persecution on the ground of religion". It aims to protect such people from proceedings of illegal migration. The amendment relaxes the requirement of naturalization from 11 years to 5 years as a specific condition for applicants belonging to these six religions. The cut-off date for citizenship is December 31, 2014, which means the applicant should have entered India on or before that date.

The Act says that on acquiring citizenship:
- Such persons shall be deemed to be citizens of India from the date of their entry into India, and
- All legal proceedings against them in respect of their illegal migration or citizenship will be closed.

It also says people holding Overseas Citizen of India (OCI) cards–an immigration status permitting a foreign citizen of Indian origin to live and work in India indefinitely–can lose their status if they violate local laws for major and minor offences and violations.

THE LOSS OF CITIZENSHIP

Under the provisions of the Constitution, Indian citizenship can be lost in three ways:

· **By renunciation**–if a person holding Indian citizenship as well as another citizenship refutes Indian citizenship voluntarily.

By termination–by operation of law as soon as an Indian citizen voluntarily acquires the citizenship of another country.

By deprivation–the Parliament can, by law, deprive any person of his citizenship by way of the provision of Article 10 of the Constitution if it is satisfied that citizenship was acquired by fraud, false representation; or concealment of material facts. If a person shows disloyalty towards the Indian Constitution; indulges in trade with enemy countries during war; is sentenced to imprisonment for a period of 2 years or more, within 5 years of registration of naturalization, or has been continuously residing out of India for more than 7 years he is liable to lose his citizenship.

SINGLE CITIZENSHIP

Though the Indian Constitution is federal and envisages a dual polity (Centre and states), it provides for only a single citizenship, that is, the Indian citizenship. The citizens in India owe allegiance only to the Union. There is no separate state citizenship. The other federal states like USA and Switzerland, on the other hand, adopted the system of double citizenship.

In USA, each person is not only a citizen of USA but also of the particular state to which he belongs. Thus, he owes allegiance to both and enjoys dual sets of rights—one set conferred by the national government and another by the state government. This system creates the problem of discrimination, that is, a state may discriminate in favour of its citizens in matters like right to vote, right to hold public offices, right to practice professions and so on. This problem is avoided in the system of single citizenship prevalent in India.

In India, all citizens irrespective of the state in which they are born or reside enjoy the same political and civil rights of citizenship all over the country and no discrimination is made between them.

OVERSEAS CITIZENSHIP OF INDIA (OCI)

The Constitution of India does not allow holding Indian citizenship and citizenship of a foreign country simultaneously. Based on the recommendation of the High Level Committee on Indian Diaspora, the Government of India decided to grant Overseas Citizenship of India (OCI) commonly known as 'dual citizenship'. Persons of Indian Origin (PIOs) of certain category as has been specified in the Brochure who migrated from India and acquired citizenship of a foreign country other than Pakistan and Bangladesh, are eligible for grant of OCI as long as their home countries allow dual citizenship in some form or the other under their local laws.

Persons registered as OCI have not been given any voting rights, election to Lok Sabha/Rajya Sabha/Legislative Assembly/Council, holding Constitutional posts such as President, Vice President, Judge of Supreme Court/High Court etc. Registered OCIs shall be entitled to following benefits:

(*i*) Multiple entry, multi-purpose life long visa to visit India;

(*ii*) Exemption from reporting to Police authorities for any length of stay in India; and

(*iii*) Parity with NRIs in financial, economic and educational fields except in the acquisition of agricultural or plantation properties. No parity shall be allowed in the sphere of political rights.

A person registered as OCI is eligible to apply for grant of Indian citizenship under section 5(1)(g) of the Citizenship Act, 1955 if he/she is registered as OCI for five years and has been residing in India for one year out of the five years before making the application.

PERSON OF INDIAN ORIGIN (PIO)

Person of Indian Origin is a person who or whose any of ancestors was an Indian national and who is presently holding another country's citizenship/ nationality *i.e.* he/she is holding foreign passport.

The Government of India has revised the PIO Card Scheme, which was launched in 1999, aimed at making the journey back to your roots, simpler, easier, flexible and absolutely hassle free. The PIO Card will entitle you to a set of privileges.

Benefits to a PIO Card Holder

- ❖ No visa required for visiting India.
- ❖ No separate "Student Visa" or "Employment Visa" required for admissions in Colleges/ Institutions or for taking up employment respectively.
- ❖ A PIO Card holder will be exempt from the requirement of registration if his stay on any single visit in India does not exceed 180 days.
- ❖ In the event of continuous stay in India of the PIO Card holder exceeding 180 days, he/she shall have to get himself/herself registered within 30 days of the expiry of 180 days with the concerned Foreigners Regional Registration Officer/Foreigners Registration Officer.
- ❖ Parity with non-resident Indians in respect of facilities available to the latter in economic, financial and educational field.
- ❖ All PIOs including PIO Card holders shall enjoy parity with NRIs in respect of all facilities in the matter of acquisition, holding, transfer and disposal of immovable properties in India except in matters relating to the acquisition of agricultural/plantation properties. No parity shall be allowed in the sphere of political rights.
- ❖ Facilities available to children of NRIs for getting admission to educational institutions in India including medical colleges, engineering colleges, Institute of Technology, Institute of Management, etc. under the general categories.
- ❖ Facilities available under the various housing scheme of LIC, State Government and other Government Agencies.
- ❖ Special counters at the immigration check posts for speedy clearance.

***

6

Fundamental Rights & Duties

The inclusion of the Fundamental Rights in Indian Constitution (Art. 12-35) had its genesis in the forces that operated in the national struggle during British rule. With the resort by the British executive to such arbitrary acts as interments and deportations without trial and curbs on the liberty of the press in the early decades of this century, it became an article of faith with the leaders of the freedom movement. Some essential rights like personal freedom, protection of one's life and limb and of one's good name derived from the common law and the principles of British jurisprudence, were well accepted and given at least in theory statutory recognition in India by various British Parliamentary enactments relating to the Government and the Constitution of India.

In a democratic set-up, people are given several rights. Some of them are essential for the all-round development of human beings. These fundamental rights are basic in the governance of the State. These rights:

(1) are given to everyone, without any discrimination. It is felt that in their absence, a person will not be able to develop his physical, spiritual and moral capabilities;

(2) are provided in the basic law or Constitution of the country. The government cannot alter them according to its wishes;

(3) cannot be ignored or suppressed. The country's executive and legislature have to respect them; and

(4) are justiciable. In case of violation of Fundamental Rights, citizens can approach the court for remedy.

The Fundamental Rights in India have some special features:

(1) Fundamental Rights are not absolute. The Parliament can put up restrictions, in the interest of the nation. They can suspend or even amend these Rights.

(2) Some Fundamental Rights, like freedom of expression are available to Indian citizens only, while some like equality before law are available to foreigners also.

(3) Fundamental Rights are both in the form of positive and negative. The negative Rights prohibit the State from doing several things while positive Rights allow people to do many things. The negative Rights are absolute while positive Rights are limited. Only those positive Rights, that are specified in the Constitution, are Fundamental Rights.

(4) Fundamental Rights put limitations on different authorities—Central Government, State Governments and Local bodies.

(5) There is no natural or unenumerated rights in India. Whatever has been specified in the Constitution, the courts can only protect those interests.

VARIOUS FUNDAMENTAL RIGHTS

Right to Equality

Articles 14, 15, 16, 17 and 18 ensure that every citizen and foreign national within the country, is treated equally before law. Article 14 says that the State shall not deny to any person equality before the law or the equal protection of the law within the territory of India. The right lays down the foundation of Rule of Law in India. Article 15 says that they shall not discriminate against any citizen on grounds only of religion, race, caste, sex, place of birth or any of them. No one can be denied access to public places on either of the above ground. However, there are two exceptions to the above Right. The Government can make special arrangements for children and women. The Government has been allowed to give special consideration to Scheduled Castes, Scheduled Tribes and others socially and educationally backward. Article 16 deals with equality of opportunity in matters of public employment. It says there shall be equality of opportunity for all citizens in matters relating to employment or appointment to any office under the State. No citizen shall, on grounds of any religion, race, caste, sex, descent, place of birth, residence, or any of them, be ineligible for, or discriminated against, in respect, of any employment or office under the State. Article 17 deals with abolition of untouchability and makes an act of untouchability cognizable offence. Article 18 deals with abolition of titles. The exceptions are titles regarding special qualification, education or given by armed forces.

Right to Freedom

These rights guaranteed under Article 19 to 22 of the Constitution, are available only to the Indian citizens. Article 19 provide six freedoms—Freedom of speech and expression; Freedom to assemble peacefully and without arms; Freedom to form associations or union; Freedom to move freely; Freedom to reside and settle; and Freedom to practise any profession or to carry on any occupation, trade or volume. These freedoms are relative and not absolute. There have been restrictions on these freedoms and these can be altered by the government as its requirement. Indian citizens are free to speak, write or print whatever they want except what is against country's unity and sovereignty; security of the country; affects friendly relations with foreign countries; against public order; contempt of court; defamatory against someone or prompts someone to commit crime. Similarly, the Government can disallow people from assembly if there is a danger to peace and order or unity and sovereignty of the country. Similarly, freedom to move freely can be restricted on the grounds of law and order or for the protection of any scheduled tribe. Freedom to reside and settle can be restricted on the similar grounds. Indian citizens are allowed freedom to carry out any occupation, trade or business but it should not be illegal or immoral. The Government can prescribe some professional or technical qualifications for some jobs or practices. The Government has been allowed to keep certain business or trade for itself and not permit private party in it.

The Right to freedom also provide protection in respect of offences. No person will be persecuted unless proved guilty. The sentence will be according to the crime. One can be sentenced only once for one crime. Nobody can be forced to give evidence against himself. Indian citizens have been given protection of life and personal liberty. So, no person can be deprived of his life or personal liberty except according to procedure established by law.

Right Against Exploitation

Article 23 of the Constitution prohibits traffic in human beings and different forms of forced labour. However, the Government, in special circumstances, can force people to work in the people's interest. Article 24 prohibits the employment of children under the age of 14 in any factory or in any other hazardous work.

Right to Freedom of Religion

India is a secular country and every religion and community is equal in the eyes of the State. Article 25 of the Constitution provides freedom of conscience and free profession and propagation of religion. However, everyone must respect public order, health and morality. Article 26 provides that every religion or its section, subject to public order, morality and health, has the right to maintain its own institutions for religious and charitable purposes, to manage its own affairs in matters of religion and to own, acquire and administer movable and immovable property in accordance with law.

Article 27 prohibits levying of any tax on the proceeds which are meant to be spent for the maintenance or promotion of any religious activity. Article 28 states that no religious instruction can be given in any educational institution which is wholly maintained out of State funds. Person attending an educational institution recognised and aided by the State cannot be compelled to take part in any religious instruction or worship conducted by it.

Cultural and Educational Rights

These rights, under Articles 29 and 30, provide every opportunity to the minority communities to protect and enrich their language, script, and culture. No one can be denied admission to an educational institution that is run by the State or funded by the State. Every minority group can establish, administer or develop an educational institution to protect their language, script or culture and the Government will not discriminate in any manner in giving aid on the ground that it is managed by a religious or linguistic minority.

Right to Constitutional Remedies

Article 32 is the most important Article, as far as Fundamental Rights are concerned because it ensures their compliance. Every citizen has the right to move the Supreme Court for the enforcement of his constitutionally guarded rights. The Supreme Court or High Courts can issue writs of Habeas Corpus, Mandamus, Prohibition, Quo Warranto and Certiorari for the compliance of Fundamental Rights.

Fundamental Rights (FR) of Citizens and Foreigners

FR available only to citizens and not to foreigners

1. Prohibition of discrimination on grounds of religion, race, caste, sex or place of birth (Article 15).
2. Equality of opportunity in matters of public employment (Article 16).
3. Protection of six rights regarding freedom of : (i) speech and ex-pression, (ii) assembly, (iii) association, (iv) movement, (v) residence, and (vi) profession (Article 19).
4. Protection of language, script and culture of minorities (Article 29).
5. Right of minorities to establish and administer educational institutions (Article 30).

FR available to both citizens and foreigners (except enemy aliens)

1. Equality before law and equal protection of laws (Article 14).
2. Protection of life and personal liberty (Article 21).
3. Prohibition of traffic in human beings and forced labour (Article 23).
4. Prohibition of employment of children in factories etc., (Article 24).
5. Freedom of conscience and free profession, practice and propagation of religion (Article 25).
6. Freedom to manage religious affairs (Article 26).

SIGNIFICANCE OF FUNDAMENTAL RIGHTS

The Fundamental Rights are significant in the following respects :

1. They facilitate the establishment of rule of law in the country.
2. They strengthen the secular fabric of the Indian State.
3. They lay down the foundation stone of social equality and social justice.
4. They facilitate the participation of people in the political and administrative process.
5. They constitute the bedrock of democratic system in the country.
6. They provide necessary conditions for the material and moral protection of man.
7. They serve as a formidable bulwark of individual liberty.
8. They protect the interests of minorities and weaker sections of society.
9. They check the absoluteness of the authority of the government.
10. They ensure the dignity and respect of individuals.

RIGHTS OUTSIDE PART III

Besides the Fundamental Rights included in Part III, there are certain other rights contained in other parts of the Constitution. These rights are known as constitutional rights or legal rights or non-fundamental rights. They are :

1. The elections to the Lok Sabha and the State Legislative Assembly shall be on the basis of adult suffrage (Article 326).
2. No person shall be deprived of his property save by authority of law (Article 300-A).
3. No tax shall be levied or collected except by authority of law (Article 265).
4. Trade, commerce and intercourse throughout the territory of India shall be free (Article 301).

Even though the above rights are also equally justiciable, they are different from the Fundamental Rights. In case of violation of a Fundamental Right, the aggrieved person can directly move the Supreme Court for its enforcement under Article 32, which is in itself a fundamental right. But, in case of violation of the above rights, the aggrieved person cannot avail this constitutional remedy. He can move the High Court by an ordinary suit or under Article 226 (writ jurisdiction of high court).

SUSPENSION OF FUNDAMENTAL RIGHTS

The fundamental rights guaranteed under the Indian Constitution can be suspended by the President during emergencies rising out of threat to the security of India or any part of its territory, or due to actual external aggression. It may be noted that the President has to issue specific orders for the suspension of the fundamental rights and such orders must be placed before the Parliament at the earliest possible. The President can also suspend the right to move the courts for the enforcement of these fundamental rights, except the rights available under Articles 20 and 21. When such orders have been issued, the State has the authority to make any law or take any executive action with regard to the fundamental rights. But such law shall, to the extent of incompetency, cease to have effect as soon as the orders aforesaid cease to operate.

HUMAN RIGHTS COMMISSION

The real test of the rights given by any constitution is in their actual implementation. The poor, illiterate and the deprived sections of the society must be able to exercise their rights. Independent organisations like the People's Union for Civil Liberties (PUCL) or People's Union for Democratic Rights (PUDR) have been working as watchdogs against the violations of rights. In this background, the government has established in 2000 an institution, the National Human Rights Commission.

The National Human Rights Commission (NHRC) is composed of a former chief justice of the Supreme Court of India, a former judge of the Supreme Court, a former chief justice of a High Court and two other members who have knowledge and practical experience in matters relating to human rights.

The commission's functions include inquiry at its own initiative or on a petition presented to it by a victim into complaint of violation of human rights; visit to jails to study the condition of the inmates; undertaking and promoting research in the field of human rights etc. The commission receives complaints in thousands every year. These relate to custodial death, custodial rape, disappearances, police excesses, failure in taking action, indignity to women etc. Its most significant intervention has been on disappeared youth in Punjab and investigation and trial of Gujarat riot cases where its intervention proved effective. The commission does not have the power of prosecution. It can merely make recommendations to the government or recommend to the courts to initiate proceedings based on the inquiry that it conducts.

VARIOUS WRITS

Habeas Corpus

Habeas corpus literally means 'you shall produce the body'. A writ of habeas corpus is in the nature of an order calling upon the person who has detained another to produce the latter before the court in order to let the court know on what ground he has been confined and to set him free if there is no legal justification for the imprisonment. By this writ, the court secures the body of a person who has been imprisoned to be brought before itself to obtain knowledge of the reason why he has been imprisoned and to set him free if there is no lawful justification for the imprisonment. By this writ, the court secures the body of a person who has been imprisoned to be brought before itself to obtain knowledge of the reason why he has been imprisoned and to set him free if there is no lawful justification for the imprisonment. The writ may be addressed to an official or a private person who has another person in his custody and disobedience to the writ is met with punishment for contempt of court. The writ of habeas corpus is a very powerful safeguard to the subject against arbitrary acts not only of private individuals but also of the executive.

The writ of habeas corpus is available for the enforcement of fundamental rights and where imprisonment or detention is ultra vires in the statute. The writ is not issued to secure the release of a person who has been imprisoned by a court of law on a criminal charge or to interfere with a proceeding for contempt by a court of record or by Parliament.

Mandamus

Mandamus literally means a command. It demands some activity on the part of the body or person to whom it is addressed. It commands the person to whom it is addressed to perform some public or quasi-public legal duty which he has refused to perform and the performance of which cannot be enforced by any other adequate legal remedy. It is a discretionary remedy. In the matter of enforcement of fundamental rights, the question of alternative remedy does not weigh so much with the court since it is the duty of the Supreme Court or the High Court to enforce the fundamental rights. In India, *mandamus* will lie against the Government itself, appropriate proceedings may be brought against the Government concerned. The writ is also available against inferior courts or other judicial bodies when they have refused to exercise their jurisdiction and thus to perform their duty.

The chief uses of *mandamus* are to compel public official and public bodies to carry out their legal duties, to compel delivery, production and inspection of documents, to compel restoration to a public office or franchise of which the holder has wrongfully been dispossessed, to ensure exercise of jurisdiction by inferior courts and quasi-judicial tribunals, etc. *Mandamus* is granted to command the performance of ministerial duty in which the official concerned has no discretion. It is not to control the exercise of discretion. It may ask officers charged with discretionary duties to act, but not to exercise their discretion in a particular way. *Mandamus* is not issued to compel legislative officials to perform their purely legislative functions.

Prohibition

The writ of *prohibition* has been defined as an extraordinary judicial writ, issuing out of a court of superior jurisdiction and directed to an inferior court for the purpose of preventing the inferior tribunal from usurping a jurisdiction with which it is not legally vested.

The differences between *mandamus* and *prohibition* are:

A. while *mandamus* calls for action, *prohibition* commands inactivity or maintenance of status quo,

B. the existence of alternative remedies does not fetter the issue of *prohibition* while the issue of *mandamus* is discretionary,

C. while *mandamus* is available against any public authority, prohibition can be issued only against judicial and quasi-judicial tribunals and is not available against purely administrative or legislative authorities or acts.

Prohibition cannot be issued against a club, trade union or political party. It may be granted not only on the application of parties concerned but also of a stranger.

Injunction

Injunction is not expressly mentioned in the list of writs which the Indian constitution empowers the Supreme and High courts to issue. It is not on par with other writs in our country. The Indian courts have powers to issue injunctions and freely do so in appropriate circumstances.

Injunction is a judicial process, operating in persona and requiring the person to whom it is directed to do, or refrain from doing, a particular thing.

The *injunction* is not a common law but an equity writ in England and the U.S.A., it is granted by courts of equity or courts processing equity jurisdiction.

Injunction is of two kinds, mandatory and preventive, resembling both *mandamus* and *prohibition*. Mandatory injunction resembles *mandamus*, for they both command the respondent to do a thing. But *mandamus* cannot be issued against private persons while injunction is primarily a process of private law and only rarely a remedy in administrative law. *Mandamus* is a remedy of common law while *injunction* is that of equity.

Certiorari

Certiorari means *'to be certified'* or *'to be made certain'*. It is a writ issued by a superior to an inferior court of record or othe ibunal or officer, ercising a judicial function, requiring the ification and return to the former of some cause ady terminated, in cases where the procedure is t according to the course of common law. It is generally issued only after the judgement of the inferior court or tribunal whose proceedings are to be reviewed.

The effect of *certiorari* is either to quash or affirm the proceedings of the lower court or tribunal. It lies only against substantial errors.

Though prohibition and *certiorari* are both issued against courts or tribunals exercising judicial or quasi-judicial powers, *certiorari* is issued to quash the order or decision of the tribunal while prohibition is issued to prohibit the tribunal from making the *ultra vires* order or decision. If follows, therefore, that while prohibition is available during the pendency of the proceedings and before the order is made *certiorari* can be issued only after the order has been made.

Quo Warranto

Quo Warranto is proceeding whereby the court enquires into the legality of the claim which a party asserts to a public office and to oust him from its enjoyment if the claim be not well founded.

The conditions necessary for the issue of a writ of *quo warranto* are as follows:

(i) The office must be public and it must be created by a statute or by the constitution itself.

(ii) The office must be a substantive one and not merely the function or employment of a servant at the will and during the pleasure of another.

(iii) There has been a contravention of the constitution or a statute or statutory instrument in appointing such a person to that office.

The fundamental basis of the proceeding of quo warranto is that the public has an interest to see that an unlawful claimant does not usurp a public office. It is a discretionary remedy which the court may grant or refuse according to the facts and circumstances of each case. The writ may be refused where it is vexatious or where it would be futile in its result or where the petitioner is guilty of laches or where there is an alternative remedy for ousting the usurper. Where the application challenges the validity of an appointment to a public office, it is maintainable at the instance of any person, whether any fundamental or other legal right of such person has been infringed or not.

FUNDAMENTAL DUTIES

In modern times generally there is no provision for Fundamental Duties in the constitutions of the world. There are hardly a few constitutions that have such a provision. In ancient times, however, the position was very different. In those days emphasis was laid on duties, rather than rights. It was felt that if everyone performs his duties, then the rights would automatically be safeguarded. But in 1976 the Indian Parliament felt that there was a need for inclusion of a list of Fundamental Duties in the Indian Constitution.

Accordingly, Constitution (Forty-Second Amendment) Act, 1976, was passed which added a new part, viz. Part IV A, and a new Article, 51 A, to the Constitution of India. The new Part was entitled as Fundamental Duties and it gives a list of ten Fundamental Duties.

The ten duties are as follows:

1. to abide by the Constitution and respect its ideals and institutions, the National Flag and the National Anthem;
2. to cherish and follow the noble ideals which inspired our national struggle for freedom;
3. to uphold and protect the sovereignty, unity and integrity of India;
4. to defend the country and render national service when called upon to do so;
5. to promote harmony and the spirit of common brotherhood amongst all the people of India transcending religious, linguistic and regional or sectional diversities, to renounce practices derogatory to the dignity of women;
6. to value and preserve the rich heritage of our composite culture;
7. to protect and improve the natural environment including forests, lakes, rivers and wildlife, and to have compassion for living creatures;
8. to develop the scientific temper, humanism and the spirit of inquiry and reform;
9. to safeguard public property and to abjure violence; and
10. to strive towards excellence in all spheres of individual and collective activity so that the nation constantly rises to higher levels of endeavour and achievement.

Eleventh Duty : In 2002, the 86th Amendment Act added the eleventh fundamental duty to the existing ten duties. According to this Act, it shall be the duty of every citizen who is a parent or guardian to provide opportunities for education to his child or ward between the age of 6 and 14 years.

Implications of Fundamental Duties

Now, let us examine these duties and find out the implications for the citizens of India. Abide by the Constitution: It implies that every citizen should act according to the provisions of the Constitution. He should not do any thing that is prohibited by the Constitution. Some of the important prohibitions by the Constitution are as follows: the practice of untouchability (Article 17), traffic in human beings (Article 23), abusing the health and strength of workers and the tender age of children (Article 39) and slaughter of cows, calves and other milch and draught animals (Article 48).

Respect its Ideals: The ideals of the Constitution are given in the Preamble. The Preamble aims at securing Justice (social, economic and political), Liberty (of thought, expression, belief, faith and worship), Equality (of status and of opportunity) and Fraternity (assuring the dignity of the individual and the unity and integrity of the Nation).

Respect its Institutions: Some of the important institutions of the Constitutions are President, Vice President, Cabinet , Prime Minister, Parliament, Supreme Court, Attorney General, Comptroller and Auditor General, Union Public Service Commission, Election Commission, Governor, Chief Minister, High Court etc.

Respect the National Flag and the National Anthem: There are certain rules framed by the Government with regard to respecting the National Flag and the National Anthem. Every citizen is expected to follow these rules. One of the rules requires that when the National Flag is unfurled or the National Anthem is sung, every citizen should remain in the position of attention and no one should make any move or murmur anything to anyone.

Cherish and Follow Noble Ideals of National Struggle: During our national struggle our leaders laid down certain noble ideals. Some of the important ideals are removal of untouchability, emancipation of women, national integrity, unity in diversity, anti-colonialism, antiimperialism, anti-racialism, democracy, secularism etc.

Uphold and Protect Sovereignty, Unity and Integrity of India: It implies that every citizen should give priority to the national interest. All other considerations such as religion, race, language, caste, sex, and place of birth should get a subordinate position. He should do nothing which endangers the Nation.

Defend the Country: Whenever there is a war or an external aggression, every citizen should come forward to defend the country and if there is a need, he should join armed forces.

Promote Harmony and Spirit of Common Brotherhood: India is a multi-racial, multi-linguistic, multi religious and multi-cultural country. In spite of various diversities, there is a need for developing harmony between different races, languages, religions and cultures. We should promote the spirit of common brotherhood.

Renounce Practices Derogatory to Women: Since ages women in India are being given a very low status in society. Infanticide, dowry and sati system are some of the most derogatory practices that bring down the dignity of women. It is the duty of every citizen to renounce these evil practices.

Value and Preserve Rich Heritage of our Composite Cultures: Though we have varieties of cultures prevalent in different parts of India based on race religion, language, region and customs, there prevails a fundamental basic unity amongst all the cultures.

It is because of the accommodative character of the Indian people that culture of one section of society has been greatly influenced by the cultures of other sections of people. This heritage needs to be preserved and valued. It is the duty of every citizen to work for and develop the composite culture of India.

Protect and Improve Natural Environment: Due to pressure of population and the greed of mankind, careless exploitation of these resources have created environmental problems. There is the need of a balanced development. This necessitates the protection and improvement of natural environments such as forests; lakes; rivers and wild life.

Develop Scientific Temper, the Spirit of Inquiry and Reform: India has been a land of superstitions and blind faith. This needs a rapid change. We should develop a rational outlook and reform our society through the spirit of inquiry. We should develop a scientific temper which could co-relate cause and effect.

Develop Humanism: While developing rational outlook and scientific temper we should not ignore humanism that is the basis of all progressive societies.

Safeguard Public Property and Abjure Violence: Of late, there has developed a tendency to destroy public property to register one's protest against a particular policy of the government. People should not forget that the property does not belong to those who are in power. It is, in fact, their own property that they are destroying. Similarly, violence has also become a weapon of protest. This needs a change. We should not forget that Mahatma Gandhi succeeded in ending an alien rule through the method of nonviolence.

Strive towards Excellence: Our nation cannot reach the top of the developed world unless every citizen individually as well as collectively strives to achieve excellence in life. Everyone should ask himself as to what has he done to achieve excellence in his own field of activity.

Utility

A question here arises as to what purpose does this inclusion of Fundamental Duties in the body of the Constitution serve? Prima facie, it does not serve any purpose unless laws are enacted to punish those who disobey them. But like the Directive Principles of State Policy, they can be useful in interpreting the various provisions of the Constitution. The judiciary can adopt the principle of harmonious construction, as it did in cases relating to Directive Principles of State Policy.

The legislatures can resort to them for legislation to implement them. The executives can rely upon them to justify actions regarding the practical application of these duties.

* * *

7

Directive Principles of State Policy

The Formulation of social and economic objectives in national constitution owes its origin essentially to the realization that the content of political freedom is impaired by the absence of social justice. Since the end of the First World War, it has become increasingly recognized that peace in the world can be established only if it is based on social justice. Accordingly, most modern Constitutions contain declarations of social and economic principles which emphasize among other things the duty of the State to strive for social security, and so provide work, education and proper conditions of employment for its citizens.

In this regard, the concept of a declaration of policy cannot be said to be foreign to the genius of India. In the fourth century B.C., we find in Kautilya's 'Arthshastra' a specific injunction to the effect that "the king shall provide the orphan, the dying, the infirm, the afflicted and the helpless with maintenance; he shall also provide subsistence to helpless expectant mothers and also to the children the give birth to."

The leader of India's freedom movement visualized that in the new dispensation following political freedom, the people should have the fullest opportunities for advancement in the social and economic spheres and that the State should make suitable provision for ensuring such progress.

Article 36 to 51 incorporate the Directive Principles of State Policy. They are in the form of instructions to the Central and State Governments which they must take into consideration while making policies and programmes. The compliance with these principles can help the Government give several social and economic rights to the citizens. The framers of the Constitution tried to incorporate social, liberal and Gandhian ideas through these directive principles. They thought that these ideals cannot be incorporated as rights or made compulsory but over a period of time, these should be compiled with. They can lead to the formation of a welfare State, give direction to the developmental policies, preserve unity and promote efforts to international security and peace. These principles, covering wide area, are not justiciable but have the backing of the popular will. While Fundamental Rights concern citizens, the Directive Principles can be implemented by States. In case of conflict between the two, the Fundamental Rights contained in Articles 14 and 19 cannot stand in the way of implementation of any of Directive Principle. So, if any law is made to implement Directive Principles, it cannot be declared null and void on the ground that it conflicted with Fundamental Rights. Any country, especially a democratic one, cannot ignore these principles as they outline the salient features of good governance.

VARIOUS DIRECTIVE PRINCIPLES

Directives relating to Political Policies

According to the Directives relating to political policies (i) 'the State' is required to take steps to organize Village Panchayats and endow them with such powers and authority as may be necessary to enable them to function as units of self-government, (ii) the 'State' should endeavour to secure for the citizens a Uniform Civil Code throughout the territory of India, (iii) 'the State' is required to take steps to separate the judiciary from the executive in the public services of the 'State' and (iv) 'the State' is required to (a) promote international peace and security; (b) maintain just and honourable relations between nations; (c) foster respect for international law and treaty obligation in the dealings of organized peoples with one another and (d) encourage settlement of international disputes by arbitration.

Directive relating to Social Policies

'The State' is required to promote with special care the educational and economic interests of the weaker sections of society and, in particular, of the Scheduled Castes and the Scheduled Tribes and to protect them from social injustices and all forms of exploitations. This Directive aims at a social order where Scheduled Castes, Scheduled Tribes and other weaker section of society are given special protection so as to make them equal partners in the national life.

Directives relating to Economic Policies

'The State' is required to direct its policy towards securing that:

(*i*) the ownership and control of material resources of the community are so distributed as best to sub-serve the common good.

(*ii*) the operation of the economic system does not result in the concentration of wealth and means of production to the common detriment.

(*iii*) the citizens, men and women equally, have the right to an adequate means of livelihood.

(*iv*) there is equal pay for equal work for both men and women.

(*v*) the health and strength of workers, men and women, and the tender age of children are not abused and citizens are not forced by economic necessity to enter vocations unsuited to their age or strength.

(*vi*) the participation of workers is ensured in the management of undertakings, establishments or other organizations engaged in any industry by suitable legislation or in any other way.

(*vii*) children are given opportunities and facilities to develop in a healthy manner and in condition of freedom and dignity and that childhood and youth are protected against exploitation and against moral and material abandonment.

(*viii*) the right to work, to education and to public assistance in cases of unemployment, old age, sickness and disablement, and in other cases of undeserved want is ensured within the limits of its economic capacity and development.

(*ix*) suitable provision is made for just and humane condition of work and for maternity relief.

(*x*) all workers, agriculture, industrial or otherwise, secure work, a living wage, condition of work ensuring a descent standard of life and full enjoyment of leisure and social and culture opportunities by suitable legislation or economic organization, or in any other way and, in particular, the State should endeavour to promote cottage industries on an individual or cooperative basis in rural area.

(*xi*) that agriculture and animal husbandry are organized on modern and scientific lines and steps taken for preservation and improvement of the breeds and prohibition of the slaughter, of cows and calf and other milch and draught cattle.

(*xii*) that the operation of the legal system promotes justice, on a basis of equal opportunity, and provision is made for free legal aid, by suitable legislation or schemes or in any other way, to ensure that opportunities for securing justice are not denied to any citizen by reason of economic or other disabilities.

Directives relating to Educational and Cultural Policies

One of the Directives requires 'the State' to provide, within a period of ten years from the commencement of the Constitution, for free and compulsory education for all children until they complete the age of fourteen years. Another Directive states that it shall be the obligation of 'the State' to protect every monument or place or object of artistic or historic interest, declared by or under law made by Parliament to be of national importance, from spoliation (extortion), disfigurement, destruction, removal, disposal or export as the case may be.

Directives regarding Health Policies

There are two Directives in this category. The first requires 'the State' to regard the raising of the level of nutrition and the standard of living of its people and the improvement of the public health as among its primary duties and, in particular 'the State' is required to endeavour to bring about prohibition of the consumption, except for medical purposes of intoxicating drinks and of drugs which are injurious to health. The second requires 'the State' to endeavour to protect and improve the environment and to safeguard the forests and wild life of the country.

CONSTITUTIONAL PROVISIONS

The various articles on Directive Principles are as follows.

Article 38 instructs the state to promote the welfare of people by securing and protecting a social order in which justice (socio-economic and political) shall inform all the institutions of national life.

Article 39(a) talks about state's role in providing adequate means of livelihood to all its citizens.

Article 39(b) provides for state's direction for equitable distribution of resources.

Article 39(c) provides for prevention of concentration of wealth in fewer hands.

Artcile 39(d) provides for equal pay for equal work, for both; men and women.

Article 39(A) provides for equal justice and free legal Aid.

Article 40 says that the state shall organize village Panchayats as units of self-government.

Article 41 provides for right to work, public assistance in case of unemployment, old age, sickness and disablement keeping in view the limitations of economic resources.

Article 42 provides for just and humane conditions for work and maternity relief.

Article 43 provides for living wages for worker and a decent standard of life, leisure and social and cultural opportunities for people.

Article 43(A) provides for participation of workers in the management of industry and other undertakings. It has been added by 42nd Amendment.

Article 44 provides for a Uniform Civil Code applicable to the entire country.

Article 45 provides free and compulsory education to children till 14 years of age. It has now been made a fundamental right under Article 21A.

Article 46 provides for protection of educational and economic interests of weaker sections of the society and in particular, of the scheduled castes and scheduled tribes.

Article 47 provides for prohibition of consumption of intoxicating liquor and to raise the level of nutrition and five improvement of public health.

Article 48 provides for preserving and improving the breeds and prohibiting the slaughter of cows, calves and other milks and draught cattles.

Article 48A added by 42nd Amendment, provides for protection and improvement of the environment and to safeguard the forests and wildlife of the country.

Article 49 provides for protection of monuments of historical and national importance.

Article 50 provides for separation of judiciary from executive.

Article 51 provides for promotion of international peace and security.

Criticism

1. Not enforceable in a court of law and dubbed as 'Window dressing' or as 'pious superfinies.' According to K.C. Wheare 'they represent manifesto of aims and aspirations.'
2. There remain theoretical ambiguity and logical inconsistency in provisions on Directive principles. Most of the ideals are vaguely combined to form a whole.

3. They are more in the nature of moral precepts than of practical utility.

UTILITY OF DIRECTIVE PRINCIPLES

Sir B. N. Rau, the constitutional advisor to the Constituent Assembly, stated that the Directive Principles are intended as 'moral precepts for the authorities of the state. They have at least an educative value. The Directive Principles, although confer no legal rights and creates no legal remedies, are significant and useful in the following ways:

1. They are like an 'Instrument of Instructions' or general recommendations addressed to all authorities in the Indian Union. They remind them of the basic principles of the new social and economic order, which the Constitution aims at building.
2. They amplify the Preamble, which solemnly resolves to secure to all citizens of India justice, liberty, equality and fraternity.
3. Their implementation creates a favourable atmosphere for the full and proper enjoyment of the fundamental rights by the citizens. Political democracy, without economic democracy, has no meaning.
4. They form the dominating background to all State action, legislative or executive and also a guide to the courts in some respects.
5. They have helped the courts in exercising their power of judicial review, that is, the power to determine the constitutional validity of a law.
6. They facilitate stability and continuity in domestic and foreign policies in political, economic and social spheres in spite of the changes of the party in power.
7. They serve as a crucial test for the performance of the government. The people can examine the policies and programmes of the government in the light of these constitutional declarations.
8. They enable the opposition to exercise influence and control over the operations of the government. The Opposition can blame the ruling party on the ground that its activities are opposed to the Directives.

DISTINCTION BETWEEN FUNDAMENTAL RIGHTS AND DIRECTIVE PRINCIPLES

The Fundamental Rights are privileges of the citizens recognised by the state. They are in the nature of denial of certain authority to the Government. They are therefore, negative in nature. The Directive Principles are like the positive directives that the Government at all levels must follow so that social and economic democracy in India can be established. The Fundamental Rights aim at the development of every individual citizen and are thus for the individual good. But the Directive Principles are meant for the general welfare of the society.

While the Fundamental rights are justifiable and are enforceable by a court of law, the Directive Principles are non-justifiable. For this reason, some people call them as "merely New Years' Greetings".

This should not lead us to conclude that the Directive Principles are inferior or subordinate to the Fundamental Rights. We have seen that the Indian State has regarded the Directive Principles as fundamental in the governance of the country. It has been making attempts to apply these principles in making laws and formulating policies.

Inspite of these differences, there is a close relationship between them. Whereas the Fundamental Rights establish social equality and democracy, the Directive Principles are meant to establish economic and social democracy. Both, are complementary to each other. All organs of the Government must follow these directions to accomplish the goal of a welfare State.

The Government cannot afford to ignore them. It is responsible for all its actions to the people in general. Although there is no legal sanction behind these Principles, the ultimate sanction lies with the People. The people know that these Directives are for their welfare hence, they are bound to pressurise the Government to implement them. Such public pressure on the Government is exercised through periodic elections.

In the *Champakam Dorairajan Case* (1951), the Supreme Court ruled that in case of any conflict between the Fundamental Rights and the Directive Principles, the former would prevail. It declared that the Directive Principles have to conform to and run as subsidiary to the Fundamental Rights. But, it also held that the Fundamental Rights could be amended by the Parliament by enacting constitutional amendments acts.

The above situation underwent a major change in 1967 following the Supreme Court's judgement in the *Golaknath Case* (1967). In that case, the Supreme Court ruled that the Parliament cannot take away or abridge any of the Fundamental Rights, which are 'sacrosanct' in nature. In other words, the Court held that the Fundamental Rights cannot be amended for the implementation of the Directive Principles.

The Parliament reacted to the Supreme Court's judgement in the *Golaknath Case* (1967) by enacting the 24th Amendment Act (1971) and the 25th Amendment Act (1971). The 24th Amendment Act declared that the Parliament has the power to abridge or take away any of the Fundamental Rights by enacting Constitutional Amendment Acts. The 25th Amendment Act inserted a new Article 31C.

In the *Kesavananda Bharati Case* (1973), the Supreme Court declared the above second provision of Article 31C as unconstitutional and invalid on the ground that judicial review is a basic feature of the Constitution and hence, cannot be taken away. The 42nd Amendment Act accorded the position of legal primacy and supremacy to the Directive Principles over the Fundamental Rights conferred by Articles 14, 19 and 31. However, this extension was declared as unconstitutional and invalid by the Supreme Court in the *Minerva Mills* case (1980). In the *Minerva Mills* case (1980), the Supreme Court also held that 'the Indian Constitution is founded on the bedrock of the balance between the Fundamental Rights and the Directive Principles. They together constitute the core of commitment to social revolution. They are like two wheels of a chariot, one no less than the other. To give absolute primacy to one over the other is to disturb the harmony of the Constitution. This harmony and balance between the two is an essential feature of the basic structure of the Constitution.

IMPLEMENTATION OF DIRECTIVE PRINCIPLES

Since 1950, the successive governments at the Centre and in the states have made several laws and formulated various programmes for implementing the Directive Principles. These are mentioned below:

1. Almost all the states have passed land reform laws to bring changes in the agrarian society and to improve the conditions of the rural masses.
2. Three-tier panchayati raj system (at village, taluka and zila levels) has been introduced to translate into reality Gandhiji's dream of every village being a republic.
3. Agriculture has been modernised by providing improved agricultural inputs, seeds, fertilisers and irrigation facilities. Various steps have also been taken to organise animal husbandry on modern and scientific lines.
4. Seats are reserved for SCs, STs and other weaker sections in educational institutions, government services and representative bodies.
5. Primary health centres and hospitals have been established throughout the country to improve the public health.
6. The Planning Commission was established in 1950 to take up the development of the country in a planned manner. The successive Five Year Plans aimed at securing socio-economic justice and reducing inequalities of income, status and opportunities.
7. The Maternity Benefit Act (1961) and the Equal Remuneration Act (1976) have been made to protect the interest of women workers.
8. The Legal Services Authorities Act (1987) has established a nation-wide network to provide free and competent legal aid to the poor and to organise lok adalats for promoting equal justice.
9. Laws to prohibit the slaughter of cows, calves and bullocks have been enacted in some states.
10. The Wildlife (Protection) Act, 1972 and the Forest (Conservation) Act, 1980, have been enacted to safeguard the wildlife and the forests respectively.

* * *

8

The President and The Union Executive

According to the Indian constitution, there is a *Rashtrapati, i.e.,* the President of the Republic of India (Art. 52). The President is the head of the State and the formal Constitutional head of the Union Executive.

The executive power vests in him, although he does not constitute like the American President, the executive Government. Like the British Queen he is the head of the Parliamentary Government functioning in accordance with the provisions of the Constitution and conventions of the constitutional responsible government.

PRESIDENT

According to the Constitution, the powers of the executive lie with the President who uses them directly or through subordinate officials (Art. 53). He uses his powers as per the advise given by the Council of Ministers. The President of India is indirectly elected and anyone with following qualifications is eligible to be a candidate for the post:

- Citizen of India.
- Completed 35 years of age.
- Eligible to be elected as Member of Parliament.
- Does not hold any office of profit under the Government of India or any State Government or any local or other authority subject to the control of any Government.

Nomination and ratification of the proposal of the candidature is done by at least fifty electorates.

The President is elected by the members of an electoral college consisting of the elected members of both the Houses of Parliament and Legislative Assemblies of the States (Art. 54). Both the Parliament and Legislative Assemblies of the States have equal number of votes. The value of votes of each MLA in the election depends on the population of the State and number of elected MLAs in the State. Similarly, the value of each MP's vote depends on thetotal number of MPs and total number of votes of MLAs of all the States. The single transferable voting system is adopted so that the President-elect has more than fifty per cent support of the voters. The voters give their first,second, third and so on, preferences which are then redistributed unless thefinal selection is done. The voting at such election is by secret ballot and any dispute regarding the election, can only be sorted out by the Supreme Court.

The tenure of the President's term is five years (Art. 56). If no one is elected at the end of the term, the incumbent stays on till the election of the successor. If the President dies during the tenure or resigns or is not well or is impeached, the Vice-President takes over for the interim period till the election is held. If the Vice-President cannot take over for any reason, the Chief Justice of the Supreme Court or otherwise, the senior most judge of the Supreme Court fills the gap. The elections have to be held within six months.

The President can be re-elected any number of time (Art. 57). He can be removed from the office, before completion of the term for violation of the

Constitution, by impeachment. Any house of the Parliament can initiate the impeachment process. At least one-fourth members of the house initiating the process must sign the proposal. Fourteen days notice about the proposal is given to the President.

The President has the right to defend himself and prove innocence, either by appearing personally or sending a representative to the Parliament. If a house approves the proposal by two-thirds majority, it is sent to the second house. If that house also accepts the proposal to impeach by two-thirds majority, the President stands impeached and relieved from the office since that day. There is no provision of appeal against the impeachment in any court.

The President, upon election, cannot be a member of the Parliament or any Legislative Assembly. He cannot hold any other office of profit. He is entitled, without payment of rent, to the use of his official residence and is entitled to such emoluments, allowances and privileges. The emoluments and allowances of the President cannot be diminished during his office. Upon retirement, he gets pension, other allowances and free medical facilities.

POWERS OF THE PRESIDENT

The Constitution has vested the President with vast powers. Broadly the powers of the President can be classified as Executive, Legislative, Financial and Judicial Powers.

Executive Powers

The President is head of State and executive powers of the Union have been vested in him. The President is empowered to exercise these powers either directly or through officers subordinate to him which means through the Prime Minister and Council of Ministers also. His executive powers are given below:-

The President appoints the Prime Minister and he appoints other ministers on the advice of the Prime Minister. He allocates portfolios among the ministers on the advice of the Prime Minister. He may remove any Minister on the advice of the Prime Minister.

The President appoints the Chief Justice and other judges of the Supreme Court and High Courts. However, in all judicial appointments, the Chief Justice of India is consulted. Besides the President may also consult such other judges of the Supreme Court as the President may be deemed necessary. While appointing Chief Justice and justices of High Courts the President has to consult the State Governor also. In the appointment of High Court judges, the President also consults the Chief Justice of the State. But now in accordance with the 1993 decision of the Supreme Court as re-interpreted in 1999, the President is bound by the recommendations of a panel of senior most judges of the Supreme Court in matters of all judicial appointments. This panel headed by the Chief Justice is known as the collegium of the Supreme Court. The President appoints the Attorney General, the Comptroller and Auditor General of India, the Chief Election Commissioner and other Election Commissioners, the Chairman and Members of Union Public Service Commission (U.P.S.C.). He/she also appoints the Governors of States and Lt. Governors of Union Territories. All such appointments are made on the advice of the Union Cabinet headed by the Prime Minister.

The President is the Supreme Commander of the armed forces. As such, the President makes appointments of Chiefs of Army, Navy, and Air Force. The President can declare war and make peace. In his/her capacity as head of state, the President conducts the country's foreign affairs. The President appoints India's ambassadors and high commissioners in other countries; and the President receives foreign ambassadors and high commissiners. All diplomatic work is conducted in his/her name (by the foreign office and Indian envoys abroad), and all international treaties are negotiated and concluded in his/her name.

All laws enacted by the Union Parliament are enforced by him/her. All officials appointed by him/her (such as Governors and Ambassadors) may be removed or recalled by him/ her, on the advice of the Union Council of Ministers.

All the functions are performed by the President on the advice of the Prime Minister. All decisions of the Union Government are communicated to him/her by the Prime Minister. The President can ask the Prime Minister only once to have a recommendation of the executive reconsidered by the Cabinet. The President can also refer a minister's decision to the Cabinet for its consideration. The President cannot seek a second reconsideration.

Legislative Powers

The President being an integral part of Parliament enjoys many legislative powers. These powers are given below:

The President summons, and prorogues the Houses of Parliament. He/she may summon the Parliament at least twice a year, and the gap between two sessions cannot be more than six months. The President has the power to dissolve the Lok Sabha even before the expiry of its term on the recommendation of the Prime Minister. In normal course he/she dissolves Lok Sabha after five years. The President nominates twelve members to Rajya Sabha from amongst persons having special knowledge in the field of literature, science, art and social service. The President can call a joint sitting of the two Houses of Parliament in case of a disagreement between Lok Sabha and Rajya Sabha on a non-money bill. So far thrice such joint sittings have been summoned. The President has the right to address and send messages to Parliament. The President addresses both Houses of Parliament jointly at the first session after every general election as well as commencement of the first session every year. These addresses contain policies of the government of the day.

Every bill passed by Parliament is sent to the President for his/her assent. The President may give his/her assent, or return it once for the reconsideration of the Parliament. If passed again the President has to give her assent. Without his/her assent no bill can become a law. The President may promulgate an ordinance when the Parliament is not in session (Art. 123).

The ordinance so issued has the force of law. The ordinance so promulgated should be laid before both Houses of Parliament when they reassemble. If it is neither rejected by the Parliament nor withdrawn by the President, it automatically lapses six weeks after the commencement of the next session of Parliament. Generally a bill is moved by the Government to enact a law in place of the ordinance.

Financial Powers

Every financial year the Finance Minister, on behalf of the President, lays an Annual Financial Statement before both the Houses of Parliament. A Money Bill cannot be introduced or moved in Lok Sabha except on the recommendation of the President. A Bill involving expenditure from the Consolidated Fund of India cannot be passed by either House of Parliament unless President has recommended for it to that House. No demand for a grant can be made except on the recommendation of the President.

Judicial Powers

The President also appoints Chief Justices and other judges of the High Courts. The President appoints law officers of the Union Government including the Attorney-General of India.

The President, as head of state, can pardon a criminal or reduce the punishment or suspend, cummute or remit the sentence of a criminal convicted by the Supreme Court or High Courts for an offence against the federal laws (Art. 72). The President can pardon a person convicted by a Court Martial. His/her power of pardon includes granting of pardon even to a person awarded death sentence. But, the President performs this function on the advice of Law Ministry.

The President enjoys certain immunities. He/she is above the law and no criminal proceedings can be initiated against him/her.

Military Powers

The supreme command of the defence forces is vested in the President but its exercise is to be regulated by law. The Parliament can make any law with regard to navy, army, air force and any other armed force of the Union. The Parliament can make any law in regard to war and peace. The President cannot declare war or deploy forces of the country without the sanction of the Parliament or in anticipation of the sanction of the Parliament.

Powers regarding Foreign Affairs

All the diplomatic business is conducted in the name of the President. He appoints ambassadors and other diplomatic agents of India accredited to other countries. Diplomatic agents accredited to India present their credentials to the President. All international treaties and agreements are also conducted in his name but they are to be ratified by the Parliament later on.

Emergency Powers

The President can declare emergency in three situations:

(*a*) ***National Emergency*** **(Art. 352) :** If the President is satisfied that the security of the nation or any part thereof is threatened by war or external aggression or internal disturbances, he can issue a proclamation of emergency. The Union Cabinet must give its recommendation in writing, then only the President can issue proclamation. Parliament has to approve the President's order within a month by two-thirds majority, to continue it after a month otherwise the order lapses. If the Lok Sabha has been dissolved or its term expires within these two months, Rajya Sabha can approve the proclamation. The national emergency can be continued indefinitely if Parliament approves it every six months by two-thirds majority.

To avoid misuse of national emergency provisions, certain safeguards have been provided. Armed rebellion is the only condition for internal disturbance. The Union Cabinet has to give its recommendation in writing for the proclamation within a month and after every six months to continue it. Two-thirds majority in Parliament is required for approving the proclamation. If Lok Sabha passes a resolution by a simple majority to end the emergency, the President has to call off the emergency. One-tenth of Lok Sabha MPs can call for the Parliament session to discuss the issue of continuation of emergency. The Fundamental Rights can be superceded only in case of external aggression or war and not in case of internal armed rebellion. The Personal liberty, as given in the Constitution, cannot be taken away during the emergency.

(*b*) ***Constitutional Emergency*** **(Art. 356) :** If the President is satisfied that Governance of a State cannot be carried on in accordance with the provisions of the Constitution, emergency can be proclaimed in the State. The Governor of the State can send a report of the breakdown of Constitutional machinery or otherwise the President himself can get the information from other sources. The Constitutional emergency can be continued for one year after Parliament passes resolutions two times after every six months interval. The emergency has to be approved by Parliament, within two months of proclamation. However, the Constitutional emergency can be extended beyond one year of:

(1) That time, that is a national emergency in the country, state or its part.

(2) Election Commission certifies that free and fair polls are not possible. This way, Constitutional emergency can be extended upto three years. Beyond that, amendment to Constitution is required.

(*c*) ***Financial Emergency*** **(Art. 360) :** The President can issue a proclamation of financial emergency if he is satisfied that the financial credit of India is threatened. The proclamation can last for two months without Parliament's approval. After coming into effect, the President will have to issue a second order to cancel the proclamation. There is no maximum time limit for this emergency.

President's Position

The President is the head of the nation. The Government's actions are taken on his behalf. He represents the whole country. But his powers are limited in the sense that he acts on the advice of the Union Cabinet. The President can, however, guide the executive and restrain them from following a wrong path. He can return, veto or delay a legislation. His discretionary powers are limited but at the time of lack of clear majority in the Parliament or division in the ruling party, he plays an important role.

VICE-PRESIDENT

The Vice-President has been provided in the Constitution to act as the President during the interim period, if required. Anyone, with the following qualifications can become Vice-President:

- Should be a citizen of India.
- Should be 35 years of age.
- Should be eligible to be election as a member of Rajya Sabha.

The Vice-President is not a member of either House of Parliament or a House of the Legislature of any State. If he is a member, then after the elections, he is deemed to have vacated his seat in the house on the date on which he enters upon his office as Vice-President.

The Vice-President is elected by an electoral college, consisting of the Members of both Houses of Parliament (elected and nominated) in accordance with the system of proportional representation by means of a single transferable vote. The voting at such election is by secret ballot (Art. 66(i)). The election process for Vice-President can be challenged only in the Supreme Court.

The Vice-President holds office for a term of five years from the date on which he enters the office (Art. 67). He will continue to occupy the office even after five years if no successor has been elected. He can resign before the completion of the term. He can be removed from the office by a resolution, before the completion of five years term. A 14 days notice has to be given before introducing the resolution. If the resolution is passed by a majority of the total members of the Rajya Sabha and agreed by the Lok Sabha, the Vice-President stands removed from the office.

Power of Vice-President

Though the Vice-President is not a member of Rajya Sabha, he is its Ex-officio Chairman. He manages the affairs of the house. However, if the Vice-President is acting as the President, he ceases to be Chairman of Rajya Sabha and is not entitled to the salary of its office.

The major function of the Vice-President is to act as President or to discharge his functions during vacancy or absence of the President. In the event of the occurrence of vacancy in the office of the President by reasons of death, resignation or removal, the Vice-President can act as President until the date on which a new President is elected to fill such vacancy. When the President is unable to discharge the functions of his office, either because of illness or absence or any other reason, the Vice-President fills in the gap.

THE COUNCIL OF MINISTERS

The basic idea underlying Parliamentary system is that the head of the state is the nominal executive, the real executive power lies with the Council of Ministers. The Council of Ministers is collectively responsible to the lower house of the Parliament. As a consequence of conventions, Indian President is vested with all executive power, but he exercises these power duly on the advice of Council of Ministers. The real Executive is the Council of Ministers headed by the Prime Minister. Their collective responsibility ensures that they remain in office as long as they enjoy the confidence of the Parliament. They swim and sink together.

Appointment of Ministers

While the Prime Minister is selected by the President, the other ministers are appointed by the

President on the advice of the Prime Minister [Article 75(1)] and the allocation of portfolios amongst them is also made by him. President's power of dismissing an individual Minister is virtual power at the hands of the Prime Minister. In selecting the Prime Minister, the President must select the leader of the party in majority in the Lok Sabha, or, a person who is in a position to win the confidence of the majority in that House.

A Composite Body

The Constitution does not classify the members of the Council of Ministers into different ranks. All this has been done informally, following the English practice. Salaries and Allowances of Ministers Act, 1952, defines Minister as a "Member of the Council of Ministers, by whatever name called, and includes a Deputy Minister."

Council of Minister consists of 3 different categories of Ministers :

1. Cabinet Minister, 2. Minister of State, 3. Deputy Minister.

The Cabinet rank ministers are the head of their departments. They attend the Cabinet meetings as a matter of right. However, a person can be appointed Cabinet Minister without a portfolio. The 44th Constitution Amendment Act (1978) has conferred Constitutional status on the Cabinet Ministers.

The Ministers of State are formally of Cabinet Status and are paid the same salary as the Cabinet Ministers and they hold independent charge of their departments. But, they attend the Cabinet meeting only when invited.

The Deputy Ministers work under Minister of State and have no separate charge of a department. They get lesser salary than Minister of State or Cabinet Minister. They assist the Minister in charge of a Department or Ministry and takes no part in Cabinet deliberations.

Qualification

A Minister must be a member of either House of the Parliament. A non-member can also be appointed as Minister but he must get himself elected to either House of Parliament before the expiry of a period of six months commencing from their appointment.

Collective Responsibility

In essence, Indian Constitution follows in the British Principle except as to the legal responsibility of individual Ministers for acts done by or on behalf of the President.

According to Article 75(3) of the Constitution —"The Council of Ministers shall be collectively responsible to the House of People." So, the Ministry, as a body, shall be under a constitutional obligation to resign as soon as it loses the confidence of the popular House of the Legislature. The collective responsibility is to the House of the People even though some of the Ministers may be members of the Council of States.

Individual Responsibility

The principle of individual responsibility of the head of the State is embodied in Article 75(2)— "The Minister shall hold office during the pleasure of the President." The result is that, though the Ministers are collectively responsible to the Legislature, they shall be individually responsible to the Executive head and shall be liable to dismissal even when they may have the confidence of the Legislature. But since the Prime Minister's advice will be available in the matter of dismissing other Ministers individually, it may be expected that this power of the President will virtually be, as in England, a power of the Prime Minister. Usually, the Prime Minister exercises this power by asking an undesirable colleague to resign, which the latter readily complies with, in order to avoid the odium of a dismissal.

Powers and Functions

The Council of Ministers forms the Government of the Union. It is headed by the Prime Minister, who is the head of the Union Government. Its powers and functions may be discussed as below :

1. Legislative Functions : The Council of Ministers controls the legislature of the Union Government, i.e., Parliament. It formulates its policy, submits and explains it to Parliament for approval.

Since it holds majority in Parliament, it is always sure of the acceptance of its policy. The entire legislation of importance passed by Parliament is initiated by the Ministers.

2. Financial Powers : The Cabinet controls the financial policy of the Union. It is the Finance Minister who submits the budget to Parliament. Parliament approves the budget expenditure and revenue items in its original form with support of a subservient majority.

3. Executive Powers : The Council of Ministers is the executive of the Union. The Ministers preside over the various departments of the government and give direction to the administration. The Cabinet brings about co-ordination of policy among various departments and settles their conflicts. The Cabinet formulates foreign and defence policies of the country and executes the five year plans.

CABINET SYSTEM

In a Parliamentary form of government, the Council of Ministers is collectively responsible to the lower house of the Parliament. The Council swims and sinks together. To ensure unanimity and team work, a small but composite body within the Council i.e. Cabinet has grown into significance. With the growing instrumentality of the government, Cabinet today wields more power and is seen with suspicion. The principle of majority rule has enhanced this tendency.

Composition and Structure

The composition of the cabinet reflects a concern for a degree of regional balance and for the representation of important communities—Muslims, Sikhs, SCs, STs and OBCs. They are heads of their departments.

The Cabinet has four major functions; to approve all proposals for the legislative enactment of Government policy, to recommend all major appointments, to settle interdepartmental disputes and to co-ordinate the various activities of the Government and oversee the execution of its policies.

Only members are entitled to attend the weekly meetings of the Cabinet, but ministers of State, Chief Ministers and technical experts may be invited to attend discussions of subjects with which they have special concern. Votes are rarely taken in the Cabinet; decisions usually are reached after discussion by a sense of the meeting. Only major issues are referred to the Cabinet, and frequently even these, such as the preparation of the budget, are decided by the appropriate minister in consultation with the Prime Minister.

Speaking about merit of Cabinet system, Herman Kiner says "on the whole the Cabinet system offers quick, vigorous, thoughtful and responsible leadership."

Rise of Cabinet Dictatorship

In recent times there have been talk of decline of Parliament and rise of cabinet dictatorship. Such tendencies are seen in relation to the disciplined party system and effective majority system. In Parliamentary system, the party or coalition commanding majority in the lower House forms the Government. This ensures the Government commanded by the Cabinet to have virtually all its wishes carried by the Parliament.

While Jawaharlal Nehru promoted free discussions and debate among ministers, Mrs. Indira Gandhi tried to consolidate the position of PM. But post 1989 phase and era of coalition and minority Governments marked some decline in the authoritarian position of Prime Minister.

In India, the notion of Cabinet dictatorship is relative and not absolute. Cabinet has not shown tendencies that are contrary to the norms of democracy. Following points support the evidences.

1. **Party System :** The fragmented and increasingly federalized party system with divergent ideologies and programmes have rendered it impossible for a single political party to command absolute majority. Unlike Britain where two party system with disciplined party workers and fixed electoral votes, India has witnessed transformation in her party system from one party dominance system to multiparty coalition politics.

2. **Coalition Politics :** Closely connected to fragmented party politics is the politics of coalition which has become more than a reality in Indian context. The members of Cabinet represent different political party, region and socio-economic milieu. Hence, there has arisen a politics of compromise and accommodation. Perhaps no Government can inhibit and promote authoritarian tendencies.
3. **Position of PM :** There has increased the role and influence of PM as coordinator and leader. He remains first among equals and ensures that Government survives and continues to perform. In this perspective, he exercises restraints and accommodates different perspectives and voices.
4. **Position of Rajya Sabha :** The role of second chamber in a federal polity like India have also checked cabinet dictatorship. The Government is criticized for its acts of omission and commission. Barring few financial and money matters, the Rajya Sabha enjoys co-equals powers with the Lok Sabha. Similarly Articles 244 and 312 confer it special powers with regard to federal structure.
5. **People Oriented :** The enlightened public opinion and mass media have enhanced the mechanism of democratic control. Every issue have come to be debated to evolve national consensus and no Government can ignore them.

Despite these optimism, it can not be denied that the powers of the Parliament have been usurped by the Cabinet. Both, the constitutional provisions and the practical reality confirm to such suspicion.

Constitutional Provision

Article 74–which provides that the President shall exercise his powers only with advice of the Council of Ministers. He can return a matter for reconsideration, only once.

In Article 352, a provision was added by the 44 Amendment. It provides that the President can impose national emergency only when the Cabinet recommends it in writing.

Practical Reality

It is a matter of everyday experience wherein one witnesses that the whole business of the Parliament are allocated to affairs of Government for either policy making or its criticism through debates and discussion.

Nevertheless, the powerful position of the Cabinet in India should not be described as its 'dictatorship.' But, one can not refuse to accept that there have been continuous decline in calibre of our Ministers. They have become rubber stamp of vested interests.

PRIME MINISTER

The office of the Prime Minister which remains an integral part of the Parliamentary system is a British contribution to the realm of politics. Indians adopted Parliamentary system with the office of Prime Minister from Britain.

Position

So important is his significance that Morley described him as "Primus inter pares" or first among equals. He has also been hailed as "Inter Stellar Luna Minores" or little moon among stars and "key stone of the Cabinet Arch."

Provision

According to Article 74(1) of the Indian Constitution, "there shall be a Prime Minister to head the Council of Ministers." Hence, without the Prime Minister, the Council can not function. The very fact that he is a Prime Minister means that he is superior to others. That is why Ramsay Muir compared cabinet to the steering wheel of the state and the Prime Minister to the 'steers Man." Ivor Jennings called him as "the sun around which the planets revolve" and Hinton said that the Prime Minister was an "elected Monarch."

Powers and Functions

1. Head of the Government: While the President is head of the state, the Prime

Ministers is head of the Government. In theory all major executive functions are vested in the hands of the President, but exercises them only with aid and advice of the Council of Ministers headed by the Prime Minister.

2. Leader of the Cabinet: According to Ivor Jennings, "he is a sun around which other ministers revolve like planets." He selects ministers of his council and distributes portfolio amongst them. He acts as Chairman of the Cabinet. He can ask for resignation of an individual Minister or can get him dismissed by the President.
3. Leader of the Parliament: In this capacity, the Prime Minister :
   - determines the dates of meeting, as also its programmes for the session.
   - chief spokesperson of the government in the Parliament.
   - announces the major policy decision of the government.
   - can participate and intervene in all debates in the Parliament.
4. Leader of the Majority Party in the Lok Sabha : In Parliamentary democracy, usually the leader of majority party in the Lower House is appointed as the Prime Minister. However, in case no party gets majority, the President may appoint a person whom he may deem fit to garner the support of majority.
5. Chairman of the Planning Commission : In this capacity, he becomes a chairman of super cabinet wherein all chief ministers of states and administrators of Union Territories are represented. It covers all developmental activities undertaken by the centre as well as states.

Prime Ministerial System

The Parliamentary system of government as practised in the United Kingdom and other countries functions on the basis of majority party working under the leadership of the Prime Minister. His position is of pre-eminence and is more powerful than the President in Presidential system. In recent times, there has been increasing use of the term 'Prime Ministerial' as synonymous with 'Parliamentary' Government. This change has occurred due to continuous widening of the powers of the Prime Minister.

So important is the stature of the office, that every Parliamentary elections are the Prime Ministerial elections. Every party puts its leader as probable Prime Ministerial candidate. He is leader of majority party in the Lower House. In his capacity he garners support of his party colleagues on various issues and have his way. The whole system of Government is under his control and he is the real Executive. He is the chairman of the Cabinet which itself is formed on his advice. Apart from these provisions, the practical politics of the day have increased his discretion. The growing instrumentality of government and measures like delegated legislation have also enhanced the power of the executive. There have been instances when the Prime Minister's office resembled the U.S. President's executive office.

However, the politics of coalition, federalized political party, effective opposition and mass media have increasingly transferred the aura of PM's office. He now has to work under a lot of pull and pressure and even resort to accommodation and compromise for survival of the Government. In England, the Prime Minister wields a lot of influence because of the disciplined two party system which either forms the government or remain in opposition. On the contrary, Indian polity has been a federal one with a lot of strong regional political parties paving way for era of coalition. And, this trend is likely to survive for some time.

PARLIAMENTARY VS PRESIDENTIAL GOVERNMENT

Parliamentary Government

A parliamentary form of government is that in which the executive is responsible to the legislature. It is also called the cabinet government or responsible government.

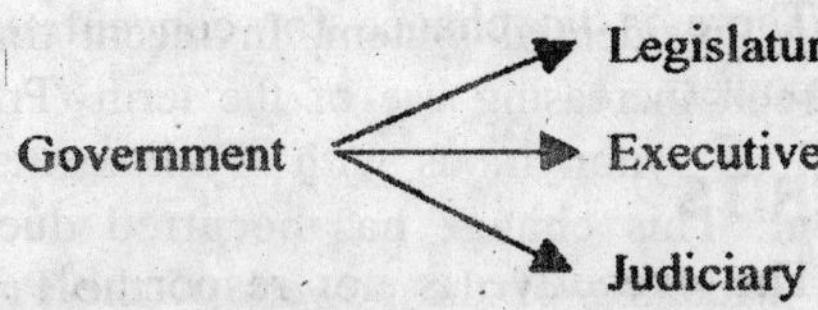

Example : India, United Kingdom (U.K)

Essential Features

1. The executive has two types of functions. One is the nominal and the other is the real. The nominal head represents the state. The real head represents the government. In Britain, head of the state is the king or queen. The head of government is the prime minister.

   Legally all the powers are vested with the nominal head. Example: President of India.

   In practice, all the powers are exercised by the real head. Example: cabinet under the leadership of the prime minister of India.
2. The ruling party should have a clear and stable majority in the legislature. In the event of a "hung parliament" a coalition government can also be formed. For example in India during the prime ministership of Mr. Deva Gowda (1996) Mr. I.K. Gujral (1998) we had hung parliament.
3. Head of a cabinet is the leader of the majority party in the legislature. He is the prime minister.
4. The prime minister and the cabinet ministers are selected from among members of parliament.
5. Each minister is responsible to the legislature for the acts of omission and commission of his own department. Likewise, all ministers are collectively responsible to the legislature for the collective policy of the ministry in power.

MERITS

1. The most important merit in a parliamentary form of government is the harmony and co-operation between the legislature and the executive.
2. It is flexible and elastic. Whenever there is a crisis, smooth change of government is possible without revolution.
3. It is responsive to public opinion.
4. Opposition political party offers a constructive criticism of governmental policies.

DEMERITS

1. It is against the theory of separation of powers. When the executive and legislature functions are combined together, there is every likelihood of prime minister becoming more powerful.
2. In the absence of majority, coalition is the only alternative. Coalition government is a weak form of government and may result in political instability.
3. If ruling party resigns from the government or defeated in the elections, the opposition party assumes office of governance. It will reverse all the decisions of the previous government. It means that there is no continuity in policy matters.

Presidential Government

The presidential form of government is that in which the executive is not responsible to the legislature.

Example: United States of America (U.S.A).

Essential Features

1. The president is the real executive. There is no nominal or ceremonial executive. All the powers are vested in the hands of the president.
2. The powers of the three organs namely, legislature, executive and judiciary are separated and vested in different persons.
3. Though the three organs of the government are kept apart, they are also connected by the system of checks and balances. Each organ of government exercises checks on the other two organs so that a sort of balance is established.
4. The tenure of the president is fixed. The tenure of office cannot be lessened or

increased under any circumstances. President can be removed by the legislature only by a process of impeachment.

MERITS

1. Stable government is possible.
2. Under a presidential form of government, experts are appointed as heads of the departments without consideration of their party affiliations. The president may appoint persons who belong to the opposition parties.
3. There is continuous and consistent policy.
4. Highly suitable during the period of national crisis.
5. There is no chance for concentration of powers.

DEMERITS

1. The executive is not responsible to the legislature and can do whatever it pleases.
2. There is always the possibility of deadlocks between the legislature and the executive.
3. It is not flexible form of government.
4. The Presidential executive finds it difficult to follow a vigorous foreign policy, as there is no harmonious relationship between the executive and the legislature. The executive may follow a policy which may not be acceptable to the legislature.

***

9

Union Legislature

LOK SABHA

The lower house of the Parliament is called Lok Sabha or House of the People. The maximum strength of the House envisaged by the Constitution is now 550 (524 members to represent States and 26 to represent Union Territories (Art. 81). The Lok Sabha at present consists of 543 members. Of these, 524 members are directly elected from States and 19 from Union Territories. By the 104th amendment of the Constitution the reservation of two members of Anglo Indian Community nominated by President have been abolished. The number remains the same until the year 2026.

State-wise Lok Sabha Seats

State	*Seats*
Andhra Pradesh	25
Nagaland	1
Arunachal Pradesh	2
Odisha	21
Assam	14
Punjab	13
Bihar	40
Rajasthan	25
Chhattisgarh	11
Sikkim	1
Goa	2
Tamil Nadu	39
Gujarat	26
Tripura	2
Haryana	10
West Bengal	42
Himachal Pradesh	4
Telangana	17
Uttarakhand	5
Jammu & Kashmir	5
Uttar Pradesh	80
Jharkhand	14
Andaman and Nicobar	1
Karnataka	28
Chandigarh	1
Kerala	20
Madhya Pradesh	29
Delhi	7
Maharashtra	48
Dadra & Nagar Haveli and Daman & Diu	2
Manipur	2
Ladakh	1
Lakshadweep	1
Meghalaya	2
Puducherry	1
Mizoram	1

Elections for the 18th Lok Sabha were held in 2024. To be a member of the Lok Sabha, a person:

(a) should be a citizen of India.

(*b*) should have completed 25 years of age.

(*c*) should not be holding any office of profit under the Union or the State or the local authority and should not have been disqualified under any law from contesting the elections.

A person can retain membership of only one seat even if elected from multiple places. If the person does not participate in the session's meeting for 60 consecutive days without any permission, he can be disqualified. There is reservation of seats for the Scheduled Castes and Scheduled Tribes. The term of the Lok Sabha, under normal circumstances is five years but can be extended by one year at a time during emergency. It can be dissolved earlier also.

Speaker of the Lok Sabha

The members of the Lok Sabha elect the Speaker (Art. 93). A voting may be held and the person receiving the highest number of votes, is declared elected. He is entitled to free residential accommodation and pay and allowances as decided by the Parliament. The Speaker can resign from the post or can be removed by passing a no-confidence vote. The Speaker is given an advance notice of 14 days before the start of discussion of no-confidence vote against him. The Speaker can personally present his point of view before the house. If the resolution is accepted by a simple majority, the Speaker is deemed to have been removed from the post. The sitting of the house during the proceedings is presided over by the Deputy Speaker. Under normal circumstances, the Speaker continues to remain in the office even if the Lok Sabha is dissolved. He continues to retain the post till the election of the new Speaker.

Though the Speaker continues to remain a member of a political party, yet he is supposed to be impartial in carrying out his duties. He presides over the house meetings and enforces order and discipline. His orders have to be accepted by one and all. He takes decisions on the bringing in of resolutions and motions in the house. All the bills are introduced with his assent. He allocates time to various members on a particular issue. He can issue warnings to errant members and can even order them to leave the house or can even ask the house marshals to take a member out. He decides on what goes into the house records and can expunge unparliamentary language. He appoints the chairmen and members of the select committees. He can regulate the presence of people in the spectators gallery. The Speaker can adjourn the house.

He decides whether the bill is a money bill or a non-money bill. After a bill is passed by Lok Sabha, the Speaker sends it to the Rajya Sabha or the President, after signing on it. The Speaker protects the special privileges provided to the members. He decides about the quorum in the house. At least ten per cent of the members must be present in the house otherwise the house has to be adjourned.

He can call for voting in the house on a bill, and if there is a tie, with both sides getting equal number of votes, the Speaker can use his casting vote to decide the fate of the bill. The Speaker also presides over the joint sitting of both the houses.

Deputy-Speaker of the Lok Sabha

The Deputy Speaker of the Lok Sabha is also elected by the members of this house (Art. 93). He assists the Speaker in his duties and in the absence of the Speaker, presides over the meetings of the house. The post of Deputy-Speaker is very often, offered to the opposition party.

Leader of the Opposition

A resolution was passed by the Parliament in 1977 whereby the leader of the opposition is given the status and facilities equivalent to the rank of cabinet ministers. The opposition party with the largest number of MPs and whose number is at least one-tenth of the total house, will have its leader elected as the leader of the opposition.

Sittings of Lok Sabha

Article 85(1) of the Constitution says that the President will call for sittings of each house regularly, at a place and time deemed fit by him, provided there is no gap of six months between the last sitting of a session and the first sitting of the forthcoming session.

RAJYA SABHA

The upper house of the Parliament is the Council of States or the Rajya Sabha. It is a permanent house. The members of the house are senior reputed persons.

The maximum strength of the house is 250, out of which 238 members are elected from state assemblies and union territories. Twelve members, who have made special contributions in the fields of art, literature, science and public service, are nominated by the President (Art. 80). Current strength of Rajya Sabha is 245.

The members from the States and Union Territories are elected by the elected members of respective assemblies. The election is on the basis of proportional representation system with a single transferable vote. The States have been given seats on the basis of their population. To qualify for the membership of Rajya Sabha, one has to: (1) be a citizen of India; (2) be at least 30 years of age; (3) fulfil the qualifications of becoming a member of Parliament; and (4) be a voter in any Lok Sabha constituency of the State.

States & their Seats in the Rajya Sabha —

S.no	*State*	*No. of Seats*
1.	Andhra Pradesh	11
2.	Arunachal Pradesh	1
3.	Assam	7
4.	Bihar	16
5.	Chhattisgarh	5
6.	Goa	1
7.	Gujarat	11
8.	Haryana	5
9.	Himachal Pradesh	3
10.	Jammu & Kashmir	4
11.	Jharkhand	6
12.	Karnataka	12
13.	Kerala	9
14.	Madhya Pradesh	11
15.	Maharashtra	19
16.	Manipur	1
17.	Meghalaya	1
18.	Mizoram	1
19.	Nagaland	1
20.	NNT of Delhi	3
21.	Nominated	12
22.	Odisha	10
23.	Puducherry	1
24.	Punjab	7
25.	Rajasthan	10
26.	Sikkim	1
27.	Tamil Nadu	18
28.	Tripura	1
29.	Uttar Pradesh	31
30.	Uttarakhand	3
31.	West Bengal	16
32.	Telangana	7
	Total	**245**

Rajya Sabha is a permanent house. All its members do not retire at the same time. Each member is elected for 6 years and after every two years, one-third of the members retire.

The Vice-President is the ex-officio Chairman of Rajya Sabha but he is not its member. The Chairman has similar duties as the Speaker of the Lok Sabha. A Deputy Chairman is elected by the Rajya Sabha members to assist the Chairman.

Unequal Status with Lok Sabha

In the following matters, the powers and status of the Rajya Sabha are unequal to that of the Lok Sabha :

1. The Rajya Sabha cannot remove the council of ministers by passing a no-confidence motion. This is because the Council of ministers is collectively responsible only to the Lok Sabha. But, the Rajya Sabha can discuss and criticise the policies and activities of the government.
2. A resolution for the discontinuance of the national emergency can be passed only by the Lok Sabha and not by the Rajya Sabha.
3. Rajya Sabha can only discuss the budget but cannot vote on the demands for grants (which is the exlcusive privilege of the Lok Sabha).
4. The Speaker of Lok Sabha presides over the joint sitting of both the Houses.
5. The Lok Sabha with greater number wins the battle in a joint sitting except when the combined strength of the ruling party in both the Houses is less than that of the opposition parties.
6. A Money Bill can be introduced only in the Lok Sabha and not in the Rajya Sabha.

7. Rajya Sabha cannot amend or reject a Money Bill. It should return the bill to the Lok Sabha within 14 days, either with recommendations or without recommendations.
8. The Lok Sabha can either accept or reject all or any of the recommendations of the Rajya Sabha. In both the cases, the Money bill is deemed to have been passed by the two Houses.
9. A financial bill, not containing solely the matters of Article 110, also can be introduced only in the Lok Sabha and not in the Rajya Sabha. But, with regard to its passage, both the Houses have equal powers.
10. The final power to decide whether a particular bill is a Money Bill or not is vested in the Speaker of the Lok Sabha.

Disqualification of Members (Art. 102)

No person can be a member of both Houses of Parliament. Neither can one be a member of either House of Parliament and any State Legislature. The person has the choice to retain any seat if elected to more than one house. A member can resign or can even be disqualified from the membership of house. One can be disqualified if:

(*a*) he holds any office of profit under the Government of India or any State Government; or

(*b*) he is of unsound mind and has been declared so by a competent court; or

(*c*) he is an undischarged insolvent; or

(*d*) he has lost citizenship of India; or

(*e*) he has been disqualified by or under any law made by Parliament; or

(*f*) he has been absent from the house for more than sixty days.

A person is not deemed to hold an office of profit if he is minister either for the Union or for States.

Quorum

Quorum is the minimum number of members required to be present in the House before it can transact any business. It is one-tenth of the total number of members in each House including the presiding officer. It means that there must be at least 55 members present in the Lok Sabha and 25 members present in the Rajya Sabha, if any business is to be conducted. If there is no quorum during a meeting of the House, it is the duty of the presiding officer either to adjourn the House or to suspend the meeting until there is a quorum.

POWERS OF PARLIAMENT

The Parliament can make laws on the subjects given in the Union List and in the Concurrent List. If Rajya Sabha passes a resolution by two-thirds majority or there is a national emergency in the country or an international treaty has to be implemented the Parliament can make laws on the subjects listed the State List also. If the two houses do not agree on a bill, the President can call for a joint sitting and the decision on the basis of majority opinion is taken.

No taxes can be levied and no expenditure can be incurred without the consent of the Parliament. In financial matters, Lok Sabha enjoys a superior position. A money bill can be introduced only in Lok Sabha. After its approval, Rajya Sabha is asked to approve it within 14 days. Rajya Sabha cannot reject the bill. It can only return it with suggestions. The bill is deemed to have been accepted by Rajya Sabha after 14 days. Lok Sabha is free to take a decision on the suggestions of Rajya Sabha.

The Parliament has control over the executive. Lok Sabha has the power to remove the executive from the office by passing a no-confidence vote. However, both the houses can question the ministers, criticise them, pass resolutions and participate in discussions involving policy matters. The Parliament decides about pay and allowances of the executive.

The Parliament has Constitutional powers. A bill providing for amendment of Constitution can be introduced in either house and both houses have to pass the bill separately. Some constitutional amendment bills have to be ratified by State legislatives also. However, the Parliament cannot alter the basic features of the Constitution. The

Parliament can initiate impeachment of the President, Vice-President, and Judges of the Supreme Court and High Courts. Both the houses of Parliament elect the Vice-President. They, along with State and Union Territory Assemblies, elect the President.

Any type of emergency cannot be continued without Parliament's approval. Both the houses have to ratify the proclamation. They can initiate proceedings to revoke the proclamation.

Rajya Sabha can also recommend constituting of an All-India Service.

PRIVILEGES OF PARLIAMENT, (ART. 105)

Parliamentary privileges are special rights, immunities and exemptions enjoyed by the two Houses of Parliament, their committees and their members. They are necessary in order to secure the independence and effectiveness of their actions. Without these privileges, the Houses can neither maintain their authority, dignity and honour nor can protect their members from any obstruction in the discharge of their parliamentary responsibilities.

Individual Privileges : The privileges belonging to the members individually are :

1. Members have freedom of speech in Parliament. No member is liable to any proceedings in any court for anything said or any vote given by him in Parliament or its committees. This freedom is subject to the provisions of the Constitution and to the rules and standing orders regulating the procedure of Parliament.
2. Members cannot be arrested during the session of Parliament and 40 days before the beginning and 40 days after the end of a session. This privilege is available only in civil cases and not in criminal cases or preventive detention cases.
3. They are exempted from jury service. They can refuse to give evidence and appear as a witness in a case pending in a court when Parliament is in session.

Collective Privileges : The privileges belonging to each House of Parliament collectively are :

1. The courts are prohibited to inquire into the proceedings of a House or its committees.
2. It can punish members as well as outsiders for breach of its privileges or its contempt by reprimand, admonition or imprisonment (also suspension or expulsion, in case of members).
3. It has the right to receive immediate information of the arrest, detention, conviction, imprisonment and release of a member.
4. It can make rules to regulate its own procedure and the conduct of its business and to adjudicate upon such matters.
5. It has the right to publish its reports, debates and proceedings and also the right to prohibit others from publishing the same.

COMMITTEE SYSTEM

The Parliament is a big body where the actions of the members are decided more or less by party affiliation. Moreover, a large rumber of responsibilities have been bestowed upon the Parliament for which the time is limited. All the issues cannot be discussed threadbare, dispassionately and objectively in the Parliament. So, committees are set up, involving Parliamentarians, to cope with the legislative work. These committees can even consult experts and question officials and concerned persons. The committees are of two types—Adhoc or Standing. The adhoc committees are set up for special assignments and are wound up when the work is over. Any bill, when introduced in the Parliament, can be sent to a select committee of a house or joint committees, set up combined by both houses. The joint committees have also been set up to undertake parliamentary investigations. The prominent standing committees are:

1. **Public Accounts Committee:** It, comprising 15 Lok Sabha and 7 Rajya Sabha MPs,

ascertains that the expenditure does not exceeds the grants and money has been spent for the same purpose for which it was sanctioned.

2. **Estimates Committee:** The 30 Lok Sabha members of this committee, examine the estimates of various ministries and departments and suggests alternative policies to the Government to ensure efficiency and economy in administration.
3. **Committee on Public Undertakings:** It, consisting of 15 Lok Sabha and 7 Rajya Sabha MPs, looks into the working of public undertakings, particularly their accounts, reports, efficiency and autonomy.
4. **Business Advisory Committee:** Such a committee of each house decides time and durations for legislative and other works.
5. **Committee on Private Members Bills:** It examines bills submitted to it by individual members and classifies them according to its importance.
6. **Committee on Petitions:** It examines the petitions made by the MPs and suggests remedial measures.
7. **Privileges Committee:** It safeguards the privileges of the members.
8. **Committee on Government Assurances:** It ensures that the assurances and promises made by the Government are fulfilled.
9. **Rules Committee:** It determines the procedure and the conduct of business in the house.
10. **Committee on Subordinate Legislations:** It examines the rules and regulations by various departments for which the powers of making laws has been delegated by the Parliament.

LEGISLATIVE PROCEDURES

Different procedures are adopted for the ordinary non-money bills and money bills. An ordinary bill can be introduced in either house of the Parliament. At the first reading, the title of the bill is read and aims of the bills are explained. At the second reading stage, general principles of the bill are discussed. At the committee stage, it is decided whether the bill has to be sent to a committee or the discussion will take place in the Parliament. Different provisions of the bill are thoroughly examined and changes suggested. At the report stage, the bill is discussed clause by clause and each clause is voted. Amendments can be moved. In the third and final reading, general discussion and voting is held. If the bill is passed by a house, it is sent to the second house where it goes through all the stages as in the first house. If the bill is approved by the second house, it is sent to the President for his signatures. However, if the two houses disagree the President calls a joint sitting and the majority view prevails. After the President's approval, the bill has to be notified for implementation.

Public Bill Vs Private Bill

Public Bill	*Private Bill*
1. It is introduced in the Parliament by a minister.	1. It is introduced by any member of Parliament other than a minister.
2. It reflects of the policies of the government (ruling party).	2. It reflects the stand of opposition party on public matter.
3. It has greater chance to be approved by the Parliament.	3. It has lesser chance to be approved by the Parliament.
4. Its rejection by the House amounts to the experession of want of parliamentary confidence in the government and may lead to its resignation.	4. Its rejection by the House has no implication on the parliamentary confidence in the government or its resignation.
5. Its introduction in the House requires seven days' notice.	5. Its introduction in the House requires one month's notice.
6. It is drafted by the concerned department in consultation with the law department.	6. Its drafting is the responsibility of the member concerned.

Ordinary Bill Vs Money Bill

Ordinary Bill	*Money Bill*
1. It can be introduced either by a minister or by a private member.	1. It can be introduced only by a minister.
2. It can be amended or rejected by the Rajya Sabha.	2. It can not be amended or rejected by the Rajya Sabha. The Rajya Sabha should return the bill with or without recommendations, which may be accepted or rejected by the Lok Sabha.
3. It can be introduced either in the Lok Sabha or the Rajya Sabha.	3. It can be introduced only in the Lok Sabha and not in the Rajya Sabha.
4. It is introduced without the recommendation of the president.	4. It can be introduced only on the recommendation of the President.
5. It does not require the certification of the Speaker when transmitted to the Rajya Sabha (if it has originated in the Lok Sabha).	5. It requires the certification of the Speaker when transmitted to the Rajya Sabha.
6. It can be detained by the Rajya Sabha for a maximum period of six months.	6. It can be detained by the Rajya Sabha for a maximum period of 14 days only.
7. Its defeat in the Lok Sabha may lead to the resignation of the government (if it is introduced by a minister).	7. Its defeat in the Lok Sabha leads to the resignation of the government.
8. It is sent for the President's assent only after being approved by both the Houses. In case of a deadlock due to disagreement between the two Houses, a joint sitting of both the houses can be summoned by the president to resolve the deadlock.	8. It is sent for the President's assent even if it is approved by only Lok Sabha. There is no chance of any disagreement between the two Houses and hence, there is no provision of joint sitting of both the Houses in this regard.
9. It can be rejected, approved, or returned for reconsideration by the President.	9. It can be rejected or approved but cannot be returned for reconsideration by the President.

The procedure adopted in money bill is a little different. These can be laid only in Lok Sabha and that too after the President's prior approval. After Lok Sabha's approval, bills are sent to Rajya Sabha which can:

(*a*) accept the bill in toto, or
(*b*) reject the bill within 14 days, or
(*c*) return with some amendments, or
(*d*) does not approve within 14 days.

Lok Sabha can discuss the amendments suggested by Rajya Sabha but is not bound to accept them. In other three circumstances, money bill is sent to the President. There is no provision of a joint sitting in case of money bill. The money bills involve expenditure or revenue generation.

JOINT SITTING OF TWO HOUSES, (ART. 108)

It is an extraordinary machinery provided by the Constitution to resolve a deadlock between the two Houses over the passage of a bill. A deadlock is deemed to have taken place under any one of the following three situations after a bill has been passed by one House and transmitted to the other House:

1. If the Houses have finally disagreed as to the amendments to be made in the bill.
2. If the bill is rejected by the other Houses.
3. If more than six months have elapsed from the date of the receipt of the bill by the other House without the bill being passed by it.

In the above three situations, the president can summon both the Houses to meet in a joint sitting for the purpose of deliberating and voting on the bill. It must be noted that the provision of joint sitting is applicable to ordinary bills or financial bills only and not to money bills or constitutional amendment bills. In the case of a money bill, the Lok Sabha has overriding powers, while a

Constitutional amendment bill must be passed by each House separately.

If the bill (under dispute) has already lapsed due to the dissolution of the Lok Sabha, no joint sitting can be summoned. But, the joint sitting can be held if the Lok Sabha is dissolved after the president has notified his intention to summon such a sitting (as the bill does not lapse in this case). After the President notifies his intention to summon a joint sitting of the two Houses, none of the Houses can proceed further with the bill. The Speaker of Lok Sabha presides over a joint sitting of the two Houses and the Deputy Speaker, in his absence. If the Deputy Speaker is also absent from a joint sitting, the Deputy Chairman of Rajya Sabha presides.

If the bill in dispute is passed by a majority of the total number of members of both the Houses present and voting in the joint sitting, the bill is deemed to have been passed by both the Houses. Normally, the Lok Sabha with greater number wins the battle in a joint sitting.

Since 1950, the provision regarding the joint sitting of the two Houses has been invoked only thrice. The bills that have been passed at joint sittings are:

Joint Sittings (Till now)

1. Dowry Prohibition Bill	1960
2. Banking Service Commission (Repeal) Bill	1977
3. Prevention of Terrorism Bill	2002

MOTIONS IN THE PARLIAMENT

A. Adjournment Motion: A motion for adjournment is meant to draw the attention of the house to a matter of urgent public importance. Such a motion is intended to focus the attention of the house to a specific act or Commission or Omission of the Government. The motion compels the Government to act quickly in an appropriate manner, otherwise it runs the risk of losing the confidence of the House. Adjournment motions are unusual features and restored to sparingly.

B. No-Confidence or Censure Motion: A censure motion is an expression of lack of confidence in the ministry. Resort to a no-confidence motion is not made under normal circumstances. Only if the opposition feels it has a reasonable chance of defeating the Government, they press for it. Sometimes, this motion is moved to stress a very important point or score a political victory. Sometimes, no voting is done and the motion is allowed to fall through voice vote only. The motion is an important political weapon in the hand of the opposition and can lead to fall of the Government.

C. Call Attention Motion: Any member, with the permission of the chair, can move the motion for discussion on a matter of general public interest. The motion must be supported by at least ten per cent of the members. If allowed by the Speaker, discussion is held for a fixed period. The adoption of motion is no reflection on the Government as they themselves bring it to initiate the discussion.

D. Closure Motion: When the time set for a particular measure is over, although the discussion is incomplete a vote may be taken on the motion before the house after adopting the closure motion. Any member can move it and if adopted, discussion is stopped immediately and vote is taken. This process is also called "Guillotine".

FINANCIAL PROCEDURE

Parliament has the unquestioned and unique right not only to ensure that public funds are raised only with its consent but also to exercise total control over the way in which the country's revenues are spent by the Government. The main principles governing the financial provisions of the Constitution are as follows:

(*a*) There can be no expenditure without the authority of Parliament.

(b) There can be no levy of tax without a law authorising it.

(c) All revenues received by the Union Government should form the 'Consolidated Fund of India' — the Government shall withdraw money for its expenditure from this fund alone.

(d) A reserve fund called 'Contingency Fund of India' is placed at the disposal of Government to meet unforeseen requirements.

(e) The Lok Sabha has supremacy over the Rajya Sabha in all financial matters.

(f) The President even cannot withhold his assent from a Money Bill passed by Parliament.

(g) Income and property of the Union is exempted to a certain extent from taxation by the State Governments.

(h) At the beginning of every financial year, the President causes to be laid before both the houses a statement of the estimated receipts and expenditure of the Government in respect of the forthcoming year. This financial statement is called the Budget.

(i) The Railway Budget is presented separately from the General Budget.

(j) Among the expenditures planned, no voting takes place on certain items as their payments are guaranteed by the Constitution. These are salaries and allowances of the President, Presiding Officers of the Houses of Parliament, Judges of Supreme Court and High Courts and Comptroller and Auditor General of India and debt charges of India.

(k) With regard to items other than the non-votable ones, the Government submits estimates in the form of demands for grants. These are discussed and the Lok Sabha even has the powers to vote on it. After the approval of both houses of Parliament, the papers are sent for President's signatures. All the expenditures are incurred in the name of President.

***

10

The Governor and The State Legislature

There are twenty eight States of Union of India *vis* Andhra Pradesh, Assam, Bihar, Gujarat, Kerala, Madhya Pradesh, Tamil Nadu, Maharashtra, Karnataka, Odisha, Punjab, Rajasthan, Uttar Pradesh, West Bengal, Nagaland, Haryana, Himachal Pradesh, Manipur, Tripura, Meghalaya, Sikkim, Mizoram, Arunachal Pradesh, Goa, Chhattisgarh, Jharkhand, Uttarakhand and Telangana.

Constitutions of these States are prescribed in the Constitution after the description of the Constitution of the Union. Unlike the American and Australian Constitution and very much like the Canadian Constitution, our Constitution lays down the Constitutions of all the States of the Union.

It is provided in the Constitution that "That shall be a Governor for each State" (Art. 153). The same person may also be appointed as Governor for two or more States.

THE GOVERNOR

The State executive consist of a Governor and the Council of Minister with the Chief Minister as its head. The Governor is the nominal executive head while the Council of Ministers the real executive authority in the State.

Appointments and Tenure

The Governor of a State is appointed by the President of India (Art. 155). There is no bar on reappointment of a Governor either in the same State or in different States. This shows that the Governor is not elected but is appointed.

The Governor is appointed for a term of five years but normally holds office during the pleasure of the President. He/she may resign before the expiry of the term or may be removed by the President earlier. As a matter of fact while appointing or removing the Governor the President goes by the advice of the Prime Minister. He/she is entitled to a rent-free residence which is called Raj Bhawan. His/her emoluments, allowances and privileges are specified by the law. However, the emoluments and allowances of the Governor cannot be reduced during his tenure.

Qualifications

To be eligible for appointment as Governor of a State (a) a person should be a Citizen of India and (b) must have completed the age of 35 years (Art. 157). The Governor cannot be a member of either House of Parliament or of a State Legislature. Nor can he hold any office of Profit under any Government. If a person who is a member of a legislature is appointed as Governor, he is deemed to have vacated his seat in the legislature the date on which he enters upon his office as Governor.

Powers and Functions of the Governor

The Constitution .confers on the Governors large number of functions which may be grouped under four heads:

(1) Executive (2) Legislative, (3) Financial, (4) Judicial.

Executive Powers

The executive power of the state is vested in the Governor who is empowered to exercise either directly or through officials subordinate to him.

(*i*) All executive actions of the State Government are also taken in his name and he is authorised to make rules regarding the way in which orders and instructions made and executed in his name are to be authenticated.

(*ii*) He appoints the Chief Minister of the State and other members of the Council of Ministers who hold office during his pleasure.

(*iii*) He allocates the business of the Government among the Minister and makes rules for the convenient transactions of such business.

(*iv*) The Governor also appoints the Advocate General, the Chairman and other members of the State Public Service Commission.

(*v*) He is consulted in the appointment of the Judges of the High Court of the State. The Governor of Jharkhand, Chhatisgarh and Orissa have a special responsibility to see that the Councils of Ministers in their respective States have a Minister incharge on Tribal welfare. The Governor of Assam has certain special powers with respect to the administration of Tribal areas as provided in the Six Schedule of the Constitution.

(*vi*) The Governor exercises a general supervision over the State administration.

(*vii*) He can submit for the consideration of Council of Ministers any matter which in his opinion requires consideration by it. It is the duty of the Chief Minister to communicate to the Governor all decisions of the Council of Ministers relating to the administration of the State and proposal for legislation. The executive power of the Governor extends to all matters in which the State Legislature has power to make laws.

Legislative Powers

The Governor is an integral, part of the State Legislature and performs number of functions in the legislative sphere. He also enjoys legislative powers.

(*i*) He convenes the State Legislature, addresses it in person and send messages to it.

(*ii*) he can also prorogue and dissolve it.

(*iii*) During every financial year, he causes the Budget to be laid before the House. It is only on his recommendation that demands for grant can be made in the State Legislature.

(*iv*) Every Bill passed by the State Legislature has to be present to the Governor for his assent. He may assent to it, or withhold it, may reserve it, for the consideration of the President. He may also return the Bill to the Legislature for reconsideration with a message suggesting alterations or modifications. But if it is again passed with or without amendments, he must give his assent thereto. The Governor has, however, no power to return a Money Bill.

(*v*) The Governor has also the special legislative power of promulgating ordinances during the recess of the State Legislature (Art. 213). If at any time the Governor is satisfied that there exist circumstances which render it necessary for him to take an immediate action, and the State Legislature is then not in session, he may promulgate an ordinances which will have the authority of law. Such an ordinance must be placed before the Legislature of the state when it reassembles and shall cease to be effective at the expiry of six weeks from the date on which the Legislature meets. It may be withdrawn earlier or disapproved by the Legislature before the expiry of the period of six weeks. The Governor has, however, no power to promulgate an ordinance without the previous instructions from the President (1) if the bill containing the same provisions would require the previous sanction of the President for introduction of in the State Legislature; or (2) if the Governor would have deemed it necessary to reserve a Bill containing the same provisions for the consideration of the President, or (3) of an Act of the State Legislature containing the same provisions would be invalid without the assent of the President.

Financial Powers

Before the commencement of every financial year, the Governor causes to be laid before the State Legislature the annual financial statement showing the estimated revenue and expenditure of the State for that year

(*i*) No demand for grant i.e. authority to spend any portion of the State ı venue, can be made except on the recommendation of the Governor.

(*ii*) He has also some powers with regard to Money and Financial Bills.

(*iii*) No Money Bill can be introduced in the Legislative Assembly without the recommendation of the Governor.

(*iv*) The State Contingency Fund is also at the disposal of the Governor who can make advances out of it to meet any unforeseen expenditure. Such expenditure must be subsequently authorised by the Assembly.

Judicial Powers

The Governor also enjoys certain judicial powers (Art. 161). Like the President of India,

(*i*) He, too, is empowered to grant pardons, reprieves, respites or to remit or commute the sentence of any Person convicted of any offense against any law relating to a matter to which the executive power of the state extends.

(*ii*) He also determines the appointments, postings and promotions of the District Judges, Session Judges and judicial officials.

(iii) His consultation is also sought in the appointment of the judges of the High Court of the State.

Discretionary Powers

As has been stated earlier that while exercising the executive, legislative, financial and judicial powers the Governor is aided and advised by the Council of Ministers headed by the Chief Minister. These powers are enjoyed by him/her as the Head of State. There are a few more powers which he/she possesses as the representative of the Central or Union Government. These powers are also called discretionary powers. It is under special circumstance that the Governor may act without the advice of the Council of Ministers. In other words, such powers of the Governor are exercised in his/her own discretion. They are:

1. A situation may arise when in the opinion of the Governor there is the breakdown of the constitutional machinery in the State. In such a case, the Governor may report the situation to the President for imposition of the President's Rule in that State. As the Governor exercises this power on his/her own, it is called the discretionary power of the Governor. In case the Governor's report is accepted by the President, and he/she proclaims emergency under Article 356, the State Council of Ministers is removed, and the State Legislative Assembly is either dissolved or put under suspension. During such emergency, the Governor rules on behalf of the President.
2. A situation may also arise when the Governor may reserve a bill for the consideration of the President. As the Governor does or can do this job on his own, it again is one of his discretionary powers (Art. 200).

The discretionary powers of the Governor were meant for extraordinary and emergency situations. However, in practice these have not only been used in such situations, but have been made use of relating to normal powers in controversial manner. This has led to creating tension between Union and State relations.

Position of the Governor

From a purely theoretical point of view, the Governor is the sole executive authority in the state and the Ministers are there simply to aid and advise him in the exercise of his functions. But in reality the position is entirely different. The Governor of a state is a mere figure head. He is the nominal executive, the real executive being the Council of Ministers. Of course, the Constitution does not provide explicitly or unequivocally that the Governor must in every case accept the advice of his Ministers. But under a system of responsible government it is inevitable that he should normally be guided by his Ministers in all matters. In case the Governor does not accept the advice of the ministers commanding a stable majority in the Assembly, they will resign, thus making it difficult for the Governor to have a Council of Minister constituted from amongst the members of the Legislature and at the same time acceptable to the Lower House. Obviously, under a fully responsible system of government, it is difficult to think of a Governor to behave in an authoritarian manner. To quote M.V. Pylee, "when a Cabinet composed of popular Ministers, collectively responsible to the Legislature, is to aid and advise the Governor in the discharge of his functions occasions are almost non-existent for him to overrule them or to action manner contrary to their advice."

But all this does not mean that the Governor is a mere figure head, a rubber stamp of his Cabinet or post-office between his Cabinet and the President or between his Cabinet and the official gazette. He is, on the other hand, an important functionary designed to play a vital role in the administration of the affairs of the state. He is the agent of the President, his advises on the affairs of the state and the representative of the Union in the State. He maintains the dignity and, stability of the State Government. He gives his assent (though it is justly a formality) to all decisions, of the Council of Ministers relating to affair of the State or proposals for legislation. He is the custodian of the interest of the minorities. He is required by oath of his office to preserve, protect and defend the Constitution.

THE CHIEF MINISTER

The duties of the Chief Minister in a State are similar to those of the Prime Minister of the Union. As head of the Council of Ministers in a State, he has to communicate to the Governor all decisions of the Council relating to the administration of the affairs of the state and proposals for legislation. He has also to furnish any information which the Governor calls for and which is concerned with the administrative and legislative matters of the state. It is also one of his duties to place before the Council, if the Governor so requires, any matter on which a decision has been taken by a Minister without consulting his colleagues in the Council (Art. 167).

Procedure for Appointment of Minister

Constitution in its Article 163 provides that there shall be a Council of Ministers with the Chief Minister as its head to aid and advise the Governor in the exercise of his functions except when he is required by the constitution to act in his discretion. It also lays down the procedure for the appointment of the Ministers. The Chief Minister is appointed by the Governor who also appoints other Ministers on the advice of the Chief Minister. All Ministers are required to be the members of the State Legislature. A person, who is not a member of the State Legislature may be appointed a Minister, but he ceases to holds his office after six months unless within that period he gets elected to the State legislature. The Governor may choose the Chief Minister from the Legislative Council. There is also no bar on his selecting a nominated member of the Legislative Council as the Chief Minister, But the Council of Ministers is collectively responsible to the Legislative Assembly and this fact forces the selection of the Chief Minister from the Lower House of the Legislature.

Functions of the Chief Minister

Chief Minister is the head of the Council of Ministers of his State. The constitutional position of the Chief Minister is more or less similar to that of the Prime Minister. The Chief Minister plays an important role in the administration of the State. We can discuss his functions as follows:

1. Chief Minister is the real head of the State Government. Ministers are appointed by the Governor on the advice of the Chief Minister. The Governor allocates portfolios

to the ministers on the advice of the Chief Minister.

2. Chief Minister presides over the Cabinet meetings. He/she coordinates the functioning of different ministries. He/she guides the functioning of the Cabinet.
3. Chief Minister plays a key role in framing the laws and policies of the State Government. Bills are introduced by the ministers in the State legislature with his/her approval. He/she is the chief spokesman of the policies of his government both inside and outside the State Legislature.
4. The Constitution provides that the Chief Minister shall communicate to the Governor all decisions of the Council of Ministers relating to the administration and the affairs of the State and proposals for legislation.
5. The Chief Minister furnishes such information relating to the administration of the affairs of the State and proposals for legislation as the Governor may call for.
6. If the Governor so requires, the Chief Minister submits for consideration of the Council of Ministers any matter on which a decision has been taken by a minister but which has not been considered by the Cabinet.
7. The Chief Minister is the sole link of communication between the Cabinet and the Governor. The Governor has the right to be informed by the Chief Minister about the decisions taken by the Council of Ministers.

The above functions show that the real authority is vested with the Council of Ministers headed by the Chief Minister. The Council of Ministers is the real executive in the State.

The position of the State Council of Ministers largely depends upon the strength of the ruling party in the State Assembly and the personality of the Chief Minister. The position of the Chief Minister is more powerful when his party is in power in the Centre as well. As long as the Chief Minister and his Council of Ministers enjoy the confidence of majority in the Legislative Assembly, he exercises the real executive power in the State.

Relationship of the Governor with the Chief Minister

The Governor is the constitutional head of the State. All executive actions in the State are taken in his name. The Governor appoints the Chief Minister and on the advice of the Chief Minister he appoints other ministers. The Governor is responsible for smooth running of the State administration. It is his/her duty to see that the State administration is carried on in accordance with the provisions of the Constitution. If he/she finds that the constitutional machinery of the State has broken down or the administration cannot be carried on in accordance with the provisions of the Constitution, he/she may recommend to the Union Government to proclaim emergency in the State. The Governor in his/her report can advise the President to impose President's Rule in the State. If the President is satisfied, he/she will declare emergency under Article 356, popularly known as President's Rule in the State. After proclamation, the State comes under the control of the Centre and the Governor acts as the Centre's agent. The Council of Ministers is dismissed and Assembly (Vidhan Sabha) is dissolved or suspended.

The Constitution provides that there shall be a Council of Ministers with the Chief Minister as its head to aid and advise the Governor in the exercise of his functions, except when he/she is required by the Constitution to act on his discretion. When the Chief Minister enjoys the confidence of the majority in the State legislature, then the Governor's capacity to exercise his/her discretionary powers is reduced. In such a situation the Chief Minister is the real head of the State administration and the Governor is the constitutional head. So we see that the Governor plays a dual role. As the constitutional head of the State, he/she acts on the advice of the Council of Ministers and also serves as the agent of the Central Government. The relations between the Governor and the Chief Minister are influenced by the political and constitutional conditions in the State. In normal conditions, the Governor is the ceremonial head of the State but during the President's Rule he/she becomes the agent of the Centre and assumes control of the State administration. Keeping the spirit of the

Constitution in mind, the Governor may in a sense be the "eyes and ears" of the Central Government and as he/she is appointed, removed or transferred by the Centre he continues to be subservient to Centre as well as the party in power there. It may be emphasised that the job of the Governor would not be merely that of an umpire to see that the game is played according to the letter and spirit of the Constitutional provisions.

STATE LEGISLATURE

For every State there is a legislature comprising the Governor and one or two houses (Art. 168). The legislative assemblies have the right to pass a resolution to abolish or create the legislative council. It must be passed by a majority of the total membership of the assembly and a two-thirds majority of the members of the assembly present and voting. The resolution is then sent to the Parliament which makes law, creating or abolishing the Council.

Legislative Council

The Parliament may, by law, create or abolish a Legislative Council in a State if the Legislative Assembly of that State passes a resolution to that effect by a majority of the total number of members of the Assembly and by a majority of not less than two-thirds of the members present and voting (Art. 169). At present, six States (viz. Bihar, Karnataka, Maharashtra, Andhra Pradesh, Telangana and Uttar Pradesh) have Legislative Councils. The Legislative Council is the Upper House of a State Legislature. The total number of members in the Legislative Council of a State does not exceed one-third of the total number of members in the Legislative Assembly of that State. However, the total number of members in the Legislative Council of a State should, in no case, be less than forty.

The Vidhan Parishad is partly elected and partly nominated. Most of the members are indirectly elected in accordance with the principle of proportional representation by means of single transferable vote system. Different categories of members represent different interests. The composition of the Legislative Council (Art. 171) is as follows :

(*i*) One-third members of the Council are elected by the members of the Vidhan Sabha.

(*ii*) One-third of the members of the Vidhan Parishad are elected by the electorates consisting of members of Municipalities, District Boards and other local bodies in the State;

(*iii*) One-twelfth members are elected by the electorate consisting of graduates in the State with a standing of three years;

(*iv*) One-twelfth members are elected by the electorate consisting of teachers of educational institutions within the State not lower in standard than a secondary school who have teaching experience of at least three years;

(*v*) The remaining, i.e. about one-sixth members are nominated by the Governor from amongst the persons having special knowledge in the sphere of literature, science, arts, co-operative movement and social service.

In order to be a member of the Legislative Council the person concerned should

- be a citizen of India:
- have attained the age of 30 years;
- be a registered voter in the State;
- not hold any office of profit

The tenure of every member of the Council is six years but every second year one-third of its members retire and new members are elected. Ten or one-tenth of the total number of members, whichever is greater, forms the quorum of any meeting of the House.

The Legislative Council chooses two of its members as Chairman and Deputy Chairman respectively. A member holding office as Chairman or Deputy Chairman vacates his office if he ceases to be a member of the Council. He may resign his office or may be removed from his office by a resolution of the Council passed by a majority of members of the Council. But, before moving such a resolution, fourteen days' notice must be given.

The Chairman and the Deputy Chairman are paid such salaries and allowances as are fixed by the Legislature.

Strength of Legislative Councils

State	*Number of Seats*
Andhra Pradesh	58
Bihar	75
Telangana	40
Karnataka	75
Maharashtra	78
Uttar Pradesh	100

Legislative Assembly

The legislative assembly is the lower house and in each State, its members are directly elected by the residents of the State. Legislative Assembly (Vidhan Sabha) of a state consists of not more than 500 and not less than 60 members (Legislative Assembly of Sikkim has 32 members vide Article 371F of the Constitution) chosen by direct election from territorial constituencies in the state (Art. 170).

The candidate for assembly seats have to be 25 years of age, citizens of India, not disqualified by any court, have his name in the voter list and does not hold any office of profit in the Government. If a member of assembly abstains for 60 days without informing the house, he stands disqualified. If a person is elected from two assembly seats or from one assembly seat and a parliamentary seat, he can retain only one seat.

The tenure of the assembly is five years, but it can be dissolved earlier also. The Governor summons the house regularly, but not more than six months gap can be there between the last meeting of a session and the first meeting of the forthcoming session. Each assembly has a speaker and a deputy speaker who preside over the meetings. One-tenth of the total members or ten members form the quorum, without which the meeting cannot begin.

The State legislatures can make laws on subjects given in the State or Concurrent List. However, some laws have to be approved by the President while some need prior approval of the President, even before introduction in the legislature. During emergency all subjects, and, in case of Rajya Sabha passing a resolution, a particular subject comes under the Parliament's jurisdiction. The legislature passes all financial bills, without which the State Government cannot spend a single paisa.

The legislature controls the executive, through no-confidence motion, adjournment motion, rejecting the budget, proposing changes in the budget or asking questions. Among the two houses, the lower house or legislative assembly is mere powerful as it can even recommend abolition of the upper house. The State Government is also responsible to the assembly and in the field of legislations, its role is paramount.

Powers and Functions

The powers and functions of the Legislature can be studied under the following heads.

Legislation

The primary function of Legislature is legislation. It has an exclusive power to legislate on the subjects mentioned in the State List. It shares the power of legislation on subjects in the Concurrent List with Parliament. In case of a conflict between the law passed by the Parliament and that of a State Legislature, the law of the Parliament prevails to the extent of inconsistency.

The Bills introduced in and passed by the Legislature are of two types, non- Money or Ordinary Bills and Money Bills. The procedure for passing a Money Bill is different from that of an Ordinary Bill. An Ordinary Bill can be introduced in either of the two Houses. Every Ordinary Bill, before it becomes an Act, has to pass through the following stages.

The draft of the proposed Bill has to be sent to the Secretariat of the House. The Speaker of the Legislative Assembly or the Chairman of Legislative Council, as the case may be, after consulting the Business Advisory Committee, determines the day and time when the Bill is to be moved in the House. On the appointed day and time the mover seeks the permission of the presiding officer to move the Bill. On receiving his assent, the mover reads the title of the Bill and gives a short speech highlighting the aims and objectives of the Bill. If there is no opposition from anyone, the Bill is supposed to have been passed in the First Reading. Ordinarily there is no opposition at this stage, because it only implies that the House has consented to consider the Bill in detail. But there are some occasions when the opposition is not prepared even to consider the Bill, the presiding officer allows a full debate and then the Bill is put to vote. If the House approves it, it is supposed to have been passed in the First Reading.

After an interval of some time (generally it is of two days) the Bill is again moved by the mover. This stage is called Second Reading and the Bill is discussed and passed in detail clause by clause. Alternatively, the House may decide to circulate the Bill for eliciting the public opinion. Then, the Bill is published in the Government Gazette inviting public reactions on it. The gist of the public opinion is then circulated amongst the members of the House.

The members discuss it in detail in the light of public opinion and vote clause by clause. There is, however, another alternative. The House may decide to refer the Bill to a Select Committee consisting of such members of the House as have special interest in the subject. The presiding officer constitutes such a Committee having 20-30 members. The Committee makes a thorough scrutiny of the Bill and suggests various changes and then submits its Report to the House. The House considers the Report and then discusses and votes the Bill in detail clause by clause. If the House approves it, it is supposed to have crossed the Report Stage. After an interval of some time, the Bill is again put before the House for final or Third Reading. At this stage, there is only a general discussion and no amendment, except some verbal changes, is allowed. If the House approves the Bill at this stage the Bill goes to the other House. In the other House also the Bill has to undergo all the stages referred to above. If the other House also approves, it goes to the Governor for his assent. The Second House (Legislative Council) can reject the Bill or send it back with its recommendations. It may even sleep over the Bill for three months. If the Legislative Assembly passes the Bill again with or without changes, the Council cannot reject it. Even if it rejects; the Bill is deemed to have been passed by both the Houses after a month.

Strength of Legislative Assemblies

State	*Number of Seats*
States	
Andhra Pradesh	175
Arunchal Pradesh	60
Assam	126
Bihar	243
Chhattisgarh	90
Goa	40
Gujarat	182
Haryana	90
Himachal Pradesh	68
Jharkhand	81
Karnataka	224
Kerala	140
Madhya Pradesh	230
Maharashtra	288
Manipur	60
Meghalaya	60
Mizoram	40
Nagaland	60
Odisha	147
Punjab	117
Rajasthan	200
Sikkim	32
Tamil Nadu	234
Telangana	119
Tripura	60
Uttarakhand	70
Uttar Pradesh	403
West Bengal	294
Union Territories	
Delhi	70
Jammu and Kashmir	83
Puducherry	30

A Bill after being adopted by both the Houses, if there are two Houses or by the Legislative Assembly, if there is only one House, is presented before the Governor for his assent. The Governor either gives his assent or returns the Bill to the Legislature for reconsideration. If the Legislature passes the Bill again, whether in amended or original form, the Governor has to give his assent after which it becomes an Act. The Governor, however, has another alternative. He may reserve the Bill for the consideration of the President. The President may give his assent or withhold it or he may refer back the Bill to the Legislature for reconsideration in the light of his suggestions. If the Legislature again passes the Bill with or without amendment, it is again sent to the President for his consideration.

The Procedure Adopted for Money Bills

The State Legislature exercises full control over the finances of the State Government. In the beginning of every financial year an Annual Financial Statement or the Budget, showing the receipts and expenditure, is laid down before the State Legislature (Art. 202). The Budget shows separately the expenditure charged on the Consolidated Fund of the State, which can be discussed but not voted upon and the amount required to meet other expenditure proposed to be made from the Consolidated Fund of the State which are discussed and voted upon by the Legislature.

The Budget speech by the Finance Minister is followed by a general discussion on the Budget as a whole. After the discussion is over the Legislative Assembly proceeds to the Voting of Demands. When all the Demands have been voted by the Legislative Assembly, both the charged and non-charged expenditures are put together and incorporated in a Bill called the Annual Appropriation Bill. It is presented before and passed by the Legislative Assembly in the same manner as any other Bill. Then it is certified by the Speaker as a Money Bill and sent to the Legislative Council if there is one, for its recommendations. Money Bills can be initiated only in the Legislative Assembly and when it is sent to the Legislative Council, the Legislative Council has to send it back within fourteen days. It can make recommendations but it can neither reject, nor amend them. In any case, the Bill is considered to have been passed by both the Houses fourteen days after its final stage in the Legislative Assembly. It is then sent to the Governor for his assent who cannot withhold it.

Control over the Executive

The Council of Ministers of the State is responsible to the Vidhan Sabha only and remains in the office so long as it enjoys the confidence of the Assembly (Vidhan Sabha). Although members in the Vidhan Parishad can ask questions, introduce adjournment motions, calling attention notives, etc. yet the Vidhan Parishad cannot remove the government.

Constitutional Amendments

A Constitutional Amendment Bill proposing changes in the federal character of the Constitution requires the approval of half the State Legislatures if the same has been passed by both the Houses of the Parliament.

Electoral Functions

Only the elected members of the Vidhan Sabha are entitled to participate in the election of the President of India. The members of the Vidhan Sabha do so in their capacity as the members of the Electoral College. But the members of the Vidhan Parishad are not entitled to vote in the election of the President. Members of the Rajya Sabha from each State are elected only by the members of Assembly and not of the Council.

The above discussion makes it clear that the Vidhan Parishad is powerless and noninfluential House. It has become a secondary House. Thus many States prefer to have unicameral Legislature. But the Vidhan Parishad is not superfluous. It serves as a check on hasty Legislation made by Vidhan Sabha by highlighting the short bills comings or defects of the bill. It lessens the burden of the Vidhan Sabha, as some bill are initiated in the Vidhan Parishad.

***

11

Elections and Electoral Process

The electoral system of India is largely based on the British pattern. The Constitution did not provide any details about the electoral system and left it to the Parliament to determine. Accordingly, the Parliament passed a number of laws to regulate the electoral system. Some prominent laws enacted by the Parliament for this purpose include the Representation of People's Act, 1950; Representation of People's Act, 1951; Presidential and Vice-Presidential Election Act, 1952; Delimitation Act, 1952, etc.

The main features of the electoral system are:

1. The elections have constitutional base.
2. It is based on universal adult franchise, which means that all citizens above the age of 18 years are entitled to participate in elections provided they have registered themselves as voters and fulfil the prescribed conditions.
3. There is a single electoral body and the system of communal representation, which existed in the pre-independence period, has been done away with.
4. There is provision for reservation of seats for Scheduled Castes and Scheduled Tribes, but these members are elected through joint electorate.
5. Representation is based on the territorial principle. There is common electoral roll for each constituency.
6. Voting is held through secret ballot.
7. The Constitution provides for an independent Election Commission, which is responsible for free and impartial elections.
8. Elections are held on the basis of single member constituencies and only one representative is elected from each constituency.
9. Political parties are an indispensable part of the electoral process and serve as an important link between the people and the government.
10. There is provision for election petitions to resolve the disputes regarding elections. The aggrieved candidates can file petitions in the High Court or the Supreme Court and if the Court finds the charge correct, the election is declared invalid.

ELECTORAL PROCEDURE

Elections to Parliament and state legislature are held in accordance with the schedule decided by the Election Commission in consultation with the concerned government. After the schedule of the election is finalised, the President or the governor issues a notification. As per the rules, eight days are given for filing of nominations by the candidates. The candidate must be a voter in the constituency from which he wishes to contest. A candidate can contest from two constituencies.

After the last date of filing of nominations returning officer scrutinizes the nomination papers and rejects those which are defective. The candidates are permitted to withdraw their candidature within two days of the scrutiny. After withdrawals, the Returning Officer finalise the list of candidates and allot them symbols. The candidates contesting as party candidates are allotted reserved symbols while the other candidates are allotted free symbols.

After the finalisation of the list of candidates, 14 days are permitted for campaigning. The candidates can incur expenses on elections as per prescribed rates in each state. These rates are fixed on the basis of number of voters in the constituency. It may be noted that the expenses incurred by the political parties on behalf of the candidates are not included in the election expenses incurred by the candidate. The election campaign in a constituency has to stop 48 hours before the poll. Generally, on the eve of the election the Election Commission evolves a code of conduct, in consultation with the political leaders, for the elections. All the contestants are expected to follow the code of conduct. However in actual practice, the code is not strictly adhered to and many a time it is violated by the candidates and parties.

Role of Elections

If democratic norms are observed, election can be helpful in:

- Political Socialization and political participation.
- Providing leaders for political process.
- Ensuring legitimate government.
- Political education of the masses.
- Resolving political conflict by peaceful means.
- Peaceful transfer of power.

It is by virtue of its significant functions that S.M. Lipset hailed elections as the 'expression of democratic class struggle.'

ELECTION COMMISSION

The Election Commission is a permanent and an independent body established by the Constitution of India directly to ensure free and fair elections in the country. Article 324 of the Constitution provides that the power of super-intendence, direction and control of elections to parliament, state legislatures, the office of president of India and the office of vice-president of India shall be vested in the election commission. Thus, the Election Commission is an all-India body in the sense that it is common to both the Central govt. and the state governments.

Since its inception in 1950 and till 15 October 1989, the election commission functioned as a single member body consisting of the Chief Election Commissioner. On 16 October 1989, the president appointed two more election commissioners to cope with the increased work of the election commission on account of lowering of the voting age from 21 to 18 years. Thereafter, the Election Commission functioned as a multimember body consisting of three election commi-ssioners. However, the two posts of election commissioners were abolished in January 1990 and the Election Commission was reverted to the earlier position. Again in October 1993, the president appointed two more election commissioners. Since then the Election Commission has been functioning as a multi-member body consisting of three election commissioners.

Terms

Every Election Commissioner has a term of six years from the date he/she assumes office or till he attains the age of 65 years (whichever is earlier).

Safeguards

The Chief Election Commissioner cannot be removed from his office, except in a like manner and on like grounds as a judge of the Supreme Court. All the three members are entitled to the same salary and other facilities, as are provided to a judge of the Supreme Court.

Functions/Powers

1. Prepare, revise and maintain the voter's list.
2. Delimitation of Constituencies.
3. Advises the President and Governor regarding electoral matters.
4. Determine criteria for recognizing political parties.
5. Settle election disputes.

ANTI-DEFECTION LAW (1985)

The evil of defection, which gave rise to political instability, was sought to be curbed through the 52nd Constitutional Amendment Act passed in 1985. This amendment added Tenth Schedule of the Constitution, which contained provisions regarding disqualification of members of the Parliament or state legislature in the event of defection. A member of Parliament or state legislature was to lose membership if : (a) he gave up the membership of the party on whose ticket he was elected to the House; (b) he voted or abstained from voting in the House against any direction of the political party; (c) an independent member joined any political party after election; (d) any nominated member joined any political party after the expiry of six months from the date on which he took his seat in the House. However, the above provisions were not to apply to a member if : (i) he left the party as a result of a split in the party, *i.e.* one-third of the members of the legislature party had agreed to such a merger, (ii) he was elected as presiding officer of the House and gave up his membership of the party to become non-partisan.

The final decision on the question whether a person has incurred disqualification on grounds of defection rests with the presiding officer of the House. Earlier, the decision of the presiding officer could not be challenged in court. However in 1993, the Supreme Court gave a ruling that the decision of the Speaker/Chairman could be challenged in the Supreme Court as well as the High Courts on the grounds of jurisdictional errors.

* * *

12

Important Officials

ATTORNEY-GENERAL OF INDIA

Attorney-General is the highest legal officer of the union government and renders legal assistant to it. He is appointed by the President and holds office during his pleasure. *(Art. 76)* To be eligible for appointment as Attorney-General of India, a person must possess the qualifications prescribed for a judge of the Supreme Court. He is entitled to such salary and allowances as may be determined by the President. The Attorney-General is entitled to audience in all courts in the country and can take part in the proceedings of Parliament and its committees. However, he is not given the right to vote.

Functions

He is the chief legal adviser of the Government of India and gives it advice on all such legal matters which may be referred or assigned to him by the President. He also performs such other legal duties as are assigned to him by the President from time-to-time. The Attorney-General appears before the Supreme Court and various High Courts in cases involving the Government of India.

ADVOCATE-GENERAL FOR THE STATES

The Government of India Act, 1935 provided for an Advocate-General for the Centre as well as one for each Governor's Province. Their function was to give advice to the respective Governments on "such legal matters and perform such other duties of a legal character as may from time-to-time be referred or assigned to him".

The memoranda on the Union and Provincial Constitution prepared by the Constitutional Advisor B.N. Rau, in May 1947 proposed to continue this practice : and accordingly they contained simple provisions in regard to the Attorney-General for the Union and the Advocate-General for the Provinces.

The Provision for the Provincial Advocate-General made in the Draft Constitution prepared by the Constitutional Advisor was accepted by the Drafting Committee without any change. It read :

1. The Governor of each State shall appoint a person who is qualified to be appointed as judge of a High Court to be Advocate-General for the State (Art. 165).
2. It shall be the duty of the Advocate-General to give advice to the Government of the State upon such legal matters and to perform such other duties of a legal character as may from time-to-time be referred or assigned to him by the Governor, and to discharge the functions conferred on him by or under this Constitution or any other law for the time being in force.
3. The Advocate-General shall retire from office upon the resignation of the Chief Minister in the State, but he may continue in office until his successor is appointed or he is reappointed.

Discussion were held over provisions and the Constituent Assembly accepted the amendment of Nasiruddin Ahmed that the Advocate-General for a State would hold office during the pleasure of the Governor and would not be required to resign with the Ministry. Therefore, while clauses (1) and (2) were adopted in their original forms, clause (3) of the above given provisions was thus change :

4. The Advocate-General shall hold office during the pleasure of the Governor, and shall receive such remuneration as the Governor may determine.

These are given under Article 165 of the Constitution. It is provided that the Advocate-General has right to speak and to take part in the proceedings of, but no right to vote in, the Houses of the Legislature of the State.

COMPTROLLER AND AUDITOR-GENERAL

Office of Comptroller and Auditor-General is of great importance under Government of India, who controls entire financial system of the country at the Union and State levels.

The Government of India Act, 1935 also provided for an Auditor-General of India, who was made independent as he was irremovable, except "in like manner and on the like grounds as a Judge of the Federal Court". The office of the Comptroller and Auditor-General is substantially modelled upon that of the Auditor-General of Government of India Act, 1935.

According to Dr. Ambedkar, the Comptroller and Auditor-General of India shall be the most important officer under the Constitution of India. For, he is to be the guardian of the public purse and it is his duty to see that not a farthing is spent out of the Consolidated Fund of India or of a State without the authority of the appropriate Legislature.

Regarding the services of the Comptroller and Auditor-General of India, it is thus provided in the Constitution :

1. There shall be a Comptroller and Auditor-General of India who shall be appointed by the President by warrant under his hand and seal and shall only be removed from office in like manner and on the like grounds as a Judge of the Supreme Court (Art. 148).
2. Every person appointed to be the Comptroller and Auditor-General of India shall before he enters upon his office, make and subscribe before the President, or some person appointed in that behalf by him, an oath or affirmation according to the form set out for the purpose in the Third Schedule.
3. The salary and other conditions of service of the Comptroller and Auditor-General shall be such as may be determined by Parliament by law and until they are so determined, shall be specified in the Second Schedule :

   Provided that neither the salary of a Comptroller and Auditor-General nor his rights in respect of leave of absence, pension or age of retirement shall be varied to his disadvantage after appointed.
4. The Comptroller and Auditor-General shall not be eligible for further office either under the Government of India or under the Government of any State after he has ceased to hold his office.
5. Subject to the provisions of this Constitution and of any law made by Parliament, the conditions of service of persons serving in the Indian Audit and Accounts Department and the administrative powers of the Comptroller and Auditor-General shall be such as may be prescribed by rules made by the President after consultation with the Comptroller and Auditor-General.
6. The administrative expenses of the office of the Comptroller and Auditor-General including all salaries, allowances and pensions payable to or in respect of persons serving in that office, shall be charged upon the Consolidated Fund of India.

Duties and Powers

The Comptroller and Auditor-General shall perform such duties and exercise such powers in relation to the accounts of the Union and of the States and of any other authority or body as may be prescribed by or under any law made by Parliament and, until provision in that behalf is so made shall perform such duties and exercise such powers in relation to the accounts of the Union of the States as were conferred on or exercisable by the Auditor-General of India immediately before the commencement of this Constitution relation to the accounts of the Dominion of India and of the Provinces respectively (Art. 149).

Audit reports

1. The reports of the Comptroller and Auditor-General of India relating to the accounts of the Union shall be submitted to the President who shall cause them to be laid before each House of Parliament.
2. The reports of the Comptroller and Auditor-General of India relating to the accounts of a State shall be submitted to the Governor of the State who shall cause them to be laid before the Legislature of the State.

CENTRAL BUREAU OF INVESTIGATION (CBI)

The Central Bureau of Investigation (CBI) was set up in 1963 by a resolution of the Ministry of Home Affairs. Presently it is under the Ministry of Personnel and enjoys the status of an attached office. The Special Police Establishment set up in 1941 was also merged with the CBI.

The CBI is the main investigating agency of the central Government. It plays an important role in preventing corruption and maintaining integrity in administration. It also provides assistance to the Central Vigilance Commission.

The role of Special Police Establishment (a division of CBI) is supplementary to the state police forces. Along with state police forces, the Special Police Establishment (SPE) enjoys the concurrent powers of investigation and prosecution for offences under the Delhi Police Establishment Act, 1946. However, to avoid duplication and overlapping of cases between these two agencies, the following administrative arrangements have been made.

1. The SPE shall take up such cases which are essentially and substantially concerned with the Central Government's affairs or employees, even if they also involve certain state government employees.
2. The state police force shall take up such cases which are substantially concerned with the state government's affairs or employees, even if they also involve certain central government employees.
3. The SPE shall also take up cases against employees of public undertakings or statutory bodies established and financed by the central government.

The functions of CBI are:

(*i*) Investigating cases of corruption, bribery and misconduct of the central government employees.

(*ii*) Investigating cases relating to infringement of fiscal and economic laws, that is breach of laws concerning export and import control, customs and central excise, income tax, foreign exchange regulation and so on. However, such cases are taken up either in consultation with or at the request of the department concerned.

(*iii*) Investigating serious crimes committed by organised gangs of professional criminals, having national and international ramifications.

(*iv*) Coordinating the activities of the anti-corruption agencies and the various state police forces.

(*v*) Taking up, on the request of a state government, any case of public importance for investigation.

(*vi*) Maintaining crime statistics and disseminating criminal information.

CENTRAL VIGILANCE COMMISSION (CVC)

The CVC was established in 1964 on the recommendation of the Santhanam Committee on Prevention of Corruption. It was set up by an executive resolution of the Union Government. As such, originally it was neither a constitutional body nor a statutory body.

The Central Vigilance Commission is the main agency for preventing corruption in the Central Government. It advises the Central Government on all matters relating to the protection and maintenance of integrity in administration. Thus, its role is advisory in the same sense as that of the UPSC. In the performance of its functions, it is given the same degree of autonomy and independence as the UPSC.

The CVC falls within the jurisdiction of the Ministry of personnel. The commission submits an annual report on its activities to the Ministry which then lays it before both the Houses of Parliament.

The jurisdiction and powers of the commission extends to all those matters which fall within the purview of the executive powers of the Central Government. Its jurisdiction covers the following public servants.

(*a*) All the employees of the Central Government (*i.e.* directly employed in the various ministries/departments of the Central Government).

(*b*) All the employees of public undertakings, corporate bodies and other institutions working under the Central Government.

(*c*) All the employees of the Delhi Metropolitan Council and the New Delhi Municipal Committee.

However, its present jurisdiction is limited to the gazetted officers and officers of equivalent status only. It advises on individual vigilance cases relating to higher civil servants only. It has no power to probe into the cases of political corruption (*i.e.* against members of Parliament and ministers).

LOKPAL

Composition: The Lokpal will consist of a chairperson and a maximum of eight members.

- **Applicability:** The Lokpal will cover all categories of public servants, including the Prime Minister. But the armed forces do not come under the ambit of Lokpal.

Eligibility

- The person who is to be appointed as the chairperson of the Lokpal should be either of the following: Either the former Chief Justice of India Or the former Judge of Supreme Court Or an eminent person with impeccable integrity and outstanding ability, having special knowledge and expertise of minimum 25 years in the matters relating to anti-corruption policy, public administration, vigilance, finance including insurance and banking, law and management.
- Out of the maximum eight members, half will be judicial members. Minimum fifty per cent of the Members will be from SC/ST/OBC/Minorities and women.
- The judicial member of the Lokpal should be either a former Judge of the Supreme Court or a former Chief Justice of a High Court.
- The non-judicial member should be an eminent person with impeccable integrity and outstanding ability, having special knowledge and expertise of minimum 25 years in the matters relating to anti-corruption policy, public administration, vigilance, finance including insurance and banking, law and management.

Term of Office

- The term of office for Lokpal Chairman and Members is 5 years or till attaining age of 70 years.
- The salary, allowances and other conditions of service of chairperson are equivalent to Chief Justice of India and members is equivalent to Judge of Supreme Court. If the person is already getting the pension (for being a former judge), the equivalent pension amount will be deducted from the salary.
- The source of salary for Lokpal and Members is Consolidated Fund of India.
- If the chairperson dies in office or has resigned from the post, President can authorise the senior-most Member to act as the Chairperson until new chairperson is appointed. If chairperson is not available for certain functions due to leave, his job will be done by senior most member.

Powers

- The Lokpal will have the power of superintendence and direction over any investigation agency including CBI for cases referred to them by the ombudsman.
- As per the Act, The Lokpal can summon or question any public servant if there exists a prima facie case against the person, even before an investigation agency (such as vigilance or CBI) has begun the probe. Any officer of the CBI investigating a case referred to it by the Lokpal, shall not be transferred without the approval of the Lokpal.
- An investigation must be completed within six months. However, the Lokpal or Lokayukta may allow extensions of six months at a time provided the reasons for the need of such extensions are given in writing.
- Special courts will be instituted to conduct trials on cases referred by Lokpal.

LOKAYUKTA

While the Central Government is still debating the establishment of the institution of Lokpal, many states have already set up the institution of Lokayuktas.

Donald C. Rowat says that "India has the most populous Ombudsman jurisdiction in the world."

It must be mentioned here that the institution of Lokayukta was established first in Maharashtra in 1971, though Orissa (now Odisha) had passed the act in this regard in 1970. The Orissa act came into force in 1983.

The various aspects of the institution of Lokayukta are explained below.

Structural Variations: The structure of the Lokayukta is not same in all the states. Some states like Rajasthan, Karnataka, Andhra Pradesh and Maharashtra have created the Lokayukta as well as Uplokayukta, while some other states like Bihar, Uttar Pradesh and Himachal Pradesh have created only the Lokayukta; there being no provision for Uplokayukta. There are still other states like the Punjab and Orissa (now Odisha) which have designated officials as Lokpal.

Appointment: The Lokayukta and Uplokayukta are appointed by the Governors in most of the states. While appointing, the Governor consults :

(*i*) the Chief Minister,

(*ii*) Chief Justice of the State High Court, and

(*iii*) the leader of opposition in the State Legislative Assembly.

Qualifications: Judicial qualifications are prescribed for the Lokayukta in the states of Uttar Pradesh, Himachal Pradesh, Andhra Pradesh, Gujarat, Orissa (now Odisha), Karnataka and Assam. But no specific qualifications are prescribed in the states of Bihar, Maharashtra and Rajasthan.

Tenure: In most of the states, the term of office fixed for Lokayukta is of 5 years duration or 65 years of age, whichever is earlier. He is not eligible for reappointment for a second term.

Jurisdiction: There is no uniformity regarding the jurisdiction of Lokayukta in all the states. The following points can be noted in this regard:

(*a*) The Chief Minister is included within the jurisdiction of Lokayukta in the states of Himachal Pradesh, Andhra Pradesh, Gujarat, while he is exculded from the purview of Lokayukta in the states of Maharashtra, Uttar Pradesh, Rajasthan, Bihar and Odisha.

(*b*) Ministers and higher civil servants are included in the purview of Lokayukta in almost all the states. Maharashtra has also included former Ministers and civil servants.

(*c*) Members of states legislatures are included in the purview of Lokayukta in the states of Andhra Pradesh, Himachal Pradesh, Gujarat, Uttar Pradesh and Assam.

(*d*) The authorities of the local bodies, corporations, companies and societies are included in the jurisdiction of the Lokayukta in most of the states.

* * *

13

Judiciary

The Constitution of the Republic of India guarantees, besides other rights, protection of life and personal liberty and provides adequate safeguards against the arbitrary deprivation thereof by the State. Adoption of a Constitution by India in 1950 did not disturb continuity of existing laws and unified structure of courts. Unity and uniformity of the judicial structure were preserved by placing such areas of law as criminal law and procedure, civil procedure, will, succession, contract including special form of contract, but not including contract relating to agricultural land, registration of deeds and documents, evidence, etc., in the Concurrent List.

SUPREME COURT

The Supreme Court has 33 judges and a Chief Justice. Ad hoc judges may be appointed to the Supreme Court, after the President's prior approval. The President appoints the judges and the Chief Justice (Art. 124(2)). Usually, the seniormost judge is appointed as the Chief Justice. Other judges are appointed, in consultation with the Chief Justice. To qualify for a Supreme Court judge's post, one has to be a citizen of India. He should have been working for at least five years regularly in one or more high courts of the country or should have been working as an advocate in a High Court for not less than ten years or should be a distinguished jurist, in the opinion of the President.

The Supreme Court judges remain in office till they attain 65 years of age. However, they can resign before the completion of the term or can be impeached and removed. To make judiciary independent from the control of the executive, the process of removing judges has been made difficult. Moreover, their salary and allowances are paid from the consolidated funds and no discussion is held in the Parliament on the conduct of the judiciary. The service conditions of the judges, cannot be changed to their disadvantage. In case of financial emergency, salaries of judges can be reduced.

A Supreme Court judge can be impeached for unconstitutional conduct or proven misbehaviour or incapacity. If both the houses of Parliament, in the same session, pass an address with majority of total membership of each house and that majority must not be less than two-thirds majority of the members present and voting, the President passes an order removing the judges. When the address is under consideration, the judge can present himself and defend. Since the procedure is so difficult, no judge in India has so far been impeached.

A Supreme Court judge, after retirement, resignation or removal, cannot plead or act in any court or before any authority within the territory of India.

The Supreme Court has only one seat, and that is in Delhi. It has no other branch. But a sitting can be held elsewhere, if the President approves. The Supreme Court has original and appellate jurisdiction.

Original Jurisdiction

The Supreme Court has original jurisdiction (Art. 131) in any dispute between: *(a)* the Government of India and one or more States; or *(b)* the Government of India and any State or States on one side and one or more than one State on the other; or *(c)* between two or more States. The Supreme Court has exclusive jurisdiction in regard to questions as to constitutional validity of Central laws.

Appellate Jurisdiction

An appeal against the High Court decision can be made in the Supreme Court. These cases can be constitutional, civil, criminal or special appeals. However, Supreme Court cannot be approached against the decision of military courts. If the High Court certifies that the case involves a substantial question of law or needs interpretation of Constitution, the case can be taken to the Supreme Court (Art. 132).

In the civil cases, appeal against the High Court decisions can be made if the High Court certifies that the case involves a substantial question of law and need to be decided by the Supreme Court (Art. 133).

An appeal in the criminal case lies to the Supreme Court if the High Court certifies it, fit for appeal. In cases, where the High Court has reversed the acquittal order of a lower court and sentenced the accused to death; or where the High Court, having withdrawn, for trial, a case from a lower court before it, has tried the accused and sentenced him to death, the Supreme Court can be approached even if the High Court does not certify (Art. 134).

In cases, civil or criminal, where no appeal can lie to the Supreme Court, the court may in its discretion grant special leave of appeal from any judgement, decree, sentence or order in any case made by any court or tribunal within India. This is a very wide discretion given to the Supreme Court concerning appellate cases and through this, it can ensure that no injustice is done.

Advisory Jurisdiction

The President can refer any matter of law or fact of public importance to the consideration of Supreme Court to seek its advice where it is expedient to do so. However, under Article 143 the advice is not binding upon the President. If, the advice is sought under Article 131, Supreme Court is bound to give its opinion.

Guardian of Fundamental Rights

Article 32 of the Constitution empowers Supreme Court to issue writs of various kinds for the enforcement of Fundamental Rights. This special responsibility conferred on Supreme Court makes it guardian of Fundamental Rights. Supreme Court can issue writs—*Habeas Corpus, Mandamus, Prohibition, Quo-Warranto* and *Certiorari* to protect Fundamental Rights.

Court of Record

The Supreme Court is a Court of Record (Art. 129). It has two implications. All its decisions and judgments are cited as precedents in all courts of the country. They have the force of law and are binding on all lower Courts, and indeed the High Courts. As a Court of Record, the Supreme Court can even send a person to jail who may have committed contempt of the court.

JUDICIAL REVIEW

It is a process through which judiciary examines whether a law enacted by a legislature or an action of the executive is in accordance with the Constitution or not. The power of the judicial review was first acquired by the Supreme Court of the United States. Now it is freely exercised by the Supreme Court of India and in many other countries. Our High Courts also exercise this power.

Judicial Review does not mean that every law passed by the legislature is taken up by the Supreme Court for review. It only means that the Court will review the law as and when it gets an opportunity. This is possible in two ways. First, the Court can review the law if its validity is challenged. The Supreme Court or High Court may get an opportunity to review a law in another situation also. If a person or institution feels that his/her rights are violated, or a certain benefit due to him under a law is being denied, the Court while examining such a petition may come to the conclusion that the law, under which relief is sought, is itself unconstitutional. Therefore, relief may not be granted.

The Supreme Court has used its power of judicial review and given various historic decisions to safeguard the rights of the individuals. It has stood guard of linguistic rights of minorities, religious rights of the people, welfare of the workers and daily wage earners. If has also taken action to protect bonded labour, prevent exploitation of women, children and deprived sections of society.

PUBLIC INTEREST LITIGATION (PIL)

The chief instrument through which judicial activism has flourished in India is Public Interest Litigation (PIL) or Social Action Litigation (SAL). Earlier, the judiciary, including Supreme Court, entertained litigation only from those parties that were affected directly or indirectly by it. It heard and decided cases only under its original and appellate jurisdiction. But subsequently, the Court permitted cases on the ground of public interest litigation. It means that even people, who are not directly involved in the case, may bring to the notice of the Court matters of public interest. It is the privilege of the Court to entertain the application for public interest litigation (PIL). The concept of PIL was introduced by Justice P.N. Bhagwati.

PIL is important because justice is now easily available to the poor and the weaker sections of society. The Supreme Court on the basis of letters received from journalists, lawyers and social workers and even on the basis of newspaper reports has taken up a number of matters of public interest. Under PIL, the rights of under trials held under illegal detention have been restored. The Supreme Court ordered the release of many detenues without trial on the ground of their personal liberty, which could not be curbed due to judicial or bureaucratic inefficiency. The Supreme Court has also taken up steps to free bonded labourers, tribals, slum dwellers, women in rescue homes, children in juvenile homes, child labour etc.

In case of environmental pollution, the Supreme Court has ordered closure of a few factories near Kanpur, Delhi and other places.

With more and more decisions coming from the Supreme Court, the scope of PIL has widened. Now a person can approach the Court through a letter and if the Supreme Court believes that the matter is of public interest, it can consider the letter to be a petition and direct the hearing of the matter so that public interest may be protected. The process of PIL has led to increased judicial activism.

The Value of PIL

1. Provides effective judicial protection of weaker sections of community.
2. Makes officialdom accountable.
3. Makes real the considerations of transparency in decision-making processes.
4. Remedies democracy deficit.
5. Creates structures for change: force the pace.
6. Allows the most effective proponents to bring cases: promotes effectivity in use of judicial institutions.
7. Allows diffused interests to be represented: air, water, environment, biodiversity, and such like.
8. Ensures access to justice.
9. Allows for participative justice.
10. Ensures government acts according to its established duty to abide by and enforce legal norms.
11. Protects and sustains democratic governance and the rule of law.

HIGH COURTS

The Constitution provides for a High Court for every State (Art. 214). However, the Parliament can provide for one High Court for two or more States. The Parliament can provide for a separate High Court for a Union Territory or include a Union Territory in the jurisdiction of a High Court of a State.

Each High Court has a Chief Justice and several judges whose number is decided by the President. The State Governor is consulted in their appointment. In the appointment of other judges, Chief Justice of the High Court is also consulted. The judges hold office upto the age of 62. The salaries and allowances of the judges once fixed cannot be changed to their disadvantage except in financial emergency. Their salaries are charged to the consolidated fund of India.

The Government can appoint additional and acting judges, if required. The President has the powers to transfer a judge from one High Court to the other. This provision in the Constitution was made to ensure impartiality and unbiasedness by the judges. However, these transfers cannot be used as punishments. Effective consultation with the Chief Justice of Supreme Court is essential before ordering the transfer.

The qualifications required for judges of a High Court are: (1) He must be a citizen of India; (2) He must have held a judicial office in India, or must have practised as an advocate of a High Court for at least 10 years. A High Court judge can resign before the retirement age of 62 years or can be promoted to Supreme Court. He can also be removed from his office by the President on an address presented to him by the Parliament after having passed it in each house by a majority of its total membership as well as by two-thirds of those present and voting. The only ground on which such an address can be passed by the Parliament is either proven misbehaviour or incapacity.

Jurisdictions

Ordinarily, the jurisdiction of a High Court of a State or of a Union Territory is coterminus with the territorial limits of that State or Union Territory. However, the Parliament has powers to extend the jurisdiction of one High Court to an adjoining State or Union Territory. Usually, High Courts are courts of appeal and their area of original jurisdiction is limited. In the presidency towns of Kolkata, Mumbai and Chennai, High Courts had some original jurisdiction, *e.g.*, they could hear the cases, involving Christians and Parsis. After the independence also, these High Courts have retained these powers. Cases, involving marriage laws, divorce, inheritance or contempt of High Court can be directly taken to the High Court.

Otherwise, High Courts have wide powers in appeal cases. In the criminal cases, an appeal against the Session Court judgement can be made in a High Court. In civil cases, an appeal can go to the High Court if the amount involved in the case exceeds the limits. In the economic offences, appeals against tribunal can be made in the High Courts. High Courts have power to issue writs, for the enforcement of fundamental rights and other purposes. High Courts have the power to transfer cases either to themselves or from one court to another. If a case involves interpretation of Constitution, High Court can transfer the case to itself. High Court acts as a court of record. Its decisions are published and can be referred to. It can sentence anyone for the contempt of Court.

High Courts have superintendence overall courts and tribunals throughout the territories in relation to which it exercises jurisdiction except military courts. This is a wide power because it includes all courts or tribunals whether an appeal against its decision lies to the High Court or not. High Courts can intervene and revise the decisions where it feels gross injustice or non-exercise or abuse of jurisdiction. High Courts have administrative control over the subordinate judiciary in the State which includes district judges, judges of city civil courts as well as Metropolitan magistrates and members of the judicial service of the State. This control is exercised in the manner of appointments, posting, promotion and administrative controls. They can make and issue general rules and prescribe forms for regulating the practice and proceedings of lower courts.

INDEPENDENCE OF JUDICIARY

The Supreme Court and High Courts are the pillars of our democratic set up. It is very essential that they work without any fear or favour. Therefore, Judges postings are done by the President and is for a fixed tenure. They cannot be easily removed from their posts. Their salaries and allowances cannot be ordinarily reduced and is debited to the consolidated fund of India for which there is no voting. Any law, limiting the powers of High Court, can be referred to the President by the Governor for his advice. Supreme Court judges cannot practice after retirement while High Court judges cannot practice in the Courts where they have worked.

Jurisdiction and Seats of High Courts in India

Name of High Court	Year Estd	Jurisdiction	Seat
Calcutta	1862	West Bengal, Andaman and Nicobar	Kolkata
Bombay	1862	Maharashtra, Goa, Dadra & Nagar Haveli and Daman & Diu	Mumbai (Bench at Panji and Aurangabad)
Madras	1862	Tamil Nadu and Puducherry	Chennai
Allahabad	1866	Uttar Pradesh	Prayagraj (with Bench at Lucknow)
Karnataka	1884	Karnataka	Bengluru
Patna	1916	Bihar	Patna
Jammu and Kashmir and Ladakh	1928	Jammu and Kashmir, Ladakh	Srinagar and Jammu
Guwahati	1948	Assam, Nagaland, Mizoram and Arunachal Pradesh	Kohima, Aizawl Circuit Bench at Itanagar
Orissa	1948	Orissa	Cuttack
Rajasthan	1949	Rajasthan	Jodhpur (Bench at Jaipur)
Andhra Pradesh	2019	Andhra Pradesh	Amaravati
Kerala	1956	Kerala and Lakshadweep	Ernakulam
Madhya Pradesh	1956	Madhya Pradesh	Jabalpur (Benches at Gwalior and Indore)
Gujarat	1960	Gujarat	Ahmedabad
Delhi	1966	Delhi	Delhi
Himachal Pradesh	1971	Himachal Pradesh	Shimla
Punjab and Haryana	1975	Punjab, Haryana and Chandigarh	Chandigarh
Sikkim	1975	Sikkim	Gangtok
Jharkhand	2000	Jharkhand	Ranchi
Chhattisgarh	2000	Chhattisgarh	Bilaspur
Uttarakhand	2000	Uttarakhand	Nainital
Manipur	2013	Manipur	Imphal
Meghalaya	2013	Meghalaya	Shilong
Tripura	2013	Tripura	Agartala
Telangana	2019	Telangana	Hyderabad

SUBORDINATE JUDICIARY

The organisation of the subordinate judiciary varies from State-to-State but the essential feature is that there is a separation of civil and criminal cases. Some States have Panchayat Courts at the lowest level. Munsiff's courts are the next higher Civil courts, with limited financial jurisdiction. Above them, come subordinate judges who have unlimited financial jurisdiction over civil suits and can hear first appeals against Munsiffs courts. District judges hear appeals from the decisions from subordinate judges. They also have criminal jurisdiction. District judge is the highest judicial authority in the district. There are additional sessions judges to look into serious criminal cases. In metropolitan areas, there are Metropolitan magistrates.

To deal with economic offences and service matters of Government employees, tribunals have been set up. These tribunals have not only reduced the burden on conventional courts but also has enabled authorities to appoint experts in the economic fields. These persons are well suited to comprehend the matter and give proper judgements. In these tribunals, the set procedure of the courts is avoided, thereby expediting the judgements.

ADMINISTRATIVE TRIBUNALS

The provisions regarding Administrative Tribunals did not form part of the original Constitution and were incorporated in the Constitution through the addition of two articles-Articles 323A and 323 B- by the 42nd amendment in 1976. Article 323 A provided for the establishment of Administrative Tribunals by a Parliamentary law for the adjudication or trial of disputes and complaints relating to the recruitment and conditions of service of government servants under the Central Government and the state government, including the employees of any local or other authority within the territory of India. In pursuance of this provisions, the Parliament enacted the Administrative Tribunal Act, 1985 under which the Central Administrative Tribunal was set up in November 1985. This tribunal seeks to provide speedy and inexpensive justice to Central Government Employees with respect to their service matters. In addition to the Central Administrative Tribunal, (CAT) the Central Government may also establish an administrative tribunal for one or more states on the request of the state government. The Central Administrative Tribunal is located at Delhi and has 17 benches located in the states.

The jurisdiction of the Central Tribunal extends to all the powers and authority enjoyed by the High Courts before the establishment of the tribunal with regard to : (a) recruitment to any All India Service or Civil Services of the Union, or a civil post under the Union or civilian employees of the defence services; (b) all service matters of the above mentioned employees; and (c) all service matters in respect of persons whose services have been placed at the disposal of the Central Government by the state government or local authorities.

FAMILY COURTS

The family courts can be set up by the state government under the Family Courts Act 1984. Such courts are usually set up in cities or towns with a population of more than 10 lakh. The main aim of these courts is to promote conciliation and to secure speedy settlement of disputes relating to marriage and family affairs.

LOK ADALATS

The Lok Adalat is a forum where the disputes/cases pending in the court of law or at pre-litigation stage are settled/compromised amicably. The Lok Adalat has been given statutory status under the Legal Services Authorities Act, 1987. Under this Act, an award made by a Lok Adalat is deemed to be a decree of a civil court and is final and binding on all parties and no appeal lies against thereto before any court.

The following types of matters are being taken up:

1. Matrimonial/Family disputes.
2. Criminal Compoundable Offence cases.
3. Land Acquisition cases.
4. Labour Disputes.
5. Workmen's compensation.
6. Bank Recovery cases.
7. Pension cases.
8. Housing Board and slum clearance cases & Housing Finance cases.
9. Consumer Grievance cases.
10. Electricity matters.
11. Telephone Bills disputes.
12. Municipal matters including House Tax cases.
13. Disputes with Cellular Companies viz. Airtel, Hutch, Tata Tele services, etc.

***

14

Emergency Provisions

President is assigned three kinds of emergency powers under Article 352, 356 and 360. When the Constitution of India was being drafted, India was passing through a period of stress and strain. Partition of the country, communal riots and the problem concerning the merger of princely states including Kashmir were major issues to be tackled. Thus, the Constitution-makers thought to equip the Central Government with the necessary authority, so that, in the hour of emergency, when the security and stability of the country is threatened by internal and external threats.

Therefore, some emergency provisions were made in Constitution to safeguard and protect the security, integrity and stability of the country and effective functioning of State Governments.

NATIONAL EMERGENCY

The Constitution of India has provided for imposition of emergency caused by war, external aggression or internal rebellion (Art. 352). This is described as the National Emergency. This type of emergency can be declared by the President of India if he is satisfied that the situation is very grave and the security of India or any part thereof is threatened or is likely to be threatened either :

(i) by war or external aggression or

(ii) by armed rebellion within the country. The President can issue such a proclamation even on the ground of threat of war or aggression. According to the 44th Amendment of the Constitution, the President can declare such an emergency only if the Cabinet recommends in writing to do so.

Such a proclamation of emergency has to be approved by both the Houses of Parliament by absolute majority of the total membership of the Houses as well as 2/3 majority of members present and voting within one month, otherwise the proclamation ceases to operate. In case the Lok Sabha stands dissolved at the time of proclamation of emergency or is not in session, it has to be approved by the Rajya Sabha within one month and later on by the Lok Sabha also within one month of the start of its next session. Once approved by the Parliament, the emergency remains in force for a period of six months from the date of proclamation. In case it is to be extended beyond six months, another prior resolution has to be passed by the Parliament. In this way, such emergency continues indefinitely. But if the situation improves the emergency can be revoked by another proclamation by the President of India. The 44th Amendment of the Constitution provides that ten per cent or more members of the Lok Sabha can requisite a meeting of the Lok Sabha and in that meeting, it can disapprove or revoke the emergency by a simple majority. In such a case emergency will immediately become inoperative. National Emergency has been declared in our country three times so far. For the first time, emergency was declared on 26 October, 1962 after China attacked our borders in the North East. This National Emergency lasted till 10 January 1968, long after the hostilities ceased.

For the second time, it was declared on 3 December, 1971 in the wake of the second India-Pakistan War. The third National Emergency (called internal emergency) was imposed on 25 June, 1975.

This emergency was declared on the ground of 'internal disturbances'.

National Emergencies till now

First	1962	Jawaharlal Nehru
Second	1971	Indira Gandhi
Third	1975	Indira Gandhi

Effects of National Emergency

The declaration of National Emergency has far-reaching effects both on the rights of individuals and the autonomy of the states in the following manner:

(i) The most significant effect is that the federal form of the Constitution changes into unitary. The authority of the Centre increases and the Parliament assumes the power to make laws for the entire country or any part thereof, even in respect of subjects mentioned in the State List.

(ii) The President of India can issue directions to the states as to the manner in which the executive power of the states is to be exercised.

(iii) During this period, the Lok Sabha can extend its tenure by a period of one year at a time. But the same cannot be extended beyond six months after the proclamation ceases to operate. The tenure of State Assemblies can also be extended in the same manner.

(iv) During emergency, the President is empowered to modify the provisions regarding distribution of revenues between the Union and the States.

The Fundamental Rights under Article 19 are automatically suspended and this suspension continues till the end of the emergency.

But according to the 44th Amendment, Freedoms listed in Article 19 can be suspended only in case of proclamation on the ground of war or external aggression. From the above discussion, it becomes quite clear that emergency not only suspends the autonomy of the States but also converts the federal structure of India into a unitary one. Still it is considered necessary as it equips the Union Government with vast powers to cope up with the abnormal situations. The exigencies of the situation prevailing in the period 1975-77 necessitated certain changes in the Constitution regarding emergency provisions. Therefore, the 44th amendment was passed on 30th April 1979 to strengthen the democratic features of the Indian Constituion and to protect citizens' rights even during the national emergency.

EMERGENCY DUE TO FAILURE OF CONSTITUTIONAL MACHINERY IN A STATE

It is the duty of the Union Government to ensure that governance of a State is carried on in accordance with the provisions of the Constitution. Under Article 356, the President may issue a proclamation to impose emergency in a state if he is satisfied on receipt of a report from the Governor of the State, or otherwise, that a situation has arisen under which the Government of the State cannot be carried on smoothly. In such a situation, proclamation of emergency by the President is called 'proclamation on account of the failure (or breakdown) of constitutional machinery.' In popular language it is called the President's Rule. Like National Emergency, such a proclamation must also be placed before both the Houses of Parliament for approval. In this case approval must be given within two months, otherwise the proclamation ceases to operate. If approved by the Parliament, the proclamation remains valid for six months at a time. It can be extended for another six months but not beyond one year. However, emergency in a State can be extended beyond one year if:

(*a*) a National Emergency is already in operation; or if

(*b*) the Election Commission certifies that the election to the State Assembly cannot be held.

This type of emergency has been imposed in most of the States at one time or the other for a number of times. It was in 1951 that this type of emergency was imposed for the first time in the Punjab State. In 1957, the Kerala State was put under the President's Rule.

In 1986, emergency was imposed in Jammu and Kashmir due to terrorism and insurgency.

In all, there are more than hundred times that emergency has been imposed in various States for one reason or the other. However, after 1995 the use of this provision has rarely been made.

Effects of Imposition of President's Rule

The declaration of emergency due to the breakdown of Constitutional machinery in a State has the following effects:

(*i*) The President can assume to himself all or any of the functions of the State Government or he may vest all or any of those functions with the Governor or any other executive authority.

(*ii*) The President may dissolve the State Legislative Assembly or put it under suspension. He may authorise the Parliament to make laws on behalf of the State Legislature.

(*iii*) The President can make any other incidental or consequential provision necessary to give effect to the object of proclamation.

The way President's Rule was imposed on various occasions has raised many questions. At times the situation really demanded it. But at other times, President's Rule was imposed purely on political grounds to topple the ministry formed by a party different from the one at the Centre, even if that particular party enjoyed majority in the Legislative Assembly. Suspending or dissolving assemblies and not giving a chance to the other political parties to form governments in states has been due to partisan consideration of the Union Government, for which Article 356 has been clearly misused. In view of the above facts, Article 356 has become very controversial. In spite of the safeguards provided by the 44th Amendment Act, this provision has been alleged to be misused by the Union Government. That is why, there is a demand either for its deletion or making provision in the Constitution to restrict the misuse of this Article. The Sarkaria Commission which was appointed to review the Centre-State relations also recommended that Article 356 should be used only as a last resort. The Commission also suggested that the State Legislative Assembly should not be dissolved unless the proclamation is approved by the Parliament. It further suggested that all possibilities of forming an alternative government should be fully explored before the Centre imposes emergency in a State on grounds of breakdown of Constitutional machinery. The Supreme Court held in the Bommai case that the Assembly may not be dissolved till the Proclamation is approved by the Parliament. On a few occasions such as when Gujral Government recommended use of Article 356 in Uttar Pradesh, the President returned the recommendation for reconsideration. The Union Government took the hint and dropped the proposal.

FINANCIAL EMERGENCY

The third type of Emergency is Financial Emergency provided under Article 360. It provides that if the President is satisfied that the financial stability or credit of India or any of its part is in danger, he may declare a state of Financial Emergency. Like the other two types of emergencies, it has also to be approved by the Parliament. It must be approved by both Houses of Parliament within two months. Financial Emergency can operate as long as the situation demands and may be revoked by a subsequent proclamation.

Effects of Financial Emergency

The proclamation of Financial Emergency may have the following consequences:

(*a*) The Union Government may give direction to any of the States regarding financial matters.

(*b*) The President may ask the States to reduce the salaries and allowances of all or any class of persons in government service.

(*c*) The President may ask the States to reserve all the money bills for the consideration of the Parliament after they have been passed by the State Legislature.

(*d*) The President may also give directions for the reduction of salaries and allowances of the Central Government employees including the Judges of the Supreme Court and the High Courts. So far, fortunately, financial emergency has never been proclaimed.

***

15

Constitutional Amendments

The Constitution of a country is the fundamental law of the country and on the basis of which all other laws in the country are made and enforced. An adequate provision for its amendment is considered implicit in the very nature of a Constitution. A democratic Constitution has to be particularly responsive to the varying conditions since a government founded on the principle of popular sovereignty "must make possible the fresh assertion of the proper will as that will change".

The flexibility or rigidity of any Constitution depends on whether it can be amended by the legislature through the same process as any other law or by a special process laid down for that purpose. The Constitution of India may be described as partly flexible and partly rigid.

PROCEDURES FOR CONSTITUTIONAL AMENDMENT

Indian freedom fighters, while framing the Constitution, realised that the basic document of the nation must reflect the spirit and character of the country. It must change with the changing time and should be able to cope up with changing environment. But they did not relish the Constitution to be a loosely bound set of rules which could be broken very easily. To amalgam the freedom to change with the rigidity of sticking to basic guidelines, they provided different procedures for Constitutional amendment (Art. 368). Today, we have made more than 100 amendments yet the basic features are still intact.

Some provisions of the Constitution can be changed by the simple majority of the Parliament. These include creation of new states, change of name of states and change in the state boundaries. But a legislation to this effect can only be introduced with the President's approval and the President can consult the concerned states. The creation or abolition of legislative council in a state can be done by passing a legislation in the Parliament by a simple majority. Parliament is empowered to pass an amendment bill, regarding administration of union territories. All these amendments, which are approved by Parliament's simple majority, are usually not listed in the Constitutional amendment.

The Constitutional amendment bills related to the method of election of the President, the Vice-President's election, representation of states in the Parliament, jurisdiction of the Supreme Court and High Courts, distribution of executive and legislative powers between the Union and states, method of the constitutional amendment and change in the list given in the seventh schedule, have to be amended in a special way. The bills pertaining to them have to be passed by two-third majority by each house of the Parliament and subsequently approved by the legislatures of not less than half of the states' legislatures.

All other provisions of the Constitution except those mentioned above can be amended if a bill to that effect is passed by each house of the Parliament by two-third majority of the members present and voting which should not be less than the majority of all the members of the house. If such a bill is not passed by either house the bill falls as there is no provision of joint sitting to pass the constitutional amendment bill.

The Constitutional amendment bills, after being passed by the Parliament and state legislatures, if necessary, are presented to the President for his assent. The President has no choice but to give assent to the Constitutional amendment bill.

IMPORTANT AMENDMENTS

1. **The Constitution (First Amendment) Act, 1951:** This amendment aimed to impose restrictions on the right to freedom of expression and the right to practise or to carry out any trade or business contained in Article 19. These restrictions were concerned with public order, friendly relationships with foreign States or incitement to an offence in relation to the right of freedom of speech. This amendment also empowered the State to prescribe professional or technical qualifications or conduct of any trade, business, industry or service by the State in relation to the right to carry on any trade or business. The State was also allowed to impose restrictions on the rights of the citizens to carry on any trade, business, industry or service. Two new Articles (31A and 31B) and the Ninth Schedule were added in this amendment.
2. **The Constitution (Second Amendment) Act, 1952:** This amendment aimed at the readjustment of the scale and representation for election to the Lok Sabha.
3. **The Constitution (Third Amendment) Act, 1954:** Substituted Entry 33 of List III (*i.e.*, the concurrent List) of the Seventh Schedule to make it correspond to Article 369.
4. **The Constitution (Fourth Amendment) Act, 1955:** Under this amendment, Article 31(2) of the constitution was amended to restate the power of the State of compulsory acquisition and requisition of private property. Article 31A was also amended in order to abolish *Zamindaris,* effect planning of urban and rural areas and assume complete control over the mineral and oil resources of the country. Six Acts were included in the Ninth Schedule. Article 305 was amended to save some laws which gave monopolies to the State.
5. **The Constitution (Fifth Amendment) Act, 1955:** It changed Article 3 so that the President was empowered to specify a time limit for state legislatures to convey their views on central laws which made impact upon areas and boundaries of the states.
6. **The Constitution (Sixth Amendment) Act, 1956:** This amendment altered Article 269 and Article 286 which were related to sales taxes and purchase taxes during the interstate trading activities. A new entry (92A) was added to the Union List.
7. **The Constitution (Seventh Amendment) Act, 1956:** Under this amendment, the existing states were changed to have a two-fold classification of States and UTs. Further, the House of the People was formed and readjustment was accepted after every census. It also provided the provisions for establishment of new High Courts and High Court Judges etc.
8. **The Constitution (Eighth Amendment) Act, 1960:** Article 334 was amended with a view to extending the period of reservation of seats of SCs, STs and the reservation of Anglo-Indians by nomination in the Parliament and in the State Legislatures for 10 years.
9. **The Constitution (Ninth Amendment) Act, 1960:** This amendment was done in order to transfer some territories to Pakistan as this was not possible under Article 3.
10. **The Constitution (Tenth Amendment) Act, 1961:** It changed the Article 240 and the First Schedule to include Dadra and Nagar Haveli as a UT.
11. **The Constitution (Eleventh Amendment) Act, 1961:** It aimed at amending Article 66 and Article 71 under the aegis of which the

election of the President or the Vice-President could not be challenged on the ground of any vacancy in the appropriate electoral college.

12. **The Constitution (Twelfth Amendment) Act, 1962:** Article 240 was amended and as a consequence Goa, Daman and Diu was included in Indian Union as a UT.
13. **The Constitution (Thirteenth Amendment) Act, 1962:** A new Article 371A was added to make provisions for Nagaland in accordance with an agreement between Government of India and Naga People's Convention.
14. **The Constitution (Fourteenth Amendment) Act, 1962:** Pondicherry was included in the First Schedule as a UT. Further legislatures were created by the Parliamentary law for Himachal Pradesh, Manipur, Tripura, Goa, Daman and Diu and Pondicherry.
15. **The Constitution (Fifteenth Amendment) Act, 1963:** It aimed for increasing the retirement age of the High Court Judges and for provision of compensatory allowances to the Judges who were transferred from one High Court to another. Further, it provided for the appointment of retired Judges act as the Judges of High Court. Article 226 was amended to empower the High Court so that it could issue direction, orders or writs to a government authority. The Act also allowed one of the members of the Service Commissions to exercise the powers of the Chairman if the latter was absent.
16. **The Constitution (Sixteenth Amendment) Act, 1963:** Article 19 was amended by this Act to impose more restrictions on the rights to freedom of speech and expression, to assemble peacefully and to form associations in the interest of national integrity. The oath of affirmation to be subscribed by the candidate for Parliamentary and state legislature elections was modified and it was added that the Candidates would uphold the integrity of the nation.
17. **The Constitution (Seventeenth Amendment) Act, 1964:** Article 31A was amended again to prohibit the acquisition of land under personal cultivation unless the market value of the land is paid as compensation. The definition of 'estate' in that Article was enlarged. The Ninth Schedule was amended to include 44 more Acts.
18. **The Constitution (Eighteenth Amendment) Act, 1966:** Article 3 was amended by this Act to specify that 'State' would include a UT as well. Further, the amendment asserted that the power to form a new state under this article includes a power to form a new state or a UT by uniting a part of a state or a UT to another State or UT.
19. **The Constitution (Nineteenth Amendment) Act, 1966:** Article 324 was amended to effect a change as a result of decision to abolish Election Tribunals and let the election petitions be heard by High Courts.
20. **The Constitution (Twentieth Amendment) Act, 1966:** A new Article 233A was added. The appointments made by the Governor were validated.
21. **The Constitution (Twenty-first Amendment) Act, 1967:** Sindhi language was included in the Eighth Schedule.
22. **The Constitution (Twenty-second Amendment) Act, 1969:** Formation of Meghalaya within the state of Assam was facilitated.
23. **The Constitution (Twenty-third Amendment) Act, 1969:** Article 334 was amended in order to safeguard the reservation of seats of SCs and STs and Anglo-Indians in Parliament and the state legislatures, for a period of another 10 years.
24. **The Constitution (Twenty-fourth Amendment) Act, 1971:** Article 13 and Article 368 were amended to remove doubts regarding the power of Parliament to amend

the Constitution including the Fundamental Rights.

25. **The Constitution (Twenty-fifth Amendment) Act, 1971:** It amended Article 31 again in the wake of bank nationalization in the country. The word 'Compensation' was replaced with the word 'amount'.

26. **The Constitution (Twenty-sixth Amendment) Act, 1971:** The privy and privileges of the former rulers of Indian States were abolished.

27. **The Constitution (Twenty-seventh Amendment) Act, 1971:** This amendment was passed to provide for some matters which resulted due to reorganization of north-eastern states. A new Article 239B was inserted which allowed the administrators of some UTs to promulgate the Ordinances.

28. **The Constitution (Twenty-eighth Amendment) Act, 1972:** The special privileges of members of Indian Civil Services in the matters of leave, pension and their rights regarding disciplinary matters were abolished.

29. **The Constitution (Twenty-ninth Amendment) Act, 1972:** The Ninth Schedule was amended to include the acts of Kerala regarding land reforms.

30. **The Constitution (Thirtieth Amendment) Act, 1972:** A valuation test of Rs. 20,000 under article 133 was removed and instead of the same, an appeal to the Supreme Court in civil proceedings was allowed to be provided only on a certificate issued by a High Court (that the matter deserves the scrutiny of the Supreme Court).

31. **The Constitution (Thirty-first Amendment) Act, 1973:** The upper limit of representation of states was raised from 500 to 525. The upper limit for representation of the UTs was reduced from 25 to 20.

32. **The Constitution (Thirty-second Amendment) Act, 1973:** Constitutional authority was granted for granting equal opportunities to different areas of Andhra Pradesh. An Administrative Tribunal was also allowed to be constituted which had the Jurisdiction to deal with the grievances relating to public services. The parliament was also empowered to legislate for establishment of a central university in the State.

33. **The Constitution (Thirty-third Amendment) Act, 1974:** Articles 101 and 190 were amended to streamline the procedure for resignation of MPs and State legislatures.

34. **The Constitution (Thirty-fourth Amendment) Act, 1974:** Twenty more land tenure and land reforms laws enacted by various state legislatures were included in the Ninth Schedule under this amendment.

35. **The Constitution (Thirty-fifth Amendment) Act, 1974:** A new Article 2A was added and Sikkim was declared an associate of the Indian Union. Article 80 and Article 81 were amended and a new Schedule (Tenth Schedule) was added which laid down terms for association of the Sikkim with the Union.

36. **The Constitution (Thirty-sixth Amendment) Act, 1975:** Sikkim was made a full-fledged state of Indian Union and it was included in the First Schedule. Sikkim was allotted one seat in the council of States and one seat in the House of the People. Article 2A and the Tenth Schedule (inserted under Thirty-fifth Amendment) were deleted. Article 80 and Article 81 were suitably amended due to these changes.

37. **The Constitution (Thirty-seventh Amendment) Act, 1975:** The UT of Arunachal Pradesh was provided with a legislative assembly. Article 240 was amended under which it was provided that the power of the President to make regulations for the UT of Arunachal Pradesh may be exercised only when the assembly is either dissolved or its functions remain suspended.

38. **The Constitution (Thirty-eighth Amendment) Act, 1975:** This Act led to the amendment of Article 123, Article 213 and Article 352 which stated that the satisfaction of President or of Governor contained in these Articles would be called in question in any court of law.

39. **The Constitution (Thirty-ninth Amendment) Act, 1975:** According to this amendment, the disputes relating to the election of President, Vice-President, PM and Speaker are to be determine by such authority as may be determined by Parliamentary law. Some central enactments were also included in the Ninth Schedule.

40. **The Constitution (Fortieth Amendment) Act, 1976:** This amendment gave all the powers to the Union with respect to all mines, minerals and items of value lying in the ocean within the territorial waters or on the continental shelf or within the exclusive economic zone of India. The Act also stated that the limits of territories waters, continental shelf, exclusive economic zone and the maritime zones of India shall be as specified from time to time or under any law made by Parliament. Further, some Acts were added to the Ninth Schedule.

41. **The Constitution (Forty-first Amendment) Act, 1976:** Article 316 was amended to raise the retirement age of the members of Public Service Commissions and Joint Public Service Commissions from 60 years to 62 years.

42. **The Constitution (Forty-second Amendment) Act, 1976:** This amendment was done in accordance with the recommendations of Swaran Singh Committee and included a number of amendments. These amendments included the clear delineation of socialistic ideals, secularism and national integrity. Further, Directive Principles were made more comprehensive and were given precedence over the Fundamental Rights. A new chapter on Fundamental Duties of the citizens was added. Special provisions were made for dealing with anti-national activities. For declaring any law to be constitutionally invalid, the requirements of a minimum number of Judges were also laid down. Further, Administrative and other Tribunals were constituted for preserving the jurisdiction of Supreme Court Under Article 136. Amendments were also made for reducing arrears in High Courts, for securing speedy disposal of service matters, for revenue issues and other vital issues related to socio-economic development (Tribunals were created for ensuring these developments in the country). Article 226 was modified.

43. **The Constitution (Forty-third Amendment) Act, 1977:** It provided for the restoration of the Jurisdiction of the Supreme Court and High Courts, curtailed by the enactment of the Constitution (Forty-second Amendment) Act, 1976. Therefore, Article 32A, Article 131A, Article 144A, Article 226A and Article 228A were deleted by this amendment. It also deleted Article 31D which gave special powers to Parliament to enact some laws in connection with anti-national activities.

44. **The Constitution (Forty-fourth Amendment) Act, 1978:** The right to property was deleted as Fundamental Right and was made a legal right. Article 352 was amended to provide "armed rebellion" as one of the circumstance for declaration of emergency. The right to personal liberty (as contained in Article 21 and Article 22) was strengthened by the provision that a law for preventive detention cannot authorize the detention for a period longer than two months unless an Advisory Board has reported that there is a sufficient cause for such a detention. Further, the amendment confirmed that the Chairman of the Advisory Board shall be a serving Judge of the appropriate High Court and that the Board shall be constituted in accordance with the recommendations of the Chief Justice of

that High Court. Through this amendment, Article 132 and Article 134 were amended and a new Article 134A was inserted. Some amendments were made for removing or correcting the distortions which had crept into the constitution due to amendments effected during internal emergency.

45. **The Constitution (Forty-fifth Amendment) Act, 1980:** This amendment was due to safeguard the interests of SCs, STs and Anglo-Indians in Parliament and the State Assemblies for another 10 years.

46. **The Constitution (Forty-sixth Amendment) Act, 1982:** Article 269 was amended so that the tax levied on the consignment of goods during the interstate trade or commerce could be assigned to the states. Further, amendment was done to enable the Parliament to formulate the principle for determining when a consignment of goods takes place in the course of interstate trade or commerce. A new entry 92B was added in the Union List which ensured the levy of tax on the consignment of goods where such a consignment took place in the course of interstate trade or commerce.

    Further, Clause (3) of Article 286 was amended for specifying conditions of levy rates, taxes on goods transfer involved in the execution of a works contract, delivery of goods on hire-purchase or payment system through instalment etc.

    Further, Article 366 was amended and a definition of "tax on the sale or purchase of goods" to include the transfer for consideration of controlled commodities, transfer of property in goods involved in the execution of a works contract, delivery of goods on hire-purchase or any system of payment by instalments etc.

47. **The Constitution (Forty-seventh Amendment) Act, 1984:** Some land reforms Acts were included in the Ninth Schedule.

48. **The Constitution (Forty-eighth Amendment) Act, 1984:** Article 356 was amended keeping in mind the situation in Punjab.

49. **The Constitution (Forty-ninth Amendment) Act, 1984:** The amendment gave a constitutional security to the autonomous District Council functioning in the State.

50. **The Constitution (Fiftieth Amendment) Act, 1984:** By Article 33, Parliament can enact laws for determining to what extent any of the rights conferred by Part III of the Constitution shall (In their application to members of Armed forces or the Forces charged with the maintenance of public order), be restricted or abrogated so that they could discharge their duties.

51. **The Constitution (Fifty-first Amendment) Act, 1984:** Article 330 has been amended and seats for the STs in Meghalaya, Nagaland, Arunachal Pradesh and Mizoram have been ensured. Further, Article 332 has been amended to provide similar reservation in the Legislative Assemblies of Nagaland and Meghalaya for reservation of the seats of tribals.

52. **The Constitution (Fifty-second Amendment) Act, 1985:** This amendment states that a MP or a State Legislature, who defects or is expelled from the party which set him up as a candidate (or an independent member of the house), joins a political party after the expiry of six months from the date on which he takes seat in the House, shall be disqualified to remain a member of the House.

53. **The Constitution (Fifty-third Amendment) Act, 1986:** The Memorandum of Settlement of Mizoram was given effect (this memorandum was signed on June 30, 1986). For this purpose, a new Article 371G was inserted *Inter alia* preventing application of any Act of Parliament in Mizoram with respect of religions or social practices of Mizos, their civil and criminal practices and

laws regarding land transfers (unless a resolution was passed in the Legislative Assembly to this effect). The new Article make the minimum number of members of Legislative Assembly as 40.

54. **The Constitution (Fifty-fourth Amendment) Act, 1986:** The salary of Chief Justice of India was increased to Rs. 10,000 per month. Similarly, the salaries of Judges of Supreme Court, Chief Justice of High Court, Judges of High Court were increased to Rs. 9,000 per month, Rs. 9,000 per month and Rs. 8,000 per month respectively. This Act also amended Part D of the Second Schedule and made enabling provisions in Articles 125 and Article 221 for changes in the salaries of Judges in future through a law of Parliament.
55. **The Constitution (Fifty-fifth Amendment) Act, 1986:** The proposal to give statehood to Arunachal Pradesh was given effect. A new Article 371H was added that the governor shall discharge his functions in consultation with the Council of Ministers. Further, the Act amended the minimum seats of the Assembly to be thirty in number.
56. **The Constitution (Fifty-sixth Amendment) Act, 1987:** The UT of Goa converted into Goa state through this amendment whereas Daman and Diu were organized under a new UT. The number of members of Goa Legislative Assembly was fixed at 40 and two members of the UT of Daman and Diu were excluded from this Assembly.
57. **The Constitution (Fifty-seventh Amendment) Act, 1987:** It was amended to provide reservation of seats in the House of the People for STs in the States of Nagaland, Meghalaya, Mizoram and Arunachal Pradesh. Article 330 and Article 332 were amended for reservation of seats for STs in Legislative Assemblies of Nagaland and Meghalaya.
58. **The Constitution (Fifty-eighth Amendment) Act, 1987:** The Constitution was amended to empower the President to publish the translation of Constitution of India in Hindi with modifications which may be necessary (including the translation of the Amendments).
59. **The Constitution (Fifty-ninth Amendment) Act, 1988:** It amends Article 365(5) of the Constitution so as to facilitate the extension of a Presidential Proclamation issued under Clause (1) of Article 356 beyond a period of one year (if necessary upto a period of three years), as permissible under Clause (4) of Article 356 with respect to Punjab.
60. **The Constitution (Sixtieth Amendment) Act, 1988:** This Act amends Clause (2) of Article 276 to increase the ceiling of taxes on professions, trades, callings and employment from Rs. 250 pm to Rs. 2,500 pm.
61. **The Constitution (Sixty-first Amendment) Act, 1989:** It reduces the voting age from 21 years to 18 years and amends Article 326 to this effect.
62. **The Constitution (Sixty-second Amendment) Act, 1989:** Article 334 continues the reservation of Seats for SCs, STs and Anglo-Indian Community by nomination in the Lok Sabha and in the Legislative Assemblies for a further period of 10 years.
63. **The Constitution (Sixty-third Amendment) Act, 1989:** The Clause (5) of Article 356 and Article 359 A of the constitution were omitted which were enacted earlier in March, 1988 through Fifty-ninth Amendment. The proclamation of emergency in Punjab was thus no longer deemed necessary.
64. **The Constitution (Sixty-fourth Amendment) Act, 1990:** It amends Clause (4) and Clause (5) of Article 356 for facilitating the extension of the proclamation issued under the Clause (1) of Article 356 on May 11, 1987, upto a period of three years and six months in relation to the state of Punjab.
65. **The Constitution (Sixty-fifth Amendment) Act, 1990:** Article 338 provides for a special officer for SCs and STs to investigate into the matters related to safeguards provided for them. This officer reports to the President.

This Article has been amended for the Constitution of a National Commission for SCs and STs comprising a Chairperson, Vice Chairperson and five other members to be appointed by the President. The Article delineates the powers of the Commission and states that its reports should be presented to the Parliament and to the Legislatures of the states.

66. **The Constitution (Sixty-sixth Amendment) Act, 1990:** This Act protects 55 State Acts relating to land reforms and ceiling an agricultural land holdings enacted by states of Andhra Pradesh, Bihar, Gujarat, Himachal Pradesh, Karnataka, Kerala, Madhya Pradesh, Maharashtra, Orissa, Rajasthan, Tamil Nadu, Uttar Pradesh, West Bengal and the administration of Pondicherry (UT), from challenge in courts, by including them in the Ninth Schedule.

67. **The Constitution (Sixty-seventh Amendment) Act, 1990:** The three year period in the case of proclamation issued on May 11, 1987, with respect to the State of Punjab was extended to three years and six months by the Constitution (Sixty-fourth Amendment) Act, 1990. This Act also amends Clause (4) of Article 356 so as to extend the period upto a period of four years.

68. **The Constitution (Sixty-eighth Amendment) Act, 1991:** The three year period in the case of proclamation issued on May 17, 1987, with respect to the State of Punjab was further increase upto a total period of five years and Clause (4) of Article 356 was modified to this effect.

69. **The Constitution (Sixty-ninth Amendment) Act, 1991:** A committee was set up which gave the recommendations that Delhi should be retained as a UT and may be provided with a Legislative Assembly and a Council of Ministers. The committee also recommended that Delhi should be accorded the Status of UT. Sixty-ninth amendment was passed to give effect to these aforementioned recommendations.

70. **The Constitution (Seventieth Amendment) Act, 1992:** An explanation was inserted in Article 54 to provide that reference to 'State' in Article 54 and Article 55 would include the National Capital Territory of Delhi and Pondicherry (UT) for constituting the electoral college for the election of the President. The provisions of Article 239A would allow the members of Legislative Assembly of Pondicherry to cast their votes in the process for election of the President. Similarly Article 239AA provides similar powers to the Legislatures of Delhi.

71. **The Constitution (Seventy-first Amendment) Act, 1992:** Konkani, Manipuri and Nepali languages were added in the Eighth Schedule.

72. **The Constitution (Seventy-second Amendment) Act, 1992:** A Memorandum of Settlement was signed by the Government of India with Tripura National Volunteers on August 12, 1988 for restoring peace in Tripura. In order to implement this Memorandum, Article 332 was amended and temporary provision for the determination of the number of seats for STs in the State Assembly of Tripura until the readjustment of the seats is made in 2000 AD under Article 170.

73. **The Constitution (Seventy-third Amendment) Act, 1993:** Article 40 is related to the organization of Panchayats. A new Part IX relating to the Panchayats has been inserted in the Constitution to provide for, among other things, *Gram Sabha* in a village or in a group of villages, constitution of Panchayats at village and other levels direct elections to all the seats in Panchayats at the village and the intermediate level; reservation of seats of SCs and STs in proportion to their population for the membership of Panchayats and offices of Chairpersons in Panchayats at each level; reservation of not less than one-third of seats for women; fixing tenure of five years for Panchayats and holding elections within a period of six months in the event of supersession of any Panchayat.

74. **The Constitution (Seventy-fourth Amendment) Act, 1993:** A new Part IX-A relating to Municipalities has been incorporated to provide for, among other things, constitution of Nagar Panchayats, Municipal Councils and Municipal Corporations.

75. **The Constitution (Seventy-fifth Amendment) Act, 1994:** This Act amends Article 323 B in Part XIV-A of the Constitution to give timely relief to the rent litigants by providing for setting up of state-level Rent Tribunals in order to reduce the tiers of appeals and to exclude the Jurisdiction of all courts, except that of Supreme Court, under Article 136 of the Constitution.

76. **The Constitution (Seventy-sixth Amendment) Act, 1994:** The Tamil Nadu government enacted a legislation known as Tamil Nadu Backward Classes, Scheduled Castes and Scheduled Tribes Bill, 1993 and send it to Government of India for consideration of the President in terms of Article 31-C of the Constitution. The President gave his assent to the Bill. As a corollary to this decision, it was necessary that the Tamil Nadu Act 45 of 1994 was brought within the purview of Ninth Schedule so that it could be protected under Article 31B of the Constitution. This Act amends the Constitution to amend the aforementioned objectives.

77. **The Constitution (Seventy-seventh Amendment) Act, 1995:** For protecting the interests of SCs and STs, the government decided to continue the existing policy of reservation in promotion for the SCs and STs. Article 16 was therefore, amended by inserting a new clause (4A) in the said Article to provide for reservation in promotion for the SCs and STs. This act seeks to achieve the aforementioned objective.

78. **The Constitution (Seventy-eighth Amendment) Act, 1995:** The inclusion of land reform laws in the Ninth Schedule was effected so that they were not challenged before the courts. Further, since the amendment to Acts which are already placed in the Ninth Schedule are not automatically immunized from legal challenge, a number of amending Acts along with a few principal Acts have been included in the Ninth Schedule so as to ensure that implementation of these Acts is not adversely affected by litigation.

79. **The Constitution (Seventy-ninth Amendment) Act, 1999:** Extends the reservations for SC/ST in the House of people and in the Legislative Assemblies of the states as also nomination of 2 Anglo-Indians to Lok Sabha up to 2010.

80. **The Constitution (Eightieth Amendment) Act, 2000:** Relates to the tenth finance commission, an alternative scheme for sharing taxes between the union and the states.

81. **The Constitution (Eighty-first Amendment) Act, 2000:** Empowered the state to consider the unfilled reserved vacancies of a year as a separate class of vacancies to be filled up in any succeeding year or years. Such class of vacancies are not to be combined with the vacancies of the year in which they are being filled up to determine the ceiling of 50 per cent reservation on total number of vacancies of that year. In brief, this amendment ended the 50 per cent ceiling on reservation in backlog vacancies.

82. **The Constitution (Eighty-second Amendment) Act, 2000:** Provides that states can make any provisions in favour of the members of the Scheduled Castes and Scheduled Tribes for relaxation in qualifying marks in any examination or lowering the standards of evaluation for reservation in matters of promotion to any class of services in connection with affairs of the union or of a state.

84. **The Constitution (Eighty-fourth Amendment) Act, 2001:** Extended the ban on readjustment of seats in the Lok Sabha and the state legislative assemblies for

another 25 years (i.e., up to 2026) with the same objective of encouraging population limiting measures. In other words, the number of seats in the Lok Sabha and the assemblies are to remain same till 2026. It also provided for the readjustment and rationalisation of territorial constituencies in the states on the basis of the population figures of 1991 census.

86. **The Constitution (Eighty-sixth Amendment) Act, 2002:** Made elementary education a fundamental right. The newly-added Article 21-A declares that "the State shall provide free and compulsory education to all children of the age of six to fourteen years in such manner as the State may determine".

87. **The Constitution (Eighty-seventh Amendment) Act, 2003:** Provided for the readjustment and rationalisation of territorial constituencies in the states on the basis of the population figures of 2001 census and not 1991 census as provided earlier by the 84th Amendment Act of 2001.

89. **The Constitution (Eighty-ninth Amendment) Act, 2003:** Bifurcated the erstwhile combined National Commission for Scheduled Castes and Scheduled Tribes into two separate bodies, namely, National Commission for Scheduled Castes (Article 338) and National Commission for Scheduled Tribes (Article 338-A). Both the Commissions consist of a Chairperson, a Vice-Chairperson and three other members. They are appointed by the President.

91. **The Constitution (Ninety-first Amendment) Act, 2003:** The numbers of council of ministers is limited by this amendment act. The number shall not exceed fifteen per cent.

92. **The Constitution (Ninety-second Amendment) Act, 2003:** Included four more languages in the Eighth Schedule. They are Bodo, Dogri (Dongri), Mathili (Maithili) and Santhali. With this, the total number of constitutionally recognised languages increased to 22.

93. **The Constitution (Ninety-third Amendment) Act, 2006:** Relates to reservation of Scheduled Castes, Scheduled Tribes and other socially and educationally backward classes in higher and professional education.

100. **The Constitution (One hundredth Amendment) Act, 2015:** Amended the first schedule of the Constitution, for the purpose of giving effect to the acquiring of territories by India and transfer of territories to Bangladesh through retaining of adverse possession and exchange of enclaves, in pursunace of the Agreement between India and Bangladesh concerning the demarcation of the land boundary, signed on 16th May, 1974 and its Protocal, signed on 6th September, 2011.

101. **The Constitution (One hundredth and first Amendment) Act, 2016:** The act amends the constitution to introduce "The Goods and Services Tax (GST).

103. **The Constitution (One hundredth and third Amendment) Act, 2019:** Provides 10 per cent reservation to Economically Weaker Sections of General Community.

104. **The Constitution (One hundred and fourth Amendment of 2019):** The 104th Amendment to the Indian Constitution has extended the time limit for terminating SC and ST seats in the House of People and State Legislatures from 70 to 80 years. It removed the seats reserved for the Anglo-Indian community in the Lok Sabha and the State Legislatures.

105. **The Constitution (One hundred and fifth Amendment of 2021):** The 105th Amendment Act restores the power of State Governments and Union Territories to identify the Socially and Educationally Backward Classes (SEBCs). The Constitution 105th amendment act Amended Articles 338B, 342A and 366 of the Constitution.

106. **The Constitution (One hundred and sixth Amendment of 2023):** The Constitution (106th Amendment) Act, 2023, reserves one-third of all seats for women in Lok Sabha, State legislative assemblies and the Legislative Assembly of the National Capital Territory of Delhi, including those reserved for SCs and STs.

AMENDMENTS AND SOCIAL CHANGE

The Constitution owes its continuity to continuous process of changes. The Constitution cannot make itself, somebody make it, not at once, but at several times. It is changeable. The amendments are made on the basis of general consensus.

Since 1950, the Constitution of India is amended more than 100 times. These amendments have been variable in importance. The important amendments are those related to right to property, which exempt from judicial process determination of compensation for property re-distributed under the land reform legislation and even abolishing right to property-from Chapter III of the Constitution. Art. 19(1), (6) and Art. 31 were the most controversial articles of our constitution. These Articles had provided for Right to Property. The constitution had allowed the people to hold, acquire or dispose of property. This applies both to movable and immovable property. Art. 31 had allowed the state to deprive a person of this property for a public purpose. Thus, the State could acquire private property for general interest of the community. The State could deprive a person of his property on payment of adequate compensation. It was open for the Courts to determine whether or not the property was being acquired for public purpose. The Constitution has provided elsewhere that no law, acquiring private property, passed by a state legislature could become a law unless it receives the assent of the President. Thus, the Centre must agree before such a law could be enacted. But, soon after the inauguration of the Constitution laws enacted by different states for abolition of Zamindari and Jagirdari were challenged and certain provisions of these laws were declared void. It was felt that judiciary was causing hindrance in the way of establishment of economic justice. Therefore, a number of amendments were made in right to property, from time-to-time. The first amendment declared all those laws constitutional which had been declared void by the Courts. The 4th amendment dropped the word 'Adequate', and provided that: "No such law (acquiring property) shall be called in question in any Court on the ground that the compensation provided by law is not adequate." Thus, the courts were told that they had not business to go into the question of adequacy of the amount of compensation. The legislature had the final word in this respect. Earlier the Court had held that compensation must have, some relation with 'market value'. The 4th amendment reversed it.

In Golakh Nath case, the Supreme Court said that rights of the people could not be curtailed or abridged even by a constitutional amendment. In the Bank Nationalization case, the Court held that the 'compensation' should not be illusionary. The 24th amendment gave the power of amending the fundamental rights to the Parliament. Thus, the Parliament reasserted its power of amending all parts of the Constitution. The 25th amendment removed the word 'compensation' from the Constitution and replaced it by the word 'amount'. Thus, when property was acquired only some amount of money had to be paid, and the court could not question about this. The 42nd amendment took away the power from the Supreme Court to question the validity of constitutional amendments.

The country had, time and again, asserted its goal of socialism. This word was even added in the Preamble. Thus, the 44th amendment deleted right to property from chapter III. It was felt that economic justice and right to property could not co-exist. Property is no more a fundamental right. It has been made a legal right which can be restricted by an ordinary law of the Parliament. It is not justified from an examination of the reasons for amending the constitution many a times and of the nature, context, scope and effect of the amendments it would appear that the Parliament has used the amending provision reasonably and fairly in the interests of the country keeping in mind the social goal to be achieved.

***

16

System of Panchayati Raj

The term 'Panchayati Raj' in India signifies the system of rural local self-government. It is created in all the states in India by the acts of the state legislatures to establish democracy at the grass roots level. It is entrusted with the duties and responsibilities in the field of rural development. It was constitutionalised through the 73rd Constitutional Amendment Act of 1992. At the central level, the Ministry of Rural Development looks after the matters relating to the Panchayati Raj bodies.

In the scheme of division of powers between the centre and the states in the Indian federal system, the item of *'Local Government'* is given to the states. Thus the fifth entry of the State List of the seventh schedule to the constitution of India deals with 'local government'.

73RD AMENDMENT ACT OF 1992

This Act has added Part-IX to the Constitution of India. It is entitled as 'The Panchayats' and consists of provisions from Articles 243 to 243-O. In addition, the Act has also added Eleventh schedule to the Constitution. It contains 29 functional items of the Panchayats and deals wih Article 243-G.

The Act has given a practical shape to Article 40 of the Constitution which says that, "The state shall take steps to organise village Panchayats and endow them with such powers and authority as may be necessary to enable them to function as units of self-government." This article forms a part of the Directive Principles of State Policy.

The salient features of the Act are:

1. **Gram Sabha:** The Act provides for a Gram Sabha as the foundation of the Panchayati Raj system. It is a body consisting of persons registered in the electoral rolls of a village comprised within the area of Panchayat at the village level. Thus, it is a village assembly consisting of all the registered voters in the area of a Panchayat. It shall exercise such powers and perform such functions at the village level as the legislature of a state determines.
2. **Three-Tier System:** The Act provides for a three-tier system of Panchayati Raj in every state, that is Panchayats at the village, intermediate and district levels. The Act defines all these terms in the following manner:
   (*a*) Panchayat means an institution (by whatever name called) of self-government for rural areas.
   (*b*) Village means, a village specified by the Governor by public notification to be a village for this purpose, and includes a group of villages so specified.
   (*c*) Intermediate level means a level between the village and district levels specified by the Governor by public notification for this purpose.
   (*d*) District means a district in a state.

   Thus, the Act brings about uniformity in the structure of Panchayati Raj throughout the country. However, a state having a population not exceeding 20 lakhs may not constitute panchayats at the intermediate level.

3. **Election of Members and Chairpersons:** All the members of Panchayats at the village, intermediate and district levels shall be elected directly by the people. Further, the chairperson of Panchayats at the intermediate and district levels shall be elected indirectly—by and from amongst the elected members thereof. However, the chairperson of a Panchayat at the village level shall be elected in such manner as the state legislature determines.

4. **Reservation of Seats:** The Act provides for the reservation of seats for scheduled castes and scheduled tribes in every Panchayat in proportion of their population to the total population in the Panchayat area. Further, the state legislature shall provide for the reservation of offices of chairpersons in the Panchayat at the village or any other level for the SC and ST.

   The Act provides for the reservation of not less than one-third of the total number of seats for women. Further, not less than one-third of the total number of offices of chairpersons in the Panchayat at each level shall be reserved for women.

   The Act also authorises the legislature of a state to make any provision for reservation of seats in any Panchayat or offices of chairperson in the Panchayat at any level in favour of backward classes.

5. **Duration of Panchayats:** The Act provides for a five-year term of office to the Panchayat at every level. However, it can be dissolved before the completion of its term. Further, fresh election to constitute a Panchayat shall be completed: *(i)* before the expiry of its duration of five years; or *(ii)* in case of dissolution, before the expiry of a period of six months from the date of its dissolution.

6. **Disqualifications:** A person shall be disqualified for being chosen as or for being a member of Panchayat if he is so disqualified: *(i)* under any law for the time being in force for the purpose of elections to the legislature of the state concerned, or *(ii)* under any law made by the state legislature. However, no person shall be disqualified on the ground that he is less than 25 years of age if he has attained the age of 21 years. Further, all questions of disqualifications shall be referred to such authority as the state legislature determines.

7. **State Election Commission:** The superintendence, direction and control of the preparation of electoral rolls and the conduct of all elections to the Panchayats shall be vested in the State Election Commission. It consists of a State Election Commissioner to be appointed by the Governor. His conditions of service and tenure of office shall also be determined by the Governor. He shall not be removed from the office except in the manner and on the grounds prescribed for the removal of a judge of the state High Court, and his conditions of service shall not be varied to his disadvantage after his appointment.

8. **Powers and Functions:** The state legislature may endow the Panchayats, with such powers and authority as may be necessary to enable them to function as institutions of self-government. Such a scheme may contain provisions for the devolution of powers and responsibilities upon Panchayats at the appropriate level with respect to: *(i)* the preparation of plans for economic development and social justice; *(ii)* the implementation of schemes for economic development and social justice as may be entrusted to them, including those in relation to the 29 matters listed in the Eleventh Schedule.

9. **Finances:** The state legislature may: *(i)* authorise a Panchayat to levy, collect and appropriate taxes, duties, tolls and fees; *(ii)* assign to a Panchayat taxes, duties, tolls end fees levied and collected by the state

government; *(iii)* provide for making grants-in-aid to the Panchayats from the Consolidated Fund of the state; and *(iv)* provide for constitution of funds crediting all moneys of the panchayats.

10. Finance Commission: The Governor of a state shall, after every five years, constitute a Finance Commission to review the financial position of the Panchayats. If shall make the following recommendations to the Governor.

(*i*) The principles which should govern: (*a*) The distribution between the state and the Panchayats of the net proceeds of the taxes, duties, tolls and fees levied by the state. (*b*) The determination of taxes, duties, tolls and fees which may be assigned to the Panchayats. (*c*) The grant-in-aid to the Panchayats from the consolidated fund of the state.

(*ii*) The measures needed to improve the financial position of the Panchayats.

(*iii*) Any other matter referred to the Finance Commission by the Governor in the interests of sound finance of the Panchayats.

The State Legislature may provide for the composition of the Commission, the required qualifications of its members and the manner of their selection.

The Governor shall place the recommendations of the Commission along with the action taken report before the state legislature.

The Central Finance Commissioner shall also suggest the measures needed to augment the Consolidated Fund of a state supplement the resources of the Panchayats in the states (on the basis of the recommendations made by the Finance Commission of the state).

URBAN LOCAL GOVERNMENT

The term *'Urban Local Government'* in India signifies the governance of an urban area by the people through their elected representatives. The jurisdiction of an urban local government is limited to a specific urban area which is demarcated for this purpose by the state government.

74th Amendment Act of 1992

This Act has added Part IX-A to the Constitution of India. It is entitled as "The Municipalities' and consists of provisions from articles 243-P to 243-ZG. In addition, the Act has also added Twelfth Schedule to the Constitution. It contains 18 functional items of municipalities and deals with Article 243-W.

The Act gave constitutional status to the municipalities. It has brought them under the purview of justiciable part of the constitution. In other words, state governments are under constitutional obligation to adopt the new system of municipalities in accordance with the provisions of the Act.

The Act aims at revitalising and strengthening the urban governments so that they function effectively as units of local government.

The salient features of the Act are:

1. Three Types of Municipalities: The Act provides for the constitution of the following three types of municipalities in every state.

(*a*) A Nagar Panchayat (by whatever name called) for a transitional area, that is, an area in transition from a rural area to an urban area.

(*b*) A Municipal Council for a smaller urban area.

(*c*) A Municipal Corporation for a larger urban area.

A transitional area, a smaller urban area or a larger urban area means such area as the Governor may specify by public notification for this purpose with regard to the following factors. These are:

(*a*) Population of the area;

(*b*) Density of population;

(*c*) Revenue generated for local administration;

(*d*) Percentage of employment in non-agricultural activities; and

(*e*) Economic importance or such other factors as the Governor may deem fit.

2. **Composition:** All the members of a municipality shall be elected directly by the people of the municipal area. For this purpose, each municipal area shall be divided int territorial constituencies to be known as wards. The state legislature may provide the manner of election of the chairperson of a municipality. It may also provide for the representation of the following persons in a municipality.

   (*i*) Persons having special knowledge or experience in municipal administration without the right to vote in the meetings of municipality.

   (*ii*) The members of the Lok Sabha and the State Legislative Assembly representing constituencies which comprise wholly or partly the municipal area.

   (*iii*) The members of the Rajya Sabha and the State Legislative Council registered as electors with the municipal area.

   (*iv*) The chairpersons of committees (other than wards committees).

3. **Wards Committees:** There shall be constituted a wards committee, consisting of one or more wards, within the territorial area of a municipality having population of three lakhs or more. The state legislature may make provision with respect to the composition and the territorial area of a wards committee and the manner in which the seats in a wards committee shall be filled. It may also make any provision for the constitution of committees in addition to the wards committees.

4. **Reservation of Seats:** The Act provides for the reservation of seats for the scheduled castes and the scheduled tribes in every municipality in proportion of their population to the total population in the municipal area. Further, it provides for the reservation of not less than one-third of the total number of seats for women (including the number of seats reserved for women belonging to the SCs and the STs).

   The state legislature may provide for the manner of reservation of offices of chairpersons in the municipalities for the SCs, the STs and the women. It may also make any provision for the reservation of seats in any municipality or offices of chairpersons in municipalities in favour of backward classes.

5. **Duration of Municipalities:** The Act provides for a five-year terms of office for every municipality. However, it can be dissolved before the completion of its term. Further, the fresh election to constitute a municipality shall be completed : (*i*) before the expiry of its duration of five years; or (*ii*) in case of dissolution, before the expiry of a period of six months from the date of its dissolution.

6. **Disqualifications:** A person shall be disqualified for being chosen as or for being a member of a municipality if he is so disqualified :

   (*i*) under any law for the time being in force for the purposes of elections to the legislature of the state concerned; or

   (*ii*) under any law made by the state legislature.

   However, no person shall be disqualified on the ground that he is less than 25 years of age if he has attained the age of 21 years. Further, all questions of disqualifications shall be referred to such authority as the state legislature determines.

7. **State Election Commission:** The superintendence, direction and control of the preparation of electoral rolls and the conduct of all elections of the municipalities shall be vested in the State Election Commission.

8. **Powers and Functions:** The state legislature may endow the municipalities with such powers and authority as may be necessary to enable them to function as institutions of self-government. Such a scheme may contain provisions for the devolution of powers and responsibilities upon municipalities at the appropriate level with respect to: (*i*) the preparation of plans for economic development and social justice; (*ii*) the implementation of schemes for economic development and social justice as may be entrusted to them including those in relation to the 18 matters listed in the Twelfth Schedule.

9. **Finances:** The state legislature may:
   (*i*) authorise a municipality to levy, collect and appropriate taxes, duties, tolls and fees;
   (*ii*) assign to a municipality taxes, duties, tolls and fees levied and collected by state government;
   (*iii*) provide for making grants-in-aid to the municipalities from the Consolidated Fund of the state; and
   (*iv*) provide for constitution of funds for crediting all moneys of the municipalities.

10. **Finance Commission:** The Finance Commission (which is constituted for the Panchayats) shall also, for evey five years, review the financial position of municipalities and make recommendation to the Governor as to:
   (*i*) The principles which should govern:
      (*a*) The distribution between the state and the municipalities, the net proceeds of the taxes, duties, tolls and fees levied by the state.
      (*b*) The determination of the taxes, duties, tolls and fees which may be assigned to the municipalities.
      (*c*) The grants-in-aid to municipalities from the Consolidated Fund of the state.
   (*ii*) The measures needed to improve the financial position of the municipalities.
   (*iii*) Any other matter referred to the Finance Commission by the Governor in the interests of sound finance of municipalities.

   The Governor shall place the recommendations of the Commission along with the action taken report before the state legislautre.

   The Central Finance Commission shall also suggest the measures needed to augment the Consolidated Fund of a state to supplement the resources of the municipalities in the state (on the basis of the recommendations made by the Finance Commission of the state).

11. **District Planning Committee:** Every state shall constitute at the district level, a District Planning Committee to consolidate the plans prepared by Panchayats and municipalities in the district, and to prepare a draft development plan for the district as a whole. The state legislature may make provision with respect to the following points:
   (*i*) The composition of such committees;
   (*ii*) The manner of election of members of such committees;
   (*iii*) The functions of such committees in relation to district planning; and
   (*iv*) The manner of the election of the chairpersons of such committees.

   The Act lays down that four-fifths of the members of a District Planning Committee should be elected by the elected members of the district panchayat and municipalities in the district from amongst themselves. The representation of these members in the committee should be in proportion to the ratio between the rural and urban populations in the district.

   The chairpersons of such committees shall forward the development plan to the state government.

* * *

17

The Jammu and Kashmir Reorganisation Act, 2019

The Jammu and Kashmir Reorganisation Bill, 2019 was passed by Parliament on August 6, 2019. The Act provides for reorganisation of the state of Jammu and Kashmir into the Union Territory of Jammu and Kashmir and Union Territory of Ladakh.

- **Reorganisation of Jammu and Kashmir:** The Act reorganises the state of Jammu and Kashmir into:

  (*i*) the Union Territory of Jammu and Kashmir with a legislature, and

  (*ii*) the Union Territory of Ladakh without a legislature.

  The Union Territory of Ladakh will comprise Kargil and Leh districts, and the Union Territory of Jammu and Kashmir will comprise the remaining territories of the existing state of Jammu and Kashmir.

- **Lieutenant Governor:** The Union Territory of Jammu and Kashmir will be administered by the President, through an administrator appointed by him known as the Lieutenant Governor.

  The Union Territory of Ladakh will be administered by the President, through a Lieutenant Governor appointed by him.

- **Legislative Assembly of Jammu and Kashmir:** The Act provides for a Legislative Assembly for the Union Territory of Jammu and Kashmir. The total number of seats in the Assembly will be 107. Of these, 24 seats will remain vacant on account of certain areas of Jammu and Kashmir being under the occupation of Pakistan.

  Further, seats will be reserved in the Assembly for Scheduled Castes and Scheduled Tribes in proportion to their population in the Union Territory of Jammu and Kashmir.

  In addition, the Lieutenant Governor may nominate two members to the Legislative Assembly to give representation to women, if they are not adequately represented.

- The Assembly will have a term of five years, and the Lieutenant Governor must summon the Assembly at least once in six months. The Legislative Assembly may make laws for any part of the Union Territory of Jammu and Kashmir related to:

  (*i*) any matters specified in the State List of the Constitution, except "Police" and "Public Order", and

  (*ii*) any matter in the Concurrent List applicable to Union Territories.

  Further, Parliament will have the power to make laws in relation to any matter for the Union Territory of Jammu and Kashmir.

- **Council of Ministers:** The Union Territory of Jammu and Kashmir will have a Council of Ministers of not more than ten per cent of the total number of members in the Assembly. The Council will aide and advise the Lieutenant Governor on matters that the

Assembly has powers to make laws. The Chief Minister will communicate all decisions of the Council to the Lieutenant Governor.

- **High Court:** The High Court of Jammu and Kashmir will be the common High Court for the Union Territories of Ladakh, and Jammu and Kashmir.

  Further, the Union Territory of Jammu and Kashmir will have an Advocate General to provide legal advice to the government of the Union Territory.

- **Legislative Council:** The Legislative Council of the state of Jammu and Kashmir will be abolished. Upon dissolution, all Bills pending in the Council will lapse.

- **Advisory Committees:** The central government will appoint Advisory Committees, for various purposes, including:

  (*i*) distribution of assets and liabilities of corporations of the state of Jammu and Kashmir between the two Union Territories,

  (*ii*) issues related to the generation and supply of electricity and water, and

  (*iii*) issues related to the Jammu and Kashmir State Financial Corporation.

  These Committees must submit their reports within six months to the Lieutenant Governor of Jammu and Kashmir, who must act on these recommendations within 30 days.

* * *

18

Union Territories

The union territories are those areas which are under the direct control and administration of the Central government. Hence, they are also known as 'centrally administered territories'. 'In this way, existence of these territories constitutes a conspicuous departure from federalism in India; the Government of India is plainly unitary in so far as the relationship between New Delhi and these Central enclaves is concerned.

At present, there are 8 Union Territories. They are:

1. Andaman and Nicobar Islands
2. Delhi
3. Lakshadweep
4. Dadra & Nagar Haveli and Daman & Diu
5. Puducherry
6. Chandigarh
7. Jammu & Kashmir
8. Ladakh

Till 1973, Lakshadweep was known by the name of Laccadive, Minicoy and Amindivi Islands. In 1992, Delhi was redesignated as the National Capital Territory of Delhi. Till 2006, Puducherry was known as Pondicherry.

The Union territories have been created for a variety of reasons. These are mentioned below :

1. Political and administrative consideration–Delhi and Chandigarh.
2. Cultural distinctiveness–Puducherry, Dadra and Nagar Haveli and Daman and Diu.
3. Strategic importance–Andaman and Nicobar Islands and Lakshadweep.
4. Special treatment and care of the backward and tribal people–Mizoram, Manipur, Tripura and Arunachal Pradesh which later became states.

The administration of the Union Territories lies with the Union Government. According to Article 238 (1). "Save as otherwise provided by the Parliament by law, every Union Territory shall be administered by the President acting, to such an extent as he thinks fit, through an administrator appointed by him with such designation as he may specify. Thus Andaman and Nicobar Islands, Delhi, Jammu & Kashmir, Ladakh and Puducherry have Lieutenant Governors and Chandigarh, Lakshdweep and Dadra & Nagar Haveli and Daman & Diu have Administrators.

Under the pattern of Government administered by Administrator/Chief Commissioner, the legislations are made by regulations as there is no provision for a legislative assembly and a Council of Ministers. There are advisory committees attached with the Home Ministry to help the administrators in respect of policy, legislative proposals, budgeting matters, development plans and other matters of importance. There is another advisory committee attached with the administrator of the Union Territory similar in all respects.

The legislature-cum-cabinet pattern prevailing in Puducherry is based on the provisions by the Government of Union Territories Act, 1963. There are two sources of power, one coming from the Central Government and the other from the Union Territory Government. The executive head, known as Lieutenant Governor, is appointed by the President. He is aided and advised by the Council of Ministers which is also appointed by the President. The pattern of Government is different from those at the States. The administrator is not a constitutional and formal head but a real head with the power to override the decisions of the ministers.

Delhi which is a Union Territory as well as the national capital has a unique arrangement. The National Capital Territory region has an assembly and an elected government.

The strength of the assembly is fixed at 70 members, directly elected by the people. The elections are conducted by the election commission of India. The assembly can make laws on all the matters of the State List and the Concurrent List except the three matters of the State List, that is, public order, police and land. But, the laws of Parliament prevail over those made by the Assembly.

The chief minister is appointed by the President (not by the Lt. governor). The other ministers are appointed by the president on the advice of the chief minister. The ministers hold office during the pleasure of the president. The council of ministers is collectively responsible to the assembly.

The council of ministers headed by the chief minister aid and advise the Lt. governor in the exercise of his functions except in so far as he is required to act in his discretion. In the case of difference of opinion between the Lt. governor and his ministers, the Lt. governor is to refer the matter to the president for decision and act accordingly.

When a situation arises in which the administration of the territory cannot be carried on in accordance with the above provisions, the president can suspend their (above provisions) operation and make the necessary incidental or consequential provisions for administering the territory. In brief, in case of failure of constitutional machinery, the president can impose his rule in the territory. This can be done on the report of the Lt. governor or otherwise. This provision resembles Article 356 which deals with the imposition of President's Rule in the states.

The Lt. governor is empowered to promulgate ordinances during recess of the assembly. An ordinance has the same force as an act of the assembly. Every such ordinance must be approved by the assembly within six weeks from its reassembly. He can also withdraw an ordinance at any time. But, he cannot promulgate an ordinance when the assembly is dissolved or suspended. Further, no such ordinance can be promulgated or withdrawn without the prior permission of the President.

States Vs Union Territories

States	Union Territories
1. Their executive head is known as governor.	1. Their executive head is known by various designations–administrator or lieutenant governor or chief commissioner.
2. A governor is a constitutional head of the state.	2. An administrator is an agent of the president.
3. Their relationship with Centre is federal.	3. Their relationship with Centre is unitary.
4. They have autonomy.	4. They do not have any autonomy.
5. Parliament cannot make laws on the subjects of the state list in relation to the states except under extraordinary circumstances.	5. Parliament can make laws on any subject of the three lists in relation to the union territories.
6. There is uniformity in their administrative set-up.	6. There is no uniformity in their administrative set-up.
7. They share a distribution of power with the Centre.	7. They are under the direct control and administration of the Centre.

***

19

Scheduled and Tribal Areas

The Fifth Schedule of the Constitution deals with the administration and control of scheduled areas and scheduled tribes in any state except the four states of Assam, Meghalaya, Tripura and Mizoram. The Sixth Schedule of the Constitution, on the other hand, deals with the administration of the tribal areas in the four northeastern states of Assam, Meghalaya, Tripura and Mizoram.

The expression "Scheduled Areas" in the Constitution means such areas as the President may by order declare to be scheduled areas. The President can order that the whole or any scheduled parts of a scheduled area ceases to be a scheduled area or a part of such an area. He can increase the area of any scheduled area in a state after consultation with the Governor of the state. The President can rectify or alter the boundaries of scheduled areas. On any alteration of the boundaries of a state or on the admission into the union or the establishment of a state, the President can declare any territory not previously included in any state to be, or to form part of, a scheduled area.

To safeguard the interests of the people staying in scheduled areas, the Governor of the state, can issue a public notification, directing that any particular Act of the Parliament, or the state legislature is not applicable to a scheduled area or any part thereof in the state. He can also make exceptions and modifications to the Acts before making them applicable to the scheduled areas or parts thereof. He can also issue directions to give retrospective effect to the Acts.

The Governor can make regulations for the peace and good governance of any area, or part of the scheduled area. He can prohibit or restrict the transfer of land by or among members of the Scheduled Tribes in such area. He can regulate the allotment of land to members of the Scheduled Tribes in such area. He can regulate the carrying on of the business as money-lender by persons who lend money to members of the Scheduled Tribes in such area. All such regulations, however, are submitted to the President and are applicable only after his assent.

The various features of administration contained in the Sixth Schedule are as follows :

1. The tribal areas in the four states of Assam, Meghalaya, Tripura and Mizoram have been constituted as autonomous districts. But, they do not fail outside the executive authority of the state concerned.
2. If there are different tribes in an autonomous district, the governor can divide the district into several autonomous regions.
3. Each autonomous district has a district council consisting of 30 members, of whom four are nominated by the governor and the remaining 26 are elected on the basis of adult franchise. The elected members hold office for a term of five years (unless the council is dissolved earlier) and nominated members hold office during the pleasure of the governor. Each autonomous region also has a separate regional council.
4. The district and regional councils within their territorial jurisdictions can constitute village councils or courts for trial of suits and cases between the tribes. They hear

appeals from them. The jurisdiction of high court over these suits and cases is specified by the governor.

5. The district and regional councils are empowered to assess and collect land revenue and to impose certain specified taxes.
6. The district and regional councils administer the areas under their jurisdiction. They can make laws on certain specified matters like land, forests, canal water, shifting cultivation, village administration, inheritance of property, marriage and divorce, social customs and so on. But all such laws require the assent of the governor.
7. The acts of Parliament or the state legislature do not apply to autonomous districts and autonomous regions or apply with specified modifications and exceptions.

Tribal Areas at a Glance

States	Tribal Areas
1. Meghalaya	1. Khasi Hills District.
	2. Jaintia Hills District.
	3. The Garo Hills District.
2. Tripura	1. Tripura Tribal Areas District.
3. Assam	1. The North Cachar Hills District.
	2. The Karbi Anglong District.
	3. The Bodoland Territorial Areas District.
4. Mizoram	1. The Chakma District.
	2. The Mara District.
	3. The Lai District.

* * *

20

Public Services & Public Service Commissions

The Public Services (civil services or government services) in India are classified into three categories–all-India services, Central services and state services. All-India services are those services which are common to both Central and state governments. The members of these services occupy top positions (or key posts) under both the Centre and the states and serve them by turns.

At present, there are three all-India services. They are :

1. Indian Administrative Service (IAS)
2. Indian Police Service (IPS)
3. Indian Forest Service (IFS)

The All-India Services Act of 1951 authorised the Central government to make rules in consultation with the state governments for the regulation of recruitment and service conditions of the members of all-India services. The members of these services are recruited and trained by the Central government but are assigned to different states for work. They belong to different state cadres; the Centre having no cadre of its own in this regard. They serve the Central government on deputation and after completing their fixed tenure they go back to their respective states.

The all-India services are controlled jointly by the Central and state governments. The ultimate control lies with the Central government while the immediate control is vested in the state governments. Any disciplinary action (imposition of penalties) against these officers can only be taken by the Central government.

Sardar Vallabhbhai Patel was the chief protagonist of all-India services in the Constituent Assembly. Hence, he came to be regarded as the 'Father of all-India Services.'

The personnel of Central services work under the exclusive jurisdiction of the Central government. The hold specialised (functional and technical) positions in various departments of the Central government. At present, there are 58 group A Central services.

The Indian Foreign Service (IFS) is the highest central service in terms of prestige, status, pay and emoluments. In fact, it (though a central service) competes with the all-India services in position, status and pay scales. It comes next to the IAS in ranking and its pay scale is higher than the IPS.

The personnel of state services work under the exclusive jurisdiction of the state government. They hold different positions (general, functional and technical) in the departments of the state government. However, they occupy lower positions (in the administrative hierarchy of the state) than those held by the members of the all-India services (IAS, IPS and IFS).

Safeguards to Civil Servants : Article 311 places two restriction on the above 'doctrine of pleasure'. In other words, it provides two safeguards to civil servents against any arbitrary dismissal from their posts:

(*a*) A civil servant cannot be dismissed or removed by an authority subordinate to that by which he was appointed.

(*b*) A civil servant cannot be dismissed or removed or reduced in rank except after an inquiry in which he has been informed of the charges against him and given a reasonable opportunity of being heard in respect of those charges.

The above two safeguards are available only to the members of the civil services of the Centre, the all-India services, the civil services of a state or to persons holding civil posts under the Centre or a state and not to the members of defence services or persons holding military posts.

PUBLIC SERVICE COMMISSION

There is a Union Public Service Commission (UPSC) to recruit people to serve under the Central Government and a Public Service Commission (PSC) for each state to recruit people for the State Civil Services. If two or more states agree to have a Common Public Service Commission and a resolution to that effect is passed by both the houses, the Parliament may by law provide for the appointment of a joint State Public Service Commission (Art. 315). The UPSC, if requested by the Governor of a state may with the approval of the President, agree to serve all or any of the needs of the state.

The Chairman and other members of Union Public Service Commission or Joint Public Service Commission are appointed by the President. For State Public Service Commission, appointment are made by the Governors (Art. 316). Usually, senior and eminent persons are made members of such Commissions. The appointment is usually for a six-year term or until they attain the age of 65 years in Union Public Service Commission or 62 years in case of State or Joint Commission. The members of the Commissions can retire before the end of the tenure. To ensure the integrity and independence of the Commission, the Constitution debars the members or the Chairman to seek further employment after retirement, either under the Central Government or any state Government.

The Chairman or any member of a PSC can only be removed from his office by order of the President on the ground of misbehaviour, after the Supreme Court, on reference being made to it by the President, inquires and reports that the concerned person ought to be removed from the post (Art. 317). Till the enquiry report is received, the concerned Chairman or the member may be suspended. Any Chairman or member of the Public Service Commission can be removed on the ground, if he

(1) is adjudged to be an insolvent, or

(2) engages during his term of office in any paid employment outside the duties of his office, or

(3) in the opinion of the President, is unfit to continue in office by reason of infirmity of mind or body.

The Public Service Commissions conduct examinations for appointments to the Services of the Union and the Services of the State respectively. They may assist in framing and operating schemes for any service for which candidates with special qualifications are required. The Public Service Commissions are consulted:

(1) on all matters relating to methods of recruitment to Civil Services and for civil posts;

(2) on the principles to be followed in making appointments, promotions and transfers from one service to another;

(3) on all disciplinary matters; and

(4) on all claims by or in respect of person who is serving or has served under the Government in a civil capacity, that any cost incurred by him in respect of acts done or purporting to be done in the execution of his duty should be paid by the Central or State Government.

However, in any particular class of cases or in any particular circumstances, the necessity to consult Public Service Commission may be overruled by the President or a Governor.

The annual report of the Union Public Service Commission (UPSC) is presented to the President, giving details of the work done by the Commission. The President causes the report to be laid in the Parliament. In respect of the cases, where advice of the Commission was not accepted, the Government attaches an explanation, giving reasons thereof.

Similarly, the Governor of the State causes the annual report of the State Public Service Commission (SPSC) to be laid before the legislature.

***

MULTIPLE CHOICE QUESTIONS

1. A special session of the Constituent Assembly was held at midnight on 14-15 August 1947 in connection with the :
(*a*) Independence resolution
(*b*) Partition of India
(*c*) Transfer of Power
(*d*) None of the above

2. Which committee was appointed to prepare guidelines for the Constituent Assembly?
(*a*) Drafting committee
(*b*) Congress Expert Com. ittee
(*c*) Advisory Committee
(*d*) Union powers Committee

3. The elections to the Constituent Assembly were :
(*a*) Indirect
(*b*) Held twice
(*c*) Direct
(*d*) None of the above

4. Members of the Constituent Assembly were elected by the elected members of the :
(*a*) Legislative Councils
(*b*) Parliament
(*c*) Legislative Assemblies of the provinces
(*d*) All of the above

5. Who described Constituent Assembly as "a body of Hindus" in the House of Lords?
(*a*) Churchill (*b*) V. Simon
(*c*) Mountbatten (*d*) Attlee

6. Who Labelled the Drafting Committee as a drifting Committee?
(*a*) Jinnah
(*b*) Kunzru
(*c*) Naziruddin Ahmed
(*d*) Jayakar

7. The demand for the establishment of a Constituent Assembly was first embodied in a resolution of the Indian National Congress passed at its Faizpur session on :
(*a*) December 8, 1936 (*b*) July 5,1938
(*c*) January 2, 1936 (*d*) August 4, 1936

8. Which committee was set up to prepare a draft constitution on August 29, 1947?
(*a*) Staff Committee
(*b*) Union Constitution Committee
(*c*) Drafting Committee
(*d*) Union powers committee

9. The constitution-making body was not in Fact a...body.
(*a*) Democratic (*b*) Legal
(*c*) Temporary (*d*) Sovereign

10. One of the earliest demands for Constituent Assembly was by the :
(*a*) Cripps Mission
(*b*) Nehru Report
(*c*) Cabinet Mission
(*d*) Simon Commission

11. The elections to the Constituent Assembly were held in :
(*a*) June 1946 (*b*) July 1946
(*c*) August 1946 (*d*) July 1947

12. Who acted as president of the Constituent Assembly on 9 December, 1946?
(*a*) Rajendra Prasad
(*b*) Sardar Patel
(*c*) Sachidanand Sinha
(*d*) K.M. Munshi

13. Which of the following is included in the Committees on procedural Affairs?
(*a*) Training and staff committee
(*b*) Credentials committee
(*c*) Hindi Translation Committee
(*d*) All of the above

14. Which of the following resolutions forms the basis of the new constitution passed in second plenary session?
(*a*) Objective Resolution

(*b*) Independence Resolution
(*c*) August Resolution
(*d*) None of the above

15. Which of the following is one of the main principles of the objectives Resolution?
(*a*) To frame a constitution which should secure for India, a due place in the comity of nations.
(*b*) That India is to be an independent, sovereign, republic
(*c*) That India is to be a democratic union with an equal level of self- government in all the constituent parts.
(*d*) All of the above

16. Which of the following is included in the Committees on Substantive Affairs?
(*a*) Union powers committee
(*b*) Drafting committee
(*c*) Advisory committee on minorities
(*d*) All of the above

17. The Constituent Assembly had a total of more than...Committees with a membership of greater than eighty individuals.
(*a*) Sixteen (*b*) Twenty
(*c*) Fifteen (*d*) Thirteen

18. Sir Krishnaswami Ayyangar, K.M. Munshi, B.L. Mittar, Saiyad Mohammed Sadulla were the members of the :
(*a*) Advisory committee
(*b*) Drafting committee
(*c*) Union powers committee
(*d*) Committee on minorities

19. Which of the following is a criticism of the Constituent Assembly?
(*a*) Congress Domination
(*b*) An unrepresentative Body
(*c*) Dominated by the legal Luminaries
(*d*) All of the abaove

20. The total number of seats fixed in the proposed Constituent Assembly for British India, Chief Commissioner's provinces, and the Indian states respectively are :
(*a*) 290, 6 and 93 seats
(*b*) 280, 16 and 93 seats
(*c*) 292, 4 and 93 seats
(*d*) 292, 7 and 90 seats

21. Who said that the father of the Indian Constitution conceived of a Constituent Assembly as something dynamic, not merely a body of representatives but "a nation on the move"?
(*a*) Ivor Jennings (*b*) J.L. Nehru
(*c*) Sardar Patel (*d*) B.R. Ambedkar

22. Who referred to the philadelphia convention, the French experiment and the Russian revolution as sources of inspiration?
(*a*) Rajendra Prasad
(*b*) Jawahar Lal Nehru
(*c*) Sardar Patel
(*d*) B.R. Ambedkar

23. Which of the following is a representative body chosen for the purpose of considering and either adopting or proposing a new constitution or changes in the existing constitution?
(*a*) Legislative
(*b*) Cabinet
(*c*) Election Commission
(*d*) Constitutent Assembly

24. The modern concept of Constituent Assembly is a/an...political contribution to the science of government.
(*a*) Eastern (*b*) Southern
(*c*) Western (*d*) Northern

25. Whose idea of the general will influenced the rise of the concept of Constitutional Government?
(*a*) Laski's (*b*) Mill's
(*c*) Rousseau's (*d*) MacIver's

26. The earliest Constituent Assemblies the philadelphia convention of 1787, which framed the constitution of the USA, and the National Assembly of France were the products of...and registered a break with the past.
(*a*) Evolution (*b*) Revolutions
(*c*) Revivalism (*d*) None of the above

27. The demand for a Constituent Assembly was for the first time authoritatively conceded by the British Government, though in an indirect way and with important reservations,in what is known as the :
(*a*) August offer, 1940
(*b*) Cripps mission, 1942
(*c*) Cabinet mission, 1946
(*d*) Quit India movement, 1942

28. "The Constituent Assembly declares its firm and solemn resolve the proclaim India as an Independent sovereign Republic and to draw up for her future governance a constitution". This statement is related to :
(*a*) Independence Resolution
(*b*) August Resolution
(*c*) Cabinet Resolution
(*d*) Objectives Resolution

29. Which of the following is one of the features of the working process of the Constituent Assembly, according to G. Austin?
(*a*) Decision-making by consensus
(*b*) The principle of Accommodation
(*c*) The act of selection and modification
(*d*) All of the above

30. Which of the following proposal were recommended by the Cabinet mission during its stay in India?
1. To form a Constituent Assembly
2. To form an interim government
3. To introduce adult Franchise
4. To form an Estimates Committee

Choose the correct answer using the codes given below :
(*a*) 1 and 2 (*b*) 2 and 4
(*c*) 1, 2 and 3 (*d*) 3 and 4

31. The demand for a Constituent Assembly was for the first time authoritatively conceded by the British Government, though in an indirect way, through :
(*a*) Shimla Conference
(*b*) August Offer
(*c*) Wavell Plan
(*d*) None of the above

32. Broadly, the duration during which the Constituent Assembly drafted the constitution for India was :
(*a*) December 1945 to December 1949
(*b*) December 1946 to December 1949
(*c*) November 1946 to January 1949
(*d*) November 1947 to January 1950

33. Over how many sessions the Constituent Assembly drafted the Constitution for India?
(*a*) 11 (*b*) 12
(*c*) 13 (*d*) 14

34. While drafting the Constitution for India how many days of actual work was undertaken by the Constituent Assembly?
(*a*) 900 days (*b*) 200 days
(*c*) 188 days (*d*) 165 days

35. How many Articles and schedules were there in the draft Constitution?
(*a*) 355 Articles and 8 schedules
(*b*) 315 Articles and 13 schedules
(*c*) 295 Articles and 13 schedules
(*d*) None of the above

36. First attempt by Indians to frame a constitution of their country was in the form of :
(*a*) Round Table conference
(*b*) Nehru Report
(*c*) Macdonald Award
(*d*) Government of India Act, 1919

37. The elections to the Constituent Assembly were :
(*a*) Indirect
(*b*) Held Twice
(*c*) Direct
(*d*) None of the above

38. The Nehru committee was appointed and the Nehru Report was submitted respectively on :
(*a*) May 19, 1928 and 10 August, 1928
(*b*) May 19, 1928 and 10 August, 1929
(*c*) May 19, 1927 and 10 August, 1928
(*d*) June 1, 1929 and August 31, 1929

39. Jawaharlal Nehru's proposal of a Constituent Assembly was for the first time formally accepted by the Congress in the year :
(*a*) 1934 (*b*) 1935
(*c*) 1936 (*d*) 1937

40. Which of the following most influenced the Constitution of India?
(*a*) Government of India Act, 1919
(*b*) Indian Independence Act, 1947
(*c*) Government of India Act, 1935
(*d*) All of the above

41. Fundamental duties have been introduced in the Constitution by :
(*a*) 42nd Amendment Act, 1976
(*b*) 44th Amendment Act, 1978
(*c*) 73rd Amendment Act, 1993
(*d*) None of the above

42. The Dominion status of India was established under :
(*a*) Government of India Act, 1919
(*b*) Government of India Act, 1935
(*c*) Both (*a*) and (*b*)
(*d*) Indian Independence Act, 1947

43. Parts XVII, XVI and XVIII of the constitution of India are related respectively to :
(*a*) Official language, SCs, STs and OBCs and Emergency provisions
(*b*) SCs, STs and OBCs, official language and Emergency provisions
(*c*) SCs, STs and OBCs, emergency provisions and official language
(*d*) None of the above

44. The work 'Constituent Assemblies of the World' is authored by :
(*a*) Subhash Kashyap
(*b*) T.S. Venkataraman
(*c*) Pattabhi Sitaramaiyya
(*d*) None of the above

45. Which of the following is one of the features of the working process of the Constituent Assembly, according to Granville Austin?
(*a*) Decison-making by consensus
(*b*) The principle of Accomodation
(*c*) The act of selection and modification
(*d*) All of the above

46. 'Politbureau is a term associated with—
(*a*) Communist Party
(*b*) Samajwadi Party
(*c*) Congress Party
(*d*) Bhartiya Janta Party

47. The Constitution of India superimposes an elected president upon the parliamentary system of responsible government. Another constitution which prescribes a similar governmental pattern is :
(*a*) The Constitution of France
(*b*) The Constitution of Germany
(*c*) The Constitution of Eire
(*d*) All of the above

48. Article 51 A which constitutes the part IVA of the constitution of India and which contain the fundamental duties was introduced in the constitution in the year :
(*a*) 1976 (*b*) 1977
(*c*) 1978 (*d*) 1979

49. Which of the following need to be considered to have a full view of the law of citizenship in India?
(*a*) The citizenship Act, 1955
(*b*) Articles 5, 6, 7 and 8
(*c*) Article 11
(*d*) All of the above

50. Protection of Civil Rights Act, 1955 pertains to :
(*a*) Human rights
(*b*) Citizenship
(*c*) Untouchability
(*d*) Freedom of expression

51. Which of the following articles made a mention of the sueability of the state :
(*a*) Article 100 (*b*) Article 200
(*c*) Article 300 (*d*) All of these

52. Prior to Independence the territory of India was divided into :
(*a*) 9 Governor's provinces, 600 states and some Centrally Administered areas
(*b*) 12 Governor's provinces, 552 states and 15 centrally Administered areas
(*c*) 6 Governor's provinces, 562 states and 2 centrally Administrated areas
(*d*) 552 provinces, 12 states and 10 centrally Administered Areas.

53. For preparing the draft, who was the advisor of the constituent Assembly?
(*a*) B.N. Rao (*b*) B.R. Ambedkar
(*c*) K.M. Munshi (*d*) J.L. Nehru

54. For the consitituent Assembly, who was the chairman of the steering Committee?
(*a*) B.N. Rao (*b*) B.R. Ambedkar
(*c*) K.M. Munshi (*d*) J.L. Nehru

55. According to the Constituent Assembly Debates Directive principles is merely another name for the :
(*a*) Bill of Rights
(*b*) Human Rights Character
(*c*) Instruments of Instructions
(*d*) Governmental Accountability

56. Which Article of the Constitution states that the state shall organise village panchayats as units of self-government?
(*a*) Article 43 (*b*) Article 40
(*c*) Article 45 (*d*) Article 42

57. In which of the following cases, the Directive principles were accorded a more subsidiary and subordinate position than was contemplated by the founding father of the constitution?
(*a*) Cow Slaughter case
(*b*) Kerala Education Bill case
(*c*) Champakam Dorairajan's case
(*d*) All of the above

58. The Golak Nath case was heard by a special Bench of 11 judges as the validity of three constitutional amendments------- , -------- and ----- was challenged.
(*a*) 3rd, 4th, 5th (*b*) 1st, 4th, 17th
(*c*) 1st, 2nd, 8th (*d*) 2nd, 3rd, 4th

59. The case of Gopalan Vs. State of Madras was relevant to :
(*a*) Article 21 (*b*) Article 12
(*c*) Article 16 (*d*) Article 14

60. In Bijoy cotton mills Vs. State of Ajmer case, the supreme court upheld the constitutional validity of minimum wages Act, 1948 by taking into consideration Article 43 which provides for :
(*a*) "Minimising inequalities in income"
(*b*) "Eliminating inequalities in status"
(*c*) "Living wages for workers"
(*d*) None of the above

61. In state of Bombay Vs. F.N. Balasara case, the supreme court gave full weight to ------, which directs the state to bring about prohibition of intoxicating drinks.
(*a*) Article 43 (*b*) Article 47
(*c*) Article 29 (*d*) Article 13

62. Which of the following Articles deals with the right to property has already been deleted by the 44th Amendment Act of 1978?
(*a*) Article 30 (*b*) Article 29
(*c*) Article 31 (*d*) Article 32

63. The expression "procedure established by law" has been taken from Article XXXI of the:
(*a*) British Constitution, 1946
(*b*) American Constitution, 1963
(*c*) German Constitution, 1987
(*d*) Japanese Constitution, 1946

64. How can a citizen protect his Fundamental Rights?
(*a*) By a writ in the Supreme court of India
(*b*) By approaching the president of India
(*c*) Through police action
(*d*) They are already protected

65. Which of the following is not a Fundamental Rights?
(*a*) Right against exploitation
(*b*) Equal pay for equal work
(*c*) Equality before law
(*d*) Right to freedom of religion

66. The Supreme Court of India gave the verdict that the original structure of the constitution as embodied in the preamble, could not be changed under any circumstances, in the case of :
(*a*) Sajjan Singh (*b*) Minerva Mills
(*c*) Keshvananda (*d*) Golaknath

67. The Gandhian principles have been enumerated in the :
(*a*) Fundamental Rights

(*b*) Preamble
(*c*) Directive Principles
(*d*) Fundamental Duties

68. An interpretation of the Indian constitution is based on the spirit of the :
(*a*) Preamble
(*b*) Fundamental Duties
(*c*) Fundamental Rights
(*d*) None of the above

69. Fundamental Duties were incorporated in the Constitution of India by the :
(*a*) 43rd Amendment Act
(*b*) 42nd Amendment Act
(*c*) 41st Amendment Act
(*d*) None of the above

70. Which of the following rights provided the necessary guidance to the framers of our constitution in selecting a set of rights which could best suit the social and political conditions in India?
(*a*) The French Declaration of Rights
(*b*) The Bill of Rights of the U.S.
(*c*) The Universal Human Rights charter
(*d*) All of the above

71. Which of the following are those conditions of social life without which no man can seek to be himself at his best?
(*a*) Duties
(*b*) Rights
(*c*) Sociability
(*d*) Civilised behaviour

72. In which of the following cases the question of amendability of Fundamental Rights came before the supreme court of India?
(*a*) Shankari prasad Vs. Union of India
(*b*) Sajjan Singh Vs. State of Rajasthan
(*c*) Golak Nath Vs. State of Punjab
(*d*) All of the above

73. In which of the following cases the validity of the first constitutional Amendment Act was challenged?
(*a*) Golak Nath's case
(*b*) Shankari Prasad's case
(*c*) Sajjan Singh's case
(*d*) Maneka Gandhi's case

74. Which of the following articles not only lays down the procedure but also confers power on the parliament to abridge or modify Fundamental Rights?
(*a*) Article 360 (*b*) Article 358
(*c*) Article 368 (*d*) Article 362

75. In which of the following cases the competence of parliament to enact 17th amendment was challenged before the constitution Bench comprising of five judges?
(*a*) Minerva mill's case
(*b*) Sajjan Singh's case
(*c*) Golak Nath's case
(*d*) None of the above

76. In which of the following decisions supreme court held that parliament's amending power is limited?
(*a*) Sajjan Singh's case
(*b*) Shankari Prasad's case
(*c*) Minerva Mills, case
(*d*) Keshvananda Bharti's case

77. Which part of the constitution provides the Directive principles of state policy?
(*a*) Part IV (*b*) Part II
(*c*) Part III (*d*) Part V

78. The Directive principles represent some what the pattern of instrument of instructions provided in the :
(*a*) Government of India Act, 1935
(*b*) Government of India Act, 1919
(*c*) Independence Act, 1947
(*d*) None of the above

79. Who among the following declared that the Indian Constitution is "First and Foremost a social document"?
(*a*) Jawaharlal Nehru
(*b*) Granville Austin
(*c*) M.K. Gandhi
(*d*) None of the above

80. Which of the following components of the Constitution has also been referred to as "the conscience of the constitution"?
(*a*) Preamble

(*b*) Fundamental Rights
(*c*) Directive principle of state policy
(*d*) Both (*b*) and (*c*)

81. In which of its sessions the congress party passed a resolution which declared that "the basis of the future constitution of India must be a declaration of Fundamental Rights"?
(*a*) Surat session of 1907
(*b*) Lucknow session of 1916
(*c*) Madras session of 1927
(*d*) Both (*a*) and (*b*)

82. Right to property has been eliminated from the fundamental rights by :
(*a*) 42nd Constitutional Amendment Act of 1976
(*b*) 44th Constitutional Amendment Act of 1978
(*c*) 43rd Constitutional Amendment Act of 1977
(*d*) 24th Constitutional Amendment Act of 1971

83. Which year does the "Golak Nath Vs the state of Punjab" case belong to?
(*a*) 1962 (*b*) 1965
(*c*) 1969 (*d*) 1967

84. Which of the following document rejected the idea of Fundamental Rights?
(*a*) Nehru Report
(*b*) Simon Commission and joint parliamentary committee which were responsible for the Government of India Act, 1935
(*c*) Objectives Resolution of Pt. Jawaharlal Nehru
(*d*) Both (*a*) and (*b*)

85. Article 300 A has :
(*a*) The vestiges of the erstwhile right to property
(*b*) Provision for the machinery of audit and account
(*c*) The power to review the acts of the state legislature
(*d*) All of the above

86. The terminology "equality before law and equal protection of laws" is found under :
(*a*) Article 13 (*b*) Article 14
(*c*) Article 15 (*d*) Article 16

87. The fundamental duties have been incorporated in Article 51A of the constitution. At present, the total number of Fundamental duties are :
(*a*) 9 (*b*) 10
(*c*) 11 (*d*) 12

88. Fundamental duties enjoin upon a person to respect :
(*a*) Mother Tongue (*b*) National Flag
(*c*) National Anthem (*d*) Both (*b*) and (*c*)

89. The people residing in India are asked by Constitution via its part IVA to preserve :
(*a*) National monuments
(*b*) Communal Harmony
(*c*) Political structure
(*d*) Rich heritage of the composite culture of the country

90. Which of the following comments are correct about enforcement of the Fundamental Duties?
(*a*) They can be only indirectly enforced
(*b*) They can be enforced if a proper suit is brought before the highest court of the country
(*c*) There is no provision in the constitution for direct enforcement of any of the Fundamental Duties
(*d*) All of the above

91. The constitution enjoins upon a person via Article 51A to protect and improve :
(*a*) Natural environment
(*b*) Unity and integrity of the nation
(*c*) Public property
(*d*) Ethnic composition of society

92. As part of the fundamental duties that a resident of India is expected to fulfill she or he should cherish and follow :
(*a*) Gandhian values and Nehruvian principles
(*b*) Noble ideals which inspired our national struggle for freedom

(c) Congress ideology
(d) None of the above

93. Article 51A makes it incumbent upon a person residing in India to promote :
(a) Communal harmony
(b) The spirit of common brotherhood amongst all the people of India
(c) Economic well-being of the nation
(d) All of the above

94. Which of the following is the country that has adopted the western model of liberal democracy and has also included a number of basic duties in its constitution.
(a) France (b) U.S.A.
(c) Germany (d) Japan

95. A committte that was appointed by the Government of India to make recommendations about Fundamental Duties was headed by :
(a) Sardar Swaran Singh
(b) Manmohan Singh
(c) Khushwant Singh
(d) Sanjay Gandhi

96. It is a fundamental Duty of a citizen of India to develop :
(a) Her or his economic status and social standing
(b) The understanding between different communities
(c) Scientific temper and spirit of enquiry
(d) All of the above

97. Which of the following works are authored by K.R. Bombwall?
(a) Constitutional law of India
(b) Indian political system
(c) Foundations of political science
(d) All of the above

98. The constitution of India through its part IVA enjoins upon the citizens of India of strive towards excellence in :
(a) One's occupational area
(b) One's economic and social endeavours
(c) All spheres of individual and collective activity
(d) None of the above

99. The power to issue writs for the enforcement of the fundamental rights is given by the constitution to the High Courts under :
(a) Article 32 (b) Article 123
(c) Article 226 (d) Article 339

100. Article 23, among other things, prohibits traffic in human beings. This expression includes :
(a) Slavery
(b) Use of women and children for immoral purposes
(c) Conscription
(d) Both (a) and (b)

101. Special provision for the protection of children is made in :
(a) Article 23 (b) Article 24
(c) Article 39(b) (d) All of these

102. Which among the following constitutional offices are to a certain extent immune from the impact of Article 14?
(a) President
(b) Governor
(c) Speaker of Lok Sabha,
(d) Both (a) and (b)

103. Which of the following cases is popularly known as Mandal Commission case?
(a) Indra Sawhney V. Union of India, 1992
(b) Bommai V. Union of India, 1994
(c) Ramsharan V. Union of India, 1989
(d) None of the above

104. Which of the following Articles provides for abolition of untouchability?
(a) Article 17 (b) Article 18
(c) Article 26 (d) Article 27

105. Who raised protest in 1970s against conferment of decorations like Bharat Ratna by the Government?
(a) Jai Prakash Narayan
(b) Ram Manohar Lohia
(c) Acharya Kripalani
(d) Vinobha Bhave

106. Freedom to reside and settle in any part of the territory of India is conferred by :
(a) Article 19(1)(e) (b) Article 18(4)
(c) Article 19(1)(d) (d) Article 19(1)(F)

107. Which of the following does not compose a ground for restriction on the freedom of speech and expression as given under the constitution?
(*a*) Defamation (*b*) Insolvency
(*c*) Contempt of court (*d*) Public order

108. 'Equality before the law', is an expression of
(*a*) English common law
(*b*) French Administrative law
(*c*) American Constitutional law
(*d*) None of the above

109. The expression 'equal protection of laws' owes its origin to :
(*a*) French Constitution
(*b*) English Constitution
(*c*) American Constitution
(*d*) None of the above

110. Equality before the law is a corollary of the concept of the rule of law given by :
(*a*) Dicey (*b*) Lord Bryce
(*c*) Lincoln (*d*) Churchill

111. Under Article 14 if there is any reasonable basis for classification, the legislature would be entitled to make a different treatment. In order to be 'reasonable' a classification must be :
(*a*) Unarbitrary (*b*) Rational
(*c*) Both (*a*) and (*b*) (*d*) Fair and just

112. Which of the following articles provides for prohibition of discrimination on grounds of religion, race, caste, sex and place of birth?
(*a*) Article 16
(*b*) Article 19(1)(C)
(*c*) Article 15
(*d*) None of the above

113. Under the constitution of India freedom of the press is deemed as included under :
(*a*) Article 19 (*b*) Article 19(1)
(*c*) Article 19(1)(a) (*d*) Article 19(2)

114. The term 'double jeopardy' pertains to :
(*a*) Article 19 (*b*) Article 20
(*c*) Article 21 (*d*) Article 22

115. Freedom of a person or personal liberty is sought to be ensured by the constitution of India by means of :
(*a*) Article 19 (*b*) Article 20
(*c*) Article 21 (*d*) Article 21 and 22

116. Which of the following chapters of the Indian constitution is the most comprehensive and detailed one?
(*a*) Chapter III (*b*) Chapter IV
(*c*) Chapter V (*d*) Chapter VII

117. Who among the following is the guardian of the fundamental rights guaranteed by the constitution of India?
(*a*) Parliament (*b*) Judiciary
(*c*) Lok Sabha (*d*) President

118. Which of the following rights is guaranteed to every person whether citizen or foreigner?
(*a*) Rights relating to protection of life
(*b*) Freedom of religion
(*c*) Right against exploitation
(*d*) All of the above

119. Equal protection of laws implies equal treatment in :
(*a*) Privileges conferred
(*b*) Liabilities imposed
(*c*) Both privileges conferred and liabilities by the law imposed
(*d*) Neither privileges conferred nor liabilities imposed

120. Which article provides for residential qualification in certain catagory of public employment?
(*a*) Article 16 (3)
(*b*) Article 16 (2)
(*c*) Article 15 (4)
(*d*) None of the above

121. Which article deals with the Right to Freedom?
(*a*) Article 15 to 18
(*b*) Article 19 to 22
(*c*) Article 17 to 21
(*d*) None of the above

122. Which of the following is included in the Union Executive?
(*a*) President
(*b*) Council of ministers
(*c*) Prime Minister
(*d*) All of the above

123. Which Article states that the Prime Minister shall be 'at the head' of the council of ministers?
(*a*) Article 57 (*b*) Article 74
(*c*) Article 72 (*d*) Article 73

124. The real executive in India is the :
(*a*) Prime Minister
(*b*) Speaker of Lok Sabha
(*c*) President
(*d*) Governor

125. Which of the following Articles of the constitution defines the duties of the prime minister in the discharge of which he acts as a link between the president and the cabinet?
(*a*) Article 75 (*b*) Article 78
(*c*) Article 77 (*d*) Article 73

126. Which of the following commission is an extra-constitutional advisory body under the chairmanship of the PM?
(*a*) Finance Commission
(*b*) Sarkaria Commission
(*c*) NITI Aayog
(*d*) Pay Commission

127. The Council of Ministers comprises of :
(*a*) Cabinet Ministers
(*b*) Ministers of State
(*c*) Deputy Ministers
(*d*) All of the above

128. A/An------ is a quasi-judicial procedure in parliament.
(*a*) Prorogation
(*b*) No-confidence motion
(*c*) Impeachment
(*d*) Censure motion

129. The vice-president shall be elected by an electoral college consisting of member of :
(*a*) State legislatures
(*b*) Both houses of parliament
(*c*) Lok Sabha and Vidhan Sabha
(*d*) None of the above

130. A veto is suspensive when the executive veto can be overridden by the legislature by an :
(*a*) Ordinary majority
(*b*) Two-third majority
(*c*) Absolute majority
(*d*) None of the above

131. The veto power of the Indian president is categorised as :
(*a*) Absolute (*b*) Suspensive
(*c*) Pocket (*d*) All of these

132. The president shall have the pardoning power in respect of :
(*a*) All cases of punishment by a court martial
(*b*) Offences against laws made under the Union and concurrent lists
(*c*) A sentence of death
(*d*) All of the above

133. Who said that "it is most useful to look upon the executive as the residuary legatee, for that explains the mixed nature of its functions and parts"?
(*a*) Finer (*b*) Laski
(*c*) Gilchrist (*d*) White

134. Who cannot be a member of parliament or a state legislature?
(*a*) Prime Minister (*b*) President
(*c*) Minister (*d*) Speaker

135. According to which article of the constitution the executive power of the Union is vested in the President who is empowered to exercise it either directly or through officers subordinate to him?
(*a*) Article 52 (*b*) Article 51
(*c*) Article 54 (*d*) Article 53

136. Who is empowered to declare three different types of emergency?
(*a*) President (*b*) Prime Minister
(*c*) Parliament (*d*) Governor

137. The President of India is elected by :
(*a*) Direct election
(*b*) Nomination
(*c*) Indirect election
(*d*) None of the above

138. Which of the following is included in the electoral college for electing the President?
(*a*) The elected members of the both Houses of Parliament

(*b*) The elected members of the Legislative Assemblies of the States
(*c*) The elected members of the Legislative Assemblies of Union Territories of Delhi and Pondicherry
(*d*) All of the above

139. Which of the following Articles of the constitution talks about the President's term of office?
(*a*) Article 52-53 (*b*) Article 56-57
(*c*) Article 51-52 (*d*) Article 57-58

140. Which Article of the constitution lays down a detailed procedure for the impeachment of the President?
(*a*) Article 57 (*b*) Article 58
(*c*) Article 62 (*d*) Article 61

141. The President is elected by the system of proportional representation by means of :
(*a*) Single transferable vote
(*b*) Single non-transferable vote
(*c*) Double transferable vote
(*d*) None of the above

142. Who nominates the Chairman of the Public Account Committee of Indian Parliament?
(*a*) The Prime Minister
(*b*) The President
(*c*) The Speaker of the Lok Sabha
(*d*) The Chairman of the Rajya Sabha

143. In case of 'private' member's Bills the President of India enjoys the powers of :
(*a*) Suspensive veto (*b*) Pocket veto
(*c*) Absolute veto (*d*) Qualified veto

144. The President of India is a :
(*a*) Real executive
(*b*) Titular executive
(*c*) De-facto executive
(*d*) None of the above

145. The President can dissolve the Lok Sabha on :
(*a*) Advice of the Chief Justice of India
(*b*) Recommendation of the Lok Sabha
(*c*) Advice of the Prime Minister
(*d*) Recommendation of the Rajya Sabha

146. The following have held office of the President of India :
(1) V.V. Giri
(2) N. Sanjiva Reddy
(3) Dr. Zakir Hussain
(4) Fakhruddin Ali Ahmed
The Chronological order in which they held office is :
(*a*) 3, 1, 4 and 2 (*b*) 2, 1, 3 and 4
(*c*) 1, 2, 3 and 4 (*d*) 1, 3, 4 and 2

147. Who was the first Vice-President of India?
(*a*) Dr. S. Radhakrishnan
(*b*) V.V. Giri
(*c*) Dr. Zakir Hussain
(*d*) N. Sanjiva Reddy

148. Who among the following prime ministers of India did not face the Lok Sabha even once?
(*a*) Indira Gandhi (*b*) Rajiv Gandhi
(*c*) Charan Singh (*d*) V.P. Singh

149. In which year Ladakh become a Union Territory?
(*a*) 2015
(*b*) 2016
(*c*) 2019
(*d*) None of the above

150. Who among the following describes the position of the prime minister as 'primus inter pares', i.e. 'first among equals.
(*a*) Morely (*b*) Appleby
(*c*) Leacock (*d*) White

151. Which of the following Acts defines "Minister" as a "Member of the Council of Ministers, by whatever name called, and includes a Deputy Minister"?
(*a*) Customs Act, 1962
(*b*) Salaries and Allowances of Minister Act, 1952
(*c*) Income-tax Act, 1961
(*d*) Monopolies and Restrictive Trade Practices Act, 1969

152. The ordinance-making power will be available to the President only when :
(*a*) The two Houses of Parliament have been prorogued
(*b*) The two Houses of Parliament are not in session

(c) Either (a) or (b)
(d) None of the above

153. The Rajya Sabha can take initiative in—
(a) Censuring a Minister
(b) Creating a New All India Service
(c) Considering Money Bill
(d) Appointing Judges

154. A veto is .... when the executive veto can be overridden by the legislature by an ordinary majority.
(a) qualified (b) absolute
(c) pocket (d) suspensive

155. The executive vetoes from the stand-point of effect on the legislation can be classified as :
1. Absolute veto 2. Qualified veto
3. Suspensive veto 4. Pocket veto
5. Multiple veto
Which of the above correct? Choose the correct answer from the codes given below :
(a) 1, 2, 3 and 4 (b) 2, 3 and 4
(c) 1, 2 and 4 (d) 2, 4 and 5

156. Which of the following steps is taken by the President when a Bill is presented to him, after its passage in both Houses of Parliament?
(a) He may declare his assent to the Bill
(b) He may declare that he withholds his assent to the Bill
(c) He may, in the case of Bills other than Money Bills, return the Bill for reconsideration of the Houses, with or without a message suggesting amendments
(d) All of the above

157. Which of the following vetoes is a useful device in the United States where the executive has no power of control over the legislature, by prorogation, dissolution or otherwise?
(a) Absolute veto (b) Pocket veto
(c) Suspensive veto (d) Qualified veto

158. The Vice-President acts as the President of India when :
(a) President is sick
(b) President is unable to discharge his duties
(c) President is absent from the country
(d) All of the above

159. Every Proclamation issued under Article 352 is to be laid before :
(a) Lok Sabha
(b) Each House of Parliament
(c) Rajya Sabha
(d) Vice-President

160. Who among the following represents Indian in international affairs?
(a) Union Minister for external affairs
(b) Prime Minister
(c) President
(d) All of the above

161. Which of the following amendments substituted the words 'armed rebellion' for 'internal disturbance' in the Article 352?
(a) 42nd Amendment, 1976
(b) 44th Amendment, 1978
(c) 24th Amendment, 1971
(d) None of the above

162. To whom the President can refer any matter of constitutional law for advice?
(a) Attorney-General
(b) Union Law Minister
(c) Supreme Court
(d) Any of the above

163. No Money Bill can be introduced in Parliament with the previous recommendation of :
(a) Prime Minister
(b) President
(c) Lok Sabha Speaker
(d) Public Accounts Committee

164. What is the period within which an ordinance promulgated by the President should be laid before both Houses of Parliament after they assemble?
(a) Six months (b) Six weeks
(c) Six days (d) Two months

165. The President has the power to summon or prorogue :
(a) Only Lok Sabha

(*b*) Only Rajya Sabha
(*c*) Any House of the Parliament
(*d*) None of the above

166. When a Bill is presented to the president after its passage in both Houses of Parliament, he shall be entitled to :
(*a*) Declare his assent
(*b*) Declare that he withholds his assent
(*c*) Return the non-money bills for reconsideration of the Houses
(*d*) Take any of the steps enumerated in (*a*) (*b*) and (*c*)

167. Who summons a joint sitting of both Houses of Parliament in case of a deadlock between them?
(*a*) Lok Sabha Speaker
(*b*) President of the Republic
(*c*) Prime Minister
(*d*) Either (*a*) or (*b*)

168. Which of the following Articles lays down that "the executive power of the Union shall be vested in the President"?
(*a*) Article 53 (*b*) Article 63
(*c*) Article 73 (*d*) Article 83

169. Which of the following Articles lay down the Ministers can be appointed by the President only on the advice of the Prime Minister?
(*a*) Article 62 (*b*) Article 71
(*c*) Article 74 (*d*) Article 75

170. The executive power which is vested by the Constitution on the President, means :
(*a*) Execution of the laws enacted by the lagislature
(*b*) The power of carrying on the business of government
(*c*) The administration of the affairs of the state
(*d*) All of the above

171. Which article lays down that all officers of the Union shall be President's subordinates?
(*a*) Article 75
(*b*) Article 53
(*c*) Article 78
(*d*) None of the above

172. Disputes cannot be raised in connection with the election of a President or Vice-President on the ground of :
(*a*) Age of the incumbent
(*b*) Domicile status of the incumbent
(*c*) Any vacancy in the electoral college
(*d*) All of the above

173. Who among the following is neither appointed, nor removed by the President?
(*a*) Attorney-General of India
(*b*) Comptroller and Auditor-General
(*c*) Speaker of State Assembly
(*d*) Chairman of a State Public Service Commission

174. In order to be Vice-President, a person must be qualified for election as :
(*a*) A member of the Council of States
(*b*) Speaker of Lok Sabha
(*c*) Chief Election Commissioner
(*d*) None of the above

175. Which of the following Articles prescribed the qualifications for election as Vice-President of India?
(*a*) Article 65 (*b*) Article 66
(*c*) Article 72 (*d*) Article 78

176. The election of the Vice-President shall be indirect and in accordance with :
(*a*) The first-past the post system
(*b*) The list system
(*c*) The system of proportional representation
(*d*) None of the above

177. Which of the following bodies will have no part to play in the election of the Vice-President?
(*a*) Rajya Sabha (*b*) State Legislatures
(*c*) Lok Sabha (*d*) None of the above

178. In which of the following ways a vacancy may arise in the office of the President?
(*a*) Loss of an essential qualification by the incumbent
(*b*) Long and unaccounted absence from the office
(*c*) Setting a side of his election as President
(*d*) All of the above

179. What will happen if the sitting President's term expires while his successor is yet to enter upon his office?
(*a*) Vice-President shall begin to act as President
(*b*) The incumbent shall continue to hold office
(*c*) The incumbent's term shall be increased for one year
(*d*) None of the above

180. Who was the first Vice-President to have been elected for a second term?
(*a*) Dr. S. Radhakrishnan
(*b*) B.D. Jatti
(*c*) Neelam Sanjeeva Reddy
(*d*) Shanker Dayal Sharma

181. Which of the following Articles lay down the norms for the Vice-President?
(*a*) Article-66 (*b*) Article-67
(*c*) Article- 68 (*d*) Article-78

182. When the Vice-President discharges the functions of the President he gets the emoluments :
(*a*) Of the President only
(*b*) Of the Vice-President only
(*c*) Both (*a*) and (*b*)
(*d*) None of the above

183. Determination of doubts and disputes relating to the election of a President or Vice-President is dealt within :
(*a*) Article 71 (*b*) Article 72
(*c*) Article 73 (*d*) Article 74

184. When the Vice-President acts as President his duties as Chairman of the Council of State are performed by :
(*a*) Speaker of Lok Sabha
(*b*) Deputy Speaker of Lok Sabha
(*c*) Deputy Chairman of the Council of States
(*d*) None of the above

185. Under which article of the Constitution, the qualifications for election to the office of the President find mention?
(*a*) Article 55 (*b*) Article 56
(*c*) Article 57 (*d*) Article 58

186. Which article of the Constitution lay down that the President's term of office is five years though he is eligible for re-election?
(*a*) Article-56 (*b*) Article 57
(*c*) Article 56-57 (*d*) Article 58

187. Which of the following Articles prescribe that the President shall not hold any other office of profit?
(*a*) Article 50 (*b*) Article 57
(*c*) Article 59 (*d*) Article 60

188. Which of the following is not a manner in which a vacancy may arise in the office of the President?
(*a*) President's demise
(*b*) President's resignation
(*c*) President's long absence
(*d*) President's removal by impeachment

189. The normal function of the Vice-President is to act as :
(*a*) President, when the President is not able to discharge the duties of his office
(*b*) Deputy Chief of Indian Armed forces
(*c*) Ex-officio Chairman of the Council of States
(*d*) None of the above

190. Article 91 lays down :
(*a*) Conditions necessary for the office of the speaker of the Lok Sabha
(*b*) The situation when the Vice-President may discharge the functions of the President
(*c*) The role of the Deputy Chairman of the Council of States when Vice-President acts as President
(*d*) None of the above

191. President's office may terminate within the term of five years due to his resignation. President has to address the resignation to :
(*a*) Vice-President
(*b*) Prime Minister
(*c*) Speaker of Lok Sabha
(*d*) Any of the above

192. Which Schedule of the Constitution lists the languages recognised by it?
(*a*) Eighth Schedule (*b*) Sixth Schedule
(*c*) Seventh Schedule (*d*) Ninth Schedule

193. Which of the following Union Territories has a Chief Minister?
(*a*) Andaman and Nicobar Islands
(*b*) Puducherry
(*c*) Chandigarh
(*d*) Dadra & Nagar Haveli and Daman & Diu

194. Who among the following administers the Oath of Office to the President of India?
(*a*) The Vice-President of India
(*b*) The Chief Justice of India
(*c*) The Chairman of Rajya Sabha
(*d*) The Prime Minister

195. Parliament of India consists of
(*a*) Directly elected members only
(*b*) Directly elected and nominated members
(*c*) Directly elected and indirectly elected members
(*d*) Directly elected, indirectly elected and nominated members

196. In a Unitary Government
(*a*) All powers are vested in the Centre
(*b*) Powers are divided between the Centre and the States under a Constitution
(*c*) Powers are divided by mutual consent of the Centre and the States through Parliamentary statute
(*d*) The Judiciary must be independent

197. Article 360 of the Constitution of India relates to
(*a*) National Emergency
(*b*) Emergency in a State
(*c*) To conduct Parliament Elections
(*d*) Financial Emergency

198. Panchayati Raj was recommended by
(*a*) Sarkaria Commission
(*b*) Fazlali Commission
(*c*) Balwantrai Mehta Committee
(*d*) Rajamannar Committee

199. Name the first woman Governor of an Indian State
(*a*) Padmaja Naidu
(*b*) Lakshmi N. Menon
(*c*) Sarojini Naidu
(*d*) Sucheta Kriplani

200. Gangtok is the capital of
(*a*) Nagaland
(*b*) Meghalaya
(*c*) Sikkim
(*d*) Arunachal Pradesh

201. Who appoints the Chief Justice of a High Court in India?
(*a*) The President of India
(*b*) The Governor of the State concerned
(*c*) The Chief Justice of the Supreme Court
(*d*) An Appointment Committee in the Union Ministry of Law

202. In India, how did the Planning Commission come into existence?
(*a*) By an Act of Parliament
(*b*) By an executive order
(*c*) Under the provisions of the Constitution
(*d*) As an attached office of the Union Ministry of Finance

203. Which is the first executive tier of the Panchayati Raj system from below?
(*a*) Gram Sabha (*b*) Gram Panchayat
(*c*) Mandal Parishad (*d*) Panchayat Samiti

204. After the Constitution of India, came into force, when did the Parliament enact the Untouch-ability (Offences) Act?
(*a*) 1953 (*b*) 1954
(*c*) 1955 (*d*) 1956

205. Which of the following pairs is ***not*** correctly matched?

	State/U.T.		**High Court**
(*a*)	Goa	—	Bombay
(*b*)	Andaman and Nicobar Islands	—	Calcutta
(*c*)	Sikkim	—	Guwahati
(*d*)	Puducherry	—	Madras

206. The procedure for the Amendment of the Constitution of India is given under
(*a*) Article 315 (*b*) Article 358
(*c*) Article 360 (*d*) Article 368

207. Which of the following Articles of the Constitution of India has provision for the President to proclaim emergency?

(*a*) Article 352 (*b*) Article 355
(*c*) Article 356 (*d*) Article 360

208. Which of the following offices is held during the pleasure of the President of India?

(*a*) Vice-President
(*b*) Chief Justice of India
(*c*) Governor of a State
(*d*) Chairman of the Union Public Service Commission

209. Article 371-A of the constitution is applicable to the state of

(*a*) Jammu & Kashmir
(*b*) Mizoram
(*c*) Manipur
(*d*) Nagaland

210. In the parliamentary practices when did the "Zero-hour" interventions emerge in India?

(*a*) 1952 (*b*) 1962
(*c*) 1972 (*d*) 1982

211. "Vote on Account" means legislative vote

(*a*) On the Appropriation Bill
(*b*) On the Finance Bill
(*c*) On the accounts and audit report submitted by the CAG
(*d*) Authorising expenditure in respect of the demands for grants pending the passing of the Appropriation Bill

212. Which of these words is not in the preamble of the constitution of India?

(*a*) Socialist (*b*) Sovereign
(*c*) Secular (*d*) Public Welfare

213. Which of the following has ***not*** been mentioned in the Indian Constitution as a Right?

(*a*) Political and Social Rights
(*b*) Educational Rights
(*c*) Economic Rights
(*d*) Religious Rights

214. Which one of the following is ***not*** stated in the Preamble of the Indian Constitution?

(*a*) Justice (*b*) Fraternity
(*c*) Adult franchise (*d*) Equality of status

215. In framing the Constitution of India, from which country did we borrow the scheme of the federal set up?

(*a*) Canada (*b*) U.K.
(*c*) U.S.A. (*d*) Switzerland

ANSWERS

1	**2**	**3**	**4**	**5**	**6**	**7**	**8**	**9**	**10**
(*c*)	(*b*)	(*a*)	(*c*)	(*b*)	(*c*)	(*a*)	(*c*)	(*d*)	(*b*)
11	**12**	**13**	**14**	**15**	**16**	**17**	**18**	**19**	**20**
(*b*)	(*c*)	(*d*)	(*a*)	(*d*)	(*d*)	(*c*)	(*b*)	(*d*)	(*c*)
21	**22**	**23**	**24**	**25**	**26**	**27**	**28**	**29**	**30**
(*b*)	(*b*)	(*d*)	(*c*)	(*c*)	(*b*)	(*a*)	(*d*)	(*d*)	(*a*)
31	**32**	**33**	**34**	**35**	**36**	**37**	**38**	**39**	**40**
(*b*)	(*b*)	(*a*)	(*d*)	(*b*)	(*b*)	(*a*)	(*a*)	(*a*)	(*c*)
41	**42**	**43**	**44**	**45**	**46**	**47**	**48**	**49**	**50**
(*a*)	(*d*)	(*c*)	(*b*)	(*d*)	(*a*)	(*c*)	(*a*)	(*d*)	(*c*)
51	**52**	**53**	**54**	**55**	**56**	**57**	**58**	**59**	**60**
(*c*)	(*a*)	(*a*)	(*c*)	(*c*)	(*b*)	(*d*)	(*b*)	(*a*)	(*c*)
61	**62**	**63**	**64**	**65**	**66**	**67**	**68**	**69**	**70**
(*b*)	(*c*)	(*d*)	(*a*)	(*b*)	(*d*)	(*c*)	(*a*)	(*b*)	(*d*)

71	72	73	74	75	76	77	78	79	80
(*b*)	(*d*)	(*b*)	(*c*)	(*b*)	(*d*)	(*a*)	(*a*)	(*b*)	(*d*)
81	**82**	**83**	**84**	**85**	**86**	**87**	**88**	**89**	**90**
(*c*)	(*b*)	(*d*)	(*d*)	(*a*)	(*b*)	(*c*)	(*c*)	(*d*)	(*c*)
91	**92**	**93**	**94**	**95**	**96**	**97**	**98**	**99**	**100**
(*a*)	(*b*)	(*b*)	(*d*)	(*a*)	(*c*)	(*c*)	(*c*)	(*c*)	(*d*)
101	**102**	**103**	**104**	**105**	**106**	**107**	**108**	**109**	**110**
(*b*)	(*d*)	(*a*)	(*a*)	(*c*)	(*a*)	(*b*)	(*a*)	(*c*)	(*a*)
111	**112**	**113**	**114**	**115**	**116**	**117**	**118**	**119**	**120**
(*c*)	(*c*)	(*c*)	(*b*)	(*c*)	(*a*)	(*b*)	(*d*)	(*c*)	(*a*)
121	**122**	**123**	**124**	**125**	**126**	**127**	**128**	**129**	**130**
(*b*)	(*d*)	(*b*)	(*a*)	(*b*)	(*c*)	(*d*)	(*c*)	(*b*)	(*a*)
131	**132**	**133**	**134**	**135**	**136**	**137**	**138**	**139**	**140**
(*d*)	(*d*)	(*a*)	(*b*)	(*d*)	(*a*)	(*c*)	(*d*)	(*b*)	(*d*)
141	**142**	**143**	**144**	**145**	**146**	**147**	**148**	**149**	**150**
(*a*)	(*c*)	(*c*)	(*b*)	(*c*)	(*a*)	(*a*)	(*c*)	(*c*)	(*a*)
151	**152**	**153**	**154**	**155**	**156**	**157**	**158**	**159**	**160**
(*b*)	(*c*)	(*b*)	(*d*)	(*a*)	(*d*)	(*d*)	(*d*)	(*b*)	(*c*)
161	**162**	**163**	**164**	**165**	**166**	**167**	**168**	**169**	**170**
(*b*)	(*c*)	(*b*)	(*b*)	(*c*)	(*d*)	(*b*)	(*a*)	(*d*)	(*d*)
171	**172**	**173**	**174**	**175**	**176**	**177**	**178**	**179**	**180**
(*b*)	(*c*)	(*c*)	(*a*)	(*b*)	(*c*)	(*b*)	(*c*)	(*b*)	(*a*)
181	**182**	**183**	**184**	**185**	**186**	**187**	**188**	**189**	**190**
(*b*)	(*a*)	(*a*)	(*c*)	(*d*)	(*c*)	(*c*)	(*c*)	(*c*)	(*c*)
191	**192**	**193**	**194**	**195**	**196**	**197**	**198**	**199**	**200**
(*a*)	(*a*)	(*b*)	(*b*)	(*d*)	(*a*)	(*d*)	(*c*)	(*c*)	(*c*)
201	**202**	**203**	**204**	**205**	**206**	**207**	**208**	**209**	**210**
(*a*)	(*b*)	(*b*)	(*c*)	(*c*)	(*d*)	(*a*)	(*c*)	(*d*)	(*b*)
211	**212**	**213**	**214**	**215**					
(*d*)	(*d*)	(*c*)	(*c*)	(*a*)					

2408

LEGAL APTITUDE

LAW AND JUDICIARY

Law is a set of rules or body of rules which follow certain custom and regulate human conduct in a society and enforced by penalties or punishments.

The fundamental source of law in India is the Indian Constitution. The Constitution of India is the basic of all governmental organs and institutions, establishes a federal form of government. Constitution establish single set of judiciary which administers both Central as well as State laws. The present Indian law mainly classified into Civil law and Criminal law.

The basic distinction between civil law and criminal law is that former relates to restoration of rights of private individuals and later concern with public wrongs or offences against society.

CLASSIFICATION OF LAW

Law can be classified into different categories like:

- National or municipal law and international law
- Public law and private law
- Criminal law and civil law

I. National or Municipal and International law

The law which is applied within a state to the individuals and corporate entities. For example: the rule or the statutes passed by the Parliament and state legislative is bound to people of India or in other sense, it is applied to only people of that country.

International law is a body of rules which regulate the relationship between the States. Therefore, States have chosen to follow the theory which they themselves considered more appropriate in accordance with their political, social and economic systems for International Law— customary as well as treaties are applied by them in different from state to state/Practice of India in relation to municipal and International law define in Constitution under Art. 51 (Directive principles).

It says that: State shall endeavour to :

a) Promote International peace and security,

b) Maintain just and honourable relations between the States,

c) Foster respect for international law and treaty obligations in the dealings of organized people with one another, and

d) Encourage settlement of international disputes by arbitration.

II. Criminal law and Civil law

Criminal law deal with conduct of a person or public wrongs or offence against the state or society. State prosecutes for criminal offence against wrong doer which is defined in Indian Penal Code, 1860 and Criminal Procedure Code, 1973.

Civil Law involve restoration of right of private individuals or juristic persons like — Companies.

For example:—

Law of Contract

Law of Tort etc.

III. Public law and Private law

Public law deal with the relationship between state and individuals. For example:—

Criminal Law

Constitutional law

Administrative Law

Private Law deals with relations among subjects.

For example:

Hindu Law—deals relations in Hindu

Mohammedan Law—deals relations in Muslim

INDIAN LEGAL SYSTEM

In Ancient India the Main Courts are following:

Kula—Family Court

Shreni—Guild Court

Gana—Area Court

Adikrita—Court appointed by king

Nripa—King's Court

In Modern India, during Muslim Rule, Islamic Courts were established which is mainly derived from the rule and law given in the Quran and the Sunnah (the practice and tradition of the prophet).

After the end of Muslim rule and under British rule the present Indian Judicial Systems were start establishing. Some of the main landmarks development during British region were:

1. Establishment of Mayor's Court 1726
2. Establishment of Supreme Court at Calcutta in 1773
3. Judicial Plan of 1787
4. Judicial Plan of 1790
5. Judicial Plan of 1793
6. Establishment of Provincial Court 1801under this first time Court is recognized as Sadar Diwani Adalat—Civil Court, Sadar Nizamat Adalat—Criminal Court.
7. Privy Council as Court of Appeal in 1883
8. Establishment of High Courts in 1861.

Government of India Act, 1935

Under this Act 'The Federal Court' in 1937 was established and later on this court is the fore runner of the Supreme Court of India in 1950.

Important Feature

1. Supremacy of the Constitution
2. Fundamental Rights to its Citizen
3. A Federal Structure
4. A Sovereign, secular, socialist democratic republic
5. An independent judiciary
6. Rule of Law
7. Common Law system
8. Adversary system of Law
9. Equality before law.

Constitution

Constitution is a set of laws and rules setting up the relationship between Center and state, state and state, define legislative, administrative and judiciary.

Federal Polity

Legislatives are law making body which are existed in both union as well as state.

Common Law System

Common law system recognize precedent as a sources of law.

Adversary System of Law

Judge has the power to only decide the case. He does not take part in the trial.

Rule of Law

The rule of law in the sense of supremacy of law. In a recent judgement of the Supreme Court, Ray, C.J. said that the Constitution is the rule of law and that no one can rise above the rule of law in the Constitution. So, Rule of Law means every action particularly of those of power must be justified by law.

Sources of Law

In primary sense, a source of law means either the manufacture or origin of a law or the ability to impart a rule or norm the equality of law. Sources of law may differ from system to system and society to society. Thus while in common law system Constitution, legislation, precedents and custom are recognized as the legal sources of law, in civil law. Countries legislation, customary law, treaty are recognized as the legal sources of law. So, India governed by Common Law System Constitution. Legislation, precedents and custom are our legal sources of law. In addition to that Hindus and Muslims are governed with their personal laws.

Constitution:—A Constitution may be fundamental law of land. It covered under the generic term legislation but it differs from legislation in so far as legislation find its authority in the Constitution while Constitution is the ultimate source and its authority lies in the political fact that it has been so accepted by the people.

Legislation:—It is the most important and biggest source of law. It consists in making of law by formal and express declaration of new rules by some authority like Parliament, state legislature by passing Acts and ordinances.

Types of legislation:—

Legislation
- Supreme
  - Parliament
  - State Legislatures
- Subordinate (delegated)

Parliament:—Parliament has the power to make laws for whole country on matters assigned to it by the Constitution under Union legislative list contained in the Seventh Schedule of the Constitution.

State Legislatures:—State Legislatures has the power to make laws for a state on the matter assigned to it by the Constitution under State legislative list contained in the Seventh Schedule of the Constitution. On certain matters, both Parliament and state legislatures have power to make laws. These are listed under concurrent list in the seventh schedule of the Constitution. But in certain exception cases, Parliament has the power to make laws for matter in the state list or overrides state laws.

Acts and ordinances

Parliament consists of

President

Rajya Sabha — Lok Sabha

State Legislative consist of

Governor

Legislative Assembly — Legislative Council

Legislative Council only present in six States Bihar, Karnataka, Maharashtra, Uttar Pradesh, Andhra Pradesh and Telangana.

An Act of Parliament is an Act passed by both the Houses of Parliament and assented to by the President.

An Act of State is an Act passed by both the Houses of State and assented to by the Governor.

Ordinance

Ordinance are temporary laws. It promulgated by the President (for the Union) and by the Governor (for the state) when circumstances makes immediate action necessary and Parliament in Union and state legislative is not in session. It is valid only for six months. An act must then be passed to replace the ordinance. Under Article 123 of Constitution, President can promulgate ordinances when parliament is not in session and remains in force for six months.

Delegated Legislation

The legislation made by various authorities such as Universities, Government Departments, Municipalities, Corporations etc. under the authority of the supreme legislation are called subordinate or delegated legislation. In other sense Supreme Legislative made the delegated legislation with some power by rules and order made by the executive. The main reason behind it that legislative can not forsees all situations or may not possess the expertise needed to set out technical matter or may not have time to provide all the details. Therefore for the convenience, out of necessity some power entrusted to executive and called delegated legislation.

Some important feature of delegated legislation

(a) Rules (made by the Central or State Government)
(b) Regulation (usually made by the delegated legislation like Corporations or Board etc.)
(c) Orders and notifications (usually issued by Central or State legislative)
(d) Statutes, Act, ordinance and regulations made by a Universities under the Act.
(e) By laws (made by Local Body)
(f) Schemes

Precedent

In common law system like Indian law precedent constitutes a very important source of law. In law, when Supreme Court or High Court decide a case and decision of these Supreme Court or High Courts as guides is the moulding of future decisions. The law laid down by the Supreme Court has been made binding on all courts in India by express Provision in Article 141 of the Constitution. The decision of Supreme Court is binding upon all the courts in India. So, in India there is no duality in judiciary and for a successful operation of the doctrine of precedent as a source of law it is absolute necessary that there should be a hierarchy of court and it proper reporting of their decisions the hierarchy of courts makes the precedents of the higher courts binding on the lower ones and the system of reporting makes these precedents easily accessible. At the apex is the Supreme Court, below that the High Courts and below that the district courts and other Courts.

The High Courts are not subject to the administrative control of the Supreme Court but certainly there are inferior to it while the lower judiciary is also within the administrative control of different High Courts within whose jurisdiction they fall.

Custom

Custom is the most ancient sources of law and held most important place in the developing the law system of any country. Custom means uniformity of conduct of people under like circumstances. It is an unwritten law of the place and the people where it obtains, certain practices are accepted by the people as good or beneficial or apt and they go on practicing them which in course of time acquire the force of law.

Custom has significance in the following branches of law:—

i. In the law relating to certain commercial transactions like negotiable instruments.

ii. Usage has also recognition in the law of lease.

iii. In family law like:

Hindu Marriage Act, 1955

Hindu Succession Act, 1956

adopted custom as a rule of law.

Law Commission of India

The Law Commissions of India is a non-statutory body. Commission recommend to the Government, reform of important law, particularly those of general application and importance. The commission is an advisory body. The Commission prepared the draft on all subjects like criminal or civil matters but could not impress the Government to get them passed. Final decision is taken by the Government.

The First Law Commission was appointed in 1835. Lord Macauley was its Chairman. First time the recommendations of the Commission was accepted in 1850. The Caste Disabilities Removal Act, 1850 was passed which abrogated the Hindu and the Mohammedan laws to the extent to which they affected any right of inheritance on the ground that a person had renounced his religion or caste.

After independence Law Minister, Shri C.C. Biswas, on 5 August 1955 announced in the Lok Sabha the Government of India's decision to appoint a law commission, its membership and the terms of reference. The Commission consisted of seven member with Shri M.C. Setalvad as its Chairman.

Initially the Commission was appointed upto 31 December 1956 but later its term was extended upto 30 September 1958. The Commission was asked

1. To review the system of judicial administration in all its aspects and suggest ways and means for improving it and making it speedy and less expensive.

2. To examine the Central Acts of general application and importance, and recommend the line on which they should be amended, revised.

INDIAN JUDICIAL SYSTEM

The present day judicial system in India is divided into mainly two part, higher judiciary such as Supreme Court and High Court and the lower judiciary such as District Court, Subordinate Court etc.

Hierarchy of Courts

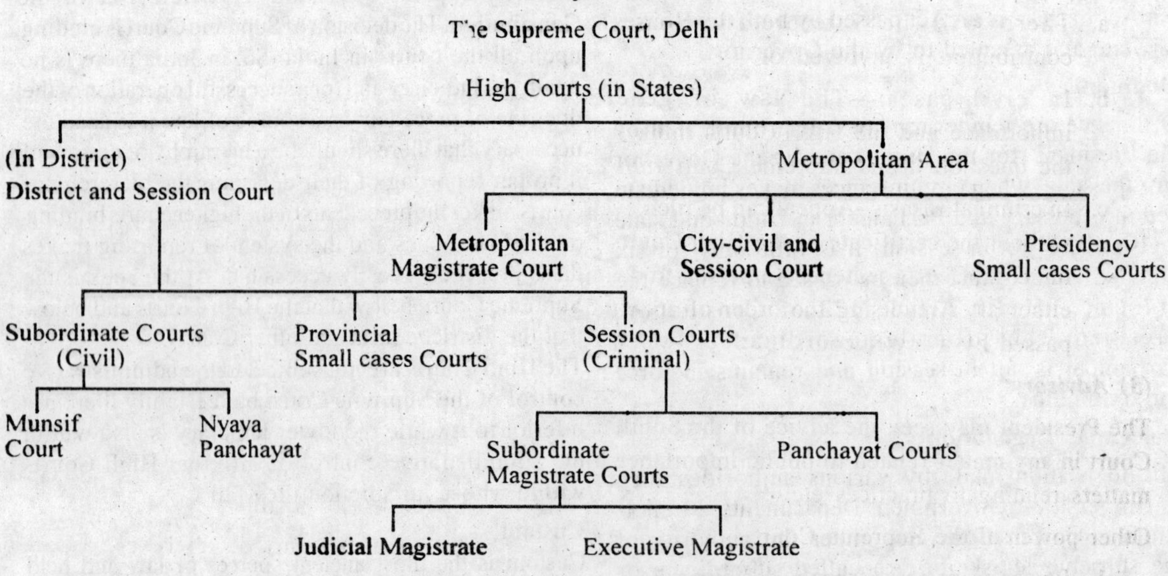

The Supreme Court

Supreme Court seat in New Delhi is the highest court of the land. It was inaugurated on 28th January 1950. The Supreme Court consists of the Chief justice and 33 other judges. The salary and perquisites are provided in the Constitution and fixed by the Parliament. The Chief Justice and other judges to be appointed by the President of India from amongst the Indian citizens who have been in one or more High Courts as judge for 5 years or advocates for ten years or one distinguished jurists in the opinion of the President. A judge holds his office upto the age of sixty-five years unless he resigns earlier or is removed. The jurisdiction and power of the Supreme Courts are very wide. Its jurisdiction may be classified as follows:

(1) Original

a. Exclusive original jurisdiction—Dispute between the Centre and the States and between the States.

b. To enforce fundamental rights.

(2) Appellate

It has the jurisdiction to hear appeals against the decision of the High Courts if High Courts certified it and if

a. There will be interpretation of the contribution is involved or

b. In civil cases:—The law of general importance and the High Courts think that the question needs Supreme Court ruling.

c. In criminal cases:—Appeal can be filed even without the certificate of the High Courts if the High Courts sentenced a person to death either after reversing the order of acquittal passed by a lower court.

(3) Advisory

The President may seek the advice of the Supreme Court in any matter related to public importance or matters relating to practices etc.

Other power of the Supreme Court

1. Power to review its own decisions.
2. Jurisdiction of the Supreme Court may further be enlarge by a law of Parliament.
3. The Supreme Court is a Court of record.
4. The law declared by it is binding on all courts within the territory of India.
5. Jurisdiction to decide election petitions in President and Vice-President.

The High Courts

The Constitution said that there must be a High Court for each State but a common High Court may also be established for two or more States and its jurisdiction may be extended to any union territory. Every High Court consists of a Chief Justice and such other judges as the President may from time to time appoint. An India citizen who has been for ten years either in the judicial service or an advocate in any High Court can be appointed as a judge and hold this office till the age of sixty two years unless he resigns earlier or is removed.

Jurisdiction of the High Courts

1. Some High Courts have both original as well as appellate jurisdiction but some other High Courts have only appellate jurisdiction.
2. High Court is a Court of record.
3. It has the power of superintendence over all courts within its territorial jurisdiction.
4. The decisions of the High Court and the law laid down by it are binding upon all courts subordinate to that High Court although for other High Courts and the courts subordinate to such other High Courts these decisions or laws have only persuasive value.
5. Jurisdiction to decide election petition.
6. Acting as a court of confirmation in all cases where the court of session has passed a sentence of death.
7. Acting as a court of reference under the matter related to direct taxes.
8. Acting as a court of reference under the matter related to the validity of Act.

Case:—

(*Keshavananda Bharati* v. *State of Kerala,* AIR 1773 SC 2299)

The Controversy regarding amendment of fundamental rights and the Preamble was settled by the Supreme Court. Under this case Supreme Court held that:—

a. The preamble can not be amended in exercise of power under Article 368 of Constitution

b. Preamble is a part of Constitution

c. Parliament cannot amend the Basic Principle of the Constitution

Further in *Minerva Mills'* case 1980 the doctrine of basic principle reaffirmed.

(*Minerva Mills* v. *Union of India,* AIR 1980 SC 1789)

Writs

There is provision in the Constitution for empowering the Supreme Court or the High Courts to issue the writs. The incidents of the several kinds of writs which our Supreme Court and the High Courts are authorized by the Constitution- to issue may be noted.

(1) Habeas Corpus

A writ of habeas corpus is in the nature of an order, the court secures the body of a person who has been imprisoned to be brought before itself to obtain knowledge of the reason why he has been imprisoned and to set him free if there is no lawful justification for the imprisonment.

The word habeas corpus means to have a body:

It may be addressed to any person like an official or a private person

Disobedience to the writ is met with the punishment for contempt of court.

For the enforcement of Fundamental rights. Under Article 21 which says that no person shall be deprived of his life or personal liberty except according to procedure established by law.

It will be issued where the order of imprisonment or detention is ultra vires.

The writ can not be issued in following cases:

1. When the person against whom the writ is issued is not within jurisdiction of the court.
2. To interfere with a proceeding for contempt by a court of record or by Parliament.
3. To secure the release of a person who has been imprisoned by a court of law on a criminal charge.

(2) Mandamus

It commands the person to whom it is addressed to performs some public or quasi public legal duty which he has refused to perform and the performance of which cannot be enforced by any other adequate legal remedy.

- Mandamus literally means a command.
- Mandamus will enforce against officers and other persons who are bound to do a public duty.
- It issued against Government order Article 226 and Article 361 of the Constitution.
- It issued against inferior court or other judicial body when they have refused to exercise their jurisdiction.
- For the enforcement of fundamental rights, when a public officer or a Government has done some act which violates the fundamental right of a person.

Mandamus for High Court

i. The Court may issue mandamus directing the public officer to perform or to exercise the power in case he refuses to do it.

ii. It directing or to compel any person to perform his public duty where duty is given him by the Constitution or a statute.

iii. To compel a court or judicial tribunal to exercise its jurisdiction when it has refused to exercise it.

iv. To direct a public official or the Government not to expose a law which is unconstitutional.

Mandamus will not be granted to the following persons:

- The President or the Governor of the State
- Mandamus does not lie against a private individual or body whether incorporated or not except where the state is in collusions with such private party.

(3) Prohibition

The writ of prohibition is issued by the Supreme Court or High Court to lower court forbidding the latter to continue proceedings therein in excess of its jurisdiction. The object of the writ is to compel lower court to keep themselves within the limits of their jurisdiction.

The difference between Mandamus and prohibition is that Mandamus can be issued against any person, government or judicial body but prohibition is issued only against judicial body.

(4) Certiorari

The prohibition is available against at an earlier stage but certiorari is available at a later stage on the similar ground.

- The Prohibition and certiorari are both issued against courts or tribunals or quasi-judicial powers.
- Certiorari is issued to quash the order or decision of judicial or quasi-judicial bodies.
- Prohibition is issued to prohibit the judicial bodies from making ultra vires order.
- Prohibition is available during the pendency of the proceedings and before the order is made, certiorari can be issued only after the order has been made.

(5) Quo Warranto

Quo Warranto is proceeding whereby the court enquires into the legality of the claim or with what authority or warrant. It classifies in public interest the legal position in regard to claim of a person to hold a public office.

SYSTEM OF TRIAL IN INDIAN JUDICIAL SYSTEM

The system of trial a case in India is the adversary system in contrast with inquisitorial system. Under the adversary system the judge does not take an active part in the trial and most of the questioning in done by the counsel for the opposite parties. Both in civil as well as criminal cases. In the inquisitorial system on the other hand. the judge plays an active role in the conduct of the trial and in the examination of witnesses.

Civil Courts and Criminal Courts

Each state is divided into District. The District Judge is the highest judicial authority (civil and criminal) in the district. He hears appeals from the decisions of the superior Magistrates and also tries the more serious criminal cases, known as the sessions courts. A subordinate judge is sometimes vested also with the powers of an Assistance session judge, in which cases he contributes in his hands both civil and criminal power like a District Judge.

There are special arrangements for civil judicial administration in the metropolitan areas. The original side of the High Courts tries the biggest civil suits arising within the area of metropolitan areas. Suits of lower value within the city are tried by the city civil courts and the presidency small cause court.

The criminal court is enacted by the enactment of the Criminal Procedure Code, 1973, the trial of criminal cases is done exclusively by judicial Magistrate except in Jammu & Kashmir and Nagaland to which that codes does not apply.

The following criminal courts are constituted:

(i) The court of session.

(ii) The courts of Metropolitan Magistrates in metropolitan area headed by the Chief Metropolitan Magistrate.

(iii) The courts of Magistrates of the First class outside the metropolitan area headed by the Chief Judicial Magistrate.

(iv) The court of magistrates of the second class under the Chief Judicial Magistrate.

(v) The courts of Executive Magistrate headed by the District Magistrate.

Judicial Review

Judicial review is a kind of power that the court exercise in examining the legality of legislative and executive actions.

Natural Justice

This doctrine is adopted by the court for fair trial and administrative action which affects private rights is taken after a fair hearing.

Two essential conditions:

a. No one can be condemned unheared, and

b. No person can be a judge in his own cause

Family Court

Family courts have been established under the Family Court Act, 1984. The main aim to promote family court for securing speedy settlement of dispute relating to marriage and family affairs. A peculiar feature of the family court is that they exclude representation by lawyers.

Legal Aid

Under Article 39A of the Constitution, it has been inserted to enjoin the state to provide free legal aid to the poor and to take other suitable steps to ensure equal justice to all which is offered by the preamble.

The Constitutional guarantee of political, economical, social and cultural justice are meaningless unless there is some mechanism whereby the poor and downtrodden sections of society are informed about their legal rights and have a means to enforce them.

Legal aid has following advantages:

i. Creation of legal awareness among the masses about their legal rights.

ii. It would spread among the people a consciousness of their rights and duties.

iii. It will strengthen respect for law which is a great asset in a democratic society.

iv. It would act as a shield against exploitation.

v. It may enhance the respect for the rule of law.

Lok Adalats

Lok Adalats were initiated by ex-Chief Justice of Supreme Court, P.N. Bhagwati. Lok Adalats are para-judicial institutions which resolve disputes outside the traditional judicial system and provide a speedy and inexpensive justice. The institution of Lok-Adalat falls within the broad ambit of legal aid and meant for the masses-the poor, down trodden and even the middle classes. These Adalats are organized by public spirited social workers. The Lok-Adalat judges come from amongst retired judges, Public spirited lawyers and Law teachers. The inspiration for these courts have come from the functioning of Nyaya Panchayats.

In Lok Adalats, technical court procedures are not followed. No fee to be paid and there is no limitation period regarding filing of cases. But they are still comparable to courts because of the sanctity of their decisions. The decisions are final and binding on the parties with no right to appeal.

Nyaya Panchayat

With the advent of independence the village Panchayats, which had strong roots in our ancient political legal system, and remained at a very low level during the British rule, were revived with full zeal. A provision was made in Article 40 of the Constitution (Directive Principle) asking the state to take steps to organise village Panchayats and endow them with such powers and authority as may be necessary to enable them to function as units of self-government. With the 73rd Amendment to the Constitution, the village Panchayats have been given a Constitutional status.

With the result almost every state has enacted legislation to regulate the composition, Constitution and powers of village Panchayats. The Nyaya Panchayats are the judicial component of the Panchayat System. They are the lowest rung of our judiciary created for the dispensation of justice at the local rural level. But, unfortunately the Constitution does not talk about Nyaya Panchayats as part of the Panchayat system. According to the latest reports, they are functioning only in a handful of States and even in them the composition and powers of this institution varies.

Advantages of Nyaya Panchayats

i. Relief to regular Courts

ii. Speedy Justice

iii. Inexpensive Justice

iv. Convenient Justice

v. Recognition of local customs and tradition

vi. No financial burden on the state

vii. Improvement in the quality of justice

LEGAL PROFESSION

Development of Legal Profession

The development of legal profession in India can be classified under two broad categories.

1. Pre-Independence development.
2. Post-Independence development.

Pre-Independence Development

Legal profession in its modern form really began during the British regime—

1. Establishment of Mayor's Court
2. Charter of the Supreme Court, 1774
3. Company's Court under Judicial Plan, 1793
4. High Court Act, 1861
5. The Legal Practitioners Act, 1879
6. The Legal Practitioners (Women) Act, 1923
7. Chamier Committee, 1923
8. Indian Bar Council Act-1926

Post-Independence Development

1. All India Bar Committee-1951
2. The Advocates Act-1961

Bar Council of India

Composition:—The Bar Council of India consists of:

1. The Attorney-General of India
2. The Solicitor-General of India
3. One member elected by each State Bar Council from amongst its members.

Committees:—The Bar Council of India has been authorized to constitute one or more of the following Committees:

a. Executive Committee

b. Disciplinary Committee

c. Enrolment Committee

d. Legal Education Committee

e. Legal Aid Committee

f. One or more Committee for the purpose of carrying out the provisions of the Act.

State Bar Councils

Composition:—A State Bar Council consists of 15-25 members elected from amongst advocates on the electoral roll of that Bar Council.

Committees:—Every States bar council has the following Committees:

a. Executive Committee

b. Enrolment Committee

c. One or more disciplinary committees

d. One or More Legal aid Committees

e. Committees for special projects.

Points to Remember

- Basic sources of law is the Constitution.
- Federal structure government but single structure judiciary.
- Indian Law mainly classified in civil law and criminal law.
- Main sources of law is Constitution, Legislation, Precedents and customs.
- The First Law Commission is appointed in 1835.
- Law Commission is an advisory body.
- First recommendation of the Law Commission was accepted in 1850.
- The Caste Disabilities Removal Act, 1850 is accepted by the Government.
- After independence First Law Commission Committee appointed in 1950 under the Chairmanship of the M.C. Setalvad.
- Supreme Court is the Apex Court of India.
- Supreme Court is inaugurated on 28th January 1950.
- Supreme Court consists of one Chief Justice and 33 other judges.
- The Chief Justice and other judges are appointed by the President.
- Judge of Supreme Court hold his office upto the age of sixty-five years.
- Supreme Court has jurisdictions—original, appellate and advisory.

- Decision of Supreme Court binding upon all other lower courts.
- Supreme Court has the power to decide election petitions in President and Vice-President election.
- Judge of the High Court hold his office upto the age of sixty-two years.
- There are five types of writ like Habeas Corpus, Mandamus, Prohibition, Certiorari and Quo Warranto.
- System of trial in Indian Judicial System is the adversary system.
- The criminal court is enacted by the Criminal Procedure Code 1973.
- The civil court is enacted by Civil Procedure Code 1908.
- Criminal Procedure Code 1973 apply in all over India except Jammu & Kashmir and Nagaland.
- Family court establish under the Family Court Act 1984.
- Legal Aid is inserted under article 394 of the Constitution.
- Lok Adalats were initiated by Ex-Chief Justice of Supreme Court P.N. Bhagwati.
- Lok-Adalats are para-judicial institutions.

MULTIPLE CHOICE QUESTIONS

1. How many High Courts are functioning in India?

A. 25 B. 20
C. 18 D. 19

2. Delegated legislation is also known as ....

A. Presidential legislation
B. State legislation
C. Subordinate legislation
D. Legislation by the judiciary

3. How many States have legislative Council?

A. 4 B. 6
C. 3 D. 5

4. In Delegated Legislation, the power of legislation is entrusted to:

A. Prime Minister
B. President
C. The organ other than the Legislation
D. All of the above

5. First Law Officer of India:

A. Chief Justice of India
B. President
C. Chairman of Law Commission of India
D. Attorney-General of India

6. Writ of Prohibition and Certiorari are available against:

A. the Legislative
B. the Act passed by the Central government
C. the decision of administrative tribunals
D. None of these

7. Child labour is prohibited in India for:

A. Any type of employment
B. Hazardous Industries
C. Both (A) and (B)
D. None of these

8. The State can be sued and sue in its own name under:

A. Article 74
B. Article 300
C. Article 299
D. Article 51

9. Jai Hind at first time used by:

A. Mahatma Gandhi
B. Bhagat Singh
C. Chandra Shekhar Azad
D. Subhash Chandra Bose

10. In which among the following cases the Supreme Court held that incorporation of National Anthem in the film "*Kabhi Khushi Kabhi Ghum*" is unprecented:

A. *M.A. Murthy* v. *State of Karnataka*, AIR 2003 SC 45

B. *Shyam Narayan Cherksey* v. *Union of India*, AIR 2003 MPL 33

C. *Karan Johar* v. *Union of India* (2003) 8 SSC 717

D. *Abdul Ghaffar Khan* v. *Vasan Raghunath Bhosle* (2003) 7 SSC 749

11. India has borrowed the concept of Parliamentary form of government from:

A. USA

B. Germany

C. Switzerland

D. United Kingdom

12. State function consist of:

A. Sovereign function

B. Non-Sovereign function

C. Both (A) and (B)

D. None of these

13. The Ordinance used by the Governor are subject to the approval of:

A. Parliament

B. President

C. Advocate-General

D. State Legislative

14. The first Constitutional amendment related to:

A. Preamble

B. Directive Principles

C. Fundamental Duties

D. Ninth Schedule

15. Can the Governor has power to reserve certain state Bill for Presidential assent:

A. It depends upon the President's prior approval

B. It depends upon the Parliament's prior approval

C. Yes

D. Both (A) and (B)

16. In which of the following cases Supreme Court laid down extensive guidelines on sexual harassment?

A. *Shyam Narayan Chaubey* v. *Union of India* AIR 2003 SC 233

B. *D.K. Basu* v. *State of West Bengal*

C. *Vishakha* v. *State of Rajasthan*

D. None of these

17. In which of the following cases Supreme Court held that the right of an Advocate to appear and conduct cases in courts is still within the control and jurisdiction of courts:

A. *Radhe Mohanlal* v. *Rajasthan High Court*, (2003) 3 SCC 427

B. *Ex-Capt Harish Uppal* v. *Union of India*, AIR 2003 SC 739

C. *Ram Narayan Popli* v. *C.B.I.*, (2003) 3 SCC 641

D. *Dr. Chanchal Goyal* v. *State of Rajasthan*, (2003) 3 SCC 485

18. Income tax in India is:

1. Progressive tax
2. Indirect tax
3. Proportional tax
4. Direct tax

A. 1 and 4 B. 1 and 2

C. 1, 2 and 3 D. All of the above

19. The Speaker of Lok Sabha can be removed from his office before the expiry of his term:

A. if the Lok Sabha passes a resolution to this effect

B. by the President on the recommendation of Prime Minister

C. if the Lok Sabha and the Prime Minister so decide

D. if both the Houses of Parliament pass a resolution to this effect

20. Which among the following are two classes of advocates in India?

A. Lawyer and trainee advocates

B. Advocates and Senior advocates

C. Lawyers and Attorneys

D. Barristers and Solicitors

21. In which of the following cases Supreme Court recognized Right Against Torture and laid down extensive 'Prison Guidelines'?

A. *Vishakha* v. *State of Rajasthan*

B. *D.K. Basu* v. *State of West of Bengal*

C. *CPI (M)* v. *Bharat Kr.*

D. None of these

22. Which among the provisions provides for right of Pre-audience of Senior advocates among others?

A. Sec. 23 of Bar Council Act

B. Art. 23 of the Constitution

C. Sec. 23 of the Advocates Act

D. Rule 23 of Supreme Court Rule

23. In which year the National Flag of India was first displayed?

A. 1935 B. 1907

C. 1906 D. 1936

24. In which of the following cases Supreme Court upheld the ban imposed on 'Bandhs' by Kerala High Courts?

A. *Vishakha* v. *State of Rajasthan*

B. *D.K. Basu* v. *State of West Bengal*

C. *CPI (M)* v. *Bharat Kumar*

D. None of these

25. In which of the following Article of the Constitution of India Specifies the ordinance making power of President?

A. Article 300 B. Article 213

C. Article 113 D. Article 299

26. Citizenship by Descent means

A. On or after 10th December 1992 if either of the parents is an Indian Citizen at the time of his birth

B. A person born outside India on or after 26th January 1950 and 10th December 1992 and if father is Indian Citizen

C. (a) is correct

D. Either (A) or (B)

27. In the advice given by the Supreme Court on matter to it by the President binding under Advisory opinion

A. Yes

B. No

C. Depend upon the matter of the advice

D. None of the above

28. Who headed the 9 (nine) judge bench of Supreme Court advisory opinion upon the 9 (nine) questions referred to by President with regard to the controversy regarding appointment of judges raised by Justice M.M. Punchhi, the then Chief Justice of India?

A. A.S. Anand J.

B. G.T. Nanavati J.

C. Sujata V. Manohar J.

D. None of these

29. Lawyers are officers of the court and are constituted into an independent profession under the

A. Advocates Act, 1961

B. Bar Council Act, 1926

C. The Legal Practitioners Act, 1879

D. Advocates Act, 1951

30. Which article empowers the Supreme Court to determine disputes between Union and States and between States:

A. Article 142 B. Article 132

C. Article 141 D. Article 131

31. Who introduced public Litigation in India?

A. Justice A.S. Anand

B. Justice P.N. Bhagwati

C. Justice G.T. Nanavati

D. Justice M.N. Venkatachaliah

32. In which of the following posts there is no provision under the Constitution of India

A. Governor

B. Vice President

C. Deputy Prime Minister

D. Deputy Speaker

33. For which among the following States who organized on a linguistic basic in India:

A. Andhra Pradesh

B. Karnataka

C. Madhya Pradesh

D. Tamil Nadu

34. Though the Constitution of India provides for the federal system of Government, India has:

A. Multiple judiciary system

B. Single judiciary system

C. Dual judiciary system

D. None of the above

35. Under the Public Interest Litigation who can move the Court?

A. Only authorised person

B. Any Public spirited person

C. A recognized Social workers

D. None of the above

36. Gram Sabha means:

A. A body consisting of persons registered in the electoral rolls of a block

B. A body consisting of persons registered in the electoral roll of a village within the area of Gram Panchayat

C. Both (A) and (B)

D. None of the above

37. What is the minimum number of judges of Supreme Court who must sit together to constitute a Constitutional Bench?

A. 4 B. 5

C. 6 D. 7

38. What is true about banker's cheque?

A. A cheque is a bill of exchange and includes the electronic image of truncated cheque and a cheque in an electronic form

B. a cheque given by bank to a customer

C. a cheque is a bill of exchange only

D. None of these

39. An appeal from the decision of Supreme Court lies to:

A. Privy Council

B. King's Bench

C. Tribunal

D. None of these

40. Total number of judge in the Supreme Court including the Chief Justice of India:

A. 25 B. 34

C. 27 D. 28

41. National Income estimates are prepared by:

A. NITI Aayog

B. By Census Department

C. Central Statistical Organization

D. Indian Statistical Institute

42. Minimum age to qualify for the President's post is:

A. 35 years B. 21 years

C. 25 years D. 30 years

43. Which article of the Constitution deals with the amendment Provision?

A. Article 374

B. Article 369

C. Article 375

D. Article 368

44. Once appointed judges of Supreme Court serve till they attain the age of:

A. 62 B. 63

C. 65 D. 66

45. Zonal councils are:

A. Para-judiciary body

B. Judiciary body

C. Advisory body

D. Power to settle the dispute between States

46. Citizen by birth means a person who has taken birth in India:

A. On or after 26th January 1950 but before 1st July 1987

B. On or after 1st July 1987 and either of parents is a citizen of India by birth

C. Only (A) is correct

D. Both (A) and (B) are correct

47. Eligibility of a person who enrolled as an advocate, he must be:

A. 25 years of age after passing his LL.B. degree

B. 21 years of age after passing his LL.B. degree

C. Only after passing his LL.B. degree

D. 30 years of age after passing his LL.B. degree

48. The Supreme Court is situated at New Delhi, but it can meet elsewhere if:

A. Parliament give the assent

B. President so orders

C. Majority of judges so decide

D. Case fall under the belonging state

49. An elected candidate to Parliament or State legislative has to furnish information about:

A. His assets, liabilities to public financial institution and liability to Central or State Government

B. Only criminal charge is furnished

C. Only his assets and debt

D. None of these

50. Who is the sources of legal authority of India?

A. Parliament

B. President

C. People of India

D. Constitution of India

51. Mukherjee Commission formed under the subject for:

A. Indira Gandhi Assassination Case

B. Disappearance of Subhash Chandra Bose

C. Assassination of Rajiv Gandhi

D. Bofors Case

52. The Symbol (v.) in case names stand for:

A. versus B. for

C. and D. Both (A) and (B)

53. Ossification test is done to determine:

A. Blood group of a person

B. Sex of a person

C. Age of a person

D. Physical condition of a person

54. Name of a Union territory which has a High Court of its own:

A. Delhi

B. Dadar & Nagar Haveli and Daman & Diu

C. Chandigarh

D. Andaman & Nicobar Islands

55. Right of Education under the Constitution of India is fall under the:

A. Directive Principle of state policy

B. Fundamental Right

C. Both (A) and (B)

D. None of these

56. What is the minimum age prescribed by law to drive a vehicle at any public place?

A. 16 years

B. 18 years

C. 16 years in case of motor cycle of blow 50CC capacity and 18 years for any other vehicle

D. 21 years

57. The Rule of Basic structures was propounded by the Supreme Court in:

A. Keshavanand Bharati case

B. Maneka Gandhi case

C. A.K. Gopalan case

D. Golak Nath case

58. The Advocates Act is suffixed by the year:

A. 1961 B. 1962

C. 1981 D. 1982

59. It is the Fundamental rights of the Consumers to know whether the food products, cosmetics and drugs are of non-vegetarian or vegetarian origin otherwise it will violate the Fundamental right of the article 19(1)(a), 21 and 25 of the Constitution of India. This decision of Supreme Court related to the case

A. *Madhya Pradesh* v. *Ghanshyam Singh* (2003) 8 SCC 13

B. *Bhupender Sharma* v. *State of Himachal Pradesh* (2003) 8 SCC 551

C. *Ozair Hussain* v. *Union of India* AIR 2003 SC 447

D. *Justice K.P. Mohapatra* v. *Shri Ram Chandra Nayak* (2002) 8 SCC 1

60. Supreme Court decided that legislative power of a state or Union is subject to the fundamental rights and the legislature cannot indirectly take away or abridge fundamental rights which it could not do directly for granting either recognition or aid to minority institution. In which case above decision relates to

A. TMA Pai Foundation v. *Union of India*

B. Ozair Hussain v. *Union of India* 2003

C. Vikash Despandey v. *Bar Council of India* 2003

D. TMA Pai Foundation v. *State of Karnataka* 2003

61. A sentence of death by a lower Court

A. must be approved by the President of India

B. must be confirmed by the High Court of that state

C. must be continued by the Supreme Court

D. None of the above

62. Who said " Law is not in intellectual legerdemain to make black appear white and white appear black but it is careless endeavour to enthrone justice."

A. M.K. Gandhi

B. Jawahar Lal Nehru

C. Justice Oliver W. Holmes

D. Subhash Chandra Bose

63. Ancient treatise on law is given in

A. Vedas B. Shrutis

C. Upanishads D. Smritis

64. Who said, "Law and sense are not the same thing."

A. M.K. Gandhi

B. Jawahar Lal Nehru

C. Subhash Chandra Bose

D. Lala Lajpat Rai

65. "Interpretation of Statutes" falls under .... jurisdiction of Supreme Court of India"

A. Appellate jurisdiction

B. Original jurisdiction

C. Advisory jurisdiction

D. Civil Jurisdiction

66. "Ultra Vires" is a term which means

A. An illegal act

B. A document contains corruption Act

C. An act beyond the authority of law

D. An act by the authority of law which is legal

67. All plans formulated by planning commission must be approved by

A. President

B. Chief Justice of Supreme Court

C. Parliament

D. National Development Council

68. In which of the following cases the Supreme Court declared unconstitutional that the 39th Constitutional Amendment laid that election of any person to Lok Sabha holding the office of Prime Minister cannot be challenged before a Court of law but only before an authority established by Parliament.

A. Maneka Gandhi Case

B. Keshavananda Bharti Case

C. Golaknath Case

D. *Indira Gandhi* v. *Raj Narain Case*

69. In which case, Supreme Court held that preamble is a basic feature of the Constitution and Parliament has no power to amend Fundamental Rights?

A. Keshavananda Bharti case

B. Minerva Mill case

C. Golaknath Case

D. Shankari Prasad case

70. Which of the following ancient books can be explained as legal code?

A. Vedas B. Smritis

C. Arthashastra D. Upanishads

71. The National Judicial Academy which provides training to judicial officers is situated at

A. Delhi B. Kolkata

C. Mumbai D. Hyderabad

72. The President of India forms an integral part of the legislative process of Central Government because

A. Without his assent no Central Bill can become law

B. He is executive head of Union

C. He appoint/administers oath member of Parliament

D. None of these

73. President is the executive head of the Union such power has given to him by

A. Parliament

B. Supreme Court of India

C. Constitution of India

D. None of these

74. Supreme Court can grant special leave to appeal against decisions of lower courts and tribunals by virtue of

A. Section 25 of the Supreme Court Rule

B. Article 174 of the Constitution

C. Section 20 of the Supreme Court Rule

D. Article 136 of the Constitution

75. Each High Court is called a Court of Record which means

A. Keeps records of various decisions in the state

B. It has power to determine questions about its own jurisdiction

C. The High Court have no such type of Court

D. None of the above

76. Which of the following is not a source of law in India?

A. Legislation

B. Precedent

C. Custom

D. Public Opinion

77. A wrongful assumption of public office is vacated by writ of

A. Certiorari

B. Prohibition

C. Quo warranto

D. Mandamus

78. A command by Court asking a public authority to perform its public duty is called by writ of

A. Certiorari

B. Prohibition

C. Mandamus

D. Quo Warranto

79. Which writ quashes the order of a lower Court which has been without jurisdiction?

A. Certiorari B. Prohibition

C. Mandamus D. Quo Warranto

80. Who was the first Chief Justice of Independent India?

A. H.J. Kania B. S.R. Das

C. S.M. Sikri D. M.H. Beg

ANSWERS

1	2	3	4	5	6	7	8	9	10
A	C	B	C	D	C	B	B	D	B
11	**12**	**13**	**14**	**15**	**16**	**17**	**18**	**19**	**20**
D	C	D	D	C	C	B	A	A	B
21	**22**	**23**	**24**	**25**	**26**	**27**	**28**	**29**	**30**
B	C	B	C	B	D	B	A	A	D
31	**32**	**33**	**34**	**35**	**36**	**37**	**38**	**39**	**40**
B	C	A	B	B	B	B	C	D	B
41	**42**	**43**	**44**	**45**	**46**	**47**	**48**	**49**	**50**
C	A	D	C	C	D	B	C	A	D
51	**52**	**53**	**54**	**55**	**56**	**57**	**58**	**59**	**60**
B	A	C	A	B	C	A	A	C	A
61	**62**	**63**	**64**	**65**	**66**	**67**	**68**	**69**	**70**
B	A	D	B	A	C	D	D	A	C
71	**72**	**73**	**74**	**75**	**76**	**77**	**78**	**79**	**80**
B	A	C	D	B	D	C	C	A	A

SOME IMPORTANT LAWS

THE LAW OF TORTS

Nature

The word "tort" is derived from the Latin word tortum meaning "twist".

Definition

Salmond defined "A tort is a civil wrong for which the remedy is an action for damages and which is not exclusively the breach of contract or the breach of trust or breach of merely equitable obligation".

Winfield defined " Tortuous liability arise from the breach of a duty primarily fixed by the law : this duty is towards the persons generally and its breach is redressible by an action for unliquidated damages"

So, in order to constitute a tort, the following conditions are to be satisfied:

(1) There must be wrongful act by the defendant.

(2) The wrongful act must cause legal damage to the plaintiff.

(3) Some legal remedy in the from of an action for damages must be available.

The basic principle behind it is "*ubi jus ibi remedium*" (where there is a right there is a remedy). Therefore, to ensure there is right with a remedy if there is infringement of right.

Legal Damages

It is not every harm or damage which is the basis for an action in tort, it must be a harm or damage is the eyes of law. The two maxims:

a) Injuria Sine Damnum and

b) Damnum Sine Injuria;

explain the real nature of legal damage.

Injuria Sine Damnum

Injuria means a wrongful act ***Sine*** means is thought ***Damnum*** means damages in a wide sense. So it means injury or violation of a legal right without causing any damage, harm or loss to the plaintiff.

Damnum Sine Injuria

It means that the plaintiff may suffer actual or substantial loss without any violation or infringement of legal right and therefore no action lies in such cases.

General defences

There are certain defences provided against the tortuous liability. There are:

Volenti non fit injuria

It is the general policy of law that everyone is the best judge of his interest and therefore the one who voluntarily agree to suffer harm is not allowed to complain for that and one's consent is a good defense against oneself. This is so because the harm voluntarily suffered does not constitute the legal injury. No one can enforce a right which he has voluntarily waived or abandoned.

Essential conditions:

a. Free Consent

b. Consent must not be Illegal

c. Knowledge

"*Ex trupi causa oritur non actio*" means no actions arise if the act is unlawful.

Defamation

Defamation is a harm or an injury to a person's reputation, his status, his honour, his prestige, his professional image and so on. In fact, the word touches upon the affected man's total social life and professional life. It is not only the injury which a man may himself suffer, it includes any injury to the reputation of his wife, his sons or dependants if the injury suffered by them has a direct bearing on the reputation of the man who alleges to have suffered an injury. Defamation is described under two heads:

Libel and slander

Libel consists of some tangible form, such as writing or a permanent speech before a large gathering; making an effigy, writing an article. Anything which has a permanent and visible character is known as libel.

Slander is abstract, insubstantial or invisible form of defamatory words, speech directed against another. Slander is like rumours and gossips addressed to the ears of the listeners. Both libel and slander are treated as a crime. Section 499 of the I. P.C. treats them as an offence.

General conditions of defamation

a. The statement (spoken or written) must be defamatory
b The statement must refer to the person defamed
c. The statement must be published by the person
d. The statement must be false

Defences against defamation

a. The statement must be justified if it is proved that the statement is true then it is complete defence
b. Fair comment
c. Privileges
d. Absolute privilege

It covers the following:

i. Parlimentary/legislative proceedings under Article 105(3).
ii. Judicial proceedings.
iii. State communications.
iv. Military proceedings.

Qualified privilege

i. reports of Parliamentary proceedings.
ii. newspaper reports of public meetings.
iii. fair and accurate report of judicial proceedings.
iv. statements made is the interest of the general public.

Vicarious Liability

The general rule is that a person is liable for his own acts but in many cases he may be held responsible for the torts committed by others. This knows as the vicarious liability that is liability incurred, or instead of, another.

The doctrine of vicarious liability is based on certain principles which may be summed up as in the following two maxims:

1. *Qui facit per alium fruit per se* this means that he who acts through another is deemed in law as doing it himself. This is especially true in the case of an agent where his act is that of principal.

2. Respondent Superior

It means the superior must be responsible. The doctrine of liability of the master for the act of his servant is based on the maxim "*Respondent Superior*" which means let the principal be liable and it puts the master in the same position as if he had done the act himself.

Modes of vicarious liability

In torts it happens that a particular person is held liable for acts of others because of certain relationship between them. It is known as vicarious liability like person is held liable for acts of others. It arises namely in references to the following relationship:

i. Principle liability for wrongs of agent
ii. Liability of one partner for wrongs of other partners and
iii. Master's liability for the wrongs of his servant.

Liability of the State

Article 300 of the constitution reads that the Government of India may sue or be sued by the name of the Union of India and Government of state may sue or be sued by the name of the state and may subject to any provisions which may be made by Act of Parliament or of the legislature of such state enacted by virtue of powers conferred by this constitution; sue or be sued in relation to respective affairs.

Negligence

It means one is responsible for the direct consequences of his negligent acts where he is placed in such a position with regard to another that it is obvious that if he does not use due care in his own conduct he will cause injury to another. In a case of negligence the person has to prove that the person negligent.

a. did not owed a duty of care towards him.
b. made a breach of that duty
c. that he suffered damage as a result of it.

Duty to take care means that one should take reasonably care to ensure that no harm will suffer. *For ex:* A manufacturer of products which he sells in such a form as to show that he intends them to reach the ultimate consumer in the form in which they left him with no reasonable possibility of any negligence.

Res Ispa Loquitur

It means the things speaks for itself. In this situation the person is not required to prove negligence. For ex: in case of accident etc.

Defences

The defence against negligent are :

a. Contributory negligence.
b. Express contract.
c. Voluntary assumption of issue.

Nuisance

Nuisance defined as an unlawful interference with a person's use or some right over or enjoyment of land or in connection with it. It also means interacting with a person's comfort, health or safety.

Kinds of nuisance

Nuisance is of two kinds:

1. Public nuisance and
2. Private nuisance

Public nuisance is a crime, of interference with the rights of public in general and is punishable as an offence.

Private nuisance with which the law of torts is concerned, there are three essentials of tort of nuisance.

a. There must be an unreasonable interference
b. Such interference must be with the use or enjoyment of land and
c. It must cause damage to the plaintiff it is a civil wrong.

Point to Remember

- Tort is derived form the Latin word *tortum* which means twist.
- *Ubi jus ibi remedium* means where there is a right, there is a remedy.
- Unliquidated damage means which is not pre-estimated.
- *Damanum sine injuiria* means damage suffered without any legal injury.
- *Injuria sine damnum* means legal injury has been suffered with no damage caused.
- There are defences against tortuous liability
- Important defence is *volentis non fit injuria* means voluntarily suffering harm.
- *Ex turpi causa oritur non actio* means no action arises if the act is unlawful.
- Defamation means harm or injury to a person's reputation.
- The injury is more to the reputation than to the self respect of the person.
- Defamation is described by two ways that is libel and slander.
- Libel is in permanent form like by print etc.
- Slander is a transient from like by uttering words.
- In India defamation is both tort as well as crime.
- Under section 499 of I.P.C. provides for punishment for defamation.
- Defence against defamation are justification of the statement, fair comment, privileges.
- Innuendo are those words, which appear innocent but contain some secondary or latent meaning which is defamatory.
- Vicarious liability means a person is liable for the act of another.
- Vicarious liability plays under the relation-principal-agent, master-servant, between partners.
- *Qui facit per alium facit per se* means he who acts through another persons acts for himself.
- *Respondent superior* means let the principal be liable.
- Article 300 of the Constitution provides that the state can be sued and can sue in its name.
- Negligence means a person's act is such that it might cause damage to another.
- Duty to take care means to be careful and behave reasonably.
- *Res ispa loquitor* means things speaks for itself.
- Defence under negligence are contributory negligence, Express contract and voluntary assumption of risk.

- Nuisance means unlawful interference with persons right over the land
- It also means interfering with comfort, safely or health of the person
- *Nuisance is of two types—*
Public nuisance and private nuisance
Defences in nuisance is presumption and statutory authority

MULTIPLE CHOICE QUESTIONS

1. Tortum is a:
A. English word
B. Hindi word
C. German word
D. Latin word

2. The term tort has been derived from tortum means:
A. twisted
B. lawful
C. wrong
D. broken

3. Tort is a ....
A. criminal wrong
B. civil wrong
C. both A and B
D. none of these

4. *Injuria sine damnum* stands for:
A. Injury with damage
B. Injury without damage
C. Wrongful act
D. Actionable claim

5. *Damnum sine injuria* stands for:
A. Damage without injury
B. Injury without damage
C. Damage with injury
D. Injury with damage

6. *Ubi jus ibi remedium* stands for:
A. harm suffered can be enforced
B. It gives right to legal remedy
C. Who commits offence should be punished
D. Where there is right, there is a remedy

7. In tort a person can claim for:
A. liquidated damage
B. unliquidated damage
C. punishment under IPC
D. none of these

8. unliquidated damage stands for
A. not pre-estimated
B. pre-estimated
C. according to the rule
D. according to the IPC

9. *Volenti non fit injuria* stands for:
A. Damage without injury
B. Injury suffered voluntarily can not be enforced
C. It is not actionable in law
D. It is enforced by the court

10. *Ex turpi causa oritur non actio* stands for:
A. no action arise if act is unlawful
B. action arise if act is unlawful
C. action arise if act is lawful
D. no action arise if act is lawful

11. Consent defines as:
A. given by words
B. given by conduct
C. both A and B
D. none of the above

12. Act of God is a:
A. non actionable claim
B. actionable claim
C. a good defence
D. none of the above

13. Defamation means:
A. attack on the persons reputation
B. attack on the person self respect
C. both A and B
D. none of the above

14. Defamation consist of

A. Libel B. Slander

C. Innuendo D. Both (A) and (B)

15. Libel is a defamation in the

A. permanent form

B. transient form

C. both (A) and (B)

D. none of the above

16. Slander is a defamation in the

A. permanent form

B. strict form

C. transient form

D. none of the above

17. In India, Defamation is

A. criminal offence

B. Tort

C. Both (A) and (B)

D. None of the above

18. Defamation is an offence under

A. section 300 of IPC

B. section 302 of IPC

C. section 304 of IPC

D. section 400 of IPC

19. Defences under defamation is

A. fair comment

B. privileges

C. justification

D. all the above

20. Privilege is a defence in the nature of

A. qualified

B. absolute

C. both (A) and (B)

D. none of the above

21. Absolute privilege consists of

A. judicial proceedings

B. Parliamentary proceedings

C. both (A) and (B)

D. none of the above

22. Vicariously Liability stands for

A. not responsible for the act of another

B. responsible for own act

C. not responsible for own act

D. responsible for the act of another

23. Match the Vicariously Liability

(a) master 1. agent

(b) principle 2. servant

(c) one partner 3. partner

	(a)	(b)	(c)
A.	1	2	3
B.	2	1	3
C.	3	1	2

D. None of the above

24. *Qui facit per alium facit per se* stands for

A. to act for another

B. to act independently

C. let the principle liable

D. None of the above

25. *Respondent Superior* stands for

A. let the partner be liable

B. let the principal be liable

C. let the agent be liable

D. let the police be liable

26. The state can be sued and can sue in its own name this has laid town under constitution in the article

A. Article 301 B. Article 300

C. Article 200 D. Article 201

27. The purpose of Article 300 under the constitution is

A. state is a sovereign power

B. state is a non-sovereign power

C. state is a non-juristic person

D. state is a juristic person

28. The master is liable for his servants act done

A. during the course of employment

B. during the course of his work

C. during the course of another person

D. out of course of another person

29. Negligence stands for

A. the conduct is safe to cause damage

B. the conduct is not safe to cause damage

C. the conduct is not cause damage

D. the conduct cause damage

30. *Res Ipsa Loquitor* means

A. a person has right to do negligent work

B. a person has not to prove negligent act

C. a person has no prove negligent act

D. a person has to prove his act

31. Duty to take care stands for

A. to be reasonable

B. to be careful

C. to be dutiful

D. all the above

32. In negligence defences are

A. Express contract

B. Voluntary taking of risk

C. Contributory negligence

D. All the above

33. Contributory negligence stands for

A. non voluntarily getting hurt

B. voluntarily getting hurt

C. both (A) and (B)

D. none of the above

34. Nuisance stands for

A. unlawful interference with a person's use of his land

B. unlawful interference with a person's office

C. lawful interference with a person's house

D. none of the above

35. nuisance means interfering with a person's

A. safety B. comfort

C. health D. all the above

36. Nuisance consist of

A. Public nuisance B. Private nuisance

C. Both (A) and (B) D. None of the above

37. Public nuisance, is a act in a nature of

A. tort B. crime

C. both (A) and (B) D. none of the above

38. Private nuisance is an act in a nature of

A. tort B. crime

C. both (A) and (B) A. none of the above

39. Public nuisance include

A. digging trench on a highway

B. brothel keeping

C. both (A) and (B)

D. none of the above

40. Defence under nuisance are

A. Statutory action

B. Prescription

C. Both (A) and (B)

D. None of the above

ANSWERS

1	2	3	4	5	6	7	8	9	10
D	A	B	B	C	D	B	A	B	A
11	**12**	**13**	**14**	**15**	**16**	**17**	**18**	**19**	**20**
C	C	C	D	A	C	C	D	D	C
21	**22**	**23**	**24**	**25**	**26**	**27**	**28**	**29**	**30**
C	D	B	B	B	B	D	A	D	B
31	**32**	**33**	**34**	**35**	**36**	**37**	**38**	**39**	**40**
D	D	B	A	D	C	B	A	C	C

CRIMINAL LAW

In the uncivilized society no person was said to be safe from attack of his opponent. In India the law of crime came into existence from the our civilization. But different laws came into existence in the reins of different rulers. In British time, Britishers adopted a different set of law which has not uniform through out the country. So, there was a need of a good codified criminal law.

In order to bring uniformity throughout India the first law commission appointed under the Chairmanship of Lord Macaulay prepared the draft Penal Code which was revised twice by subsequent Commissions. The final draft Code was presented in the legislative council in 1856 and then in 1857 and was finally passed and received the Governor General assent on October 6, 1860.

The Indian Criminal Law is basically based on:

(a) Indian Penal Code, 1860

(b) Criminal Procedure Code, 1973 and

(c) The Indian Evidence Act, 1872

The Indian Penal Code is subjective in nature whereas Criminal Procedure Code is adjective in nature. All the offences mentioned under the Indian Penal Code is to be investigated, tried and dealt as per the provision of the Criminal Procedure Code. Indian Evidence Act is a kind of supportive law, which helps in establishing the facts during any criminal or judicial investigation under the Criminal Procedure Code.

Definition of Crime

Crime is a social phenomenon. Law regulates the social interest, arbitrates conflicting claims and demands. The security of persons and property is an essential function of the state. Therefore when security of persons and property, the breaking of which is an act called crime.

Black Stone define crime "an act committed or omitted in violation of a Public Law forbidding or commanding it."

FUNDAMENTAL ELEMENTS OF CRIME

Physical element, *actus reus* and mental element, *mens rea* are two tests of criminality known to our law which is based on English law. Other then this in there are also many elements that go to constitute a crime like intention, motive, knowledge, of human being etc.

Mens Rea

Mens rea means guilty mind or evil intent. There can be no crime of any nature without an evil mind. Every crime requires a mental element. Mens rea is considered a fundamental principle of penal liability. So, a person with innocent mind cannot commit a crime. The maxim *actus non facit reum, sine mens sit rea* (the intent and act must both concur to constitute the crime).

Actus Reus

Actus reus means wrongful act. *Actus reus* defined as some illegal act must take place in pursuance of the guilty intention.

The *actus reus* is constituted by the event and not by the activity which caused the event.

Intention

Intention of a person shows his mental stage. It is the purpose of design with which an act is done. It is actually conduct of a person by which he design and act accordingly. The burden of proving intention lies upon the prosecution.

Motive

Like intention, motive is also a mental stage of a person. Motive intended a person to help in framing an intention. Motive of a person shows his mental status that he does a crime or not or form an intention for unlawful act.

Knowledge

Knowledge in comparison to intention is a strong word and imports certainty and not mere a probability, knowledge is an awareness of the consequences of the act.

OFFENCE AFFECTING THE HUMAN BODY

Homicide

The word homicide is a Latin word. Homicide : homo+cide

Homo means *man*

Cide means *I cut*

Homicide actually means killing of a human being by a human being. It may be lawful or unlawful. Lawful homicides is of two types:

(1) excusable homicide

(2) justified homicide

Unlawful homicide includes

(a) culpable homicide not amounting to murder

(b) Murder and

(c) Homicide by rash or negligent acts

Culpable homicide:

Culpable homicide is defined under the section 299 of Indian Penal Code, 1860. Whoever causes death, by doing an act with the intention of causing death or with the intention of causing such bodily injury as is likely to cause death or with the knowledge that he is likely by such act to cause death. Commits the offence of culpable homicide.

Murder

Murder is defined under the section 300 of Indian Penal Code, 1860.

Except in the cases hereinafter excepted culpable homicide is murder, if the act by which the death is caused is done with the intention of causing death or

Secondly if it is done with the intention of causing such bodily injury as the offender knows to be likely to cause the death of the person to whom the harm is caused or

Thirdly If it is done with the intention of causing bodily injury to any person and the bodily injury intended to be inflicted is sufficient is the ordinary course of nature to cause death or

Fourthly If the person committing the act knows that it is so imminently dangerous that it must, in all probability, cause death or such bodily injury as is likely to cause death, and commits such act without any excuse for incurring the risk of causing death or such injury as aforesaid.

Distinction between Culpable Homicide and Murder

(1) culpable homicide is genus and murder is species

(2) all murder is culpable homicide but all murder does not fall under section 300

(3) culpable homicide is actually capable homicide not amounting to murder

Punishment for culpable homicide

Punishment for culpable homicide not amounting to murder describe under the section 304 of IPC.

Punishment for murder

Punishment for murder described under the section 302 of IPC.

Suicide

Suicide is defined under the section 309 of IPC:- Whoever attempts to commit suicide and does any act towards the commission of such offence shall be punished with simple imprisonment for a term, which may extend to one year or with fine or with both.

Exceptions to Offence of Murder

Exception 1 :—Culpable homicide is not murder if the offender, whilst deprived of the power of self control by grave and sudden provocation, causes the death of the person who gave the provocation or causes the death of any other person by mistake or accident.

Exception 2 :—Culpable homicide is not murder if the offender, in the exercise in good faith of the right of private defence of person or property, exceeds the power given to him by law and causes the death of the person against whom he is exercising such right of defence without premeditation, and without any intention of doing more than is necessary for the purpose of such defence.

Exception 3 :—Culpable homicide is not murder if the offender, being a public servant or aiding a public servant acting for the advancement of public justices, exceeds the powers given to him by law, and causes death by doing an act which he, in good faith, believes to be lawful and necessary for the due discharge of his duty as much public servant and without ill-will towards the person whose death is caused.

Exception 4:—Culpable homicide is not murder if it is committed.

(1) without premeditation

(2) in a sudden fight

(3) in the heat of passion upon a sudden quarrel and

(4) without the offender having taken undue advantage or acted in a cruel or unusual manner.

Exception 5:—Culpable homicide is not murder when the person whose death is caused, being the age of eighteen years, suffer death or takes the risk of death with his own consent

Kidnapping and Abduction

Kidnapping actually defined under section 361 of IPC:—

Whoever takes or entices any minor under sixteen years of age if a male, or under eighteen years of age if a female or any person of unsound mind, out of the keeping of the lawful guardian of such minor or person of unsound mind, without the consent of such guardian, is said to kidnap such minor or person from lawful guardianship.

Abduction

Abduction is defined under section 362 of IPC:

Whoever by force compels, or by any deceitful means induces any person to go from any place, is said to abduct that person.

Differences between Kidnapping and Abduction

- A girl of 18 years of age or over can only be abducted and not kidnapped
- A girl below 18 years of age can be kidnapped as well as abduction provided the other conditions are satisfied.

OFFENCE AGAINST PROPERTY

Theft

Theft is defined under section 378 of IPC as:

whoever intending to take dishonestly any moveable property out of the possession of any person without that person's consent, moves that property in order to such taking, is said to commit theft.

Punishment

Section 379 of IPC defines punishment for theft as whoever commits theft shall be punished with imprisonment of either description for a term which may extend to three years or with fine or with both.

Extortion

Extortion is defined under section 383 of IPC: Whoever, intentionally puts any person in fear of any injury to that person, or to any other, and thereby dishonestly induces the person so put in fear to deliver to any person any property or valuable security, or anything signed or sealed which may be converted into a valuable security commits extortion.

Punishment

Section 384 of IPC defines punishment for extortion as whoever commits extortion shall be punished with imprisonment for a term which may extend to three year or with five or with both

Differences between Extortion and Theft

(1) under theft a person take the property without the owner's consent but under extortion it is committed by wrongful obtaining of owner's consent.

(2). theft is limited only to movable property but extortion is for both moveable and immoveable property.

(3) under theft property is taken away but in extortion it is delivered to the offender.

- Extortion is almost equal to the offense of black mail under English law.

Points to Remember

- For the uniformity of law in India the First Law Commission appointed under the Chairmanship of Lord Macaulay.
- The Indian Criminal Law basically base on—
  Indian Penal Code, 1860:
  Criminal Procedure Code, 1973
  The Indian Evidence Act, 1872
- Indian Penal Code is objective in nature whereas Criminal Procedure Code is adjective in nature.

- Indian Evidence Act is a supportive law which helps in establishing the fact during any judicial investigation.
- Two test of criminality—

  Actus reus—physical element

  Mans rea—mental element.
- Mens rea means guilty mind.
- Actus rews means wrongful act.
- For constitute a crime actus reus, mens rea, motive, knowledge, intention etc. are main elements.
- Intention, motive and knowledge are the mental stage of offender.
- Homicide means killing of a human being by a human being.
- Lawful homicide is of two types—

  Excusable homicide

  Justified homicide.
- Unlawful homicide includes—

  Culpable homicide not amounting to murder.

  Murder and Homicide by rash or negligent act.
- culpable homicide defined under section 299 of IPC.
- Punishment for culpable homicide not amounting to murder defined under section 304 of IPC.
- Murder is defined under section 300 of IPC.
- Punishment for murder is defined under section 302 of IPC.
- Suicide is defined under section 309 of IPC.
- Kidnapping is defined under section 301 of IPC.
- Abduction is defined under section 362 of IPC.
- A girl of 18 years of age or above can only be abducted not kidnapped.
- A girl below 18 years of age can be kidnapped.
- A boy of 16 years of age or above can only be abducted not kidnapped.
- A boy below 16 years of age can be kidnapped.
- Theft is defined under section 378 of IPC.
- Punishment for theft is defined under section 379 of IPC.
- Extortion is defined under section 363 of IPC.
- Punishment for extortion is defined under 384 of IPC.
- Under theft, property is taken away without the consent of owner.
- Under extortion property is taken away by wrongful consent of owner.
- Theft is limited only to movable property.
- Extortion is for both moveable as well as immoveable property
- Extortion is almost equal to the offence of Black Mail under English Law.

MULTIPLE CHOICE QUESTIONS

1. First Law Commission appointed under the Chairmanship of:

A. Lord Macaulay
B. Lord Irbin
C. Lord Itley
D. Lord William

2. The Indian Penal Code was enacted in:

A. 1973 B. 1872
C. 1860 D. 1926

3. The Indian Criminal Law consist of:

A. I.P.C. and Contract Law
B. I.P.C. and Cr.P.C.
C. I.P.C. and Evidence Law
D. C.P.C. and I.P.C.

4. The Code of Criminal Procedure was enacted in:

A. 1860 B. 1926
C. 1872 D. 1973

5. The Indian Evidence Act was enacted in:

A. 1860 B. 1973
C. 1872 D. 1926

6. The Indian Evidence Act, 1872 helps in
   A. Procedural of crime
   B. Subjective nature
   C. Police enquiry
   D. Judicial enquiry

7. The Criminal Procedure Code is of
   A. Subjective in nature
   B. Procedural nature
   C. Supportive in nature
   D. None of the above

8. *Actus reus* means
   A. Wrongful act
   B. Lawful act
   C. Unlawful act
   D. Act that is justified

9. *Mens rea* means
   A. Guilty mind
   B. With intention
   C. Wrongful act
   D. None of the above

10. The maxim *actus non facit reum, nisi mens sit rea* means
    A. intention along constitute the crime
    B. the intent and act must both concur to constitute the crime
    C. motive and intention are main element to constitute the crime
    D. none of the above

11. which of the following constitutes a crime
    A. Mens rea B. Motive
    C. Intention D. All the above

12. Criminal intention is equivalent to
    A. Mens rea
    B. Motive
    C. Actus reus
    D. Intention

13. The burden of proving guilty intention lies upon
    A. Judges
    B. Police
    C. Offender
    D. Prosecution

14. A person with innocent mind
    A. can commit a crime
    B. cannot commit a crime
    C. may commit a crime
    D. depend upon the fact

15. Ignorance of law is
    A. excusable
    B. not excusable
    C. a lawful wrong
    D. none of the above

16. *Ignoratia juris non excusat* means
    A. Ignorance of law excuses no one
    B. Ignorance of law is excused
    C. Depend upon the fact
    D. Depend upon the person

17. Homicide means killing of a human being by
    A. a human being
    B. by accident
    C. by natural disaster
    D. by some kind of animal

18. Section 299 IPC provides for
    A. Culpable homicide
    B. Extortion
    C. Murder
    D. Theft

19. Section 300 IPC provides for
    A. Culpable homicide
    B. Extortion
    C. Murder
    D. Theft

20. Which of the following is lawful homicides?

A. excusable

B. justified

C. both (A) and (B)

D. none of the above

21. Unlawful homicide includes

A. culpable homicide not amounting to murder

B. murder

C. homicide by rash or negligent

D. All of the above

22. Section 302 IPC defines

A. Punishment for theft

B. Punishment for murder

C. Punishment for extortion

D. None of the above

23. Section 304 IPC defines

A. Punishment for culpable homicide not amounting to murder

B. Punishment for murder

C. Punishment for theft

D. Punishment for extortion

24. Section 304 of IPC provide punishment for

A. Murder B. Suicide

C. Theft D. Extortion

25. Section 361 of IPC defines

A. Kidnapping B. Abduction

C. Theft D. Extortion

26. Section 362 of IPC defines

A. Kidnapping B. Abduction

C. Theft D. Extortion

27. Taking of a male under the age of 16 years and a female under the age of 18 years is defined as

A. Abduction

B. Kidnapping

C. Both (A) and (B)

D. None of the above

28. Taking of a male above the age of 16 years and a female above the age of 18 years is defined as

A. Abduction B. Kidnapping

C. Extortion D. None of the above

29. Section 378 of IPC defines

A. Abduction B. Theft

C. Extortion D. Kidnapping

30. Section 383 of IPC defines

A. Abduction

B. Theft

C. Extortion

D. Kidnapping

31. Section 379 of IPC defines punishment for

A. Abduction B. Theft

C. Kidnapping D. Murder

32. Section 384 of IPC defines punishment for

A. Abduction

B. Theft

C. Kidnapping

D. Extortion

33. Extortion is almost equal to offence of

A. Black mail

B. Theft

C. Demand of money

D. None of the above

34. Theft is defined only for

A. moveable property

B. immoveable property

C. both (A) and (B)

D. none of the above

35. Extortion is defined only for

A. moveable property

B. immoveable property

C. both (A) and (B)

D. none of the above

36. Extortion means seeking delivery of the persons property by putting him under

A. fear

B. a contract

C. without fear

D. humiliation

37. Robbery is in aggravated form of

A. theft

B. extortion

C. both (a) and (b)

D. none of the above

38. Under theft removal of property

A. with the consent of owner

B. without the consent of owner

C. with the consent of other person

D. without the consent of police

39. If the things removed temporarily with dishonest intention amount to

A. robbery

B. extortion

C. theft

D. none of the above

40. Match the following

(a) Section 299 — 1. Murder

(b) Section 300 — 2. Punishment for murder

(c) Section 302 — 3. Punishment for culpable homicide

(d) Section 304 — 4. Culpable homicide

	(a)	(b)	(c)	(d)
A.	4	1	2	3
B.	4	1	3	2
C.	1	4	2	3
D.	4	1	2	3

41. Match the following

(a) First Law Commission of India — 1. 1856

(b) Indian Penal Code — 2. 1860

(c) The Indian Evidence Act — 3. 1973

(d) Criminal Procedure Code — 4. 1872

	(a)	(b)	(c)	(d)
A.	1	2	4	3
B.	1	2	3	4
C.	2	1	3	4
D.	2	1	4	3

42. Mistake of fact is other than

A. Intention

B. Mistake of law

C. Knowledge of act

(d) Mens rea

43. Match the following

(a) Kidnapping — (1) Section 383

(b) Abduction — (2) Section 378

(c) Theft — (3) Section 362

(d) Extortion — (4) Section 361

	(a)	(b)	(c)	(d)
(a)	3	2	4	1
(b)	3	4	2	1
(c)	4	3	1	2
(d)	4	3	2	1

44. Match the following

A. Section 379 — 1. Punishment for culpable homicide

B. Section 384 — 2. Punishment for murder

C. Section 302 — 3. Punishment for theft

D. Section 304 — 4. Punishment for extortion

	(a)	(b)	(c)	(d)
(a)	3	4	2	1
(b)	3	4	1	2
(c)	4	3	1	2
(d)	4	3	2	1

45. Mens rea is a

A. English maxim

B. Latin maxim

C. French maxim

D. Greek maxim

46. If an unlawful act is done under the mistake of fact

A. person is not guilty

B. person is guilty

C. person has good defence

D. depend upon the fact of cases

47. Section 107 of IPC defines

A. Abduction B. Theft

C. Extortion D. Murder

48. The word entice means in kidnapping

A. desire in the other

B. to provoke

C. sentimentally attachment

D. none of the above

49. If a person committed murder under sudden provocation that amount to

A. murder

B. culpable homicide not amounting to murder

C. depend upon the fact

D. none of the above

50. Match the following

(a) Mistake of fact under certain circumstances

(b) *Actus non facit reum nisi sit rea*

(c) First Law Commission

(d) *Ignoratia juris non excusat*

(1) Ignorance of law is not excusable

(2) Ignorance of law is excusable

(3) Uniformity of law

(4) The intent and act must both concur to constitute the crime

	(a)	(b)	(c)	(d)
A.	2	4	3	1
B.	1	3	2	4
C.	4	2	3	1
D.	1	3	4	2

ANSWERS

1	2	3	4	5	6	7	8	9	10
A	C	B	D	C	D	B	A	A	B
11	**12**	**13**	**14**	**15**	**16**	**17**	**18**	**19**	**20**
D	A	D	B	B	A	A	A	C	C
21	**22**	**23**	**24**	**25**	**26**	**27**	**28**	**29**	**30**
D	B	A	B	A	B	B	A	B	A
31	**32**	**33**	**34**	**35**	**36**	**37**	**38**	**39**	**40**
B	D	A	A	C	A	C	B	C	A
41	**42**	**43**	**44**	**45**	**46**	**47**	**48**	**49**	**50**
A	D	D	A	B	C	A	A	B	A

LAW OF CONTRACT

The law related to breach of commercial activity is governed by the Indian Contract Act, 1872. According to section 2 (h) of the Indian Contract Act, 1872 defines the term contract as an agreement enforceable by law is contract. Thus every contract is made up of, a proposal from one side and its acceptance by the other. So, in business agreement it is usual that the parties intend legal consequences to follow. On the other hand there are certain agreement which do not create obligation: *for ex:* —

a. Agreement between husband and wife

b. Agreement relating to social matters

According to section 2 (a), 2 (b) and 2 (d) of the Indian Contract Act, 1872, contract consists of

a. Proposal or offer

b. Acceptance of proposal or offer

c. Consideration

Promissor: The person making the proposal is called the promisor

Promisee : The person accepting the proposal is called the promisee

Promise : A proposal when accepted becomes a promise .

Essential Elements of a Contract

A valid contract has following conditions:

i. An agreement

ii. Free consent

iii. Object is lawful

iv. The parties are competent to contract

v. Not declared to be void

ESSENTIAL FOR CREATING A CONTRACT

Offer or Proposal

When a person offer to another person his willingness to do with a view to enter into a contract with promise. This offer must be communicated to other party.

Acceptance

When a person to whom the proposal said to be made is accepted, result in an agreement. It is only after the acceptance of the proposal that a contract between the two parties can arise.

Intention

The parties must show interest to give rise a legal consequences to follow. It also depends upon the circumstances of the contract.

Consideration

Consideration is a necessary element of the contract. Consideration is the cause of the promise and in its absence the promise is only bare promise. A consideration show that promise is contemplated for creation of legal obligations. Consideration is defined under the section 2 (d) of the Indian Contract Act, 1872. The purpose of this definition is to emphasise the simple act that consideration is some act, done or promised to be done, at the desire of the promisor.

Pollock defined "consideration as the price for which the promise of the other is bought and the promise thus given for value is enforceable."

Privity of Contract

The doctrine of privity of contract means that a contract between the parties only. No third person can enforce it. In general rule that no third person can sue.

Capacity to Contract

According to section 10 and section 11 of Indian Contract Act, 1872 minor, persons of unsound mind and persons disqualified by law are incompetent to contract.

Void, Voidable, Illegal Contract

Under many circumstances the agreement between the parties may not be a valid contract due to certain unlawful object in it.

Void Contract

Section 2 (g) of Indian Contract Act, 1872 defines: An agreement not enforceable by law is said to be void. Void agreement has no legal effect for ex: A minor's agreement being void, ordinarily. It should be wholly devoid of all effects.

Voidable Contract

Section 2 (i) of Indian Contract Act, 1872 defines. An agreement which is enforceable by law at the option of one or more of the parties thereto, but not at the option of the other or others is a voidable contract.

The distinction between void and voidable extract is that former is not enforceable from the very beginning but later is depend upon the act of the parties. Voidable out is that which is good unless avoided.

Illegal Contract

In this type of contract, there is no legal remedy between the parties, as object of the contract is unlawful. If there will be some transaction or any agreement between the parties but it can not be enforced from a court of law.

Some Illegal contract by

i. Mistake
ii. Fraud
iii. Misrepresentation
iv. Coercion
v. Under influence
vi. In capacity
vii. Impossibility

Doctrine of frustration

When the performance of the contract become impossible, the purpose which the parties have in mind is frustrated. If the performance become impossible because of a supervening event, the parties are excused from the performance of the contract. Section 56 of Indian Contract Act, 1872 defines "Agreement to do impossible act—an agreement to do an act impossible is itself is void."

Illustrations

a. A agrees with B to discover treasure by magic. The agreement is void.

b. A and B contract to marry each other. Before the time fixed for the marriage. A goes mad the contract becomes void.

c. A contracts to act at a theatre for six months in consideration of sum paid in advance by B. On several occasion A is too ill to act. The contract to act on these occasions become void.

A contract to do an act which after the contract is made, becomes impossible or by reason of some event which the promisor could not prevent, unlawful, becomes void when the act becomes impossible or unlawful.

According section 56 of Indian Contract Act, 1872 there can be two types of impossibility.

a. *Initial impossibility:*—It provides that if a contract is impossible of being performed, the parties to it will never able to fulfill their object and hence such an agreement is void. *For ex*:- Illustration (a).

b. *Subsequent impossibility:*—It provides that the performance of contract may be possible when entered upon but because of some event it become impossible to perform it, then becomes void. *For ex*:- Illustration (b).

Frustration of contract means an intervening event or charge of circumstances so fundamental as to be impossibility of performance there are certain grounds making the performance of contract impossible. These are:

a. Destruction of the subject matter
b. Change of circumstances
c. Non-occurrence of a contemplated event
d. Death or Incapacity of party
e. Government or legislative intervention
f. Intervention of war

Quasi-Contracts

Section 68 to 72 of Indian Contract Act, 1872 deals certain relations created by contract. These obligations are known as quasi-contract. It describes where the obligation to pay arises neither on the basis of a contract nor a tort, but because a person has obtained an unjust benefit at the cost of another.

The quasi-contractual obligations are based on a person to return the benefit that he was desired from another because of a certain relationship existing between the persons.

Supply of Necessaries

Section 68 of Indian Contract Act, 1872 defines if a person like minor (minor's agreement is void) incapable of contract are made liable to reimbursement to a person who supplies necessaries to a minor even though the contract is void. Such duty to reimburse is not there because of any valid contract with the minor but because the law recognizes this to be a quasi contractual obligation.

Payment by an Interested Person

Section 69 of Indian Contract Act, 1872 defines a person who is interested in the payment of money which another is bound by law to pay and who therefore pays it, is entitled to be reimbursed by the other.

Finder of Goods

Section 71 of Indian Contract Act, 1872 defines a person who finds goods belonging to another and takes them into his custody, is subject to the same responsibility as a bailee.

Points to Remember

- Law related to branch of commercial activity governed by the Indian Contract Act, 1872.
- Under Article 2 (h) of Indian Contract Act, 1872 agreement enforceable by law is contract.
- Here are certain agreement which do not create obligation for it:- Agreement between husband wife; social matters.
- The person making the proposal is called the promisor.
- The person accepting the proposal is called the promisee.
- A proposal when accepted becomes a promise.
- A valid contract contains an agreement, free consent, object is lawful, the parties are competent to contract, not declared to be void.
- An offer is proposal.
- Acceptance means giving assent to acceptance of proposal.
- The parties must show interest to give rise a legal consequences to follow.
- No contract without consideration.
- Privity of contract define no stranger can enforce the contract.
- Minor, persons of unsound mind and persons disqualified by law are incompetent to contract.
- Under many circumstances the agreement between the parties is not valid due to certain unlawful object in it.
- According to section 2 (g) of Indian Contract Act, 1872, an agreement not enforceable by law is to be void.
- Voidable contract is enforceable at the option of either parties.
- Illegal contract can not be enforceable by the court of law.
- A minor's contract is void.
- From Illegal contract may by mistake, fraud and misrepresentation. coercion, under influence, incapacity, impossibility, etc.
- If performance of contract become impossible due to some supervening event, the parties are excused form the performance of the contract.
- According to section 56 of Indian Contract Act, 1872 – an agreement to be impossible act is void.
- There are two types of impossibilities—initial impossibilities and subsequent impossibility.
- There are certain grounds making the performance of contract impossible. These are destruction of the subject matter, change of circumstances, non-occurrence of a contemplated event, death or incapacity of party, Government or legislative Intervention, intervention of war.
- Section 68 to 72 of Indian Contract Act, 1872 deals with quasi-contract.
- Quasi-contract is not a contract but it resembles a contract.
- Section 68 of Indian Contract Act, 1872 defines supply of necessaries.
- Section 64 of Indian Contract Act, 1872 defines payment by an interested person.
- Section 71 of Indian Contract Act, 1872 defines finder of goods

MULTIPLE CHOICE QUESTIONS

1. The law of contract is governed by:

A. Indian Contract Act, 1872

B. Indian industrial Act, 1926

C. Indian Evidence Act, 1872

D. Indian Companies Act, 1956

2. An agreement enforceable by law is called:

A. business agreement

B. quasi-contract

C. contract

D. tort

3. Indian Contract Act passed in the year:

A. 1972 B. 1872

C. 1962 D. 1862

4. According to section 2 (a) of Indian Contract Act, 1872 lays down provision regarding what is a:

A. offer

B. consideration

C. acceptance

D. privity of contract

5. According to section 2 (b) of Indian Contract Act, 1872 lays down provision regarding what is a:

A. offer

B. consideration

C. acceptance

D. privity of contract

6. According to section 2 (d) of Indian Contract Act, 1872 lays down provision regarding what is a:

A. offer

B. consideration

C. acceptance

D. privity of contract

7. Promisor is a person

A. who does not makes the proposal

B. who makes the proposal

C. who accepts the proposal

D. who does not accept the proposal

8. promisee is a person

A. Who accept the proposal

B. Who does not accept the proposal

C. Who does not makes the proposal

D. Who makes the proposal

9. A proposal when accepted becomes a

A. Promisee B. Promisor

C. Promise D. None of the above

10. Agreement between .... do not create obligation

A. husband and wife

B. social activity

C. both a and b

D. none of the above

11. A valid contract contains

A. An agreement

B. Free consent

C. Object is lawful

D. All the above

12. When an offer is accepted, it becomes a

A. Agreement

B. Proposal

C. Valid contract

D. None of the above

13. Intention must give rise to create

A. Legal relationship

B. An agreement

C. For consideration

D. Lawful agreement

14. The object of valid contract must be

A. unlawful

B. considerable

C. accepted

D. lawful

15. Person who cannot enter into valid contract are

A. minor

B. person of unsound mind

C. persons disqualified by law

D. All of the above

16. Match the following

(a) Section 2 (a)	(1) Proposal		
(b) Section 2 (b)	(2) Valid contract		
(c) Section 2 (d)	(3) Acceptance		
(d) Valid contract	(4) Consideration		

	(a)	(b)	(c)	(d)
A.	1	3	4	2
B.	1	3	2	4
C.	3	1	4	2
D.	3	2	4	1

17. Consideration is a necessary element of the

A. Valid agreement

B. Valid contract

C. Valid business activity

D. None of the above

18. Contract is valid only if

A. Parties are competent

B. There is some consideration

C. Both (a) and (b)

D. None of the above

19. An offer is a proposal to enter a contract in return for a

A. contract

B. promise

C. for business agreement

D. set of promises

20. The principal that no third party can sue is known as

A. doctrine of frustration

B. doctrine of privity

C. both A and B

D. none of the above

21. An agreement not enforceable by law is defined under

A. Section 2 (g) of Indian Contract Act, 1872

B. Section 2 (a) of Indian Contract Act, 1872

C. Section 2 (c) of Indian Contract Act, 1872

D. Section 2 (l) of Indian Contract Act, 1872

22. Section 2 (c) of Indian Contract Act, 1872 defines

A. void contract

B. contract

C. voidable contract

D. consideration

23. A void contract is

A. Not enforceable by law

B. Enforceable by law

C. Not a contract

D. Illegal contract

24. A voidable contract is

A. Not enforceable by law

B. Enforceable by law

C. Not a contract

D. None of the above

25. An agreement is not enforceable from the very beginning

A. valid B. void

C. voidable D. none of the above

26. An agreement entered upon by a minor is

A. voidable B. illegal

C. void D. none of the above

27. An agreement which has no legal effect is called

A. voidable contract

B. illegal contract

C. void contract

D. valid contract

28. An agreement enforceable by law is

A. voidable contract

B. illegal contract

C. void contract

D. valid contract

29. An agreement can not enforceable by law is

A. Voidable contract

B. Illegal contract

C. Void contract

D. Both (A) and (B)

30. Which of the following are Illegal contract

A. Mistake

B. Misrepresentation

C. Fraud

D. All the above

31. The performance of the contract become impossible is called

A. doctrine of privity

B. doctrine of frustration

C. doctrine of misrepresentation

D. None of the above

32. An agreement to do impossible act defined under

A. Section 56 of Indian Contract Act, 1872

B. Section 46 of Indian Contract Act, 1872

C. Section 68 of Indian Contract Act, 1872

D. Section 71 of Indian Contract Act, 1872

33. An agreement to do an impossible act is

A. voidable contract

B. valid contract

C. void contract

D. none of the above

34. The maxim *lex non cogit ad impossibilia* is related to

A. subsequent impossibility

B. invalid impossibility

C. doctrine of privity

D. none of the above

35. If a contract is impossible to perform from the very beginning is called

A. Subsequent impossibility

B. Initial impossibility

C. Doctrine of privity

D. None of the above

36. If a contract possible but because of some event it become impossible to perform is called

A. subsequent impossibility

B. initial impossibility

C. doctrine of privity

D. none of the above

37. Grounds of frustration are

1. destruction of the subject matter
2. change of circumstances
3. death or in capacity of party
4. intervention of war

(a) only (1) and (2)

(b) only (1), (2) and (3)

(c) only (1), (3) and (4)

(d) all of the above

38. Doctrine of Impossibility is dealt in

A. section 60

B. section 61

C. section 56

D. section 55

39. According to section 63 of Indian Contract Act, 1872 contract can discharged by

A. natural consent

B. depend upon the party

C. depend upon the third party

D. depend upon the agent

40. Under Indian Contract Act, 1872, Quasi-contractual obligations are mentioned in

A. sections 68 to 72

B. sections 69 to 72

C. sections 59 to 61

D. only section 71

41. Quasi-contract is a

A. Contract

B. Tort

C. Both contract as well as tort

D. Resembles a contract

42. Bailee means

A. finder of lost goods

B. one who gets the bail

C. who perform the quasi contract

D. none of the above

43. Section 68 of Indian Contract Act, 1872 defines

A. payment by an interested person

B. supply of necessaries

C. finder of goods

D. none of the above

44. Section 69 of Indian Contract Act defines

A. finder of goods

B. supply of necessaries

C. payment by an interested person

D. none of the above

45. An agreement creating an obligation is

A. Contract

B. Tort

C. Promise

D. Quasi contract

46. Section 71 of Indian Contract Act defines

A. finder of goods

B. supply of necessaries

C. payment by an interested person

D. none of the above

47. Match the following

(a) Section 71 (1) Agreement to be impossible as is void

(b) Section 68 (2) finder of goods

(c) Section 69 (3) Payment by an interested person

(d) Section 56 (4) Supply of necessaries

	(a)	(b)	(c)	(d)
A.	4	1	3	2
B.	4	1	2	3
C.	1	4	2	3
D.	1	4	3	2

ANSWERS

1	2	3	4	5	6	7	8	9	10
A	C	B	A	C	B	B	A	C	C
11	**12**	**13**	**14**	**15**	**16**	**17**	**18**	**19**	**20**
D	C	A	D	D	A	B	C	B	B
21	**22**	**23**	**24**	**25**	**26**	**27**	**28**	**29**	**30**
A	C	A	A	B	C	C	A	D	D
31	**32**	**33**	**34**	**35**	**36**	**37**	**38**	**39**	**40**
B	A	C	A	B	A	D	C	A	A
41	**42**	**43**	**44**	**45**	**46**	**47**			
D	A	B	C	D	A	D			

ADMINISTRATVE LAW

Administrative law is that branch of public law which deals in the organization and powers of administrative and quasi-administrative agencies like Corporation, Boards, Universities etc., and prescribes principles and rules by which an official action is reached and reviewed in relation to individual liberty and freedom.

From the definition it is clear that administrative law is not a general law dealing in the court but it is a law which includes rule, making action, administrative directions, rule application action.

Development of Administrative Law

The main factors responsible for the growth of administrative law are:—

(1) Modernisation and Globlisation create structural change and create problems.

(2) The inadequacy of the tradition type judicial system to give and settle all the disputes.

(3) The inadequacy of the tradition legislative organs cannot pass rules of every day.

Administrative law includes the following features:—

(1) Administrative discretion

(2) Provision for administrative appeal or review

(3) Delegated legislation

(4) Right and liabilities of the state

(5) Power to issue licences and power to control and inspection

(6) Judicial review of administrative action

Rule of Law

The doctrine of rule of law is one of the fundamental principles of administrative law. Rules of law means that the law rules.

For ex.:—The Constitution of India was made the supreme law of the land.

So, ruler of law means

(1) Supermacy of law

(2) A system of fixed rule

(3) Equality before the law

(4) Due process of fairness of law

(5) Natural law

(6) Right of individual/ protection of individual liabilities

(7) Judicial review

(8) Legal spirit

Droit Administratif

The system of *droit administratif* prevailing in France where two types of legal system. So, there exist two types of court which are independent of each other

1. between administrative tribunal and government
2. between administrative tribunal and citizens.

Delegated Legislation

The doctrine of separation of power assign exclusive the function to administer the law enacted by legislature, but in reality the executive besides administration performs many legislative function also. It is the concept of delegated legislation which has empowered the executive to perform functions of other two organs.

One of the most significant developments of the present century is the growth in the legislative powers of the executive. With the growth in the functions of the state and the consequent growth in the number of laws enacted by the legislature, the executive has come to play a much more dominant role.

Delegated legislation in simple terms means when the function of legislature is entrusted to organs other than the legislature by the legislature itself the legislation made by such organs is called delegated legislation."

According to Salmond "delegated legislation is that which proceeds from any authority other than the sovereign power and therefore is dependent for the continued existence and validity on more superior or supreme authority.

Delegated legislation is also called as sub-ordinate legislation.

Need for delegated legislation

(1) Pressure upon Parliamentary time

(2) Emergency

(3) Technicality

(4) Secrecy

(5) Discretion

Principles of Natural Justice

The purpose of the rules of Natural Justice is to prevent miscarriage of justice. In India, the principles of Natural Justice are grounded in articles 14 and 21 of constitution. So, principles of Natural Justice is that justice is simple and elementary not complex. Principle of Natural Justice is also known as substantial justice, universal justice, fundamental justice.

Two basic principles of Natural Justice

(1) *Nemo debet esse judex in propria cause* :—no man shall be a judge in his own cause, and

(2) *Audi alteram partem*:—no men should be condemned unheard.

Points to Remember

- Administrative law mainly deals with administrative and quasi administrative.
- Factors responsible for growth and development of administrative law are :- modernisation, globalisation, inadequacy of court, legislation do not have much more time.
- There is a close relationship between the constitutional law and administrative law.
- Administrative law deals with power of executive while constitutional law deals with legislative, Parliament and civil servant.
- The law made by the executive should not be contrary to the constitutional provisions.
- Doctrine of rule of law is fundamental principle of administrative law.
- Rules of law means that the law rules
- Rules of law attributes to :—

  Supremacy of law, equality before law, fairness in law, natural law, protection of individual liabilities, etc.
- *Droit administratif* prevailing in France where two types of courts are existed.
- Delegated legislation is an authority given by legislation to delegated legislation.
- Power of delegated legislation includes all rules, orders, regulations, by law, etc.
- Delegated legislation is also known as subordinate legislation.
- The reason for development of delegated legislation is that, Parliament has not too much time to discuss about all things, certain legislation are quite technical so it needs expert, in emergency situation quick decision is required, etc.
- Main purpose of the rules of Natural Justice is to prevent the miscarriage.
- The principle of Natural Justice describe in article 14 and 21 of the Constitution.
- Basic principle of Natural Justice are:

Nemo debet esse judex in propria causa : —No man shall be a judge in his own cause.

Audi alteram partem :—no man should be condemned unheard

- principles of Natural Justice is also known as substantial justice.

MULTIPLE CHOICE QUESTIONS

1. Administrative law mainly deals with:

A. Court and legislative

B. Administrative and quasi-administrative

C. Administrative and court

D. Administrative and legislative

2. There is a close relationship between:

A. Law and justice

B. Administrative law and Constitutional law

C. Constitution law and law of Evidence

D. None of the above

3. Administrative law is concerned with the power of the:

A. Legislative

B. Judge

C. President

D. Executive

4. One of the important factor responsible for the growth and development of administrative law is:

A. Changing work of office

B. Changing role of executive

C. Changing role of state

D. Changing role of authority

5. Rule of law means:

A. Law rules

B. Depend upon the legislative

C. Law depend upon person to person

D. None of the above

6. Who is the Supreme *law of land* in India:

A. People

B. Police

C. Legislative

D. Constitution

7. Fundamental principle of administrative law is:

A. Legislative

B. Constitution

C. Rule of law

D. Supreme Court

8. Rule of law puts control over the power of:

A. Legislative

B. Judiciary

C. President

D. Executive

9. No person can be unheard or arrested except by:

A. Legislative

B. Due process in law

C. Judges

D. President

10. Main attributes to rule of law are:

A. Due process or fairness of law

B. Equality before law

C. Supremacy of law

D. All of the above

11. Droit administratif is prevailing in:

A. American system of law

B. Indian system of law

C. French system of law

D. British system of law

12. *Droit administratif* defines:

A. Two types of court which are independent

B. Two types of court which are not independent

C. Single judiciary system

D. None of the above

13. In French system of two types of court are:

A. Civil Court and Criminal Court

B. Administrative Court and Ordinary Court

C. Administrative court and Criminal court

D. Martial court and Administrative court

14. The doctrine under which delegated legislative formed by own legislative is

A. Doctrine of separation of power

B. Doctrine of rule of law

C. Both (A) and (B)

D. None of the above

15. Delegated legislation is also known as

A. Legislation by judiciary

B. Subordinate legislative

C. Only legislative

D. None of these

16. Delegated legislation means

A. Rules and regulations

B. Orders

C. By laws

D. All the above

17. Delegated legislation is administered by

A. Legislative

B. Executive authority

C. Judge

D. All the above

18. Need for development of delegated legislative are

A. Pressure upon Parliamentary time

B. Emergency

C. Technicality

D. All the above

19. In delegated legislation power of legislation entrusted to

A. President

B. Parliament

C. Organ other than the legislative

D. Judiciary

20. Principle of Natural Justice is given in our Constitution under

A. Art 14 and 21

B. Art 21 and 20

C. Art 14 and 27

D. Art 15 and 16

21. Principle of Natural Justice corresponds to the constitutional provisions of

A. Right of life

B. Right of equality

C. Right of education

D. Right of work

22. The principal of Natural Justice is also known as

A. Natural Justice

B. Fair justice

C. Substantial justice

D. Fairness in law

23. Principle of Natural Justice is

A. Simple and elementary

B. Complex

C. Sophisticated

D. None of these

24. *Audi Alteram partem* means

A. No person should be judges of his own cause

B. A person should be judges of his own cause

C. Every one should be heard before being condemned

D. Every one should not be heard before being condemned

25. *Nemo debet ess judix in propria causa* means

A. No person should be judges of his own cause

B. A person should be judges of his own cause

C. Every one should be heard before being condemned

D. Every one should not be heard before being condemned

ANSWERS

1	2	3	4	5	6	7	8	9	10
B	B	D	C	A	D	C	D	B	D
11	**12**	**13**	**14**	**15**	**16**	**17**	**18**	**19**	**20**
C	A	B	A	B	D	B	D	C	A
21	**22**	**23**	**24**	**25**					
B	C	A	C	A					

MIXED BAG

MULTIPLE CHOICE QUESTIONS

1. Which section of Indian Penal Code was struck down by Supreme Court, while making attempt to commit suicide non-punishable?

A. Section 302 of IPC
B. Section 304 of IPC
C. Section 309 of IPC
D. Section 310 of IPC

2. Muslim religious foundations are known as:

A. Diya B. Wakfs
C. Ulema D. Quzat

3. Article 361 of the constitution exempts the following from jurisdiction of t. e Penal Code:

A. Governor
B. President
C. Both A and B
D. None of the above

4. Words which appear to be innocent but contain some hidden meaning which may sense defamation is:

A. Innuendo
B. Slander
C. Libel
D. All of the above

5. What is true with rights of private defence in criminal law?

A. Private defence of only property
B. Private defence of only body of self
C. Private defence of property and body of self
D. Private defence of property of self or any other person and private defence of body of self or of any other

6. Central Vigilance Commission is to inquire offences committed by Central Government employees under:

A. Prevention of Corruption Act, 1988
B. General Clause Act 1897
C. Central Vigilance Act, 1985
D. None of the above

7. Central Vigilance Commission is constituted under:

A. Parliament action
B. Prevention of Corruption Act, 1988
C. Central Vigilance Commission Act 2003
D. All the above

8. Central Vigilance Commissioner shall be appointed by:

A. Home Minister of India
B. Prime Minister of India
C. President of India
D. Chief Justice of India

9. 'The Family Courts Act' was passed in the year:

A. 1988 B. 1978
C. 1984 D. 1974

10. Dowry prohibition Act, 1961 prohibit:

A. both giving and taking of dowry either directly or indirectly by a party to marriage
B. giving of dowry either directly or indirectly by a party to marriage
C. taking of dowry either directly or indirectly by a party to marriage
D. none of the above

11. Dissolution of Muslim Marriage Act, 1939 provides grounds of dissolution of Muslim marriage to:

A. Males and female
B. All family
C. Only male
D. Only female

12. Can a couple who has adopted a son, adopt another son legally?

A. yes
B. No, because law prohibits it
C. No, because they have already a child
D. None of these

13. The term wakf Muslim law means:

A. Temporary dedication by a person professing Islam of any property

B. Permanent dedication by a person professing Islam of any movable or immovable property for any purpose recognized by Muslim Law as pious, religious or charitable

C. Both A and B

D. None of these

14. Under the Workmen's Compensation Act, 1923 the amount of compensation in respect of death or injury or in respect of woman or a person under a legal disability shall not be made:

A. otherwise than by deposit with concerned court

B. otherwise than by deposit with Compensation Commissioner

C. otherwise than payment made directly by employer

D. all the above

15. The so-called provision in the Central Vigilance Commission Act 2003 envisages that CBI before conducting an enquiry into an offence committed by officers of the rank of joint secretary or above in any government department or in any public sector undertaking has to take prior approval of:

A. Central Vigilance Commission

B. Police Chief of that state

C. Central Government

D. State Government

16. Under the Repatriation of Prisoners Act, 2003 repatriation means:

A. Migration of offenders from one country to another country

B. Reception of certain prisoners from the country or place outside India only

C. Transfer of certain prisoners from India to country or place outside India and reception in India of certain prisoners from country or place outside India

D. Transfer of certain prisoners from India to country or place outside India only

17. The term prisoner under the Repatriation of Prisoners Act, 2003 means:

A. A person undergoing a sentence of imprisonment before the year 2000

B. A person undergoing a sentence of imprisonment passed by criminal court of India only

C. A person undergoing a sentence of imprisonment under an order passed by a criminal court including the courts established under the law for the time being in force in contracting courts

18. A child offender who commits any crime can be tried and prosecuted under the Juvenile Justice Act, 2000 only when his:

A. Age is below 12 years

B. Age is below 16 years

C. Age is below 18 years

D. Age is below 14 years

19. Copyright subsists for:

A. 50 years B. 40 years

C. 70 years D. 60 years

20. A person whose guardian has been appointed attains the age of majority at:

A. 16 years B. 18 years

C. 21 years D. 20 years

21. A major is a person who has attain the age of .... according to Indian Majority Act.

A. 16 years

B. 17 years

C. 18 years

D. 21 years

22. A Hindu wife can marry immediately after divorce but for Muslim wife

A. She also can marry immediately

B. According to decision of the court

C. Has to wait till period of seclusion (Iddat) is over

D. Has to wait for seven years

23. Fidilliary relationship means relationship based on:

A. Faith B. Trust

C. Contract D. Money

24. When the age of child accused cannot be proved by birth certificate, educational certificate or any other legal source, then court can order the test of:

A. Ossification test

B. Truth test

C. Blood test
D. All the above

25. Who is regarded as 'corporate sole'?
A. Prime Minister
B. President
C. King of England
D. Member of Parliament

26. Under which offence a police officer can arrest a person without a warrant:
A. Cognizable offence
B. Non-cognizable offence
C. Bailable offence
D. Non-bailable offence

27. .... are those offences which are punishable with imprisonment for two years or less. These offences can be compromised between the parties.
A. Cognizable offences
B. Non-cognizable offences
C. Compoundable offences
D. Non-compoundable offences

28. The meaning of unliquidated damage under law of torts is:
A. A certain money
B. Not as certainable
C. Penal and example
D. None of the above

29. ..... is an act which is twisted, crooked, which is not straight and lawful.
A. Crime B. Contract
C. Tort D. Wrong

30. Contract is said to have three essentials. Which one among the following is not an essential in the formation of contracts?
A. Offer
B. Acceptance
C. Damage
D. Consideration

31. A husband is obliged to maintain his divorced wife:
A. Till she gets remarried
B. Forever
C. Decided by court
D. Till the children grow up

32. The Indian Contract Act enacted in the year:
A. 1870 B. 1872
C. 1772 D. 1770

33. Public holidays are declared under:
A. Negotiable Instrument Act, 1881
B. Public Holiday Act, 1967
C. Public Employees Act, 1967
D. Contract Act, 1872

34. According to section 138 of Negotiable Instrument Act, 1881 the dishonour of cheque results in awarding punishment of:
A. six months
B. two years imprisonment or with fine
C. only imprisonment of a year
D. depends on discretion of the court

35. Under which Act, it was provided that women doing similar work to men, would qualify for equal pay:
A. Gender Equality Act, 1976
B. Protection of Women's Right Act, 1980
C. Equal Remuneration Act, 1976
D. Workmen's Compensation Act, 1948

36. Muslim Marriage is a:
A. Civil Contract
B. Sacrament
C. Both A and B
D. None of the above

37. A doctor has a .... relationship with his patient.
A. Personal B. Business
C. Financial D. Fiduciary

38. Large majority of Indian Muslims are covered under the:
A. Ismaili school of law
B. Hanafi School of law
C. Ithana school of law
D. Ashmi school of law

39. Euthanasia means:
A. Mercy killing
B. Murphy's death
C. Final exist
D. None of the above

40. Consider the following statements:
A. Felonies are major crime
B. Misdemeanors are major crime

C. Felonies are minor crime
D. Misdemeanors are minor crime

41. You send your employee with a computer to be delivered to your customer. The employee takes the computer home and uses it over a period of time. You find out a fortnight later and report him for:
A. Forgery B. Embezzlement
C. Cheating D. Fraud

42. .... is the law of place.
A. *Lex Loci*
B. National law
C. Both national law and municipal law
D. Both A and B

43. The rule of evidence which forbids a person from denying the truth of some statement formerly made by him:
A. Estoppel
B. Estreat
C. Estray
D. Et seq

44. When the Muslim husband and wife mutually consent to a divorce, it is known as
A. Khula
B. Mubarrat
C. Both A and B
D. None of the above

45. Which law ensures settlement of disputes in the industries in India?
A. The Industrial Dispute Act, 1947
B. The Trade Union Act, 1945
C. The Factories Act, 1947
D. Minimum Wages Act, 1948

46. The law related to marriage, succession, divorce of various communities:
A. under various personal laws which is codified or uncodified
B. under common civil code
C. is entirely uncodified
D. none of the above

47. Guideline for protection of witness which has issued by Delhi High Court in Neelam Katara case on 14th October 2003 shall remain in effect till:
A. Protection given to the witness of this case only
B. Case refer to Supreme Court
C. A suitable law is enacted for witness protection
D. None of the above

48. A right available against world at large is:
A. In rem B. In site
C. In personam D. All of the above

49. The truncated cheque which can be signed using digital signature is the provision under:
A. Banker's Books Evidence Act, 1891
B. State Bank of India Act, 1955
C. Banking Regulation Act, 1949
D. Negotiable Instruments Act, 1881

50. Innuendo hints at:
A. Defamation
B. Libel
C. Slander
D. All of the above

51. The application for monthly allowance for interim maintenance and expenses under section 125 of the Criminal Procedure Code as per the Criminal Laws (Amendment) Act, 2001 shall be disposed of):
A. Within 60 days from the date of notice of application to party
B. Within 15 days from the date of notice of application to party
C. Within 45 days from the date of notice of application to party
D. Within 90 days from the date of notice of application to party

52. Match the following:
I. Indemnity
II. In cast
III. Indictment
IV. Inadvertence
a. Carelessness
b. Sexual intercourse between members of a family
c. Written accusation of crime
d. Exemption from penalty
A. I-d, II-b, III-c, IV-a
B. I-d, II-b, III-a, IV-c
C. I-b, II-d, III-a, IV-c
D. I-b, II-d, III-c, IV-a

53. A triable offence committed by an adult is:
A. Civil wrong
B. Criminal offence
C. Indictable offence
D. None of these

54. Homicide is killing of a human being by another human being. It may be:
A. Lawful
B. Unlawful
C. Both A and B
D. None of the above

55. One of the following cannot be taken as Intellectual property:
A. Copyright
B. Discovery
C. Patents
D. None of these

56. When a witness repeats another person's statement the evidence is called:
A. Ideal evidence
B. Secondary evidence
C. Subsidiary evidence
D. Hearsay evidence

57. Ignorantia juris sine reum excusat stands for:
A. Ignorance of fact is no excuse
B. Ignorance of law is no excuse
C. Ignorance of law has excuse
D. None of the above

58. The killing of new born child by its parents:
A. Infanticide B. Foeticide
C. Malfeasance D. Abortion

59. A written acknowledgement of debt is abbreviated at IOU. It stands for:
A. I owe you
B. Promissory note
C. Instrument of understanding
D. All the above

60. An order of the court directs a person to do something or refrain from doing a particular thing is called:
A. Injunction B. Inhibition
C. Intortunuim D. Infans

61. Risk of conviction and punishment is called:
A. Justification B. Jeopardy
C. Antrefois D. Jetram

62. Bail means a method:
A. Under which accused person release from police custody
B. Under which accused person release from suit or case
C. To procure the release of a person from legal custody by undertaking that he shall appear at the trial before judgement
D. Under which accused person release for a period of 90 days

63. Match the following:
I. Ipso facto
II. Ultra vires
III. Intra vires
IV. Inter country
a. A. By the trust
b. Within powers
c. Not final
d. Beyond power
A. I-a, II-d, III-b, IV-c
B. I-a, II -d, III-c, IV-b
C. I-d, II -a, III-c, IV-b
D. I-d, II -a, III-b, IV-c

64. The execution of death sentence can be postponed in case of
A. Possibility of appeal in the Supreme Court or in case of pregnant women
B. Possibility of appeal in the High Court
C. Possibility of inspiration by the Session Court
D. All the above

65. The expression dying intestate refers to:
A. dying without leaving a will
B. dying with leaving a will
C. dying without a debt
D. dying with a debt

66. In a criminal trial the burden of proof means:
A. To prove the existence of any fact and when a person is bound to prove the existence of any fact, is said that the burden of proof lies on that person
B. To prove the existence of fact by court
C. To prove the existence of a particular section of the act under which the case is tried
D. To prove the existence of any law and when an authority of law is bound to prove

the existence of any law then it is said that the burden of proof lies on that authority

67. Extortion means:

A. Dishonestly including a person. So put in fear to deliver to any person any property or valuable security or anything signed or sealed which may be converted into valuable security

B. Intentionally putting any person in fear of any injury to him or to any other person

C. Both A and B

D. None of the above

68. Who among the following names is associated with drafting of Indian Penal Code 1860?

A. Lord Macaulay

B. Warren Hastings

C. Lord Lytton

D. Lord Rypen

69. Which one of the following legislations does not deal with the protection of environment?

A. Public Liability Insurance Act, 1991

B. Port Laws Amendment Act, 1997

C. Water Cess Act, 1977

D. Forest Conservation Act, 1980

70. Anticipatory bail under section 438 of the Criminal Procedure Code, 1972 means:

A. a direction to release a person on parole issued even before a person is appeared for arrest

B. a direction to release a person on bail issued after a person arrested

C. a direction to release a person on bail when he is in police custody after being arrested

D. a direction to release a person on bail issued even before a persons is appeared for arrest

71. The maxim Res Ispa Loquitor means:

A. things speak themselves

B. things do not speak themselves

C. justice is blind

D. there is remedy for every wrong

72. A National Environment Appellate Authority to deal with complaints, petition, appeals against the Government on environment clearance projects was created by the Act in the year:

A. 1990 B. 1992

C. 1995 D. 1997

73. In criminal law the burden of proving the guilty of an accused lies upon the:

A. Defence B. Prosecution

C. Accused D. Victim

74. Indian Criminal Law consists of:

A. Indian Penal Code and Indian Evidence Act

B. Indian Evidence Act and Criminal Procedure Code

C. Criminal Procedure Code and Indian Penal Code

D. Indian Penal Code

75. Which among the following statement is true with Indian Penal Code?

A. Indian Penal Code is to prevent lawlessness and punish offenders

B. Indian Penal Code is a procedural law

C. Indian Penal Code makes the procedure to punish offender

D. Indian Penal Code is to punish offender

76. "Local Law" under Indian Penal Code refers to:

A. as a law applicable to all over India

B. as a law applicable to a particular part of India

C. as a law applicable to Jammu and Kashmir

D. none of these

77. When an offer is accepted by other party, it becomes:

A. Contract B. Consideration

C. Agreement D. Proposal

78. Which day is celebrated as National Consumer's Day as the Consumer Protection Act was enacted on that day in 1986?

A. 24 December B. 24 October

C. 21 May D. 21 December

79. Whoever has sexual intercourse with a person who is and whom he knows or has reason to believe to be the wife of another man, without the consent of that man, such sexual intercourse amount to:

A. Bigamy
B. Abatement of rape
C. Unnatural sex
D. Adultery

80. The maxim *Ubi jus ibi remedium* means
A. In law there is a remedy for every wrong
B. In law there is a remedy for every one
C. In law justice is according to damage
D. None of there

81. The Central Pollution Control Board (CPCB) was set up under the provisions of:
A. The Environment Protection Act
B. The Water Act
C. The Water (Prevention and Control of Pollution) Act
D. The Central Pollution Control Act

82. Cruelty to a women by husband or relative of husband is deprived under:
A. Section 304 of Indian Penal Code
B. Section 498 of Indian Penal Code
C. Section 498-A of Indian Penal Code
D. Section 302 of Indian Penal Code

83. In 2002, India satisfied the protocol on:
A. Bio-Chemistry B. Bio-safety
C. Bio-physics D. Bio-diversity

84. 'Defamation' infringes a person right to:
A. life B. reputation
C. pride D. status

85. Match the following:
I. Alive
II. Adultery
III. Adulteration
IV. Alteration
a. Adding of a substance to food which renders it dangerous to health
b. Sleeping with a married partner
c. A dispute
d. An excuse
A. I-d, II-b, III-a, IV-c
B. I-d, II-a, III-b, IV-c
C. I-b, II-c, III-a, IV-b
D. I-c, II-c, III-d, IV-a

86. An insolvent person is:
A. Bankrupt
B. Mad
C. Infirm
D. Financially unsound

87. A crime of unlawfully damaging or destroying property by fire is called:
A. Arson B. Affray
C. Adultery D. Advownon

88. Injury under Indian Penal Code refers to:
A. any act illegally caused to any person, in body, mind, reputation or property
B. any act illegally caused to any person on his body
C. any act illegally caused to any person, in body and mind
D. any act illegally caused to any person in body and reputation

89. Right of private defence under section 97 of the Indian Penal Code extends to:
A. Private defence of body of himself and self property
B. Private defence of body of himself and any other person and private defence of property to himself and any other person
C. Private defence of self property
D. None of these

90. If a witness makes a statement in court, knowing it to be false he commits the offence of:
A. false evidence B. perils
C. perjury D. all of the above

91. Which law takes care of the Stock Exchanges and their operation in India?
A. The Securities and Exchange Board of India Act
B. The Depositories Act
C. The Companies Act
D. The Controller of Capital Issues Act

92. Which statement is true?
A. Hindi is the official language of the union as per constitution of India
B. English is the official of the union as per constitution of India
C. Both A and B
D. None of these

93. Punishment as provided for the offences under Indian Penal Code reads as:
I. Fine

II. Imprisonment for life
III. Capital punishment
IV. Forfeiture of property
A. only I
B. only I and IV
C. only I, II and III
D. all of the above

94. Law of Contract deals with:
A. Proposal and acceptance
B. Ownership and transfer of obligation
C. Enforcement of obligations as per agreements and promise
D. All the above

95. Which Hindu Law is being amended to give equal property rights to women in the society?
A. Hindu succession Act
B. Hindu maintenance and adoption Act
C. Hindu Marriage Act
D. All the above

96. "Closure" the word used in Parliament means:
A. end of zero hour
B. end of session
C. closure of adjournment motion
D. stop of further debate on a motion under consideration

97. Contempt of Court means:
A. civil wrong
B. criminal wrong
C. both civil as well as crimnal wrong
D. none of the above

98. The delimitation commission was established in 2002. The chairman of this commission was:
A. Justice Y.B. Chandrachud
B. Justice Kuldip Singh
C. Justice Nanavati
D. Justice V.R. Krishan Iyer

99. For a valid contract which of the following conditions must be satisfied:
I. Intention to contract
II. Consenous ad idem
III. Must be set out in writing
IV. Legality of object
A. I, II and IV
B. I, II and III
C. III and IV
D. I, II, III and IV

100. What is the meaning of culpable?
A. Involving a breach of legal duty
B. Blame worthy
C. Both A and B
D. None of these

101. An order of a court proclaimed on the hearing of a suit is called:
A. Decree B. Degree
C. Deed D. Dehor

102. Punishment for rape reads as:
A. Imprisonment which shall not be less than 5 years but which may be for life for a term which may extend to 13 years and also with fine
B. Imprisonment which shall not be less than 7 years but which may be for life or for a term which may extend to 10 years and also with fine
C. Imprisonment which shall not be less than 14 years but which may be for life or for a term which may extend to 12 years and also with fine
D. Only capital punishment

103. Electoral right in respect of section 171 of Indian Penal Code means:
A. the right of a person to vote a candidate in election
B. the right of a person to stand as a candidate in election
C. the right of a person to stand or not to stand as or to withdraw from being, a candidate or to vote or refrain from voting at any election
D. the right of a person to stand, or not to stand as or to withdraw from being a candidate

104. What is true with mistake of law and mistake of fact is commiting a criminal offence?
A. Mistake of law and mistake of fact both have no excuse
B. Mistake of law and mistake of fact both are not defence
C. Mistake of law is a defence whereas mistake of fact is no defence

D. Mistake of law is no defence whereas mistake of fact may be treated as defence

105. Damages are awarded except crime case:
A. Breach of contract B. Tort
C. Criminal conduct D. Libel suit

106. Property of a female Hindu according to the Hindu Succession Act of 1952 shall be held:
A. to be her absolute property
B. to be her conditional property
C. to be her contingent property
D. to be her limited property

107. The first cyber police station viz. a cyber crime cells whose jurisdiction covers all offences committed under Information Technology Act, 2000 offences relating to intellectual property and cyber crimes was set up in 1995 at:
A. New Delhi B. Mumbai
C. Bangalore D. Madras

108. According to Freedom of Information Act, 2002, the freedom of information means:
A. All citizens have right to get information
B. Public authorities have right to get information
C. Certain citizens have right to obtain information from public authority
D. Specified citizens have rights to get information

109. Which among the following relates to capital punishments?
A. Sentence of life imprisonment
B. Sentence of rigorous life imprisonment
C. Sentence of death
D. Sentence of death with fine

110. Joint heirs to a property are called:
A. Ancestral B. Father
C. Coparcener D. Co-owners

111. According to the Hindu Succession Act, 1956, a child in mother's womb at the time of death of an intestate and sequently born alive shall:
A. have right subject to age of intestate
B. have same right to inherit to intestate as if born before death of intestate
C. have not same right as others have
D. none of the above

112. Under the Contempt of Courts Act, 1971 the accused may be discharged or punishment may be remitted on:
A. apology that educes punishment
B. apology made to the satisfaction of court
C. apology has no place in the Act
D. none of these

113. Punishment for person illegally practicing in courts and before other authorities amounts to:
A. Imprisonment upto 2 years
B. Imprisonment upto 1½ years
C. Imprisonment upto 1 year
D. Imprisonment upto 6 months

114. Match the following:
I. Consumer Protection Act
II. Workmen's Compensation Act
III. Industrial Disputes Act
IV. Hindu Marriage Act
a. 1986
b. 1947
c. 1955
d. 1923
A. I-a, II-b, III-c, IV-d
B. I-d, II-c, III-b, IV-a
C. I-a, II-d, III-c, IV-b
D. I-a, II-d, III-b, IV-c

115. To permit operations of private life Insurance Companies, the Government of India enacted the Insurance Regulatory and Development Authority Act in the year:
A. 2000 B. 1999
C. 1998 D. 1997

116. According to the Negotiable Instruments (Amendment and Miscellaneous Provisions) Act, 2002 the cheque includes:
A. Electronic image of a truncated cheque and a cheque in the electronic form
B. Electronic image only
C. Electronic device only
D. Cheque in the electronic form only

117. Except in case of court of judicial commissioner the hearing of cases of criminal contempt to be by:
A. Bench of not less than 9 judges
B. Bench of not less than 7 judges

C. Bench of not less than 5 judges
D. Bench of not less than 2 judges

118. The Competition Commission of India is established under:
A. Monopolies and Restrictive Trade Practice Act, 1969
B. Competition Act, 2002
C. Consumer Protection Act, 1986
D. None of these

119. In year 2002 the Competition Act was enacted by the replacement of:
A. Monopolies and Restrictive Trade Practice Act, 1969
B. Consumer Protection Act, 1986
C. Prevention of Corruption Act, 1999
D. Protection of Civil Right Act, 1955

120. National conference on rivers interlinking; a win-win situation 2003:
A. India will get benefit for kharif crops
B. India will get benefit for farming of any type
C. India will get benefit facilities from least irrigated area
D. India will get benefit by Rs. 5,60,000 cross project by way of providing drinking water and irrigation

121. To ensure minimum 100 days employment to the rural population of the country, the Central government tabled before the Parliament during December, 2004:
A. National Rural Employment Guarantee Bill, 2004
B. Rural Employment Bill, 2004
C. India Rural Employment Bill, 2004
D. None of these

122. Law of torts deals with:
A. Defamation
B. Negligence
C. Trespass
D. All the above

123. The law of contract allows parties to :
A. Enforce contract
B. Make law for themselves
C. Both A and B
D. None of these

124. The provision of Indian Succession Act, 1956 do not apply to:
A. Hindu
B. Muslim
C. Christian
D. Both B and C

125. The word due process of law means:
A. In course through courts
B. Justice by tribunals
C. As ordained by statue law
D. In course of time

126. A mode of transfer of property, including mortgage, lease etc. but excluding will:
A. Conversion
B. Conveyance
C. Contumacy
D. Conusance

127. In order of the following, employment is not covered by the right to equality of opportunity for all citizens enshrined in the Constitution of India:
A. Local bodies
B. Co-operative societies
C. Public sector undertaking
D. Government department

128. .... is an established defence when it is proved that the plaintiff failed to take reasonable care of himself and thus contributed to his injuries.
A. Self injury
B. Volenti non fit injuria
C. Contributory negligence
D. None of these

129. The time limit for filling different kinds of suits is contained in:
A. Court rules in India
B. Under Bar Council of India
C. Limitation Act
D. Arbitration Act

130. The Maxim "*in causit probatio equi dict, non qui negat*" what does it mean?
A. Guilt must be proven beyond reasonable doubt
B. Where there is a guilty then there is a remedy

C. The burden of proof is on him who denies
D. No man is guilty without proof

131. Sales of Goods Act, 1930, contains provisions regarding:
A. Sales and purchase of goods
B. Movable property
C. Immovable property
D. All of the above

132. What is the legal name given to the repairs needed to a house at the end of a tenancy?
A. Dies netasti
B. Dilapidations
C. Dies utids
D. Dies fasi

133. The relief provided under Specific Relief Act, 1963:
A. Pro rata B. Pari passu
C. Mandatory D. Discretionary

134. Decit is:
A. a tort B. a crime
C. both A and B D. none of these

135. Which type of statement is made by law?
I. If murder is committed, the murderer will be punished with death or life imprisonment
II. Murder is wrong, do not commit it
A. only II
B. only I
C. both I and II
D. neither I nor II

136. The Indian Succession Act, 1956 contains provisions regarding:
A. Intestate succession
B. Testamentary succession
C. Both A and B
D. None of these

137. Stay order has the effect of:
A. Status quo B. Sine die
C. Pari passu D. Pro rata

138. Transfer of Property Act, 1882 covers:
A. Immovable property
B. Movable property
C. Both A and B
D. None of these

139. A nominal sum given as a token that the parties are eager about concluding the sale is called:
A. Earnest money B. Debt
C. Security D. Advance money

140. Though there is provision under section 146 of the Evidence Act, 1872 that a witness can be cross examined to discover who he is and what is his position in life, in the case of rape or attempt to rape the prosecutrix cannot be asked as to her general immoral character. This provision was made in:
A. Indian Penal Code (Amendment) Act, 1990
B. Criminal Procedure (Amendment) Act, 1999
C. Indian Evidence (Amendment) Act, 2002
D. All of the above

141. The phrase 'duty to care' means you must take reasonable care to avoid acts or omissions which you can reasonably foresee would be likely to injure your neighbour. In this definition, the word 'neighbour' means:
A. All person whom I know
B. All people of that state
C. All persons living in any vicinity, whom I owe a duty of care
D. All persons who can be so closely and directly affected, that I ought to reasonably have them in contemplation

142. What is the diminished responsibility?
A. When death is caused by a person
B. When death is caused by an insane person
C. When death is caused by an accident
D. When death is caused by duress

143. Parties may refers their disputes to an independent third party, instead of regular courts, under the provision of:
A. Limitation Act
B. Arbitration Act
C. Negotiable instrument Act
D. Arbitration & Conciliation Act

144. Crime is an act or omission which is perceived as harmful to society at large. This is proved:
A. by punished him
B. by trial is by court
C. by the state government
D. by one party to criminals suit being state

145. A mortgage is of immovable property while a pledge is of ...... property:
A. Immovable property
B. Movable property
C. Both A and B
D. None of these

146. .... is a general pardon:
A. Amnesty B. Remission
C. Reprieve D. Suspension

147. Family law comprises of laws governing:
A. Family relation
B. Property matter
C. Matrimonial property
D. Matrimonial relations

148. The act of unlawfully entering into another's property:
A. trespass
B. bailiff
C. supra
D. breach of property

149. Offence of breaking a divine idol:
A. trespass B. sacrilege
C. blasphemy D. crime

150. The act of having anal intercourse is the offence of:
A. Slander B. Sodomy
C. Adultery D. Sedition

151. When the master is held liable for the wrongful act of his servant, the liability is:
A. Strict
B. Absolute
C. Vicarious
D. All the above

152. Match the following:
I. Vis major
II. Volenti non fit injuria
III. Void
IV. Voidable
a. Irresistible force
b. An act illegal from very beginning
c. An act until rescinded, legal
d. Consent is defence
A. I-a, II-d, III-c, IV-b
B. I-d, II-a, III-c, IV-b
C. I-b, II-c, III-d, IV-a
D. I-a, II-d, III-b, IV-c

153. The term heir under the Hindu Succession Act, 1956 defines:
A. any person, male or female, who is entitled to succeed to the property of an intestate
B. any person, male or female, who is entitled to succeed to the property under a will
C. any male who is entitled to succeed to the property under an intestate
D. only son of the deceased and is entitled to succeed to property, of intestate

154. The term 'half blood' under Hindu succession Act, 1956 defines:
A. When two persons are descended from a common ancestor but by different wives
B. When two persons are descended from a common mother but different husbands
C. When two person are descended from a separate ancestors by different wives
D. When two persons are descended from a common ancestor but by same wife

155. The term "full blood" under the Hindu succession Act, 1956 defines:
A. When two persons are descended from a common ancestor by the same wife
B. When two persons are descended from a common ancestor but by different wives
C. When two persons are descended from a common wife but different husbands
D. When two persons one descended from a separate ancestor by same wife

156. According to Indian Law a man is presumed to be dead if he is not heard of as alive for:
A. 9 years B. 7 years
C. 5 years D. 2 years

157. A women who institute and carries on proceeding in a criminal court of law is:
A. Prosecutrix B. Prosecutor
C. Advocate D. Fallen

158. An act in excess of the authority conferred by law:
A. Intra virus B. Ultra virus
C. Illegal D. All the above

159. What is testament?
A. court order
B. evidence (oral)

C. evidence (documentary)
D. will

160. Which among the following states have ground water regulation laws in India?
A. Gujarat and Maharashtra
B. Haryana and Punjab
C. Kerala and Tamil Nadu
D. Himachal Pradesh and Punjab

161. The term consumer means a person:
A. who buys the goods
B. who buys the goods and service for a consideration
C. who sells the goods and give service for a consideration
D. who buys goods and service and consideration is irrelevant

162. "A civil wrong for which the remedy is a common law action for unliquidated damages, and which is not exclusively the breach of contract, or the breach of trust". This definition of tort is given by:
A. Dicey B. Williams
C. Salmond D. Winfield

163. Right to life and personal liberty is:
A. physical rights
B. fundamental rights
C. equality rights
D. constitutional rights

164. The maxim –"*salus populi suprema lex*" means:
A. Welfare of people is paramount law
B. Law is supreme in society
C. Everyone is equal before law
D. Law is equal for everyone

165. An act done under threat or fear is done under:
A. Compulsion B. Duress
C. Dunress D. All the above

166. Husband and wife have a right to each other's company. This right is called:
A. conjugal right
B. legal right
C. matrimonial right
D. consortium right

167. A lawyer appointed by court to represent a poor litigant is:
A. Amicus curiae
B. Advocate
C. Public prosecutor
D. None of these

168. When property is in possession of a person other than the owner, the owner is in:
A. Adverse possession
B. Dispossession
C. Unpossession
D. None of these

169. Defamation by means of writing, print etc. is legally called:
A. Slander B. Liable
C. Libel D. Liber

170. Liability is:
A. Responsibility
B. Subjection to legal obligation
C. Duty
D. To take care of other

171. The offence of inciting disaffection, hatred or contempt against government is:
A. Not an offence
B. Defamation
C. Sedition
D. Treason

172. An exclusive right conferred on one who invents a machine, to make, use, sell or assign it for a certain period is called:
A. Copyright B. Inquents
C. Patent D. Deed

173. In which of the following a man is liable independently of the existence of either wrongful in act or negligence?
A. Strict liability
B. Vicarious liability
C. Both A and B
D. None of these

174. When a judge makes certain remarks in the course of his judgement, which are said " by the way" and do not have direct bearing on the facts at hand. Such remarks are called:
A. Comments ordinaralis
B. Observation
C. Obiter dictum
D. Judicial dictum

175. In some primitive tribes, an alleged óffender is made to walk on a network of red hot iron rod. If he burns himself, it is taken as guilty and killed and if he crosses the network unharmed he is taken as innocent and is acquitted. This method of trial is called:
- A. Arbitrio judicis
- B. Trial by god
- C. Trial by ordeal
- D. Trial by conscience

176. The reason (or ground) of a judicial decision is known as:
- A. obiter dicta
- B. ratione sole
- C. ratione tenural
- D. ratio decidendi

177. Negligence means:
- A. doing something which a prudent and reasonable
- B. causing damage
- C. both A and B
- D. omission to do something which a reasonable

178. A person who takes proceeding against the accused on behalf of the state:
- A. Procator — B. Prosecutor
- C. Judge — D. Lawyer

179. Mens rea is translated as :
- A. Evil — B. Guilty mind
- C. Unlawful act — D. Intention

180. Who is a recidivist?
- A. Rash person
- B. Saint
- C. Habitual criminal
- D. Reserved person

181. A marriage between an unmarried woman and a married man is:
- A. valid — B. null
- C. void — D. voidable

182. What is plea bargaining?
- A. A procedure by which an accused pleads
- B. A conference between opposing lawyers to settle claim
- C. A proud term between opposing lawyers and judge to determine the time a case should take place
- D. A procedure by which a defendant pleads

183. Law of contract is a:
- A. International law
- B. Conflict of law
- C. Public law
- D. Private law

184. A person who attests copies of original documents, to render them authentic is called:
- A. Notary public
- B. Advocate
- C. Public prosecutor
- D. All the above

185. A borrows money from B and pledges some land as security for repayment of debt. The arrangement is called:
- A. Hundi — B. Pledge
- C. Mortgage — D. None of these

186. X filed a suit for breach of contract against Y. The district court decided in X's favour. However, appealed to the High Court, the legal terminology for X is appellant , which X would be called:
- A. Respondent — B. Accused
- C. Defendant — D. Plaintiff

187. One of the following is not a negotiable instrument :
- A. Promissory note
- B. Will
- C. Bill of exchange
- D. Cheque

188. When an on-going case is adjourned to a future date and defendant is ordered to be kept in custody in the meantime, the defendant is said to:
- A. decreed — B. ordered
- C. remanded — D. condemned

189. A rule of inheritance which favours the eldest son:
- A. *primus inter pares*
- B. *ultimogeniture*
- C. *ux ori local*
- D. *primogeniture*

190. A child born after father's death:
- A. Bastard — B. Postea
- C. Postliminits — D. Posthumous

191. The early release of a prisoner is called:
A. Parole B. Bail
C. Lien D. Lease

192. One who bring an action at law?
A. Party B. Plaintiff
C. Plaint D. Defendant

193. An exclusive right conferred on one who invents a machine, to make, use sell or assign it for a certain period is called:
A. Deed B. Patent
C. Invent D. Copyright

194. The gifts or ornaments, clothes etc. given to a woman by her husband are legally called:
A. Parcels
B. Paraphernalia
C. Bride wealth
D. Dowry

195. Consider the following statements:
I. consanguinity implies relationship of blood as between father and sons
II. affinity implies relations by marriage as between husband and wife's brother
A. I is true, II is true
B. I is false II is true
C. Both are false
D. Both are true

196. criminal law is .... law, while administrative law is .... law
A. Private, private
B. Public, private
C. Private, public
D. Public, public

197. Consider the following statements:
I. piracy is an act of robbery on the sea
II. piracy is the infringement of copyright
A. only II is correct
B. both are incorrect
C. both I and II are correct
D. only I is correct

198. A deed is a written statement which is:
A. Sealed
B. Delivered
C. Signed
D. All of the above are necessary

199. The mistaken decision of a court:
A. Per curian B. Pepper cort
C. Per curiam D. Per intorrunium

200. Who said "Litigation is a game in which the court is umpire"?
A. Pollock B. Austin
C. Blackstone D. Salmond

ANSWERS

1	2	3	4	5	6	7	8	9	10
C	B	C	A	D	A	D	C	B	A
11	**12**	**13**	**14**	**15**	**16**	**17**	**18**	**19**	**20**
D.	C	B	B	C	C	C	C	D	C
21	**22**	**23**	**24**	**25**	**26**	**27**	**28**	**29**	**30**
C	C	B	A	C	A	C	B	C	C
31	**32**	**33**	**34**	**35**	**36**	**37**	**38**	**39**	**40**
A	B	A	B	C	A	D	B	A	B
41	**42**	**43**	**44**	**45**	**46**	**47**	**48**	**49**	**50**
B	A	A	C	A	A	C	A	C	A
51	**52**	**53**	**54**	**55**	**56**	**57**	**58**	**59**	**60**
A	A	C	C	B	D	B	A	A	A
61	**62**	**63**	**64**	**65**	**66**	**67**	**68**	**69**	**70**
B	C	A	A	A	A	C	A	C	D
71	**72**	**73**	**74**	**75**	**76**	**77**	**78**	**79**	**80**
A	D	B	C	A	B	C	A	D	A

81	82	83	84	85	86	87	88	89	90
C	C	B	B	A	A	A	A	B	C
91	**92**	**93**	**94**	**95**	**96**	**97**	**98**	**99**	**100**
A	A	D	D	A	D	C	B	B	C
101	**102**	**103**	**104**	**105**	**106**	**107**	**108**	**109**	**110**
C	B	C	D	C	A	C	A	C	C
111	**112**	**113**	**114**	**115**	**116**	**117**	**118**	**119**	**120**
B	B	D	A	B	A	C	B	A	D
121	**122**	**123**	**124**	**125**	**126**	**127**	**128**	**129**	**130**
A	D	C	D	A	B	B	B	C	C
131	**132**	**133**	**134**	**135**	**136**	**137**	**138**	**139**	**140**
B	B	D	C	B	C	A	A	C	D
141	**142**	**143**	**144**	**145**	**146**	**147**	**148**	**149**	**150**
B	D	D	B	A	D	A	B	B	B
151	**152**	**153**	**154**	**155**	**156**	**157**	**158**	**159**	**160**
C	D	A	A	A	B	A	C	A	A
161	**162**	**163**	**164**	**165**	**166**	**167**	**168**	**169**	**170**
B	C	A	A	B	A	A	A	C	B
171	**172**	**173**	**174**	**175**	**176**	**177**	**178**	**179**	**180**
C	C	A	C	C	D	C	B	B	C
181	**182**	**183**	**184**	**185**	**186**	**187**	**188**	**189**	**190**
C	D	D	A	D	A	B	C	D	D
191	**192**	**193**	**194**	**195**	**196**	**197**	**198**	**199**	**200**
A	B	B	B	D	D	C	D	C	A

LEGAL TERMS

— A —

Abandonment Relinquishment of an interest, claim of right voluntarily.

Abduction The wrongful taking away of a person. A male above the age of 16 and a female above the age of 18 is abducted below that age, they are kidnapped. Section 352 of Indian Penal Code deals with this offence.

Abet To aid in the commission of an offence.

Abettor One who encourages or aid the commission of an offence.

Abide To act in accordance with rule of law.

Ab initio From the very beginning.

Abscond One who hide oneself in order to escape arrest of legal proceeding for a crime or avoid arrest.

Accessory A person who is concerned in the crime but does not actually commit the crime.

Accomplice A person who is associated with another person in the commission of any offence.

Accused A person becomes an accused immediately after he has been arrested by the police for an offence which forms the subject matter of investigation by them.

Acquittal The order of discharge of courts if a court satisfied with the evidence that the accused is not guilty, he shall record an order of acquittal (Cr,P.C., 1973, Secs. 248 and 255).

Act of God An accident which occurs due to the operation of natural forces, which no human foresight could provide against.

Act of State Act done by Government in the exercise of its sovereign powers.

Actionable Wrong A wrongful act which an action lies in a court of law.

Actus Reus Wrongful act.

Adjourn To defer the hearing of a case to another date in the court.

Adjudication Decision of the court, e.g., The order of a court which declares a debtor to be a bankrupt.

Ad Idem With a common understanding.

Ad Valorem According to the valuation.

Administrative Law That branch of public law which deals with the various organs of the sovereign power and rules made by him.

Adultery Adultery is voluntary sexual intercourse between a married man and some other than his wife or between a married woman and some other than her husband.

Adverse Claim A claim put forward against the interest of another person.

Affidavit A written statement under a oath, which is sworn to by person making it, as true.

Affray Unlawful fighting or use of force to intimidate others.

Age of Capacity The age at which a person becomes legally capable of entering into a contract, executing a will, maintaining a law suit etc.

Age of Majority The age at which a person attains full legal rights e.g. 18 years in India.

Agnates Relatives whose relationship can be traced exclusively through males.

Alibi (Elsewhere) A defence where an accused alleges that at the time when the offence with which he is charged was committed, he was elsewhere.

Alien Enemy A person owing allegiance to an adverse belligerent state.

Alimony The maintenance given by husband to his divorced wife.

Assault Sudden violent attack to hurt another person by striking at him with or without weapon.

Amicus Curiae The friend of the court is the name is given to the lawyer appointed by a court to represent a poor litigant.

Amnesty A general pardon given by Government.

Annuity An amount that is payable yearly after a certain period.

Appeal Application to a higher court to examine against a case decided by a lower court and possibly given a different decision.

Arbitration Settling disputes by referring them to independent third parties.

Arrest Arrest means the lawful restraining of the liberty of a person in order to compel obedience to the order of a court or to prevent the commission of a crime.

Arson Crime of unlawfully damaging or destroying by fire.

Assay Usually used to denote examination of weight and measures by officials.

Attach To take, seize or apprehend property by order of court.

Autrefois A person cannot be tried for the same offence twice.

— B —

Bail Releasing an arrested person after taking sureties that he will regularly attend the court and face the trail.

Bailiff A subordinate officer of the court who executes writs and other court orders such as serving summons.

Bailment When goods are left by one person with another to hold accordance with instructions.

Barter To exchange one commodity for another.

Bastard A child born by unlawful wedlock, an illegitimate child.

Battery Crime of actual or intended use of physical force on a person.

Bench Name of the judge sit in court.

Bestiality Act of having intercourse with an animal. It is prohibited and punishable.

Bequeath To dispose of personal property by will.

Bigamy Entering into a marriage with one person while still legally married to another. It is an offence, punishable by seven years in prison.

Blasphemy The public or criminal libel of speaking matter relating to God Jesus Christ, the Bible or the book of common prayer, intending to wound the feelings of mankind or to excite contempt and hatred against the church.

Body Corporate An association or collection of persons having rights and duties distinct from those of the individual persons who form it from time to time.

Bona Fide In good faith.

Bona Vacantia Goods that do not have an owner. Generally they go to the finder.

Bond A legal instrument by which a person undertakes to do or not to do something.

Borstal A reformatory where young offenders are kept.

Breach The infringing or violation of a right, duty or law, agreement etc.

Breach of Contract Breach of contract is failure to perform the obligation under the contract.

Brief An abbreviated statement of acts and points of law drawn up for counsel in charge of a case.

Breach of Trust 'Breach of trust' means a breach of any duty imposed on a trusted. As such, by any law for the time being in force (Indian Trust Act, 1882, sec.3).

Buggery Sodomy; the offence committed by a person consisting of anal penetration punishable by the Sexual offences Act, 1956. It is prohibited by law as an unnatural offence.

Burden of Proof The duty of a party to prove a disputed assertion or charge.

By Stander One who is present at the place of occurrence but does not participate in it.

By Law Regulations made by the local authority or corporation or company for its members for their day to day work.

— C —

Case A legal action or trial, argument put in legal proceedings.

Caveat A warning..

Caveat Emptor Let the purchaser beware.

Cede To assign or transfer, To transfer territory.

Certiorari A writ from Superior Court which quashes the decision of a lower court because it is based on irregular procedure.

Charge-Sheet It is the process in which the officer in charge of a police station or lock-up enters the accusation or charges against person brought there in custody whether arrested with or without warrant.

Chattel Movable property.

Circumstantial Evidence A series of circumstances from which an inference of suit can be drawn.

Class Action A law suit brought by a representative member of a group of person on behalf of all others.

Cognate Blood relation other than an agnate and includes a female relation only.

Cognizable Offence An offence in which arrest can be made without a warrant.

Cognizance Cognizance means the acceptance of a cause for hearing and decision to take notice of a dispute or controversy, taking judicial notice by court.

Cohabitation Living together as husband and wife even if not married.

Commutation The change of a penalty or punishment from a greater to a less punishment.

Confession Confession is a written acknowledgement of guilt by a party accused of an offence.

Condonation The Pardoning of an offence.

Conjugal Rights Right of husband/wife to the consortium of the other.

Consanguinity Relationship by blood.

Consideration The price for the promise to do or not to do something. Every contract requires consideration to be legally enforceable.

Consummation Voluntarily sexual intercourse to make marriage complete.

Contempt of Court Willful disregard, disobedience or disrespect to a court of law.

Contraband Goods Goods prohibited by law.

Contract A legally binding agreement between two or more parties.

Conversion The action of wrongfully converting something to one's own use.

Conveyance A written document transferring ownership of land from one person to another.

Conviction Conviction is the act of a court awarding a person guilty of a criminal offence and awarding a punishment.

Coparcener One who shares (equally) with other inheritance in the estate of a common ancestor.

Copyright The exclusive right of printing or otherwise multiplying copies of published literary work; That is, the right of preventing all others from doing so. The infringement of this right is called piracy. Copyright extends to original, artistic, dramatic and musical works and to recordings films and broadcast, etc.

Coroner An officer who inquires into any violent of unnatural death.

Corpus A body; human body.

Court Fee The fee payable on filing of a suit, application, appeal, etc. in the court of law.

Court Martial A tribunal for the administration of military law.

Covenant An agreement in writing between two persons, whereby, one is enjoying to do or not to do something.

Culpable Criminal, blameworthy.

Custody Confinement or imprisonment e.g. Remand (of accused person) in custody, Control and possession of something or person e.g. To surrender ourself into the custody of the court.

Custom An unwritten law dating back to civilization. This is a conduct which is observed uniformly and voluntarily by the people.

— D —

Damages A sum of money paid to the plaintiff as compensation for breach of contract or tort.

De Facto In fact, actually.

De Jure According to the law.

Declaratory Decree A decree which simply declares the rights of the parties to express the opinion of the court on any question without ordering to be done.

Decree A judgement delivered by a court.

Deed A written statement which is signed, sealed and delivered.

Defamation Publication of a false or derogatory statement regarding a person, which lowers his reputation in the eyes of members of the society.

Defendant A person sued in a court of law.

Delegated Legislation This consists of orders, rules regulations, directions, by laws etc. which is made by a person or body other than the legislative authority by virtue of powers conferred by the statute. It is also called subordinate legislation or administrative legislation.

Demise The grant of lease.

Deposition The giving of testimony upon oath in a court of law.

Deponent A person who makes an affidavit or deposition.

Desertion Abandonment by one spouse or the other.

Devise A gift of land in a will.

Disclaimer Disclaimer is an express denial, or complete renouncing one's legal right or claim.

Diplomatic Privilege Legal immunity accorded to ambassadors and representatives of foreign governments.

Distress The seizure chattel to satisfy out of the proceeds of its sale, some debt or claim.

Divorce Dissolution of marriage.

Domicile The place where one has his permanent residence to which, if absents, he has the intention of returning.

Donee To whom gift is made.

Donor One who makes a gift.

— E —

Easement	Right which an owner of land has over land of another person, e.g. Right of light, right of way.
Embezzlement	Dishonest misappropriation of property by a person, who comes in possession thereof lawfully.
Eminent Domain	Power of the state to acquire private property for public use.
Enactment	Act of Parliament.
Encumbrance	A liability on property.
Encroachment	Unlawfully entering upon another's rights or possessions.
Equity	Fair and right, the recourse to general principles of justice to correct and supplement the ordinary law.
Escheat	The lapsing of property of the sovereign or state on the death of the owner intestate and without heir.
Estate	An interest in land.
Estoppels	A rule of evidence preventing a person from denying truth of statement which he has made previously by which he has led another to believe and act upon.
Eviction	Dispossession; recovery of land by the application law.
Ex Gratia	Payment as a favour without any legal obligation.
Evidence	The legal means exclusive of more argument, which tend to prove or disprove any matter of fact, the truth of which is submitted to judicial investigation.
Ex Officio	By virtue of office.
Ex Parte Order	An order granted after hearing one party only.
Execution	Enforcing a court's judgement with the force of law.
Executor	A representative appointed in a will to execute the will after the testator's death.
Expert Witness	One who gives an opinion on a particular subject due to his special knowledge.
Extradition	A process by which an offender is transferred from one country to another for a trial.

— F —

False Imprisonment	The confinement of a person without just cause or excuse. There must be a total restraint of the person, and the onus of proving reasonable cause is on the defendant.
Felony	Crime of any kind, legally graver than misdemeanors.
Feme Sole	Unmarried woman.
Fiat	A command, a decree, a short order or warrant of a judge or public officer that certain steps should be taken.
Fiduciary	A relationship based on trust or good faith.
FIR	First information report of grievance which is given to police.
Force Majeure	Irresistible force, circumstances beyond one's control.
Fore Closure	A decree determines the equitable right of a mortgagor to redeem after the mortgagee's estate has become absolute at law.
Forfeiture	A punishment whereby the offender lost all his interests in his property.
Forma Pauperis	A suit may be instituted by a pauper who is person not possessed to sufficient means to enable him to pay the fee prescribed by law for the plaint in such suit.
Franchise	The right of voting.

Freehold The absolute ownership of land.

Frustration of the contract The cancellation of a contract due to impossibility of performance.

Full Blood Two persons are said to be related to each other by full blood when they are descended from a common ancestor by the same wife.

Functus Officio An authority who has performed the act authorized so that the authority is exhausted.

— G —

Good will The benefit which arises from the establishment of particular business or occupations. Intrinsic value of the good repute and customs of an established trade or business.

Gratuitous Without valuable or legal consideration.

Gratuity A lump sum paid by an employer to retiring employee.

Ground Rent The rent paid by the holder of a lease to do the freeholder.

Group Litigation A law suits, instituted on behalf of or against a group of person recognized as one litigating entity.

Guardian A person having right and duty to protect the property or right of a minor person.

Genocide Mass killing of a group of people belonging to a particular religion, race etc.

— H —

Habeas Corpus It means have the body to present. A writ issued to bring person before a court, to ensure that his imprisonment is not illegal.

Half Blood The children of the same mother, but have different fathers.

Hearsay It is not admissible as an evidence under Evidence Act because witness makes statements of another, who was a direct witness to the event in question.

Heresy A deliberate and over denial of some accepted dogma of Christian Church.

Hiba Perfect gift, one accompanied be delivery and acceptance (under Mohammadan Law).

Homicide Killing of a human being by another human being.

Hostile Witness The witness who makes statements adverse to the party calling and examining him.

Hypothecation A right of a creditor in which the pleader retains possession of the thing pledges.

— I —

Ibid At the same place or from the same sources, in the same book or passage.

Imbezzle To steal, where a person entrusted with goods, wastes and diminishes them.

Immovable Property Property attached or embedded to the land.

Immunity The condition of being exempt from some liability to which other are subject, *For ex*:—The immunity of a judge in respect of things done or said when exercising his judicial function.

Impeach Bring a charge against a person.

In Camera Not in open court, in private.

In Cest Sexual intercourse between persons related with blood. For ex. Brother and Sister etc.

In Limnie At the outset, preliminary.

In Pari Delicto In equal fault, culpable or criminal.

In Pari Materia Upon the some matter or subject or in an analogous case.

In Re In the matter of.
Indictment A written accusation, read out in court at the beginning of a criminal trial.
Indemnity Formal legal acceptance of responsibility against damage or loss.
Injunction An order or judgement by which a party to an action is required to do or refrain from doing a particular thing.
Innuendo Defamatory hint or reamark.
Insolvent A person whose assets are sufficient to pay his debt.
Inter Alia Among other things.
Inter Vivos Between living persons.
Inter Locutory Order Order which is made pending the cause and before a final hearing on the merit.
International Law The body of rules regulating the relations among the nations, resolving the conflict between laws of different nations.
Interrogatories In the course of civil suit, these are particular permission in writing demanded of witnesses or parties brought in to be examined in a case.
Intestate A person who dies without making a will.
Intra Vires Within the powers.
Ipso Facto By the fact itself.

— J —

Judgement Debtor A person against whom a decree has been passed.
Judgement In Rem A judgement in rem binds not only the parties of the action but all other persons.
Joint Tenancy Where property is ancestral is owned by two or more persons under one instrument or act of the parties.
Jointly and Severally When persons jointly as well individually liable for their actions.
Judgement A decision of a court with legal reasoning in a legal proceeding.
Judicial Review The power of the courts to review the legislative and executive section and determine their validity.
Jump Bail Failure of the accused person to appear before court at the time after getting a bail.
Jurat That part of an affidavit that it was sworn before him.
Jurisprudence The Science or Philosophy of law.
Juristic Person A legal entity other than a natural person such as corporations, association, idols etc.
Juvenile Courts Magistrates exercising jurisdiction over offences committed by and other matters related to children and young persons.
Juvenile Delinquency An offence committed by a person who is under 16 years of age.

— K —

Kidnapping An act of taking away or abducting a person out of another's custody or from lawful guardianship for unlawful purpose.
Kin Blood relatives.

— L —

LL.B. Legum Baccalaureus, Bachelor of Laws.
Laches Neglect of a person to promptitude in pursuing a legal remedy.

Laissez Faire Government non-interference in the economic matters.

Larceny The taking and carrying away of mere personal goods of another with intent to steal the goods.

Law A body of rules which regulates human conduct governs the relationship between two or more person.

Lease The contract between owner of property and a tenant who agrees to pay money for the use and possession of the property for a fixed period of time.

Legacy A gift of property by will.

Libel A defamatory statement especially in writing but it includes also pictures, signs, or electronic broadcast.

Lien A right by which a person in possession of the property holds and retains it against the other is satisfied of a demand due to the party retraining it.

Liquidated Fixed or certained.

Litigation The taking of legal action by a party who is known as a litigant.

Lunatic An idiot or person of unsound mind or insane.

— M —

Mala Fides With bad faith, with wrong intention.

Malfeasance Wrongful conduct, especially by a public official, an important act.

Malice Ill will, intent to commit an unlawful act.

Mandamus A writ issued by the Supreme Court or the High Court and directed a Governmental or semi governmental, a judicial or quasi judicial and private bodies performing public function to perform their duties.

Manslaughter It is a crime of unlawful killing but not amounting to murder under English law.

Mercy Killing (Euthanasia) A painless killing of a person who is convicted for death penalty by the court of Law.

Mens Rea A guilty mind.

Mc Naghten Rule A rule which determine whether a person is legally insane or not under English Law.

Mesne Profits Damages payable by trespassers who have stayed in possession after their right to occupy land has ended.

Minor A person below 18 years but where guardian appointed for a minor, then such person remains minor upto age 21 years.

Miscarriage Failure in the administration of justice, synonym for abortion.

Misfeasance The improper doing of an act which a person might lawfully do.

Moratorium A legal authorization to a debtor to postpone payment for a certain time.

Mortgage A loan of money taken after giving security bond of immoveable property.

— N —

Natural Justice Justice which is founded in equity, honesty and good conscience.

Naturalization It is the act by which a foreigner requires the status of a natural born citizen.

Negligence A tort, actionable at the suit of a person suffering damage from the defendant's breach of duty to take care to refrain from injuring him.

Negotiable Instrument A negotiable instrument means a promissory note, bills of exchange or cheque payable either to order or to bearer.

Next Friend A person who is admitted or appointed by a court as a special guardian to act for the benefit of a minor or insane person.

Non-Cognizable Offence This is an offence where the police has no legal authority to arrest the accused person without a warrant from the court.

Nominee A person who has been selected by a party as its candidate for a public office.

Notary A solicitor who attests deeds, or one, who in the case of a dishonoured bills, notes or deeds or protests it. Notary is also known as notary public.

— O —

Obiter Dicta Remarks of a judge, which are said by the way and are not directly relevant to the case at hand.

Offender An accused person, one who is under accusation of having committed an offence, one who is guilty of an offence.

Onus A burden.

Order The formal expression of any decision of a civil court which is not a decree.

Original Jurisdiction Jurisdiction to entertain cases is the first instance as distinguished from appellate jurisdiction.

Ownership An absolute right over property for something based on rightful title.

— P —

Pardon Decision of the Head of state to forgive a person who has given punishment incurred for some offence.

Parole Process by which a prisoner is allowed to be conditionally released during the term of imprisonment.

Passing Off A tort, where by a wrong committed by person who sells goods or carries on business etc, thereby making the buyers believe that the good actually come from the former.

Patent Exclusively privilege granted by the authority to an inventor who invent something new.

Per Incurrium A mistaken decision by a court.

Perjury An offence of giving a false statement before the court which a person known to be false.

Plaint The statement in writing of the cause of action in a suit.

Plaintiff A person, who brings a suit to a court of a law.

Plea Bargaining Where the accused instead of defending his case in proper defence simply pleaded guilty under a promise or assurance that he would be let off lightly and then in appeal or revision to enhance the sentence.

Pledge It is a contract where a bailment of personal property as security for some debt or engagement.

Polygamy Having more than one wife or husband.

Post Mortem An examination of dead body to ascertain the actual cause of death.

Power of Attorney An authority given by one person to another to act on his behalf.

Pre-emption A right to purchase property before other persons.

Prescription Method of acquiring rights over another's land by long period of adverse possession.

Presumption of Death — If a person has not been heard of as alive, for seven years, there is presumption in law that he is dead.

Prima Facie — On the face of it, based on the first impression.

Private Law — That part of law which deals with relations between private individuals.

Probate — The copy of a will ratified under the seal of a court of competent jurisdiction with a grant of administration to the estate of the testator.

Prohibition — An order of a higher court (Supreme Court, High Court) preventing an interior court from doing something.

Pro-rata — Proportionately.

Prorogation — The act of bringing a session of Parliament or other legislative assembly to an end.

Proviso — A condition.

Public Law — That body of laws which deals with the relations between private individuals and the governments.

Public Policy — A policy that is in the interest of the state and community.

—Q—

Quash — To render null or void by a superior court, to set aside or put an end to by an order of a higher court.

Quasi — It were analogous to, semi.

Quasi Contract — A quasi contract is an act for event from which, though not consensual contract, an obligation arises from a contract.

Quo Warranto — A writ of quo warranto issued by the Supreme Court or the High Court against a person who claims or who usurps any office, franchise or liberty to enquire by what authority he supports his claim.

Quorum — Minimum number of persons necessary for conduct of proceeding.

—R—

Ratification — Approval by word or writing or conduct.

Ratio Decidendi — Opinion given by the judge and such opinion is necessary for the decision of particular case.

Recognizance — Sum of money will be forfeited by the accused person who falls to answer his bail.

Redemption — The paying off a loan by a mortgagor, a buying back of the legal estate after it has passed to the mortgagee.

Rejoinder — A reply to the plaintiff replication.

Remand — A committal of an accused to prison.

Repeal — To rescind to revoke.

Repudiate — The renunciation of a right, contract or obligation.

Repugnant — In consistent.

Res judicata — A cause or suit already decided.

Retrospective Legislation — An act that applies to a period before the act was passed.

Right of Re-entry — Right of landlord to take possession if tenant breaks the terms of tenancy.

Robbery — Crime of using force or causing fear of force in order to steal.

— S —

Sale Transfer of ownership in exchange of price paid.

Sedition The inducing of a girl or women to part with her virtue.

Setting Aside Cancelling, making void.

Sine Die Indefinitely.

Slander Defamatory words spoken of another.

Sovereignty Apex authority or higher authority, Indian possess the sovereignty as union of states but state does not possess sovereignty.

Speaking Order An order which contains matters which is explanatory or illustrative of the direction which is given by it.

Specific Performance The performance of a contract exactly or substantially according to its terms.

Stare Decisis The principle that decisions of courts in previous cases must be followed in subsequent cases of similar nature.

Status Quo The existing state of things.

Statute An act of Parliament.

Subpoena An order of a court to a person to appear and give evidence before it.

Substantive Law That part of a law which creates and defines right.

Suit A process instituted in a court of justice for recovery of protection of a right.

Summary Proceedings A proceeding without following the strict rules of procedure for trials.

Summons An order by which a person is called to appear before a court, judicial officer etc.

Surety The person who gives the guarantee.

Surrogate Mother A woman who carries a child pursuance of an arrangement made before she began to carry the child, and with a view to any child carried is pursuance of it being handed over to and the parental rights being exercised by another person or persons.

— T —

Tenant One who hold lands by any kind of title, whether for years, for life.

Testae Dying after having made a will.

Testator He who makes will.

Testimony Statement made by witness under oath.

Tort A civil wrong which is not exclusively the breach of contract or the breach of trust.

Tort-Feasor One who commits or is guilty of a tort.

Trade Mark A mark used by a manufactures or traders to distinguish his goods from the goods for other.

Treason Betrayal of a nation attempt to overthrow the government of the state of which one owes allegiance by resorting to war against it or by helping enemies.

Trespass To pass beyond.

Trial It means any hearing before the court at which evidence is taken.

— U —

Uberrimae Fides Abundant faith, mutual good faith between persons in a particular relationship. *For ex:* Physician and patient, guardian and ward, attorney and client.

Unicameral Legislat A legislature consisting only one house.
For ex: State like Bihar, U.P., Maharashtra, J&K Karnataka has bi-cameral legislative and other remaining state consists of uni-cameral legislative.

Unilateral One sided.

Unilateral Contract When the party to whom an engagement is made, makes no express agreement on his part, the contract is called unilateral contract, binding only one party.

Uterine Blood Two persons are said to be uterine blood when they are descended from a common ancestral but by different husband.

Ultra Vires Outside the powers of.

— V —

Vacantia Bona Goods unclaimed or without an owner.

Versus Against or prefix symbol of opposite part written as (vs) or (v.) e.g. *Golaknath* vs. *Union of India* or *Golaknath* v. *Union of India.*

Veto This power has given to the permanent member of security council who have power of any permanent member of the security of the United Nations to refuse to agree to a proposed course of action; Power to prohibit or refuse; refusal to assent to a Parliamentary Bill.

Vicarious Liability Liability incurred upon a person for acts of another.
For ex : Principle's liability for act of his agent.

Vis-Major Act of god, irresistible force.

Void Not valid, of no effect.

Voidable Capable of being set aside as void at the opinion of a party.

— W —

Wager A bet or something laid down and hazarded on the issue of an uncertain event.

Waiver The intentional or voluntary relinquishment of a known right.

Wakf Permanent dedication of property for religious or charitable purpose under Muslim Law.

Warranty A promise by the seller to repair goods during the specified period. However, the purchaser here does not have a right to ask for replacement of goods.

Will A person's declaration in writing of his intention as to disposal of his property after his death.

Writ A judicial process of written command or order issued by a court, directing or enjoining the person or persons to whom it is addressed to do or restrain from doing some act specified therein.

Witness A person who is a reporter of a crime. He has personal knowledge of occurrence. His name is recorded in chargesheet and helps the court in trial stage.

LEGAL MAXIM

— A —

A Fortiori	With strong reason
A Priori	From the cause to the effect
Ab Antiquo	From ancient times
Ab Initio	From the very beginning
Abiure	To renounce on oath or affirmation
Acta Extoriora Indicant Interiora Secreta	Acts indicate the intention
Actus Legis Nemini Facit Injuriam	Law holds no man responsible for the act of god
Actus Non Facit Reum Nisi Mens Sit Rea	A guilty mind is necessary to constitute a crime
Actus Reus	Wrongful act, the physical act of involving in the crime
Ad Hoc	For a particular purpose
Ad Idem	Of the same mind
Ad Referendum	For further consideration
Ad Rem	To the point
Ad Valorem	According to the value
Addenda	List of additions
Alias	Otherwise called
Alibi	Elsewhere
Alimony	Maintenance given by a husband to his divorced wife
Amicus Curiae	A friend of court, the name is given to lawyer appointed by a court to represent a poor litigant
Animus Attestandi	The intention of attesting
Animus Deserendi	The intention of deserting
Antenuptial	Before marriage
Assumpsit	He promised or undertook
Au Fait	Conversant with
Audi Alteram Partem	Hear the other side
Auterefois	A person cannot be tried for the same offence twice
Auterefois Acquit	Formerly acquitted
Auterefois Convict	Formerly convicted

— B —

Bailiff	A subordinate officer of the court who executes writs and other court orders
Bona Fide	In good faith, honestly
Bona Vacantia	Goods that do not have an owner. Generally they go to the finder
Boni Judici Est Ansliare Jurisdictioness	It is the part of a good judge to enlarge his jurisdiction.

— C —

Causa Celebre	A celebrated case
Causa Causans	The immediate cause
Carte Fide	In good faith, honesty
Causa Sine Qua Non	Factor essential to the occurring of event
Caveat	An order given to officers may "let him beware"
Caveat Emptor	Let the buyer beware
Caveat Venditor	Let the seller beware
Canveat Viator	Let the traveller beware
Certiorari	An order of a higher court which quashes the decision of lower court
Compos Mentis	Of sound mind
Consensus, Non Concubitus, Facit Matrimonium	It is the consent of the parties, not their cohabitation which constitutes a valid marriage
Consensus Ad Idem	Agreement as to the same thing
Corpus Delicti	The substance of the crime
Coup D'etat	Violent or illegal change
Coup D'grace	Finishing stroke
Culpa	Wrongful default

— D —

Damnum Sine Injuria	Damage without legal injury
De Die In Diem	From day to day
De Facto	In fact
De Jure	In law
De Novo	New
Decree	Order of court pronounced after hearing the case
Decree Nisi	A conditional decree
Defeasible Right	Right which can be defeated
Doli Capax	Capable of crime
Doli Incapex	Incapable of crime
Double Jeopardy	A second prosecution for the same offence
Durante Absentia	During absence
Durante Vita	During life

— E —

Ejusdem Generis	Of the same kind, the rule that where particular words are followed by general words.
Emeritus	Retired after long service
En Bloc	All at the same time
En Masse	In a body
Ex Aequo Et Bono	In justice and good faith

Ex Contractu	Arising out of contract
Ex Curia	Out of court
Ex Delicto	Arising out of wrong
Ex Gratia	As a favour
Ex Nudo Pacto – Non Oitur Actio	An action does not arise from a bare promise
Ex Officio	By virtue of office
Ex Parte	In the absence of one party
Ex Post Facto	Acting retrospectively
Expressio Unius Est Exclusio Alterius	Express mention of one thing implies the exclusion of another
Extra Vires	Beyond powers

— F —

Factum	An act or deed
Factum Probantia	Facts which are given in evidence to prove other facts in crime
Faux Pas	Tactless mistake
Flagrante Delicto	In the commission of the offence
Force Majeure	Beyond one's control

— H —

Habeas Corpus	A court order which directed the person to produce before a court who illegally detained beyond twenty four hours before
Honoris Causa	As mark of esteem

— I —

Ibid	In the same place
Ignorantia Facti Excusat - Ignorantia Juris Non Excusat	Ignorance of the fact is an excuse but ignorance of the law does not excuse
Ignoratia Juris Non Excusat	Ignorance of law has no excuse
Impasse	An insoluble difficulty
In Curia	In open court
In Loco Parentis	In the place of a parent
In Memoriam	In memory of
In Pari Delicto	Where both parties are equally in fault
In Pari Materia	Where two enactments have a common purpose in an analogous case
In Personam	Proceeding or directed against or reference to a specific person
In Re	In the matter of
In Rem	Right available against the world at large

It Situ	In its original situation
In Toto	Wholly
Infra	Below
Injuria Sine Damunum	Legal injury without actual damage
Innuendo	An innocent statement which a hidden defamatory meaning
Inter Alia	Among other things
Inter Vivos	Made between people who are alive
Intestate	Dying without leaving will
Intra Vires	Within power
Ipso Facto	By reason of that fact

— J —

Jus	Right
Jus Naturale	Law of nature, natural justice

— L —

Laissez Faire	Doctrine of non-interference by state in economy
Lex	Statute
Lex Fori	The law of the court in which the case is tried
Lex Loci	The law of a place
Lex Non Cogit Ad Impossibilia	Law cannot compel a person who is not possible to perform
Lis Pendens	A pending suit
Locus Standi	Right to be heard in court

— M —

Mala Fide	With bad faith
Mandamus	We command
Manifesta Probatione Non Indiget	Things manifest do not require proof.
Mens Rea	Guilty mind
Mesne	Intermediate
Mesne Profits	Damage payable by trespassers who have stayed in possession after their right to occupy land has ended
Modus Operandi	Mode of operating
Mutatis Mutandis	With necessary changes being made

— N —

Nemo Debet Esse Judex In Propria Sua Causa	No man can be judge in his own cause
Nemo Tenetur Seipsum Accusore	No man can be compelled to incriminate himself
Nisi	Ineffective unless person affected fails to show cause
Non Assumpsit	He did not promise
Non Compos Mentis	Not of sound mind

Non Obstante	Notwithstanding
Noscitur A Sociis	Meaning of word can be gathered from context
Noscitur A Socvis	Meaning of a doubtful word may be ascertained by reference to the meaning of words associated with it
Nota Bene (Nb)	Take notice
Nudum Pactum	An enforceable contract
Nullus Commodum Capere Potest De Injuria Sua Propria	No man can take advantage of his own wrong

—O—

Obiter Dicta	Remark of a judge
Obiter Dictum	Judge's opinion

—P—

Par Excellence	Eminently
Pendente Lite	Pending litigation
Per	As stated by
Per Annum	By the year
Per Capita	Individually
Per Curiam	By the court
Per Incuriam	Wrong decision by court, by oversight
Per Se	By itself
Prima Facie	On the first sight
Pro Bono Publico	For the good of the public
Pro Rata	In proportion

—Q—

Quantum Merit	As a person earned
Quash	Making null or invalid or making end to a legal proceeding
Quasi Contract	A contract between a party comes
Quasi Judicial	Sharing of qualities of and approximating to what is judicial
Qui Facit Per Alium Facit Per Se	He who acts through another is deemed to act in person
Qui Per Alium Facit Per Seipsum Facere Videtur	He who does an act through another is deemed in law to do it himself
Quid Pro Quo	Something for something
Quo Warranto	Order of a court in the form of writ directed the person in authority to show by what right he claim it
Quorum	Minimum number of persons necessary for conduct of proceeding of parliament
Quo Jure	By what right

— R —

Raison D'etre	Reason for the existence of a thing
Rapprochement	Restoration of harmonious relations
Ratio Decidendi	Principal laid down by the court in deciding a case
Rebus Sic Stantibus	Binding bill circumstances remain the same
Res Gestae	The facts so connected with a fact in issue so as to explain its nature
Res Judicata	A case already decided
Res Nullis	A things which has no owner
Respondent Superior	Let the principle be held responsible
Responsa Prudentuim	The answer of the learned in law. The opinions and decisions of learned lawyers

— S —

Salus Populi Est Suprema Lex	The welfare of the people is the paramount law
Sine Die	Indefinitely
Sine Qua Non	Indispensable condition.
Spes Successionis	Mere hope of succeeding to property
Stare Decisis	The principle that decision of courts in previous cases must be followed in subsequent cases of similar nature
Status Quo	To maintain the present state of affairs
Statute	An act of parliament
Sub Judice	Under judicial consideration or in course of trial
Subpoena	An order of a court to a person to appear and give evidence before it
Sui Generis	The only one of its kind
Suo Moto	On its own
Supra	Above

— T —

Tort	Civil wrong
Trespass	To pass beyond
Turpis Causa	A base on which no action can be founded, the maxim being ex turpi causa non oritur actis

— U —

Uberrinae Fide	Of the utmost good faith
Ubi Jus Remedium	Where there is a right there is a remedy
Ultra Vires	Beyond the power

— V —

Vide	Refer to
Vigilantibus, Non Dormientibus, Jura Subveniunt	The law assists those who are vigilant, not those who sleep over their rights
Vis Major	Irresistible force
Void	Have no legal effect
Void Ab Initio	Void from very beginning
Volenti Non-fit Injuria	Damage suffered by consent is not a cause of action
Voluntas In Delictis Non Exitus Spectatur	In crimes, the intention, and not the result, is looked into

ABBREVIATIONS

A

ADB	Asian Development Bank
AID	Agency for International Development
AIR	All India Reporter
AITUC	All India Trade Union Congress

B

BCI	Bar Council of India
BPE	Bureau of Police Enetrprises

C

CAT	Central Administrative Tribunal
CAG	Comptroller and Auditor General
CBDT	Central Board of Direct Taxes
CHOGM	Commonwealth Head of Governments Meeting
CIA	Central Intelligence Agency
CID	Criminal investigation Department
CJI	Chief Justice of India
CIB	Company Law Board
COFEPOSA	Conservation of Foreign Exchange and Prevention of Smuggling Activities Act
CBR	Central Board of Revenue
CEC	Chief Election Commission
COPRA	Consumer Protection Act, 1986
CPC	Civil Procedure Code
Cr. P.C.	Criminal Procedure Code
CRY	Child Relief and Youth
CVC	Chief Vigilance Commissioner

D

DA	Dearness allowance

E

ECAFE	Economic Commission for Asia and Far East
ECOSOC	Economic and Social Council
ESMA	Essential Survives and Maintenance Act
EEC	European Economic Community
ESCAP	Economic and Social Commission for Asia and the Pacific

F

FBI	Federal Bureau of Investigation
FEMA	Foreign Exchange Management Act
FERA	Foreign Exchange Regulation Act
FIR	First Information Report
FCRA	Foreign Contribution Regulation Act
FLC	Foreign Legal Consultant
FTC	Fast Track Court

G

GATT	General Agreement on Tariffs and Trade
GOI	Government of India

H

HC	High Court

I

IAAS	Indian Audit and Accounts Service
ICAO	International Civil Aviation Organization
ICJ	International Court of Justice
ICRC	International Committee of Red Cross
ICWA	Indian Council of World Affairs
IDA	International Development Agency
IDC	International Development Corporation
ILI	Indian Law Institute
ILO	International Labour Organization
IMF	International Monetary Fund
INTERPOL	International Police Organization
IOCU	International Organization of Consumer Union
IPC	Indian Penal Code
IPR	Intellectual Property Rights
IPU	International Parliamentary Union
IRDA	Insurance Regulatory and Development Authority

J

JD	Juris Doctor

L

LLM	Legum Majister, Master of Laws

M

MCOCA	Maharashtra Control of Organised Crime Act
MISA	Maintenance of Internal Security Act
MLA	Member of Legislative Assembly
MLC	Member of Legislative Council
MP	Member of Parliament
MODVAT	Modified Value Added Tax
MRTPC	Monopolies and Restrictive Trade Practices Commission

N

NALSA	National Legal Services Authority
NATO	North Atlantic Treaty Organization
NCDRC	National Consumer Dispute Redressal Commission
NETA	National Environmental Tribunal Act
NJS	National Judicial Service
NNT	Nuclear Non-Proliferation Treaty
NPT	Nuclear Proliferation Treaty
NRC	Nuclear Regularity Commission

O

OIGS	On India Government Service
OSP	Open Sky Policy

P

PDA	Preventive Detention Act
PIB	Press Information Bureau
PFA	Prevention of Food Adulteration Act
PIL	Public Interest Litigation
POTA	Prevention Of Terrorism Act
POW	Prisoner Of War

R

RAW	Research and Analysis Wing
ROC	Registrar of Companies

S

SAPTA	South Asian Preferential Trade Agreement
SC	Supreme Court
SETAO	South East Asia Treaty Organization
SEBI	Securities and Exchange Board of India
SICA	The Sick Industries Control Act
SITA	Suppression of Immoral Traffic in Women and Girls Act

T

TADA	Terrorists and Disruptive Activities (Prevention) Act
TRIMS	Trade Related Investment Measures
TRIPS	Trade Related Intellectual Property Rights

U

UNCE	Conference on Environment and Development
UNCTAD	United Nation Conference on Trade and Development
UNEP	United Nations Environment Programme
UNESCO	United Nations Education, Scientific and Cultural Organization
UNICEF	United Nations International Children's Emergency Fund
UNIDO	United Nations Industrial Development Organisation

V

VAT	Value Added Tax

W

WFP	World Food Programme
WIPO	World Intellectual Property Organization
WTO	World Trade Organization
WWF	World Wide Fund
WWW	World Wide Web

INTERNATIONAL LAW AND INTERNATIONAL ORGANISATIONS

NATURE OF INTERNATIONAL LAW

International law or law of Nations deals the relation between states. Actually It consists of a body of rules and it applies to all the states equally without any regard to their size and power. It has been used in contradiction to the National Law or Municipal Law. National law or Municipal law deals with the law of country on the other hand International law deals above and outside the national laws of the various states and to some extent operates on the territories of all the states.

The term International law was used for first time by British Jurist, J. Bentham in 1780.

DEFINITION OF INTERNATIONAL LAW

Oppenheim's Definition

Oppenheim defined "law of nations or International law is the name of body of customary and treaty rules which are considered legally binding by civilized state in their intercourse with each other."

Modern Definition

Starke—"International law may be defined as that body of law which is composed for its greater part of the principles and rules of conduct which states fell themselves bound to observe and therefore do commonly observe in their relations with each other and which includes also :

> "the rule of law relating to the functioning of international institutions or organizations their relation with each other and their relations with state and individuals and certain rules of law relating to individuals and non-state entities so far as the rights and duties of such individuals and non-state entities are the concern of the international community."

Branches of International Law

International law has two main branches:

(a) Public International Law
(b) Private International Law

Public International Law mainly deals with the states but private International Law mainly deals with the individuals.

Sources of International Law

Sources means historical fact out of which rules of conduct come into existence. It refers to the method and procedure by which international law is created. The main sources of International law are :-

(1) International Convention /Treaty
(2) International custom
(3) General principles of law recognized by civilized nations
(4) Judicial Decisions and Juristic Works
(5) Resolution of General Assembly

International Conventions/Treaties

In the modern time, International conventions or treaties are the most important sources of international law. Treaties whether general or particular. establishing rules expressly recognized by the contesting states as the first source of international law. Treaties may be classified into two categories

(a) Law Making Treaties

These treaties have a large number of parties and create general or universal norms. The provisions of there treaties are directly the source of international law. Thus these treaties perform the same functions in the international field as legislations does in the state field.

(b) Treaty Contracts

It is a treaty between two or only a few states dealing with a special matter concerning these states exclusively. Treaty contracts are not directly a source of international law, but they help the formation of international law through the operation of the principles governing the development of customary rules.

International Customs

International custom is the oldest and most original source of international law. Customary rules of international law are the rules which have been developed in a long process of historical development. When a clear and continuous habit of doing certain actions grow up under the aegis of the conviction that these actions are right.

Actually custom emerges from the usage. Usage means those actions which are often repeated by the states. So when states in their international relations start behaving in a particular way in certain circumstances. It is expected that in the similar circumstances they will behave is the same way. But when this usage receives the general acceptance of recognition by the states in their relations with each other, there develops a conception that such a habit or behaviour has become right as well as obligation of the state and in this way usage becomes the custom.

Opinio juris et necessitatis

It implies a feeling on the part of the states that is acting as they do they are fulfilling a legal obligation. Thus when a general usage is international sphere, or state practice, is connected with opinion *juris et necessitates* international customary law exists.

General Principles of Law

General principles of law recognized by civilized states as the third source of international law. It constitutes an important landmark in the history of international law. It is a principle which has been found to be generally accepted by certain civilized legal systems may fairly presumed to be so reasonable as to be necessary to the maintenance of justice under any system.

OTHER IMPORTANT TREATIES

Pacta sunt servanda

It is basis of the binding force of treaties. It means states are bound to fulfill in good faith the obligations assumed by them under treaties.

In nearly all the cases the object of the treaty is to impose binding obligations on the states who are parties to it. There is a great controversy amongst the jurists in regard to the binding force of a treaty-some find it in the law of nature, others in becoming a party to the treaty

Exceptions to the Principle

Rebus sic stantibus

The maxim *rebus sic stantibus* means that a treaty may be terminated if there occurs a fundamental change in the circumstances under which it was concluded.

Jus logens

There are certain principles in international law which all the states must observe, their non-observance may affect the very foundation of the legal system to which they belong. They, therefore cannot be altered by concluding treaties. These basic values possess the character of jus logens.

The evolution of jus logens traced to Roman law doctrine "Jus publicum privatorum pactis mutari not potest" which means that a public law or right cannot be altered by the agreement of private persons.

RECOGNITION

According to jurist, recognition means that an existing state acknowledge the political entity of another state, by overt or covert act.

In other way, recognition means the members of the international community formally acknowledge that the state has acquired international personality.

Theories of Recognition

There are mainly two theories of recognition

(a) Constitutive Theory

Any country does not became a state whenever other state constitute the personality of a state by granting recognition.

(b) Declaratory/ Evidently Theory

A country of the new government exists as such prior to and independently of recognition. Recognition is merely a formal acknowledge by declaration or evidence of an existing fact that a particular state or government possesses the essential element as required under international law.

Legal Effect of Recognition

(a) Recognised state becomes entitled to sue in the courts of another recognizing state

(b) Recognized state becomes entitled to the succession and possession of property situated in the territory of another recognising state

(c) Recognized state may enter into diplomatic and treaty relationship with the other recognizing state

Forms of Recognition

A state may be recognized in two ways

(a) Express Recognition

When an existing state recognize the new state by a notification or declaration, announcing the intention of recognition, the recognition is said to be express.

(b) Implied Recognition

Implied recognition is expressed in two ways

(a) *Unilateral acts :* When a state enters into a bilateral treaty or establishes diplomatic relation with an unrecognized state it may be inferred that the former has granted recognition to the latter

(b) *Collective acts :* When an unrecognized state participates in a multilateral treaty the other participants or parties are regarded to have recognized the new state if the intention has been indicated.

Modes of Recognition

Recognition may be of two kinds

(1) De facto Recognition

De facto recognition means that the state recognized possesses the essential elements of statehood and is fit to be a subject of international law, but it is doubted that it may be able and willing to fulfill its obligation under international law.

(2) De jure Recognition

When an existing state considers that the new state is capable of possessing all the essential attributes of statehood with stability and permanency, the recognition granted is known as de jure recognition. Three essential conditions are required for the grant of de jure recognition.

(a) A reasonable assurance of stability and permanence .

(b) The government should command the general support of the population and

(c) It should be able and willing to fulfill its international obligations

UNITED NATIONS ORGANIZATION (UNO)

- Prior to the UNO, the league of nations was established under the Treaty of Versailles, 1919
- Main aim of the league of nations to promote international peace and security
- Under the Atlantic Charter, 1991 first time the idea of creating an effective organization
- The United Nations Declaration, 1942 followed at Franklin Roosevelt is associated with the phrase United Nations
- The UNO finally came into existence on October 24, 1945. The organization was formed in San Francisco in 1945 under a permanent charter which was ratified by 50 countries.
- The headquarters of UNO has been in New York city since 1946 and the membership on 2021 consists of 193 nations.
- South Sudan being the latest entry

Aims and Objectives

The aims/objectives of the U.N. are set forth in the preamble which states that "we the people of the United Nations" are determined:

(i) to save the succeeding generations from the scourge of war.

(ii) to reaffirm faith in fundamental human rights and in the dignity and worth of the human person.

(iii) to reaffirm faith in the equal rights of men and women, and all nations large and small

(iv) to establish conditions under which justice and respect for international law and international obligations can be maintained .

(v) to promote social progress etc

(vi) to maintain international peace and security

(vii) to ensure that armed forces shall not be used, save in the common interest and

(viii) to promote economic and social advancement of all the people.

Purpose and Principles

Article 1 of the charter enunciates the purpose of the UNO:

(1) to maintain international peace and security

(2) develop friendly relations among nations

(3) foster international cooperation in social, economic, cultural and humanitarian matters

(4) develop respect for human rights and freedom

(5) take necessary steps to achieve these objectives

Article 2 lays down the following basic principles:

(1) basis of UN shall be sovereign equality of its members

(2) the member state shall fulfill in good faith their obligations under the charter

(3) the member states shall be settle their disputes by peaceful means

(4) member states shall not use force against territorial integrity/political independence of another member state

(5) all member states are to assist the UN when it takes preventive or enforcement actions against a state

(6) UNI to ensure that non member states act in accordance with these principles, so far as may be necessary for the maintenance, of international peace and security.

Membership

These are two types of members :-

(a) *Original members* : Those states who participated in the San Francisco Conference (1945) and signed and ratified the charter

(b) M*embers subsequently admitted* : A state can be member of UNO when it is first recommended by a majority of seven members, including all five permanent member of Security Council and later approved by 2/3 majority of General Assembly

The Organs of UNO

The following are the major organs of the UNO:

(1) the General Assembly

(2) the Security Council

(3) the Economic and Social Council

(4) The Trusteeship Council

(5) The International Court of Justice

(6) The Secretariat

(i) General Assembly

It is the principle organ of the UNO consisting of all members. Each member states has one vote and five representatives. The General Assembly regularly meets once a year in the third week of the month of September. But special session can also be called by the Secretary General either on the request of security council or on the request of majority of member states. Decision on important problems are taken by a 2/3 majority of members present and voting

(ii) Security Council

It is a continuously functioning body, originally consisted of 11 members, but since 1965 of 15 member as following:

(a) five permanent members are China, UK, USA, France and Soviet Union (Russia)

(b) ten non-permanent members elected by the General Assembly for a period of 2 years. Among these ten non-permanents members, 5 members from Afro Asian nations, one from Eastern Europe, two from Latin America and two from western countries, are elected.

Voting Procedure in Security Council

Each member state of the security council has one vote. Decissions of the security council on procedural matters are to be made by an affirmative vote of 9 members and decissions on all other substantive matters are to be made by an affirmative vote of 9 members including the concurring votes of five permanent members.

If a permanent members casts a negative vote on a substantive matter, the decision is blocked or vetod i.e. does not come into existence. USSR used veto for the first time is security council.

(iii) The Economic and Social Council (ECOSOC)

The charter of UN in order to achieve the economic and social advancement of all people, created the ECOSOC as a permanent organ of UN with a view to rescue international prosperity, stability and justice. The council originally has 18 members but now composed of 54 members, elected by General Assembly for a term of 3 years.

(iv) The Trusteeship Council

The charter of UN provides for an International Trusteeship system with the objective of furthering international peace and security to promote the advancement of the inhabitants of the Trust territories and their progressive development towards self government or independence

(v) The Secretariat

For smooth making of UN, for execution of its decision, and for administering of its policies and programmes, the charter created a secretariat headed by a Secretary General – appointed for a term of 5 years the General Assembly on the recommendation supported by nine affirmative votes of the security council.

There are six official languages recognized by the UNO :

(1) Arabic

(2) Chinese

(3) English

(4) French

(5) Russian

(6) Spanish

THE INTERNATIONAL COURT OF JUSTICE (ICJ)

The Permanent Court of International Justice (PCIJ) was established in1921 under the covenant of the league of nations. After its dissolution, the new International Court of Justice (ICJ) started functioning on 18 April 1946 with the head quarters at the Hague. ICJ is the principal judicial organ of the UNO. The rules concerning the ICJ are set out, in a statute anne-xed to the UN charter. All members of the UN are ispo facto parties to the statute of ICJ. The member states are under an obligation to comply with the decision of ICJ in the case to which they are parties. The function of the ICJ was conceived primarily to decide legal disputes between state parties when they agree to submit their dispute to it. The ICJ was not given the power of judicial review over the actions taken by other international organs. Thus, the absence of compulsory jurisdiction over states and lack of power of judicial review makes it a weaker court

Organisation of ICJ

The Court consists of 15 judges who are elected from among persons of high moral character who possess the qualification required for the appointment to the highest judicial office of their own states. But two judges shall not be elected from the same state.

Jurisdiction of ICJ

The access to the court is open to the states which are parties to the statute and charter, as well as to the non-members who are admitted to UN under Art. 92 (2) of the charter. The states, which are not parties to the statute, can have access to the court if they fulfill the conditions laid down by the General Assembly in each case and upon the recommendation made by the security council.

INTERNATIONAL CRIMINAL COURT (ICC)

The U.N. General Assembly in 1989 requested the International Law Commission to address the question of establishing an international criminal court. The commission prepared a Draft statute. The Rome conference U.N. Diplomatic conference of pleni potentiaries, in Italy, adopted the statute known as the "Rome statute of the International Criminal Court" on 17 July 1998. The conference was attended by 162 countries.

Establishment of the Court

Article 1 of ICC, which establishes the ICC, provides that it shall be a Permanent institution and shall have power to exercise jurisdiction over persons for the most serious crime of international concern.

Jurisdiction

The court has jurisdiction is accordance with the statue with respect to the following crime :

(a) crime of genocide

(b) crime against humanity

(c) war crimes and

(d) crime of aggression

MULTIPLE CHOICE QUESTIONS

1. International law governs the relations between:
A. states
B. individuals
C. both A and B
D. none of the above

2. The term International law was coined by:
A. J. Starke
B. Austin
C. Bentham
D. Estrade

3. Public International law deals with matters relating to:
A. individuals
B. states
C. only for public
D. international organization

4. Private International law mainly deals with:
A. States
B. Individuals
C. Both A and B
D. None of the above

5. Principal behind International law is:
A. Individual sovereignty
B. State sovereignty
C. Sovereign equality
D. None of the above

6. Main sources of International law are:
A. International conventions
B. Custom
C. Treaties
D. All the above

7. Direct sources of international law are:
I. treaties
II. custom
III. judicial decisions
IV. general principles recognized by civilized nations
A. only I
B. only I, III, IV
C. only I, II, IV
D. only I, II, III, IV

8. Pacta Sunt Servanda means:
A. obligation on the parts of the states to honour the treaty
B. obligation to pass to some other country
C. obligation to United Nation Organization
D. None of these

9. Direct sources of international law are:
A. Treaties
B. Judicial decisions
C. Customs
D. Both A and C

10. Judicial decisions are the..............of International law.
A. direct sources
B. indirect sources
C. no sources
D. relative sources

11. Equity and justice means:
A. consideration of fairness and equitable sense
B. mutual relations of nations
C. judicial reasons
D. all the above

12. Modes of recognition are:
A. De facto recognition
B. De jure recognition
C. Both A and B
D. None of the above

13. Recognition means:
A. Acknowledgement of political entity with statehood
B. Non-acknowledgement
C. Both A and B
D. None of these

14. Collective recognition means recognition by:
A. Number of states
B. United State organization
C. International conventions
D. None of these

15. Main theories of recognition are:
A. declamatory theory
B. constitutive theory

C. treaties
D. both A and B

16. Insurgency means:
A. Inherent struggle
B. Political revolt
C. Revolt citizen
D. Change of Government

17. Treaties are:
A. International Conventions
B. International agreement
C. Both A and B
D. Customs

18. Ratification means:
A. signing the treaty
B. approval of the head of the state
C. approval given by the state representative
D. all the above

19. The United Nation is:
A. Association of International organization
B. A human right body
C. An association of sovereign states
D. An adjudicatory body

20. The main purpose of U.N. is to:
A. Maintain peace and security
B. Develop friendly relations among nations
C. Centre for attainment of common ends
D. All the above

21. Principle behind the United Nations:
A. Sovereign equality among nations
B. Non-intervention
C. Peaceful settlement of disputes
D. All the above

22. The member who signed the charter of United Nations in San Francisco conference are:
A. Original member
B. Permanent member
C. Temporary member
D. Real member

23. Condition prescribed for the U.N. membership are:
A. statehood
B. acceptance of charter obligations
C. peace loving country
D. all the above

24. An individual is governed by:
A. United Nations Organization
B. Human Right Commission
C. State Law
D. International law

25. The headquarters of ICJ is located at:
A. The Hague
B. New York
C. Washington D.C.
D. Geneva

26. The parties before the ICJ are:
A. State only
B. Individual only
C. International organization
D. Organs of UNO and states

27. Total number of judges on ICJ is:
A. 15 judges B. 12 judges
C. 25 judges D. 10 judges

28. The judges of ICJ is elected by:
A. General Assembly
B. The Secretariat
C. The Security Council
D. All the above

29. The statute of the ICJ is same as the statute of:
A. Supreme Court of USA
B. Supreme Court of India
C. Permanent court of International Justice
D. None of these

30. The decision of I.C.J. affects:
A. All the organs of U.N.O.
B. All the members of U.N.O.
C. The General Assembly
D. State party to dispute

31. The decisions of International Court of justice:
A. has become law in International sphere
B. has a binding force
C. does not have a binding force
D. none of these

32. The term of the I.C.J. judges for:
A. 15 years B. 10 years
C. 9 years D. 7 years

33. India become the member of United Nations in the year:
A. 1947 B. 1950
C. 1952 D. 1945

34. United Nations International Day for National Disaster reduction is observed on:
A. 24 October B. 13 October
C. 30 October D. 12 October

35. The general Assembly is the:
A. Independent body
B. Supplemental organ of United Nations
C. Main deliberative organ of United Nation
D. Not as organ of the United Nation

36. In 2002, a country guaranteed the criminal rights in its constitution, the country is:
A. India B. U.S.A
C. Canada D. Germany

37. In the annual meeting of the General Assembly the member state can take:
A. 10 delegates B. 5 delegates
C. 6 delegates D. 15 delegates

38. The international law consists of:
A. Public International Law
B. Private International law
C. Public International law and Municipal Law
D. Public International law and Private International law

39. The permanent International Criminal Court was set up in 2002, its seat is at:
A. New York B. Hague
C. Vienna D. New Delhi

40. The decision of the General Assembly of UNO have no legally binding effect for the Governments because there is no provision for the:
A. World opinion is sufficient
B. Because states are independent
C. Intention enforcing authority
D. Moral authority of world community prevails

41. World Environment Day is observed on:
A. 25 October B. 25 June
C. 15 October D. 5 June

42. The Antarctic Treaty was held in Washington in the year 1959 and came into force on:
A. 23rd June 1961 B. 22nd June, 1951
C. 23rd June, 1951 D. 22nd June 1961

43. United Nation Day (UN Day) is observed on:
A. 24 November B. 24 October
C. 21 November D. 21 October

44. Match the following books with their **authors:**

1. Henry Maine	a. Concept of law
2. A.V. Diecy	b. leaning the law
3. H.L.A. Hart	c. Ancient law
4. G. Williams	d. Law and public opinion in 19th century England

A. I-c, II-d, III-a, IV-b
B. I-c, II-d, III-b, IV-a
C. I-d, II-c, III-b, IV-a
D. I-d, II-c, III-a, IV-b

45. United Nations Millenium Declaration was made at:
A. New Delhi, September 2000
B. Tokyo, September 2000
C. Washington D.C., September 2000
D. New York, September 2000

46. The Father of International law is:
A. Grobius B. A.V. Dicey
C. H.L.A. Hart D. G. Williams

47. The law relating to diplomatic relations is codified in:
A. San Francisco Convention
B. Vienna Convention
C. Hague Convention
D. Geneva Convention

48. The law relating to prisoners of war has been codified by:
A. San Francisco Convention
B. Vienna Convention
C. Hague Convention
D. Geneva Convention

49. The law relating to nobilities has been codified by:
A. San Francisco Convention
B. Vienna Convention
C. Hague Convention
D. Geneva Convention

50. Who is the author of the work "The Devil's dictionary"?
A. Grotius B. A.V. Dicey
C. H.L.A. Hart D. Ambrose Bierce

51. 'The law is its majestic equalitarianism, forbids the rich as well as the poor to sleep under bridges, to beg in the streets and to steal bread'. Who said the this statement?

A. Grotius B. Anatole France
C. A.V. Dicey D. Ambross Bierce

52. Which country became first one to legalise euthanasia?
A. Netherlands B. Belgium
C. Switzerland D. France

53. Which country became second one to legalise euthanasia?
A. Netherlands B. Belgium
C. Switzerland D. France

54. Which of the following statements can be attributed to Montesquieu?
A. Liberty is absolute
B. Liberty is deprived by a circumstance of law
C. Liberty is the right to do whatever the laws permit
D. Man is born free, and everywhere he is in chains

55. 'The Universal Declaration of Human Rights' was adopted by the UN in:
A. 1945 B. 1946
C. 1947 D. 1948

56. Match the following:
1. Public opinion is always in advance of the law
2. Law are meant to be broken
3. Who profits by crime is guilty of it
4. It is better to risk saving a guilty person than to condemn innocent one

I. Seneca
II. John Milton
III. Voltaire
IV. John Gabworth

A. 1-I, 2-II, 3-III, 4-IV
B. 1-II, 2-I, 3-III, 4-IV
C. 1-II, 2-I, 3-IV, 4-III
D. 1-I, 2-II, 3-IV, 4-III

57. England has four voluntary association which have the sole right to call to the Bar. They are called Inns of courts. The Inns of court are:
I. Acqusith Inn
II. Gray's Inn
III. Inner Temple
IV. Middle Temple
V. Lincoln's Temple

A. I, II, III & IV
B. I, II, IV & V
C. I, III, IV & V
D. II, III, IV & V

58. Who is the author of these immortal words "Mastering the lawless science of our law, that codeless myriad or precedent that wilderness of single instances thro' which a few, by writ or fortune led may beat a pathway out to wealth and fame."
A. Rousseau B. Disraeli
C. Tennyson D. Dickens

59. "Ignorance of the law excuses no man, not that all men know the law, but because it is an excuse every man will plead". Who said these words?
A. Rousseau B. John Selden
C. Dickens D. Tennyson

60. Genocide occurred in all but one case:
A. Rwanda B. Bosnia
C. Gulf war D. Nazi Germany

61. The international treaty becomes binding on India when:
A. General Assembly of U.N.O. give their assent
B. International organization passes or accepting the treaty
C. Parliament makes special legislation for accepting the treaty
D. Prime Minister signs the treaty

62. The Hague Convention of 1899, 1904 and 1907 delineated:
A. Rule for non-use of chemical weapons
B. Rule for no war
C. Rule of human rights
D. Rules of public International law

63. Match the following:
I. De Montmorency II. Salmond
III. Hobbes IV. Austin

a. Law is body of principle recognized and applied by state in the administration of justice
b. Law is rule of conduct imposed and enforced by a sovereign state
c. Coercion is weapon of law but not the basis of law

d. Law is the command of him who has coercive power

A. I-c, II-a, III-d, IV-b
B. I-a, II-c, III-d, IV-b
C. I-a, II-c, III-b, IV-d
D. I-c, II-a, III-b, IV-d

64. The chief representative of United Kingdom or the chief representative of a Common Wealth Country is called:

A. Chairperson
B. High Commissioner
C. Ambassador
D. Charge de 'Affairs

65. Match the following:

I. Public International law
II. Conflict of laws
III. State law
IV. National law

a. Between sovereign states
b. Body of rights and duties of citizens of different sovereign states towards one another
c. Maharashtra Industries Act
d. Indian Penal Code

A. I-a, II-c, III-d, IV-b
B. I-a, II-b, III-c, IV-d
C. I-d, II-c, III-b, IV-a
D. I-c, II-d, III-b, IV-a

66. High sea is:

A. sea beyond 200 km of a coast of any country
B. sea lying more than 5 km beyond the cost of a country
C. sea lying beyond a distance of 3 miles from the coast of any country
D. none of these

67. "Law is an ass" was said by:

A. Marx B. Locke
C. Charles Dickens D. Abraham Lincoln

68. ....defines right as an interest which is recognized and protected by law.

A. Marx B. Salmond
C. Pullock D. Ihering

69. "Law is a jealous mistress".......this often quoted phrase is attributed to.

A. John Selden B. Dryden
C. Francies Bacon D. Joseph Story

70. Who is the author of these immortal words "Democracy is kingless regime, interested by many kings who are sometimes more exclusive, tyrannical and destructive than one, if he be a tryant":

A. Abraham Lincoin
B. Charles Dickness
C. Benito Mussolini
D. Adolf Hitler

ANSWERS

1	2	3	4	5	6	7	8	9	10
A	C	B	B	C	D	D	A	D	B
11	**12**	**13**	**14**	**15**	**16**	**17**	**18**	**19**	**20**
D	C	A	A	D	B	B	B	C	D
21	**22**	**23**	**24**	**25**	**26**	**27**	**28**	**29**	**30**
D	A	D	C	A	D	A	A	C	D
31	**32**	**33**	**34**	**35**	**36**	**37**	**38**	**39**	**40**
C	C	D	B	C	D	B	D	B	C
41	**42**	**43**	**44**	**45**	**46**	**47**	**48**	**49**	**50**
D	A	B	A	D	A	B	D	C	D
51	**52**	**53**	**54**	**55**	**56**	**57**	**58**	**59**	**60**
B	A	B	C	D	B	D	C	B	C
61	**62**	**63**	**64**	**65**	**66**	**67**	**68**	**69**	**70**
C	D	A	B	B	A	C	B	B	C

LEGAL REASONING

Legal reasoning is a test to solve legal problem. It involves application of legal principle to legal problem and derive the correct answer. The problems of legal reasoning based on the factual situation and it makes you thinking like a lawyer in a given situation. Legal reasoning gives you a prior knowledge of some legal principle and their correct application. Therefore, it is only to be expected that the LL.B Entrance test should examine you for this ability.

Legal Principle

However, intending to take dishonesty any moveable property out of the possession of any person without that person's consent, moves that property in order to such taking, is said to commit theft.

Factual Situation

A sees a ring belonging to Z lying on a table in Z's house. Not venturing to misappropriate the ring immediately for fear of search and detection. A hides the ring in a place where it is highly improbable that it will ever be found by Z, with the intention of taking the ring from the hiding place and selling it when the loss is forgotten.

Decision

Is A guilty of theft :

(a) No, because A had only changed the place so not guilty of theft

(b) Yes, because A had the intention of taking movable property from Z's possession, and with this intention he removed the ring

(c) Yes, because A had the only intention of removing the ring from Z's possession

To answer the above question, you have to first read the legal principle and break into parts to understand and then apply it on factual situation.

The different part of Legal Principles are:

(1) Whoever

(2) Intending to take dishonestly

(3) Any moveable property

(4) Out of the possession of any person

(5) Without that person's consent

(6) Moves that property

(7) In order to such taking

(8) Is said to commit theft

Factual Situation

(1) A sees a ring belonging to Z lying on a table in Z's house.

(2) Not venturing to misappropriate the ring immediately for fear of search and detection.

(3) A hides the ring under the sofa cover, where it is highly improbable that it will even be found by Z.

(4) A has the intention of taking the ring from the hiding place and selling it when the loss is forgotten.

Now analyse the legal principle and factual situation

1. whoever - A
2. intending to take dishonestly – A's intention is dishonestly because he hide the ring
3. any movable property- ring is movable property
4. out of the possession of any person – A's intention is to take the ring out of Z's possession
5. without that person's consent – here Z does not know about that A hide the ring so consent is absent
6. moves the property – A hide the ring under the sofa cover from the table
7. in order to such taking – Here A hide the ring under sofa cover it means the ring was taken
8. is said to commit theft – A committed the theft because he took the ring with dishonest intention from Z's possession

Therefore, A committed theft

So, answer to the question is (b)

Some Other Situations

A. A takes an article belonging to Z out of Z's possession without Z's consent, with the intention of keeping it until he obtains money from Z as a reward for its restoration. Here A takes dishonestly. A has therefore committed theft.

B. A, being on friendly terms with Z, goes into Z's library in Z's absence, and takes away a book without Z's express consent for the purpose merely of reading it, and with the intention of returning it. Here, it is probable that A may have conceived that he had Z's implied consent to use Z's book. If this was A's impression, A has not committed theft.

Areas of Testing in Legal Reasoning

Problems in the legal reasoning generally come from the following areas :

(a) Law of Torts
(b) Contract Act
(c) Criminal law
(d) Constitutional law etc.

A. Law of Torts

The word tort is derived from the Latin word tortum meaning twisted or crocked. Therefore tort means wrong. Tort is a civil wrong as well as private wrong. In tort, damages are unliquidated means not fixed or not pre-determined or which are determined by the court and also damage is fixed according to facts and circumstances. The basic principle behind the action for tort is "*Ubi jus ibi remedium*" means where there is a right, there is a remedy.

The essentials to constitute a tort are following :

(1) There must be some wrongful act or omission done by defendant
(2) Some damage or harm suffered by plaintiff
(3) Legal remedy is there for causing such legal damage

(1) Damnum sine Injuria : It means damage without injury. Under this maxim a person suffered damage or loss but no violation of legal right is caused to him. So, no action lie under the law of torts.

EXAMPLE - 1

PRINCIPLE : No, action lies for mere damage or loss, however substantial, caused by an act which does not infringe some legal rights of a person

FACTS : A number of steamship companies acting in combination agreed to regulate the cargoes and freight charges between China and Europe. A general rebate of 5 per cent was allowed to all suppliers who shipped with the members of the combination. As a result of this action, the plaintiff had to bring down their rates to that level which was unremunerative to them. Can plaintiff who suffered loss claim compensation?

(a) Yes, companies are adopted unlawful combination.
(b) No, companies are acting lawful and exercise of one's right.
(c) Yes, plaintiff suffered loss in business.

Answer : Though plaintiff suffered loss but his legal rights were not violated by the companies. There is no illegal point in the combination of defendants. So answer is (b).

EXAMPLE - 2

PRINCIPLE : If there is infringement of legal right of a person, he can sue under torts for compensation even if he has not suffered any harm or loss.

For example :

Glucestor Grammar School case : Where a school master set up a rival school near the plaintiff's school and students from plaintiff's school migrated to that school.

The court held that the plaintiff had no remedy for loss suffered by them because defendant exercise his own legal right, so that was no cause of action in the exercise of one's right without hindrance and freely competing with one's rival.

(2) Injuria sine damnum : It means injury without damage. So plaintiff suffered infringement of his legal right without damage or loss. Plaintiff can sue defendant under tort.

For example : Ashby v. *White* case

Where the defendant, a returning officer wrongfully refused to register the vote of the plaintiff who was a qualified voter at a parliamentary election. In fact the candidate for whom the vote was intended was elected and did not suffer any damage. So plaintiff suffered no harm but his legal right was violated. Court held that defendant was held liable. So, plaintiff was awarded damages.

FACTS : Mr. A, a bank Manager refuses to honour a cheque presented by B, a customer. He knows that B has sufficient funds in his account. Can B sue A under torts and claim compensation.

(a) Yes Mr. A has violated legal right of B. So B can be need under torts to pay compensation.

(b) No because B suffered no damage, so he should not get any compensation.

(c) No, because C plead extraordinary situation is the bank at that point of time due to which he could not honour the cheque.

Answer : B has suffered a legal wrong, he has been deprived of a right recognized by law and he has against the person so depriving him, a remedy, that is, an action on the case, so answer is (a)

General Defence to Tort

Volenti non fit injuria **:** It is the general policy of law that everyone is the best judge of his interest and therefore the one who voluntarily agrees to suffer harm is not allowed to complain for that and one's consent is a good defence against oneself. This is so because the harm. Voluntarily suffered does not constitute the legal injury. Therefore, the Latin maxim "*volenti non fit injuria*" means no breach of a legal right.

Is committed against one who is a willing part or voluntarily suffered harm does not constitute an injury and is not actionable. This, there are two basic essential conditions of this maxim.

(a) Free consent

(b) Knowledge of risk

EXAMPLE - 3

PRINCIPLE **:** No legal remedy exists for an injury caused by an act, for which one has consented.

FACTS **:** The driver of a van with restive horses cried for help. The plaintiff went and attempted to hold the horse but it throw him on the ground causing him injuries, in respect of which he sued the defendant.

(a) The suit is dismissed because the plaintiff must have known that his attempt to hold the horse with the risk.

(b) The suit is not dismissed and plaintiff must be compensated because driver cry for help and he is in problem.

(c) Plaintiff should be able to recover as the driver failed to take precautions of horse.

(d) Plaintiff should not be able to recover as he consented to the risk.

Answer is (a) because the maxim "*volenti non fit injuria*" can be applied and plaintiff must know that by his attempt there will be danger.

EXAMPLE - 4

PRINCIPLE **:** No legal remedy exists for an injury caused by an act, for which one has consented

FACTS **:** In the one day International cricket match between India and Pakistan, Sehwag hit a full toss delivery of Shoaib Akhtar over the boundary for a six. The ball fell on the body of one of the spectator and injured him. Spectator sues organiser of the match for reimbursement of the medical bill he paid fc treatment.

(a) Spectator can recover the costs of his medical expense from Sehwag.

(b) Spectator should be compensated as he purchased the ticket to get entertainment and not to get injured.

(c) No body would be liable to pay anything to spectator because he voluntarily exposed himself to risk.

(d) Organiser is liable as it did not ensure that the spectators were protected from the risks of such injuries.

Answer is (c) the principle of *volenti non fit injuria* shall apply. Spectator has no remedy as he has impliedly consented to such injury which may be caused in watching a cricket match.

EXAMPLE - 5

PRINCIPLE **:** Damages cannot be claimed against a risk to which consent has been given. The principle does not apply to rescue cases.

FACTS **:** A and B brought tickets to have a view of a football match. During the course of the game a hand kick from one of the players caused the ball to hit A on his face, causing bleeding and nausea from nose. After half time the organizers allowed entry of more spectators then the seating capacity of the stadium. In the resulting stampede C and D who were watching the match since the beginning got injured.

(a) A shall not be able to recover as by purchasing a seat in a football game he consented to all the risks of such watching.

(b) A shall not be able to recover as he consented to the risk of the ball.

(c) A shall be able to recover as he consented to watch the game not to be injured in it.

(d) A shall be able to recover as the organizers failed to take precautions against the ball.

Answer is (a).

EXAMPLE - 6

PRINCIPLE : When a person consents to the infliction of some harm upon himself, he has no remedy in tort.

FACTS : A person at a motor car race being held on a track owned by the company. During the race there was a collision between two cars. One of which was thrown among the spectator thereby injuring the person. Person filed a suit against the company.

(a) company is not liable because person impliedly took the risk of injury.

(b) company is not liable becau. › it owned duty of care towards the person.

(c) company is liable.

(d) company is liable because it owned to being of case towards fhe person.

Answer is (a)

EXAMPLE - 7

PRINCIPLE : There is no liability is tort in cases of inevitable accidents

FACTS : The defendant who was one of a showing party, fixed on a peasant. One of the bullets from his gun glanced off the brought of a tree and accidentally wounded the plaintiff who was engaged in carrying cartridges and game for the party.

(a) Defendant is liable.

(b) Defendant is not liable because it is an inevitable accident and could not possible to prevent.

(c) Defendant is liable because he had not act in this way.

(d) None of these.

Answer is (b).

EXAMPLE - 8

PRINCIPLE : A master is liable for the wrongs committed by the servant in the course of his employment.

FACTS : During the poonam celebrations which was attended by lakhs of people, the plaintiff was seriously injured by the explosion caused by igniting explosive powder filled coconut shells. During the festival, all sorts of explosion are fired and fire-works mark the poonam celebrations. Many contractor are engaged to make the explosive devices. During the celebrations, one shell, instead of going vertically into the sky fell tangentially on the crowd and injured the plaintiff.

(a) Master is liable because it is fault of employees who had made the coconut shells known as Minnal gundus.

(b) Master is not liable because plaintiff is a volunteer and that he has come to watch the celebrations.

(c) Master is not liable because it is fault of employees.

(d) Master is not liable because employees had been taken care in handling the explosive.

Answer is (a) because master is liable for the acts of his servant only when the act done by the servant during the course of his employment.

EXAMPLE - 9

PRINCIPLE : A master is liable for the wrongful acts of his servants committed in the course of employment.

FACTS : The plaintiff had dispatched hundreds of cannisters full of mustard oil which was manufactured by them and sold under their brand. At the railway station, a few hundred cannisters were seized by the Sanitary Inspector and were loaded in a truck which was used for carrying rubbish and night soil. By this act plaintiff suffered a huge loss because their customers refused to take delivery of the tins on the ground that they had been carried in municipal vehicle which was used to carry rubbish and night soil and unfit for human consumption.

(a) Sanitary Inspector is liable for his act.

(b) Plaintiff cannot succeed because it is duty of sanitary Inspector to check the quality of oil.

(c) Municipality held to be liable because his employees handled the cannisters negligently.

(d) No any one liable.

The answer is (c).

EXAMPLE - 10

PRINCIPLE : A master is liable for the wrongful acts of his servants committed in the course of employment.

FACTS : A person opened an account with a Bank, where under he agreed to deposit Rs. 500/- every month in the Bank. Shyam an agent of the Bank used to come every months to collect the amount from the person and deposit in the Bank. The Bank paid commission to Shyam for the money deposited. It was discovered one day that Shyam had not deposited the amount for more than two months and had disappeared with the money. Person filed a suit against the Bank.

(a) Bank would not be liable because Shyam was not its employee.

(b) Bank would not be liable because as it was person's responsibility to check his passbook regularly.

(c) Bank would be liable because Shyam was paid commission by the Bank for doing work on its behalf.

Answer is (c).

EXAMPLE - 11

PRINCIPLE : An employer shall be liable to the injuries caused to his employee by the negligence of a fellow employee in the course of employment.

FACTS : Sita Ram was the owner of a car which he entrusted to one Mohammad Yakub for playing it as a taxi. He was not merely a driver but was in sole charge of the taxi and he employed M as a cleaner of the taxi. M trained the cleaner to drive the car and gave him the taxi for taking the driving test and obtaining the driver's license. While taking the test, the cleaner took a sudden turn without giving any signal and seriously injured the plaintiff's leg.

(a) Sita Ram shall be liable because M was in the course of their employment at the time of accident.

(b) Sita Ram shall not be liable. M was not is the course of employment when he took the taxi for driving test.

(c) No any person liable in this act.

Answer is (b).

EXAMPLE - 12

PRINCIPLE : A careless person becomes liable for his negligence when he owed a duty of care to others.

FACTS : As the bus was leaving the bus stop. A person rushed and boarded the bus keeping the door open, another person who was standing near the bus stop was hit by the door of the moving bus and injured. Can another person claim compensation from that person.

(a) Person is not liable to that person, as it was the duty of a person to take sufficient care while standing on the bus stop.

(b) Person is not liable because it is duty of the conductor of the bus to close the door.

(c) Person is liable for not taken care to close the door of the moving bus.

(d) Person is not liable because it is a duty of the driver of the bus to take care while driving a bus.

Answer is (c) because it is a duty of last men who board the bus, has a duty to take care to close the door.

EXAMPLE - 13

PRINCIPLE : Everybody is under a legal obligation to take reasonable care to avoid act or omission which he can foresee would injure his neighbour. The neighbour for this purpose is any person whom he should have in his mind as likely to be affected by his act.

FACTS : A widow had filed an appeal through her counsel claiming compensation because her husband had been killed in motor accident. The case remained on the daily list of court for three weeks and then it has dismissed on default. Widow filled a case of compensation against the counsel.

(a) Counsel is liable to widow for having taken care.

(b) Counsel is not liable because it was duty of the widow to take care.

(c) Counsel is not liable because it was duty of the court to inform widow.

(d) None of the above.

Answer is (a).

Vicarious Liability

The maxim *"Qui facit per alium facit per se"* provides the general principle of vicarious liability. This means that he who acts through another is deemed in law as doing it himself. This is especially true in the following cases :

(i) Principal and agent
(ii) Partners
(iii) Master and servant
(iv) Independent contractor

"Respondent Superior"

It means the superior must be responsible. The doctrine of liability of the master for the act of his servant is based on maxim respondent superior which means the principal be liable and it puts the master in the same position as if he had done the act himself.

Negligence

It means one is responsible for the direct consequences of his negligent act where he is placed in such a position with regard to another that it is obvious that if he does not use due care in his own conduct he will cause injury to another. In a case of negligence the person has to prove that the person negligent.

(a) did not owed a duty of care towards him.
(b) made a breach of that duty.
(c) that he suffered damage as a result of it.

"Res Ispa Loquitor"

It means the things speaks for itself. In this situation the person is not required to prove negligence.
For ex : in the case of accident etc.

Defences

The defences against negligence are :

(a) contributory negligence.
(b) express contract.
(c) voluntary assumption of risk.

Nuisance

Nuisance defined as an unlawful interference with a person's use or some right over or enjoyment of land or some right over or enjoyment of land or in connection with it. It also means interfering with a person's comfort, health or safety.

Kind of Nuisance

Nuisance is of two kinds:

(1) Public nuisance
(2) Private nuisance

There are three essential of tort of nuisance:

(a) There must be an unreasonable interference
(b) Such interference must be with the use or enjoyment of land and
(c) It must cause damage to the plaintiff

EXAMPLE - 14

PRINCIPLE : A farm house belong to Raja Ram Chandra had its fencing electrified. The main object was to ensure the farm was secured from any animals. There was a clear warning about electrified fencing. In near to the farm house a summer camp of school children was carried by the cricket coach Rajender. A cricket ball hit by a student fell within the farm. One student attempted to jump the fence to take the ball but got injured by the electric shock. Rajender files a suit against Raja Ram Chandra

(a) Raja will not be liable because he had given sufficient warning.
(b) Raja will not be liable because student was a trespasser.
(c) Raja will liable because he must have taken note of the adjacent playground.

Answer is (c) because occupier of the premises owes duty to take such reasonable care to see that the entrant does not suffer injury on the premises by reasons of the danger concerned.

EXAMPLE - 15

PRINCIPLE : The occupier of a premise owes a duty of care to all his invitees and visitors.

FACTS : Ramesh, a owner of bungalow was constructing a swimming pool is his compound. Since the work was incomplete, he asked his workers to cover it with plastic. Next day, The postman who came inside the bungalow to deliver a telegram and fell into his unfinished pool. The postman filed a suit against Ramesh.

(a) Ramesh is liable because the postman came into the bungalow in the course of his duty.
(b) Ramesh is not liable because postman was trespasser.
(c) Ramesh is not liable because postman did not take care of himself.

(d) Ramesh is not liable because he did not called the postman to his house.

The answer is (a)

EXAMPLE - 16

PRINCIPLE : If, as a result of carelessness, one injures another, he is legally liable to the injured victim for resulting damages, unless the victim's own carelessness also contributes to causing the accident.

FACTS : 'X' carelessly left an iron pole across a public road. 100 metres from the spot was a traffic signal where indicating the speed limit of a two-wheeler as 40 kmph but 'M' riding a scooter at speed of 65 kmph notified the iron pole from a distance but would not avoid it and collided with the pole and got injured. Y sued X for compensation.

(a) Y will succeed because X did the act carelessly.

(b) Y will not succeed as he was driving more speed to that of limit speed.

(c) Y will not succeed because it was mistake from the Y side.

(d) Y will succeed because X could void the accident by putting up a warning.

Answer is (b)

EXAMPLE - 17

PRINCIPLE : An unlawful interference with a person's use or enjoyment of land, or some right over, or in connection with it, is a nuisance is tort.

FACTS : A suit was filed by X to seek in injunction from the court in order to the defendant Y from installing and running floor mill in their premises. According to X it created nuisance to them as they were put on the first floor of the same premises.

(a) X will not succeed because Y installing floor mill for the economic reasons.

(b) X will succeed because in a residential area it create nuisance.

(c) X will not succeed because of any other rule of law.

Answer is (b).

EXAMPLE - 18

PRINCIPLE : The owner of immoveable property is entitled to a column of air space above the surface. But the owner's right to air space above his land is restricted to such height as is necessary foı the ordinary use and enjoyment of his land and the structures on it.

FACTS : Yamuna cable company provides cable facility to its customers. One such cable wire passes over the house of Mr. Sharma who is not a subscriber of Yamuna cable company. The cable wire which was passed over the Mr. Sharma's storeyed house is 15 feet above to top floor. Aman, son of Mr. Sharma is unable to fly a kite on the terrace. Mr. Sharma requested the cable company to alter the portion of cable wire but to no avail. One day Mr. Sharma cut the cable wire and thus cleared the airspace above his house. The Yamuna cable company filed a suit against Mr. Sharma.

(a) The cable company is succeed because ordinarily cable wire is above 15 feet so cable wire is not interfering to any enjoyment of Mr. Sharma.

(b) The cable company is not succeed because Mr. Sharma has every right to enjoyment of his property by removing objects causing obstruction is the airspace above his property to a reasonable extent.

(c) The company is succeed because it is for public use like electricity and telephone cable etc.

Answer is (a)

EXAMPLE - 19

PRINCIPLES

(1) If a persons makes a statement that lowers the reputation of another person in the eyes of right thinking people, then it is defamation.

(2) The person above reputation is affected can sue the culprit and recover damages.

FACTS : The plaintiff was an amature golfer. The defendants published an advertisement in which there appeared a caricature of Mr. Tolly. The defendant neither consulted nor had paid money to plaintiff. Mr. Tolly sued the defendants.

(a) Mr. Tolly succeed because by caricature it is liable.

(b) Mr. Tolly cannot succeed because he only published the advertisement.

(c) Mr. Tolly cannot succeed because it is not liable.

(d) Both (b) and (c)

Answer is (a).

CRIMINAL LAW

In the uncivilized society no person was said to be safe from attack of his opponent. In India, the law of crime came into existence from our civilization. But different law came into existence in the reins of different rulers. In British time, Britishers adopted a different set of law which was not uniform throughout the country. So, there was a need of a good codified criminal law.

In order to bring uniformity throughout India, the First Law Commission was appointed under the Chairmanship of Lord Macauly prepared the draft penal code which was revised twice by subsequent commission. The final draft code was presented in the legislative council in 1856 and then in 1857 and was finally passed and received the Governor General's assent on October 6, 1860.

The Indian Criminal law basically based on

(a) Indian Penal Code, 1860

(b) Criminal Procedure Code, 1973

(c) The Indian Evidence Act, 1872

The Indian Penal Code is subjective in nature whereas Criminal Procedure Code is adjective in nature. All the offences mentioned under the Indian Penal Code is to be investigated, tried and dealt as per the provision of the Criminal Procedure Code. The Indian Evidence Act is a kind of supporting law, which helps in establishing the facts during any criminal or judicial investigation under the Criminal Procedure Code.

Mens Rea

Mens rea is one of the essential element of crime. It covers a wide range of mental states and conditions, the existence of which would give a criminal here to actus reus. A criminal offence is only committed when an act is done voluntarily. "*Actus non facit reum nisi mens sit rea*" is a Latin maxim which lays down a fundamental principle of criminal law this means the act does not make one guilty unless the mind is also guilty.

EXAMPLE - 1

There was ship wreck on the high seas. A, the husband of W, was also on a voyage on this ship. Most of the people on this ship died because of the mishap. After about five years of this mishap, W believing that her husband A is dead, married another person Y. Then about six months after the marriage, A, came back, and prosecuted W for the offence of bigamy.

The question before the court was whether W committed the offence of bigamy with a guilty intention. The court decided on the basic of mens rea and took the view that at the time of second marriage she in good faith and on reasonable grounds believed her husband to be dead and that this bonafide belief afforded a good defence.

Group Liability

If two or more Persons intend to do a thing, jointly, it is just the same as if each of them had done it individually. If the intention or purpose is common, so must be the responsible.

EXAMPLE - 2

PRINCIPLE : When a criminal act is done by one person in furtherance of the common intention of himself and some other persons, each of such persons is liable for the act is the same manner as if it is done by him alone.

FACTS : A, B and C decided to commit burglary. They broke into a locked house. However, a domestic servant appeared from the out-house before they had finished, he started shouting. A, B and C left the house and started running away. They were pursued by a small crowd. A, on being caught by X, one of the person pursuing them, stabbed him and run away by that time B and C had disappeared. X died on account of the stab wounds. Later the police could arrest all the three. They were charged for attempted burglary and murder of X.

(a) Along with A, the person who stabbed X, B and C are also guilty of murder because A stabbed X in furtherance of common intention to commit murder.

(b) Along with A, B and C be also guilty of murder because A, at the time of stabbing X, was acting on behalf of B and C and he wanted to save not only himself but B and C as well.

(c) A alone is guilty of murder because though there was common intention to commit the offence of burglary, there was no common intention to commit the offence of murder.

The answer is (c).

General Exceptions

There are various kinds of act done under the circumstances mentioned in section 76 to 106 which will not amount to offences under the code.

The general exceptions are mainly:

1. Mistake (section 76, IPC)
2. Unsoundness of mind or Insanity (section 84, IPC)
3. Intoxication (section 85, IPC)
4. Right of private defence (section 97, IPC)

Mistake

Section 76 Act done by a person bound, or by mistake of fact believing himself bound by law. Nothing is an offence which is done by a person who is, or who by reason of a mistake of fact and not by reason of mistake of law in good faith believes himself to be bound by law to do it.

Illustrations:

(a) A, a soldier fires on a mob by order of his superior officer in conformity with the commands of the law, A was committed no offence.

(b) A, an officer of a court of justice, being ordered by the court to arrest Y, and after due inquiry, believing Z to Y, arrests Z. A has committed no offence.

EXAMPLE - 3

The appellant's wife was taking a bath over the grave of her child in the belief that she would in this way get a son along with her husband. It was a dark night and a villager took the husband to be a ghost and killed him by beating him from a stick. He was held not liable for murder because he believed in good faith at the time of the attack that the object of his assault was not a living human being, but a ghost or some object other than a living human being. The court made it clear that the ground for its opinion was that mens rea or an intention to do wrong or commit an offence did not exist in the case.

Unsoundness of Mind

Section 84 : Act of person of unsound mind.—Nothing is an offence which is done by a person who at the time of doing it, by reason of unsoundness of mind is incapable of knowing the nature of the act or that he is doing what is either wrong or contrary to law.

EXAMPLE - 4

A, was suffering under an insane delusion the X and Y were harassing him. He bought a knife in order to revenge himself on them, and that very evening he went to their club and stabbed them dead. The fact that he actually bought a knife and went to the club of his victims shows that he knew what he was going to do, namely, an act contrary to law, he had an intention to kill. Thus, A would be guilty of murder. But this would not be so if at the time of committing the act, A is so deranged as not to know what he was doing or that he was doing an act contrary to law.

Intoxication

Nothing is an offence which is done by a person who, at the time of doing it, by reason of intoxication, incapable of knowing the nature of the act, or that he is doing what is either wrong, or contrary to law: provided that the thing which intoxicated him, was administered without his knowledge or against his will. Two important legal points to take the defence of intoxicated.

1. Intoxication must be not voluntary or without knowledge and.
2. The level of intoxication must be such as to make a person incapable of knowing the nature of his act.

For Ex. : X became very drunk, but knew what he was doing. He went to his home, took hold of sword and glint along the road shocked his intention to kill with whom he had a dispute, Z, a passer by gently tried to pacify X, who thereupon inflicted wound on Z, of which Z died within a few minutes. In the circumstances, X would be guilty of culpable homicide.

EXAMPLE - 5

PRINCIPLE : Any person who interferes with the discharge of duties by a public servant is liable for punishment.

FACTS : Mohandass got drunk of his own volition and on his way back home he assaulted a policeman. He is prosecuted for intimidating a public servant.

DECISION : Mohandass would be liable for punishment because according to section 85 of IPC intoxication. He has been intoxicated voluntarily. He cannot take the defence of intoxication to avoid liability.

Right of Private Defence

Section 96 of IPC define things done in private defence: "Nothing is an offence which is done in the exercise of the right of private defence."

The right of private defence is the right to protect one's own person and property against the unlawful aggression of others. It is right inherent in man and based on the principle that it is the first duty of man to help himself.

The doctrine of right of private defence is founded in following ten points:

(i) A private citizen whose life is threatened by a grave danger, need not wait for the state aid. However, where aid is available it must be obtained.

(ii) The right of defence is protective or preventive and not punitive.

(iii) The right cannot be availed of for the sake of self gratification, to satisfy one's ego or to satisfy one's malicious or sadistic urges.

(iv) The right must be exercised when there is:

(a) real and immediate threat.

(b) a reasonable apprehension of such threat.

(v) The apprehension must be reasonable and not fanciful. And present and imminent danger should be present.

(vi) The right of private defence commences as soon as a reasonable apprehension of danger to the body arises from an attempt.

(vii) The protective measures employed must be relative to the danger ahead.

(viii) The right of defence ends with the necessity of it.

(ix) The law does not require that a person should not exercise his right to self defence if by running away he can avoid injury.

(x) The law does not require that a person placed in such circumstances should weigh the arguments for and against an attack.

The right of private defence is not available in the following situations:

1. The aggressors cannot claim the right of private defence.
2. There cannot be private defence against private defence.
3. In a case when two parties are having a free fight without disclosing as to who is the initial aggressor.

EXAMPLE - 6

PRINCIPLE : (1) Any person may use reasonable force in order to protect his property or person.

(2) However, the force employed must be proportionate to the apprehended danger.

FACTS : A person walking at a night on a lonely road. A robber came with a knife and said to the person, "your life or your purse". Person pulled out his revolver. On seeing it, robber ran. Person shot robber in his leg.

(a) Person will not be punished as the force he used was proportionate to the apprehended injury.

(b) As robber ran to escape there was no longer a threat to person's property so person will be punished.

(c) Person will not be punished as there was danger to his property.

(d) Person will be punished as the force employed was disproportionate to the apprehended injury.

The answer is (b) because the right of private defence ends with the necessity of it and here also robber ran so danger or threat to a property or body is end.

EXAMPLE - 7

PRINCIPLE : An aggressor cannot claim the right of private defence in criminal law.

FACTS : The robbers, armed with knives and crowbars, broke the access door of a house and entered into it. The owner of the house took out his gun and threatened to shot them. The robbers ran out of the house and started pelting stones. The owners opened the fire. Having heard the gun shot, the police rushed to the place and announced that the owner must stop firing. The owner, suspecting mischief continued to fire and a policeman was injured by a shot. The robbers meanwhile fled away. The owner was sued for attacking the police servant on duty.

(a) The owner shall be liable for causing him harm, in excess of what is necessary for self defence.

(b) The owner shall not be liable for attacking the public servant as such though he may be held liable otherwise.

(c) The owner's action is justified by the consideration of self defence.

The answer is (c).

EXAMPLE - 8

PRINCIPLE : One has right to defend his life and property against criminal harm provided it is not possible to approach public authorities and more harm than is necessary has not been caused to avert the danger.

FACTS : On one night, D was sleeping on the roof of his building, while other member of his family were sleeping inside their rooms. He got awakened by vibrations and repeated sound of beating on the wall. He saw that some armed men, were entering his room after making a hole in the wall of his house. He has his gun and mobile with him and at first he warned the robbers by firing in the air but not informed to police. As they were fleeing from the house, he fired and killed one of them. Decide.

(a) D can avail the right of private defence as he was defending his life and property.

(b) D cannot avail the right of private defence as he caused more harm than was necessary to ward off the danger.

(c) D can avail of the right as at first he only fired in the air.

The answer is (b) he kills a robber while armed man was fleeing away. It means there was no apprehension of death or grievous hurt to him.

EXAMPLE - 9

PRINCIPLE : Every person has a right to defend his own body and the body of any other person, against any offence committed by anybody

FACTS : Z, under the influence of madness, attempts to kill A, A defending himself against Z's attacks kill Z. A takes the plea of right of private defence. Decide.

(a) A can avail the right of private defence as he was defending his life

(b) A cannot avail the right as he caused more harm then was necessary because Z under the influence of madness

(c) A cannot avail the right of private defence as he knows that Z was mad.

The answer is (a) because right of private defence is also applied against a person of unsound mind.

Criminal Conspiracy

EXAMPLE - 10

PRINCIPLE : When two or more persons agree to do, or cause to be done.

(1) An illegal act or

(2) An act which is not illegal by illegal means, such an agreement is designated a criminal conspiracy.

FACTS : A, B and C went to Budkal lake for a picnic and there was pre-planned in mind of A to kill C. A conspires along with B to kill C. Decide.

(a) Both of them guilty of murder because he has conspired to kill C.

(b) Both of them are not guilty because A has planned in mind..

(c) There were no cause of criminal conspiracy because there need A two or more person.

The answer is (a).

Sedition

EXAMPLE - 11

PRINCIPLE : Whoever by words, signs or otherwise brings into hatred or contempt or excites disaffection toward the government established by law in India shall be punished with imprisonment for life.

FACTS : In a public meeting, Yashpal Reddy, the leader of an opposition party thunders "This is a government of scoundrel, bootleggers and scamsters. They deserve to be unseated. Teach them a lesson in the coming elections by voting them out of power. The government is contemplating to prosecute Yashpal Reddy.

(a) Yashpal Reddy is guilty of sedition for having made irresponsible and inflammatory statement against the government.

(b) Yashpal Reddy is not guilty of sedition as he is only exercising his freedom of speech in public.

(b) Yashpal Reddy is guilty of sedition as his statement would incite people to violence leading in break down of law and order.

The answer is (b).

Culpable Homicide

Homicide means killing of a human being by a human being.

Culpable homicide defined under section 299 of IPC:

(a) Whoever causes death.

(b) By doing an act with the intention of causing death.

(c) With the intention of causing such bodily injury as is likely to cause death.

(d) With the knowledge that he is likely by such act to cause death.

EXAMPLE - 12

PRINCIPLE : A man is guilty of culpable homicide amounting to murder, if the act by which the death is caused is done without the intention of causing murder.

FACTS : A is suffering from jaundice and inflammation of the brain and B know his condition very well. Once they had a heated argument on some issue and A slapped B in anger, B lost his self- control and dealt a service blow on A's head. As a result, A died. The police sought to prosecute B for murder.

(a) B was liable for murder, because he knew A's delicate condition.

(b) B was not liable for murder, because he acted in self defence.

(c) B was not liable for murder because he did not have the intention to kill A.

The answer is (c).

EXAMPLE - 13

PRINCIPLE : A man is guilty of culpable homicide amounting to murder, if the act by which the death is caused is done without the intention of causing murder.

FACTS : A, intending to kill his wife W, gave her a poisoned chocolate which she left on the table and herself went to attend a telephone call meanwhile, their child C came in, picked up, and ate the chocolate. A, who was standing nearby, got quite upset by the sudden turn of events but kept quite due to fear of being exposed of his evil designs to kill W. C died of poisoning and A is being tried for C's murder. Decide.

(a) W is causing death of her children as she gave them chocolate.

(b) A is not guilty because he did not intend to kill his son.

(c) A is guilty of committing culpable homicide in as much as he had the intention to cause death.

The answer is (c)

EXAMPLE - 14

PRINCIPLE : Whoever causes death by doing an act with the intention of causing death commits culpable homicide, punishable under Indian Penal Code.

FACTS : In this case, there was no previous enmity between the accused and deceased. There was a scuffle and sudden quarrel that preceded the occurrence. The accused alongwith other inflicted two injuries on the head and some bruises on other part of the body of deceased by a ringed stick and on ordinary stick. Medical report said that the injury was sufficient in the ordinary course of nature to cause death. Decide.

Answer : The accused had no intention to cause particular injury which was sufficient to cause death. The accused, however, might have knowledge that said injury is likely to cause death. Thus accused is guilty of culpable homicide not amounting to murder.

Murder

Murder is defined under section 300 of IPC:—
Except in the case hereinafter excepted

(a) culpable homicide is murder if the act by which the death is caused is done with the intention of causing death or.

(b) if it is done with the intention of causing such bodily injury as the offender knows to be likely to cause the death of the person to whom the harm is caused or.

(c) if it is done with the intention of causing bodily injury to any person and the bodily injury intended to be inflicted is sufficient in the ordinary course of nature to cause death or

(d) if the person committing the act knows that it is so imminently dangerous that it must, in all probability cause death or such bodily injury as is likely to cause death, and commits such act without any excuse for incurring the risk of causing death or such injury as aforesaid.

EXAMPLE - 15

PRINCIPLE : Culpable homicide is murder, if the act by which the death is caused is done with the intention of causing death.

FACTS : X is in cultivating possession of agricultural land belonging to Z. A suit is pending before the court for recovery of the said land X alongwith Y intending to kill Z to keep the disputed land in possession, plan and set fire to his house by locking Z from outside just before midnight and by preventing other from coming to his rescue. Z is roasted alive. Decide.

(a) X and Y guilty of murder.

(b) X and Y are not guilty of murder.

(c) X and Y are guilty of culpable homicide not amounting to murder.

(d) None of the above.

The answer is (a).

Wrongful Restraint

Section 339 of IPC define wrongful restraint- whoever voluntarily obstructs any person so as to prevent that person from proceeding in any direction in which that person has a right to proceed is said wrongfully to restrain that person.

Exception: The obstruction of a private way over land or water which a person in good faith believes himself to have a lawful right to obstruct, is not an offence in the meaning of this section.

EXAMPLE - 16

PRINCIPLE : Whoever prevents any person from proceeding beyond certain circumscribing being limits, is said to have wrongfully confined the person.

FACTS : A obstructs a path along which Z has a right to pass. A not believing in good faith that he has a right to stop the path. Z is thereby prevented from passing. Decide.

(a) A cannot be said to have wrongfully restrains Z.

(b) A can be said to have wrongfully restrains Z.

(c) None of the above.

The answer is (b).

Kidnapping

EXAMPLE - 17

PRINCIPLE : If any person entices or allures any minor, out of the custody of the lawful guardian of such minor, without the consent of such lawful guardian, is said to have kidnapped such minor.

FACTS : A, a youngman resided in Delhi in the neighbourhood of X and had developed cordial relations with X. A presented a costly gift for G, a 17 years old daughter of X on her birthday. X sensed this growing intimacy between A and G. X shifted place but A tracked G and persuaded her to meet him at the railway station. A took G to Kanpur and married her A is being prosecuted for kidnapping. Decide.

(a) A is guilty of kidnapping, as he persuaded G to go with him.

(b) A is not guilty of kidnapping because consent was there.

(c) A is not liable of any offence.

The answer is (a).

Rape

EXAMPLE - 18

PRINCIPLE : A man is said to commit 'rape' who has sexual intercourse with a women without her will consent by fraud or she is under sixteen years of age.

FACTS : A person has a sexual intercourse with a girl below sixteen years of age with her consent. Decide, is the person is tried for the offence of rape?

(a) Person is not guilty as there was consent from the girl.

(b) Person is guilty of rape because due to age factor, her consent was not valid defence for him.

(c) None of the above.

The answer is (b).

Theft and Extortion

Theft defines under section 378 of IPC- whoever

(1) Intending to take dishonestly

(2) Any moveable property

(3) Taking out of the possession of another person

(4) Taking without consent

(5) Moving property in order to such taking

EXAMPLE - 19

A sees a ring belonging to Z lying on a table in Z's house. Not venturing to misappropriate the ring immediately for fear of search and detection. A hides the ring in a place where it is highly improbable that it will ever be found by Z, with the intention of taking the ring from the hiding place and selling it when the loss is forgotten. Here A, at the time of first moving the ring, commit theft.

EXAMPLE - 20

PRINCIPLE : When any person dishonestly takes any moveable property out of the possession of any other person without his consent, he is guilty of theft.

FACTS : A entered the drawing room of Y. A picked up the H.M.T. Quartz wrist watch lying on the table and hide it in a corner and left immediately whether A was committed theft?

(a) A commits theft because he has moved the watch from Y's table without his consent.

(b) A does not commit theft because he has not left Y's house with watch.

(c) A does not commit theft because Y is careless with his valuables.

(d) A commits theft at the moment he picks up the watch dishonestly and intended to keep it.

The answer is (d).

EXAMPLE - 21

PRINCIPLE : When any person dishonestly takes any moveable property out of the possession of any other person without his consent, he is guilty of theft

FACTS : A entered the study room of Y and takes away a book with the intention to return it.

(a) A commit theft because the book has been taken without Y's consent.

(b) A does not commit theft because he intends to return the book.

(c) A commit theft because he has moved the book from Y's house.

(d) A commit theft because he has taken a book which is moveable property.

The answer is (b).

EXAMPLE - 22

PRINCIPLE : When any person dishonestly takes away moveable property out of the possession of any other person without his consent, he is guilty of theft.

FACTS : A finds a mobile on the road and he keeps it.

(a) A commit theft because he does not report to owner of the mobile.

(b) A does not commit theft because the mobile was not taken away from the possession of any body.

(c) A commit theft because he does not report to police.

(d) None of the above.

The answer is (b).

EXAMPLE - 23

PRINCIPLE : Theft is the dishonest moving of property with the intention of taking it out for the person's possession without his consent.

FACTS : A gives the woolen coat to Dry Cleaner along with his wife's sarees for the purpose of dry cleaning. He is told to collect the clothes after two days. When he comes after two days, he finds that he does not have enough money to pay to the Dry Cleaners. But since due to the winter, he needs the coats discriptively, he immediately placed the coat near his goods so that he can quickly take it without the knowledge of the dry cleaner.

(a) A is guilty of theft

(b) A is not guilty of theft

(c) A is not guilty of theft but has to pay compensation to the Dry Cleaner

The answer is (a).

Extortion

Extortion is defined under section 383 of IPC :— Whoever intentionally

(1) Puts any person in fear of injury

(2) Dishonest inducement

(3) Delivery of property or valuable security by the person put in fear to any person.

For Ex : A, by putting Z in fear of grievous hurt, dishonestly induces Z to sign or affix his real to a blank paper and deliver it to A. Z signs and delivers the paper to A. Here as the paper so signed may be converted into a valuable property. A has committed extortion.

EXAMPLE - 24

PRINCIPLE : Whoever, intentionally puts any person in fear of physical or mental injury and thereby induces the person so put in fear to deliver any property to any person, commits extortion.

FACTS : X saw Y removing a stereo from a car parked in Kamla Nagar. X demands Rs. 200 from Y, giving him a threat that if he did not give the money, he would inform the police. Y gave the money. Has X committed extortion?

(a) X is the guilty of Extortion because he dishonestly induces Y to deliver money.

(b) X is not guilty of any offence.

(c) None of the above.

The answer is (a).

EXAMPLE - 25

A refused to register the marriage of B and C and to enter their marriage in the register unless he was paid Rs. 50. B paid the money. Can A convicted for extortion.

Answer : A cannot be convicted for extortion, as there is no fear of injury as essential requirement of extortion under section 383 of IPC. The fear must be of such a nature and extent as to unsettle the mind of the person to whom it operates and takes away from his acts that element of free voluntary action which alone constitutes consent.

Misappropriation

Section 403 of IPC defines misappropriation of property:— Whoever, dishonestly misappropriates or converts to his own use any moveable property, shall be punished with imprisonment of either description for a term which may extend to two years or with fine, or with both.

Illustrations : A finds a Government promissory note belonging to Z, bearing a blank endorsement. A, knowing that the note belong to Z, pledges it with a banker as a security for a loan, intending at a future time to restore it to Z. A has committed an offence under this section.

EXAMPLE - 26

PRINCIPLE : Whoever dishonestly misappropriates or converts to his own use any moveable property shall be punishable.

FACTS : A, with B's consent, lodged his hundred sheep in B's field overnight and the next moring drove his flock to the market for sale. At the time of the sale when the sheep were counted the presence of an extra sheep belonging to B was brought to A's notice. A sold it with the rest. Decide whether A is being tried for criminal misappropriation.

(a) A has committed the offence of misappropriation of property.

(b) A is guilty of theft because he has sell the sheep without B's consent.

(c) A is guilty of theft because he take the sheep intentionally.

The answer is (a).

Cheating

Section 415 of IPC defines cheating- whoever, by deceiving any person, fraudulently or dishonestly induces the person to deliver any property to any person, or to consent that any person shall retain any property, or intentionally induces the person so deceived to do or omit to do anything which he would not do or omit if he were not so deceived, and which act or omission causes or is likely to cause damage or harm to that person in body, mind, reputation or property is said to cheat.

Illustration : A intentionally deceives Z into a belief that A means to deliver to Z a certain quantity of indigo plant which he does not intend to deliver, and thereby dishonestly induces Z to advance money upon the faith of such delivery. A cheats, but if A at the time of obtaining the money, intends to deliver the indigo plant, and afterwards breaks his contract and does not deliver it, he does not cheat, but is liable only to a civil action for breach of contract.

EXAMPLE - 27

PRINCIPLE : A person is guilty of cheating, when he fraudulently induces another person to deliver the latter's property to him.

FACTS : 'A' falsely represented to 'B', a shop owner that he was an officer from the commercial Tax Department, while examining the account of the shop 'A' showed interest in buying a microwave oven on instalment basis. B readily agreed with the hope that he would get a favorable assessment from A regards his tax liability. A paid the first instalment took the microwave oven and disappeared from the scene. The police, however, manged to catch hold of A and prosecuting him for cheating.

(a) A committed cheating, because he induced B to part with microwave oven, passing as through that he was from the Commercial Tax Department.

(b) A committed cheating, because he did not pay the subsequent instalments.

(c) A did not commit cheating, because B handed over the article in order to get a favourable assessment from A.

The answer is (a).

Mischief

Mischief defined under section 425 IPC: Whoever with intent to cause, or knowing that he is likely to cause, wrongful loss or damage to the public or to any person, causes the destruction of any property or any such damage in any property or in the situation thereof as destroys or disminishes it value or utility, or affects it injuriously commits mischief.

Explanation 1: It is not essential to the offence of mischief that the offender should intend to cause or damage to the owner of the property injured or destroyed. It is sufficient if he intends to cause or knows that he is likely to cause, wrongful loss or damage to any person by injuring any property, whether it belong to that person or not.

Explanation 2 : Mischief may be committed by an act affecting property belonging to the person who commits the act or to that person and other jointly.

EXAMPLE - 28

PRINCIPLE : Whoever with the intent to cause, or knows that he is likely to cause, wrongful loss or damage to the public or to any person, causes the destruction of any property, or any such change in any property or in the situation thereof or destroys or diminishes its value or utility or affect it injuriously, commit mischief.

FACTS : A knowing that his effects are about to be taken in execution in order to satisfy a debt due from him to Z, destroys those effects, with the intention of thereby preventing Z from obtaining satisfaction of the debt and of thus causing damage to Z. He knowingly destroy the property. Decide whether A has committed mischief or not?

(a) A commit mischief, because he knowingly destroy the property to caused the damage to Z.

(b) A does not commit mischief because his act cannot be proved on the ground of law and evidence in its support.

(c) A cannot be punished because his assets are not sufficient to obtain satisfaction of debt.

(d) None of the above.

The answer is (a).

Defamation

EXAMPLE - 29

PRINCIPLE : According to section 499 of IPC: Whoever, by words either spoken or intended to be read, or by signs or by visible representations, make or publishes any imputation concerning any person intending to harm, or knowing or having reason to believe that such imputation will harm, the reputation of such person is said except in the cases hereinafter excepted, to defame that person.

Illustration : A draws a picture of Z running away with B's watch, intending it to be believed that Z stole B's watch, this is defamation.

FACTS : A says – Z is an honest man, he never stole B's watch, intending to cause it to be believed that Z did steal B's watch. Decide A will defame or not.

(a) A is guilty as he is intending to cause it to be believed that Z did steal b's watch

(b) A is not guilty because he is talking about only Z for his honestly

(c) None of the above.

The answer is (a).

Attempt

Section 511 of IPC defines attempt-Whoever attempts to commit an offence punishable by this code with imprisonment for life or imprisonment, or to cause such an offence to be committed and in such attempt does any act towards the commission of the offence, shall, where no express provision is made by this code for the punishment of such attempt be punished with imprisonment of any description provided for the offences or a term which may extend to one half of the imprisonment for life, one half of the longest imprisonment provided or that offence or with such fine as is provided for the offence, or with both.

Illustration : A makes an attempt to steal some Jewels by breaking open a box, and finds that there is no Jewel in it. He has born an act towards the commission of theft, and therefore is guilty under this section.

EXAMPLE - 30

PRINCIPLE : After one has finished preparation to commit an offence, any act done towards committing the offence with intention to commit it, is an attempt to commit the offence which is by itself an offence.

FACTS : A wants to kill B. He buys a gun and catridges for committing the murder. He then sets out searching B and when he sees B, he loads his gun and takes him at B and pulls the trigger. The gun did not fire. Which of the answer you will feel more appropriate.

(a) A is guilty of attempt to murder B from the time he sets out in search of B.

(b) A is guilty of attempt to murder from the time he loads his gun.

(c) A is guilty of attempt to murder from the moment he takes aims at B.

The answer is (c).

EXAMPLE - 31

PRINCIPLE : Preparation to commit an offence is not an offence. After making the preparation any act done towards committing the offence with intention to commit it is an attempt to commit the offence. Which is by itself an offence.

FACTS : The accused, on quarrelling with his brother, he gone to market and buys a gun and cartridges to kill his brother. He loads his gun and takes aim at him and pulls the trigger. The gun did not fire. Decide from when he is charged for the attempting to murder.

(a) Accused is guilty of attempt of murder from the time he fired at his brother.

(b) Accused is guilty of attempt of murder from the time he takes aim at his brother.

(c) Accused is guilty of attempt of murder from the time when he loads the gun.

The answer is (b).

LAW OF CONTRACT

Introduction

The law related to contract is governed by the Indian Contract Act, 1872

According to section 2 (h) of the Indian Contract Act, 1872 defines the term contract as an agreement enforceable by law is contract. Thus every contract is made up of a proposal from one side and its acceptance by the other. So in business agreement it is usual that the parties intend legal consequences to follow.

According to section 2 (a), 2 (b) and 2 (d) of the Indian contract Act, 1872 contract consists of

(a) Proposal or offer
(b) Acceptance of proposal of offer
(c) Consideration

Essential Elements of a Contract

Section 10 of the Indian Contract Act, 1872 provides for the essential elements of a valid contract. To constitute a valid contract, following elements are essential:

(1) Offer and Acceptance
(2) Intention to create legal relationship
(3) Consideration
(4) Parties must be competent to contract
(5) Lawful consideration is a must
(6) There must be free consent among the parties entering into contract
(7) The object of contract must be lawful or legal

(8) Agreement must not be expressly declared void by the contract Act.

Offer and Acceptance

The first essential for ceating a contract is valid offer or proposal.

Sec. 2 (a) defines proposal as follows :

> "When one person signifies to another his willingness to do or abstain from doing anything, with a view to obtaining the assent of that other to such act or abstinence, he is said to make a proposal."

Section 3 defines signify means that the proposal must be communicated to the other party.

Section 9 provides that a valid proposal may be made by words (spoken or written).

Section 4 : The communication of a proposal is complete when it comes to the nowledge of the person to whom it is made. If an offer has not yet been communicated, even if somebody acts according to the terms of the offer, he cannot be deemed to be acceptor of that offer. Acting if ignorance of an offer does not amount to the acceptance of the same.

For Ex : It was held that even if the acceptor had once know of the offer but had completely forgotten about it at the time of acceptance, he would be in no better position than a person who had not heard of the offer at all. In that case, the government offered a reward for giving information about some murderers. The offer further added that if the information was given by an accomplish being himself the murderer, he would also be entitled to a free pardon. The plaintiff, being an accomplice, saw the offer and having been so much excited by the hope of pardon, that he gave the information to save himself. Completely forgetting the reward. So he could not recover the reward.

An offer must be made with an intention to create legal relationship. An offer is not a valid offer if it does not create a legal obligation upon the other party. Merely trifles do not constitute an offer. For Ex:-

(a) A and B contract to marry each other. Before the time fixed for the marriage A goes mad. The contract becomes void.

(b) A contracts to B to discover treasure by magic. The agreement is void.

An offer is different from an invitation to offer. Sometimes a person may not offer to sell his goods, but make some statement or give some information with a view to invitation others to make offers on that basis. For ex:- a book seller sends catalogue of books indicating prices of various books to many persons. This is an invitation of offer. If any person is interested in purchasing the books, he may make an offer and the person circulating the catalogue has a discretion to accept or reject the offer.

EXAMPLE - 1

PRINCIPLES

(i) When one person signifies to another his willingness to do or abstain from doing anything, with a view to obtaining the assent of that other to such act or abstinence, he is said to make a proposal.

(ii) The proposal must be communicated to the other party.

(iii) A valid proposal may be made by words (written or spoken).

FACTS : A fire broke out in the defendant's firm believing that he was entitled to the free service of Uptron. Fire Brigade, he summoned it. The defendant's firm was not within the free service zone of the Uptron. Uptron claimed compensation for its services.

(a) Defendant can succeed in the court of law

(b) Uptron can recover the compensation from the defendant

(c) There is no intention to enter into legal relations

(d) None of the above answer is correct

The answer is (b) because the defendant asked for the service of Uptron and Uptron provides them. Hence the service were rendered an implied promise to pay for them.

EXAMPLE - 2

PRINCIPLES : No one can accept a proposal without any knowledge thereof.

FACTS : The plaintiff, who was defendant's servant, was sent to search of missing boy. After the plaintiff had left in search of the boy, the defendant issued a reward of Rs 500 to any one who might find out the boy. The plaintiff came to know of this offer only when he had already traced, and informed defendant about the boy. The plaintiff brought an action to claim this reward.

(a) Defendant has to pay the amount, because he had promised to pay the reward to anyone giving the information about the boy.

(b) Defendant need not pay the amount, because he had given the information without knowing the reward.

(c) Defendant need not pay the amount because the promise was made only to other than his family related persons.

The correct answer is (b) because the plaintiff was ignorant of the offer of reward, his act of bringing the lost boy did not amount to the acceptance of the offer, and therefore he was not entitled to claim the reward.

EXAMPLE - 3

PRINCIPLE : Law does not take notice of trifles.

FACTS : Ram and Shyam decided that they both should go together to their office. Both of them agrees to the proposal and it is decided that both of them would meet at a particular bus stop at 9 a.m from where they would take the bus for the office. Inspite of agreement Shyam does not turn up. Ram waits for him at 9 a.m. at bus stop everyday for a continuous period of one week. Thereafter Ram files a suit against Shyam claiming damage for mental tension and agony suffered by him.

(a) The matter is too small and court will refuse to go into it.

(b) There is no intention to create legal relationship.

(c) Shyam is guilty of breach of contract so he is liable to pay damage.

(d) Ram is not guilty of break of contract so he is not liable to pay damage.

The correct answer is (a) because law does not take notice of trifles and also there is no intention to create legal relationship and there is no consideration.

EXAMPLE - 4

PRINCIPLE ; When the parties to an agreement agree on the same thing in the same sense, there arising a legally binding obligation between them.

FACTS : Ganesh gallery was a well known antique shop in the city. Shakuntala who had penchant for collecting articles of rare beauty, was taken up by an intricately designed flower vase in the shop. The shopkeeper explained to her the vase belonged to the Vijayanagar Empire period and although very delicate, it was quite strong and not easily breakable. Shakuntala said that he was attracted to it only for the aesthetic pleasure it gave her and its other characteristics were immaterial to her and brought piece. She later discovered that it was not a period piece and noticed it developing cracks as well. She proceeds against the proprietor of Ganesh Gallery for monetary relief.

(a) Ganesh Gallery must compensate Shakuntala, since both the characteristics attributed to the article were proved wrong.

(b) Ganesh Gallery need not compensate, since Shakuntala was unconcerned about what was attributed to the article.

(c) The proprietor must compensate her for irresponsible statement made by him.

The answer is (a) because there is no any intention to create legal relationship and also do not agree upon his statement.

EXAMPLE - 5

PRINCIPLES

(1) An agreement enforceable in a court of law is a contract

(2) In order for an agreement to be enforceable in a court of law, there must be a meeting of minds between both the parties.

(3) Parties to a contract should do something for the other party. The obligation to do something for the other party is mutual. This is called consideration and absence of consideration renders the contract unenforceable.

FACTS : Mohan promised to take Sunder out for a dinner in Taj Coromendal. Even after two weeks, Mohan did not fulfil the promise. Sunder wants to sue the Mohan to enforce that promise. If Sunder goes to court.

(a) He can compel Mohan to buy him a dinner at Taj Coromandal.

(b) He can recover the value of dinner from Mohan.

(c) This promise will not be enforced by a court of law as there is no consideration from Sunder.

The answer is (c) because there is no evidence or intention to create legal relationship in this case.

EXAMPLE - 6

PRINCIPLE : If both the parties agree upon to same thing in the same sense, the parties are bound by their agreement.

FACTS : Sanjay wrote to Hrithik offering to sell his horse for Rs. 30,000. Hrithik wrote back, I agree to purchase your black horse for Rs. 30,000.

(a) The parties are bound by their agreement as they agree on the price and also on the goods for sale.

(b) The parties are not bound by the agreement as the object is uncertain.

(c) The parties are bound by their agreement as the colour of the horse is only a question of detail.

The answer is (b).

EXAMPLE - 7

PRINCIPLE : A clear offer and acceptance lead to a contractual relationship.

FACTS : The plaintiff offered to purchase the lodge owned by the defendants for Rs. 6000. He wrote the defendant's agent asking whether his offer has been accepted and saying that he was prepared to accept any higher price if found reasonable. The agent replied "would not accept less than Rs. 10,000". The plaintiff accepted this and ask to send all legal documents.

(a) Defendant becomes bound to sell the lodge to plaintiff after quoting the price of it.

(b) Mere quotation of price will not bind the defendant to sell the lodge to plaintiff.

(c) The defendant may argue that it did not desire to sell the lodge to plaintiff but plaintiff prevent the defendant from selling the same to anybody else.

The answer is (b) because defendants gave only the lowest price and did not expressed their willingness to sell. Thus they had made no offer therefore no concluded contract.

EXAMPLE - 8

PRINCIPLE : A person who rightfully rescinds a contract is entitled to compensation for any damage which he has sustained through the non-fulfilment of the contract.

FACTS : A singer final his contract with a five star hotel. The terms and condition of the contract was that the singer sing at his hotel for five days a week for next one year, who engages to pay her 15,000 rupees each month. After a week singer willfully absents herself from the hotel and manager in consequences. rescinds the contract. Singer sue the hotel manager for compensation.

(a) singer can recover claim because contract is for one year.

(b) singer can not recover the claim because he willfully absent himself form the hotel.

(c) singer can recover because he has rightfully rescinded the contract.

(d) None of the above.

The answer is (b).

EXAMPLE - 9

PRINCIPLE

(i) Acceptance of an offer is complete when the acceptance is put into the course of transmission so as to be out of power of the acceptor.

(ii) Acceptance once completed makes the agreement binding on both the parties.

FACTS : A accepts to buy B's offer of his motor car for Rs. 4 lakhs. The acceptance was put into e-mail. Unfortunately, when e-mail was put, there is distortions as a result of which B is not in a position to really read what A has written.

(a) B is bound to perform the agreement but not A.

(b) Both the parties are bound to perform their part of the agreement.

(c) Nobody is bound to perform the agreement.

(d) A is bound to perform the agreement but not B.

The answer is (d).

Consideration

Consideration constitutes the very foundation of the contract. An agreement without consideration is void.

Consideration is the cause of the promise and in its absence the promise would only be a bare promise. The fact that a promise has been made for consideration goes to show that parties contemplated the creation of a legal obligation.

For ex : If a man promises a charitable institution that he will pay Rs. 1 lakh into its funds if it procures him other nine persons to do the same, justice requires that his promise should be held binding on him as soon as it has procured the nine offer to pay Rs. 1 lakh each, but the act done by the institution is either a benefit to him or a detriment to the institution.

Act done at the promisor's desire furnishes a good consideration for his promise even though it is of no personal significance or benefit to him.

For ex : In the leading case of *Kedar Nath* v. *Gorie Mohamed* 1886 ILR 14 Calcutta 64, on the basis of promised subscription of defendant, plaintiff entered into a contract with contractor for the purpose of building the hall. The court held that the defendant liable. The court observed that the persons were asked to subscribe knowing the purpose for which money was to be applied, they knew that on the faith of their subscription an obligation has to be issued to pay the contractor for the work. In another leading case *Doraswami Iyer* v. *Arunachala Ayyar,* AIR 1936 Madras 135, the repair of a temple was in progress. As the work proceeds, more money was required and to raise this money subscriptions were invited. The defendant became a subscriber for Rs. 1000. It was to recover that the suit was filed. But no recovery was allowed.

In *Kedar Nath* case the construction of the hall began on the faith of the promised subscriptions, but in the present case, temple repairs were already in progress when the subscription were invited. The action was not induced by the promise to subscribe but was rather independent of it.

EXAMPLE - 10

PRINCIPLE : A contract without consideration is void

FACTS : Ram owes Shyam Rs. 1100 put the debt is barred by limitation. Shyam cannot file a suit. Ram signs a written promise to pay Shyam Rs. 500 on account of this debt. Shyam now files a suit for the recover of Rs. 500. Decide.

(a) The contract is enforceable as it has sufficient consideration.

(b) The contract is not enforceable as consideration is inadequate.

(c) Time barred debt is no consideration.

The answer is (a).

EXAMPLE - 11

PRINCIPLE : A contract is an agreement which the law will enforce. All agreements are contract if they are made with free consent by parties competent to contract for a lawful consideration and with a lawful object.

FACTS : A, a young man, a 30 years old business man of sound mind without any consideration agrees to give B Rs. 10,000. A fails to fulfil his promise. B sues A for the amount.

(a) B will succeed as A has the capacity to make the contract

(b) B will succeed as A made the promise of his own free will

(c) B will succeed as the money is not being paid for any illegal object

(d) B will fail as the agreement is without consideration.

The answer is (d).

EXAMPLE - 12

PRINCIPLE : A contract without consideration is void. When at the desire of one party, the other party does something the consideration is said to flow from the latter to the former.

FACTS : A house was on fire and a child was trapped inside the house, everyone was shouting for help. A brave on lookers, hearing the shouting of child, went inside the house and brought it out the grateful father, of the child promised to pay the rescuer Rs. 10,000 subsequently be rendered the promise. The rescuer sued the promisee for the breach.

(a) Commercial consideration can not be applied to humanitarian help.

(b) The father of the child must pay for the service rendered by the rescuer.

(c) The recover is not entitled to the payment, since he acted on his own.

The answer is (c).

EXAMPLE - 13

PRINCIPLE : An agreement is contract if it is made by the free consent of the parties competent to contract, for a lawful consideration and with a lawful object, and they are not hereby expressly declared to be void.

FACTS : Ram agrees to sell Shyam a house worth Rs. 15 lakhs for Rs 5000. Is the agreement between Ram and Shyam a contract. Decide.

(a) No, because Shyam has played foul on Ram.

(b) Yes, because inadequacy of consideration does not make an agreement void.

(c) No, because there is no free and express consent.

(d) No, because consideration inadequate.

The answer is (b).

EXAMPLE - 14

PRINCIPLE :

(1) No consideration – no contract.

(2) Consideration is something done or abstinence of a party at the desire of another party.

(3) Consideration must have value in the eye of law.

FACTS : Innovative Educational Trust manages a school named Bharat Vidyaniketan. Ram, the parent of a student in the school suggested to the trust that it could build a new library building for which he would bear a part of the cost. The school authority accepted the suggestion and started construction of the building. Ram have suffered a loss in business, now he refuses to pay the part he had offered earlier which of the decision you think is appropriate.

(a) Ram is liable to pay because based upon his promise, the school authority started construction of the building.

(b) Ram is not liable to pay because as the building was for the benefit of the school and he has nothing to do with it by way of enjoying and benefit.

(c) Ram is liable to pay because Ram's child is a student in the same school.

(d) None of the above.

The answer is (a).

Competency of Parties

Section 10 of the Indian Contract Act, 1872 requires that the parties must be competent to contract.

Section 11 of the Indian Contract Act, 1872 defines who are competent to contract:

> "Every person is competent to contract who is the age of majority according to the law to which he is subject, and who is of sound mind and is not disqualified from contracting by any law to which he is subject, therefore, the following persons are parties incompetent to contract:
>
> (a) A minor, a person below the age of 18 years
>
> (b) A person of unsound mind or insane
>
> (c) A person disqualified by any law to contract

For Ex : In leading case *Mohiribibi* v. *Bharmodas Ghose* (1903) 30 Cal 539 - The Plaintiff a minor mortgaged his house in favour of the defendant, a money lender and to secure a loan. A part of this amount was actually advanced to him. While considering the proposed advanced, money lender received the information that the plaintiff was still a minor. Subsequently the minor commenced this action stating that he was under age when he executed the mortgage and the same should therefore be cancelled. The court held that a minor's agreement is absolutely void. In other side, a situation may arise where a minor has declared or intentionally caused or permitted another person to believe him to be a person who has attained the age of majority.

For Ex : In a case, *Khan Gul* v. *Lakha Singh,* AIR 1928 Lah 60 a minor by fraudulently concealing his age, contracted to sell a plot of land to the plaintiff. He received the consideration of said amount and then refused to perform this part of the bargain. The court held that the doctrine of restitution would be apply to it and found sufficient reason of this application. The doctrine rests upon the salutary principle that an infant cannot be allowed by a court of equity to take advantage of his own fraud.

Persons of unsound mind

Section 12 of Indian Contract Act, 1872 said that, a person is said to be of sound mind for the purpose of making a contract if at the time when he makes it, he is capable of understanding it and of forming a rational judgement as to its effects upon his interests. A person who is usually of unusal mind, but occasionally of sound mind, may take a contract when he is of sound mind. A person who is usually of sound mind, but occasionally of unsound mind, may not make a contract when he is of unsound mind.

Illustration : (a) A patient in a lunatic asylum, who is at interval of sound mind, may contract living those intervals.

(b) A sane man, who is delirious from fever. Or who is so drunk that he cannot understand the terms of a contract, or from a national judgement as to its effect on his interests, cannot contract whilst such delirious or drunkenness last.

Case : Inder Singh v. *Parmeshwardhri Singh,* AIR 1957 Pat 491, a property worth Rs. 25,000 was agreed to be sold by a person for Rs. 7000 only. His mother proved that he was a born a idiot incapable of understanding the transaction. The court held that sale to be void.

EXAMPLE - 15

PRINCIPLE : A minor's agreement is absolutely void.

FACTS : Ram aged 16 is a stamp collector he is particularly anxious to get a rare stamp belonging to Shyam who agrees in writing to sell this to Ram for Rs. 500 but subsequently refuses to deliver it to Ram though Ram pays Rs. 500. Ram now wants to sue Shyam. Will Ram succeed?

(a) Ram cannot succeed as Shyam is not liable.

(b) Ram can succeed as he has paid Rs. 500 for the stamp.

(c) Ram can succeed as Shyam agreed in writing to sell the stamp.

The answer is (b).

EXAMPLE - 16

PRINCIPLE : A minor is not competent to contract.

FACTS : The plaintiff a minor mortgage his house in favour of the defendant, a money lender, to secure a loan of Rs. 20,000. The part of this amount was actually advanced to him. While considering the proposed advance, the attorney received information that the plaintiff was still a minor. The mortgage files a suit against the minor to recover the money advanced by him. The minor mortgager take the plea that the suit is not maintain as there was no valid contract. Decide.

(a) The minor is liable to return the money received by him as advance.

(b) The minor is not liable to return the money because an agreement with minor is absolutely void.

(c) It is voidable at the option of the parties.

The answer is (b).

EXAMPLE - 17

PRINCIPLE : (1) A person who is usually of sound mind, but occasionally of unsound mind may not make a contract when he is of unsound mind.

(2) A person who is usually of unsound mind but occasionally of sound mind may make a contract when he is of sound mind.

FACTS :- A property worth about Rs. 25000 was agreed to be sold by a person for Rs. 7000 only. His mother proved that he was a born idiot incapable of understanding the transaction. Decide.

(a) Sale is void

(b) Sale is not void because he was idiot but know about the money

(c) Sale is not vaid because money was already accepted

The answer is (a).

EXAMPLE - 18

PRINCIPLE : An agreement is enforceable at law if parties competent to contract enter into it with free consent, for consideration. And the contract is not contrary to law and against public policy.

FACTS : A minor enter into an agreement to sell his flat at Delhi for a sum of Rs. 10 lakhs. Minor's father is very annoyed with minor at the transaction and does not allow to delivers. The buyer files a suit for a specific performance:

(a) The buyer will not succeed because A's father does not approve of the contract.

(b) The buyer will succeed because A freely entered into the contract.

(c) The buyer will not succeed because A is minor.

(d) The buyer will succeed because the agreement is with consideration.

The answer is (c).

Free Consent

A mere consent is not enough for a valid contract. One of the essentials of a valid contract is that the parties should enter into the contract with their free consent.

Consent is said to be free when it is not caused by

(i) coercion
(ii) undue influence
(iii) fraud
(iv) misrepresentation
(v) mistake

Where the consent to an agreement is caused by coercion, undue influence, fraud or misrepresentation, the agreement is a contract voidable at the option of the party whose consent was so caused. For example a person is induced to sign an agreement by fraud, be may, on discovering the truth, either uphold the contract or reject it. Where consent is caused by mistake, the agreement is void.

For Ex :

(a) A agree to buy from B a certain house. It turns out that the house was dead at the time of the bargain, though neither party was aware of the fact. The agreement is void on account of mistake.

(b) A husband persuaded his illiterate wife to sign certain documents telling her that by them he was going no mortgage her two lands to secure his indebtedness and in fact mortgaged four lands belonging to her. This was an act done with the intention of deceiving her and a case of fraud.

(c) A, a man inferbled by disease or age, is induced, by B's influence over him as his medical attendant, to agree to pay B an unreason able sum for his professional services, B employees undue influence.

(d) A threates to shoot B if B does not agree to sell his property A at a stated price. B's consent was been obtained by coercion.

Undue Influence

(1) Where the relations subsisting between the parties are such that one of the parties is in a position to dominate the will of the other, and uses that position to obtain an unfair advantage over the other, there is said to be undue influence.

(2) A person is said to be able to dominate the will of another.

(a) Where he holds a real or apparent authority over the other, or where he stands in a fiduciary relation to the other.

(b) Where he makes a contract with a person where mental capacity is or permanently affected by reason of age, illness, or mental or bodily distress.

(3) Where a person who is in a position to dominate the will of another enter into a contract with him and the transaction appears, on the face of it or on evidence adduced, to be unconscionable, the burden of proving that such contract was not induced by undue influence shall lie upon the person in a position to dominate the will of the other.

Illustration : A having advanced money to his son B, during his minority, upon B's coming of majority age obtain, by misuse of parental influence, a bond from B for a greater amount than the sum due in respect of the advance. A employs undue influence.

EXAMPLE - 19

PRINCIPLE : Where both the parties to an agreement are under a mistake as to a matter of fact essential to the agreement, the agreement is void.

FACTS : Ram is a supplier of electric goods. Shyam agrees to buy from Ram some electrical goods. The goods for which Shyam agrees to buy was already sold to another party, though neither party was aware of it. Decide, is the agreement between Ram and Shyam void?

(a) Yes, because Ram and Shyam were relatives.

(b) Yes, because Ram and Shyam were under a mistake as to matter of fact which is cosential to the agreement.

(c) No, because shyam was enforced the goods were already sold.

(d) No, because Ram was informed of the fact.

The answer is (b).

EXAMPLE - 20

PRINCIPLE : When a person represents to another something as a true fact knowing fully well that it is not true, he is guilty of fraud. The person subjected to fraud may void an agreement.

FACTS : A presents a horse for sale. The horse is kept on display so that anyone interested could examine it. The horse has a cracked hoof and it is cleverly concealed by the owner. B tells A "if you do not deny it, I shall assume that the horse is sound." A keeps silent, B purchases the horse. Decide.

(a) B can void the agreement on discovery of the defect.

(b) B cannot void the agreement, as the horse was on display and he could have satisfied himself of its soundness by personal examination.

(c) B cannot avoid the agreement as A did not make any representation to mislead him. He merely kept silent so that B could find things out by himself.

The answer is (c).

EXAMPLE - 21

PRINCIPLE :

(i) If there is undue influence on a party to an agreement, he may refuse to perform the agreement.

(ii) When one party in an agreement is in a position to dominate the will of the other party and he uses his position over the other party to get the other party's consent to the agreement, this is undue influence.

FACTS : A son forged his father's signature on several promissory notes and paid them into his banking account. When the truth discovered, the bank's manager threatened prosecution of the son if a satisfactory solution were not found. To avert this threat, the father agreed to give an equitable mortgage to the bank on his property in return for promissory notes. The father sought to cancel the agreement on the ground that he was influenced by the threat. Decide.

(a) Father has to pay for the promissory notes.

(b) Father can cancelled the agreement on the used undue influence to force.

(c) Father has to give mortgage to the bank.

The answer is (b). The fears of the father were stimulated and operated on to an extent to deprive him of free agency. There was inequality between the parties and one of them took unfair advantage of the situation of the other and used undue influence to free an agreement from hi,.

EXAMPLE - 22

PRINCIPLE : When a person is in a position to dominate another's will and uses that position to procure an unfair contract such contract can be avoided.

FACTS : Ram was preparing for medical entrance exam and he wanted to do his M.B.B.S. but unfortunately he could not get the seat in any government college. But one private college offered him for M.B.B.S. under certain conditions and agreement, provided that he would pay a hefty sum as capitation fee and he would serve the college after completing his M.B.B.S degree. Ram paid the capitation fee and completed his degree. But he refused to serve the college, claiming that he could avoid the contract. Decide.

(a) Ram can avoid the contract because the private college was in a position to dominate the will of Ram.

(b) Ram cannot avoid the contract because agreement is done before the 5 years and given by him under free will.

(c) Ram can avoid the contract because there were no consideration.

The answer is (a) because the agreement was signed by him under undue influence which is a sufficient ground to void the contract.

EXAMPLE - 23

PRINCIPLE : A contract procured by coercion is bad under Indian Contract Act. Coercion is defined as committing or threatening to commit any act forbidden by Indian Penal Code. Attempt to commit suicide is an offence under Indian Penal Code.

FACTS : Ram wanted his wife Savitri to part with some agricultural property given to her by her father at the time of marriage. Savitri resisted fearing that her husband would sale it away. Ram threatned her that if she does not sign the deed transferring the property to him, he would commit suicide. Savitri signed the deed and subsequently challenged the deed on the ground that the deed was under the undue influence of force.

(a) Savitri will not succeed because the deed was valid.

(b) Savitri will succeed because the deed was not valid.

(c) Savitri will not succeed because she work under emotion.

(d) Savitri will succeed because the land was not given as a dowry.

The answer is (b) because it was signed under the threat of suicide by her husband which amounts to coercion and is violate the contract.

EXAMPLE - 24

PRINCIPLE :- A person to whom money has been paid, or anything delivered, by mistake or under coercion must repay or return it.

FACTS : Ram and Shyam jointly owe 100 rupees to Savitri. Ram alone pays the amount to Savitri, Shyam not knowing of this fact, pays 100 rupees over agian to Savitri. Decide whether savitri bound to repay Shyam?

(a) No

(b) Facts not clear

(c) Yes because Shyam has paid Savitri under mistake or unknowingly.

The answer is (c).

OTHER IMPORTANT LAWS

EXAMPLE -1

PRINCIPLE : All minorities, whether based on religion or language shall have the rights to establish and administer educational institution of their choice.

FACTS : Md. Yusuf wants to establish an educational institution to held the poor person of his community and to educate the children of community. Yusuf being a very rich man has no problem regarding finance for institution. Therefore he applies to state government to grant him permission to establish and administer the institution. State government reject his plea on ground that said institution will create communal tension in the proposed area. Yusuf has following remedies:

(a) He should file a civil suit in District Court.

(b) He should file a special leave petition before Supreme Court.

(c) He has no remedy under the law.

(d) He should file a writ petition before the High Court or Supreme Court.

The answer is (d).

EXAMPLE - 2

PRINCIPLE : Under the Workmen's Compensation Act an employer is liable to compensate his workmen for injuries sustained by them in the course of and out of employment.

FACTS : APCO Pvt. Ltd. is a company manufacturing corrugated boxes in New Mumbai. It has about 2000 worker, it sends its buses to being its workers to the factory site from different parts of New Mumbai. Once a strike was called by one group of workers of APCO Pvt. Ltd. another group of workers, who belonged to a rival trade union, did not support the strike. When a bus carrying non striking workers was going towards the factory, a group of striking workers hurled stones at bus. One of the stone hit Mr. Laxman, a worker in the bus. He sustain a major head injury. Later he claimed compensation from the management of APCO Pvt. Ltd. for injuries sustained by him.

(a) The employers are liable to compensate Mr. Laxman because the injury was sustained by him in the course of employment. For this purpose it may be presumed that he was in the course of employment the moment he boarded the company bus.

(b) The employers are liable to compensate Mr. Laxman because the injury was caused by their workers who was not on a strike and it was caused by a striking workers who was against the interest of the company.

(c) The employers may pay some compensation to Mr. Laxman on account of moral obligation to do so, but there is no legal obligation on the employers because the injury was sustained outside the factory limits and hence it was not sustained in course of and out of employment.

The answer is (a).

EXAMPLE - 3

PRINCIPLE : Limitation bars are remedy, not the right.

FACTS : After the expiry of the period of limitation of three years, debtor Rohan makes a part payment of debt to creditor Sohan. Then Sohan files a suit against Rohan for recovery of the debt after two years from the date of part payment. Decide.

(a) the part payment extends the period of limitation.

(b) the suit is time barred as part payment is made after the expiry of period of limitation.

(c) fresh period of limitation begins from the date of part payment.

The answer is (c).

EXAMPLE - 4

PRINCIPLE : No person can be judge in his own cause.

FACTS : An admission test is to be held to select the best students for admission on merit. The father of a candidate without disclosing that his son is appearing in the test is involved in conducting test. Objections are taken on the ground that the sanctity of the test is vitiated as a person indirected in the test has taken part in conducting it. Decide.

(a) Test is valid because father of candidate is not a judge in this case.

(b) Admission test is vitiated because father is a party of conducting the test and hence in a position to affect the result.

(c) Objection not on sound ground.

The answer is (b).

EXAMPLE - 5

PRINCIPLE : Under the constitution no body can be convicted twice for the same offence

FACTS : The students of a college went on strike against the fee hike by the college. A student X in the ensuing confusion assaulted a staff member and injured him grievously. For this offence, he was rusticated form the college. Subsequently, the police arrested him and charge sheeted him for causing grievous hurt. X pleads that he is being convicted for the same offence twice.

(a) X is not yet convicted is only a court can convict and rustication from the colleges does not amount to conviction.

(b) X should not be punished twice for same offence. This is unconstitutional.

(c) X has not committed an intentional crime. He should be acquitted as rustication is itself enough punishment.

(d) X cannot plead double conviction as the two authorities are different.

The answer is (d).

EXAMPLE - 6

PRINCIPLE : Liability of a person depends upon his act.

FACTS : One evening a delivery boy from M/s K.T. Dass and Co. delivered a carton of sweets at Mr. Chatterjee's residence. The delivery boy told Mrs. Chatterjee that the sweets were ordered by her husband. When Mr. Chatterjee came home in the evening, he told his wife that he did not order any sweets. Neverthless, the entire family finished all the sweets. Next day morning the delivery boy came again to Mr. Chatterjee's residence and explained that by mistake he delivered to the carton to them, in fact it was to be delivered to their next door neighbour, Mr. Banerjee. When Mr. Chatterjee told him that they had already consumed the sweets, the boy on behalf of his employer asked Mr. Chatterjee to pay the price of sweets.

(a) M/s. K.T. Dass and Co. have no right to claim the price because there was a serious mistake on the part of their employee

(b) M/s. K.T. Dass and Co. cannot claim the price because the sweets were not ordered by Mr. and Mrs. Chatterjee at all.

(c) M/s. K.T. Dass and Co. cannot claim the price because there was no contract or agreement between them and Mr. or Mrs. Chatterjee.

(d) M/s. K.T. Dass and Co. are entitled to claim the price from Mr. and Mrs. Chatterjee because they consumed the sweets without ascertaining why they were delivered to them and because they enjoyed the sweets though they did not order them.

The answer is (d).

Example - 7

PRINCIPLE : Whoever by words, signs or otherwise brings into hatred or contempt or excites disaffections towards the government established by law in India shall be punished in the imprisonment for life.

FACTS : In public meeting, Yashpal Reddy, the leader of an opposition party thunders, "This is a government of scoundrels, bootleggers and scamsters. They deserve to be unseated. Teach them a lesson in the coming election by voting them out of power." The government is contemplating to prosecute Yashpal Reddy.

(a) Yashpal Reddy is guilty of sedition for having made irresponsible and inflammatory statement against the government.

(b) Yashpal Reddy is not guilty of sedition as he is only exercising his freedom of speech in public.

(c) Yashpal Reddy is guilty of sedition, as this statement would invite people to violence leading to breakdown of law and order.

The answer is (b).

EXAMPLE - 8

PRINCIPLE : A promissory note is an instrument in writing signed by the maker to pay a certain sum of money only to do or to the order of a certain person.

FACTS : Anand promises to pay Yogesh a sum of Rs. 5000 through e-mail. Later, Anand refuse to pay. Can Yogesh sue him?

(a) Yogesh can sue him as Anand made a promise to pay him Rs. 5000.

(b) Yogesh cannot sue him as this is not a promissory note.

(c) Yogesh can sue him as this is a promissory note.

The answer is (b).

EXAMPLE - 9

PRINCIPLE : (1) The constitution is supreme and all the laws in violation of provision of the constitution are void.

(2) A client can exercise his Fundamental Right to have a lawyer of his choice, provided that particular lawyer is in a position to defend him.

FACTS : The constitution of a country A, confers upon its citizens the fundamental right to be represented by a lawyer of their own choice in the criminal proceedings. A citizen, Yogesh, assumed a crime, engaged a famous criminal lawyer Jaitely to defend him. Just one day before the trial was to begin Jaitely's house was raided by income tax authorities, and he was detained by them is that connection. Yogesh moved a petition in the court that he was entitled to be represented by Jaitely, and therefore, the later should be released so as to enable him to argue the former's case.

(a) Yogesh can hire any other lawyer, may other are available.

(b) Yogesh will succeed because his Fundamental Right of legal representation is being violated due to detention of the criminal lawyer.

(c) The lawyer is not in a reasonable position to defend him, so his petition would be rejected.

The answer is (c).

EXAMPLE - 10

PRINCIPLE : When any industry producing such materials which is hazardous to the public health then the management is strictly liable for the injury caused by it.

FACTS : Konark Industries Ltd. is a large industry manufacturing industrial chemicals and enzymes used in training process. It is located in Sambalpur, Orissa. It was found recently that the industry is discharging industrial toxic waste in the river Mahanadi. As a result the water is highly polluted, the Orissa Pollution Control Board decided to keep legal action against the company for violation of applicable Environment Laws. They obtain an order from the court to prevent the industry from discharging pollutants in the river. Now the Pollution Control Board is considering whether the directors of the company may be prosecuted and punished with imprisonment for violating the Pollution Control Laws which make such a pollution a criminal offence.

(a) It is unreasonable to punish the higher like directors of a company by sending them to jail. Instead of that company may be asked to pay the large amount of fine only.

(b) Although directors are not responsible for the day to day management of a company, their control amounts to responsibility hence they must be prosecuted and punished even with imprisonment.

(c) A company may be asked to pay compensation for polluting the environment. But there need not be any criminal responsibility as far as the higher officials of a company are concerned.

(d) It would be unreasonable to read official of a company to fail violation of pollution control laws because that will affect industrial production and economic growth of the nation and the people will suffer because of such harsh action against industrialists.

The answer is (b).

EXAMPLE - 11

PRINCIPLE : Legal aid is a right and not a charity.

FACTS : A person facing a criminal charge in a criminal trial pleads that he is unable to engage an advocate for reasons of poverty and that he should be provided with a lawyer at state expenses to defend him. Decide.

(a) State is bound to provide him a lawyer as it is a matter of his right.

(b) State may refuses to pay the expenses of lawyer to a criminal person.

(c) State may deny on the ground of unavailability of lawyer or lack of finance.

The answer is (a).

EXAPMLE - 12

PRINCIPLE : A partner has implied authority to raise a loan on behalf of the partnership business. If it is necessary in the usual course of business.

FACTS : A, B and C are partners in a firm of Chartered Accounts. They had agreed that some of them would contract a loan in the name of the firm without consent of all partners. Nevertheless, A took a loan from a bank in the name of the firm and spent the money for his personal purpose. The bank demanded the repayment from the partnership firm.

(a) The partnership firm is not liable, because the partners had unanimously argued that none of them would raise a loan in the name of the firm.

(b) The partnership firm is not liable, because raising a loan is not in the usual course of business in this case.

(c) The partnership firm is liable because A had acted as a partner while raising the loan.

The answer is (c).

EXAMPLE - 13

PRINCIPLE : Marriage of minors under the Hindu Marriage Act, 1955 is not null and void.

FACTS : A petition is filed by a wife claiming maintenance from her husband in 1989. The husband opposed the claim on the ground that at the time of marriage, the wife was five years of age and he himself was 10 years and that their marriage was illegal. Will the wife succeed?

(a) The wife will succeed as the marriage was valid.

(b) The wife will not succeed because both of them were minor.

(c) The wife will not succeed because the marriage was illegal.

The answer is (a).

EXAMPLE - 14

PRINCIPLE : A law taking away Fundamental Right is unconstitutional.

FACTS : The forty-fourth amendment of the constitution has removed fundamental right to property forever from the constitution decide whether it is constitutional.

(a) Yes, because right to property is not a Fundamental Right to life.

(b) No, because when right to property is declared a Fundamental Right by constitution a law taking away it unconstitutional.

(c) Yes, state can amended any Fundamental Right.

The answer is (c).

EXAMPLE - 15

PRINCIPLE : Under Indian Constitution, everybody shall be equal before law. The Income Tax Act happens to provide that those whose annual income is upto Rs. 60,000 shall pay 10% of their income as tax, and those whose annual income exceeds Rs. 60,000 shall pay the tax at the rate of 20% those citizen whose annual income exceeds Rs. 60,000 challenge the legislation on the ground that it is a violation of the principle of equality before law.

(a) They will succeed because the law discriminate against the people who earn more than Rs. 60,000 per annum.

(b) They will not succeed, because the people who earn more than Rs. 60,000 are not equal to the people who earn less than Rs 60,000.

(c) They will not succeed, because this law enables the government to equalites the incomes of all the people in the country.

The answer is (b).

EXAMPLE - 16

PRINCIPLE : A partner shall share with each other partners whatever profits he makes in the course of partnership business.

FACTS : A, B and C are partners doing business in sarees. When A went to the manufactures to buy sarees, he was told that if he brought 600 sarees, he would get discount of Rs. 100 on each saree, the partnership business required only 500 sarees. However, A bought 600 sarees and kept 100 sarees for himself. He accounted for the sale of 500 sarees to his partners and pocketed the profit he made from the sale of the 100 sarees to himself. On finding this out, B and C are demanding a share in the profits made from the sale of the 100 sarees as well.

(a) A is bound to share the profit over sale of the 100 sarees also, as it was made in the course of partnership business only.

(b) A is not bound to share the additional profit as he was accountable only for Rs. 500 shares to his partners.

(c) A need not share the additional profit, because his additional buying of 100 sarees was to get the discount and help the firm.

The answer is (a).

EXAMPLE - 17

PRINCIPLE : An adopted child shall be deemed to be the child of the adoptive parents with effect from the date of adoption, and from this date, the child's relations in the natural parents shall be replaced by its relations with the adopted parents.

FACTS : X was born is a prosperous Hindu Joint Family under Hindu Law. X is entitled to a share in the property inherited by his (i.e. X's) father from his (i.e.X's) grandfather. X was given in adoption to another person, namely M. After this adoption, there were partition in the erstwhile family of X. X claimed a share in the course of partition.

(a) X will succeed, because by virtue of being born into the family, X should get a share in the family property.

(b) X will not succeed because he is entitled to the property of the adoptive parents only.

(c) None of the above.

The answer is (b).

EXAMPLE - 18

PRINCIPLE : An unfair trade practice includes a trade practice which for the purpose of sale, falsely represents that the goods are of a particular standard, quality or grade.

FACTS : P & Co. issues an advertisement that their tooth paste is 102% better than the tooth paste of C & Co. Is this can an unfair trade practice?

(a) No, this is not unfair trade practice as this is a normal practice is trade.

(b) No, because the facts in this advertisement are correct.

(c) Yes, because the fact relating to the product are not correct.

The answer is (c).

EXAMPLE - 19

PRINCIPLE : No state has right to injure the interest of the other states.

FACTS : Torina and Perina are adjoining nations. In Torina, just across the International boundary, a smelting industry is set up. The sulphur fumes discharged by this industry are seriously polluting air near the town Petro in Perina. Perina complains to Torina about the discharge of fumes. The dispute between Torina and Parina is submitted to arbitration for settlement. The following claims are being considered by the arbitrators which do you think is the most reasonable and fair.

(a) Torina is a sovereign and independent state. It may use its territory in whatsoever manner it likes.

(b) Torina says Perina will have to suffer from sulpher because it is unavoidable in the industrial area.

(c) All states a must ensure that their territories must be used in such a manner as not to cause injury to the interests of other states. Hence Torina must relocate the industry.

(d) Perina agrees that Torina may use its territory in whatsoever manner it likes insists that Torina should pay some compensation to Perina for loss they are continually suffering.

The answer is (c).

EXAMPLE - 20

PRINCIPLE

(i) Any law made by the Parliament that infringes the fundamental rights of the citizens is invalid and unenforceable.

(ii) Freedom to carry on trade or profession of one's own choice is a fundamental right.

(iii) The parliament is competent to impose reasonable restrictions on the exercise of this right.

(iv) If the restrictions, of fundamental rights imposed by the parliament, totally removes or nullifies any fundamental right then it will be construed as an unreasonable restriction.

FACTS : In order to ensure that people live in an amicable atmosphere the government of India decided to abolish courts and constituted Dispute settlement Boards. Further, to achieve this objective, the law stipulated that lawyers should not be allowed to espouse the claims of parties, and instead their claims be espouse by social workers.

(a) The law made by the parliament is valid as it does not infringe any fundamental right.

(b) The law made by the parliament is valid as was though there is restriction of fundamental right, such a restriction is reasonable.

(c) The law made by parliament is invalid as it constitutes an infringement of fundamental rights and the restriction imposed is not reasonable.

(d) None of the above.

The answer is (c).

MODEL QUESTIONS

DIRECTIONS : Given below is a statement of legal principle, followed by a factual situation. Apply the principle to the facts and select the most appropriate answer among the alternatives given. Encircle your choice.

1. *PRINCIPLE :* Where the owner of a vehicle, being himself in possession and occupation of it, requests or allows another person to drive, the owner is liable as principal for damage caused by the person actually driving.

FACTS : Dr. Ramayya took his car to Dolphin Co. Ltd. a garage which he had been frequenting for servicing. Since Dolphin Co. Ltd. was out of the way. Dr. Ramayya requested the owners to drop him near a bus terminal so that he may get back to his work. The owner directed a machanic by name Shankar to drop Dr. Ramayya in the same car which he had brought for servicing and being the car back. On the way, the car collided with a lorry, due to the negligence of Shankar. The owner of the lorry, James, is seeking the legal advice on to the course of action.

(a) Dr. Ramayya is liable, because the car belongs to him and he requested for assistance of Shankar.

(b) Dolphin Co. Ltd., is liable, because Shankar is their driver.

(c) Dr. Ramayya is liable, because he would have asked Shankar to drive carefully.

(d) Dolphin Co. Ltd. is liable because the car is entrusted to their care.

2. *PRINCIPLE :* Whoever delivers to any other person as genuine any counterfeit currency which he knows to be counterfeit. But which he did not know to be counterfeit at the time when he received it is guilty of an offence.

FACTS : Mr. Ramchandran is a Cashier in a school. One evening his wife returned home from market. While she was counting the remaining money.

Mr. Ramchandran notice counterfeit currency note of Rs. 100, his wife told him that it was given to her by way of change when she gave a Rs. 500 note in the grocery shop by the person at the cash counter. Mr. Ramchandran goes to the same shop with a view to get rid of the counterfeit note. He buys a shaving cream for Rs. 32.50 and give the counterfeit note at the cash counter. The cashier inspects the notes and realize that it is counterfeit. He calls the police.

(a) Mr. Ramchandran is not guilty of any offence because he neither manufacture the counterfeit note nor did he circulate it with a view to deceive anybody.

(b) Mr. Ramchandran is not guilty because he was attempting to return the counterfeit note to the same person from whom he received it.

(c) Mr. Ramchandran is guilty because he attempt to deliver a counterfeit currency note as genuine as which he know was counterfeit.

3. ***PRINCIPLE :*** A master shall be liable for the acts of his servants done in the course of employment.

FACTS : HMT, a public sector undertaking is operating a number of bus services for its employers in Bangalore. These buses are quite distinct in their appearance and carry the board, " for HMT employees only" M. a villager from neighbouring state, was waiting for a regular bus in one of the bus stops in Bangalore. A bus belonging to HMT happened to stop nearby and a number of people get into the bus M without realising that it was HMT bus got into the bus is soon thereafter, the bus met with an accident due to the drivers negligence. M along with several others, was injured, M seeks to file a suit against HMT claiming damages.

(a) As will succeed, because he got into the bus without realizing that it was HMT bus.

(b) M will not succeed, because it was for him to find out whether it was a public transport.

(c) M will succeed, because the driver was anyhow dot bound to drive carefully.

4. ***PRINCIPLE :*** In a contract of agency, no liability exists upon the agent towards his principal (master), if he acts with reasonable diligence in the matter of agency.

FACTS : Ganesh, the owner of an estate, instructed Dinesh, an estate agent to find a buyer for his estate. Dinesh, got an offer from Krishna Bhat to buy the estate for Rs. 9,50,000 and the same was promptly communicated to Ganesh. Before the contract of sale was concluded, the agent got an offer of 10,25,000. from Dayanand. Dinesh did not communicate the information to Ganesh. The latter brings an action over the former for not having performed his function as an agent.

(a) Dinesh is not liable to Ganesh as his job was only to find a buyer and no more.

(b) Dinesh is not liable to Ganesh as he got good price for the estate which under the prevailing market conditions, was a bonanza.

(c) Dinesh is liable to Ganesh as he did not completely perform the function of an agent.

5. ***PRINCIPLE :*** A person, intentionally causing harm to others, is liable for battery. A person is safe have intended the harm, in so far as he brings about the harm purposefully or knowingly.

FACTS : A teacher suffering from arthritis problem was moving around the class room in the course of teaching. As she was moving backwards to reach her chair, a student saw a scorpion moving underneath the chair and immediately rushed to attack the scorpion and in that process, moved the chair. Meanwhile, the teacher fell down in the process of taking her seat and broke her hips. A suit was filed against the students for battery.

(a) The student is not liable, since he wanted to save the teacher and others from the scorpion.

(b) The student is liable, since he knew that the teacher would be taking her seat.

(c) The student should be held additionally liable for back of attention to the teaching.

6. ***PRINCIPLE :*** A partner shall share with other partners whatever profit he makes in the course of partnership business.

FACTS : P, a partner in a Bangalore firm engaged in textile business, went to a nearby place to buy some silk sarees. The manufacturer therein told him, " if you buy 500 sarees, you will get discount of Rs. 50 each sarees". P infact required only 400 sarees for his firm, nevertheless he brought 500 sarees and kept 100 sarees for himself. After sometime, he on his own sold 100 sarees and made a good profit. Other partners demand that he should share these profit with them.

(a) P has to share the profits, because he bought there 100 sarees in the course of partnership business.

(b) P need not share it, because he has already benefited the firm by getting a substantial discount in the purchases.

(c) P need not share the profit, because his additional buying of 100 sarees was to get the discount and help the firm.

7. ***PRINCIPLE :*** The owner of a property, who allows its use by another person, become liable, for the damaged caused by its use, by the latter.

FACTS : Tataiah takes his car to the garage for servicing. Since his office is a couple of kilometers away from the garage, he requests the owner of the garage to get him dropped to his office in his car by one of the latter's assistants. The owner of the garage ask Jaggah, an employee, to do the needful. On the way of dropping Tataiah, the car collide with a motor cycle owing to negligent driving by Jaggah and injure its rider The motor cyclist brings a legal action against. Tat..iahs seeking monetary relief.

(a) Motorcyclist will in his action, as he should have brought an action against the garage owner, in whose employment was Jaggah.

(b) Motorcyclist will not succeed to Jaggah, who is not the agent of Tataiah, is driving the vehicle.

(c) Motorcyclist will succeed as the car was driven by Jaggah with the consent of Tataiah.

8. ***PRINCIPLE***

(i) Whoever is under a duty of care to another shall be liable for any injury to the latter directly resulting from the breach of that duty.

(ii) Harm suffered voluntarily does not constitute legal injury.

FACTS : Hanuman stores sent certain items in a horse carriage to a customers house, which happened to be by the side of a main road and near a school zone. The driver of a the carriage delivered the items to the customer and went inside the house to collect the receipt, leaving the carriage unattended on the road. Some naughty children of nearby school threw stones at the horses. The horse ran in confusion and they were about to run over an old women. A traffic policeman, at great risk of his life, some how seized the horses and stopped the carriage. He suffered serious personal injuries in the process. The policeman seeks compensation from Hanuman stores.

(a) (i) Hanuman stores is not liable, because they do not owe a duty of care to the old woman or policeman.

(ii) Hanuman stores is liable, because they owe a duty of care to all the user of the road.

(iii) Both old woman and policeman could have taken reasonable care to protect themselves.

(b) (i) Hanuman stores is not liable because some naughty children scared away their horses.

(ii) The school management ought to have care to discipline the children.

(iii) The Hanuman stores is liable because the driver ought to have anticipated the naughty conduct on the part of the children.

(c) (i) The policeman cannot succeed, because he suffered injury voluntarily.

(ii) The policeman can succeed, because he owed a duty of care to old woman.

(iii) The old woman was under a duty to take care of himself.

9. ***PRINCIPLE***

(i) A principal shall be liable for all the acts of his agent done in the course of employment.

(ii) A shall be considered as an agent of B, provided that:

(a) B remunerates A and

(b) B has direction and control over what A is doing.

FACTS : The Consolidated Motors was a firm dealing with second hand cars. Suresh came to the office of the firm and offered to sell their cars, provided he would get 8% commission on cars sold by him. The Consolidated Motors agreed to the proposition. One day, Suresh took out a car for the purpose of demonstration to a prospective client and in course of demonstration, he knocked down Ramesh and injured him. Ramesh is seeking legal remedy. The main issue is whether Suresh is an agent of Consolidated Motors.

(a) Suresh is the agent of Consolidated Motors because he gets remuneration by way of commission.

(b) Suresh is not the agent of Consolidated Motors, the commission is not the same as remuneration.

(c) Suresh is not the agent of Consolidated Motors because the latter do not have control over his activities.

10. *PRINCIPLE :* A master shall be liable for the fraudulent acts committed by his servant in the course of employment.

FACTS : Shila Devi opened a S.B. Account with Oriental Bank, and a cousin of her by name Mohan, who was a clerk in the bank, helped her to complete the formalities. Subsequently she used to entrust whatever money she was getting to Mohan along with her passbook and Mohan used to return the passbook with the relevant entries. One day Shila Devi discovered that Mohan, instead of crediting the money to her account, had been misappropriating it and the entries in the pass book were made by him without authorisation. Shila Devi seeks Compensation from Oriental Bank.

(a) Oriental Bank shall be liable because Mohan was acting in the course of employment.

(b) Oriental Bank shall not be liable because Mohan was not acting in the course of employment.

(c) Oriental Bank shall not be liable because Shila Devi was negligent.

11. *PRINCIPLE :* A master is liable for the acts committed by his servant in the course of employment.

FACTS :- Mahesh was a driver working in a company Lipton and Co. One day, the Manager asked him to drop a customer at the airport and get back at the earliest. On his way back from the airport, he happened to see his fiancé Roopa waiting for a bus to go home. He offered to drop her at home which happened to be close to his office. She got into the car and soon thereafter, the car somersaulted due to the negligence of Mahesh. Roopa was thrown out of the car and suffered multiple injuries. She seeks compensation from Lipton and Co.

(a) Lipton and Co. shall be liable because Mahesh was in course of their employment at the time of accident.

(b) Lipton and Co. shall not be liable because Mahesh was not in the course of employment when he took Roopa inside the car.

(c) Roopa got in to the car at her own risk, and therefore, she cannot sue anybody.

12. *PRINCIPLE*

(i) Manufacturer is liable for the latent defects in the goods manufactured by him.

(ii) A seller is relieved of any liability for the defects in goods sold by him, if the purchaser chooses his goods by trade name and not by relying upon the judgement and skill of the seller.

FACTS : Krishnan went to Rama stores and asked the shop keeper to give him a good bread, the shop keeper replied " people normally buy Mohan Bread from me". Krishnan brought a packet of Mohan Bread. It so happened that there was a stone embedded in one of the bread slice and it broke Krishnan's teeth, while eating, the bread, Krishnan seeks compensation from Rama Stores and Modern Bread company.

(a) Mohan Bread company alone will be liable.

(b) Rama stores alone will be liable.

(c) Both Mohan Bread company and Rama stores will be liable.

(d) None of them will be liable, since Krishnan ought to have checked the bread before eating it.

13. *PRINCIPLE*

(i) Master is liable for the wrongful acts committed by servants, in the course of their employment if third parties suffer damages in consequence.

(ii) However the master is not liable if the wrongful act was committed by the servant has no connection whatsoever with the servants contract of employment.

(iii) If a person by an act lower the reputation of another in the eye of right thinking people, then the person who suffered loss of reputation can sue for damages.

FACTS : Rajiv is a servant of Jawahar. On his way to Jawahar's house to report for duty, he goes to have a cup of coffee. There he sees Singh and accuses Mr. Singh being a dishonest person. Mr. Singh wants to sue Jawahar, as Rajiv is Jawahar's servant.

(a) Jawahar is liable because Rajiv defamed Singh.

(b) Jawahar is not liable as the defamation was not in the course of Rajiv's employment.

(c) Rajiv is liable even though the defamation was not in the course of employment.

(d) None of the above answer is correct

14. *PRINCIPLE*

(i) An agreement enforceable in a court of law is a contract.

(ii) In order for an agreement to be enforceable in a court of law, there must be a meeting of minds between both the parties.

(iii) Parties to a contract should do something for the other party. The obligation to do something for the other party is mutual. This is called consideration and absence of consideration renders the contract unenforceable.

FACTS : Mohan promised to take Sunder for a dinner in Taj Coromandal. Even after two weeks, Mohan did not fulfil the promise. Sunder wants to sue Mohan to enforce that promise. If Sunder goes to court.

(a) He can compel Mohan to buy him a dinner at Taj Coromandal.

(b) He can recovers the value of dinner form Mohan.

(c) This promise will not be enforced by a court of law as there is no consideration from Sunder.

(d) None of the above answer is correct.

15. *PRINCIPLE :*

(i) Any person may use reasonable force in order to protect his property or person.

(ii) However, the force employed must be proportionate to the apprehended danger.

FACTS : Ravi was walking on a lonely road. Maniyan came with a knife and said to Ravi, your life or your purse." Ravi pulled out his revolver. One seeing it, maniyan ran. Ravi shot Maniyan in his legs

(a) Ravi will not be punished as there was danger to his property.

(b) Ravi will not be punished as the force he used was proportionate to the apprehended injury.

(c) Ravi will be punished to the force employed was misappropriate to the apprehended injury.

(d) As Maniyan ran away to escape there was no longer a threat to Ravi's property. so Ravi will be punished.

16. *PRINCIPLE :*

(i) Under Indian Constitution, if a person is convicted of an offence, he cannot be prosecuted again.

(ii) Under criminal procedure code, if a person is prosecuted in an offence and if the prosecution results with in an acquittal or in conviction, than he cannot be prosecuted for the same offence.

FACTS : Maniyan was prosecuted for an offence of murder and he was acquitted. Thereafter additional evidence came to light pointing to maniyan's complicity is the same offence so the police want to prosecute him again

(a) Maniyan cannot be prosecuted as he enjoys the right under our constitution not be prosecuted twice for the same offence.

(b) Maniyan cannot be prosecuted as he enjoys the right under criminal procedural code not to be prosecuted twice for the same offence.

(c) Maniyan cannot be prosecuted as he is protected both by the constitution and criminal procedure code.

(d) None of the above is correct.

17. ***PRINCIPLE :***

(i) Any law made by the parliament that infringes the fundamental rights of the citizens is invalid and unenforceable.

(ii) Freedom to carry on trade or profession of one's own choice is a fundamental right.

(iii) The parliament is competent to impose reasonable restrictions on the exercise of this right.

(iv) If the restrictions, of fundamental rights imposed by the parliament, totally removes or nullifies any fundamental right then it will be construed as an unreasonable restriction.

FACTS : In order to ensure that people live in an amicable atmosphere the Government of India decided to abolish courts and constituted Dispute Settlement Boards. Further, to achieve this objective, the law stipulated that lawyers should not be allowed to espouse the claims of parties, and instead their claims be espoused by social workers.

(a) The law made by the parliament is valid as it does not infringe any fundamental right.

(b) The law made by the parliament is valid as even though there is restriction of fundamental right, such a restriction is reasonable.

(c) The law made by the parliament is invalid as it constitutes an infringement of fundamental rights and the restriction imposed is not reasonable.

(d) None of the above answers is correct.

18. *PRINCIPLE*

(i) If a person makes a statement that lowers the reputation of another person in the eyes of right thinking people, the it is defamation.

(ii) The person whose reputation as affected can sue the culprit and recover damages.

FACTS : Rama told Sita, "you are thief, you stole my heart", Sita has furious and she felt that she was defamed:

(a) Rama has defamed Sita and hence he is liable to pay damages.

(b) Rama is liable to pay as Sita's reputation was lowered in the eyes of right thinking people.

(c) Ram is not responsible, as right thinking people will not mistake his statement.

(d) None of the above answers is correct.

19. *PRINCIPLE*

(i) In order to succeed in an action for damages, the person who files the case must prove that the defendant is at fault.

(ii) However, if the factors which caused the accident were in the normal course of the defendant and if the accident is of such a nature that it would not have happened, in the normal then the law presumes, fact on the part of the persons who had control over the factors that caused the accident.

FACTS : Vasu was walking on a street. When Vasu was crossing Venkan's house a bag of rice fell on Vasu and he was injured. But he did not know what caused the bag of rice to fall on him. In an action for damages brought by Vasu.

(a) Vasu cannot succeed as he could not prove that Vankan was at fault.

(b) Vasu can succeed because the law will presume that Venkan is at fault.

(c) Vasu can succeed as the rice bag fell on him.

(d) None of the above answer is correct.

20. *PRINCIPLE :* An adopted child shall be deemed to be the child of the adoptive parents with effect from the date of adoption, and from this date, the child's relations with the natural parents shall be replaced by its relations with the adopted parents.

FACTS : X was born into prosperous Hindu Family. Under Hindu Law, X is entitled to a share as the property inherited by his (i.e. X's) father from his (i.e. X's) grandfather. X was given in adoption to another person, namely M. After the adoption, there was partition in the erstwhile family of X. X claimed a share in the course of partition.

(a) X will succeed because by nature of being born into the family, X should get a share in the family property.

(b) X will not succeed, because he is entitled to properties of the adoptive parents only.

21. *PRINCIPLE :* No one can accept a proposal without any knowledge thereof.

FACTS : Ramesh proposed to give a reward of Rs 1000 to anyone informing him the whereabouts of his lost dog. The proposal was printed in a daily newspaper by name "The Daily Observer", on 1.1.1994. On 3rd January, Rahim a friend of Ramesh happened to see the dog and informed Ramesh about it. Ramesh immediately rushed to the spot and collected the dog. At that time, neither Rahim knew about the reward (since he was not a regular reader of the Daily Observer)", nor Ramesh mentioned anything about the award. On the 5th January, Rahim came to know about the announcement of the award through a friend of him and he demanded the reward of Rs. 1000 from Ramesh. Ramesh refused to pay.

(a) Ramesh has to pay the amount because he had promised to pay the amount to anyone giving the information about the dog.

(b) Ramesh need not pay the amount, because he had given the information without knowing about the reward.

(c) Ramesh need not pay the amount becaue the promise was made only to the reader of "the Daily Observer".

22. *PRINCIPLE :* Whoever, intending to take dishonestly any property out of the possession of another person, moves that property for such taking, is said to commit theft.

FACTS : Suresh went into the house of his friend Ramesh to discuss some important matter. Since Ramesh was not at home, Suresh waited for him in the later's drawing room. When Ramesh did not turn up. Suresh took out a pen from Ramesh's table and wrote down a message and went home. While going back, by force of habit, he just dropped the pen into the pocket. Subsequently, he forgot about it. Since the pen happened to be very valuable one, Ramesh complained to the police and the police traced the pen in Suresh's house.

(a) Suresh committed theft because he took the pen without Ramesh's consent.

(b) Suresh committed theft, because he failed to return the pen.

(c) Suresh did not commit theft, because he did not have the dishonest intention.

23. *PRINCIPLE :* A person, who through his words or actions leads others to belief that he is associated with a partnership business shall be liable to the acts of partnership firm.

FACTS : A and B were running a partnership business in a small town when the business ran into difficulties. A and B raised a loan from a local bank and R, an influential man of the locality stood as a guarantor. D came to know of this transaction, and subsequently D happened to advance Rs. 50,000 to the partnership business believing that R was associated with the business as partner. But when the firm failed to repay the amount, D brought a suit against R for the repayment.

(a) R is liable, because through his conduct as a guarantor, he led to believe that he was associated with the partnership business.

(b) R is not liable, because the act of guaranting extends only to a particular transaction.

(c) R is not liable, because he never intended D to associate him (i.e. R) with the business.

24. *PRINCIPLE :* A partner has implied authority to raise a loan on behalf of the partnership business, it is necessary in the usual course of business.

FACTS : A, B and C are partners in a firm of Chartered Accountants. They had agreed that none of them would contract a loan in the name of the firm without the consent of all the partners. Nevertheless, A took a loan from a Bank in the name of the firm and spent the money for his personal purposes. The Bank demanded the repayment from partnership firm.

(a) The partnership firm is not liable, because the partners had unanimously agreed that none of them would raise a loan in the name of the firm.

(b) The partnership firm is not liable, because raising a loan is not in the usual course of business in this case.

(c) the partnership firm is liable because A had acted as a partner while raising the loan.

25. *PRINCIPLE :* "*Volenti non fit injuria*" a well established legal principle, mean that a person has no remedy for the injury caused by an act to which he has consented.

FACTS : An old lady was walking in a narrow one way lane in the opposite direction. It was night time, and there was no street light. A car moving in right direction but without headlights knocked her down since the driver could not see her. She filed a suit against the driver.

(a) She would lose, because she violated the traffic rules in the first instance.

(b) She would loss, because she voluntarily exposed herself to the risks.

(c) The driver would loss, because he drove without proper headlights.

26. *PRINCIPLE :* A master will be liable for the wrongful acts of his servants in the course of employment.

FACTS : Raman has a regular S. B. Account in Karnataka Bank in which he used to deposit money from time to time. One day, when he wanted to withdraw some big amount, he discovered that two entries in his pass book, immediately prior to the date of withdrawal, were not authenticated by the manager, as required under Banking Rulers. The Bank declined the responsibility for these entries and the manager disclaimed any knowledge in this regard. Raman filed a suit against the Bank.

(a) Raman will loss, because he should have taken care that the entries were authenticated.

(b) Raman will loss, because the manager was not aware of the issue.

(c) Raman will win, because it was for the manager to ensure the authentication.

27. *PRINCIPLE :* An employer shall be liable to the injuries caused to his employee by the negligence of a fellow employee in the course of employment

FACTS : Kannappa and Veerappa were two employees working in the textile factory of Gokuldas. One day, Kannappa came to the factory in an inebriated stage and his hands were not steady while operating the machine. As a result, Veerappa who just happened to go near the machine for some work got injured. He filed a suit against Gokuldas for compensation.

(a) Gokuldas will be liable, because Veerappa was injured by Kannappa's act in the course of employment.

(b) Gokuldas will not be liable because he was not responsible for Kannappa's inebriated condition.

(c) Gokuldas will not be liable, because Veerappa himself should have been careful while going near Kannappa.

28. *PRINCIPLE :* A master will be liable to the act of his servants in the course of employment.

FACTS : Hanuman was a driver employed by Hindustan Petroleum to drive their petrol lorries. He was strictly forbidden from smoking in the course of employment. That warning was printed on the body of the vehicle, he was driving. One day when he was transferring petrol from his tank to the underground tank of Maruti filling station, he struck a match to light a cigarette and he threw it on the floor. It caused an explosion damaging the properties of Maruti filling station. Maruti filling station filled a suit against Hindustan Petroleum claiming damages.

(a) Hindustan Petroleum will have to pay, because Hanuman struck the match in the course of employment.

(b) Hindustan Petroleum will not liable, because he was clearly forbidden from showing by them.

(c) Hindustan Petroleum will not be liable, because Maruti filling station should have prevented him from smoking.

29. *PRINCIPLE :* A master will be liable for the negligent acts of his servant in the course of employment.

FACTS : Samuel was a driver employed by Kohinoor company to drive their luxury buses during the night. Mohammad has been his assistant over a period of time. One night, when he was driving he felt terribly sleepy and he handed over the steering-wheel to Mohammed and dozed off. The bus hit against a car coming from the opposite side due to the inexperience of Mohammad. The owner of the car filled suit against Kohinoor.

(a) Kohinoor will be liable, because it was improper on the part of Samuel to ask Mohammad to drive.

(b) Kohinoor will not be liable to pay, because Samuel was not supposed to ask Mohammed to drive.

(c) Kohinoor will be liable, because Mohammed was also an employee of Kohinoor.

30. *PRINCIPLE :* A person is guilty of culpable homicide amounting to murder, if the act by which the death is caused is done with the intention of causing death.

FACTS : A was hiding behind a bush to catch some rabbits. B also came to same place for hunting with his gun. When B discovered some movements near the bush, he though that it was an animal and fired a shot. A was killed by the shot. The police sought to prosecute B for murder.

(a) B would not be liable for murder, because he has not intention to kill A.

(b) B would be liable for murder because he should have taken care to find out the target before shooting.

(c) B would not be liable for murder because it was too much to expect B to identity the target before shooting.

31. *PRINCIPLE :* A person commits cheating, when he fraudulently induces another person to deliver the latter's property to him.

FACTS : A falsely represented to B, a shop owner that he was an officer from the sales tax department. In the course of going through the vouchers, A expressed his interest to buy, a costly television on installment basis. B readily agreed hoping that he would get a favourable assessment from a regarding his tax liability. A pay the first instalment and took the T.V. and disappeared. The police somehow managed to arrest him and sought to prosecute him for cheating.

(a) A committed cheating, because he induced B to part with the T. V. posing himself as a sales tax officer.

(b) A committed cheating, because he did not pay the subsequent installment.

(c) A did not commit cheating, because B handed over the T.V. to him in order to get favourable assessment.

32. *PRINCIPLE :* A men would be responsible for all direct consequences of his act, in so far as he could reasonably foresee them as arising from his act.

FACTS : A ship carrying petroleum was moving on the high sea on a short halt in a port, the master of ship engaged some stevedores to lead some metallic planks onto the ship. While loading the planks, a plank slipped from the hands of stevedor and the spark, emitted thereby, ignited petroleum vapour and caused considerable damage to the goods. The owner of the goods filled a suit against the master of the ship.

(a) The master of the ship is not liable, because he was not responsible for the act of stevedore.

(b) The master of the ship is liable, because he is responsible for the acts of the stevedor since he engaged them.

(c) The master is liable, because he should have foreseen the consequence of the stevedor act.

33. *PRINCIPLE :* A man is guilty of culpable homicide amounting to murder, if the act which the death is caused or done with the intention of causing death.

FACTS : A is suffering from jaundice and inflammation of the brain and B know his condition very well. Once they had a heated argument on some issue and A slapped B in anger. B lost his self-control and dealt a severe below on A's head. As a result, A died, the police sought to prosecute B for murder.

(a) B was liable for murder, because he knew A's delicate condition.

(b) B was not liable for murder, because he acted in self-defence.

(c) B was not liable for murder, because he did not have the intention to kill A.

34. *PRINCIPLE :* An occupier is liable to a trespasser in respect to some willful act intended to cause harm or done with reckless disregard.

FACTS : Sakalchand, the owner of a warehouse, got the fence electrified on account of his legitimate fear of dacoity. There was a clear warning about the electrified fencing. There was playground nearby wherein the children had been playing over a period of time. One day, the cricket ball of the children went into the fence and a child running after the ball touched the fence inadvertently. The child suffered from the shock. The parents of the child filed a suit against Sakalchand.

(a) Sakalchand will not be liable, because the child was a trespasser.

(b) Sakalchand will not be liable, because his fencing was legitimate.

(c) Sakalchand will be liable, because he must have taken note of the adjacent playground.

35. *PRINCIPLE :* Everybody is under a legal obligation to take reasonable care to avoid act or omission which he can foresee would injure his neighbour. The neighbour for this purpose is any person whom he should have in his mind as likely to be affected by this act.

FACTS : Ram, while rushing to board a moving train, pushed Shyam who was walking along with a heavy package, containing fire crackers. As a result, the package ripped from his hand and the crackers exploded injuring a boy standing closely. A suit was filed against Ram by the boy claiming damages.

(a) Ram is not liable, because he did not know anything about the contests of the package.

(b) Ram is not liable, because Shyam would not have carried such a package in a crowded place like railway station.

(c) Ram is liable, because Ram is under an obligation not to push Shyam.

36. *PRINCIPLE :* Everybody is under a legal obligation to take reasonable care to avoid act or omission which he can foresee would cause his neighbour. The neighbour for this purpose is any person whom he should have in his mind as likely to be affected by this act.

FACTS : Anant, while driving his scooter at a high speed, knocked down Shankar, a middle aged person, walking on the road. Shankar broke his leg as a result of the accident. But since Shankar was suffering from diabetes, the leg had to be amputated. Shankar filed a suit against Anant for the loss of leg.

(a) Anant is liable, since the loss of the leg is directly attributable to this act.

(b) Anant is not liable for the loss of leg, since he did not know Shankar was suffering from diabetes.

(c) Anant is not liable, since a diabetes patient like Shankar should not have walked on the road.

37. *PRINCIPLE :* A person is liable for all direct consequences of his act, which he could have reasonably foreseen us naturally flowing from his act.

FACTS : Krishna while driving his car at a high speed in a crowded road, knocked down a cyclist. The cyclist died on the spot with a lot of blood spilling around. Lakshmi, a pregnant woman was passing by, suffered from a nervous shock, leading to abortion. Lakshmi filled a suit against Krishna claiming damages.

(a) Krishna will be liable, because he owed a duty of reasonable care to everybody on the road including Lakshmi.

(b) Krishna will not be liable, because he cannot have foreseen Lakshmi suffering from nervous shock as a result of his act.

(c) Krishna will be liable, to Lakshmi because he failed to drive carefully.

38. *PRINCIPLE :* Nobody shall unlawfully interfere with a person's use or enjoyment of land, or some right over, or in connection with it. The use or enjoyment, envisaged herein, should be normal and reasonable taking into account surrounding situation.

FACTS : Krishna and Kannan were neighbours in a residential locality. Kannan started a typing class in a part of his house and this typing sound disturbed Krishna who could not put up with any kind of continuous noise. He filed a suit against Kannan.

(a) Kannan is liable, because he should not have started typing classes in his house.

(b) Kannan is liable, because as a neighbour, he should have realized Krishna's delicate nature.

(c) Kannan is not liable, because typing sound did not disturb anyone else other than Krishna.

39. *PRINCIPLE :* An occupier is not normally liable to a trespasser except in respect of willful act intended to cause harm or done with reckless disregard.

FACTS : Jaspal, a rich man of the locality had kept a ferocious dog to guard his house he strictly instructed all his servant not to go near that dog and there was a special attendant who was to take care of the dog. There was a prominent board warning the visitors about the ferocious dog. One day a twelve year old boy playing in the neighbourhood, running after his ball got into the house the dog attacked him and killed him. Jaspal was sued for damages.

(a) Jaspal is not liable, because the boy was a trespasser.

(b) Jaspal is not liable, because a twelve year ought to have know about the presence of the ferocious dog.

(c) Jaspal is liable for the negligence of his servant to keep watch on such a ferocious dog. during the day time.

40. *PRINCIPLE :* A master will be liable for the wrongful acts of his servants in the course of employment.

FACTS : Ramadevi was an old widow who opened an account with the Syndicate Bank, where under she would deposit Rs. 5 everyday in the Bank. Sunder was the neighbour who used to collect the amount and deposit them in the Bank. Sunder would get a small commission from the Bank for the money deposited. It was discovered one day that Sunder for more than three months did not deposit the money and vanished with the money. Ramadevi filed a suit against Syndicate Bank.

(a) Syndicate Bank would not be liable, because Sunder was not its employee.

(b) Syndicate Bank would not be liable, because for the failure of Ramadevi to check the status of her accounts.

(c) Syndicate Bank would be liable, because Sunder was paid commission by the Bank for doing its work.

41. ***PRINCIPLE :*** Contract is an agreement freely entered into between the parties.

FACTS : Ramlal was dealer in cement. The Government of India, by an order issued under the Essential Commodities Act, fixed the price of cement, and also the quantity which a person can buy from the dealer. Ramlal carried on his business under this new order sometime, but he requested to pay the sales tax on his sale transaction on the ground that there were not the contracts truly entered into by him.

(a) Ramlal would succeed, because the price and quantity were not negotiated by him.

(b) Ramlal would not succeed, because free consent between the parties were there despite the restriction on price and quantity.

(c) Ramlal would succeed, because the Government under the new order forced him to enter into contracts.

42. ***PRINCIPLE :*** The occupier of a premise owes a duty of care to all his invitees and visitors.

FACTS : Sakalchand who was owing a big house, with a compound wall, constructed an underground tank to store water, this was covered by gunny bags since the work was not complete. The postman who came inside to deliver a registered letter fell into this tank and got hurt. It may be noted that there was a box outside the compound wall, wherein all the mails could have been deposited. The postman filed a suit against Sakalchand claiming compensation.

(a) Sakalchand is not liable, because he did not invite the postman to the house.

(b) Sakalchand is not liable, because it was for the postman to take care of himself.

(c) Sakalchand is liable, because the postman came into the premises in the course of his duty.

43. ***PRINCIPLE :*** The occupier of a premise owes a duty of care to all his invitees and visitors.

FACTS : Kishanlal was running a dairy farm in his house. A part of his farm was used by the people as a short cut to get into the nearby railway station. Kishanlal never liked it and put up a board that "All trespassers will be prosecuted". But he actually tolerated them, because quite a few of them patronised his business. One day, a person who was crossing the farm to get into the railway station was attacked by a bull belonging to the farm. The injured person filed a suit against Krishanlal.

(a) Krishanlal is not liable in view of the clear notice against trespassers.

(b) Kishanlal is liable because he in fact allowed the people to use his premises.

(c) Kishanlal is not liable to the people other than his customers.

44. ***PRINCIPLE :*** The owner of immoveable property is entitled to the column of airspace above the surface. However, the owner's right to air and space above his land is restricted to such height it is necessary for the ordinary use and enjoyment of his land and the structure on it.

FACTS : Galaxy Cable TV Network Company is providing cable connections to their customers. One of the cables passes over the house of Mr. Vasanth Bhat. He is not a customer of the Network Company. The cable is neither attached to his house nor to any projection thereof. It is at a distance of 20 feet above the terrace of Mr. Bhat's two storeyed house. Because of the cable, Mr. Bhat's son Sachin is unable to fly kite from the terrace. Mr. Bhat requested the Network Company to change the position of the cable. But the company did not bother to change it. One evening Mr. Bhat cut the cable and cleared the airspace above his house.

A network company suffered a loss of about Rs. 1000. They bring a local action against Mr. Bhat for recovery of loss suffered.

(a) The Network Company will succeed because the cable was not interfering with the ordinary use and enjoyment of Mr. Bhat's property.

(b) The Network Company will not succeed because Mr. Bhat has every right to ensure proper enjoyment of his property by removing objects causing trespass in the air above his property to a reasonable extent.

(c) The network company will succeed because laying such cables in widely practiced in all cities like electricity and telephone wires.

45. *PRINCIPLE :* Every person has a right to defend his own persons, property or possession against an immediate harm, and to that end, may use reasonable amount of force.

FACTS : Mr. Kaul was passing by Mrs. Mattoo's house. At that time, Mrs. Mattoo's dog ran out and bite Mr. Kaul's overcoat. Mr. Kaul turned around and raised the pristol he was carrying in the pocket of his overcoat. The dog ran away, and Mr. Kaul shot the dog as it was running away. Mr. Kaul know that the dog had attacked so many other people in that locality of Jammu. Mrs. Mattoo claims that her dog was of a rare breed and it was worth Rs. 5000. She is planning to bring a legal action against Mr. Kaul for compensation.

(a) She will succeed in getting the compensation from Mr. Kaul because he killed the dog which was not actually attacking him at the time of shooting.

(b) She will not succeed because Mr. Kaul was justified in shooting the dog to protect himself.

(c) She will not succeed because Mr. Kaul had took the action to protect himself as well as many other members of public in future.

46. *PRINCIPLE :* In case of a breach of contract, compensation can be awarded for the personal inconvenience suffered by a party by reason of the breach, which naturally arose in the usual course of things from such breach, or which the parties know, whom they made the contract to be likely to result from the breach of it.

FACTS : Mr. Anil and Mrs. Seema Shah bought bus tickets for a journey from Bhavnagar to Amreli a small town in Gujarat from a private bus company. The bus was to got Jamnagar via Amreli. The bus driver, by mistake took them in a somewhat wrong direction and dropped them at a distance of 3 miles from Amreli on the state highway. Finding no other conveyance and no place to stay Mr. and Mrs. Shah had to walk the distance of 3 miles in midnight. Later they filed a case against the bus company and claimed Rs. 2500 as damages for inconvenience suffered in being obliged to walk and Rs. 5000 in respect of Mrs. Seema Shah's illness caused by catching cold during that night.

(a) The bus company is liable to pay both the amount claimed because the loss was suffered on account of the fault of the bus company and the inconvenience suffered and illness arose in the usual course of things from breach of contract.

(b) The bus company s liable to pay both the amounts claimed because the loss was suffered by Mr. and Mrs. Shah for no fault of theirs.

(c) The bus company is liable to pay only Rs. 2500 by way of compensation for inconvenience suffered by them for being obliged to walk during the night. They are not liable to pay Rs. 5000 in respect of Mrs. Seema Shah's illness because the bus company did not expect her to catch cold on account of the breach of contract.

47. *PRINCIPLE :* A bailment is the delivery of goods by one person to another for some purpose, upon a contract that they shall, when the purpose is accomplished, be returned. In all cases of bailment the person whom the goods are delivered is expected to take as much care of the goods as a man of ordinary prudence would, under similar circumstances take of his own goods of similar nature.

FACTS : Mrs. Basanti gave 25 grams of pure gold to M/s Hiralal Shroff and company a firm of jewelers to make two bangles of a particular design out of that gold. The jewellers kept the gold in an almirah in their shop. There was burglary in the shop and the gold given by Mrs Basanti was stolen along with other jewellery belonging to the firm. The burglar broke open one of the shop in windows. The firm had not employed a watchman to guard their valuables during the night, Now Mrs. Basanti brings an action against the firm for compensation.

(a) The firm of jewelers is not liable to compensate Mrs. Basanti because they took as much care as they took in respect of their own goods which is established by the fact that their own goods were also stolen along with the gold belonging to Mrs. Basanti.

(b) In the firm is liable to compensate Mrs. Basanti because it failed to take as much care as a man of ordinary prudence ought to have taken in respect of the goods entrusted.

(c) The firm is not liable to compensate Mrs. Basanti because it took reasonable came in respect of the goods instead to it and the burglary could not have avoided under any circumstances.

48. *PRINCIPLE :* Under the workmen's compensation Act an employer is liable to compensate his workmen for injuries sustained by them in the course of and out of employment.

FACTS : Apco Pvt. Ltd is a company manufacturing corrugated boxes in New Mumbai., it has about 2000 workers. It sends its buses to bring its workers to the factory site form different parts of New Mumbai. Once a strike was called by one group of workers of Apco Pvt. Ltd. Another group of workers who belonged to rival trade union did not support the strikes. When a bus carrying non-striking workers was going towards the factory. A group of striking workers hurled stones at the bus, one of the stones hit Mr. Lakshman More, a worker in the bus. He sustained a major head injury. Later he claimed compensation from the management of Apco Pvt. Ltd. for injuries sustained by him.

(a) The employers are liable to compensate Mr. More because the injury was sustained by him in the course of employment. For this purpose it may be presumed that he was in the course of employment the moment he boarded the company vehicle.

(b) The employers are liable to compensate Mr. More because the injury was caused to one of their legal workers who was not on strike and it was caused by a striking workers who was acting against the interest of the company.

(c) The employer may pay some compensation to Mr. more on account of moral obligation to do so, but there is no legal obligation on the employers because the injury was sustained outside the factory limits and hence it was not sustained in the course of and out of employment.

49. *PRINCIPLE :* When a criminal act is done by the person in furtherance of the common intention of himself and some other persons, each of such persons is liable for the act in the same answer as it were done by each one of them.

FACTS : A, B and C decided to council burglary. They broke into a locked house. However, a domestic servant appeared from the out-house before they had finished, and started shouting. A, B and C left the house and started running away. They were pursued by a small crowed. A on being caught by X, one of the persons pursuing them, stabbed him and ran away. By that time B and C had disappeared. X died on account of the stabs wounds. Later the police would arrest all the three. They were charged for attempted burglary and murder of X.

(a) Along with A the person who stabbed X, B and C are also guilty of murder because A stabbed X in furtherance of common intention to commit murder.

(b) Along with A, B and C are also guilty of murder because A, at the time of stabbing X, was acting on behalf of B and C and he wanted to save not only himself but B and C as well.

(c) A alone is guilty of murder because though there was common intention to commit the offence of burglary, there was no common intention to commit the offence of murder.

50. *PRINCIPLE :* A right of action cannot arise out of an illegal activity.

FACTS : A and B were thieves engaged in stealing cars and other vehicles. Once they stole a car, and while driving off, they had to cross a city. They engaged a driver to drive them through the city they did not know the route inside. The indicator lamp of the car was not working and the thieves had not realized this, and therefore, had not told about it to the driver. Which driving through the city, the car was hit by another vehicle because of the faulty indicator. In the accident, the driver was injured and he filed a suit against A and B.

(a) the driver would lose, because he was driving a stolen car.

(b) the driver would win because he was not a party to the stealing.

(c) the driver would win, because he did not know anything about the stealing.

ANSWERS

1	2	3	4	5	6	7	8	9	10
A	C	B	C	A	C	C	C	B	A
11	**12**	**13**	**14**	**15**	**16**	**17**	**18**	**19**	**20**
B	A	B	C	D	D	B	C	A	B
21	**22**	**23**	**24**	**25**	**26**	**27**	**28**	**29**	**30**
B	C	C	C	C	C	A	A	C	A
31	**32**	**33**	**34**	**35**	**36**	**37**	**38**	**39**	**40**
A	B	A	C	C	A	C	A	B	C
41	**42**	**43**	**44**	**45**	**46**	**47**	**48**	**49**	**50**
B	C	A	A	A	A	B	A	C	C

TEST PAPER-I

MULTIPLE CHOICE LEGAL QUESTIONS

1. ***PRINCIPLE :*** Marriage of minors under the Hindu Marriage Act 1955, is not null and void.

FACTS : A petition is filed by a wife claiming maintenance from her husband in 1989. The husband opposed the claim on the ground that at the time of marriage, the wife was five years of age and he himself was 10 years and that their marriage was illegal. Will the wife succeed?

A. The wife will succeed as the marriage was valid.

B. The wife will succeed because both of them were minors.

C. The wife will not succeed because the marriage was illegal.

2. ***PRINCIPLE :*** A Promissory Note is an instrument in writing signed by the maker to pay a certain sum of money only to or to the order of a certain person.

FACTS : Anand promises to pay Yogesh a sum of Rs. 5,000/- through e-mail. Later, Anand refuses to pay. Can Yogesh sue him?

A. Yogesh can sue him as Anand made a promise to pay him Rs. 5,000/-

B. Yogesh cannot sue him as this is not a promissory note

C. Yogesh can sue him as this is a promissory note

3. ***PRINCIPLE :*** A contract is an agreement enforceable by law.

FACTS : Amita invited Beena to her house for dinner. Beena accepted the invitation but later did not go. On Beena's failure to attend, Amita filed a suit against Beena for the price of non-consumed food. Can this agreement be enforced by law?

A. This agreement cannot be enforced as it is just a social agreement.

B. This agreement can be enforced as Amita can recover the price of non-consumed food.

C. This agreement cannot be enforced as Beena did not accept the invitation in writing.

4. ***PRINCIPLE :*** An unfair trade practice includes a trade practice which for the purpose of sale, falsely represents that the goods are of a particular standard, quality or grade.

FACTS : P & Co. issues an advertisement that their toothpaste is 102% better than the toothpaste of C & Co. Is this an unfair trade practice?

A. No, this is not an unfair trade practice as this is a normal practice in trade.

B. No, because the tests in this advertisements are correct.

C. Yes, because the facts relating to the product are not correct.

5. ***PRINCIPLE :*** A master is liable for the wrongful acts of his servants committed in the course of employment.

FACTS : Lakshmi was a housewife who opened an account with the Maharashtra Bank, whereunder she agreed to deposit Rs. 300/- every month in the Bank. Krishna, an agent of the Bank used to come every month, to collect the amount and deposit in the Bank. The Bank used to give a small commission to Krishna for the money deposited. It was discovered one day that Krishna had not deposited the amount for more than three months and had disappeared with the money. Lakshmi filed a suit against Maharashtra Bank.

A. Maharashtra Bank would not be liable because Krishna was not its employee.

B. Maharashtra Bank would be liable because Krishna was paid commission by the bank for doing work on its behalf.

C. Maharashtra Bank would not be liable as it was Lakshmi's responsibility to check her passbook regularly.

6. ***PRINCIPLE :*** A bailment is the delivery of goods by one persons to another for some purpose, upon a contract that they shall, once the purpose fulfilled, be returned. Further, the person to whom the goods are delivered is obliged to take as much care of the goods as a man of ordinary prudence would, under similar circumstances take of his own goods.

FACTS : Mrs. Sita gave a gold bar to M/s. Zaveri Lall & Co., jewellers to make a necklace of a certain pattern. The jewellers kept the gold bar in an almirah. Unfortunately the shop was burgled and Mrs. Sita's gold bar was also stolen. The jewellers had not employed a watchman to guard their valuables. Advise Mrs. Sita on proposed legal action.

A. The jewellers are not liable to make compensation because they took reasonable care in respect of the goods entrusted to them and the burglary could not have been avoided under any circumstances.

B. The jewellers are liable to compensate Mrs. Sita because they failed to take as much care as a man of ordinary prudence ought to have taken in respect of goods entrusted.

C. The jewellers are not liable to compensate Mrs. Sita because they took as much care as they took in respect of their own goods which is established by the fact that their own goods were also stolen.

D. Both A and C.

7. *PRINCIPLE :* Whoever delivers to any other person as genuine any counterfeit currency which he knows to be counterfeit, but which he did not know to be counterfeit at the time when he received it is guilty of an offence.

FACTS : On returning home from the market one day, Mrs. X notices a counterfeit currency note of Rs. 50 while counting the remaining money. Mrs. X returns to the same shop where she got the counterfeit currency with a view to get rid of the counterfeit note. She buys a shampoo worth Rs. 32.00 and passes the fake note at the cash counter. The Cashier inspects the note and realizes that it is counterfeit. He calls the police:

A. Mrs. X is not guilty because she was attempting to return the counterfeit note to the same person from whom she received it.

B. Mrs. X is not guilty of any offence because she neither manufactured the counterfeit note nor did she circulate it with a view to deceive anybody.

C. Mrs. X is guilty because she attempted to deliver a counterfeit currency note as genuine which she knew was counterfeit.

D. None of the above.

8. *PRINCIPLE :* In case of a breach of contract, compensation can be awarded for the personal inconvenience suffered by a party by reason of the breach, which naturally arose in the usual course of things from such breach, or which the parties knew, when they made the contract to be likely to result from the breach of it.

FACTS : Sunita and Sushmita bought bus tickets for a journey from Adyar to Mandaveli. The bus was to go to St. Thomas Mount via Mandaveli. However, the driver mistakenly took a wrong direction and the two girls were dropped of a distance of 2½ miles from Mandaveli on the highway. With no other transportation in sight nor a place to stay, the two had to walk 2½ miles at midnight.

Later they filed a case against the bus company and claimed Rs. 5000 as damages for inconvenience caused in having to walk and Rs. 6500 for Sushmita having fallen ill by catching cold during the night.

A. Both the amounts are liable to be paid because Sunita and Sushmita suffered loss for no fault of theirs.

B. The bus company is liable to pay both the amounts claimed because the loss was suffered on account of the fault of the bus company and the inconvenience suffered and illness arose in the normal course of things from breach of contract.

C. The compensation for inconvenience suffered by being forced to walk at night is liable to be paid by the bus company. However no compensation for Sushmita's illness because this was not expected on account of breach of contract.

D. The bus company is not liable to pay any amount, because it was the driver's fault.

9. *PRINCIPLE :* Every person has a right to defend his own person, property or possession against immediate harm, and for the same purpose, may use a reasonable amount of force.

FACTS : While Andrew was passing Joe's house one day, Joe's dog ran out and bit his pant. When Andrew turned around with a pistol in his hand, the dog ran away. Andrew shot the dog as it was running away. Andrew was well aware that the dog had attacked others in the same locality. Joe claimed that the dog was of a rare breed and worth Rs. 10,000 Help Joe decide for against bringing legal action against Andrew.

A. Joe will not succeed because Andrew was justified in shooting the dog to protect himself.

B. Joe will not succeed because Andrew took the action to protect himself as well as many other members of public in future.

C. Joe will succeed in getting compensation from Andrew because he killed the dog which was not actually attacking him at the time of shooting.

D. Both B and C.

10. ***PRINCIPLE :*** The owner of immovable property is entitled to a column of air space above the surface. But, the owner's right to air space above his land is restricted to such height as is necessary for the ordinary use and enjoyment of his land and the structures on it.

FACTS : Ark Cable TV Company provides cable facility to its customers. One such cable connection passes over the house of Mr. Bajaj, who is not a customer of Ark Cable TV Company. The cable is neither attached to his house not to any projection thereof, further it is at 15 feet above the terrace of Mr. Bajaj's 3 storeyed house. Because of the cable, Aditya the son of Mr. Bajaj is unable to fly a kite on the terrace. Mr. Bajaj requested the cable company to alter the position of the cable, but to no avail. One day, Mr. Bajaj cut the cable and thus cleared the airspace above his house. The Cable company having suffered a loss of Rs. 1000 brings legal action against Mr. Bajaj.

A. The company will not succeed because Mr. Bajaj has every right to ensure proper enjoyment of his property by removing objects causing obstruction in the airspace above his property to a reasonable extent.

B. The company will succeed because like electricity, telephone cables, laying of such cables is a common practice in all cities.

C. The company will succeed because the cable was not interfering with the ordinary use and enjoyment of Mr. Bajaj's property.

D. Both B and C.

11. ***PRINCIPLE :*** The occupier of a promise owes a duty of care to all his invitees and visitors.

FACTS : Suresh was a owner of big bunglow with a compound wall. He was constructing a swimming pool in his compound. Since the work was incomplete, he asked his workers to cover it with gunny bags. Next morning, the post-man who came inside to deliver a telegram fell into his unfinished pool. The post-man filed a suit against Suresh claiming compensation.

A. Suresh is not liable because he did not invite the postman to his house.

B. Suresh is not liable because it was for the postman to take care of himself.

C. Suresh is liable because the postman came into the premises in the course of his duty.

12. ***PRINCIPLE :*** A minor's agreement is absolutely void.

FACTS : Cuckoo aged 16 is a stamp collector. He is particularly anxious to get a rare stamp belonging to Manoj who agrees in writing to sell this to Cuckoo for Rs. 100/- but subsequently refuses to deliver it to Cuckoo though Cuckoo pays Rs. 100/-. Cuckoo now wants to sue Manoj. Will he succeed?

A. Cuckoo cannot succeed as Manoj is not liable.

B. Cuckoo can succeed as he has paid Rs. 100/- for the stamp.

C. Cuckoo can succeed as Manoj agreed in writing to sell the stamp.

13. ***PRINCIPLE :*** An incorporated company under the Companies Act has a separate legal entity and corporate liability.

FACTS : Certain persons transferred a tea estate to an incorporated company and claimed exemptions from "ad valorem" duty on the ground that they themselves were shareholders in the company.

A. The shareholders are liable to pay as the company is a separate legal person.

B. The shareholders are not liable to pay it is a transfer from them in one name to themselves under another name.

C. The shareholders are liable because everybody has to pay duty on a transfer or conveyance.

14. ***PRINCIPLE :*** Ignorance of law is no excuse.

FACTS : A fails to fill his income tax returns for five years. The Income Tax department issues to him notice to show cause as to why proceedings should not be initiated against him for the recovery of the income tax due from him with penalty and interest. Advise A.

A. A may request the department to waive the interest and penalty as he was not aware.
B. A must pay the tax dues as ignorance cannot be pleaded as a ground of defence.
C. A may request the Court to excuse him as his advocate had told him that he is not liable to pay taxes.

15. ***PRINCIPLE*** **:** The obligation to maintain parents who are unable to maintain themselves which was moral upto 1973 has now been made legal.

FACTS **:** After her marriage Dr. Vijaya continued her medical practice but she no longer maintained her old parents who were sick and bedridden and had no other means. They sued their daughter for maintenance.

A. They will not succeed as Dr. Vijaya is now married.
B. They will not succeed because Vijaya's responsibility is now towards her husband and his parents.
C. They will succeed because a daughter after her marriage does not cease to be the daughter of her father or mother.

16. The first permanent Global Criminal Court which was established in the year 2002 will sit in:

A. Hague B. New Delhi
C. London D. New York

17. Punishment as provided for the offences under Indian Penal Code read as:

1. Death sentence
2. Imprisonment for life (both rigorous and simple)
3. Forefeiture of property
4. Fine

A. Only 1 and 2
B. Only 2, 3, 4
C. Only 3 and 4
D. All of the above.

18. Cruelty to a women by husband or relative of husband is defined under:

A. Section 498A of Indian Penal Code
B. Section 498 of Indian Penal Code
C. Section 497 of Indian Penal Code
D. Section 496 of Indian Code

19. Who among the following had the longest tenure as the Chief Justice of India?

A. H.J. Kania B. P.N. Bhagwati
C. Y.V. Chandrachud D. M.H. Beg

20. For Hindus.....is an offence, punishable with seven years imprisonment, even though a Muslim can have four wives:

A. Monogomy B. Polyandry
C. Polygamy D. Adultery

21. In law, a man is presumed to be dead if he is not heard of as alive for:

A. 5 years B. 7 years
C. 9 years D. 10 years

22. The burden of proof in a criminal case generally rest on the:

A. Accused B. Plaintiff
C. Judge D. Prosecution

23. Which of the following gives the buyer right to reject goods, repudiate the contract and claim damages?

A. Breach of promise B. Warranty
C. Guarantee D. Breach of trust

24. Socialism stands for:

A. State ownership of all property
B. Equal distribution of wealth to all citizens
C. International peace
D. None of these

25. Security Council in the U.N.O. has:

A. 11 members B. 9 members
C. 15 members D. 12 members

26. The number of Elected Members in the Lok Sabha is:

A. 500 B. 525
C. 543 D. 542

27. Who is considered the father of politics?

A. Plato B. Socratese
C. Aristotle D. Periclose

28. Federal State is a:

A. Union of States
B. Combination of States
C. Group of States
D. None of these

29. Plan expenditure in India is met from:

A. Internal borrowings and other measures
B. External aid from other countries
C. External aid from IMF
D. External aid and assistance from OECD countries

30. A promise made without the intention of performing it amounts to:
A. Innocent misrepresentation
B. Fraud
C. Negligent misrepresentation
D. Wrongful misrepresentation

31. A contingent contract is:
A. Void B. Voidable
C. Valid D. Illegal

32. Match the following:
I. M. Hidayatullah
II. M.C. Setalvad
III. Nani Palkhiwala
IV. Lord Denning
a. The family story
b. We, the people
c. My life
d. My own Boswell

	I	II	III	IV
A.	d	c	b	a
B.	a	b	c	d
C.	b	a	d	c
D.	c	a	b	d

33. Whoever has sexual intercourse with a person who is said and whom he knows or has reason to believe to be the wife of another man, without the consent of that man, such sexual intercourse amounts to:
A. Rape
B. Adultery
C. Unnatural offence
D. Abatement of rape

34. If a constable has reasonable cause to suspect that a motorist is drunk, he:
I. Checks the motorist's breath with an Alcometer
II. Makes an arrest
III. Impounds the vehicle
IV. Lets the person off with a bribe
A. It is a constable's discretion to do any of the four
B. First I if it is affirmative, then II & III, no legal authority to do IV
C. Invariably IV
D. Only III

35. When a person speaks slanderously about God or Religion, it is called:
A. Buggery B. Blasphemy
C. Bestiality D. Bingoism

36. Where are juvenile delinquents sent?
A. Borstal
B. Asylums
C. Protective custody
D. Reformation Centre

37. The number of judges in the International Court of Justice are:
A. 10 B. 15
C. 20 D. 18

38. The International Treaty becomes binding on India when:
A. Prime Minister signs the treaty
B. Parliament makes special legislation for accepting the treaty
C. Both A and B
D. None of the above

39. The law of torts deals with:
A. Injuries to person or property caused by failure to take reasonable care
B. Money transactions
C. Partnerships
D. Industrial Production

40. Child Labour (Prohibition and Regulation) Act, 1986 prohibits:
A. child labour in hazardous occupations and processes,
B. child labour in non-hazardous occupations
C. child labour completely
D. none of the above

41. The Parliament amended the Constitution in 1992 and introduced the Panchayati Raj and Nagar Palikas by the:
A. 54th & 56th Amendments
B. 45th and 46th Amendments
C. 89th & 90th Amendments
D. 73rd & 74th Amendments

42. By which Constitutional Amendment Bill, the voting age was reduced from 21 years to 18 years?
A. 48th B. 57th
C. 61st D. 63rd

43. Guidelines of Election Commission in March 2003 mandating the declaration of candidate's criminal antecedent, assets, liabilities and educational qualifications to safeguard the right to information of voters relates to:

A. Declaration of Supreme Court that representation of People Amendment Act of 2002 unconstituuional

B. Declaration of Supreme Court that Representation of People Act, 1950 unconstitutional

C. Declaration of Supreme Court that Representation of People Act of 1951 unconstitutional

D. None of the above

44. The basic distinction between Civil and Criminal laws is:

A. Civil laws deal with matters of restoration of right

B. Criminal laws deal with punishment

C. Criminal laws deal wit wrongs which are harmful to society at large

D. Both A and C

45. A prerogative writ used to command a person who is detaining another in custody to produce that person before the court:

A. Habeas Corpus B. Ceritorari

C. Quo Warranto D. Mandamus

46. The Hague Convention of 1899, 1904 & 1907 delineated:

A. Rules of public international law

B. Rules of human rights

C. Rules for non-use of chemical weapons

D. None of the above

47. ……is a general pardon:

A. Remission B. Reprieve

C. Amnesty D. Suspension

48. Husband and wife have a right to each other's company. This right is called:

A. Legal right

B. Matrimonial right

C. Consortium right

D. Conjugal right

49. An act done under threat or fear is done under:

A. Duress B. Dunress

C. Compulsion D. None of these

50. A deed is a written statement which is:

A. Signed B. Sealed

C. Delivered D. All of the above

51. The base of the Indian parliamentary system is:

A. adult franchise

B. universal adult franchise

C. male franchise

D. proportional representation of the population

52. Finance Commission is constituted by:

A. Parliament

B. Prime Minister

C. Lok Sabha Speaker

D. President

53. Parliament is a:

A. Unicameral legislature

B. Bicameral legislature

C. Tricameral legislature

D. None of the above

54. The Parliament of India meets at an interval of:

A. three months

B. four months

C. not more than six months

D. nine months

55. How many members of Lok Sabha are represented by the States and Union territories?

A. 540 B. 543

C. 550 D. 552

56. The maximum gap between two sessions of parliament is:

A. three months B. six months

C. four months D. nine months

57. The power to establish new states or change the boundaries of any state is vested in:

A. the President

B. the Parliament

C. the Union Cabinet

D. the President on the recomendation of the Union Council of Ministers

58. The minimum age to get elected a member of the Rajya Sabha is:

A. 30 years B. 35 years

C. 40 years D. 25 years

59. A person can not be elected a member of the Lok Sabha unless he attains the age of:

A. 26 years B. 30 years

C. 32 years D. 25 years

60. Who can disolve the Rajya Sabha?
A. the Chairman, Rajya Sabha
B. the Speaker, Lok Sabha
C. the President
D. It can not be dissolved

61. The Lok Sabha can be dissolved before the expiry of its normal term of five years by:
A. the Prime Minister
B. the President
C. the Speaker, Lok Speaker
D. the President on the recommendation of Prime Minister

62. What is the maximum strength of Lok Sabha?
A. 540 B. 548
C. 542 D. 550

63. The maximum strength of the Rajya Sabha is:
A. 230 B. 240
C. 250 D. 245

64. What is the duration of the Rajya Sabha?
A. 2 years
B. 4 years
C. its duration is of permanent nature as after individual terms of six years each, one-third members retire after two years
D. none of the above

65. Who has the sole power to control the expenditure of the Government?
A. the Prime Minister
B. the Comptroller and Auditor General
C. the President
D. the Parliament

66. The members of the Lok Sabha are:
A. nominated by the President
B. appointed by the Speaker, Lok Sabha
C. directly elected by the people
D. none of the above

67. During a national emergency, the President can extend the life of the Lok Sabha in the first instance for a period of:
A. one year B. nine months
C. six months D. one month

68. The Council of States, i.e., Rajya Sabha is a permanent house, but:
A. one-third of its members retire every year
B. one-half of its members retire every year
C. one-third of its members retire every two years
D. one-third of its members retire every four years

69. In Rajya Sabha, the States are represented:
A. on the basis of size
B. on the basis of language
C. equal representation
D. on the basis of population

70. The members of Rajya Sabha are elected by:
A. members of the present Rajya Sabha
B. the Vice-President statewise
C. elected members of State Legislative Assemblies
D. the people directly

71. The ex-officio Chairman of Rajya Sabha is:
A. senior-most member of the Rajya Sabha
B. leader of the House in Rajya Sabha
C. the Vice-President
D. elected by the members

72. The nominated members of Rajya Sabha are:
A. the freedom fighters and senior political leaders
B. retired bureaucrats or armed-forces officers
C. the men of learning and wide experience such as artists, scientists and social-workers
D. none of the above

73. The number of schedules in the constitution is:
A. 395 B. 100
C. 8 D. 12

74. The Deputy Chairman of the Rajya Sabha is:
A. The leader of the largest party in the house
B. The senior – most member of the house
C. Elected from amongst the members of the Rajya Sabha
D. Appointed by the Chairman

75. Each member of the Rajya Sabha enjoys the term of :
A. Four years B. Five years
C. Six years D. Two years

ANSWERS

1	2	3	4	5	6	7	8	9	10
A	B	A	C	B	B	C	C	C	D
11	**12**	**13**	**14**	**15**	**16**	**17**	**18**	**19**	**20**
C	C	C	B	C	C	A	A	C	C
21	**22**	**23**	**24**	**25**	**26**	**27**	**28**	**29**	**30**
B	D	C	A	C	C	B	A	B	B
31	**32**	**33**	**34**	**35**	**36**	**37**	**38**	**39**	**40**
A	A	B	B	B	A	B	B	A	A
41	**42**	**43**	**44**	**45**	**46**	**47**	**48**	**49**	**50**
D	C	C	D	A	A	C	D	A	D
51	**52**	**53**	**54**	**55**	**56**	**57**	**58**	**59**	**60**
B	D	B	C	B	B	B	A	D	D
61	**62**	**63**	**64**	**65**	**66**	**67**	**68**	**69**	**70**
D	D	C	C	D	C	D	C	D	C
71	**72**	**73**	**74**	**75**					
C	C	D	C	C					

TEST PAPER-II

MULTIPLE CHOICE LEGAL QUESTIONS

1. ***PRINCIPLE :*** A master is liable for the wrongs committed by the servant in the course of his employment.

FACTS : Obalesh works as a clerk in a pharmaceutical company Bio-Pharma Ltd. He is required to take stock of the goods supplied and maintain the accounts of the company. Ramachandra, a friend of Obalesh, from the neighbouring village, came to meet Obalesh in the office. Since Ramachandra did not have any other acquaintance in the city he gave Rs. 10000/-, he had with him, to Obalesh for safe keeping. When Ramachandra returned to the office the next morning to collect the money from Obalesh. He learnt that the latter had disappeared with his money. Ramachandra brings a legal action against Bio-Pharma Ltd. For the recovery of the money.

A. Bio-Pharma Ltd., would be liable, since Obalesh received the money while being in the office.

B. Bio-Phrama Ltd., would not bel liable, as Ramachandra had no business transactions with the company

C. Bio-Pharma Ltd., would not be liable, as safekeeping of money was not part of Obalesh's duty.

2. ***PRINCIPLE :*** The occupier of a premise owes a duty of care to all his invites and visitors.

FACTS : Suresh was a owner of big bunglow with a compound wall. He was constructing a swimming pool in his compound. Since the work was incomplete, he asked his workers to cover it with gunny bags. Next morning, the post-man who came inside to deliver a telegram fell into his unfinished pool. The post-man filed a suit against Suresh claiming compensation.

A. Suresh is not liable because he did not invite the postman to his house.

B. Suresh is not liable because it was for the postman to take to himself.

C. Suresh is liable because the postman came into the premises in the course of his duty.

3. ***PRINCIPLE :*** The owner of immovable property is entitled to the column of airspace above the surface. However, the owner's right to air and space above his land is restricted to such height as is necessary for the ordinary use and enjoyment of his land and the structures on it.

FACTS : Galaxy Cable TV Network Company is providing cable connection to their customers. One of the cable passes over the house of Mr. Vasanth Bhat. He is not a customer of the Network Company. The cable is neither attached to his house nor to any projection thereof. It is at a distance of 20 feet above the terrace of Mr. Bhat's son Sachin is unable to fly a kite from the terrace. Mr. Bhat requested the Network Company to change the position of the cable. But company did not bother to change it. One evening Mr. Bhat cut the cable and cleared airspace above his house. The Network company suffered a loss of about Rs. 1000. They bring a legal action against Mr. Bhat for recovery of loss suffered.

A. The Network Company will succeed because the cable was not interfering with the ordinary use and enjoyment of Mr. Bhat's property.

B. The Network Company will not succeed because Mr. Bhat his every right to ensure proper enjoyment of his property by removing objects causing trespass in the air above his property to a reasonable extent.

C. The Network Company will succeed because laying cable is widely practiced in all cities like electricity and telephone wires.

4. ***PRINCIPLE :*** Whoever takes or entices any minor under sixteen year of age if a male, or under eighteen years of age if a female out of the keeping of the lawful guardian of such male, or female without the consent of guardian is said to kidnap such minor.

FACTS : M, very fond of ice cream, grew up into a well-build, tall and charming girl. She topped in

Pre-Engineering Entrance test and got admission in a prestigious Delhi Engineering College. She developed intimacy with her classmate N of 17 years of age, who often offered her lavish gifts. During course of chit-chat M stated herself to be nineteen, she was actually just under eighteen but looked almost nineteen years old. M asked N to meet her the next day at the New Delhi Railway station. The boy accordingly went to the station and met the girl when she showed two tickets to Jaipur. Both of them gone to Pink City. A fortnight later, N arrested by police on the charged with kidnapping.

A. N is guilty of kidnapping the M
B. N is not guilty of kidnapping the M
C. N can be prosecuted with another charge
D. None of the above

5. *PRINCIPLE* : A principle shall be liable for any damage caused by the agent in the course of employment. The scope of an agent authority is conditioned not only by the power conferred by the principal, but by the reasonable public perception of such authority.

***FACTS* :** Omega is a well-known hospital, offering specialized facilities. When a patient comes to the hospital, the general physician examines him and refers him to the specialist concerned. The brochure of hospital describes all the doctors as Omega's doctors. But in fact all of them including the general physician are independent people, using Omega's facilities under contractual arrangements.

Gokul, having gone through the brochure, came to the hospital seeking a cure for a rare kind of disease. He was admitted into the hospital and operated upon for some heart problem. Among the various documents he signed at the time of admission, there was a form there under Omega disclaimed liability for the negligence of any doctor. Gokul signed all the documents mechanically as most of the patients tend to do under those agonising circumstances. Due to the negligence of operating surgeon. Gokul died. When his kin filed a suit against Omega alleging negligence, Omega resisted the claim on the basis of document, signed by Gokul.

A. Omega shall not be liable, since the contract signed by Gokul, exempted it from any liability.
B. Omega shall not be liable, since it is not really in a position to control the specialists surgeon in the course of a complicated operation.
C. Omega shall be liable, because Gokul was drawn into the hospital by its brochure describing the various facilities available.

6. *PRINCIPLE* : Law do not take notice of trifles.

***FACTS* :** A proposes to his neighbour 'B' that they both should go together for a morning walk. 'B' agrees to the proposal and it is decided the both of them would meet at a particular point at 6 a.m. from where they would set off for the morning walk. Inspite of the agreement 'B' does not turn up. 'A' waits for him at 6 a.m. every day for a continuous period of seven days. Thereafter he files a suit against 'B' claiming damages for the agony and mental fortune suffered by him.. Decide

A. 'B' is guilty of breach of contract and is liable to pay damages.
B. There is no intention to enter into legal relations.
C. The matter is too small and the court will refuse to go into it.

7. *PRINCIPLE 1* : No consideration—No contract

***PRINCIPLE 2* :** Consideration is something done or abstinence of a party at the desire of another party.

***PRINCIPLE 3* :** Consideration must have value in the eye of law.

***FACTS* :** Innovative Education Trust manages a School named Bharat Vidyaniketan. Ashok, the parent of a student in the school suggested to the trust that it could build a new library building for which he would bear a part of the cost. The School authority accepted the suggestion and started construction of the building. Ashok have suffered a loss in business, now refuses to pay the part he had offered earlier.

Which of the decision you think is appropriate?

A. Ahsok is not liable to pay as the building was for the benefit of the School and he has nothing to do with it by way of enjoying and benefit.
B. He is not liable to pay as Ashok's child is a student in the same school.
C. Ashok is liable to pay because based upon his promise, the School authority started construction of the building.

8. *PRINCIPLE :* Whoever, intend to take dishonestly any movable property out of the possession of any person without that person's consent, moves that property in order to such taking, is said to commit theft.

FACTS : A sees a ring belong to Z lying on a table in Z's house. Not venturing to misappropriate the ring immediately for fear of search and detection, A hides the ring in a place where it is rightly improbable that it will be found by Z, with the intention of taking the ring from the hiding place and selling it when the loss is forgotten.

A. A is not guilty of commits theft because he only hide the ring and not taking

B. A is not guilty of commit theft because he just want to hide the ring.

C. A is guilty of commit theft because at the time of first moving the ring.

9. *PRINCIPLE :* The legal principle is the same as above.

FACTS : Krishnan, while driving his car at a high speed in a crowded road, knocked down a cyclist. The cyclist died on the spot with a lot of blood spilling around. Lakshmi, a pregnant woman passing by, suffered from nervous shock, leading an abortion. Lakshmi flled a suit against Krishnan claiming damages.

A. Krishnan will be liable, because he owed a duty a reasonable care to everybody on the road including the Lakshmi.

B. Krishnan will not be liable, because he could not have forseen Lakshmi suffering from nervous shock as a result of his act.

C. Krishnan will be liable, to Lakshmi because he failed to drive carefully.

10. *PRINCIPLE :* A contract with consideration is void.

FACTS : A owes B Rs. 1100 but the debt is barred by limitation. B cannot file a suit. A signs a written promise to pay B Rs. 500 on account of this debt. B now files a suit for the recovery of Rs. 500/-. Decide.

A. The contract is not enforceable as consideration is inadequate.

B. Time barred debt is no consideration.

C. The contract is enforceable as it has sufficient consideration.

11. *PRINCIPLE :* Whoever, intend to take dishonestly any movable property out of the possession of any person without that person's consent, moves that property in order to such taking, is said to commit theft.

FACTS : A delivers his watch to Z, a jewellers to be regulated. Z carries it to his shop. A, not owing to the jewellers any debt for which the jewellers might lawfully detain the watch as a security, enters the shop openly, takes his watch by force out of Z's hand, and carries it away.

A. A commits the theft because he takes away his watch.

B. A does not commits the theft but committed criminal trespass and assault.

C. A neither commits theft nor any other crime, he simple take away his watch.

12. *PRINCIPLE :* Everybody is under a legal obligation to take reasonable care to avoid act or omission which he can forsee would injure his neighbour. The neighbour for this purpose is any person whom he should have in his mind as likely to be affected by his act.

FACTS : Ram, while rushing to board a moving train, pushed Shyam who was walking along with a heavy package, containing fire crackers. As a result, the package slipped from his and crackers exploded injuring a boy standing closely. A suit was filed against Ram, by the boy, claiming damages.

A. Ram is not liable, because he did not know anything about the contents of the package.

B. Ram is not liable, because Shyam should not have carried such a package in a crowded place like Railway Station.

C. Ram is liable, because Ram is under an obligation not to push Shyam.

13. *PRINCIPLE :* A master is liable for the wrongful acts of his servants committed in the course of employment.

FACTS : Lakshmi was a housewife who opened an account with Maharashtra Bank whereunder she agreed to deposit Rs. 300/- every month in the bank. Krishna an agent of the bank used to come every month, to collect the amount and deposit in the bank. The Bank used to give a small commission to Krishna for the money deposited. It was discovered one day that Krishna had not deposited the amount for more than three months and had disappeared with the money. Lakshmi filed a suit against Maharashtra Bank.

A. Maharashtra Bank would not be liable because Krishna was not its employee.
B. Maharashtra Bank would be liable because Krishna was raise commission by the Bank for doing work on its behalf.
C. Maharashtra Bank would not be liable as it was Lakshmi's responsibility to check her passbook regularly.

14. ***PRINCIPLE :*** An occupier is liable to a trespasser in respect of some willful act intended to cause harm or done with reckless disregard.

FACTS : A farm house belonging to Thotappa had its fencing electrified. The object was to ensure that the farm was secured from any wild animals in the vicinity. There was a clear warning about the electrified fencing. A cricket ball, hit from a nearby play ground, fell within the farm, Muthanna, the coach conducting the summer camp for school going children there, attempted to jump the fence to retrieve the ball, got injured on account of the electric shock sustained. Muthanna files a suit against Thotappa for relief.

A. Thotappa will not be liable, because Muthanna was a trespasser.
B. Thotappa will not be liable, because he had given sufficient warning about electric fence.
C. Thotappa will be liable because he must have taken note of the adjacent playground.

15. PRINCIPLE : A careless person becomes liable for his negligence when he owed a duty of care to others.

FACTS : As the bus was leaving the platform, Basappa rushed and boarded the bus keeping the door open. Beerappa, who was standing at the edge of the platform, was hit by the door of the moving bus and injured, Beerappa takes Basappa to court demanding monetary compensation.

A. Basappa is liable to Beerappa for not having taken care to close the door of the moving bus.
B. Basappa is not liable to Beerappa, as it was the duty of the conductor of the bus to close the door.
C. Basappa is not liable to Beerappa, as it was the duty of the latter to take sufficient care, while standing on the platform, as not to expose oneself to such accidental harm.

16. In this famous case, the Supreme Court said "the President means, for all practical purposes, the Prime Minister or Council of Ministers and his opinion, satisfaction or decision is constitutionally secured when Minister arrives at such opinion, satisfaction or decision?

A. Ram Jawaya Kapur v. State of Punjab
B. Maneka Gandhi v. Union of India
C. Dr. M. Ismail Faruqui v. Union of India
D. None of the above

17. After 86th Amendment to the Constitution article 45 of the Constitution includes:

A. Provision for the right to education of children.
B. Provision for early childhood care and protection against any offence.
C. Provision for early childhood care and education to children below the age of six years.
D. Provision for children for care and education upto age of 18 years.

18. Ancient treatise on law?

A. Vedas B. Upanishads
C. Smritis D. Shrutis

19. Which of following books can be regarded as a legal code:

A. Arthashastra B. Geet Govinda
C. Mahabharata D. Ramayana

20. Lawyer's ethics demands:

A. Not to defend a person known to him to have committed a crime
B. To defend everyone including a criminal who approaches him for legal services.
C. To refer the criminal to another lawyer who has no personal knowledge of his crime
D. To refuse his services on the ground that it is against his sense of morality.

21. You are being interviewed for a senior position in a Company, which is seeking a license for producing electricity. The license is available if a bribe of Rs. 10 lakhs is paid to the license issuing authority. The company believes that it stands to gain ten times more profit if it gets the license. It seeks your advice on:

A. Whether the amount should be paid
B. Whether they should bargain for a lesser amount
C. Whether they should refuse payment and ignore the profit
D. Whether they should pay it by crossed cheque only.

22. MLAs and MPs should have freedom to air their views in the legislature. Their action should not be open to question in a court of law. Therefore, if the ruling party paid money to some opposition members for voting in their favour, law should take the position:

A. The bribe givers may be prosecuted, but not the bribe takers
B. Both givers and takers should be exempted from any liability
C. Law should not take cognizance of such activity of elected representatives.
D. Whatever happens in such situations is protected by the privileges of legislators.

23. Equality cannot be achieved through reservation because:

A. it creates vested interests
B. it cannot be ended, once granted
C. it sacrifices merit and promotes mediocrity
D. historical wrongs cannot be corrected by unequal treatment

24. Copying in examination is wrong because:

A. it results in unequal competition
B. it puts a premium on dishonesty
C. it is not open to everybody
D. it makes one feel guilty

25. The Headquarters of ICJ is at:

A. London B. New York
C. Washington D. Hague

26. In the annual meeting of the General Assembly the member State can have:

A. 5 representatives
B. 10 representatives
C. 7 representatives
D. 15 representatives

27. The International Law consist of:

A. Public International Law only
B. Private International Law
C. Public International Law and Domestic Law
D. Public International Law and Private International Law.

28. Central Vigilance Commission is to be constituted under:

A. Prevention of Corruption Act of 1988
B. Central Vigilance Commission Act of 2003
C. Special Commission appointed by Central Government
D. Special direction of Supreme Court.

29. How many judges are there in the Supreme Court (including the Chief Justice)?

A. 24 B. 34
C. 25 D. 27

30. "Injury" under Indian Penal Code refers to:

A. any act illegally caused to any person
B. any act illegally caused to any person, in body and mind
C. any act illegally caused to any person in body, mind and reputation
D. any act illegally caused to any person, in body, mind reputation or property

31. "Special Law" under the Indian Penal Code refers to:

A. as a law applicable to a particular subject
B. as a law applicable to particular area
C. as a law applicable to Union Territories
D. as a law applicable to National Capital Region

32. India is:

A. Sovereign, Secular democracy
B. Sovereign, secular democratic republic
C. Sovereign, secular socialists democratic republic
D. None of the above

33. The Union Council of Ministers hold office:

A. During the pleasure of the Prime Minister
B. During the pleasure of the President of India
C. During the pleasure of the Vice-President of India
D. During the pleasure of the Lok Sabha Speaker

34. An unlawful act without criminal intention is:
A. Vicarious liability
B. Strict liability
C. No offence in itself
D. Abetment

35. A finds a watch on the floor of the class-room. A picks it up and put it in his pocket instead of returning it to the college authorities. Next day he sold it. A is liable for:
A. Theft
B. Extortion
C. Criminal misappropriation
D. Criminal breach of trust

36. A lawyer appointed by court to represent a poor litigant is:
A. Amicus Curiae
B. Legal Aidman
C. Lok Nyaya Pradayak
D. None of the above

37. The act of having anal intercourse is the offence of:
A. Sodomy B. Sedition
C. Libel D. Slander

38. The United Nations was established on:
A. 24 October, 1944
B. 24 October, 1947
C. 24 October, 1946
D. 24 October, 1945

39. The Headquarters of the International Criminal Court is at:
A. New York B. Geneva
C. The Hague D. Washington D.C.

40. Judges of the Supreme Court are selected by:
A. The Chief Justice of India
B. The Union Law Minister
C. A panel of Senior-most Judges of the Supreme Court:
D. The Prime Minister

41. Members of the Constituent Assembly of India were:
A. elected by the people
B. elected by the Provincial Assemblies
C. nominated by the Congress Party
D. nominated by the Viceroy

42. Right to Property was dropped from Part III of the Constitution by:
A. 25th Amendment B. 42nd Amendment
C. 44th Amendment D. 39th Amendment

43. The Union Executive is responsible to:
A. Rajya Sabha
B. Supreme Court
C. President
D. Lok Sabha

44. Which one of the following writs is issued in case of illegal detention:
A. Certiorari B. Mandamus
C. Habeas Corpus D. Quo Warranto

45. National emergency can not be imposed in case of:
A. Armed rebelion
B. Political Crisis
C. International aggression
D. War

46. The concept of 'Sarvodaya' is associated with:
A. M.K. Gandhi
B. Vinobha Bhave
C. Jayaprakash Narayan
D. Jawaharlal Nehru

47. Universal Declaration of Human Rights was adopted by U.N. in:
A. 1948 B. 1968
C. 1937 D. 1951

48. Indian citizenship cannot be terminated by:
A. Renunciation B. Termination
C. Imprisonment D. Deprivation

49. The concept of Judicial Review in India is inspired by Constitution of:
A. Britain B. France
C. U.S.A. D. Switzerland

50. Who was the Chairman of the Constituent Assembly?
A. B.R. Ambedkar B. Vallabhai Patel
C. Rajendra Prasad D. Pandit Nehru

51. When a new state is to be created by separating a territory from any state of Indian Union:
A. Both the houses of parliament pass a bill in this regard
B. The Governor of the said state on the recom-

mendation of Chief Minister gives consent

C. The Presidential ordinance is issued in this regard

D. The parent state gives approval to the President and after that the parliament passes a bill by simple majority in this regard

52. A joint session of both the houses of parliament can be called by the President

A. if any of the house does not take any action for six months on a bill remitted by the other

B. if the amendment to a bill proposed by one house is not acceptable to the other house

C. if a bill passed by one house is rejected by the other house.

D. all the above conditions

53. The Quorum of the Parliament is fixed at:

A. one-half of the membership of the house

B. one-third of the membership of the house

C. one-fourth of the membership of the house

D. one-tenth of the membership of the house

54. No taxes can be levied or expenditure incurred without the approval of

A. The Union Finance Minister

B. The Chairman Finance Commission

C. The Parliament

D. The President

55. The maximum number of days, within which the Rajya Sabha has to return back a bill to the Lok Sabha after rejection or acceptance is:

A. two days B. ten days

C. one month D. two months

56. The Lok Sabha and Rajya Sabha sit jointly when

A. it is necessary

B. both the houses have to discuss some matter jointly

C. there is a disagreement between the two houses

D. none of the above

57. A Bill is sent to the select committees after:

A. the formal introduction

B. the first reading

C. the second reading

D. none of the above

58. If the President think that the Anglo-Indian Community has not been adequately represented in the Lok Sabha, he may nominate:

A. not more than five members from this community

B. not more than two members from this community

C. one member

D. none of the above

59. The minimum age for casting vote in India is:

A. 20 years B. 22 years

C. 18 years D. 25 years

60. Article 1 of the Constitution declares India as:

A. Federation of states

B. Quasi federation

C. Union of states

D. None of the above

61. Who presides over the joint-sitting of Lok Sabha and Rajya Sabha?

A. The President

B. The Speaker, Lok Sabha

C. The Chairman, Rajya Sabha

D. The Minister for Parliament Affairs

62. Who certifies that whether a particular Bill is a money Bill or not

A. The Speaker, Lok Sabha

B. The Chairman, Estimates Committee

C. The Chairman, Public Accounts Committee

D. The Union Finance Minister

63. A money Bill can originate:

A. only in joint sitting of both the Houses of Parliament

B. either of the House

C. only in Lok Sabha

D. only in Rajya Sabha

64. The Rajya Sabha exclusively enjoys the power:

A. to return the money Bill

B. to recommend suspension of any minister

C. to recommended the creation of new All India Services

D. to call its special session

65. The members of numerios committees of Parliament are:

A. elected by the people directly

B. nominated by the parties concerned

C. appointed by the Prime Minister

D. either appointed by the Speaker or elected by the House

66. Which one of the following is not the legislative power of the Parliament

A. appointment the Prime Minister

B. law-making or Legislation

C. approval of ordinances

D. none of the above

67. The various subjects of legislation are enumerated in the Seventh Schedule of the Constitution in:
A. Four lists B. Two lists
C. One lists D. Three lists

68. President does not appoint:
A. Election Commissioner
B. Comptroller and Auditor-General
C. Prime Minister
D. Lok Sabha Speaker

69. The decision on dispute regarding the disqualification of Members of Parliament is taken by:
A. The Speaker, Lok Sabha
B. The Chief Election Commissioner
C. The Chairman, Rajya Sabha
D. The President in consultation with the Election Commission

70. Which legislative body is presided over by a non-member:
A. State Legislative Council
B. Rajya Sabha
C. Lok Sabha
D. State Legislative Assembly

71. The Committee which has some associate members form Rajya Sabha is :
A. The Committee on Public Enterprises
B. The Committee on Privileges
C. The Public Accounts Committee
D. The Estimates Committee

72. The exclusive legislative power with regard to defence forces and war and peace is vested in :
A. The President
B. The Defence Minister
C. The Cabinet Committee on Defence Matters
D. The Parliament

73. The power to amend the Constitution is vested in :
A. The President
B. The Parliament
C. The Council of Ministers
D. The President on the recommendation of the Prime Minister

74. The power to vote the demands for grants presented by the government is exclusively vested in:
A. Rajya Sabha
B. Lok Sabha
C. The Joint Sitting of both the Houses
D. None of the above

75. The right to pass a vote of no-confidence is exclusively vested in :
A. The Lok Sabha
B. The Rajya Sabha
C. The Joint Sitting of both the house
D. None of the above

ANSWERS

1	2	3	4	5	6	7	8	9	10
C	C	A	B	C	C	C	A	B	C
11	**12**	**13**	**14**	**15**	**16**	**17**	**18**	**19**	**20**
B	A	B	C	A	A	C	C	A	B
21	**22**	**23**	**24**	**25**	**26**	**27**	**28**	**29**	**30**
C	C	C	D	D	A	C	A	B	A
31	**32**	**33**	**34**	**35**	**36**	**37**	**38**	**39**	**40**
B	C	B	B	D	A	A	D	C	C
41	**42**	**43**	**44**	**45**	**46**	**47**	**48**	**49**	**50**
B	C	D	C	B	B	D	C	C	C
51	**52**	**53**	**54**	**55**	**56**	**57**	**58**	**59**	**60**
D	D	D	C	B	C	B	B	C	C
61	**62**	**63**	**64**	**65**	**66**	**67**	**68**	**69**	**70**
B	A	C	C	D	A	D	D	D	B
71	**72**	**73**	**74**	**75**					
C	D	B	B	A					

TEST PAPER-III

MULTIPLE CHOICE LEGAL QUESTIONS

1. *PRINCIPLE :* Everybody is under a legal obligation to take reasonable care to avoid act or omission which he can foresee would injure his neighbour. The neighbour for this purpose is any person whom he should have in his mind as likely to be affected by his act.

FACTS : Ram, while rushing to board a moving train, pushed Shyam who was walking along with a heavy package, containing fire crackers. As a result, the package slipped from his hand and the crackers exploded injuring a boy standing closely. A suit was filed against Ram, by the boy, claiming damages.

A. Ram is not liable, because he did not know anything about the contents of the package.

B. Ram is not liable, because Shyam should not have carried such package in a crowded place like Railway station.

C. Ram is liable, because Ram is under an obligation not to push Shyam.

2. *PRINCIPLE :* Everybody is under a legal obligation to take reasonable care to avoid act or omission which he can foresee would injure his neighbour. The neighbour for this purpose is any person whom he should have in his mind as likely to be affected by his act.

FACTS : Krishnan, while driving his car at a high speed in a crowded road, knocked down a cyclist. The cyclist died on the spot with a lot of blood spilling around. Lakshmi, a pregnant woman was passing by, suffered from a nervous shock, leading to abortion. Lakshmi filed a suit against Krishnan claiming damages.

A. Krishnan will be liable, because he owed a duty a reasonable care to everybody on the road including Lakshmi.

B. Krishnan will not be liable, because he could not have foreseen Lakshmi suffering from nervous shock as a result of his act.

C. Krishnan will be liable, to Lakshmi because he failed to drive carefully.

3. *PRINCIPLE :* A person is liable for all direct consequences of his act, which he could have reasonably foreseen as naturally flowing from his act.

FACTS : Anant, while driving his scooter at a high speed, knocked down Shankar, a middle-aged person, walking on the road. Shankar broke his leg as a result of the accident. But since Shankar was suffering from diabetes, the leg had to be amputated. Shankar filed a suit against Anant for the loss of leg.

A. Anant is liable, since the loss of the leg is directly attributable to his act.

B. Shankar is not liable for the loss of leg, since he did not know Shankar was suffering from diabetes.

C. Shankar is not liable, since a diabetes-patient like Shankar should not have walked on the road.

4. *PRINCIPLE :* Whoever, intend to take dishonestly any movable property out of the possession of any person without that person's consent, moves that property in order to such taking, is said to commit theft.

FACTS : A, being on friendly terms with Z, goes into Z's liabrary in Z's absence, and takes away a book without Z's express consent for the purpose merely of reading it and with the intention of returning it. Here it is probable that A may have conceived that he has Z's implied consent to use Z's book. If this was A's impression.

A. A has committed theft

B. A has not committed theft

C. Can't say about it

D. None of these

5. *PRINCIPLE :* An occupier is not normally liable to a trespasser except in respect of willful act intended to cause harm or done with reckless disregard.

FACTS : Jaspal, a rich man of the locality had kept a ferocious dog to guard his house. He strictly instructed all his servants not to go near that dog and there was a special attender who was to take care of the dog. There was a prominent board warning the visitors about the ferocious dog. One day, a twelve year old boy playing in the neighbourhood, running after his ball got into the house. The dog attacked him and killed him. Jaspal was sued for damages.

A. Jaspal is not liable because the boy was a trespasser

B. Jaspal is not liable because a twelve year boy ought to have known about the presence of the ferocious dog.

C. Jaspal is liable for the negligence of his servant to keep watch on such a ferocious dog during the day time.

6. *PRINCIPLE :* A master will be liable for the wrongful acts of his servants in the course of employment.

FACTS : Ramadevi was an old widow who opened an account with the Syndicate Bank, where under she would deposit Rs.5 everyday in the Bank. Sundar was the neighbour who used to collect the amounts and deposit them in the Bank. Sundar would get a small commission from the Bank for the money deposited. It was discovered one day that Sundar for more than three months did not deposit the money and vanished with that money. Ramadevi filed a suit against Syndicate Bank.

A. Syndicate Bank would not be liable, because Sundar was not its employee

B. Syndicate Bank would not be liable, for the failure of Ramadevi to check the status of her accounts.

C. Syndicate Bank would be liable, because Sundar was paid commission by the Bank for doing its work.

7. *PRINCIPLE :* Contract is an agreement freely entered into between the parties.

FACTS : Ramlal was the dealer in cement. The Government of India, by an order issued under the Essential Commodities Act, fixed the price of cement, and also the quantity which a person can buy from the dealer. Ramlal carried on his business under this new order for sometime, but he refused to pay the sales tax on his sale transactions on the ground that these were not the contracts freely entered into by him.

A. Ramlal would succeed, because the price and quantity were not negotiated by him;

B. Ramlal would not succeed, because free consent between the parties were there despite the restriction on price and quantity.

C. Ramlal would succeed, because the Government under the new order, forced him to enter into contracts.

8. *PRINCIPLE :* Whoever, dishonestly misappropriates or converts to his own use any movable property, shall be punished with imprisonment of either description of a term which may extend to two years, or with fine or with both.

FACTS : A and B, being joint owners of a horse, A takes the horse out of B's possession, intending to use it. Here, as A has a right to use the horse. But, A sells the horse and appropriates the whole proceeds to his own use. Decide.

A. A is guilty of an offence of dishonesty misappropriation

B. A is not guilty of any offence because he has right to use the horse

C. Can't say about it

D. None of these

9. *PRINCIPLE :* The occupier of a premise owes a duty of care to all his invitees and visitors.

FACTS : Kishanlal was running a dairy farm in his house. A part of his farm was used by the people as a short cut to get into the nearby railways station. Kishanlal never liked it and put up a board that "All trespassers will be prosecuted". But he actually tolerated them, because quite a few of them patronized his business. One day, a person who was crossing the farm to get into the railway station was attacked by a bull belonging to the farm. The injured person filed a suit against Kishanlal.

A. Kishanlal is not liable in view of the clear notice against trespassers.

B. Kishanlal is liable, because he in fact allowed the people to use his premises.

C. Kishanlal is not liable to the people other than his customers.

10. *PRINCIPLE :* The occupier of a premise owes a duty of care to all his invitees and visitors.

FACTS : Kishanchand arranged a cocktail for his friends in his farm house with nice gardens and a swimming pool. The area of swimming pool was brightly lit and the pool had sufficient enclosures. But one of the guest, in his inebriated condition, strayed into the area of swimming pool and fell into the pool, suffered injuries. He filed a suit against Kishanchand claiming damages.

A. Kishanchand is not liable, because he invited the guests only for the party and not for the swimming

B. Kishanchand cannot be held responsible for the drinking propensities of his friends.

C. Kishanchand as a host would be responsible to take care of his guests when they are in his premises.

11. ***PRINCIPLES :*** (I) Under Indian Constitution, if a person is convicted of an offence, he cannot be prosecuted again.

(II) Under Criminal Procedure Code, if a person is prosecuted in an offence and if the prosecution results either in an acquittal or in conviction, then he cannot be the prosecuted for the same offence.

FACTS : Maniyan was prosecuted for an offence of murder and he was acquitted. Thereafter additional evidence came to light pointing to Maniyan's complicity in the same offence. So the police went to prosecute him again.

A. Maniyan cannot be prosecuted as he enjoys the right under our Constitution not be prosecuted twice for the same offence.

B. Maniyan cannot be prosecuted as he enjoys the right under Criminal Procedure Code not to be prosecuted twice for the same offence.

C. Maniyan cannot be prosecuted as he is protected both by the Constitution and Criminal Procedure Code.

D. None of the above answers is correct.

12. In order to ensure that people live in an amicable atmosphere the Government of India decided to abolish courts and constituted Dispute Settlement Boards. Further, to achieve this objective, the law stipulated that lawyers should not be allowed to espouse the claims of parties, and instead their claims be espoused by social workers.

PRINCIPLES : (I) Any law made by the Parliament that infringes the fundamental rights of the citizens is invalid and unenforceable.

(II) Freedom to carry on trade or profession of one's own choice is a fundamental right.

(III) The Parliament is competent to impose reasonable restrictions on the exercise of this right.

(IV) If the restrictions, of fundamental rights imposed by the Parliament, totally removes or nullifies any fundamental right then it will be construed as an unreasonable restriction.

A. The law made by the Parliament is valid as it does not infringe any fundamental right.

B. The law made by the Parliament is valid as even though there is restriction of fundamental right, such a restriction is reasonable.

C. The law made by the Parliament is invalid as it constitutes an infringement of fundamental rights and the restriction imposed is not reasonable.

D. None of the above answers is correct.

13. ***PRINCIPLES :*** (I) If a person makes a statement that lowers the reputation of another person in the eyes of right thinking people, then it is defamation.

(II) The person whose reputation is affected can sue the culprit and recover damages.

FACTS : Rama told Sita "You are a thief. You stole my heart". Sita was furious and she felt that she was defamed.

A. Rama has defamed Sita and hence he is liable to pay damages.

B. Rama is liable to pay as Sita's reputation was lowered in the eyes of right thinking people

C. Rama is not responsible, as right thinking people will not mistake this statement.

D. None of the above answers is correct.

14. ***PRINCIPLES :*** (I) In order to succeed in an action for damages, the person who files the case must prove that the defendant is at fault.

(II) However, if the factors which caused the accident were in the normal course of the defendant and if the accident is of such a nature that it would not have happened, in the normal then the law presumes fault on the part of the persons who had control over the factors that caused the accident.

FACTS : Vasu was walking on a street. When Vasu was crossing Venkat's house, a bag of rice fell on Vasu and he was injured. But he did not know what caused the bag of rice to fall on him.

In an action for damages brought by Vasu

A. Vasu cannot succeed, as he could not prove that Venkat was at fault.

B. Vasu can succeed, because the law will presume that Venkat is at fault.

C. Vasu can succeed, as the rice bag fell on him

D. None of the above answers is correct.

15. ***PRINCIPLE :*** Whoever takes or entices any minor under sixteen years of age if a male, or under eighteen years of age if a female, out of the keeping of the lawful guardian of such male or female without the consent of guardian is said to kidnap such minor.

FACTS : M, very fond of ice cream, grew up into a well built, tall and charming girl. She topped in a Pre-Engineering Entrance Test and got admission in a prestigious Delhi Engineering College. She developed intimacy with her class-mate N of 17 years of age, who often offered her lavish gifts. During course of chit-chat M stated herself to be nineteen whereas she was actually just under eighteen but looked almost nineteen years old. M asked N to meet her the next day at the New Delhi Railway Station. The boy accordingly went to the station and met the girl when she showed two tickets to Jaipur. Both of them gone to Pink city. A fortnight later, N arrested by police on the charged with kidnapping.

A. N is guilty of kidnapping the M.

B. N is not guiilty of kidnapping the M.

C. N can be prosecuted with another charge.

D. None of the above.

16. A study of the background of toppers in different professional colleges concludes that the students who studied in their mother tongue as a medium of instruction in schools fare as well as those who studied in English medium schools. So we can conclude that parents must be encouraged to give their children primary education in their mother tongue. It is more natural for a person to study in his or her mother tongue rather that in an alien language. Which of the following would strengthen the above argument?

A. As far as possible parents should send their children to schools using their mother tongue as medium of instruction.

B. The medium of instruction in a school where a child is studying does not make any difference in so far as intellectual growth of the child is concerned.

C. The teachers in non-English medium schools are equally competent like teachers in English medium schools because they can contribute to the intellectual growth of the students although they do not study in English medium.

D. The parents of children going to non-English medium schools need not suffer from inferiority complex.

17. The importance of scientific knowledge has increased greatly over the past thirty years, yet in the same period, the communication gap between scientists and non-scientists has grown considerably. If the vast majority of citizens is not to lose touch with crucial public issues, this gap should be bridged.

The underlying assumption in the above passage is that:

A. No effort to bridge the communication gap has been made so far

B. An understanding of science is necessary to solve social problems

C. The rate of scientific discovery has been increasing in leaps and bounds over the past thirty years.

18. Women's reservation in the Parliament is the need of the hour because they represent the voice of nearly 50% of the population.

Which of the following statements contradicts the above?

A. There is no right to stand for elections or to be elected

B. A legislator is supposed to represent his constituency and not a section of it.

C. The constituents of a constituency have a right to elect any person from among the eligible who contest for elections.

19. If as a result of the exercise of executive power, rights of the citizens are restricted or infringed, the exercise of power must be supported by legislation. Where there is no such restriction or infringement of the right the executive is competent to exercise power.

On the above premises, which of the following is the best conclusion?

A. If a decision adds to the rights of citizens, it is enforceable directly
B. Executive is competent to restrict rights
C. Legislation is always required to exercise power.

20. Indian citizenship is based on the principle of:

A. Birth in Indian Territory
B. Long stay in Indian territory
C. Birth through Indian parents
D. Meritorious Service to Indian nation

21. Supreme Court of India is a court of record, because:

A. All its judgments are recorded
B. All its judgments are reported in Law Reports
C. All its orders are self-executing
D. It has power to punish for contempt of court

22. Powers of Panchayats under Indian legal system are:

A. Determined by State legislatures
B. Laid down by the Constitution
C. Laid down by the Governor as per the direction of State Legislatures
D. Determined by State Legislature subject to the provision of the Constitution

23. A public interest litigation can be initiated by:

A. Any public spirited individual
B. Any person whose right is infringed
C. Any lawyer
D. Any recognized leader

24. The International Court of Justice adjudicates the disputes between:

A. States and foreign corporations
B. States only
C. States and International Institutions
D. States and private individuals

25. The World Trade Organisation is located at:

A. New York B. Washington, D.C.
C. Rome D. Geneva

26. The phrase 'duty of care' means you must take reasonable care to avoid acts or omissions which you can reasonably foresee would be likely to injure your neighbour. In this definition the word 'neighbour' indicates:

A. All persons who can be so closely and directly affected, that you ought to reasonably have them in contemplation.
B. All people living in your vicinity, whom you owe a social duty
C. Your next door resident

27. Property can be divided into movable property, immovable property and intellectual property. An exclusive right conferred on one who has developed a new thing with the use of his intellect and faculty is his intellectual property.

A person then enjoys an exclusive right to make use, sell, assign that property.

When such a right is given in relation to invention of a machine it is known as:

A. Inquests B. Deed
C. Patent D. Copyright

28. Every person has freedom of speech and expression. Constitution attaches great importance to this freedom. It is believed that this freedom is indispensable to the operation of any democratic system. This freedom is guaranteed as:

A. Directive principle of state policy
B. Fundamental duty
C. Fundamental right
D. Legal right

29. Dowry is a social evil. Every person recognizes it to be so and yet it cannot be eradicated because:

A. Dowry Prohibition Act is ineffective
B. Women are the vulnerable section of the society
C. Women have no right to property
D. Patriarchal Society

30. When an on going case is adjourned to a future date, and the defendant is ordered to be kept in custody in the meantime:

A. The defendant is said to be remanded to custody
B. The defendant is said to be condemned to custody
C. The defendant is said to be ordered to custody
D. The defendant is said to be decreed to custody

31. Absconder in the eye of law means:
A. Run away from Home
B. Run away after killing
C. Hide to evade the process of law
D. Challenge the executive

32. 'Accomplice' in legal terms means:
A. Partner in a Crime
B. Eye Witness
C. On looker
D. Criminal Mind

33. Any court of Tribunal in the Territory of India means – Court which:
A. Have Judicial Right
B. Must be within the Territory of India
C. Working under International Court
D. None of these

34. Countersign means:
A. Take Signature
B. Unauthenticated Signature
C. To add one's Signature to the document
D. Attempt to suicide

35. 'Delinquent Child' is one who:
A. Has no parents
B. No education
C. Has no legs
D. Has committed an offence

36. 'Habeas corpus' is a:
A. Greek term B. Latin term
C. English term D. French term

37. 'Burden of proof' means:
A. Take allegation
B. Contradictory statement
C. Prove an allegation
D. Clean judgment

38. Hindu Marriage Act was passed in:
A. 1950 B. 1952
C. 1955 D. 1959

39. 'Capacity' in legal term means:
A. Natural Power B. Physical Power
C. Moral Power D. Legal Power

40. 'Rule of Law' a term in Indian constitution is taken from:
A. U.K. B. U.S.A
C. Russia D. Ireland

41. *Quid Pro Quo* means:
A. One for the other B. Illegal action
C. Moral values D. lawlessness

42. Immunity denotes:
A. Freedom from infection
B. From interference
C. From power of the state
D. No control

43. Detention denotes:
A. Confiscating goods
B. Arrest
C. Defects
D. No freedom to move

44. Law:
A. Follows human behaviour
B. Prescribes rules
C. Is supreme will
D. None of these

45. Waqf is a:
A. Charitable institution
B. Gift
C. One man's property
D. Institution for pardanashin ladies

46. Relations between Fundamental Rights and Directive Principles is of:
A. Harmony but imbalance
B. Harmony and balance
C. Only harmony
D. Only of conflict

47. Untouchability (Offences) Act was Passed in
A. 1955 B. 1957
C. 1959 D. 1962

48. What is a 'moot'?
A. A basic point of law
B. A basic fact of case
C. Mock court for practice by students
D. Another name for magistrate's court

49. The early release of a prisoner is called:
A. Bail B. Parole
C. Lease D. Lien

50. …………… is a general pardon:
A. Remission B. Reprieve
C. Amnesty D. Suspension

51. The judges of Supreme Court and High Courts can be removed by the President:
A. when the Lok Sabha recommends so
B. when the Joint Sitting of both the Houses recommend so

C. when a request for their removal is made in the form of address adopted by a special majority of both the Houses
D. when the Council of Minister recommends so

52. The power to promulgate ordinance during recess of parliament has been given to:
A. The Speaker, Lok Sabha
B. The Chairman, Rajya Sabha
C. The Union Law Minister
D. The President

53. The Constitution emphasizes two major priviliges to the Members of Parliament, viz:
A. freedom of speech and right to property
B. freedom of speech and freedom of writing
C. freedom of speech and right of publication
D. freedom to travel anywhere and freedom of expression

54. The Members of Parliament enjoy the freedom from arrest. But this privilege is not available to members in:
A. FERA violation case
B. economic offences case
C. criminal cases
D. cases of legal nature

55. The following parliamentary committee has the largest membership:
A. The Committee on privileges
B. The Estimates Committee
C. The Public Accounts Committee
D. The Committee on Public Enterprises

56. The parliamentary Committee concerned with the regularity and economy of expenditure of government is:
A. The Estimates Committee
B. The Committee on Privileges
C. The Public Accounts Committee
D. None of the above

57. Who acts as the friend, philosopher and guide of the Public Accounts Committee?
A. Chairman, Finance Commission
B. Comptroller and Auditor General
C. Union Finance Minister
D. None of the above

58. The Parliament can make a law on a subject in the State List when:
A. the Rajya Sabha passes a resolution that such subjects are of national importance
B. the proclamation of Emergency is in force
C. two or more states make a request to the parliament to make a law on the subject
D. all the above conditions

59. A certain Bill passed by parliament becomes a law when:
A. the Speaker agrees to it
B. the Joint Sitting of Parliament approves it
C. the President gives his consent
D. the Council of Ministers approves it

60. The powers of the Upper House are limited in matters of finance, if the legislature happens to be:
A. Unicameral B. Bicameral
C. Multicameral D. None of the above

61. The President can return a bill to the Houses of Parliament:
A. any numer of lines B. thrice
C. twice D. only once

62. The session of Parliament begins with:
A. the Speaker, lok Sabha address
B. the address of the President to a Joint Sitting of both the Houses
C. the President's message
D. the Prime Minister's address

63. In both the Houses of Parliament, the first item of business is :
A. The Private Members bills
B. The Debate on Naitonal Issues
C. The Question Hour
D. The Zero Hour

64. During Question Hour, the starred questions are:
A. the question with star mark
B. the questions which are answered by the minisers orally
C. the questions which need greater attention
D. none of the above

65. Through the Calling Attention Notice the Members of Parliament
A. can call the attention of the Speaker

B. can elicit information on important matters of urgent public importance
C. can call the attention of the President on national issues
D. none of the above

66. Through the Adjournment motion, the Members of Parliament
A. can not adjourn the House
B. can bring an urgent matter, which brooks no delay, for discussion
C. try to adjourn the House
D. none of the above

67. Through the no-confidence motion:
A. the members can express no-confidence in the House
B. the members can express no-confidence in the government
C. the members of the oppo. 'ion can critically examine the policies of the government
D. none of the above

68. A bill introduced by a member or a minister, goes through:
A. one reading
B. two readings
C. three readings
D. unlimited readings

69. A Money Bill can not be introduced in:
A. the Rajya Sabha
B. the Lok Sabha
C. the Joint Sitting of both the Houses
D. none of the above

70. All the expenditure which is charged upon the Consolidated Fund of India, is not submitted to the Vote of Parliament, but these are open to discussion by:
A. only Lok Sabha
B. only Rajya Sabha
C. only Joint Sitting of both the Houses
D. either of the House

71. Who presents the Union Budget in Lok Sabha?
A. The Prime Minister
B. The Union finance Minister
C. The Chairman, Finance Commission
D. The Dy. Chairman, Planning Commission

72. The Constitution provides that a House of Parliament may declare a seat vacant:
A. if a member is guilty of breach of privilege of the House
B. if a member is absent for 60 days without the permission of the House
C. if a member is unable to perform properly
D. none of the above

73. The difference between a Money Bill and a Finance Bill is that:
A. a Finance Bill can be introduced in the Rajya Sabha
B. a Finance Bill is an ordinary Bill
C. a Finance Bill can be rejected by Rajya Sabha, whereas Money Bill can not be
D. none of the above

74. The relation between parliament and president is that the:
A. President has nothing to do with Parliament
B. President is superior to Parliament
C. President is a wing of Parliament
D. None of the above

75. Which of the following union territories is represented in the Rajya Sabha?
A. Andaman and Nicobar Islands
B. Puducherry
C. Chandigarh
D. Dadra & Nagar Haveli and Daman & Diu

ANSWERS

1	2	3	4	5	6	7	8	9	10
C	A	A	A	C	C	B	C	A	B
11	**12**	**13**	**14**	**15**	**16**	**17**	**18**	**19**	**20**
D	B	C	A	B	B	B	C	A	A
21	**22**	**23**	**24**	**25**	**26**	**27**	**28**	**29**	**30**
A	B	A	C	D	A	C	B	C	A

31	32	33	34	35	36	37	38	39	40
C	A	A	C	D	A	C	C	D	B
41	**42**	**43**	**44**	**45**	**46**	**47**	**48**	**49**	**50**
A	D	B	C	B	B	C	C	B	B
51	**52**	**53**	**54**	**55**	**56**	**57**	**58**	**59**	**60**
C	D	C	C	B	C	B	D	C	B
61	**62**	**63**	**64**	**65**	**66**	**67**	**68**	**69**	**70**
D	B	C	B	B	B	C	C	A	C
71	**72**	**73**	**74**	**75**					
B	B	C	C	B					

TEST PAPER-IV

MULTIPLE CHOICE LEGAL QUESTIONS

1. ***PRINCIPLE :*** Whoever, being in any manner entrusted with property, or with any dominion over property, dishonestly misappropriates or converts to his own that property in violation law is commits criminal breach of trust.

FACTS : A residing in Kolkatta, is agent of Z, residing at Delhi. There is an express or implied contract between A and Z, that all sums remitted by Z to A shall be invested by A according to Z's directions. Z remits a lakh of rupees to A, with directions to A to invest the same in company's paper. A dishonestly disobeys the direction and employs the money in his own business. Decide.

A. A has committed breach of trust.
B. A has committed misappropriation of property.
C. A has committed both the crime.
D. None of these.

2. ***PRINCIPLE :*** Whoever delivers to any other person as genuine any counterfeit currency which he knows to be counterfeit, but which he did not know to be counterfeit at the time when he received it is guilty of an offence.

FACTS : Mr. Ramachandran is a cashier in a school. One evening his wife returned home from market. While she was counting the remaining money, Mr. Ramachandran noticed a counterfeit currency note of Rs.100. His wife told him that it was given to her by way of change when she gave a Rs.500 note in the grocery shop by the person at the cash counter. Mr. Ramachandran goes to the same shop with a view to get rid of the counterfeit note. He buys a shaving cream worth Rs. 32.50 and gives the counterfeit note at the cash counter. The cashier inspects the note and realizes that it is counterfeit. He calls the police.

A. Mr. Ramachandran is not guilty of any offence because he neither manufactured the counterfeit note nor did he circulate it with a view to deceive anybody.
B. Mr. Ramachandran is not guilty because he was attempting to return the counterfeit note to the same person from whom he received it.
C. Mr. Ramachandran is guilty because he attempted to deliver a counterfeit currency note as genuine, which he knew was counterfeit.

3. ***PRINCIPLE :*** Every person has a right to defend his own person, property or possession against an immediate harm, and to that end, may use reasonable amount of force.

FACTS : Mr. Kaul was passing by Mrs. Mattoo's house. At that time, Mrs. Mattoo's dog ran out and bit Mr. Kaul's overcoat. Mr. Kaul turned around and raised the pistol he was carrying in the pocket of his overcoat. The dog ran away, and Mr. Kaul shot the dog as it was running away. Mr. Kaul knew that the dog had attacked so many other people in that locality of Jammu. Mrs. Mattoo claims that her dog was of a rare breed and it was worth Rs.5000/-. She is planning to bring a legal action against Mr. Kaul for compensation.

A. She will succeed in getting compensation from Mr. Kaul because he killed the dog which was not actually attacking him at the time of shooting.
B. She will not succeed because Mr. Kaul was justified in shooting the dog to protect himself.
C. She will succeed because Mr. Kaul took the action to protect himself as well as many other members of public in future.

4. ***PRINCIPLE :*** In case of a breach of contract, compensation can be awarded for the personal inconvenience suffered by a party by reason of the breach, which naturally arose in the usual course of things from such breach or which the parties knew, when they made the contract to be likely to result from the breach of it.

FACTS : Mr. Anil and Mrs. Seema Shah bought bus tickets for a journey from Bhavnagar to Amreli, a small town in Gujarat, from a private bus company. The bus was to go to Jamnagar via Amreli. The bus driver, by mistake, took them in a somewhat wrong direction and dropped them at a distance of 3 miles from Amreli on the state highway. Finding no other conveyance and no place to stay, Mr. and Mrs. Shah had to walk the distance of 3 miles at midnight. Later they filed a case against the bus company and claimed Rs.2,500/- as damages for inconvenience suffered in being obliged to walk and Rs.5,000/- in respect of Mrs. Seema Shah's illness caused by catching cold during that night.

A. The bus company is liable to pay both the amounts claimed because the loss was suffered on account of the fault of the bus company and the inconvenience suffered and illness arose in the usual course of things from breach of contract.

B. The bus company is liable to pay both the amounts claimed because the loss was suffered by Mr. and Mrs. Shah for no fault of theirs.

C. The bus company is liable to pay only Rs.2,500/- by way of compensation for inconvenience suffered by them for being obliged to walk during the night. They are not liable to pay Rs.5,000/- in respect of Mrs. Seema Shah's illness because the bus company did not expect her to catch cold on account of the breach of contract.

5. *PRINCIPLE :* A bailment is the delivery of goods by one person to another for some purpose, upon a contract that they shall, when the purpose is accomplished, be returned. In all cases of bailment the person whom the goods are delivered is expected to take as much care of the goods as a man of ordinary prudence would, under similar circumstances take of his own goods of similar nature.

FACTS : Mrs. Basanti gave 25 gms of pure gold to M/s. Hiralal Shroff and Company – a firm of jewellers to make two bangles of a particular design out of that gold. The jewellers kept the gold in an almirah in their shop. There was burglary in the shop and the gold given by Mrs. Basanti was stolen along with other jewellery belonging to the firm. The burglars broke open one of the shop windows. The firm had not employed a watchman to guard their valuables during the night. Now Mrs. Basanti brings an action against the firm for compensation.

A. The firm of jewellers is not liable to compensate Mrs. Basanti because they took as much care as they took in respect of their own goods which is established by the fact that their own goods were also stolen along with the gold belonging to Mrs. Basanti.

B. The firm is liable to compensate Mrs. Basanti because it failed to take as much care as a man of ordinary prudence ought to have taken in respect of the goods entrusted.

C. The firm is not liable to compensate Mrs. Basanti because it took reasonable care in respect of the goods entrusted to it and the burglary could not have been avoided under any circumstances.

6. *PRINCIPLE :* Under the Workmen's Compensation Act an employer is liable to compensate his workmen for injuries sustained by them in the course of and out of employment.

FACTS : Apco Pvt. Ltd., is a company manufacturing corrugated boxes in New Mumbai. It has about 2000 workers. It sends its buses to bring its workers to the factory site from different parts of New Mumbai. Once a strike was called by one group of workers of Apco Pvt. Ltd. Another group of workers – who belonged to a rival trade union – did not support the strike. When a bus carrying non-striking workers was going towards the factory, a group of striking workers hurled stones at the bus. One of the stones hit Mr. Laxman More, a worker in the bus. He sustained a major head injury. Later he claimed compensation from the Management of Apco Pvt. Ltd., for injuries sustained by him.

A. The employers are liable to compensate Mr. More because the injury was sustained by him in the course of employment. For this purpose it may be presumed that he was 'in the course of employment' at the moment he boarded the company vehicle.

B. The employers are liable to compensate Mr. More because the injury was caused to one of their loyal workers who was not on a strike and it was caused by striking worker who was acting against the interest of the company.

C. The employers may pay some compensation to Mr. More on account of a moral obligation to do so, but there is no legal obligation on the employers because the injury was sustained outside the factory limits and hence it was not sustained 'in the course of and out of employment'.

7. *PRINCIPLE :* When a criminal act is done by one person in furtherance of the common intention of himself and some other persons, each of such persons is liable for the act in the same manner as if it were done by each one of them.

FACTS : A, B and C decided to commit burglary. They broke into a locked house. However, a domestic servant appeared from the out-house before they had finished, he started shouting. A, B and C left the house and started running away. They were pursued by a small crowd. A, on being caught by X, one of the persons pursuing them, stabbed him and ran away. By that time B and C had disappeared. X died on account of the stab wounds. Later the police could arrest all the three. They were charged for attempted burglary and murder of X.

A. Along with A – the person who stabbed X – B and C are also guilty of murder because A stabbed X in furtherance of common intention to commit murder.

B. Along with A, B and C are also guilty of murder because A, at the time of stabbing X, was acting on behalf of B and C and he wanted to save not only himself but B and C as well.

C. A alone is guilty of murder because though there was common intention to commit the offence of burglary, there was no common intention to commit the offence of murder.

8. *PRINCIPLE :* Any person who interferes with the discharge of duties by a public servant is liable for punishment.

Nothing is an offence if the person who committed it, was unable to appreciate the consequences of his act, due to intoxication, provided such intoxication was administered against his will and without his consent.

FACTS : Krishna got drunk of his own volition and on his way back home he assaulted a policeman. He is prosecuted for intimidating a public servant.

Is Mr. Krishna liable for punishment?

A. Yes B. No

C. Cannot say

9. *PRINCIPLE :* Whoever, dishonestly misappropriates or converts to his own use any movable property, shall be punished with imprisonment of either description for a term which may extend to two years, or with fine or with both.

FACTS : A, with B's consent, lodged his hundred sheep in B's field overnight and the next morning drove his flock to the market for sale. At the time of the sale when the sheep were counted the presence of an extra sheep belonging to B was brought to A's notice. A sold it with the rest. Decide.

A. A is being tried for the theft

B. A is being tried for dishonest misappropriation of property

C. A is being tried for both theft as well as dishonest misappropriation of property.

10. *PRINCIPLE :* 1. Master is liable for the wrongful acts committed by servants, in the course of their employment if third parties suffer damages in consequences.

2. However the master is not liable if the wrongful act committed by the servant has no connection whatsoever with the servant's contract of employment.

3. If a person by an act lowers the reputation of another in the eye of right thinking people, then the person who suffered loss of reputation can sue for damages.

FACTS : Tiwari is a servant of Ajit. On his way to Ajit's house to report for duty, he goes to have a cup of coffee. There he sees Singh and accuses Mr. Singh of being a dishonest person. Mr. Singh wants to sue Ajit, as Tiwari is Ajit's servant.

A. Ajit is liable because Tiwari defamed Singh.

B. Ajit is not liable as the defamation was not in the course of Tiwari's employment.

C. Ajit is liable even thought he defamation was not in the course of employment.

D. None of the above answers is correct.

11. *PRINCIPLES :* (1) Whoever is under a duty of care to another shall be liable for any injury to the latter directly resulting from the breach of that duty. (2) Harm suffered voluntarily does not constitute legal injury

FACTS : Hanuman Stores sent certain items in a horse carriage to a customer's house, which happened to be by the side of a main road and near a school zone. The driver of the carriage delivered the items to the customers and went inside the house to collect the receipt, leaving the carriage unattended on the road. Some naughty children of nearby school threw stones at the horses. The horses ran in confusion and they were about to run over an old woman. A traffic police man, at great risk to his life, somehow seized the horses and stopped the carriage. He suffered serious personal injuries in the process. The policeman seeks compensation from Hanuman Stores.

A. Hanuman Stores is not liable, because they do not owe a duty of care to the old woman or policeman.
B. Hanuman Stores is not liable because some naughty children scared away their horses.
C. The policeman cannot succeed, because he suffered injury voluntarily.
D. The policeman can succeed, because he owed a duty of care to old woman.

12. *PRINCIPLES :* (I) An agreement enforceable in a court of law is a contract

(II) In order for an agreement to be enforceable in a court of law, there must be a meeting of minds between both the parties.

(III) Parties to a contract should do something for the other party. The obligation to do something for the other party is mutual. This is called 'consideration' and absence of consideration renders the contract unenforceable.

FACTS : Mohan promised to take Sundar out for a dinner in Chola Sheraton. Even after two weeks, Mohan did not fulfill the promise. Sundar wants to sue Mohan to enforce that promise.

If Sundar goes to court:

A. He can compel Mohan to buy him a dinner at Chola Sheraton.
B. He can recover the value of dinner from Mohan.
C. This promise will not be enforced by a Court of Law as there is no consideration from Sundar.
D. None of the above answers is correct.

13. *PRINCIPLE :* Theft is the dishonest moving of property with the intention of taking if out from the person's possession without his consent.

FACTS : Naman wants to put on Levis jeans and a Monte Carlo sweatner on Christmas Night. But, both the clothes are dirty. He therefore gives them to a dry cleaner for dry cleaning. He is told to collect the clothes after two days from the shop. When he reaches the shop after two days, he finds that he does not have enough money to pay to the dry cleaner. But due to winter he needs the sweatner desperately. So he surreptitiously places the sweatner near his other goods so that he can quickly take it without the knowledge of the dry cleaner.

A. Naman is guilty of theft.
B. Naman is not guilty of theft.
C. Naman is not guilty or theft but he must pay the dry cleaning charges.
D. Naman is partly guilty of theft.

14. *PRINCIPLE :* A careless person becomes liable for his negligence when he owed a duty of care to others.

FACTS : As the bus was leaving the platform, Kashish rushed and boarded the bus keeping the door open. Ashish, who was standing at the edge of the platform, was hit by the door of the moving bus and injured. Ashish claims compensation from Kashish.

A. Kashish is liable to Ashish for not having taken care to close the door of the moving bus.
B. Kashish is not liable to Ashish as it was the duty of the conductor of the bus to close the door.
C. Kashish is not liable to Ashish, as it was the duty of the latter, to take sufficient care, while standing on the platform as not to expose oneself to such accidental harm.
D. None of the above.

15. *PRINCIPLE* : Whoever, dishonestly misappropriates or converts to his own use, any movable property, shall be punished with imprisonment of either description for a term which may extend of two years, or with fine or with both.

FACTS : A lost his brief-case containing valuables. Z, as friend of A informed him that his brief-case was seen lying in J's shop. Thereupon, A reached J's shop and finding his brief-case lying there pulled out his revolver and asked J to hand over the brief-case to him under the fear of injury, J gave the brief-case to A. However, on reaching home he discovered that the brief-case did not belong to him but decide to retain it. Decide.

A. A is guilty of criminal misappropriation only.
B. A is guilty of extortion only.
C. A is guilty of both criminal misappropriation as well as extortion.
D. None of these.

16. Can a child under seven years of age be arrested?
A. Yes
B. No
C. Circumstantial
D. None of the above

17. Sexual intercourse with a girl under... is rape even if she had given her consent.
A. 15 years B. 16 years
C. 17 years D. 18 years

18. 'Homicide' is killing of a human being by another human being. It may be
A. Lawful
B. Unlawful
C. Both A and B
D. Neither A nor B

19. Honest vivex, alterum non Laedere sueem cuique tribuere means 'to live honestly, not to harm another and give every man his due' is a summary of the basic precepts of law coined by .... in A.D. 533:
A. Ulpian B. Blackstone
C. Odepus D. Austin

20. The execution of death sentence can be postponed in case of:
A. Possibility of appeal in the Supreme Court and in case of pregnant woman.
B. Possibility of appeal in the High Court and not in case of pregnant woman.
C. Possibility of continuation in the special court.
D. Possibility of confirmation by the session's court.

21. Secularism means a religion:
A. Non-propagation of religion
B. Propagation of all religion
C. Propagation of atheism
D. None of the above.

22. A person who makes a will is also called a ....
A. Executor B. Beneficiary
C. Writer D. Testator

23. A right enjoyed by an owner of land over adjoining land, of another such as a right of way, of light, of support or of a flow of air or water is called as:
A. Permission
B. Easement
C. Lease
D. Licence

24. The relation between a Turstee and a Beneficiary is also called .... relationship.
A. Friendly
B. Fiduciary
C. Master and Servant
D. Employer and Employee

25. Which country does not have a written constitution?
A. India
B. United Kingdom
C. United States of America
D. Pakistan

26. Resignation of the President of India is addressed to:
A. Vice President of India
B. Prime Minister of India
C. Speaker of Lok Sabha
D. Chief Justice of India

27. 'Rio Declaration' relates to:
A. United Nations Women Convention
B. World Trade Organisation
C. United Nations Human Right
D. International Legal Framework for Bio Diversity and Sustainable Development

28. Democracy does not stand for:
A. Rule of Law
B. Equal Right for all
C. Liberty of the individual
D. Unrestricted freedom of the people

29. Who is the final Sovereign in India?
A. President B. Prime Minister
C. Parliament D. People

30. Panchayati Raj is organized at the:
A. Village level
B. Village and Block levels
C. Village, Block and District levels
D. Village, Block, District and State levels

31. The Union Territories get representation in:
A. Only Lok Sabha
B. Both Lok Sabha and Rajya Sabha
C. Only Rajya Sabha
D. Neither Lok Sabha nor Rajya Sabha

32. Judges of the International Court of Justice are appointed by:
A. General Assembly
B. Security Council
C. General Assembly and the Security Council
D. Permanent Members of the Security Council

33. The Supreme court of India has the power of:
A. Nominal Review
B. Judicial Review
C. Legal Review
D. Political Review

34. Section 361 of Indian Penal Code define:
A. Extortion
B. Kidnapping
C. Abduction
D. Cheating

35. Criminal law is ..... law, while administrative law is .... law.
A. Public, private B. Private, public
C. Public, public D. Private, private

36. Genocide occurred in all but one case:
A. Bosnia B. Nazi German
C. Rwanda D. Gulf War

37. Lokayukta in States investigates:
A. Any action taken by a Minister or a Secretary or any public servant including a public servant notified for the purpose by State Government
B. Any action taken by a Minister or a Secretary or any public servant including a public servant notified for the purpose by Central Government
C. Any action taken by Prime Minister Cabinet Secretary notified for purpose by Supreme Court
D. None of the above

38. In a famous book "The Nuer" a society without law has been described. The regulation of relation is by the institution of 'blood feud'. The author of the book is:
A. Henry Maine
B. Dicey
C. E.E. Evans Pritichard
D. Morgret Mead

39. If the Supreme Court can be asked by the President to give advice on a question of law or fact, under Article 143, the Supreme Court:
A. Is bound to give advice
B. May refuse to give advice
C. May dismiss the Presidential Reference as nonsense.
D. None of the above

40. Dowry Prohibition Act of 1961 prohibits:
A. Giving of dowry either directly or indirectly by a party to marriage
B. Taking of dowry either directly or indirectly by a party to marriage
C. Both giving and taking of dowry either directly or indirectly by a party to marriage
D. None of the above

41. Which writ quashes the order of a lower Court which has been without jurisdiction?
A. Mandamus B. Quo Warranto
C. Prohibition D. Certiorari

42. Central Vigilance Commission is to inquire offences committed by Central Government employees under:
A. Prevention of Corruption Act of 1988
B. Indian Penal Code of 1860
C. Indian Evidence Act of 1872
D. General Clauses Act of 1897

43. Who was the first Chief Justice of independent India?
A. S.R. Das B. M.H. Beg
C. H.J. Kania D. S.M. Sikri

44. The First State in India which was created on linguistic basis:

A. Madhya Pradesh
B. Andhra Pradesh
C. Gujarat
D. Maharashtra

45. A joint sitting of two Houses may be called in all but one situation:
A. When one House rejects a Bill
B. Both Houses disagree on amendments suggested by other
C. When more than 6 months elapse and a House neither passes nor returns a Bill
D. When Rajya Sabha fails to return a Money Bill

46. After 50 years of Constitution coming into force the Government of India set up a National Commission for Review of Working of Constitution under the Chairmanship of a retired Chief Justice of the Supreme Court. The judge is:
A. A.M. Ahmadi
B. Ranganath Mishra
C. M.N. Venkatachaliah
D. J.S. Verma

47. Who was the first Attorney General of India?
A. C.K. Daphtary
B. M.C. Setalvad
C. Nani A. Palkhiwala
D. Niren Dey

48. A wrongful assumption of public office is vacated by writ of:
A. Mandamus
B. Quo Warranto
C. Prohibition
D. Certiorari

49. A command by court asking a public authority to perform in public duty is called the writ of:
A. Mandamus
B. Quo Warranto
C. Prohibition
D. Certiorari

50. The so-called provision in the Central Vigilance Commission Act of 2003 envisages that CBI before conducting an enquiry into an offence committed by officers of the rank of joint secretary or above in any government department or in any public sector undertaking has to take prior approval of:
A. Central Government
B. Concerned State Government
C. Concerned State Vigilance Commission
D. Police Chief of Concerned State.

51. When the two Houses of Parliament differ over a Bill and a joint session of parliament is called, where decision is taken by majority vote. In case of a tie, how is the same resolved?
A. The Bill is shelved for the session for consideration
B. The President can use his discretion
C. The Bill is re-submitted after one month at the joint sitting
D. The Speaker, Lok Sabha can make use of his casting-vote

52. Sometimes back 55 new land reform laws were included in the Ninth Schedule by the:
A. 74th amendment B. 73rd amendment
C. 66th amendment D. 70th amendment

53. How many regional languages are included in the Eighth Schedule of the Constitution?
A. 9 B. 12
C. 15 D. 22

54. The freedom of speech of a member of parliament is:
A. almost absolute
B. subject to normal restrictions
C. similar to that of a citizen
D. none of the above

55. If any Government is defeated on the floor of the Rajya Sabha:
A. Parliament is dissolved
B. The Prime Minister submits his resignations
C. President's rule is imposed
D. Nothing happens

56. The President can spend out of the Contingency Fund of India:
A. with the approval of Parliament
B. with the approval of Public Accounts Committee
C. in case of natural calamities
D. without the approval of Parliament

57. The meetings of Parliament are summoned by:
A. The leaders of respective houses
B. The Speaker in Lok Sabha and Chairman in Rajya Sabha

C. The Prime Minister
D. The President

58. A Select or Joint Committee can be appointed by:
A. The Union Minister for Parliamentary Affairs
B. The Prime Minister
C. The President
D. The Speaker, Lok Sabha

59. Why is the Government of India called "Parliamentary" because:
A. the parliament is a sovereign body
B. the executive is accountable to the legislature
C. the people elect the democratic government
D. none of the above

60. The Public Accounts Committee comprises of:
A. 25 members B. 22 members
C. 12 members D. 24 members

61. The Estimates Committee of Parliament consists of:
A. 40 members elected directly
B. 40 members nominated by the President
C. 40 members appointed by the parliament
D. 30 members elected through the system of proportional representation

62. The President has the discretion in the selection of the Prime Minister, when:
A. no party has clear majority in either house of the parliament
B. no political party has clear majority in the Lok Sabha
C. two different political parties enjoy the majority in two differnt houses
D. none of the above

63. The greatest advantage of the democratic rule is that it:
A. represents the largest number of people
B. regards votes of every person as equal
C. avoids the risk of people being exploited by a reigning government aristocracy
D. none of the above

64. The main objective of the Cultural and Educational right granted to the citizen under the Fundamental Rights is:
A. to help the minorities to conserve their culture
B. to evolve a single integrated Indian culture
C. to preserve the rich cultural heritage of India
D. none of the above

65. A motion for no-confidence can be moved in Lok Sabha if it is supported by atleast:
A. 120 members B. 90 members
C. 60 members D. 50 members

66. The "Vote on Account" is passed by the Lok Sabha to:
A. assert its supremacy over finance matters
B. enable the government to fulfil its financial demands
C. meet the expenditure during the period till the budget is passed
D. meet the expenditure on secret mission

67. The Bharat Ratna and Padam Shri awards have been constituted by the government under:
A. Article 17 B. Article 18
C. Article 22 D. Article 24

68. The mind and ideals of the farmers of the Constitution are reflected in:
A. The Fundamental Duties
B. The Fundamental Rights
C. The Directive Principles of State Policy
D. The Preamble

69. Which of the following is not a standing joint committee of both the houses of parliament
A. Estimates Committee
B. Committee on Officers of Profit
C. Committee on Salaries and Allowances of Members of Parliament
D. Committee on welfare of SCs and STs

70. The value of a vote of a member of Parliament for the election of President is determined by dividing the:
A. Total value of votes of all state legislative assembly members by the elected members of both the houses of parliament
B. Particular state population as per the latest census by the number of members of parliament elected from that state

C. Countries population as per the latest census by the number of the Lok Sabha members
D. Countries population as per the latest census by the total number of members of both the houses of parliament

71. Who presides over the Lok Sabha if neither the Speaker nor the Deputy-Speaker is available?
A. a member of the panel of chairmen announced by the Speaker
B. a member nominated by the President
C. the senior-most member of the house
D. the Union Minister for parliament affairs

72. The Chief of the Lok Sabha Secretariat, the Secretary-General is:
A. elected by the members of the Lok Sabha
B. nominated by the President
C. appointed by the Speaker
D. appointed by the Prime MInister

73. The competent authority to prescribe the conditions for acquiring citizenship is:
A. The Census Commissioner
B. The Chief Election Commissioner
C. The President
D. The Parliament

74. India is a republic because:
A. it's policies are those of Republican
B. it has an elected head of state
C. it is a socialist, secular and democratic country
D. it has a sovereign parliament

75. When for the first time, the President made Proclamation of Emergency under Article 352?
A. in 1962 B. in 1965
C. in 1971 D. in 1975

ANSWERS

1	2	3	4	5	6	7	8	9	10
A	C	A	C	B	A	C	A	A	B
11	**12**	**13**	**14**	**15**	**16**	**17**	**18**	**19**	**20**
C	C	A	A	A	B	B	C	A	A
21	**22**	**23**	**24**	**25**	**26**	**27**	**28**	**29**	**30**
A	A	B	B	B	A	C	D	A	C
31	**32**	**33**	**34**	**35**	**36**	**37**	**38**	**39**	**40**
B	C	B	C	C	D	A	C	B	C
41	**42**	**43**	**44**	**45**	**46**	**47**	**48**	**49**	**50**
A	A	C	B	D	C	B	B	A	A
51	**52**	**53**	**54**	**55**	**56**	**57**	**58**	**59**	**60**
D	C	D	A	D	D	D	D	B	B
61	**62**	**63**	**64**	**65**	**66**	**67**	**68**	**69**	**70**
D	B	C	A	D	C	B	D	A	B
71	**72**	**73**	**74**	**75**					
A	C	D	B	A					

TEST PAPER-V

MULTIPLE CHOICE LEGAL QUESTIONS

1. ***PRINCIPLE :*** Where the owner of a vehicle, being himself in possession and occupation of it, requests or allows another person to drive, the owner is liable as principle for damage caused by the person actually driving.

FACTS : Dr. Ramayya took his car to Dolphin Co. Ltd., a garage which he had been frequenting, for servicing. Since Dolphin Co. Ltd., was out of the way, Dr. Ramayya requested the owner to drop him near a bus terminal so that he may get back to his work. The owner directed a mechanic by name Shankar to drop Dr. Ramayya in the same car which he had brought for servicing and bring the car back. On the way, the car collided with a lorry, due to the negligence of Shankar. The owner of the lorry, James is seeking the legal advice as to the course of the action.

A. Dr. Ramayya is liable, because the car belongs to him and he requested for the assistance of Shankar.

B. Dolphin Co. Ltd., is liable, because Shankar is their driver.

C. Dr. Ramayya is liable, because he could have asked Shankar to drive carefully.

D. Dolphin Co. Ltd., is liable, because, the car is entrusted to their care.

2. ***PRINCIPLES :*** 1. Whoever is under a duty of care to another shall be liable for any injury to the latter directly resulting from the breach of that duty.
2. Harm suffered voluntarily does not constitute legal injury

FACTS : Hanuman Stores sent certain items in a horse carriage to a customer's house, which happened to be by the side of a main road and near a school zone. The driver of the carriage delivered the items to the customers and went inside the house to collect the receipt, leaving the carriage unattended on the road. Some naughty children of nearby school threw stones at the horses. The horses ran in confusion and they were about to run over an old woman. A traffic policeman, at great risk to his life, somehow seized the horses and stopped the carriage. He suffered serious personal injuries in the process. The policeman seeks compensation from Hanuman Stores.

I A. Hanuman Stores is not liable, because they do not owe a duty of care to the old woman or policeman

B. Hanuman Stores is liable, because they owe a duty of care to all the users of the road.

C. Both old woman and policeman could have taken reasonable care to protect themselves.

II A. Hanuman Stores is not liable because some naughty children scared away their horses.

B. The School Management ought to have taken care to discipline the children.

C. The Hanuman Stores is liable because the driver ought to have anticipated the naughty conduct on the part of the children.

III A. The policeman cannot succeed, because he suffered injury voluntarily.

B. The Policemen can succeed, because he owed a duty of care to old woman

C. The old woman was under a duty to take care of herself.

3. ***PRINCIPLES :*** (1) A principal shall be liable for all the acts of his agent done in the course of employment.

(2) A shall be considered as an agent of B, provided that

a. B remunerates A and

b. B has direction and control over what A is doing.

FACTS : The Consolidated Motors was a firm dealing with second hand cars. Suresh came to the office of the firm and offered to sell their cars, provided he would get 8% commission on cars sold by him. The Consolidated Motors agreed to the proposition. One day, Suresh took out a car for the purpose of demonstration to a prospective client and in the course of demonstration, he knocked down Ramesh and injured him. Ramesh is seeking legal remedy. The main issue is whether Suresh is an agent of Consolidated Motors.

A. Suresh is the agent of Consolidated Motors, because he gets remuneration by way of commission.

B. Suresh is not the agent of Consolidated Motors, because the commission is not the same as remuneration

C. Suresh is not the agent of Consolidated Motors because the latter do not have control over his activities.

4. ***PRINCIPLE :*** A master shall be liable for the fraudulent acts committed by his servant in the course of employment

FACTS : Shaila Devi opened a S.B. Account with Oriental Bank, and a cousin of her by name Mohan, who was a clerk in that Bank, helped her to complete the formalities. Subsequently she used to entrust whatever money she was getting to Mohan along with her pass book and Mohan used to return the pass book with relevant entries. One day Shaila Devi discovered that Mohan, instead of crediting the money to her account, had been misappropriating it and the entries in the pass book were made by him without authorization. Shaila Devi seeks compensation from Oriental Bank.

A. Oriental Bank shall be liable because Mohan was acting in the course of employment.

B. Oriental Bank shall not be liable, because Mohan was not acting in the course of employment.

C. Oriental Bank was not liable, because Shaila Devi was negligent.

5. ***PRINCIPLE :*** A master is liable for the acts committed by his servant in the course of employment.

FACTS : Mahesh was a driver working in a company Lipton and Co. One day, the Manager asked him to drop a customer at the airport and get back at the earliest. On his way back from the airport, he happened to see his fiancé Roopa waiting for a bus to go home. He offered to drop her at home which happened to be close to his office. She got into the car and soon thereafter, the car somersaulted due to the negligence of Mahesh. Roopa was thrown out of the car and suffered multiple injuries. She seeks compensation from Lipton and Co.

A. Lipton & Co. shall be liable, because Mahesh was in the course of their employment at the time of accident.

B. Lipton & Co. shall not be liable, Mahesh was not in the course of employment when he took Roopa inside the car.

C. Roopa got into the car at her own risk, and therefore, she cannot sue anybody.

6. ***PRINCIPLES :*** (i) Manufacturer is liable for the latent defects in the goods manufactured by him. (ii) A seller is relived of any liability for the defects in goods sold by him, if the purchaser chooses his goods by trade name and not by relying upon the judgment and skill of the seller.

FACTS : Krishnan went to Rama Stores and asked the shop-keeper to give him a good bread. The shopkeeper replied: "People normally buy Modern Bread from me". Krishnan bought a packet of Modern Bread. It so happened that there was a stone embedded in one of the bread slices and it broke Krishnan's teeth, while eating the bread. Krishnan seeks compensation from Rama Stores and Modern Bread Company.

A. Modern Bread Company alone will be liable.

B. Rama Stores alone will be liable

C. Both Modern Bread Company and Rama Stores will be liable.

D. None of them will be liable, since Krishnan ought to have checked the bread before eating it.

7. ***PRINCIPLE :*** A master will be liable to the act of his servants in the course of employment.

FACTS : Hanuman was a driver employed by Hindustan Petroleum to drive their petrol lorries. He was strictly forbidden from smoking in the course of employment. That warning was printed on the body of the vehicle he was driving. One day when he was transferring petrol from his tank to the underground tank of Maruthi Filling Station, he struck a match to light a cigarette and threw it on the Floor. It caused an explosion damaging the properties of Maruthi Filling Station. Maruthi Filling Station filed a suit against Hindustan Petroleum claiming damages.

A. Hindustan Petroleum will have to pay, because Hanuman struck the match in the course of employment.

B. Hindustan Petroleum will not be liable because he was clearly forbidden from smoking by them.

C. Hindustan Petroleum will not be liable, because Maruthi Filling Station should have prevented him from smoking.

8. *PRINCIPLE :* A master will be liable for the negligent acts of his servant in the course of employment.

FACTS : Samuel was a driver employed by Kohinoor Company to drive their luxury buses during the night. Mohammed has been his assistant over a period of time. One night, when he was driving he felt terribly sleepy and he handed over the steering – wheel to Mohammed and dozed off. The bus hit against a car coming from the opposite side due to the inexperience of Mohammed. The owner of the car filed a suit against Kohinoor.

A. Kohinoor will be liable, because it was improper on the part of Samuel to ask Mohammed to drive.

B. Kohinoor will not be liable to pay, because Samuel was not supposed to ask Mohammed to drive

C. Kohinoor will be liable, because Mohammed was also an employee of Kohinoor.

9. *PRINCIPLE :* A person is guilty of culpable homicide amounting to murder, if the act by which the death is caused is done with the intention of causing death.

FACTS : A was hiding behind a bush to catch some rabbits. B also came to the same place for hunting with his gun. When B noticed some movements near the bush, he thought that it was an animal and fired a shot. A was killed by the shot. The police sought to prosecute B for murder.

A. B would not be liable for murder, because he did not have the intention to kill A

B. B would be liable for murder because he should have taken care to find out the target before shooting.

C. B would not be liable for murder, because it was too much to expect B to identify the target before shooting.

10. *PRINCIPLE :* A person commits cheating, when he fraudulently induces another person to deliver the latter's property to him.

FACTS : A falsely represented to B, a shop-owner that he was an officer from the Sales Tax Department. In the course of going through the vouchers, A expressed his interest to buy, a costly television on installment basis. B readily agreed hoping that he would get a favourable assessment from A regarding his tax liability. A paid the first installment and took the T.V. and disappeared. The police somehow managed to arrest him and sought to prosecute him for cheating.

A. A committed cheating, because he induced B to part with the T.V., posting himself as a sales-tax officer.

B. A committed cheating, because he did not pay the subsequent instalment.

C. A did not commit cheating, because B handed over the T.V. to him in order to get favourable assessment.

11. *PRINCIPLE :* A man would be responsible for all direct consequences of his act, in so far as he could reasonably foresee them as arising from his act.

FACTS : A ship carrying petroleum was moving on the high sea. On a short halt in a port, the master of the ship engaged some stevedors to load some metallic planks onto the ship. While loading the planks, a plank slipped from the hands of stevedor and the spark, emitted thereby, ignited petroleum vapour and caused considerable damage to the goods. The owner of the goods filed a suit against the master of the ship.

A. The master of the ship is not liable, because he was not responsible for the act of stevedor.

B. The master of the ship is liable, because he is responsible for the acts of stevedor since he engaged them.

C. The master is liable, because he should have foreseen the consequences of the stevedor's act.

12. *PRINCIPLE :* A man is guilty of culpable homicide amounting to murder, if the act which the death is caused is done with the intention of causing murder.

FACTS : A is suffering from jaundice and inflammation of the brain and B know this condition very well. Once they had a heated argument on some issue and A slapped B in anger. B lost his self-control and dealt a severe blow on A's head. As a result, A died. The police sought to prosecute B for murder.

A. B was liable for murder, because he knew A's delicate condition

B. B was not liable for murder, because he acted in self defence.

C. B was not liable for murder, because he did not have the intention to kill A

13. ***PRINCIPLE :*** An occupier is liable to a trespasser in respect of some wilful act intended to cause harm or done with reckless disregard.

FACTS : Sakalchand, the owner of a warehouse, got the fence electrified on account of his legitimate fear of dacoity. There was a clear warning about the electrified fencing. There was a playground nearby wherein the children had been playing over a period of time. One day, the cricket ball of the children went into the fence and a child running after the ball touched the fence inadvertently. The child suffered from the shock. The parents of the child filed a suit against Sakalchand.

A. Sakalchand will not be liable, because the child was a trespasser.

B. Sakalchand will not be liable, because his fencing was legitimate

C. Sakalchand will be liable, because he must have taken note of the adjacent playground.

Directions : *In question 14-17, Choose the answer you feel to be correct marking (✓) against correct one. Each question carries one mark.*

14. Corruption persists in India because:

A. Failure of the law enforcement machinery

B. There are no laws to prevent corruption.

C. Corruption is now a socially accepted norm

D. Corruption is inevitable in a democracy

15. Ignorance of law is not excused because:

A. Law is a part of civilized life

B. Knowledge of law gives social strength

C. One can then dictate the terms in life

D. So that one may ignore law.

16. The reason for all young people migrating to other countries is:

A. There is more money to be made in the West

B. India has noting to offer to its young people

C. Western culture is better than Indian culture

D. Western countries offer better opportunities than India

17. How will you eradicate child labour?

A. You will construct more schools and make schooling compulsory

B. You will take school to the door step of children and make schooling compulsory

C. You will adopt policy for eradication of poverty

D. You will take B and C steps

18. Police Chief: 'Police functions invariably infringe the rights of wrong doers and occasionally innocent citizens. But, this is permitted by the law in the interest of law and order and protection of life and property. If they are to be looked at by an independent state agency other than a court, policemen will not be able to perform their duties properly.'

Chief Minister: 'Well, your job is to enforce the law, Powers are given to you for using them to achieve the goals. In the process, if you commit bonafide mistake, do not worry about it, I am here to defend you. Use violence if you have to. Moderate the force that you use. Do not mix up with criminals. Protect life and property of citizens.

From the above conversation one can draw the following conclusion, namely—

A. Chief Minister gave the police license to kill without worrying about consequences.

B. Police Chief wanted to say that human rights protection and law and order are two contradictory things and state can seek only one of the two.

C. Police Chief and Chief Minister are of the view that within the boundaries of law, policemen are free to use force to curb wrongdoing and if harm results, State will not treat it as human rights violations.

D. Police and criminals are united in perpetrating wrong doing and the police advance human rights concerns as a shield to avoid acting against their benefactors, the criminals.

19. The 'Universal Declaration of Human Rights' was adopted by the UN in:
A. 1946 B. 1947
C. 1948 D. 1949

20. Which among the following articles of Constitution of India provides that the Superintendence, direction and the control of elections in India are vested in an independent body called the Election Commission?
A. Article 324 B. Article 368
C. Article 356 D. Article 256

21. In India Right to Property is now a:
A. Legal right
B. Moral right
C. Fundamental right
D. None of these

22. What is true with mistake of law and mistake of fact in committing a criminal offence?
A. Mistake of law is no defence whereas mistake of fact may be treated as defence
B. Mistake of law is a defence whereas mistake of fact is no defence
C. Mistake of fact and mistake of law both are defence
D. Mistake of law and mistake of fact both are not defence

23. Attorney General for India means:
A. Advisor to Central Government and State Governments
B. Supreme judicial authority
C. Topmost Legal Advisor to Central Government
D. Advisor to President of India

24. .... is an inquiry into cause of death
A. Coroneration B. Inquest
C. Investigation D. Cannot say

25. A filed a suit for breach of contract against B. The District Court decided in A's favour. B then appealed to the High Court. The legal terminology for B is appellant, while A would be called
A. Defendant B. Plaintiff
C. Respondent D. Accused

26. A, B and C enter into an agreement to divide amongst themselves gains acquired by fraud or to be acquired by fraud in future. The agreement is:
A. lawful B. Unlawful
C. Immoral D. Adequate

27. Article 40 of the Constitution calling for establishment of village Panchayat has given constitutional status with 73rd Amendment. Now the governance system consists of –
A. Two Tier B. Three Tier
C. Four Tier D. None of the above

28. Preservation of environment is an on going debate. On one hand the traditional environmentalists are in favour of preserving the pristine environment and not to welcome any developmental or industrial activities. On the other hand staunch development lobby believes that only development and industrialization can keep the nation's economy strong. Under these circumstances:
A. India should concentrate on preservation of environment alone
B. India should go all out for industrialization
C. Follow a middle path where developmental activities are managed in such a way that environment is also protected and preserved.
D. Ignore the debate and make a case to case choice

29. The term legislation refers to:
A. making of law of both Central Government or state Government
B. making of law of State Government only
C. making of law of Central Government only
D. making of law by local-self government

30. Court of law means:
A. Institutions wherein disputes are adjudicated and justice is administered
B. Institutions wherein the law is made
C. Institutions wherein law is amended
D. Institutions wherein law is repealed

31. Except in case of court of judicial commissioner the hearing of cases of criminal contempt to be by:

A. Bench of not less than two judges
B. Bench of not less than ten judges
C. Bench of not less than five judges
D. Single judge only

32. Under the Contempt of Courts Act, 1971 the accused may be discharged or punishment may be remitted on:
A. Apology made to the satisfaction of court
B. Apology has no place in the Act
C. Apology that reduces punishment
D. None of the above

33. Contempt of court means:
A. Both civil contempt and criminal contempt
B. Only criminal contempt
C. Only civil contempt
D. None of the above

34. The offence of inciting disaffection, hatred or contempt against government is:
A. Treason B. Sedition
C. Defamation D. Election

35. When a witness repeats 'another person's statement', the evidence is called:
A. Hearsay
B. Heresay
C. Secondary evidence
D. Presumptive evidence

36. The Chief representative of United Kingdom in/and the Chief Representative of a Common Wealth Country is called:
A. Ambassador
B. Charge de' Affairs
C. High Commissioner
D. None of the above

37. High sea is:
A. Sea lying more than 5 km beyond the coast of a country
B. Sea lying beyond a distance of 3 miles from the coast of any country
C. Sea beyond 200 km of a coast of any country
D. Both A & B

38. Bail means a method:
A. to procure the release of a Person from legal custody by undertaking that they shall appear at the trial before judgment
B. to procure permanent release from the suit or case
C. to process the release for a period of 90 days during the trial
D. to process a release from police custody.

39. Methods of pressure group do not include:
A. Collective bargaining
B. Strike
C. Behind the screen method
D. Contesting elections

40. Who among the following is fourth Pillar of Indian Constitution?
A. Comptroller and Auditor General
B. Attorney General
C. Advocate General
D. Lieutenant General

41. A 'History Sheet' is maintained in:
A. The Police Station
B. The Session Court
C. The Office of Police Commissioner
D. None of these

42. When did Constituent Assembly adopt a National Flag?
A. 22nd August, 1947
B. 22nd July, 1947
C. 22nd Setember, 1947
D. 22nd June, 1947

43. The International Court of Justice is situated at:
A. Hague B. New York
C. Washington D. None of these

44. In criminal case the burden of proof is lies upon:
A. Eye witness B. Prosecution
C. Complainant D. None of these

45. The voting right is a:
A. Constitutional right
B. Personal right
C. Fundamental right
D. All of the above

46. Which of the following is known as the Guardian of the Constitution of India?
A. Prime Minister
B. President of India
C. Supreme Court of India
D. Parliament of India

47. What is mean of secularism?
A. Propagation of any one religion

B. Propagation of all religion
C. Non-propagation of any religion
D. None of these

48. The Constitution of India contains:
A. Twelve Schedules
B. Ten Schedules
C. Nine Schedules
D. Fifteen Schedules

49. The meaning of 'Mens rea' is:
A. Criminal Act
B. Civil Wrongful Act
C. Guilty mind
D. Preparation of a crime

50. The Consumer Protection Act is related to:
A. The supplies to Indian Army
B. The supplies to Indian Railway
C. Consumers
D. None of these

51. When for the first time, the President made Promulgation of Emergency on grounds on Internal disturbances?
A. in 1952 B. in 1962
C. in 1975 D. in 1988

52. The Right to Property was removed from the list of Fundamental Rights during the tenure of :
A. Ch. Sharan Singh
B. Smt. Indira Gandhi
C. Shri Lal Bahadur Shastri
D. Shri Morarji Desai

53. Which Lok Sabha enjoyed a term of more than five years:
A. Second Lok Sabha
B. Fifth Lok Sabha
C. Seventh Lok Sabha
D. Ninth Lok Sabha

54. The Proportional Representation System is used in the election of:
A. The Speaker, Lok Sabha
B. The Chairman, Rajya Sabha
C. The President of India
D. The Deputy Speaker, Lok Sabha

55. The salary/emoluments of which one of the following is exempted from Income Tax?
A. The Chief Election Commissioner
B. The Chief Justice of Supreme Court
C. The Chairman, Finance Commission
D. The President

56. For the success of democracy there must be:
A. cent-per-cent literacy in the country
B. corruption-free society
C. devotion for duty among the people
D. the creation of an intelligent educated public

57. The greatest disadvantage of the Parliamentary form of Government in India is that:
A. it is open to the public always
B. elected members are superior to the non-elected ones
C. in practical terms, the executives control the parliament instead of parliament controlling the executives
D. none of the above

58. The final authority to expound the meaning of Indian constitution is:
A. The Parliament
B. The Supreme Court
C. The President
D. The Union Law Minister

59. In the election of the President possible, if one or more state assemblies stand dissolved:
A. Yes
B. No
C. only under very special circumstances
D. none of the above

60. When a member of parliament casts his vote without regard to party affiliation it is called:
A. Cross-Voting
B. Defection
C. Crossing the Floor
D. Free Voting

61. The term "autonomy" means:
A. the power to manage financial matters
B. the power to manage internal matters
C. the power to manage law and order
D. none of the above

62. Which part of the Constitution proclaims India as a secular nation?
A. The Directive Principles of State Policy
B. The Fundamenal Rights
C. The Fundamental Duties
D. The Preamble

63. The report of the Public Accounts Committee of Parliament is submitted to:
A. The Union Finance Minister
B. The Union Minister for Parliamentary Affairs
C. The Speaker, Lok Sabha
D. The President

64. The Committee on Privileges of Lok Sabha is nominated by:
A. The Leader of the House
B. The Prime Minister
C. The Union Minister for Parliamentary Affairs
D. The Speaker, Lok Sabha

65. The Foreign Exchange Regulation Act (FERA) came into force on:
A. January 1, 1971 B. January 1, 1974
C. January 28, 1978 D. January 1, 1975

66. The Maintenance of Internal Security Act (MISA) was passed by the parliament in:
A. May, 1978 B. June, 1975
C. January, 1977 D. January, 1975

67. In voting in parliament; the simple majority is enough to amend:
A. Administration of SCs and STs
B. Provisions relating to citizenship
C. Creation and isolation of a state
D. All the above

68. Time gap between two sessions of Parliament cannot exceed:
A. 3 months B. 1 year
C. 6 months D. no fixed gap

69. The special provision with regard to the state of Jammu and Kashmir is contained in the Constitution in:
A. Part VI B. Part IX
C. Part XI D. Part XXI

70. The Ninth Schedule of the Constitution was:
A. A original part of the Constitution
B. Added by the 42nd amendment
C. Added by the 24th amendment
D. Added by the 1st amendment

71. If the government does not enforce the Directive Principles of State Policy a citizen approaches:
A. The President
B. The Supreme Court
C. The High Court
D. None of the above

72. The President enjoys the discretionary powers with regard to:
A. The appointment of Attorney General
B. The Promulgation of Emergency
C. Imposition of President's rule in a State
D. None of the above

73. The first linguistic state is:
A. Tamil Nadu
B. Kerala
C. Karnataka
D. Andhra Pradesh

74. The government had appointed the first commission in 1948 to examine the case for the reorganization of states on a linguistic basis under the Chairmanship of:
A. Justice Chandrachud
B. Justice S.K. Dhar
C. Justice Mahajan
D. None of the above

75. In 1948 the Indian National Congress appointed the famous JVP committee comprising of Jawaharlal Nehru, Vallabh Bhai Patel and Pattabhi Sitaramayya, 1948 to:
A. Examine the issue of reorganization of states on the basis of religion
B. Examine the issue of reorganization of states on linguistic basis
C. Examine the secular credentials of the country
D. None of the above

ANSWERS

1	2	3	4	5	6	7	8	9	10
A	C	B	A	B	A	A	C	A	A
11	**12**	**13**	**14**	**15**	**16**	**17**	**18**	**19**	**20**
B	A	C	A	A	D	D	C	C	C

21	**22**	**23**	**24**	**25**	**26**	**27**	**28**	**29**	**30**
A	A	C	B	C	B	B	C	A	A
31	**32**	**33**	**34**	**35**	**36**	**37**	**38**	**39**	**40**
A	A	A	A	A	C	C	A	D	A
41	**42**	**43**	**44**	**45**	**46**	**47**	**48**	**49**	**50**
A	A	A	B	A	C	C	A	C	C
51	**52**	**53**	**54**	**55**	**56**	**57**	**58**	**59**	**60**
C	D	B	C	D	D	C	B	A	D
61	**62**	**63**	**64**	**65**	**66**	**67**	**68**	**69**	**70**
B	D	C	D	D	B	D	C	D	D
71	**72**	**73**	**74**	**75**					
D	C	D	B	B					

YOUR SPACE

GENERAL INTELLIGENCE & REASONING

1. LETTER SERIES

In letter series, the letters follow a definite order. The given series of letters can be in natural order or in reverse order or combination of both. The letters may be skipped or repeated or consecutive. The given series may be single or may even comprise of two different series merged at alternate positions. While attempting questions on letter series one should note the pattern of alphabet series.

Alphabets in natural series are :

A B C D E F G H I J K L M N O P Q R S T U V W X Y Z

A ↓ 1st, E ↓ 5th, J ↓ 10th, O ↓ 15th, T ↓ 20th, Y ↓ 25th

Alphabets in reverse series are :

Z Y X W V U T S R Q P O N M L K J I H G F E D C B A

Z ↓ 1st, V ↓ 5th, Q ↓ 10th, L ↓ 15th, G ↓ 20th, B ↓ 25th

Note : On reaching Z, the series restarts from A and on reaching A, it restarts from Z.

EXERCISE

Directions : *In each of the following series determine the order of the letters. Then from the given options select the one which will complete the given series.*

1. B Y C X D W E ?
(*a*) S (*b*) T
(*c*) U (*d*) V

2. B A F E J I P O ? U
(*a*) V (*b*) T
(*c*) S (*d*) Q

3. B A D C ? H G J I
(*a*) EF (*b*) FE
(*c*) FG (*d*) DF

4. ADG, XVT, BEH, WUS, ?
(*a*) VTR (*b*) CFI
(*c*) DFJ (*d*) STU

5. GMSY, IOUA, KQWC, ?
(*a*) MSYE (*b*) NSYE
(*c*) MTYE (*d*) MSYF

6. ADG, GJM, ?, SVY
(*a*) MPS (*b*) MQR
(*c*) MQS (*d*) SPM

7. XYZ, UVW, ?, OPQ
(*a*) RST (*b*) STU
(*c*) QRS (*d*) TUV

8. JOBS, KMEO, LKHK, ?, NGNC
(*a*) MJLH (*b*) LIKG
(*c*) MIKG (*d*) MNGM

9. AZ, GT, MN, ?, YB
(*a*) KF (*b*) TS
(*c*) RX (*d*) SH

10. BMY, DNW, FOU, ?
(*a*) HPT (*b*) HPS
(*c*) HQS (*d*) GPS

11. AZ, CX, EV, ?
(*a*) HU (*b*) GS
(*c*) GT (*d*) HT

12. DMP, FLN, HKL, JJJ, ?
(*a*) MIH (*b*) III
(*c*) LIH (*d*) MII

13. ECA, JHF, OMK, ?, YWU
(*a*) TRP (*b*) LNP
(*c*) QPN (*d*) RPT

14. ABP, CDQ, EFR, ?
(*a*) GHS (*b*) HGS
(*c*) GHR (*d*) GHT

15. BEH, KNQ, TWZ, ?
(*a*) IJL (*b*) BDF
(*c*) CFI (*d*) ADG

EXPLANATORY ANSWERS

1. (*d*) : There are two alternate series.

+1 +1 +1

B Y C X D W E V

−1 −1 −1

Series I : BCDE (natural order)
Series II : YXWV (reverse order)

2. (*a*) : Each vowel (AEIOU) is preceded by the letter that comes next to it in the natural alphabetical series.

B A F E J I P O V U

3. (*b*) : The letters in natural series are divided into sections of two letters each. The letters in each section are written backward.

BA DC FE HG JI

4. (*b*) : There are two alternate series.

ADG XVT BEH WUS CFI

Series I : ADG BEH CFI

+1 +1
+1 +1
+1 +1

Series II : XVT WUS

−1
−1
−1

5. (*a*) : The series is formed by moving each letter two steps forward from one group to the next.

GMSY IOUA KQWC MSYE

+2 +2 +2
+2 +2 +2
+2 +2 +2
+2 +2 +2

(The series restarts from A on reaching Z)

6. (*a*) : In each group of three letters the alphabet is in the succession of +3. The next group begins with the last alphabet of the previous group.

A D G G J M M P S S V Y

+3 +3 +3 +3 +3 +3 +3 +3

7. (*a*) : The alphabet from one group to the next are in recession of −3, *i.e.*,

XYZ UVW RST OPQ

−3 −3 −3
−3 −3 −3
−3 −3 −3

8. (*c*) : The alphabets in each group follow the pattern +1, −2, +3 and −4 respectively from one group to the next group.

JOBS KMEO LKHK MIKG NGNC

+1 +1 +1 +1
−2 −2 −2 −2
+3 +3 +3 +3
−4 −4 −4 −4

9. (*d*) : The letters in one group correspond to the letters in the next group in the manner +6, −6 respectively, *i.e.*,

AZ GT MN SH YB

+6 +6 +6 +6
−6 −6 −6 −6

10. (*b*) : The letters in one group correspond to the letters in the next group in the manner +2, +1, -2 respectively, *i.e.*,

BMY DNW FOU HPS

+2 +2 +2
+1 +1 +1
−2 −2 −2

11. (*c*) : The letters in each group correspond to the letters in the next group in the manner +2, –2 respectively, *i.e.,*

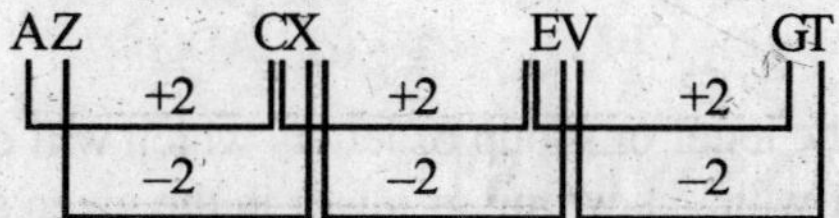

12. (*c*) : The alphabets in each group correspond to the alphabets in the next group in the manner +2, –1, –2 respectively, *i.e.,*

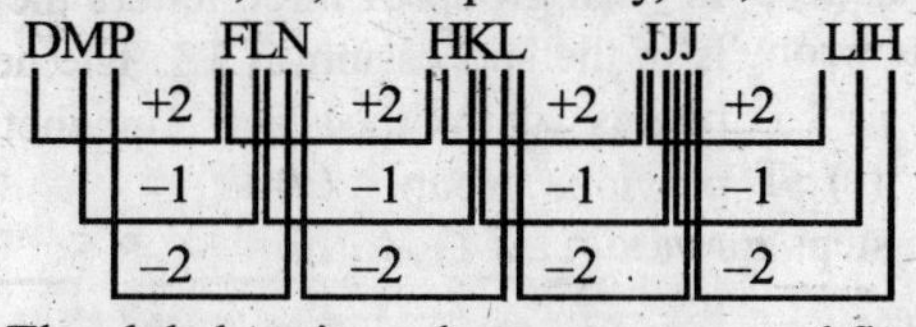

13. (*a*) : The alphabets in each group are moved five steps forward, *i.e.,*

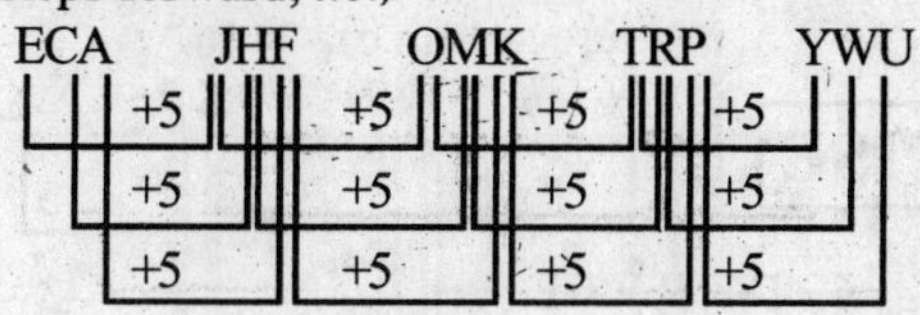

14. (*a*) : The letters in one group correspond to the letters in the next group in the manner +2, +2, +1 respectively, *i.e.,*

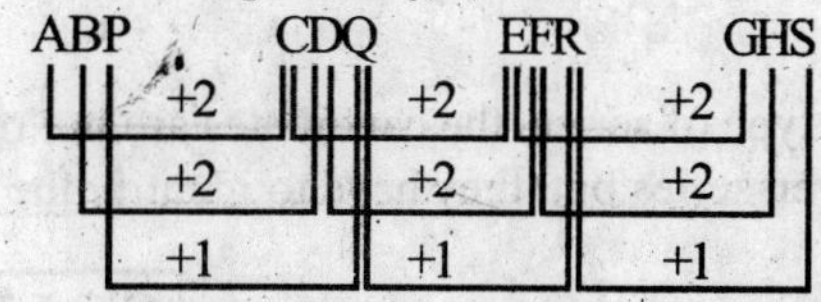

15. (*c*) : All the letters in each group are moved nine steps forward.

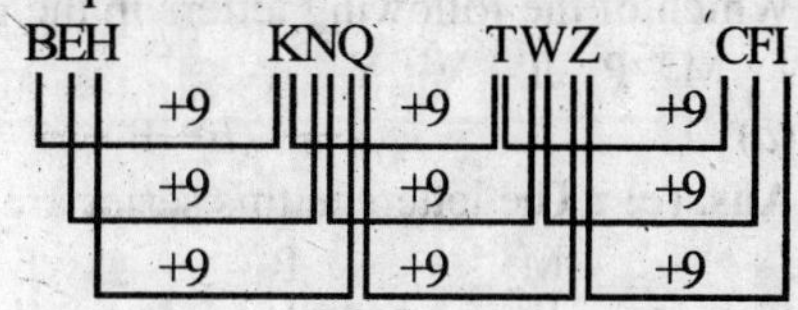

2. WRONG LETTER SERIES

In this type of series, the candidates are not required to find the letter or group of letters which will complete the given series but, they have to identify the letter or number which is wrong or misfit in the given series.

SOLVED EXAMPLE

1. Which of the following letters in the given series is wrong?

J M P T V Y

(*a*) J (*b*) P (*c*) T (*d*) Y

Ans. (*c*) : The letters in this series are moved three steps forward, *i.e.*,

J M P S V Y

+3 +3 +3 +3 +3

Letter 'T' should have been 'S'.

EXERCISE

Directions : *Which letter(s) in each of the following series is wrong or is misfit in the series?*

1. AEHOU

(*a*) U (*b*) O

(*c*) H (*d*) E

2. CHMSWB

(*a*) C (*b*) S

(*c*) B (*d*) W

3. XSNICY

(*a*) Y (*b*) C

(*c*) S (*d*) I

4. ZAWBXC

(*a*) D (*b*) C

(*c*) X (*d*) W

5. MLONQPR

(*a*) R (*b*) O

(*c*) Q (*d*) L

6. DKRYFL

(*a*) L (*b*) D

(*c*) R (*d*) Y

7. LNQTWZCF

(*a*) C (*b*) Q

(*c*) L (*d*) F

8. XW, DC, CB, NM, PQ

(*a*) NM (*b*) CB

(*c*) PQ (*d*) XW

9. BEINSAI

(*a*) A (*b*) E

(*c*) S (*d*) I

10. ZTPKHF

(*a*) Z (*b*) P

(*c*) T (*d*) F

EXPLANATORY ANSWERS

1. (*c*) : The series is made with vowels only. AEIOU. I should be in place of H.

2. (*b*) : The letters in the series are moved five steps forward.

C H M R W B

+5 +5 +5 +5 +5

R should be in place of S

(The series restarts from A on reaching Z)

3. (*b*) : The pattern in the series is –5, *i.e.,*

X S N I D Y

–5 –5 –5 –5 –5

D should be in place of C.

4. (*d*) : There are two alternate series

+1 +1

Z A Y B X C

–1 –1

Series I : ZYX (reverse series)

Series II : ABC (natural series)

Y should be in place of W.

5. (*a*) : Two consecutive letters are written backwards.

ML ON QP SR

S should be in place of R.

6. (*a*) : The pattern in this series in moving the letters seven steps forward.

D K R Y F M

+7 +7 +7 +7 +7

M should be in place of L.

7. (*c*) : The pattern in the series is +3

K N Q T W Z C F

+3 +3 +3 +3 +3 +3 +3

K should be in place of L.

8. (*c*) : The series is made with any two consecutive letters written backwards.

XW DC CB NM QP

← ← ← ← ←

Q should come before P in the series.

9. (*c*) : The difference between the letters is increased by one at each step.

B E I N T A I

+3 +4 +5 +6 +7 +8

T should be in place of S.

10. (*b*) : The difference between the letters is decreased by one at each step.

Z T O K H F

–6 –5 –4 –3 –2

O should be in place of P.

3. REPEAT SERIES

In this type of series, small letters of the alphabet are used to make a set of letters which are repeated. The candidate has to find the set of letters which will fit the blanks left in the given series in such a manner that one section of the series is further repeated in the same manner.

SOLVED EXAMPLE

1. Which of the following groups of letters will complete the given series?
ba-b-aab-a-b
(*a*) baab (*b*) abba (*c*) abaa (*d*) babb
Ans. (*b*) : The series is baab, baab, baab. Here the section 'baab' is repeated in the series.

***Solving steps* :** The candidate has to look for clues to solve such series pattern. 'aab' in the Series indicates that 'b' in this series is preceded by two 'a' so, the first blank and the last blank will be filled by 'a'. Now the first set is formed, *i.e.,* 'baab' in the beginning. This set is repeated, so the second and third blanks will have 'b' filling them. Now, solve the exercise given below to know the different ways in which these series are formed.

EXERCISE

Directions : *Which of the following groups of letters will complete the given series?*

1. ab---b-bbaa-
(*a*) babba (*b*) abaab
(*c*) abbab (*d*) baaab

2. aa-ab--aaa-a
(*a*) baaa (*b*) abab
(*c*) aaab (*d*) aabb

3. -baa-aab-a-a
(*a*) baab (*b*) abab
(*c*) aaba (*d*) aabb

4. -a cca-ccca-acccc-aaa
(*a*) ccaa (*b*) acca
(*c*) caac (*d*) caaa

5. c-bbb--abbbb-abbb-
(*a*) abccb (*b*) bacbb
(*c*) aabcb (*d*) abacb

6. ac-cab-baca-aba-acac
(*a*) bcbb (*b*) aacb
(*c*) babb (*d*) acbc

7. --aba--ba-ab
(*a*) abbab (*b*) bbaba
(*c*) baabb (*d*) abbba

8. --babbba-a--
(*a*) bbaba (*b*) babbb
(*c*) baaab (*d*) ababb

9. k-mk-lmkkl-kk-mk
(*a*) lklm (*b*) lkmk
(*c*) lkmm (*d*) lkml

10. abc-d-bc-d-b-dd
(*a*) decdb (*b*) dadac
(*c*) cdabe (*d*) bacde

11. b-abbc-bbca-bcabb-ab
(*a*) acba (*b*) acaa
(*c*) cacc (*d*) cabc

12. aca-ac--a-ac
(*a*) babc (*b*) aaac
(*c*) cacc (*d*) caca

13. ba-cb-b-bab-?
(*a*) acbb (*b*) bcaa
(*c*) cabb (*d*) bacc

14. ab-aa-caab-aab-a
(*a*) bcbc (*b*) bbca
(*c*) cbcc (*d*) caba

15. -bbcaa-bcaa-bc-a-bca
(*a*) bacab (*b*) abbab
(*c*) abcba (*d*) bcaab

16. a-bccb-ca-cca-baab-c
(*a*) accab (*b*) abcaa
(*c*) bacaa (*d*) ababc

17. b-dabbcd-b-c-ab
(*a*) cabd (*b*) bcad
(*c*) dcba (*d*) acbd

18. a-ba-caacb-bc-
(*a*) acbb (*b*) cbab
(*c*) cbaa (*d*) cbba

19. c-baa-aca-cacab-acac-bca
(*a*) acbaa (*b*) cbaac
(*c*) bccab (*d*) bbcaa

20. -bcc-ac-aabb-ab-cc
(*a*) bacab (*b*) abaca
(*c*) aabca (*d*) bcaca

21. ab-ccca-bccc-bbcc-
(*a*) abbc (*b*) bbac
(*c*) bbca (*d*) cabc

22. -cbc-a-bcaac-ca
(*a*) aaba (*b*) caab
(*c*) bcab (*d*) aacb

23. ab-ba--ba-
(*a*) abba (*b*) baab
(*c*) baba (*d*) abab

24. yx-yx-yxz-xzy-zyxz
(*a*) zzyx (*b*) xxzy
(*c*) yyzx (*d*) yzxz

25. xxxy-y-xxy-yxx-
(*a*) xyxy (*b*) yxyx
(*c*) yyxx (*d*) xxyy

EXPLANATORY ANSWERS

1. (*d*) : The series is abbaab, abbaab.
2. (*c*) : The series is aaaaba, aaaaba.
3. (*b*) : The series is aba, aba, aba, aba.
4. (*d*) : The series is c,a,cc,aa, ccc, aaa, cccc, aaaa.
5. (*a*) : The series is cabbbb, cabbbb, cabbbb.
6. (*b*) : The series is acac, abab, acac, abab, acac.
7. (*a*) : The series is ab, ab, ab, ab, ab, ab.
8. (*b*) : The series is bababb, bababb.
9. (*d*) : The series is klmk, klmk, klmk, klmk.
10. (*b*) : The series is abcdd, abcdd, abcdd.
11. (*d*) : The series is bcab, bcab, bcab, bcab, bcab.
12. (*c*) : The series is ac, ac, ac, ac, ac, ac.
13. (*d*) : The series is babc, babc, babc.
14. (*c*) : The series is abca, abca, abca, abca.
15. (*b*) : The series is abbca, abbca, abbca, abbca.
16. (*d*) : The series is aabcc, bbcaa, ccabb, aabcc.
17. (*a*) : The series is bcdab, bcdab, bcdab.
18. (*c*) : The series is acbabca, acbabca.
19. (*a*) : The series is cabaac, acabca, cabaac, acabca.
20. (*a*) : The series is bbccaa, ccaabb, aabbcc.
21. (*b*) : The series is abbccc abbccc.
22. (*d*) : The series is acbca acbca acbca.
23. (*d*) : The series is ab ab ab ab ab.
24. (*a*) : The series is yxz yxz yxz yxz yxz yxz.
25. (*b*) : The series is xxx yyy xxx yyy xxx.

4. NUMBER SERIES

In this type of series, the set of given numbers in a series are related to one another in a particular pattern or manner. The relationship between the numbers may be (i) consecutive odd/even numbers; (ii) consecutive prime numbers; (iii) squares/cubes of some numbers with/without variation of addition or subtraction of some number; (iv) sum/product/difference of preceding numbers; (v) addition/subtraction/multiplication/division by some number; and (vi) many more combinations of the relationships given above.

EXERCISE

Directions : *In the following questions, select the number(s) from the given options for completing the given series.*

1. 7776, 1296, 216, 36, 6, ?
(*a*) 6 (*b*) 0
(*c*) 3 (*d*) 1

2. 29282, 2662, 242, 22, ?
(*a*) 1 (*b*) 2
(*c*) 0 (*d*) 11

3. 1, 2, 2, 4, 16, ?, 65536
(*a*) 276 (*b*) 64
(*c*) 256 (*d*) 198

4. 3, 5, 9, 15, 23, ?, 45
(*a*) 37 (*b*) 35
(*c*) 31 (*d*) 33

5. 7, 21, 35, 49, 63, ?
(*a*) 70 (*b*) 77
(*c*) 81 (*d*) 108

6. 10, 14, 23, 39, 64, ?, 149
(*a*) 78 (*b*) 128
(*c*) 103 (*d*) 100

7. 6, 24, 29, 116, 121, ?, 489
(*a*) 468 (*b*) 484
(*c*) 243 (*d*) 363

8. 5, 50, 45, 450, 445, ?, 4445
(*a*) 4450 (*b*) 4600
(*c*) 4550 (*d*) 4500

9. 6.25, 9, 12.25, 16, 20.25, 25, 30.25?
(*a*) 36 (*b*) 32
(*c*) 28.25 (*d*) 40.25

10. 243, 5, 81, 15, 27, 45, 9, ?
(*a*) 5 (*b*) 15
(*c*) 135 (*d*) 27

11. 2, 7, 14, 23, ?, 47
(*a*) 31 (*b*) 38
(*c*) 28 (*d*) 34

12. 0, 1, 8, 27, 64, ?
(*a*) 125 (*b*) 128
(*c*) 256 (*d*) 121

13. 37, 47, 58, ?, 79, 95
(*a*) 71 (*b*) 69
(*c*) 68 (*d*) 67

14. 4, –8, 14, –22, 32, ?
(*a*) –44 (*b*) 42
(*c*) –42 (*d*) 44

15. 6, 7, 9, 11, 15, 15, 24, 19, ?
(*a*) 32 (*b*) 34
(*c*) 36 (*d*) 37

EXPLANATORY ANSWERS

1. (*d*) : The numbers in this sequence are divided by 6 each time.

2. (*b*) : The numbers in the series are divided by 11 at each step.

3. (*c*) : The number in the series is product of all the numbers preceding it.

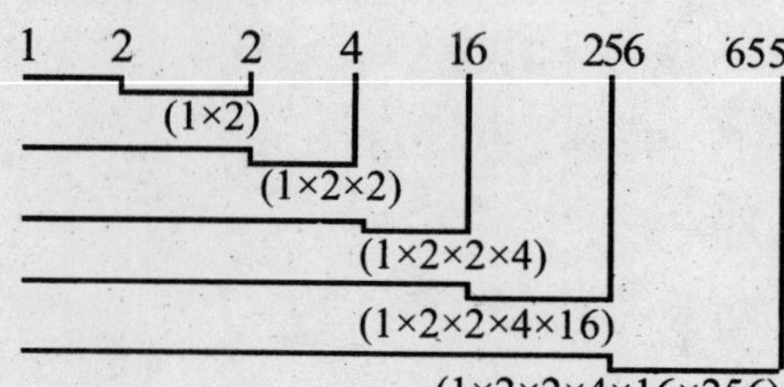

4. *(d)* : The difference between consecutive numbers increases by 2 at each step.

3 5 9 15 23 33 45

+2 +4 +6 +8 +10 +12

5. *(b)* : The series is multiplication of 7 by odd numbers starting from 3.

7 21 35 49 63 77

×3 ×5 ×7 ×9 ×11

6. *(d)* : The number plus the square of numbers in natural order starting from 2 gives the next number in the series.

10 14 23 39 64 100 149

$+2^2$ $+3^2$ $+4^2$ $+5^2$ $+6^2$ $+7^2$

7. *(b)* : The sequence in the series is ×4, +5, which is repeated.

8. *(a)* : The sequence in the series is ×10, –5, which is repeated.

9. *(a)* : There are two alternate series :

+6 +8 +10

6.25 9 12.25 16 20.25 25 30.25 36

+7 +9 +11

Series I : 6,25, 12.25, 20.25, 30.25 (sequence is +6, +8, +10)

Series II : 9, 16, 25, 36 (sequence is +7, +9, +11)

10. *(c)* : There are two alternate series :

÷3 ÷3 ÷3

243 5 81 15 27 45 9 135

×3 ×3 ×3

Series I : 243, 81, 27, 9 (division by 3)

Series II : 5, 15, 45, 135 (multiplication by 3)

11. *(d)* : The difference between two consecutive numbers is increasing by 2 starting from 5.

2 7 14 23 34 47

+5 +7 +9 +11 +13

12. *(a)* : The numbers are cubes of numbers in natural order.

13. *(a)* : The sum of the digits of the number is added to the number to obtain the next number in the series.

37 47 58 71 79 95

+(3+7) +(4+7) +(5+8) +(7+1) +(7+9)

14. *(a)* : Alternate numbers are marked positive and negative, but the difference between their magnitude increases by 2 at each step.

4 –8 14 –22 32 –44

4 6 8 10 12

15. *(c)* : There are two alternate series :

+3 +6 +9 +12

6 7 9 11 15 15 24 19 36

+4 +4 +4

Series I : 6, 9, 15, 24, 36 (sequence is +3, +6, +9, +12)

Series II : 7, 11, 15, 19 (addition of 4 at each step)

5. WRONG NUMBER SERIES

In this type of series, the given series may be complete but what needs to be identified is the number in the given completed series which is disturbing the sequential pattern of that series and does not fit in with the relationship shared between the other numbers.

EXERCISE

Directions : *In the given series find the number which is wrong.*

1. 5, 25, 120, 625, 3125, 15625
(*a*) 15625 (*b*) 625
(*c*) 120 (*d*) 5

2. 4, 8, 11, 22, 18, 36, 24, 50
(*a*) 8 (*b*) 22
(*c*) 36 (*d*) 24

3. 2, 4, 12, 24, 72, 142, 432
(*a*) 432 (*b*) 12
(*c*) 142 (*d*) 72

4. 2, 3, 4, 4, 6, 8, 9, 12, 16
(*a*) 3 (*b*) 9
(*c*) 6 (*d*) 12

5. 97, 91, 86, 83, 79, 77, 76, 76
(*a*) 86 (*b*) 76
(*c*) 91 (*d*) 83

6. 7, 11, 11, 9, 15, 7, 19, 5, 23, 1
(*a*) 5 (*b*) 7
(*c*) 1 (*d*) 9

7. 3, 7, 12, 28, 48, 118, 192, 448
(*a*) 12 (*b*) 118
(*c*) 28 (*d*) 7

8. 10, 100, 1100, 11000, 111000, 1210000
(*a*) 1210000 (*b*) 11000
(*c*) 100 (*d*) 111000

9. 24576, 6144, 1536, 386, 96, 24
(*a*) 386 (*b*) 6144
(*c*) 96 (*d*) 1536

10. 11, 13, 15, 17, 19, 23, 29, 31, 37
(*a*) 13 (*b*) 23
(*c*) 15 (*d*) 31

11. 36, 43, 49, 54, 60, 61, 63, 64
(*a*) 60 (*b*) 63
(*c*) 54 (*d*) 43

12. 3, 10, 41, 206, 1236, 8660
(*a*) 10 (*b*) 41
(*c*) 206 (*d*) 1236

13. 17, 25, 37, 50, 65, 82, 101
(*a*) 25 (*b*) 17
(*c*) 101 (*d*) 65

14. 12, 20, 38, 42, 56, 72
(*a*) 20 (*b*) 38
(*c*) 56 (*d*) 72

15. 5, 6, 11, 22, 42, 88, 176
(*a*) 5 (*b*) 42
(*c*) 176 (*d*) 11

EXPLANATORY ANSWERS

1. (*c*) : The numbers in the series are multiplied by 5 to get the next number.
∴ 125 should be in place of 120.

2. (*d*) : Two numbers form a pair. The first number increases by 7 for the next pair and the second number is the double of first number.

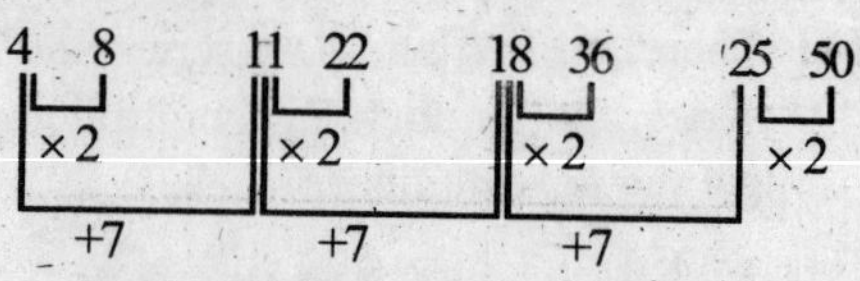

∴ 25 should be in place of 24.

3. (c) : There are two alternate series and in each series, the numbers are multiplied by 6 to get the next number.

$\times 6 \quad \times 6 \quad \times 6$

2 4 12 24 72 144 432

$\times 6 \quad \times 6$

$\therefore$ 144 should be in place of 142.

4. (b) : There are three alternate series and in each series, the numbers are multiplied by 2 to get the next number.

$\times 2 \quad \times 2$

2 3 4 4 6 8 8 12 16

$\times 2 \quad \times 2$

$\times 2 \quad \times 2$

Series I : 2, 4, 8 *Series II* : 3, 6, 12

Series III : 4, 8, 16

$\therefore$ 8 should be in place of 9.

5. (d) : The difference between the consecutive numbers in the series decreases by 1 at each step.

97 91 86 82 79 77 76 76

$-6 \quad -5 \quad -4 \quad -3 \quad -2 \quad -1 \quad -0$

$\therefore$ 82 should be in place of 83.

6. (c) : There are two alternate series :

$+4 \quad +4 \quad +4 \quad +4$

7 11 11 9 15 7 19 5 21 3

$-2 \quad -2 \quad -2 \quad -2$

Series I : 7, 11, 15, 19, 23 (addition of 4)

Series II : 11, 9, 7, 5, 3 (subtraction of 2)

$\therefore$ 3 should be in place of 1.

7. (b) : There are two alternate series and in each series, the numbers are multiplied by 4 to get the next number.

$\times 4 \quad \times 4 \quad \times 4$

3 7 12 28 48 112 192 448

$\times 4 \quad \times 4 \quad \times 4$

$\therefore$ 112 should be in place of 118.

8. (d) : The numbers in this series are multiplied by 10 and 11 alternately is, *i.e.*, $\times 10, \times 11$.

10 100 1100 11000 121000 1210000

$\times 10 \quad \times 11 \quad \times 10 \quad \times 11 \quad \times 10$

$\therefore$ 121000 should be in place of 111000.

9. (a) : The numbers in this series are divided by 4 to get the next number.

24576 6144 1536 384 96 24

$\div 4 \quad \div 4 \quad \div 4 \quad \div 4 \quad \div 4$

$\therefore$ 384 should be in place of 386.

10. (c) : The series comprises of prime numbers in increasing order. Only 15 is an exception.

11. (a) : The difference between two consecutive numbers is decreasing by 1 at each step.

36 43 49 54 58 61 63 64

$+7 \quad +6 \quad +5 \quad +4 \quad +3 \quad +2 \quad +1$

$\therefore$ 58 should be in place of 60.

12. (d) : The sequence followed in this series is :

$3 \times 3 + 1 = 10,\ 10 \times 4 + 1 = 41$

$41 \times 5 + 1 = 206,\ 206 \times 6 + 1 = 1237$; and

$1237 \times 7 + 1 = 8660$

$\therefore$ 1237 should be in place of 1236.

13. (a) : The numbers in the series are 1 plus the squares of numbers in natural order starting from 4.

17 26 37 50 65 82 101

$\downarrow$

$4^2 + 1 \quad 5^2 + 1 \quad 6^2 + 1 \quad 7^2 + 1 \quad 8^2 + 1 \quad 9^2 + 1 \quad 10^2 + 1$

$\therefore$ 26 should be in place of 25.

14. (b) : The sequence followed in this series is :

$3 \times 4 = 12,\ 4 \times 5 = 20,\ 5 \times 6 = 30,$

$6 \times 7 = 42,\ 7 \times 8 = 56,\ 8 \times 9 = 72$

$\therefore$ 30 should be in place of 38.

15. (b) : The numbers in the series are the sum of all the numbers preceding them.

5 6 11 22 44 88 176

$(5+6)$

$(5+6+11)$

$(5+6+11+22)$

$(5+6+11+22+44)$

$(5+6+11+22+44+88)$

$\therefore$ 44 should be in place of 42.

6. WORD ANALOGY

In Analogy Tests, the relationship between two given words is established and then applied to the other words. The type of relationship may vary, so while attempting such questions the first step is to identify the type of relationship, which can be any one of the following.

EXERCISE

Directions : *In the questions given below one term is missing. Based on the relationship of the two given words find the missing term from the given options.*

1. HUNGER : FOOD : : THIRST ?
(*a*) Water (*b*) Drink
(*c*) Tea (*d*) Coffee

2. HUNTER : GUN : : WRITER : ?
(*a*) Book (*b*) Pen
(*c*) Poem (*d*) Page

3. WOOL : SHEEP : : SILK : ?
(*a*) Saree (*b*) String
(*c*) Silkworm (*d*) Moth

4. FOOD : STOMACH : : FUEL : ?
(*a*) Engine (*b*) Automobile
(*c*) Rail (*d*) Aeroplane

5. WATER : SAND : : OCEAN : ?
(*a*) Island (*b*) River
(*c*) Desert (*d*) Waves

6. ADULT : BABY : : FLOWER : ?
(*a*) Seed (*b*) Bud
(*c*) Fruit (*d*) Butterfly

7. WRITER : READER : : PRODUCER : ?
(*a*) Creator (*b*) Contractor
(*c*) Creature (*d*) Consumer

8. ENTRANCE : EXIT : : LOYALTY : ?
(*a*) Treachery (*b*) Patriotism
(*c*) Fidelity (*d*) Reward

9. MOTHER : MATERNAL : : FATHER : ?
(*a*) Eternal (*b*) Detrimental
(*c*) Paternal (*d*) Formidable

10. PEARL : NECKLACE : : FLOWER : ?
(*a*) Plant (*b*) Garden
(*c*) Petal (*d*) Bouquet

11. ALPHABET : WORD : : WORD : ?
(*a*) Sound (*b*) Music
(*c*) Sentence (*d*) Dictionary

12. LIFE : DEATH : : HOPE : ?
(*a*) Cry (*b*) Pain
(*c*) Despair (*d*) Sad

13. GOOD : BAD : : VIRTUE : ?
(*a*) Blame (*b*) Sin
(*c*) Despair (*d*) Vice

14. BIRD : FLY : : SNAKE : ?
(*a*) Timid (*b*) Clatter
(*c*) Crawl (*d*) Hole

15. CAT : MOUSE : : BIRD : ?
(*a*) Cage (*b*) Trap
(*c*) Eagle (*d*) Worm

16. STATE : EXILE
(*a*) Police : Arrest
(*b*) Judge : Convict
(*c*) Constitution : Amendment
(*d*) Church : Excommunicate

17. CAPRICIOUSNESS : RELIABILITY
(*a*) Extemporaneous : Predictability
(*b*) Unreliable : Inhuman
(*c*) Tenacious : Practicality
(*d*) Arbitrary : Whimsical

18. LOATH : COERCION
(*a*) Detest : Caressing
(*b*) Irritate : Caressing
(*c*) Irate : Antagonism
(*d*) Reluctant : Persuasion

19. SCALES : FISH
(*a*) Lady : Dress (*b*) Tree : Leaves
(*c*) Bird : Feather (*d*) Skin : Man

20. TREE : SAPLING
(*a*) Hut : Mansion
(*b*) Giant : Dwarf
(*c*) Horse : Foal
(*d*) Ant : Elephant

21. CHALK : BLACKBOARD
(*a*) Door : Handle
(*b*) Table : Chair
(*c*) Ink : Paper
(*d*) Type : Paint

22. PRIMEVAL : MEDIEVAL
(*a*) Dinosaur : Dragon
(*b*) Gorilla : Soldier
(*c*) Evolution : Revelation
(*d*) Thorn : Rose

23. TRILOGY : NOVEL
(*a*) Rice : Husk
(*b*) Milk : Cream
(*c*) Fabric : Weaving
(*d*) Serial : Episode

24. PEDANT : ERUDITION
(*a*) Prude : Modesty
(*b*) Blunt : Politician
(*c*) Diplomats : Tactless
(*d*) Enemy : Friendly

25. FURY : IRE
(*a*) Convulsion : Spasm
(*b*) Amusement : Happiness
(*c*) Joke : Laugh
(*d*) Dispassion : Emotion

EXPLANATORY ANSWERS

1. *(a)* : Hunger is satiated by food, thirst by water.

2. *(b)* : Weapon of a hunter is a gun, weapon of a writer is a pen.

3. *(c)* : Wool is obtained from sheep, silk is obtained from silkworm.

4. *(a)* : Food is consumed in stomach, fuel is consumed in engine.

5. *(c)* : The related words are near opposites.

6. *(b)* : The youngone of an adult is a baby and that of a flower is a bud.

7. *(d)* : A writer aims to please the readers by his writings, a producer aims to please the consumers by his products.

8. *(a)* : The related words are opposites.

9. *(c)* : Relations on the mother's side are maternal and on the father's side paternal.

10. *(d)* : Many pearls make a necklace, many flowers make a bouquet.

11. *(c)* : More than one alphabet make a word, more than one word make a sentence.

12. *(c)* : The related words are opposites.

13. *(d)* : The related words are opposites.

14. *(c)* : Birds fly, snakes crawl.

15. *(d)* : Cat chases the mouse, bird chases the worm.

16. *(d)* : Punishment of leaving the State is exile, punishment of leaving the Church is excommunication.

17. *(c)* : The related words are antonyms.

18. *(d)* : Loathing is the result of constant coersion, reluctance is the result of constant persuasion.

19. *(d)* : Covering of the fish is scales, covering of man is skin.

20. *(c)* : Young tree is a sapling, young horse is a foal.

21. *(c)* : Chalk is used to write on blackboard, ink is used to write on paper.

22. *(a)* : The related words represent almost the same time period and answer option represents almost the same sized creatures.

23. *(d)* : Trilogy is section of a novel, episode is a section of a serial.

24. *(a)* : The related words are synonyms.

25. *(b)* : Fury causes ire, amusement causes happiness.

7. NUMBER ANALOGY

In number analogy also, the relationship between the given numbers is detected and then applied to the second part to find the missing numbers. This relationship between the numbers can be based on any of the following patterns : *(i)* numbers can be odd/even/prime numbers; *(ii)* numbers can be multiples of one number; *(iii)* numbers can be squares/cubes of different numbers; *(iv)* some numbers can be added to/ subtracted from/multiplied to/divided into the first number to get the second number; *(v)* the second number can be the sum/product/difference of the digits of first number; and *(vi)* combinations of any mathematical calculations given above can apply to the relationship between the two given numbers.

EXERCISE

Directions : *In the following questions, select the number from the given options which follows the same relationship as shared between the first two numbers.*

1. 1 : 11 : : 2 : ?
(*a*) 20 (*b*) 22
(*c*) 24 (*d*) 44

2. $\frac{1}{7}:\frac{1}{14}::\frac{1}{9}:?$
(*a*) $\frac{1}{88}$ (*b*) $\frac{1}{80}$
(*c*) $\frac{1}{81}$ (*d*) $\frac{1}{18}$

3. 0.16 : 0.0016 : : 1.02 : ?
(*a*) 10.20 (*b*) 0.102
(*c*) 0.0102 (*d*) 1.020

4. 663 : 884 : : 221 : ?
(*a*) 332 (*b*) 554
(*c*) 773 (*d*) 442

5. 16 : 0.16 : : ?
(*a*) 2 : 0.02 (*b*) 7 : 0.007
(*c*) 1.3 : 0.13 (*d*) 0.01 : 0.001

6. $3:\frac{1}{3}::?$
(*a*) 6 : 12 (*b*) 5 : 2/15
(*c*) 8 : 1/8 (*d*) 9 : 27

7. 65 : 13 : : 180 : ?
(*a*) 93 (*b*) 36
(*c*) 133 (*d*) 102

8. 125 : 27 : : 343 : ?
(*a*) 729 (*b*) 64
(*c*) 216 (*d*) 512

9. 357 : 73 : : ?
(*a*) 429 : 94
(*b*) 201 : 21
(*c*) 138 : 38
(*d*) 93 : 39

10. 731 : 902 : : 655 : ?
(*a*) 646 (*b*) 800
(*c*) 793 (*d*) 556

11. 162 : 9 : : 310 : ?
(*a*) 33 (*b*) 27
(*c*) 16 (*d*) 4

12. 13 : 17 : : 15 : ?
(*a*) 19 (*b*) 11
(*c*) 21 (*d*) 16

13. 225 : 15 : : 256 : ?
(*a*) 26 (*b*) 16
(*c*) 20 (*d*) 28

14. 46 : 48 : : 54 : ?
(*a*) 59 (*b*) 40
(*c*) 67 (*d*) 62

15. 33 : 36 : : 21 : ?
(*a*) 9 (*b*) 18
(*c*) 25 (*d*) 32

EXPLANATORY ANSWERS

1. (b) : The first number is repeated to obtain the second number.

2. (d) : The first fraction is multiplied by half to obtain the second fraction.

$\frac{1}{7} : \frac{1}{14} :: \frac{1}{9} : \frac{1}{18}$

$\times\frac{1}{2}$ $\quad\times\frac{1}{2}$

3. (c) : The decimals are divided by 100.

0.16 : 0.0016 :: 1.02 : 0.0102

÷ 100 ÷ 100

4. (d) : The digits at tens and hundreds place is same but the digit at the units place is half the other identical digits.

<u>66</u> <u>3</u> : <u>88</u> <u>4</u> :: <u>22</u> <u>1</u> : <u>44</u> <u>2</u>

5. (a) : Of the two related numbers, the second number is the result of first number divided by 100.

16 : 0.16 :: 2 : 0.02

÷ 100 ÷ 100

6. (c) : Of the two related numbers, the second number is the part fraction of the first number, *i.e.* 3 is related to one-third $\left(\frac{1}{3}\right)$. Similarly, 8 will be related to one-eighth $\left(\frac{1}{8}\right)$.

7. (b) : The first number is divided by 5 to get the second number.

65 : 13 :: 180 : 36

÷ 5 ÷ 5

8. (a) : The numbers are cubes of different odd numbers.

125 : 27 :: 343 : 729

↓ ↓ ↓ ↓

5^3 3^3 7^3 9^3

9. (a) : The central digit of the first number is left out and the corner digits written in reverse order to get the second number.

357 : 73 :: 429 : 94

10. (a) : The sum of the digits of both the numbers is same.

$731 : 902 \rightarrow 7+3+1$
$= 9+0+2$ *i.e.* $11 = 11$

$655 : 646 \rightarrow 6+5+5$
$= 6+4+6$ *i.e.* $16 = 16$

11. (d) : The sum of the digits of the first number is the second number.

162 : 9 :: 310 : 4

1 + 6 + 2 3 + 1 + 0

12. (a) : First number plus 4 gives the second number.

13 : 17 :: 15 : 19

+4 +4

13. (b) : The root of first number is the second number.

225 : 15 :: 256 : 16

$\sqrt{225}$ $\sqrt{256}$

14. (b) : The product of the digits of first number is multiplied by 2 to get the second number.

46 : 48 :: 54 : 40

(4 × 6) 2 (5 × 4) 2

15. (a) : The square of the sum of the digits of the first number is the second number.

33 : 36 :: 21 : 9

$(3+3)^2$ $(2+1)^2$

8. ODD ONE OUT

In this type of classification, four words are given out of which three are almost same in matter or meaning and only one word is different from the common three. One has to find out the word which is different from the rest.

EXERCISE

Directions : *In each of the following questions, three words are alike in some manner. Spot the odd one out.*

1. (*a*) Green (*b*) Red (*c*) Colour (*d*) Orange
2. (*a*) Stable (*b*) Hole (*c*) Canoe (*d*) Sty
3. (*a*) Nose (*b*) Eyes (*c*) Skin (*d*) Teeth
4. (*a*) Venus (*b*) Moon (*c*) Pluto (*d*) Mars
5. (*a*) Happy (*b*) Gloomy (*c*) Lively (*d*) Cheerful

Directions : *Three of the following four in each question are alike in a certain way and so form a group. Select the group of letters that does not belong to that group.*

6. (*a*) ACE (*b*) LOR (*c*) GIK (*d*) VXZ
7. (*a*) TSR (*b*) LKJ (*c*) PQO (*d*) HGF
8. (*a*) EF LM (*b*) KJ SR (*c*) XW HG (*d*) ED YX
9. (*a*) JOPK (*b*) BOPC (*c*) QOPR (*d*) TOPS
10. (*a*) DfH (*b*) MoQ (*c*) UwY (*d*) lnO

Directions : *In each of the following questions, there are four options. Three numbers, in these options, are alike in certain manner. Only one number does not fit in. Choose the one which is different from the rest.*

11. (*a*) 1948 (*b*) 2401 (*c*) 966 (*d*) 1449
12. (*a*) 182 (*b*) 169 (*c*) 130 (*d*) 158
13. (*a*) 129 (*b*) 130 (*c*) 131 (*d*) 132
14. (*a*) 3215 (*b*) 9309 (*c*) 4721 (*d*) 2850
15. (*a*) 1776 (*b*) 2364 (*c*) 1976 (*d*) 3776

Directions : *In the following questions select the pair which is different from the other three.*

16. (*a*) Chair - Furniture
    (*b*) Shirt - Garment
    (*c*) Necklace - Jewellery
    (*d*) Bogie - Engine
17. (*a*) Crayon - Paper
    (*b*) Pencil - Lead
    (*c*) Pen - Ink
    (*d*) Brush - Paint
18. (*a*) War - Peace
    (*b*) Real - Natural
    (*c*) Premiere - First
    (*d*) Wrath - Anger
19. (*a*) Finger - Thimble
    (*b*) Head - Cap
    (*c*) Waist - Tiara
    (*d*) Foot - Shoe
20. (*a*) Day - Night
    (*b*) Clever - Foolish
    (*c*) Clear - Blurred
    (*d*) Arrive - Come

Directions : *In the following questions, which of the following pair of letters is different from the other three?*

21. (*a*) FGH - HIJ (*b*) PQR - RST (*c*) MNO - OPQ (*d*) CDE - DEF

22. (*a*) JuM - jUm (*b*) iLo - Ilo (*c*) PSa - psA (*d*) ZeX - zEx

23. (*a*) NQT - JMP (*b*) CFI - RUX (*c*) ADG - FGH (*d*) SVY - ORU

24. (*a*) DXD - XDX (*b*) KUK - UKU (*c*) FHF - EHE (*d*) RSR - SRS

25. (*a*) AYT - BZU (*b*) FNG - EMF (*c*) RWO - QVN (*d*) HJD - GIC

EXPLANATORY ANSWERS

1. (*c*) : All others are types of colour.

2. (*c*) : Canoe is a boat. Others are resting places of birds/animals.

3. (*d*) : All others are sense organs.

4. (*b*) : All others are planets.

5. (*b*) : All others are expressions of joy.

6. (*b*) : The sequence in each group is +2. Only option (*b*) has sequence in +3, *i.e.,*

ABCDE (+2, +2) LMNOPQR (+3, +3)

G H I J K (+2, +2) VWXYZ (+2, +2)

7. (*c*) : The sequence of alphabet in each group is in reverse order. Only option (*c*) has sequence in disturbed order.

8. (*a*) : Two consecutive alphabet in each group are in reverse sequence (–1), *i.e.,*

KJ SR ; XW HG ; ED YX (–1 –1 –1 –1 –1 –1)

Only in option (*a*) the sequence is in natural order (+1), *i.e.,*

E F (+1) L M (+1)

9. (*d*) : In each group, letters 'OP' are common. The two corner alphabet are in natural order (+1); *i.e.,*

JOPK (+1) ; BOPC (+1) ; QOPR (+1)

Only in option (*d*) they are in reverse order (–1); *i.e.,*

TOPS (–1)

10. (*d*) : In other groups, only the alphabet in the centre is of lower case. In this option letter 'L' on the left is also in lower case.

11. (*a*) : Other numbers are divisible by 7.

12. (*d*) : Other numbers are multiples of 13.

13. (*c*) : 131 is a prime number.

14. (*b*) : In other numbers, no digit is repeated.

15. (*b*) : In other numbers, the last two digits are same.

16. (*d*) : Bogie is a part of train which is a type of conveyance. Chair, Shirt and Necklace are types of furniture, garment and jewellery respectively.

17. (*a*) : The medium used for writing with pencil is lead, with pen it is ink and with brush, it is paint. With crayon it should be wax.

18. (*a*) : The pair of words are opposite. Other pairs are synonyms.

19. (*c*) : Tiara is worn on the head.

20. (*d*) : Other words are opposite to each other.

21. (*d*) : In all other groups, the letters are in natural series and the last letter of first part is the first letter of the second part.

22. (*b*) : In all other groups, only the vowel is in lower case in the first part and in second part the case is reversed.

23. (*c*) : In all other groups, the letters jump two letters in between them.

24. (*c*) : In all other groups, the single letter in first part is repeated in the second and vice versa.

25. (*a*) : In all other groups, the letters in the first part are one step forward than the corresponding letters in the second part.

9. CODING AND DECODING

Coding is a secretive language which is used to change the representation of the actual term/word/value. This coded language can be framed by *(i)* moving the letters one or more steps forward or backward; *(ii)* substituting numbers for letters and vice–versa; *(iii)* writing the letters of the given word in reverse order in part or in whole; and *(iv)* replacing the letters in their natural series by the same positioned letters in their reverse series.

There is variety in ways of coding. Coding language is not only for words and numbers but also for hiding a group of words, statements or even sentences. This form of coding pattern may appear to be confusing but after solving only a few questions it is very easy to understand. Questions based on this coding pattern require no moving of steps or straining efforts of calculations, but only quick tallying or comparing ability. The codes can be letters or numbers.

EXERCISE

Directions : *In the following questions select the right option which indicates the correct code for the word or letter given in the question.*

1. If MUSK is coded as 146816, then ZERO will be coded as :

(*a*) 113811 (*b*) 122912
(*c*) 15915 (*d*) 2651815

2. If BAD is coded as 7, HIS as 9, LOW will be coded as :

(*a*) 50 (*b*) 8
(*c*) 23 (*d*) 5

In a certain code LIBERATE is written as 56403170, TRIBAL will be written in the same code as :

(*a*) 734615 (*b*) 736415
(*c*) 136475 (*d*) 034615

4. In certain military code, SYSTEM is written as SYSMET, and NEARER as AENRER, what will be the code for FRACTION?

(*a*) CRAFNOIT (*b*) FRCAITNO
(*c*) CARFNOIT (*d*) FRACNOIT

5. If CRUDE is written as BSTED, then MOIST will be coded as :

(*a*) NNJRU (*b*) LNHRS
(*c*) NPJTU (*d*) LPHTS

6. In a certain code ALPACA is written as ACAPLA. How will ANIMAL be written in that code?

(*a*) LAMINA (*b*) ALAMIN
(*c*) LAMNIA (*d*) AAMLIN

7. In a certain code FINGER is written as DGLECP. What will be the code for KIDNEY?

(*a*) IGBLCW (*b*) IGCLBW
(*c*) IBCGLE (*d*) IGBKCV

8. In a certain code QUESTION is written as NXBVQLLQ. How will REPLY be coded?

(*a*) YHMOV (*b*) OBMVI
(*c*) VHSOB (*d*) OHMOV

9. If in a certain code SKEW is coded as PNCY, then what will JXQV will stand for?

(*a*) MUTS (*b*) MUST
(*c*) MTSU (*d*) STUM

10. In a certain code LONDON is written as MPOEPO. What will IVOHSZ mean in the same code?

(*a*) HUNGRY (*b*) HUNDRY
(*c*) GRUNHY (*d*) HONDUS

11. In a certain code language 8514 is a code for HEAD, 3945 for RIDE and 057 for BEG. What will be the code for GRADE?

(*a*) 71345 (*b*) 73415
(*c*) 74135 (*d*) 73145

12. If MOTHERLAND is coded as 9501623748, how will DREAM be coded?
(*a*) 82697 (*b*) 86297
(*c*) 82769 (*d*) 82679

13. If OATH is coded in a certain language as TEYL, then how will WORD be coded?
(*a*) BWRH (*b*) HRWB
(*c*) BSWH (*d*) CSXI

14. If FINANCE is coded as GKQESIL, then how will BANK be coded in the same manner?
(*a*) CBOL (*b*) CDRP
(*c*) CCQO (*d*) CCPN

15. PLANNING is coded in a certain language as UFFHSCSA. How will AUTHORITY be coded in the same language?
(*a*) FOYBTLNND
(*b*) FYOTBNNLT
(*c*) FBOYTLNTN
(*d*) FBOYTNLTN

EXPLANATORY ANSWERS

1. (*b*) : The coded number signifies the position of the alphabet in its reverse order of the alphabetical series (ZYXW...)

M U S K –> MUSK
↓ ↓ ↓ ↓
14th 6th 8th 16th → 146816

Similarly,

Z E R O → ZERO
↓ ↓ ↓ ↓
1st 22nd 9th 12th → 122912

2. (*d*) : The coded number is the sum of number digits signifying the position of the alphabet in the natural order.

B A D
↓ ↓ ↓
2nd 1st 4th *i.e.*, 2 + 1 + 4 = 7

Similarly,

H I S
↓ ↓ ↓
8th 9th 19th *i.e.*, 8 + 9 + 19 = 36
further, 3 + 6 = 9

Also,

L O W
↓ ↓ ↓
12th 15th 23rd *i.e.*, 12 + 15 + 23 = 50
further, 5 + 0 = 0

3. (*b*) : The letters of the word TRIBAL are picked from LIBERATE. So will be the coded numbers.

L I B E R A T E → given word
5 6 4 0 3 1 7 0 → codes

Similarly,

T R I B A L → word to be coded
7 3 6 4 1 5 → answer codes

4. (*c*) : The word is divided into two equal parts and the letters of each part are written in reverse order.

SYS TEM SYS MET NEA RER AEN RER

Similarly,

FRAC TION CARF NOIT

5. (*d*) : The code is formed by moving the letters one step backwards and one step forward alternately.

CRUDE BSTED
–1
+1
–1
+1
–1

Similarly,

MOIST LPHTS
–1
+1
–1
+1
–1

6. (*a*) : The letters of the word are written backwards.

ALPACA ACAPLA

Similarly,

ANIMAL LAMINA

7. *(a)* : The word is coded by moving the letters two steps backwards.

FINGER DGLECP

−2
−2
−2
−2
−2
−2

Similarly,

KIDNEY IGBLCW

−2
−2
−2
−2
−2
−2

8. *(d)* : The letters of the word are coded by moving three steps backward and three steps forward alternately.

QUESTION NXBVQLLQ

−3
+3
−3
+3
−3
+3
−3
+3

Similarly,

REPLY OHMOV

−3
+3
−3
+3
−3

9. *(b)* : The letters are decoded by moving the letters +3, −3, +2 and −2 steps respectively.

PNCY SKEW

+3
−3
+2
−2

Similarly,

JXQV MUST

+3
−3
+2
−2

10. *(a)* : The letters of the coded word are moved one step backward.

MPOEPO LONDON

−1
−1
−1
−1
−1
−1

Similarly,

IVOHSZ HUNGRY

−1
−1
−1
−1
−1
−1

11. *(d)* : The word GRADE is framed by letters in the given words. So, in order to find the code for GRADE select the respective number codes.

H E A D R I D E B E G → letters
8 5 1 4 3 9 4 5 0 5 7 → codes

So,

G R A D E → letters
7 3 1 4 5 → answer codes

12. *(d)* : The letters of the word are coded by numbers. So to find the code for DREAM select the respective numbers.

M O T H E R L A N D → letters
9 5 0 1 6 2 3 7 4 8 → codes

So, D R E A M → letters
8 2 6 7 9 → answer codes

13. *(c)* : The letters are coded by moving five and four steps forward alternately.

OATH TEYL
+5
+4
+5
+4

Similarly,

WORD BSWH
+5
+4
+5
+4

14. *(c)* : The letters of the word are coded by moving one step ahead and increasing the difference by one.

FINANCE GKQESIL
+1
+2
+3
+4
+5
+6
+7

Similarly,

BANK CCQO
+1
+2
+3
+4

15. *(a)* : The letters of the word are coded by moving five steps forward and six steps backward alternately.

PLANNING UFFHSCSA
+5
−6
+5
−6
+5
−6
+5
−6

Similarly,

AUTHORITY FOYBTLNND
+5
−6
+5
−6
+5
−6
+5
−6
+5

10. STATEMENT ANALYSIS

In these type of questions, a few statements are given. Certain facts are broken up and mentioned in these statements. What is required is to analyse the statements, arrange and sort out the given facts and then answer the questions related to the given statements.

EXERCISE

1. Among five friends, A is heavier than B; C is lighter than D; B is lighter than D but heavier than E. Who among them is the heaviest?

(*a*) B (*b*) C
(*c*) A (*d*) Can't say

2. Pune is bigger than Jhansi, Sitapur is bigger than Chittor. Raigarh is not as big as Jhansi, but is bigger than Sitapur. Chittor is not as big as Sitapur. Which is the smallest?

(*a*) Jhansi (*b*) Pune
(*c*) Chittor (*d*) Sitapur

3. Ajay works more than Ram. Alok works as much as Raju. Pankaj works less than Alok. Ram works more than Alok. Who works the most of all?

(*a*) Ajay (*b*) Ram
(*c*) Alok (*d*) Raju

4. Among five friends P, Q, R, S and T, who is the youngest? To arrive at the answer which of the following information given in the statements (A) and (B) is sufficient?

(A) R is younger than P and T.
(B) S is younger than Q.

(*a*) Only A alone is sufficient
(*b*) Either A or B is sufficient
(*c*) Both A and B together are needed
(*d*) Both A and B together are not sufficient

5. A is elder to B while C and D are elder to E who lies between A and B. If C be elder to B, which one of the following statements is necessarily true?

(*a*) E is elder to B
(*b*) A is elder to C
(*c*) C is elder to D
(*d*) D is elder to C

6. Suresh is as much older than Kamal as he is younger than Prabodh. Navin is as old as Kamal. Which of the following statements is wrong?

(*a*) Suresh is older than Navin
(*b*) Kamal is younger than Suresh
(*c*) Prabodh is not the oldest
(*d*) Navin is younger than Prabodh

Directions (Qs. 7 to 9) : *Ram, Sohan and Mohan play football, hockey and cricket. Ram, Ramesh and Mohan play hockey, cricket and basketball. Ram, Sohan, Rahim and Mohan play football and cricket. Now answer the following questions based on the above statements :*

7. Which game is played by all the boys?

(*a*) Football (*b*) Hockey
(*c*) Cricket (*d*) Basketball

8. Which two boys play all the games?

(*a*) Ram, Sohan (*b*) Ram, Ramesh
(*c*) Sohan, Mohan (*d*) Ram, Mohan

9. Who does not play football?

(*a*) Ramesh (*b*) Sohan
(*c*) Rahim (*d*) Mohan

Directions (Qs. 10 to 12) : *Read the following directions and answer the questions given below :*

There are five persons in a group. Out of these two are men. Only three persons know swimming, of which one is a man. There is a couple, of which the husband knows swimming. A is the younger sister of D and B is the husband of E. C is a swimming champion.

10. Who is the other man in the group?
(*a*) C (*b*) B
(*c*) A (*d*) D

11. The two women who know how to swim are:
(*a*) A and C (*b*) C and D
(*c*) D and E (*d*) A and E

12. The two persons who do not know how to swim are :
(*a*) B and D (*b*) D and E
(*c*) A and E (*d*) A and D

Directions (Qs. 13 to 15) : *Read the following statements and answer the questions given below :*

Rajat, Sushil and Nagesh play football, hockey and cricket. Rajat, Ramu and Nagesh play hockey, cricket and basketball. Rajat, Sushil, Mayank and Nagesh play football and cricket.

13. Which game is played by all the boys?
(*a*) Hockey (*b*) Basketball
(*c*) Football (*d*) Cricket

14. Who does not play football?
(*a*) Rajat (*b*) Nagesh
(*c*) Sushil (*d*) Ramu

15. Which of the following two boys play all the games?
(*a*) Nagesh, Rajat (*b*) Mayank, Ramu
(*c*) Ramu, Nagesh (*d*) Sushil, Mayank

EXPLANATORY ANSWERS

1. (*d*) : The five friends in descending order of weight are : A/D, B/C, E or A/D, B, C/E. Either A or D is the heaviest.

2. (*c*) : The order of cities in descending order of size is : Pune, Jhansi, Raigarh, Sitapur, Chittor.

3. (*a*) : On the basis of doing work, the descending order will be : Ajay, Ram, Alok/Raju, Pankaj.

4. (*d*) : Statements are not inter-related.

5. (*a*) : The order in descending seniority will be : A/C/D, E, B.

6. (*c*) : On the basis of age the descending order will be : Prabodh, Suresh, Kamal/Navin.

Chart for Answers 7 to 9

Boy	*Games Played*
Ram	Football, Hocky, Cricket, Basketball
Sohan	Football, Hockey, Cricket
Mohan	Football, Hockey, Cricket, Basketball
Ramesh	Hockey, Cricket, Basketball
Rahim	Football, Cricket.

7. (*c*) **8. (*d*)** **9. (*a*)**

For Answers 10 to 12 the information chart will be :

A. Woman ((younger sister of D); knows swimming.
B. Man (husband of E); knows swimming
C. Woman; Swimming champion
D. Man (brother of A)
E. Woman (wife of B)

From the couple B & E, B (husband) knows swimming. C is a swimming champion. Three persons know how to swim of which only B is a man. So, the two women who know how to swim are C and A (the younger sister of D). There are two men in the group of five. One is B and the other will be D.

10. (*d*) **11. (*a*)** **12. (*b*)**

Chart for Answers 13 to 15

Boy	*Games Played*
Rajat	— Football, Hockey, Cricket, Basketball
Sushil	— Football, Hockey, Cricket, Basketball
Nagesh	— Football, Hockey, Cricket, Basketball
Ramu	— Hockey, Cricket, Basketball
Mayank	— Football, Cricket

13. (*d*) **14. (*d*)** **15. (*a*)**

11. PLACE ARRANGEMENT

Place arrangement generally refers to the positioning of persons or objects in a manner indicated by set of information given. One has to understand the order of placement and then attempt questions following the given information.

EXERCISE

Directions : *In the following questions, understand the arrangement pattern and then select the right answer from the given options :*

1. Five boys are sitting in a row. Raghu is not adjacent to Shyam or Amit. Ajay is not adjacent to Shyam. Raghu is adjacent to Mayank. If Mayank is at the middle in the row, then Ajay is adjacent to whom out of the following?

(*a*) Amit (*b*) Raghu
(*c*) Mayank (*d*) Shyam

2. Mini is to the right of Rajni but to the left of Ananta. Saya is to the right of Mini but to the left of Jaya. Who is on the extreme left if all the girls are facing North?

(*a*) Jaya (*b*) Mini
(*c*) Rajni (*d*) Saya

3. O, P, Q, R, S and T are standing on a bench according to their height. P is taller than O but shorter than S. Only S is taller than T. R is shorter than P but taller than Q. Who is the shortest?

(*a*) O (*b*) Q
(*c*) P (*d*) Cannot be said

4. Five personalities are living in a multistoried building. Mr. Effortless lives in a flat above Mr. Active, Mr. Charge lives in a flat below Mr. Diligent, Mr. Active lives in a flat above Mr. Diligent and Mr. Behaved lives in a flat below Mr. Charge. Who lives in the topmost flat?

(*a*) Mr. Charge (*b*) Mr. Diligent
(*c*) Mr. Effortless (*d*) Mr. Behaved

5. Six friends are sitting in a circle and playing cards. Kenny is to the left of Danny. Michael is in-between Bob and John. Roger is in between Kenny and Bob. Who is sitting to the right of Michael?

(*a*) Danny (*b*) John
(*c*) Kenny (*d*) Bob

6. Four girls A, B, C and D are sitting in a circle. B and C are facing each other. Which of the following is definitely true?

(*a*) A is to the left of C
(*b*) D is to the left of C
(*c*) A and D are facing each other
(*d*) A is not between B and C

7. Brijesh, Jayesh, Amar and Praveer are playing a game of cards. Amar is to the right of Jayesh who is to the right of Brijesh. Who is to the right of Amar?

(*a*) Brijesh
(*b*) Praveer
(*c*) Brijesh or Praveer
(*d*) Jayesh

8. In a pile of 10 books there are 3 of History, 3 of Hindi, 2 of Maths, and 2 of English. Taking from above there is an English book between a History and Maths book, a History book between a Maths and an English book, a Hindi book between an English and a Maths book, a Maths book between two Hindi books, and two Hindi books between a Maths and a History book. Book of which subject is at the sixth position from the top?

(*a*) English (*b*) Hindi
(*c*) History (*d*) Maths

9. Five persons A, B, C, D and E are sitting in a row facing you such that D is on the left of C and B is on the right of E. A is on the right of C and B is on the left of D. If E occupies a corner position, then who is sitting in the centre?

(*a*) A (*b*) B
(*c*) C (*d*) D

10. Six friends A, B, C, D, E and F are standing in a circle. B is between F and C; A is between E and D; F is to the left of D. Who is between A and F?

(*a*) C (*b*) B
(*c*) D (*d*) E

EXPLANATORY ANSWERS

1. *(b)* : The order of sitting is :
Amit, Shyam, Mayank, Ajay, Raghu
or
Ajay, Raghu, Mayank, Amit, Shyam

2. *(c)* : The order in which the girls are positioned is :
Rajni, Mini, Ananta, Saya, Jaya
or
Saya, Jaya, Ananta
or
Saya, Ananta, Jaya

3. *(d)* : In descending order of height, the standing positions are :

S		S
T		T
P	*or*	P
R		R
O		Q
Q		O

Either O or Q is the shortest. The informa-tion given is not enough to clarify the answer.

4. *(c)* : The personalities living in flats in multi-storied building are in order given below :
Mr. Effortless
Mr. Active
Mr. Diligent
Mr. Charge
Mr. Behaved

5. *(d)* : The order in which the friends are sitting is :

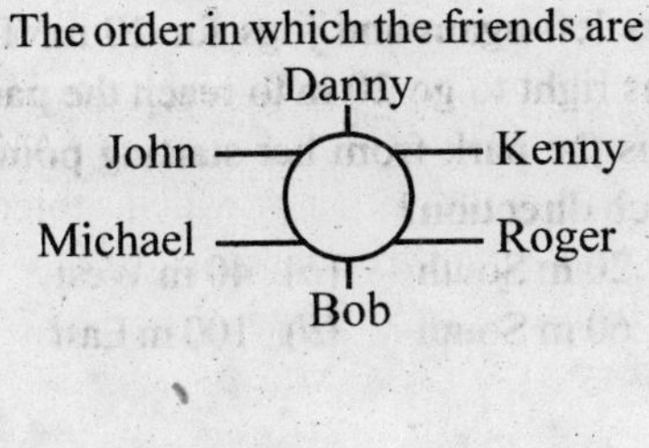

6. *(c)* : The sitting positions are :

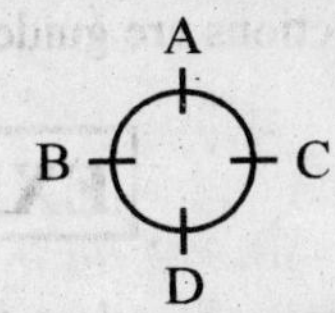

or

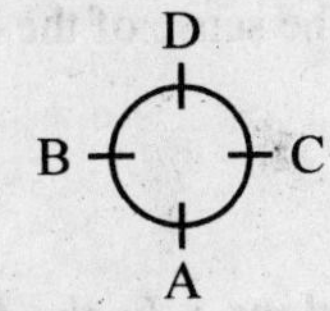

7. *(b)* : The order from left to right is :
Brijesh, Jayesh, Amar, Praveer

8. *(b)* : The pile of books is in the order :

1st — History
English
Maths
History
English
6th — Hindi
Maths
Hindi
Hindi
10th — History

9. *(d)* : Sitting order while facing us is :
A, C, D, B, E

10. *(c)* : The pattern of standing is :

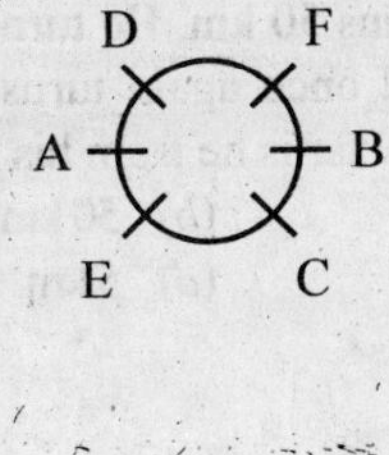

12. DIRECTION SENSE

In these type of tests, the directions in questions needs to be perceived. Such questions are based on the direction chart.

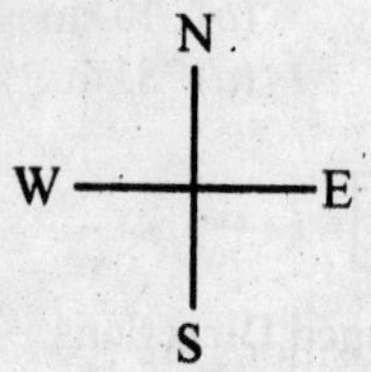

N = North S = South E = East W = West

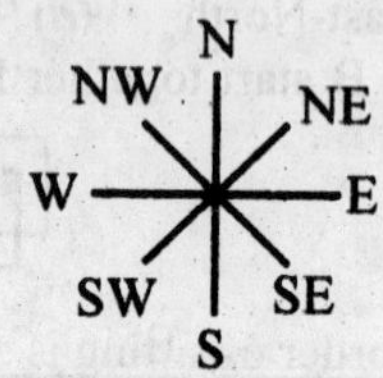

The sense of the different directions are guided by the left and right turns or angular turns.

EXERCISE

Directions : *In the following questions, select the right answer from the given options to depict the correct direction/distance.*

1. Kittu walks towards East and then towards South. After walking some distance he turns towards West and then turns to his left. In which direction is he walking now?
   (*a*) North (*b*) South
   (*c*) East (*d*) West
2. A person is driving towards West. What sequence of directions should he follow so that he is driving towards South?
   (*a*) left, right, right
   (*b*) right, right, left
   (*c*) left, left, left
   (*d*) right, right, right
3. Richa drives 8 km to the South, turns left and drives 5 km. Again, she turns left and drives 8 km. How far is she from her starting point?
   (*a*) 3 km (*b*) 5 km
   (*c*) 8 km (*d*) 13 km
4. Dingi runs 40 km towards North then turns right and runs 50 km. He turns right and runs 30 km, and once again turns right and runs 50 km. How far is he from his starting point?
   (*a*) 90 km (*b*) 50 km
   (*c*) 10 km (*d*) 5 km
5. If North is called North-West, North-West is called West, West is called South-West and so on. What will South-East be called?
   (*a*) East (*b*) West
   (*c*) North-East (*d*) South-East
6. A man travels 100 km towards South. From there he turns right and travels 100 km and again turns right to travel 50 km. Which direction is he in from his starting point?
   (*a*) North (*b*) North-East
   (*c*) East (*d*) South-West
7. A train runs 120 km in West direction, 30 km in South direction and then 80 km in east direction before reaching the station. In which direction is the station from the train's starting point?
   (*a*) South-West (*b*) North-West
   (*c*) South-East (*d*) South
8. Facing the West direction, Priya jogs for 20 m, turns left and goes further 40 m. She turns left again and jogs for 20 m. Then she turns right to go 20 m to reach the park. How far is the park from her starting point and in which direction?
   (*a*) 20 m South (*b*) 40 m West
   (*c*) 60 m South (*d*) 100 m East

9. If all the directions are rotated, *i.e.*, if North is changed to West and East to North and so on, then what will come in place of North-West?

(*a*) South-West (*b*) North-East

(*c*) East-North (*d*) East-West

10. A and B start together from one point. They walk 10 km towards North. A turns left and covers 5 km whereas B turns right and covers 3 km. A turns left again and covers 15 km whereas B turns right and covers his 15 km. How far is A from B?

(*a*) 18 km (*b*) 10 km

(*c*) 5 km (*d*) 8 km

EXPLANATORY ANSWERS

1. (*b*) :

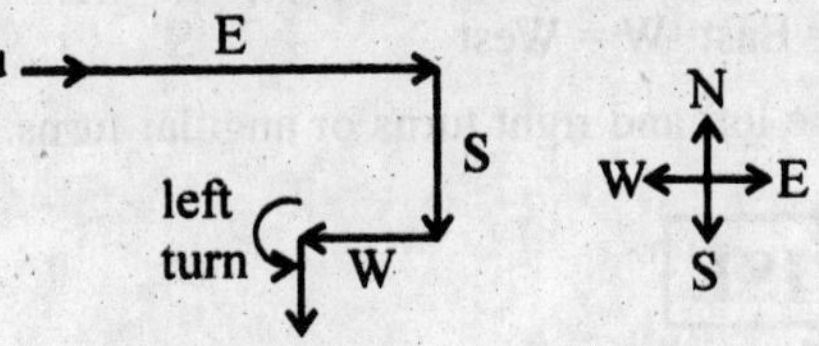

2. (*d*) :

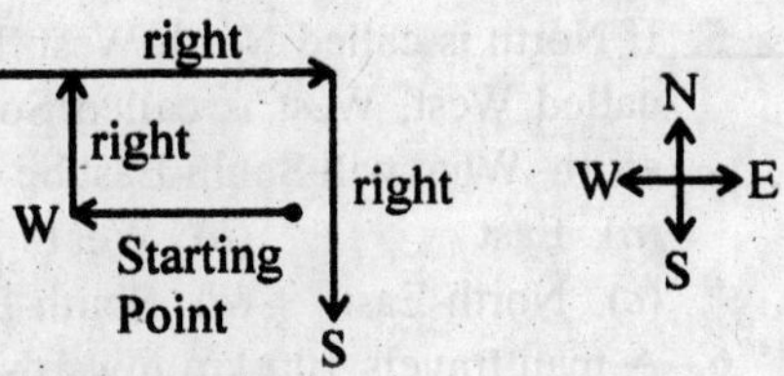

3. (*b*) :

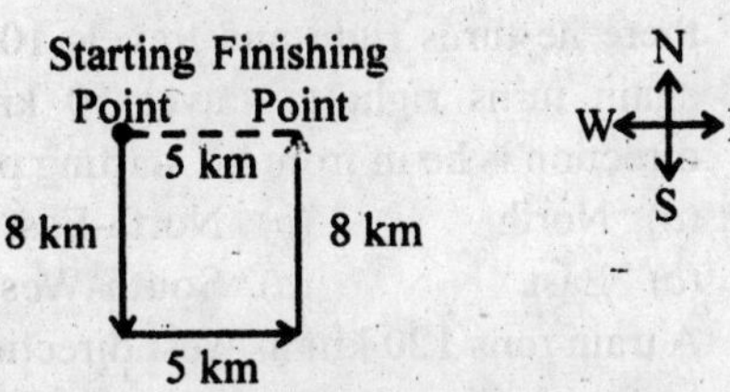

4. (*c*) :

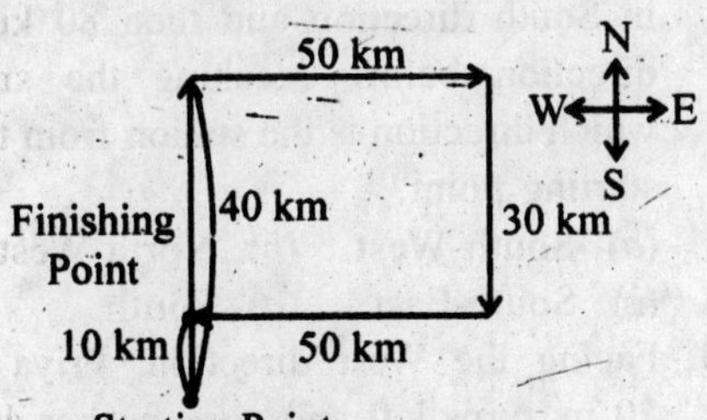

5. (*a*) : **Original Directions**

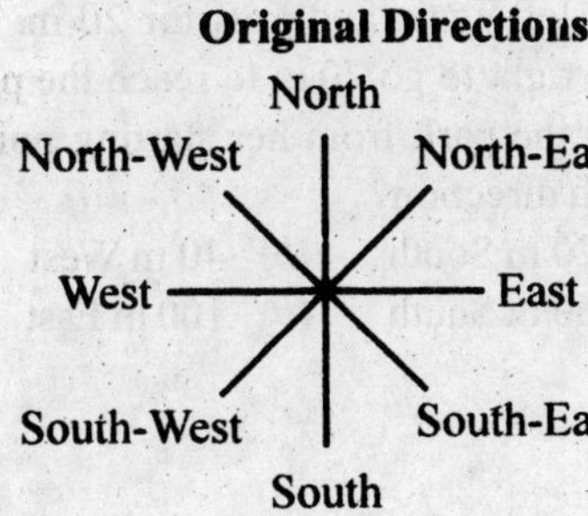

Changed Directions

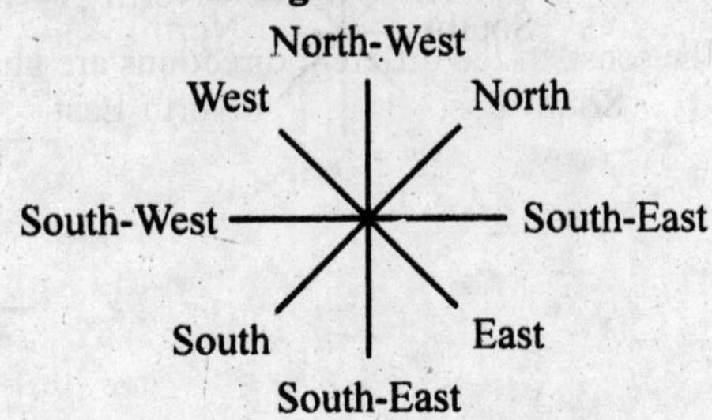

6. (*d*) :

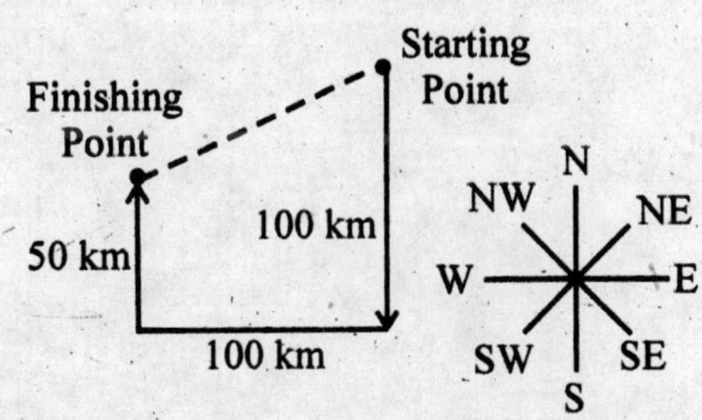

7. (*a*) :

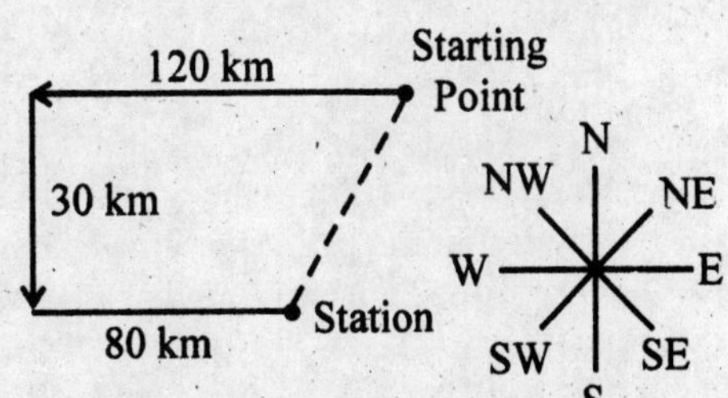

8. (*c*) : (40 + 20) = 60 metres South

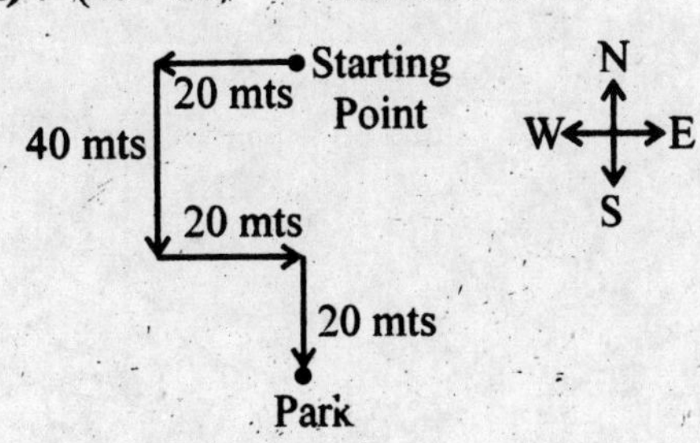

9. *(a)* : Original Directions

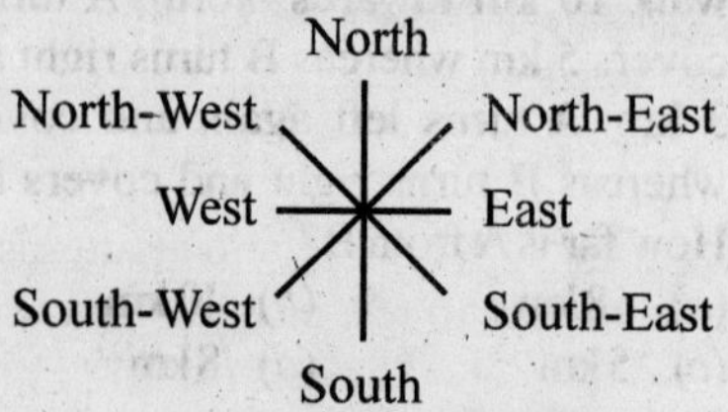

Changed Directions

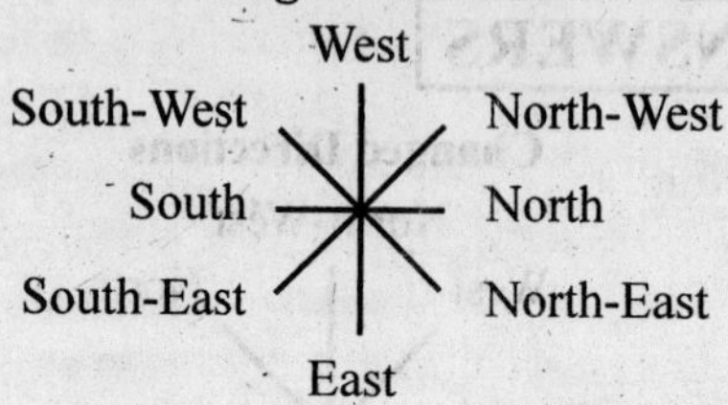

10. *(d)* :

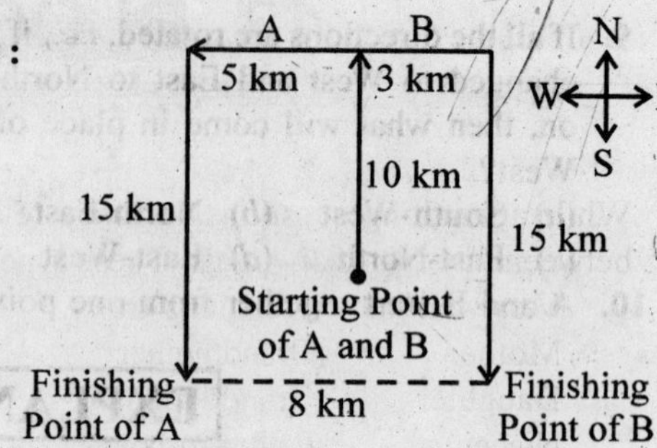

13. BLOOD RELATIONSHIPS

While attempting questions on blood relations, one should be clear of all the relation patterns that can exist between any two individuals. These type of questions are given mainly to test one's relationship ability.

Very well-known relations are :

Mother	Grandmother	Father	Grandfather	Son	Grandson
Daughter	Granddaughter	Brother	Brother-in-law	Sister	Sister-in-law
Niece	Father-in-law	Nephew	Mother-in-law	Uncle	Son-in-law
Aunt	Daughter-in-law	Husband	Cousin	Wife	

The patterns of some relationships which help in solving questions in these tests are :

Father's *or* Mother's Father	—	Grandfather (Paternal *or* Maternal)
Father's *or* Mother's Mother	—	Grandmother (Paternal *or* Maternal)
Father's *or* Mother's Son	—	Brother
Father's *or* Mother's Daughter	—	Sister
Father's Brother	—	Paternal Uncle
Father's Sister	—	Paternal Aunt
Mother's Brother	—	Maternal Uncle
Mother's Sister	—	Maternal Aunt
Uncle *or* Aunt's Son *or* Daughter	—	Cousin
Son's Wife	—	Daughter-in-law
Daughter's Husband	—	Son-in-law
Husband's *or* Wife's Brother	—	Brother-in-law
Husband's *or* Wife's Sister	—	Sister-in-law
Brother's Wife	—	Sister-in-law
Sister's Husband	—	Brother-in-law
Brother's Son	—	Nephew
Brother's Daughter	—	Niece

EXERCISE

Directions : *In each of the following questions keenly study the relationship mentioned between the persons, and then from the given options select the right relationship as the answer.*

1. A lady said, "The person standing there is my grandfather's only son's daughter". How is the lady related to the standing person?
(*a*) Sister (*b*) Mother
(*c*) Aunt (*d*) Cousin

2. Ajay is the brother of Vijay. Mili is the sister of Ajay. Sanjay is the brother of Rahul and Mehul is the daughter of Vijay. Who is Sanjay's Uncle?
(*a*) Rahul (*b*) Ajay
(*c*) Mehul (*d*) Data inadequate

3. A man introduced the boy coming with him as "He is son of the father of my wife's daughter". What relation did the boy bear to the man?
(*a*) Son-in-law (*b*) Son
(*c*) Brother (*d*) Father

4. If Amit's father is Billoo's father's only son and Billoo has neither a brother nor a daughter, what is the relationship between Amit and Billoo?

(*a*) Uncle — Nephew
(*b*) Father -- Daughter
(*c*) Father — Son
(*d*) Cousins

5. Pointing to a woman in the photograph a man said, "She is the daughter of my grand-mother's only son." How is the woman related to the man?

(*a*) Mother (*b*) Daughter
(*c*) Sister-in-law (*d*) Sister

6. Pointing to a photograph, a woman said, "She is the only daughter of my mother's father." How is the woman related to the person in the photograph?

(*a*) Mother
(*b*) Grandmother
(*c*) Daughter
(*d*) Cannot be determined

7. Ram is the brother of Shyam and Mahesh is the father of Ram. Jagat is the brother of Priya and Priya is daughter of Shyam. Who is the uncle of Jagat ?

(*a*) Shyam (*b*) Mahesh
(*c*) Ram (*d*) Data insufficient

8. Introducing a man, a woman said, "His wife is the only daughter of my father". How is the man related to the woman?

(*a*) Husband (*b*) Father
(*c*) Father-in-law (*d*) Brother

9. If Maya is the only daughter of Richa's grandmother's brother, how is Maya's daughter related to Richa?

(*a*) Niece (*b*) Cousin
(*c*) Aunt (*d*) Mother

10. Pointing to a woman, a man said, "Her husband's mother is the wife of my father's only son". How is the man related to the woman?

(*a*) Son (*b*) Brother-in-law
(*c*) Uncle (*d*) Father-in-law

EXPLANATORY ANSWERS

1. (*a*) :

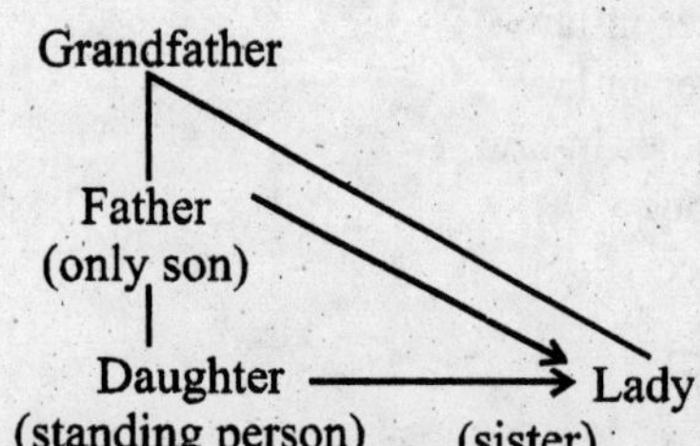

Lady's grandfather's son is lady's father and father's daughter will only be lady's sister.

2. (*d*) : 1. Mili ⟶ (sister) Ajay ⟶ (brother) Vijay ↓ Mehul (daughter)

2. Sanjay ⟶ (brother) Rahul

There are two sets of relationship. Information given is incomplete and no relation can be established between the two sets.

3. (*b*) : The relationship chart based on problem is :

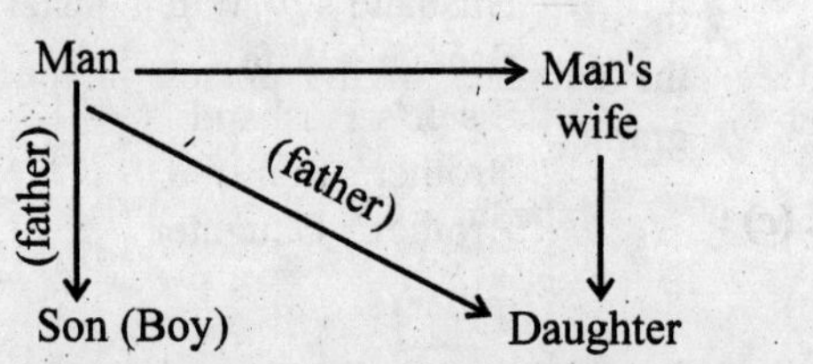

'Father of the man's wife's daughter' is the man himself and the boy in question is the man's son.

4. (*c*) : The relationship chart based on problem is :

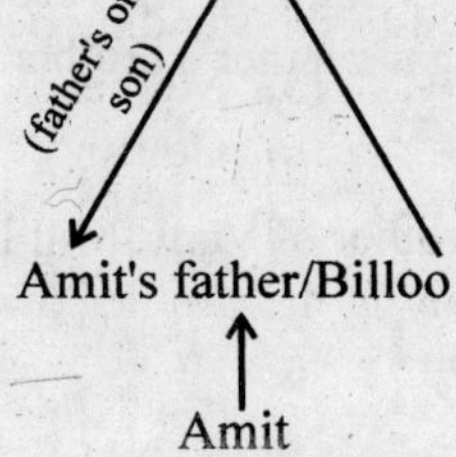

Amit's father is Billoo's father's only son means Billoo is the only son in question also, he is the father of Amit. It must be noted that Billoo has no brother which means he is single and also, when he has no daughter, Amit is his only son.

5. (*d*) :

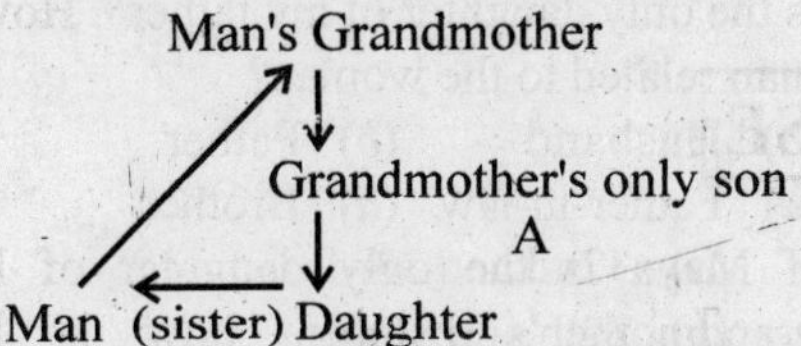

'My grandmother's only son' is the father of the man, and 'daughter of my grandmother's only son' is the sister of the man.

6. (*c*) :

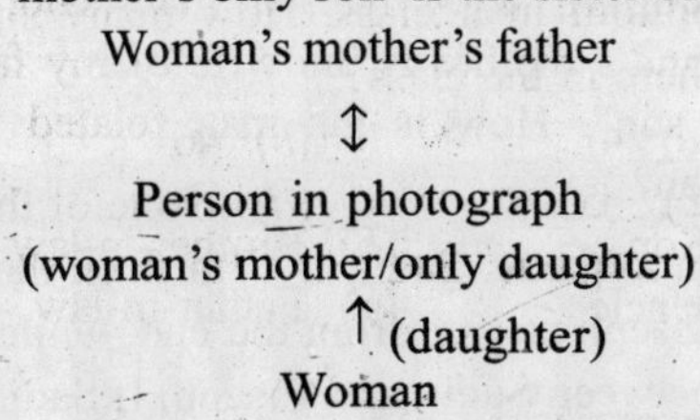

'Only daughter of my mother's father' is the person in the photograph and she is also the mother of the woman. So, the woman is the daughter of the person in the photograph.

7. (*c*) :

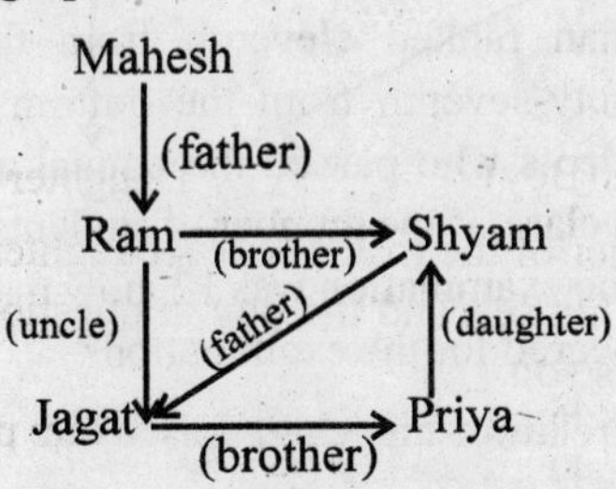

Jagat is brother of Priya and Priya is daughter of Shyam. So Shyam is also the father of Jagat. Ram is the brother of Shyam. So, Jagat's father's brother Ram is the uncle of Jagat.

8. (*a*) :

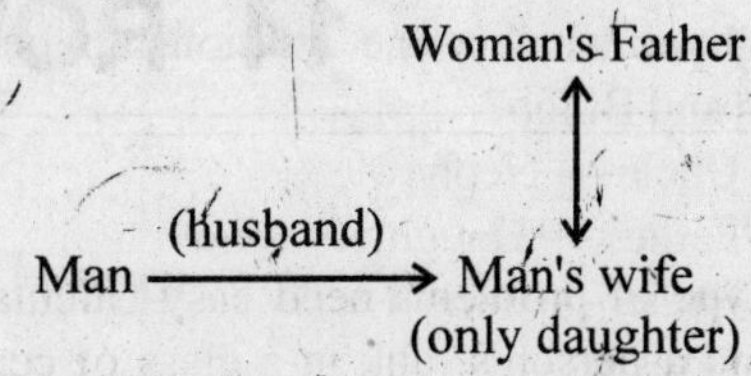

'Only daughter of my father' is the woman herself and the man is her husband.

9. (*b*) :

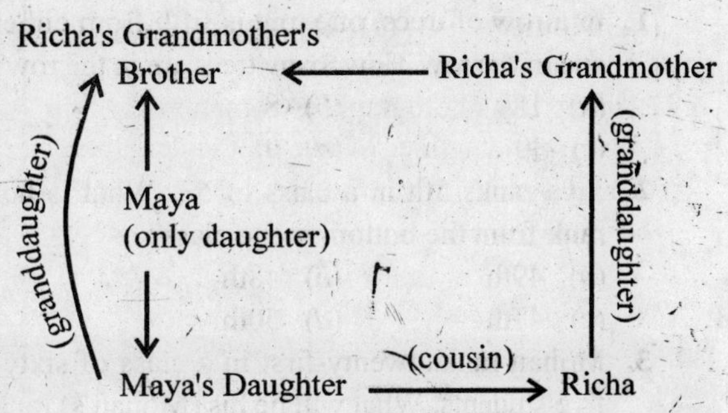

Both Maya's Daughter and Richa are granddaughters of a brother and a sister respectively. So Maya's daughter is the cousin of Richa.

10. (*d*) :

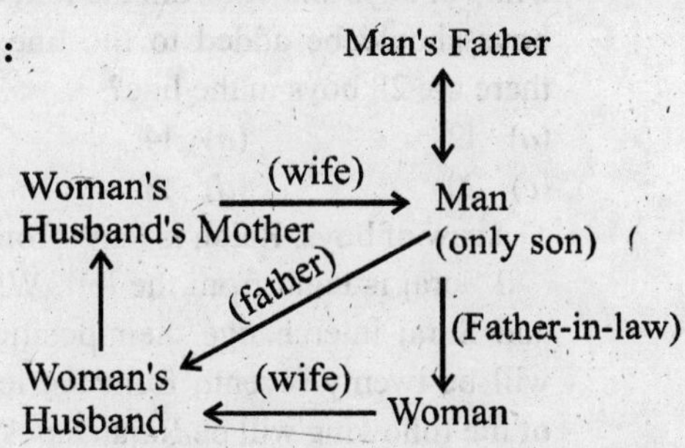

'My father's only son' is the man himself. 'Her husband's mother' is the wife of the man and so the man is the father of the woman's husband. As the woman is the wife of man's son, the man is the father-in-law of the woman.

14. ROWS AND RANKS

These type of problems need easy calculations to find out the number of objects in a row, lane or queue or to find a person's rank in a class of certain number of students; or to find the total number of students.

EXERCISE

1. In a row of trees, one tree is fifth from either end of the row. How many trees are in the row?
(*a*) 11 (*b*) 8
(*c*) 10 (*d*) 9

2. Jaya ranks 5th in a class of 53. What is her rank from the bottom in the class?
(*a*) 49th (*b*) 48th
(*c*) 47th (*d*) 50th

3. Mohan ranks twenty-first in a class of sixty-five students. What will be his (Mohan's) rank if the lowest candidate is assigned rank 1?
(*a*) 44th (*b*) 45th
(*c*) 46th (*d*) Data inadequate

4. If Rahul finds that he is 12th from the right in a line of boys and 4th from the left, how many boys should be added to the line such that there are 28 boys in the line?
(*a*) 12 (*b*) 14
(*c*) 20 (*d*) 13

5. In a row of boys, Rajan is tenth from the right and Suraj is tenth from the left. When Rajan and Suraj interchange their positions, Suraj will be twenty-seventh from the left. Which of the following will be Rajan's position from the right?
(*a*) Tenth
(*b*) Twenty-sixth
(*c*) Twenty-ninth
(*d*) None of these

6. Mahesh and Suresh are ranked 11th and 12th respectively from the top in a class of 41 students. What will be their respective ranks from the bottom?
(*a*) 32nd and 33rd
(*b*) 29th and 30th
(*c*) 30th and 31st
(*d*) 31st and 30th

7. Uma ranked 8th from the top and 37th from bottom in a class. How many students are there in the class?
(*a*) 47 (*b*) 46
(*c*) 45 (*d*) None of these

8. In a queue, Sadiq is 14th from the front and Joseph is 17th from the end, while Jane is in between Sadiq and Joseph. If Sadiq be ahead of Joseph and there be 48 persons in the queue, how many persons are there between Sadiq and Jane?
(*a*) 5 (*b*) 6
(*c*) 7 (*d*) 8

9. Rohan ranked eleventh from the top and twenty-seventh from the bottom among the students who passed the annual examination in a class. If the number of students who failed in the examination was 12, how many students appeared for the examination?
(*a*) 48
(*b*) 49
(*c*) 50
(*d*) Cannot be determined

10. Some boys are sitting in a row. P is sitting fourteenth from the left and Q is seventh from the right. If there are four boys between P and Q, how many boys are there in the row?
(*a*) 19 (*b*) 21
(*c*) 25 (*d*) 23

EXPLANATORY ANSWERS

1. (*d*):

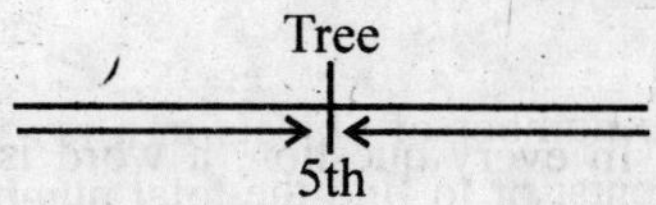

Total number of trees in the row are :
$(5+5)-1=9$.

2. (*a*) :

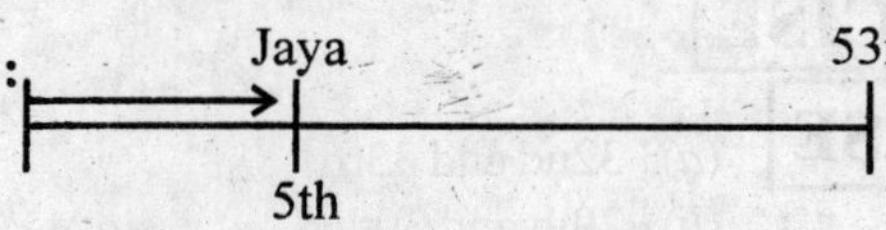

Jaya's rank from the bottom is :
$(53-5)+1=49$th.

3. (*b*) :

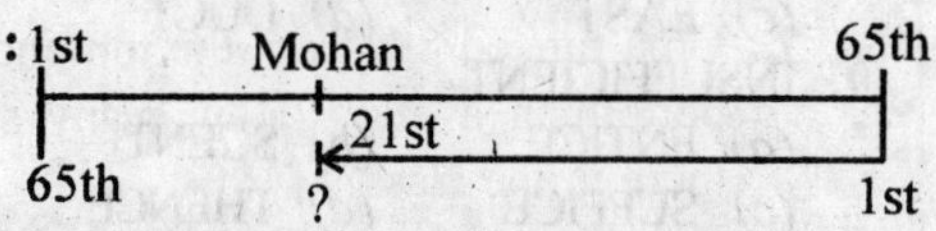

Note : Mohan's rank from the last or the question asked means the same.
Mohan's rank is $(65-21)+1=45$th.

4. (*d*) :

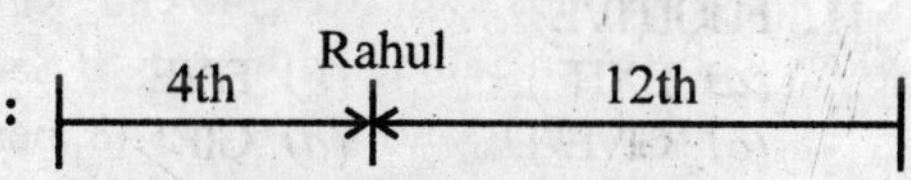

The number of boys in the line are :
$(4+12)-1=15$
To make a line of 28 boys, $(28-15)$ *i.e.* 13 more boys are needed.

5. (*d*) :

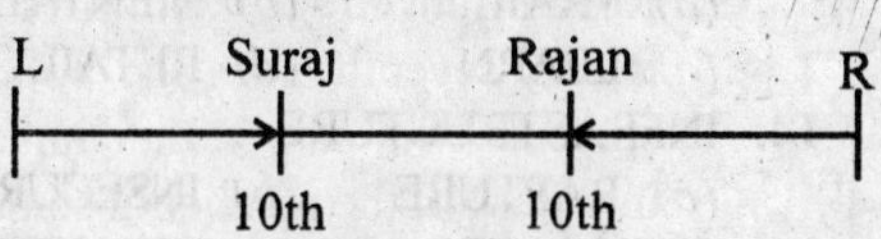

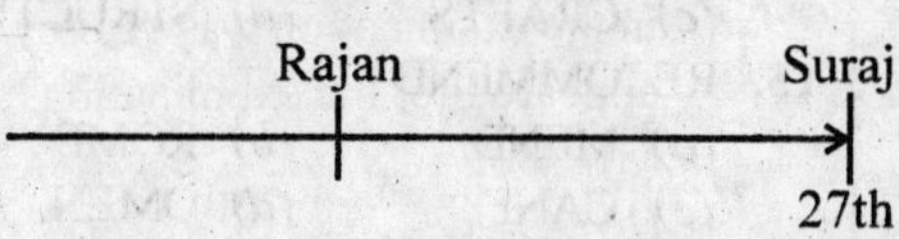

As the position of boys is equal from both ends, Rajan will also be 27th from the right after changing positions.

6. (*d*) :

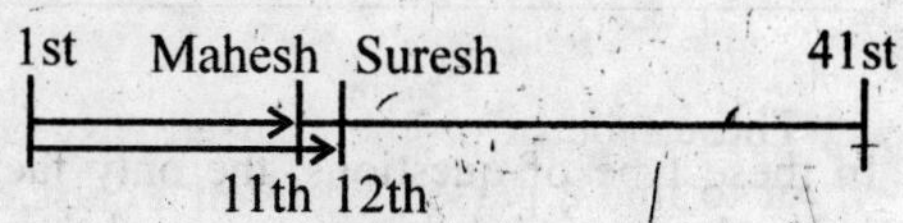

Mahesh's position from bottom is :
$(41-11)+1=31$st
Suresh's position from bottom is :
$(41-12)+1=30$th.

7. (*d*) :

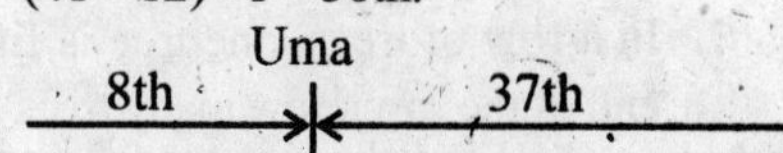

Total number of students in the class are :
$(8+37)-1=44$.

8. (*d*) :

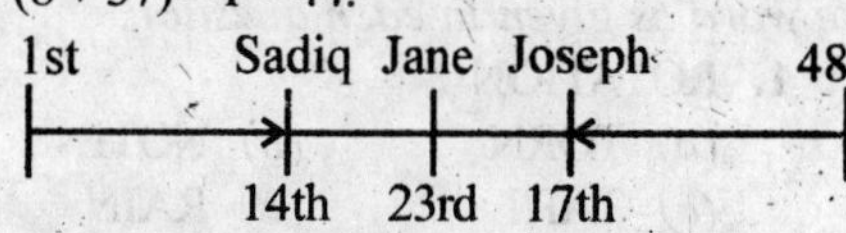

Sadiq's position from front : 14th
Joseph's position from last :
17th or $48-17+1=32$nd from front.
Middle postion between Sadiq & Joseph

$$=\frac{(32-14)}{2}+14=23 \text{ rd.}$$

Hence, Jane position is 23rd from front
Person between Sadiq & Jane
$=23-14-1=8$.

9. (*b*) :

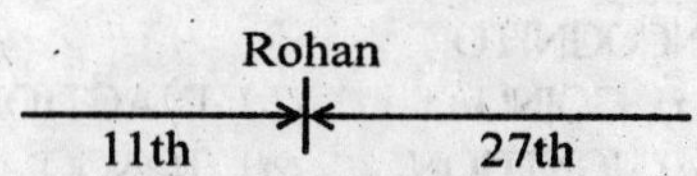

Number of students who passed the examination $(11+27)-1=37$
Those who failed = 12
Total number of students who appeared in the examination $=37+12=49$.

10. (*c*) :

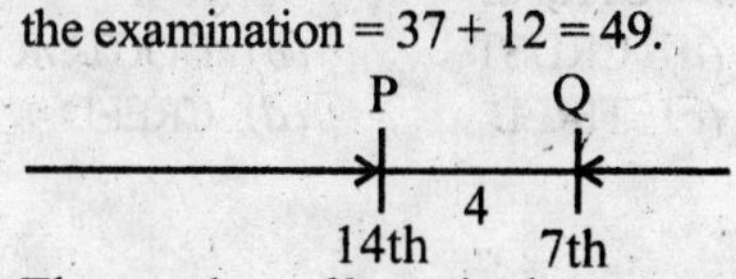

The number of boys in the row are :
$(14+4+7)=25$.

15. PERMUTATIONS AND COMBINATIONS

In these type of questions, the only factor essential is alertness. In every question, a word is given. By using the letters of this given word the options are formed. The candidates are required to find from the given options the word *(i)* which cannot be formed by using the letters of the given word or *(ii)* which can be formed by using the letters of the given word.

EXERCISE

Directions : *Find out the one word among the options which cannot be formed by using the letters of the word as given in each question.*

1. ROTATION
   (a) TORN (b) NOTE
   (c) TART (d) RAIN
2. PHILOSOPHY
   (a) SOIL (b) SHIP
   (c) SOLO (d) SPIN
3. SLAVATION
   (a) SNORT (b) LATVIA
   (c) SALIVA (d) AVAIL
4. ACADEMY
   (a) DEMY (b) MACE
   (c) DIRE (d) MADE
5. INCOGNITO
   (a) GOING (b) INACTION
   (c) IGNITION (d) TONGO
6. JUDICIARY
   (a) INJURY (b) CADDY
   (c) DICY (d) ACRID
7. DOCTRINE
   (a) CRUST (b) DOCTOR
   (c) TIRED (d) CREED
8. EDUCATED
   (a) DATE (b) CUTE
   (c) EAST (d) DUCT
9. INSUFFICIENT
   (a) ENTICE (b) SCENT
   (c) SUFFICE (d) THENCE
10. DECEMBER
    (a) REDEEM (b) DECREE
    (c) BRACED (d) MEMBER
11. FUGITIVE
    (a) EXIT (b) FIVE
    (c) GIVE (d) GIFT
12. CATASTROPHE
    (a) TASTE (b) CHEAP
    (c) POUCH (d) STARE
13. TORRENTIAL
    (a) TRAIL (b) MENTAL
    (c) LEARN (d) RETAIL
14. INFRASTRUCTURE
    (a) RAPTURE (b) INSECURE
    (c) CRAFTS (d) STRUCTURE
15. RECOMMEND
    (a) MEND (b) ROME
    (c) CANE (d) OMEN

ANSWERS

1	2	3	4	5	6	7	8	9	10
(b)	(d)	(a)	(c)	(b)	(a)	(a)	(c)	(d)	(c)
11	**12**	**13**	**14**	**15**					
(a)	(c)	(b)	(a)	(c)					

16. SYMBOL SUBSTITUTION

Questions in these category are easy to attempt. Candidates must be quick in substituting symbols and calculations. The common pattern of questions asked are given below.

EXERCISE

1. If "+" means "−"; "−" means "×"; "×"means "÷" and "÷" means "+", then
$15 \times 5 \div 10 + 5 - 3 = ?$
(a) 9.5 *(b)* 0
(c) −2 *(d)* 24

2. If "+" means "×"; "−" means "÷"; "÷"means "+" and "×" means "−", then what will be the value of $20 \div 40 - 4 \times 5 + 6 = ?$
(a) 60 *(b)* 1.67
(c) 150 *(d)* 0

3. If × stands for addition, < for subtraction, + stands for division, > for multiplication, − stands for equal to, ÷ for greater than, and = stands for less than, state which of the following is true?
(a) $5 \times 3 < 7 \div 8 + 4 \times 1$
(b) $3 \times 4 > 2 - 9 + 3 < 3$
(c) $5 > 2 + 2 = 10 < 4 \times 8$
(d) $3 \times 2 < 4 \div 16 > 2 + 4$

4. If → stands for subract, ← stands for add, ↓↑↑ stands for multiply, ↓↓ stands for divide, ↔ for greater than, ⟷ stands for equal to, then which of the following alternatives is true?
(a) 4 ← 6 ↑↑ 2 ⟷ 3 → 12 ← 12
(b) 10 ↓↓ 5 ↑↑ 5 ⟷ 9 → 3 ← 4
(c) 15 ↑↑ 2 → 5 ⟷ 12 ↓↓ 4 ← 3
(d) 13 ↓↓ 13 ← 1 ↔ 20 → 5 ↑↑ 2

5. If Δ denotes =; + denotes >, − denotes <, □ denotes ≠, × denotes > and ÷ denotes < then a + b − c denotes
(a) b Δ c □ a
(b) b □ a ÷ c
(c) a ÷ b × c
(d) b − a + c

6. If '✱' denotes '×', 'Δ' denotes '÷', '□' denotes '−', '●' denotes '+', 'α' denotes '=' and 'β' denotes ≠, then which of the following euations is correct?
(a) 2 □ 10 ✱ 4 Δ 5 α 5 ● 12 Δ 6
(b) 27 Δ 9 ● 6 β 3 ✱ 6 □ 9
(c) 4 Δ 2 ✱ 0 α 7 Δ 1 ✱ 0
(d) 5 ● 6 Δ 3 □ 2 α 8 Δ 4 ✱ 3

7. If ↓ stands for '÷', ↑ stands for '×', → stands for '+' and ← stands for '−', then
25 ↓ 5 → 3 ↑ 6 ← 8 = ?
(a) 9 *(b)* 12
(c) 16 *(d)* 15

8. If the + and × signs of the following equations are interchanged, which will be the correct equation?
(a) $7 \times 5 + 3 = 20$
(b) $4 + 9 \times 1 = 42$
(c) $6 \times 5 + 8 = 46$
(d) $2 + 11 \times 4 = 28$

9. If '+' stands for multiplication, '×' stands for addition, '÷' stands for subtraction and '−' stands for division, then what will be the result of the following equation?
$7 \times 4 \div 10 \times 2 + 5 = ?$
(a) 7 *(b)* 0
(c) 11 *(d)* 15

10. If 'A' means '÷', 'B' means '+', 'C' means '×' and 'D' means '−', then
12 C 4 A 24 D 10 B 1 = ?
(a) $11\frac{1}{3}$ *(b)* 23
(c) −7 *(d)* $16\frac{4}{5}$

EXPLANATORY ANSWERS

1. (c) : $15 \div 5 + 10 - 5 \times 3$
$3 + 10 - 15 = -2$

2. (d) : $20 + 40 \div 4 - 5 \times 6$
$20 + 10 - 30 = 0$

3. (c) : *(a)* $5 + 3 - 7 > 8 \div 4 + 1$
$1 > 3$
(b) $3 + 4 \times 2 = 9 \div 3 - 3$
$11 = 0$
(c) $5 \times 2 \div 2 < 10 - 4 + 8$
$5 < 14$
(d) $3 + 2 - 4 > 16 \times 2 \div 4$
$1 > 8$

4. (b) : *(a)* $4 + 6 \times 2 = 3 - 12 + 12$
$16 = 3$
(b) $10 \div 5 \times 5 = 9 - 3 + 4$
$10 = 10$
(c) $15 \times 2 - 5 = 12 \div 4 + 3$
$25 = 6$
(d) $13 \div 13 + 1 > 20 - 5 \times 2$
$2 > 10$

5. (d) : What is given is a > b < c
The equations are :
(a) b = c ≠ a which is wrong
(b) b ≠ a < c which is wrong
(c) a < b > c which is wrong
(d) b < a > c which is correct
Therefore, *(d)* is the answer.

6. (c) : The solved equations will be :
(a) $2 - 10 \times 4 \div 5 = 5 + 12 \div 6$
$2 - 8 = 5 + 2$
$-6 = 7$ which is wrong
(b) $27 \div 9 + 6 \neq 3 \times 6 - 9$
$3 + 6 \neq 18 - 9$
$9 \neq 9$ which is wrong
(c) $4 \div 2 \times 0 = 7 \div 1 \times 0$
$2 \times 0 = 7 \times 0$
$0 = 0$ which is correct
(d) $5 + 6 \div 3 - 2 = 8 \div 4 \times 3$
$5 = 6$ which is wrong

7. (d) : $25 \div 5 + 3 \times 6 - 8$
$5 + 18 - 8 = 15$

8. (c) : After interchanging the signs the equations are :
(a) $7 + 5 \times 3 = 22$ which is wrong
(b) $4 \times 9 + 1 = 37$ which is wrong
(c) $6 + 5 \times 8 = 46$ which is correct
(d) $2 \times 11 \div 4 = 26$ which is wrong

9. (c) : $7 + 4 - 10 + 2 \times 5$
$7 + 4 - 10 + 10 = 11$

10. (c) : $12 \times 4 \div 24 - 10 + 1$
$2 - 10 + 1 = -7$

17. MISSING NUMBERS

Playing with numbers and mathematical skills are needed to attempt these type of tests. The candidates have to work out the right combination of arithmetical symbols to arrive at the answer options which will take the place of the interrogation sign in the given questions.

EXERCISE

Directions: *In each question given below which one number can be placed at the sign of interrogation?*

1.

(*a*) 693 (*b*) 939
(*c*) 981 (*d*) 993

2.

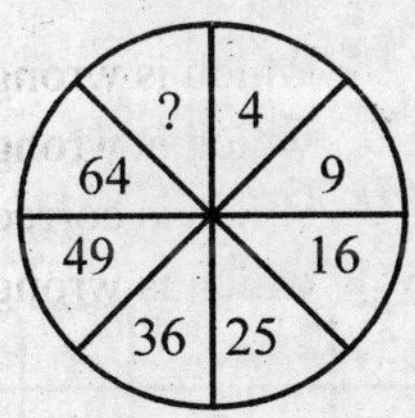

(*a*) 68 (*b*) 100
(*c*) 72 (*d*) 81

3.

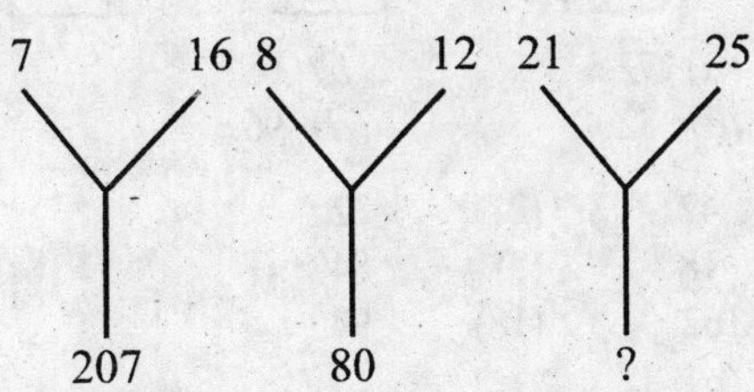

(*a*) 425 (*b*) 184
(*c*) 241 (*d*) 210

4.

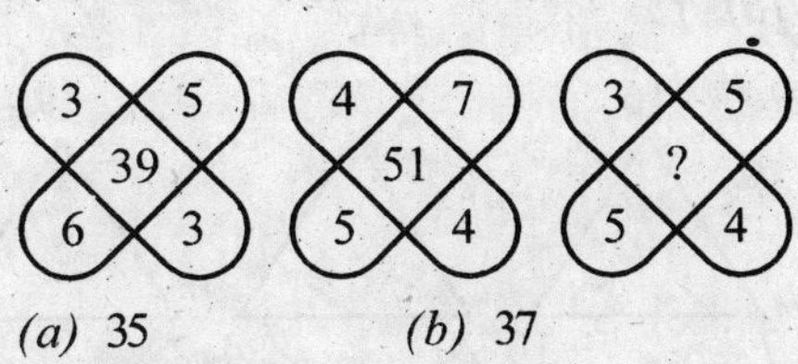

(*a*) 35 (*b*) 37
(*c*) 45 (*d*) 48

5.

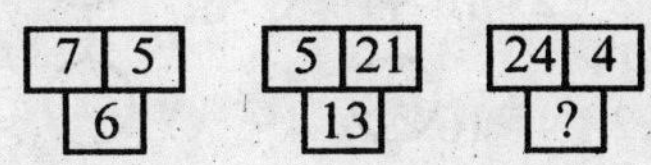

(*a*) 4 (*b*) 8
(*c*) 20 (*d*) 14

6.

14	9	4
12	7	2
10	5	0
16	11	?

(*a*) 9 (*b*) 6
(*c*) 3 (*d*) 7

7.

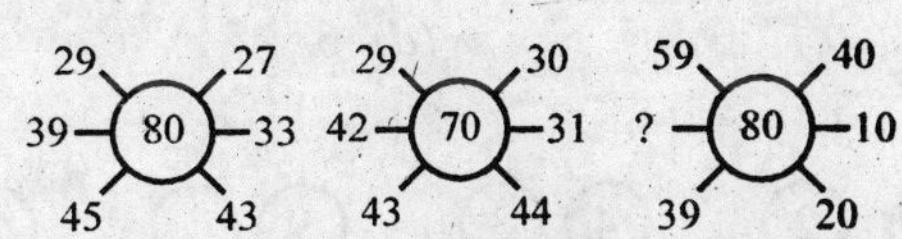

(*a*) 69 (*b*) 49
(*c*) 50 (*d*) 60

8.

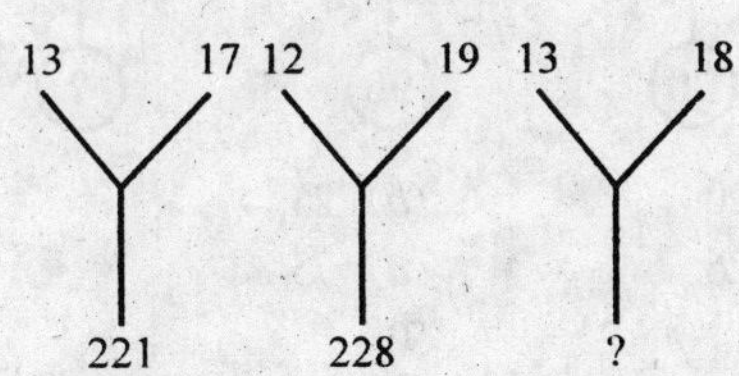

(*a*) 31 (*b*) 229
(*c*) 234 (*d*) 312

9.

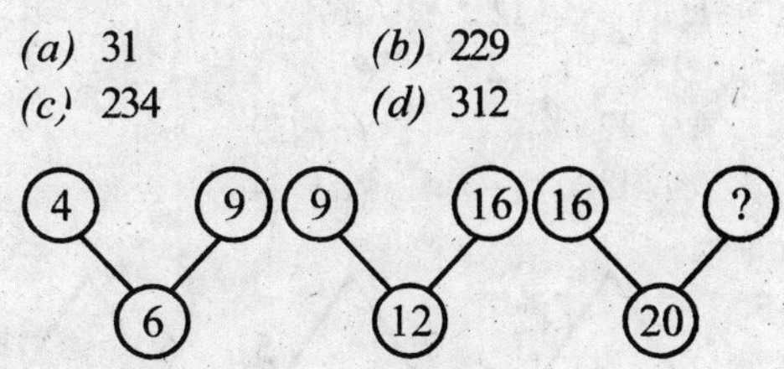

(*a*) 21 (*b*) 25
(*c*) 50 (*d*) 60

10.

51	(11)	61
64	(30)	32
35	(?)	43

(*a*) 25 (*b*) 27
(*c*) 32 (*d*) 37

11.
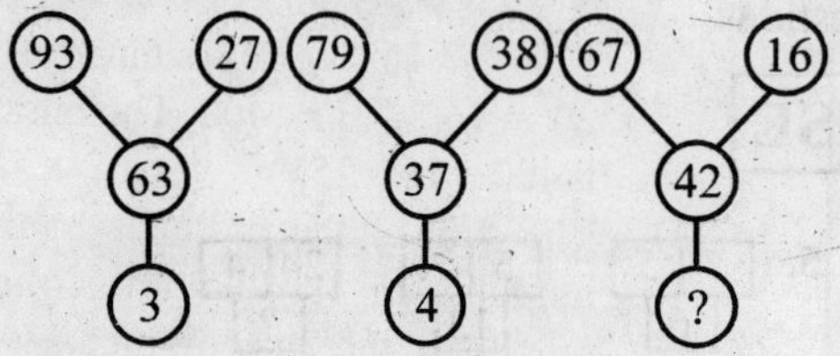

(*a*) 5 (*b*) 6
(*c*) 8 (*d*) 9

12.
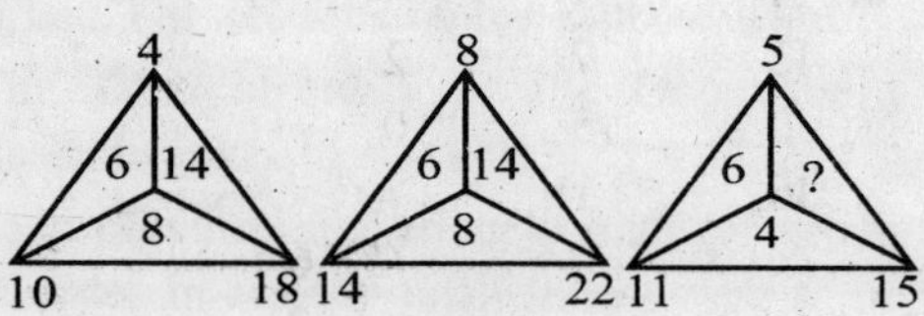

(*a*) 8 (*b*) 14
(*c*) 10 (*d*) 6

13.
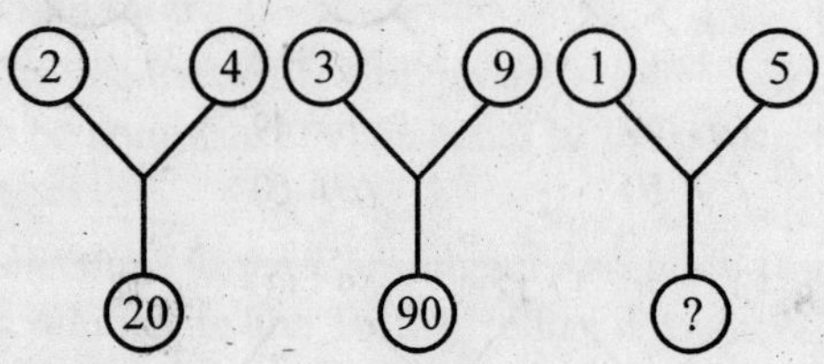

(*a*) 20 (*b*) 25
(*c*) 26 (*d*) 75

14.

27	22	50
13	12	26
9	2	?

(*a*) 12 (*b*) 39
(*c*) 18 (*d*) 24

15.
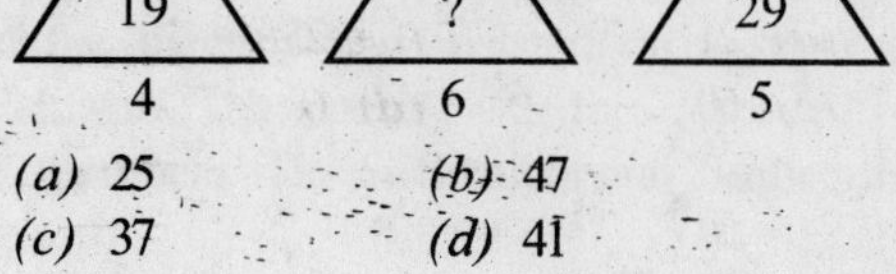

(*a*) 25 (*b*) 47
(*c*) 37 (*d*) 41

16.
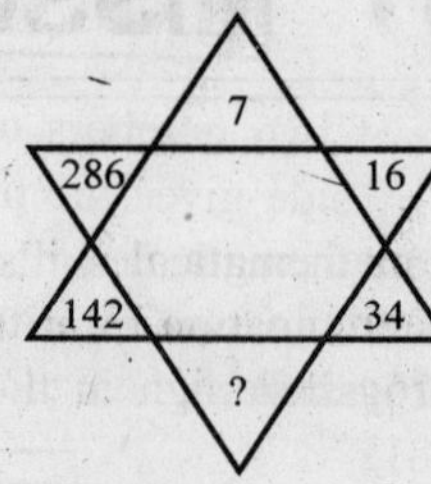

(*a*) 70
(*b*) 68
(*c*) 56
(*d*) 92

17.
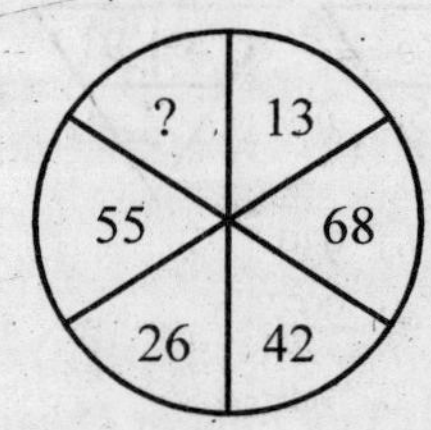

(*a*) 41 (*b*) 37
(*c*) 29 (*d*) 25

18.
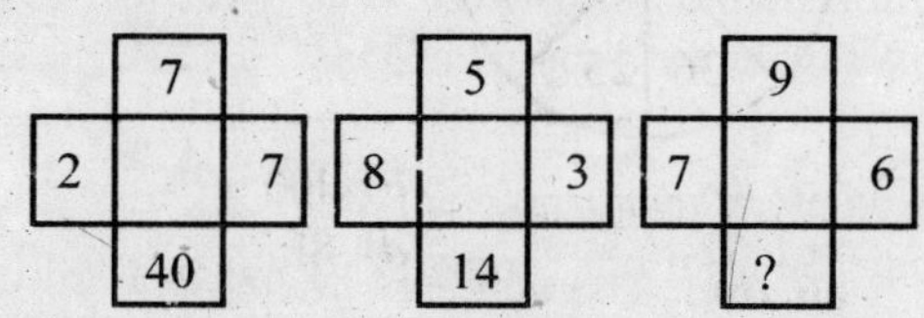

(*a*) 72 (*b*) 68
(*c*) 82 (*d*) 96

19.

42	(21)	22
78	(?)	84
162	(18)	99

(*a*) 12
(*b*) 13
(*c*) 60
(*d*) 72

20.
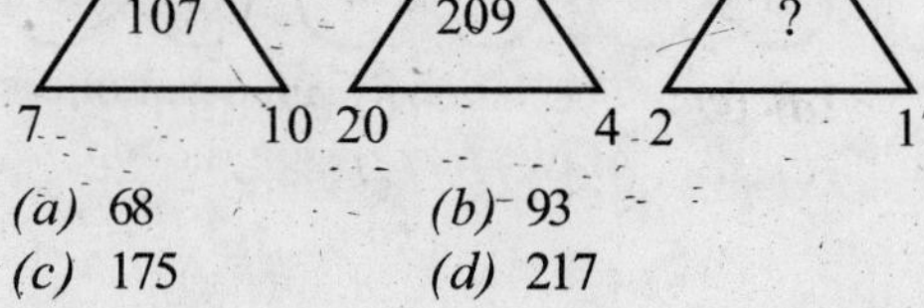

(*a*) 68 (*b*) 93
(*c*) 175 (*d*) 217

EXPLANATORY ANSWERS

1. (c) : The squares of two numbers on the top placed side by side gives the number inside the bottom triangle, *i.e.,*
6^2 and $3^2 = 369$.
2^2 and $5^2 = 425$, similarly
3^2 and $9^2 = 981$.

2. (d) : Starting from number 4 the numbers are the squares of numbers in natural order *i.e.,* $2^2 = 4, 3^2 = 9, 4^2 = 16 \ldots\ldots 9^2 = 81$.

3. (b) : The number at the bottom is the difference of the squares of two numbers at the top, *i.e.,*
$16^2 - 7^2 = 256 - 49 = 207$
$12^2 - 8^2 = 144 - 64 = 80$, similarly
$25^2 - 21^2 = 625 - 441 = 184$.

4. (b) : The number in the centre is the sum of the products of diagonal numbers, *i.e.,*
$(3 \times 3) + (5 \times 6) = 39$
$(4 \times 4) + (7 \times 5) = 51$, similarly
$(3 \times 4) + (5 \times 5) = 37$.

5. (d) : Sum of two numbers on the top divided by 2 gives the third number, *i.e.,*
$(7 + 5) \div 2 = 6$
$(5 + 21) \div 2 = 13$, similarly
$(24 + 4) \div 2 = 14$.

6. (b) : The numbers in 2nd and 3rd columns are 5 less than the nunbers in 1st and 2nd columns respectively, *i.e.,*
$14 - 5 = 9$ and $9 - 5 = 4$
$12 - 5 = 7$ and $7 - 5 = 2, \ldots$ similarly
$16 - 5 = 11$ and $11 - 5 = 6$.

7. (a) : The sum of 3 numbers in each line in one figure is same, *i.e.,*
$29 + 80 + 43$ or $39 + 80 + 33$
or $45 + 80 + 27 = 152$
$29 + 70 + 44$ or $42 + 70 + 31$
or $43 + 70 + 30 = 143$,
similarly $59 + 80 + 20$ or $39 + 80 + 40 = 159$.
The missing number is :
$159 - (80 + 10) = 69$.

8. (c) : The number at the bottom is the product of two numbers at the top, *i.e.,*
$13 \times 17 = 221$
$12 \times 19 = 228$, similarly
$13 \times 18 = 234$.

9. (b) : Square of number at the bottom is equal to the product of two numbers at the top, *i.e.,*
$6^2 = 4 \times 9$, *i.e.,* 36
$12^2 = 9 \times 16$, *i.e.,* 144, similarly.
$20^2 = 16 \times ?$, *i.e.,* 400. The missing number is $400 \div 16 = 25$.

10. (b) : The sum of the products of the digits of numbers in 1st and 3rd columns is the number in the 2nd column, *i.e.,*
$(5 \times 1) + (6 \times 1) = 11$
$(6 \times 4) + (3 \times 2) = 30$, similarly
$(3 \times 5) + (4 \times 3) = 27$.

11. (d) : The sum of numbers on right and centre subtracted from the number on the left gives the number at the bottom, *i.e.,*
$93 - (27 + 63) = 3$
$79 - (38 + 37) = 4$, similarly
$67 - (16 + 42) = 9$.

12. (c) : The number inside each triangle is the difference of the numbers at its base *i.e.*
$10 - 4 = 6$, $18 - 4 = 14$ and $18 - 10 = 8$
$14 - 8 = 6$, $22 - 8 = 14$ and $22 - 14 = 8$, similarly
$11 - 5 = 6$, $15 - 5 = 10$ and $15 - 11 = 4$.

13. (c) : The sum of squares of two numbers at the top gives the third number below, *i.e.,*
$2^2 + 4^2 = 20$
$3^2 + 9^2 = 90$, similarly
$1^2 + 5^2 = 26$.

14. (a) : The sum of numbers in 1st and 2nd column plus 1 is the number in the 3rd column, *i.e.,*
$27 + 22 + 1 = 50$
$13 + 12 + 1 = 26$, similarly
$9 + 2 + 1 = 12$.

15. (d) : The product of numbers on either side of the triangle plus the number at the base is the number inside the triangle, *i.e.,*
$(5 \times 3) + 4 = 19$
$(6 \times 4) + 5 = 29$, similarly
$(7 \times 5) + 6 = 41$.

16. *(a)* : Clockwise starting from number 7, the next number is obtained by doubling the number and adding 2, *i.e.,*
$(7 \times 2) + 2 = 16$
$(16 \times 2) + 2 = 34$ . . . , similarly
$(34 \times 2) + 2 = 70$
$(70 \times 2) + 2 = 142$
$(142 \times 2) + 2 = 286$.

17. *(c)* : The difference between the numbers in opposite sectors is 13, *i.e.,*
$26 - 13 = 13$
$68 - 55 = 13$, similarly
The missing number is $42 - 13 = 29$
($42 + 13 = 55$ is not given as option).

18. *(b)* : The number at the bottom is obtained by subtracting the sum of two numbers in the centre grid line from the square of the number at the top, *i.e.,*
$7^2 - (2 + 7) = 40$
$5^2 - (8 + 3) = 14$, similarly
$9^2 - (7 + 6) = 68$.

19. *(b)* : The number inside the brackets is obtained by multiplying the number on the left by 2 and then dividing the product by the sum of digits of number on the right, *i.e.,*
$(42 \times 2) \div (2 + 2) = 21$
$(162 \times 2) \div (9 + 9) = 18$, similarly
$(78 \times 2) \div (8 + 4) = 13$.

20. *(a)* : Subtracting the sum of squares of two numbers at the base from the square of number at the apex gives the number inside the triangle, *i.e.,*
$16^2 - (7^2 + 10^2) = 107$
$25^2 - (20^2 + 4^2) = 209$, similarly
$19^2 - (2^2 + 17^2) = 68$.

18. ALPHABET PROBLEMS

Alphabet problems are fun to attempt. They are based on alphabetical series in natural as well as reverse order.

Natural Order

A B C D E F G H I J K L M N O P Q R S T U V W X Y Z

Reverse Order

Z Y X W V U T S R Q P O N M L K J I H G F E D C B A

Note : The series starts from A on reaching Z and from Z on reaching A. Of these A E I O U are vowels and the rest are consonants.

EXERCISE

1. Which letter should be ninth letter to the left of ninth letter from the right if the first half of the alphabet is reversed?

(a) I *(b)* D
(c) F *(d)* E

2. Starting from the fifth letter from the left, if twelve letters are written in reverse order, then which letter will be the seventh to the left of the fourteenth letter from the right?

(a) N *(b)* H
(c) L *(d)* O

3. What letter will come in the centre of sixth letter from the right and thirteenth letter from the left?

(a) Q *(b)* R
(c) P *(d)* S

4. If in the word "DISTURBANCE", the first letter is interchanged with the last letter, the second letter is interchanged with the tenth letter and so on, which letter would come after the letter "T" in the newly formed word?

(a) I *(b)* U
(c) N *(d)* S

5. If it is possible to make a meaningful word with the third, the fifth, the seventh and the tenth letters of the word PROJECTION. If no such word can be made, give 'O' as the answer. If more than one such word can be made, give 'M' as the answer.

(a) T *(b)* N
(c) O *(d)* M

6. A meaningful word is made if we take the first, fourth, fifth, seventh, tenth, eleventh and the twelfth letters of the word "FELICITATIONS". Which of the following will be the fifth letter of that word from the right end of that word?

(a) T *(b)* C
(c) N *(d)* I

7. On rearranging the jumbled spelling of the word SKARTINS, a language is obtained. What is the fifth letter from the right of the rearranged word?

(a) N *(b)* K
(c) R *(d)* S

8. If the 1st, 3rd, 5th, 7th, 10th and 13th letters of the word "ENTERTAINMENT" are used to make a meaningful word, then what two letters will come in the centre?

(a) A M *(b)* T T
(c) RE *(d)* N A

9. On rearranging the jumbled spelling of the word GRUBY a sport is obtained. What is the letter in the centre?

(a) R *(b)* B
(c) G *(d)* U

10. If the letters 'ERVSECI' can be rearranged to form a meaningful word what will be the fifth letter from the right?

(a) R *(b)* V
(c) E *(d)* None of these

11. From the word HASTEN how many independent meaningful English words can be made without changing the order of the letters and using each letter only once?

(a) 1 *(b)* 2
(c) 3 *(d)* 4

EXPLANATORY ANSWERS

1. *(d)* : MLKJIGHFEDCBANOPQRSTUVWXYZ

9th 9th

2. *(d)* : ABCDPONMLKJIHGFEQRSTUVWXYZ

7th 14th

3. *(a)* :

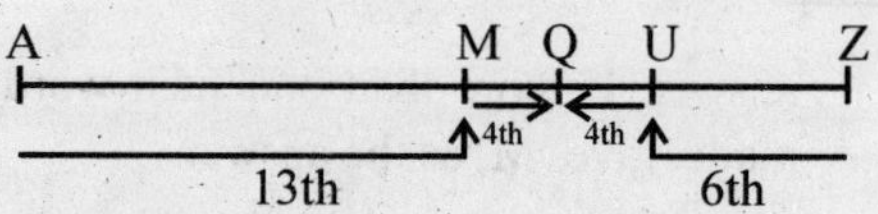

13th letter from left is 'M' and 6th letter from right is 'U'. The letter in the centre of 'M' and 'U' is 'Q'.

4. *(d)* : ECNABRUTSID

5. *(d)* : PROJECTION

The 3rd, 5th, 7th and 10th letters are OETN.

The words formed are TONE and NOTE.

6. *(b)* : FELICITATIONS

The 1st, 4th, 5th, 7th, 10th, 11th and 12th lettes are FICTION.

The word is FICTION and 5th letter from right is 'C'.

7. *(d)* : The word is SANSKRIT and 5th letter from right is 'S'.

8. *(b)* : ENTERTAINMENT

The 1st, 3rd, 5th 7th, 10th and 13th letters are ETRAMT.

The word formed is MATTER.

9. *(c)* : The sport is RUGBY. The letter in the centre is 'G'.

10. *(a)* : The word is SERVICE and fifth letter from right is 'R'.

11. *(b)* : The words formed are : HAS, TEN.

19. LOGICAL DIAGRAM

In these type of questions, a set of five different figures is given as options. Each figure represents a logical pattern of certain groups of related words wherein each word represents a class. One has to identify the most appropriate logical figure for the set of words given. Some of the relationships represented by these diagrams are given below. Understand the relationship patterns and then attempt the exercise following the explanation.

EXERCISE

Directions : *From the five logical Diagrams, select one which best illustrates the relationship among three given classes in the questions 1 to 10.*

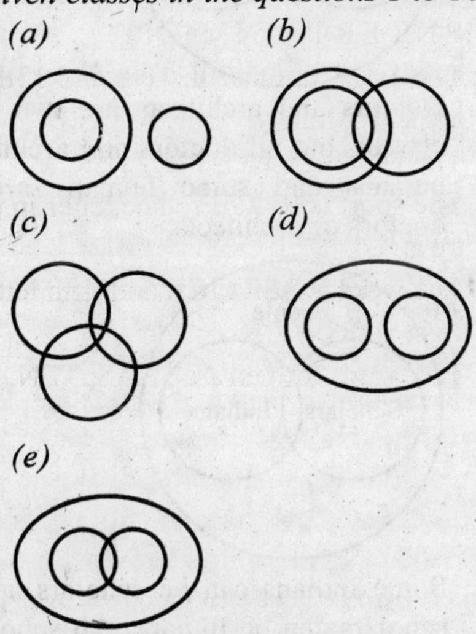

1. Birds, fruits, mangoes
2. Criminals, lawyers, bandits
3. Swimmers, bachelors, men
4. Smart, engineers, women
5. Vegetables, potatoes, brinjals
6. Grapes, sweet, fruit
7. Doctors, architects, humans
8. Scholars, people, Indians
9. Children, naughty, studious
10. Pens, pencils, stationery

Directions : *From the five logical diagrams select one which best illustrates the relationship among three given classes in questions 11 to 20.*

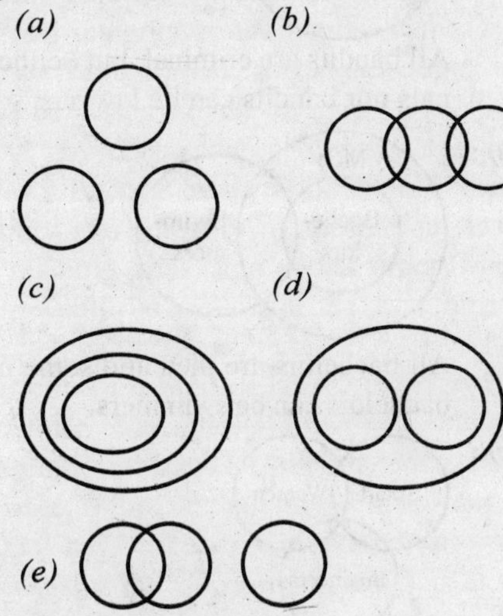

11. Ink, crayons, red
12. Canines, dogs, pups
13. Table, chair, stool
14. Ripe, mangoes, basket
15. Scholars, studious, illiterates
16. Cars, ships, means of conveyance
17. Age, number, thirteen
18. Country, state, continent
19. Father, parent, mother
20. Iron, metal, mercury

EXPLANATORY ANSWERS

1. *(a)* :

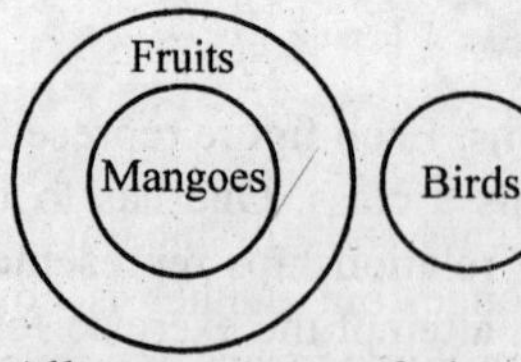

All mangoes are fruits, but neither fruits, nor mangoes can be birds.

2. *(a)* :

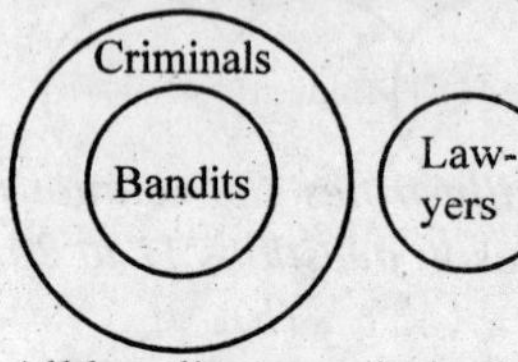

All bandits are criminal, but neither criminals nor bandits can be lawyers.

3. *(b)* :

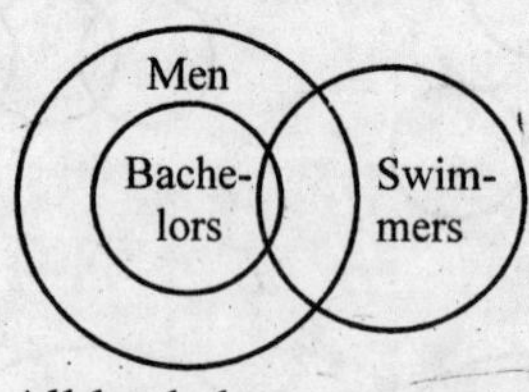

All bachelors are men and some men and bachelors can be swimmers.

4. *(c)* :

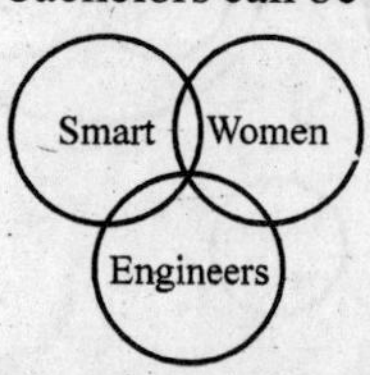

Some women can be smart and some women can be engineers and vice–versa. Some engineers can be women and some engineers can be smart and vice–versa.

5. *(d)* :

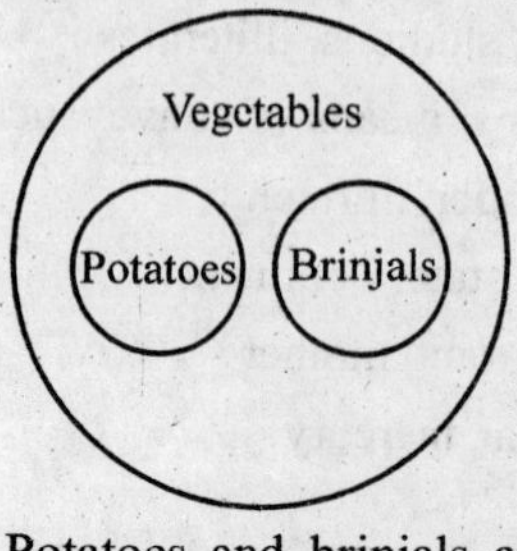

Potatoes and brinjals are vegetables but they have nothing in common. Some vegetables are potatoes and some are brinjals.

6. *(b)* :

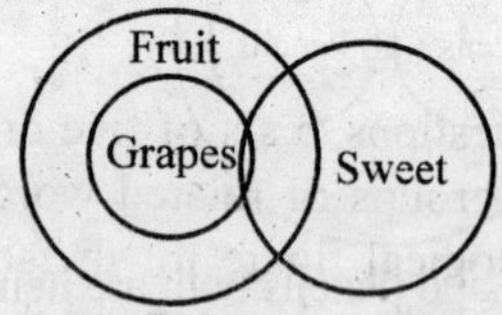

Some grapes are sweet and all grapes are fruit. But not all that is sweet is fruit.

7. *(d)* :

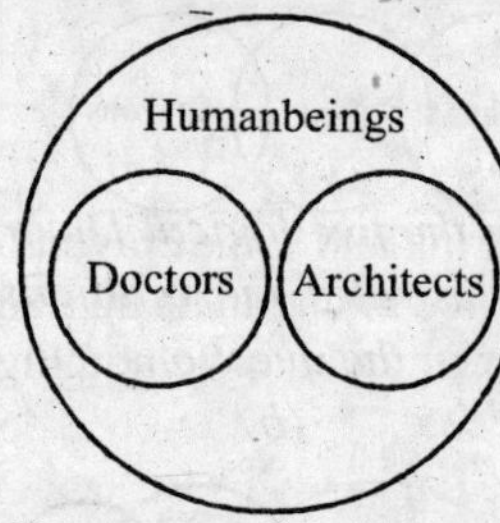

Doctors and architects are two separate classes, but all doctors and architects are humans and some humans are either doctors or architects.

8. *(e)* :

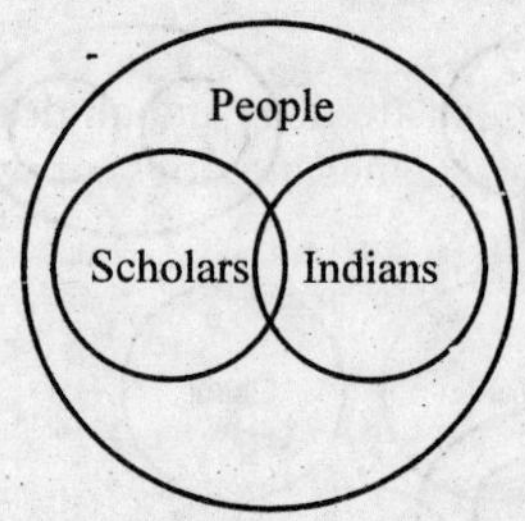

Some Indians can be scholars and some scholars can be Indians. All scholars and Indians are people.

9. *(c)* :

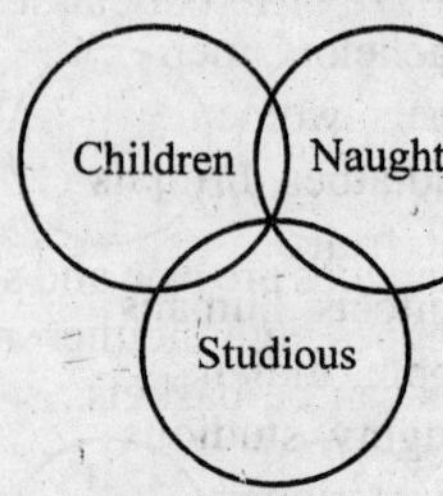

Some children can be naughty and some can be studious, some studious can be children and some naughty. Some naughty can be studious and some children.

10. ***(d)*** **:**

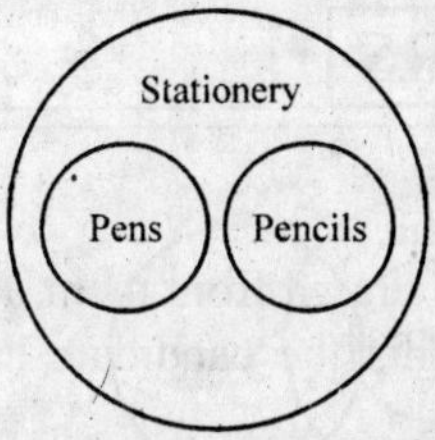

Pens and pencils both are items of stationery and some stationery is pens and pencils, but pens and pencils are two separate classes.

11. ***(b)*** **:**

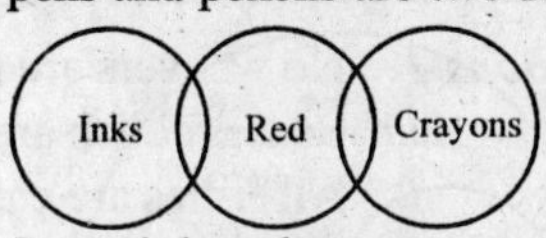

Some ink and some crayons can be red and some red units can be inks and crayons, but ink and crayon have nothing in common.

12. ***(c)*** **:**

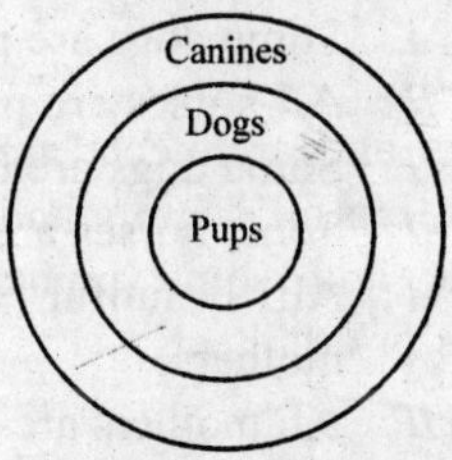

All pups are dogs and all dogs are canines. Some canines are dogs, of which some are pups.

13. ***(a)*** **:**

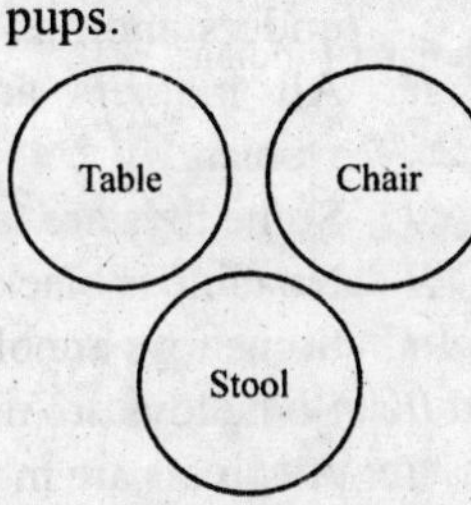

All three are different classes.

14. ***(e)*** **:**

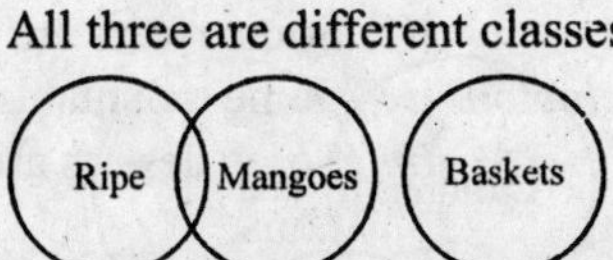

Some mangoes are ripe and some ripe units are mangoes, but neither ripe units nor mangoes can be baskets.

15. ***(e)*** **:**

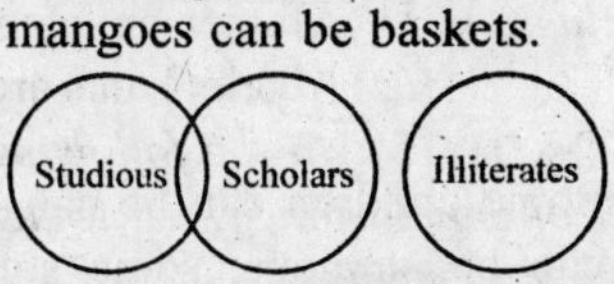

Some studious can be scholars and some scholars can be studious, but neither studious nor scholars can be illiterates.

16. ***(d)*** **:**

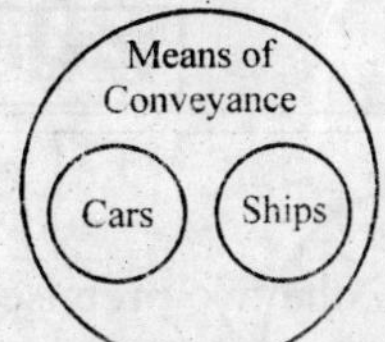

All cars and all ships are means of conveyance, but neither is contained in the other. Some means of conveyance are cars and some ships.

17. ***(b)*** **:**

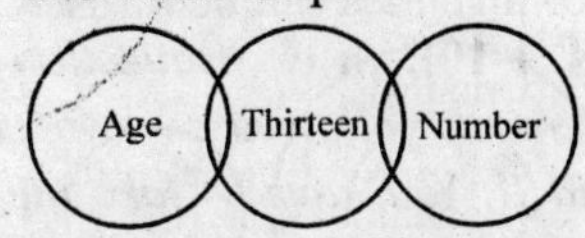

Some are aged thirteen and some numbers are thirteen. Some thirteen units are numbers and some ages. Age and number have nothing in common.

18. ***(c)*** **:**

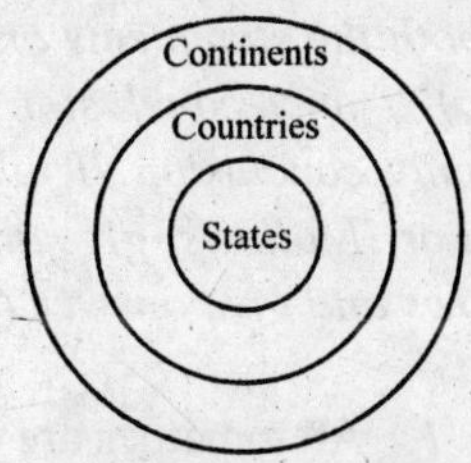

All continents contain countries within it and each country contains states within it.

19. ***(d)*** **:**

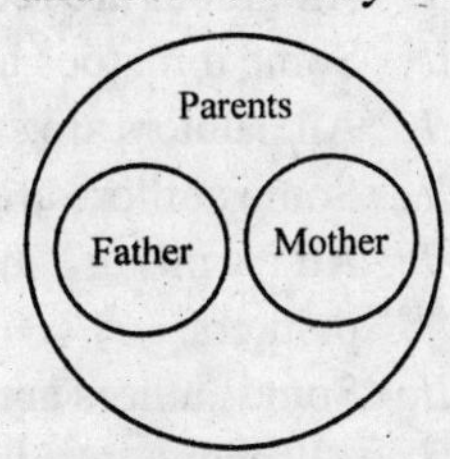

All fathers and mothers are parents, but they are two separate classes. Some of the parents are fathers and some are mothers.

20. ***(d)*** **:**

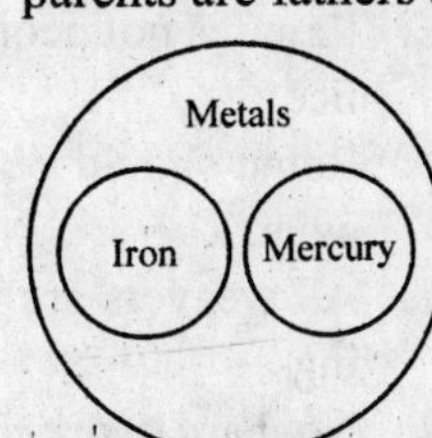

Iron and mercury are metals, but they have nothing in common. Some metals are iron and some mercury.

20. SYLLOGISM

In this reasoning pattern, the two premises are followed by two conclusions drawn from them. Five options *(a)*, *(b)*, *(c)*, *(d)* and *(e)* are given as answers. Based on the two statements the candidate has to select the right option as answer.

EXERCISE

Directions (Qs. 1-10): *In each question below are given two statements followed by two conclusions numbered I and II. You have to take the two given statements to be true even if they seem to be at variance from commonly known facts and then decide which of the given conclusions logically follows from the two given statements, disregarding commonly known facts. Read both the statements and—*

Give answer (a) if only conclusion I follows; give answer (b) if only conclusion II follows; give answer (c) if either I or II follows; give answer (d) if neither I nor II follows and give answer (e) if both I and II follows.

1. *Statements* *I*: All tomatoes are red.
II: All grapes are tomatoes.
Conclusions I: All grapes are red.
II: Some tomatoes are grapes.

2. *Statements* *I*: All painters are smilling.
II: Some authors are painters.
Conclusions I: All smiling authors are painters.
II: Some authors are smiling.

3. *Statements* *I*: All peons in this office are efficient.
II: Ramu is not efficient.
Conclusions I: Ramu is not peon in this office.
II: Ramu should be more efficient.

4. *Statements* *I*: All weavers are hard working.
II: No hard working men are foolish.
Conclusions I: No weavers are foolish.
II: Some foolish are weavers.

5. *Statements* *I*: All fishes are cars.
II: All cars are vegetables.
Conclusions I: Some vegetables are cars.
II: Some vegetables are fishes.

6. *Statements* *I*: Some dogs are pups.
II: All horses are pups.
Conclusions I: Some dogs are horses.
II: Some horses are dogs.

7. *Statements* *I*: All beautiful women are mothers.
II: All mothers are understanding.
Conclusions I: All beautiful women are understanding.
II: All mothers are beautiful women.

8. *Statements* *I*: Some toys are tables.
II: No table is black.
Conclusions I: Some toys are black.
II: Some toys are not black.

9. *Statements* *I*: All rivers are mountains.
II: Some rivers are deserts.
Conclusions I: Some mountains are deserts.
II: Some deserts are not mountains.

10. *Statements* *I*: All men are horses.
II: All horses are elephants.
Conclusions I: All men are elephants.
II: All elephants are men.

Directions (Qs. 11-15): *In the following questions, select the set of conclusion which logically follows from the given statements.*

11. *Statements* *I* : All foxes are plates.
II : All plates are trees.
Conclusions *I* : All foxes are trees.
II : All trees are foxes.
III : Some trees are foxes.
IV : Some trees are plates.
(a) All conclusions are correct.
(b) Only conclusions I, III, and IV follow.
(c) Only conclusions II, III, and IV follow.
(d) Only conclusions I and IV follow.
(e) None of the above.

12. *Statements* *I* : Some cubes are squares.
II : All squares are circles.
Conclusions *I* : All cubes are circles.
II : Some circles are cubes.
III : Some circles are squares.
IV : All squares are cubes.
(a) Only conclusion I follows.
(b) Only conclusion I, II and III follow.
(c) All conclusions are correct.
(d) Only conclusions II and III follow.
(e) None of the above.

13. *Statements* *I* : All cups are goats.
II : All goats are tins.
Conclusions *I* : All goats are cups.
II : All tins are goats.
III : No cups are tins.
IV : No tins are cups.
(a) Only conclusions III and IV follow.
(b) Only conclusios I and II follow.
(c) Only conclusions I, II and III follow.
(d) All conclusions are correct.
(e) None of the above.

14. *Statements* *I* : All bombs are bags.
II : Some bags are jets.
Conclusions *I* : All bombs are jets.
II : All jets are bombs.
III : Some jets are bombs.
IV : Some bombs are jets.
(a) Only conclusion III follows.
(b) Only conclusions I and II follow.
(c) All conclusions are correct.
(d) Only conclusions III and IV follow.
(e) None of these.

15. *Statements* *I* : Some thorns are jackets.
II : Some jackets are boats.
Conclusions *I* : No thorns are boats.
II : All jackets are boats.
III : Some boats are thorns.
IV : No jackets are thorns.
(a) Either conclusion I or IV follows.
(b) Either conclusion I or II follows.
(c) Either conclusion I or III follows.
(d) No conclusion is correct.
(e) All conclusions are correct.

EXPLANATORY ANSWERS

1. *(e)* : When all tomatoes are red and all grapes are tomatoes, then all grapes are also red. When all grapes are tomatoes, then some tomatoes must be grapes. Therefore, both conclusions I and II are correct.

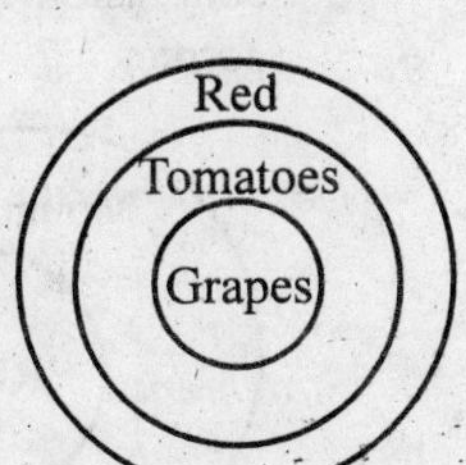

2. *(b)* : When all painters are smiling and some authors are painters, then some authors are smiling. Therefore, only conclusion II is correct.

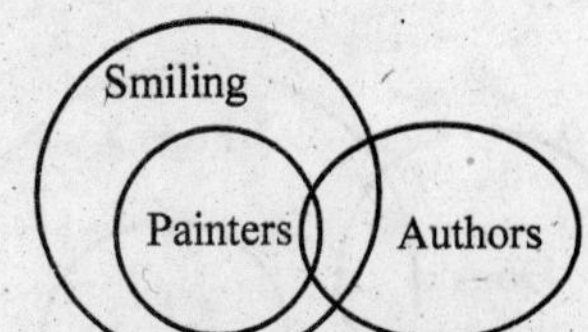

3. *(a)* : When all the peons of the office are efficient, then Ramu cannot be a peon in this office. Therefore, only conclusion I is correct.

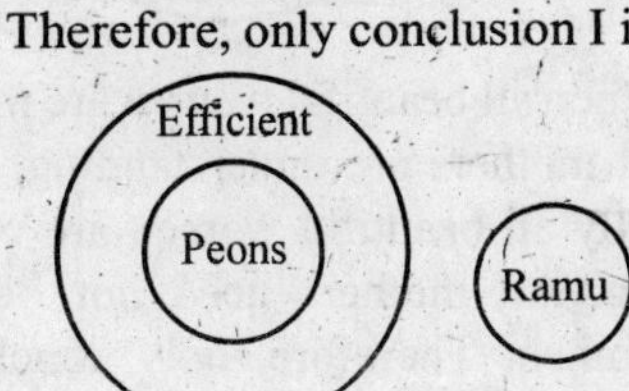

4. *(a)*: When all weavers are hardworking and no hardworking men are foolish, then no weavers are foolish. Therefore, only conclusion I is correct.

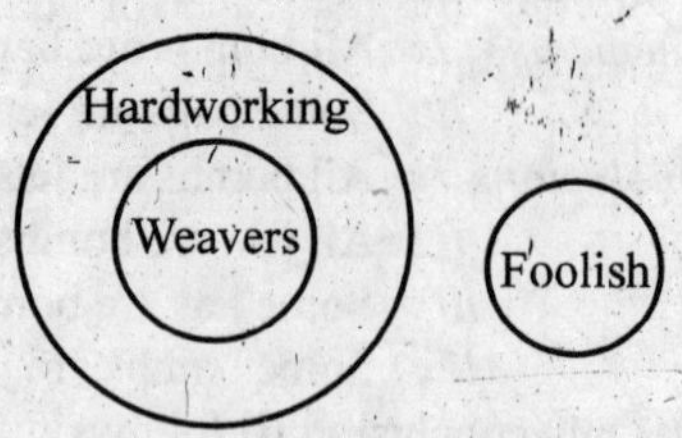

5. *(e)*: When all fishes are cars and all cars are vegetables, then all fishes will naturally be vegetables. This means that some vegetables are fishes. And when all cars are vegetables, then some vegetables will be cars naturally. Therefore, both the conclusions I and II are correct.

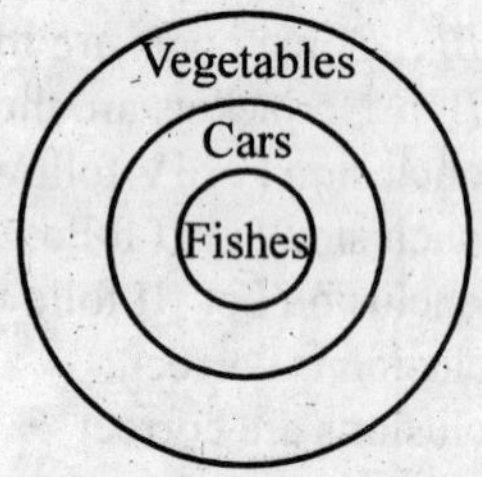

6. *(d)*: No relationship can be established between the two statements. Therefore, neither conclusion I nor conclusion II is correct.

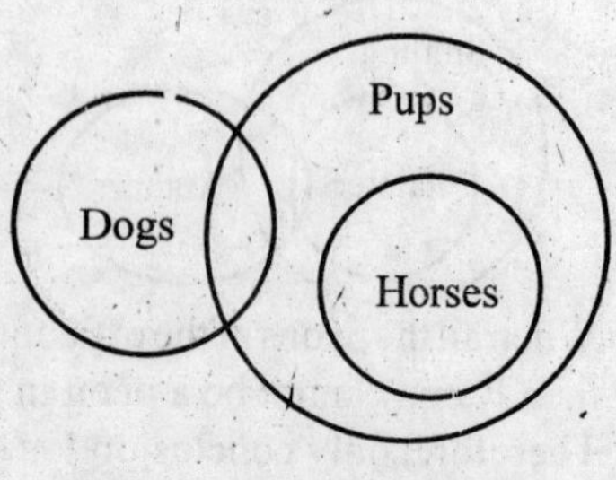

7. *(a)*: When all beautiful women are mothers and all mothers are understanding, then naturally all beautiful women are understanding. All mothers need not be beautiful women. Therefore, only conclusion I is correct.

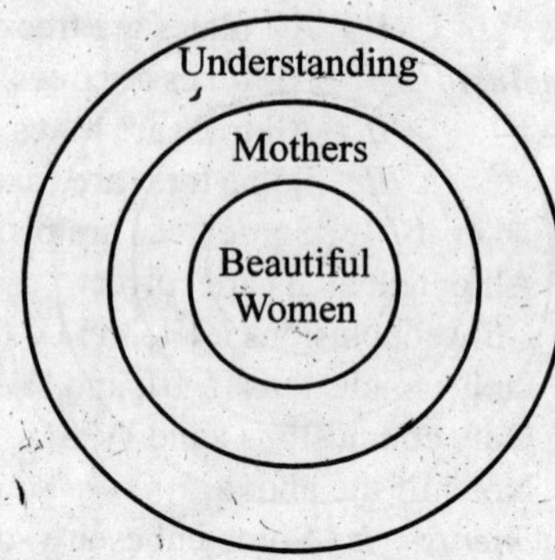

8. *(c)*: When some toys are tables and no table is black, then it is indicated that some toys can be black, as all toys are not tables. On the other hand, some toys may not be black. Therefore, there is a possibility that some toys may or may not be black. As such, either conclusion I or conclusion II can be correct.

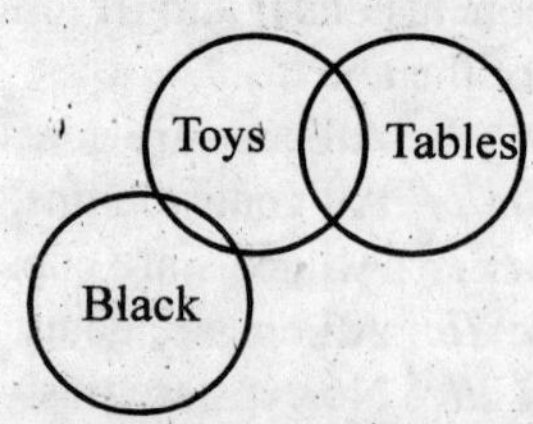

9. *(e)*: When all rivers are mountains and some rivers are deserts, then some deserts cannot be mountains and also, some mountains need not be deserts. Therefore, both conclusion I and conclusion II are correct.

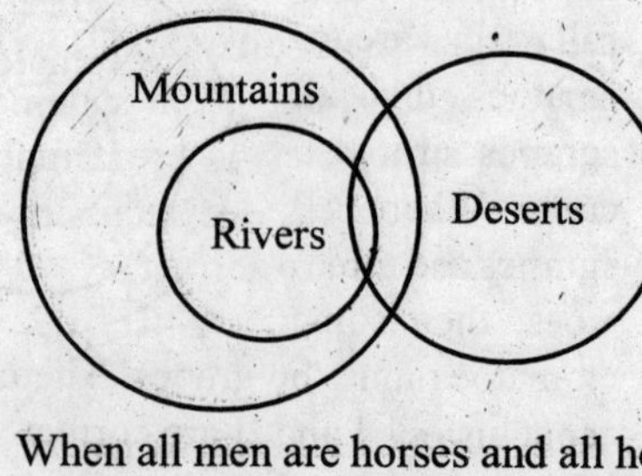

10. *(a)*: When all men are horses and all horses are elephants then, naturally all men are elephants, but all elephants need not be men. Therefore, only conclusion I is correct.

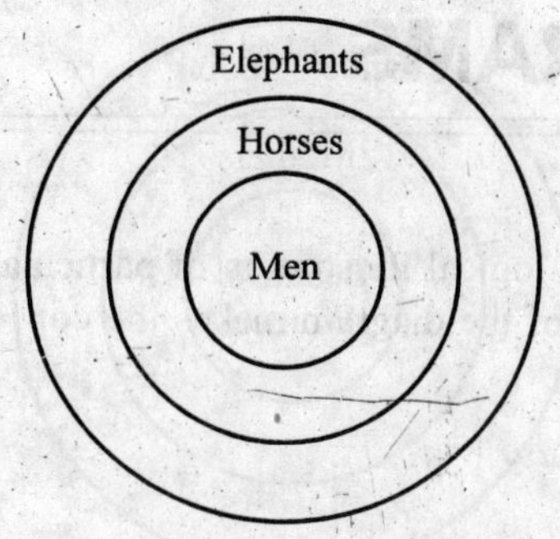

11. ***(b)*** **:**

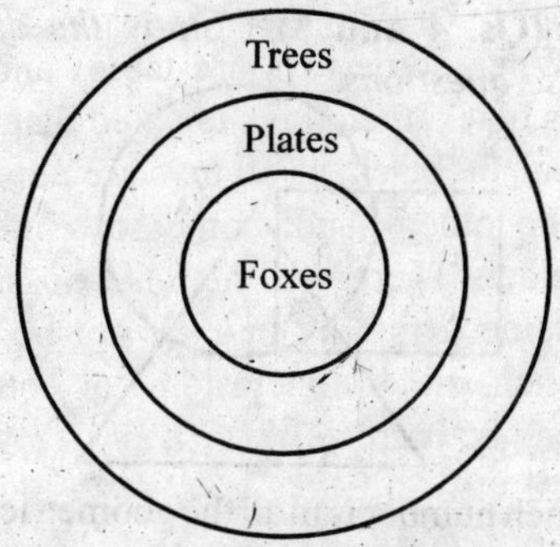

When all foxes are plates and all plates are trees, then naturally all foxes will be trees and some trees will then have to be foxes. And when all plates are trees then some trees will have to be plates. Therefore, only conclusions I, III and IV are correct.

12. ***(d)*** **:** When it is given that some cubes are squares and all squares are circles, then some cubes will naturally be circles, though all cubes cannot be circles. When some cubes are circles, then some circles will have to be cubes. And when all squares are circles, then some circles will have to be squares. As per given statement II, all squares are circles. Therefore all squares cannot be cubes. As such only conclusions II and III are correct.

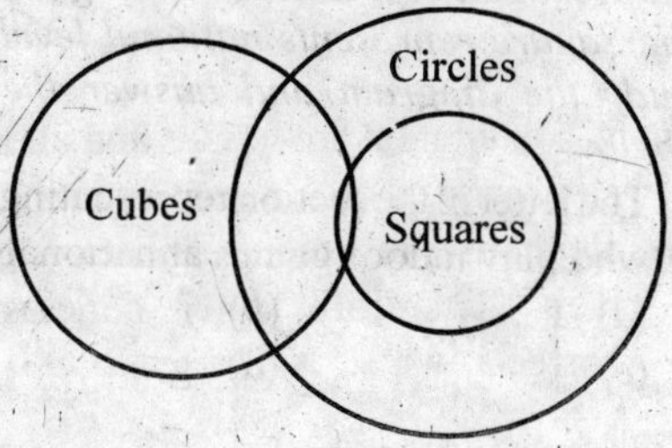

13. ***(e)*** **:** When all cups are goats, then only some goats can be cups. When all goats are tins, then only some tins can be goats. When all cups are goats and all goats are tins, then naturally all cups are tins and some tins must be cups. Therefore, all the conclusions are incorrect.

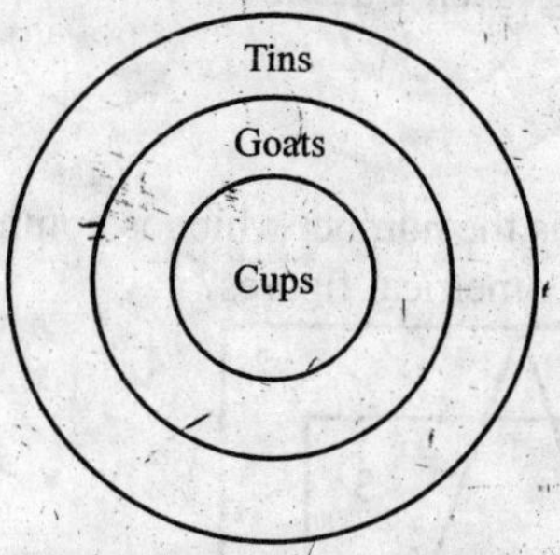

14. ***(e)*** **:** When all bombs are bags and some bags are jets then all bombs cannot be jets. 'Some bags' indicate that there is no chance of some bombs being jets, or some jets being bombs. Further all jets cannot be bombs. Therefore, all conclusions are incorrect.

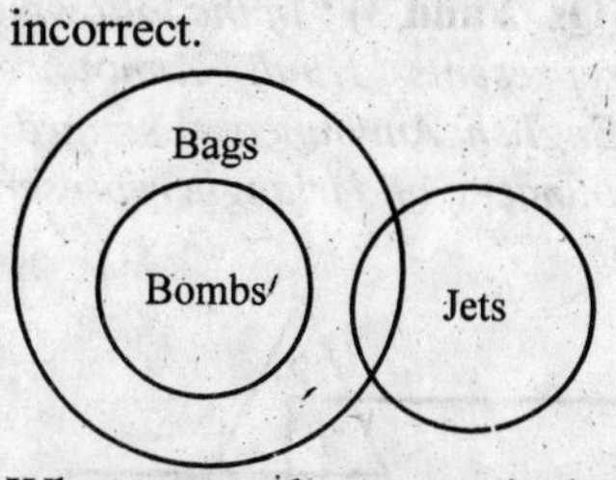

15. ***(d)*** **:** When some thorns are jackets and some jackets are boats, then some thorns may be boats but some boats cannot be thorns. As per Statement I, some thorns are jackets, some jackets need to be thorns. When Statement II conveys that some jackets are boats, then it is clear that all jackets cannot be boats. Therefore, no particular given conclusion can be drawn from the given statements.

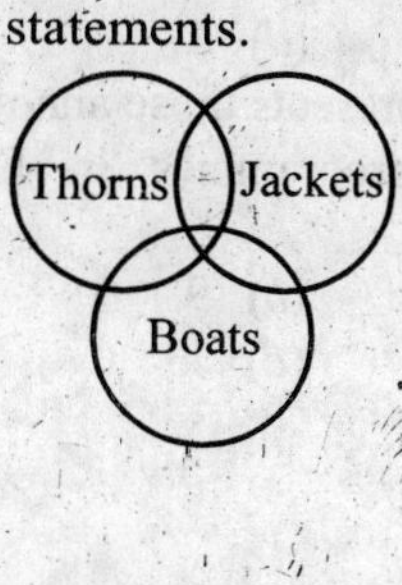

21. VENN DIAGRAMS

In these type of questions, diagrammatic representation presents a logical illustration of particular class or statements based on which the questions are asked. A clear view of the diagram makes the concepts clear for attempting such questions.

EXERCISE

1. What is the number which is common to only two geometrical figures?

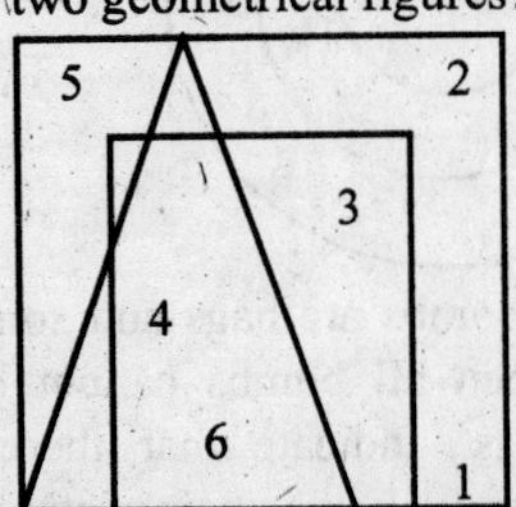

(*a*) 4 (*b*) 3
(*c*) 5 (*d*) 2

Directions (Qs. 2 and 3) : *In the following diagram, rectangle represents Hindi Announcers, circle represents English Announcers, square represents French Announcers, and triangle represents German Announcers.*

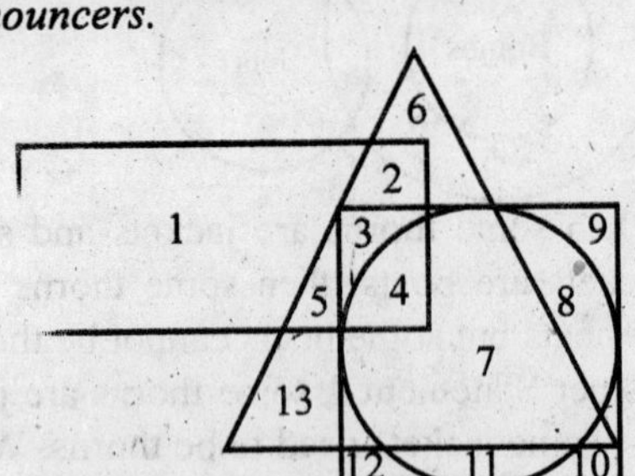

2. Which area represents those announcers who can present programmes in Hindi, French and German only?

(*a*) 1 (*b*) 2
(*c*) 3 (*d*) 4

3 Which area represents those announcers, who can present programmes in French and English only?

(*a*) 7 (*b*) 9
(*c*) 11 (*d*) 13

Directions (Qs. 4 and 5) : *Study the diagram to answer these questions.*

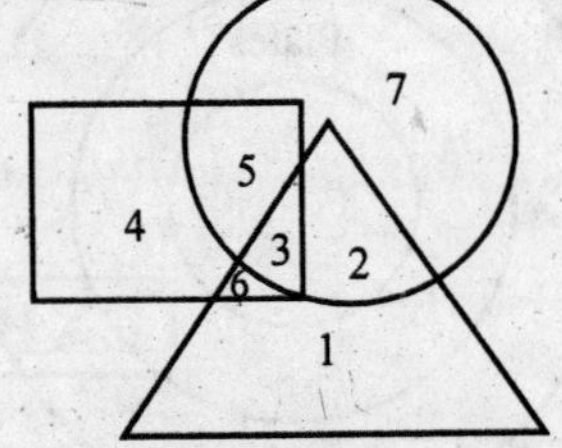

4. Which number is in all the geometrical figures?

(*a*) 5 (*b*) 6
(*c*) 2 (*d*) 3

5. Number 6 is in :

(*a*) Rectangle and triangle
(*b*) Circle and traingle
(*c*) Rectangle and circle
(*d*) Rectangle only

Directions (Qs. 6 to 9) : *In the following diagram*

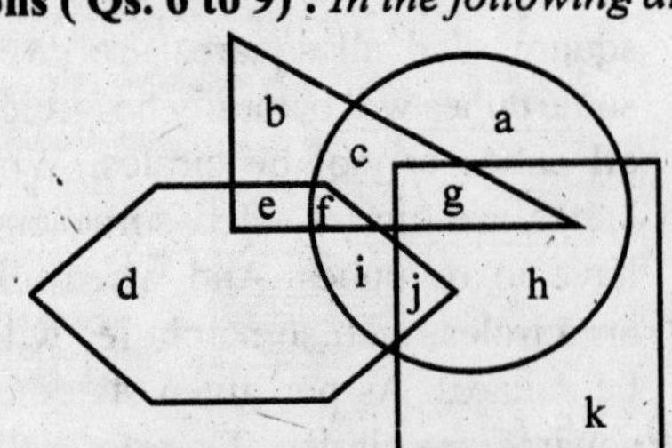

The Circle represents players
The Triangle represents outdoor games
The Hexagon represents indoor games and
The Square represents national level players
Study the diagram and answer the questions given below :

6. The letter in the section representing the players who play indoor games at national level is :

(*a*) f (*b*) i
(*c*) j (*d*) g

7. The letter representing the section of outdoor as well as indoor game players who do not play at the national level is :
(*a*) c (*b*) f
(*c*) e (*d*) i

8. The section representing national level players who do not play either outdoor or indoor games but still come under the category of players is :
(*a*) k (*b*) g
(*c*) c (*d*) h

9. Persons who play outdoor games but do not come under the category of players are represented in the section marked :
(*a*) b (*b*) c
(*c*) a (*d*) d

Direction (Qs. 10) : *Study the diagram given below.*

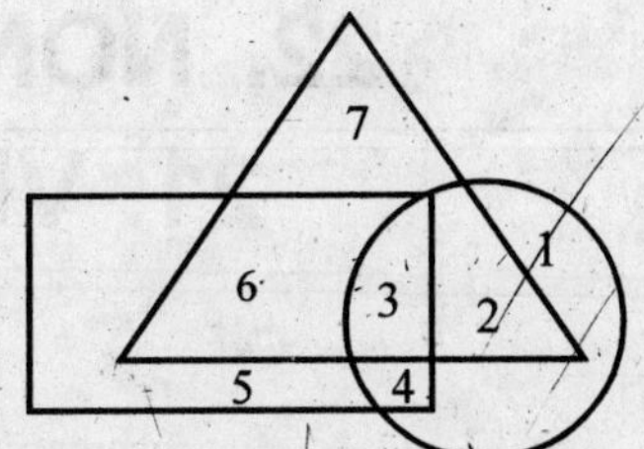

A college provides three different activities, students union represented by triangle, literary society represented by rectangle and social service league represented by circle.

10. Those who take part in both literary society and social service league but not in students union are represented by :
(*a*) 3 & 4 (*b*) 5 & 6
(*c*) 5 & 1 (*d*) 4

EXPLANATORY ANSWERS

1. (*b*) :

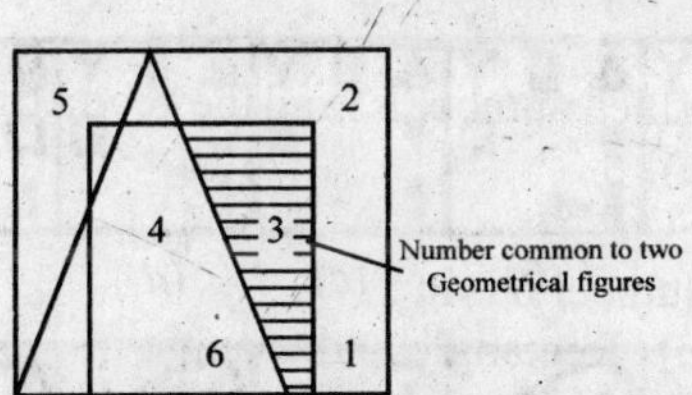

Note : Numbers 4 and 6 are common to all three geometrical figures.

2. (*c*), 3. (*c*) :

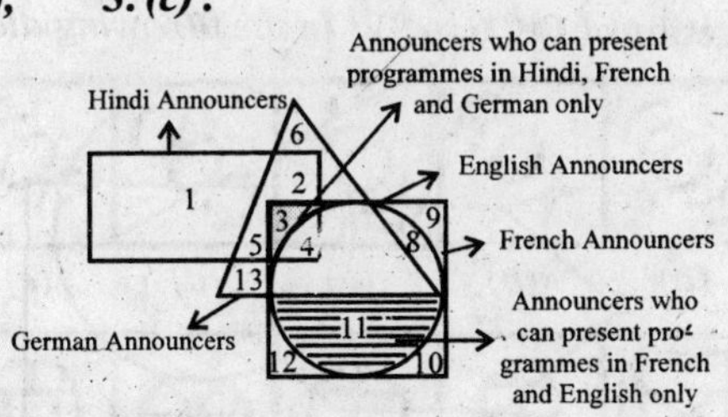

4. (*d*), 5. (*a*) :

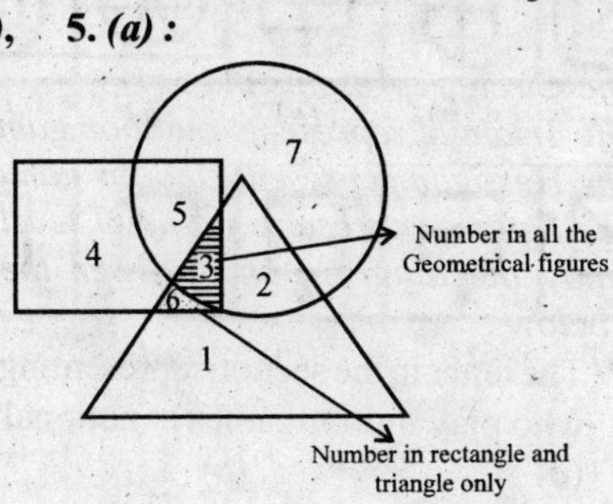

6. (*c*), 7. (*b*), 8. (*d*), 9. (*a*) :

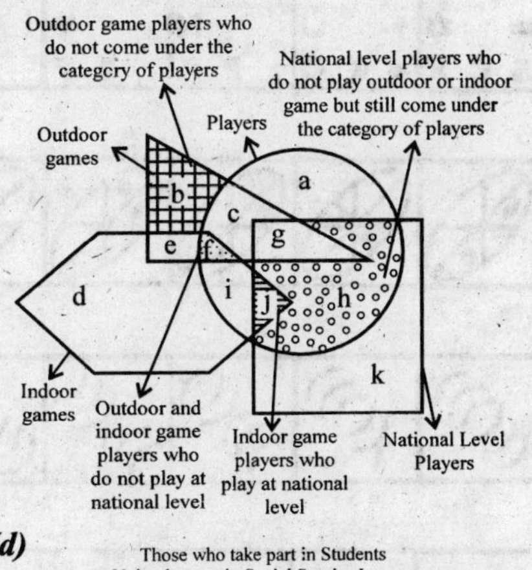

10. (*d*)

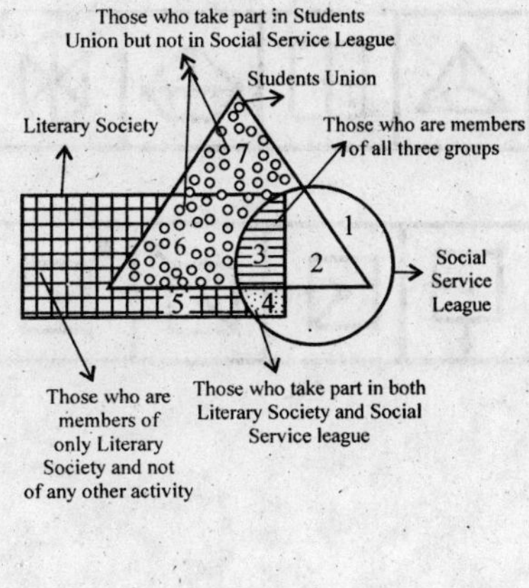

22. NON-VERBAL SERIES

EXERCISE

Directions (Q. 1–10) : *In each of the following questions which one of the five answer figures given below should come after the problem figures if the sequence are continued?*

Problem Figures | **Answer Figures**

1.  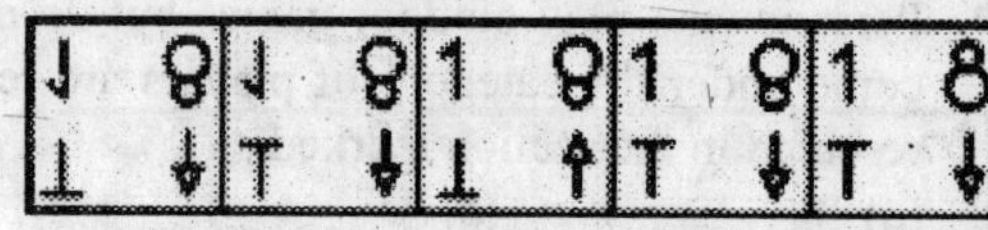

(a) (b) (c) (d) (e)

2.  

(a) (b) (c) (d) (e)

3.  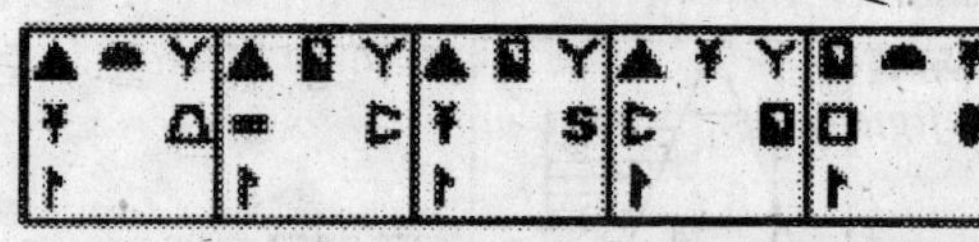

(a) (b) (c) (d) (e)

4.  

(a) (b) (c) (d) (e)

5.  

(a) (b) (c) (d) (e)

6.  

(a) (b) (c) (d) (e)

7.  

(a) (b) (c) (d) (e)

Problem Figures **Answer Figures**

8. 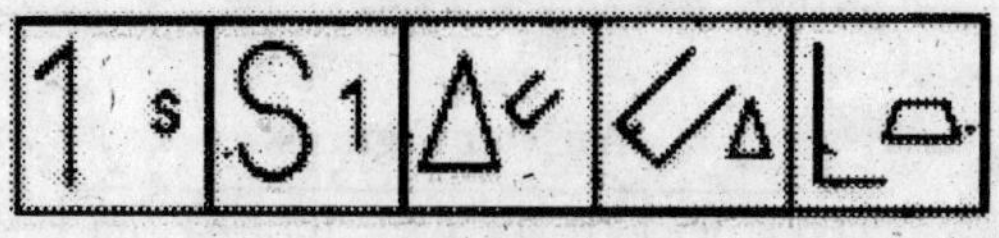 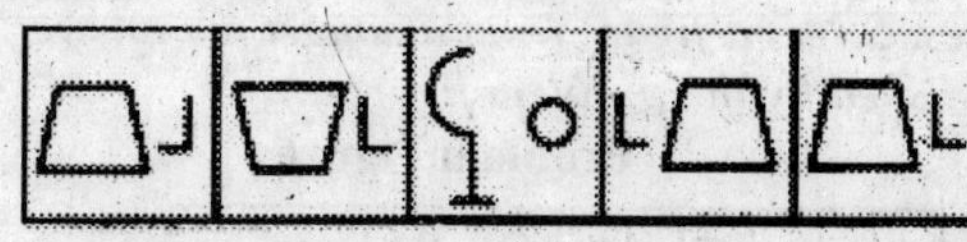

(a) (b) (c) (d) (e)

9.  

(a) (b) (c) (d) (e)

10.  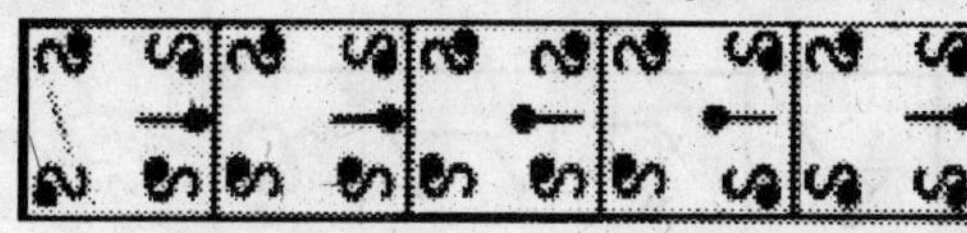

(a) (b) (c) (d) (e)

Directions (Q. 11-20) : *In each of these questions, a series begins with an unmarked figure on the extreme left in the row of figures. One and only one of the five lettered figures in the series does not fit into the series. The two unmarked figures, one on the extreme left and the other on the extreme right fit into the series. Take as many aspects into account as possible of the figures in the series and find out the one and only of the five marked figures which does not fit into the series. The letter of that figure is the answer.*

11. 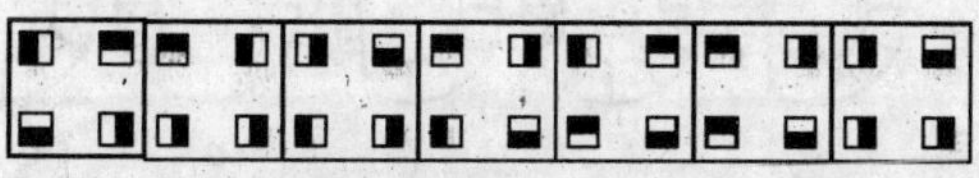

(a) (b) (c) (d) (e)

12. 

(a) (b) (c) (d) (e)

13. 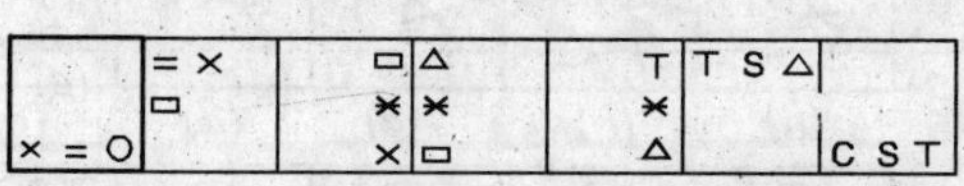

(a) (b) (c) (d) (e)

14. 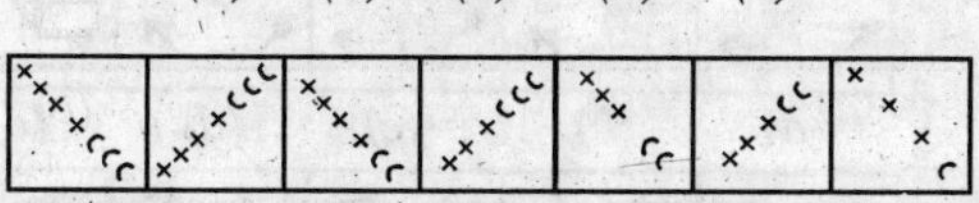

(a) (b) (c) (d) (e)

15. 

(a) (b) (c) (d) (e)

16. 

(a) (b) (c) (d) (e)

17. 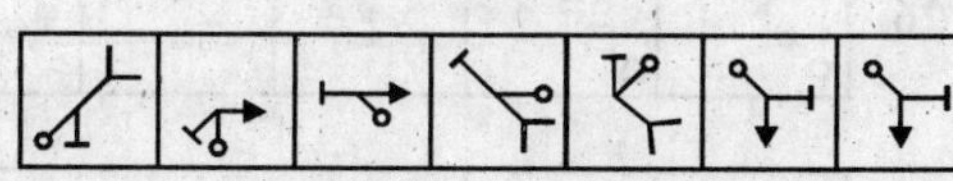

(a) (b) (c) (d) (e)

18. 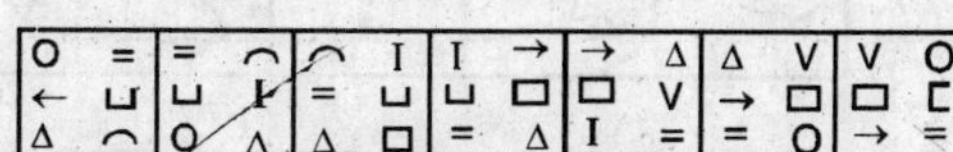

(a) (b) (c) (d) (e)

19. 

(a) (b) (c) (d) (e)

20. 

(a) (b) (c) (d) (e)

Directions (Q. 21–30) : *Each of the following questions consist of problem figures followed by answer figures. Select a figure from amongst the answer figures which will continue the same series or pattern as established by the problem figures.*

Problem Figures | **Answer Figures**

21. 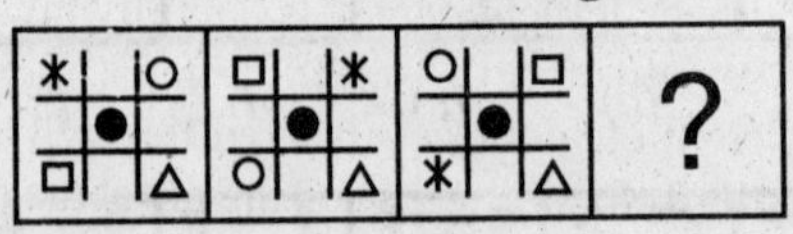

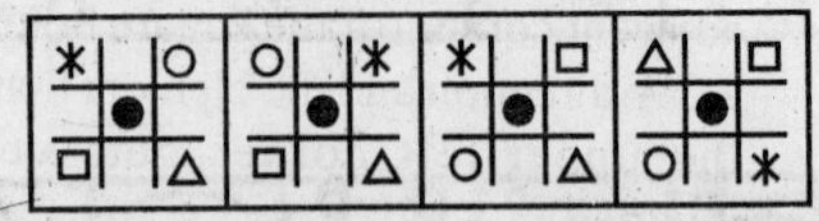

(a) (b) (c) (d)

22. 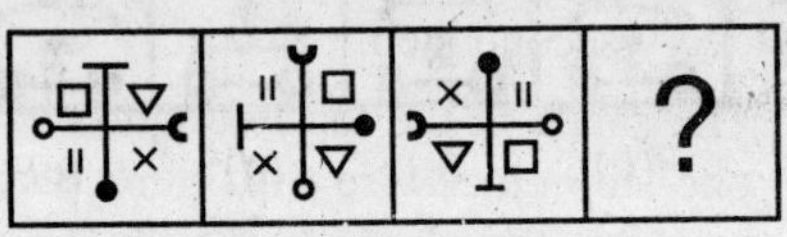

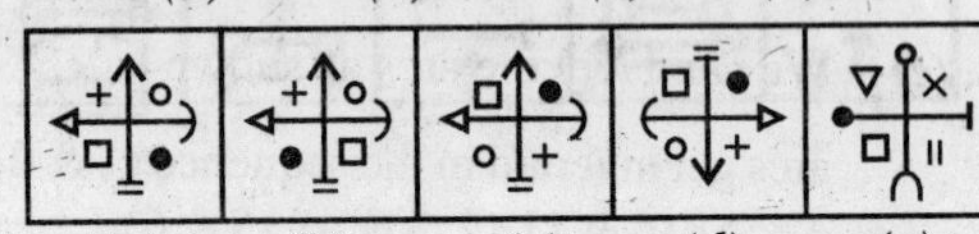

(a) (b) (c) (d) (e)

23. 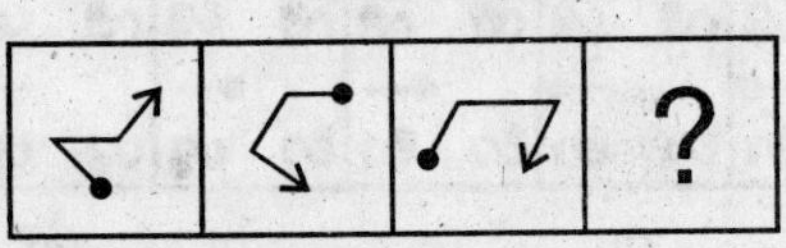

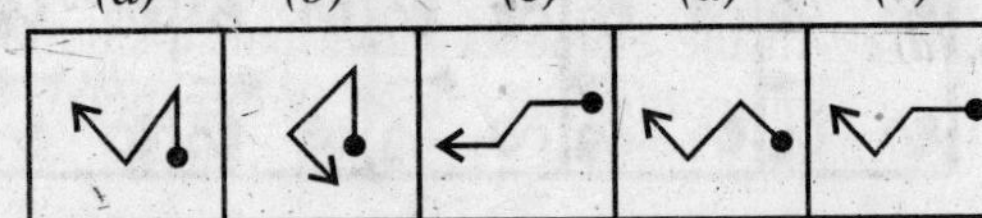

(a) (b) (c) (d) (e)

24. 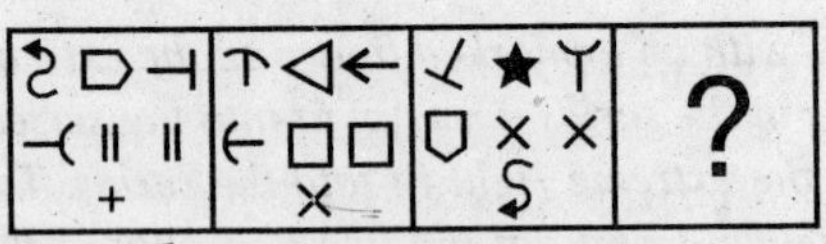

(a) (b) (c) (d) (e)

25. 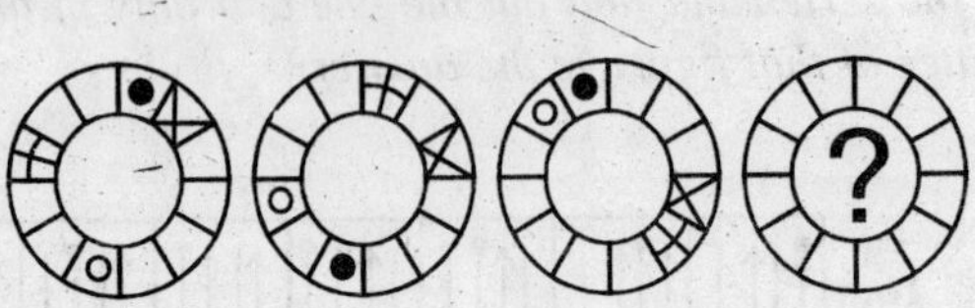

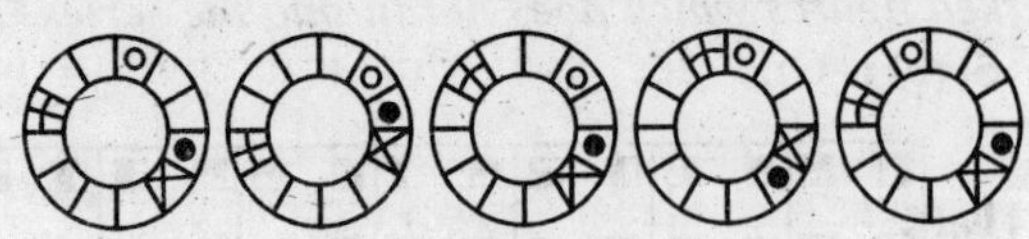

(a) (b) (c) (d) (e)

26. 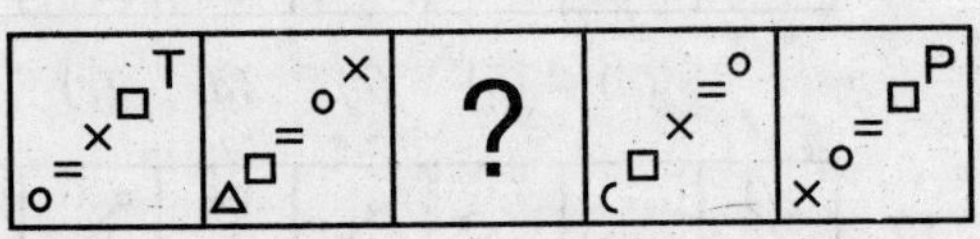

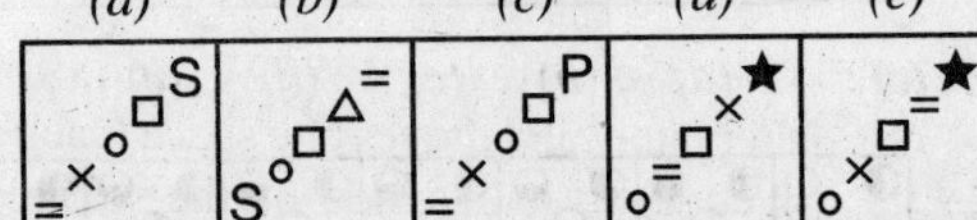

(a) (b) (c) (d) (e)

27. 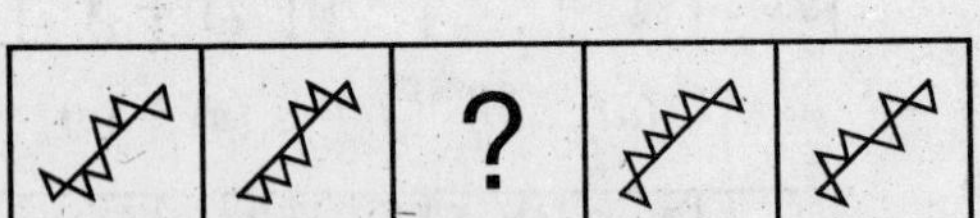

(a) (b) (c) (d) (e)

28. 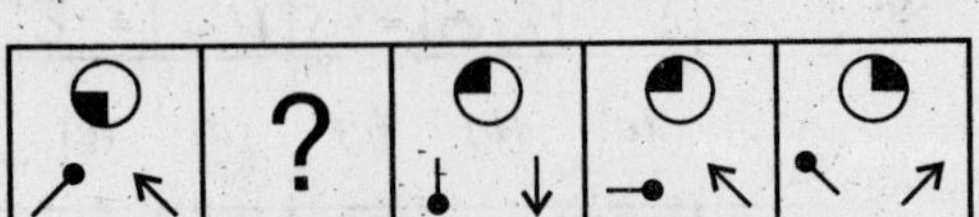

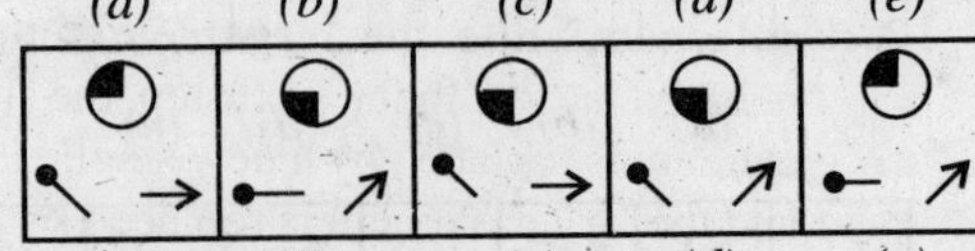

(a) (b) (c) (d) (e)

29. 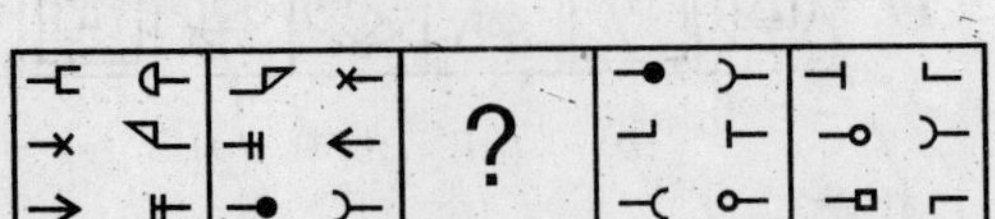

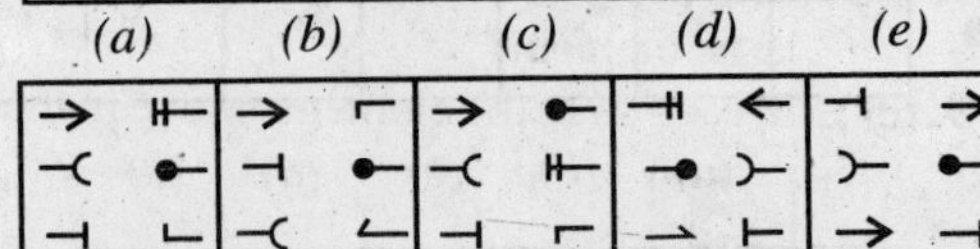

(a) (b) (c) (d) (e)

30. 

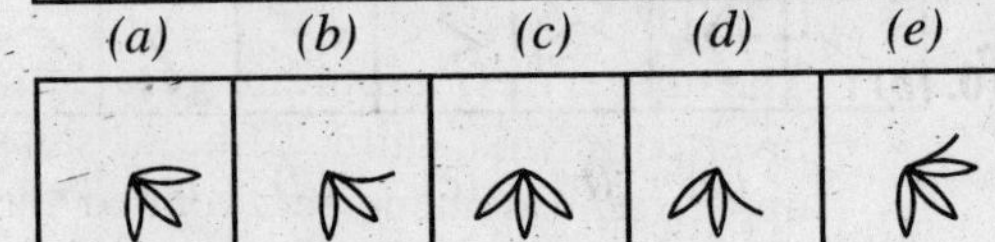

(a) (b) (c) (d) (e)

EXPLANATORY ANSWERS

1. (d) : In each step, all the elements move to the adjacent corner (of the square boundary) in a CW direction and the element that reaches the upper-left corner gets vertically inverted.

2. (c) : We can label the arcs as shown 

. The arcs get inverted in the sequence (1 & 2), (3, 4 & 5), (6 & 1), (2, 3 & 4), (5 & 6), ...

3. (d) : All the elements move half-a-side of the square boundary in ACW direction in each step. Also, first, third and fifth elements are replaced by new elements in one step and second, fourth and sixth elements are replaced by new elements in the next step. The two steps are repeated alternately.

4. (a) : In each step, the dot moves one space CW and the arrow moves two spaces CW.

5. (c) : One arc and four arcs get inverted alternately.

6. (e) : The number of parts increases by one along with the number of sides in the figure.

7. (c) : The pin rotates 45°CW and 90°CW alternately and moves one space (each space is equal to half-a-side of the square) and two spaces CW alternately. The arrow rotates 90°ACW and 45°ACW alternately and moves two spaces and one space.

8. (e) : In one step, the two elements interchange positions and the smaller element gets enlarged while the larger element gets reduced in size. In the next step, the smaller element is replaced by a new small element and the larger element is replaced by a new large element.

9. (c) : In each step, the elements move in the order

.

10. (b) : The upper-left element gets laterally inverted in first, third, fifth. .... steps; the upper-right element gets rotated through 180° is first, fourth, seventh,.... steps; the lower-left element gets laterally inverted in second, fourth, sixth, ... steps; the lower-right element gets rotated through 180° in third, sixth,... steps and the pin at the middle-right position gets laterally inverted in every second step.

11. (a) : The shade in the top left square is moved one step clockwise till figure B and then reversed, the process is repeated. The shade in the top right square is moved one step anticlockwise till figure D and then reversed. The shade in the bottom left square is moved one step clockwise in alternate figures and the shade in bottom right square is moved one step clockwise after two figures. In figure 'A' the rule is isolated by the shade in the bottom left square.

12. (e) : In alternate figures a new circle is shaded clockwise. The pattern of the shade is also moved clockwise. In figure 'E' right half of the circle in the centre should have been shaded.

13. (a) : The three elements are placed either horizontally or vertically. In option 'A' neither of the placements can be applied.

14. (c) : The placement of elements is same in alternate figures. The number and type of elements is same in two subsequent figures. In this manner, figure 'C' should have four crosses and two C shapes.

15. (c) : The element is moved one step anticlockwise and the arc at one end is turned outside and inside alternately. In figure 'C' the element should be on the right side with the arc turned outside on the top side.

16. (e) : The left most element, line segment with the dot is moved one step towards right till figure C where it reaches the extreme right position. This process is repeated from figure D where the element on the extreme left, line segment with a circle, is moved. In figure 'E' the placement of the elements does not follow the rule of the series.

17. (e) : The 'T' line is rotated 45° clockwise and the line with the circle 45° anticlockwise. The 'Y' shape and the arrow are repeated twice after two figures. In option E, the 'T' shape and the line with the circle are rotated by 90°.

18. (e) : First the elements in the four corners are moved one step anticlockwise, next the four elements from the top are moved one step anticlockwise and then the four elements from the bottom are moved one step anticlockwise. Of the remaining two elements, the one on the left is made new each time and then their places are interchanged. This process is repeated from figure D. In option 'E' open square should have been in place of circle to continue the series.

19. (a) : At each step the outermost figure is removed and a new figure is placed right in the centre of other two figures. In option 'A' the triangle is turned upside down, which violates the rule of the series.

20. (a) : The arrow is moved one step anticlockwise and the triangle one step clockwise. In figure 'A' the triangle should have been on the left side of the figure.

21. (a) : The places of star, circle and square are moved one step clockwise at each step.

22. (e) : The elements in the four quadrants are moved one step clockwise and the elements at the ends of the cross are moved one step anticlockwise in this series.

23. (a) : In alternate figures, the line with the dot is turned 90° clockwise and the arrow 180° clockwise.

24. (e) : In alternate figures, the element in the top left position is horizontally inverted and moved one and half steps anticlockwise, the top middle element is turned 90° clockwise and moved one step anticlockwise, the top right element is turned 135° clockwise and moved one step anticlockwise, the element at the bottom is replaced by a new element and moved to the top middle position, and the two identical elements are replaced by two new identical elements.

25. (a) : The cross and the circle move one and two steps clockwise respectively (at each step), the plus moves 3, 4 and 5 steps clockwise, and the dot 6, 5 and 4 steps clockwise.

26. (a) : At first step, the fifth or the bottom most element is moved to the second place from top, the second element moved to the fourth place, the fourth element is moved to the third place, the third element is moved to the first or the topmost place and the element on the top, which is made new, is moved to the last or the fifth place. At second step i.e., from second problem figure to third problem figure the above process is reversed. The bottom most element is the first and the top most element is the last or fifth. Hereafter, the process is repeated from the beginning. Option 'A' is the right answer.

27. (c) : Starting from the bottom, one triangle is moved to the opposite side at each step in upward order. Option 'C' fits into the question marked space.

28. (c) : The shade inside the circle is rotated clockwise in alternate figures; the line segment with a dot is rotated 135° clockwise in alternate figures and the arrow is rotated 135° anticlockwise in alternate figures. By this process answer figure 'C' completes the series.

29. (a) : At each step the elements are moved diagonally upward and then laterally inverted, and the top two elements are made new and placed at the bottom line. By this process, option figure 'A' completes the series.

30. (a) : The number of arcs making the petals of the flower are increased by one, one and half, two, two and half respectively at each step. Also, the flower is turned 45° anticlockwise. By this process, option 'A' is the right answer.

23. NON-VERBAL ANALOGY

EXERCISE

TYPE-I

Directions (Q. 1-15): *The second figure in the first unit of the Problem Figures bears a certain relationship to the first figure. Similarly, one of the figures in the Answer Figures bears the same relationship to the first figures in the second unit of the Problem Figures. Locate the figure which would fit the questions marks.*

Problem Figures | **Answer Figures**

1.

1 2 3 4

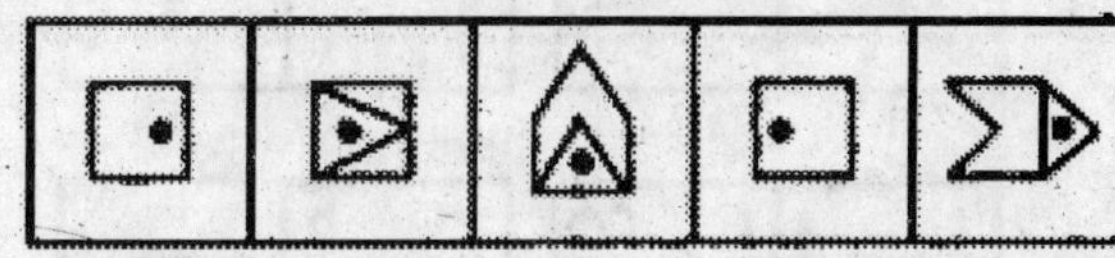

(a) (b) (c) (d) (e)

2.

1 2 3 4

(a) (b) (c) (d) (e)

3.

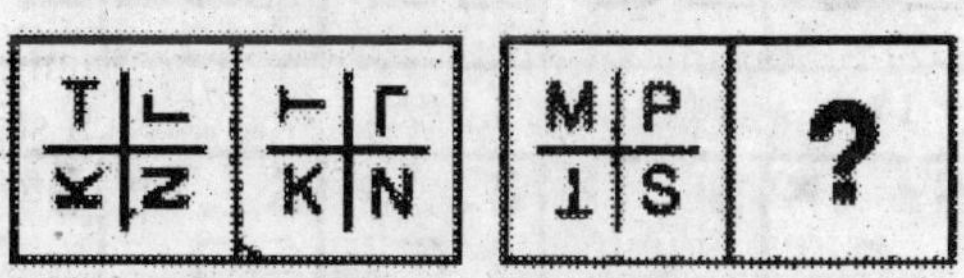

1 2 3 4

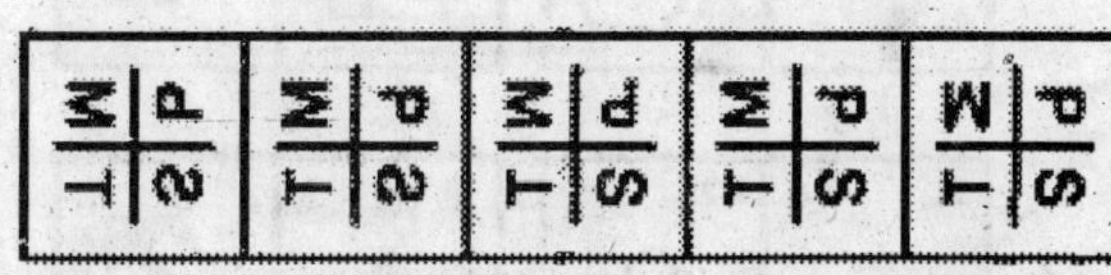

(a) (b) (c) (d) (e)

4.

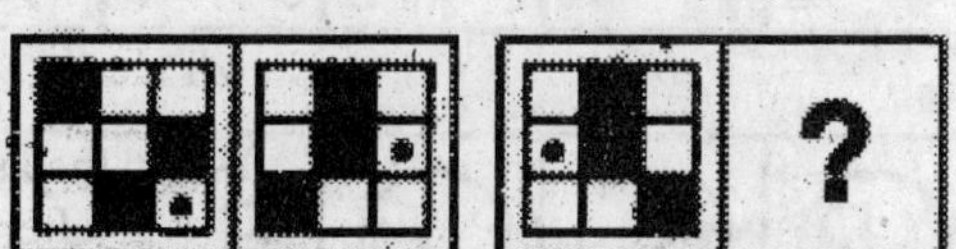

1 2 3 4

(a) (b) (c) (d) (e)

5.

1 2 3 4

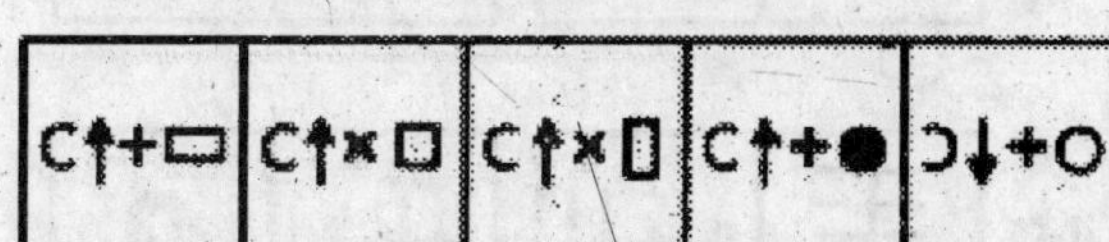

(a) (b) (c) (d) (e)

6.

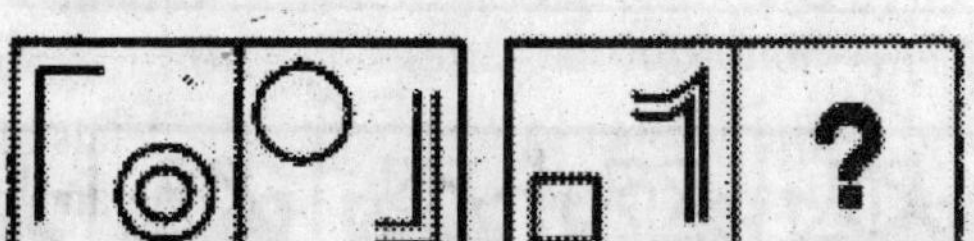

1 2 3 4

(a) (b) (c) (d) (e)

Problem Figures **Answer Figures**

7.

1 2 3 4

(a) (b) (c) (d) (e)

8.

1 2 3 4

(a) (b) (c) (d) (e)

9.
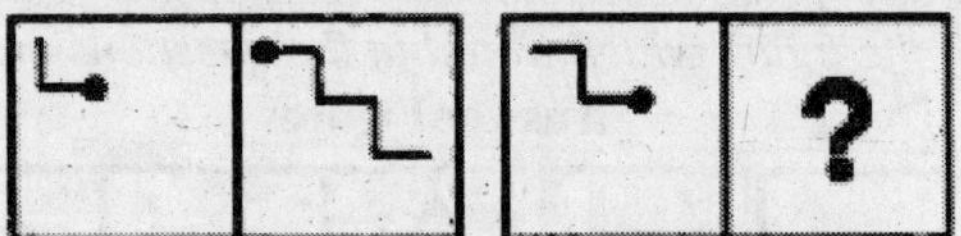
1 2 3 4

(a) (b) (c) (d) (e)

10.

1 2 3 4

(a) (b) (c) (d) (e)

11.

1 2 3 4

(a) (b) (c) (d) (e)

12.
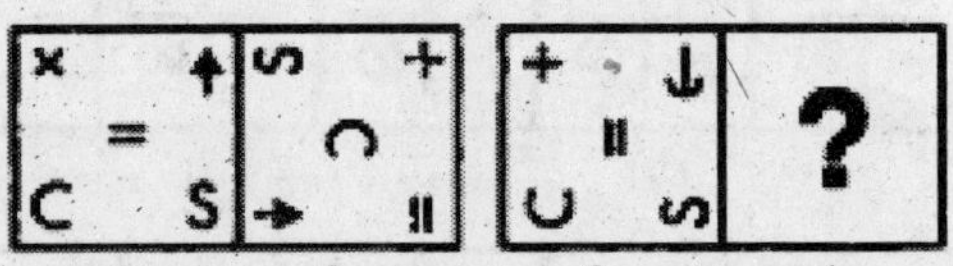
1 2 3 4
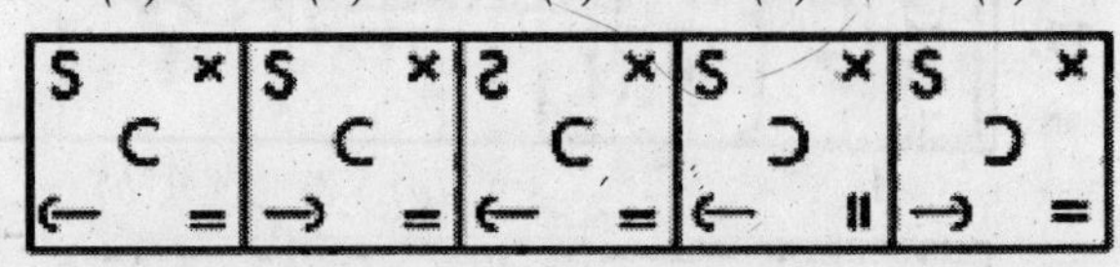
(a) (b) (c) (d) (e)

13.

1 2 3 4

(a) (b) (c) (d) (e)

14.

1 2 3 4

(a) (b) (c) (d) (e)

15.

1 2 3 4

(a) (b) (c) (d) (e)

TYPE-II

Directions (Q. 16–30): *In each of the following questions, a related pair of figures is followed by five numbered pairs of figures. Select the pair that has a relationship* **similar** *to that in the unnumbered pair.*

Problem Figure **Answer Figures**

16. 

(a) (b) (c) (d) (e)

17. 

(a) (b) (c) (d) (e)

18. 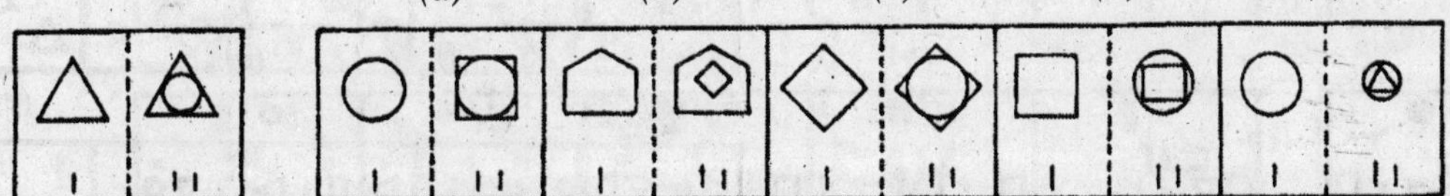

(a) (b) (c) (d) (e)

19. 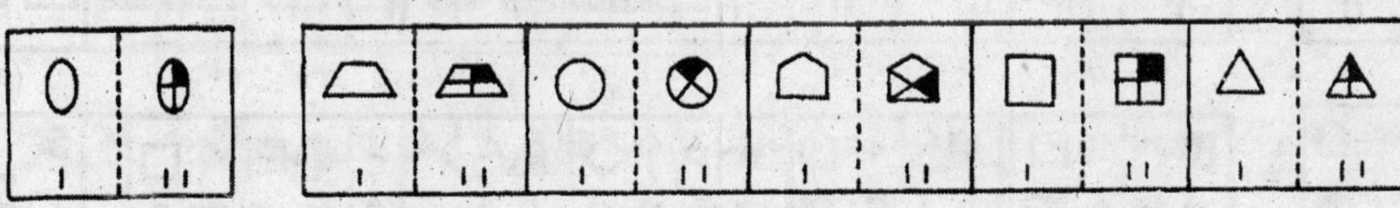

(a) (b) (c) (d) (e)

20. 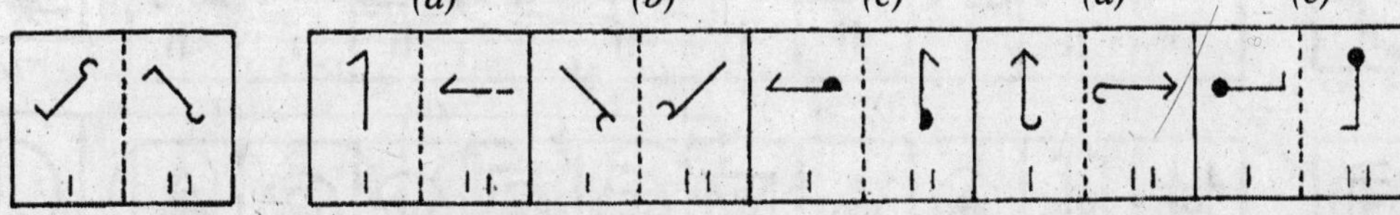

(a) (b) (c) (d) (e)

21. 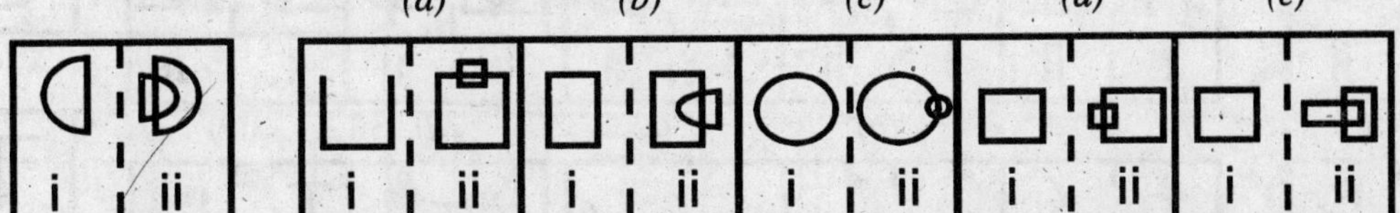

(a) (b) (c) (d) (e)

22. 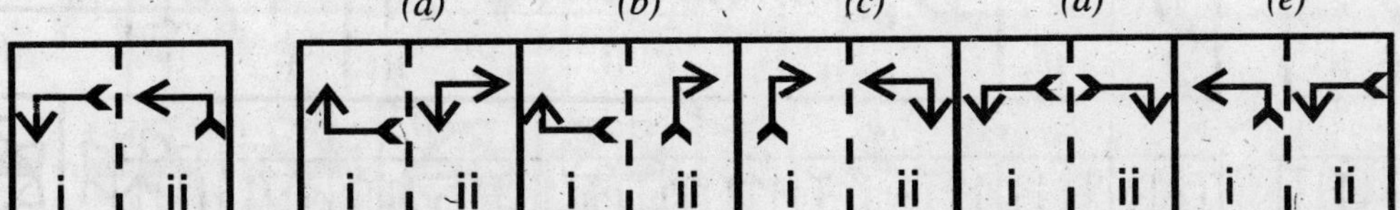

(a) (b) (c) (d) (e)

Problem Figure | **Answer Figures**

23.

(a) (b) (c) (d) (e)

24.

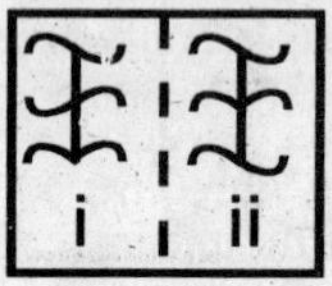

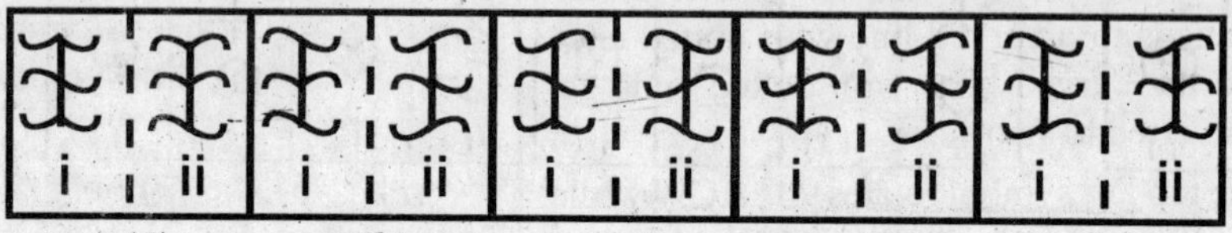

(a) (b) (c) (d) (e)

25.

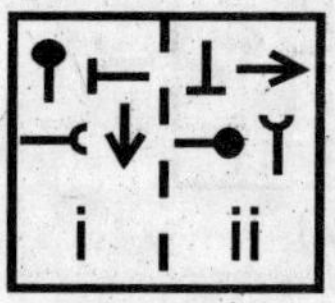

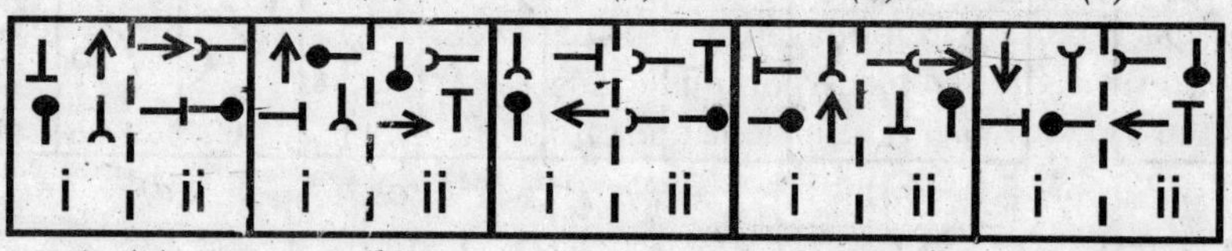

(a) (b) (c) (d) (e)

26.

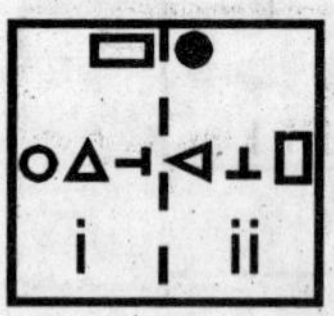

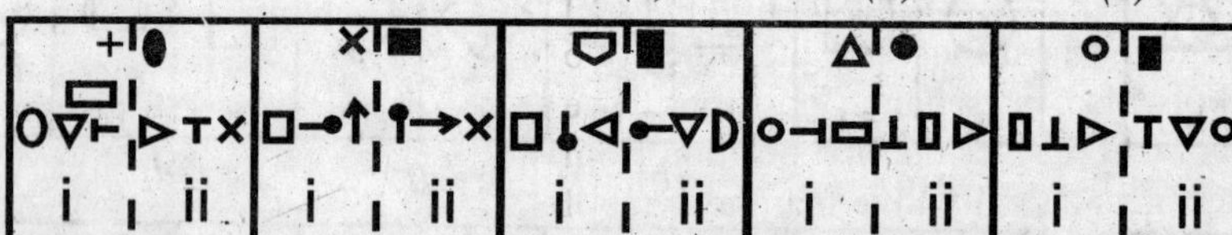

(a) (b) (c) (d) (e)

27.

(a) (b) (c) (d) (e)

28.

(a) (b) (c) (d) (e)

29.

(a) (b) (c) (d) (e)

30.

(a) (b) (c) (d) (e)

EXPLANATORY ANSWERS

1. (b) : The R.H.S. figure is fitted into the L.H.S. figure and the resulting figure is rotated 90° CW.

2. (b) : The figure rotates 45° ACW, the arrow changes to a curved line with dotted ends and the curved lines with dotted ends get converted to arrows.

3. (d) : The top left symbol rotates 90° ACW while all other symbols rotate 90° CW.

4. (e) : The black portion in top layer moves one step to the right; the black portions in the middle and the lower layers move one step to the left and the dot moves one step upwards.

5. (d) : The first and second symbols from the left interchange positions and the other two symbols also interchange positions. The symbol that reaches the first position from the left gets laterally inverted; the symbol that reaches the second position gets inverted, the third symbol rotates 90° CW and the fourth symbol gets replaced by a new one.

6. (d) : The single figure is replaced by a figure similar to the double figures and the double figures are replaced by figures similar to the single figure.

7. (e) : The figure rotates 135° ACW; a 'T' appears diagonally opposite to the black leaf and a 'Y' appears diagonally opposite to the white leaf.

8. (c) : The square rotates through 45°. The arrow moves 90° ACW and the pin moves 45° ACW.

9. (b) : The figure rotates through 180° and three lines forming a zig-zag, get attached to its lower end.

10. (d) : The symbols move in the order

The symbol that reaches the central position rotates 90° CW and its arc gets inverted; the 'P' shaped symbol rotates through 180°; the 'C' shaped symbol rotates 90° CW; the 'S' Shaped symbol gets laterally inverted and the fifth symbol gets replaced by a new one.

45°, the symbol that reaches the lower right corner rotates 90° ACW and a new symbol appears in middle-left position.

11. (e) : The upper and the lower parts of the figure get separated. Shading is removed from the upper part and the lower part is inverted. The two parts are then placed side by side.

12. (a) : The symbols move in the order

The symbol that reaches the top-left corner rotates 90° ACW; the symbol in the top-right corner rotates through 45°; the symbols in the lower-left corner and in the central positions rotates 90° CW and the symbol that reaches the lower-right corner rotates through 90°.

13. (e) : The figure gets laterally inverted. The dot on the larger arc, the pin and the small arc rotate 90° ACW. Also, the pin gets inverted.

14. (c) : The figure rotates 90° CW. One half of one of the lines on the arrow is lost. The figure in front of the arrowhead rotates through 45°.

15. (d) : The missing line segment in the first figure is replaced in second. Then moving ACW, the third line segment is removed along the two next consecutive sides of the square. Shaded portion in the first figure moves three steps ACW. Similarly, the third figure gives figure (D).

16. (b) : The uppermost design enters into innerside side of the lower design from Ist figure to the IInd figure.

17. (a) : In element I to II upper left design comes at lower right rotating 135° C.W. Middle design goes to upper left and rotates 90° CW. While lower right design goes to middle and it also rotates 90° C.W. The same changes occur in option A.

18. (e) : In element I to II and ellipse is put in the triangle. Similarly in option E a triangle is put in the ellipse.

19. (d) : From first figure to IInd figure, design is divided into four equal parts and right side of the upper portion becomes shaded.

20. (e) : From Ist figure to IInd figure, design is reversed after moving 90° anticlockwise direction.

21. (d) : The figure in the first part is laterally inverted and a similar but smaller design is placed on its left side in the second part.

22. (e) : The element in first part is moved by 90° and the places of short and long line segments are interchanged.

23. (c) : The number of sides making the top left figure is increased by one and a new figure is made, shaded and moved to the top right position. The element in the centre is turned 90° anticlockwise and the small line on the other side is turned by 180°. The element in the bottom right is turned upside down and moved to the bottom left position.

24. (a) : The direction of both arcs on the top, are on the middle right and arc on the bottom left in first part are turned to the other side in the second part.

25. (b) : From part one to part two, the element in the top left is turned 90° clockwise and the other three 90° anticlockwise, also the elements are moved one step anticlockwise.

26. (b) : From part one to part two, the top right element is turned by 90° and moved down, the lower right and middle elements are turned 90° clockwise and 90° anticlockwise respectively and moved to the left and the lower left element is shaded and moved up.

27. (a) : All the four elements exchange place diagonally and in doing so the top left element is laterally inverted, the top right element is horizontally inverted, the bottom right element is turned 90° anticlockwise and the number of lines making the element in bottom left is increased by one.

28. (e) : The innermost figure is removed and the new innermost figure also encloses the other two figures. The innermost and smallest figure is then shaded.

29. (b) : The design in the first part is horizontally inverted in the second.

30. (b) : All the elements in the first part are turned upside down and then, 1st, 2nd, 3rd and 4th positioned elements become 3rd, 4th, 1st and 2nd elements in the second part.

24. ODD MAN OUT

In this type of reasoning a statement is followed by inferences drawn from it. From these inferences only one definitely follows which is the hidden proposition of the sentence and it is the right answer to the question.

EXERCISE

Directions (Q. 1–10) : *In each question below five figures are given. Four are similar in a certain way and so form a group. The question is— which one of the figures* **does not** *belong to that group?*

1. 

(a) (b) (c) (d) (e)

2. 

(a) (b) (c) (d) (e)

3. 

(a) (b) (c) (d) (e)

4. 

(a) (b) (c) (d) (e)

5. 

(a) (b) (c) (d) (e)

6. 

(a) (b) (c) (d) (e)

7. 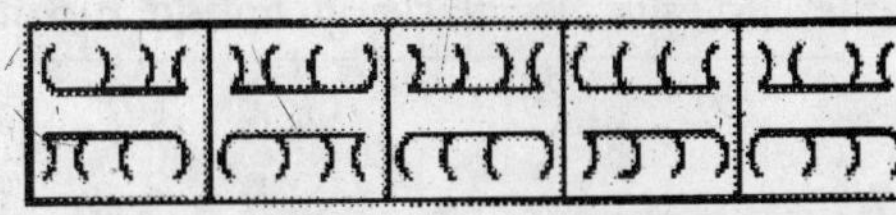

(a) (b) (c) (d) (e)

8. 

(a) (b) (c) (d) (e)

9. 

(a) (b) (c) (d) (e)

10. 

(a) (b) (c) (d) (e)

Directions (Q. 11–20) : *In each of the following questions, in four out of the five figures, element I is related to element II in the same particular way. Find out the figure in which the element I is* **not** *so related to element II.*

11. 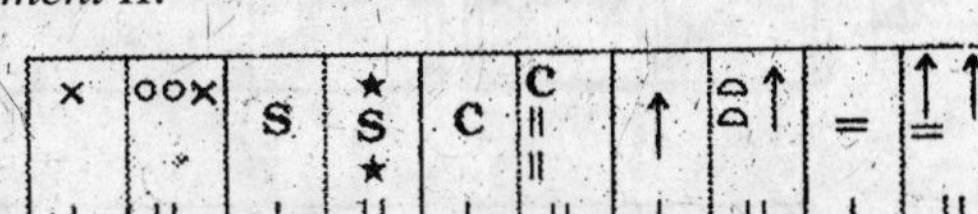

(a) (b) (c) (d) (e)

12. 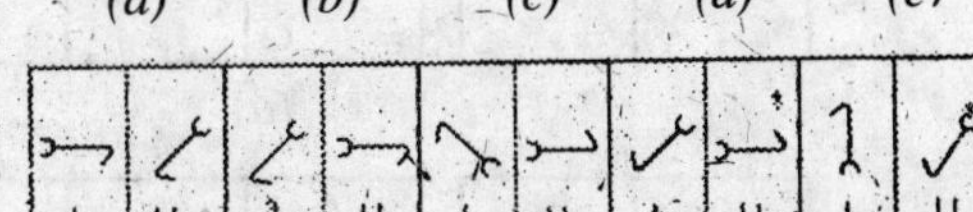

(a) (b) (c) (d) (e)

13. 

(a) (b) (c) (d) (e)

14. 

(a) (b) (c) (d) (e)

15. 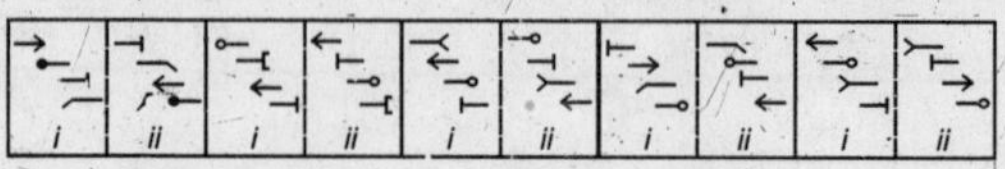

(a) (b) (c) (d) (e)

16. 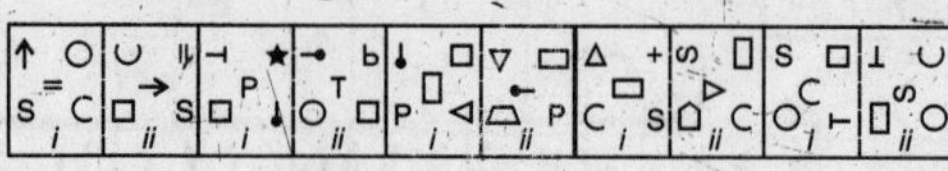

(a) (b) (c) (d) (e)

17. 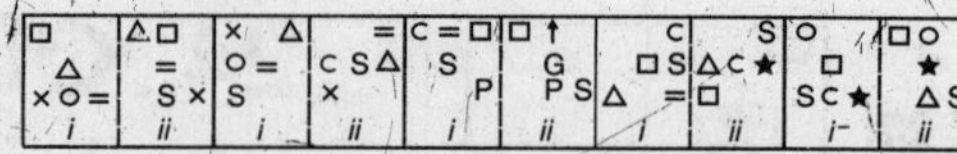

(a) (b) (c) (d) (e)

18. 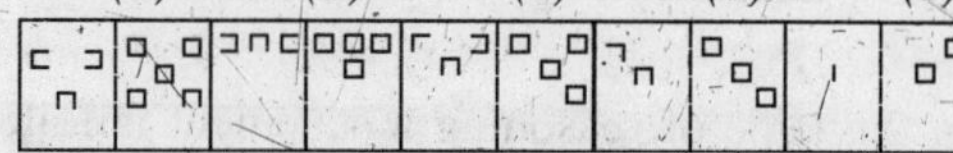

(a) (b) (c) (d) (e)

19. 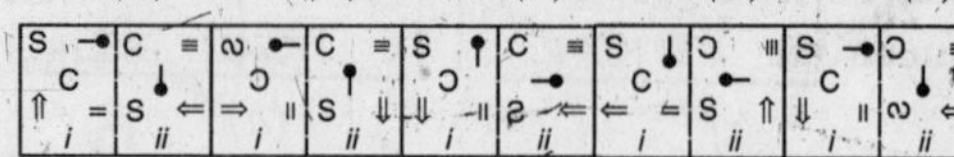

(a) (b) (c) (d) (e)

20. 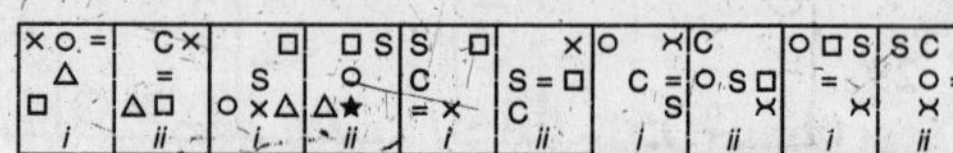

(a) (b) (c) (d) (e)

Directions (Q. 21–30) : *In each of the following questions, a related pair of figures (unnumbered) is followed by five numbered pairs of figures. Out of these five, four have relationship similar to that in the unnumbered pair. Only one pair of figures does not have similar relationship. Select that pair of figures which does not have a similar relationship to that in the unnumbered pair. Number of that pair is your answer.*

21. 

(a) (b) (c) (d) (e)

22. 

(a) (b) (c) (d) (e)

23. 

(a) (b) (c) (d) (e)

24. 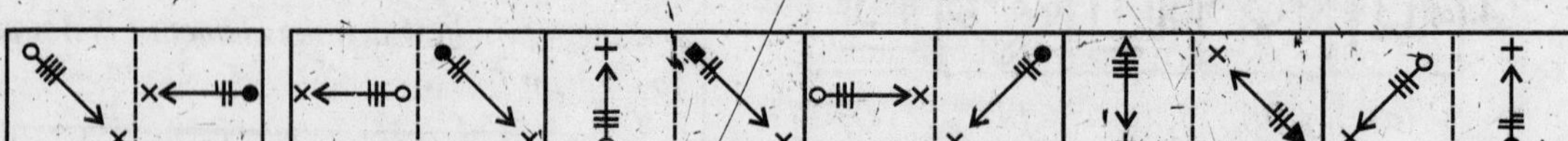

(a) (b) (c) (d) (e)

25. 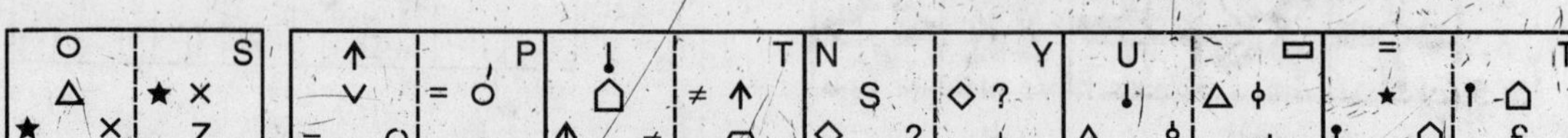

(a) (b) (c) (d) (e)

26. 

(a) (b) (c) (d) (e)

27. 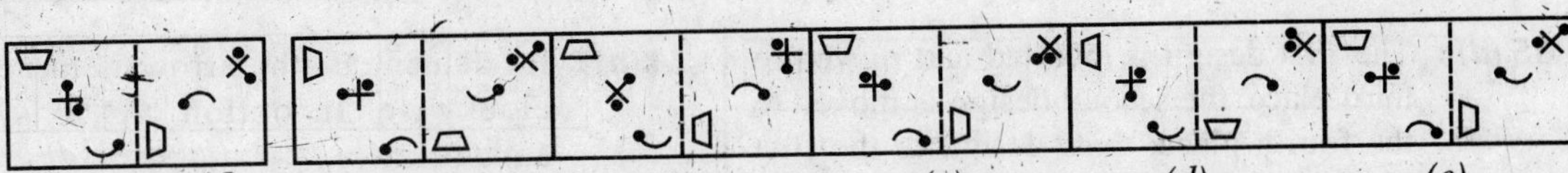

(a) (b) (c) (d) (e)

28. 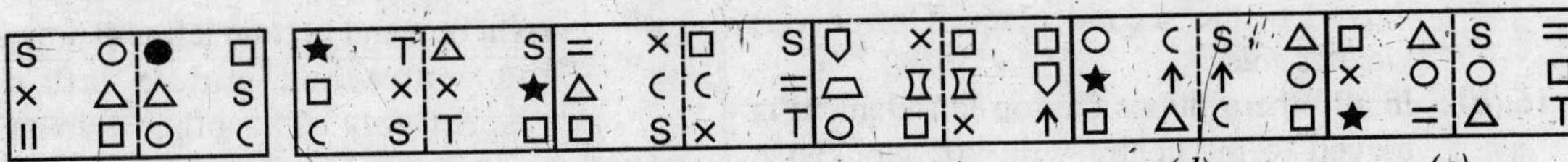

(a) (b) (c) (d) (e)

29. 

(a) (b) (c) (d) (e)

30. 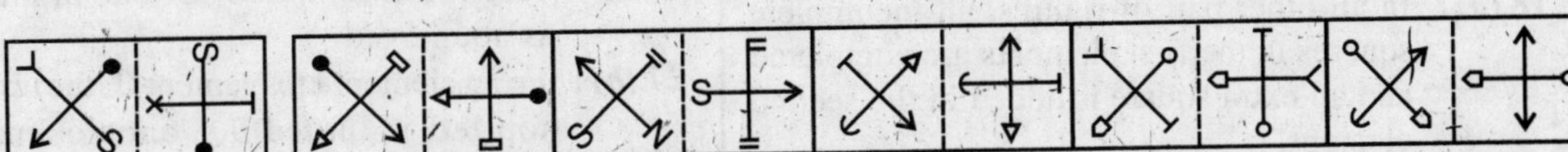

(a) (b) (c) (d) (e)

EXPLANATORY ANSWERS

1. *(d)*: In all other figures, the arrow and the + sign lie towards the black end of the main figure.

2.*(a)*: The pins, equal in number of sides in the main figure are attached to the midpoint of a side of the main figure in case of figures (B), (C), (D) and (E). In figure (A), these pins are attached to a vertex of the main figure.

3.*(c)*: In all other figures, the dot appears in the angle formed between the arrow and the pin.

4.*(a)*: All other figures can be rotated into each other. (In each figure except figure (A), the middle element is obtained by rotating the outer element through 90° CW and the inner element is obtained by rotating the middle element through 90° CW).

5.*(c)*: All other figures have at least one line of symmetry.

6.*(c)*: All other figures can be rotated into each other.

7.*(e)*: In each one of the other four figures, four arcs are curved towards the left and four other arcs are curved towards the right.

8.*(c)*: All other figures can be rotated into each other.

9.*(d)*: In all other figures, the number of dots outside the main figure is one more than the number of dots inside the main figure.

10.*(a)*: In all other figures, one of the dots lies outside the triangle as well as the circle.

11.*(e)*: Except in figure (B), in all other figures, from element I to II two new designs are added in one side of the main design.

12.*(c)*: In each figure from element I to II the main design rotates through 135° clockwise or anticlockwise. Except in figure (C), in all other figures, the smaller line segment moves to other side from element I to II.

13.*(a)*: In all other figures the element II can be obtained by the lateral inversion of the element I. In figure (A), the lower design has not been inverted.

14.*(b)*: In figure (B), the small segment is on the same side as that of the half shaded circle in both the elements.

15.(*d*) : The first design is inverted and moved to third place, the second design is moved to the fourth place, third design to the first place and fourth design is inverted and moved to the seeond place. Option (D) violates this.

16.(*b*) : In all other options the top-left element is moved to the centre with 90° clockwise rotation. Here, it is rotated anticlockwise.

17.(*d*) : All the designs are shifted in a set pattern one behind the other. The fourth design in all others is changed and placed in the last. Here, the fifth and last designs are changed.

18.(*a*) : In all other pair of figures, all incomplete squares in the first elements are completed and an extra square is added in the second element.

19.(*a*) : From element I to element II, the 'S' shape is turned 90° clockwise and moved down, the double arrow shape '⇒' is turned 90° clockwise and moved to the right, the two parallel lines one turned by 90°; one parallel line is added and all three lines are moved up, the line with a dot is turned 90° clockwise and moved to the centre and the 'C' shape in the centre is turned by 180° and moved to top left position. Here, the double arrow is turned anticlockwise.

20.(*c*) : Starting from one unit, all units are moved in a set pattern, the places of last two units moved are interchanged and the last unit is then made new. Here, no changes are made in the last two units.

21.(*d*) : From element I to element II clockwise the first unit is moved 2 steps forward, the second unit 1 step forward, the third unit 2½ steps forward and the fourth unit 3 steps forward. In option 'D' the third unit violates the rule.

22.(*e*) : From element I to element II, the horizontal bar is turned 135° anticlockwise and the unit at the lower end is turned by 180°. The vertical bar is turned 90° anticlockwise and the unit at the lower end is turned by 180°. In option 'E' one more unit at the top is turned by 180°.

23.(*e*) : In element II, the shade is moved two sections clockwise and shifted from the centre to the base. In option 'E' it is not so.

24.(*a*) : In element II, the arrow is turned 135° clockwise. In option 'A'' it is turned anticlockwise.

25.(*b*) : From element I to element II, the bottom right unit and bottom left unit are moved to the centre and middle left position respectively. The other two units are removed and two new elements are placed in the top right and bottom centre position respectively. In option 'B' the placement of bottom right and left elements is not right.

26.(*c*) : In element II, the shades are shifted one petal clockwise. In option 'C' one of the shades is not moved.

27.(*b*) : From element I to element II, the unit on the top left is turned 90° anticlockwise and moved to the bottom right corner position, the unit in the centre is turned 135° anticlockwise and moved to the top right position, and the unit in the bottom right is turned by 180° and moved to the centre. In option 'B', the middle unit is turned 135° clockwise.

28.(*a*) : From element I to element II, a new unit is placed in the top left position, the top left unit is moved to the middle right position, the middle right unit is moved to the left position, the middle left unit is replaced by a new unit and placed in bottom right position, the bottom right unit is moved to the top right position, and the top right unit is moved diagonally to replace the bottom left unit. In option 'A', the middle left unit is not changed when moved to the bottom right position.

29.(*e*) : From element I to element II starting anticlockwise, the first and second units are moved 1½ steps clockwise respectively, the third unit ½ step anticlockwise, the fourth unit 2 steps clockwise, and a new unit is placed ahead of the first unit. Option 'E' violates the rules.

30.(*e*) : In element II, the cross is turned 135° clockwise and then the positions of left and top units on the cross are interchanged. In option 'E' it is not so.

ENGLISH LANGUAGE

1. Comprehension Passages

ENGLISH LANGUAGE COMPREHENSION

The objective of language comprehension test is to ascertain the ability of the candidates to understand the passage properly. Therefore candidates are required to take notice of the following points:

1. Read the full passage very attentively and intelligently.
2. Try to comprehend the gist of it.
3. Make a mental note of all the important details and points given in the passage.
4. Read the passage for the second time in case you have not been able to understand it satisfactorily.
5. Divide the time proportionately for all the passages.
6. Answer the questions on the basis of facts, as given in the paragraph.
7. Don't waste much time in answering the questions of any one passage.
8. Check all the answers once again, very carefully, to see whether any question is left unanswered by mistake.

MODEL QUESTIONS (FOR PRACTICE)

Directions: *Each of the following passages is followed by five questions. Read the passage carefully and then answer the questions that follow each. For each question, four probable answers A, B, C and D are given. Only one out of these is correct. Choose the correct answer.*

PASSAGE-1

The use of words like 'welcome', 'thank you', 'please', etc., at the right moment reflects a polite nature. The civic sense also lies within the scope of good manners. We should not shout or talk loudly in public places like hospitals and libraries and create disturbance. We should not cheat people or make fun of them. Cleanliness is also necessary. We must not throw the waste on roads and make use of dustbins. We should not harm the public property as it belongs to all of us. While in a queue, discipline should be maintained. We must give fair chance to others.

1. Expressions like 'welcome' 'thank you' and 'please' reflect
   A. happiness B. discipline
   C. civic sense D. polite nature
2. While in a library, we should
   A. respect others B. avoid arguments
   C. talk in low tone D. be courteous
3. A public property belongs to
   A. nobody
   B. all of us
   C. government
   D. one who maintains it

4. Discipline is
   A. the rule of proper conduct or action
   B. the rule of road sense
   C. making use of dustbins
   D. forming a queue
5. The most appropriate title for this passage would be
   A. Polite Nature
   B. Courtesy
   C. Good Manners
   D. Civic Sense

PASSAGE-2

There is an old proverb 'Early to bed and early to rise makes a man healthy and wise.' I am in the habit of getting up early in the morning and have formed the habit of taking long morning walks in the past two years. It is a light exercise and best for physical fitness. The morning air which is fresh and pure is beneficial for the lungs. The early rays of the rising sun are good for healthy skin. 'Health is wealth' and doctors also recommend morning walk to their patients for gaining sound health and freshness of energy.

1. What is good for lungs?
   A. Sunrays B. Fresh air
   C. Sound sleep D. Light exercise
2. What is a light exercise?
   A. Early to bed
   B. Early to rise
   C. Morning walk
   D. Gaining sound health
3. What is good for skin?
   A. Fresh air
   B. Morning air
   C. Morning walk
   D. Rising sun's rays
4. What is best for physical fitness?
   A. Light exercise
   B. Long morning walk
   C. Early to rise
   D. Fresh and pure air
5. Long morning walk
   A. bring sound sleep
   B. ensures physical fitness
   C. ensures healthy skin
   D. keeps healthy, wealthy and wise

PASSAGE-3

Mahatma Gandhi lived a splendid long life and has set great moral standards before us. He showed to the world the true way to peace. He wished to see India prosper but he became a martyr for the noble cause of Hindu-Muslim unity at the time of partition when a religious fanatic, Nathuram Godse, shot him dead on January 30, 1948. His last words were 'Hey Ram'. He lived and died for his country and countryman.

1. Mahatma Gandhi showed the world the true way to
   A. prosperity B. love
   C. truth D. peace
2. Mahatma Gandhi became a martyr for the noble cause of
   A. truth
   B. non-violence
   C. freedom of India
   D. Hindu-Muslim unity
3. Mahatma Gandhi was shot dead
   A. before India achieved independence
   B. by a mad man
   C. by an intolerant religious person
   D. by a non-religious person
4. Mahatma Gandhi set great moral standards. It means
   A. he was a great religious teacher
   B. he was a great moralist
   C. he made India morally stronger
   D. moral was everything to him
5. Gandhiji lived and died for his country and countryman. It means
   A. he was born in India and died in India
   B. he was a patriot
   C. he was a great moralist
   D. he sacrified his life for India and her people

PASSAGE-4

On one hot day a crow felt very thirsty. He flew from one place to another in search of water. After long hours of labour he found a pitcher. Eagerly, he perched on the mouth of the pitcher. He found that the water was at the bottom of the vessel. He tried his best to dip his beak but did not succeed. He did not know what to do. Suddenly some pebbles lying nearby gave him an idea. One by one he dropped the pebbles with his beak into the pitcher. The level of water slowly came up to the mouth of the pitcher. The crow then drank the water and quenched his thirst.

1. The crow found a pitcher
A. as it flew
B. after many hours of labour
C. full of water
D. which was empty

2. What is the moral of the passage?
A. No pains, no gains
B. God helps those who help themselves
C. Necessity is the mother of invention
D. Try and try again, you will succeed at last

3. The crow flew from place to place
A. in search of pitcher
B. in search of pebbles
C. in search of water
D. in search of a vessel

4. The pitcher, the crow found
A. was full of water
B. was dry
C. had little water in the bottom
D. had water up to its mouth

5. As the crow dropped pebbles into the pitcher, what happend?
A. The pitcher broke down
B. The water leaked one of the pitcher
C. The level of water into the pitcher rose up slowly
D. Water level immediately rose to the mouth of the pitcher

PASSAGE-5

Once upon a time a crane and a fox lived in a forest. They were good friend. One day the fox invited the crane to a feast. He made a tasty food and served it before the crane on a plate. The crane could not eat anything because of the long beak. But the fox licked all his food. The crane felt insulted. He decided to teach the fox a lesson. Next day he invited the fox. He prepared the same tasty food and placed it in front of the fox inside a narrow glass. The crane ate easily while the fox looked on. Now, it was the fox's turn to remain hungry.

1. What is the moral of the passage?
A. Beware of the wicked
B. One good turn deserves another
C. Be contented with what you have
D. Tit for tat

2. The crane could not eat tasty food because the
A. food was served in a shallow plate
B. food was very hot
C. food was served in a long jar
D. crane was not hungry

3. The fox had to remain hungry because
A. the food served was not enough in quantity
B. the food was served inside a narrow glass
C. the food served was not tasty
D. the food was all liquid

4. Why did the crane feel insulted?
A. Because he was invited to feast but he could not eat anything
B. Because the food was served in a shallow plate and he could not eat
C. Because the food was too hot
D. Because the fox gulped all the food quickly

5. The crane successfully taught a lesson to the fox when he invited the fox to a feast and served the food
A. in a narrow glass
B. in a large plate
C. in a broken plate
D. in a long jar

PASSAGE-6

The family set down at the table and began to talk about the summer holidays. They had to decide a place to visit during the vacation. Should they go to their village or to a hill station? The parents preferred the village while the children wished to go the hill station. After few moments of discussion the elders decided to visit both the places. First they shall go to the village for a week and then stay at the hill station for the remaining days. For the first time the family shall be together during the holidays. The children were happy with the holiday plan.

1. The purpose for which the family set down at the table was
   A. to decide a place to visit during the vacation
   B. to educate the children how to carry articles during a visit to a hill station
   C. to decide the date when they should start their journey
   D. to tell the children that they will visit a hill station during this vacation
2. The final plan was to visit
   A. their village
   B. a hill station
   C. their village as well as a hill station
   D. their home town
3. The final decision was made by
   A. the boys B. the girls
   C. the women D. the elders
4. They decided first to go to their village and stay there for
   A. a day B. a week
   C. ten days D. a fortnight
5. Why were children happy?
   A. Because a hill station was included in their holiday plan
   B. Because a visit to their village was excluded from their holiday plan
   C. Because their choice prevailed
   D. Because they were going all alone to the hill station

PASSAGE-7

Once Govind intended to go on pilgrimage with his family. He asked Mirind to accompany. But for his trade's reason, he did not go with him. So Govind thought it safe to leave the box of his jewellery with him, as it was dangerous to leave it in a lone house or take it on the journey. So he went to him with the box. He took him to a lonely place under a tree and handed it over to him. He told Mirind, "Keep it safe with you. I shall return from the journey after six month then I shall take it back from you." Mirind said, "Don't worry, I shall keep it as safe as own."

1. Govind intended to go
   A. for a business trip
   B. to a hill station
   C. on a long journey to a sacred place
   D. to his home town for a long period
2. Why did Govind leave his box of jewellery with Mirind?
   A. Because it was not safe to take the box with him on a long journey
   B. Because Mirind was his fast friend
   C. Because the box was very heavy
   D. Because his house was unsafe
3. Why did Govind take Mirind to a lonely place?
   A. To tell him that the box contained valuable jewellery
   B. So that no third person could see box
   C. To show him what was within the box
   D. To tell him that the box will remain with him
4. Where did Govind hand over the box of jewellery to Mirind?
   A. At Mirind's house
   B. At his own house
   C. In a lonely place
   D. In a lonely place under a tree
5. It was not safe to leave the box in a lone house. Here the word 'lone house' means
   A. a house in a deserted place
   B. a house where none lives
   C. a house without door and lock
   D. a house near the forest

PASSAGE-8

Zahir-ud-din Babar was the first Mughal emperor of India. A descendent of Timur on father's side and Changez Khan on his mother's side, Babar was a brave warrior. After defeating Ibrahim Lodhi in the First Battle of Panipat in 1526 he entered Delhi and soon gained control over Agra. After many more battles with Rajputs he extended his empire over Punjab, Uttar Pradesh and north Bihar. He died at a young age of 48 years in 1530 at his capital Agra without getting much time to consolidate his victories.

1. Zahir-ud-din Babar was the first
   A. Muslim ruler of India
   B. Mughal ruler of India
   C. Afghan ruler of India
   D. Turk ruler of India
2. Babar was born in the years
   A. 1480 B. 1482
   C. 1492 D. 1962
3. Babar first occupied
   A. Punjab B. Agra
   C. Delhi D. Panipat
4. Babar was a brave warrior. Here brave warrior means
   A. courageous soldier
   B. a kind hearted soldier
   C. a clever fighter
   D. a victorious general
5. Babar extended his empire over Punjab and Uttar Pradesh after many more battles with the
   A. Afghans B. Rajputs
   C. Mughals D. Lodhies

PASSAGE-9

Our National Flag is tricolour. It has three equal horizontal strips. The strip at the top is saffron, in the middle is white and at the bottom is green. The ratio of width to length of the flag is 2 : 3. In the centre of the white strip is a wheel in navy blue. The wheel represents the *chakra.* Its design is similar to the wheel which appears on the abacus of the Sarnath Lion Capital of Ashoka. Its diameter approximates to the width of the white strip. The wheel has 24 spokes. It was adopted by Constituent Assembly on July 22, 1947. We love our national flag. We respect it. We are ready to sacrifice our life to protect its honour. It represents the nation. So it is a symbol of national honour.

1. In our national flag the wheel is located in the centre of
   A. saffron strip B. white strip
   C. green strip D. blue strip
2. In our national flag which of the strips is at the bottom in our national flag
   A. blue C. saffron
   B. white D. green
3. Why do we love our national flag?
   A. Because it is tricolour
   B. Because it has three strips
   C. Because it has a wheel at the centre
   D. Because it is a symbol of national honour
4. Our national flag was approved by
   A. President
   B. Lok Sabha
   C. Parliament
   D. Constituent Assembly
5. The diameter approximates to the width of the white strip. Here the word 'approximates' means
   A. is more or less equal
   B. is exactly equal
   C. is not equal
   D. is related

PASSAGE-10

Distance in large cities are long. All the people do not have their own means of transport. They have to depend upon the state or private buses. The number of bus users is very large. Every bus stop is, therefore, crowded. The number of buses is not adequate. Thus people suffer the torture of long wait at the bus stop. Some bus stops are quite orderly. People form queues and get into the buses turn by turn. However, often this order is forgotten and confusion spreads when the bus comes and the law of jungle prevails.

1. Why are the bus stops crowded?
   A. Because they are small is size
   B. Because the number of passengers is very large
   C. Because they are situated at some busy centre
   D. Because people do not form queues
2. Long wait at the bus stop is the result of
   A. over-crowding in the buses
   B. late running of buses
   C. shortage of buses
   D. slow speed of buses
3. Some bus stops are quite orderly where
   A. there is no crowd
   B. the number of buses is adequate

C. people do not have to wait for long
D. people form queues and enter the buses one by one

4. Most of the people who travel by buses are
A. non-working
B. do not have their own vehicles
C. have to go a long distance
D. live in large cities

5. What happens when people do not have their own transport?
A. They have to wait for a bus at a bus stop
B. They have to depend upon the state or private buses
C. They have to travel long distances
D. They form queues and get into buses one by one

PASSAGE-11

A certain king once fell ill and doctors said that only a sudden fright would restore his health but the king was not a man for anyone to play tricks on, except his fool. One day, when the fool was with him in his boat he cleverly pushed the king into water but he was rescued and put to bed. The fright, the bath and bed cured the diseased king, but he was so angry with the fool that he turned him out of the country.

1. What did the doctor say about the king?
A. Only a sudden fright would restore the king's health
B. Only fool would cure the king
C. Only a boat trick could cure the king
D. The king had suffered a sudden fright

2. He cleverly pushed the king into water but *he* was rescued and put to bed. In this sentence *he* refers to
A. the king B. the fool
C. the doctor D. the river

3. When the fool pushed the king into water they were
A. in the palace B. in the bed
C. in the garden D. in a boat

4. Who played the trick on the king?
A. The doctor B. The boatman
C. The fool D. The fright

5. The fool who cured the king was
A. rewarded
B. thrown into water
C. turned out of the country
D. put into jail

ANSWERS

	1	2	3	4	5
Passage 1.	D	C	B	A	C
Passage 2.	B	C	D	B	B
Passage 3.	D	D	C	B	D
Passage 4.	B	C	C	C	C
Passage 5.	D	A	B	B	A
Passage 6.	A	C	D	B	A
Passage 7.	C	A	B	D	B
Passage 8.	B	B	C	A	B
Passage 9.	B	D	D	D	A
Passage 10.	B	C	D	B	B
Passage 11.	A	A	D	C	C

2. English Grammar

PARTS OF SPEECH

Part of speech	Definition or Function	Examples
Noun	Name of a person, place, animal, quality or thing	Ram, boy, dog pen, sun, Delhi, truth, honesty
Pronoun	Used in place of a noun	I, you, he she, they
Articles & Determiners	Points out indefinite and definite nouns	a, an, the, few, some
Adjective	Describes a noun or pronoun	big, honest, wooden valuable, quiet, deep, soft, narrow
Adverb	Describes a verb, an adjective or another adverb	silently, widely, softly, quietly, very, carefully
Verb	Tells about action or state of something or someone	is, am, was, have, do, like, walk, work, make, throw, tell
Conjuction	Joins words, clauses or sentences	and, but, when, yet, while, else
Preposition	Links a noun or pronoun to another word	at, to, after, on for, under, over, with
Interjection	Expresses sudden feelings or emotions	Ah!, Alas!, oh!, ouch!, hi!, well!, Hurrah!

NOUNS

A word which denotes a person, a thing, an animal or a place is said to be a noun.

There are two noun numbers in English — the *Singular* and the *Plural*.

Singular Numbers : A noun that denotes one person or one thing, is said to be in the Singular number. For example — book, pencil, bird, dog, hen etc. are in singular number.

Plural Number : A noun that denotes more than one person or one thing is said to be in plural number. For example — boys, pens, lions, girls, men etc. are in plural number.

REMEMBER

Singular	*Plural*
Cat	Cats
Book	Books
Pen	Pens
Room	Rooms
Tree	Trees
Bus	Buses
Bush	Bushes
Box	Boxes
Glass	Glasses
Dish	Dishes
Judge	Judges
Tax	Taxes
Watch	Watches
Calf	Calves
Thief	Thieves
Knife	Knives

Singular	*Plural*
Scarf	Scarves
Wife	Wives
Leaf	Leaves
Wolf	Wolves
Half	Halves
Monarch	Monarchs
Roof	Roofs
Hoof	Hoofs
Gulf	Gulfs
Staff	Staffs
Radio	Radios
Bamboo	Bamboos
Folio	Folios
Hero	Heroes
Volcano	Volcanoes
Mango	Mangoes
Potato	Potatoes
Photo	Photos
Piano	Pianos
Baby	Babies
Fly	Flies
Country	Countries
Lady	Ladies
Boy	Boys
Monkey	Monkeys
Ox	Oxen
Child	Children
Man	Men
Woman	Women
Tooth	Teeth
Axis	Axes
Basis	Bases
Foot	Feet
Goose	Geese
Englishman	Englishmen
Radius	Radii
Vertex	Vertices
Stimulus	Stimuli

1. Note the plurals of the following nouns:

Singular	*Plural*	*Singular*	*Plural*
copy	copies	cry	cries
baby	babies	duty	duties
body	bodies	country	countries
family	families	diary	diaries
fly	flies	fairy	fairies
city	cities	spy	spies
army	armies	storey	storeys
bay	bays	monkey	monkeys

2. The following nouns do not undergo any change in plural form, in general.

Singular	*Plural*	*Singular*	*Plural*
deer	deer	sheep	sheep
thousand	thousand	pair	pair
hundred	hundred	score	score
dozen	dozen	gross	gross

Note: We can write—

(*a*) thousands of men; (*b*) two pairs of shoes; (*c*) dozens of mangoes; (*d*) scores of people etc.

But—

(*a*) two thousand rupees; (*b*) three hundred men; (*c*) five dozen eggs, etc.

3. The following nouns are usually used in plural forms. They take a plural verb after them—

eatables	fetters	surroundings
riches	alms	spectacles
trousers	pants	scissors
premises	thanks	annals
congratulations	goods	shorts
tongs	pains	arms
breeches	(for troubles)	

4. The following are the nouns which are plural in appearance but are usually used in singular number. They are followed by a singular verb—

news	politics	physics
mathematics	economics	ethics
politics	classics	gallows
statistics	athletics	innings
mechanics	summons	mumps

5. Collective nouns often used as plurals—

public	police	cattle
audience	clergy	folk
people	poultry	nation
elite	gentry	glitterati

6. The nouns that are usually used in singular forms—

advice	hair	rice
fuel	alphabet	machinery
offspring	issue	furniture
mischief	stationery	luggage
bedding	information	abuse

7. Material nouns are always used in singular number—

gold	copper	milk
water	silk	wool

Note: They may be used in plural with a different meaning.

copper coins (coppers), chains or fetters (irons), cans made of tin (tins).

GENDERS

The difference in sex is denoted by Gender in grammar. The various genders are as follows :

1. **Masculine Gender :** A noun that denotes a male is said to be of the masculine gender, as man, uncle, ox, boy etc.
2. **Feminine Gender :** A noun that denotes a female is said to be of feminine gender, as woman, aunt, princess, cow etc.
3. **Common Gender :** Nouns which denote both males and females are said to be of the common gender, as friend, cousin, person, parent, baby etc.
4. **Neuter Gender :** A noun that denotes the name of object without life is said to be of neuter gender, as file, table, pencil.

REMEMBER

Masculine	*Feminine*
Boy	Girl
Son	Daughter
Brother	Sister
Murderer	Murderess
Sorcerer	Sorceress
Son-in-law	Daughter-in-law
Father-in-law	Mother-in-law
Man-servant	Maid-servant
Land-lord	Land-lady
Bachelor	Maid
Gentleman	Lady
Monk	Nun
Earl	Countess
Lad	Lass
Sir	Madam
Duke	Dutchess
Emperor	Empress
Milk-man	Milk-maid
Pea-cock	Pea-hen
Step-father	Step-mother
Hero	Heroine
Viceroy	Vicerine
Mr.	Mrs.
Governor	Governess
Master	Mistress
Wizard	Witch
Heir	Heiress
Host	Hostess
Lion	Lioness
Mayor	Mayoress
Actor	Actress
Buck	Doe
Colt	Filly
Dog	Bitch
Horse	Mare
Count	Countess
Hunter	Huntress
Prince	Princess
Abbot	Abbess
God	Goddess
Author	Authoress
Ox	Cow
Widower	Widow
Grand-father	Grand-mother
He-goat	She-goat
Milk-man	Milk-woman
Bridegroom	Bride
Tiger	Tigress
Priest	Priestess
Poet	Poetess
Shepherd	Shepherdess
Nephew	Niece
Stag	Hind

PRONOUNS

The repetition of a noun in a sentence or a set of sentences is really boring. So, instead of repeating the noun, we can use a word (for that noun) called the pronoun.

"A pronoun is a word that we use instead of a noun".

Example:

This is *Sachin. He* plays cricket.

Note: *He* is the pronoun used in place of *Sachin.*

Kinds of Pronouns

1. **Personal pronouns :** A pronoun which is used instead of the name of a person is known as a 'Personal Pronoun'. A list of the 'Personal pronouns' is listed below :

I, my, mine, me, we (First Person)
You, your, yours (Second Person)
He, his, him, she, her, hers, it,
its, they, their, theirs, them (Third Person)

2. **Demonstrative, Indefinite and Distributive Pronouns :**

(a) **Demonstrative Pronouns :** Pronouns used to point out the objects to which they refer are called Demonstrative Pronouns.

Examples :
(i) *This* is a present from my uncle.
(ii) *These* are merely excuses.
(iii) Bembay mangoes are better than *those* of Bangaluru.

(b) **Indefinite Pronouns :** All pronouns which refer to persons or things in a general way and do not refer to any particular person or thing are called Indefinite Pronouns.

Examples :
(i) *Somebody* has stolen my watch.
(ii) *Few* escaped unhurt.
(iii) Did you ask *anybody* to come?

(c) **Distributive Pronouns :** Each, either, neither are called distributive pronouns because they refer to persons or things one at a time. For this reason they are always singular and followed by the verb in singular.

Examples :
(i) *Each* of the men received a reward.
(ii) *These* men received *each* a reward.
(iii) *Either* of you can go.

3. **Relative Pronouns :** A relative pronoun refers or relates to some noun going before, which is called its Antecedent.

Examples :
(i) I met Hari *who* used to live here.
(ii) I have found the pen *which* I had lost.
(iii) Here is the book *that* you lent me.

4. **Interrogative Pronouns :** These pronouns, are used for asking questions.

Examples :
(i) *Whose* book is this?
(ii) *What* will all the neighbours say?
(iii) *Which* do you prefer, tea or coffee?

Note : Interrogative pronouns can also be used in asking indirect questions. Consider the following examples :
(i) I asked *who* was speaking.
(ii) Tell me *what* you have done.
(iii) Say *which* you would like best.

Behaviour of the Pronouns

1. If three pronouns are used together in the same sentence they are arranged in the following order :

2	+	3	+	1
↓		↓		↓
Second Person		Third Person		First Person

Examples :
I, you and he must help *that* poor man. (Incorrect)
You, he and I must help *that* poor man. (Correct)

2. When two or more singular nouns are joined by and, the pronoun used for them should be plural.

Examples :
Mohan and Sohan are friends. *They* play football. *They* live at Lajpat Nagar.

3. But if these nouns joined by and refer to the same person or thing, the pronoun used should be singular.

Examples :
(i) Delhi, the beautiful city and the capital of India, is famous for *its* historical monuments.
(ii) The manager and owner of the firm expressed *his* views on the demands of the workers.

4. When two nouns are used with as well as, the pronoun agrees with the first subject.
Examples :
(a) Mohan as well as his friends is doing *his* work.
(b) The students as well as their teachers are doing *their* work.
5. When two singular nouns joined by 'and' are preceded by *each* or *every,* the pronoun used must be singular and should agree in gender with the second noun.
Examples :
(a) Every man and every woman will do *her* best for the nation.
(b) Each boy and each girl went to *her* house.
6. When two nouns are joined by using 'with', the pronoun agrees with the noun coming before 'with'.
Examples :
(a) The boy with *his* parents has gone to see a movie.
(b) The children with *their* parents have gone to picnic.
7. When two different nouns are joined by either.......... or; neither .... nor, the pronoun is used according to the number and gender of the second noun.
Examples :
(a) Either your sister or you have done *your* work.
(b) Neither the students nor the teacher was in *his* class.
8. The pronoun coming after '*than*' must be in the same case as that coming before '*than*'.
Examples :
(a) She plays better than *me.* (Incorrect)
She plays better than *I.* (Correct)
(b) His elder brother is more intelligent than *him.* (Incorrect)
His elder brother is more intelligent than *he.* (Correct)
9. 'Many a' always takes a singular pronoun and singular verb.
Example :
Many a soldier has met *his* death in the battle field.
10. 'Who', 'Whose', 'Whom' are used only for persons.
Examples :
(a) *Who* is knocking at the door?
(b) *Whose* pen is this?
(c) *What* do you want?
11. 'Which' is used for things.
Example :
Which game do you like?

MULTIPLE CHOICE QUESTIONS

Directions: *In the following questions choose the correct options to fill the blanks.*

1. The place was so dirty that ..... wished to run away from there.
A. everybody B. anybody
C. few D. some

2. ..... was there to help me.
A. Somebody B. Anything
C. Anybody D. Nobody

3. Is there ...... to eat?
A. some B. something
C. any D. few

4. ..... of the students were making a great noise.
A. Anyone B. Somebody
C. Many D. Nobody

5. ..... of the students can solve this sum.
A. Someone B. Anybody
C. Somebody D. None

6. ...... of us should try our best to make India a heaven.
A. Any B. Somebody
C. Anybody D. All

7. ...... of us do not know the real meaning of our lives.
A. Any B. Something
C. Several D. Many

8. My .... black.
A. hairs are B. hair is
C. hairs shall D. hair will

9. She saw two .... on the last Sunday.
A. thiefs B. theifs
C. thieves D. theives

10. My sister is a ....
A. bacheloress B. bachelor
C. unmaried D. spinster

11. One is supposed to do ....
A. our duty B. their duty
C. one's duty D. his duty

12. Take anything .... you want.
A. that B. which
C. than D. then

13. I cannot tolerate ....
A. separated you
B. your separation
C. separation from you
D. you separated

14. He is .... faithful partner.
A. Yours B. You
C. Your D. Your's

15. Ajay is more smart than ....
A. her B. hers
C. herself D. she

16. Vivek works harder than ....
A. me B. I
C. her D. his

17. They should help ....
A. the poor people B. the poor
C. the poor persons D. the poor peoples

18. .... are mad.
A. All his sons B. His all sons
C. Sons all his D. All sons his

19. The poor fellow .... to fate.
A. resigned
B. resigned himself
C. resigned itself
D. resigned themselves

20. Nobody will help you but ....
A. I B. me
C. ours D. his

21. It is a good chance, You must avail .... this opportunity.
A. of B. yourself of
C. for D. from

22. The person who is elected .... my relative.
A. is B. he is
C. his D. him

23. He made ....
A. yours mention B. mention of you
C. mention for you D. mention about you

24. .... I know, he is quite faithful.
A. As far as B. So far as
C. So far this D. So far so

25. It is a duty of a person to take .... for his family.
A. pain B. pains
C. pain-killers D. pained

26. She does not love .... husband.
A. his B. her
C. its D. their

27. Let .... work together.
A. him and me B. he and I
C. he and him D. I and me

28. Copper, Silver and Gold ....
A. each will do B. either will do
C. any one will do D. any will do

29. Jessica and Roma are very irregular .... habits.
A. in her B. in their
C. in its D. in every

30. One likes to enjoy .... who was a great poet.
A. The sonnets of Shakespeare
B. Shakespeare's sonnets
C. Sonnets
D. Shakespeare

31. That is the boy .... everybody loves.
A. whom B. who
C. that D. whose

32. That is the girl .... won the first prize.
A. whom B. who
C. whose D. which

33. That is the man .... purse was lost.
A. who B. whom
C. whose D. their

ANSWERS

1	2	3	4	5	6	7	8	9	10
A	D	B	C	D	D	D	B	C	D
11	12	13	14	15	16	17	18	19	20
C	A	C	C	D	B	B	A	B	B
21	22	23	24	25	26	27	28	29	30
B	A	B	A	B	B	A	C	B	A
31	32	33							
A	B	C							

ARTICLES

The family of the articles has only three members. They are : A, An and The. However, they fall under two groups :

(a) Definite Article *(b)* Indefinite Article

'The' is known as definite article whereas 'a' and 'an' are known as indefinite articles.

Use of the Definite Article 'The'

'The' is used before

1. The superlative degree :
   He is the ablest man of the town.
   (ablest is a superlative degree)
2. The name of states, countries etc. having a descriptive name :
   (i) The J & K is a small state. (J & K is a descriptive name)
   (ii) He lives in the U.S.A. (U.S.A. is a descriptive name)
   (But the Delhi and the America are wrong because neither Delhi nor America is a descriptive name)
3. The names of the scriptures :
   The Gita is a holy book. (Gita is a scripture)
4. Name of newspapers :
   The Tribune is published from Chandigarh.
5. Name of rivers, canals, seas, oceans, bays, gulfs, groups of islands etc. :
   (i) The Ganga is a holy river.
   (ii) The Indian Ocean is the deepest ocean.
   (iii) The Persian Gulf is a narrow gulf.
6. The name of famous buildings :
   The Taj is one of the best buildings in India.
7. The names of nationals, sects and communities:
   (i) The English defeated the Germans in the World War.
   (ii) The rich should help the poor.
   (iii) The Hindus believe in the caste system.
8. Proper nouns used as common nouns :
   (i) Kalidas is the Shakespeare of India.
   (ii) Delhi is the London of India.
9. Famous historical events :
   The Industrial Revolution changed the face of England.
10. The directions and the celestial bodies:
    The sun rises in the east.
11. Titles :
    Akbar, the Great was loved by his subjects.

Do not use 'the'

1. Before languages :
   The English is an international language. (Incorrect)
   English is an international language. (Correct)
2. Before the names of games :
   The hockey is a popular game. (Incorrect)
   Hockey is a popular game. (Correct)

Use of the Indefinite Articles 'A' and 'An'

'A' is used before :

1. All singular common nouns beginning with a consonant :
   (i) A boy sings a song.

(ii) A black and a white cow were grazing in the field.

2. If a word begins with a vowel but gives the sound of a consonant, 'a' should be used before it :
   (i) He was helped in his work by a European.
   (ii) He is a one-eyed man.
   (iii) It is a useful work.

'An' is used as follows :

1. All singular common nouns beginning with a vowel (*i.e.*, a, e, i, o, u) :
   (i) He is an artist.
   (ii) He is an old man.
   (iii) I intend to buy an umbrella.
2. If a word starts with a consonant but gives the sound of a vowel, "an" should be used before it :
   (i) Brutus is an honourable man.
   (ii) He is an honour to his profession.
   (iii) He is an L.L.B.
   (iv) He is an M.A.
   (v) You will reach there in an hour.

Demonstratives, that, these and those

1. The demonstrative adjectives and pronouns are for objects nearby the speaker:
   this (singular) those (plural)
   and for objects far away from the speaker.
   That (singular) those (plural)
2. Demonstratives are the only adjectives that agree in number with their nouns.
   That hat is nice.
   Those hats are nice.
3. When there is the idea of selection, the pronoun "one" (or "ones") often follows the demonstrative.
   I want a book. I'll get this (one).
   If the demonstrative is followed by an adjective, "one"(or "ones") must be used.
   I want a book. I'll get this big one.

MULTIPLE CHOICE QUESTIONS

Directions: *In the following questions choose the correct options to fill the blanks.*

1. .... will have to be paid for this material.
A. Half rupee B. Half a rupee
C. A half rupee D. An half rupee

2. .... is taking keen interest in India.
A. The USA B. USA
C. An USA D. A USA

3. Only .... can save our country.
A. the Hitler B. a Hitler
C. Hitler D. an Hitler

4. I can run for ....
A. hundred miles B. the hundred miles
C. a hundred miles D. an hundred miles.

5. .... man-eater has been killed.
A. The B. A
C. An D. Either A or B

6. What .... fine idea!
A. the B. an
C. a D. No article

7. .... earth is moving around the sun.
A. An B. A
C. The D. No article

8. This is .... first example while I got.
A. the B. a
C. an D. No article

9. This is .... house which was built during earthquake.
A. a B. an
C. the D. No article

10. .... America is a rich country.
A. The B. An
C. A D. No article

11. .... U.S.A. is a developed country.
A. A B. An
C. The D. No article

12. .... Bible is a holy book.
A. A B. The
C. An D. No article

13. .... rich should help the poor.
A. The B. A
C. An D. No article

14. .... Gold is a costly metal.
A. The B. A
C. An D. No article

15. Kalidas is .... Shakespeare of India.
A. a B. an
C. the D. No article

16. I cannot do .... difficult work.
A. a such B. the such
C. such the D. such a

17. How foolish .... plan it is!
A. a B. an
C. the D. No article

18. An ink is .... useful article.
A. an B. a
C. the D. No article

19. There are .... husband and wife.
A. a B. an
C. the D. No article

20. He is learning .... French
A. the B. a
C. an D. No article

ANSWERS

1	2	3	4	5	6	7	8	9	10
B	A	B	C	D	C	C	A	C	D
11	**12**	**13**	**14**	**15**	**16**	**17**	**18**	**19**	**20**
C	B	A	D	C	D	A	B	D	D

ADJECTIVES & ADVERBS

An Adjective is a word which adds something to the meaning of a noun or a pronoun.

Mridula is an *intelligent* girl.
He has a *black* goat.
He is a *brilliant* student.
She is a *clever* girl.
It is a *beautiful* picture.

In the sentences given above, the words in italics are adjectives.

An Adverb is a word which qualifies the meaning of a Verb, an Adjective or another Adverb.

(*i*) He talks *slowly*.
(*ii*) He is a *very* good student.
(*iii*) He talks *very* slowly.

In sentence (*i*), *slowly* qualifies the verb *talks*.

In sentence (*ii*), *very* qualifies the adjective *good*.

In sentence (*iii*), *very* qualifies the adverb *slowly*.

Adjectives have three degrees of comparison :

1. **Positive Degree :** It expresses the common form of an adjective.

   Example :

   Ram is a *tall* boy.

   In the above sentence *tall* is an adjective and expresses the common form.

2. **Comparative Degree :** It expresses the more of the same form.

   Example :

   Ram is *taller* than Mahesh.

   In the above sentence *taller* is an adjective that expresses the more of the common form of the adjective *tall*.

"When and How to Use" Comparative Degree?

(a) Comparative Degree is used when two persons or two groups of persons or things are compared.

Examples :

(a) He is *wiser* than his younger brother.
(b) This glass is *cleaner* than the other.

(b) When two different qualities in the same person are compared, more is used instead of 'er' to form the comparative. The formula used in this case should be :

More + Positive Degree

She is *fairer* than polite. (Incorrect)
She is *more fair* than polite. (Correct)

(c) When selection of one out of two persons or things is meant, the degree of comparison is followed by of and *the* is used before it.

Example :

Zia is abler of *the* two sisters.

(d) If two comparatives are used in the same sentence to impress upon an idea, both should be preceded by the definite article.

Examples :

(i) The higher you go, the cooler it is.

(ii) The more we get, the more we desire.

(e) When one person or thing is compared with another of the same kind, other is used after the comparative degree. In such sentences other is normally preceded by any or all.

Examples :

(i) Kalidas is greater than any dramatist. (Incorrect)

Kalidas is greater than any other dramatist. (Correct)

(ii) Lead is heavier than all metals. (Incorrect)

Lead is heavier than all other metals. (Correct)

(f) Senior, junior, superior, inferior, prior, anterior (earlier than) and posterior (later than) are always followed by 'to'.

Examples :

(i) Ram is senior *to* Mohan by three years.

(ii) That pen is inferior *to* that.

(iii) He is junior *to* me in rank.

(iv) This event was posterior *to* that.

Note: Never use *than* after the above mentioned adjectives.

Important Information

(a) 'Preferable' is also used as an adjective of the comparative degree. As such, it is always followed by *to* and not *a*.

Death is preferable than dishonour. (Incorrect)

Death is preferable *to* dishonour. (Correct)

(b) To intensify the Degree of comparison, we use *far* or *much* before the comparative.

Examples :

(i) This book is *far* better than that.

(ii) His performance was *much* better than Mohan's.

Warning : Always avoid the use of double comparatives.

Don't say : Ram is more cleverer than his younger brother.

Say: Ram is cleverer than his younger brother.

3. **Superlative Degree :** It expresses the most of the common form of an adjective.

Example :

He is the ablest man of the town.

How and when to use the Superlative Degree?

(a) The Superlative Degree is used when more than two persons or things are compared.

(b) The Superlative Degree is generally preceded by 'the' and followed by 'of' in most of the cases or otherwise.

(c) When an adjective of the superlative degree is preceded by a Possessive Adjective or a Noun in the Possessive case, 'the' should not be used before it.

Example :

Which is Kalidas' best play?

It will be a blunder to use 'the' before the Superlative Degree in such cases.

Don't say : Which is Kalidas' the best play.

(d) To intensify the degree of comparison, *by far* is used before the superlative degree.

Example :

India is *by far* the most beautiful country of the world.

Note: Always avoid the use of double superlatives.

Don't say : He is the most strongest boy in the class.

Say : He is the strongest boy in the class.

Use of some Important Adjectives

1. (a) '**Some**' is used as follows :

(i) With countable nouns where it means—a little, a small quantity.

(ii) In a question which shows some request.

Examples :

(i) There is some water in the bottle.

(ii) Some of the students were absent yesterday.

(iii) Will you have some milk?

(iv) Will you buy some fruit for me?

(b) '**Any**' is used as follows :

(i) In negative sentences.

(ii) In interrogative sentences.

(iii) After 'Hardly', 'Scarcely' and 'Barely'.
(iv) After 'If'.

Examples :

(i) There is not any sugar in the pot.
(ii) We haven't any rice in the house.
(iii) I have hardly any money.
(iv) There are scarcely any plants in this field.
(v) If there is any danger, blow the whistle.

2. (a) **Older :** Older (and oldest) are used for persons animals and things. But 'Older' and 'Oldest' refer to the persons who do not belong to the same family.

Examples :

(i) Radha is older than Shyama.
(ii) John is the oldest member of the staff. 'Older' and 'Oldest' refer to the persons who do not belong to the same family.

(b) **Elder** (and **eldest**) are used in respect of the members of the same family like sons, daughters, brothers, sisters.

Examples :

(i) My elder sister is a lecturer.
(ii) Meenakshi is the eldest of the three sisters.

Note :

(i) 'Elder' is not followed by 'than'.
(ii) 'Elder' and 'Eldest' cannot be used for things.

3. (a) **'Few'** is negative and is the opposite of 'Many'. It means 'not many'.

(b) **'A few'** is positive and means 'some at least'. It is the opposite of 'None'.

(c) **'The few'** means 'minority' and suggests 'whether there is'.

Examples :

(i) We have few holidays in school.
(ii) Only a few boys will fail in the examination.
(iii) The few poems that he wrote are very popular.

4. (a) **Further** means 'something additional'.

(b) **Farther** means 'a greater distance'.

Examples :

(i) Further discussion will be held in the office of the principal.
(ii) Amritsar is farther from Delhi than Ambala.

5. (a) **Little** is negative. It means, 'not much', or 'hardly any'.

(b) **A little** is positive. It means 'some quantity'.

(c) **The little** denotes quantity. It means, 'not much but all that is, or whatever quantity there is'.

Examples :

(i) There is little hope of his success.
(ii) He knows a little of everything.
(iii) I have spent the little money I had.
(iv) The little knowledge of shoe-making proved very useful to me.

6. (a) **'Much'** expresses 'quantity'.

(b) **'Many'** expresses 'number'.

(c) **'Many a'**—'Singular noun' and 'Singular verb' are used with 'many a'.

Examples :

(i) There is not *much* water in the jug.
(ii) *Many* boys are absent today.
(iii) *Many* a battle has been fought on the soil of India.

7. (a) **'Less'** denotes 'in a small degree'.

(b) **'Fewer'** denotes 'number'.

Examples :

(i) He devotes less time to his studies.
(ii) There are no fewer than ten chairs in this room.

8. (a) **'Each'** is used for a single number of 'two persons' or 'things'.

(b) **'Every'** is used for a single number of 'many persons' or 'things'.

Examples :

(i) Each boy must take part in games.
(ii) There are only two poets. Each poet recited his poem.
(iii) Every man dies in this world.
(iv) Every man is expected to do his duty.

9. (a) **'Either'** means one of the two or both.

(b) **'Neither'** is negative of the either.

Examples :

(i) You may buy either of these two chairs.
(ii) Neither of them could speak on the stage.

10. (a) **'Later'** expresses 'late in time'.

(b) **'Latter'** means 'second in position or order'.

Examples :

(i) My father reached later than I expected.

(ii) The latter position was better than the former.

Use of some Important Adverbs

1. (a) Also, too, enough:

(i) He taught English. Also, he edited the school magazine

(ii) He is a writer and also he is a painter.

(iii) He is too obstinate to listen to any reason.

(iv) This is too difficult a piece for the junior students.

(v) Sarla was kind enough to help the poor.

(vi) He is brave enough to help the truth.

Note: 'Too' is used in a negative sense, but enough is used in a positive sense.

(b) Fairly and rather: Both suggest the meaning 'moderately'. But, mainly 'fairly' is used with the words that denote a positive meaning and rather is used with the words that denote a negative meaning:

(i) Rita did fairly well in that competition, but her performance was rather poor in sports.

(ii) Mona is fairly rich, but she is rather stingy.

Note: 'Rather' can also be used in a positive sense.

(i) This is a rather interesting job.

(ii) That boy is rather smart.

(c) Hardly, barely, scarcely: These words mostly convey the negative suggestions and are almost similar.

(i) I have hardly any strength now.

(ii) There was barely any supply to the township,

(iii) There were scarcely a hundred guests present.

Note: With slight variance in the meaning, the words given above convey the idea of 'very little', 'not enough', 'lack of quantity and number'.

(d) Yet, Still: These adverbs can often be used to connect the sentence units:

(i) He has been defeated many times in the contest; still he wants to be a competitor.

(ii) Mona was sick; yet she went on doing her work.

(e) Alone:

(i) He alone (none else) is capable of handling that fire,

(ii) He hunted all alone in the forest. (not in any company)

Special Note:

(a) Apart from their conventional positions the adverbs might be used in different positions with different meanings and angles.

(i) He had only four books.

(ii) John only contacted his friend in need.

(iii) He greeted me only.

(iv) Only he greeted me there.

(b) Inversion: Some adverbs can be inverted *i.e.* placed in the beginning of the sentence and then be followed by an interrogative form. The most common of these adverb are: so, seldom, never, nowhere, under no circumstances, hardly, scarcely etc.

(i) So big was the bus that it could not enter the narrow lane.

(ii) Hardly had he reached the station when he received the message.

MULTIPLE CHOICE QUESTIONS

Directions: *In the following questions choose the correct options to fill the blanks.*

1. The girl whom you met is the .... sister of Ravi.

A. eldest B. elder
C. older D. oldest

2. The historical place is ....

A. seeing worth

B. worthy of seeing
C. worth seeing
D. worthy seeing

3. These flowers smell ....
A. sweet B. sweetly
C. more sweetly D. sweetest

4. .... aspirant cannot pass the entrance examination.
A. Each B. Every
C. All D. No

5. Harivansh Rai .... second Shakespeare.
A. is a B. is
C. is the D. is an

6. .... student in the class got prizes.
A. Each and every B. Every and each
C. Every D. Never

7. It is .... picture than the one we saw last Monday.
A. interesting B. much interesting
C. more interesting D. most interesting

8. She is clever ....
A. that her mother is
B. as her mother is
C. to her mother is
D. than her mother is

9. They will get ....
A. Red, green and black paper
B. Red, green black paper
C. Red and green and black paper
D. Red green black paper

10. Health is .... wealth.
A. preferable to
B. more preferable than
C. more preferable to
D. most preferable then

11. .... water that was in the jug evaporated.
A. Little B. The little
C. Small D. A small

12. He has not sung .... songs.
A. much B. most
C. more D. many

13. Srishti has searched .... office.
A. whole the B. the whole
C. a whole D. some whole

14. Premchand was .... best and .... famous writer.
A. a, the most B. the, a most
C. the, more D. the, the most

15. William Shakespeare is famous as ....
A. a poet and a dramatist
B. a poet and dramatist
C. the poet and the dramatist
D. a poet and the dramatist

16. What does .... leader suggest?
A. other B. another
C. others D. anothers

17. He .... money.
A. has few B. have few
C. has little D. have little

18. The .... boys are rewarded.
A. first two B. two first
C. firsts two D. two's first

19. He is .... brave.
A. stronger than
B. stronger then
C. more strong then
D. more strong than

20. No sooner said ....
A. so done B. and done
C. then done D. but done

21. She returned .... than I had thought.
A. quickly B. more quicker
C. more quickly D. quicker

22. He is .... foolish person.
A. rather the B. a rather
C. rather a D. rather

23. This pen .... rupees.
A. costs twenty
B. twenty costs only
C. costs only twenty
D. only costs twenty

24. It is .... pride.
A. nothing else but
B. nothing else than
C. else nothing than
D. but

25. This tea is .... to drink.
A. too hot B. very hot
C. enough hot D. much hot

ANSWERS

1	2	3	4	5	6	7	8	9	10
A	C	A	B	A	C	C	C	A	A
11	**12**	**13**	**14**	**15**	**16**	**17**	**18**	**19**	**20**
B	D	B	D	B	B	C	A	D	C
21	**22**	**23**	**24**	**25**					
C	C	C	A	A					

DETERMINERS

Determiners are actually Adjectives. They are always followed by nouns.

Determiners are of the following kinds:

1. Demonstrative Determiners
this, that, these, those

2. Possessive Determiners
my, our, your, his, her, its, their

3. Quantitative Determiners
some, any, much, enough, sufficient, whole, a little, the little, little, all, both

4. Numerical Determiners
a few, some, few, the few, any, several, many, no, etc.

One, two, three ... (Cardinals)

First, second, third ... (Ordinals)

5. Distributive Determiners
either, neither

6. Articles

Indefinite: a, an

Definite: the

MULTIPLE CHOICE QUESTIONS

Directions: *In the following questions choose the correct options to fill the blanks.*

1. Give me .... rice.
A. some B. few
C. a few D. any

2. .... sheep grazing on the slope of the hill had gone away.
A. Any B. The few
C. This D. Much

3. Have you got .... magazines to read?
A. all B. much
C. some D. little

4. I have .... money that I want to spend on shares.
A. any B. much
C. less D. some

5. There is .... owl on the branch of the tree.
A. a B. the
C. an D. some

6. My brother is .... MBA.
A. a B. an
C. the D. any

7. Have you got .... cheese?
A. some B. many
C. a few D. few

8. No, I have not got .... cheese.
A. many B. few
C. any D. some

9. There is only .... milk left in the bottle.
A. enough B. few
C. much D. a little

10. There is .... hope of his recovery.
A. any B. little
C. many D. few

11. .... dogs were barking at the strangers.
A. Some B. Any
C. Much D. Less

12. The girl bought her father .... juice.
A. few B. some
C. any D. many

13. You should take .... honey everyday.
A. any B. many
C. a little D. a few

14. .... boy was punished by the teacher.
A. Either B. All
C. Any D. Many

15. .... girl was asked to join the army.
A. None B. Neither
C. All D. Any

16. .... water in the jug has been drunk by Mohan.
A. The little B. The few
C. A few D. Few

17. I shall play .... piano at the party.
A. some B. any
C. the D. few

18. .... labourers were found dead in the mine.
A. Any B. Fewer
C. Many D. Less

19. Could I borrow .... umbrella?
A. our B. your
C. yours D. my

20. My brother is standing in the .... row.
A. any B. many
C. some D. first

ANSWERS

1	2	3	4	5	6	7	8	9	10
A	B	C	D	C	B	A	C	D	B
11	**12**	**13**	**14**	**15**	**16**	**17**	**18**	**19**	**20**
A	B	C	A	B	A	C	C	B	D

THE VERB

A Verb is a word that tells something about the action or state of or happenning to a person or thing.

A Verb tells the following:

1. What a person or thing does.
Sachin goes to school daily.
The bell *rang* loudly.
Many birds fly in the sky.
She *sang* a song.

2. What a person or thing is.
India *is* the biggest democracy in the world.
Ram Mehar *is* very rich.
They *are* happy.

3. What is done to a person or thing.
You *are liked* by all.
Two thieves *were arrested.*
Four students *were punished* by the teacher.

4. What happens to a person or thing.
His maternal uncle *died* last week.
Two ships *sank* yesterday.
Leaves *turn* yellow in autumn.

5. What a person or thing has, had, and so on.
I *have* a new car.
He *had* a scooter last year.
He *has* several cows and goats.

It goes without saying that a verb is the most important part of a sentence. No sentence is complete without a Verb.

Important Information

1. If two or more singular nouns are joined by 'and' the verb used will be plural.

Example:
(i) He and I were going to the market.
(ii) Ram and Mohan are friends.

2. If two singular nouns joined by 'and' points out to the same thing or person, the verb used must be singular.

Example:
(i) Rice and curry is the favourite food of the Punjabis.
(ii) The Collector and District Magistrate is away.

3. In case two subjects are joined by 'as well as' the verb agrees with the first subject.

Example :
(i) Kanta as well as her children is playing.
(ii) Children as well as their mother are playing.

In the case of first sentence the verb (is) agrees with Kanta and in the case of second sentence the verb (are) agrees with the children.

4. 'Neither', 'Either', 'Every', 'Each', 'Everyone', and 'Many a' are followed by a singular verb.
Example :
(i) Either of the plans is to be adopted.
(ii) Neither of the two brothers is sure to pass.
(iii) Every student is expected to be obedient.
(iv) Everyone of them desires this.
(v) Many a person is drowned in the sea.

5. If two subjects are joined by 'Either .... or' / 'Neither .... nor', the verb agrees with the subject near to it.
Example :
(i) Either my brother or I am to do this work.
(ii) Neither he nor they are prepared to do this work.

6. 'A great many' is always followed by a 'plural noun' and a 'plural verb'. For example :
A great many students have been declared successful.

7. Similarly if two subjects are joined by 'with', 'together with', 'no less than', in addition to 'and not', etc. the verb agrees with the first subject.
Example :
(i) The boy with his parents has arrived.
(ii) He, no less than I, is to blame.

8. Nouns, plural in form, but singular in meaning, take a singular verb.
Example :
This news was broadcast from television yesterday.

MULTIPLE CHOICE QUESTIONS

Directions: *In the following questions choose the correct options to fill the blanks.*

1. The bus with all its passengers .... lost.
A. were B. was
C. are D. would

2. You as well as I .... responsible for this work.
A. am B. are
C. was D. is

3. Raghava like all his companions .... a spoiled child.
A. are B. were
C. is D. will be

4. Pen and ink .... required for me.
A. are B. were
C. is D. has required

5. Every girl and every boy .... attended the seminar.
A. have B. has
C. is D. are

6. Not only she but all her sisters ...... been married.
A. has B. have
C. is D. are

7. There .... nothing but miseries in life.
A. is B. are
C. were D. will be

8. Neither prose nor poem .... given.
A. were B. was
C. has D. have

9. Either he or I .... wrong.
A. is B. are
C. am D. were

10. Either Sulekha or Rekha .... coming here.
A. are B. is
C. were D. have

11. .... the child or his parents to blame?
A. Is B. Are
C. Were D. Has

12. You and I .... neighbours.
A. am B. are
C. was D. has

13. The house with all its belongings ..... sold away.
A. were B. are
C. was D. must

14. Either water or juice .... required.
A. is B. are
C. were D. has

15. There were not as many tables as .... required.
A. was B. were
C. is D. are

16. They each .... a book.

A. have B. are

C. has D. is

17. He and I .... class friends.

A. is B. am

C. was D. are

18. She as well as I .... guilty.

A. is B. are

C. am D. must be

19. Purushottam .... not read more on this chapter.

A. needs B. has been need

C. need D. had been need

20. He came .... to his aunt.

A. run B. running

C. to run D. in run

21. She dislikes .... meat.

A. eat to B. to eat

C. eating D. to eating

22. He likes ....

A. sing to B. singing

C. to sing D. to singing

23. We are ready .... the match.

A. play to B. to playing

C. playing D. to play

24. .... is injurious to health.

A. Smoking B. To smoke

C. To smoking D. Smoke to

25. He loves .... raw vegetables.

A. eaten B. eating

C. to eating D. eat to

26. He seemed .... finished his homework.

A. have to B. to have

C. having D. to having

ANSWERS

1	2	3	4	5	6	7	8	9	10
B	B	C	C	B	B	A	B	C	B
11	**12**	**13**	**14**	**15**	**16**	**17**	**18**	**19**	**20**
A	B	C	A	B	A	D	A	C	B
21	**22**	**23**	**24**	**25**	**26**				
C	B	D	A	B	B				

CONJUNCTIONS

A conjunction is a word which connects words, clauses or sentences.

Look at the following sentences.

(i) He bought apples *and* mangoes.

(ii) God made the country *and* man made the town.

(iii) The door was open *but* there was no one in the house.

(iv) He knows that I am here *and* that I want to see him.

In the sentence (i), *and* connects two words—*apples* and *mangoes.*

In the sentence (ii), *and* connects two sentences—*God made the country* and *man made the town.*

In the sentence (iii), *but* connects two sentences—*The door was open* and *there was no one in the house.*

In the sentence (iv), *and* connects two clauses—*that I am here* and *that I want to see him.*

The main coordinating conjunctions are: and, but, for, or, nor, also, either ..... or, neither ..... nor.

There are some conjunctions which are used in pairs. They are:

either .... or, ... neither .... nor, both .... and, though .... yet, whether .... or, not only .... but also.

Example: *Either* take it *or* leave it.

It is *neither* useful *nor* ornamental.

They *both* like *and* respect me.

Though he is suffering from high fever, *yet* he does not cry.

He does not care *whether* you go *or* stay.

He is *not only* doltish, *but also* obstinate.

The conjunctions which are used in pairs in this way, are called correlative conjunctions, or merely correlatives.

Use of Important Conjunctions

1. **As soon as :** As soon as denotes simultaneous time.
   Example : As soon as he saw his enemy, he took to his heels.
2. **No sooner .... than :**
   (a) 'No sooner' is always followed by 'than'.
   (b) Please remember that 'No sooner' is always followed by do/does/did. As such only first form of the verb should be used after the subject.
   Example :
   No sooner did he see his enemy than he took to his heels.
3. **Hardly :** Hardly is followed by when.
   Examples :
   (i) Hardly had I left the house when it started raining.
   (ii) We had hardly come into the room when his father began chastising him.
   Note :
   A. Hardly is never followed by than.
   B. 'Scarcely' can also be used in the sense and manner of 'Hardly'.
4. **Lest :** Lest is used in the sense of so that .... not. It is always followed by should. Lest is negative in sense. Hence 'not' should never be used with it.
   Example :
   Work hard lest you should fail.
   Note : 'Lest' is always followed by 'should' and not 'may'.
5. **Unless :** Unless expresses condition. It is also used in the negative sense. Use of 'not' is not allowed with unless because unless is already in the negative sense.
   Example :
   Unless you labour hard you will not pass.
6. **Until :** 'Until' expresses time. It means 'till not'.
   Example :
   Wait here until I return.
   Note : Until is in the negative sense. So 'not' should not be used with it. Example :
   Wait here until I do not return. (Incorrect)
   Wait here until I return. (Correct)
7. **As well as :** When two subjects are joined by 'as well as', the verb always agrees with the first subject.
   Examples :
   (i) The teacher as well as students is playing.
   (ii) Students as well as the teacher are playing.
   Note : 'Both' and 'as well as' cannot be used together in the same sentence.
   Examples :
   Both Sita as well as Kanta are beautiful. (Incorrect)
   Sita as well as Kanta is beautiful. (Correct)
   Both Sita and Kanta are beautiful. (Correct)
8. **As if :** 'As if' is used in the sense of pretension. While using 'as if' in a sentence, we should see that even the third person singular subject gets 'were'.
   Example :
   He talks as if he were mad.
9. **Till :** Till expresses time. Till is always used in the affirmative.
   Example :
   We did not come back till sunset.
10. **Rather than :** 'Rather than' is used in the sense of 'preference'. 'Rather' is always followed by 'than'.
    Example :
    I would rather die than submit.
11. **As long as/so long as :** Both express time during which an action or event takes place.
    Example :
    As long as there is life, there is hope.
12. **However :** It is both a subordinate and co-ordinate clause.
    Examples :
    (a) Mala worked hard, she however, failed.
    (b) However hard he may work, he cannot pass.
13. **Such as :** 'Such as' gives us the sense of 'like'. Such is always followed by 'as'.
    Example :
    Life is such a puzzle as cannot be solved.

MULTIPLE CHOICE QUESTIONS

Directions: *In the following questions choose the correct options to fill the blanks.*

1. Neither he .... his friend is good.
A. or B. and
C. but D. nor

2. The officer asked the peon .... why he was late.
A. that B. if
C. but D. No word needed

3. Both Ajay .... Vijay are intelligent.
A. or B. nor
C. and D. No word needed

4. No Sooner did the thief see the public .... he ran away.
A. then B. and
C. but D. than

5. Abhinav .... his brothers was going to Mumbai.
A. but B. yet
C. No word needed D. together with

6. He behaves .... he were the captain of the team.
A. as if B. as
C. No word needed D. that

7. Either Rupali .... Sonali is going to attend the meeting.
A. and B. but
C. nor D. or

8. Neither Nirmal .... Ashwinee is going to listen the speech.
A. and B. but
C. nor D. or

9. Ravi .... Prakash are going to Kolkata.
A. or B. nor
C. but D. and

10. Rice .... curry is my usual breakfast.
A. and B. but
C. then D. than

11. Hardly had he left .... his brother came.
A. then B. than
C. when D. that

12. I would rather have a copy .... a book.
A. then B. than
C. when D. that

13. He is no other .... my friend.
A. then B. than
C. when D. but

14. He saw a snake ....he awoke.
A. then B. when
C. than D. No word needed

15. Ten years have passed .... my grandmother died.
A. since B. when
C. then D. than

16. She is .... good .... bad.
A. either, not B. neither, or
C. neither, nor D. neither, than

17. The cellphone is both cheap .... best.
A. than B. and
C. then D. or

18. No sooner did the rogue see the police .... he disappeared.
A. then B. than
C. so D. because

19. Srishti will go .... Sanju goes.
A. if B. than
C. then D. although

20. She is wise .... timid.
A. and B. yet
C. but D. however

21. Make hay .... the sun shines.
A. though B. while
C. after D. before

22. He is so weak .... he cannot walk.
A. but B. that
C. then D. so

23. Although he is rich, ... he is unhappy.
A. but B. yet
C. so D. still

24. Wait here .... I come back.
A. till B. until
C. before D. after

25. He is my friend .... I shall help him.
A. so
B. hence
C. that is why
D. therefore

26. He must go away .... he will be beaten.
A. otherwise B. and
C. or D. else

27. God loves good men .... good men love God.
A. and B. or
C. that D. those

28. He was late .... he was not punished.
A. but B. yet
C. still D. therefore

29. Walk slowly ...., you may fall.
A. and B. or
C. so D. otherwise

30. Work hard, ... you will fail.
A. and B. or
C. otherwise D. else

ANSWERS

1	2	3	4	5	6	7	8	9	10
D	D	C	D	D	A	D	C	D	A
11	**12**	**13**	**14**	**15**	**16**	**17**	**18**	**19**	**20**
C	B	B	B	A	C	B	B	A	C
21	**22**	**23**	**24**	**25**	**26**	**27**	**28**	**29**	**30**
B	B	B	A	B	C	A	C	D	D

PREPOSITIONS

A *Preposition* is a word which is placed before a noun or a pronoun to show its relation to some other word in the sentence.

1. I saw a goat *in* the field.
2. I am fond *of* hot coffee.

In sentence 1, the word *in* shows the relation between two things—*goat* and *field.*

In sentence 2, the word *of* shows the relation between the attribute expressed by the adjective *found* and *tea.*

The words *in* and *of* are here used as prepositions.

The noun or pronoun which is used with a preposition is called its object. The noun or pronoun is in the objective case. It is governed by the preposition. Now it is absolutely clear that in sentence 1, the noun *field* is in the objective case. The word *field* is governed by the preposition *in.*

A preposition may have two or more objects.

The road runs over *hill* and *plain.*

Here, the words *hill* and *plain* are used as objects.

Use of Important Prepositions

1. Among, Between

'**Among**' is used for more than two persons or things; '**Between**' is used only for two.

Examples :

(i) Distribute these sweets *among* the poor students of the class.

(ii) Distribute these books *between* Ram and Shyam.

2. Among, In

'**Among**' is used before collective plural nouns. '**In**' is used before collective singular nouns.

Examples :

(i) I found him standing *among* the crowd.

(ii) I saw him in the crowd.

3. Beside, Besides

'**Beside**' means 'by the side of'. '**Besides**' means 'in addition to'.

Examples :

(i) The daughter was sitting *beside* her mother.

(ii) *Besides* his relatives, he invited his friends also.

4. In, Within

'**In**' means at the expiry of a period of time in future, '**Within**' means before the expiry of a period of time in any tense.

Examples :

(i) She will return *in* a week.

(ii) I shall finish my work *within* a weak.

5. On, Upon

'**On**' is used for things at rest; '**Upon**' is used for things in motion.

Examples :

(i) He is sitting *on* the floor.

(ii) The dog sprang *upon* the table.

6. By, With

'**By**' denotes the agent or doer, '**With**' denotes the instrument with which anything is done.

Examples :

(i) The bird was killed *by* the hunter with an arrow.

(ii) He beat the dog *with* a stick.

(iii) I shall reach here *by* five o'clock.

7. After, In

'**After**' means at the end of a period of time in the past. '**In**' means at the end of a period of time in future.

Examples :

(i) I shall return your book *in* a week.

(ii) He returned the book *after* a week.

8. For, From, Since

'**For**' is used before a noun denoting a period of time with all the tenses. '**From**' is used before a noun or phrase denoting a point of time, it is used in all the tenses. '**Since**' is used before a noun or phrase denoting some point of time and is always produced by a verb in the perfect continuous tense or third form of a verb.

Examples :

(i) We have been playing cards *for* two hours.

(ii) She stayed with her uncle *from* the 15th of March to the 15th of May.

(iii) I have been reading this book *since* morning.

9. Above, Over

'Above' means 'higher from', **Over** is used in the following four senses :

(i) In the sense of 'above' :
At noon, the sun is *over* our heads.

(ii) In the sense of 'beyond' :
I cannot get *over* my disappointment.

(iii) In the sense of 'Superiority' :
God *over* all blesses for ever more.

(iv) In the sense of 'Conclusion' :
It is all *over* with me.

10. At, Towards

'**At**' denotes the idea of aim, '**Towards**' denotes the idea of destination.

Examples :

(i) He threw the stone *at* the cat.

(ii) He went *towards* the house.

11. At, In, On

'At' is used as follows :

(i) **'At'** is used with small towns and villages.

Examples :

(a) He was born *at* Sonepat.

(b) He lives *at* village Bangra. (Bangra is a village)

(ii) **'At'** is used before a noun denoting a definite point of time.

Example :

He called on me *at* 9 p.m. yesterday.

'In' is used as follows :

(iii) **'In'** is used with the names of big cities, provinces and countries.

Examples :

(a) His father lives *in* England.

(b) His younger brother lives *in* Calcutta.

(iv) **'In'** is used before the names of months and years.

Example :

His elder sister was born *in* 1972 *in* the month of May.

'On' is used with dates and names of days.

Examples :

(a) I joined college *on* the 26th April.

(b) He will leave for Kolkata *on* Wednesday next.

Important Information

1. **'In'** is also used in the following phrases :
In the morning; In the evening, In winter, In summer.

2. '**In**' also denotes a place inside anything.
   He travelled *in* a crowded bus.
3. '**At**' is used in the following phrases :
   At home, *At* the station, *At* work, *At* play.

12. Below, Beneath

Below means 'of lower level in position, dignity and expectation' etc. *Beneath* means 'under'.

Examples :

(i) It is *below* my dignity to talk to her.
(ii) They rested *beneath* the shade of a tree.

13. In, Into, To

'**In**' expresses Rest or Motion inside anything. '**Into**' expresses Motion towards the inside of anything or change from one medium to another. '**To**' denotes motion from one place to another.

Examples :

(i) The boys are *in* the room.
(ii) Translate this passage from English *into* Hindi.
(iii) Every morning he goes *to* the temple.

14. Till, By, Of, Off

- 'Till' means upto or not earlier than.
- 'By' means not later than.
- 'Of' shows cause, source, separation, quality, contents, possession, apposition, point of reference, space in time etc.
- 'Off' shows separation at a near distance, and detached condition.

Consider the following examples:

(i) I shall work *till* 5 a.m.
(ii) Madhu died *of* cancer.
(iii) The nib *of* the pen is made *of* gold.
(iv) He presented me a bottle *of* perfume.
(v) Our principal is a man *of* principle.
(vi) He lived in the house *of* his friend.
(vii) *By* this time tomorrow, I'll have finished my job.
(viii) My house is *off* the road.
(ix) The book fell *off* the table.

MULTIPLE CHOICE QUESTIONS

Directions: *Tick the correct preposition for the blank in each of the following sentences.*

1. He applied ...... the manager.
A. for B. to
C. with D. by

2. Trust ...... God and do the right.
A. in B. for
C. to D. with

3. She is worthy ...... a prize.
A. with B. for
C. to D. of

4. Mr. Gomes has no taste ...... music.
A. of B. for
C. with D. to

5. You are hard ...... hearing.
A. at B. of
C. with D. for

6. He is sure ...... his success
A. for B. with
C. on D. of

7. Preeti was warned ...... the danger ahead.
A. for B. at
C. of D. about

8. I am thankful ...... you for a good advice.
A. for B. with
C. to D. of

9. Deepak would not surrender ...... the police.
A. with B. to
C. for D. on

10. The small plant in your lawn is very sensitive ...... touch.
A. on B. with
C. to D. about

11. Divya was sure to succeed ..... the examination.
A. for B. in
C. to D. with

12. Geeta was jealous ...... Ravina's beauty.
A. to B. with
C. for D. of

13. He was ignorant ..... what was happening there.
A. for B. of
C. to D. with

14. Your pen is inferior ...... mine.
A. than B. with
C. from D. to

15. Reenu is no match ...... Meenu.
A. to B. for
C. with D. upon

16. It is necessary ...... you to apply for this job.
A. on B. with
C. for D. to

17. Be loyal ...... your country.
A. for B. to
C. on D. with

18. Mukesh is junior ...... me.
A. than B. to
C. from D. of

19. Deepika was innocent ...... the crime.
A. of B. with
C. from D. to

20. I am desirous.... joining the Indian cricket team.
A. for B. of
C. to D. on

ANSWERS

1	2	3	4	5	6	7	8	9	10
B	A	D	B	B	D	D	D	B	D
11	**12**	**13**	**14**	**15**	**16**	**17**	**18**	**19**	**20**
B	D	B	D	B	D	B	B	A	B

SYNONYMS

A synonym is a word which conveys a meaning similar to the given word.

REMEMBER

Words	*Synonyms*
Add	Increase
Adequate	Enough
Adjust	Adapt
All	Aggregate
Allow	Permit
Abode	Dwelling
Apt	Proper
Assess	Appraise
Accuse	Calumniate
Abashed	Timid
Annoy	Displease
Ample	Enough, Sufficient
Amplify	Increase
Apathetic	Unenthusiastic
Accost	Address
Authentic	True

Words	*Synonyms*
Adjust	Fit
Approve	Assent, Allow, Accept
Adapt	Conform
Adversary	Opponent, Rival, Competitor
Beat	Whack
Benign	Kind
Breeze	Zephyr
Baffle	Puzzle
Booty	Spoil
Beauty	Charm
Beast	Animal
Bandit	Robber
Blaze	Shine
Bond	Tie
Bend	Twist
Bate	Diminish
Beg	Plead
Barbaric	Wild, Savage
Bashful	Shy, Reserved

Words	*Synonyms*	*Words*	*Synonyms*
Begin	Start	Dwell	Live, Dilate
Blend	Mix, Mingle	Declare	Pronounce
Bizarre	Funny	Drunk	Flushed
Below	Under	Deficient	Lacking
Bedevil	Confuse	Damn	Condemn, Curse
Bemoan	Lament	Decrease	Diminish
Babble	Nonsense	Destruction	Devastation
Blame	Fault	Efficient	Competent
Behaviour	Demeanour	Ethnic	Racial
Call	Accost	Enthral	Enslave
Copy	Imitate	Earnest	Serious
Close	Shut	Envious	Jealous
Caress	Love	Ending	Final
Camp	Stay	Egg	Incite
Connect	Attach	Extempore	At once
Cut	Injure, Curtail	Extensive	Far-ranging
Cling	Stick	Extra	Surplus
Conical	Funny	Existence	Life
Convey	Carry	Exceed	Overstep
Conspicuous	Prominent	Enormous	Vast
Cheerful	Happy, Pleasant	Excessive	Superfluous
Curtail	Decrease	Free	Unhindered
Cheerless	Sad, Dejected	Frigid	Cold
Curious	Strange	Feed	Cater
Circumstance	Factor, Situation, Condition	Fame	Reputation
		Frame	Make
Competent	Capable	First	Initial
Congruent	Overlapping	Frighten	Terrorise, Intimidate
Cope	Deal, Endure	Fervent	Fervid
Confident	Sure	Fall	Decline
Complex	Intricate	Feeble	Frail
Cajole	Coax, Flatter	Fickle	Changeable
Cunning	Crafty	Finish	Conclude
Delectable	Joyful, Delightful	Fraud	Deception
Devilish	Diabolical	Forgiving	Placable
Delicate	Soft	Grow	Develop
Devil	Fiend	Greed	Avidity
Delay	Postpone	Greet	Welcome
Dislike	Repugnance	Grave	Serious
Destroy	Ruin	Group	Constellation

Words	*Synonyms*
Given	Bestowed
Gratitude	Thankfulness
Have	Possess
Hire	Rent
Hit	Strike
Handsome	Beautiful
Hinder	Prevent
Heap	Pile
Hope	Expect
Hard	Harsh
Help	Aid
Hymn	Song
Henpecked	Enslaved
Hoodwink	Mystify, Cheat
Humble	Polite, Urbane, Modest
Harass	Vex, Trouble
Impart	Instil
Intact	Untouched
Instal	Establish
Indict	Impeach
Imitate	Ape
Instigate	Incite
Initiate	Start, Introduce
Inimical	Unfriendly
Insufferable	Intolerable
Impartiality	Justice
Jolly	Merry
Joyful	Delectable
Join	Conjoin
Kind	Benign
Kill	Murder
Kindred	Similar
Kinship	Relationship
Keen	Sharp
Knowledge	Scholarship
Lazy	Slothful
Large	Substantial, Gargantuan
Listless	Careless, Lackadaisical
Lax	Loose
Little	Small
Lifelike	Realistic

Words	*Synonyms*
Lofty	High
Lenient	Soft, Gentle
Lacking	Deficient, Wanting
Lessen	Decrease
Middleclass	Bourgeois
Mitigate	Lessen, Abate
Modesty	Humility, Lowliness
Mix	Mingle, Blend
Mixture	Mingling
Mixed	Assorted
Modify	Decrease
Mean	Imply
Multifarious	Varied
Miscarry	Abort
Note	Notice
Noble	Stately
Native	Indigenous
Needful	Necessary
Notify	Declare
Nervous	Shaky, Tremulous, Timid
Natural	Spontaneous
Near	Close
Normal	Natural
Offend	Displease
Oppress	Persecute, Tyrannize
Opponent	Adversary
Obstruct	Hinder, Check
Offence	Fault
Offender	Villain
Overstep	Exceed
Overlapping	Congruent
Occult	Mystic
Profane	Unholy
Patience	Forbearance
Pornographic	Obscene
Plenitude	Abundance
Prominent	Important
Prodigal	Spender
Procrastinate	Postpone
Promote	Develop, Honour
Persecute	Tyrannise

Words	Synonyms
Profess	Claim
Pliant	Flexible
Plebian	Common
Polished	Sophisticated
Quake	Shake
Quit	Leave
Queer	Eccentric
Quell	Suppress
Quantify	Allot
Reply	Answer
Relinquish	Retire
Read	Peruse
Relation	Reference
Render	Do
Remainder	Residuals
Repeat	Reiterate
Repentant	Contrite
Retaliative	Retaliatory
Rumour	Hearsay
Reveal	Divulge
Ritualistic	Ceremonious
Soft	Delicate
Sort	Kind, Choose, Select
Selfish	Egoistic
Sensual	Earthly
Suppress	Quell, Check
Stimulate	Provoke
Tasteless	Insipid
Travel	Journey
True	Authentic, Faithful, Truthful
Turbulence	Turmoil
Tragedy	Calamity
Tasteful	Tasty, Delicious
Touching	Painful
Thankful	Grateful
Tremendous	Great, Huge
Tough	Strong
Terminate	Conclude, End
Theory	Doctrine
Tell	Relate
Tremble	Shake, Shiver
Urge	Spur
Unbeaten	Unsubdued
Use	Utilize, Practise
Underhand	Unfair, Undue
Unfair	Unjust
Unravel	Reveal, Divulge
Unimportant	Common
Unconcerned	Apathetic
Unimitated	Inimitable
Unfortunate	Unlucky
Understand	Perceive, Comprehend
Vain	Proud, Haughty, Conceited, Shameless
Vale	Valley, Dale, Dell
Vice	Fault
Virtue	Quality
Veracity	Reality
Value	Price, Prize
Vex	Tease
Vibrate	Quiver, Shake
Violent	Excessive
Vivid	Clear, Lucid
Victory	Triumph
Vulgar	Indecent
Virtuous	Honest
Variegated	Varied, Multifarious
Well	Good
Yell	Cry, Shout
Yonder	There
Yearn	Wish, Desire
Yoke	Slavery
Zest	Earnestness, Enthusiasm
Zealous	Earnest

ANTONYMS

A antonym is a word which conveys a meaning opposite to the given word.

REMEMBER

Words	Antonyms
Abhor	Love
Abnormal	Normal
Able	Unable
Acceptable	Unacceptable
Adequate	Inadequate
Amusing	Boring

Words	*Antonyms*
Angry	Calm
Apex	Bottom
Attract	Repel
Bad	Good
Barren	Fertile
Beautiful	Ugly
Bitter	Sweet
Brave	Cowardly
Brief	Lengthy
Bright	Dull
Calm	Violent
Careful	Careless
Clear	Vague, Cloudy
Cold	Hot
Cruel	Kind
Dear	Cheap
Deep	Shallow
Difficult	Easy
Direct	Indirect
Dishonest	Honest
Disobey	Obey
Encourage	Discourage
Enormous	Tiny
Excellent	Bad
Expensive	Cheap
Eat	Fast
Fair	Unfair
Fake	Authentic
False	True
Famous	Notorious
Fool	Genius
Generous	Miserly
Genius	Fool
Genuine	Unauthentic
Gigantic	Tiny
Glad	Depressed
Good	Bad
Great	Little
Happy	Sad

Words	*Antonyms*
Hard	Soft
Hate	Love
Honest	Dishonest
Idle	Busy
Immoral	Moral
Include	Exclude
Incorrect	Correct
Intelligent	Unintelligent
Kind	Cruel
Like	Dislike
Long	Short
Lucid	Vague
Major	Minor
Naive	Experienced
Nadir	Apex
Neat	Clumsy
Obedient	Disobedient
Obscure	Clear
Oppose	Support
Optimistic	Pessimistic
Out	In
Patience	Impatience
Peaceful	Belligerent
Pious	Impious
Polite	Impolite
Potent	Impotent
Prominent	Unimportant
Proper	Improper
Pure	Impure
Quick	Slow
Quiet	Disturbance
Real	False, Unreal
Reject	Select, Choose
Reliable	Unreliable
Respect	Disrespect
Right	Wrong
Robust	Feeble, Weak
Sad	Happy

Words	Antonyms
Secret	Open
Sensible	Insensible
Severe	Mild
Sharp	Blunt
Simple	Complex
Sociable	Unsociable
Tall	Short
Tidy	Untidy
Uncanny	Canny
Violent	Calm
Vivid	Vague

Words	Antonyms
Strong	Weak
Big	Small
Easy	Difficult
Fast	Slow
High	Low
Catchy	Unattractive
Ugly	Handsome, Beautiful, Tidy
Tasty	Insipid
Sonorous	Harsh

MULTIPLE CHOICE QUESTIONS

Directions (Qs. 1 to 20): *In the following questions choose the word which best expresses the meaning of the given word.*

1. ABSURD
A. Foolish B. Simple
C. Courageous D. Silly

2. ABANDON
A. Lose B. Profit
C. Vacate D. Foil

3. CAJOLE
A. Pause B. Lenient
C. Blast D. Lure

4. COMBAT
A. Fight B. Conflict
C. Shoot D. Quarrel

5. LAMENT
A. Condone B. Console
C. Complain D. Contribution

6. DEBACLE
A. Disgrace B. Defeat
C. Collapse D. Decline

7. SHIVER
A. Fear B. Tremble
C. Shake D. Ache

8. TORTURE
A. Terror B. Harassment
C. Torment D. Tranquility

9. LAUDABLE
A. Lovable B. Commendable
C. Profitable D. Oblivious

10. FIXED
A. Sterile B. Static
C. Stubborn D. Parennial

11. QUEER
A. Unfamiliar B. Cute
C. Curious D. Strange

12. SUFFICIENT
A. Fit B. Proper
C. Adequate D. Vast

13. GLOSS
A. Brightness B. Soothing
C. Rubbing D. Miracle

14. LONGING
A. Prune B. Apathy
C. Curtail D. Craving

15. JEER
A. Applaud B. Magnanimity
C. Avoid D. Scoff

16. ZENITH
A. Minimum B. Nadir
C. Plant D. Peak

17. GARB
A. Distort B. Dress
C. Trivial D. Rage

18. ABHOR
A. Rude B. Reconcile
C. Crave D. Detest

19. YIELD
A. Shum B. Incisive
C. Retain D. Surrender

20. YOKE
A. Twist B. Release
C. Link D. Extra

Directions (Qs. 21 to 38): *In the following questions choose the word which best expresses the opposite of the given word.*

21. TRAGIC
A. Dramatic B. Strong
C. Gentle D. Comic

22. ORAL
A. Verbal B. Sane
C. Minor D. Written

23. ADMIRE
A. Hate B. Unlike
C. Dislike D. Enough

24. VIOLENT
A. Gentle B. Savage
C. Haughty D. Decline

25. ADVERSITY
A. Windfall B. Inprosperity
C. Prosperity D. Slave

26. GENUINE
A. Spurious B. Obscure
C. Countless D. Apathetic

27. GRUDGE
A. Essence B. Guile
C. Goodwill D. Ill-will

28. STIFF
A. Soft B. Courteous
C. Lively D. Flexible

29. VANITY
A. Conceit B. Pride
C. Ostentious D. Humility

30. FRONT
A. Upper B. Unusual
C. Back D. Rear

31. ATTRACT
A. Lured B. Longing
C. Repel D. Disguise

32. COMFORT
A. Discomfort B. Discontent
C. Uncomfort D. Miscomfort

33. WELCOME
A. Repel B. Accept
C. Resist D. Fight

34. TACTFUL
A. Naive B. Loose
C. Strict D. Uncivilized

35. DUTIFUL
A. Harmful B. Watchful
C. Forgetful D. Remiss

36. RIGID
A. Flux B. Adoptable
C. Yielding D. Adaptable

37. RARE
A. Petty B. Poor
C. Small D. Common

38. ZEAL
A. Despair B. Calmness
C. Passiveness D. Indifference

ANSWERS

1	2	3	4	5	6	7	8	9	10
D	C	D	A	C	C	B	C	B	B
11	**12**	**13**	**14**	**15**	**16**	**17**	**18**	**19**	**20**
D	C	A	D	D	D	B	D	D	C
21	**22**	**23**	**24**	**25**	**26**	**27**	**28**	**29**	**30**
D	D	C	A	C	A	C	D	D	D
31	**32**	**33**	**34**	**35**	**36**	**37**	**38**		
C	A	C	A	D	D	D	D		

3. Sentence Completion

It is such an exercise which starts with the primary schools and continues in the highest level of competitive examinations. One must practise it regularly to score well.

Directions (Qs. 1 to 15): *Pick out the most effective word(s) from the given words to fill in the blanks to make the sentence meaningfully complete.*

1. The student ...... that book from the library to study at home.
A. issued B. borrowed
C. hired D. lent

2. I wish I ...... a king.
A. was B. am
C. should be D. were

3. He ...... to listen to my arguments and walked away.
A. denied B. disliked
C. objected D. refused

4. The flow of blood was so ...... that the patient died.
A. intense B. adequate
C. profuse D. extensive

5. When I met her yesterday, it was the first time I ...... her since Christmas.
A. saw B. have seen
C. had seen D. have been seing

6. Can you pay ...... all these articles?
A. for B. of
C. off D. out

7. I ...... you to be at the party this evening.
A. expect B. hope
C. look forward to D. desire

8. ...... being a handicapped person, he is very cooperative and self-reliant.
A. Because B. Although
C. Since D. Despite

9. The child broke ...... from his mother and ran towards the painting.
A. away B. after
C. down D. with

10. With his ...... income, he finds it difficult to live a comfortable life.
A. brief B. sufficient
C. meagre D. huge

11. He could ...... a lot of money in such a short time by using his intelligence and working hard.
A. spend B. spoil
C. exchange D. accumulate

12. Though the brothers are twins, they look ......
A. alike B. handsome
C. indifferent D. different

13. Unfavourable weather conditions can ...... illness.
A. cure B. detect
C. treat D. enhance

14. No sooner did the bell ring, ... the actor started singing.
A. when B. than
C. after D. before

15. If I ...... realised it, I would not have acted on his advice.
A. was B. had
C. were D. have

Directions (Qs. 16 to 25): *In each question, an incomplete statement (Stem) followed by four fillers* *is given. Pick out the best one which can complete the incomplete stem correctly and meaningfully.*

16. Unless you work harder you will fail, means .....

A. if you fail you will work harder.
B. you must at least plan well than you will not fail.
C. hardly you will fail if you do not desire so.
D. if you do not put more efforts, then you will fail.

17. Even if it rains I shall come, means .....

A. if I come it will not rain.
B. if it rains I shall not come.
C. I will certainly come whether it rains or not.
D. whenever there is rain I shall come.

18. Dinesh is as stupid as he is lazy means .....

A. Dinesh is stupid because he is lazy.
B. Dinesh is lazy because he is stupid.
C. Dinesh is either stupid or lazy.
D. Dinesh is equally stupid and lazy.

19. He is so lazy that he .....

A. cannot depend on others for getting his work done.
B. cannot delay the schedule of completing the work.
C. can seldom complete his work on time.
D. dislike to postpone the work that he undertakes to do.

20. He always stammers in public meetings, but his today's speech .....

A. was fairly audible to everyone present in the hall.
B. was not received satisfactorily.
C. could not be understood properly.
D. was free from that defect.

21. In order to raise the company's profit, the employees .....

A. demanded two additional increments.
B. decided to go on paid holidays.
C. requested the management to implement new welfare schemes.
D. offered to work overtime without any compensation.

22. Although, he is reputed for making very candid statements, ...

A. his today's speech was not fairly audible.
B. his promises had always been realistic.
C. his speech was very interesting.
D. his today's statements were very ambiguous.

23. I felt somewhat more relaxed .....

A. but tense as compared to earlier.
B. and tense as compared to earlier.
C. as there was already no tension at all.
D. and tension-free as compared to earlier.

24. With great efforts his son succeeded in convincing him not to donate his entire wealth to an orphanage .....

A. and lead the life of a wealthy merchant.
B. but to a home for the forsaken children.
C. and make an orphan of himself.
D. as the orphanage needed a lot of donations.

25. Even though it is a very large house, ...

A. there is a lot of space available in it for children.
B. there is hardly any space available for children.
C. there is no dearth of space for children.
D. the servants take a long time to clean it.

ANSWERS

1	2	3	4	5	6	7	8	9	10
B	D	D	C	C	A	A	D	A	C
11	**12**	**13**	**14**	**15**	**16**	**17**	**18**	**19**	**20**
D	D	D	B	B	D	C	D	C	D
21	**22**	**23**	**24**	**25**					
D	D	D	C	B					

4. Spotting Errors

The most common errors in English are of spellings, grammar and usage of words. By regular practice, the errors can be easily spotted and minimised.

MULTIPLE CHOICE QUESTIONS

Directions: *In the following questions some of the sentences have errors and some are correct. Find out which part of a sentence has an error, the number of that part is your answer. If a sentence is free from errors, then your answer is D i.e., No error.*

1. (A) Either Ram or/(B) you is responsible/(C) for this action./(D) No error.

2. (A) The student flatly denied/(B) that he had copied/(C) in the examination hall./(D) No error.

3. (A) By the time you arrive tomorrow/(B) I have finished/(C) my work./(D) No error.

4. (A) The captain with the members of his team/(B) are returning/(C) after a fortnight./(D) No error.

5. (A) After returning from/(B) an all-India tour/(C) I had to describe about it./(D) No error.

6. (A) The teacher asked his students/(B) if they had gone through/(C) either of the three chapters included in the prescribed text./(D) No error.

7. (A) Do you know/(B) how old were you/(C) when you came here?/(D) No error.

8. (A) Beware of/(B) a fair-weather friend/(C) who is neither a friend in need nor a friend indeed./(D) No error.

9. (A) Copernicus proved/(B) that Earth/(C) moves round the Sun./(D) No error.

10. (A) The property/(B) was divided/(C) among the two brothers./(D) No error.

11. (A) I am quite certain/(B) that the lady is not only greedy/(C) but miserly./(D) No error.

12. (A) The brilliant success in the examination/(B) as well as his record in sports/(C) deserves high praise./(D) No error.

13. (A) I cannot find/(B) where has he gone/(C) though I have tried may best./(D) No error.

14. (A) If I was/(B) the Prime Minister of India/(C) I would work wonders/(D) No error.

15. (A) If it weren't/(B) for you,/(C) I wouldn't be alive today./(D) No error.

16. (A) He looked like a lion/(B) baulked from/(C) its prey./(D) No error.

17. (A) Widespread flooding/(B) is affecting/(C) large areas of the villages./(D) No error.

18. (A) If we really set to/(B) we can get the whole house/(C) cleaned in an afternoon./(D) No error.

19. (A) It's arrogant for you/(B) to assume you'll/(C)win every time./(D) No error.

20. (A) The two books are the same/(B) except for the fact that this/(C) has an answer in the back./(D) No error.

21. (A) Your husband doesn't/(B) believe that you are older/(C) than I./(D) No error.

22. (A) I could not/(B) answer to/(C) the question./(D) No error.

23. (A) Two years passed/(B) since/(C) my cousin died./(D) No error.

24. (A) I am learning English/(B) for ten years/(C) without much effect./(D) No error.

25. (A) Ramesh has agreed/(B) to marry with the girl/(C) of his parent's choice./ (D) No error.

26. (A) When he was arriving./(B) the party was/(C) in full swing./(D) No error.

27. (A) The most studious boy/(B) in the class/(C) was made as the captain./(D) No error.

28. (A) I am participating/(B) in the two-miles race/(C) tomorrow morning./(D) No error.

29. (A) When the boy committed a mistake/(B) the teacher made him to do/(C) the sum again./(D) No error.

30. (A) Whenever a person lost anything/(B) the poor folk around/(C) are suspected./(D) No error.

ANSWERS

1	2	3	4	5	6	7	8	9	10
B	D	B	B	C	C	D	D	B	C
11	**12**	**13**	**14**	**15**	**16**	**17**	**18**	**19**	**20**
C	D	B	A	C	C	C	A	A	C
21	**22**	**23**	**24**	**25**	**26**	**27**	**28**	**29**	**30**
C	B	A	A	B	A	C	B	B	A

EXPLANATORY ANSWERS

1. Replace 'is' by 'are'.

2. No error.

3. Replace 'have' by 'would have'.

4. Replace 'are' by 'is'.

5. Replace 'had to describe' by 'described'.

6. Replace 'either' by 'any'.

7. No error.

8. No error.

9. Omit 'that'.

10. Replace 'among' by 'between'.

11. Add 'also'.

12. No error.

13. Replace 'has he' by 'he has'.

14. Replace 'was' by 'were'.

15. Replace 'wouldn't be' by 'would not have been'.

16. Replace 'its' by 'his'.

17. Replace 'areas' by 'area'.

18. Replace 'set to' by 'set on'.

19. Replace 'for' by 'of'.

20. Replace 'in' by 'on'.

21. Replace 'I' by 'me'.

22. Omit 'to'.

23. Replace 'passed' by 'have passed'.

24. Replace 'am' by 'have been'.

25. Omit 'with'.

26. Replace 'was arriving' by 'arrived'.

27. Omit 'as'.

28. Replace 'in' by 'at'.

29. Omit 'to'.

30. Replace 'lost' by 'loses'.

5. One Word Substitution

There are many single words in English language which can be perfectly used for a number of words. These words help in expressing ideas in a short and correct manner for the right occasion. Such words not only increase the vocabulary but also enable you to economise in the use of words to a great extent.

Multiple Word Expression	*Substitution*
One who always looks towards the bright side of things	Optimist
One who always looks towards the dark side of things	Pessimist
The time when one develops from a child into an adult	Adolescence
The process of growing more plants in order to form a forest.	Afforestation
The science which deals with farming	Agriculture
From some other country or place etc.	Alien
A term, etc. giving more than one meaning	Ambiguous
A vehicle which is used to carry sick persons	Ambulance
An animal which can live both in water and on land	Amphibian
A lawless situation when there is no government	Anarchy
Belonging to the history of thousands of years old	Ancient
Once a year	Annual
A very old object but still valuable	Antique
Words of opposite meanings	Antonyms
Words of similar meanings	Synonyms
Signatures of a famous person	Autograph
A government led by one person with absolute authority	Autocracy
A written work of one's own life history	Autobiography
A person who has never been married	Bachelor
A person usually having no hair on his head	Bald
A place where one can deposit money and get interest	Bank
A person who cuts our hair	Barber
A building/group of buildings where soldiers live	Barracks
A person who makes buns and biscuits	Baker
A person who lives by asking people for food and money without doing any useful job	Beggar
The crime of having married to two persons at the same time	Bigamy
The branch of science which deals with the study of plants	Botany
Able to speak two languages	Bilingual

Multiple Word Expression	*Substitution*
Able to speak more than two languages	Polyglot
The branch of science which deals with the living organisms	Biology
A powerful snow storm	Blizzard
A great successful book or movie	Blockbuster
A short news on the radio or TV	Bulletin
A system in which the most important works are organised by the government officials	Bureaucracy
A person who has no vision in his eyes	Blind
A page or a series of pages on which the information of days, weeks, months, etc. is given	Calendar
A person who eats human flesh	Cannibal
A complete list of items often arranged alphabetically	Catalogue
A sudden disaster	Catastrophe
A period of 100 years	Century
A branch of science which deals with chemicals	Chemistry
A printed leaf usually issued by banks that we sign to carry certain financial deal	Cheque
A person who makes or mends shoes	Cobbler
A group of people who has been chosen by others to make decisions on their own	Committee
A building in which nuns live	Convent
An animal which feeds on other animals	Carnivorous
A person who does criticism	Critic
A person who cannot hear	Deaf
A condition in which one loses a lot of water from one's body because of vomiting, etc.	Dehydration
A system of government in which the people cast their votes to elect their leaders	Democracy
The study of skin problems	Dermatology
A long piece of land covered with sand	Desert
The art of managing relationships between countries	Diplomacy
A piece of information about the words in a book form	Dictionary
A piece of information about the telephone numbers of the people in a book from	Directory
A person in charge of a newspapers, magazine etc.	Editor
A person who thinks he is better than the others	Egoist
To leave your country and settle in some other country	Emigrate
A book or series of books giving almost all knowledge about an area or some persons etc.	Encyclopaedia
Study of insects	Entomology
Time when day and night are of the same duration	Equinox
To sell things out of the country	Export
To purchase things from some other country	Import
A plant or animal no longer in existence	Extinct
A situation when there is a shortage of food for a long period of time	Famine
An amount of money that we pay for some action or services	Fee
Related to women	Feminine
An animal strong and aggressive	Ferocious

Multiple Word Expression	*Substitution*
A piece of land where plants grow easily from the soil that is favourable to them	Fertile
A work of literature having some imaginary events	Fiction
A large amount of water covering certain area	Flood
A person who sells flowers	Florist
A religious ceremony for burying or cremating a dead person	Funeral
A substance which kills fungus	Fungicide
A person studying or having studied the diseases and the related things of female reproductory system	Gynaecologist
The murder of the person of the same group race or country	Genocide
A substance which kills germs	Germicide
A situation in which many people die because of fire during war	Holocaust
The act of killing a person deliberately	Homicide
A word having the pronunciation as the other one does but it differs in meaning	Homophone
A word having the same spelling as the other one does but it is pronounced in some other way	Homonym
A person who is attracted towards the person of the same sex	Homosexual
Go across and parallel to the ground	Horizontal
A substance which kills the insects	Insecticide
That cannot be corrected	Incorrigible
That cannot be defeated	Invincible
That cannot be eaten	Inedible
That cannot be seen	Invisible
A place in a school or college where books are kept for the benefit of students, teachers etc.	Library
A place in a school or college where scientific experiments are performed	Laboratory
An official who is a judge in the lowest court	Magistrate
A piece of music or a book before it is printed	Manuscript
Related to men	Masculine
One who believes in the existence of God	A theist
One who does not believe in the existence of good	An atheist
That can be believed	Credible
That cannot be believed	Incredible
That which dissolves in a solvent	Soluble
That which does not dissolves in a solvent	Insoluble
Hard writing that can be read	Legible
Hard writing that cannot be read	Illegible
A person who does jobs beneficial to mankind	Philanthropist
A person who goes on foot	Pedestrian
A person who fights for his own country	Patriot
An act of killing oneself	Suicide
A woman whose husband is dead	Widow
A man whose wife is dead	Widower
A person who eats vegetarian and non-vegetarian diets	Omnivorous

Multiple Word Expression	*Substitution*
Something which is everywhere at the same time	Omnipresent
One who knows everything	Omniscient
A child who does not have parents	Orphan
An award etc. given after the death of the person	Posthumous
The place where animals are kept for amusement and to increase the knowledge of the public	Zoo
The science which deals with the study of animals	Zoology

MULTIPLE CHOICE QUESTIONS

Directions: *In questions given below, out of the four alternatives, choose the one which can be substituted for the given words/sentences.*

1. Something that relates to everyone in the world
A. General B. Common
C. Usual D. Universal

2. An expression of mild disapproval
A. Warning B. Denigration
C. Impertinence D. Reproof

3. One who is not easily pleased by anything
A. Maiden B. Medieval
C. Precarious D. Fastidious

4. Murder of a king
A. Infanticide B. Matricide
C. Genocide D. Regicide

5. A remedy for all diseases
A. Stoic B. Marvei
C. Panacea D. Recompense

6. A dramatic performance
A. Mask B. Mosque
C. Masque D. Mascot

7. Study of birds
A. Orology B. Optology
C. Ophthalmology D. Ornithology

8. Ready to believe
A. Credulous B. Credible
C. Creditable D. Incredible

9. Incapable of being seen through
A. Ductile B. Opaque
C. Obsolete D. Potable

10. One who eats everything
A. Omnivorous B. Omniscient
C. Irresistible D. Insolvent

11. A place where bees are kept is called
A. An apiary B. A mole
C. A hive D. A sanctuary

12. One who cannot be corrected
A. Incurable B. Incorrigible
C. Hardened D. Invulnerable

13. One who is in charge of a museum
A. Curator B. Supervisor
C. Caretaker D. Warden

14. Continuing fight between parties, families, clans, etc.
A. Enmity B. Feud
C. Quarrel D. Skirmish

15. A voice loud enough to be heard
A. Audible B. Applaudable
C. Laudable D. Oral

16. A paper written by hand
A. Handicraft B. Manuscript
C. Handiwork D. Thesis

17. Habitually silent or talking little
A. Serville B. Unequivocal
C. Taciturn D. Synoptic

18. To slap with a flat object
A. Chop B. Hew
C. Gnaw D. Swat

19. A person who speaks many languages
A. Linguist B. Monolingual
C. Polyglot D. Bilingual

20. A light sailing-boat built specially for racing
A. Canoe B. Yacht
C. Frigate D. Dinghy

21. A fixed orbit in space in relation to earth
A. Geological B. Geo-synchronous
C. Geo-centric D. Geo-stationary

22. A style in which a writer makes a display of his knowledge

A. Pedantic B. Verbose
C. Pompous D. Ornate

23. A religious discourse

A. Preach B. Stanza
C. Sanctorum D. Sermon

24. A place that provides refuge

A. Asylum B. Sanatorium
C. Shelter D. Orphanage

25. Detailed plan of a journey

A. Travelogue B. Travelkit
C. Schedule D. Itinerary

26. A person who insists on something

A. Disciplinarian B. Stickler
C. Instantaneous D. Boaster

27. A drawing on transparent paper

A. Red print B. Blue print
C. Negative D. Transparency

28. One who believes that all things and events in life are predetermined is a

A. Fatalist B. Puritan
C. Egoist D. Tyrant

29. A school boy who cuts classes frequently is a

A. Defeatist B. Sycophant
C. Truant D. Martinet

30. The act of violating the sanctity of the church is

A. Blasphemy B. Heresy
C. Sacrilege D. Desecration

31. A place where monks live as a secluded community

A. Cathedral B. Diocese
C. Convent D. Monastery

32. One who is fond of fighting

A. Bellicose B. Aggressive
C. Belligerent D. Militant

33. Tending to move away from the centre or axis

A. Centrifugal B. Centripetal
C. Axiomatic D. Awry

34. Words inscribed on tomb

A. Epitome B. Epistle
C. Epilogue D. Epitaph

35. Leave or remove from a place considered dangerous

A. Evade B. Evacuate
C. Avoid D. Exterminate

36. Original inhabitants of a country

A. Abroge B. Aborger
C. Aborgory D. Aborigins

37. Government by the officials

A. Theocracy B. Plutocracy
C. Bureaucracy D. Democracy

38. Incapable of being exhausted

A. Inexhaustible B. Inaexhaustible
C. Exhaustable D. Non-tired

39. A person of good understanding, knowledge and reasoning power

A. Expert B. Intellectual
C. Snob D. Literate

40. One absorbed in his own thoughts and feelings rather than in things outside

A. Scholar B. Recluse
C. Introvert D. Intellectual

ANSWERS

1	2	3	4	5	6	7	8	9	10
D	D	D	D	C	C	D	A	B	A
11	**12**	**13**	**14**	**15**	**16**	**17**	**18**	**19**	**20**
A	B	A	B	A	B	C	D	A	B
21	**22**	**23**	**24**	**25**	**26**	**27**	**28**	**29**	**30**
D	A	D	A	D	B	D	A	C	C
31	**32**	**33**	**34**	**35**	**36**	**37**	**38**	**39**	**40**
D	A	A	D	B	B	C	A	B	C

6. Spelling Errors

There are thousands of words in English language. It is difficult to remember the spellings and meanings of all at once. Try to learn as many as you can. Use a dictionary regularly.

Directions: *Find the correctly spelt words.*

1. A. Damage B. Dammage C. Damaige D. Dammege
2. A. Efficiant B. Effecient C. Efficient D. Eficient
3. A. Schedule B. Schdule C. Schedale D. Schedeule
4. A. Occurad B. Occurred C. Ocurred D. Occured
5. A. Grieff B. Grief C. Grieef D. Grrief
6. A. Guarantee B. Garuntee C. Guaruntee D. Gaurantee
7. A. Meddicine B. Medicine C. Medicene D. Medicinne
8. A. Benefeted B. Benefitted C. Benifited D. Benefited
9. A. Acommodation B. Acomodation C. Accomodation D. Accommodation
10. A. Querrelsome B. Quarrelsame C. Quarrelsome D. Querralsome
11. A. Sympathetic B. Smypathetic C. Sympothetic D. Sympethetic
12. A. Prograssive B. Progressive C. Progresive D. Prograsive
13. A. Uncivilized B. Uncevilized C. Uncivillized D. Uncevelized
14. A. Extravagant B. Extreragent C. Extreregant D. Extravegent
15. A. Missunderstood B. Miesunderstood C. Misunderstood D. Misunderstod
16. A. Belligerent B. Beligirent C. Belligarant D. Belligerrent
17. A. Astonished B. Astronished C. Astoneshed D. Asstonished
18. A. Sincerely B. Sencerely C. Sincerelly D. Sincerrely
19. A. Rigourous B. Rigerous C. Rigorous D. Regerous
20. A. Satellite B. Sattellite C. Satelite D. Sattelite
21. A. Pesanger B. Passenger C. Pessenger D. Pasanger
22. A. Humurous B. Humorous C. Humoreus D. Humorrous
23. A. Exeggerate B. Exaggerate C. Exadgerate D. Exagerate
24. A. Fariegn B. Forein C. Foriegn D. Foreign
25. A. Excesive B. Excessive C. Exccessive D. Exccesive
26. A. Forcaust B. Forcast C. Forecast D. Forecaste
27. A. Paralleted B. Paralelled C. Parralleled D. Parallelled

28. A. Ocasion B. Occassion
C. Occasion D. Ocassion

29. A. Boquet B. Bouquet
C. Bouquete D. Bouquette

30. A. Chettering B. Chaterring
C. Chattering D. Chatering

31. A. Discourage B. Disscourage
C. Discourege D. Discaurage

32. A. Curageous B. Courageous
C. Courrageous D. Couregeous

33. A. Abandon B. Abanddon
C. Abendon D. Abbandon

34. A. Embarassment
B. Emberrassement
C. Embarrassment
D Embbaresment

35. A. Eccintric B. Eccentrie
C. Eccentric D. Eccintrie

36. A. Occasional B. Occassional
C. Occesional D. Occessional

37. A. Querrel B. Querral
C. Quarrel D. Quarel

38. A. Contrebution B. Contribution
C. Contributtion D. Conterbution

39. A. Desgrace B. Disgrece
C. Disgrice D. Disgrace

40. A. Harassment B. Herassment
C. Harasment D. Harassmient

41. A. Imaginative B. Imeginative
C. Imagenative D. Imaginetive

42. A. Suficient B. Suficiant
C. Sufficient D. Sufficiant

43. A. Adequate B. Edequate
C. Adaquete D. Edaquete

44. A. Exparienced B. Experianced
C. Experienced D. Experrienced

45. A. Flatering B. Fletering
C. Flattering D. Fletaring

46. A. Cuttiveted B. Culltrivated
C. Cultivated D. Caltivated

47. A. Praiceworthy B. Peiseworthy
C. Praiseworthy D. Praisaworthy

48. A. Profesional B. Professionel
C. Professional D. Profissional

49. A. Ameteur B. Amateur
C. Amataur D. Amateor

50. A. Unfevourable B. Unfevaurable
C. Unfavourable D. Unfivourable

ANSWERS

1	2	3	4	5	6	7	8	9	10
A	C	A	B	B	A	B	B	D	C
11	**12**	**13**	**14**	**15**	**16**	**17**	**18**	**19**	**20**
A	B	A	A	C	A	A	A	C	A
21	**22**	**23**	**24**	**25**	**26**	**27**	**28**	**29**	**30**
B	B	B	D	B	C	A	C	B	C
31	**32**	**33**	**34**	**35**	**36**	**37**	**38**	**39**	**40**
A	B	A	C	C	A	C	B	D	A
41	**42**	**43**	**44**	**45**	**46**	**47**	**48**	**49**	**50**
A	C	A	C	A	C	C	C	B	C

GENERAL AWARENESS

NATIONAL SYMBOLS

STATE EMBLEM

State Emblem of India is an adaptation from the Sarnath Lion Capital of Ashoka. It was adopted by the Government of India on January 26, 1950. In the adapted form, only three lions are visible, the fourth being hidden from the view. The wheel (Dharma Chakra) appears in relief in the centre of the abacus with a bull on the right and a horse on the left.

The bell-shaped lotus has been omitted. The words ''Satyameva Jayate'' meaning ''Truth alone triumphs'' are inscribed below the Emblem in Devanagari script.

NATIONAL FLAG

The National Flag of India is a horizontal tricolour of deep saffron (Kesari), white and dark green in equal proportion. In the centre of the white band there is a wheel in navy blue colour. It has 24 spokes. The ratio of the length and the breadth of the flag is 3 : 2. Its design was adopted by the Constituent Assembly of India on July 22, 1947.

NATIONAL ANTHEM

Rabindranath Tagore's song 'Jana-gana-mana' was adopted by the Constituent Assembly as the National Anthem of India on January 24, 1950.

Jana-gan-mana-adhinayaka jaya he, Bharata-bhagya-vidhata
Punjab-Sindh-Gujarat-Maratha-Dravida-Utkala-Banga
Vindhya-Himachala-Yamuna-Ganga Uchhala-jaladhi-taranga.
Tava subha name jage, Tava subha asisa mange, Gahe tava jaya gatha,
Jana-gana-mangala-dayak, jaya he Bharata bhagya vidhata,
Jaya he, jaya he, jaya he, Jaya jaya jaya, jaya he.

NATIONAL SONG

Bankim Chandra Chatterji's 'Vande Mataram' which was a source of inspiration to the people in their struggle for freedom, has been adopted as National Song. It has an equal status with the National Anthem.

Vande Mataram
Sujalam, suphalam, malayaja-shitalam,
Shasya shyamalam, Mataram
Shubhrajyotsna,pulkita yaminim,
Phulla kusumita drumadalashobhinim,
Subhasinim sumadhura—bhashinim,
Sukhadam, Varadam, Mataram.

NATIONAL CALENDAR

It is based on the Saka era with Chaitra as its first month and a normal year of 365 days. It was adopted from March 22, 1957. Dates of the national calendar have a permanent correspondence with dates of Gregorian calendar as Chaitra I falls on March 22 in a normal year and March 21 in a leap year. In official communications, both Saka and Gregorian calendar dates are written. Months of the national calendar are Chaitra, Vaishakha, Jaishtha, Ashada, Shrâvan, Bhadra, Ashvina, Kartika, Margashirsha, Pausha, Magha and Phalguna.

NATIONAL ANIMAL

The magnificent tiger — Panthera tigris (Linnaeus) is the national animal of India. Tiger is found in several parts of the country and is known for its grace, strength, agility and enormous power. 'Project Tiger' was launched in 1973 to check their dwindling population in India.

NATIONAL BIRD

The Indian Peacock — Pavo Christatus (Linnaeus) is the national bird of India. It is a colourful, swan-sized bird with a fan-shaped crest of feathers on its head and a long-slander neck. The male species is more colourful with blue breast and a spectacular bronze-green train of around 200 elongated feathers.

National Flower—Lotus

National Tree—Banyan

National Fruit—Mango

National Currency—Rupee '₹'

(One Rupee = 100 Paise)

National Aquatic Animal—Dolphin

BOOKS AND AUTHORS

Name of Book	Author
Ain-e-Akbari	Abul Fazal
Anand Math	Bankim Chandra Chatterjee
An Unknown Indian	Nirad C. Chaudhuri
Arthshastra	Kautilya
Coolie	Mulk Raj Anand
Das Kapital	Karl Marx
Discovery of India	Jawaharlal Nehru
Eternal India	Mrs. Indira Gandhi
Godan	Prem Chand
Gitanjali	Rabindranath Tagore
Gora	Rabindranath Tagore
Geet Govinda	Jayadeva
Harsha Charit	Bana Bhatta
Hindu View of Life	Dr. S. Radhakrishnan
India Wins Freedom	Maulana Abul Kalam Azad
Jobs of Millions	V.V. Giri
Jungle Book	Rudyard Kipling
Kamayani	Jai Shankar Prasad
Kadambari	Bana Bhatta
Life Divine	Sri Aurobindo
Last days of Netaji	G.D. Khosla
Les Miserables	Victor Hugo
Mahabharat	Veda Vyas
Macbeth	William Shakespeare
Mein Kempf	Hitler
Meghduta	Kalidas

Name of Book	Author
Mother (Maa)	Maxim Gorky
Mother India	Katherine Mayo
My Experiments with Truth	Mahatma Gandhi
My Presidential Years	R. Venkataraman
Neeti Shatak	Bhartrihari
Nehru and His Vision	Dr. K.R. Narayanan
Old Man and the Sea	Ernest Hemingway
One World	Wendell Wilkie
Panchtantra	Vishnu Sharma
Paradise Lost	John Milton
Ramayana	Valmiki (in Sanskrit)
Raghuvansham	Kalidas
Rajtarangini	Kalhan
Ram Charit Manas	Tulsi Das
Abhijnan Shakuntalam	Kalidas
Satanic Verses	Salman Rushdie
Saket	Maithili Sharan Gupta
Speed Post	Shobha De
The God of Small Things	Arundhati Roy
Treasure Island	R.L. Stevenson
Twelfth Night	William Shakespeare
Train to Pakistan	Khuswant Singh
Uttara Ram Charitra	Bhava Bhuti
Vanity Fair	W.M. Thackeray
War and Peace	Leo Tolstoy
Wealth of Nations	Adam Smith
Wake up India	Annie Besant

INVENTIONS AND DISCOVERIES

Geographical Discoveries

Discovery	Discoverer
America	Columbus
Brazil	Cabral
North Pole	Robert Peary
Everest (Conquered)	Tabie Junko
Planetary Motion	Kepler
Hawaiian Islands	Captain Cook
South Pole	Amundsen
Solar System	Copernicus

Chemistry and Physics

Discovery	Discoverer
Atom Bomb	Otto Hahn
Atomic Theory	Dalton
Atomic Numbers	Moseley
Cosmic Rays	R.S. Millikan
Dynamite	Alfred Nobel
Electrons Theory	Bohr
Electricity (current)	Volta
Electric Telegraphy (Code)	S. Morse

Discovery	Discoverer
Gravitation	Newton
Gas Light	Murdock
Oxygen	J. Priestly
Photography	L. Daguerre
Printing for the blind	Louis Braille
Radium	Madame Curie
Telegraph	Samuel Morse
Television	J.L. Baird
Telephone	Graham Bell
Wireless	G. Marconi
X-rays	W.K. Roentgen
Mechanical	
Aeroplane	Wright Brothers
Bicycle	Macmillan
Computer	Charles Babbage
Dynamo	Michal Faraday
Diesel Engine	Rudolf Diesel
Engine (Railway)	Stephenson
Fountain Pen	Waterman
Gramophone	Edison
Locomotive Power of Steam	James Watt
Helicopter	Brequet
Life Boat	Henry Greathead

Discovery	Discoverer
Microscope	Z. Jansen
Printing Press	Gutenberg
Revolver	Colt
Sewing Machine	Elias Howe
Thermometer	Fahrenheit
Transistor	W. Shockley
Typewriter	Sholes
Telescope	Hans Lippershey
Tank (Military)	Swinton
Medical	
Antiseptic Surgery	Lord Joseph Lister
Bacteria	Leeuwenhock
Circulation of Blood	William Harvey
Homoeopathy (Discovered)	Hahnemann
Insulin	F. Banting
Penicillin	Alexander Flemming
Malaria Parasite	Dr. Ronald Ross
Stethoscope	Laennec
Vitamins	Funk
Anti-Rabies Treatme[illegible]	Pasteur
General	
Nylon	Carouthers
Science of Geometry	Euclids

WORLD'S GEOGRAPHICAL SURNAMES

• City of Sky-scrapers—New York • City of Seven Hills—Rome • City of Dreaming Spires—Oxford • City of Golden Gate—San Francisco • City of Magnificent Buildings—Washington D.C. • City of Eternal Springs—Quito (S. America) • China's Sorrow—Hwang Ho • Cockpit of Europe—Belgium • Dark Continent—Africa • Emerald Isle—Ireland • Eternal City—Rome • Empire City—New York • Forbidden City—Lhasa (Tibet) • Garden City—Chicago • Gate of Tears—Strait of Bab-el-Mandeb • Gift of the Nile—Egypt • Granite City—Aberdeen (Scotland) • Hermit Kingdom—Korea • Herring Pond—Atlantic Ocean • Holy Land—Jerusalem • Island Continent—Australia • Islands of Cloves—Zanzibar • Isle of Pearls—Bahrein (Persian Gulf) • Key to the Mediterranean—Gibralter • Land of Cakes—Scotland • Land of Golden Fleece—Australia • Land of Maple Leaf—Canada • Land of Morning Calm—Korea • Land of Midnight Sun—Norway • Land, of the Thousand Lakes—Finland • Land of the Thunderbolt—Bhutan • Land of White Elephant—Thailand • Land of Thousand Elephants—Laos • Land of Rising Sun—Japan • Loneliest Island—Tristan De Gunha (Mid-Atlantic) • Manchester of Japan—Osaka • Pillars of Hercules—Strait of Gibraltar • Pearl of the Antilles—Cuba • Playground of Europe—Switzerland • Quaker City—Philadelphia • Queen of the Adriatic—Venice • Roof of the World—The Pamirs, Central Asia • Sugar bowl of the world—Cuba • Venice of the North—Stockholm • Windy City—Chicago • Whiteman's grave—Guinea Coast of Africa • Yellow River—Huang Ho (China) • Sickman of Europe—Turkiye

CAPITALS AND CURRENCIES OF COUNTRIES

Country	Capital	Currency
Afghanistan	Kabul	Afghani
Algeria	Algiers	Dinar
Angola	Luanda	New Kwanza
Argentina	Buenos Aires	Peso
Armenia	Yeravan	Dram
Australia	Canberra	Dollar
Austria	Vienna	Euro
Azerbaijan	Baku	Monat
Bahrain	Manama	Dinar
Bangladesh	Dhaka	Taka
Barbados	Bridgetown	Dollar
Belgium	Brussels	Euro
Bhutan	Thimphu	Ngultrum
Bolivia	La paz	Boliviano
Brazil	Brasilia	Cruzeiro
Bulgaria	Sofia	Lev
Byelorussia	Minsk	Zaichik
Cambodia	Phnom-Penh	Riel
Canada	Ottawa	Dollar
Chile	Santiago	Peso
China	Beijing	Yuan
Colombia	Bogota	Peso
Congo	Brazzaville	Franc
Croatia	Zagreb	Kuna
Cuba	Havana	Peso
Cyprus	Nicosia	Euro
Czech Republic	Prague	Crown
Denmark	Copenhagen	Krone
Egypt	Cairo	Pound
Estonia	Tallinn	Kroon
Ethiopia	Addis Ababa	Birr
Fiji	Suva	Dollar
Finland	Helsinki	Euro
France	Paris	Euro
Georgia	Tbilisi	Lari
Germany	Berlin	Euro
Ghana	Accra	Cedi
Greece	Athens	Euro
Guatemala	Guatemala City	Quetzal
Hong Kong	Victoria	Dollar
Hungary	Budapest	Forints
Iceland	Reykjavik	Krona
India	New Delhi	Rupee
Indonesia	Jakarta	Rupiah
Iran	Teheran	Rial
Iraq	Baghdad	Dinar
Ireland	Dublin	Euro
Israel	Jerusalem	Shekel
Italy	Rome	Euro
Jamaica	Kingston	Dollar
Japan	Tokyo	Yen
Jordan	Amman	Dinar
Kazakhstan	Akmola	Tenge
Kenya	Nairobi	Shilling
Korea (S)	Seoul	Won
Korea (N)	Pyongyang	Won
Kyrgyzstan	Bishkek	Som
Kuwait	Kuwait City	Dinar
Laos	Vientiane	Kip
Latvia	Riga	Lat
Lebanon	Beirut	Pound
Libya	Tripoli	Dinar
Lithuania	Vilnius	Litas
Malaysia	Kuala Lumpur	Ringgit
Maldives	Male	Rufiyya
Mauritius	Port Louis	Rupee
Moldavia	Chisinau	Leu
Mexico	Mexico City	Peso
Morocco	Rabat	Dirham
Mozambique	Maputo	Metical
Myanmar (Burma)	Nay Pyi Taw	Kyat
Nepal	Kathmandu	Rupee
Netherlands	Amsterdam	Euro
New Zealand	Wellington	Dollar
Nigeria	Abuja	Naira
Norway	Oslo	Krone
Oman	Muscat	Rial
Pakistan	Islamabad	Rupee
Philippines	Manila	Peso
Poland	Warsaw	Zloty
Portugal	Lisbon	Euro
Qatar	Doha	Riyal
Romania	Bucharest	Leu
Russia	Moscow	Ruble
Saudi Arabia	Riyadh	Rial

Country	Capital	Currency	Country	Capital	Currency
Slovakia	Bratislava	Euro	Turkmania	Ashikabad	Manat
Spain	Madrid	Euro	Uganda	Kampala	Shilling
Sri Lanka	Colombo	Rupee	Ukraine	Kiev	Hyrvna
Sudan	Khartoum	Dinar	United Arab Emirates	Abu Dhabi	Dirham
Sweden	Stockholm	Krona	U.K.	London	Pound Sterling
Switzerland	Berne	Swiss Francs	U.S.A.	Washington	Dollar
Syria	Damascus	Pound	Uzbekistan	Tashkent	Som
South Africa	Capetown (Legislative) Pretoria (Administrative)	Rand	Vietnam	Hanoi	Dong
			Yemen	Sana'a	Rial/Dinar
			Zimbabwe	Harare	Dollar
Tajikistan	Dushanbe	Somoni	Congo (Democratic Republic)	Kinshasa	Franc
Taiwan	Taipei	Dollar			
Tanzania	Dodoma	Shilling			
Thailand	Bangkok	Baht			
Turkiye	Ankara	Turkish Lira	Zambia	Lusaka	Kwacha

INDIAN CITIES AND THEIR RIVERS

City	State	River	City	State	River
Agra	U.P.	Yamuna	Patna	Bihar	Ganga
Ahmedabad	Gujarat	Sabarmati	Prayagraj	U.P.	Confluence of the Ganga, Yamuna and invisible Saraswati
Alwaye	Kerala	Periyar			
Kolkata	West Bengal	Hooghly			
Cuttack	Odisha	Mahanadi			
Delhi	Delhi	Yamuna	Srinagar	J & K	Jhelum
Haridwar	Uttarakhand	Ganga	Surat	Gujarat	Tapti
Kanpur	Uttar Pradesh	Ganga	Tiruchirapally	Tamil Nadu	Kaveri
Ludhiana	Punjab	Sutlej	Ujjain	Madhya Pradesh	Shipra
Lucknow	Uttar Pradesh	Gomati	Vijayawada	Andhra Pradesh	Krishna
Nasik	Maharashtra	Godavari	Varanasi	Uttar Pradesh	Ganga

WONDERS OF THE WORLD

Seven Wonders of the Ancient World: (1) the Pyramids of Egypt, built in approximately 2700 BC; (2) the Hanging Gardens at Babylon; (3) the temple of Artemis at Emphesus; (4) the statue of Zeus at Olympia; (5) the tomb of Mausolus at Halicarnassus, built in nearly 350 BC; (6) the Colossus of Rhodes, built in nearly 280 BC; (7) the Pharos Lighthouse at Alexandria.

Seven Wonders of the Medieval World: (1) the Colosseum of Rome; (2) the Great Wall of China; (3) the Porcelain Tower of Nanking; (4) the Mosque at St. Sophia (Constantinople); (5) Stonehenge; (6) the Catacombs of Rome; (7) the Leaning Tower of Pisa.

Seven New Wonders of the World: (1) Taj Mahal of Agra (India); (2) Pyramid at Chichen Itza (Mexico); (3) Machu Picchu (Peru); (4) Statue of Christ The Redeemer (Brazil); (5) Great Wall of China; (6) Roman Colosseum, Italy; (7) Ruins of Petra, Jordan.

STATES & UNION TERRITORIES OF INDIA (CAPITALS, PRINCIPAL LANGUAGES)

States & Union Territories	*Capitals*	*Principal Languages*
■ Andhra Pradesh	Amravati	*Telgu and Urdu*
■ Arunachal Pradesh	Itanagar	*Monpa, Adi, Nissi etc.*
■ Assam	Dispur	*Assamese and Bengali*
■ Bihar	Patna	*Hindi and Maithili*
■ Chhattishgarh	Raipur	*Hindi*
■ Goa	Panaji	*Konkani*
■ Gujarat	GandhiNagar	*Gujarati*
■ Haryana	Chandigarh	*Hindi*
■ Himachal Pradesh	Shimla	*Hindi and Pahari*
■ Jharkhand	Ranchi	*Hindi*
■ Kerala	Thiruvananthpuram	*Malyalam*
■ Karnataka	Bengluru	*Kannada*
■ Madhya Pradesh	Bhopal	*Hindi*
■ Maharashtra	Mumbai	*Marathi*
■ Meghalaya	Shillong	*Khashi, Jayantia and Garo*
■ Manipur	Imphal	*Manipuri*
■ Mizoram	Aizawl	*Mizo and English*
■ Nagaland	Kohima	*Naga, Assamese and English*
■ Odisha	Bhubaneshwar	*Odiya*
■ Punjab	Chandigarh	*Punjabi*
■ Rajasthan	Jaipur	*Hindi, Rajasthani*
■ Sikkim	Gangtok	*Sikkimese and Gorkhali*
■ Tamil Nadu	Chennai	*Tamil*
■ Tripura	Agartala	*Bengali, Tripuri*
■ Uttar Pradesh	Lucknow	*Hindi*
■ Uttarakhand	Dehradun	*Hindi*
■ West Bengal	Kolkata	*Bengali*
■ Telangana	Hyderabad	*Telgu and Urdu*
■ Jammu & Kashmir	Srinagar/Jammu	*Kashmiri, Dongri, Urdu, Dardi and Pahari*
■ Andaman and Nicobar Islands	Port Blair	*Hindi, Nicobarese, Bengali, Malayalam, Tamil, Telugu*
■ Chandigarh	Chandigarh	*Hindi, Punjabi, English*
■ Dadar and Nagar Haveli and Daman and Diu	Daman	*Gujarati, Hindi*
■ Delhi	Delhi	*Hindi, Punjabi*
■ Lakshadweep	Kavaratti	*Malayalam*
■ Puducherry	Puducherry	*Tamil, Telugu, Malayalam, English and French*
■ Ladakh	Leh	*Ladakhi*

HIGH COURTS IN INDIA

Name	*Territorial Jurisdiction*	*Seat*
Allahabad	Uttar Pradesh	Prayagraj (Bench at Lucknow)
Andhra Pradesh	Andhra Pradesh	Amaravati
Bombay	Maharashtra, Goa Dadar and Nagar Haveli and Daman and Diu	Mumbai (Benches at Nagpur, Panaji, and Aurangabad)
Calcutta	West Bengal and Andaman & Nicobar Islands	Kolkata (Circuit Benches at Port Blair and Jalpaiguri)
Chhattisgarh	Chhattisgarh	Bilaspur
Delhi	New Delhi	NCT of Delhi
Gauhati	Assam, Nagaland, Mizoram and Arunachal Pradesh	Guwahati (Benches at Kohima, Aizawl and Itanagar)
Gujarat	Gujarat	Ahmedabad
Himachal Pradesh	Himachal Pradesh	Shimla
Jammu & Kashmir and Ladakh	Jammu & Kashmir/Ladakh	Srinagar and Jammu
Jharkhand	Jharkhand	Ranchi
Karnataka	Karnataka	Bengaluru (Circuit Benches at Dharwar and Gulbarga)
Kerala	Kerala & Lakshadweep	Ernakulam
Madhya Pradesh	Madhya Pradesh	Jabalpur (Benches at Gwalior and Indore)
Madras	Tamil Nadu & Puducherry	Chennai (Bench at Madurai)
Orissa	Odisha	Cuttack
Patna	Bihar	Patna
Punjab and Haryana	Punjab, Haryana and Chandigarh	Chandigarh
Rajasthan	Rajasthan	Jodhpur (Bench at Jaipur)
Sikkim	Sikkim	Gangtok
Uttarakhand	Uttarakhand	Nainital
Tripura	Tripura	Agartala
Meghalaya	Meghalaya	Shillong
Manipur	Manipur	Imphal
Telangana	Telangana	Hyderabad

FAMOUS HILL STATIONS

Hill Station	State/UT
1. Almora, Mussoorie Nainital	: Uttarakhand
2. Cherrapunji (Shillong), Khasi Hills (Shillong)	: Meghalaya
3. Ooty, Kodaikanal Yereaud	: Tamil Nadu
4. Dalhousie, Kassauli	: Himachal Pradesh
5. Darjeeling	: West Bengal
6. Gulmarg, Srinagar	: Jammu and Kashmir
7. Mahabaleshwar	: Maharashtra
8. Mt. Abu	: Rajasthan
9. Panchmarhi	: Madhya Pradesh

FAMOUS NATIONAL PARKS

1. Corbett National Park	: Nainital, Uttarakhand
2. Dudhwa National Park	: Lakhimpur Kheri, Uttar Pradesh
3. Kaziranga National Park	: Jorhat, Assam
4. Kanha National Park	: Jabalpur, Bhedaghat
5. Gir National Park	: Rajkot, Junagarh, Gujarat
6. Guindy National Park	: Guindy, Chennai, Tamil Nadu
7. Nagairhole National Park	: Coorg, Karnataka
8. Bandipur National Park	: Mysore, Karnataka

FAMOUS NATIONAL WILDLIFE SANCTUARIES

1. Dachigam Wildlife Sanctuary	: Srinagar, Jammu and Kashmir
2. Sariska	: Alwar, Rajasthan
3. Hazaribagh Wildlife Sanctuary	: Hazaribagh, Jharkhand
4. Tiger Project	: Sawai Madhopur, Rajasthan
5. Mudhumali Wildlife Sanctuary	: Mudhumalia, Nilgiri, Tamil Nadu
6. Periyar Wildlife Sanctuary	: Idukki, Kottayam, Kerala

HOLY PLACES IN INDIA

1.	Amarnath	Jammu and Kashmir
2.	Ayodhya	Uttar Pradesh
3.	Badrinath	Uttarakhand
4.	Dwarka	Gujarat
5.	Haridwar	Uttarakhand
6.	Kancheepuram	Tamil Nadu
7.	Kedarnath	Uttarakhand
8.	Mathura	Uttar Pradesh
9.	Puri	Odisha
10.	Rameswaram	Tamil Nadu
11.	Tirupati	Andhra Pradesh
12.	Ujjain	Madhya Pradesh
13.	Varanasi	Uttar Pradesh
14.	Bodh Gaya	Bihar

SPORTS

Terms Associated With Sports :

Cricket : Ashes, Bye, Bodyline, Bowling, Break, Cover-point, Creases, Chinaman, Chucker, Drive, Duck, Follow on, Googly, Hit-Wicket, Hat-trick, Leg-before-wicket, Leg break, Leg-bye, Maiden over, No ball, Night-watchman, Runner, Run-out, Stumped, Silly-point, Slip.

Football : Handball, Corner kick, Dribble, Free Kick, Hat-trick, Off-side, Penalty Kick, Try, Throw in, Wembley.

Hockey : Bully, Carry, Corner kick, Corner, Penalty stroke, Off-side, Penalty, Roll in scoop, Sticks, Sudden death, Striking circle, Short Corner, Scoop, Tie-breaker, Under-cutting, Hat-trick.

Tennis : Backhand drive, Deuce, Fault, Half-volley, Net, Let, Volley, Smash, Service.

Billiards : Break, Cannons, Cue, Pot, Jigger, Scratch, In Bauk, In, Off.

Bridge : Dummy, Finesse, Grand-slam, Little Slam, Revoke, Ruff slam, Trump, Tricks, Vulnerable.

Volley Ball : Booster, Love, Service, Volley, Smasher.

Badminton : Smash, Drop, Let.

Chess : Check, Checkmate, Gambit, State-mate.

Golf : Bogy, Caddie, Hole, Links, Stymie, Tee, Put.

Polo : Chukker, Mallet, Bunder.

Baseball : Bunting, Diamond, Pitcher, Put-out, Strike, Home.

Boxing : Knockout, Punch, Upper-cut, Jab, Hook.

FAMOUS TROPHIES

Agha Khan Cup	Hockey
Beighton Cup	Hockey
Corbillion Cup	World Table Tennis (Women)
Davis Cup	Lawn Tennis
Duleep Trophy	Cricket
Durand Cup	Football
Ezra Cup	Polo
I.F.A. Shield	Football
Irani Cup	Cricket (India)
Jayalaxmi Cup	Table Tennis (Women)
Lady Rattan Tata Trophy	Hockey (Women)
Nehru Cup	Hockey (India)
Obaidullah Cup	Hockey
Ranji Trophy	Cricket (India)
Rangaswamy Cup	Hockey (India)
Rovers Cup	Football (India)
Santosh Trophy	Football (India)
Subroto Cup	Football
Thomas Cup	Badminton
Uber Cup	Badminton (Women)
Wellington Trophy	Rowing (India)

BIGGEST, LARGEST, TALLEST OF THE WORLD

Airport, *Largest*—King Fahd International Airport, Dammon (Saudi Arabia)

Animal, *Tallest*—Giraffe (Average height 6.09 m); *Largest and Heaviest*—Blue Whale (190 tonnes)

Longest recorded Animal—Boot lace Worm (55 m); *Fastest*—Cheetah (Approximately 100 km/hr)

Bay, *Largest*—Bay of Bengal

Continent, *biggest*—Asia (31,845,872 km^2); *Smallest*—Australia Mainland (Area 76,17,930 km^2)

Desert, *Largest*—Sahara (N. Africa; maximum length 5,150 km EW; maximum width 3,200 km NS)

Dome, *Largest*—Singapore National Stadium (310 m)

Fish, *Largest fresh water*—Plabeuk (China, Laos and Thailand); *Most abundant*—Bristle mouth; *Most venomous*—Stone Fish (Indo-Pacific Waters)

Fountain, *Tallest*—King Fahd's Fountain (Jeddah, Saudi Arabia)

Gulf, *Largest*—Gulf of Mexico (1,544,000 sq. km)

Island, *Biggest*—Greenland (Kalaatdlit Nunaat-2,175,000 sq km)

Lake, *Largest*—Caspian Sea (Azerbaijan, Russia, Iran border: 37.18 lakh km^2); *Deepest*—Baikal (Siberia); *Largest (fresh water)*—Superior Lake (USA---Canada border: 82,350 km^2)

Mountain, *Highest peak*—Mt. Everest (8848 m; Nepal); *Highest range*—Himalayas, Asia (upto 4200 m); *Greatest mountain range*—Himalaya-Karakoram (96 out of 109 peaks over 7315 m are here)

Museum, *Largest*—American Museum of Natural History, New York

Ocean, *Largest and Deepest*—The Pacific (Area: 166,240,000 km^2; Depth: 10,924 m)

Platform, *Longest (rail)*—Shri Siddharoodha Swamiji Railway Station, Hubballi (Karnataka; India, 1507 m. long)

Railway Station, *Largest*—Grand Central Terminal (New York City; 19 hc)

Rivers, *Longest*—(i) Nile (6650 km) (ii) Amazon (6437 km)

Sea, *Largest*—Philippine Sea (5,695,000 sq. km)

Star, *Brightest*—Sirius A (also called Dog Star)

Temple, *Largest*—Angkor Vat (Cambodia: 402 acres)

Tunnel, *Longest (railway)*—Gotthard Base Rail Tunnel (Switzerland; 57.1 km); *Largest (road)*—Laerdal, Norway (24.51 km)

FIRST IN INDIA

Governor General of Independent India — Lord Mountbatten

Cosmonaut — Sq. Ldr. Rakesh Sharma

Field Marshal — S.H.F.J. Manekshaw

Indian Governor General of Indian Union — C. Rajagopalachari

Indian I.C.S. Officer — Satyendra Nath Tagore

Indian to swim across English Channel — Mihir Sen

Indian Women to swim across English Channel — Miss Arti Saha

Man to climb Mount Everest — Tenzing Norgay

Man to climb Mount Everest without Oxygen — Phu Dorjee

Man to climb Mount Everest twice — Nwang Gombu

Nobel Prize Winner — Rabindra Nath Tagore

President of Indian National Congress — W.C. Banerjee

President of Indian Republic — Dr. Rajendra Prasad

Talkie Film — Alam Ara (1931)

Test Tube Baby (Documented) — Indira

Viceroy of India — Lord Canning

Woman Minister of Indian Union — Rajkumari Amrit Kaur

Woman Governor — Mrs. Sarojini Naidu

Woman President of Indian National Congress — Dr. Annie Besant

Woman Prime Minister — Mrs. Indira Gandhi

Woman Speaker of a State Assembly — Mrs. Shanno Devi

Prime Minister of India — Pt. Jawaharlal Nehru

Muslim President of Indian Union — Dr. Zakir Hussain

Speaker of Lok Sabha — G.V. Mavlankar

Women to Climb Mount Everest — Bachhendri Pal

Woman Judge in Supreme Court — Mrs. Meera Sahib Fatima Biwi

Women Chief Justice of a High Court — Smt. Leela Seth

The First Indian Weightlifter to Win bronze medal in Olympics — Karnam Malleshwari (Sydney, in 2000)

Chief of Defence Staff (CDS) —General Bipin Rawat

World Chess Champion — Vishwanathan Anand

India's First Woman Merchant Navy Officer — Sonali Banerjee

The First Woman Air Vice-Marshal — P. Bandopadhyaya

The First Indian to be appointed as United Nations Civilian Police Advisor — Ms. Kiran Bedi

The First Women to be appointed Deputy Governor of Reserve Bank of India — K.J. Udeshi

The First Indian Lady to win a medal in World Athletic Championship — Anju Bobby George

The First Sikh Prime Minister of India — Dr. Manmohan Singh

IMPORTANT DAYS

15th January — Army Day
26th January — Republic Day
30th January — Leprosy Eradication Day/ Martyr's Day
28th February — National Science Day
8th march — International Women's Day
15th March — World Consumer's Day
21st March — World Disabled Day
5th April — National Marine Day
7th April — World Health Day
18th April — World Heritage Day
22nd April — International Earth Day
Ist May — Worker's Day
3rd May — International Sun Day
21st May — Anti-Terrorism Day
24th May — Commonwealth Day
31st May — World No Tobacco Day
5th June — World Environment Day
21st June — World Yoga Day
26th June — International Day against Drug Abuse
11th July — World Population Day
15th August — Independence Day
24th August — Sanskrit Day
5th September — Teacher's Day
8th September — World Literacy Day
27th September — World Tourism Day
1st October — World Elder's Day
4th October — World Animal Day
8th October — Air Force Day
10th October — National Solidarity Day
16th October — World Food Day
24th October — U.N. Day
14th November — World Diabetes Day
14th November — Children's Day
19th November — National Integration Day
26th November — Law Day
1st December — World AIDS Day
4th December — Navy Day
7th December — Flag Day
10th December — Human Rights Day

PARLIAMENTS OF IMPORTANT COUNTRIES

Afghanistan — Shora
Britain — Parliament House of Commons, House of Lords
Denmark — Folketing
The Netherlands — States General
India — Sansad
Israel — Knesset
Iran — Majlis
Ireland — Airetann
Iceland — Althing
Japan — Diet
Norway — Storting
Russia — Supreme Soviet
Spain — Cortes
Sweden — Riksdag
U.S.A. — Congress Senate
Germany — Bundestag

MINERAL RESOURCES OF THE WORLD

Mineral	Largest Producers
Iron Ore	China, Japan, Russia
Tin	China, Indonesia, Peru
Lead	China, Australia, U.S.A.
Zinc	China, Australia, Peru
Manganese	South Africa, Brazil, Australia
Aluminium	China, Russia, Canada
Petroleum	Saudi Arabia, Russia, USA
Silver	Peru, Mexico, China
Coal	China, USA, India

WORLD'S LARGEST PRODUCERS

Articles	Producers	Articles	Producers
Carpets	Iran	Cheese	USA
Cocoa	Cote d'Ivoire	Coffee	Brazil
Copper	Chile	Cotton	China
Diamonds	Russia	Jute	India
Rice	China	Rubber	Thailand
Silk	China	Steel	China
Sugar	Brazil	Tea	China
Tin	China	Wheat	China
Wool	Australia		

TEN LARGEST COUNTRIES BY AREAS

Rank by Area	Country	Area (sq. km.)
1.	Russia	17,075,400
2.	Canada	9,976,139
3.	China	9,561,000
4.	U.S.A.	9,363,123
5.	Brazil	8,511,965
6.	Australia	7,686,848
7.	India	3,287,263
8.	Argentina	2,776,889
9.	Kazakhstan	2,724,900
10.	Algeria	2,381,741

PRESIDENT OF INDIA

He is the constitutional head of the Republic but not the real executive.

Qualifications: (1) Indian citizen; (2) age not less than 35 years; (3) should have qualifications for election to Lok Sabha; (4) should not hold any office of profit; (5) should not be a Member of Parliament or State Legislature.

Election: He is elected by the elected Members of Parliament and State Legislative Assemblies in accordance with the system of proportional representation by means of single transferable vote.

Powers: He makes appointment to all the Constitutional posts. He can address either House of Parliament and send message to them. He can summon and prorogue either House of Parliament and dissolve Lok Sabha. All Bills passed by Parliament must receive his assent to become an Act. He issues Ordinance when Parliament is not in session. No money Bill can be introduced in Lok Sabha without his recommendation. He can grant pardon, reprieve or remit punishment and he can commute death sentences. He can declare national emergency, state emergency and financial emergency.

VICE-PRESIDENT OF INDIA

The Vice-President acts as the ex-officio Chairman of Rajya Sabha and acts as the President when the latter is unable to discharge his functions due to illness, absence or any other reason, or till the election of a new President when a vacancy is caused by the death, resignation or removal of the President.

The Vice-President is elected by an electoral college consisting of the members of both Houses of Parliament in accordance with the system of proportional representation by means of the single transferable vote. He must be a citizen of India, not less than 35 years of age, and should be eligible for election as a member of the Council of States.

PRIME MINISTER OF INDIA

The Prime Minister is the leader of the majority party in the Parliament and the President cannot exercise his discretion in the appointment of the Prime Minister. He stays in office till the majority of the members of Lok Sabha has confidence in him. He occupies an important posi-tion in relation to the council of Ministers. He recommends the names of the persons to be included in the Council of Ministers. He allocates portfolios among them and can ask any minister to tender resignation. He can drop a minister while reshuffling the ministry. He coordinates the administration of various departments. He is the chief link between the President and the Council. He is the leader of the majority party and so, he has a great influence on the Parliament and the party. The Prime Minister enjoys such extensive powers as have been described as the virtual ruler of the country.

THE SOLAR SYSTEM: SOME FACTS

Number of Planets: 8—Mercury, Venus, Earth, Mars, Jupiter, Saturn, Uranus and Neptune.

Largest most

Massive planet .... Jupiter
Brightest planet .... Venus
Brightest star .... Sirius
Fastest orbiting planet .... Mercury
Longest (Synodic) day .... Mercury
Planet with largest moon .... Jupiter
Greatest average density .... Jupiter
Tallest mountain .... Earth
Strongest magnetic fields .... Jupiter
Most circular orbit .... Venus
Shortest (synodic) day .... Jupiter
Hottest planet .... Venus
No moons .... Mercury, Venus
Planet with moon with most eccentric orbit .... Neptune
Lowest average density .... Saturn
Deepest Oceans .... Jupiter
Greatest amount of liquid on the surface .... Earth

THE EARTH: FACTS AND DATA

Composition of the Earth: Aluminium (0.4%), Sulphur (2.7%), Silicon (13%), Oxygen (28%), Calcium (1.2%), Nickel (2.7%), Magnesium (17%), Iron (35%)

Surface area	: 510100500 sq km
Land Surface (29.1%)	: 148950800 sq km
Ocean Surface (70.9%)	: 361149700 sq km
Type of water	: 97% salt, 3% fresh
Total area of water	: 382672000 sq km
Equatorial diameter	: 12753 km
Equatorial Circumference	: 40066 km
Polar Circumference	: 39992 km
Polar diameter	: 12710 km
Equatorial radius	: 6376 km
Polar radius	: 6335 km
Mass (estimated weight)	: 594×10^{19} metric tons
Mean distance from the Sun	: 149407000 km

Earth's orbit speed (around sun)	: 107320 kmph	Time of Rotation (on its axis)	: 23 hrs 56 min 4.09 seconds
Period of Revolution (round the sun)	: 365 days 5 hrs 48 min. 45.51 seconds	Inclination of the axis (to the plane of the ecliptic)	: 23°27'

PRINCIPAL MOUNTAIN PEAKS OF THE WORLD

Mountains	Height in Metres	Range	Date of First Ascent
1. Mount Everest	8,848	Himalayas	May 29, 1953
2. K-2 (Godwin Austen)	8,611	Karakoram	July 31, 1954
3. Kanchenjunga	8,597	Himalayas	May 25, 1955
4. Lhotse	8,511	Himalayas	May 18, 1956
5. Makalu I	8,481	Himalayas	May 15, 1955
6. Dhaulagiri I	8,167	Himalayas	May 13, 1960
7. Mansalu I	8,156	Himalayas	May 9, 1956
8. Chollyo	8,153	Himalayas	Oct. 19, 1954
9. Nanga Parbat	8,124	Himalayas	July 3, 1953
10. Annapurna I	8,091	Himalayas	June 3, 1950
11. Gasherbrum I	8,068	Karakoram	July 5, 1958
12. Broad Peak I	8,047	Karakoram	June 9, 1957
13. Gasherbrum II	8,034	Karakoram	July 7, 1956
14. Shisha Pangma (Gosainthan)	8,014	Himalayas	May 2, 1964
15. Gasherbrum III	7,952	Karakoram	Aug. 11, 1975

POPULAR NICK NAMES OF SOME FAMOUS PERSONALITIES

Andhra Kesari	T. Prakasam	Lal, Bal, Pal	Lala Lajpat Rai, Bal Gangadhar Tilak, Bipin Chandra Pal
Anna	C.N. Anna Durai	Little Corporal	Napoleon Bonaparte
Bang Bandhu	Sheikh Mujibur Rehman	Lokmanya	Bal Gangadhar Tilak
Bapu	Mahatma Gandhi	Mahamana	Pt. Madan Mohan Malaviya
Bard of Avon	William Shakespeare	Maid of Orleans	Joan of Arc
Chachaji	Jawaharlal Nehru	Maiden Queen	Queen Elizabeth I
Desh Bandhu	C.R. Das	Missile Man	A.P.J. Abdul Kalam
Frontier Gandhi	Khan Abdul Gaffar Khan	Man of Destiny	Napoleon Bonaparte
Fuhrer	Adolf Hitler	Netaji	Subhash Chandra Bose
G.B.S.	George Bernard Shaw	Nightingale of India	Sarojini Naidu
Grand Old Man of India	Dadabhai Naoroji	Panditji	Jawaharlal Nehru
Grand Old Man of Britain	Gladstone	Punjab Kesari	Lala Lajpat Rai
Guru Dev	Rabindra Nath Tagore	Shastriji	Lal Bahadur Shastri
Guruji	M.S. Golwalkar	Uncle Ho	Ho Chi Minh
Iron Man of India	Sardar Patel	Wizard of the North	Walter Scott
Lok Nayak	Jayaprakash Narayan		
Lady with the Lamp	Florence Nightingale		

FAMOUS INTERNATIONAL ORGANISATIONS, HEADQUARTERS

International Organisations	*Headquarters*
United Nations Organisations (U.N.O.)	New York
International Monetary Fund (I.M.F.)	Washington D.C.
World Health Organisation (W.H.O.)	Geneva
Food & Agricultural Organisation (FAO)	Rome
International Labour Organisation (ILO)	Geneva
UNESCO	Paris
International Court of Justice	The Hague
Universal Postal Union (UPU)	Berne
International Civil Aviation Organisation (ICAO)	Montreal
UNIDO	Vienna
International Atomic Energy Agency (IAEA)	Vienna
International Finance Corporation (IFC)	Washington
United Nations Development Programme (UNDP)	New York
UNICEF	New York
International Maritime Organisation (IMO)	London
World Meteorological Organisation (WMO)	Geneva
International Telecommunication Union (ITU)	Geneva
Arab League	Cairo
Commonwealth of Nations	London
World Trade Organisation (WTO)	Geneva
International Development Association (IDA)	Washington D.C.
International Bank for Reconstruction and Development (IBRD)	Washington D.C.
World Intellectual Property Organisation (WIPO)	Geneva
Organisation of Islamic Conference (OIC)	Jeddah (Saudi Arabia)
European Union	Brussels
Red Cross	Geneva
Interpol	Lyons (France)
Asian Development Bank (ADB)	Manila
North Atlantic Treaty Organisation (NATO)	Brussels
Association of South East Asian Nations (ASEAN)	Jakarta

BHARAT RATNA AWARD WINNERS

No.	Name	Year
1.	C. Rajagopalachari	1954
2.	Dr. S. Radhakrishnan	1954
3.	Dr. C.V. Raman	1954
4.	Dr. Bhagwan Das	1955
5.	Dr. M. Visvesvaraya	1955
6.	Jawaharlal Nehru	1955
7.	Govind Ballabh Pant	1957
8.	Dr. D.K. Karve	1958
9.	Dr. Bidhan Chandra Roy	1961
10.	Purushottam Das Tandon	1961
11.	Dr. Rajendra Prasad	1962
12.	Dr. Zakir Hussain	1963
13.	Dr. Pandurang Vaman Kane	1963
14.	Lal Bahadur Shastri*	1966
15.	Indira Gandhi	1971
16.	V.V. Giri	1975
17.	K. Kamraj*	1976
18.	Mother Teresa	1980
19.	Acharya Vinoba Bhave*	1983
20.	Khan Abdul Ghaffar Khan	1987
21.	M.G. Ramachandran*	1988
22.	Dr. B.R. Ambedkar*	1990
23.	Dr. Nelson R. Mandela	1990
24.	Rajiv Gandhi*	1991
25.	Sardar Vallabhbhai Patel*	1991
26.	Morarji R. Desai	1991
27.	Maulana Abdul Kalam Azad*	1992
28.	Jehangir Ratanji Dadabhai Tata	1992
29.	Satyajit Roy	1992
30.	Gulzari Lal Nanda	1997
31.	Mrs. Aruna Asaf Ali*	1997
32.	Dr. A.P.J. Abdul Kalam	1997
33.	M.S. Subbalakshmi	1998
34.	C. Subramaniam	1998
35.	Jaya Prakash Narayan*	1999
36.	Prof. Amartya Sen	1999
37.	Pt. Ravi Shankar	1999
38.	Gopinath Bardoloi	1999
39.	Lata Mangeshkar	2001
40.	Bismillah Khan	2001
41.	Bhimsen Joshi	2009
42.	C.N.R. Rao	2014
43.	Sachin Tendulkar	2014
44.	Madan Mohan Malaviya*	2015
45.	Atal Bihari Vajpayee	2015
46.	Nanaji Deshmukh*	2019
47.	Bhupen Hazarika*	2019
48.	Pranab Mukherjee	2019
49.	Karpoori Thakur*	2024
50.	Lal Krishna Advani	2024
51.	Charan Singh*	2024
52.	P.V. Narasimha Rao*	2024
53.	M.S. Swaminathan*	2024

* Posthumous

ART AND CULTURE

☞ Classical Dances

Dance	*State*	*Famous Artists*
Bharat Natyam	Tamil Nadu	Yamini Krishnamurthy, Rukmini Devi Arundale, Swapna Sundari, Sonal Mansingh, Vaijanti Mala, Mrinalini Sarabhai, Chandralekha, Indrani, Ram Gopal, Bal Saraswati
Kathakali	Kerala	Gopinath, K.K. Nayar, Kunju-Kurup, T.K. Chandu
Kuchipudi	Andhra Pradesh/ Telangana	Sapna Sundari, Raja Reddy, Shobha Nayar, Radha Reddy, Vedantam Satyanarayan, Vimpanti Chinna Satyam.
Kathak	North India	Birju Maharaj, Gopi Krishna, Shambhu Maharaj, Sitara Devi, Vishnu Sharma, Durga Lal, Shobhana Narayan
Odissi	Odisha	Kelucharan Mahapatra, Indrani Rehman, Madhavi Mudgal, Pratima Bedi, Samyukta Panigrahi, Sonal Mansingh, Debudas
Manipuri	Manipur	Uday Shankar, Bipin Singh, Suryamukhi, Darohra Jhaveri

☞ Famous Folk Dances

State/UT	*Folk Dance*	*State/UT*	*Folk Dance*
Andhra Pradesh/ Telangana	Dandari, Banjara	Kerala	Mohini Attam, Padayuni
Assam	Bihu, Keli Gopal, Sataria	Madhya Pradesh	Lota Nritya, Jawara
Bihar	Chhau, Magahi, Durga dance	Maharashtra	Tamasha, Dahi Handi, Gof. Deepak Dindi
W. Bengal	Kirtan, Kalatri, Asweabadh, Brita, Kalidance	Manipur	Dhol Cholam
Chhattisgarh	Saila, Karama, Bhagoria	Meghalaya	Nongakarem
Gujarat	Garba, Rasalila, Tippani, Dandia,	Nagaland	Bamboo dance
		Odisha	Chhau, Maya Shabari, Dalachai
Haryana	Damyal, Lahoor	Punjab	Gidda, Bhangra, Panihari
Himachal Pradesh	Dussehra dance, Hikat, Notio	Rajasthan	Thumar, Kathaputali, Tera Tali
		Tamil Nadu	Terukalathu, Kabalatam, Kargam, Pulivesham
Jammu & Kashmir	Dumhal	Tripura	Hazagiri
Jharkhand	Jhau, Ghumakudia, Jadur, Sarhul, Soharai, Karama, Vaima, Loojhari, Jat-Jatin, Vidayat	Uttar Pradesh	Rasalila, Nautanki, Thali, Dhurang, Jhumela, Huraka, Bol.
		Uttarakhand	Kajari, Karan
Karnataka	Yakshagan, Dolu Kunitha	Goa	Dhode Modini

MUSIC

Main Schools of Classical Music

- There are two main schools of classical music, namely, the Hindustani and the Carnatic. The Hindustani school of classical music is in vogue in north-western India, eastern India and northern parts of the South India.

Musical Instruments

- ***They are:*** Tabla, Mridangam, Pakhawaj, Chandai, Dholak, Veena, Sitar, Sarod, Gootuvadhyam, Sarangi, Flute, Nadaswaram, Shehnai, Shringi and Turahi.

FAMOUS INTERNATIONAL AIR SERVICES

Air Service	*Name of Country*	*Air Service*	*Name of Country*
Air India	India	Lufthansa Airlines	Germany
British Overseas Airways Corporation	Britain	Iraqi Airways	Iraq
Trans World Airlines	America	National Airlines	Iran
Russian Airlines	Russia	Quantas Airlines	Australia
Japan Airlines	Japan	Hong-Kong Airlines	Hong-Kong
Pakistan International Airlines	Pakistan	Egypt Airlines	Egypt
Malaysia Airlines	Malaysia	Slovak Airlines	Slovakia
Royal Nepal Airlines	Nepal	S.I.A.	Singapore
Swiss Airways	Switzerland	Garuda Airways	Indonesia
Air France	France	Bangladesh Viman Sewa	Bangladesh
Kuwait Airways	Kuwait	Air Lanka	Sri Lanka
Pan American World Airways	America	Elitalia Airlines	Italy
K.L.M. Royal Airlines	The Netherlands (Holland)	Air Canada	Canada

FAMOUS RELIGIONS, FOUNDERS, HOLY BOOKS & PLACES OF WORSHIP

Religion	*Founder*	*Holy Books*	*Place of Worship*
Hinduism	Hinduism has no one Founder. (This religion is based upon the religion of original Aryan Settlers)	Ramayan, Vedas, Puranas and Geeta	Temple
Sikh	Guru Nanak Dev	Guru Grantha Sahib	Gurdwara
Christianity	Jesus Christ	Bible	Church
Islam	Prophet Mohammed	Koran (Quran)	Mosque
Parsi	Zoroaster	Zend Avesta	Fire Temple
Jainism	Adinath Rishavdev	Jain Granth	Jain Temple
Buddhism	Gautam Buddha	Tripitaka	Buddha Temple
Jew	Moosa	Torah	Synagogue

INTELLIGENCE AGENCIES OF SOME PROMINENT COUNTRIES

Country	*Intelligence Agency*
India	Research & Analysis Wing (RAW), Intelligence Bureau (I.B.), Central Bureau of Investigation (C.B.I.)
Pakistan	Inter Service Intelligence (I.S.I.)
U.S.A.	Central Intelligence Agency, Federal Bureau of Investigation
Britain	Military Intelligence (M.I.)-5 and 6, Special Branch, Ultra, Joint Intelligence Organisation
Israel	Mosad
Egypt	Mukhabarat
Japan	Nicho

Country	*Intelligence Agency*
Russia	K.G.B. (Komitel Gosudarstvennoy Bezopasnosty) (Committee for State Security)
Canada	Security Intelligence Service
S. Africa	Bureau of State Security
Iran	Sabak
Iraq	Al-Mukhabarat
Australia	Australian Security and Intelligence Organisation
France	S.D.E.C.E.
Spain	C.E.S.I.D.
Cuba	D.G.I.

SOME PROMINENT RACES OF THE WORLD

Races	Country/Area	Races	Country/Area	Races	Country/Area	Races	Country/Area
Veddas	Sri Lanka	Pygmy	Congo Basin	Eskimo	Canada, Tundra Region	Bushman	Kalahari Desert
Somaid	West Siberia	Bantu	Central and South Africa	Lapps	European Tundra	Red Indian	North America
Masai	East Africa						
Muree	New Zealand	Tartars	Siberia				
Yakoot	Russian Tundra	Baddu	Arab's Desert	Hausa	Nigeria		
Papuans	New Guyana	Semang	Malaysia	Kirghiz	Steppes (Russia)		

FAMOUS STRAITS OF THE WORLD

Strait	Between	Country
Malacca Strait	Andaman Sea and South China Sea	Indonesia
Palk Strait	Mannar and Bay of Bengal	India-Sri Lanka
Magellan Strait	Pacific and South Atlantic Ocean	Chile
Dover Strait	English Channel and North Sea	England-France
Berring Strait	Berring Sea and Chukasi Sea	Alaska-Russia
Sugaroo Strait	Japan Sea and Pacific Ocean	Japan
Sunda Strait	Java and Indian Ocean	Indonesia
Gibralter Strait	Mediterranean Sea and Atlantic Ocean	Spain
Harmuj Strait	Persia and Bay of Oman	Oman-Iran
Hudson Strait	Bay of Hudson and Atlantic Ocean	Canada

FAMOUS NEWSPAPERS OF THE WORLD

Newspaper	Place of Publishing	Language	Newspaper	Place of Publishing	Language
Daily News	New York (America)	English	Hindu, Hindustan, Times of India, Tribune, Statesman, Indian Express, Economic Times	India	English
Guardian	London (Britain)	English			
Pravada	Moscow (Russia)	Russian			
Al-Ahram	Cairo (Egypt)	Arabic			
Merdeca	Jakarta (Indonesia)	Indonesian			
Times	London (Britain)	English	Hindustan, Nav Bharat Times, Dainik Bhaskar, Dainik Jagaran, Punjab Kesari	India	Hindi
People's Daily	Beijing (China)	Chinese			
New Statesman	Britain	English			
Daily Mirror	Britain	English			

IMPORTANT BOUNDARY LINES

Boundary Line	Countries	Boundary Line	Countries
Durand Line	Pakistan and Afghanistan	17th Parallel	The line which defined the boundary between North Vietnam and South Vietnam before the two were united.
Hindenberg Line	Germany-Poland		
Maginot Line	France and Germany		
Mannerhein Line	Russia-Finland		
Mc Mahon Line	India-China		
Order Niesse Line	Germany-Poland		
Radcliff Line	India-Pakistan	38th Parallel	North Korea and South Korea
Seigfrid Line	Germany-France		
24th Parallel	India-Pakistan	49th Parallel	U.S.A. and Canada

SIGNALS/SIGNS AND MEANING

Signal/Sign	Meaning	Signal/Sign	Meaning
Red Triangle	Family Planning	White Flag	Treaty or Surrender
Red Cross	Medical Help	Yellow Flag	Vehicles with patients of contagious diseases
Red Light	Danger, 'Stop' for the movement of vehicles	Two Bones across with a Skull	Danger of electricity
Green Light	Go		
Olive Branch	Peace	Half mast flown Flag	National mourning
White Pigeon or Dove	Peace	Lotus and culture	Sign of civilization
Black Strip on Arm	(i) Opposition (ii) Sorrow	Wheel (Chakra)	Sign of Progress
Black Flag	Opposition	A blind folded woman with scale in hand	Sign of Justice
Red Flag	(i) Danger (ii) Revolution	Reversed flown	National calamity flag

NATIONAL EMBLEMS OF IMPORTANT COUNTRIES

Country	National Emblem	Country	National Emblem
America	Golden Rod	New Zealand	Kiwi, Fern Southern Cross
Australia	Kangaroo	Norway	Lion
Ireland	Shamrock	Nepal	Kukri
Italy	White Lily	Pakistan	Crescent
Israel	Candelabrum	Poland	Eagle
Iran	Rose	France	Lily
Canada	White Lily	Belgium	Lion
Great Britain	Rose	Bangladesh	Water Lily
Chile	Candor and Huemul	Mongolia	The Soyombo
Germany	Corn Flower	Russia	Double headed eagle
Japan	Chrysanthemum	Lebanon	Cedar Tree
Zimbabwe	Zimbabwe Bird	Sudan	Secretary Bird
Denmark	Beach	Syria	Eagle
Turkiye	Crescent and Star	India	Lioned Capital
The Netherlands	Lion		

THE CONTINENTS OF THE WORLD

Name	Population (2021) (In million)	Per cent of the world's population
Asia	4,584	59.1
Africa	1,375	17.4
Europe	747	9.8
North America	373	4.8
South America	651	8.4
Australia	41.66	0.5
Antarctica	NA	NA

COMPUTER

The computer is the system of that electronic device through which various informations are processed on the basis of a definite set of instructions called program and mathematical (numerical) and non-mathematical both types of informations are processed.

The first mechanical computer was composed or fabricated by Blaise Pascal in 1642 and it is called Pascalene. But in 1833, Charles Babbage first time conceived an automatic calculator or computer. Charles Babbage is called the father of modern computer. Herman made an electronic tabulating machine based on punch cards which operates automatically.

In 1937, first mechanical computer mark-I was fabricated by Howard Akeen. The most outstanding contribution in the development of modern computer goes to John Wan Newmaan who brought the 2nd revolution in the area of computer in 1951. He discovered EDVAC (Electronic Discrete Variable Automatic Computer) and utilised the stored program and the binary number system in the computer.

FUNCTIONS OF COMPUTER

1. Collection and composition (input) of datas;
2. Storage of datas.
3. Processing of datas.
4. Retrieval or output of the proccessed informations and datas.

UNITS OF COMPUTER

1. Input unit.
2. Central processing unit–CPU.
3. External Memory unit.
4. Output unit.

The CPU of the computer is called brain of the computer and sometimes CPU is also called Micro Processor of the computer. The data is entered through the input unit in the computer and through the central processing unit with the help of External Memory Unit datas are arranged and processed. Ultimately by the output unit these datas or informations are issued or released.

PARTS OF COMPUTER

- **Monitor :** The monitor of the computer is like a television in which the picture appears in the form of doted points on the screen and these are called pixcels.
- **Hard Disc and Floppy Disc :** The Hard Disc is the permanent disc in the computers while the Floppy Disc is the disc utilised when datas or informations are to be transferred from one computer to another.
- **Mouse :** The mouse of the computer is like the remote control of TV through which computer is directly regulated or controlled without utilising the key-board.
- **Printer :** The printer is a device which prints any documents or processed informations of the computer.

SOME HIGH LEVEL LANGUAGES

1. **FORTRAN :** This language was developed for solving the mathematical formulae very quickly and conveniently.
2. **COBOL :** This language was developed for the commerical purposes. For the processing of this language a group of sentences is selected called paragraph and all paragraphs composed are called a section, while all sections composed are called a division.
3. **BASIC :** In basic a definite part of the prescribed instruction is only inserted in the computer.
4. **ALGOL :** This was basically fabricated and designed for the complex algebraic calculations.
5. **PASCAL :** It is an amplified and modified form of ALGOL.
6. **COMAL :** This computer language is used for the students of secondary level.
7. **LOGO :** This language is used for children and kids for drawing Graphic line diagrams.
8. **PROLOG :** This language is developed in 1973 in France and this language is used for Artificial Intelligence which is capable and equivalent to the logical program.

9. **FORTH :** This language was invented by Charles Mure which is frequently used in all types of the works in the computer.

COMPUTER VIRUS

The computer virus is an electronic code which is used to abolish or erradicate the inclusive informations or programs of the computer. Some important computer viruses are Micheleanjalo, Dork Avangor, kilo, filip, Macmug, Scores, Casecade, Jeruslem, Date crime, Coloumbs crime, Internet virus, Pachcom, Pach EXE, COM-EXE, Marizuana, C-brain, bloody, Chenge Mungu and Desi etc.

COMPUTER NETWORKING

There are two types of networkings which are usually occur—Local Area Networking (LAN) and Wide Area Networking (WAN). By LAN all the computers of the same buildings are connected like the computers of university premises, computers of offices etc.

By WAN all the comptuers of a large area are connected like the computers of all the offices of a city or town etc. In India a very large computer network namely INDONET has been installing through which all the main towns and cities has to be interlinked.

COMPUTER TERMINOLOGY

- **Bit :** The bit is a unit of measurement of the electronic data. One bit is either 0 or 1 but not both. On composing 8 bits, 1 byte is formed.
- **Bug :** The Bug is the error in the computer program or system and its eradication is called Debug.
- **Byte :** Total eight bits compose a byte. Thus 8 bits = 1 byte.
- **CD-ROM :** A CD like of music CD in which data can be stored substantially called CD-ROM. In a CD with comparison to floppy extremely more datas can be stored but one problem in it is that one time recorded data can not be deleted or modified.
- **Chip :** It is a thin slice on which by a special mechanism a circuit is designed which is normally made from Silicon.
- **Memory System :** The place where computer data and program are temporarily kept is called Memory system. Usually memory is implied from RAM.
- **Modem :** The device which converts digital signals into analogue signals and vice-versa is called Modem.
- **RAM :** It is Random Access Memory (a place) where datas to be processed are kept temporarily and it is unstable memory.
- **ROM :** It is Read Only Memory and it is stable or Non-valatile memory which doesn't ended after power off.
- **Scanner :** It is a device through which graphic image is transformed to digital image and the scanners are of usually two types one desktop and another hand operating.

PROGRAMING

Computers perform phenomenal feats of calculation, but they do not do so in a complicated way. They actually carry out very simple operations, such as addition and subtraction. They achieve their fantastic computing power by carrying out these operations at incredible speed.

The programme, or set of instructions for operating the computer, is therefore written as a sequence of very simple steps. (See box below) Several computer languages have been developed for different applications, including BASIC, COBOL, FORTRAN and PASCAL. Writing programmes is very skilled and time-consuming work. But for most typical computer applications ready-written programmes are available, called "packages".

☞ How A Programme Works

Without a programme to tell it what to do and how to do it, a computer is unable to function. If, for example, you wanted to know how many times the word 'the' appears in this paragraph, or in the whole book, it would not be enough merely to put the text into a computer and then ask it how many times the word appears. For the computer to accomplish the calculations it has to be told what to do in simple steps. The instructions might be:

1. Scan the text until a space followed by 'T' or 't' is found.
2. If the next letter is not 'h', go back to step 1.
3. If the letter is 'h', is the next letter 'e'?
4. If not, go back to step 1. If it is, go to step 5.
5. If 'e' is followed by a space, add 1 to the total.
6. Go back to step 1.

A full computer programme for this operation would need to be broken down into even more simple steps, but a series of such programmes could enable a computer to analyse any amount of text in great detail.

DEFENCE

The Supreme Command of the Armed Forces is vested in the hands of the President of the Country. The responsibility for national defence, however, rests with the Cabinet. All important questions having a bearing on defence are decided by the Cabinet Committee on Political Affairs, which is presided over by the Prime Minister. The Defence Minister is responsible to Parliament for all matters concerning the Defence Services. All the administrative and operational control of Armed Forces are exercised by the Ministry of Defence. The three services – Army, Navy and Air Force function through their respective service headquarters headed by the chief of Staff.

COMMISSIONED RANKS IN DEFENCE SERVICES

Army	Navy	Air Force
General	Admiral	Air Chief Marshal
Lieutenant-General	Vice-Admiral	Air Marshal
Major-General	Rear-Admiral	Air Vice-Marshal
Brigadier	Commodor	Air Commodor
Colonel	Captain	Group Captain
Lieutenant-Colonel	Commander	Wing Commander
Major	Lt.Commander	Squadron Leader
Captain	Lieutenant	Flight Lieutenant
Lieutenant	Sub-Lieutenant	Flying Officer

INTERNAL SECURITY ORGANISATIONS OF INDIA

S. No.	Name of Organisation	Year of Creation	Headquarters
1.	Assam Rifles (A.R.)	1835	Shillong
2.	Central Reserve Police Force (C.R.P.F.)	1939	New Delhi
3.	National Cadet Corps (N.C.C.)	1948	New Delhi
4.	Territorial Army	1948	In different States
5.	Indo-Tibetan Border Police	1962	New Delhi
6.	Home Guard	1962	In different States
7.	Coast Guard	1978	New Delhi
8.	Border Security Force (B.S.F.)	1965	New Delhi
9.	Central Industrial Security Force (C.I.S.F.)	1969	New Delhi
10.	National Security Guard	1984	New Delhi
11.	Police	—	In different States

COMMANDER-IN-CHIEFS OF INDIA

	Name	Tenure
1.	General Sir Rob Lockhart	Aug. 15, 1947 — Dec. 31, 1947
2.	General Sir Roy Bucher	Jan. 1, 1948 — Jan. 14, 1949
3.	General K. M. Kariappa	Jan. 15, 1949 — Jan. 14, 1953
4.	General Maharaj Rajendra Sinhji	Jan. 15, 1953 — March 31, 1955

FIRST INDIAN CHIEFS OF STAFF OF INDIAN FORCES

	Name	Tenure
1.	General Maharaj Rajendra Sinhji (Army Staff)	April 1, 1955 — May 14, 1955
2.	Vice Admiral R.D. Katari (Naval Staff)	April 22, 1958 — June 4, 1962
3.	Air Marshal S. Mukherjee (Air Staff)	April 1, 1954 — Nov. 8, 1960

ARMY INSTITUTES

	Institute	Location
1.	Sainik Schools upto +2 Level	33 places in India
2.	Rashtriya Indian Military College (prepare for entrance to N.D.A)	Dehradun
3.	National Defence Academy (three services)	Khadakwasla, Pune
4.	Indian Military Academy (Army)	Dehradun
5.	Officers Training Academy (3 services) Short Courses	Chennai
6.	National Defence College	New Delhi
7.	The College of Combat	Mhow
8.	The College of Military Engineering	Kirkee
9.	Military College of Telecommunication Engineering	Mhow
10.	The armoured Corps Centre and School	Ahmed Nagar
11.	The School Artillery	Deolali
12.	The Infantry School	Mhow and Belgaum
13.	College of Material Management	Jabalpur

AIR FORCE INSTITUTIONS

Institution	Location
Air Force Academy	Hyderabad
Helicopter Training School	Hakimpet
Flying Instructors School	Tambaram, Chennai
The College of Air Warfare	Secunderabad
Air Force Administrative College	Coimbatore
Air Force Technical College	Jalahalli

DEFENCE PRODUCTION UNITS

	Unit	Location
1.	Bharat Dynamites Ltd.	Hyderabad
2.	Praga Tools	Hyderabad
3.	Mishra Dattu Nigam	Hyderabad
4.	Bharat Electronics Ltd.	Bangalore
5.	Bharath Earthmovers Ltd.	Bangalore
6.	Heavy Vehicles Ltd.	Avadi, Chennai
7.	Garden Reach Ship Builders and Engineers Ltd.	Kolkata
8.	Mazagaon Dock	Mumbai
9.	Goa Shipyard	Marmugao
10.	Hindustan Shipyard Ltd.	Vishakhapatnam
11.	Hindustan Aeronautics Ltd.	Bangalore, Hyderabad, Nasik, Koraput, Kanpur, Lucknow

☞ Indian Army Commands

Command	HQ Location	Command	HQ Location
Eastern Command	Kolkata	Western Command	Chandigarh
Northern Command	Udhampur	Southern Command	Pune
Central Command	Lucknow	Training Command	Shimla
South-Western Command	Jaipur		

☞ Indian Air Force Commands

Command	HQ Location	Command	HQ Location
Western Air Command	New Delhi	South-Western Air Command	Gandhinagar
Central Air Command	Prayagraj	Eastern Air Command	Shillong
Southern Air Command	Thiruvananthapuram	Training Command	Bengaluru

☞ Indian Navy Commands

Command	HQ Location	Command	HQ Location
Eastern Naval Command	Vishakhapatnam	Western Naval Command	Mumbai
Southern Naval Command	Kochi		

☞ Missile and Other Weapons

Name	Class	Range
✶ Agni I	SRBM	850 km
✶ Agni II	MRBM	2500 km
✶ Agni III	IRBM	3500 km-5500 km
✶ Agni IV *or* Agni II Prime	IRBM	4000 km
✶ Agni V	ICBM	5000 km-6000 km
✶ Agni VI	ICBM	8000 km-10000 km
✶ Agni 3SL	ICBM	5200 km-11600 km
✶ Dhanush	SRBM	350 km
✶ Nirbhay	Subsonic Cruise Missile	1000 km

Name	Class	Range
✶ Brahmos	Supersonic Cruise Missile	290 km
✶ Brahmos 2	Hypersonic Cruise Missile	290 km
✶ Prithvi I	SRBM	150 km
✶ Prithvi III	SRBM	350 km
✶ Sagarika	SLBM	700 km-2200 km
✶ Shaurya	TBM	700 km-2200 km
✶ Astra	Air to Air Missile	80 km-100 km
✶ Barak-I	SRSAM	12 km
✶ Barak-8	SRSAM	90 km

☞ Chief of Defence Staff (CDS)

To bring in reform in higher defence management in the country, the post of Chief of Defence Staff (CDS) was created in the rank of a four-star General with salary and prerequisites equivalent to a Service Chief. The Chief of Defence Staff will also head the Department of Military Affairs (DMA), to be created within the Ministry of Defence and functions as its Secretary. Gen. Bipin Rawat was the first CDS of the country from January 1, 2020 to December 08, 2021. Gen. Anil Chauhan assumed the charge of the second CDS on September 30, 2022.

MULTIPLE CHOICE QUESTIONS

1. Match List-I with List-II and select the correct answer from the codes given below the lists:

List-I

(*a*) Napoleon Bonaparte
(*b*) Jean Jacques Rousseau
(*c*) Croce
(*d*) Madame Roland

List-II

1. 'A history is contemporary history'
2. 'Liberty what crimes are committed in thy name'
3. 'Man is born free but everywhere he is in chains.'
4. 'I am the Child of Revolution'

Codes :

	(*a*)	(*b*)	(*c*)	(*d*)
A.	1	2	3	4
B.	4	3	1	2
C.	3	4	2	1
D.	3	4	1	2

2. Abraham Lincon was elected the President of United States in:
A. 1862 B. 1860
C. 1875 D. 1855

3. Who was known as the 'Prince of Humanists'?
A. Francisco Petrarch B. Dante
C. Boccacio D. Erasmus

4. D-Day is the day when:
A. Germany declared war on Britain
B. US dropped the atom bomb on Hiroshima.
C. Allied Troops landed in Normandy
D. Germany surrendered to the allies

5. Whose teachings inspired the French Revolution?
A. Locke
B. Rousseau
C. Hegel
D. Plato

6. At a time when empires in Europe were crumbling before the might of Napoleon which one of the following Governor-Generals kept the British flag flying high in India?
A. Warren Hastings B. Lord Cornwallis
C. Lord Wellesley D. Lord Hastings

7. Which one of the following statements regarding Fascism in Italy is *not* true?
A. The Fascists came to power as a result of popular uprising
B. In 1926, all political parties except Mussolini's party were banned
C. The Fascists suppressed the Socialist movement
D. The Fascists were hostile to the Communists

8. The fall of Czar Nicholas-II is known as:
A. Bloody Sunday
B. Bolshevik Revolution
C. February Revolution
D. October Revolution

9. Industrial Revolution took place first in:
A. France B. Germany
C. United Kingdom D. Japan

10. The British Prime Minister at the outbreak of World War II was :
A. Churchill B. Baldwin
C. Attlee D. Chemberlain

11. The 'Great Depression' (1929) economic crisis was met by adopting the policy of
A. Stimulus B. Marshall Plan
C. New Deal D. Open Door

12. The slogan "No taxation without representation" was raised during the:
A. American War of Independence
B. Russian Revolution
C. French Revolution
D. Indian Freedom struggle

13. In the nineteenth century the people of Europe started moving from the villages to the cities due to the impact of :
A. Epidemics
B. War
C. Industrialisation
D. Population explosion in villages

14. The important cause of the Civil War in America was:
A. Abolition of slavery
B. Quest for freedom
C. Industrialisation
D. Rebellion by the native Americans

15. Industrial Revolution could not have come about without:
A. Merchant capitalism
B. The Enclosure Movement
C. The services of the proletariat class
D. An agricultural revolution

16. Consider the following statements :
The French Revolution came about mainly due to the :
1. Extreme poverty of the people
2. Impact of the works of great writers
3. Cruelty of the rulers
4. Impact of impulsive reaction
Which of the above statements are correct?
A. 1, 2 and 4 B. 2 and 3
C. 1, 3 and 4 D. 1, 2, 3 and 4

17. Asia's oldest and largest Buddhist monastery is situated in :
A. Tawang (Arunachal Pardesh)
B. Lhasa (Tibet)
C. Trincomallee (Sri Lanka)
D. Ulan Bator (Mongolia)

18. Who was the main architect of the Russian Revolution?
A. Karl Marx B. Lenin
C. Stalin D. Tolstoy

19. V.I. Lenin is associated with :
A. Russian Revolution of 1917
B. Chinese Revolution of 1949
C. German Revolution
D. French Revolution of 1789

20. Which one of the following statements is *not* correct?
A. Voltaire believed in Natural Religion
B. Rousseau wrote *Social Contract*
C. Montesquieu authored *The Spirit of Laws*
D. Necker believed in 'General Will'

21. 6th April, 1930 is well known in the history of India because this date is associated with...........
A. Dandi March by Mahatma Gandhi
B. Quit India Movement
C. Partition of Bengal
D. Partition of India

22. Which ruler enforced the system of 'Price Control' in India?
A. Mohammad Tughlak
B. Razia Begum
C. Alauddin Khilji
D. Sher Shah Suri

23. The concept of 'Din-e-Elahi' was founded by which king?
A. Dara Shikoh B. Akbar
C. Sher Shah Suri D. Shahjahan

24. Who are supposed to be the earliest inhabitants of India? Where did they come from?
A. Aryans from Central Asia
B. Dravidians from Mediterranean
C. Negroids from Africa
D. Bhils and the Santhals from West Asia

25. The one chief characteristic of temple architecture of the Gupta Age was :
A. Absence of dome
B. Huge size
C. Beautiful carvings
D. absence of a covered courtyard for the gathering of worshippers

26. The Rigveda consists of :
A. 1000 hymns B. 2028 hymns
C. 1028 hymns D. 1038 hymns

27. The central point in Ashoka's dharma was :
A. royalty to kings
B. peace and non-violence
C. respect to elders
D. religious tolerance

28. The social evil which was conspicuously absent during ancient India was :
A. *Sati*-System
B. *Devadasi*-System
C. Polygamy
D. *Purdah*-System

29. Which, among the following, can be accepted as a novelty introduced by Mughal emperors to their buildings?
A. Domes
B. Minarets
C. Arches
D. Attached gardens

30. The first ruler of India who defeated Muhammud of Ghur was :
A. Mularaja II of Gujarat
B. Prithviraja Chauhan of Delhi
C. Jayachand of Kannauj
D. Parmaldeva of Bundelkhand

31. What important event happened in India in 1911?
A. Bengal was partitioned
B. Non-Cooperation movement was launched
C. India's capital was shifted from Calcutta to Delhi
D. Mahatma Gandhi presided over the Congress session

32. The first phase of the Congress Party (1885-1905) was characterized by its efforts to secure:
A. limited independence
B. complete freedom
C. Indianization of services
D. constitutional reforms

33. The Muslim League demanded a separate homeland for the Indian Muslims openly for the first time at its annual session held in Lahore in the year :
A. 1931 A.D.
B. 1936 A.D.
C. 1940 A.D.
D. 1941 A.D.

34. Under whose governorship did the East India Company secure the Diwani Rights in Bengal, Bihar and Odisha from Emperor Shah Alam?
A. Lord Cornwallis
B. Lord William Bentinck
C. Lord Clive
D. Lord Wellesley

35. The Simon Commission was generally boycotted by the Indian political parties. What was the reason for this general non-cooperation?
A. the Commission aimed at dividing the people
B. it was an 'all white' Commission
C. it came after the Jallianwala Bagh carnage
D. it was an eye wash

36. Aligarh Muslim University was founded by :
A. Dr. Saifuddin Kitchlu
B. Mohammad Ali Jinnah
C. Sir Syed Ahmed Khan
D. Maulana Mohammad Ali

37. Ibn Batutah was an African traveller visiting India during the time of :
A. Alivardi Khan
B. Ala-ud-din Khalji
C. Iltutmish
D. Mohammad-bin-Tughlaq

38. The battle of Wandiawash was fought in :
A. 1726
B. 1760
C. 1818
D. 1857

39. The abolition of *Sati* by government regulation was at the time of :
A. Warren Hastings
B. Lord Wellesley
C. Lord Bentinck
D. Lord Ahmerst

40. Pick out the wrong combination :
A. Dilwara Temple : Mt. Abu
B. Pashupati Temple : Kathmandu
C. Padmanabh Temple : Bangalore
D. Minakshi Temple : Madurai

41. Match the following:
(a) Chanhudaro
(b) Kalibangan
(c) Lothal
(d) Surkotada
1. Alleged discovery of the skeleton of horse.
2. Bead making.
3. Traces of a dock and ship on seal.
4. Evidence of ploughing the fields.

The Correct code is :

	(a)	*(b)*	*(c)*	*(d)*
A.	2	4	3	1
B.	2	1	3	4
C.	1	2	3	4
D.	2	1	4	3

42. Match the Harappan settlements with the banks of rivers on which they were located :

(*a*) Harappa — 1. Ravi
(*b*) Mohenjodaro — 2. Indus
(*c*) Ropar — 3. Sutlej
(*d*) Kalibangan — 4. Ghaggar
(*e*) Lothal — 5. Bhogava

Codes :

	(*a*)	(*b*)	(*c*)	(*d*)	(*e*)
A.	1	2	3	4	5
B.	1	2	3	5	4
C.	2	1	3	5	4
D.	2	1	4	3	5

43. The Goddess 'Kannagi' whose many temples were erected during the 'Sangam Age' was the goddess of :

A. Chastity B. Love
C. Prowess D. Wisdom

44. The Jain goal of life is to attain deliverance from the fetters of mudane existence, the way to which lies through three jewels. Which one of the following was not included among the 'three jewels' of Jainism?

A. Right faith B. Right action
C. Right knowledge D. Right conduct

45. The most striking feature of the Ashokan pillar is polish. Name the Ashokan pillar which is considered to be the most graceful of all Ashokan pillars.

A. Sarnath
B. Rampurva
C. Laurya-Nandangarh
D. Rummindei

46. Which are the correct statements?

1. The land grants, started in Satavahana period, paved the way for feudal developments in India.
2. Silk and spices were the Chief Indian export articles of Indo-Roman trade.
3. The Guptas issued the largest number of gold coins in ancient India.
4. The first memorial of a 'SATI' dated 510 A.D. is found at Eran in Madhya Pradesh.

A. 1 and 2 B. 1, 3, and 4
C. 1 and 4 D. 1, 2, 3 and 4

47. Who among the following patronised the 'Gandhara' (Indo-Greek style) School of Art?

A. Ashoka, the Great
B. Harsha Vardhana
C. Kanishka
D. Chandragupta Vikramaditya

48. The Sultanate of Delhi had five ruling dynasties. The dynasty having longest and shortest period were :

A. Ilbari and Khalji
B. Tughlaq and Khalji
C. Tughlaq and Sayyid
D. Ilbari and Lodis

49. Which one of the following events took place at the last during reign of Muhammad-bin-Tughlaq?

A. Introduction of token currency
B. Increase of land-revenue in Doab
C. Transfer of Capital from Delhi to Devagiri.
D. Conquest of Khurasan and Iraq

50. The most learned medieval Muslim ruler who was well versed in various branches of learning including astronomy, mathematics and medicine was :

A. Jalaluddin Khilji
B. Sikander Lodi
C. Ghiyasuddin Tughlaq
D. Muhammad-bin-Tughlaq

51. The 'Sufis' had 12 silsilas. They propounded the idea of Union with God through:

A. Love B. Rituals
C. Fasts D. Prayers

52. Match the following:

(*a*) Peshwa — 1. Foreign affairs
(*b*) Panditrao — 2. Audit and accounts
(*c*) Amatya — 3. Providing grants to scholars
(*d*) Sumant — 4. General supervision
5. Military affairs

Select the correct code :

	(*a*)	(*b*)	(*c*)	(*d*)
A.	2	3	4	5
B.	4	1	2	3
C.	4	3	2	1
D.	3	1	4	2

53. The Regulating Act of 1773 can be regarded as the first measure to :
A. assert the right of British Parliament to legislate for India
B. separate the legislature from the executive
C. separate the judiciary from the executive
D. centralise law-making

54. What was the exact constitutional status of the Indian Republic on 26th January, 1950?
A. A Democratic Republic
B. A Sovereign, Democratic Republic
C. A Sovereign, Secular, Democratic Republic
D. A Sovereign, Socialist, Secular, Democratic Republic

55. When the British obtained the grant of Diwani of Bengal, Bihar and Odisha they acquired the right to :
A. maintain law and order in these territories
B. administer civil justice and collect revenue in these territories
C. collect revenue and establish revenue administration in these territories
D. militarily defend these territories

56. Which of the following were responsible for the growth of nationalism in India during the British rule?
1. Economic exploitation of India.
2. Impact of western education.
3. Role of the Press.
Select the correct answer using the codes given below :
Codes:
A. 1, 2 and 3 B. 1 and 2
C. 2 and 3 D. 1 and 3

57. Which one of the following nationalist leaders has been described as being radical in politics but conservative on social issues?
A. G.K. Gokhale
B. B.G. Tilak
C. Lala Lajpat Rai
D. Madan Mohan Malviya

58. Provincial Autonomy in British India was envisaged by the :
A. Act of 1909 B. Act of 1919
C. Act of 1935 D. Act of 1947

59. Dyarchy means :
A. double government
B. a government in which the centre is very powerful
C. a government based on division of power between centre and provinces
D. None of the above

60. The Indian National Congress observed 'Independence Day' for the first time on 26th January in :
A. 1920 B. 1925
C. 1930 D. 1947

61. ....is situated near the banks of Sabarmati River
A. Bhavnagar B. Aurangabad
C. Ahmedabad D. Rajkot

62. Sericulture is:
A. science of the various kinds of serum
B. artificial rearing of fish
C. art of silkworm breeding
D. study of various cultures of a community

63. The most abundant constituents of earth's crust are:
A. Igneous rocks
B. Sedimentary rocks
C. Metamorphic rocks
D. Granite

64. Indian Standard Time is based on:
A. 80°E longitude B. 82½°E longitude
C. 110°E longitude D. 25°E longitude

65. Tides in the oceans are caused by :
A. Gravitational pull of the moon on the earth's surface including sea water
B. Gravitational pull of the sun on the earth's surface only and not on the sea water
C. Gravitational pull of the moon and the sun on the earth's surface including the sea water
D. None of these

66. Nagarjunasagar Project is situated on the river:
A. Tungabhadra
B. Cauvery
C. Krishna
D. Godavari

67. The difference between the Indian Standard Time and the Greenwich Mean Time is:
A. – 3½ hours B. + 3½ hours
C. – 5½ hours D. + 5½ hours

68. Which of the following dams is not on Narmada river?
A. Indira-Sagar Project
B. Maheshwar Hydel Power Project
C. Jobat Project
D. Koyna Power Project

69. Which of the following statements is **not true** about the availability of water on the earth, the crisis for which is going to increase in the years to come?
A. About 97.5 per cent of the total volume of water available on the earth is salty
B. 80 per cent of the water available to us for use comes in bursts as monsoons
C. About 2.5 per cent of the total water available on the earth is polluted water and cannot be used for human activities
D. Possibility is that some big glaciers will melt in the coming ten-fifteen years and sea level will rise by 3-4 metres all over the earth

70. Which of the following is **not** a cash crop?
A. Jute B. Paddy
C. Cashewnut D. Sugarcane

71. Through which States does Cauvery River flow?
A. Gujarat, M.P., Tamil Nadu
B. Karnataka, Kerala, Tamil Nadu
C. Karnataka, Kerala, Andhra Pradesh
D. M.P., Maharashtra, Tamil Nadu

72. Indian Standard Time is the local time of 82½°E which passes through :
A. Guntur B. Delhi
C. Allahabad D. Kolkata

73. The 17th parallel defines the boundary between:
A. North and South Korea
B. USA and Canada
C. North and South Vietnam
D. China and Russia

74. During the period of south-west monsoon, Tamil Nadu remains dry because:
A. the winds do not reach this area
B. there are no mountains in this area
C. it lies in the rain shadow area
D. the temperature is too high to let the winds cool down

75. Which country does top in producing cocoa?
A. Cote d'Ivoire B. Brazil
C. Croatia D. Nigeria

76. The biggest reserves of thorium are in :
A. India B. China
C. The Soviet Union D. U.S.A.

77. The Girnar Hills are situated in which of the following states?
A. Gujarat B. Karnataka
C. Madhya Pradesh D. Maharashtra

78. During December 22nd the sun is vertically over:
A. Tropic of Cancer
B. Tropic of Capricorn
C. The Equator
D. None of the above

79. Photosphere is described as the :
A. Lower layer of atmosphere
B. Visible surface of the sun from which radiation emanates
C. Wavelength of solar spectrum
D. None of the above

80. Broadly, there are three layers of the earth of the crust, the mantle and the core. The crust forms what percentage of the volume of the earth?
A. 0.5% B. 2.5%
C. 7.5% D. 12.5%

81. The grassland of Argentina is known as :
A. Pampas B. Campos
C. Savanna D. None of the above

82. Different seasons are formed because :
A. Sun is moving around the earth
B. of revolution of the earth around the Sun on its orbit
C. of rotation of the earth around its axis
D. All of the above

83. Eskers and Drumlins are features formed by:
A. underground water
B. running water
C. the action of wind
D. glacial action

84. Match List-I and List-II and select the correct answer using the codes given below the Lists :

List-I *(Rivers)*	**List-II** *(Towns)*
(*a*) Ghaghara	1. Lucknow
(*b*) Brahmaputra	2. Hoshangabad
(*c*) Narmada	3. Ahmedabad
(*d*) Sabarmati	4. Guwahati
	5. Ayodhya

	(*a*)	(*b*)	(*c*)	(*d*)
A.	4	5	1	2
B.	5	4	2	3
C.	5	4	3	1
D.	3	5	2	1

85. Which of the statements as regards the consequences of the movement of the earth is not correct?
A. Revolution of the earth is the cause of the change of seasons.
B. Rotation of the earth is the cause of days and nights.
C. Rotation of the earth causes variation in the duration of days and nights.
D. Rotation of the earth effects the movement of winds and ocean currents.

86. The world is divided into :
A. 12 time zones
B. 20 time zones
C. 24 time zones
D. 36 time zones

87. The 'Kiel' canal links the :
A. Pacific and Atlantic Oceans
B. Mediterranean Sea and Red Sea
C. Mediterranean Sea and Black Sea
D. North Sea and Baltic Sea

88. Match the following :

List-I	**List-II**
(*a*) Himadri	1. Outer Himalayas
(*b*) Shivalik	2. Inner Himalayas
(*c*) Himanchal	3. Middle Himalayas
(*d*) Sahyadri	4. Western Ghats

Codes:

	(*a*)	(*b*)	(*c*)	(*d*)
A.	1	2	3	4
B.	4	2	3	1
C.	2	1	3	4
D.	1	2	3	4

89. The term 'Regur' refers to:
A. Laterite soils
B. Black Cotton soils
C. Red Soils
D. Deltaic Alluvial Soils

90. Location of sugar industry in India is shifting from north to south because of:
A. cheap labour
B. expanding regional market
C. cheap and abundant supply of power
D. high yield and high sugar content in sugarcane

91. Consider the following statements :
1. Ozone is found mostly in the Stratosphere.
2. Ozone layer lies 55-75 km above the surface of the earth.
3. Ozone absorbs ultraviolet radiation from the Sun.
4. Ozone layer has no significance for life on the earth.

Which of the above statements are correct?
A. 1 and 3 B. 2 and 4
C. 2 and 3 D. 1 and 4

92. Match List-I with List-II and select the correct answer using the codes given below the Lists :

List-I *(Crops)*	**List-II** *(Producer)*
(*a*) Banana	1. Brazil
(*b*) Cocoa	2. Cote d'Ivoire
(*c*) Coffee	3. India
(*d*) Tea	4. China

Codes :

	(*a*)	(*b*)	(*c*)	(*d*)
A.	2	3	1	4
B.	3	2	1	4
C.	3	2	4	1
D.	2	3	4	1

93. Darjeeling and Dharamsala would be the right places to visit if one wanted to get a clear view respectively of :
A. Kanchanjunga and Dhauladhar ranges
B. Nandadevi and Dhauladhar ranges
C. Kanchanjunga and Nandadevi ranges
D. Nandadevi and Nanga Parvat

94. Atmosphere exists because:
A. The Gravitational force of the Earth
B. Revolution of the Earth
C. Rotation of the Earth
D. Weight of the gases of atmosphere

95. Victoria lake is located in the continent:
A. Africa
B. Asia
C. North America
D. South America

96. The famous Lagoon Lake of India is :
A. Dal Lake B. Chilka Lake
C. Pulicat Lake D. Mansarover

97. Where are most of the earth's active volcanoes concentrated?
A. Indian Ocean B. Pacific Ocean
C. Aral Sea D. Atlantic Ocean

98. Through which of the following states does the river Chambal flow?
A. U.P., M.P., Rajasthan
B. M.P., Gujarat, U.P.
C. Rajasthan, M.P., Bihar
D. Gujarat, M.P., U.P.

99. Which country is called the sugar bowl of the world?
A. Cuba B. India
C. Argentina D. USA

100. The area covered by forest in India is about:
A. 46% B. 33%
C. 23% D. 21.71%

101. A closed economy is the one which :
A. does not permit emigration or immigration
B. permits emigration but no immigration
C. engages in no foreign trade
D. engages in no foreign and domestic trade or transit

102. In a developed economy the major share of employment originates in the :
A. primary sector B. tertiary sector
C. secondary sector D. any of the above

103. The Economic and Social Commission for Asia and Pacific (ESCAP) is located at :
A. Bangkok B. Kuala Lumpur
C. Manila D. Singapore

104. Commercial vehicles are not produced by which of the following companies in India?
A. TELCO B. Ashok Leyland
C. DCM Daewoo D. Birla Yamaha

105. In India, the Public Sector is most dominant in:
A. transport
B. steel production
C. commercial banking
D. organised term-lending financial institutions

106. The main argument advanced in favour of small scale and cottage industries in India is that:
A. cost of production is low
B. they require small capital investment
C. they advance the goal of equitable distribution of wealth
D. they generate a large volume of employment

107. The most serious economic problems of India are:
A. Poverty and unemployment
B. Stagnation, not poverty
C. Unemployment, not poverty
D. Underdevelopment, not poverty

108. Which of the following is not one of the three central problems of an economy?
A. What to produce
B. How to produce
C. When to produce
D. For whom to produce

109. If saving exceeds investment, the national income will:
A. fall B. rise
C. fluctuate D. remain constant

110. In which of the following industries in India are the maximum number of workers employed?
A. Sugar B. Jute
C. Textiles D. Iron and Steel

111. Terrace Cultivation is practiced mostly:
A. in urban areas
B. on slopes of mountains
C. on tops of hills
D. in undulating tracts

112. Which of the following is a Selective Credit Control method?
A. Bank Rate
B. RBI directives
C. Cash Reserve Ratio
D. Open market operations

113. Which of the following taxes is not shared by the Central Government with the States?
A. Union excise duties
B. Customs duty
C. Income tax
D. Estate duty

114. ICICI is the name of a:
A. Financial Institution
B. Chemical Industry
C. Cotton Industry
D. Chamber of Commerce and Industry

115. Structural Unemployment arises due to
A. Deflationary conditions
B. Heavy industry bias
C. Shortage of raw material
D. Inadequate productive capacity

116. Which Commission replaced the Planning Commission in 2015?
A. NIYAM Aayog
B. NAGRIK Aayog
C. NITI Aayog
D. Jan Aayog

117. The largest public sector bank in India is:
A. Central Bank of India
B. Punjab National Bank
C. State Bank of India
D. Indian Overseas Bank

118. Which of the following statements best explains the term contraband goods?
A. Goods produced only for exports
B. Goods produced in joint sector only
C. Goods for the trading of which licence is not required
D. Goods that are forbidden, from export, import or even possession, by law

119. Price in the market is fixed by:
A. Stock exchange rates
B. The demand and supply ruling in the market at a particular time
C. The Finance Minister
D. None of the above

120. Devaluation of currency helps to promote:
A. National Income
B. Savings
C. Imports at lower cost
D. Exports

121. Balanced economic growth can be achieved only if:
A. All the sectors of economy grow at the same rate
B. Population growth is arrested
C. All the inter dependent sectors grow in harmony
D. Basic and heavy industries are assigned highest priority

122. P.V. Sindhu is associated with which of the following sports?
A. Badminton
B. Weightlifting
C. Swimming
D. Tennis

123. 'MODVAT' stands for:
A. Modified Value Added Tax
B. Deduction of cost of inputs from the value of output
C. Reduction in import duties
D. Imposition of tax on professions

124. Who among the following is the first to receive 'Dada Saheb Phalke' award?
A. Shivaji Ganeson B. Devika Rani
C. Dr. Raj Kumar D. None of the above

125. The term 'devaluation' means:
A. Reducing the value of a currency in terms of another currency
B. Increasing the value of a currency
C. Revising the value of a currency
D. None of the above

126. Per capita net availability of pulses has shown a tendency of:
A. Increase over time
B. Decrease over time
C. Constant over time
D. First increase then decrease

127. National Income is the same as:
A. Net national product at market price
B. Net domestic product at market price
C. Net national product at factor cost
D. Net domestic product at factor cost

128. Which one of the following is not an example of indirect tax?
A. Sales tax B. Excise duty
C. Customs duty D. Expenditure tax

129. The major aim of devaluation is to:
A. encourage imports
B. encourage exports
C. encourage both exports and imports
D. discourage both exports and imports

130. Structural unemployment arises due to:
A. deflationary conditions
B. heavy industry bias
C. shortage of raw materials
D. inadequate productive capacity

131. When was the Family Planning Programme officially started in India?
A. 1950 B. 1952
C. 1956 D. 1962

132. When was the Reserve Bank of India nationalised?
A. 1947 B. 1949
C. 1950 D. 1951

133. Which of the following is *not* a feature of the Indian economy?
A. High rate of population growth
B. Disguised unemployment
C. Lowest rate of adult literacy
D. High rate of exports

134. The 'Relative Deprivation' approach for measuring poverty has been adopted by:
A. developing countries
B. developed countries
C. under-developed countries
D. None of the above

135. One of the main factors that led to rapid expansion of Indian exports is:
A. Imposition of import duties
B. Liberalisation of the economy
C. Recession in other countries
D. Diversification of exports

136. Sustainable economic development means an increase in the rate of growth of real:
A. total and per capita product
B. total and per capita product and level of literacy rate
C. total and per capita product and life expectancy at birth
D. total and per capita product, taking into account the cost of degradation of the quality of environment in this process

137. Functional unemployment occurs when:
A. unemployed have no qualification for job
B. people frequently change their job
C. people were thrown out from job due to recession
D. None of these

138. Which among the following does **not** have a 'free trade zone'?
A. Kandla B. Mumbai
C. Visakhapatnam D. Thiruvanantpuram

139. Sun Belt of USA is important for which one of the following industries?
A. Cotton textile
B. Petrochemicals
C. Hi-tech electronics
D. Food Processing

140. Commercial banking system in India is
A. unit banking B. branch banking
C. mixed banking D. None of the above

141. Who gives recognition to political parties in India?
A. Parliament

B. President

C. Supreme Court

D. Election Commission

142. The Quorum of the Legislative Council is :

A. one-fourth of its total membership

B. one-third of its membership

C. one-tenth of its membership

D. 25

143. The Indian Constitution is:

A. federal

B. unitary

C. a happy mixture of the federal and unitary

D. federal in normal times and unitary in times of emergency

144. Universal adult franchise implies a right to vote to all:

A. adult residents of the State

B. adult male citizens of the State

C. residents of the State

D. adult citizens of the State

145. When a resolution prefering a charge against the President has been passed by a specified majority in the House, it is sent to the other House for investigation. If, as a result of such an investigation, a resolution is passed through a specified majority by the other House, declaring that the charge has been sustained, the President shall leave his office. The specified special majority must not be less than :

A. two-third of the members present and voting

B. one-third of the members present and voting

C. three-fourth of the members present and voting and two-third of the total membership

D. two-third of the total membership

146. Which one of the following judicial powers of the President of India has been *wrongly* listed?

A. he appoints the Chief Justice and other judges of the Supreme Court

B. he can remove the judges of the Supreme Court on grounds of misconduct

C. he can consult the Supreme Court on any question of law or fact which is of public importance

D. he can grant pardon, reprieves and respites to persons punished under Union Law

147. The Vice-president of India can be removed from his office before the expiry of his term if :

A. the Rajya Sabha passes a resolution by a majority of its members and the Lok Sabha agrees with the resolution

B. if the Supreme Court of India recommends his removal

C. the President so desires

D. None of the above

148. The Chief Justice of a High Court in India is appointed by the :

A. Governor of the State

B. Prime Minister of India

C. Chief Justice of the Supreme Court

D. President of India

149. Which of the following statements is constitutionally not true about the passing of the Union Budgets, Railway Budgets and Finance Bill in India?

1. Under the law, Finance Bill should be adopted by both the Houses of the Parliament within 45 days of its introduction.
2. If the Finance Bill is not adopted within specified period, the government loses its authority to levy the taxes proposed in the budgets.
3. In the absence of full budget, a vote-on-account gives the power to the government to spend.
4. Government cannot raise revenues without a proper approval of the Finance Bill

A. Only 2 B. Only 3

C. Only 4 D. Only 1, 2 and 3

150. Normally, on whose advice the President's Rule is imposed in a State?

A. Chief Minister

B. Legislative Assembly

C. Governor

D. Chief Justice of High Court

151. Which Article of the Indian Constitution deals with Amendment procedure?
A. Article 368 B. Article 358
C. Article 367 D. All of these

152. Government is the agency through which the will of :
A. the state is expressed
B. the people is expressed
C. the head of the state is expressed
D. the majority is expressed

153. In a unitary system of government :
A. The centre is all powerful
B. The centre is weaker than the states
C. The centre and states stand at par
D. The states and centre are supreme in their respective spheres

154. In Cabinet System of Government the real executive authority rests with :
A. The Council of Ministers
B. The Prime Minister
C. The Constitution
D. The Parliament

155. The Head of the State under a parliamentary government:
A. is an elected representative
B. is a hereditary person
C. is a nominated person
D. may be any one of the above

156. In the event of a ministerial proposal being defeated on the floor of the legislature, under the parliamentary system :
A. the government waits for a general no-confidence motion
B. the minister concerned is taken to task by the Prime Minister
C. the minister is forced to resign
D. the whole Council of Ministers resign

157. The "due process of law" is an essential characteristic of the judicial system of:
A. UK B. France
C. USA D. India

158. Under the Constitution it is :
A. obligatory for the President to accept the advice of the Council of Ministers but is not obliged to follow it
B. obligatory for the President to accept the advice of the Council of Ministers
C. not obligatory for the President to seek or accept the advice of the Council of Ministers
D. obligatory for the President to seek the advice of the Council of Ministers if his own party is in power

159. Which one of the following statements is correct?
A. the Presiding Officer of Rajya Sabha is elected every year
B. the Presiding Officer of Rajya Sabha is elected for a term of two years at a time
C. the Presiding Officer of Rajya Sabha is elected for a term of six years
D. the Vice-President of India is the ex-officio Presiding Officer of Rajya Sabha

160. The introduction of "no confidence" motion in the Lok Sabha requires the support of at least:
A. 50 members B. 70 members
C. 60 members D. 80 members

161. The High Court comes under :
A. State List B. Union List
C. Concurrent List D. None of the above

162. Which one of the following has been wrongly listed as a Fundamental Duty of the Indian citizens?
A. to develop scientific temper, humanism and spirit of inquiry and reform
B. to work for raising the prestige of the country in the international sphere
C. to protect and improve the natural environment
D. to strive towards excellence in all spheres of individual and collective activity

163. Which one of the following is not a Fundamental Duty as outlined in Article 51A of the Constitution?
A. to abide by the Constitution and respect its ideals
B. to defend the country and render national service when called upon to do so

C. to work for the moral upliftment of the weaker sections of society
D. to preserve the rich heritage

164. The main characteristics of the Directive Principles of State Policy given in the Indian Constitution are :
A. not enforceable by any court
B. fundamental in the governance of the country
C. 'Like instruments, instructions, political manifesto and a code of moral precepts which have to guide governors of the country'
D. no law can be passed, which is opposed to these principles

165. Of the following which are true?
A. In a State, the Legislative Council is dominant with regard to non-financial bills and the Legislative Assembly with regard to financial (money) bills
B. Vidhan Parishad can virtually block legisla-tion even if the same is passed by the Vidhan Sabha
C. In case of a tie between the two Houses, the Governor is duty-bound to call a joint session of the two Houses to have the issue settled on a majority verdict
D. If a Bill is twice approved by the Vidhan Sabha, it becomes law even if rejected by the Vidhan Parishad

166. Which one of the following types of emergency can be declared by the President?
A. Emergency due to threat of war and external aggresion
B. Emergency due to break-down of constitutional machinery in a State
C. Financial emergency on account of threat to the financial credit of India
D. all the three emergencies

167. The chairman of which of the following parliamentary committees is invariably from the members of ruling party?
A. Committee on public undertakings
B. Public accounts committee
C. Estimates committee
D. Committee on delegated legislation

168. Which of the following is not a formally prescribed device available to the members of parliament?
A. Question hour
B. Zero hour
C. Half-an-hour discussion
D. Short duration discussion

169. Which of the following is not a tool of executive control over public administration?
A. Power of appointment and removal
B. Line agencies
C. Appeal to public opinion
D. Civil services code

170. If the Speaker of the State Legislative Assembly decides to resign, he should submit his resignation to the:
A. Judges of the High Court
B. Deputy Speaker
C. Chief Minister
D. Finance Minister

171. Who was the first Home Minister of Independent India?
A. Rajendra Prasad
B. Jawahar Lal Nehru
C. B.R. Ambedkar
D. Sardar Vallabh Bhai Patel

172. India is a Federal State because of:
A. dual judiciary
B. dual citizenship prevalent here
C. share of power between the Centre and the States
D. rigid Constitution

173. Residuary Subjects are those subjects which are:
A. contained in the State list
B. contained in the Union list
C. contained in the Concurrent list
D. not covered by any of the three lists

174. Which of the following writs can be issued, by the Supreme Court, to enforce Fundamental Rights?
A. Writ of Habeas Corpus
B. Writ of Mandamus
C. Writ of Quo Warranto
D. All of these

175. When the offices of both the President and the Vice-President of India are vacant, who will discharge their functions?
A. Prime Minister
B. Home Minister
C. Chief Justice of India
D. The Speaker

176. The Supreme Court tenders advice to the President of India on a matter of law or fact:
A. on its own
B. only when such advice is sought
C. only if the matter relates to some basic issue
D. only if the issue poses a threat to the unity and integrity of the country

177. Six months shall **not** intervene between two sessions of the Indian Parliament because :
A. it is the customary practice
B. it is the British convention followed in India
C. it is an obligation under the Constitution of India
D. None of the above

178. The States of the Indian Union can be recognised or their boundaries altered by:
A. the Union Parliament by a simple majority in the ordinary process of legislation
B. two-thirds majority of both the Houses of Parliament
C. two-thirds majority of both the Houses of Parliament and the consent of the legislatures of concerned States
D. an executive order of the Union government with the consent of the concerned State governments

179. The Basic Feature theory of the Constitution of India was propounded by the Supreme Court in the case of :
A. Minerva Mills Vs. Union of India
B. Golaknath Vs. State of Punjab
C. Maneka Gandhi Vs. Union of India
D. Keshavananda Vs. State of Kerala

180. Which one of the following writs is issued by a court in case of illegal detention of a person?
A. Habeas corpus B. Mandamus
C. Certiorari D. Quo-warranto

181. Name the instrument with the help of which a sailor in a submarine can see the objects on the surface of the sea.
A. Telescope B. Periscope
C. Gycroscope D. Stereoscope

182. 'HEMOPHILLIA' is the disease of ....
A. liver B. blood
C. brain D. bones

183. Vitamin A is abundantly found in ....
A. Brinjal B. Tomato
C. Carrot D. Cabbage

184. .... is not soluble in water.
A. Vitamin A B. Vitamin B
C. Vitamin C D. None of these

185. The blood vessels with the smallest diameter are called ....
A. capillaries B. arterioles
C. venules D. lymphatics

186. Out of the following .... has the greatest elasticity.
A. steel B. rubber
C. aluminium D. annealed copper

187. Cooking gas is a mixture of which of the following two gases?
A. Carbon Dioxide and Oxygen
B. Butane and Propane
C. Carbon Monoxide and Carbon Dioxide
D. Methane and Ethylene

188. The substance most commonly used as a food preservative is:
A. sodium carbonate B. tartaric acid
C. acetic acid D. benzoic acid

189. Normally, the substances that fight against diseases in human systems are known as:
A. dioxyribonucleic acids
B. carbohydrates
C. enzymes
D. antibodies

190. The SI unit of temperature is ....
A. Kelvin B. Celsius
C. Fahrenheit D. None of the above

191. One of the common fungal diseases of man is :
A. plague B. ringworm
C. cholera D. typhoid

192. A clear sky is blue because:
A. red light is scattered more than blue
B. ultraviolet light has been absorbed
C. blue light is scattered more than red
D. blue light has been absorbed

193. Jenner introduced the method of making people immune to :
A. small pox B. rabies
C. cholera D. polio

194. The largest cell in the human body is :
A. Nerve cell B. Live cell
C. Muscle cell D. Kidney cell

195. What is the device that steps up or steps down the voltage?
A. Dynamo B. Conductor
C. Inductor D. Transformer

196. The protein deficiency disease is known as :
A. Kwashiorker B. Cirrhosis
C. Eczema D. Clycoses

197. Iron deficiency causes :
A. rickets B. anaemia
C. cirrhosis D. goitre

198. Blood group of an individual is controlled by :
A. Haemoglobin B. Shape of RBC
C. Shape of WBC D. Genes

199. In a normal man the amount of blood pumped out by the heart per minute is about :
A. 1 litre B. 3 litres
C. 4 litres D. 5 litres

200. Red/green colour blindness in man is known as :
A. Protanopia
B. Deutetanopia
C. Both A and B above
D. Marfan's syndrome

201. The blue colour of the water in the sea is due to :
A. Reflection of the blue light by the impurities in sea water
B. Reflection of the blue sky by sea water and scattering of blue light by water molecules
C. Absorption of other colours by water molecules
D. None of the above

202. The image formed on the retina of the eye is:
A. upright and real
B. larger than the object
C. small and inverted
D. enlarged and real

203. Unit of loudness of sound is:
A. bel B. decibel
C. phon D. none of these

204. Oil rises up the wick in a lamp :
A. because oil is volatile
B. due to the capillary action phenomenon
C. due to the surface tension phenomenon
D. because oil is very light

205. The 'stones' formed in human kidney consist mostly of :
A. calcium oxalate
B. sodium acetate
C. magnesium sulphate
D. calcium

206. We hear the sound later, while the light is seen earlier:
A. because light's speed is more than that of sound
B. because lights travel in a straight direction while sound in a zigzag direction
C. because sound's frequency is lower than light
D. All of the above

207. Which part of an eye is transplanted?
A. Cornea B. Retina
C. Iris D. Sciera

208. The Universal donor group of blood is:
A. O B. A
C. B D. AB

209. The green colour of the leaf is due to :
A. Presence of Chloroplast
B. Presence of Chromium
C. Presence of Nicoplast
D. Presence of excess of oxygen

210. Voice of a child is more shrill than that of an elderly person because:
A. the pitch of the child's voice is higher than that of the person
B. the pitch is lower
C. the child is more energetic
D. None of the above

ANSWERS

1	2	3	4	5	6	7	8	9	10
B	C	D	C	B	C	A	C	C	D
11	12	13	14	15	16	17	18	19	20
C	A	C	A	A	D	A	B	A	D
21	22	23	24	25	26	27	28	29	30
A	C	B	C	D	C	B	D	D	B
31	32	33	34	35	36	37	38	39	40
C	D	C	C	B	C	D	B	C	C
41	42	43	44	45	46	47	48	49	50
A	A	A	B	C	D	C	B	B	D
51	52	53	54	55	56	57	58	59	60
A	C	A	B	B	A	B	C	A	C
61	62	63	64	65	66	67	68	69	70
C	C	B	B	C	C	D	D	D	B
71	72	73	74	75	76	77	78	79	80
B	C	C	C	A	A	A	B	B	A
81	82	83	84	85	86	87	88	89	90
A	B	D	B	C	C	D	C	B	D
91	92	93	94	95	96	97	98	99	100
A	B	A	A	A	B	B	A	A	D
101	102	103	104	105	106	107	108	109	110
C	B	A	D	D	D	A	C	D	C
111	112	113	114	115	116	117	118	119	120
B	B	B	A	D	C	C	D	B	D
121	122	123	124	125	126	127	128	129	130
C	A	A	B	A	D	C	D	B	D
131	132	133	134	135	136	137	138	139	140
B	B	D	A	B	D	B	D	D	C
141	142	143	144	145	146	147	148	149	150
D	C	D	D	D	B	A	D	C	C
151	152	153	154	155	156	157	158	159	160
A	B	A	A	A	D	C	B	D	A
161	162	163	164	165	166	167	168	169	170
B	B	C	B	D	D	C	B	B	B
171	172	173	174	175	176	177	178	179	180
D	C	D	D	C	B	C	A	D	A
181	182	183	184	185	186	187	188	189	190
B	B	C	A	A	A	B	D	D	A
191	192	193	194	195	196	197	198	199	200
B	C	A	A	D	A	B	D	D	A
201	202	203	204	205	206	207	208	209	210
B	B	B	B	A	A	A	A	A	A